TREATIES

AND OTHER

INTERNATIONAL ACTS
OF THE UNITED STATES
OF AMERICA

EDITED BY

HUNTER MILLER

VOLUME 3

DOCUMENTS 41–79 : 1819–35

UNITED STATES

GOVERNMENT PRINTING OFFICE

WASHINGTON : 1933

For sale by the Superintendent of Documents, Washington, D. C.   -   -   -   Price $5.00 (cloth)

PUBLICATIONS OF THE DEPARTMENT OF STATE

No. 453

TREATIES AND OTHER INTERNATIONAL ACTS
OF THE UNITED STATES OF AMERICA

1942

Gift of U. S. State Department

PREFACE

16332

The scheme of this work as a whole is fully described in Volume 1. It may be said here that the arrangement of the documents is chronological according to date of signature; each document has a serial number, but the numbers are merely for convenience and have no other significance. All international acts of the United States which have gone into force are in general included, whether now in force or not; but postal conventions and treaties with Indian tribes are not included. Extrinsic and related papers which are referred to in the documents proper are also printed, so far as possible.

The headnote to each document gives the relevant dates; the notes which follow each document are mainly textual and procedural but treat to some extent of the diplomatic history of the document.

As the document volumes are to be globally indexed, there is no separate index for this volume.

The print of the documents and of the quotations in the notes is literal and thus includes any peculiarities and even any errors of the original. Certain texts are reproduced in facsimile.

This volume contains thirty-nine documents of the treaty edition, numbered 41 to 79, inclusive. The period covered is from 1819 to 1835.

A facsimile reproduction of the Steuben-Webster copy of the famous Mitchell's Map (see pp. 338–40, 350–51) is contained in a pocket inside the back cover of this volume.

H. M.

MARCH 21, 1933.

v

CONTENTS OF VOLUME 3

vii

LIST OF DOCUMENTS IN VOLUME 3

LIST OF DOCUMENTS IN VOLUME 3—Continued

MAPS IN VOLUME 3

xi

WRITINGS CITED IN VOLUME 3

(Citations abbreviated in the text are included, with cross references where necessary.)

Adams, Charles Francis. The Works of John Adams, Second President of the United States, with a Life of the Author, Notes, and Illustrations. Boston, Little, Brown & Co., 1850–56. 10 vols.

Adams, Herbert B. The Life and Writings of Jared Sparks, Comprising Selections from His Journals and Correspondence. Boston and New York, Houghton, Mifflin & Co., 1893. 2 vols.

American Historical Review, The. Vol. XXXIII, October, 1927–July, 1928. New York, The Macmillan Co.

American Journal of International Law, The. Vol. 12. New York, Oxford University Press, 1918.

American State Papers. Foreign Relations. Washington, Gales & Seaton, 1832–59. 6 vols.

Anderson, Chandler P. Canadian Questions. Northern Boundary of the United States. The Demarcation of the Boundary between the United States and Canada, from the Atlantic to the Pacific, with Particular Reference to the Portions Thereof Which Require More Complete Definition and Marking. Report Prepared for the Department of State. Washington, Government Printing Office, 1906. iv+85 pp.

Annual Report of the American Historical Association for the Years 1884–. New York and London, G. P. Putnam's Sons, 1885–89; Washington, Government Printing Office, 1890–.

Annual Report of the Secretary of the Treasury on the State of the Finances for the Fiscal Year Ending June 30, 1908. Washington, Government Printing Office, 1908. xii+539 pp.

Ashley, Percy. Modern Tariff History: Germany, United States, France. 2d ed. London, John Murray, 1910. x+447 pp.

Baasch, Ernst. "Beiträge zur Geschichte der Handelsbeziehungen zwischen Hamburg und Amerika." In Hamburgische Festschrift zur Erinnerung an die Entdeckung Amerika's (q.v.), I.

Bancroft, George. Histoire de l'action commune de la France et de l'Amérique pour l'indépendance des Etats-Unis. Translated by Count Adolphe de Circourt. Paris, F. Vieweg, 1876. 3 vols.

——— History of the United States of America, from the Discovery of the Continent [to 1789]. "The Author's Last Revision." New York, D. Appleton & Co., 1883–85. 6 vols.

Bases de constitucion federal [de los estados federados del Centro de América. Guatemala, 1824.] (Pamphlet in the Library of the Department of State, endorsed as received August 5, 1824, from the "Minister from Guatemala.")

Bittner, Ludwig. Die Lehre von den völkerrechtlichen Vertragsurkunden. Berlin and Leipzig, Deutsche Verlags-Anstalt Stuttgart, 1924. 14+314 pp.

Boletim da agência geral das colónias. No. 69, March, 1931. Lisbon.

Boston Evening Daily Transcript, September, 1830.

Bowring, Sir John. The Kingdom and People of Siam; with a Narrative of the Mission to That Country in 1855. London, John W. Parker & Son, 1857. 2 vols.

Bremisches Jahrbuch. Herausgegeben von der historischen Gesellschaft des Künstlervereins. Vol. X. Bremen, C. E. Müller, 1878.

British and Foreign State Papers, 1812-. London, 1825[?]-.

Bulletin des lois du Royaume de France, 7e série, contenant les lois et ordonnances rendues pendant le second semestre de l'année 1820. Vol. XI. Paris, L'Imprimerie Royale, 1821.

Burrage, Henry Sweetser. Maine in the Northeastern Boundary Controversy. Portland, printed for the State, 1919. xiv+398 pp.

Canada and Its Provinces: A History of the Canadian People and Their Institutions, by One Hundred Associates. Edinburgh ed. Edited by Adam Shortt and Arthur G. Doughty. Toronto, T. and A. Constable at the Edinburgh University Press for the Publishers Association of Canada, Ltd., 1914-17. 23 vols.

Carter, Clarence E. "The Beginnings of British West Florida." _In_ The Mississippi Valley Historical Review (q.v.), December, 1917.

Code of the Laws of the United States of America of a General and Permanent Character in Force December 7, 1925, The. Volume 44—part 1 of the United States Statutes at Large. Washington, Government Printing Office, 1926.

Codificación nacional de todas las leyes de Colombia desde el año de 1821, hecha conforme a la ley 13 de 1912, por la Sala de Negocios Generales del Consejo de Estado. Bogotá, Imprenta Nacional, 1924-.

Congressional Debates. _See_ Register of Debates in Congress.

Congressional Globe, The. [23d Congress to 42d Congress, December 2, 1833, to March 3, 1873.] Washington, Office of the Globe, 1834-73. 46 vols. in 111.

Constitucion de la república federal de Centro-América dada por la asamblea nacional constituyente en 22 de noviembre de 1824. "De orden del supremo poder executivo de la republica." Guatemala, J. J. de Arév [1824?].

Coues, Elliott. The Expeditions of Zebulon Montgomery Pike to Headwaters of the Mississippi River, through Louisiana Territory, and in New Spain, during the Years 1805-6-7. Rev. ed. New York, Francis P. Harper, 1895. 3 vols.

Crandall, Samuel Benjamin. Treaties, Their Making and Enforcement. 2d ed. Washington, John Byrne & Co., 1916. xxxii+663 pp.

Cuerpo de leyes de la República de Colombia, que comprende todas las leyes, decretos y resoluciónes dictados por sus congresos desde el de 1821 hasta el último de 1827. Reimpreso cuidadosamente por la edición oficial de Bogotá publicada en tres volúmenes. Caracas, Valentin Espinal, 1840. xlii+592 pp.

Curtis, George Ticknor. Life of Daniel Webster. 2d ed. New York, D. Appleton & Co., 1870. 2 vols.

—— Life of James Buchanan, Fifteenth President of the United States. New York, Harper & Bros., 1883. 2 vols.

Daily National Intelligencer, Washington, June 26, 1822; October 31, 1833.

Douglas, Edward M. Boundaries, Areas, Geographic Centers, and Altitudes of the United States and the Several States. (U. S. Geological Survey Bulletin 817.) 2d ed. Washington, Government Printing Office, 1930. viii+265 pp.

D. S. (Archives of the Department of State.) *See* Manuscript, Department of State Archives, for a list of the volumes cited.

Elliot, Jonathan. The American Diplomatic Code, Embracing a Collection of Treaties and Conventions between the United States and Foreign Powers from 1778 to 1834. Washington, Jonathan Elliot, jr., 1834. 2 vols.

Encyclopædia Britannica, The. 14th ed. London, The Encyclopædia Britannica Co., Ltd.; New York, Encyclopædia Britannica Inc., 1929. 24 vols.

Executive Journal. *See* Journal of the Executive Proceedings of the Senate of the United States of America.

Final Report of George H. Shields, Agent and Counsel of the United States before the United States and Chilean Claims Commission, Held under Treaty Signed at Santiago, Chile, August 7, 1892, The. Washington, Gibson Bros., 1894. 188+10 pp.

Fitzmaurice, Edmond George Petty-Fitzmaurice. Life of William, Earl of Shelburne, Afterwards First Marquess of Lansdowne, with Extracts from His Papers and Correspondence. London, Macmillan & Co., 1875–76. 3 vols.

Foreign Relations. *See* Papers Relating to the Foreign Relations of the United States.

Fur Seal Arbitration: Proceedings of the Tribunal of Arbitration Convened at Paris under the Treaty between the United States of America and Great Britain Concluded at Washington February 20, 1892, for the Determination of Questions between the Two Governments Concerning the Jurisdictional Rights of the United States in the Waters of Bering Sea. Washington, Government Printing Office, 1895. 16 vols.

Gallatin, Albert. A Memoir on the North-eastern Boundary, in Connexion with Mr. Jay's Map, . . . together with a Speech on the Same Subject, by the Hon. Daniel Webster . . . Delivered at a Special Meeting of the New-York Historical Society, April 15th, 1843. Illustrated by a Copy of the "Jay Map." New York, "Printed for the Society," 1843. (2)+74 pp.

Gallatin, Albert. The Right of the United States of America to the North-eastern Boundary Claimed by Them. Principally Extracted from the Statements Laid before the King of the Netherlands. New York, Samuel Adams, 1840. x+180 pp.

Ganong, William F. "A Monograph of the Evolution of the Boundaries of the Province of New Brunswick." *In* Proceedings and Transactions of the Royal Society of Canada (q.v.), 2d series, VII.

Graham, Walter Armstrong. Siam. 3d ed. London, De la More Press, 1924. 2 vols.

Greville, Charles Cavendish Fulke. A Journal of the Reign of Queen Victoria from 1837 to 1852. (The Greville Memoirs, second part.) Edited by Henry Reeve. London, Longmans, Green & Co., 1885. 3 vols.

Hamburgische Festschrift zur Erinnerung an die Entdeckung Amerika's. Herausgegeben vom wissenschaftlichen Ausschuss des Komités für die Amerika-Feier. Hamburg, L. Friederichsen & Co., 1892. 2 vols.

Hansard's Parliamentary Debates, Third Series, Commencing with the Accession of William IV. Comprising the period from [October 26, 1830, to August 5, 1891]. London, 1831–91. 356 vols.

Haswell, John H. Treaties and Conventions Concluded between the United States of America and Others Powers since July 4, 1776. Washington, Government Printing Office, 1889. xiv+1434 pp.

Heffening, W. Das islamische Fremdenrecht bis zu den islamisch-frankischen Staatsverträgen. Hanover, 1925.

Hildt, John C. "Early Diplomatic Negotiations of the United States with Russia." *In* Johns Hopkins University Studies in Historical and Political Science (q.v.), XXIV, May–June, 1906.

Hill, Lawrence F. Diplomatic Relations between the United States and Brazil. Durham, Duke University Press, 1932. x+322 pp.

House of Representatives Report No. 25, 19th Congress, 1st session, 1825–26 (serial 141).

—— Document No. 92, 20th Congress, 2d session, 1828–29 (serial 186).

—— Documents Nos. 3 and 22, 21st Congress, 2d session, 1830–31 (serial 206).

—— Document No. 129, 21st Congress, 2d session, 1830–31 (serial 209).

—— Document No. 46, 22d Congress, 1st session, 1831–32 (serial 217).

—— Documents Nos. 249, 250, 303, and 304, 22d Congress, 1st session, 1831–32 (serial 221).

—— Document No. 147, 22d Congress, 2d session, 1832–33 (serial 235).

—— Document No. 242, 24th Congress, 1st session, 1835–36 (serial 291).

—— Documents Nos. 32 and 42, 25th Congress, 1st session, 1837 (serial 311).

—— Document No. 351, 25th Congress, 2d session, 1837–38 (serial 332).

House of Representatives Document No. 35, 27th Congress, 3d session, 1842–43 (serial 420).

——— Report No. 92, 28th Congress, 2d session, 1844–45 (serial 468).

——— Executive Document No. 139, 41st Congress, 2d session, 1869–70 (serial 1417).

——— Executive Document No. 129, 48th Congress, 1st session, 1883–84 (serial 2207).

International Boundary Commission: Joint Report upon the Survey and Demarcation of the Boundary between the United States and Canada from the Source of the St. Croix River to the St. Lawrence River in Accordance with the Provisions of Article III of the Treaty Signed at Washington April 11, 1908. Washington, Government Printing Office, 1925. xvi+512 pp.

Johns Hopkins University Studies in Historical and Political Science. Baltimore, The Johns Hopkins Press, 1883–.

Journal of the Executive Proceedings of the Senate of the United States of America. Washington, Duff Green and Government Printing Office, 1828–.

Journals of the Continental Congress, 1774–1789. Edited by Worthington Chauncey Ford and Gaillard Hunt. Washington, Government Printing Office, 1904–.

Judicial Code, The. (36 Statutes at Large, pt. 1, 1087–1169.)

Kapp, Friedrich. The Life of Frederick William von Steuben, Major General in the Revolutionary Army. 2d ed. New York, Mason Bros., 1859. xvi+37–735 pp.

Laws of the Republic of Texas. . . . Houston, Printed at the Office of the Telegraph [etc.], 1838–39. 4 vols. in 1.

Laws of the United States of America. Philadelphia, John Bioren & W. John Duane; Washington, R. C. Weightman [etc.], 1815–45. 10 vols. in 11.

Letter from the Secretary of State, Transmitting, Pursuant to a Resolution in the House of Representatives, of the Nineteenth Ultimo, a Copy of the Maps and Report of the Commissioners under the Treaty of Ghent, for Ascertaining the Northern and Northwestern Boundary between the United States and Great Britain.

Lindeman, Moritz. "Zur Geschichte der älteren Handelsbeziehungen Bremens mit den Ver. Staaten von Nordamerika." *In* Bremisches Jahrbuch (q.v.), X.

Lossing, Benson J. The Pictorial Field-Book of the War of 1812; or, Illustrations, by Pen and Pencil, of the History, Biography, Scenery, Relics, and Traditions of the Last War for American Independence. New York, Harper & Bros., 1869. 1084 pp.

Malloy, William M. Treaties, Conventions, International Acts, Protocols, and Agreements between the United States of America and Other Powers, 1776–1909. Washington, Government Printing Office, 1910. 2 vols.

Manning, William R. "An Early Diplomatic Controversy between the United States and Brazil." *In* American Journal of International Law (q.v.), XII.

Manning, William R. Diplomatic Correspondence of the United States Concerning the Independence of the Latin-American Nations. New York, London, etc., Oxford University Press, 1925. 3 vols.

——— Early Diplomatic Relations between the United States and Mexico. Baltimore, The Johns Hopkins Press, 1916. xii+406 pp.

Manuscript, Department of State Archives. Colombian Claims (unbound manuscript).

——— Communications to Foreign Sovereigns and States. Vol. 1.

——— Consular Despatches, Constantinople. Vol. 1.

——— Consular Despatches, Copenhagen. Vol. 3.

——— Consular Despatches, Lisbon. Vol. 5.

——— Consular Despatches, Montevideo. Vol. 1.

——— Consular Despatches, Rio de Janeiro. Vol. 4.

——— Consular Despatches, Tunis. Vol. 5.

——— Credences. Vols. 1, 2.

——— Despatches, Brazil. Vols. 5, 6, 7, 8, 9.

——— Despatches, Central American Federation. Vol. 1.

——— Despatches, Chile. Vol. 3.

——— Despatches, Colombia. Vols. 3, 6, 7, 8, 10.

——— Despatches, Denmark. Vol. 1B.

——— Despatches, France. Vol. 25.

——— Despatches, Great Britain. Vols. 24, 25, 33, 34, 35, 50.

——— Despatches, Italy (Naples). Vol. 1.

——— Despatches, Mexico. Vols. 1, 3, 4, 5.

——— Despatches, Naples and Sweden. Vol. 5.

——— Despatches, Netherlands. Vols. 8, 9.

——— Despatches, Portugal. Vols. 9, 10, 11, 13, 14.

——— Despatches, Russia. Vols. 7, 8, 9, 10, 11, 12.

——— Despatches, Spain. Vols. 10, 15, 16, 17, 18, 31, 32, 33, 41.

——— Despatches, Turkey. Vols. 1 (pts. 1 and 2), 2, 3, 6, 25.

——— Despatches, Venezuela. Vol. 1.

——— Domestic Letters. Vols. 24, 66.

——— Instructions, American States. Vol. 14.

——— Instructions, France. Vol. 14.

——— Instructions, Mexico. Vol. 15.

Manuscript, Department of State Archives. Instructions, Netherlands. Vol. 14.

——— Instructions, Spain. Vol. 14.

——— Instructions to Consuls. Vols. 1, 2.

——— Instructions, Turkey. Vols. 1, 2, 3.

——— Instructions, United States Ministers. Vols. 5, 8, 9, 10, 11, 12, 13.

——— Instructions, Venezuela. Vol. 1.

——— Journal of All the Proceedings of the Commissioners on the Part of His Britannic Majesty and of the United States of America Appointed to Carry into Effect the Sixth and Seventh Articles of the Treaty of Peace and Amity Made and Concluded at Ghent on the Twenty-fourth Day of December in the Year of Our Lord One Thousand Eight Hundred and Fourteen in Execution of the Sixth Article.

——— Letters of William Tudor Minister U. S. to Rio de Janeiro.

——— Manuscript. Unbound manuscript in the archives of the Department of State.

——— Miscellaneous Letters, January–March, 1825; January–March, 1831; April–June, 1832; April–July, 1845.

——— Northeastern Boundary. Envelopes 7, 8, 17.

——— Notes from the Austrian Legation. Vol. 1.

——— Notes from the British Legation. Vols. 16, 18.

——— Notes from the Central American Legation. Vol. 1.

——— Notes from the Colombian Legation. Vol. 1 (pt. 2).

——— Notes from the Danish Legation. Vol. 1.

——— Notes from the French Legation. Vol. 7.

——— Notes from the Hanseatic Legation. Vol. 1.

——— Notes from the Mexican Legation. Vols. 1, 2.

——— Notes from the Neapolitan Legation. Vol. 1.

——— Notes from the Portuguese Legation. Vol. 3.

——— Notes from the Prussian Legation. Vol. 1.

——— Notes from the Russian Legation. Vol. 1.

——— Notes from the Spanish Legation. Vols. 5, 7, 12.

——— Notes from the Swedish Legation. Vol. 3.

——— Notes from the Turkish Legation. Vols. 3, 5.

——— Notes to Foreign Legations. Vols. 2, 3, 4, 5.

——— Notes to Legations of Italian States. Vol. 6.

——— Notes to the Spanish Legation. Vol. 6.

Manuscript, Department of State Archives. Papers Relative to the Commissioners under the Fifth Article of the Treaty with England, Northeastern Boundary, 1796.

———— Portuguese Claims (unbound manuscript).

———— Record of the Proceedings of the Brazilian Commission [under the Convention of January 27, 1849].

———— Report Book. Vols. 4, 5, 6.

———— Report of the Commissioners with a List of Awards, etc. Commission under the Treaty with Spain, February 22, 1819. No. VI.

———— Russian Claims (unbound manuscript).

———— Special Agents. Vol. 10.

———— Special Missions. Vol. 1.

———— Unperfected. Original treaties in the archives of the Department of State which have not gone into force.

Manuscript, Department of State Library. Bills, 1896–99.

Manuscript, Library of Congress. 58 Continental Congress Papers.

———— 9 Franklin Papers, Miscellaneous.

———— 58 Thomas Jefferson Papers.

Manuscript, Naval Records and Library. Cruises of U.S.S. *Cyane*, 1826; U.S.S. *Franklin*, 1821–1824; U.S.S. *Ontario*, 1818–; U.S.S. *Peacock*, 1826–1827; U.S.S. *United States*, 1825.

———— General Letter Book. Vol. 17.

———— Officers of Ships of War. Vols. 15, 16.

Manuscript, New York Historical Society. Bradish Papers. Box 7.

Manuscript, Public Record Office, London. Foreign Office Records, America, series 2, now class 5. Vol. 5.

Marshall, Thomas Maitland. A History of the Western Boundary of the Louisiana Purchase, 1819–1841. (University of California Publications in History.) Berkeley, University of California Press, 1914. xiv + 266 pp.

Martens. *See* Von Martens.

Martin, Lawrence. Mitchell's Map, an Account of the Origin and Uses of the Most Important Map in American History. [Draft of an unpublished book.]

———— Noteworthy Maps, with Charts, Views, and Atlases, Accessions [of the Division of Maps, Library of Congress] for the Fiscal Year Ending June 30, 1926. Washington, Government Printing Office, 1927. iv + 28 pp.

Martin, Lawrence, and Clara Egli. Noteworthy Maps, No. 2, Accessions [of the Division of Maps, Library of Congress] for the Fiscal Year Ending June 30, 1927. Washington, Government Printing Office, 1929. vi + 36 pp.

Martin, Lawrence, and Clara Egli. Noteworthy Maps, No. 3, Accessions [of the Division of Maps, Library of Congress] for the Fiscal Year Ending June 30,1928. Washington, Government Printing Office, 1930. vi+33 pp.

Mémoires des Commissaires du Roi et de ceux de Sa Majesté Britannique, sur les possessions et les droits respectifs des deux Couronnes en Amérique; avec les actes publics et pièces justificatives. Paris, L'Imprimerie Royale, 1755–57. 4 vols.

Memoirs of John Quincy Adams, Comprising Portions of His Diary from 1795 to 1848. Edited by Charles Francis Adams. Philadelphia, J. B. Lippincott & Co., 1874–77. 12 vols.

Mesgnien Meninski, Franciscus a. Lexicon Arabico-Persico-Turcicum adjecta ad singulas voces et phrases significatione Latina ad usitatiores etiam Italica. Nunc secundis curis recognitum et auctum [by B. von Jenisch and F. von Klezl]. Vienna, 1780 [–1802]. 4 vols.

Mississippi Valley Historical Review, The. Cedar Rapids, Iowa, 1914–.

Moniteur Universel, Le, Paris, July 29, 1820.

Moore, John Bassett. A Digest of International Law. Washington, Government Printing Office, 1906. 8 vols.

—— History and Digest of the International Arbitrations to Which the United States Has Been a Party. Washington, Government Printing Office, 1898. 6 vols.

—— International Adjudications, Ancient and Modern: History and Documents, Together with Mediatorial Reports, Advisory Opinions, and the Decisions of Domestic Commissions, on International Claims. Modern series. New York, London, etc., Oxford University Press, 1929–.

—— The Works of James Buchanan, Comprising His Speeches, State Papers, and Private Correspondence. Philadelphia and London, J. B. Lippincott Co., 1908–11. 12 vols.

Myers, Denys Peter. Manual of Collections of Treaties and of Collections Relating to Treaties. Cambridge, Harvard University Press; London, Oxford University Press, 1922. xlviii+685 pp.

Niles' Weekly Register, Containing Political, Historical, Geographical, Scientific, Statistical, Economic, and Biographical Documents, Essays, and Facts: Together with Notices of the Arts and Manufactures, and a Record of the Events of the Times. Baltimore, 1811–48. 73 vols.

North Eastern Boundary Arbitration, American Statements and Appendices. [The first title-page reads: "Statement on the Part of the United States, of the Case Referred, in Pursuance of the Convention of 29th September, 1827, between the Said States and Great Britain, to His Majesty, the King of the Netherlands, for His Decision Thereon. Printed, but not published."] Washington, Office of the United States Telegraph, 1829. 46+vi+96+x+ 448+16 pp. (A printed volume in the archives of the Department of State, Northeastern Boundary, envelope 7.)

Northeastern Boundary Pamphlets, 1814–42. (A volume in the library of the Department of State consisting of eleven pamphlets published between 1814 and 1842.)

Papers Relating to the Foreign Relations of the United States, with the Annual Message of the President, 1861–. Washington, Government Printing Office, 1862–.

Paullin, Charles O. Atlas of the Historical Geography of the United States. Edited by John K. Wright. Washington, Carnegie Institution; New York, American Geographical Society, 1932. xvi+162 pp.+166 plates.

Pereira Pinto, Antonio. Apontamentos para o direito internacional, ou collecção completa dos tratados celebrados pelo Brasil com differentes nações estrangeiras, acompanhada de uma noticia historica, e documentada sobre as convenções mais importantes. Rio de Janeiro, F. L. Pinto & cª. and Typographia Nacional, 1864–69. 4 vols.

Proceedings and Transactions of the Royal Society of Canada. Ottawa, 1883–.

Register of Debates in Congress [18th Congress, 2d session, to 25th Congress, 1st session]. Washington, Gales & Seaton, 1825–37. 14 vols. in 29.

Regular Confidential Printed Documents before the Senate of the United States in Executive Session during the 18th . . . Congresses, from December 15, 1824, to . . . . Washington, Government Printing Office, 1914–.

Report of the International Waterways Commission upon the International Boundary between the Dominion of Canada and the United States through the St. Lawrence River and the Great Lakes as Ascertained and Re-established Pursuant to Article IV of the Treaty between Great Britain and the United States Signed 11th April, 1908. Ottawa, Government Printing Bureau, 1916. ii+286 pp. Box volume of maps.

Report of the Librarian of Congress for the Fiscal Years Ending June 30, 1926, 1927, 1929, 1930, 1931, 1932. Washington, Government Printing Office, 1926–32.

Resolves of the . . . Legislature of the State of Maine [1831–33]. Augusta, I. Berry & Co., 1831–33.

Revised Statutes of the United States, Passed at the First Session of the Forty-third Congress, 1873–'74. 2d ed. Washington, Government Printing Office, 1878. xvi+1394 pp.

Richardson, James D. A Compilation of the Messages and Papers of the Presidents, 1789–1897. Washington, Government Printing Office, 1896–99. 10 vols.

Roberts, Edmund. Embassy to the Eastern Courts of Cochin-China, Siam, and Muscat; in the U. S. Sloop-of-War Peacock, David Geisinger, Commander, during the Years 1832-3-4. New York, Harper & Bros., 1837. 432 pp.

Robertson, William Spence. "Francisco de Miranda and the Revolutionizing of Spanish America." *In* Annual Report of the American Historical Association for the Year 1907 (q.v.), I.

Robertson, William Spence. History of the Latin-American Nations. Rev. ed. New York and London, D. Appleton & Co., 1925. xxiv+630 pp.

Said-Ruete, Rudolph. Said bin Sultan (1791–1856), Ruler of Oman and Zanzibar: His Place in the History of Arabia and East Africa. London, Alexander-Ouseley, Ltd., 1929. xviii+200 pp.

Senate Confidential Documents. *See* Regular Confidential Printed Documents before the Senate of the United States.

Senate Documents Nos. 118, 121, and 132, 22d Congress, 1st session, 1831–32 (serial 214).

——— Document No. 70, 22d Congress, 2d session, 1832–33 (serial 230).

——— Document No. 147, 23d Congress, 2d session, 1834–35 (serial 269).

——— Document No. 351, 25th Congress, 2d session, 1837–38 (serial 317).

——— Document No. 431, 25th Congress, 2d session, 1837–38 (serial 318).

——— Document No. 1, 25th Congress, 3d session, 1838–39 (serial 338).

——— Document No. 1, 28th Congress, 1st session, 1843–44 (serial 431).

——— Miscellaneous Document No. 55, 36th Congress, 1st session, 1859–60 (serial 1038).

——— Committee Report No. 93, 36th Congress, 1st session, 1859–60 (serial 1039).

——— Executive Document No. 38, 44th Congress, 2d session, 1876–77 (serial 1720).

[Session Laws.] Acts Passed at the . . . Session of the . . . Congress of the United States. 1789–.

Sherman, William Roderick. The Diplomatic and Commercial Relations of the United States and Chile, 1820–1914. Boston, The Gorham Press, 1926. 224 pp.

Sparks, Jared. The Works of Benjamin Franklin; Containing Several Political and Historical Tracts Not Included in Any Former Edition, and Many Letters Official and Private Not Hitherto Published; with Notes and a Life of the Author. Boston, Hilliard, Gray & Co., 1836–40. 10 vols.

——— The Writings of George Washington; Being His Correspondence, Addresses, Messages, and Other Papers, Official and Private, Selected and Published from the Original Manuscripts; with a Life of the Author, Notes, and Illustrations. New York, Harper & Bros., 1847. 12 vols.

Statutes at Large of the United States of America, The. Boston, Little, Brown & Co.; Washington, Government Printing Office, 1846–.

Statutes of the United Kingdom of Great Britain and Ireland . . . Containing the Acts of 6 George IV (1825) and 7 George IV (1826), The. Vol. X. London, George Eyre and Andrew Strahan, 1826. (*Cited* 6 George IV.)

Times Law Reports, The. London, The Times Publishing Co., 1885–.

Treaty Series. Washington, Government Printing Office, 1908–.

Treitschke, Heinrich Gotthard von. Treitschke's History of Germany in the Nineteenth Century. Translated by Eden and Cedar Paul. New York, McBride, Nast & Co., 1915–19. 7 vols.

United States Code. *See* Code of the Laws of the United States.

United States Reports: Cases Adjudged in the Supreme Court. Vol. 32 (*cited* 7 Peters).

Vignoles, Charles Blacker. Observations upon the Floridas. New York, 1823. 197 pp.

Von Martens, Georg Friedrich. Nouveau recueil de traités. Gottingue, Librairie de Dieterich, 1817–42. 16 vols. in 20.

—— Nouveau recueil général de traités. 2d series. Gottingue, Librairie de Dieterich, 1876–1908. 35 vols.

Weber, W. Der deutsche Zollverein. Geschichte seiner Entstehung und Entwickelung. 2d rev. ed. Leipzig, Veit & Co., 1871. x+503 pp.

Wharton, Francis. The Revolutionary Diplomatic Correspondence of the United States. Washington, Government Printing Office, 1889. 6 vols.

White, James. "Boundary Disputes and Treaties." *In* Canada and Its Provinces (q.v.), VIII.

Wriston, Henry Merritt. Executive Agents in American Foreign Relations. (The Albert Shaw Lectures on Diplomatic History, 1923.) Baltimore, The Johns Hopkins Press; London, Oxford University Press, 1929. xii+874 pp.

Writings and Speeches of Daniel Webster, The. National ed. Boston, Little, Brown & Co., 1903. 18 vols.

Wyke, W., and H. Keuchenius. State Papers of the Kingdom of Siam, 1664–1886. Compiled by the Siamese Legation in Paris. By order of H. H. Prince Presdang. London, William Ridgway, 1886. viii+242 pp.

DOCUMENTS 41–79 : 1819–35

Treaty Series No. 327
8 Statutes at Large, 252–73
18 *ibid.*, pt. 2, Public Treaties, 712–18

41

SPAIN : FEBRUARY 22, 1819

Treaty of Amity, Settlement, and Limits, signed at Washington February 22, 1819. Original in English and Spanish.
Submitted to the Senate February 22, 1819. Resolution of advice and consent February 24, 1819. Ratified by the United States February 25, 1819. Ratified by Spain October 24, 1820. The Spanish instrument of ratification was submitted to the Senate February 14, 1821. (Message of February 13, 1821.) Resolution of advice and consent February 19, 1821. Ratified by the United States February 22, 1821. Ratifications exchanged at Washington February 22, 1821. Proclaimed February 22, 1821.
The text of the Spanish instrument of ratification follows the treaty texts; then are printed, with translations, the three Spanish land grants.

Original

Treaty of Amity, Settlement and Limits between The United States of America, and His Catholic Majesty.

The United-States of America and His Catholic Majesty desiring to consolidate on a permanent basis the friendship and good correspondence which happily prevails between the two Parties, have determined to settle and terminate all their differences and pretensions by a Treaty, which shall designate with precision the limits of their respective bordering territories in North-America.

With this intention the President of the United-States has furnished with their full Powers John Quincy Adams, Secretary of State of the said United-States;

Original.

Tratado de Amistad, arreglo de diferencias, y Limites entre S. M. C^ca^ y los Estados-Unidos de America.

Deseando S. M. Catolica y los Estados Unidos de America, consolidar de un modo permanente la buena correspondencia y amistad que felizmente reyna entre ambas partes, han resuelto transigir y terminar todas sus diferencias y pretensiones por medio de un Tratado que fixe con precision los limites de sus respectivos y confinantes territorios en la America Septentrional.

Con esta mira han nombrado, Su M. C^ca^ al Exmo Sor D^n^ Luis de Onis, Gonsalez, Lopez y Vara, Señor de la Villa de Rayaces, Regidor perpetuo del Ayunta-

3

and His Catholic Majesty has appointed the Most Excellent Lord Don Luis de Onis, Gonsalez, Lopez y Vara, Lord of the Town of Rayaces, Perpetual Regidor of the Corporation of the City of Salamanca, Knight Grand-Cross of the Royal American Order of Isabella, the Catholic, decorated with the Lys of La Vendée, Knight-Pensioner of the Royal and distinguished Spanish Order of Charles the Third, Member of the Supreme Assembly of the said Royal Order; of the Counsel of His Catholic Majesty; his Secretary with Exercise of Decrees, and his Envoy Extraordinary and Minister Plenipotentiary near the United-States of America.

And the said Plenipotentiaries, after having exchanged their Powers, have agreed upon and concluded the following Articles.

miento de la Ciudad de Salamanca, Caballero Gran Cruz de la Real orden Americana de Isabel la Católica, y de la decoracion del Lis de la Vendea, Caballero Pensionista de la Real y distinguida orden Española de Carlos III, Ministro Vocal de la Suprema Asamblea de dicha R! orden, de su consejo, su Secretario con exercicio de Decretos y su Enviado Extraordinario y Ministro Plenipotenciario cerca de los Estados-Unidos de America: Y el Presidente de los Estados-Unidos, á Don Juan Quincy Adams, Secretario de Estado de los mismos Estados-Unidos.

Y ambos Plenipotenciarios, despues de haver cangeado sus Poderes, han ajustado y firmado los Articulos siguientes.

ARTICLE. 1.

There shall be a firm and inviolable peace and sincere friendship between the United-States and their Citizens, and His Catholic Majesty, his Successors and Subjects, without exception of persons or places.

ARTICULO 1.

Habrá una paz solida e inviolable, y una amistad sincera entre S. M. C^{ca} sus sucesores y subditos, y los Estados-Unidos y sus ciudadanos sin excepcion de personas ni lugares.

ART. 2.

His Catholic Majesty cedes to the United-States, in full property and sovereignty, all the territories which belong to him, situated to the Eastward of the Mississippi, known by the name of East and

ART. 2.

S. M. C. cede á los Estados-Unidos, en toda propiedad y soberania, todos los territorios que le pertenecen situados al Este del Misisipi, conocidos bajo el nombre de Florida Occidental y

West Florida. The adjacent Islands dependent on said Provinces, all public lots and Squares, vacant Lands, public Edifices, Fortifications, Barracks and other Buildings, which are not private property, Archives and Documents, which relate directly to the property and sovereignty of said Provinces, are included in this Article. The said Archives and Documents shall be left in possession of the Commissaries, or Officers of the United-States, duly authorized to receive them.

Art. 3.

The Boundary Line between the two Countries, West of the Mississippi, shall begin on the Gulph of Mexico, at the mouth of the River Sabine in the Sea, continuing North, along the Western Bank of that River, to the 32^d degree of Latitude; thence by a Line due North to the degree of Latitude, where it strikes the Rio Roxo of Nachitoches, or Red-River, then following the course of the Rio-Roxo Westward to the degree of Longitude, 100 West from London and 23 from Washington, then crossing the said Red-River, and running thence by a Line due North to the River Arkansas, thence, following the Course of the Southern bank of the Arkansas to its source in Latitude, 42. North, and thence by that parallel of Latitude to the

Florida Oriental. Son comprehendidos en este Articulo las Yslas adyacentes dependientes de dichas dos Provincias, los Sitios, Plazas publicas, terrenos valdios, edificios publicos, fortificaciones, casernas y otros edificios que no sean propiedad de algun Yndividuo particular, los Archivos y documentos directamente relativos á la propiedad y soberanía de las mismas dos Provincias. Dichos archivos y documentos se entregarán á los Comisarios ú Oficiales de los Estados-Unidos debidamente autorizados para recibirlos.

Art. 3.

La Linea divisoria entre los dos paises al Occidente del Misisipi arrancará del Seno Mexicano en la embodacura del Rio Sabina en el Mar, seguirá al Norte por la Orilla Occidental de este Rio hasta el grado 32 de latitud; desde alli por una linea recta al Norte hasta el grado de latitud en que entra en el Rio Roxo de Natchitochez (Red River), y continuará por el curso del Rio Roxo al Oeste hasta el grado 100. de longitud Occidental de Londres y 23. de Washington, en que cortará este Rio, y seguirá por una linea recta al Norte por el mismo grado hasta el Rio Arkansas, cuya orilla Meridional seguirá hasta su nacimiento en el grado 42. de latitud Septentrional; y desde dicho punto se tirará una linea recta por el mismo paralelo de

South-Sea.[1] The whole being as laid down in Melishe's Map of the United-States, published at Philadelphia, improved to the first of January 1818. But if the Source of the Arkansas River shall be found to fall North or South of Latitude 42, then the Line shall run from the said Source due South or North, as the case may be, till it meets the said Parallel of Latitude 42, and thence along the said Parallel to the South Sea:[1] all the Islands in the Sabine and the said Red and Arkansas Rivers, throughout the Course thus described, to belong to the United-States; but the use of the Waters and the navigation of the Sabine to the Sea, and of the said Rivers, Roxo and Arkansas, throughout the extent of the said Boundary, on their respective Banks, shall be common to the respective inhabitants of both Nations. The Two High Contracting Parties agree to cede and renounce all their rights, claims and pretensions to the Territories described by the said Line: that is to say.— The United States hereby cede to His Catholic Majesty, and renounce forever, all their rights, claims, and pretensions to the Territories lying West and South of the above described Line; and, in like manner, His Catholic Majesty cedes to the said United-States, all his rights, claims, and pretensions to any Territories,

latitud hasta el Mar del Sur.[1] Todo segun el Mapa de los Estados-Unidos de Melish, publicado en Philadelphia y perfecionado en 1818. Pero si el nacimiento del Rio Arkansas se hallase al Norte ó Sur de dicho grado 42. de latitud, seguirá la linea desde el origen de dicho Rio recta al Sur ó Norte, segun fuese necesario hasta que encuentre el expresado grado 42 de latitud, y desde alli por el mismo paralelo hasta el Mar del Sur.[1] Pertenecerán á los Estados-Unidos todas las Yslas de los Rios Sabina, Roxo de Natchitochez, y Arkansas, en la extension de todo el curso descrito; pero el uso de las aguas y la navegacion del Sabina hasta el Mar y de los expresados Rios Roxo y Arkansas en toda la extension de sus mencionados limites en sus respectivas orillas, sera comun á los habitantes de las dos Naciones.

Las dos Altas partes contratantes convienen en ceder y renunciar todos sus derechos, reclamaciones, y pretensiones sobre los territorios que se describen en esta linea; á saber, S. M. Cᶜᵃ renuncia y cede para siempre por si, y á nombre de sus herederos y sucesores todos los derechos que tiene sobre los territorios al Este y al Norte de dicha linea; y los Estados-Unidos en igual forma ceden á S. M. Cᶜᵃ y renuncian para siempre todos sus derechos,

[1] Or Pacific Ocean.

East and North of the said Line, and, for himself, his heirs and successors, renounces all claim to the said Territories forever.[1]

Art. 4.

To fix this Line with more precision, and to place the Land marks which shall designate exactly the limits of both Nations, each of the Contracting Parties shall appoint a Commissioner, and a Surveyor, who shall meet before the termination of one year from the date of the Ratification of this Treaty, at Nachitoches, on the Red River, and proceed to run and mark the said Line from the mouth of the Sabine to the Red River, and from the Red River to the River Arkansas, and to ascertain the Latitude of the source of the said River Arkansas, in conformity to what is above agreed upon and stipulated, and the Line of Latitude 42. to the South Sea: they shall make out plans and keep Journals of their proceedings, and the result agreed upon by them shall be considered as part of this Treaty, and shall have the same force as if it were inserted therein. The two Governments will amicably agree respecting the necessary Articles to be furnished to those persons, and also as to their respective escorts, should such be deemed necessary.[2]

reclamaciones y pretensiones á qualesquiera territorios situados al Oeste y al Sur de la misma linea arriba descrita.[1]

Art. 4.

Para fixar esta linea con mas precision y establecer los Mojones que señalen con exactitud los límites de ambas Naciones, nombrará cada una de ellas un Comisario y un Geómetra que se juntarán antes del termino de un año, contado desde la fecha de la ratificacion de este Tratado, en Natchitochez, en las orillas del Rio Roxo, y procederán á señalar y demarcar dicha linea, desde la embocadura del Sabina hasta el Rio Roxo, y de este hasta el Rio Arkansas, y á averiguar con certidumbre el origen del expresado Rio Arkansas, y fixar segun queda estipulado y convenido en este Tratado, la linea que debe seguir desde el grado 42 de latitud hasta el Mar Pacifico. Llevaran diarios y levantarán planos de sus operaciones, y el resultado convenido por ellos se tendrá por parte de este Tratado, y tendrá la misma fuerza que si estuviese inserto in el; deviendo convenir amistosamente los dos Gobiernos en el arreglo de quanto necesiten estos Yndividuos, y en la escolta respectiva que deban llevar, siempre que se crea necesario.[2]

---

[1] See the note regarding Article 3.
[2] See the note regarding Article 4.

Art. 5.

The Inhabitants of the ceded Territories shall be secured in the free exercise of their Religion, without any restriction, and all those who may desire to remove to the Spanish Dominions shall be permitted to sell, or export their Effects at any time whatever, without being subject, in either case, to duties.

Art. 6.

The Inhabitants of the Territories which His Catholic Majesty cedes to the United-States by this Treaty, shall be incorporated in the Union of the United-States, as soon as may be consistent with the principles of the Federal Constitution, and admitted to the enjoyment of all the privileges, rights and immunities of the Citizens of the United-States.

Art. 7.

The Officers and Troops of His Catholic Majesty in the Territories hereby ceded by him to the United-States shall be withdrawn, and possession of the places occupied by them shall be given within six months after the exchange of the Ratifications of this Treaty, or sooner if possible, by the Officers of His Catholic Majesty, to the Commissioners or Officers of the United-States, duly

Art. 5.

A los habitantes de todos los territorios cedidos se les conservará el exercicio libre de su Religion, sin restriccion alguna; y á todos los que quisieren trasladarse á los Dominios Españoles se les permitirá la venta ó extraccion de sus efectos en qualquiera tiempo, sin que pueda exigirseles en unó ni otro caso derecho alguno.

Art. 6.

Los habitantes de los territorios que S. M. C^{ca} cede por este Tratado á los Estados-Unidos seran incorporados en la Union de los mismos Estados lo mas presto posible, segun los principios de la Constitucion Federal, y admitidos al goce de todos los privilegios, derechos é immunidades de que disfrutan los ciudadanos de los demas Estados.

Art. 7.

Los Oficiales y tropas de S. M. C^{ca} evacuarán los territorios cedidos á los Estados-Unidos seis meses despues del cange de la ratificacion de este Tratado, ó antes si fuese posible, y darán posesion de ellos á los Oficiales, ó Comisarios de los Estados-Unidos debidamente autorizados para recibirlos: Y los Estados-Unidos proveerán los transportes y escolta necesarios para llevar á la

appointed to receive them; and the United-States shall furnish the transports and escort necessary to convey the Spanish Officers and Troops and their baggage to the Havana.[1]

Habana los Oficiales y tropas Españoles, y sus equipages.[1]

Art. 8.

All the grants of land made before the 24th of January 1818. by His Catholic Majesty or by his lawful authorities in the said Territories ceded by His Majesty to the United-States, shall be ratified and confirmed[2] to the persons in possession of the lands, to the same extent that the same grants would be valid if the Territories had remained under the Dominion of His Catholic Majesty. But the owners in possession of such lands, who by reason of the recent circumstances of the Spanish Nation and the Revolutions in Europe, have been prevented from fulfilling all the conditions of their grants, shall complete them within the terms limited in the same respectively, from the date of this Treaty; in default of which the said grants shall be null and void. All grants made since the said 24th of January 1818. when the first proposal on the part of His Catholic Majesty, for the cession of the Floridas was made, are hereby declared and agreed to be null and void.[3]

Art. 8.

Todas las concesiones de terrenos hechas por S. M. C^{ca} ó por sus legitimas autoridades antes del 24. de Enero de 1818. en los expresados territorios que S. M. cede á los Estados-Unidos, quedarán ratificadas y reconocidas[2] á las personas que esten en posesion de ellas, del mismo modo que lo serian si S. M. hubiese continuado en el dominio de estos territorios; pero los propietarios que por un efecto de las circunstancias en que se ha hallado la Nacion Española y por las revoluciones de Europa, no hubiesen podido llenar todas las obligaciones de las concesiones, seran obligados á cumplir las segun las condiciones de sus respectivas concesiones desde la fecha de este Tratado, en defecto de lo qual seran nulas y de ningun valor. Todas las concesiones posteriores al 24. de Enero de 1818, en que fueron hechas las primeras proposiciones de parte de S. M. C^{ca} para la cesion de las dos Floridas, convienen y declaran las dos Altas partes contratantes que quedan anuladas y de ningun valor.[3]

---

[1] See the note regarding Article 7.
[2] See the note regarding Article 8.
[3] See the note regarding the Spanish land grants.

ART. 9.

The two High Contracting Parties animated with the most earnest desire of conciliation and with the object of putting an end to all the differences which have existed between them, and of confirming the good understanding which they wish to be forever maintained between them, reciprocally renounce all claims for damages or injuries which they, themselves, as well as their respective citizens and subjects may have suffered, until the time of signing this Treaty.

The renunciation of the United-States will extend to all the injuries mentioned in the Convention[1] of the 11th of August 1802.

2. To all claims on account of Prizes made by French Privateers, and condemned by French Consuls, within the Territory and Jurisdiction of Spain.

3. To all claims of indemnities on account of the suspension of the right of Deposit at New-Orleans[2] in 1802.

4. To all claims of Citizens of the United-States upon the Government of Spain, arising from the unlawful seizures at Sea, and in the ports and territories of Spain or the Spanish Colonies.

5. To all claims of Citizens of the United-States upon the Spanish Government, statements of

ART. 9.

Las dos altas partes contratantes animadas de los mas vivos deseos de conciliacion y con el objeto de cortar de raiz todas las discusiones que han existido entre ellas y afianzar la buena armonia que desean mantener perpetuamente, renuncian una y otra reciprocamente á todas las reclamaciones de daños y perjuicios que asi ellas como sus respectivos subditos y ciudadanos hayan experimentado hasta el dia en que se firme este Tratado.

La renuncia de los Estados-Unidos se extiende á todos los perjuicios mencionados en el Convenio[1] de 11. de Agosto de 1802.

2. A todas las reclamaciones de presas hechas por los Corsarios Franceses, y condenadas por los Consules Franceses dentro del territorio y jurisdiccion de España.

3. A todas las reclamaciones de indemnizaciones por la suspension del derecho de Deposito en Nueva Orleans[2] en 1802.

4. A todas las reclamaciones de los Ciudadanos de los Estados-Unidos contra el Gobierno Español procedentes de presas y confiscaciones injustas asi en la mar como en los puertos y territorios de S. M. en España y sus Colonias.

5. A todas las reclamaciones de los Ciudadanos de los Estados-Unidos contra el Gobierno de

[1] Document 27.
[2] See the note regarding the right of deposit at New Orleans.

which, soliciting the interposition of the Government of the United-States have been presented to the Department of State, or to the Minister of the United-States in Spain, since the date of the Convention[1] of 1802, and until the signature of this Treaty.

The renunciation of His Catholic Majesty extends,

1. To all the injuries mentioned in the Convention of the 11th of August 1802.

2. To the sums which His Catholic Majesty advanced for the return of Captain Pike[2] from the Provincias Internas.

3. To all injuries caused by the expedition of Miranda[3] that was fitted out and equipped at New-York.

4. To all claims of Spanish subjects upon the Government of the United-States arizing from unlawful seizures at Sea or within the ports and territorial Jurisdiction of the United-States.

Finally, to all the claims of subjects of His Catholic Majesty upon the Government of the United-States, in which the interposition of His Catholic Majesty's Government has been solicited before the date of this Treaty, and since the date of the Convention of 1802, or which may have

España, en que se haya reclamado la interposicion del Gobierno de los Estados-Unidos antes de la fecha de este Tratado, y desde la fecha del Convenio[1] de 1802, ó presentadas al Departamento de Estado de esta Republica, ó Ministro de los Estados-Unidos en España.

La renuncia de S. M. C^{ca} se extiende:

1. A todos los perjuicios mencionados en el Convenio de 11. de Agosto de 1802.

2. A las cantidades que suplió, para la vuelta del Capitan Pike[2] de las Provincias Internas.

3. A ios perjuicios causados por la expedicion de Miranda,[3] armada y equipada en Nueva-York.

4. A todas las reclamaciones de los subditos de S. M. C^{ca} contra el Gobierno de los Estados-Unidos procedentes de presas y confiscaciones injustas asi en la mar como en los puertos y territorios de los Estados-Unidos.

5. A todas las reclamaciones de los subditos de S. M. C^{ca} contra el Gobierno de los Estados-Unidos, en que se haya reclamado la interposicion del Gobierno de España antes de la fecha de este Tratado, y desde la fecha del Convenio de 1802, ó que hayan sido presentadas al Departamento de Estado

---

[1] Document 27.
[2] See the note regarding Captain Pike.
[3] See the note regarding the expedition of Miranda.

been made to the Department of Foreign Affairs of His Majesty, or to His Minister in the United-States.

And the High Contracting Parties respectively renounce all claim to indemnities for any of the recent events or transactions of their respective Commanders and Officers in the Floridas.

The United-States will cause satisfaction to be made for the injuries, if any, which by process of Law, shall be established to have been suffered by the Spanish Officers, and individual Spanish inhabitants, by the late operations of the American Army in Florida.[1]

Art. 10.

The Convention[2] entered into between the two Governments on the 11. of August 1802, the Ratifications of which were exchanged the 21st December 1818, is annulled.

Art. 11.

The United-States, exonerating Spain from all demands in future, on account of the claims of their Citizens, to which the renunciations herein contained extend, and considering them entirely cancelled, undertake to make satisfaction for the same, to an amount not exceeding Five Millions of Dollars. To ascertain the full amount and validity of

de S. M. ó á Su Ministro en los Estados-Unidos.

Las altas partes contratantes renuncian reciprocamente todos sus derechos á indemnizaciones por qualquiera de los ultimos acontecimientos y transacciones de sus respectivos Comandantes y Oficiales en las Floridas.

Y los Estados-Unidos satisfarán los perjuicios, si los hubiese habido, que los habitantes y Oficiales Españoles justifiquen legalmente haber sufrido por las operaciones del exercito Americano en ellas.[1]

Art 10.

Queda anulado el Convenio[2] hecho entre los dos Gobiernos en 11. de Agosto de 1802, cuyas ratificaciones fueron cangeadas en 21. de Diciembre de 1818.

Art. 11.

Los Estados-Unidos descargando á la España para lo sucesivo de todas las reclamaciones de sus Ciudadanos á que se extienden las renuncias hechas en este Tratado, y dandolas por enteramente canceladas, toman sobre si la satisfaccion ó pago de todas ellas hasta la cantidad de cinco Millones de pesos fuertes. El Sor Presidente nombrará, con con-

[1] See the note regarding the final paragraphs of Article 9.
[2] Document 27.

those claims, a Commission,[1] to consist of three Commissioners, Citizens of the United-States, shall be appointed by the President, by and with the advice and consent of the Senate; which Commission shall meet at the City of Washington, and within the space of three years, from the time of their first meeting, shall receive, examine and decide upon the amount and validity of all the claims included within the descriptions above mentioned. The said Commissioners shall take an oath or affirmation, to be entered on the record of their proceedings, for the faithful and diligent discharge of their duties; and in case of the death, sickness, or necessary absence of any such Commissioner, his place may be supplied by the appointment, as aforesaid, or by the President of the United-States during the recess of the Senate, of another Commissioner in his stead. The said Commissioners shall be authorized to hear and examine on oath every question relative to the said claims, and to receive all suitable authentic testimony concerning the same. And the Spanish Government shall furnish all such documents and elucidations as may be in their possession, for the adjustment of the said claims, according to the principles of Justice, the Laws of

sentimiento y aprobacion del Senado, una Comision[1] compuesta de tres Comisionados, Ciudadanos de los Estados-Unidos, para averiguar con certidumbre el importe total y justificacion de estas reclamaciones; la qual se reunirá en la Ciudad de Washington, y en el espacio de tres años, desde su reunion primera, recibirá, examinará, y decidirá sobre el importe y justificacion de todas las reclamaciones arriba expresadas y descritas. Los dichos Comisionados prestarán juramento, que se anotará en los quadernos de sus operaciones, para el desempeño fiel y eficaz de sus deberes; y en caso de muerte, enfermedad ó ausencia precisa de alguno de ellos, será reemplazado del mismo modo, ó por el Sor. Presidente de los Estados-Unidos, en ausencia del Senado. Los dichos Comisionados se hallaran autorizados para oir y examinar bajo juramento qualquiera demanda relativa á dichas reclamaciones, y para recibir los testimonios autenticos y convenientes relativos á ellas. El Gobierno Español subministrará todos aquellos documentos y aclaraciones que esten en su poder para el ajuste de las expresadas reclamaciones, segun los principios de justicia, el derecho de gentes, y las estipulaciones del Tratado[2] entre las dos partes de 27. de

---

[1] See the note regarding Article 11.
[2] Document 18.

Nations, and the stipulations of the Treaty[1] between the two Parties of 27th October 1795; the said Documents to be specified, when demanded at the instance of the said Commissioners.

The payment of such claims as may be admitted and adjusted by the said Commissioners, or the major part of them, to an amount not exceeding Five Millions of Dollars, shall be made by the United-States, either immediately at their Treasury or by the creation of Stock bearing an interest of Six per Cent per annum, payable from the proceeds of sales of public lands within the Territories hereby ceded to the United-States, or in such other manner as the Congress of the United-States may prescribe by Law.

The records of the proceedings of the said Commissioners, together with the vouchers and documents produced before them, relative to the claims to be adjusted and decided upon by them, shall, after the close of their transactions, be deposited in the Department of State of the United-States; and copies of them or any part of them, shall be furnished to the Spanish Government, if required, at the demand of the Spanish Minister in the United-States.

Octubre de 1795, cuyos documentos se especificarán quando se pidan á instancia de dichos Comisionados.

Los Estados-Unidos pagarán aquellas reclamaciones que sean admitidas y ajustadas por los dichos Comisionados, ó por la mayor parte de ellos, hasta la cantidad de Cinco Millones de pesos fuertes, sea inmediatamente en su Tesoreria, ó por medio de una Creacion de fondos con el interés de un seis por ciento al año, pagaderos de los productos de las ventas de los terrenos valdios en los territorios aqui cedidos á los Estados-Unidos, ó de qualquiera otra manera que el Congreso de los Estados-Unidos ordene por Ley.

Se depositarán, despues de concluidas sus transacciones, en el Departamento de Estado de los Estados-Unidos, los quadernos de las operaciones de los dichos Comisionados, juntamente con los documentos que se les presenten relativos á las reclamaciones que deben ajustar y decidir; y se entregarán copias de ellos ó de parte de ellos al Gobierno Español, y á peticion de su Ministro en los Estados-Unidos, si lo solicitase.

---

[1] Document 18.

Art. 12.

The Treaty[1] of Limits and Navigation of 1795. remains confirmed in all and each one of its Articles, excepting the 2, 3, 4, 21 and the second clause of the 22[d] Article, which, having been altered by this Treaty, or having received their entire execution, are no longer valid.

With respect to the 15th Article of the same Treaty of Friendship, Limits and Navigation of 1795, in which it is stipulated, that the Flag shall cover the property, the Two High Contracting Parties agree that this shall be so understood with respect to those Powers who recognize this principle; but if either of the two Contracting Parties shall be at War with a Third Party, and the other Neutral, the Flag of the Neutral shall cover the property of Enemies, whose Government acknowledge this principle, and not of others.

Art. 13.

Both Contracting Parties wishing to favour their mutual Commerce, by affording in their ports every necessary Assistance to their respective Merchant Vessels, have agreed, that the Sailors who shall desert from their Vessels in the ports of the other, shall be arrested and delivered up, at the instance of the Consul—who shall

Art. 12.

El Tratado[1] de limites y navegacion de 1795. queda confirmado en todos y cada uno de sus articulos, excepto los articulos 2, 3, 4, 21, y la segunda clausula del 22, que habiendo sido alterados por este Tratado, ó cumplidos enteramente, no pueden tener valor alguno.

Con respecto al Articulo 15 del mismo Tratado de amistad, limites y navegacion de 1795 en que se estipula, que la bandera cubre la propiedad, han convenido las dos altas partes contratantes en que esto se entienda asi con respecto á aquellas Potencias que reconozcan este principio; pero que, si una de las dos partes contratantes estuviere en guerra con una tercera, y la otra Neutral, la bandera de esta Neutral cubrirá la propiedad de los enemigos, cuyo Gobierno reconozca este principio, y no de otros.

Art. 13.

Deseando ambas Potencias contratantes favorecer el Comercio reciproco prestando cada una en sus puertos **to**dos los auxilios convenientes á sus respectivos buques Mercantes, han acordado en hacer prender y entregar los Marineros que desierten de sus buques en los puertos de la otra, á instancia del Consul; quien sin embargo deberá

---

[1] Document 18.

prove nevertheless, that the Deserters belonged to the Vessels that claimed them, exhibiting the document that is customary in their Nation: that is to say, the American Consul in a Spanish Port, shall exhibit the Document known by the name of *Articles*, and the Spanish Consul in American Ports, the Roll of the Vessel; and if the name of the Deserter or Deserters, who are claimed, shall appear in the one or the other, they shall be arrested, held in custody and delivered to the Vessel to which they shall belong.

probar que los desertores pertenecen á los buques que los reclaman, manifestando el documento de costumbre en su Nacion; esto es, que el Consul Español en puerto Americano exhibirá el Rol del buque, y el Consul Americano en puerto Español, el documento conocido bajo el nombre de *Articles;* y constando en uno ú otro el nombre ó nombres del desertor ó desertores que se reclaman, se procederá al arresto, custodia y entrega al buque á que correspondan.

Art. 14.

The United-States hereby certify, that they have not received any compensation from France for the injuries they suffered from her Privateers, Consuls, and Tribunals, on the Coasts and in the Ports of Spain, for the satisfaction of which provision is made by this Treaty; and they will present an authentic statement of the prizes made, and of their true value, that Spain may avail herself of the same in such manner as she may deem just and proper.[1]

Art. 14.

Los Estados-Unidos certifican por el presente que no han recibido compensacion alguna de la Francia por los perjuicios que sufrieron de sus Corsarios, Consules y Tribunales en las costas y puertos de España, para cuya satisfaccion se provee en este Tratado, y presentarán una relacion justificada de las presas hechas, y de su verdadero valor, para que la España pueda servirse de ella en la manera que mas juzgue justo y conveniente.[1]

Art. 15.

The United-States to give to His Catholic Majesty, a proof of their desire to cement the relations of Amity subsisting between the two Nations, and to favour the

Art. 15.

Los Estados-Unidos para dar á S. M. C^{ca} una prueba de sus deseos de cimentar las relaciones de Amistad que existen entre las dos Naciones, y de favorecer el

---

[1] See the note regarding Article 14.

Commerce of the Subjects of His Catholic Majesty, agree that Spanish Vessels coming laden only with productions of Spanish growth, or manufactures directly from the Ports of Spain or of her Colonies, shall be admitted for the term of twelve years to the Ports of Pensacola and S[t] Augustine [1] in the Floridas, without paying other or higher duties on their cargoes or of tonnage than will be paid by the vessels of the United-States. During the said term no other Nation shall enjoy the same privileges within the ceded Territories. The twelve years shall commence three months after the exchange of the Ratifications of this Treaty.

Comercio de los subditos de S. M. C[ca], convienen en que, los buques Españoles que vengan solo cargados de productos de sus frutos ó manufacturas directamente de los puertos de España ó de sus Colonias, sean admitidos por el espacio de doce años en los puertos de Panzacola y San Augustin [1] de las Floridas, sin pagar mas derechos por sus cargamentos, ni mayor derecho de tonelage, que el que paguen los buques de los Estados-Unidos. Durante este tiempo ninguna Nacion tendrá derecho á los mismos privilegios en los territorios cedidos. Los doce años empezaran á contarse tres meses despues de haberse cambiado las ratificaciones de este Tratado.

Art. 16.

The present Treaty shall be ratified in due form by the Contracting Parties, and the Ratifications shall be exchanged in Six Months from this time or sooner if possible.

In Witness whereof, We the Underwritten Plenipotentiaries of the United-States of America and of His Catholic Majesty, have signed, by virtue of Our Powers, the present Treaty of Amity, Settlement and Limits, and have thereunto affixed our Seals respectively.

Art. 16.

El presente Tratado sera ratificado en debida forma por las partes contratantes, y las ratificaciones se cangearán en el espacio de seis meses desde esta fecha, ó mas pronto si es posible.

En fé de lo qual nosotros los Infrascritos Plenipotenciarios de S. M. C[ca], y de los Estados-Unidos de America, hemos firmado en virtud de nuestros Poderes, el presente Tratado de Amistad, Arreglo de diferencias, y Limites, y le hemos puesto nuestros sellos respectivos.

---

[1] See the note regarding Article 15.

Done at Washington, this Twenty-Second day of February, One Thousand Eight Hundred and Nineteen.

[Seal] JOHN QUINCY ADAMS
[Seal] LUIS DE ONIS

Hecho en Washington, á veinte y dos de Febrero de mil ochocientos diez y nueve.

[Seal] LUIS DE ONIS
[Seal] JOHN QUINCY ADAMS

[The Spanish Instrument of Ratification]

[Translation]

Dⁿ Fernando Septimo por la gracia de Dios, y por la Constitucion de la Monarquia Espanola, Rey de las Españas.

Por cuanto en el dia Veinte y dos de Febrero del año proximo pasado de mil ocho cientos diez y nueve, se concluyó y firmó en la Ciudad de Washington entre Dⁿ Luis de Onis, mi Enviado Extraordinario y Ministro Plenipotenciario, y Dⁿ Juan Quincy Adams, Secretario de Estado de los Estados Unidos de America, autorizados competentemente por ambas partes, un tratado compuesto de diez y seis articulos, que tiene por objeto el arreglo de diferiencias, y de limites entre ambos Gobiernos y sus respectivos territorios; cuya forma y tenor literal es el siguiente.

Ferdinand the Seventh, by the Grace of God and by the Constitution of the Spanish Monarchy, King of the Spains.

Whereas on the twenty-second day of February of the year one thousand eight hundred and nineteen last past, a treaty was concluded and signed in the city of Washington between Don Luis de Onis, My Envoy Extraordinary and Minister Plenipotentiary, and John Quincy Adams, esq., Secretary of State of the United States of America, competently authorized by both parties, consisting of sixteen articles, which had for their object the arrangement of differences and of limits between both Governments and their respective territories; which are of the following form and literal tenor:

[Here follow both texts of the treaty]

Por tanto: haviendo visto y examinado los referidos diez y seis articulos, y habiendo precedido la anuencia y autorizacion de las Cortes generales de la Nacion por lo respectivo á la cesion que en los articulos 2? y 3? se menciona y

Therefore, having seen and examined the sixteen articles aforesaid, and having first obtained the consent and authority of the General Cortes of the Nation with respect to the cession mentioned and stipulated in the second and

estipula, he venido en aprobar y ratificar todos y cada uno de los referidos articulos y clausulas que en ellos se contiene; y en virtud de la presente los apruebo y ratifico; prometiendo en fé y palabra de Rey cumplirlos y observarlos, y hacer que se cumplan y observen enteramente como si Yo mismo los hubiese firmado: sin que sirva de obstaculo en manera alguna la circunstancia de haber transcurrido el termino de los seis meses prefijados para el cange de las ratificaciones en el articulo 16; pues mi deliberada voluntad es que la presente ratificacion sea tan valida y subsistente y produzca los mismos efectos que si hubiese sido hecha dentro del termino prefijado. Y deseando al mismo tiempo evitar qualquiera duda ó ambiguidad que pueda ofrecer el contenido del articulo 8° del referido tratado con motivo de la fecha que en él se señala como termino para la validacion de las concesiones de tierras en las Floridas, hechas por Mi ó por las autoridades competentes en Mi Real nombre, á cuyo señalamiento de fecha se procedió en la positiva inteligencia de dejar anuladas por su tenor las tres concesiones[1] de tierras hechas á favor del Duque de Alagon, Conde de Puñonrostro, y Dⁿ Pedro de Vargas; tengo a bien declarar que las referidas tres concesiones han quedado y quedan enteramente anula-

third articles, I approve and ratify all and every one of the articles referred to, and the clauses which are contained in them; and, in virtue of these presents, I approve and ratify them, promising, on the faith and word of a King, to execute and observe them and to cause them to be executed and observed entirely as if I Myself had signed them; and that the circumstance of having exceeded the term of six months fixed for the exchange of the ratifications in the sixteenth article may afford no obstacle in any manner, it is My deliberate will that the present ratification be as valid and firm, and produce the same effects, as if it had been done within the determined period. Desirous at the same time of avoiding any doubt or ambiguity concerning the meaning of the eighth article of the said treaty in respect to the date which is pointed out in it as the period for the confirmation of the grants of lands in the Floridas, made by Me or by the competent authorities in My royal name, which point of date was fixed in the positive understanding of the three grants[1] of land made in favor of the Duke of Alagon, the Count of Puñonrostro, and Don Pedro de Vargas, being annulled by its tenor; I think proper to declare that the said three grants have remained and do remain entirely

---

[1] See the texts of the land grants, which follow, and also the notes thereon.

das è invalidadas; sin que los tres individuos referidos, ni los que de estos tengan titulo ó causa, puedan aprovecharse de dichas concesiones en tiempo ni manera alguna: bajo cuya explicita declaracion se ha de entender ratificado el referido articulo 8.º En fé de todo lo cual mandé despachar la presente firmada de mi mano, sellada con mi sello secreto, y refrendada por el infrascripto Mi Secretario del Despacho de Estado. Dada en Madrid á veinte y quatro de Octubre de Mil ochocientos veinte.

FERNANDO.
EVARISTO PEREZ DE CASTRO.

annulled and invalid, and that neither the three individuals mentioned, nor those who may have title or interest through them, can avail themselves of the said grants at any time or in any manner; under which explicit declaration the said eighth article is to be understood as ratified. In the faith of all which I have commanded to despatch these presents, signed by My hand, sealed with My secret seal, and countersigned by the underwritten, My Secretary of Despatch of State. Given at Madrid the twenty-fourth of October, one thousand eight hundred and twenty.

FERNANDO.
EVARISTO PEREZ DE CASTRO.

[The Spanish Land Grants]

[Translation]

Dⁿ Antonio Porcél Caballero pensionista de la Real y distinguida Orden de Carlos 3º, del Consejo de Estado, y Secretario de Estado y del Despacho de la Gobernacion de Ultramar &ª

Certifico que con fecha seis de Febrero de mil ochocientos diez y ocho, se espidieron por el estinguido Consejo de las Indias, Reales Cedulas de igual tenor, al Gobernador Capitan General de la Ysla de Cuba y su distrito, al Intendente de Exercito y Real Hacienda de la Havana y su distrito, y al Gobernador de las Floridas, para que Cada uno en la parte que le tocare dispusiese lo conveniente á que tuviese efecto la gracia concedida al

Don Antonio Porcel, Knight Pensioner of the Royal and Distinguished Order of Charles the Third, of the Council of State, and Secretary of State and of Despatch of the Ultramarine Government, etc.

I certify that under date of the sixth of February, one thousand eight hundred and eighteen, royal letters patent of the same tenor were sent by the late Council of the Indies to the Governor Captain General of the island of Cuba and its dependencies, to the Intendant of the Army and Royal Business of the Habana and its district, and to the Governor of the Floridas, that each should do his utmost, in his particular department, to give effect to the

Duque de Alagon de varios terrenos en la Florida oriental, cuyo contenido es el siguiente.

"El Rey.

Mi Gobernador y Capitan General de la Ysla de Cuba y su distrito. El Duque de Alagon Baron de Espes, me hizo presente en esposicion de doce de Julio del año ultimo lo que sigue—Señor—El Duque de Alagon Baron de Espes, Capitan de Guardias de la Real Persona De V. M. con el mayor respeto espone: Que siendo un interes de la Corona, que se dén à grandes Capitalistas los terrenos incultos para que se pueblen y cultiven, en lo que resultan unas ventajas demostradas y aconsejadas por todos los Politicos, en cuyo caso se hallan muchos, ò casi los mas del fertil suelo de las Floridas; y siendo tambien un derecho De V. M. como dueño absoluto, el distribuirlos en obseguio de la Agricultura, y en premio y recompensa de los servicios interesantes que se le hacen con utilidad De V. M. y de su Reyno todo. Deseoso de merecer estas señales de aprecio de su magnanimo corazon, y de contribuir por mi parte à llenar las miras del poblacion tan interesantes al bien comun: à V. M. suplica se digne concederle el terreno inculto que no se halle cedido en la Florida oriental, situado entre las Margenes de los Rios Santa Lucia y San Juan, hasta sus embocaduras en el mar, y la Costa del Golfo de la Florida, é Yslas adyacentes, con la embocadura en el Rio Hijuelos, por el grado veinte y seis de latitud, siguiendo su orilla izguienda hasta su nacimiento, tirando una linea

grant made to the Duke of Alagon of various lands in East Florida, of the following tenor:

"The King

"My Governor and Captain General of the island of Cuba and its dependencies: The Duke of Alagon, Baron de Espes, has manifested to Me, on the twelfth of July last, as follows: 'Sire: The Duke of Alagon, Baron de Espes, Captain of Your Majesty's Royal Body Guards, with the greatest respect exposes that, it being the interest of the Crown that the uncultivated lands should be given to great capitalists, in order that they may be peopled and cultivated, from which flow the advantages pointed out and advised by all politicians, and by means of which much or nearly the most of the fertile soil of the Floridas has been discovered, and it being a right of Your Majesty, as absolute lord, to distribute them for the benefit of agriculture and in reward and recompense of the eminent services which have been rendered to Your Majesty and your whole Kingdom; being desirous of deserving those marks of the value of his magnanimous courage and of contributing as far as possible to fulfil the designs of population, so interesting to the commonweal, he humbly requests Your Majesty that you would deign to grant him all the uncultivated land not ceded in East Florida which lies between the Rivers Saint Lucia and Saint Johns, as far as the mouths by which they empty themselves into the sea, and the coast of the Gulf of Florida, and the adjacent islands, with the mouth of the River

ala Laguna Macaco, bajando luego por el Camino del Rio de San Juan hasta la laguna Valdés, cortando por otra linea desde el estremo norte de esta laguna hasta el nacimiento del Rio Amarima, siguiendo la orilla derecha hasta su embocadura por los veinte y ocho ù veinte y cinco de latitud, y continuando por la costa del mar, con todas sus Yslas adyacentes, hasta la embocadura del Rio Hijuelos, en plena propiedad para si y sus herederos, y permitiendose la introducion de Negros para el travajo y cultivo de las tierras libre de derechos: gracia que espera merecer de la innata piedad de V. M. Enterado del contenido de esta esposicion, y atendiendo al distinguido merito de este sugeto, y a su acreditado celo por mi Real servicio, como tambien a las ventajas que resultaràn al Estado del aumento de poblacion de los citados paises que pretende, he tenido à bien acceder ala gracia que solicita en quanto no se oponga à las Leyes de esos mis Reynos; y comunicarlo al mi Consejo de las Indias para su execucion, en Real orden de diez y siete de Diciembre del referido año. En su consecuencia os mando y encargo por esta mi Real Cedula que con arreglo a las Leyes que rigen en la materia, auxilieis eficazmente la execucion de la espresada gracia, tomando todas las disposiciones que se dirigan asu devido efecto, sin perjuicio de tercero, y para que el espresado Duque de Alagon pueda desde luego poner en execucion su designio conforme en todo con mis beneficos deseos en obsequio de la agricultura y comercio de dhas posesiones, que claman por una poblacion pro-

Hijuelos, in the twenty-sixth degree of latitude, following the left bank up to its source, drawing a line from Lake Macaco, then descending by the way of the River Saint Johns to the Lake Valdés, crossing by another line from the extreme north of said lake to the source of the River Amarima, following its right bank as far as its mouth, in the twenty-eighth or twenty-fifth degree of latitude, and running along the seacoast, with all the adjacent islands, up to the mouth of the River Hijuelos, in full property to himself and his heirs; allowing them also to import negroes, for the labor and cultivation of the lands, free of duties—a gift which I hope to obtain from Your Majesty's innate goodness.'

"Having taken the premises into consideration and bearing in mind the distinguished merit of the memorialist and his signal zeal for My royal service, as well as the benefits to be derived by the state from an increase of population in the countries the cession whereof he has solicited, I have judged fit to grant him the same, in so far as is conformable to the laws of these My Kingdoms, and to make it known to My Council of the Indies, for its due execution, by a royal order of the seventeenth of December in the year aforementioned. Wherefore I charge and command you, by this My royal *cédula*, with due observance of the laws to such cases pertaining, to give full and effectual aid to the execution of the said cession, taking all requisite measures for its accomplishment, without injury to any third party; and in order that the said Duke of Alagon may forthwith carry his plans

porcionada ala feracidad de su suelo, y ala defensa y seguridad de las costas, dando cuenta successivamente de su progreso; entendiendose que la introduccion de negros que comprende la misma gracia, deve sujetarse en quanto al trafico de ellos, a las reglas prescriptas en mi Real Cedula de diez y nueve de Diciembre ultimo, que asi es mi voluntad; y que de esta cedula se tome razon en la Contaduria general de Indias, fecha en Palacio à seis de Febrero de mil ochocientos diez y ocho.

Yo EL REY.

Por mandado del Rey Nuestro Señor.

ESTEBAN VAREA."

Y para que conste firmo esta Certificacion en Madrid à quince de Octubre de mil ochocientos veinte

(L. S.)   (Sig.)

ANTONIO PORCEL

Don Evaristo Perez de Castro, Caballero de número de la órden de Carlos 3º, del Consejo de Estado, y Secretario del Despacho de Estado &º

Certifico que la firma que antecede del Exmo Sᵒʳ Dⁿ Antonio Porcel Secretario del Despacho de la Gobernacion de Ultramar, es la que acostumbra poner en todos sus escritos. Y para los efectos convenientes doy el presente certificado, firmado de mi

into execution, in conformity with My beneficent desires in favor of the agriculture and commerce of the said territories, which require a population proportioned to the fertility of the soil and the defense and security of the coasts, he giving regular accounts of his proceedings; it being understood that the introduction of negroes, which the same cession comprehends, ought, as far as relates to the traffic in them, to be subject to the regulations prescribed in My royal *cédula* of the nineteenth of December last, for such is My will, and that due note be taken of the present *cédula* in the office of the Accountant General of the Indies.

"Dated at the Palace the sixth of February, one thousand eight hundred and eighteen.

"I, THE KING.

"By command of the King our Lord,

"ESTEBAN VAREA."

And I confirm this exemplification at Madrid the fifteenth of October, one thousand eight hundred and twenty.

[Seal]   (Signed)

ANTONIO PORCEL

Don Evaristo Perez de Castro, Knight of the Order of Charles the Third, of the Council of State, and Secretary of Despatch of State, etc.

I certify that the foregoing signature of His Excellency Don Antonio Porcel, Secretary of Despatch of the Ultramarine Government, is that which he is accustomed to put to all his writings. And, for the proper purposes, I give the present certificate,

mano y sellado con el escudo de mis armas en Madrid à veinte y uno de Octubre de mil ochocientos y veinte.

(L. S.) (Sig.)
EVARISTO PEREZ DE CASTRO.

Dⁿ Antonio Porcel, Caballero pensionista de la Real y distinguida orden de Carlos tercero, del Consejo de Estado, y del Despacho de la Gobernacion de Ultramar, &ª

Certifico que con fecha de seis de Febrero de mil ochocientos diez y ocho, se expedieron por el extinguido Consejo de las Indias Reales Cedulas de igual tenor al Gobernador Capitan General de la Ysla de Cuba y su distrito, al Intendente de exercito y real Hacienda de la Havana y su distrito, y al Gobernador de las Floridas, para que cada uno en la parte que le tocase dispusiese lo conveniente á que tubiese efecto la gracia concedida al Brigadier Conde de Puñonrostro de varios terrenos situados en la Florida occidental, cuyo contenido es el siguiente.

"El Rey.

Mi Gobernador y Capitan General de la Ysla de Cuba y su distrito. El Brigadier Conde de Puñonrostro me hizo presente en exposicion de tres de Noviembre del año ultimo lo que sigue— Señor—El Brigadier Conde d Puñonrostro, Grande de España de primera clase, y vuestro Gentil Hombre de Camara con exercicio &ª &ª P. A. L. R. P. de V. M. con el mas profundo respeto, expone:

signed by my hand and sealed with my seal of arms at Madrid the twenty-first of October, one thousand eight hundred and twenty.

[Seal] (Signed)
EVARISTO PEREZ DE CASTRO.

[Translation]

Don Antonio Porcel, Knight Pensioner of the Royal and Distinguished Order of Charles the Third, of the Council of State, and Secretary of State and of Despatch of the Ultramarine Government, etc.

I certify that under date of the sixth of February, one thousand eight hundred and eighteen, royal letters patent of the same tenor were sent by the late Council of the Indies to the Governor Captain General of the island of Cuba and its dependencies, to the Intendant of the Army and Royal Business of the Habana and its district, and to the Governor of the Floridas, that each should do his utmost, in his particular department, to give effect to the grant made to Brigadier the Count of Puñonrostro of various lands situated in West Florida, of the following tenor:

"The King

"My Governor and Captain General of the island of Cuba and its dependencies: The Brigadier Count of Puñonrostro submitted to Me, on the third of November last, what follows: 'Sire: The Brigadier Count of Puñonrostro, Grandee of Spain of the first class, and your Gentleman of the Bed Chamber in actual attendance, etc., etc., throws himself at Your Majesty's

que movido del anhelo de procurar por todos los medios posibles el hacer productible parte de los immensos terrenos despoblados è incultos que V. M. tiene en las Americas, y que por su feracidad prometen las mayores ventajas, tanto al que expone como al Estado, si llegase à verificarse, como lo espera, el noble proyecto que anima al exponente de convertir una pequeña parte de aquellos desiertos en morada de habitantes pacificos cristianos é industriosos, que aumentando la poblacion de vuestros reynos, fomenten la agricultura y el comercio, y por consiguiente hagan inmensos los ingresos de vuestro real Herario. Esta empresa dirigida por persona que al conocimiento del pays reune las circumstancias de poder comparar los progresos que han hecho por este medio otras Naciones, como la de los Estados Unidos, que en una epoca muy limitada ha elevado su poder à un grado extraordinario, distinguiendose la Mobila adyacente à la Florida, que en los seis años ultimos aprovechandose de la emigracion se ha convertido de un pays inculto y desierto, en una Provincia rica y comerciante, cultivada y poblada con mas de 300D habitantes. Esto mismo debe suceder à la Florida en el corto tiempo de diez y ocho ò veinte años si se adoptan las medidas conducentes à ello, y si al exemplo del exponente avandonan otros la apatia y se dedican á labrar su fortuna individual, y por consiguiente la del Estado. Confiado pues en lo re comendable de esta empresa, en los vivos deseos que animan à V. M. por la prosperidad de la Nacion, y en los servicios y sacrificios del exponente, se atreve

56006°—33——4

royal feet with the most profound respect and submits to Your Majesty that, prompted by the desire of promoting, by all possible means, the improvement of the extensive waste and unsettled lands possessed by Your Majesty in the Americas, which, by their fertility, offer the greatest advantages not only to your memorialist but to the state, provided due effect, as is hoped, be given to the noble project formed by Your Majesty's memorialist, of converting a small portion of those deserts into the abode of peaceable, Christian, and industrious inhabitants, who will increase the population of your Kingdoms, promote agriculture and commerce, and thereby add immensely to your royal revenues. This enterprise should be conducted by a person who, with a knowledge of the country, would combine the intelligence necessary for comparing the progress made by other nations in similar situations, and particularly by the United States, which, within a very recent period, have advanced their power to an extraordinary height, and especially in the instance of the Mobile country, adjoining Florida, which in the last six years has received such an influx of emigrants as to be converted from a desert waste into a rich commercial province, highly improved and peopled with more than three hundred thousand souls. A similar change would be effected in Florida within eighteen or twenty years by the adoption of judicious arrangements and by those exertions which Your Majesty's memorialist proposes to employ for the promotion of his personal

à suplicar à V. M. que en remuneracion de ellos se digne concederle en plena propiedad y con arreglo à las leyes que rigen en la materia, todas las tierras incultas que no se hallen cedidas en la Florida, comprendidas entre el rio Perdido al occidente del Golfo de Mexico, y los rios Amaruja y el Sⁿ Juan, desde Popa hasta su desague en el Mar por la parte de Oriente, por el Norte la linea de demarcacion con los Estados Unidos, y al Sur por el Golfo de Mexico, incluyendo las Yslas desiertas en la costa. Por tanto, à V. M. rendidamente suplica, que en atencion a lo expuesto, y a las includables ventajas que resultan à la Nacion, se sirva acceder à esta solicitud, y mandar al mismo tiempo se comuniquen las correspondientes ordenes a las Autoridades del Pays, prebiniendoles presten al exponente todos los auxilios y proteccion necesaria, asi para la designacion de los terrenos, como para llevar à efecto la empresa en todas sus partes: gracia que espera de la Munificencia de V. M.—Enterado del contenido de esta exposicion, y atendiendo al distinguido merito de este sugeto, y à su acreditado celo por mi real servicio, como tambien a las ventajas que resultaràn al Estado del aumento de poblacion de los citados paises que pretende, he tenido à bien acceder à la gracia que solicita en cuanto no se oponga à las leyes de esos mis reynos, y comunicarlo al mi consejo de Indias para su execucion en Real orden de diez y siete de Diciembre del referido año. En su consecuencia os mando y encargo por esta mi Real Cedula, que con arreglo à las leyes que rigen en la materia

interest, and consequently that of the state. Relying on the merits of the case and the lively interest felt by Your Majesty in the national prosperity, and in the services and sacrifices of Your Majesty's memorialist, he humbly requests Your Majesty that, taking them into consideration, you would be graciously pleased to grant and cede to him, in full right and property, and the mode and manner required by law, all the waste lands, not heretofore ceded in Florida, lying between the River Perdido, westward of the Gulf of Mexico, and the Rivers Amaruja and Saint Johns, from Popa to the point where it empties into the ocean, for the eastern limit; and, for the northern, the boundary line of the United States; and, to the south, by the Gulf of Mexico, including the desert islands on the coast. He therefore humbly prays, in consideration of the premises and the unquestionable advantages to be derived by the Nation, Your Majesty will be pleased to grant this his petition, and, thereupon, direct the necessary orders to be given to the local authorities to afford him all due aid and protection, as well in designating the territory referred to as in giving full effect to the whole enterprise. All which he hopes from the munificence of Your Majesty.'

"Having taken the premises into consideration and bearing in mind the distinguished merits of the memorialist and his signal zeal for My royal service, as well as the benefits to be derived by the state from an increase of population in the countries the cession whereof he has solicited, I have

auxilieis eficazmente la execucion de la espresada gracia, tomando todas las disposiciones que se dirijan à su debido efecto, sin perjuicio de tercero, y para que el espresado Conde de Puñonrostro pueda desde luego poner en execucion su designio, conforme en todo con mis beneficos deseos, en obsequio de la agricultura y comercio de dichas posesiones que claman por una poblacion proporcionada à la feracidad de su suelo, y à la defensa y seguridad de las costas; dando cuenta succesivamente de su progreso: que asi es mi voluntad, y que de esta cedula se tome razon en la Contaduria general de Indias. Fecha en Palacio à seis de Febrero de mil ochocientos diez y ocho.

judged fit to grant him the same, in so far as is conformable to the laws of these My Kingdoms, and to make it known to My Council of the Indies, for its due execution, by a royal order of the seventeenth of December in the year aforementioned. Wherefore I charge and command you, by this My royal *cédula*, with due observance of the laws to such cases pertaining, to give full and due effect to the said cession, taking all requisite measures for its accomplishment, without injury to any third party, and to the end that the said Count of Puñonrostro may forthwith carry his plans into execution, in conformity with My beneficent desires in favor of the agriculture and commerce of the said territories, which require a population proportioned to the fertility of the soil and the defense and security of the coasts, he giving regular accounts of his proceedings, for such is My will, and that due note be taken of the present *cédula* in the office of the Accountant General of the Indies.

"Dated at the Palace the sixth of February, one thousand eight hundred and eighteen.

Yo el Rey.
Por mandado del Rey nuestro Señor.
Estevan Varea."

"I, the King.
"By command of the King our Lord,
"Estevan Varea."

Y para que conste firmo esta Certificacion en Madrid à quince de Octubre de mil ochocientos y veinte.
(L.S.) (Sig.)
Antonio Porcel

And I confirm this exemplification at Madrid the fifteenth of October, one thousand eight hundred and twenty.
[Seal] (Signed)
Antonio Porcel

Don Evaristo Perez de Castro, Caballero de número de la órden de Carlos 3º del consejo de Estado

Don Evaristo Perez de Castro, Knight of the Order of Charles the Third, of the Council of State,

y Secretario del Despacho de Estado &ᵍ

Certifico que la firma que antecede del Exᵐᵒ Sᵒʳ Dⁿ Antonio Porcel, Secretario del Despacho de la Gobernacion de Ultramar, es la que acostumbra poner en todos sus escritos. Y para los efectos convenientes doy el presente certificado, firmado de mi mano y sellado con el escudo de mis armas en Madrid à veinte y uno de Octubre de mil ochocientos y veinte.

  (L.S.) (Sig.)
Evaristo Perez de Castro.

and Secretary of Despatch of State, etc.

I certify that the foregoing signature of His Excellency Don Antonio Porcel, Secretary of Despatch of the Ultramarine Government, is that which he is accustomed to put to all his writings. And, for the proper purposes, I give the present certificate, signed by my hand and sealed with my seal of arms at Madrid the twenty-first of October, one thousand eight hundred and twenty.

  [Seal] (Signed)
Evaristo Perez de Castro.

Dⁿ Antonio Porcel, Caballero pensionista de la real y distinguida Orden de Carlos tercero del Consejo de Estado y Secretario de Estado y del Despacho de la Gobernacion de Ultramar, &ᵍ

Certifico que con fecha de nueve de Abril de mil ochocientos diez y ocho, se espidieron por el extinguido Consejo de las Indias reales cedulas de igual tenor al Gobernador Capitan General de la Ysla de Cuba y su distrito, al Intendente de exercito y real hacienda de la Habana y su distrito, y al Gobernador de las Floridas, para que cada uno en la parte que le tocase dispusiera lo conveniente à que tubiese efecto la gracia concedida à Dⁿ Pedro de Vargas, de varios terrenos situados en las Floridas; cuyo contenido es el siguiente.

    "El Rey.

Mi Gobernador y Capitan General de la Ysla de Cuba y su distrito. Con fecha de veinte y

Don Antonio Porcel, Knight Pensioner of the Royal and Distinguished Order of Charles the Third, of the Council of State, and Secretary of State and of Despatch of the Ultramarine Government, etc.

I certify that under date of the ninth of April, one thousand eight hundred and eighteen, royal letters patent of the same tenor were sent by the late Council of the Indies to the Governor Captain General of the island of Cuba and its dependencies, to the Intendant of the Army and Royal Business of the Habana and its district, and to the Governor of the Floridas, that each should do his utmost, in his particular department, to give effect to the grant made to Don Pedro de Vargas of various lands situated in the Floridas, of the following tenor:

    "The King

"My Governor and Captain General of the island of Cuba and its dependencies: Under date

cinco de Enero ultimo, me hizo presente Dⁿ Pedro Vargas lo que sigue—Señor—Dⁿ Pedro de Vargas Caballero de la real Orden militar de Alcantara, tesorero general de la real casa y Patrimonio de V. M. con el mas profundo respeto a V. R. M. espone Que hay una porcion de tierras vacantes y despobladas en el territorio de las Floridas y deseando que si V. M. se digna premiar sus tales cuales servicios y las pruebas de lealtad que le tiene dadas, sea sin el mas minimo grabamen del Erario, ni perjuicio de tercero como puede en el dia verificarse con algunas tierras de aquel pais à V. M. suplica que por un efecto de su soberana piedad se digne concederle la propiedad del terreno que esta comprehendida en la siguiente demarcacion a saver. Desde la embocadura del rio Perdido y de su bahia en el Golfo de Mexico siguiendo la costa del mar, subir por la bahia del Buen Socorro, y de la Mobila, continuar por el Rio de Mobila hasta tocar la linea norte de los Estados Unidos y baxar por ella con una recta al origen del Rio Perdido y siguiendo por el Rio de la Mobila abaxo y la bahia de su nombre volver por la costa del Mar acia el Oeste con todas las calas entradas é Yslas adyacentes que pertenecen à la España en la epoca presente hasta llegar à la linea del Oeste de los Estados Unidos y volver por la del Norte comprehendiendo todas las tierras baldias que corresponden ò puedan corresponder à la España y están en disputa ò reclamacion con los Estados Unidos, segun el tenor de los tratados, y asimismo el terreno baldio y no cedido à otro particu-

of the twenty-fifth of January last Don Pedro de Vargas manifested to Me as follows: 'Sire: Don Pedro de Vargas, Knight of the Royal Military Order of Alcantara, Treasurer General of the Royal House and Patrimony of Your Majesty, with the most profound respect, at your royal feet, exposes that there is a quantity of vacant and unpeopled land in the territory of the Floridas, and desiring that, if Your Majesty shall deign to reward his passable services and the proofs which he has given of his loyalty, it may be without the least burden on the public treasury, or in prejudice of any third person, as may be done at present by some lands of that country, he beseeches Your Majesty that, by an effect of your sovereign goodness, you would deign to grant him the property of the land which lies comprised within the following limits: that is to say, from the mouth of the River Perdido and its bay in the Gulf of Mexico, following the seacoast, to ascend by the Bay of Buen Socorro and of Mobile, continuing by the River Mobile till it touches the northern line of the United States, and descending by that in a right line to the source of the River Perdido, and following the River Mobile in its lower part and the bay of that name, returns by the seacoast towards the west, comprehending all the creeks, entries, and islands adjacent, which may belong to Spain at the present time, till it reaches the west line of the United States, then, returning by their northern line, comprehending all the waste lands

lar que hay entre el Rio Hijuelos
en la Florida Oriental y el Rio
Santa Lucia tirando una linea *desde
el nacimiento del uno al del otro y
siguiendo por la costa del Golfo de
Mexico* desde la embocadura del
Rio Hijuelos, hasta la punta de tancha, y doblando esta por la costa
del Golfo de Florida hasta la
embocadura del Rio Santa Lucia
con las Yslas y cayos adyacentes."

Enterado del contenido de esta
esposicion, y atendiendo al merito
de este sugeto y à su acreditado
celo por mi real servicio; como
tambien à las ventajas que re-
sultarán al Estado de la poblacion
de los citados paises, he tenido
à bien acceder à la gracia que
solicita, en cuanto no se oponga à
las leyes de esos mis reinos, y
comunicarlo al mi Consejo de las
Indias para su cumplimiento en
real orden de dos de Febrero proximo pasado. En su consequencia
os mando y encargo por esta mi
real Cedula, que con arreglo a las
Leyes que rigen en la materia y
sin perjuicio de tercero auxilieis eficazmente la execucion de
la expresada gracia, tomando
todas las disposiciones que se
dirigan à su debido efecto, como
tambien al aumento de poblacion, agricultura y comercio de
las referidas posesiones; dando
cuenta succesivamente de su progreso: que asi es mi voluntad, y
que de esta Cedula se tome razon
en la Contaduria general de

which belong, or may belong, to
Spain, and are in dispute or
reclamation with the United
States, according to the tenor of
the treaties, and, also, all the
waste land not ceded to any
other individual, which is between the River Hijuelos, in
East Florida, and the River
Saint Lucia, drawing a line *from
the source of one river to the source
of the other, and following by the
coast of the Gulf of Mexico*, from
the mouth of the Hijuelos to the
point of Tancha, and doubling
this, by the coast of the Gulf of
Florida, to the mouth of the
River Saint Lucia, with the
islands and keys adjacent.'

"Considering the contents of this
exposition and attending to the
merit of the individual and his
accredited zeal for My royal service, as also to the advantages to
result to the state from peopling
the said countries, I have thought
proper to accede to the favor
which he solicits, in as far as it
be not opposed to the laws of
these My Kingdoms, and communicated it to my Council of
the Indies, for its accomplishment, in a royal order of the
second of February last. Consequently I command and charge
you, by this My royal *cédula*,
that, conforming to the laws
which regulate in these affairs,
and without prejudice to third
persons, that you efficaciously aid
the execution of the said grant,
taking all the measures which
may conduce to its due effect,
as also to the augmentation of
the population, agriculture, and
commerce of the aforesaid possessions, giving account, from time
to time, of the progress made, for

Indias. Fecha en Palacio à nueve de Abril de mil ochocientos diez y ocho.

this is My will, and that due notice shall be taken of this *cédula* in the office of the Accountant General of the Indies.

"Dated at the Palace the ninth of April, one thousand eight hundred and eighteen.

Yo EL REY.
Por mandado del Rey nuestro Señor.
ESTEVAN VAREA."

"I, THE KING.
"By command of the King our Lord,
"ESTEVAN VAREA."

Y para que conste firmo esta Certificacion en Madrid à quince de Octubre de mil ochocientos y veinte.
(L. S.) (Sig.)
ANTONIO PORCEL

I confirm this exemplification at Madrid the fifteenth of October, one thousand eight hundred and twenty.
[Seal] (Signed)
ANTONIO PORCEL

Don Evaristo Perez de Castro, Caballero de número de la órden de Carlos 3º del Consejo de Estado y Secretario del Despacho de Estado, &ᶜ

Certifico que la firma que antecede del Exᵐᵒ Sᵒ.ʳ Dⁿ Antonio Porcel, Secretario del Despacho de la Gobernacion de Ultramar, es la que acostumbra poner en todos sus ascritos. Y para los efectos convenientes doy el presente certificado, firmado de mi mano y sellado con el escudo de mis armas en Madrid à veinte y uno de Octubre de mil ochocientos y veinte.
(L. S.) (Sig.)
EVARISTO PEREZ DE CASTRO

Don Evaristo Perez de Castro, Knight of the Order of Charles the Third, of the Council of State, and Secretary of Despatch of State, etc.

I certify that the foregoing signature of His Excellency Don Antonio Porcel, Secretary of Despatch of the Ultramarine Government, is that which he is accustomed to put to all his writings. And, for the proper purposes, I give the present certificate, signed by my hand and sealed with my seal of arms at Madrid the twenty-first of October, one thousand eight hundred and twenty.
[Seal] (Signed)
EVARISTO PEREZ DE CASTRO

NOTES

In the diary of John Quincy Adams for February 22, 1819, is the following account of the signature of this treaty (Memoirs of John Quincy Adams, IV, 273–74):

Mr. Onis [the Spanish Minister] came at eleven, with Mr. Stoughton, one of the persons attached to his Legation. The two copies of the treaty made out at his house were ready; none of ours were entirely finished. We exchanged the original full powers on both sides, which I believe to be the correct course on

the conclusion of treaties, though at Ghent, and on the conclusion of the Convention of 3d July, 1815, the originals were only exhibited and copies exchanged. I had one of the copies of the treaty, and Mr. Onis the other. I read the English side, which he collated, and he the Spanish side, which I collated. We then signed and sealed both copies on both sides—I first on the English and he first on the Spanish side. Some few errors of copying, and even of translation, were discovered and rectified. It was agreed that the four other copies should be executed in two or three days, as soon as they are all prepared. Mr. Onis took with him his executed copy of the treaty, and I went over with ours to the President's. The message and documents to be sent with it to the Senate were all prepared, but the President's brother and private Secretary, Joseph Jones Monroe, was gone to the Capitol with another message to Congress, and Mr. Gouverneur, Mrs. Monroe's nephew, who also resides at the President's and acts occasionally as his secretary, was likewise abroad. The President requested me to ask Mr. D. Brent to take the message with the treaty to the Senate, which he did. As I was going home from my office I met Mr. Fromentin, a Senator from Louisiana, and asked him if the treaty had been received by the Senate. He said it had—was read, and, as far as he could judge, had been received with universal satisfaction.

The record of the execution of the other four originals on February 25 is thus given (*ibid.*, 278):

Mr. Onis came, with Mr. Stoughton, and we executed the four remaining copies of the treaty, after carefully reading and collating them with our copy already executed. Onis took two of the copies now signed and sealed, and two of them remain at the office. The treaty was sent this day by message to Congress.

Thus six originals of the treaty were executed. Three of them are now in the treaty file; they differ very slightly *inter se* in matters of capitalization, in style of punctuation and writing, and in spelling; there are also something like eighty instances in which the use of commas varies in one of the originals as compared with one or both of the others; but none of these differences appears to be in any way material. The only difference in wording that has been noticed is in Article 13, where one original has "claim them" instead of "claimed them." That original which is endorsed in pencil, "Imperfect (see p. 11)," appears to be complete and perfect, except that a piece of paper, upon which is written the last paragraph of Article 9 and the whole of Article 10 in the same handwriting as the rest of the document, has been pasted on "page 11."

In this treaty, as will be seen from the printed texts, the principle of the *alternat* was carefully observed. In each of the three originals which are in the treaty file, the English text is on the left-hand pages, the United States is named first therein throughout, and the signature of John Quincy Adams is above that of Luis de Onis; in the Spanish text His Catholic Majesty is named first throughout and the order of the signatures is reversed.

Regarding the observance of the *alternat* in general on the part of the United States, John Quincy Adams wrote as follows in his instructions of March 8, 1819, to John Forsyth, Minister to Spain (D. S., 8 Instructions, U. S. Ministers, 304–5; American State Papers, Foreign Relations, IV, 650–51):

On exchanging the ratifications certificates of the fact, will be mutually executed, by you and the Spanish Minister with whom you will make the exchange. Copies of that which passed in both languages on the exchange of the ratifications of the Convention of 11ᵗʰ August 1802. are now furnished you and will serve as forms to be used in the performance of this ceremony. On this occasion, as upon all others, in which you may have occasion to execute any document, joint or reciprocal, with a foreign Minister of State, you will be careful to preserve the right of the United States to the *alternative* of being first named, and your own right, as their Representative to sign first in the papers executed, while, in the counterparts, the other contracting party will be named first, and the foreign Minister will first sign and seal. A rigid adherence to this practice has become necessary, because it is strictly adhered to by all the European Sovereigns, in their compacts with one another and because the United States having heretofore sometimes forborne to claim this conventional indication of equal dignity, some appearance of a disposition to alledge the precedent against them, as affecting their right to it, was manifested by the British Plenipotentiaries on executing the Convention of 3ᵈ July 1815. and by Mʳ de Onis at the drawing up and signing of this Treaty. The scruple was however in both cases abandoned and the right of the United States to the alternative was conceded. It is not expected that it will hereafter be questioned, and you will consider it as a standing instruction to abide by it, in the execution of any instrument of Compact which, as a public Minister of the United States you may be called to sign.

The texts here printed have been collated with that original which is bound with a buff ribbon and which bears the following endorsement in pencil on the front cover: "Original Treaty with Spain, 22. Feb. 1819   Florida Treaty."

Following the treaty texts the Spanish instrument of ratification is printed as being part of the agreement. Its text has been collated with the original document in the Department of State file; the English translation of it is from the original proclamation, but the style of capitalization, punctuation, etc., has been revised as in other translations printed in this edition.

It appears that the first ratification by President Monroe—that dated February 25, 1819—was executed at least in duplicate (D. S., 8 Instructions, U. S. Ministers, 314–15, March 26, 1819). On October 10, 1819, John Forsyth, Minister to Spain, wrote from Madrid that he was sending back "one of the ratified copies of the Convention" (D. S., 17 Despatches, Spain, No. 7). It is doubtless that same original ratification, in a velvet cover, which is now in the file. It lacks the Great Seal, which was, it may be supposed, originally enclosed in a box "of silver, richly gilt, with the American Eagle in raised work upon the lid," according to the early custom (D. S., 1 Special Missions, 122).

While there is no duplicate of the second United States instrument of ratification—that of February 22, 1821—in the file, its final clauses are recited in the proclamation.

The Spanish instrument of ratification recites both texts of the treaty, the Spanish on the left pages and the English on the right. With it are three originals of the certificate of exchange of ratifications on February 22, 1821, two in Spanish and one in English.

The recitals of the proclamation, the original of which is in the file, are elaborate; they include not only the text of the treaty in English and Spanish, but also the Spanish instrument of ratification with an

English translation thereof, the Senate resolution of February 19, 1821, and the concluding clauses of the United States instrument of ratification of February 22, 1821. The proclamation is printed in American State Papers, Foreign Relations, V, 127–33; it is also printed below.

The file also contains an attested copy of each of the Senate resolutions, which are dated February 24, 1819, and February 19, 1821, respectively (Executive Journal, III, 178, 244).

The three originals of this treaty in the file, the original of the first United States instrument of ratification, and the original proclamation, all have the word *original* written at the head of each text of the treaty; but that word does not appear above either text of the Spanish instrument of ratification.

The Full Powers

One other document in the treaty file is a copy of the full power granted to John Quincy Adams under date of February 16, 1819, to "meet and confer" with the Envoy of His Catholic Majesty of and concerning the matters specified and "to conclude a Treaty touching the premises." The copy is headed in a different hand, which appears to be that of John Quincy Adams, "Full Power of the President of the United States, to the Secretary of State." The text of that copy of the full power follows:

James Monroe, President of the United States of America

To all whom these presents shall concern, Greeting:

Know Ye, that I have given and granted, and do hereby give and grant to John Quincy Adams, Secretary of State of the United States, full power and authority, and also general and special command to meet and confer with the Envoy Extraordinary and Minister Plenipotentiary of His Catholic Majesty residing in the United States, being furnished with the like full powers, of and concerning the limits between the Territories of the United States, and those of his said Catholic Majesty in North America, and any mutual cessions of part of the same; of and concerning all matters of difference between the said United States and His Catholic Majesty, and concerning the relations of Navigation & Commerce between the said United States, and His Catholic Majesty; and to conclude a Treaty touching the premises for the final ratification of the President of the United States, by and with the Advice and Consent of the Senate thereof, if such advice and consent be given.

In Testimony whereof I have caused the seal of the United States to be hereunto affixed.

Given under my hand at the City of Washington the sixteenth day (L S) of February A. D. 1819, and of the Independence of the United States the Forty third.

(Signed)   JAMES MONROE.

By the President
(Signed)   JOHN QUINCY ADAMS
Secy of State.

It is to be observed that the foregoing full power contains not even a conditional promise of ratification.

In the later diplomatic exchanges regarding the fact that the treaty was not ratified on the part of Spain within the time limited,

very decided language was used concerning the duty of ratification by the Spanish Government in view of the wording of the full power given to Don Luis de Onis.

A copy of that full power, which is dated September 10, 1816, was transmitted to Secretary of State Adams on February 17, 1819 (D. S., 5 Notes from the Spanish Legation), following the communication to the Spanish Envoy of the full power of Adams on the same day (D. S., 2 Notes to Foreign Legations, 363). The original Spanish full power is also in D. S., 5 Notes from the Spanish Legation, with a translation thereof as follows:

Don Ferdinand, by the Grace of God King, etc., etc., desiring to consolidate the friendship and good understanding which happily prevails between My Kingdoms and the United States of America through the mutual interests existing between the two Governments, and reposing full confidence in you, Don Luis de Onis, Knight of the royal and distinguished Order of Charles the Third and My Minister Plenipotentiary to the United States of America, by reason of your fidelity, distinguished zeal, and approved capacity in the arduous concerns committed to you, have granted and by these presents do grant to you full power, in the most ample form, to treat, of yourself and without other intermediate authority, with such person or persons as may be authorized by the President of the United States, and, on the principles of the most perfect equality and fitness, to conclude and sign a treaty of amity, whereby past differences may be adjusted and a firm and lasting peace established between the two Governments— obliging ourselves, as we do hereby oblige ourselves and promise, on the faith and word of a King, to approve, ratify, and fulfil, and to cause to be inviolably observed and fulfilled, whatsoever may be stipulated and signed by you, to which intent and purpose I grant you all authority and full power, in the most ample form, thereby and of right required.

In faith whereof We have given command to issue the present, signed with Our royal hand, sealed with Our privy seal, and countersigned by Our underwritten First Secretary of State and of Universal Despatch.

Given at Madrid the tenth day of September, one thousand eight hundred and sixteen.

[Seal] FERDINAND

PEDRO CEVALLOS

In instructions to Forsyth of August 18, 1819 (D. S., 8 Instructions, U. S. Ministers, 343–48; American State Papers, Foreign Relations, IV, 657–58), the substance of which was repeated in the American note dated at Madrid October 2, 1819 (D. S., 17 Despatches, Spain, No. 7, enclosure 9 with Forsyth's despatch of October 10, 1819; American State Papers, Foreign Relations, IV, 662–63), Secretary of State John Quincy Adams wrote as follows:

The only reason assigned by the Minister of State ad interim for the postponement of the Spanish ratification, was the determination of the King, founded upon the great importance of the Treaty, to act upon it with full deliberation. this may have been sufficient to justify delay within the period stipulated by the Treaty, but after the expiration of that period, can no longer be alledged. Delay beyond that period will be a breach of faith; for the Treaty in all its parts, became from the moment of its signature by Mᵏ Onis and the ratifications of the United States, as binding upon the honour and good faith of the Spanish King and nation, as it would be after the ratification. It is scarcely supposable that Spain will contest this position, or that it should be necessary to present it to her view, in the following terms of the full power of Mᵏ Onis, the original of which, signed by the King of Spain, was delivered to me before the signature of the Treaty. The words of His Catholic Majesty are, after authorizing Mᵏ Onis to treat,

negotiate and conclude a Treaty, whereby past differences may be adjusted; and a firm and lasting peace established between the two Governments—"Obliging "ourselves, as we do hereby oblige ourselves, and promise on the faith and words "of a King, to approve, ratify and fulfill and to cause to be inviolably observed "and fulfilled; *whatsoever may be stipulated and signed by you,* to which intent and "purpose I grant you all authority and full power in the most ample form thereby "as of right required ("oligandonos y prometemos en fe y palabra de Rey que "aprobaremos ratificaremos, Compliremos, y haremos observar y Cumplir "inviolablemente quanto por vos fuere estipulado y firmado paro lo qual os "concedo todas las facultades y plenos poderes en la forma mas amplia que de "derecho se requieren.") If language so explicit and Unqualified were, in regard to its import, susceptible of any doubt founded on the usage which requires the ratification of the Sovereign for the full Consummation of a Treaty, there is nothing dubious or uncertain in the extent of the obligation resting upon him by the signature of his Minister vested with such a full power. . . .

The obligation of the King of Spain therefore in honour and in justice to ratify the Treaty signed by his Minister is a perfect and unqualified as his royal promise in the power, and it gives to the United States, the right equally perfect to compel the performance of that promise.

Should it be suggested that the United States themselves have on more than one occasion withheld or annexed Conditions to the ratification of Treaties, signed by their Plenipotentiaries in Europe, it will readily occur to you that by the nature of our Constitution, the full powers of our Ministers never are, or can be unlimited. That whatever they conclude, must be and by the other Contracting power is always known and understood to be subject to the deliberation and determination of the Senate, to whose consideration it must be submitted before its ratification. That our full powers never contain the solemn promise of the nation to ratify whatever the Minister shall Conclude, but reserve expressly not only the usual right of ratification, but the Constitutional privilege of the Senate, to give or withhold their assent to the ratification, without which Assent by a majority of two thirds of the Members present at the Vote taken after Consideration of the Treaty, the President has no Authority to ratify. In withholding, or refusing the ratification, therefore no promise or engagement of the State is violated. But neither the same reason, nor the same principle applies to the King of Spain, who possesses the sole, entire and exclusive power of ratifying Treaties made by his Ministers, and therefore by the promise on the faith and word of a King to ratify whatever a Minister shall sign, commits his own honour, and that of the nation to the fulfilment of his promise. This distinction is well known and clearly recognized by the Law of nations. The Spanish Government cannot alledge either that Mr Onis transcended his secret instructions, or that the ratification of the United States has been refused, or that any unfair advantage was taken on the part of the United States in the negotiation, or that Spain was not fully aware beforehand of the full extent of the engagements Contracted by Mr Onis. It is too well known and they will not dare to deny it, that Mr Onis' last instructions authorized him to concede much more than he did. That these instructions had been prepared by Mr Pizarro; that after the appointment of the Marquis de Casa-Yrujo to the Ministry, they were by him submitted to the Kings Council and with their full sanction were transmitted to Mr Onis; that both in relation to the grants of land in Florida, and to the Western boundary, the terms which he obtained were far within the limits of his Instructions.

Some months later, moreover, a letter written by Adams to the Chairman of the Senate Committee on Foreign Relations (William Lowndes), gave the following opinion (American State Papers, Foreign Relations, IV, 673–74):

With reference to the question proposed by the committee, "whether the Executive considers the Florida treaty as a subsisting one, valid according to national law, and giving the same perfect rights, and imposing the same perfect obligations, as if it had been ratified," I have the honor to state that the President considers the treaty of 22d February last as obligatory upon the honor and good

faith of Spain, not as a perfect treaty, (ratification being an essential formality to that,) but as a compact which Spain was bound to ratify; as an adjustment of the differences between the two nations, which the King of Spain, by his full power to his minister, had solemnly promised to *approve, ratify,* and *fulfil.* This adjustment is assumed as the measure of what the United States had a right to obtain from Spain, from the signature of the treaty. The principle may be illustrated by reference to rules of municipal law relative to transactions between individuals. The difference between the treaty unratified and ratified may be likened to the difference between a covenant to convey lands and the deed of conveyance itself. Upon a breach of the covenant to convey, courts of equity decree that the party who has broken his covenant shall convey, and, further, shall make good to the other party all damages which he has sustained by the breach of contract.

As there is no court of chancery between nations, their differences can be settled only by agreement or by force. The resort to force is justifiable only when justice cannot be obtained by negotiation; and the resort to force is limited to the attainment of justice. The wrong received marks the boundaries of the right to be obtained.

The King of Spain was bound to ratify the treaty; bound by the principles of the law of nations applicable to the case; and further bound by the solemn promise in the full power. He refusing to perform this promise and obligation, the United States have a perfect right to do what a court of chancery would do in a transaction of a similar character between individuals, namely, to compel the performance of the engagement as far as compulsion can accomplish it, and to indemnify themselves for all the damages and charges incident to the necessity of using compulsion. They cannot compel the King of Spain to sign the act of ratification, and, therefore, cannot make the instrument a perfect treaty; but they can, and are justifiable in so doing, take that which the treaty, if perfect, would have bound Spain to deliver up to them; and they are further entitled to indemnity for all the expenses and damages which they may sustain by consequence of the refusal of Spain to ratify. The refusal to ratify gives them the same right to do justice to themselves as the refusal to fulfil would have given them if Spain had ratified, and then ordered the Governor of Florida not to deliver over the province.

By considering the treaty as the term beyond which the United States will not look back in their controversial relations with Spain, they not only will manifest a continued respect for the sanctity of their own engagements, but they avoid the inconvenience of re-entering upon a field of mutual complaint and crimination so extensive that it would be scarcely possible to decide where or when negotiation should cease, or at what point force should be stayed for satisfied right; and by resorting to force only so far as the treaty had acknowledged their right, they offer an inducement to Spain to complete the transaction on her part, without proceeding to general hostility. But Spain must be responsible to the United States for every wrong done by her after the signature of the treaty by her minister; and the refusal to ratify his act is the first wrong for which they are entitled to redress.

According to those views, the rights and duties of the two parties, owing to the differing wording of the respective full powers, were not, from the date of signature of the treaty, equal or the same; the Government of Spain was under an obligation, not perhaps strictly a legal obligation but one very close thereto, to ratify; but the Government of the United States might withhold ratification at its pleasure.

In the instructions of August 18, 1819, as well as in the extremely interesting extract from the diary of John Quincy Adams of February 22, 1819, above quoted, it is said that in this case the original full powers were exchanged. Adams believed that to be the correct practice, although he cites instances when "the originals were only exhibited and copies exchanged," a course which at the time was

more usual (Bittner, Die Lehre von den völkerrechtlichen Vertrags-urkunden, 143) and one which is now frequently, though by no means always, followed.

The Floridas

By Article 16 of this treaty it was provided that the exchange of ratifications should take place by August 22, 1819, six months from the date of signature. The place of exchange was not stated.

Not until exactly two years from the signature of the treaty did the exchange of ratifications take place at Washington on February 22, 1821.

The delay in the exchange of ratifications and the form of the Spanish instrument of ratification of October 24, 1820 (printed above after the treaty texts), have a common explanation.

While there were earlier discussions at both Capitals, the negotiations which resulted in this treaty began in the latter part of 1817 and were conducted at Washington by Secretary of State John Quincy Adams for the United States and by Don Luis de Onis for Spain; and toward their close the French Minister at Washington, G. Hyde de Neuville, was an active and friendly intermediary. The voluminous correspondence and other papers submitted to the Senate with the treaty on February 22, 1819, are in American State Papers, Foreign Relations, IV, 422–626.

If any treaty were to result, a relinquishment by Spain of all claim to the Floridas was essential. The other major questions were the boundary of the Louisiana territory and the monetary claims of the United States for its citizens. While the representative of Spain talked of an impossible alliance and sought vainly to obtain some form of restraining declaration or promise by the United States in regard to her future attitude toward the Spanish possessions in South America, no such promise could possibly be made by this Government, which was already considering recognition of the rule at Buenos Aires, where independence had been declared on July 9, 1816.

The proposals and discussions regarding the boundary of the Louisiana territory are fully treated, with valuable maps, in Marshall, A History of the Western Boundary of the Louisiana Purchase, 1819–1841, 46–70.

To the United States, relinquishment by Spain of the Floridas meant the cession of East Florida and of that portion of West Florida east of the River Perdido; for since 1803 this Government had consistently maintained that the cession of Louisiana in that year included, east of the Mississippi, not only the then island of New Orleans, but all the remaining territory south of 31° north latitude as far east as the River Perdido, the western boundary of the State of Florida today; and, accordingly, the United States held that American territory extended eastward from the Mississippi to the Perdido.

Something should be said as to the geography of the Floridas, for there has been misapprehension on the point. The division of the region into two provinces by the British Government is discussed in

the Mississippi Valley Historical Review for December, 1917 (Carter, "The Beginnings of British West Florida").

By Article 2 of the treaty of 1795 with Spain (Document 18) the north line "of the two Floridas" had been fixed; from the Mississippi at 31° north latitude it ran due east to the Chattahoochee, thence along that river to its junction with the Flint, thence straight to the head of St. Marys River, and down that river to the Atlantic Ocean. The territories south of that line and east of the Mississippi (excluding the then island of New Orleans) were the Floridas; the dividing line between East Florida and West Florida was the Apalachicola or Chattahoochee (the river intersected by the parallel of 31° is now known as the Chattahoochee, and the name Apalachicola now applies only to that portion of the stream below the junction of the Chattahoochee and the Flint).

The State of Florida now includes all of East Florida and also that part of West Florida which extends from the Apalachicola and the Chattahoochee west to the Perdido; it is the Perdido River which is now the western boundary of the State of Florida.

The United States never claimed *all* of West Florida under the cession of Louisiana; but it did claim thereunder all of West Florida west of the Perdido. In other words, what the United States claimed of West Florida was that region from 31° north latitude south, which now forms part of three States—that part of Louisiana which is east of the Mississippi and north of the Iberville and Lake Pontchartrain, and those parts of Alabama and Mississippi which extend from the Louisiana line on the west (the Pearl River) to the Florida line (the River Perdido) on the east and which have the Gulf of Mexico on the south.

Spain had contested the American position from the very beginning. Diplomatic relations between the two countries had been suspended from 1808 to 1815; but the dispute was in fact ended before the negotiations for this treaty began. The control and jurisdiction of the United States were complete throughout West Florida west of the Perdido; the western portion of that region was added to the State of Louisiana by the act of April 14, 1812 (2 Statutes at Large, 708–9); the resolution of December 10, 1817 (3 *ibid.*, 472–73), admitted Mississippi into the Union, with her present territory on the Gulf of Mexico from the Pearl River to the Alabama line; the remainder, the area thence eastwards to the Perdido, formed part of Alabama Territory, destined to be admitted as a State by the resolution of December 14, 1819 (3 *ibid.*, 608). All that the United States could obtain in this regard was a formal recognition by Spain of the accomplished fact.

The claims of American nationals against Spain which were relinquished by Article 9 of the treaty were large; to the extent of five million dollars the United States, by Article 11, agreed to pay them; and a part of the bargain was the cession of the territory from the River Perdido east, including East Florida, with ungranted Crown

lands of enormous extent, which by the cession would pass to the United States. (See the proposal of Adams to Onis of January 16, 1818, American State Papers, Foreign Relations, IV, 463–64.)

During the negotiations it was well known on both sides that three very large grants of lands in the Floridas had been made by the King of Spain during the winter of 1817–18. All the details of those grants were not known in Washington during the negotiation of this treaty, but it was evident that the grants had been sought in anticipation of a probable treaty of cession, that they had been made to favorites of the Spanish Court, and that they were made on no other consideration. Of the three grantees the Duke of Alagon was Captain of the Royal Body Guards, the Count of Puñonrostro was Gentleman of the Bed Chamber, and Don Pedro de Vargas was Treasurer General.

Map of the Floridas

A map of the Floridas, showing their boundaries in relation to the treaty of 1819, is at page 41. The plotting on that map of the three land grants, which are discussed below, is necessarily approximate and partial; and no attempt is made, either in the hachured areas or elsewhere, to indicate the extent of previous grants, which were numerous and some of which were of large area (see generally Charles Vignoles, Observations upon the Floridas, published in 1823, and the map accompanying that work). The Alagon grant was, within its stated limits, of "the uncultivated land (*terreno inculto*) which has not been ceded in East Florida"; the Puñonrostro grant was, within its stated limits, of "all the uncultivated lands (*tierras incultas*) which have not been ceded in Florida." The Vargas grant was the most vague and general of the three; it first covered the region (diagonally hachured on the map) between the Perdido on the east and Mobile Bay and River on the west, then "all the waste lands (*tierras baldias*) which belong, or may belong, to Spain and are in dispute or reclamation with the United States, according to the tenor of the treaties," in the region to the west of that previously described, as far, apparently, as the Mississippi, which seems to be intended by the language "the west line of the United States"; and finally there was included "the waste land (*terreno baldio*) not ceded to any other individual," within limits sufficiently extensive to comprise the region in the southern part of the Florida peninsula (not hachured) which was not within the description of the Alagon grant.

Accordingly, the descriptions of the three grants read together were sufficiently sweeping to cover all ungranted lands throughout the Floridas, East and West, subject, perhaps, to some argument regarding the meaning of the wording generally; and it is to be mentioned that, in the translations of the land grants above printed, the English equivalents of various Spanish expressions are not wholly consistent.

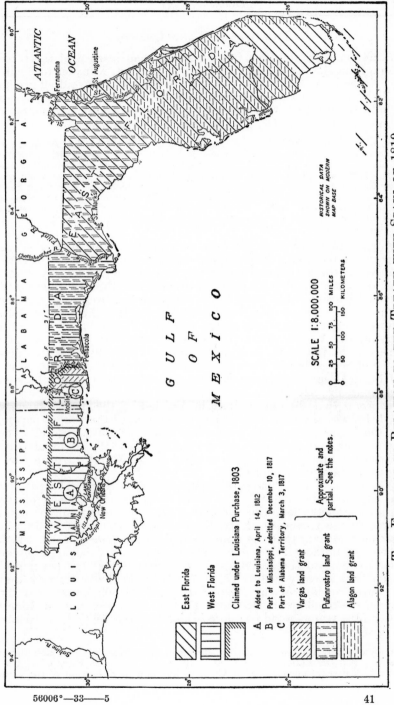

The Floridas in Relation to the Treaty with Spain of 1819

The Spanish Land Grants

Secretary of State John Quincy Adams had learned of the three grants from the despatches of George W. Erving, Minister to Spain. The clause in Article 8 of the treaty making null and void all grants made by the King of Spain since January 24, 1818, was intended to include the Alagon, Puñonrostro, and Vargas grants (Memoirs of John Quincy Adams, IV, 265, February 18, 1819):

> With regard to the article concerning the grants of lands, he claimed an entire confirmation of all grants prior to the 24th of January, 1818, with a formal annulment of those made since then—that is, those made last winter to the Duke of Alagon, Count Puñon Rostro, and Vargas. I told him we could not agree to give, by the treaty, any validity to grants which they would not have without the treaty. They should be as valid to us as they were to the King of Spain, and not more valid. We should not disturb bona fide holders, but it certainly could not be the intention of Spain that the treaty should sanction frauds.

Adams, however, had not been as careful in this matter as its importance required. The despatch of Erving of February 10, 1818, referred to the grants and mentioned two of the grantees by name. The despatch of February 26 mentioned all three grantees and enclosed extracts from the Alagon and Puñonrostro grants showing their extent. The despatch of April 5 was the first that gave specific information regarding any of the essential dates, as it enclosed a copy of the Vargas grant (D. S., 15 Despatches, Spain, No. 64; American State Papers, Foreign Relations, IV, 509–11). With a despatch of September 20 was enclosed a copy of the Puñonrostro grant (D. S., 16 Despatches, Spain, No. 93; American State Papers, Foreign Relations, IV, 524–25).

It seems that the date written in Article 8 of the treaty, January 24, 1818, was accepted after due consideration of the Vargas papers, for the Vargas grant was void under the letter of Article 8. The petition for that grant was dated January 25, 1818, the royal order February 2, and the *real cédula* or royal decree March 10, or, according to the later copy, April 9.

The dates of the Puñonrostro papers were earlier. The petition was of November 3, 1817, the royal order to the Council of the Indies was of the following December 17, and the date of the royal decree to the Governor of the Floridas was February 6, 1818. It may be said here that the dates in the Alagon papers, as to which there was nothing specific in the despatches to Adams, were the same as those of the Puñonrostro grant except that the petition of Alagon was as early as July 12, 1817. It seems the better view that the effective date of the Puñonrostro and Alagon grants was the date of the royal order, December 17, 1817. However, what Adams says on the point should be quoted (Memoirs of John Quincy Adams, IV, 287):

> I immediately hunted up all Mr. Erving's late correspondence, and found the copy and translation of the grant to the Count of Puñon Rostro, being an order to the Governor-General of Cuba to put him in possession of the land.

It is dated 6th February, 1818, which may therefore be considered as the time when the grant was *made;* and so I considered it when we signed the treaty, for I examined this very paper with a view to ascertain its date before signing the treaty. But now, upon a close examination of the paper itself, I found it was not as Mr. Erving described it in his dispatch, a *copy* of the grant, but an order to the Governor to put the grantee in possession, and referring to the grant itself as having been dated, and announced to the Council of the Indies, in December, 1817. In fair construction we have a right to consider the grant as not *made* until this order was issued. Still, if I had critically scanned this paper before signing the treaty, I should not have agreed to the 24th of January, 1818, as the date before which all grants are conditionally confirmed. I should have insisted upon some months earlier.

The Spanish texts and English translations of the three grants are printed above, following the text of the Spanish instrument of ratification, from copies of exemplifications and accompanying translations thereof which are in the archives of the Department of State. It appears that those copies and translations were made in the Department of State in February, 1821, from the original "authentic copies" which were in the possession of Vives, the Spanish Minister at Washington (Memoirs of John Quincy Adams, V, 271). From the dates of the exemplifications, October 15 and 21, 1820, it seems that Vives probably obtained them from Madrid with the Spanish instrument of ratification.

The English translations were published with the proclamation in the press of the period (e.g., Niles' Weekly Register, XX, 39–44, March 17, 1821); the Spanish texts and the translations were printed in Laws of the United States, Bioren & Duane ed., VI, 632–37, in 1822; and they were subsequently copied in Elliot's Diplomatic Code, I, 433–39, and in 8 Statutes at Large, 267–73.

It appears from the exemplifications that following the petition of the grantee a royal order for the grant issued to the Council of the Indies and that this was followed by a royal decree of similar tenor to the Governor and Captain General of the island of Cuba and its dependencies, to the Intendant of the Army and Royal Business of the Habana and its District, and to the Governor of the Floridas. The exemplification in each case includes the text of the royal decree to the Governor and Captain General of the island of Cuba and its dependencies, and in no case is the text of the previous royal order given.

The copies of the Vargas and Puñonrostro grants which were enclosed respectively in the despatches of Erving dated April 5 and September 20, 1818, and which are printed in American State Papers, Foreign Relations, IV, 510–11 and 524–25, are not exemplifications. Their substance, however, is in each case the same as that here printed. They contain certain record notations which these exemplifications do not, and in the Puñonrostro case the address of the letters patent there is to the Governor of the Floridas. There is, however, a discrepancy in a date in respect of the Vargas grant which cannot be explained. As transmitted by Erving in his despatch of April 5, 1818, the date of the royal decree is March 10, 1818. In the exemplification it is April 9, 1818, four days later than the date of Erving's despatch.

Adams was deeply chagrined when he learned of his slip and saw its possible consequences; he wrote in his diary, "Never will this treaty recur to my memory but associated with the remembrance of my own heedlessness. Should it hereafter be, as it probably will, exposed to the world, and incur from my country reproach as bitter as my own, it will be no more than I deserve" (Memoirs of John Quincy Adams, IV, 289).

The bad news about the three grants came soon after the signature of the treaty. Henry Clay, then Speaker of the House of Representatives, informed President Monroe by March 8, 1819, that the three grants were dated January 23, 1818, one day before the date fixed by Article 8 of the treaty (*ibid.*, 287). While Clay's information was inaccurate, his statement was near enough the facts to warrant attention.

In the meantime, on February 24, the Senate had given its advice and consent to the ratification of the treaty, and the instrument of ratification on the part of the United States had been executed on February 25. That ratification was in the usual form and made no reference to the three grants; and the treaty had been communicated to Congress with the presidential message of February 26, 1819 (Richardson, II, 53).

John Forsyth, formerly Chairman of the Committee on Foreign Affairs of the House of Representatives and recently elected Senator from Georgia, had been appointed Minister to Spain; to him had been entrusted the duty of exchanging the ratifications of the treaty at Madrid; his instructions were dated March 8, 1819 (D. S., 8 Instructions, U. S. Ministers, 304–7); and he was to leave Washington on March 10 with the United States ratification (Memoirs of John Quincy Adams, IV, 291). The following is an extract from his instructions:

The Treaty of Amity, Settlement and Limits between the United States and Spain concluded on the 22nd ult° and ratified on the part of the United States, having provided for the adjustment of all the important subjects of difference between the two Nations, the first object of your mission will be to obtain the ratification of the Spanish Government and to receive it in exchange for ours, the authentic instrument of which is committed to your charge. The United States Ship Hornet, Captain Read, is in readiness at Boston and orders have been despatched under which you will take passage in her for Cadiz. It is desirable that you should embark without delay. On your arrival in Spain, The Hornet will remain at Cadiz, subject to your orders, until the Exchange of the ratifications can be effected, and if, as is anticipated, no obstacle should intervene to delay that transaction, you will, upon receiving the Spanish ratified Copy, immediately forward it to Captain Read, with directions to bring it immediately to the United States.

Adams at once took steps to obtain a statement from Onis in the matter of the three grants; to this end he drafted a note to Onis as well as a declaration to be delivered by Forsyth at Madrid upon the exchange of ratifications; and these he submitted to President Monroe, whose views are thus stated by Adams (Memoirs of John Quincy Adams, IV, 290):

The President approved the drafts, but directed me to instruct Mr. Forsyth, if any difficulty should be made by the Spanish Government against receiving the declaration, he should nevertheless exchange the ratifications; for he considered the treaty of such transcendent importance to this country, that if we should not get an inch of land in Florida, the bargain would still be inexpressibly advantageous to us. The removal of all apprehension of a war with Spain, the consolidation of our territorial possessions, the command of the Gulf of Mexico, the recognized extension to the South Sea, and the satisfaction of so large an amount of the claims of our citizens upon Spain, were objects of such paramount consideration, and the attainment of them would raise our standing and character so high in the estimate of the European powers, that the land was of very trifling comparative consequence. Besides, as Onis admits that he signed the treaty with the understanding that the grants were annulled, and De Neuville certifies that such was the mutual understanding, if the fact be that they were made before the 24th day of January, the fraud will be so palpable that when we have got possession of the country we shall have the means of doing ourselves justice in our own hands.

The declaration, as drafted by Adams, was in the following terms (D. S., 8 Instructions, U. S. Ministers, 311; American State Papers, Foreign Relations, IV, 652):

The Undersigned, Minister Plenipotentiary from the United States of America, at the Court of His Catholic Majesty, is commanded by The President of the United States to explain and declare, upon the Exchange of the ratifications of the Treaty of Amity, Settlement and Limits between the United States and His Catholic Majesty, signed by the respective Plenipotentiaries, at Washington, on the twenty second day of February last, that in agreeing upon the 24th day of January 1818, as the date, subsequent to which all grants of land, made by His Catholic Majesty, or by his legitimate authorities in the Floridas, were declared to be null and void, it was with a full and clear understanding between the Plenipotentiaries, of both the high contracting parties, that among the grants thus declared null and void, were all those made or alledged to have been made in the course of the preceding winter, by His Catholic Majesty to the Duke of Alagon, the Count of Punon Rostro and Mr Vargas, and all others derived from them. And the ratifications of the Treaty are exchanged under the explicit declaration and Understanding that all the said grants are null and void and will be so held by the United States.

The note of Adams to Onis, of March 10, 1819, reads as follows (D. S., 2 Notes to Foreign Legations. 363–64; American State Papers, Foreign Relations, IV, 651):

By the 8th Article of the Treaty of Amity, Settlement and Limits signed by us on the 22^d of last month, all grants of land in the Floridas made by His Catholic Majesty or his legitimate authorities in those Provinces subsequent to the 24th of January 1818 are declared to be null and void. This date you will recollect was agreed to on the part of the United States with a full and clear understanding between us that it included the grants alledged to have been made in the course of the preceding Winter by the King to the Duke of Alagon, the Count of Punon Rostro and Mr Vargas. As these grants, however, are known to the Government of the United States only from rumour, without the knowledge of their dates, it is proper that on exchanging the ratifications, your Government should know, that whatever the date of those grants may have been, it was fully understood by us that they are all annulled by the Treaty, as much as if they had been specifically named and that they will be so held by the United States. To avoid any possible misconception your answer to this statement is requested and the exchange of the ratifications will be made under the explicit declaration and understanding that all the abovementioned grants and all others derived from them are null and void.

Onis replied to Adams, under the same date, as follows in translation (D. S., 5 Notes from the Spanish Legation; American State Papers, Foreign Relations, IV, 651–52):

I have received the note you were pleased to address to me, of this day's date, in which you state that by the eighth article of the treaty signed by us on the 22d of last month, it was agreed on the part of the United States that all grants of land in the Floridas made by His Catholic Majesty or his legitimate authorities subsequent to the 24th of January, 1818, are declared to be null and void, with a full understanding that it included the grants alleged to have been made in the course of the preceding winter, by the King, to the Duke of Alagon, the Count of Puñonrostro and Mr. Vargas; and that, therefore, you request of me a declaration that whatever the date of those grants may have been, it was fully understood by us that they are annulled by the treaty, as much as if they had been specifically named.

With the frankness and good faith which have uniformly actuated my conduct and which distinguish the character of the Spanish Nation, I have to declare to you, Sir, that when I proposed the revocation of all the grants made subsequent to the date above mentioned, it was with the full belief that it comprehended those made to the Duke of Alagon, as well as any others which had been stipulated at that period.

But at the same time that I offer you this frank, simple, and ingenuous declaration, I have to express to you that if my conception had been different or if it had appeared to me that any of those grants were prior to the above-mentioned date, I would have insisted upon their recognition, as the honor of the King, my master, and the unquestionable rights of his sovereignty, of his possessions, and the disposal of them, obviously required.

I will hasten to transmit to my Government due information of the whole; and impressed as I am with the conviction of His Majesty's most earnest desire to meet the wishes of the President, I persuade myself that he will with pleasure participate in that sentiment by admitting the explicit declaration which you have requested of me. In the meantime I beg you will favor me with your answer to the explanations I requested yesterday in relation to the late act of Congress concerning piracy.

Adams at once wrote to Forsyth under date of March 10, 1819, sending him copies of the two foregoing notes and of the declaration. His letter follows (D. S., 8 Instructions, U. S. Ministers, 310; American State Papers, Foreign Relations, IV, 652):

By the 8th Article of the Treaty of Amity, settlement and limits between the United States and Spain, signed on the 22nd of last month, all the grants of lands, made by His Catholic Majesty or by his lawful authorities, since the 24th of January 1818, in the territories ceded by His Catholic Majesty to the United States in the Floridas, are declared and agreed to be null and void. This date was proposed by Mr Onis and acceded to, on the part of the United States, with a full and clear understanding on both sides, that the grants made or alledged to have been made in the course of the preceding winter to the Duke of Alagon, the Count of Punon Rostro and Mr Vargas were among those agreed and declared to be null and void. Copies of the grants to the Count of Punon Rostro and to Mr Vargas in the form of orders to the Governor General of the Island of Cuba, and to the Governor of the Floridas had been transmitted to this Department by Mr Erving; the first of which bears date the 6th of February and the second the 10th of March 1818.—but no copy has been received of that to the Duke of Alagon. As, however, the authenticity of these documents might be denied and the grants have never been made public, it is proper that the possibility of any future question with regard to those grants should be guarded against.—for which purpose the form of a declaration is enclosed, which it will be proper for you to deliver on exchanging the ratifications of the treaty, to the Spanish Minister with whom you will make the exchange. The fact of

the mutual understanding that those grants were annulled by the Treaty is fully and explicitly admitted by Mr Onis in his answer, dated this day, to a note from me on this subject, copies of which, with a translation of his answer, are herewith enclosed. It is not anticipated that any objection will be made to receiving the declaration, if, however, there should be, you will, nevertheless, exchange the ratifications; it being sufficient to give the notice and proof of the understanding on both sides of the operation of the article and of the effect which will be given to it on the part of the United States.

Adams also obtained from the French Minister at Washington, G. Hyde de Neuville, a statement on the subject of the grants, under date of March 18, which reads thus in translation (American State Papers, Foreign Relations, IV, 653):

I was very sure, and you were of the same opinion, that to destroy the rumor which had been spread, it would suffice to inform the Minister of Spain of it. The loyalty which characterizes him did not permit the smallest uneasiness on the subject. After the declaration of Mr. Onis, mine can be of no importance; however, as you desire (in case the mistake of date should be real) that the fact resulting from the treaty should be well established, and by all those persons who took part, directly or indirectly, in the transaction, I have the honor, Sir, to declare to you in the most formal manner that it has been understood—always understood by you, by the Minister of Spain, and, I will add, by myself—that the three great grants of land made to the Duke of Alagon, to the Count of Puñonrostro, and to Mr. Vargas, were of the number of those annulled.

The date of 24th January was proposed and accepted in the complete persuasion, on one part and the other, that these three great grants were subsequent to it.

I will add, Sir, because it is the exact and pure truth, that, having been charged by Mr. Onis, during his illness, to discuss with you several articles of the treaty, particularly the eighth article, you consented to the drawing up of this article more in conformity with the desire of the Spanish Minister, only on the admission, as a fact beyond doubt, that the three principal grants were and remained null and as not having taken place. Mr. Onis has not ceased thus to understand it. He has explained himself upon it frankly and loyally as well since as before the treaty. The mistake of date, if it exists, can, then, give birth to no difficulty whatever at Madrid. The good faith of Mr. Onis and that of his Government, are guaranties too strong to render any other explanations necessary. Between Governments, as between individuals, the same laws of honor and probity govern transactions. The convention exists only by the convention; therefore, Sir, in this case the simple statement of the fact will be sufficient to rectify the mistake.

On May 9, 1819, Forsyth reached Madrid. By a note of May 12 he informed the Spanish First Secretary of State of his arrival and, on May 18, of his readiness to exchange the ratifications of the treaty (D. S., 17 Despatches, Spain, No. 3, June 10, 1819).

The treaty had become disliked in official circles in Spain; the influence of the three grantees was one feature against it; and the Spanish Government still vainly hoped for some modification of the American attitude toward independence in South America. On June 13 dismissal from office of the Marquis de Casa Yrujo, who was considered responsible for the treaty, took place.

Perhaps the difficulties might have been surmounted by a less inept negotiator than Forsyth. There was no question of the decided stand of this Government, which insisted on the ratification of the treaty

and considered that its failure would mean a worse bargain for Spain; but Forsyth wrote in language harsh and unworthy and calculated to offend. As early as June 21, when two months still remained of the time limited by the treaty for the exchange of ratifications, Forsyth used such expressions as "bad faith," "perfidy," and "the degradation of conscious baseness," and wrote (D. S., 17 Despatches, Spain, No. 5, June 22, 1819, enclosure; American State Papers, Foreign Relations, IV, 655):

No wise King will dare to do an act which would deprive him of the respect of all nations, sully the reputation of his Kingdom in the eyes of the civilized world and deprive his people of the strongest incentive to virtuous exertions under every dispensation of Heaven, the confidence in the integrity of their government.

President Monroe, according to Adams, disapproved "of Forsyth's conduct and of the style of his official notes at Madrid" and wanted "to express his positive disapprobation." Adams considered that Forsyth "had neither the experience, nor the prudence, nor the sincerity, nor the delicacy of sentiment suited for such a station"; he adds, as to a Cabinet meeting of February 10, 1820 (Memoirs of John Quincy Adams, IV, 521–22):

Calhoun said that Forsyth's diplomatic notes were exactly like his speeches in Congress—ironical; that he gave more personal offence to his opponents by indulging himself in that style than any other member with whom he ever sat in a deliberative assembly. Now, the great faults of Forsyth at Madrid have been indiscretion and indecorum, faults quite sufficient to show that he was not qualified for the office of a public Minister on a highly critical mission, but which ought not to be severely punished by those who appointed him, knowing his character.

The six months' period allowed for the exchange of the ratifications expired on August 22, 1819, without action taken. Forsyth continued to write notes at Madrid; one of these, that of October 18, called a remonstrance and containing a long discussion of the three land grants, was regarded by the Spanish Government as so insulting to the King of Spain that it was returned on November 12 (American State Papers, Foreign Relations, IV, 668–72). The Government of Spain decided to transfer the negotiations to Washington by sending here as its Envoy General Don Francisco Dionisio Vives; but by this time the only real question for Spain was not the land grants, but South America. On November 27 the French Minister at Washington, G. Hyde de Neuville, thus stated the case (Memoirs of John Quincy Adams, IV, 453–54):

At the office De Neuville was with me nearly two hours. He told me that De Mun had arrived, and brought him voluminous dispatches, among which was an instruction to postpone his journey to France. He said that the French Government, finding that the ratification of the treaty by Spain was likely to fail, had made the strongest remonstrances to the Spanish Cabinet, and had finally called upon them in the most explicit manner to declare what they intended to do; that the King of Spain had given the strongest assurances that it was his most earnest desire and his settled determination to finish this transaction amicably with the United States; that he would immediately send out a Minister to obtain the desired explanations, and the French Government had been informed what

was the real obstacle to the ratification. It was not the affair of the grants. The Minister would say something on that subject, but it would ultimately make no real difficulty. The great stumbling-block was South America. The proposition which we had made to England, and were ready to make to France and Russia, for a joint recognition of the independence of Buenos Ayres, had been made use of to persuade the King of Spain that if he should ratify the treaty, the next day we should recognize the South Americans and make a common cause with them. His jealousy, being thus excited, had been much strengthened by exaggerated representations from this country of a miserable plundering expedition into the province of Texas, which has been carried on the last summer by people from the United States. De Neuville's instructions are, therefore, to use all his influence with the Government of the United States to prevail upon them to take no precipitate measure which might produce war, but to wait until the Spanish Minister shall come, with the perfect assurance that we shall obtain the ratification without needing the application of force. De Neuville added that however short of full and explicit candor Onis's conversation here had been, he had been clear and unequivocal in his declarations at Paris and at Madrid. His talk here, therefore, was undoubtedly inspired by the fear of being harshly treated, perhaps exiled or imprisoned, upon his return to Spain; and the order to arrest him had actually been signed by the King. He was at large, but without employment, and had not been consulted upon anything that was done. De Neuville urged, therefore, with all possible earnestness, that the President should wait to hear what this Spanish Minister has to say, before recommending to Congress that any further step should be taken, and expressed the wish that the President would also, in the message, say something which Spain might receive as a pledge that the United States would not, immediately after the ratification of the treaty, recognize the South Americans, or make common cause with them.

So far as concerned the land grants and South America, Adams' answer was direct and brief (*ibid.*, 455):

As to the grants, we could not negotiate about them. It was disgusting even to discuss a subject upon which Spain could not even advance a pretension without the grossest outrage upon good faith. And with regard to South America, no such pledge as that which the Minister was to ask for could or would be given. We had invariably refused to make any stipulation upon that subject; we should certainly make none, express or implied, now.

There is little doubt, however, that the views of the French Minister had some influence in softening the terms of the President's message to Congress of December 7, 1819, which, instead of recommending to Congress to authorize the immediate occupation of Florida, proposed that course only if the coming negotiations with the Spanish Envoy proved unsatisfactory (American State Papers, Foreign Relations, IV, 627); see also the messages of March 27 and May 9, 1820, Richardson, II, 69–72).

The Exchange of Ratifications

General Vives did not arrive in Washington until April, 1820. In the meantime a military revolt in Spain had temporarily restored there the Constitution of 1812, which the King of Spain had accepted and according to which it was necessary that the treaty should be submitted to the Cortes before ratification.

The negotiations between Vives and Secretary of State John Quincy Adams were in part in writing and in part verbal (for the

notes written, see American State Papers, Foreign Relations, IV, 680–89); the full power of Vives did not authorize him to exchange the ratifications of the treaty; it was under date of December 15, 1819, and its clause of substance was as follows (translation, *ibid.*, 681):

We have authorized and by these presents We do authorize you, granting you full power in the most ample form, to meet and confer with such person or persons as may be duly authorized by the Government of the United States, and with him or them to settle, conclude, and sign whatsoever you may judge necessary to the best arrangement of all points depending between the two Governments; promising, as We do hereby promise upon the faith and word of a King, to approve, ratify, and fulfil such articles or agreements as you may conclude and sign.

In his note of April 14, 1820, making no mention of the land grants, Vives brought forward these three points (translation, *ibid.*, 680):

That the United States, taking into due consideration the scandalous system of piracy established in and carried on from several of their ports, will adopt measures, satisfactory and effectual, to repress the barbarous excesses and unexampled depredations daily committed upon Spain, her possessions, and properties, so as to satisfy what is due to international rights and is equally claimed by the honor of the American people.

That in order to put a total stop to any future armaments and to prevent all aid whatsoever being afforded from any part of the Union which may be intended to be directed against and employed in the invasion of His Catholic Majesty's possessions in North America, the United States will agree to offer a pledge (*á dar una seguridad*) that their integrity shall be respected.

And, finally, that they will form no relations with the pretended Governments of the revolted provinces of Spain situate beyond sea, and will conform to the course of proceeding adopted in this respect by other powers in amity with Spain.

The answers on behalf of the United States on the first two points were regarded as satisfactory; the flat refusal of this Government to contract any engagement "not to form any relations with those [South American] provinces" was referred to Madrid. The United States continued willing to exchange the ratifications of the treaty despite the lapse of time, assuming that the Senate again consented to that course; and while the question of the land grants was brought forward by Adams, it was not debated; Vives wrote on May 5, 1820 (translation, *ibid.*, 685):

In the event of the King's receiving as satisfactory the answer of your Government to the third point of my proposals, the abrogation of the grants will be attended with no difficulty; nor has that ever been the chief motive for suspending the ratification of the treaty; for the thorough comprehension of which I waive at present any reply to the remarks which you are pleased to offer on that topic. I cannot, however, refrain from stating to you that, in discussing with you the validity or the nullity of the grants above mentioned, I merely said that "in my private opinion they were null and void through the *inability* of the grantees to comply with the terms of the law."

The result was that on October 5, 1820, the Cortes "advised the King to cede the Floridas to the United States" and also declared null and void the three land grants in question even if the treaty should not be ratified (*ibid.*, 694; D. S., 18 Despatches, Spain, October 5,

1820); and the ratification by His Catholic Majesty followed under date of October 24, 1820.

That instrument of ratification, in original and translation, is printed above following the treaty texts; it is a part of the agreement, explanatory of the treaty and particularly of the provisions of Article 8 thereof; its elaborate clauses regarding that article are clear and positive in their declaration that the Alagon, Puñonrostro, and Vargas grants "have remained and do remain entirely annulled and invalid."

On February 12, 1821, the Spanish instrument of ratification was delivered to Secretary of State Adams by General Vives, who then declared his readiness to make the exchange, making at the same time a plea (which met with refusal) for some recognition of the claims of Spanish subjects provided for by the convention of 1802 (Document 27) but abandoned by Articles 9 and 10 of this treaty (D. S., 2 Notes to Foreign Legations, 415–18).

The Spanish instrument of ratification was submitted to the Senate on February 14, 1821, with the following presidential message of the previous day (Executive Journal, III, 242–43):

The ratification by the Spanish government, of the treaty of amity, settlement, and limits, between the United States and Spain, signed on the 22d of February, 1819, and on the 24th of that month ratified on the part of the United States, has been received by the Envoy Extraordinary and Minister Plenipotentiary of that power at this place, who has given notice that he is ready to exchange the ratifications.

By the sixteenth article of that treaty, it was stipulated, that the ratifications should be exchanged within six months from the day of its signature; which time having elapsed, before the ratification of Spain was given, a copy, and translation thereof, are now transmitted to the Senate, for their advise and consent to receive it in exchange for the ratification of the United States, heretofore executed.

The treaty was submitted to the consideration of the Cortes of that kingdom, before its ratification, which was finally given with their assent and sanction. The correspondence between the Spanish Minister of Foreign Affairs, and the Minister of the United States at Madrid, on that occasion, is also herewith communicated to the Senate; together with a memorandum by the Secretary of State, of his conference with the Spanish Envoy here, yesterday, when that Minister gave notice of his readiness to exchange the ratifications.

The return of the original papers, now transmitted, to avoid the delay necessary to the making of copies, is requested.

The papers accompanying the presidential message of February 13, 1821, are printed in American State Papers, Foreign Relations, IV, 650–703; they cover the period between signature and exchange of ratifications (see also *ibid.*, V, 263–82).

The resolution which the Senate passed on February 19, by a vote of forty to four, was in the following form (*ibid.*, 244):

Resolved, (two-thirds of the Senators present concurring therein,) That the Senate having examined the treaty of amity, settlement, and limits, between the United States of America and his Catholic Majesty, made and concluded on the twenty-second day of February, 1819, and seen and considered the ratification thereof, made by his said Catholic Majesty, on the 24th day of October, 1820, do consent to, and advise the President of the United States to ratify the same.

The comments of Secretary of State Adams on the Senate resolution are in his diary for February 19, 1821 (Memoirs of John Quincy Adams, V, 285–86):

While I was with the President, Mr. Charles Cutts, the Secretary of the Senate, came in with their resolution advising to the ratification, but drawn up in a special form, differing from that which had been presented as the question in the message from the President. The treaty had been ratified by and with the advice and consent of the Senate on the 24th February; but the last article stipulated that the ratifications should be given on both sides and exchanged within six months from the date. As the King of Spain withheld his ratification beyond that period, the United States were no longer bound to accept it after the expiration of the time, and when it was ratified the question arose, whether the tardy ratification should be accepted by us. By the letter of the Constitution it was perhaps not necessary to submit this question to the Senate; but the disposition of the President is to consult them whenever there is any plausible Constitutional motive for so doing; and I was especially desirous that the sense of the Senate should again be deliberately taken upon the merits of the treaty, because a continued systematic and laborious effort has been making by Mr. Clay and his partisans to make it unpopular. In the pursuit of this project, resolutions against the treaty had been introduced into the Legislatures of Kentucky and of Louisiana, and the Western newspapers have been indefatigably filled with essays and dissertations to the same effect. Among the rest, T. B. Robertson, Governor of Louisiana, one of Clay's puppets, made an attack upon the treaty in his speech to the Legislature. After two years of this work, I was glad to see how the Senate would vote upon the treaty when brought before them again. But the question in the President's message was for their advice and consent to receive the Spanish ratification in exchange for that of the United States, heretofore given. From mere inattention to the form of the question in the message, and not from any objection to it, they took the other course, of an advice and consent to a second ratification of the treaty. And against this there were only four votes—Brown, of Louisiana, who married a sister of Clay's wife; Richard M. Johnson, of Kentucky, against his own better judgment, from mere political subserviency to Clay; Williams, of Tennessee, from party impulses, connected with hatred of General Jackson; and Trimble, of Ohio, for some maggot in the brain, the cause of which I do not yet perfectly know. At the ratification of the treaty two years ago there was no formal opposition made, but the real opposition was greater to it than now. On this event I will not attempt to describe my feelings.

The ratification by the United States, the exchange of ratifications, and the proclamation took place on February 22, 1821, just two years after the signature of the treaty. The procedure is thus described (*ibid.*, 288–89):

Ratifications of the Florida Treaty exchanged. General Vivés came, according to appointment, at one o'clock, to the office of the Department of State, with Mr. Salmon, his Secretary of Legation. Our preparations were not entirely completed when he came, but were ready within half an hour. I then took the treaty with the King of Spain's ratification myself; the General took the treaty with the President's ratification; Mr. Ironside held one of the originals executed by me and Mr. Onis, and Mr. Salmon another. Mr. Brent held the printed copy with the President's proclamation. Mr. Salmon read, from the original in his hand, the treaty, all the rest comparing their respective copies as he proceeded. I read in like manner the English, from the treaty which we retain with the Spanish ratification. Both the ratifications were then examined and found correct. The triplicate certificates of the exchange were then signed and sealed, observing the alternative precedence of signature, as had been done with Mr. Onis. General Vivés and Mr. Salmon then withdrew, taking with them the treaty ratified by the President, and leaving that with the ratification of the King of Spain. I went immediately to the President's. He signed the proclamation of the ratified

treaty and the messages to the two Houses communicating it to them as proclaimed. The messages were sent, and that to the House of Representatives was received while the House were in session. The Senate had just adjourned when Mr. Gouverneur, who carried the message, reached the Capitol.

There are three originals of the certificate of exchange of ratifications in the treaty file, two in Spanish and one in English. The document is in customary form, and it is stated therein that it was signed "in triplicates," that is, in triplicate for each Government.

THE PROCLAMATION

The presidential message of February 22, 1821, communicating the treaty to Congress, is in American State Papers, Foreign Relations, V, 127–33, where the full text of the proclamation of the same date is printed. In view of the unusually elaborate form of the proclamation, its text, from the original document, follows:

By the President of the United States,

A PROCLAMATION.

Whereas a Treaty of Amity, Settlement, and Limits, between the United States of America and His Catholic Majesty was concluded and signed between their Plenipotentiaries in this city, on the 22ᵈ day of February, in the year of our Lord one thousand eight hundred and nineteen, which Treaty, word for word, is as follows:

[Here follows the text of the treaty in English and Spanish]

And whereas his said Catholic Majesty did on the twenty fourth day of October, in the year of our Lord one thousand eight hundred and twenty, ratify and confirm the said Treaty, which ratification is in the words and of the tenor following:

[Here follows the Spanish instrument of ratification with an English translation]

And whereas the Senate of the United States did, on the nineteenth day of the present month, advise and consent to the ratification, on the part of these United States, of the said Treaty in the following words:

"IN SENATE OF THE UNITED STATES
February 19th. 1821.

Resolved, two thirds of the Senators present concurring therein, that the Senate having examined the treaty of Amity, Settlement and Limits between the United States of America and his Catholic Majesty made and concluded on the twenty second day of February 1819, and seen and considered the Ratification thereof, made by his said Catholic Majesty on the 24ᵗʰ day of October 1820, do consent to, and advise the President of the United States to ratify the same."

And whereas in pursuance of the said advice and consent of the Senate of the United States I have ratified and confirmed the said Treaty in the words following, viz.

"Now, therefore, I, James Monroe, President of the United States of America, having seen and considered the Treaty above recited, together with the Ratification of His Catholic Majesty thereof, do in pursuance of the aforesaid advice and consent of the Senate of the United States, by these Presents, accept, ratify, and confirm the said Treaty and every clause and article thereof as the same are herein before set forth."

"In faith whereof I have caused the Seal of the United States of America to be hereto affixed."

"Given under my Hand at the City of Washington this twenty second day of February in the year of our Lord one thousand eight hundred and twenty one, and of the Independence of the said States the forty fifth.

(Signed)   JAMES MONROE

By the President
   (Signed)   JOHN QUINCY ADAMS,
                  Secretary of State."

And whereas the said Ratifications, on the part of the United States, and of His Catholic Majesty, have been this day duly exchanged at Washington, by John Quincy Adams Secretary of State of the United States, and by General Don Francisco Dionisio Vives Envoy Extraordinary and Minister Plenipotenciary of His Catholic Majesty: Now, therefore, to the end that the said Treaty may be observed and performed with good faith on the part of the United States, I have caused the premises to be made public, and I do hereby enjoin and require all persons bearing office, civil or military, within the United States, and all others, citizens or inhabitants thereof, or being within the same, faithfully to observe and fulfil the said Treaty and every clause and article thereof.

In testimony whereof I have caused the seal of the United States to be affixed to these presents, and signed the same with my hand.

        Done at the city of Washington, the twenty second day of February, in the year of our Lord one thousand eight hundred and twenty one,
[Seal] and of the sovereignty and independence of the United States the forty fifth.

                             JAMES MONROE

By the President
   JOHN QUINCY ADAMS
       Secretary of State

ARTICLE 3

"Longitude 100 West from London" and "23 from Washington" are not exactly the same. The following statement in the matter is from Douglas, Boundaries, Areas, Geographic Centers, and Altitudes of the United States (U. S. Geological Survey Bulletin 817, 2d ed.), 36, note:

The zero point of the London meridian is the cross on St. Paul's Cathedral in London, which is $0° 05' 48.356''$ (4.17 miles) west of Greenwich (Ordnance Survey of Great Britain, letter of Sept. 6, 1927). For reference to the establishment of the meridians of London and Greenwich see The Mariner's Mirror, vol. 13, No. 2, London, Cambridge Press, April, 1927. Longitudes on the Mitchell map of 1755 are referred to the London meridian. The Melish map of 1818 has the degrees west of London indicated along the lower edge, and the degrees west of Washington near the upper edge; the $0°$ of the Washington meridian coincides with $77°$ west of London. In 1804 a line through the center of the White House was run out and marked for the zero of the Washington meridian. This line is $76° 56' 25''$ west of London. It will be seen from these statements that the location of this boundary was somewhat uncertain, but the position was recognized as the 100th degree west of Greenwich in acts of Sept. 9, 1850, and June 5, 1858 [9 Statutes at Large, 446–52; 11 *ibid.*, 310].

There is an example of "Melishe's" map in the treaty file, noted as having been filed with the treaty on October 9, 1893. This map is about 35½ by 55 inches (85 by 140 cm.) and is entitled "Map of the United States with the contiguous British & Spanish Possessions Compiled from the latest & best Authorities by John Melish Engraved by

J. Vallance & H. S. Tanner. Entered according to Act of Congress the 6ᵗʰ day of June 1816. Published by John Melish Philadelphia. Improved to the 1ˢᵗ of January 1818."

The location of the source of the Arkansas River was unknown at the time. The treaty provided that from that source (if not in latitude 42° north) the line should run north or south, as the case might be, to the forty-second parallel of north latitude, and thence west to the Pacific.

Assuming that the Tennessee Fork of the Arkansas River constitutes the headwaters thereof, the source of the Arkansas lies in Lake County, Colorado, not far from Leadville, in approximately 39° 20′ north latitude, 106° 25′ west longitude. This point is about 183 miles south of latitude 42° north.

ARTICLE 4

No commissioners and surveyors met to "fix this Line" under Article 4. By the treaty with Mexico of January 12, 1828 (Document 60), the "Line" was formally adopted as the boundary between the United States and Mexico. While Article 4 of this treaty provided that the commissioners and surveyors should meet before the end of one year from the exchange of ratifications, or by February 22, 1822, at Natchitoches, Louisiana, on the Red River, nothing had been done during that period, although the subject had been discussed at the exchange of ratifications and Forsyth had received instructions thereon (D. S., 9 Instructions, U. S. Ministers, 91–92, June 13, 1821).

On March 8, 1822, President Monroe advised Congress that the Spanish Provinces "which have declared their independence and are in the enjoyment of it ought to be recognized" (Richardson, II, 116–18). Mexico was one of the countries named.

By this time Mexico was *de facto* independent. The army of Iturbide had entered the city of Mexico on September 27, 1821, and the Provisional Junta was formally installed the next day (Manning, Early Diplomatic Relations between the United States and Mexico, 1). On April 9, 1822, the Spanish Minister at Washington, Don Joaquin de Anduaga, wrote to Secretary of State Adams regarding Article 4 of the treaty. He enclosed a list of the agents nominated by Spain, who had orders "to proceed to the execution" (D. S., 7 Notes from the Spanish Legation).

In view of the situation with Mexico, the matter was discussed in the Cabinet on April 19 at a meeting called primarily for the purpose of considering "the recognition of the new Southern Governments." Adams' account of the discussion is as follows (Memoirs of John Quincy Adams, V, 493–94):

Another question was much discussed. I have received official notice, first through Mr. Forsyth, and lately from the Spanish Minister, Anduaga, of the appointment of a Commissioner, Surveyor, Astronomer, &c., on the part of Spain to run the boundary line according to a stipulation in the late treaty. The House of Representatives struck out of the appropriation bill the sum which had been estimated for the expense of this Commission during the present year, on the ground of the proposed recognition of Mexico. The appropriation was said,

however, to have been restored by the Senate. If the House should agree to the amendment, and the appropriation should pass, the question was whether the Commission should be appointed and the line run.

Mr. Calhoun thought it could not be done; that it would be inconsistent with the recognition of Mexico; that it would give offence and rouse the indignation of the new empire; and that if the line is to be run at all, it must be with Mexican instead of Spanish Commissioners. The President and all the other members of the Cabinet, however, thought otherwise; that, as it was the mere mechanical execution of a compact already consummate, we are still bound to the execution of the treaty, notwithstanding the subsequent recognition of Mexico, which is a recognition of independence, but not of boundary; that we should proceed to the fulfilment of the stipulation unless objection should be made on the part of Mexico—in which case the Commissioners must of course cease. By the article, the Commissioners were to meet within one year from the exchange of the ratifications at Natchez, which, by the delay of Spain to appoint her Commissioner, became impossible.

Mr. Calhoun thought this released us from the obligation of this engagement, especially considering the subsequent engagements in Mexico.

I thought it would have the appearance of subterfuge to allege this ground for non-performance. The conclusion was to wait and see how the House will dispose of the Senate's amendment in the appropriation bill.

The "conclusion" of "the President and all the other members of the Cabinet" was a singularly inconclusive one. If by the recognition of Mexico the United States regarded Mexico as her neighbor, the boundary between the two countries, whether that of the treaty or any other, was a question with Mexico alone. Only on the theory that the territory west and south of the "Line" was Spanish, could Spain have any possible interest in it; and that Mexico would regard the "Line" as her boundary and would object to a commissioner of Spain's having anything to do with it or with its delimitation and demarcation, was inevitable.

By the act of May 4, 1822 (3 Statutes at Large, 678), an appropriation was made for "such missions to the independent nations on the American continent, as the President of the United States may deem proper"; but an appropriation had also been voted by the act of April 30 for the "two commissions under the treaty with Spain" (*ibid.*, 673).

On May 17, 1822, Adams answered the Spanish note, declining to proceed under Article 4 of the treaty, under the mistaken idea that Congress had made no appropriation, although he said that "great and important changes had occurred in the Provinces to be affected" (D. S., 3 Notes to Foreign Legations, 79); but, finding that there was an appropriation, Adams wrote again on May 29 that "this Government is now ready to proceed to the execution of the Article," inquired when the commissioner and surveyor on the part of Spain would be at Natchitoches, and gave assurance that "the Commissioner and Surveyor on the part of the United States, will be instructed to meet them at that place, and at the time which you shall designate" (*ibid.*, 81). The Spanish Minister answered on June 1 that he could not then say "when the said Spanish Commissaries will be able to reach Natchitoches" (D. S., 7 Notes from the Spanish Legation); and this ended the correspondence with the Government of Spain

(see the report of the Secretary of State of February 25, 1823, American State Papers, Foreign Relations, V, 241–42).

Recognition of Mexico by the United States became complete on December 12, 1822, when José Manuel Zozaya was formally received by President Monroe as the first Minister of Mexico at Washington (Manning, Early Diplomatic Relations between the United States and Mexico, 12; Niles' Weekly Register, XXIII, 240, December 14, 1822).

As was to be expected, Mexico from the beginning had taken the position that Article 3 of this treaty fixed the boundary between the United States and Mexico; and the fears and suspicions of Mexico regarding the intentions of the United States were not lessened by the delay in the formal statement of the attitude of this Government (see generally Manning, *op. cit.*, ch. IX).

In the instructions of March 26, 1825, when Henry Clay had become Secretary of State under President John Quincy Adams, Articles 3 and 4 of this treaty were mentioned, and Joel R. Poinsett, Minister to Mexico, was informed that the treaty "having been concluded when Mexico composed a part of the dominions of Spain, is obligatory upon both the United States and Mexico" (D. S., 10 Instructions, U. S. Ministers, 233). On July 12, 1825, the Mexican Government was informed that the United States held itself bound to carry the treaty into effect (D. S., 1 Despatches, Mexico, Poinsett to Clay, No. 7, July 18, 1825); but the binding character of the treaty did not lessen the increasing desire of the United States for the acquisition of Texas. The real position of the two Governments toward the close of 1825 is summed up by Manning (*op. cit.*, 297) as follows:

Thus within a few months after the negotiations had begun each government discovered that the other, while claiming to be willing to ratify and abide by the treaty of 1819, was really wishing to secure the extreme limits claimed by the United States on the one side and by Spain on the other before that treaty was concluded. Each had also discovered that the other was determined not to give up anything which that treaty secured to it. But each hoped something would happen to break down the determination of the other.

As above mentioned, the result for the time being was the treaty with Mexico of January 12, 1828 (Document 60), although the going into force of that treaty was delayed until April 5, 1832.

ARTICLE 7

By Article 7 of the treaty, possession of the Floridas was to be given to the United States within six months after the exchange of ratifications, or by August 22, 1821. The royal order of the King of Spain for the delivery of possession was dated October 24, 1820 (translation in American State Papers, Foreign Relations, IV, 702–3).

The papers regarding the delivery of the Floridas, which were transmitted to Congress with the message of President Monroe on December 5, 1821, and at various times in 1822, are in American State Papers, Foreign Relations, IV, 740–808. They include some of the corre-

spondence regarding the difficulties as to the archives, which arose after the possession of the Floridas had been received by officers of the United States (see Moore, Digest, I, 445).

The act of March 3, 1821 (3 Statutes at Large, 637–39), provided for the execution of this treaty. Less complete provisions had been contained in the act of March 3, 1819 (*ibid.*, 523–24), which was to take effect when the ratifications had been exchanged "and the King of Spain shall be ready to surrender said territory to the United States."

On March 10 Major General Andrew Jackson was appointed Commissioner to receive possession of the Floridas and also Governor of the Floridas, and on March 20 he was given a special commission to administer the government (American State Papers, Foreign Relations, IV, 751–52).

The formal delivery of East Florida to the United States took place at St. Augustine on July 10, 1821. The record of the transaction was signed by Colonel Robert Butler for the United States and by Colonel José Coppinger for Spain. Possession of West Florida was similarly delivered on July 17 at Pensacola, and the *procès-verbal* of the delivery was signed by General Jackson and Colonel José Callava. The originals of the documents are in the archives of the Department of State; the texts of them are printed in American State Papers, Foreign Relations, IV, 749–50, 764–65.

In connection with the delivery of the Floridas a controversy arose as to whether the "fortifications" of Article 2 included their artillery or not. The United States did not finally press its contention (see Moore, Digest, I, 282–84).

ARTICLE 8

The English text of the first sentence of Article 8 is to the effect that land grants made prior to January 24, 1818, by proper Spanish authority, "shall be ratified and confirmed" to those in possession; the Spanish is "quedarán ratificadas y reconocidas," meaning "shall remain ratified and confirmed."

In an opinion by Chief Justice Marshall, the Supreme Court said in 1833 regarding this language (*United States* v. *Percheman*, 7 Peters, 51, 89):

No violence is done to the language of the treaty by a construction which conforms the English and Spanish to each other. Although the words "shall be ratified and confirmed," are properly the words of contract, stipulating for some future legislative act; they are not necessarily so. They may import that they "shall be ratified and confirmed" by force of the instrument itself. When we observe that in the counterpart of the same treaty, executed at the same time by the same parties, they are used in this sense, we think the construction proper, if not unavoidable.

In the case of Foster v. Elam, 2 Peters, 253, this court considered these words importing a contract. The Spanish part of the treaty was not then brought to our view, and it was then supposed that there was no variance between them. We did not suppose that there was even a formal difference of expression in the same instrument, drawn up in the language of each party. Had this circum-

stance been known, we believe it would have produced the construction which we now give to the article.

The argument of counsel for the appellee in the case cited gives (*ibid.*, 69) the following as the equivalent of the Spanish phraseology of the first sentence of Article 8, "fairly rendered":

All concessions of lands made by his catholic majesty, or by his legitimate authorities, before the 24th January 1818, in the aforesaid territories, which his majesty cedes to the United States, shall remain confirmed and acknowledged to the persons in possession of them (i.e. the concessions), in the same manner that they would have been if the dominion of his catholic majesty over these territories had continued.

The Right of Deposit at New Orleans

The "right of Deposit at New Orleans," mentioned in Article 9 of this treaty, refers to Article 22 of the treaty with Spain of 1795 (Document 18), which granted to citizens of the United States the right to deposit merchandise and effects in the port of New Orleans and to export them without payment of duty. The right was granted for three years and was either to continue thereafter or an equivalent establishment was to be assigned elsewhere on the Mississippi.

On October 16, 1802, the privilege was suspended by a decree of the Intendant of the Province of Louisiana (American State Papers, Foreign Relations, II, 469–71). The suspension was continued until the following April, when the right was restored by order of the King of Spain (Moore, International Arbitrations, V, 4493).

Captain Pike

The "return of Captain Pike from the Provincias Internas," mentioned in Article 9, refers to the expedition of Captain Zebulon Montgomery Pike, of the United States Army, which is described in Coues, The Expeditions of Zebulon Montgomery Pike, II.

Captain (then Lieutenant) Pike left St. Louis on July 15, 1806, with a party consisting of one lieutenant, one surgeon, one sergeant, two corporals, sixteen privates, one interpreter, and fifty-one Indians. Ascending the Missouri River and its tributary, the Osage, Pike passed through Missouri to Kansas and, after crossing east central Kansas, proceeded north to Nebraska. Turning south, the party reached and crossed the Arkansas River near the present city of Great Bend, Kansas. Pike then went up the Arkansas; he passed Pueblo, Colorado, and made a trip to Pike's Peak, which bears his name but the summit of which he did not reach. A month or more was spent in the region of the headwaters of the Arkansas River; Pike went nearly to its source; then he turned back and camped again near the present site of Cañon City, Fremont County, Colorado; thence a south and southwest course was taken, and Pike reached the Rio Grande or Rio del Norte near what is now Alamosa, Alamosa County, Colorado, on January 30, 1807.

Pike supposed that he had there reached the Red River and thought that he was in American territory. While there was no definitive boundary in 1807, such occupation of that region as existed was that of Spain; and by the "Line" of this treaty, the territory south of the Arkansas River and west of 100° longitude west from London was Spanish. Pike was well south of the Arkansas and at nearly 106° west longitude.

It was here that Pike and such of his party as had remained with him were detained by Spanish forces; they were taken first to Santa Fe and then to Chihuahua. During his detention Pike was well treated by the Spanish authorities, but his papers were taken from him. Receiving permission to return to his own country under escort, Pike reached Natchitoches, Louisiana, on July 1, 1807, and reported his arrival to General Wilkinson.

Captain Pike was killed in action on April 27, 1813, during the attack on York (Toronto).

THE EXPEDITION OF MIRANDA

The "expedition of Miranda" is mentioned in the second clause 3 of Article 9 of this treaty.

A full and reasoned account of the expedition of Francisco de Miranda in 1806 against the Spanish dominions in South America is in chapter IX of "Francisco de Miranda and the Revolutionizing of Spanish America," by Dr. William Spence Robertson (Annual Report of the American Historical Association for the Year 1907, I, 361–98). That account of Miranda is replete with citations and has a valuable bibliography. The author considers that the expedition of 1806, "although originally fitted out in a port of the United States, was in many respects more of a British than an American enterprise" (p. 396).

The following statement regarding the expedition of 1806 is largely based on the work of Dr. Robertson above mentioned.

Miranda reached the United States from England in November, 1805. Rufus King, who had been Minister at London, was in New York at the time. Colonel William S. Smith, surveyor at New York, entered into relations with Miranda. These and many others attended a dinner in his honor. After this reception he went on to Washington. While in Washington Miranda had interviews with President Jefferson and Secretary of State Madison. When he returned to New York, about two hundred recruits were gathered, and the expedition sailed on February 2, 1806, on the *Leander*.

The Spanish Minister at Washington, Yrujo, kept his home Government informed of Miranda's activities. He notified the Spanish Consul in the port of New York to watch Miranda and sent warning to the Spanish colonial officials.

When the matter of the equipment and departure of this expedition became public, Colonel William S. Smith, surveyor at New York, and Samuel G. Ogden, a West Indian merchant, were brought to trial for violation of neutrality laws, but were acquitted.

Miranda failed to secure the assistance which he was expecting in Haiti and remained for a time at the Dutch island of Aruba (or Oruba), just off the coast of Venezuela. In April, 1806, Miranda approached the mainland; but his attempt to force a landing was resisted and failed. Some sixty of his men fell into Spanish hands and for years remained prisoners; among them were thirty-six Americans (American State Papers, Foreign Relations, III, 256–59). After the failure of this first attack, Miranda passed to Barbados, where he expected aid from the British commander, Admiral Cochrane.

About two months after his first attempt, Miranda left Barbados, stopping at Trinidad, where he gathered recruits. His vessel was accompanied by several British vessels of war and by one brig under the American flag. On August 3, 1806, a landing was effected near Coro, in Venezuela. The next day the town of Coro was occupied; proclamations were issued calling on the people to rise and strike for their independence; but there was almost no response. Appeals for additional forces and supplies were sent by Miranda to Cochrane and to British officers at Jamaica; but no help came from either of these sources. Miranda then evacuated Coro, going again to the island of Aruba. Warned by the commander of a British ship, in September, that he should leave the Dutch island, Miranda went back to Trinidad and finally to Barbados; but after some months his force gradually dwindled, and in the next year (1807) he abandoned his enterprise.

Protests had been made at Washington regarding the Miranda expedition as early as February, 1806 (Robertson, *op. cit.*, 370–73), and on July 18, 1806, the Spanish Government informed the Minister at Madrid that the expedition would be the basis of reclamation against the United States, on account of the injuries, expenses, and prejudices which it had caused to Spain (D. S., 10 Despatches, Spain, No. 9, July 25, 1806).

THE FINAL PARAGRAPHS OF ARTICLE 9

By the next to the last paragraph of Article 9 of the treaty the two parties respectively renounced their claims "to indemnities for any of the recent events or transactions of their respective Commanders and Officers in the Floridas."

The final paragraph of Article 9 provided that the United States would cause satisfaction to be made for such injuries as "by process of Law, shall be established to have been suffered by the Spanish Officers, and individual Spanish inhabitants, by the late operations of the American Army in Florida."

The act of March 3, 1823 (3 Statutes at Large, 768), made it the duty of the judges of the superior courts in the Territory of Florida to "receive and adjust" all such claims. Section 2 of that statute provided that all cases in which decisions were rendered in favor of the claimants should be reported to the Secretary of the Treasury, who, "on being satisfied that the same is just and equitable, within the provisions of the said treaty," should pay the amount adjudged.

There were three invasions of the Floridas; a graphic account
of them is in Moore, International Arbitrations, V, 4519–24.   In
March, 1812, a force which was under the direction of General
George Matthews, who had been appointed Commissioner under
the secret statute of January 15, 1811 (3 Statutes at Large, 471),
and which included a detachment of the regular Army, took possession of Fernandina and the country thence to St. Augustine,
to which siege was laid.   The measures taken by Matthews were
disavowed by the United States and he was recalled; the American
troops were withdrawn and the country restored to the Spanish
authorities in May, 1813.

During the War of 1812 with Great Britain, and in part because
of military demonstrations of the British, General Andrew Jackson
took possession of Pensacola on November 7, 1814, and that night
the British forces abandoned and blew up Fort Barrancas, on the
west side of the entrance to Pensacola Bay (Lossing, Pictorial Field-
Book of the War of 1812, 1022–23).

During the Seminole War in 1818, General Jackson, who was in
command of the forces of the United States, occupied St. Marks and
Pensacola and, after a brief siege, obtained the surrender of Fort
Barrancas on May 27, 1818.   While the United States assumed
responsibility for the acts of General Jackson, the occupied places
were ordered restored to Spanish authority later in the same year.

During those operations, and in particular during those of 1812–13
and 1818, private property was taken, plundered, or destroyed.
Regarding the first invasion—that of East Florida by General Matthews—Judge Bronson wrote (Senate Miscellaneous Document
No. 55, 36th Congress, 1st session, serial 1038, p. 40):

> Suffice it to say, that before or when the United States troops finally evacuated
> the country, the whole inhabited part of the province was in a state of utter
> desolation and ruin.   Almost every building outside of the walls of St. Augustine
> was burned or destroyed; farms and plantations laid waste; cattle, horses, and
> hogs driven off or killed, and movable property plundered or destroyed; and in
> many instances slaves dispersed or abducted.   So far as the destruction of
> property of every kind was concerned, the desolation of the Carnatic by Hyder
> Ali was not more terrible and complete.

That claims which arose, based on the invasion of 1818, were
within the treaty, was undoubted; but in respect of the earlier claims
various questions arose as to the English and Spanish texts.   The
English text speaks of "the late operations of the American Army";
the Spanish text has no equivalent for the word "late."   The opposing
views were that the word "late" was to be read as meaning "recent"
(used in the previous paragraph) and thus included operations of
1812–13 and of 1814.   On the other hand, it was said that the
word signified "latest" or "last" and was thus limited to operations
in 1818 (see Senate Committee Report No. 93, 36th Congress, 1st
session, serial 1039).

It was because of the word "late" that Secretary of the Treasury
Rush in 1826 rejected all claims for losses due to the invasion in
1812–13.   The awards for 1814 had been previously disallowed by
Secretary of the Treasury Crawford on the ground that the invasion

of 1814 by General Jackson was not contrary to the law of nations and that the claims were not within the treaty.

Appealing to Congress, the claimants also pointed out that the last words of Article 9 in the English text are "in Florida," whereas the last words in the Spanish are "en ellas"—"in them" or "in the Floridas"—and consequently argued that the intention could not have been to limit the claims to those for losses in 1818, "which were almost wholly confined in West Florida" (Moore, *op. cit.*, 4526).

By the act of June 26, 1834 (6 Statutes at Large, 569), provision was made for the adjudication of the claims of 1812–13; but the action of the judges in allowing interest at 5 per cent during the period when no provision of law existed for the satisfaction of the claims, was overruled in 1836 by Secretary of the Treasury Woodbury; and another question as to the texts was raised.

The English text refers to such claims as "by process of Law, shall be established"; the Spanish refers to those claims which the Spanish inhabitants and officers "justifiquen legalmente," or shall legally establish. Here it was argued that the text intended to provide for finality of judicial decision and accordingly that adverse executive determination by the Secretary of the Treasury was contrary to the treaty. On the other hand, it was said that the term "process of Law" was not used in any technical sense in the treaty, but generally, as the equivalent of laws passed for the purpose (see Senate Miscellaneous Document No. 55, 36th Congress, 1st session, serial 1038).

For a detailed account of the East and West Florida claims, bringing their history up to 1884, see Moore, International Arbitrations, V, 4519–31, and the numerous authorities there cited.

ARTICLE 11

The statute for carrying this treaty into effect (act of March 3, 1821, 3 Statutes at Large, 637–39) contained provisions in respect of the Commissioners to act pursuant to the terms of Article 11 (see also the acts of April 30, 1822, and March 3, 1823, *ibid.*, 673, 762). The Commissioners duly appointed were Hugh Lawson White, William King, and Littleton Waller Tazewell; they took the oath of office on June 9, 1821, and made their final report on June 8, 1824.

By the act of May 24, 1824 (4 Statutes at Large, 33–34), an appropriation of five million dollars was made for the payment of the claims allowed. As the total of the sums awarded was $5,454,545.13, each allowed claim was abated to the extent of 8⅓ per cent thereof.

An account of the origin of the claims before the Commissioners and of their proceedings, with numerous citations and including the text of the final report of the Commissioners, is in Moore, International Arbitrations, V, 4487–4518.

ARTICLE 14

Among the claims passed on by the Commissioners under Article 11 of the treaty were those mentioned in the first clause 2 of Article 9

as "all claims on account of Prizes made by French Privateers, and condemned by French Consuls, within the Territory and Jurisdiction of Spain."

The final report of the Commissioners appointed under Article 11 of the treaty was made on June 8, 1824. One of the schedules to this report was schedule E, which was certified as containing "an authentic statement of all the prizes made of Vessels and cargoes belonging to Citizens of the United States, by French privateers, for which any allowance hath been made by them the said Commissioners; together with an authentic statement annexed of their true value." The total amount of this schedule was $3,075,338.19. However, an abatement of 8⅓ per cent was made in order to reduce the total amount of these claims and of all others allowed, the aggregate being $5,454,545.13, to the $5,000,000 specified in Article 11 of the treaty. The original report, with the schedules annexed, is in the archives of the Department of State, in a volume entitled "Report of the Commissioners with a List of Awards, &c. Commission under the Treaty with Spain Feb. 22, 1819. No. VI."

Printed copies of the report and the awards of the Commissioners were transmitted by the Secretary of State to Don Hilario de Rivas y Salmon, Chargé d'Affaires of Spain, on August 31, 1824 (D. S., 3 Notes to Foreign Legations, 186–87).

The chapter on the "Indemnity under the Florida Treaty," Moore, International Arbitrations, V, 4487–4518, with numerous citations, includes the text of the report (without the schedules) made by Commissioners Hugh Lawson White, William King, and Littleton Waller Tazewell under date of June 8, 1824.

The paragraph of the report of the Commissioners which refers particularly to schedule E thereof is as follows:

In order to enable the U. S. to comply completely with the provision of the 14th Article of this Treaty, and to present to Spain an authentic statement of the prizes made from Citizens of the U. S. by French privateers, for which injuries Spain was regarded by the Commission as having been liable, the undersigned have annexed hereto a fifth schedule, marked E (extracted from that marked C), in which is contained a list of all the vessels of the U. S. captured by French privateers, for which any allowance has been made by this board, and of the true value so allowed. For the particulars of such captures, the Commission begs leave to refer to the vouchers and documents produced before the Commissioners, relative to the claims on this account. These vouchers and documents, together with the records of their proceedings, the undersigned Commissioners have directed their Secretary to deposit in the Department of State of the U. S. in pursuance of the provisions of the 11th Article of the Treaty aforesaid.

ARTICLE 15

The terms of Article 15 regarding the entry of Spanish vessels into the ports of Pensacola and St. Augustine for twelve years, commencing three months after the exchange of ratifications, or until May 22, 1833, were recognized in section 2 of the act of March 3, 1821 (3 Statutes at Large, 637–39). By section 3 of the act of March 30, 1822 (*ibid.*, 660–61), the treaty provisions were more specifically made statutory.

Treaty Series No. 113
8 Statutes at Large, 274–77
18 *ibid.*, pt. 2, Public Treaties, 300–2

42

GREAT BRITAIN : JUNE 18, 1822

Declaration of the Commissioners under Article 6 of the Treaty of Ghent (Document 33), signed at Utica June 18, 1822.   Original in English.

The Undersigned, Commissioners, appointed, sworn, and Authorized, in Virtue of the Sixth Article of the treaty of Peace and Amity [1] between His Britannic Majesty and the United States of America, concluded at Ghent, on the twenty fourth day of December, in the year of our Lord, One thousand eight hundred and fourteen, impartially to examine, and, by a Report or Declaration, under their hands & seals, to designate, "that portion of the boundary of the United "States, from the point where the 45th degree of North latitude, strikes "the river Iroquois, or Cataraqua, [2] along the middle of said river into "Lake Ontario, through the middle of said Lake until it strikes the "communication by water, between that lake and lake Erie, thence, "along the middle of said Communication, into Lake Erie, through the "Middle of said Lake, until it arrives at the water communication "into Lake Huron, thence through the middle of said water commu-"nication into Lake Huron, thence, through the middle of said Lake, "to the water Communication between that lake and lake Superior," and, to "decide to which of the two Contracting parties the several "islands, lying within the said rivers, lakes and water Communications, "do respectively belong, in conformity with the true intent of the "treaty [3] of 1783": Do Decide and Declare, that the following described line (which is more clearly indicated, on a series of Maps [4] accompanying this report, exhibiting correct surveys and delineations of all the rivers, lakes, water communications and islands, embraced by the Sixth Article of the Treaty of Ghent, [5] by a black line, shaded on the British side with red, and on the American side with blue; and each

---

[1] Document 33.
[2] Now the St. Lawrence River.
[3] Document 11.
[4] See the note regarding the original maps.
[5] Document 33.

sheet of which series of Maps is identified by a Certificate, subscribed by the Commissioners and by the two principal Surveyors employed by them) is the true boundary intended by the two before mentioned treaties: That is to say,

Beginning at a Stone Monument, erected by Andrew Ellicott Esquire, in the year of our Lord one thousand eight hundred and seventeen, on the South bank or Shore of the said river Iroquois or Cataraqua, (now called the St Lawrence,) which Monument, bears South seventy four degrees and forty five minutes west, and is eighteen hundred and forty yards distant, from the Stone Church in the Indian village of St Regis, and indicates the point at which the forty fifth parallel of North latitude strikes the said river: Thence running North thirty five degrees and forty five minutes west, into the river, on a line at right angles with the southern Shore, to a point one hundred yards south of the opposite island, called Cornwall Island: Thence, turning westerly, and passing around the southern and western sides of said island, keeping one hundred yards distant therefrom, and following the curvatures of its shores, to a point opposite to the North west corner or angle of said Island: Thence, to and along the middle of the main river, until it approaches the eastern extremity of Barnhart's Island: Thence, northerly, along the channel which divides the last mentioned island from the Canada Shore, keeping one hundred yards distant from the island, until it approaches Sheiks Island: Thence, along the middle of the strait which divides Barnhart's and Sheiks' Islands, to the channel, called The long Sault, which separates the two last mentioned islands from the lower Long Sault Island: Thence, westerly (crossing the centre of the last mentioned channel) until it approaches within one hundred yards of the north shore of the Lower Sault Island: Thence, up the North branch of the river, keeping to the North of, and near, the Lower Sault Island, and also North of, and near, the Upper Sault (sometimes called Baxter's) Island, and south of the two small islands, marked on the Map A and B to the western extremity of the Upper Sault, or Baxter's Island: Thence, passing between the two islands called The Cats, to the middle of the river above: Thence, along the middle of the river, keeping to the North of the small islands marked C and D; and North also of Chrystlers Island, and of the small island next above it, marked E, until it approaches the north east angle of Goose Neck Island; Thence, along the passage which divides the last mentioned island from the Canada Shore, keeping one hundred yards from the Island, to the upper end of the same; Thence, South of, and

near, the two Small islands called The Nut Islands: Thence, North of, and near, the island marked F. and also of the island called Dry, or Smuggler's, Island: Thence, passing between the islands marked G and H,[1] to the North of the island called Isle au Rapid Plat: Thence, along the North side of the last mentioned island, keeping one hundred yards from the shore, to the upper end thereof: Thence, along the middle of the river, keeping to the South of, and near, the islands called Cousson (or Tussin) and Presque Isle: Thence, up the river, keeping north of, and near, the several Gallop Isles, numbered on the Map 1. 2. 3. 4. 5. 6. 7. 8. 9 & 10, and also of Tick, Tibbets' and Chimney Islands: and south of, and near, the Gallop Isles numbered 11. 12. & 13, and also of Duck. Drummond, and Sheep, Islands Thence, along the middle of the river, passing North of Island No. 14, South of 15. & 16, North of 17, South of 18. 19. 20. 21. 22. 23. 24. 25 & 28, and North[2] of 26 & 27: Thence, along the middle of the river, north of Gull Island, and of the islands N? 29. 32. 33. 34. 35, Bluff Island, and N? 39. 44. & 45, and to the South of N? 30. 31. 36. Grenadier Island, & N? 37. 38. 40. 41. 42. 43. 46. 47. & 48, until it approaches the east end of Well's Island; Thence, to the North of Well's Island, and along the Strait which divides it from Rowe's Island, keeping to the North of the small islands N? 51. 52. 54. 58. 59. & 61, and to the south of the small islands numbered and marked 49. 50. 53. 55. 57. 60 & X, until it approaches the North east point of Grindstone Island: Thence, to the North of Grindstone Island, and keeping to the North also of the small islands N? 63. 65. 67. 68. 70. 72. 73. 74. 75. 76. 77. & 78, and to the South of N? 62. 64. 66. 69 & 71, until it approaches the southern point of Hickory Island: Thence, passing to the South of Hickory Island and of the two small islands lying near it's southern extremity Numbered 79. & 80: Thence, to the South of Grand or Long Island, keeping near its southern shore, and passing to the North of Carlton Island, until it arrives opposite to the south western point of said Grand Island in lake Ontario: Thence, passing to the North of Grenadier, Fox, Stony, and the Gallop, Islands, in lake Ontario, and to the South of, and near, the islands called The Ducks, to the middle of the said lake: Thence, Westerly, along the middle of said lake, to a point opposite the Mouth of the Niagara River: Thence, to and up the middle of the said river, to the Great Falls: Thence, up the Falls, through the point of the Horse Shoe, keeping to the west of Iris or Goat Island, and of

[1] Islands G and H are marked G and I on original map 3.
[2] The line on original map 6 runs south of island 26 and north of island 27.

the group of small islands at it's head, and following the bends of the river, so as to enter the strait between Navy, and Grand Islands: Thence, along the middle of said strait, to the head of Navy Island: Thence, to the west and south of, and near to, Grand and Beaver Islands, and to the west of Strawberry, Squaw and Bird Islands, to Lake Erie: Thence, Southerly and Westerly, along the middle of Lake Erie, in a direction to enter the passage immediately south of Middle Island, being one of the easternmost of the group of islands lying in the western part of said lake: Thence, along the said passage, proceeding to the North of Cunningham's Island, of the three Bass Islands, and of the Western Sister, and to the south of the Islands, called The Hen and Chickens, and of the Eastern & Middle Sisters: Thence, to the Middle of the Mouth of the Detroit river, in a direction to enter the channel which divides Bois blanc and Sugar Islands: Thence, up the said Channel to the West of Bois Blanc Island, and to the east. of Sugar, Fox and Stony, Islands, until it approaches Fighting or Great Turkey Island: Thence, along the western side, and near the shore, of said last mentioned island, to the middle of the river above the same: Thence, along the middle of said river, keeping to the south east of, and near, Hog Island, and to the North-west of, and near, the island called Isle a la Pache, to Lake St. Clair: Thence, through the middle of said lake, in a direction to enter that mouth or channel of the river St. Clair which is usually denominated The old Ship Channel: Thence, along the middle of said channel, between Squirrel Island on the South east, and Herson's Island on the North west, to the upper end of the last mentioned island, which is nearly opposite to Point aux Chenes on the American Shore: Thence, along the middle of the river St Clair, keeping to the west of, and near, the islands called Belle Rivierè Isle and Isle aux Cerfs, to Lake Huron: Thence, through the middle of lake Huron, in a direction to enter the strait or passage between Drummond's Island on the West, and The little Manitou Island on the east: Thence, through the middle of the passage which divides the two last mentioned islands: Thence, turning Northerly and Westerly around the eastern and Northern Shores of Drummonds island, and proceeding in a direction to enter the passage between the island of St Joseph's and the american Shore, passing to the North of the intermediate islands[1] N⁰ 61. 11. 10. 12. 9. 6. 4. & 2, and to the South of those Numbered 15. 13. 5 & 1: Thence, up the

---

[1] Original maps 24 and 25 omit all the numbers of the "intermediate" and "small" islands.

said last mentioned passage, keeping near to the Island St. Joseph's, and passing to the North and east of Isle a la Crosse, and of the small islands numbered 16. 17. 18. 19 & 20, and to the south and west of those numbered 21. 22. & 23, until it strikes a line (drawn on the Map with black ink, and shaded on one side of the point of intersection with blue and on the other with red) passing across the river at the head of St Joseph's Island, and at the foot of the Neebish Rapids; Which line denotes the termination of the boundary directed to be run by the Sixth Article of the Treaty of Ghent.[1]

And the said Commissioners Do further decide and declare, That all the Islands lying in the Rivers, Lakes and Water Communications, between the before described Boundary Line and the adjacent shores of Upper Canada, Do, and each of them Does, belong to his Britannic Majesty: and that all the Islands, lying in the rivers, lakes, and water Communications, between the said Boundary Line and the adjacent shores of the United States, or their Territories, Do, and each of them Does, belong to the United States of America, in Conformity with the true intent of the Second Article of the said Treaty[2] of 1783, and of the Sixth Article of the Treaty. of Ghent.

In faith whereof We, the Commissioners aforesaid, have signed this Declaration, and thereunto affixed our Seals. Done, in Quadruplicate, at Utica, In the State of New York, in the United States of America, this eighteenth day of June, in the year of our Lord One thousand eight hundred and twenty two.

PETER B. PORTER   [Seal]
ANTH: BARCLAY   [Seal]

NOTES

It is stated in the declaration that it was executed in quadruplicate. One original, engrossed on parchment, is in the Department of State file.

By Article 2 of the Definitive Treaty of Peace with Great Britain of September 3, 1783 (Document 11), the boundary westward from that point where the forty-fifth degree of north latitude strikes the River St. Lawrence (near St. Regis, Franklin County, New York), is described as follows:

Thence along the middle of said River into Lake Ontario; through the Middle of said Lake until it strikes the Communication by Water between that Lake & Lake Erie; Thence along the middle of said Communication into Lake Erie; through the middle of said Lake, until it arrives at the Water Communication between that Lake & Lake Huron; Thence along the middle of said Water-Communication into the Lake Huron, thence through the middle of said Lake to

---

[1] Document 33.   [2] Document 11.

the Water Communication between that Lake and Lake Superior, thence through Lake Superior Northward of the Isles Royal & Phelipeaux to the Long Lake; Thence through the Middle of said Long-Lake, and the Water Communication between it & the Lake of the Woods, to the said Lake of the Woods; Thence through the said Lake to the most Northwestern Point thereof, and from thence on a due West Course to the River Mississippi.

No steps were taken by the two Governments to describe more in detail or to survey or map the boundary in the St. Lawrence River and through the Great Lakes until commissioners were appointed for that purpose under Articles 6 and 7 of the Treaty of Ghent (Document 33). Article 6 of that treaty dealt with the portion of that boundary from the point where the forty-fifth degree of north latitude strikes the River St. Lawrence to the water communication between Lake Huron and Lake Superior. In part that article reads as follows:

Whereas by the former Treaty of Peace that portion of the boundary of the United States from the point where the forty fifth degree of North Latitude strikes the River Iroquois or Cataraquy to the Lake Superior was declared to be "along the middle of said River into Lake Ontario, through the middle of said Lake until it strikes the communication by water between that Lake and Lake Erie, thence along the middle of said communication into Lake Erie, through the middle of said Lake until it arrives at the water communication into the Lake Huron; thence through the middle of said Lake to the water communication between that Lake and Lake Superior:" and whereas doubts have arisen what was the middle of the said River, Lakes, and water communications, and whether certain Islands lying in the same were within the Dominions of His Britannic Majesty or of the United States: In order therefore finally to decide these doubts, they shall be referred to two Commissioners to be appointed, sworn, and authorized to act exactly in the manner directed with respect to those mentioned in the next preceding Article unless otherwise specified in this present Article. The said Commissioners shall meet in the first instance at Albany in the State of New York, and shall have power to adjourn to such other place or places as they shall think fit. The said Commissioners shall by a Report or Declaration under their hands and seals, designate the boundary through the said River, Lakes, and water communications, and decide to which of the two Contracting parties the several Islands lying within the said Rivers, Lakes, and water communications, do respectively belong in conformity with the true intent of the said Treaty of one thousand seven hundred and eighty three. And both parties agree to consider such designation and decision as final and conclusive.

This declaration of the Commissioners of June 18, 1822, was made pursuant to the provisions of Article 6 of the Treaty of Ghent above quoted and was the result of the labors of some years, as the Commissioners first met at Albany on November 18, 1816. The manuscript journal of the Commissioners, from November 18, 1816, to June 22, 1822, is in the archives of the Department of State, and an account of their proceedings is in Moore, International Arbitrations, I, 162–70. The declaration was communicated to Congress with the presidential message of February 26, 1823 (American State Papers, Foreign Relations, V, 241–45).

The Original Maps

The "Maps accompanying this report" (except two which were not signed) form strictly a part of the declaration. Originals of those maps, of which there are twenty-five, are in the archives of the Department of State. As a whole the maps were not, in the first instance, serially numbered, but they have been marked in pencil with numbers 1 to 25; and those numbers will be used here for convenience of reference, as the original maps have usually been referred to by them.

Maps 1 to 10 show the line running up the St. Lawrence River to Lake Ontario. The originals are numbered I to X, and they are entitled "Iroquois or St Lawrence 1817" (I to III) or "Iroquois or St Lawrence 1818" (IV to X).

Map 11, which, in order of locational sequence, should properly be map 12, is entitled "Lake Ontario," with the legend, "Copied from the Survey made in the years 1815–16 & 17 by Capt. H. F. W. Owen of H. B. Majesty's Royal Navy." This map is of Lake Ontario as a whole. It is neither certified nor signed.

Map 12, which should properly be map 11, is entitled "Ontario 1819." It represents the northeastern portion of Lake Ontario.

Maps 13 to 16 show the line extending from Lake Ontario through the Niagara River and into Lake Erie. Maps 13, 14, and 16 are entitled "Niagara 1819" and are numbered respectively I, II, and IV. Map 15 is entitled "The Second Section of the Survey of 1819."

Map 17 is entitled "Lake Erie." It represents the entire lake. This map is not certified and is not signed. It has the following legend:

That part West of Points Pélé and Sandusky including all the Islands, is reduced from the actual Surveys, made by order of the Commissioners.

The other parts of the Lake, (except the entrance into the Niagara River) are reduced from such printed maps as were supposed to be the most accurate.

Map 18 has no title. It is a map of the southwest end of Lake Erie.

Maps 19 to 23 carry the line through the water communication between Lake Erie and Lake Huron. Maps 19 to 21 are entitled "Detroit 1820" and are numbered respectively I to III. Map 22 is entitled "Lake St Clair." While this map is duly signed, it has no certificate. Map 23 has no title. It shows the line extending from the Channels at the head of Lake St. Clair through the River St. Clair and into Lake Huron. It is twice signed, with two certificates.

Map 24 is entitled "The Fifteenth Section N$^{\circ}$ 1. Lake Huron 1820 & 21." This map represents Lake Huron as a whole and indicates the termination of the line under Article 6 of the Treaty of Ghent. It has the following legend and signed certificate:

The black Lines denote the actual Survey; and the Latitudes and Longitudes designated in the body of the Map are the actual observations made by Order of the Board.

The dotted Lines are the Shores of the Lake as laid down, and copied from the Map of Mr William Smyth, Surveyor General of Upper Canada and are not to be depended on.

The black Line of Cabotia, and Isles north of it, is copied from the naval Survey of Captain of the Royal Navy.

We certify this to be a true Map (the black Lines only included) of part of the Boundary designated by the 6th Article of the Treaty of Ghent from actual Survey by order of the Board.

Map 25 has no title.   It is a map of the upper end of Lake Huron, and on it also is marked the termination of the line under Article 6 of the Treaty of Ghent.

These originals, numbered 1 to 25, are of various sizes and scales. Measured between the innermost border lines, or including in addition any extension of the map beyond these lines, the dimensions are as follows: The two largest maps are respectively 9 feet 9 inches high by 2 feet 3 inches wide (298 by 69 cm.), and 4 feet 2 inches high by 7 feet 4 inches wide (128 by 224 cm.).   The four smallest maps, while varying slightly in size, are approximately 1 foot 11 inches high by 2 feet 11 inches wide (58 by 89 cm.).   The remaining maps are for the most part about 2 feet 6 inches high by 4 feet 3 inches wide (76 by 129 cm.).

The scale of the maps is usually expressed in terms both of a geographical mile of 6075.6 feet and of an English mile of 5280 feet in relation to units of length graphically shown on the map.   Maps 12, 18, 22, and 25 are in a scale of 1 inch to 1 geographical mile (1 : 72,900); maps 11 and 17 are in a scale of 1 inch to 3 geographical miles (1 : 219,000); map 24 is in a scale of 1 inch to 7 geographical miles (1 : 510,000); and the remaining eighteen maps are in a scale of 5 inches to 1 geographical mile (1 : 14,600).

All these twenty-five maps except maps 11 and 17 are signed by Peter B. Porter and Anthony Barclay, Commissioners, and William A. Bird and David Thompson, Surveyors, under Articles 6 and 7 of the Treaty of Ghent, and all the signed maps except map 22 have this certificate over the signatures: "We certify this to be a true Map of part of the Boundary designated by the sixth article of the Treaty of Ghent; from actual Survey by order of the Board."   Filed with these originals is a sheet entitled "The 6th Art: Tr: Ghent— Contents of the Portfolio."   This paper seems to be a list of the maps before they were finally assembled and mounted.   It has corrections and additions in pencil and is not dated.   It is signed by John Bigsby, Assistant Secretary to the Commissioners, and bears this note: "The sheets, which are not certified and signed, were intended to be united with others which have certificates and signatures."

As stated in the declaration, there is drawn on these maps, to indicate the boundary, "a black line shaded on the British side with red and on the American side with blue."

Facsimiles of these twenty-five maps, somewhat reduced in size, are in Moore, International Arbitrations, VI, numbered 1 to 25. Those facsimiles are in black and white only, so that the boundary shows as a continuous black line, without the blue and red shading of the originals.

Lithographed reproductions of eight of these maps, showing the boundary line with the blue and red shading, are in a work in the form of an atlas entitled "Letter from the Secretary of State, Transmitting, Pursuant to a Resolution in the House of Representatives, of the Nineteenth Ultimo, a Copy of the Maps and Report of the Commissioners under the Treaty of Ghent, for Ascertaining the Northern and Northwestern Boundary between the United States and Great Britain." In that work, a copy of which is in the Division of Maps, Library of Congress, is printed this declaration of June 18, 1822, with the letter of transmittal of Secretary of State Henry Clay dated March 15, 1828, which reads as follows:

The Secretary of State, in pursuance of a resolution of the House of Representatives, of the 19th ultimo, directing him to report to that House a copy of the Maps, and so much of the Reports of the Commissioners under the Treaty of Ghent, for ascertaining the Northern and Northwestern Boundary between the United States and Great Britain, as will exhibit those parts of said Boundary which are already decided upon, has the honor to report the accompanying copies of a part of a series of Maps which have been communicated to this office, exhibiting Surveys and Delineations of so much of said Boundary Line as is believed to be required by the resolution of the House; and respectfully to refer the House to the Decision, dated 18th June, 1822, of the Joint Commissioners under the sixth article of the said treaty, published at the end of the Acts of the second Session of the Seventeenth Congress, in the seventh volume of the Laws of the United States, for a further and full explanation of the said Boundary Line, as agreed upon and established.

The reproductions are somewhat reduced from the originals and comprise maps 18 to 25, inclusive, and in that order except that map 25 precedes map 24.

In 1891 the United States Lighthouse Board published a set of maps which includes those under Article 6 of the Treaty of Ghent. The maps are in a folder entitled "Northern Boundary of the United States According to the Treaty of Ghent." They consist of twenty-nine maps in thirty-two sheets. Each map bears the following notation: "U. S. Light-House Board, Washington, D. C., November, 1891. Photolithographed from original charts by permission of the U. S. State Department. Geo. W. Coffin Commander, U. S. N. Naval Secretary." The maps show the line from near St. Regis on the St. Lawrence to Pigeon River, northwestern Lake Superior. They are not numbered but correspond with maps 1–27, 35, and 56 in Moore, International Arbitrations, VI. The maps are reduced in scale to less than half that of the originals. The map sheets are of uniform size and measure 16 by 24 inches.

A very careful report on the Canadian boundary from the Atlantic to the Pacific, giving its history to 1906, will be found in Chandler P. Anderson, Canadian Questions: Northern Boundary of the United States. Pages 31 to 35 of that work treat particularly of the boundary dealt with by Article 6 of the Treaty of Ghent.

THE EXISTING BOUNDARY

The boundary between the United States and Canada through the St. Lawrence River and the Great Lakes, as now demarcated, is shown on a series of charts entitled "International Boundary between the United States and Dominion of Canada through the Saint Lawrence River and Great Lakes as Ascertained and Reestablished by the International Waterways Commission Pursuant to Article 4 of the Treaty between the United States and Great Britain Signed April 11, 1908, in 30 Sheets Including an Index Sheet." Each of the twenty-nine charts showing the boundary is signed by the members of the International Waterways Commission with the following certificate:

We certify that this is an accurate chart, prepared and adopted by us, showing a portion of the international boundary line as defined and located by us under Article IV of the treaty between the United States of America and the United Kingdom of Great Britain and Ireland, signed April 11, 1908. Adopted at Buffalo, New York, August 15, 1913.

Sheets Nos. 1 to 23, inclusive, of this series, cover that portion of the boundary dealt with by Article 6 of the Treaty of Ghent, namely, from the point where the forty-fifth degree of north latitude strikes the River St. Lawrence to the water communication between Lake Huron and Lake Superior; sheets Nos. 21 to 29, inclusive, show the boundary continuing from the water communication between Lake Huron and Lake Superior to the mouth of Pigeon River at the western shore of Lake Superior.

The scale of sheets Nos. 1 to 23 is generally 1:20,000, but Nos. 8, 14, 17, and 21 are 1:60,000; Nos. 9, 13, and 20 are 1:300,000; and No. 11 is 1:10,000.

Duplicate originals of these charts, prepared by the International Waterways Commission pursuant to Article 4 of the Treaty with Great Britain of April 11, 1908, are in the archives of the Department of State.

The "Report of the International Waterways Commission upon the International Boundary between the Dominion of Canada and the United States through the St. Lawrence River and Great Lakes as Ascertained and Re-established Pursuant to Article IV of the Treaty between Great Britain and the United States Signed 11th April, 1908," dated at Buffalo April 29, 1915, with three appendices, was printed at Ottawa in 1916, in one volume, with a box volume of maps. A detailed "Description of International Boundary Line between Canada and the United States through the St. Lawrence River, Great Lakes, and Communicating Waterways," is at pages 31–96; and the records transmitted to each of the two Governments for its archives are thus described at page 114:

There are transmitted to each Government for its archives the following records: Two leather portfolios, each containing a set of the thirty boundary charts, certified and signed by the Commissioners; thirty of the sixty engraved copper plates, 27½ inches by 43 inches, covering alternate charts along the

boundary line; and thirty of the sixty aluminum plates, 43 inches by 53 inches, consisting of fifteen black and fifteen tint plates, covering the remaining alternate charts along the boundary line.

The maps reproduced in the work mentioned are on a somewhat smaller scale than the originals and are there listed as follows:

INDEX—Montreal to Duluth, St. Lawrence river and Great lakes general index sheet to all sheets.
    1—St. Lawrence river, St. Regis to Dickinson Landing.
    2—St. Lawrence river, Dickinson Landing to head of Morrisburg canal.
    3—St. Lawrence river, head of Morrisburg canal to Prescott.
    4—St. Lawrence river, Prescott to Oak Point.
    5—St. Lawrence river, Oak point to Alexandria bay. The Rift.
    6—St. Lawrence river, Alexandria bay to east end of Wolfe island.
    7—St. Lawrence river, east end of Wolfe island to west end of Wolfe island.
    8—East end of lake Ontario, west end of Wolfe island to Main Duck island.
    9—General sheet of lake Ontario.
    10—Niagara river, lake Ontario to Niagara falls.
    11—Niagara river, Whirlpool to Navy island.
    12—Niagara river, Niagara falls to lake Erie.
    13—General sheet of lake Erie.
    14—West end of lake Erie.
    15—Detroit river, lake Erie to Fighting island.
    16—Detroit river, Fighting island to lake St. Clair.
    17—Lake St. Clair general sheet.
    18—St. Clair river, lake St. Clair to Port Lambton.
    19—St. Clair river, Marine City to lake Huron.
    20—General sheet lake Huron.
    21—North channel and St. Marys river, False Detour passage to foot of Sugar island.
    22—North channel and St. Marys river, Potagannissing bay to foot of Mud lake.
    23—St. Marys river, foot of Mud lake to middle Neebish.
    24—St. Marys river, middle Neebish to Sault Ste. Marie.
    25—St. Marys falls.
    26—Sault Ste. Marie to point Iroquois.
    27—East end of lake Superior.
    28—General sheet of lake Superior, Whitefish point to Pigeon bay.
    29—North shore of lake Superior, Spar island to head of Pigeon bay.

Treaty Series No. 87
8 Statutes at Large, 278–83
18 *ibid.*, pt. 2, Public Treaties, 243–45

43

FRANCE : JUNE 24, 1822

Convention of Navigation and Commerce, with two separate articles (the second of which was not ratified), signed at Washington June 24, 1822. Original in English and French.
Submitted to the Senate December 10, 1822. (Message of December 4, 1822.) Resolution of advice and consent January 31, 1823. Ratified by the United States February 12, 1823. Ratified by France November 6, 1822. Ratifications exchanged at Washington February 12, 1823. Proclaimed February 12, 1823.

Original.

Convention of Navigation and Commerce between the United-States of America and His Majesty the King of France and Navarre.

The United-States of America, and His Majesty the King of France and Navarre, being desirous of settling the relations of Navigation and Commerce between their respective Nations, by a temporary Convention reciprocally beneficial and satisfactory, and thereby of leading to a more permanent and comprehensive arrangement, have respectively furnished their full powers in manner following, that is to say: the President of the United-States, to John Quincy Adams, their Secretary of State; and His Most Christian Majesty, to the Baron Hyde de Neuville, Knight of the Royal and Military Order of St Louis, Commander of the

Original.

Convention de Navigation et de Commerce entre Sa Majesté le Roi de France et de Navarre, et les Etats-Unis d'Amérique.

Sa Majesté le Roi de France et de Navarre, et les Etats-Unis d'Amérique désirant régler les relations de Navigation et de Commerce entre leurs Nations respectives, par une Convention temporaire, réciproquement avantageuse et satisfaisante, et arriver ainsi à un arrangement plus étendu et durable, ont respectivement donné leurs pleins-pouvoirs, savoir: Sa Majesté Très-Chrétienne au Baron Hyde de Neuville, Chevalier de l'Ordre Royal et Militaire de St Louis, Commandeur de la Légion-d'honneur, Grand-Croix de l'Ordre Royal Américain d'Isabelle la Catholique, son Envoyé extraordinaire et Ministre plénipotentiaire près

77

Legion of Honor, Grand-Cross of the Royal American Order of Isabella the Catholic, His Envoy extraordinary and Minister plenipotentiary near the United-States; who, after exchanging their full powers, have agreed on the following Articles.

ARTICLE 1.st

Articles of the growth, produce, or manufacture of the United-States, imported into France in vessels of the United-States, shall pay an additional duty not exceeding twenty francs per ton of merchandise, over and above the duties paid on the like articles, also of the growth, produce, or manufacture of the United-States when imported in French vessels.

ARTICLE 2.

Articles of the growth, produce, or manufacture of France, imported into the United-States in French Vessels, shall pay an additional duty not exceeding three dollars and seventy five cents per ton of merchandize, over and above the duties collected upon the like articles, also of the growth, produce or manufacture of France, when imported in Vessels of the United-States.

ARTICLE 3.

No discriminating duty shall be levied upon the productions of the soil or industry of France, imported in French bottoms into the

les Etats-Unis; et le Président des Etats-Unis, à John Quincy Adams, leur sécrétaire d'Etat; lesquels, après avoir échangé leurs pleins pouvoirs, sont convenus des Articles suivans.

ARTICLE 1.er

Les produits naturels ou manufacturés des Etats-Unis importés en France sur Batimens des Etats-Unis payeront un Droit additionel qui n'excèdera point vingt francs par tonneau de marchandise, en sus des Droits payés sur les mêmes produits naturels ou manufacturés des Etats-Unis quand ils sont importés par Navires français.

ARTICLE 2.

Les produits naturels ou manufacturés de France importés aux Etats-Unis sur Batimens français payeront un Droit additionel qui n'excèdera point trois dollars soixante quinze cents par tonneau de marchandise, en sus des Droits payés sur les mêmes produits naturels ou manufacturés de France quand ils sont importés par Navires des Etats-Unis.

ARTICLE 3.

Aucun Droit différentiel ne sera levé sur les produits du sol et de l'Industrie de France qui seront importés par Navires fran-

Ports of the United-States for transit or re-exportation.

Nor shall any such duties be levied upon the productions of the soil or industry of the United-States imported in Vessels of the United-States into the Ports of France for transit or re-exportation.

ARTICLE 4.

The following quantities shall be considered as forming the ton of merchandise for each of the Articles hereinafter specified:

Wines—four 61 gallon-hogsheads or 244 gallons of 231 cubic inches American measure.

Brandies—and all other liquids, 244 gallons.

Silks, and all other dry goods, and all other articles usually subject to measurement: forty two cubic feet French in France, and fifty cubic feet American measure in the United-States.

Cotton—804 $^{lb.}$ avoir dupois or 365 Kilogrammes.

Tobacco—1,600 ^{lb} avoir dupois or 725 Kilogrammes.

Ashes, pot and pearl, 2240 ^{lb} avoir dupois or 1016 Kilog^s

Rice—1600 ^{lb} avoir dupois or 725 Kilogrammes.

And for all weighable Articles

çais dans les Ports des Etats-Unis pour transit ou ré-exportation.

Il en sera de même dans les Ports de France pour les produits du sol et de l'Industrie de l'Union qui seront importés pour transit ou ré-exportation par Navires des Etats-Unis.

ARTICLE 4.

Les quantités suivantes seront considérées comme formant le tonneau de marchandise pour chacun des Articles ci-après spécifiés:

Vins—quatre barriques de 61 gallons chaque, ou 244 gallons de 231 pouces cubes. (mesure Américaine)

Eaux de vie et tous autres liquides, 244 gallons.

Soieries et toutes autres marchandises sèches ainsi que tous autres Articles généralement soumis au mésurage, quarante deux pieds cubes, mesure française, en France; et cinquante pieds cubes, mesure Américaine, aux Etats-Unis.

Cotons—804 ^{L} avoir dupoids ou 365 Kilogrammes.

Tabacs—1600 ^{L} avoir dupoids ou 725 Kilogrammes.

Potasse et Perlasse 2240 ^{L} avoir dupoids ou 1016 Kilog.

Riz—1600 ^{L} avoir dupoids ou 725 Kilogrammes.

Et pour tous les Articles non-

not specified, 2240 $^{lb.}$ avoir dupois or 1016 Kilogrammes.

ARTICLE 5.

The duties of Tonnage, light money, Pilotage, Port-charges, brokerage and all other duties upon foreign shipping, over and above those paid by the National shipping in the two Countries respectively, other than those specified in Articles 1 and 2 of the present Convention, shall not exceed, in France for vessels of the United-States, five francs per ton of the Vessel's American Register, nor, for Vessels of France in the United-States, ninety four cents per ton of the Vessel's French passport.

ARTICLE 6.

The contracting parties, wishing to favor their mutual Commerce, by affording in their Ports every necessary assistance to their respective vessels, have agreed that the Consuls and Vice-Consuls may cause to be arrested the sailors being part of the crews of the vessels of their respective Nations, who shall have deserted from the said vessels, in order to send them back and transport them out of the Country. For which purpose the said Consuls and Vice-Consuls shall address themselves to the Courts, Judges and Officers com-

spécifiés et qui se pèsent, 2240 ^{L} avoir dupoids ou 1016 Kilogrammes.

ARTICLE 5.

Les Droits de Tonnage, de Phare, de Pilotage, Droits de Port, Courtage et tous autres Droits sur la Navigation Etrangère en sus de ceux payés respectivement par la Navigation Nationale dans les deux Pays, autres que ceux spécifiés dans les Articles 1 et 2 de la présente Convention, n'excèderont pas, en France pour les Batimens des Etats-Unis, cinq francs par tonneau d'après le Régistre Américain du Batiment, ni pour les Batimens français aux Etats-Unis, quatre vingt-quatorze cents par Tonneau d' après le Passeport français du Batiment.

ARTICLE 6.

Les parties contractantes désirant favoriser mutuellement leur Commerce, en donnant dans leurs Ports toute assistance nécessaire à leurs Batimens respectifs, sont convenues que les Consuls et Vice-Consuls pourront faire arrêter les matelôts faisant partie des Equipages des Batimens de leurs Nations respectives qui auraient deserté des dits Batimens pour les renvoyer et faire transporter hors du Pays. Auquel effet les dits Consuls et Vice-Consuls s'adresseront aux Tribunaux, Juges et Officiers compètens, et leur feront, par écrit, la demande des dits

petent, and shall demand the said deserters in writing, proving by an exhibition of the Registers of the Vessel, or ship's roll, or other official Documents, that those men were part of the said crews; and on this demand so proved (saving however where the contrary is proved) the delivery shall not be refused; and there shall be given all aid and assistance to the said Consuls and Vice-Consuls for the search, seizure and arrest of the said deserters, who shall even be detained, and kept in the prisons of the Country, at their request and expense, until they shall have found an opportunity of sending them back. But if they be not sent back within three months, to be counted from the day of their arrest, they shall be set at liberty, and shall be no more arrested for the same cause.

déserteurs, en justifiant par l'exhibition des Registres du Batiment ou rôle d'Equipage ou autres Documens officiels, que ces hommes faisaient partie des dits Equipages. Et sur cette demande ainsi justifiée, sauf toutefois la preuve contraire, l'extradition ne pourra être refusée, et il sera donné toute aide et assistance aux dits Consuls et Vice-Consuls pour la recherche, saisie et arrestation des susdits déserteurs, lesquels seront même détenus et gardés dans les Prisons du Pays, à leur réquisition, et à leurs frais, jusqu'à ce qu'ils ayent trouvé moyen de les renvoyer. Mais s'ils n'etaient renvoyés dans le délai de trois mois à compter du jour de leur arrêt, ils seront élargis, et ne pourront plus être arrêtés pour la même cause.

ARTICLE 7.

The present temporary Convention shall be in force for two years from the first day of October next, and even after the expiration of that term, until the conclusion of a definitive Treaty, or until one of the Parties shall have declared its intention to renounce it; which declaration shall be made at least six months beforehand.

ARTICLE 7.

La présente Convention temporaire aura son plein effet pendant deux ans à partir du 1er Octobre prochain, et même après l'expiration de ce terme, elle sera maintenue jusqu'à la Conclusion d'un Traité définitif, ou jusqu'à ce que l'une des Parties ait déclaré à l'autre son intention d'y renoncer; laquelle déclaration devra être faite au moins six mois d'avance.

And in case the present Arrangement should remain without such declaration of its discontinuance by either party, the extra-duties specified in the 1st and 2^{d} articles shall, from the expiration of the said two years, be on both sides diminished by one fourth of their whole amount, and afterwards by one fourth of the said amount from year to year, so long as neither party shall have declared the intention of renouncing it as above stated.

ARTICLE 8.

The present Convention shall be ratified on both sides, and the ratifications shall be exchanged within one year from the date hereof, or sooner if possible. But the execution of the said Convention shall commence in both Countries on the first of October next, and shall be effective, even in case of non-ratification, for all such vessels as may have sailed *bonâ fide*, for the Ports of either Nation, in the confidence of its being in force.

In faith whereof, the respective Plenipotentiaries have signed the present Convention, and have thereto affixed their seals at the City of Washington, this 24th day of June, A D. 1822.

JOHN QUINCY ADAMS   [Seal]
G HYDE DE NEUVILLE   [Seal]

Et dans le cas où la présente Convention viendrait à continuer sans cette déclaration par l'une ou l'autre Partie, les Droits extra-ordinaires spécifiés dans les 1er et 2^{d} Articles seront, à l'expiration des dits deux années, diminuées de part et d'autre d'un quart de leur montant, et successivement d'un quart du dit montant d'année en année, aussi longtems qu'aucune des Parties n'aura déclaré son intention d'y renoncer, ainsi qu'ils est dit ci-dessus.

ARTICLE 8.

La présente Convention sera ratifiée de part et d'autre, et les ratifications seront échangées, dans l'espace d'une année, à compter de ce jour, ou plutôt si faire se peut. Mais l'éxécution de la dite Convention commencera dans les deux Pays, le premier Octobre prochain, et aura son effet, dans le cas même de non-ratification, pour tous Batimens partis *bonâ fide* pour les Ports de l'une ou l'autre Nation, dans la confiance qu'elle était en vigueur.

En foi de quoi, les Plénipotentiaires respectifs ont signé la présente Convention, et y ont apposé leurs Sceaux, en la Ville de Washington, ce 24me jour de Juin de l'an de Notre Seigneur 1822.

[Seal]   G HYDE DE NEUVILLE
[Seal]   JOHN QUINCY ADAMS

SEPARATE ARTICLE.	ARTICLE SÉPARÉ
The extra-duties levied on either side before the present day, by virtue of the Act of Congress of 15 May 1820, and of the Ordinance of 26 July of the same year, and others confirmative thereof, and which have not already been paid back, shall be refunded.	Les Droits extraordinaires levés de part et d'autre jusqu'à ce jour, en vertu de l'Acte du Congrès du 15 Mai 1820 et de l'Ordonnance du 26 Juillet de la même année, et autres la confirmant, qui n'ont point déjà été remboursés, seront restitués.
Signed and Sealed as above, this 24th day of June 1822.	Signé et scellé comme ci-dessus, ce 24me jour de Juin 1822.
[Seal] JOHN QUINCY ADAMS	[Seal] G HYDE DE NEUVILLE
[Seal] G HYDE DE NEUVILLE	[Seal] JOHN QUINCY ADAMS

[On the last two written pages of the original appear the English and French texts of the second separate article, which was not ratified.[1]]

NOTES

The language and form of this convention were discussed shortly before its signature. The conversation between Secretary of State Adams and Baron Hyde de Neuville, the French Minister at Washington, on June 15, 1822, is thus reported (Memoirs of John Quincy Adams, VI, 20–21):

His last difficulty was, that I had in the concluding article expressed that the Convention was drawn up original in both languages. He said he was willing to do anything in that respect for which there was a precedent, but heretofore there had been a pretension on the part of France of a preference for the French language. They no longer had any such pretension; but as this express assertion, that both sides were original, was in no other treaty, he was afraid it might make some difficulty in France. I referred him to the former treaties with France, but although they were all signed in both languages, and all, except the Consular Convention of 14th November, 1788, expressly say so, yet all the rest, except the Convention of 30th September, 1800, say they were originally drawn up in French, and that says the signing in both languages shall not be drawn into precedent. He seemed to doubt the propriety of declaring the copies in both languages original.

I told him it was certainly no novelty in French diplomacy; and showed him the discussion between the French and British Commissaries previous to the war of 1755, in which the British Commissaries charge the French with having quoted the Treaty of Utrecht in the French translation instead of the *original* Latin; to which the French Commissaries replied that the French copy was original as well as the Latin.

"Well," said the Baron, "ils avoient tort" [they were wrong]. He consented, however, after I had shown him this example, to insert the word "original" at the top of the treaty on both sides, as was done in our last treaty with Spain [see Document 41].

---

[1] See the note regarding the second separate article.

There is an error in the foregoing statement of Adams, for the Consular Convention of November 14, 1788, with France (Document 15), was signed in French only, as were also the contracts of 1782 and 1783 (Documents 4 and 9).

The respective contentions of the British and French Commissaries regarding the language of the Treaty of Utrecht are to be found in Mémoires des Commissaires du Roi et de ceux de Sa Majesté Britannique, sur les possessiones et les droits respectifs des deux Couronnes en Amérique, IV, 430–34.

The documents relating to the negotiation of this convention which were transmitted to the Senate with the presidential message of December 4, 1822, are in American State Papers, Foreign Relations, V, 149–213. Some of the discussions are reported in the Memoirs of John Quincy Adams, VI, 15–23.

The signing of this convention is thus described by Secretary of State Adams (*ibid.*, 29):

At one o'clock the Baron Hyde de Neuville, the French Minister, came with De Menou, and we executed four copies of the Commercial Convention in both languages. Two copies had been made by Mr. Ironside at the office, and two at the French Legation. Some small corrections were necessary to make them all uniform. The alternative was preserved throughout. Both copies were signed and sealed by both parties, and both as originals. In the examination of the copies, the Baron held one of ours, and I one of theirs; Mr. Brent the other of theirs, and Menou the other of ours. Menou read the French copy, and Mr. Brent ours. We found the usual inconveniences of sealing the inside of the papers with wax, and in more than the usual degree, as there were two separate articles, each separately executed.

The Baron observed to Menou that this day was my festival day—St. John's day—the Baptist. He said his own name was John, too; but from the Evangelist. As we sealed on both sides of the paper, it happened in one of the copies that by the turning of a leaf his seal and mine adhered together, so that they could not be parted. I told him it was *de bon augure*—which he took as a compliment. We interchanged the copies, he taking one of his own and one of ours, and we the same.

There are two originals of this convention in the treaty file; one has the English text on the left-hand pages and the French on the right, and the other has the French text on the left-hand pages and the English on the right. From the above-quoted record it appears that one of these originals was prepared in the Department of State and the other at the French Legation. It might be supposed that the original which has the English on the left was the one prepared in the Department of State; but the evidence is to the contrary, and the handwriting of the other original—the one with the French on the left—definitely shows that it was the one prepared in the Department of State, for that writing is the same as the handwriting of the original United States instrument of ratification of this treaty, of the original proclamation (except the treaty texts) of the treaty with Spain of 1819 (Document 41), and of other documents of the same period which were written in the Department of State and are now in the archives. The handwriting appears to be that of George Edmund Ironside, a clerk in the Department of State whom Adams mentions as having made "two copies" of the treaty.

The text printed above has been collated with that original which has the English on the left pages. The two originals differ very slightly in matters of capitalization, spelling, abbreviation, and accent; and the punctuation is not altogether the same in the one as in the other, there being some thirty instances of difference in respect of the insertion or omission of commas; but none of those differences seems to be in any way material. The variant wordings are that the original with the French on the left pages omits "the" before "said crews" in Article 6 and in the French text of the same article has "occasion" for "moyen."

As may be seen from the printed texts, the principle of the *alternat* was duly observed; the United States is named before the King of France and Navarre in the English text, and the signatures of the Plenipotentiaries follow the same order, which is reversed in the French text.

THE FULL POWERS

A certified copy of the full power of the French Plenipotentiary is in D. S., 7 Notes from the French Legation, as an enclosure to the note of Baron Hyde de Neuville of February 17, 1821. Slightly revised, the English translation there written is as follows:

Louis, by the Grace of God King of France and of Navarre

To all who shall see these present letters, Greeting:

Desirous to fix and regulate in a manner respectively advantageous, the relations of commerce and navigation between France and the United States, for these causes, We having entire confidence in the capacity, prudence, and experience of Our very dear and well-beloved the Sieur Baron Hyde de Neuville, Knight of Our Royal and Military Order of St. Louis, Officer of the Legion of Honor, Grand Cross of the Royal Order of Isabella the Catholic, and Our Envoy Extraordinary and Minister Plenipotentiary at Washington, We have named and appointed him, and by these presents, signed with Our hand, We name and appoint him, Our Plenipotentiary, giving him full and absolute power to meet with the Plenipotentiary or Plenipotentiaries of the United States, equally furnished with full powers in proper form, in order to negotiate, conclude, and sign in Our name, with the same authority as We ourselves would or could do, such articles, conventions, and other acts as he may judge fit for attaining the important end which We have in mind. Promising, on the faith and word of a King, to accept, accomplish, and execute punctually all that Our said Plenipotentiary shall have stipulated, promised, and signed in Our name and in virtue of the present full powers, without ever contravening or permitting the same to be contravened, directly or indirectly, for any cause or under any pretext whatsoever; likewise to give Our letters of ratification thereof in proper form and to have them delivered for exchange within the period which shall be agreed upon. In faith whereof We have caused Our seal to be put to these presents. Given at the Palace of the Tuileries the twentieth day of the month of October in the year of grace one thousand eight hundred and twenty and in the twenty-sixth of Our reign.

LOUIS

By the King:
PASQUIER

The full power to Secretary of State Adams was dated February 20, 1821, and is in customary form (D. S., 1 Credences, 330; see also Memoirs of John Quincy Adams, V, 282–83).

THE SENATE RESOLUTION

According to the Executive Journal, III, 329–30, two resolutions were prepared on January 31, 1823, regarding this convention, the first unanimously giving the advice and consent of the Senate to the convention and the first separate article, and the second, by a vote of forty-one to three, advising and consenting to the second separate article; but the attested resolution which is in the treaty file is in the following form:

Resolved, two thirds of the Senators present concurring therein, that the Senate do advise and consent to the ratification of the Convention of Navigation and Commerce, and the two seperate articles attached thereto, made and concluded between the United States and the King of France and Navarre, on the 24ᵗʰ day of June 1822, at the City of Washington.

THE RATIFICATIONS

It is said in the second separate article that "the refusal to ratify this Article, on either side, shall in no wise affect or impair the ratification or the validity of the preceding Articles of this Convention." It appears that this clause resulted from a proposal of the French Minister during the negotiations, who "expressed the wish to make the two separate articles separate also from each other; to which I [Adams] agreed" (Memoirs of John Quincy Adams, VI, 20).

The French instrument of ratification mentions and recites only the French text of the treaty and of the first separate article. It omits the word "original" as a heading to the text and makes no mention of the second separate article at all.

A facsimile of the United States instrument of ratification, obtained from the French archives, is now in the treaty file. Preceding the text of the treaty and of the first separate article in English and French, is the following recital:

Whereas a Convention of Navigation and Commerce between the United States of America, and His Majesty the King of France and Navarre, was concluded and signed at Washington on the twenty fourth day of June last past, which Convention, with two separate Articles annexed thereto, is word for word as follows, excepting the second of the said separate Articles.

The final clauses of the ratification are somewhat unusual in form. The Senate had given its advice and consent to the second separate article, and President Monroe was prepared to ratify it. While the French instrument of ratification omitted mention of the second separate article, the Government of France had not said definitely that it would not be ratified. Accordingly, the question of future ratification of that article was reserved by the United States, although these final clauses of the instrument contain words of ratification of the second separate article:

And whereas the Senate of the United States did on the thirty-first day of January last past, two thirds of the Senators present concurring therein, advise and consent to the Ratification of the said Convention, and of the two separate Articles attached thereto;

Now therefore I, James Monroe, President of the United States of America, having seen and considered the said Convention together with the advice and consent of the Senate of the United States as aforesaid, and in pursuance thereof, do, by these Presents, accept, ratify and confirm the said Convention, and the first separate Article annexed thereto, as the same are herein before set forth.

And I do also accept, ratify and confirm the said Second separate Article of the said Convention. But inasmuch as it has not yet been ratified on the part of France; and inasmuch as no refusal to ratify the same on the part of France has been made known to me, so that the said Ratification may yet be given, and hereafter exchanged for that of the United States within one year from the 24th of June last, I do therefore reserve the said Second separate Article, and the Ratification on the part of the United States, of the same, to be separately exchanged for the Ratification on the part of France, of the said Article, should it be given in time for the Exchange within one year from the 24th day of June last.

In faith whereof I have caused the Seal of the United States to be hereto affixed at the City of Washington this twelfth day of February 1823. and in the 47th year of the Independence of the United States.

The Exchange of Ratifications

The record of the exchange of ratifications is a certificate thereof in the treaty file, which is in both English and French and was executed by the Secretary of State and the French Chargé d'Affaires. As that act shows the insistence of John Quincy Adams on the use of both languages in the convention as originals, the English text of the certificate is printed:

We the Undersigned, John Quincy Adams Secretary of State of the United States, and Charles Jules de Menou Count de Menou, Knight of the Royal order of the Legion of Honour, Chargé d'Affaires of His Majesty the King of France and Navarre, do hereby certify that the Ratifications of the Convention of Navigation and Commerce between the United States and His said Majesty, concluded on the 24th day of June last, together with the first separate Article annexed thereto, have with all suitable solemnities and after due comparison each with the other, and with the original example of the said Convention and separate Article, been exchanged by us.

But in the Ratification on the part of His Majesty the King of France and Navarre, the copy of the Convention being only in the French Language, the said John Quincy Adams Secretary of State, desired that mention thereof should be made in the present Certificate, and that in accepting the Ratification on the part of His Majesty the King of France as aforesaid, he observes that the Convention as concluded was in the two Languages, both purporting on the face of the said Convention to be *original*.

In Witness whereof we have signed this act in duplicates, and in both Languages, and have sealed the same with our respective Seals at the City of Washington, this twelfth day of February one thousand eight hundred and twenty three.

The proclamation of February 12, 1823, was dated the same day as the exchange of ratifications. The original proclamation in the treaty file contains the text of the convention and of the first separate article in both English and French. It is printed in American State Papers, Foreign Relations, V, 222–24.

Article 8

By Article 8 of the convention it was provided that "the execution of the said Convention shall commence in both Countries on the

first of October next, and shall be effective, even in case of non-ratification, for all such vessels as may have sailed *bonâ fide*, for the Ports of either Nation, in the confidence of its being in force."

On the part of the United States, this agreement that the execution of the convention should commence on October 1, 1823, even if it were not then in force as a convention, is properly to be regarded as an Executive agreement authorized by statute. Section 2 of the act of May 6, 1822 (3 Statutes at Large, 681), which, by section 3 of the same act, was to continue in force to the "end of the next session of Congress," provided as follows (see also the act of March 3, 1821, *ibid.*, 641–42):

And be it further enacted, That, in the event of the signature of any treaty or convention concerning the navigation or commerce between the United States and France, the President of the United States be, and is hereby, authorized, should he deem the same expedient, by proclamation, to suspend, until the end of the next session of Congress, the operation of the act [of May 15, 1820, *ibid.*, 605], entitled "An act to impose a new tonnage duty on French ships and vessels," and for other purposes; and also to suspend, as aforesaid, all other duties on French vessels, or the goods imported in the same, which may exceed the duties on American vessels, and on similar goods imported in the same.

Accordingly, on June 24, 1822, the date of the signature of the convention, the following proclamation, a copy of which, but not the original, is in the treaty file, was issued. It seems that the actual date of issuance was perhaps June 25 and that there was "a material error in the proclamation itself, for which I [John Quincy Adams] am myself responsible, the draft being incorrect" (Memoirs of John Quincy Adams, VI, 30, 32, 33). The text printed in the Daily National Intelligencer of June 26, 1822, shows that the error was the omission of the words "being the growth, produce and manufacture of France."

By the President of the United States

A Proclamation.

Whereas by the second section of an act of Congress of the 6th of May last, entitled "An act in addition to the act concerning Navigation, and also to authorize the appointment of Deputy Collectors," it is Provided, That in the event of the signature of any treaty or convention concerning the navigation or commerce between the United States and France, the President of the United States, if he should deem the same expedient, may suspend, by Proclamation, until the end of the next Session of Congress, the operation of the act, entitled "an act to impose a new tonnage duty on French ships and vessels, and for other purposes": and also to suspend, as aforesaid, all other duties on French vessels, or the goods imported in the same, which may exceed the duties on American vessels and on similar goods imported in the same: And whereas a convention of navigation and commerce between the United States of America and His Majesty, the King of France and Navarre, has this day been duly signed by John Quincy Adams, Secretary of State, on the part of the United States, and by the Baron Hyde de Neuville, Envoy Extraordinary and Minister Plenipotentiary from France, on the part of His Most Christian Majesty, which Convention is in the words following:

[Here follows the English text of the convention and of the two separate articles]

Now therefore be it known, that I, James Monroe, President of the United States, in pursuance of the authority aforesaid, do hereby suspend, from & after the first day of October next, until the end of the next session of Congress, the operation of the act aforesaid, entitled "An act to impose a new Tonnage duty on French Ships and vessels and for other purposes," and also all other duties on French vessels and the goods being the growth, produce and manufacture of France imported in the same which may exceed the duties on American vessels and on similar goods imported in the same, saving only the discriminating duties payable on French Vessels and on articles the growth, produce and manufacture of France, imported in the same, stipulated by the said convention to be paid.

In testimony whereof, I have caused the seal of the United States, to be affixed to these presents, & signed the same with my hand.

        Done at Washington, the 24ᵗʰ day of June in the year of our Lord
(L. S) one thousand eight hundred & twenty two, and of the Independence of the United States the forty sixth.

                      Signed   JAMES MONROE.

By the President,
    Sgnd   JOHN QUINCY ADAMS

The foregoing proclamation is not to be found in the Statutes at Large. It is printed in Richardson, II, 183–84, and also in American State Papers, Foreign Relations, V, 145–48, including in the latter, however, both the French and the English text of the convention.

THE FIRST SEPARATE ARTICLE

As the second separate article did not go into force, the first separate article became the separate article of the convention. The act of May 15, 1820, which is mentioned in the separate article, is in 3 Statutes at Large, 605. It imposed a duty of eighteen dollars a ton on all French vessels, to commence on July 1, 1820.

The French ordinance of July 26, 1820, is in Bulletin des lois du Royaume de France, 7ᵉ série, XI, 235. It provided for a special tonnage duty on American ships of ninety francs a ton, without prejudice to a supplement of 10 per cent, and with exception to such ships as had left American ports directly for France before June 15. The ordinance was not applicable to ships in ballast and was to cease to be applicable "if the act of Congress of May 15 shall be annulled, and from the moment when official knowledge of such annulment shall be received in France." On the same day another ordinance was issued (*ibid.*, 236), which provided for a bounty, from October 15, 1820, to March 31, 1821, inclusive, at the rate of ten francs per hundred kilograms, on cotton imported into France in French ships from foreign ports other than those of the United States. That ordinance also provided that the same bounty should be paid on imports of cotton into France prior to October 15, in such French ships as had paid in United States ports the duty of eighteen dollars a ton imposed by the act of May 15, 1820. The two ordinances mentioned are also printed in Le Moniteur Universel of July 29, 1820.

The Second Separate Article

As has been explained, the second separate article did not go into force. In the original that article is on the last two written pages and reads as follows in the two texts:

Separate Article.

It is agreed that the extra-duties, specified in the 1st and 2d Articles of this Convention shall be levied only upon the excess of value of the merchandize imported, over the value of the merchandize exported in the same Vessel upon the same voyage: so that if the value of the Articles exported shall equal or exceed that of the Articles imported in the same Vessel (not including however Articles imported for transit or re-exportation) no such extra-duties shall be levied; and if the Articles exported are less in value than those imported, the extra-duties shall be levied only upon the amount of the difference of their value. This Article, however, shall take effect, only in case of ratification on both sides; and not until two months after the exchange of the ratifications. But the refusal to ratify this Article, on either side, shall in no wise affect or impair the ratification or the validity of the preceding Articles of this Convention.

Signed and Sealed as above, this 24th day of June 1822.

    [Seal] John Quincy Adams.
    [Seal] G Hyde de Neuville

Article séparé.

Il est convenu que les Droits extraordinaires, spécifiés dans les 1er et 2d Articles de cette Convention, ne seront levés que sur l'excèdant de la valeur de la marchandise importée, sur la valeur de la marchandise exportée par le même Batiment dans le même voyage. En sorte que si la valeur des Articles exportés égale ou surpasse celle des Articles importés par le même Batiment (exceptant toutefois les Articles importés pour transit ou ré-exportation), aucun Droit extraordinaire ne sera levé; et, si les Articles exportés sont inférieurs en valeur à ceux importés, les Droits extraordinaires ne seront levés que sur le montant de la différence de leur valeur. Cet Article toutefois n'aura d'effet que dans le cas de ratification de part et d'autre; et seulement deux mois après l'échange des ratifications. Mais le refus de ratifier cet Article, d'une ou d'autre part, n'affectera et n'affaiblira en rien la ratification ou la validité des Articles précèdens de cette Convention.

Signé et scellé, comme ci-dessus, le 24me jour de Juin 1822.

    [Seal] G Hyde de Neuville
    [Seal] John Quincy Adams.

Execution of the Convention

The convention was communicated to the House of Representatives on February 20, 1823, with the presidential message of February 18 (American State Papers, Foreign Relations, V, 222–24). An act for carrying into effect the convention was approved March 3, 1823 (3 Statutes at Large, 747–48); that statute repealed the act of May 15, 1820, which imposed a duty of eighteen dollars a ton on French vessels (*ibid.*, 605); it authorized the refund of any extra duties levied under that act; and in section 6 it enacted the provisions of the second separate article upon condition that that article should go into force by June 23, 1823.

Under date of May 4, 1826, there was enacted a statute "to provide for the apprehension and delivery of deserters from French ships in the ports of the United States" (4 Statutes at Large, 160). A general statute on the same subject, applicable to "any foreign government, having a treaty with the United States, stipulating for the restoration of seamen deserting," became law on March 2, 1829 (*ibid.*, 359–60).

Treaty Series No. 114
8 Statutes at Large, 282–97
18 *ibid.*, pt. 2, Public Treaties, 303–8

44

GREAT BRITAIN : JULY 12, 1822

Convention for Determining the Indemnification under the Decision of the Emperor of Russia as to the True Construction of Article 1 of the Treaty of Ghent (Document 33), signed at St. Petersburg (Leningrad) July 12, 1822 (June 30, Old Style), under the mediation of the Emperor of Russia. Original in English and French; but the annexes to the convention are in French only.
Submitted to the Senate December 10, 1822. (Message of December 4, 1822.) Resolution of advice and consent January 3, 1823. Ratified by the United States January 9, 1823. Ratified by Great Britain October 4, 1822. Ratified by Russia August 4, 1822 (July 23, Old Style). Ratifications exchanged at Washington January 10, 1823. Proclaimed January 11, 1823.

In the name of the most-holy & indivisible Trinity:

The President of the United-States of America, and His Majesty the King of the United Kingdom of Great-Britain and Ireland, having agreed, in pursuance of the fifth Article of the Convention[1] concluded at London on the 20th day of October 1818. to refer the differences which had arisen between the two Governments, upon the true construction and meaning of the first Article of the Treaty of Peace and Amity,[2] concluded at Ghent on the 24th day of December 1814, to the friendly arbitration of His Majesty the Emperor of all the Russias, mutually engaging

Au nom de la Très-Sainte & indivisible Trinité

Le Président des Etats-Unis d'Amérique & Sa Majesté le Roi du Royaume uni de la Grande Bretagne & de l'Irlande ayant décidé d'un commun accord en conséquence de l'article V. de la convention[1] conclue à Londres le 20. Octobre 1818, que les différends qui se sont élevés entre les deux Gouvernemens sur la construction & le vrai sens du 1ᵉʳ Article du Traité de paix & d'amitié,[2] conclu à Gand le 24. Décembre 1814. seraient déférés à l'arbitrage amical de Sa Majesté l'Empereur de toutes les Russies; s'étant en outre engagés réciproquement à regarder Sa décision comme finale

---

[1] Document 40. [2] Document 33.

to consider His decision as final and conclusive; And His said Imperial Majesty, having, after due consideration, given His decision[1] upon these differences in the following terms: to wit:

"That the United States of "America are entitled to claim "from Great-Britain a just indem-"nification for all private prop-"erty, which the British forces "may have carried away; and as "the question relates to Slaves "more especially, for all the "Slaves that the British forces "may have carried away from "places and territories of which "the Treaty stipulates the resti-"tution, in quitting these same "places and territories."

"That the United States are "entitled to consider as having "been so carried away, all such "Slaves as may have been trans-"ferred from the above mentioned "territories to British Vessels "within the Waters of the said "territories, and who for this "reason may not have been "restored."

"But that if there should be "any American Slaves, who were "carried away from territories of "which the first Article of the "Treaty of Ghent has not stipu-"lated the restitution to the "United States, the United States "are *not* entitled to claim an "indemnification for the said "Slaves."

& définitive; & Sa Majesté Impériale après mûre considération, ayant émis cette décision[1] dans les termes suivans:

"Que les Etats-Unis d'Améri-"que sont en droit de réclamer de "la Grande-Bretagne une juste "indemnité pour toutes les pro-"priétés particulières que les "forces Britanniques auroient em-"portées; & comme il s'agit plus "spécialement d'esclaves, pour "tous les esclaves que les forces "Britanniques auroient emmenés "des lieux & territoires dont le "traité stipule la restitution, en "quittant ces mêmes lieux & "territoires."

"Que les Etats-Unis sont en "droit de regarder comme em-"menés tous ceux de ces esclaves "qui, des territoires indiqués ci-"dessus auroient été transportés "à bord de vaisseaux Britanni-"ques mouillés dans les eaux des "dits territoires, & qui par ce "motif n'auroient pas été "restitués."

"Mais que s'il y a des esclaves "Américains emmenés de terri-"toires dont l'article 1ᵉ du traité "de Gand n'a pas stipulé la resti-"tution aux Etats-Unis, les Etats-"Unis ne sont pas en droit de "réclamer une indemnité pour les "dits esclaves."

---

[1] That decision was written in French.

Now, for the purpose of carrying into effect this award of His Imperial Majesty as Arbitrator, His good offices have been farther invoked to assist in framing such convention or articles of Agreement between the United States of America and His Britannic Majesty, as shall provide the mode of ascertaining and determining the value of Slaves and of other private property, which may have been carried away in contravention of the Treaty of Ghent, and for which indemnification is to be made to the Citizens of the United States, in virtue of His Imperial Majesty's said award, and shall secure compensation to the sufferers for their Losses so ascertained and determined. And His Imperial Majesty has consented to lend His médiation for the above purpose and has constituted and appointed Charles Robert, Count Nesselrode, His Imperial Majesty's Privy Councellor, Member of the Council of State, Secretary of State directing the Imperial Department of Foreign Affairs, Chamberlain, Knight of the order of S⁺ Alexander Nevsky, Grand Cross of the order of S⁺ Vladimir of the first Class, Knight of that of the white Eagle of Poland, Grand Cross of the order of S⁺ Stephen of Hungary, of the Black and of the red Eagle of Prussia, of the Legion of Honor of France, of Charles III of Spain, of S⁺ Ferdi-

Comme il s'agit à présent de mettre cette sentence arbitrale à exécution, les bons offices de Sa Majesté Impériale ont été encore invoqués, afin qu'une convention arrêtée entre les Etats-Unis & Sa Majesté Britannique stipulât les articles d'un accord propre à établir, d'une part, le mode à suivre pour fixer & déterminer la valeur des esclaves ou autres propriétés privées qui auroient été emmenés en contravention au Traité de Gand, & pour lesquels les citoyens des Etats-Unis auraient droit de réclamer une indemnité en vertu de la décision ci-dessus mentionnée de Sa Majesté Impériale; de l'autre à assurer un dédommagement aux individus qui ont supporté les pertes qu'il s'agit de vérifier & d'évaluer. Sa Majesté Impériale a consenti à prêter Sa médiation pour le dit objet, & a fondé & nommé le Sieur Charles Robert Comte de Nesselrode, Son Conseiller privé, Membre du Conseil d'Etat, Secrétaire d'Etat dirigeant le Ministère des affaires étrangères, Chambellan actuel, Chevalier de l'Ordre de S⁺ Alexandre Nevsky, Grand-Croix de l'Ordre de S⁺ Wladimir de la 1ʳᵉ classe, Chevalier de celui de l'aigle blanc de Pologne, Grand 'Croix de l'ordre de S⁺ Etienne de Hongrie, de l'aigle noir & de l'aigle rouge de Prusse, de la Légion d'honneur de France, de Charles III d'Espagne, de S⁺ Ferdinand & du Mérite de Naples, de l'Annonciade de Sar-

nand and of Merit of Naples, of the Annunciation of Sardinia, of the Polar Star of Sweden, of the Elephant of Denmark of the golden Eagle of Wirtemberg, of Fidelity of Baden, of St Constantine of Parma, and of Guelph of Hannovre—. and John Count Capodistrias, His Imperial Majesty's Privy Counsellor, and Secretary of State, Knight of the order of St Alexander Nevsky, Grand-Cross of the order of St Vladimir of the first class, Knight of that of the White Eagle of Poland, Grand-Cross of the order of St Stephen of Hungary, of the Black and of the red Eagle of Prussia, of the Legion of Honour of France, of Charles III of Spain, of St Ferdinand and of Merit of Naples, of St Maurice and of St Lazarus of Sardinia, of the Elephant of Denmark, of Fidelity and of the Lion of Zähringen of Baden, Burgher of the Canton of Vaud, and also of the Canton and of the Republic of Geneva, as His Plenipotentiaries to treat, adjust and conclude such Articles of Agreement as may tend to the attainment of the abovementioned end, with the Plenipotentiaries of the United States and of His Britannic Majesty; That is to say; on the part of the President of the United States, with the advice and consent of the Senate thereof, Henry Middleton, a Citizen of the said United States, and their Envoy extraordinairy

daigne, de l'Etoile polaire de Suède de l'éléphant de Dannemarc, de l'aigle d'or de Würtemberg, de la Fidélité de Bade, de St Constantin de Parme & des guelfes de Hanovre;—& le Sieur Jean Comte de Capodistrias, Son Conseiller privé & Secrétaire d'Etat, Chevalier de l'Ordre de St Alexandre Nevsky, Grand'Croix de l'ordre de St Wladimir de la 1re classe, Chevalier de celui de l'Aigle blanc de Pologne, Grand'Croix de l'ordre de St Etienne de Hongrie, de l'aigle noir & de l'aigle rouge de Prusse, de la Légion d'honneur de France, de Charles III d'Espagne, de St Ferdinand & du Mérite de Naples, des Sts Maurice & Lazare de Sardaigne, de l'Eléphant de Dannemarc, de la Fidélité & du Lion de Zähringen de Bade, Bourgeois du Canton de Vaud, ainsi que du Canton & de la République de Genève,—pour Ses Plénipotentiaires à l'effet de négocier, règler & conclure tels articles d'un accord qui pourraient faire atteindre la fin indiquée plus haut, conjointement avec les Plénipotentiaires des Etats-Unis & de Sa Majesté Britannique, savoir: de la part du Président des Etats-Unis, de l'avis & du consentement de leur Sénat, le Sieur Henry Middleton, citoyen des dits Etats-Unis & Leur Envoyé extraordinaire & Ministre plénipotentiaire près Sa Majesté Impériale,—& de la part de Sa Majesté le Roi du Royaume Uni

and Minister Plenipotentiary to His Majesty the Emperor of all the Russias: and on the part of His Majesty the King of the United Kingdom of Great Britain and Ireland, the Right Honorable Sir Charles Bagot, one of His Majesty's most Honorable Privy Council, Knight Grand Cross of the most Honorable Order of the Bath, and His Majesty's Ambassador Extraordinary and Plenipotentiary to His Majesty, the Emperor of all the Russias. And the said Plénipotentiaries, after a reciprocal communication of their respective full Powers, found in good and due form, have agreed upon the following Articles.

de la Grande Bretagne & de l'Irlande, le très honorable Sir Charles Bagot, l'un des membres du très-honorable Conseil privé de Sa Majesté, Chevalier Grand' Croix du très-honorable ordre du Bain & Son Ambassadeur extraordinaire & plénipotentiaire près Sa Majesté Impériale: lesquels Plénipotentiairies, après s'être réciproquement communiqué leurs pleinpouvoirs respectifs, trouvés en bonne & due forme, sont convenus des articles suivants:

ARTICLE 1st

For the purpose of ascertaining and determining the amount of Indemnification which may be due to Citizens of the United States under the decision of His Imperial Majesty, Two Commissioners and two Arbitrators shall be appointed in the manner following: That is to say: One Commissioner and one Arbitrator shall be nominated and appointed by the President of the United States of America by and with the advice and consent of the Senate thereof; and one Commissioner and one Arbitrator shall be appointed by His Britannic Majesty—And the two Commissioners and two Arbitrators thus ap-

ARTICLE I.

Pour vérifier & déterminer le montant de l'indemnité qui pourra être dûe aux Citoyens des Etats-Unis par suite de la décision de Sa Majesté Impériale, deux Commissaires & deux arbitres seront nommés de la manière suivante, savoir: Un Commissaire & un arbitre seront nommes & accrédités, par le Président des Etats-Unis, de l'avis & du consentement de leur Sénat; l'autre Commissaire & l'autre arbitre seront nommés par Sa Majesté Britannique. Les deux Commissaires & les deux arbitres, ainsi nommés, se réuniront en Conseil, & tiendront leurs séances dans la ville de Washington. Ils

pointed, shall meet and hold their sittings as a Board in the City of Washington. They shall have power to appoint a Secretary and before proceeding to the other business of the Commission, They shall respectively take the following oath (or affirmation) in the presence of each other. Which oath or affirmation being so taken and duly attested, shall be entered on the record of their proceedings: That is to say: "I, A. B. one "of the Commissioners (or Arbi- "trators as the case may be) ap- "pointed in pursuance of the Con- "vention concluded at St Peters- "burg on the 30th/12th day of "June/July One Thousand Eight "hundred and twenty two, be- "tween His Majesty the Emperor "of all the Russias, the United "States of America, and His Bri- "tannic Majesty, do solemnly "swear (or affirm) that I will dili- "gently, impartially and carefully "examine, and to the best of my "Judgement, according to Justice "and equity, decide all matters "submitted to me as Commis- "sioner (or Arbitrator as the Case "may be) under the said Con- "vention."

All vacancies occuring by death or otherwise shall be filled up in the manner of the original appointment, and the new Commissioners or Arbitrators shall take the same oath or affirmation and perform the same duties.

auront le pouvoir de choisir un Secrétaire; & avant de procéder au travail de la Commission, ils devront prêter respectivement & en présence les uns des autres, le serment ou l'affirmation qui suit, & ce serment ou affirmation prêté & formellement attesté fera partie du protocole de leurs Actes & sera conçu ainsi qu'il suit: "Moi A: B:, l'un des Commis- "saires /:ou arbitres, suivant le "cas:/ nommés en exécution de la "convention conclue à St Péters- "bourg, le 30 Juin/12 Juillet mil- "huit-cent-vingt & deux, entre Sa "Majesté L'Empereur de toutes "les Russies, les Etats-Unis d'Amé- "rique & Sa Majesté Britannique "jure ou affirme solennellement "que j'examinerai avec diligence, "impartialité & sollicitude, & que "je déciderai d'après mon meilleur "entendement & en toute justice "& équité, toutes les réclamations "qui me seront déférées en ma "qualité de Commissaire /:ou d'ar- "bitre, suivant le cas:/ à la suite "de la dite Convention."

Les vacances causées par la mort ou autrement, seront remplies de la même manière qu'au moment de la nomination primitive, & les nouveaux Commissaires ou arbitres devront prêter le même serment ou affirmation, & s'acquitter des mêmes devoirs.

ARTICLE II^d

If at the first meeting of this Board, the Governments of the United States and of Great Britain shall not have agreed upon an average value, to be allowed as compensation for each Slave for whom Indemnification may be due; then and in that case, the Commissioners and Arbitrators shall conjointly proceed to examine the testimony which shall be produced under the authority of the President of the United States, together with such other competent testimony as they may see cause to require or allow, going to prove the true value of Slaves at the period of the exchange of the ratifications of the treaty of Ghent; and upon the evidence so obtained, they shall agree upon and fix the average value. But, in Case that the majority of the Board of Commissioners and Arbitrators should not be able to agree respecting such average value, then and in that case, recourse shall be had to the Arbitration of the Minister or other agent of the Mediating Power, accredited to the Government of the United States. A Statement of the evidence produced and of the proceedings of the Board thereupon shall be communicated to the said Minister or Agent, and his decision, founded upon such evidence and proceedings shall be final and

ARTICLE II.

Si lors de la première réunion de ce Conseil, le Gouvernement des Etats-Unis & celui de la Grande Bretagne ne sont point parvenus à déterminer d'un commun accord la valeur moyenne qui devra être assignée comme compensation pour chaque esclave, pour lequel il sera dû une indemnité, dans ce cas les Commissaires & les arbitres procèderont conjointement à l'examen de tous les témoignages qui leur seront présentés par ordre du Président des Etats-Unis, ainsi que de tous les autres témoignages valables qu'ils croiront devoir requérir ou admettre dans la vue d'arrêter la véritable valeur des esclaves à l'époque de l'échange des ratifications du traité de Gand; & d'après les preuves qu'ils auront ainsi obtenues, ils établiront & fixeront la sus dite valeur moyenne. Dans le cas où la majorité du Conseil des Commissaires & arbitres ne pourroit pas s'accorder sur cette valeur proportionnelle, alors on aura recours à l'arbitrage du Ministre ou autre Agent de la Puissance médiatrice accrédité auprès due Gouvernement des Etats-Unis. Toutes les preuves produites & tous les actes des opérations du Conseil à ce sujet, lui seront communiqués & la décision de ce Ministre ou Agent, basée, comme il vient d'être dit, sur ces preuves & sur les actes de

conclusive. And the said average value, when fixed and determined by either of the three before mentioned methods, shall in all cases serve as a rule for the compensation to be awarded for each and every Slave, for whom it may after wards be found that indemnification is due.

Article III.

When the average value of Slaves shall have been ascertained and fixed, the two Commissioners shall constitute a board for the examination of the claims which are to be submitted to them, and they shall notify to the Secretary of State of the United States, that they are ready to receive a definitive List of the Slaves and other private property, for which the Citizens of the United States claim indemnification; it being understood and hereby agreed that the Commission shall not take cognizance of nor receive, and that His Britannic Majesty shall not be required to make compensation for any claims for private property under the first Article of the treaty of Ghent, not contained in the said List. And His Britannic Majesty hereby engages to cause to be produced before the Commission, as material towards ascertaining facts, all the evidence of which His Majesty's Government may be in possession, by returns from

ces opérations, sera regardée comme finale & définitive. C'est sur la valeur moyenne fixée par un des trois modes mentionnés ci-dessus, que devra être réglée en tout état de cause la compensation qui sera accordée pour chaque esclave pour lequel on reconnoitra par la suite, qu'une indemnité est dûe.

Article III.

Lorsque le prorata aura été ainsi arrêté, les deux Commissaires se constitueront en conseil pour l'examen des réclamations qui leur seront soumises, & ils notifieront au Secrétaire d'Etat des Etats-Unis, qu'ils sont prêts à recevoir la liste définitive des esclaves & autres propriétés privées pour lesquels les Citoyens des Etats-Unis réclament une indemnité. Il est entendu que les Commissaires ne sauroient examiner ni recevoir, & que Sa Majesté Britannique ne sauroit, en vertu des clauses de l'article 1ᵉ du Traité de Gand, bonifier aucune prétention, qui ne seroit pas portée sur la dite liste. Sa Majesté Britannique s'engage d'autre part à ordonner, que tous les témoignages que Son Gouvernement peut avoir acquis par les rapports des officiers de Sa dite Majesté ou par tout autre canal sur le nombre des esclaves emmenés, soyent mis sous les yeux des Commissaires, afin de contribuer à la vérification des faits.

His Majesty's officers or otherwise, of the number of Slaves carried away. But the Evidence so produced, or it's defectiveness, shall not go in bar of any claim or claims which shall be otherwise satisfactorily authenticated.

Article IV.

The two Commissioners are hereby empowered and required to go into an examination of all the claims submitted, thro' the above-mentioned List, by the owners of Slaves or other property, or by their lawful attornies or representatives, and to determine the same respectively according to the merits of the several cases, under the rule of the Imperial decision herein above recited and having reference, if need there be, to the explanatory Documents[1] hereunto annexed marked A & B. And in considering such claims, the Commissioners are empowered and required to examine on oath or affirmation, all such persons as shall come before them, touching the real number of the Slaves or value of other property for which indemnification is claimed: and also to receive in evidence, according as they may think consistent with Equity and Justice, written depositions or

Mais soit que ses témoignages viennent à être produits, soit qu'ils manquent, cette circonstance ne pourra porter préjudice á une réclamation ou aux réclamations qui par une autre voie seront légitimées d'une manière satisfaisante.

Article IV.

Les deux Commissaires sont autorisés & chargés d'entrer dans l'examen de toutes les réclamations qui leur seront soumises au moyen de la liste ci-dessus mentionnée, par les propriétaires d'esclaves ou les possesseurs d'autres propriétés, ou par les procureurs ou mandataires de ceux-ci, & à prononcer sur ces réclamations suivant le degré de leur mérite, la lettre de la décision Impériale citée plus haut, & en cas de besoin la teneur des documens[1] ci-annexés & cotés A & B.

En considérant les dites réclamations, les Commissaires sont autorisés à interpeller sous serment ou affirmation telle personne qui se présenterait à eux, concernant le véritable nombre des esclaves ou la valeur de toute autre propriété pour laquelle il serait réclamé une indemnité; ils sont autorisés de même à recevoir autant qu'ils le jugeront conforme à l'équité & à la justice, toutes les dépositions écrites, qui seraient

---

[1] There are three annexes to the convention, marked A, A/, and B; their texts in French, with translations, are here printed following the signatures to the convention.

papers, such depositions or papers being duly authenticated, either according to existing legal forms, or in such other manner as the said Commissioners shall see cause to require or allow.

Article V[th].

In the event of the two Commissioners not agreeing in any particular case under examination, or of their disagreement upon any question which may result from the Stipulations of this Convention, then and in that Case, they shall draw by lot the name of one of the two Arbitrators, who, after having given due consideration to the matter contested, shall consult with the Commissioners and a final decision shall be given conformably to the opinion of the majority of the two Commissioners and of the Arbitrator so drawn by Lot. And the Arbitrator when so acting with the two Commissioners shall be bound in all respects by the Rules of proceeding enjoined by the IVth. Article of this Convention upon the Commissioners, and shall be vested with the same powers, and be deemed, for that case, a Commissioner.

Article VI

The decision of the two Commissioners, or of the majority of the Board as constituted by the preceding article, shall in all

duement légitimées soit d'après les formes existantes, voulues par la loi, soit dans tout autre mode que les dits Commissaires auraient lieu d'exiger ou d'admettre.

Article V.

Si les deux Commissaires ne parviennent pas à s'accorder sur une des réclamations qui seront soumises à leur examen, ou s'ils diffèrent d'opinion sur une question résultant de la présente Convention, alors ils tireront au sort le nom d'un des deux arbitres, lequel après avoir pris en mure délibération l'objet en litige, le discutera avec les Commissaires. La décision finale sera prise conformément à l'opinion de la majorité des deux Commissaires & l'arbitre tiré au sort. Dans des cas semblables l'arbitre sera tenu de procéder à tous égards d'après les règles prescrites aux Commissaires par le IVme article de la présente Convention. Il sera investi des mêmes pouvoirs & censé pour le moment faire les mêmes fonctions.

Article VI.

La décision des deux Commissaires ou celle de la majorité du Conseil formé ainsi qu'il a été dit en l'article précédent, sera

cases be final and conclusive, whether as to number, the value or the ownership of the Slaves, or other property for which indemnification is to be made. And His Britannic Majesty engages to cause the Sum awarded to each and every owner in lieu of his Slave or Slaves or other property, to be paid in specie without deduction, at such time or times, and at such place or places, as shall be awarded by the said Commissioners, and on condition of such releases or assignments to be given, as they shall direct: provided, that no such payments shall be fixed to take place sooner than twelve months from the day of the exchange of the ratifications of this Convention.

dans tous les cas finale & définitive, soit relativement au nombre & à la valeur, soit pour la vérification de la propriété, des esclaves ou de tout autre bien meuble privé, pour lequel il sera réclamé une indemnité. Et Sa Majesté Britannique prend l'engagement que la somme adjugée à chaque propriétaire en place de son esclave ou de ses esclaves, ou de toute autre propriété, sera payée en espèces sans déduction, à tel tems ou à tels termes, & dans tel lieu ou tels endroits, que l'auront prononcé les dits Commissaires & sous clause de telles exemptions ou assignations, qu'ils l'auront arrêté: pourvu seulement qu'il ne soit pas fixé pour ces payemens de terme plus rapproché que celui de douze mois à partir du jour de l'échange des ratifications de la présente Convention.

Article VII.

It is farther agreed that the Commissioners and Arbitrators shall be respectively paid in such manner as shall be settled between the Governments of the United States and Great-Britain at the time of the exchange of the ratifications of this Convention. And all other expenses attending the execution of the Commission shall be defrayed jointly by the United States and His Britannic Majesty, the same being previously ascer-

Article VII.

Il est convenu en outre, que les Commissaires & arbitres recevront de part & d'autre un traitement, dont les Gouvernemens des Etats-Unis & de Sa Majesté Britannique se réservent de déterminer le montant & le mode à l'époque de l'échange des ratifications de la présente Convention. Toutes les autres dépenses qui accompagneront les travaux de la Commission seront supportées conjointement par les Etats-Unis & par Sa

tained and allowed by the majority of the Board.

Article VIII.

A certified copy of this Convention, when duly ratified by His Majesty the Emperor of all the Russias, by the President of the United States, by and with the advice and consent of their Senate, and by His Britannic Majesty, shall be delivered by each of the contracting parties respectively to the Minister or other agent of the Mediating Power accredited to the Government of the United States, as soon as may be after the ratifications shall have been exchanged; which last shall be effected at Washington in six months from the date hereof, or sooner if possible.

In faith whereof the respective Plenipotentiaries, have signed this Convention, drawn up in two Languages, and have hereunto affixed their Seals.

Done in Triplicate at St Petersburg this Thirtieth/Twelfth day of June/July One Thousand Eight Hundred and Twenty two.

Majesté Britannique. Ces dépenses devront d'ailleurs être au préalable vérifiées & admises par la majorité du Conseil.

Article VIII.

Lorsque la présente Convention aura été duement ratifiée par Sa Majesté Impériale, par le Président des Etats-Unis de l'avis & du consentement de leur Sénat, & par Sa Majesté Britannique,—une copie vidimée en sera délivrée par chacune des Parties contractantes au Ministre ou autre Agent de la Puissance Médiatrice, accrédité près le Gouvernement des Etats-Unis, & cela le plutôt que faire se pourra, après que les Ratifications auront été échangées: cette dernière formalité sera remplie à Washington dans l'espace de six mois, de la date ci-dessous, ou plutôt s'il est possible.

En foi de quoi, les Plénipotentiaires respectifs ont signé la présente Convention & y ont apposé respectivement le cachet de leurs armes.

Fait triple à St Pétersbourg, 30 Juin/12 Juillet de l'année mil-huit-cent-vingt & deux.

[Seal]　Nesselrode
[Seal]　Capodistrias
[Seal]　Henry Middleton
[Seal]　Charles Bagot

[Annexes]

[Translation]

A.

A

Le Soussigné Secrétaire d'Etat Dirigeant le Ministère Impérial des affaires étrangères, a l'honneur de communiquer à Monsieur de Middleton, Envoyé Extraordinaire & Ministre Plénipotentiaire des Etats-Unis d'Amérique, l'opinion[1] que L'Empereur, Son Maître, a cru devoir exprimer sur l'objet des différends qui se sont élevés entre les Etats-Unis & la Grande-Bretagne relativement à l'interprétation de l'Article premier du Traité de Gand.[2]

Monsieur de Middleton est invité à considérer cette opinion comme la décision arbitrale demandée à l'Empereur par les deux Puissances.

Il se rappellera sans doute, qu'aussi bien que le Plénipotentiaire de S. M. Britannique, il a dans tous ses mémoires principalement insisté sur le sens grammatical de l'Art: I. du Traité de Gand, & que même dans sa note du 4/16 Novembre 1821; il a formellement déclaré que c'étoit sur la *signification des mots dans le texte de l'article tel qu'il existe*,[3] que devoit se fonder la décision de Sa Majesté Impériale.

The undersigned Secretary of State directing the Imperial Administration of Foreign Affairs, has the honor to communicate to Mr. Middleton, Envoy Extraordinary and Minister Plenipotentiary of the United States of America, the opinion[1] which the Emperor, his master, has thought it his duty to express upon the object of the differences which have arisen between the United States and Great Britain relative to the interpretation of the first article of the Treaty of Ghent.[2]

Mr. Middleton is requested to consider this opinion as the award required of the Emperor by the two powers.

He will doubtless recollect that he, as well as the Plenipotentiary of His Britannic Majesty, in all his memorials, has principally insisted on the grammatical sense of the first article of the Treaty of Ghent, and that, even in his note of November 4/16, 1821, he has formally declared that it was on the *signification of the words in the text of the article as it now is*,[3] that the decision of His Imperial Majesty should be founded.

---

[1] Or decision, which is annex A/ following.
[2] Document 33.
[3] See the note regarding annex A.

La même déclaration étant consignée dans la note du Plénipotentiaire Britannique en date du 8/20 Octobre 1821, L'Empereur n'a fait que se conformer aux vœux énoncés par les deux Parties, en vouant toute Son attention à l'examen de la question grammaticale.

L'opinion[1] ci-dessus mentionnée fera connoitre la manière dont Sa Majesté Impériale juge cette question; & afin que le Cabinet de Washington connoisse également les motifs sur lesquels se fonde le jugement de L'Empereur, le Soussigné joint à la présente, un extrait[2] de quelques observations, sur le sens littéral de l'Article premier du Traité de Gand.

Sous ce rapport, L'Empereur s'est borné à suivre les règles de la langue employée dans la rédaction de l'acte, par lequel les deux Puissances ont réclamé Son arbitrage, & défini l'objet de leur différend.[2]

C'est uniquement à l'autorité de ces règles, que Sa Majesté Impériale a cru devoir obéir, & Son Avis ne pouvoit qu'en être la conséquence rigoureuse & nécessaire.

Le Soussigné saisit avec empressement cette occasion, pour réitérer à Monsieur de Middleton

The same declaration being made in the note of the British Plenipotentiary dated October 8/20, 1821, the Emperor had only to conform to the wishes expressed by the two parties by devoting all his attention to the examination of the grammatical question.

The above-mentioned opinion[1] will show the manner in which His Imperial Majesty judges of this question; and in order that the Cabinet of Washington may also know the motives upon which the Emperor's judgment is founded, the undersigned has hereto subjoined an extract[2] of some observations upon the literal sense of the first article of the Treaty of Ghent.

In this respect the Emperor has confined himself to following the rules of the language employed in drawing up the act by which the two powers have required his arbitration and defined the object of their difference. [2]

His Imperial Majesty has thought it his duty, exclusively, to obey the authority of these rules, and his opinion could not but be the rigorous and necessary consequence thereof.

The undersigned eagerly embraces this occasion to renew to Mr. Middleton the assurances of

---

[1] Annex A/.
[2] See the note regarding annex A.

les assurances de sa considération très-distinguée.

St Pétersbourg, ce 22. Avril 1822.[1]

NESSELRODE

A MONSIEUR DE MIDDLETON &c

A/.

Invité par les Etats-Unis d'Amérique et par la Grande Bretagne à émettre une opinion, comme arbitre dans les différends qui se sont élevés entre ces deux Puissances, au sujet de l'interprétation de l'article premier du Traité[2] qu'elles ont conclu à Gand, le 24. Décembre 1814, l'Empereur a pris connoissance de tous les actes, mémoires et notes où les Plénipotentiaires respectifs ont exposé à Son Ministère des affaires étrangères, les argumens que chacune des Parties en litige fait valoir à l'appui de l'interprétation qu'elle donne au dit article.

Après avoir murement pesé les observations développées de part et d'autre:

Considérant que le Plénipotentiaire Américain et le Plénipotentiaire Britannique ont demandé que la discussion fût close;

Considérant que le premier dans sa note du 4/16. Novembre 1821, et le second dans sa note du 8/20. Octobre de la même année, ont déclaré, que c'est

his most distinguished consideration.

St. Petersburg, April 22, 1822.[1]

NESSELRODE

[Translation]

A/

Invited by the United States of America and by Great Britain to give an opinion, as arbitrator in the differences which have arisen between these two powers, on the subject of the interpretation of the first article of the treaty[2] which they concluded at Ghent on the 24th December, 1814, the Emperor has taken cognizance of all the acts, memorials, and notes in which the respective Plenipotentiaries have set forth to his Administration of Foreign Affairs the arguments upon which each of the litigant parties depends in support of the interpretation given by it to the said article.

After having maturely weighed the observations exhibited on both sides:

Considering that the American Plenipotentiary and the Plenipotentiary of Britain have desired that the discussion should be closed;

Considering that the former, in his note of November 4/16, 1821, and the latter, in his note of October 8/20 of the same year, have declared that it is *upon the*

---

[1] Or May 4, 1822, New Style.
[2] Document 33.

sur la construction du texte de l'article, tel qu'il existe, que la décision arbitrale doit se fonder, et que l'un et l'autre n'ont invoqué que comme moyens subsidiaires, les principes généraux de droit des gens et de droit maritime;

L'Empereur est d'avis, "que ce "n'est que d'après le sens littéral "et grammatical de l'article 1. "du Traité de Gand que la ques-"tion peut être décidée."

Quant au sens littéral et grammatical de l'article 1. du Traité de Gand:

Considérant que la période sur la signification de la quelle il s'élève des doutes, est construite ainsi qu'il suit:

"Tous les territoires, lieux et possessions quelconques, pris par l'une des Parties sur l'autre, durant la guerre, ou qui pourroient être pris après la signature du présent Traité, à l'exception seulement des isles ci-dessous mentionnées, seront rendus sans délai et sans faire détruire ou emporter aucune partie de l'artillerie ou autre propriété publique *originairement prise dans les dits forts et lieux et qui s'y trouvera au moment de l'échange des ratifications du Traité*, ou aucuns esclaves ou autres propriétés privées. Et tous archives, registres, actes et papiers, soit d'une nature publique ou appartenans à des parti-

construction of the text of the article as it stands, that the arbitrator's decision should be founded, and that both have appealed, only as subsidiary means, to the general principles of the law of nations and of maritime law;

The Emperor is of opinion "that the question can only be decided according to the literal and grammatical sense of the first article of the Treaty of Ghent."

As to the literal and grammatical sense of the first article of the Treaty of Ghent:

Considering that the period upon the signification of which doubts have arisen, is expressed as follows:

"All territory, places, and possessions, whatsoever, taken by either party from the other during the war, or which may be taken after the signing of this treaty, excepting only the islands hereinafter mentioned, shall be restored without delay and without causing any destruction or carrying away any of the artillery or other public property *originally captured in the said forts or places, and which shall remain therein upon the exchange of the ratifications of this treaty*, or any slaves or other private property; and all archives, records, deeds, and papers, either of a public nature or belonging to private persons,

culiers, qui dans le cours de la guerre peuvent être tombés entre les mains des Officiers de l'une ou de l'autre partie, seront de suite, en tant qu'il sera praticable, restitués et délivrés aux autorités propres et personnes auxquelles ils appartiennent respectivement;"

considérant que dans cette période, les mots: *originairement prise et qui s'y trouvera au moment de l'échange des ratifications*, forment une phrase incidente, laquelle ne peut se rapporter *grammaticalement* qu'aux substantifs ou sujets qui précèdent,

Qu'ainsi l'article 1. du Traité de Gand, ne défend aux Parties contractantes d'emporter des lieux dont il stipule la restitution, que les seules propriétés publiques *qui y auroient été originairement prises et qui s'y trouveroient au moment de l'échange des ratifications*, mais qu'il défend d'emporter de ces mêmes lieux, *aucune propriété particulière quelconque;*

Que d'un autre coté, ces deux défenses ne sont applicables qu'uniquement aux lieux dont l'article stipule la restitution;

L'Empereur est d'avis:

"Que les Etats-Unis d'Améri-"que, sont en droit de réclamer "de la Grande Bretagne une juste "indemnité, pour toutes les pro-

which, in the course of the war, may have fallen into the hands of the officers of either party, shall be, as far as may be practicable, forthwith restored and delivered to the proper authorities and persons to whom they respectively belong."

Considering that in this period the words *originally captured, and which shall remain therein upon the exchange of the ratifications,* form an incidental phrase, which can have respect, *grammatically,* only to the substantives or subjects which precede;

That the first article of the Treaty of Ghent thus prohibits the contracting parties from carrying away from the places of which it stipulates the restitution, only the public property *which might have been originally captured there, and which should remain therein upon the exchange of the ratifications,* but that it prohibits the carrying away from these same places *any private property whatever;*

That, on the other hand, these two prohibitions are solely applicable to the places of which the article stipulates the restitution:

The Emperor is of opinion:

"That the United States of America are entitled to a just indemnification from Great Britain for all private property car-

"priétés particulières que les "forces Britanniques auroient em- "portées, et comme il s'agit plus "spécialement d'esclaves, pour "tous les esclaves que les forces "Britanniques auroient emmenés "des lieux et territoires dont le "Traité stipule la restitution, en "quittant ces mêmes lieux et "territoires.

"Que les Etats-Unis sont en "droit de regarder comme em- "menés, tous ceux de ces esclaves "qui, des territoires indiqués ci- "dessus, auroient été transportés "à bord de vaisseaux Britanniques "mouillés dans les eaux des dits "territoires, et qui par ce motif "n'auroient pas été restitués.

"Mais que s'il y a des esclaves "Américains emmenés de terri- "toires dont l'article 1. du Traité "de Gand n'a pas stipulé la resti- "tution aux Etats-Unis, les Etats- "Unis ne sont pas en droit de "réclamer une indemnité, pour "les dits eclaves."

L'Empereur déclare en outre, qu'Il est prêt à exercer l'office de Médiateur qui Lui a été déféré d'avance, par les deux Etats, dans les négociations que doit amener entre eux, la décision arbitrale qu'ils ont demandée.

Fait à St Pétersbourg, le 22. Avril 1822.[1]

ried away by the British forces; and as the question regards slaves more especially, for all such slaves as were carried away by the British forces from the places and territories of which the restitution was stipulated by the treaty, in quitting the said places and territories.

"That the United States are entitled to consider as having been so carried away all such slaves as may have been transported from the above-mentioned territories on board of the British vessels within the waters of the said territories, and who, for this reason, have not been restored.

"But that, if there should be any American slaves who were carried away from territories of which the first article of the Treaty of Ghent has not stipulated the restitution to the United States, the United States are not to claim an indemnification for the said slaves."

The Emperor declares, besides, that he is ready to exercise the office of mediator, which has been conferred on him beforehand by the two states, in the negotiations which must ensue between them in consequence of the award which they have demanded.

Done at St. Petersburg April 22, 1822.[1]

---

[1] Or May 4, 1822, New Style.

B.

Le Soussigné Secrétaire d'Etat, dirigeant le Ministère Impérial des affaires étrangères, s'est empressé de porter à la conoissance de l'Empereur son Maître, les explications dans lesquelles Mr. l'Ambassadeur de S. M. Britannique est entré avec le Ministère Impérial, à la suite de la communication préalable et confidentielle qui a été faite à Monsieur de Middleton ainsi qu'à Mr. le Chevalier Bagot de l'opinion exprimée par l'Empereur, sur le vrai sens de l'art: 1er du Traité de Gand.[1]

Mr. le Chevalier Bagot entend qu'en vertu de la décision de Sa Majesté Impériale, "S. M. Britan-"nique n'est pas tenue à indemniser "les Etats-Unis d'aucuns esclaves "qui, venant des endroits qui n'ont "jamais été occupés par ses "troupes, se sont volontairement "réunis aux forces Britanniques, "ou en conséquence de l'encourage-"ment que les officiers de S. M. leur "avoit offert, ou pour se dérober "au pouvoir de leur maître, ces "esclaves n'ayant pas été emmenés "des lieux ou territoires pris par S. "M. Britannique durant la guerre, "et conséquemment n'ayant pas "été emmenés des lieux dont "l'article stipule la restitution."

B

The undersigned Secretary of State directing the Imperial Administration of Foreign Affairs, has without delay laid before the Emperor, his master, the explanations into which the Ambassador of His Britannic Majesty has entered with the Imperial Ministry in consequence of the preceding confidential communication which was made to Mr. Middleton, as well as to Sir Charles Bagot, of the opinion expressed by the Emperor upon the true sense of the first article of the Treaty of Ghent.[1]

Sir Charles Bagot understands that, in virtue of the decision of His Imperial Majesty, "His Britannic Majesty is not bound to indemnify the United States for any slaves who, coming from places which have never been occupied by his troops, voluntarily joined the British forces, either in consequence of the encouragement which His Majesty's officers had offered them, or to free themselves from the power of their master—these slaves not having been carried away from places or territories captured by His Britannic Majesty during the war and, consequently, not having been carried away from places of which the article stipulates the restitution."

---

[1] Document 33.

En réponse à cette observation, le Soussigné est chargé par Sa Majesté Impériale, de communiquer ce qui suit à Monsieur le Ministre des Etats-Unis d'Amérique.

L'Empereur ayant, du consentement mutuel des deux Plénipotentiaires, émis une opinion fondée uniquement sur le sens qui résulte *du texte de l'Article* en litige, ne se croit appelé à décider ici aucune question relative à ce que les loix de la guerre permettent ou défendent aux Parties belligérantes, mais toujours fidèle à l'interprétation grammaticale de l'Art: 1ᵉʳ du Traité de Gand, Sa Majesté Impériale déclare une seconde fois qu'il Lui semble, d'après cette interprétation:

"Qu'en quittant les lieux et "territoires dont le Traité de "Gand stipule la restitution aux "Etats-Unis, les forces de S. M. "Britannique n'avoient le droit "d'emmener de ces mêmes lieux "et territoires, absolument aucun "esclave, par quelque moyen qu'il "fût tombé ou venu se remettre "en leur pouvoir."

"Mais que si, durant la guerre, "des esclaves américains avoient "été emmenés par les forces "Angloises, d'autres lieux que "ceux dont le Traité de Gand "stipule la restitution, sur terri-"toire ou à bord de vaisseaux Bri-"tanniques, la Grande Bretagne

In answer to this observation, the undersigned is charged by His Imperial Majesty to communicate what follows to the Minister of the United States of America.

The Emperor having, by the mutual consent of the two Plenipotentiaries, given an opinion, founded solely upon the sense which results *from the text of the article* in dispute, does not think himself called upon to decide here any question relative to what the laws of war permit or forbid to the belligerents; but, always faithful to the grammatical interpretation of the first article of the Treaty of Ghent, His Imperial Majesty declares a second time that it appears to him according to this interpretation:

"That, in quitting the places and territories of which the Treaty of Ghent stipulates the restitution to the United States, His Britannic Majesty's forces had no right to carry away from these same places and territories, absolutely, any slave, by whatever means he had fallen or come into their power.

"But that if, during the war, American slaves had been carried away by the English forces from other places than those of which the Treaty of Ghent stipulates the restitution, upon the territory, or on board British vessels, Great Britain should not be bound to

"ne seroit pas tenue d'indemniser "les Etats-Unis de la perte de ces "esclaves, par quelque moyen "qu'ils fussent tombés ou venus "se remettre au pouvoir de ses "officiers."

Quoique convaincu, par les explications préalables dont il a été question plus haut, que tel est aussi le sens que Mr. le Chevalier Bagot attache à son observation, le Soussigné n'en a pas moins reçu de Sa Majesté Impériale, l'ordre, d'adresser aux Plénipotentiaires respectifs, la présente note, qui leur prouvera, que pour mieux répondre à la confiance des deux Gouvernemens, l'Empereur n'a pas voulu qu'il pût s'élever le plus leger doute sur les conséquences de son opinion.

Le Soussigné saisit avec empressement cette occasion de réitérer à Monsieur de Middleton, l'assurance de sa considération très-distinguée.

St: Pétersbourg le 22. Avril 1822.[1]

NESSELRODE
À MONSIEUR DE MIDDLETON &c

indemnify the United States for the loss of these slaves, by whatever means they might have fallen or come into the power of her officers."

Although convinced by the previous explanations above mentioned that such is also the sense which Sir Charles Bagot attaches to his observation, the undersigned has nevertheless received from His Imperial Majesty orders to address the present note to the r e s p e c t i v e Plenipotentiaries, which will prove to them that, in order the better to justify the confidence of the two Governments, the Emperor has been unwilling that the slightest doubt should arise regarding the consequences of his opinion.

The undersigned eagerly embraces this occasion of repeating to Mr. Middleton the assurance of his most distinguished consideration.

St. Petersburg, April 22, 1822.[1]

NESSELRODE

NOTES

For clarity it is first to be stated that "the explanatory Documents hereunto annexed, marked A & B," according to Article 4 of the convention, are not, as might be supposed, two documents, but three; their originals are marked respectively A, A/, and B. The document marked A is the covering note of Count Nesselrode, Russian Secretary of State for Foreign Affairs, addressed to Henry Middleton, American

---

[1] Or May 4, 1822, New Style.

Minister at St. Petersburg, dated April 22, Old Style, or May 4, 1822, enclosing the document marked A/, which is the decision of the Emperor of Russia under the same date. The document marked B is another communication of Nesselrode to Middleton, also of the same date. Throughout these notes, for convenience, those three documents are respectively referred to as annex A, annex A/, and annex B.

Dates in the headnote and elsewhere, except when otherwise stated, are those of the New Style or present calendar. At the time, dates in the Old Style were twelve days earlier.

As this convention between the United States and Great Britain was framed under the mediation of the Emperor of Russia, whose good offices had been invoked to that end, it was accordingly signed by the Plenipotentiaries of Russia as well as by those of the United States and Great Britain. The purpose of the convention was to carry into effect the previous decision (also called the "award" or the "opinion") of the Emperor of Russia, which is annex A/ to the convention.

Article 1 of the Treaty of Ghent of December 24, 1814 (Document 33), following the War of 1812 with Great Britain, contained the following provision:

All territory, places, and possessions whatsoever taken by either party from the other during the war, or which may be taken after the signing of this Treaty, excepting only the Islands hereinafter mentioned, shall be restored without delay and without causing any destruction or carrying away any of the Artillery or other public property originally captured in the said forts or places, and which shall remain therein upon the Exchange of the Ratifications of this Treaty, or any Slaves or other private property.

The dispute between the two Governments with regard to the construction and execution of that article arose chiefly from the carrying away of slaves by British forces. The respective contentions of the two Governments are set forth in Moore, International Arbitrations, I, 350–57. Article 5 of the convention of October 20, 1818, with Great Britain (Document 40), referring to the differences that had arisen under Article 1 of the Treaty of Ghent, provided:

Whereas under the aforesaid Article, the United States claim for their Citizens, and as their private Property, the Restitution of, or full Compensation for all Slaves who, at the date of the Exchange of the Ratifications of the said Treaty, were in any Territory, Places, or Possessions whatsoever directed by the said Treaty to be restored to the United States, but then still occupied by the British Forces, whether such Slaves were, at the date aforesaid, on Shore, or on board any British Vessel lying in Waters within the Territory or Jurisdiction of the United States; and whereas differences have arisen, whether, by the true intent and meaning of the aforesaid Article of the Treaty of Ghent the United States are entitled to the Restitution of, or full Compensation for all or any Slaves as above described, the High Contracting Parties hereby agree to refer the said differences to some Friendly Sovereign or State to be named for that purpose; and The High Contracting Parties further engage to consider the decision of such Friendly Sovereign or State, to be final and conclusive on all the Matters referred.

The proposal of the Emperor of Russia as the "Friendly Sovereign" to whom the differences of the two Governments were to be referred, was made to Great Britain pursuant to the instruction to Richard Rush, Minister at London, of November 10, 1819 (D. S., 8 Instructions, U. S. Ministers, 362), from which the following is quoted:

By the fifth article of the Convention of 20. October 1818. with Great-Britain, it is agreed, that the difference between the two Governments with regard to the restitution of or compensation for Slaves, carried away from the United-States by British Officers, after the Ratification of the Treaty of Ghent, shall be referred to some friendly Sovereign or State, to be named for that purpose, whose decision upon the subject is to be final and conclusive.

The President wishes you to name to the British Government the Emperor of Russia, as the Sovereign to whose decision it would be agreeable to the Government of the United-States that the subject should be referred. And if this proposal should be assented to, it may be proper that the proposition should be jointly made by the Ministers of the two parties at S⁺ Petersburg.

The proposal was accepted by the British Government on January 20, 1820 (D. S., 24 Despatches, Great Britain, No. 106, January 21, 1820).

The presidential message to Congress of November 14, 1820 (American State Papers, Foreign Relations, IV, 645), includes this paragraph:

The question depending between the United States and Great Britain respecting the construction of the first article of the treaty of Ghent has been referred by both Governments to the decision of the Emperor of Russia, who has accepted the umpirage.

It was known at the time that the Emperor of Russia had consented to act (D. S., 7 Despatches, Russia, No. 24, May 17, 1820), but the formal request from the two Governments was of a later date.

The invitation to the Emperor of Russia was extended by notes addressed to Count Nesselrode, Russian Secretary of State for Foreign Affairs, by Henry Middleton, United States Minister, and by Sir Charles Bagot, British Ambassador, at St. Petersburg, under date of June 21, 1821 (D. S., 8 Despatches, Russia, Middleton to the Secretary of State, No. 6, August 1, 1821, enclosures B and D). The acceptance of the Emperor of Russia was communicated in notes of Nesselrode to the representatives of the two Governments dated June 22, Old Style, or July 4, 1821 (*ibid.*, enclosures C and E). On July 30 the act or *compromis* submitting the question at issue for decision of the Emperor of Russia was signed by the representatives of the two Governments (*ibid.*, enclosure I) and on the following day was transmitted with a note of Middleton to Nesselrode (*ibid.*, enclosure H).

Regarding the form of the *compromis*, or act of submission, Middleton wrote (*ibid.*), "the *alternat* is preserved by presenting duplicates signed by both the Plenipotentiaries, each signing first & naming first his own Government in the paper presented by him." The *compromis*

was written in French; its text, from *ibid.*, enclosure I, with a translation, follows:

[Translation]

Compromis par lequel les États-Unis d'Amérique et l'Angleterre se rapportent a la décision de Sa Majesté l'Empereur de toutes les Russies dans leur différend sur l'interprétation du premier article du Traité de Gand—signé 24 Décembre 1814.

Arbitral Agreement Whereby the United States of America and England Refer the Decision of Their Difference as to the Interpretation of Article 1 of the Treaty of Ghent, Signed December 24, 1814, to His Majesty the Emperor of All the Russias.

(Here was inserted the first article of the treaty of Ghent in the original English)

Traduction. Article premier du Traité de Gand.

Article 1 of the Treaty of Ghent

"Il y aura une paix solide et "universelle entre Sa Majesté Bri-"tannique et les États-Unis, et "entre leurs pays, territoires, cités, "villes, et peuples respectifs, de "tout rang, sans exception de "lieux ou de personnes. Toutes "hostilités cesseront sur terre et "sur mer, aussitôt que ce traité "aura été ratifié par les deux "parties, ainsi qu'il est dit ci-après. "Tous les territoires, lieux, et "possessions quelconques, pris par "l'une des parties sur l'autre, du-"rant la guerre, ou qui pourraient "être pris après la signature du pré-"sent traité, à l'exception seule-"ment des isles ci-dessous men-"tionnées, seront rendus sans "délai, et sans faire détruire, ou "emporter aucune partie de l'ar-"tillerie, ou autre propriété pub-"lique originairement prise dans "les dits forts ou lieux et qui s'y "trouvera au moment de l'échange "des ratifications de ce traité, ou "aucuns esclaves ou autres pro-"priétés privées. Et tous ar-"chives, registres, actes et papiers, "soit d'une nature publique ou ap-"partenans à des particuliers, qui "dans le cours de la guerre peuvent "être tombés entre les mains des "officiers de l'une ou de l'autre par-"tie, seront de suite, en tant que "sera practicable, restitués et dé-"livrés aux autorités propres et "personnes aux quelles ils appar-"tiennent respectivement."

There shall be a firm and universal Peace between His Britannic Majesty and the United States, and between their respective Countries, Territories, Cities, Towns, and People of every degree without exception of places or persons. All hostilities both by sea and land shall cease as soon as this Treaty shall have been ratified by both parties as hereinafter mentioned. All territory, places, and possessions whatsoever taken by either party from the other during the war, or which may be taken after the signing of this Treaty, excepting only the Islands hereinafter mentioned, shall be restored without delay and without causing any destruction or carrying away any of the Artillery or other public property originally captured in the said forts or places, and which shall remain therein upon the Exchange of the Ratifications of this Treaty, or any Slaves or other private property; And all Archives, Records, Deeds, and Papers, either of a public nature or belonging to private persons, which in the course of the war may have fallen into the hands of the Officers of either party, shall be, as far as may be practicable, forthwith restored and delivered to the proper authorities and persons to whom they respectively belong. . . .

Pendant la guerre qui fut terminée par ce traité, les forces navales de Sa

During the war which was terminated by this treaty the naval forces

Majesté Britannique occupèrent plusieurs de baies et rivières des États Unis, et les forces de terre débarquèrent et prirent poste en plusieurs endroits, nommément à l'isle de Tangier dans l'État de la Virginie et à l'isle de Cumberland dans la Géorgie. Pendant le tems qu'elles occupoient ces postes, un nombre très considérable d'esclaves appartenant à des citoyens des États-Unis fut ou fait captif ou accueilli comme refugié par ces forces, les officiers commandant en chef ayant promulgué une proclamation par laquelle ils les invitoient à se rendre à bord des bâtimens, ou aux postes occupés par les troupes de Sa Majesté Britannique, avec promesse de les recevoir au service soit de terre ou de mer de Sa dite Majesté, ou, à leur choix, de les transporter comme colons libres aux possessions Britanniques sur le continent, ou dans les isles, où ils trouveroient tout encouragement convenable.

Après l'échange des ratifications du traité, le gouvernement des États-Unis nomma des Commissaires pour en surveiller l'exécution, et la restitution des propriétés et des esclaves, qu'on devoit rendre, selon leur interprétation du traité, en évacuant les forts, lieux et possessions dans le territoire des États-Unis—mais les Officiers Anglois, ayant interprété l'article premier du traité comme obligatoire seulement à l'égard des esclaves qui avoient été *originairement pris et qui restoient* encore au moment de l'échange des ratifications du traité *dans les Forts et lieux* qu'on devoit évacuer, et non point à l'égard des esclaves qui avoient été antérieurement ou mis à bord des vaisseaux ou tranférés du local où ils avoient été originairement pris:—il resulta de cette interprétation qu'un nombre assez considérable d'esclaves fut emmené.

Interprétation des États Unis.

Le Gouvernement des États-Unis soutient de son coté, que la stipulation ayant rapport aux propriétés privées a imposé aux forces britanniques l'obligation d'évacuer les forts lieux et possessions qu'elles occupoient dans les dites États, sans emporter de propriétés particulières ou emmener aucuns esclaves:—Que les Officiers Anglois n'avoient pas le droit d'émanciper des esclaves appartenans aux citoyens des

of His Britannic Majesty occupied several of the bays and rivers of the United States, and the land forces disembarked and took position at several places, especially at Tangier Island in the State of Virginia and at Cumberland Island in Georgia. During the time that they occupied these positions, a considerable number of slaves belonging to United States citizens were either made captive or received as refugees by these forces, the chief commanding officers having issued a proclamation inviting them to go on board the ships or into the positions occupied by His Britannic Majesty's troops, with the promise to receive them into the land or sea service of His Majesty aforesaid or, at their choice, to transport them as free colonists to the British possessions on the continent or on the islands, where they would find all proper encouragement.

After the exchange of ratifications of the treaty, the Government of the United States appointed commissioners to look after its enforcement and the restitution of the property and the slaves that were to be returned according to their interpretation of the treaty, on the evacuation of the forts, places, and possessions in United States territory; but the English officers having construed Article 1 of the treaty as being binding only with respect to the slaves who had been *captured originally and who still remained* at the time of exchange of ratifications of the treaty *in the forts and places* that were to be evacuated, and not with respect to the slaves who had been previously either put on board the vessels or transferred from the place where they had originally been taken, the result of this interpretation was that a considerable number of slaves were taken away.

Interpretation of the United States

The Government of the United States maintains on its part that the stipulation relating to private property imposed the obligation upon the British forces to evacuate the forts, places, and possessions which they occupied in the said United States, without carrying away any private property or taking away any slaves; that the English officers did not have a right to emancipate slaves belonging

États Unis:—Et que l'Angleterre est tenue d'indemniser les Propriétaires de tous les esclaves que ses officiers ont emmenés en contravention à la stipulation du traité en quittant les dits forts, lieux ou possessions.

Développement de cette interprétation.

1º Pour motiver cette interprétation, il n'y a qu'à prendre le sens littéral de la stipulation, pour la restitution des territoires et des propriétés en général, ayant toutefois égard à la construction elliptique du dernier membre de la période. On y voit que les territoires, lieux et possessions, qui avoient été pris pendant la guerre, devoient être rendus sans délai, et sans faire détruire ou emporter aucune partie de l'artillerie, ou autres propriétés publiques originairement prises et qui restoient encore à la paix dans les dits forts ou lieux, et *sans emporter* (car le sens de la période entière indique ces mots sous-entendus) de propriétés privées, les esclaves inclusivement. La stipulation quant aux propriétés particulières est absolue, et sans condition autre que celle contenue dans la phrase "sans emporter" c: a: d: d'être sur les lieux. La condition specifiée dans le texte, celle d'avoir été prise et de rester sur les lieux, est aussi expressément limitée à la propriété publique, que l'interdiction d'emporter est commune à toutes des deux espèces de propriété.

Il y a une distinction très marquée dans l'article, et en effet il existe une différence essentielle dans ces deux espèces de propriété. Il peut y avoir de bonnes raisons pour stipuler le droit de faire détruire les propriétés publiques, lorsqu'il n'y en a pas pour adopter la même mesure à l'égard des propriétés particulières. Il arrive souvent qu'on fait la stipulation de détruire les forts qu'on évacue, et d'emporter l'artillerie et les munitions de guerre qui s'y trouvent au moment de la paix; mais il n'y a peut être pas d'exemple d'une stipulation pour faire détruire les propriétés particulières, encore moins les esclaves; et la stipulation de ne pas les détruire ne seroit guère moins inouïe.

to citizens of the United States; and that England is under the obligation to indemnify the owners of all the slaves whom her officers took away in violation of the stipulation of the treaty on leaving the said forts, places, and possessions.

Exposition of This Interpretation

1. In order to justify this interpretation it is only necessary to take the literal sense of the stipulation prescribing restitution of territories and property in general, paying attention, however, to the elliptical construction of the last clause of the sentence. In it we see that the territories, places, and possessions which had been taken during the war were to be restored without delay, and that without destroying or carrying away any part of the artillery or other public property originally taken and which still remained in these said forts or places upon the conclusion of peace, and *without carrying away* (for the meaning of the whole sentence implies these words as being tacitly understood) any private property, including slaves. The stipulation as regards private property is absolute and without any other condition than that embodied in the phrase "without carrying away," that is, of being there (on the spot). The condition specified in the text, namely, that of having been captured and of remaining on the spot, is as expressly limited to public property as the clause prohibiting carrying away is common to both kinds of property.

There is a very marked distinction in the article, and as a matter of fact there is an essential difference between these two kinds of property. There may be good reasons for stipulating the right to cause public property to be destroyed, when there are none for adopting the same measure with respect to private property. It often happens that a stipulation is made to destroy the forts which are evacuated, and to carry away the artillery and war supplies found there at the time of concluding peace; but there is perhaps no instance of a stipulation to cause private property, much less slaves, to be destroyed, and a stipulation not to destroy them would be hardly less strange.

D'ailleurs, si l'intention des contractans avoit été de subordonner la restitution des esclaves et des autres propriétés particulières, à la limitation contenue dans les termes "originairement prises et qui se trouveront encore dans les dits forts et lieux" ils auroient mis cette phrase à la fin de la période après les mots "ou aucuns esclaves ou autres propriétés privées." Dans ce cas la restitution de toutes les propriétés quelconques eut été subordonnée aux mêmes conditions; tandis qu'au contraire on voit que la clause restrictive a été placée immédiatement après les mots "l'artillerie et autres propriétés publiques"; et par conséquent la restriction se trouve limitée aux seules propriétés publiques, sans affecter en aucune manière les propriétés particulières.

2º Il ne peut guère être nécessaire d'insister sur ce que l'émancipation des esclaves de l'ennemi n'est point parmi les moyens légitimes de faire la guerre selon les usages établis parmi les nations civilisées; car en effet il faut adhérer à cette doctrine pour peu qu'on admette des restrictions quelconques dans les moyens de se nuire en tems de guerre. L'Angleterre ayant reconnu les esclaves comme propriété particulière par les termes du traité, ne sauroit s'attribuer le droit de détruire cette propriété en leur donnant la liberté.

3º La Justice de la réclamation contenue dans la 3ᵐᵉ proposition ne peut point être douteuse.

En resumé, il paroit évident que l'Angleterre a stipulé *de ne point emporter de propriétés particulières ou emmener d'esclaves qui se trouveroient êtres au moment de l'échange des ratifications du traité dans les limites des États-Unis*, soit qu'ils fussent dans les forts, ou à bord des Vaisseaux de l'Angleterre dans les eaux des États-Unis, *territoire* ou *possession* qu'on devoit évacuer.

Interprétation de l'Angleterre.

De l'autre coté le Gouvernement de S. M. Britannique soutient que, la prohibition dans l'article d'emporter ou d'emmener des esclaves n'est qu'une prohibition de les emmener des forts lieux et possessions qui devoient être restitués à l'échange des ratifications:—
Que les termes de l'article ne permet-

Moreover, if it had been the intention of the contracting parties to make the restitution of the slaves and other private property subject to the limitation embodied in the terms "originally captured and which shall remain in the said forts and places," they would have put this phrase at the end of the sentence after the words "or any slaves or other private property." In this case the restitution of all the property, of whatever character, would have been made subject to the same conditions; whereas, on the contrary, we see that the restrictive clause was placed immediately after the words "artillery and other public property"; and consequently the restriction is limited to public property alone, without in any wise affecting private property.

2. It can hardly be necessary to insist on the fact that the emancipation of the slaves of the enemy is not among the lawful means of waging war according to the usages established among civilized nations; for, as a matter of fact, we must adhere to this doctrine if we admit any restrictions whatever in the means of injuring one another in time of war. England having recognized the slaves as being private property under the terms of the treaty, cannot claim the right to destroy this property by setting them free.

3. The justice of the claim embodied in the third proposition can admit of no doubt.

To sum up, it appears evident that England stipulated *not to carry off private property or to take away slaves which or who might be situated within the limits of the United States at the time of exchange of ratifications of the treaty*, whether they were in the forts, or on board the vessels of England in the waters of the United States, or in the *territory* or *possessions* which were to be evacuated.

England's Interpretation

On the other hand, the Government of His Britannic Majesty maintains that the provision in the article which prohibits carrying or taking away slaves merely prohibits taking them away from the forts, places, and possessions which were to be returned upon the exchange of ratifications; that

tent pas de faire de distinction entre des esclaves et toute autre espèce de propriété particulière:—que ni l'une ni l'autre des parties ne prétend qu'il y ait une différence, et que par conséquent, toutes les stipulations de l'article qui s'attachent aux esclaves comme à une espèce de propriété particulière doivent nécessairement s'attacher également à toutes les autres propriétés particulières auxquelles l'article se référe; à l'exception des archives, registres, actes et papiers, à l'égard des quels il y a une stipulation spéciale:—que si l'on soutient que la propriété particulière est exemptée de toutes les conditions aux quelles il est convenu que la propriété publique doit être restituée, il en résulteroit que la restitution des propriétés particulières ne seroit plus assujettie, selon les termes de l'article, à aucune condition; mais la restitution sans conditions de toute propriété particulière ne pouvait être dans l'intention des parties contractantes, et en effet n'a jamais été reclamée de la part des États-Unis.

La restitution de la propriété particulière est donc sujette à certaines conditions; les quelles ne sont à chercher que dans l'article du traite, et ne peuvent être conséquemment autres que celles que l'on admet être attachées à la restitution de l'artillerie, et des autres propriétés publiques.

Pour ces raisons le gouvernement de S:M:B: est d'opinion que les Officiers de S:M: étoient autorises par le traité à emporter ou emmener

1º tous les esclaves qui se trouvoient à bord des Vaisseaux de S:M: à l'époque de l'échange des ratifications du traité; et

2º tous les esclaves qui à cette même époque ne se trouvoient pas dans les forts, lieux ou possessions mêmes où ils avoient été originairement pris.

Le Gouvernement de S:M:B: ne conteste pas le fait (qui ne parôit avoir aucune relation avec la question actuelle sur le vrai sens du premier article du traité) que tandis que quelques uns des esclaves dont il s'agit, ont été pris dans les forts lieux et possessions qui ont été subséquemment restitués, d'autres ont été reçus par les Officiers de S:M: comme déserteurs ou transfuges, incités à se soustraire au pouvoir au pouvoir de leurs mâitres par de motifs particuliers, ou par des

the terms of the article do not warrant any distinction being drawn between slaves and any other kind of private property; that neither of the parties maintains that there is any difference, and that consequently all the stipulations of the article which refer to slaves as a species of private property must necessarily also refer to all other private property to which the article relates, with the exception of archives, records, deeds, and papers, in regard to which there is a special stipulation; and that if one were to hold that private property is exempt from all the conditions under which it is agreed that public property is to be restored, the result would be that the restitution of private property would no longer be subjected to any conditions under this article; however, the unconditional return of all private property could not have been within the intention of the contracting parties and has in fact never been demanded by the United States.

The restitution of private property is therefore subject to certain conditions, which are to be sought only in the article of the treaty and can consequently not be other than those which are admitted to refer to the restoration of artillery and other public property.

For these reasons the Government of His Britannic Majesty is of opinion that His Majesty's officers were warranted by the treaty in carrying or taking away:

1. All the slaves who were on board of His Majesty's vessels at the time of exchange of the ratifications of the treaty; and

2. All the slaves who were not at that time in the forts, places, or possessions where they had originally been taken.

The Government of His Britannic Majesty does not dispute the fact (which appears to have no relation with the present question as to the real sense of the first article of the treaty) that, while some of the slaves in question were taken in the forts, places, and possessions which were subsequently restored, others were received by His Majesty's officers as deserters or fugitives induced to free themselves from the power of their masters by private motives or by invitations ex-

invitations que leur avoient addressées les Officiers de S:M: en conformité aux loix et à l'usage de la guerre.

Les deux Gouvernemens ayant persisté également à s'en tenir chacun à son interprétation du premier article du traité de Gand, sont enfin convenus de s'en remettre à cet égard à l'arbitrage de Sa Majesté L'Empereur de toutes les Russies; les dits Gouvernemens s'étant en même tems engagés, de la manière la plus formelle, à considérer la decision de Sa Majesté Impériale comme obligatoire en toutes choses ayant rapport a l'objet sus-mentionné.

A l'effet que Sa Majesté Impériale puisse émettre son opinion sur le dit différend, Les Sous-Signés, plénipotentiaires des États Unis et de l'Angleterre, par ordre de leurs Gouvernemens respectifs, ont rédigé, d'un commun accord, l'état de la question ci-dessus, fait double, comme leur Compromis, en y joignant un court exposé des argumens respectifs, et en se réservant réciproquement d'y ajouter les mémoires et observations qu'ils pourront juger nécessaires, de part ou l'autre, à eclaircir et à mettre dans son vrai jour la question sur laquelle Sa Majesté Impériale est sollicitée de prononcer un jugement arbitral; et Les deux Parties se réservent également le droit réciproque, selon l'esprit de la convention du 20 Octobre 1818 d'avoir recours à l'intervention de Sa Majesté Impériale dans le cas où des difficultés, ultérieures se présenteroient dans l'exécution de Sa décision, comme "points référés" par la dite convention.

à St Petersbourg ce 18/30 Juillet 1821.

(Signed) Henry Middleton
(Signed) Charles Bagot

tended to them by His Majesty's officers in accordance with the laws and usages of war.

The two Governments, having likewise persisted in each abiding by its own interpretation of the first article of the Treaty of Ghent, finally agreed to refer the matter to the arbitration of His Majesty the Emperor of all the Russias, the said Governments having at the same time most formally pledged themselves to consider the decision of His Imperial Majesty as binding in all matters connected with the aforementioned subject.

To the end that His Imperial Majesty may give his opinion on the said difference, the undersigned Plenipotentiaries of the United States and England have, by order of their respective Governments and in common accord, drawn up a statement of the above question in duplicate as their Arbitral Agreement, appending thereto a short summary of the respective arguments and reciprocally reserving the right to add such memoranda and observations as they may deem necessary on either side in order to make clear and put in its proper light the question on which His Imperial Majesty is asked to pronounce an arbitral judgment; and the two parties likewise reserve the reciprocal right, according to the spirit of the convention of October 20, 1818, to have recourse to the intervention of His Imperial Majesty in case subsequent difficulties should arise in carrying out his decision, as "points referred" by the said convention.

St. Petersburg, July 18/30, 1821.

Henry Middleton
Charles Bagot

With the note of Middleton to Nesselrode of July 31 was also communicated a printed statement or *exposé abrégé* on the part of the United States (D. S., 8 Despatches, Russia, No. 6, August 1, 1821, enclosure); and other pleadings followed in due course. Copies of the "answer" of the British Ambassador, undated, but of October 20, and the American "replication" of November 16, are enclosures 2 and 3 to Middleton's despatch of November 17, 1821 (D. S., 8 Despatches, Russia, No. 13). The final observations of Sir Charles Bagot of December 19, 1821, and the note of Middleton of December 21, closing the arguments, are respectively enclosures 2 and 3 to the despatch of the latter of January 9, 1822 (D. S., 9 Despatches, Russia, No. 15).

The decision of the Emperor of Russia, which was in favor of the position of the United States and which is annex A/ to this conven-

tion, was rendered on May 4, 1822 (April 22, Old Style); communication of the decision of the Emperor of Russia and of other papers, including annex A to the convention, which is the covering note of Nesselrode, and annex B, was made by the despatch of Middleton to the Secretary of State dated May 6 (D. S., 9 Despatches, Russia, No. 18), and in that despatch he wrote particularly about annex B as follows:

> The several papers . . . were only delivered two days ago, as the dates will show. No communication was made to me upon the subject from the period when the written discussion was closed, until about a week since, when the British Ambassador and myself were invited to attend at the foreign office, and the decision *as it now remains* was read to us confidentially. It was upon that occasion that Sir Charles Bagot proposed the enquiry noticed in the paper No 4 [annex B]. I did not deem it necessary to say anything farther upon the subject than to remark that I believed he must have misconceived the meaning of the decision which was worded entirely in the terms of the Treaty, and could not therefore attempt to draw any line of distinction between Slaves captured and such as had voluntarily surrendered themselves; & farther, that I could not imagine it could be the Emperor's intention to countenance the doctrine that such a mode of warfare as that contended for by the adversary is legitimate. The answer which was drawn from the Emperor by this enquiry is contained in the paper No 4 [annex B], & must be considered I suppose as an *annex* to the *final decision* (No 2.) [annex A/].

Enclosure 3 to that despatch of Middleton of May 6, was a paper of "grammatical observations" which is mentioned in the fifth paragraph of annex A to the convention as "an extract of some observations upon the literal sense of the first article of the Treaty of Ghent." Further reference is made below to those "grammatical observations."

By notes of May 9 and 18, 1822, the American Minister and the British Ambassador respectively requested the mediation of the Emperor of Russia in the ensuing negotiations, following the intimation of willingness to accept that function contained in the final paragraph of the decision of May 4 (annex A/); and the Russian Plenipotentiaries were named in the note of Nesselrode of May 28 (May 16, Old Style). The three notes are enclosures 1, 4, and 5 to the despatch of Middleton of July 6 (D. S., 9 Despatches, Russia, No. 19); and the same despatch reported that agreement upon the terms of the convention had been reached on July 4, 1822.

The Full Powers

The full power to Henry Middleton dated June 6, 1820, was broader in terms than the usual form for the negotiation and signature of a treaty; it was issued before the submission of the controversy to the Emperor of Russia and granted authority in respect of the entire procedure, reading as follows (D. S., 1 Credences, 321):

> James Monroe, President of the United States of America.
>
> To all to whom these presents shall come, Greeting:
>
> Whereas a difference prevails between the United States of America and His Britannic Majesty, as to the construction of the first Article of the Treaty of peace

and amity concluded between the parties at Ghent on the 24ᵗʰ day of December, one thousand eight hundred and fourteen; and it is provided by the fifth Article of the Convention concluded at London between the said parties on the 12ᵗʰ day of October 1818, that the difference referred to should be submitted to some friendly Sovereign or State, to be named for that purpose, whose decision should be final and conclusive: And whereas His Majesty, the Emperor of all the Russias, has been designated by the parties, as the common friend of both, to whose arbitrament and decision the true construction of the said first Article of the Treaty of Ghent should be referred: Now therefore be it known, that reposing special Trust and Confidence in the integrity, prudence and abilities of Henry Middleton, Envoy Extraordinary and Minister Plenipotentiary from the United States to His said Imperial Majesty, I have authorized and empowered, and do hereby authorize and empower him to do and perform any act or acts which may be necessary, or proper on the part of the United States for giving effect to what may be determined upon, through the good offices or arbitrament of the Emperor of all the Russias, as the true Construction of the Article referred to, of the Treaty of Ghent.

> In testimony whereof I have caused the seal of the United States to be hereunto affixed. Done at the City of Washington the 6ᵗʰ day of June A. D. 1820, and of the Independence of the United States the forty fourth.

(L. S.)

JAMES MONROE.

By the President.
JOHN QUINCY ADAMS,
    Secʸ of State.

A copy of the full power of Middleton had been delivered to Lord Castlereagh in the summer of 1820 and had been assented to by him with the suggestion "that one conformable to it might be prepared for Sir Charles Bagot" (D. S., 25 Despatches, Great Britain, No. 146, September 21, 1820).

On August 1, 1821 (D. S., 8 Despatches, Russia, No. 6), Middleton wrote that the British Ambassador had not received his full power although he had communicated his instructions dated June 16, 1820 (enclosure A to the same despatch). In his next despatch, of August 19 (*ibid.*, No. 7), Middleton wrote "that a full power under the Great Seal was received by him [Sir Charles Bagot] a few days since, bearing date 22ᵈ August *1820*, of which I have the honor to enclose you herewith a Copy," which is in the following terms:

George R (manu ipsius Regis)

George the Fourth, by the Grace of God, King of the United Kingdom of Great Britain and Ireland, Defender of the Faith, King of Hanover &c. &c. To all and singular to whom these Presents shall come, Greeting! Whereas a difference prevails between Us and Our Good Friends The United States of America, as to the true Construction of the first Article of the Treaty of Peace & Amity concluded at Ghent on the 24ᵗʰ day of December 1814, between Us and Our said Good Friends: And Whereas, it is provided by the fifth Article of the Convention concluded at London on the 20ᵗʰ day of October 1818. between Us and our said Good Friends, that the said Difference should be submitted to some Friendly Sovereign or State, to be named for that purpose, whose Decision should be final and conclusive:

And Whereas, Our Good Brother the Emperor of all the Russias has been designated by Us and by Our said Good Friends The United States of America, as the common friend of both, to whose Arbitration and Decision the true construction of the said first Article of the Treaty of Ghent should be referred:— Know Ye therefore, that We reposing entire confidence in the Judgement, Skill

and Abilities of our Right Trusty and Well Beloved Councillor, Sir Charles Bagot, Knight Grand Cross of the Most Honorable Order of the Bath, and Our Ambassador Extraordinary and Plenipotentiary to Our said Good Brother, have named, made, constituted and appointed as We do by these Presents name, make, constitute and appoint him, in this matter, Our undoubted Commissioner, Procurator and Plenipotentiary, Giving unto him all and all manner of Power and Authority to treat, adjust and conclude, with such person or persons as may be vested with similar Power and Authority on the part of our said Good Brother The Emperor of all the Russias, and of our said Good Friends the United States of America, any Articles, Compacts, Convention or Agreement that may tend to the Attainment of the above mentioned End, and to sign for Us, and in our name, every thing so agreed upon and concluded, and to do and transact all such other matters, which may appertain to the finishing the aforesaid Work, in as ample Manner and Form, and with equal force and efficacy, as We Ourselves could do, if Personally Present:—Engaging and promising upon our Royal Word, that whatever Things shall be so transacted and Concluded by Our said Commissioner, Procurator, and Plenipotentiary, shall be agreed upon, acknowledged, and accepted by Us in the fullest Manner, and that We will never suffer, in the whole or in part, any person whatsoever to infringe or act contrary thereto. In witness Whereof, We have caused the Great seal of Our United Kingdom of Great Britain and Ireland, to be affixed to these Presents, which We have signed with Our Royal Hand. Given at Carlton Palace, the Twenty second day of August in the Year of Our Lord One Thousand Eight Hundred and Twenty, and in the First Year of our Reign.

(L. S.)

Nothing appears regarding the full powers granted to the Russian Plenipotentiaries to sign this convention, other than the statement in the note of Count Nesselrode of May 16, 1822, Old Style, repeated in the first protocol of June 10, Old Style, that the Emperor of Russia had named Count Nesselrode and Count Capodistrias as "Plénipotentiaires Médiateurs" (D. S., 9 Despatches, Russia, No. 20, July 16, 1822, enclosures 5 and 8).

FORM OF THE CONVENTION

In his despatch of July 16, 1822, which reported the signature of the convention on July 12 and which enclosed the original, Middleton wrote as follows regarding its form and language (*ibid.*):

It is known to you, Sir, to be the practise of this Government, when addressed by foreigners in their native tongue, other than *french*, to give the answer in the Russ language. The french is therefore willingly resorted to by all who desire to avoid this course, and is become here on this account the universal medium of communication with the Government for *all* nations. This will account for the circumstance of the correspondence & decision we are considering being *in french*. In reference to the convention being drawn up in *two languages*, it is proper that I should state to you, that the British Plenipotentiary & myself had proposed to insert in the body of the instrument a declaration "that it had been first written & agreed to in English": this was objected to by the Russian Plenipotentiaries, who observed that *we* might nevertheless if we pleased draw up an additional article for that purpose. This we have declined doing, but it is distinctly understood between the British plenipotentiary & myself, that as the instrument was first written & agreed to *by us in English*, so *we* consider the *english Copy* as entitled to a preference in case of any discrepancy appearing between the two. Sir Charles Bagot, in transmitting the Convention to his Government, acquaints the British Secretary of State with the understanding between us upon this point, & we both presume that the two Governments will instruct their Commissioners accordingly.

Upon the *form* of the Convention I have but little to remark. It is strictly such as has appeared to me to be suggested by the occasion. *The Capitation* "In the name of the most Holy & Undivided Trinity" was added at the instance of the Russian Plenipotentiaries, who informed us that *all* their treaties & conventions invariably commence in this manner.

It was thus informally agreed, upon the signature of the convention, that its English text should be controlling; and a more formal agreement regarding the documents was embodied in the protocol of signature, the original of which was one of the enclosures to Middleton's despatch of July 16, 1822. The text of that protocol, in French, with the contemporary translation which is with it, follows:

[Translation]

Protocole de Signature.

Les Soussignés Plénipotentiaires de Sa Majesté L'Empereur de toutes les Russies, des Etats Unis d'Amérique et de Sa Majesté le Roi du Royaume Uni de la Grande Brétagne et de l'Irlande, s'étant réunis ce jourd'hui en l'hotel du Ministère des affaires étrangères de Russie, ont signé dans la forme accoutumée, la convention cijointe entre Sa Majesté L'Empereur de toutes les Russies, les Etats Unis d'Amérique et Sa Majesté Britannique.

En signant la dite Convention les Plénipotentiaires soussignés ont arrêté:

1º Que le Plénipotentiaire des Etats Unis d'Amérique et celui de Sa Majesté Britannique, joindroient chacun à l'exemplaire de la Convention qui lui est destinés, les annèxes *A & B*. mentionnées dans la dite Convention, en les fesant transcrire sur les notes originales qui lui ont été adressées par le Ministère des affaires étrangeres de Russie.

2º Que les observations grammaticales jointes à l'original de l'annèxe cotée *A*. ne seroient transcrites, vû la nature de leur contenû, ni dans les instrumens, ni dans les actes de ratification de la Convention Susdite.

Fait triple à S! Petersbourg le 12 Juillet/30 Juin 1822.

NESSELRODE
CAPODISTRIAS
HENRY MIDDLETON.
CHARLES BAGOT

Protocol of Signature

The undersigned Plenipotentiaries of His Majesty the Emperor of all the Russias, of the United States of America, and of His Majesty the King of the United Kingdom of Great Britain and Ireland, having met this day at the office of the Department of Foreign Affairs of Russia, have signed, in the usual form, the subjoined convention between His Majesty the Emperor of all the Russias, the United States of America, and His Britannic Majesty.

In signing the said convention the undersigned Plenipotentiaries have agreed:

1. That the Plenipotentiary of the United States of America and that of His Britannic Majesty should each attach to the copy of the convention which is destined for him, the additions A and B mentioned in the said convention, by causing them to be transcribed from the original notes which have been addressed to them by the Department of Foreign Affairs of Russia.

2. That the grammatical observations subjoined to the original of the annex, letter A, should not be transcribed, seeing the nature of their contents, either in the instruments or in the acts of ratification of the aforesaid convention.

Done in triplicate at St. Petersburg July 12/June 30, 1822.

NESSELRODE
CAPODISTRIAS
HENRY MIDDLETON.
CHARLES BAGOT

However, and despite the language of the protocol of signature, Middleton put the originals of the annexes A, A/, and B, and not copies thereof, with the original of the convention for the United

States. This is not only twice specifically stated by Middleton in his despatch of July 16, 1822, but is shown to be the case by the documents themselves.

The designations of the annexes in the convention and the references in annex A to other papers, tend to confusion, which a summary statement of the procedure may clarify.

About April 29, 1822 ("about a week since," Middleton wrote in his despatch of May 6), the American Minister and the British Ambassador attended at the Russian Foreign Office, where Count Nesselrode read them confidentially the decision or opinion of the Emperor of Russia. At that time Sir Charles Bagot made some verbal observations regarding the meaning of the decision. On May 4 (April 22, Old Style), which is strictly the date of the decision, the papers were communicated by the Russian Foreign Office to the representatives of the two Governments concerned. The papers so communicated were four, and three of them are annexed to the convention. The one of primary importance is the decision of the Emperor of Russia, which is marked A/ (here called annex A/) and which was enclosed in a covering note signed by Count Nesselrode, which is marked A (here called annex A); but in the text of the convention (Article 4) these two annexed documents, marked respectively A and A/, are together spoken of as "marked A."

The third paper communicated is annex B to the convention. This is also a note signed by Count Nesselrode, and it was written because of, and in response to, the verbal observations of Sir Charles Bagot at the conference which took place about April 29.

The fourth paper communicated is that spoken of in the protocol of signature of the convention as "grammatical observations." This paper is not an annex to the convention, although it is referred to in annex A as "an extract of some observations" which is "subjoined" to that annex A. However, instead of the "grammatical observations" being "subjoined" to annex A, it was specifically agreed in the protocol of signature that those observations should not be annexed to the convention at all, or to any of the ratifications; and they were not.

However, as those observations were one of the documents communicated with the decision of the Emperor of Russia, their text is printed, in French and in translation, toward the close of these notes.

The File Papers

One original of this convention, which, according to the final clauses thereof, was signed in triplicate, is in the Department of State file. The convention proper is written on separate sheets of paper, with the English text in the left columns and the French in the right.

In Article 4 of the convention mention is made of "explanatory Documents hereunto annexed marked A & B." To the original convention above mentioned, however, there are in fact three annexed documents, marked respectively A, A/, and B. Annex A is the covering note of Count Nesselrode, Russian Secretary of State for Foreign Affairs, to Henry Middleton, Minister of the United States

at St. Petersburg, dated April 22, Old Style, or May 4, 1822, enclosing annex A/, which is the opinion or decision of the Emperor of Russia of the same date. Thus a reference in the text of the convention to the document "marked A" means annex A and annex A/ together. Annex B is the note of Nesselrode to Middleton of the same date, commenting on a communication of Sir Charles Bagot, the British Ambassador at St. Petersburg.

The annexes to the original convention in the Department of State file are, as stated above, the originals transmitted to Middleton by Count Nesselrode. They are in French only and are written in part on double sheets of paper. The convention and the annexes are fastened together with an unsealed ribbon. Those annexes are printed above, with a translation from the Session Laws of the second session of the Seventeenth Congress, published in 1823; that same translation is printed in American State Papers, Foreign Relations, V, 219–21, and is the one which has heretofore been printed in the Statutes at Large and in treaty collections generally.

Regarding a portion of the translation this is to be said: The convention, in its opening paragraphs, embodies a portion of the decision of the Emperor of Russia. That decision was written in French, and in the French text of the convention it is quoted. In the corresponding portion of the English text of the convention the quotation is a translation, and that translation in the text of the convention of the extract from the decision of the Emperor of Russia differs verbally from the corresponding paragraphs of the later translation of the decision itself as found in annex A/.

Among the papers in the treaty file are copies of the three annexes, certified by Count Nesselrode; the attested resolution of the Senate of January 3, 1823 (Executive Journal, III, 319); and the original proclamation of January 11. The resolution of the Senate describes the convention as "concluded between the United States and Great Britain, at St. Petersburg, on the 12th. day of July 1822, under the mediation of the Emperor of Russia." The proclamation, which is in customary form, includes the text of the convention in English and French, but the three annexes are in French only. The proclamation is printed in American State Papers, Foreign Relations, V, 214–19.

Seven other papers in the file—a facsimile of the United States instrument of ratification of January 9, 1823; the original British and Russian instruments of ratification; a French translation of the Russian ratification; the original protocol of exchange, with a minute regarding the Russian instrument of ratification; the certificate of exchange of ratifications between the United States and Great Britain; and the agreement between the United States and Great Britain under Article 7 as to the payment of the commissioners and arbitrators—are printed or described below.

Certain papers accompanied the convention when it was transmitted to the Senate with the presidential message of December 4, 1822, and were printed (Executive Journal, III, 311). There appears to be now available no copy of that Senate document.

The Invocation

At the beginning of this convention is the invocation, "In the name of the most-holy & indivisible Trinity." As was said in the despatch of July 16, 1822, above quoted (D. S., 9 Despatches, Russia, No. 20), that invocation, there styled the "Capitation," was used at the time in all treaties and conventions made by Russia. Some other states then followed the same practice; the solemn phrase is found as the opening of various other treaties of the United States; instances are the Treaty of Peace of September 3, 1783, with Great Britain (Document 11); the treaty of September 4, 1816, with Sweden and Norway (Document 36); the convention of April 17, 1824, with Russia (Document 46); the treaty of July 4, 1827, with Sweden and Norway (Document 55); the treaty of December 12, 1828, with Brazil (Document 64); and the treaty of December 18, 1832, with Russia (Document 75). Some comments on its use will be found in the notes to Document 55, the treaty of July 4, 1827, with Sweden and Norway.

The Ratifications

There is now in the Department of State file a facsimile of the United States instrument of ratification, obtained from the British archives. The ratification is in the usual form, containing the text of the convention in English and French and of the annexes in French. In its final clause is the statement that it was given "in duplicates."

The Russian instrument of ratification includes the convention only, without the annexes; the French text is in the left columns and the English in the right. The ratification itself is written in the Russian language, and there is in the treaty file a French translation thereof, certified by the Russian Chargé d'Affaires, George Ellisen.

The British instrument of ratification is also in the usual form. It includes the text of the convention in English and French, the former in the left columns, followed by the annexes in French: first comes annex A; then, following a few lines in French regarding the enclosures to that annex, annex B; and thereafter annex A/, headed "Opinion de Sa Majesté Impériale."

Annexes A and B of the British ratification, however, are the notes of April 22, Old Style, or May 4, 1822, addressed by Count Nesselrode to Sir Charles Bagot. They are identic with the two notes of the same date to Middleton; but, as the *alternat* is observed, annex A of the British ratification differs slightly in form from annex A printed above, and there is a trifling difference between the American and the British documents in the language of the concluding formal paragraph of both annex A and annex B.

The Exchange of Ratifications

According to John Quincy Adams, the tripartite exchange of the ratifications of this convention was a rather formidable ceremony,

requiring some hours for its completion.   The following account is from his diary (Memoirs of John Quincy Adams, VI, 123–24):

I went to the office at one; and, soon after, Mr. Canning came with Mr. Parish, and Mr. Ellisen, the Russian Chargé d'Affaires, with Baron Maltitz, and we exchanged the ratifications of the Convention signed at St. Petersburg the 12th of July last.   This was the first Convention ever negotiated by the United States under a mediation, and of which the exchange was accordingly tripartite. Mr. Canning was excessively punctilious upon every point of formality; Mr. Ellisen much less so.   We were employed till six o'clock before the exchange was completed.   Mr. Canning had two certificates of exchange to execute, one with me and one with Mr. Ellisen.   That which I had drawn up was tripartite, to be executed by all three, and each party to retain one.   But after five or six copies of my draft had been made, and still Mr. Canning wanted some insignificant transposition of words, requiring new copies, which there was no longer time to make out, I gave up altogether my draft, and we merely signed a protocol in French, proposed by Mr. Ellisen, and which contained all the substance of the certificate that I had drawn up.   It included, of course, an acknowledgment by Mr. Ellisen of the receipt of the certified copy of the Convention, which, by its eighth article, was to be delivered by each of the parties to the Minister or Agent of the mediating power.   We compared together all the ratified copies.   I held the English ratified copy, and Mr. Brent the Russian ratified copy, which we were to receive; Mr. Canning held our ratified copy, and Mr. Parish the Russian ratified copy, which were to be delivered to Mr. Canning; and Mr. Ellisen held our ratified copy, and Baron Maltitz the British ratified copy, which were to be delivered to Mr. Ellisen; each party thus collating the two copies which it was to retain, Mr. Ironside holding at the same time the original executed treaty, transmitted by Mr. Middleton.   There were several slight variations between the copies; none of any consequence.   But there were three explanatory documents in French only, which in the English copies, and in ours, formed part of the ratified Convention, but in the Russian were on separate papers, not within the body of the ratification—but signed and sealed as annexed copies.

Mr. Canning took great exception to this, and insisted upon having a minute of it entered upon the protocol, as it was.   I executed with Mr. Canning also the agreement for the payment of the Commissioners and Arbitrators.   He accepted the modification proposed by the President, with some slight alterations.   It was quite dark when I came home to dinner.

It thus appears that the certified copies of the annexes which are in the treaty file, were delivered with, and as part of, the Russian instrument of ratification.

The protocol of exchange, with the minute regarding the Russian ratification, is written in French.   Its text, with a translation, follows:

[Translation]

Protocole concernant l'échange des ratifications de la convention signée à St Petersbourg le 30 Juin/12 Juillet 1822 par les Plénipotentiaires de la Grande Brétagne des Etats Unis d'Amérique et de la Russie.

Mͬ John Quincy Adams, Sécrétaire d'Etat des Etats Unis d'Amérique, Monsieur Stratford Canning, Envoyé extraordinaire et Ministre plénipotentiaire de Sa Majesté Britannique et Mͬ George d'Ellisen Chargé d'affaires de

Protocol concerning the exchange of the ratifications of the convention signed at St. Petersburg June 30/July 12, 1822, by the Plenipotentiaries of Great Britain, the United States of America, and Russia.

Mr. John Quincy Adams, Secretary of State of the United States of America, Mr. Stratford Canning, Envoy Extraordinary and Minister Plenipotentiary of His Britannic Majesty, and Mr. George Ellisen, Chargé d'Affaires of

sa Majesté l'Empereur de toutes les Russies s'étant réunis le dix Janvier nouveau style 1823 à Washington, pour procéder conformement aux ordres de leurs Gouvernemens respectifs à l'échange des ratifications de la convention, signé à St Petersbourg le 30 Juin/12 Juillet 1822 par les Plénipotentiaires des dits Gouvernemens, l'échange des instrumens de ratification de la convention susmentionnée, revêtus de la signature de Sa Majesté l'Empereur de toutes les Russies, de celle de Sa Majesté Britannique et signé par Monsieur le Président des Etats Unis de l'avis et du consentement de leur Sénat s'est fait conformément à l'article 8 de la dite convention.

Des copies vidimées de la convention ratifiée ont été remises par le Sécrétaire d'Etat des Etats Unis et par l'Envoyé d'Angleterre au Chargé d'affaires de Russie.

Fait triple à Washington le dix Janvier nouveau style de l'an de grace mil huit cent vingt et trois.

> John Quincy Adams
> Stratford Canning
> George Ellisen

Monsieur le Ministre d'Angleterre ayant observé que les trois annexes inserées dans les Ratifications de Sa Majesté Britannique & des Etats Unis & qui lui ont été communiquées en Copie, vidimée par S. Ex. Monsieur le Comte de Nesselrode ne se trouvent point également inserées dans les Ratifications de Sa Majesté L'Empereur de toutes les Russies, le présent Protocole en fait mention, pour obvier à toute objection qui par la suite pourrait être causée par cette circonstance.

Fait Triple, Washington dix Janvier 1823.

> John Quincy Adams
> Stratford Canning
> George Ellisen

His Majesty the Emperor of all the Russias, having met at Washington on January 10, 1823, New Style, in order to proceed, pursuant to the orders of their respective Governments, to the exchange of the ratifications of the convention signed at St. Petersburg June 30/July 12, 1822, by the Plenipotentiaries of the said Governments, the exchange of the instruments of ratification of the above-mentioned convention, bearing the signature of His Majesty the Emperor of all the Russias, that of His Britannic Majesty, and signed by the President of the United States with the advice and consent of their Senate, took place in accordance with Article 8 of the said convention.

Collated and certified copies of the ratified convention have been delivered by the Envoy of England and by the Secretary of State of the United States to the Chargé d'Affaires of Russia.

Done in triplicate at Washington January 10, New Style, of the year of grace one thousand eight hundred and twenty-three.

> John Quincy Adams
> Stratford Canning
> George Ellisen

The Minister of England having observed that the three annexes inserted in the ratifications of His Britannic Majesty and of the United States and copies of which, collated and certified by His Excellency, Count Nesselrode, have been communicated to him, are not similarly inserted in the ratification of His Majesty the Emperor of all the Russias, the present protocol makes mention thereof in order to obviate any objection which might hereafter be caused by this circumstance.

Done in triplicate, Washington, January 10, 1823.

> John Quincy Adams
> Stratford Canning
> George Ellisen

There is also in the treaty file the certificate of the exchange of ratifications between the United States and Great Britain. This is written in English, is in customary form, and is signed and sealed by John Quincy Adams and Stratford Canning.

Article 7

The agreement between the United States and Great Britain for the payment of the commissioners and arbitrators was duly executed,

as provided in Article 7, "at the time of the exchange of the said ratifications." An original of that agreement is in the treaty file; it reads as follows;

We, the Undersigned, having this day met in the City of Washington to exchange the ratifications of the Convention concluded and signed at St. Petersburg on the 30 day of June/12 day of July 1822, by the respective Plenipotentiaries of the United States of America, His Majesty the King of the United Kingdom of Great Britain & Ireland, and His Majesty the Emperor of all the Russias, do hereby certify, that at the time of exchanging the said ratifications it was agreed by us, for our respective Governments, conformably to the seventh article of the above mentioned Convention, that the salary or compensation of the Commissioners and Arbitrators mentioned therein shall be at the rate of one thousand pounds sterling, or four thousand four hundred and forty four dollars, to each Commissioner, and of seven hundred and fifty pounds sterling, or three thousand three hundred and thirty three dollars, to each Arbitrator, per annum, from the time of the first meeting of the Commissioners at Washington until the final dissolution of the Board, to be paid quarterly; with an additional allowance, to be paid with the first quarter's salary, of six hundred pounds sterling to the Commissioner, and of the same sum to the Arbitrator, to be appointed on the part of His Britannic Majesty, in consideration of their being called upon to exercise their functions at a distance from their country; and of a sum of five hundred pounds sterling to each of them at the close of the Commission, for their return home.

It was also agreed by us, that the compensation of the Secretary of the said Board of Commissioners shall be at the rate of four hundred fifty pounds sterling, or two thousand dollars, a year, to commence from the period of his appointment, until the final dissolution of the Board.

And it was lastly agreed by us, that the said salaries and additional allowances shall, like the contingent expenses of the Commission, be defrayed jointly by the United States and His Britannic Majesty, the said expenses to be laid before the Board at the end of each quarter, and after being ascertained & allowed by a majority of the Board, to be divided, including salary, and allowance, as above, into two moieties, for each of which the Commissioners on either side shall draw respectively on the proper departments of their own Governments.

In witness whereof, we have hereunto set our hands and affixed our seals, at Washington, this tenth day of January one thousand eight hundred and twenty three.

[Seal] JOHN QUINCY ADAMS.
[Seal] STRATFORD CANNING

ANNEX A

In annex A to the convention, which is the covering note of the Russian Secretary of State for Foreign Affairs of May 4, 1822, to the American Minister at St. Petersburg, reference is made to various documents.

One of them, which is mentioned in the fourth paragraph of annex A, is the note of Sir Charles Bagot to Count Nesselrode of October 20, 1821. A copy thereof, without date, is enclosure 2 to the despatch of Middleton of November 17, 1821 (D. S., 8 Despatches, Russia, No. 13); it is there called an "answer." The phrase in that note to which reference is made in annex A may be thus translated from the French: "It is upon the signification of the words and upon the construction of the text of the article in dispute as it now exists, and not upon the alleged intentions of one or the other of the contractants, that His Imperial Majesty is invited to pronounce his decision." It was to

that phrase of the British Ambassador that the note of Middleton of November 16, 1821 (*ibid.*, enclosure 3, there styled a "replication"), mentioned in the third paragraph of annex A, referred; and the italicized words (French) in that paragraph are a literal quotation from the American note.

Another document mentioned in annex A (the fifth paragraph) and stated to be thereto "subjoined," is what was called "an extract of some observations upon the literal sense of the first article of the Treaty of Ghent."

As has been stated, those "grammatical observations," as they were styled in the protocol of signature, were not made part of the convention with annex A, although they are one of the documents communicated with the decision of the Emperor of Russia of May 4, 1822. A copy of them, in French, is enclosure 3 to Middleton's despatch of May 6 (D. S., 9 Despatches, Russia, No. 18).

The difference between the United States and Great Britain under Article 1 of the Treaty of Ghent was essentially a question of grammar; and while discussion in French of a question of grammar in a document written in English is somewhat unusual, a reference of such a question to the decision of a "Friendly Sovereign" is even more unusual; and these observations of Secretary of State John Quincy Adams, written on June 26, 1820, when he was drafting the instructions to the American Minister at St. Petersburg, are quite in point as to the whole situation (Memoirs of John Quincy Adams, V, 159–60):

It is a singular, and I apprehend will prove a very difficult and delicate, negotiation. During the late war, the British naval officers stationed in our waters and who landed on our shores received all the runaway slaves who could escape to them, and issued proclamations inviting them to join them. They enlisted numbers of them among their troops, and formed one or two regiments of them. They also took numbers of them prisoners in their predatory excursions into the country. At the conclusion of the treaty of peace the British Plenipotentiaries agreed to the article stipulating for the restoration of all places taken, without carrying away any of the artillery or other property originally taken in them and remaining in them at the time of the exchange of ratifications, or any slaves or other private property. Notwithstanding this, they actually carried away many hundred slaves, and great numbers of them within the whole description applied by the article to public property, namely, slaves who had not been removed from the places where they were originally taken. When Sir Alexander Cochrane and Admiral Cockburn were called upon after the peace to carry this article into effect, they found it obliged them to restore to their masters slaves whom they had enticed away from them by promises of freedom. They therefore set forth a violent and unnatural construction of the article to avoid compliance with it, refused to restore the slaves, and, with a very few exceptions, carried them all away. Their pretence was, that the clause limiting the promise not to carry away *public* property, to such as should have been in the places taken when captured, and remain there at the ratification of the treaty, must be extended also to slaves and other private property. They changed altogether the terms of the article to give it this construction, and the British Government have persisted in it. After a thorough discussion of the subject, first between the Commissioners who were sent by the American Government to receive the slaves and the British officers who refused to restore them; next between Mr. Monroe, when Secretary of State, and Anthony St. John Baker, the British Chargé d'Affaires; and finally between me and the Lords Liverpool, Bathurst, and Castlereagh in

England, each party adhering to its own construction of the Article, a proposal was made on our part that the question should be submitted to the decision of some friendly sovereign or State. To this the British Government, after a delay of two years, assented, and it was stipulated by the fifth article of the Convention of 20th October, 1818. It has since been agreed that the Emperor of Russia should be the umpire. This reference of a question upon the construction of an article of a treaty to a third party is unusual, but not unexampled; though there is something whimsical in the idea that the United States and Great Britain, both speaking English, should go to the Slavonian Czar of Muscovy to find out their own meaning, in a sentence written by themselves, in the language common to them both. The question is one, however, not of language, but of grammar, or rather there is no question at all; in strictness of grammar the sentence admits of no other construction than that for which we contend. In the looseness of common discourse the whole sentence might be carelessly spoken with the meaning for which the British insist, but not without a solecism. The plain truth, as I believe, is that the British Plenipotentiaries at Ghent and their Government agreed to it without reflecting upon what they promised by it. The stipulation was perfectly just and proper, and their difficulty about carrying it into execution arose from the preceding wrong of their own officers in enticing away the slaves by promises of freedom. This reference of the question is a sort of drawing lots for the event. It gives us one more chance for justice.

However, as those "grammatical observations" were officially communicated with the decision of the Emperor of Russia and are referred to in the covering note of Count Nesselrode, their text is here printed in French, with a translation:

[Translation]

La question de Grammaire à résoudre pour l'interprétation de l'article 1ᵉʳ du Traité de Gand, peut être posée comme il suit:

La phrase incidente ou modification exprimée en ces termes; "originairement prise dans les dits forts et lieux et qui s'y trouvera au moment de l'échange des ratifications"; doit-elle se rapporter à la fois aux mots; "aucune partie de l'artillerie ou autres propriétés publiques et aucuns esclaves ou autres propriétés privées"; ou seulement au premiers et non aux seconds?

Les deux parties s'accordent à reconnoître qu'il y a une ellipse dans la phrase à laquelle elles prêtent une signification différente—mais l'une soutient que pour suppléer tous les mots omis dans cette ellipse, il faut construire la phrase de la manière suivante:—"sans détruire ou emporter aucune partie de l'artillerie ou propriété publique originairement prise dans les dits forts et lieux et qui s'y trouvera au moment de l'échange des ratifications, et sans détruire ou emporter aucuns esclaves ou autres propriétés privées originairement prises dans les dits forts et lieux et qui s'y trouveront au moment de l'échange des ratifications."

The grammatical question to be solved in interpreting Article 1 of the treaty of Ghent may be propounded thus:

Should the incidental phrase or modification expressed in the following terms: "originally captured in the said forts or places and which shall remain therein upon the exchange of the ratifications," be construed as relating both to the words "any of the artillery or other public property" and "any slaves or other private property," or only to the former words and not to the latter?

Both parties agree that there is an ellipsis in the phrase to which they attach a different meaning, but one holds that in order to supply all the words omitted in this ellipsis the phrase should be constructed as follows: "without destroying or carrying away any of the artillery or public property originally captured in the said forts or places and which shall remain therein upon the exchange of the ratifications, and without destroying or taking away any slaves or other private property originally captured in the said forts or places and which shall remain therein upon the exchange of the ratifications."

L'autre prétend au contraire, qu'il n'y a de sous-entendus que les verbes "détruire et emporter," et que pour suppléer l'ellipse on doit construire la phrase ainsi qu'il suit:—"sans détruire ou emporter aucune partie de l'artillerie ou autre propriété publique originairement prise dans les dits forts el lieux et qui s'y trouvera au moment de l'échange des ratifications, et sans détruire ou emporter aucuns esclaves ou autres propriétés privées."

De ces deux constructions quelle est la plus conforme aux régles de la logique et de la syntaxe?

Les Grammairiens définissent l'Ellipse "une figure de construction." "On parle par ellipse, disent-ils, lorsqu'on retranche des mots qui seroient nécessaires pour rendre la construction pleine" (voyez le Dictionnaire des difficultés de la langue française par Laveaux 1818.)

Les Logiciens enseignent que toute proposition pour être complête *doit offrir un sens fini.*

D'après ces principes, il faut suppléer dans la phrase dont il s'agit, les mots qui sont *nécessaires* pour rendre la construction pleine, et pour que la proposition offre *un sens fini*—(voyez Condillac Cours d'Étude Tome V. Ch X. Edᵃ 8º.)

Or ces mots paraissent être ceux-ci: "sans détruire ou emporter" verbes qu'il faut nécessairement placer avant les substantifs: "aucuns esclaves ou autres propriétés privées," puisque ces verbes régissent incontestablement ce dernier membre de phrase. Avec la répétition des verbes *sans détruire ou emporter* la construction est pleine, et la proposition offre un sens fini. On pourrait en conclure que ces mots sont les seuls nécessaires à suppléer et que la construction pleine de la période doit être telle qu'il suit:

"*Sans détruire ou emporter* aucune partie de l'artillerie ou autre propriété publique originairement prise dans les dits forts et lieux et qui s'y trouvera au moment de l'échange des ratifications, et *sans détruire ou emporter* aucuns esclaves ou autres propriétés privées."

Cependant pour se convaincre s'il faut ou s'il ne faut pas répéter après *aucuns esclaves ou autres propriétés privées,* la

The other contends, on the contrary, that the only words tacitly understood are the verbs "destroy and carry away," and that in order to supply the ellipsis the phrase should be constructed as follows: "without destroying or carrying away any of the artillery or other public property originally captured in the said forts or places and which shall remain therein upon the exchange of the ratifications, and without destroying or carrying away any slaves or other private property."

Which of these two constructions is most in conformity with the rules of logic and syntax?

Grammarians define ellipsis as being "a figure of construction." "We speak elliptically," they say, "when we leave out words which would be necessary to render the construction complete" (see the Dictionnaire des difficultés de la langue française, by Laveaux, 1818).

Logicians teach that every proposition, in order to be complete, *must present a finished thought.*

According to these principles those words must be supplied in the phrase in question which are *necessary* in order to render the construction complete and in order that the proposition may embody a *finished thought* (see Condillac, Cours d'étude, vol. V, ch. X, 8vo ed.).

Now these words appear to be the following: "without destroying or carrying away," which verbs must necessarily be placed before the substantives "any slaves or other private property," since these verbs undeniably govern this last group of words. With the repetition of the verbs "*without destroying or carrying away,*" the construction becomes complete and the proposition presents a finished thought. It might be concluded from this that these words are the only ones that need be supplied and that the full construction of the period should be as follows:

"*Without destroying or carrying away* any of the artillery or other public property originally captured in the said forts or places and which shall remain therein upon the exchange of the ratifications, and *without destroying or carrying away* any slaves or other private property."

However, in order to convince one's self whether it is necessary or not to repeat, after the words *any slaves or*

modification *originairement prise dans les dits forts et lieux et qui s'y trouvera au moment de l'échange des ratifications*, il est bon de voir comment les grammairiens qualifient cette modification, et quelle place ils lui assignent dans l'ordre du discours.

Le mot *prise* qui suit ceux de *propriété publique*, est incontestablement le participe passé du verbe prendre.

Les participes passés employés de cette manière, et destinés à modifier ou à déterminer le sujet ou substantif auquel ils se rapportent, sont appelés par les grammairiens *adjectifs verbaux* (Laveaux ubi supra)

En fixant la place que les adjectifs verbaux doivent occuper dans le discours, ces mêmes grammairiens posent en principe général "qui les adjectifs verbaux formés du participe présent et du participe passé des verbes se mettent toujours *après* leurs substantifs, *et que cette règle est sans exception* pour les adjectifs formés des participes passés." (Laveaux ibidem).

On est donc forcé de reconnoître, que suivant l'autorité de la grammaire, la modification *originairement prise &c.* ne peut se rapporter qu'aux substantifs *après* lesquels elle a été placée, et par conséquent qu'à *l'artillerie et à la propriété publique*.

D'autre part, considérée dans son ensemble, cette modification porte les caractères distinctifs que les grammairiens attribuent aux *propositions incidentes*. "une proposition incidente, dit l'Académie, est celle qui est inserée dans une proposition principale dont elle fait partie." "On peut dire que c'est une proposition particulière liée à un mot *dont elle est le supplément explicatif ou determinatif;*" ajoutent les grammairiens. (Laveaux ibidem).

Ici encore il s'agit évidemment de voir, quels sont la place et le genre de rapports que les régles de la logique et de la grammaire assignent aux propositions incidentes dans l'ordre du discours.

Condillac répond: "que *les propositions incidentes n'ont jamais qu'une place* dans le discours, parcequ'elles *doivent toujours être à la suite du mot dont elles développent ou déterminent l'idée.*" (Cours d'Etude Tom V. Ch. X.)

other private property, the modifying words *originally captured in the said forts or places and which shall remain therein upon the exchange of the ratifications*, it is well to note how grammarians characterize such a modification and what place they assign thereto in the order of discourse.

The word *captured*, which follows the words *public property*, is incontestably the past participle of the verb *capture*.

Past participles used in this way and intended to modify or determine the subject or substantive to which they relate, are called by grammarians *verbal adjectives* (Laveaux, *ubi supra*).

In fixing the place which verbal adjectives should occupy in discourse, these same grammarians lay it down as a general principle "that verbal adjectives formed from the present and past participles of verbs are always placed *after* their substantives, *and that this rule is without exception* with respect to adjectives formed from past participles" (Laveaux, *ibid.*).

We are therefore compelled to recognize that, according to the rules of grammar, the modifying words *originally captured, etc.*, can relate only to the substantives *after* which they were placed, and consequently only to *artillery and public property*.

Furthermore, considered as a whole, this modification bears the distinctive characteristics which grammarians attribute to *incidental clauses*. "An incidental clause," says the Academy, "is one inserted in a principal clause of which it forms a part." "One may say that it is a special clause connected with a word *of which it is the explanatory or determining supplement,*" add the grammarians (Laveaux, *ibid.*).

Here again it is evidently a question of ascertaining the place and kind of relations which the rules of logic and grammar assign to incidental clauses in the order of discourse.

Condillac answers "that *incidental clauses never have more than one place* in discourse, for they *must always be after the word the sense of which they develop or determine*" (Cours d'étude, vol. V, ch. X).

Le même auteur répéte dans un autre endroit (Tom VII. Ch. VIII.) *"la place d'une proposition incidente est après le substantif qu'elle modifie."*

Enfin Laveaux donne aussi la même règle, et se fonde sur l'autorité d'autres grammairiens pour observer encore "que la proposition incidente, soit explicative soit déterminative, forme avec son *antécédant* un tout qui est une partie logique de la proposition principale, et que *l'antécédant en est la partie grammaticale correspondante.*"

Il résulte de ces définitions que, dans l'article 1ᵉʳ du traité de Gand, la modification *originairement prise* étant *liée aux mots précédans:* "propriété publique": et *formant le supplément explicatif et déterminatif de ces mots*, doit être considérée comme proposition incidente, et que la place d'une proposition incidente étant *après* le substantif qu'elle modifie, cette même proposition ne sauroit modifier les substantifs *avant* lesquels elle se trouve placée. Ou, en d'autres termes, que dans la construction logique et grammaticale de la phrase: "sans emporter aucune partie de l'artillerie ou autre propriété publique originairement prise dans les dits forts et lieux, et qui s'y trouvera au moment de l'échange des ratifications, ou aucuns esclaves ou autres propriétés privées": les mots *originairement prise &cᵃ* supplement déterminatif de ceux de *propriété publique*, ne peuvent être sous-entendus après ceux de *aucuns esclaves &cᵃ:* c'est à dire que par l'article 1ᵉʳ du traité de Gand la défense d'emmener des esclaves ou d'emporter des propriétés privées, n'a point été assujettie à la même limitation d'origine et de tems, que la défense d'emporter l'artillerie ou les propriétés publiques.*

The same author repeats in another place (vol. VII, ch. VIII): *" The place of an incidental clause is after the substantive which it modifies."*

Finally, Laveaux also gives the same rule, relying on the authority of other grammarians in observing further "that an incidental clause, whether explanatory or determinative, forms with its *antecedent* a whole which is a logical part of the main clause, and that the *antecedent is the corresponding grammatical part thereof.*"

It follows, as a result of these definitions, that in Article 1 of the Treaty of Ghent the modifying words *"originally captured,"* being *connected with the preceding words* "public property" and *forming the explanatory and determinative supplement of these words*, should be considered as an incidental clause, and that since the place of an incidental clause is *after* the substantive which it modifies, this incidental clause cannot modify the substantives *before* which it is placed; or, in other words, that in the logical and grammatical construction of the phrase "without carrying away any of the artillery or other public property originally captured in the said forts or places and which shall remain therein upon the exchange of the ratifications, or any slaves or other private property," the words *originally captured, etc.*, as determinative supplement of the words *public property*, cannot be tacitly understood after the words "*any slaves, etc.*"; that is to say that under Article 1 of the Treaty of Ghent the prohibition to take away slaves or to carry away private property was not made subject to the same limitation as to origin and time as the prohibition to take away artillery or public property.*

---

* On essayera de rendre cette vérité plus sensible par deux exemples. La phrase même qu'on vient de citer renferme une modification qui peut être également applicable à plusieurs sujets. Cette modification est précisément celle de *originairement prise &cᵃ* Ces mots peuvent se rapporter à ceux de: *aucune partie de l'artillerie:* et à ceux de: *propriété publique:* On peut parfaitement comprendre: aucune partie de l'artillerie *originairement prise;* aucune propriété publique *originairement prise:* car ici la phrase incidente est *après* les substantifs qu'elle modifie.

*We will try to render this truth more palpable by two examples. The very phrase which has just been cited embodies a modification which may be equally applicable to several subjects. This modification is precisely that represented by the words *originally captured, etc.* These words may relate to the words *any of the artillery* and to the words *public property.* We may perfectly well understand: any of the artillery *originally captured;* any public property *originally captured,* for here the incidental phrase is *after* the substantives which it modifies. In the case under

Les mémoires britanniques objectent à cette interprétation la différence que l'on remarque entre la clause rélative aux esclaves, et celle qui concerne les régistres et papiers. Quand on a parlé de restitution pure, simple et inconditionnelle, on s'est autrement exprimé, disent-ils; on a eu soin de mettre: *Et tous archives régistres &c.ª seront restitués sans délai &c.ª* phrase qu'on a même fait succéder immédiatement à celle qui a rapport aux esclaves.

C'est encore l'autorité seule de la grammaire qui peut résondre cette objection.

Entre la clause qui défend d'emporter les esclaves, et celle qui ordonne la restitution des archives et régistres, on trouve la conjonction *Et*.

L'Académie dit, que cette conjonction lie les parties de l'oraison, telles que les noms, pronoms, verbes. "Il faut ajouter, dit Laveaux, qu'elle lie aussi les phrases d'un discours. *Cette conjonction marque l'action de l'esprit qui*

Dans le cas que l'on discute, l'identité d'origine et de rapports qui existe entre la propriété publique et la propriété particulière, fait qu'en répétant la modification *originairement prise &c.ª* après le second membre de phrase: *ou aucuns esclaves ou autres propriétés privées:* On obtient un sens qui ne présente en lui même rien de contradictoire. Mais pour faire sentir le motif de la régle de logique et de grammaire, qui veut que le substantif modifié par une proposition incidente *précéde* nécessairement *cette proposition,* supposons qu'on ait dit:—"sans emporter aucune imposition originairement prélevée sur les contribuables des États-Unis, et qui se trouveroit dans les caisses publiques au moment de l'échange des ratifications, ni aucuns esclaves ou autres propriétés privées:"—cela voudrait-il dire qu'on n'est tenu de restituer que les esclaves ou autres propriété privées originairement prélevées sur les contribuables des États-Unis et qui se trouveroient dans les caisses publiques au moment de l'échange des ratifications? On a cité de préférence Condillac et Laveaux, parceque le premier de ces auteurs pose le plus souvent des principes de grammaire générale, applicables à toutes les langues, et que le second en facilitant les recherches par la forme de Dictionnaire qu'il a donnée à son ouvrage, rapporte toujours les opinions des grammairiens les plus célébres.

The objection made to this interpretation in the British memoranda is based on the difference to be noted between the clause relating to slaves and that concerning records and papers. In speaking of pure and simple and unconditional restitution a different mode of expression was used; they say, for care was taken to say: *and all archives, records, etc., shall be forthwith restored, etc.,* which phrase was made to follow immediately that relating to slaves.

Grammar is once more the only authority that can dispose of this objection.

Between the clause which forbids taking away slaves and that ordering the return of the archives and records, we find the conjunction *and*.

The Academy says that this conjunction joins the parts of speech such as nouns, pronouns, and verbs. "It must be added," says Laveaux, "that it also joins the phrases of a discourse. *This conjunction marks the action of the*

discussion the identity of origin and of relations existing between public and private property leads to the result that, by repeating the modifying words *originally captured, etc.,* after the second phrase, *or any slaves or other private property,* we obtain a sense which has nothing contradictory in itself. But in order to demonstrate the reason for the rule of logic and grammar which prescribes that the substantive modified by an incidental clause necessarily *precedes such clause,* let us suppose that one had said: "without taking away any contribution originally levied on the taxpayers of the United States and which might remain in the public coffers upon the exchange of the ratifications, or any slaves or other private property," would this mean that one is obliged to restore only the slaves or other private property originally levied on the taxpayers of the United States and which might remain in the public coffers upon the exchange of the ratifications? Condillac and Laveaux have been cited by preference because the former of these authors most often lays down principles of general grammar, applicable to all languages, while the second facilitates research by the dictionary form which he has given to his work and always quotes the opinions of the most celebrated grammarians.

considère sous un même rapport les mots et les phrases qu'elle lie." . . . "Elle sert à unir deux propositions affirmatives, ou à lier une proposition affirmative avec une proposition négative." Si donc on avoit voulu établir entre les deux clauses la différence dont parlent les mémoires britanniques, au lieu de les lier l'une à l'autre par une conjonction copulative, en disant: *et tous régistres &cᵃ seront restitués &cᵃ* c'est à dire *en outre, de plus,* tous régistres seront restitués; ou bien, tous régistres seront restitués *de même, pareillement;* il auroit fallu marquer une opposition, par l'emploi d'une autre tournure ou d'une particule adversative.

"Une proposition se lie-t-elle à une précédente *comme apposée,* (dit Condillac Tom. V. Ch. XXIII.) nous avons les conjonctions *Mais, Cependant, Pourtant;*—affirment-elles ensemble, nous avons la conjonction *Et.*"

mind which considers in the same relation the words and phrases which it joins. . . . It serves to unite two affirmative propositions, or to join an affirmative with a negative proposition." If, therefore, it had been desired to establish between the two clauses the difference spoken of in the British memoranda, then, instead of joining them together with a copulative conjunction by saying *and all records, etc., shall be restored, etc.,* that is to say, *besides, moreover,* all records shall be restored, or else, all records shall *likewise, also* be restored, it would have been necessary to indicate an opposition by using another mode of expression or an adversative particle.

"If a proposition is joined to a preceding one *as being opposed thereto,*" says Condillac, vol. V, ch. XXIII, "we have the conjunctions *but, however,* or *nevertheless;* if the propositions are jointly affirmative, we have the conjunction *and.*"

Fin.   End

Finally, reference is made in annex A (the sixth paragraph) to "the act by which the two powers have required his arbitration and defined the object of their difference." That act is the *compromis* or act of submission of July 30, 1821, signed by Henry Middleton and Sir Charles Bagot, which has been described and the text of which, in French and in translation, has been printed above in these notes.

Procedure under the Convention

In view of the fact that the procedure laid down by this convention, in so far as it concerned the determination of the average value of the slaves, pursuant to Article 2, was carried out, and, so far as it concerned the determination of the particular claims, pursuant to Articles 3–6, completely failed to work (see Moore, International Arbitrations, I, 366–82), the preliminary discussions leading up to those clauses of this convention will be noticed.

It is indeed curious that those discussions took place nearly two years prior to the decision of the Emperor of Russia in favor of the American contention regarding the construction of Article 1 of the Treaty of Ghent. This meant indeed that long before the question of the construction of the Treaty of Ghent had been submitted to the Arbitrating Sovereign for his decision, the representatives of the two Governments, acting upon the hypothesis that that decision would be in favor of the contention of the United States, came to a provisional accord upon the procedure then and in such case to be followed.

Henry Middleton, who had been appointed Minister to Russia and who was on his way to St. Petersburg, acting under instructions from the Department of State (D. S., 9 Instructions, U. S. Ministers, 18–36, July 5, 1820), was in London from July 12 to September 20, 1820, where he and Richard Rush, American Minister at London, conferred with Lord Castlereagh, British Secretary of State for Foreign Affairs, regarding the submission of the question of the meaning of the first article of the Treaty of Ghent to the Emperor of Russia for his decision.

In the course of those conferences the question was brought up, in accordance with the above-mentioned instructions to Middleton (*ibid.*, 29), of the means of "ascertaining the facts, and of awarding the indemnity" to the individual claimants, in the event that the decision should be in favor of the United States. Middleton was authorized to suggest to Lord Castlereagh (*ibid.*):

> . . . the appointment of a Commission of three persons; one to be appointed by the President, by and with the advice and consent of the Senate, one by His Britannic Majesty, and the third by the Emperor of Russia, to sit in the United States, and with the usual powers of the Commissions which have heretofore sat upon questions between the United States and Great Britain, modified to the circumstances of the case; and to determine definitively upon all claims brought before them.

This proposal was made to Lord Castlereagh on August 10, 1820 (enclosure B with the despatch of Rush of September 21, 1820, D. S., 25 Despatches, Great Britain, No. 146).

That American proposal was in form a very simple one; but Castlereagh found objections to it, one of which at least was very weighty. Some hundreds of slaves were in question, and if such a commission were required to take evidence as to the particular value of each individual slave, its task would have been one of enormous labor and difficulty.

Of a conference at the Foreign Office on August 22, attended by Middleton, Rush, Castlereagh, and also by Mr. Goulburn, of the Foreign Office, Rush wrote as follows (*ibid.*, despatch of September 21, 1820):

> His Lordship next objected to the commission proposed. . . . Such commissions he said were both expensive and dilatory. This government had had experience of them, and felt reluctant to having more. The commissioners had always the strong motive of interest, and thence a natural tendency, to prolong their own existence. The third commissioner, to be chosen by the Emperor of Russia, would, moreover, in effect, decide every thing. His Lordship thought also, that great embarrassments would attend their attempts to determine the true value of each individual slave. It would leave room for great uncertainties and inevitably cause great delays. . . . He then said, that he thought a mode more simple and appropriate would be, to fix upon a given sum as the value of each slave. The whole number carried off being next known, an aggregate sum could be paid by this government, leaving to our own the duty of distribution among the owners by such rules as it might deem just. He proposed, as a part of this plan, that the Emperor should be called upon by the parties to say what the average value of each slave ought to be.

It seems that Castlereagh considered that if a fixed sum as the value of each slave could be determined, there could then be without difficulty a determination, possibly even an agreement, regarding the total number of slaves, leaving the liability of the British Government a mere matter of calculation to be discharged by a lump-sum payment, the distribution of which would be for the Government of the United States. But the suggestion of Castlereagh did not prove acceptable as a whole, although as far as it proposed the fixing of an average value of the slaves, it was in principle adopted in Article 2 of this convention.

Of a conference on August 30 "at 5 o'clock in the afternoon," which Rush also attended, Middleton wrote to the Secretary of State as follows (D. S., 8 Despatches, Russia, No. 2, September 15, 1820; see also the despatch of Rush of September 21, D. S., 25 Despatches, Great Britain, No. 146):

> Lord Castlereagh once more objected to the nature of the Commission proposed by us. . . .
>
> His Lordship finally proposed that if we continued to object to the substitute already offered for our Commission; to wit; that the Emperor should be allowed to fix a sum as the average value of each Slave; he would suggest for our approbation a Tribunal to be constituted in the mode settled in the Treaty of 1817 between England & Spain respecting the Slave Trade. This tribunal consists of Two Judges & two Arbitrators; the two former to settle all differences if they can agree, & in the case of the disagreement of the Judges, one of the Arbitrators is called in by Lot to decide between them. He dwelt upon the advantages of this plan & said they would have no objection to such a Commission to sit at Washington.

That second suggestion of Castlereagh was in substance the procedure adopted in Articles 3–6 of this convention. It was taken, as he said, from the treaty between Great Britain and Spain signed at Madrid on September 23, 1817 (Von Martens, Nouveau recueil de traités, IV, 492–511). The procedure under Article 12 of that treaty between Great Britain and Spain and under the "Regulations for the Mixed Commissions," annexed thereto, is essentially similar to that adopted in this convention.

Still another conference was held on September 8, this time not at the Foreign Office but at Cray Farm, the country residence of Lord Castlereagh. At that conference there was drawn up a statement or memorandum of "the points fixed in our late conversations," which is enclosure F to Middleton's despatch of September 15, 1820 (D. S., 8 Despatches, Russia, No. 2). A copy of that memorandum is as follows, the "points fixed" being in the right-hand column and Castlereagh's observations in the left:

Sept: 8ᵗʰ 1820.

> Memorandum of a Conversation held between Lord Castlereagh, Mʳ Rush & Mʳ Middleton on the Subject of the Slave question with reference to points to be hereafter decided in the event of the decision of the Emperor of Russia being in favor of the claim of the Governmᵗ of the U: S:

(observations.)

On the first paragraph Lord Castlereagh desires to observe, that the British Government at present regards the claims of the American Government as limited within the number of Slaves set forth in a List delivered by Mr Adams to Ld Castlereagh on the 5th day of Septr 1815. Should the decision on the general principle of the reference be against G^t Britain & in favor of the U: S: & should the Amer^n Gov^t deny the above position & have any reasons to alledge for extending this List or for taking measures still to receive claims, the british Gov^t is not disposed to refuse itself to a fair examination of this claim, but they feel it essential before any Commission shall actually sit, to take cognizance of such claims, that their precise extent and nature should be ascertained by the Amer^n Gov^t calling upon their Citizens to make such claims as they may have to bring forward within a reasonable time to be named, and that an average value per head shall be fixed upon as the rate at which indemnity for Slaves improperly withdrawn is to be paid by the British Gov^t.

Lord Castlereagh (subject to the opinion however of his Gov^t) has no objection to assert to the three last articles, it being his wish to give every facility to the speedy & equitable adjustment of these claims & that whatever differences of opinion may prevail between the british & american Governments as to the best mode of accomplishing this purpose, should be submitted to the consideration and arbitration of his Imperial majesty the Emperor of Russia.

First: That the American Government should make known the whole number of the Slaves for which compensation is to be claimed, before the sitting of the Commission, or alledge farther reasons why it should not be incumbent upon them to do so. On the british Government not acceding to the sufficiency of the reasons alledged, the Emperor of Russia to decide between the parties, it being understood that the American Gov^t claims the right of compensation for all the Slaves that can be actually proved to have been carried off in contravention of the Treaty without being held to a previous List.

Secondly. That the Commission shall consist of Two Judges and two Arbitrators (to be appointed in the manner settled in the Treaty between Great Britain & Spain relative to the Slave Trade) and that it may sit in Washington.

Thirdly. It is agreed on the part of the British Gov^t that all the evidence of which it may be in possession by returns from its own officers of the number of Slaves carried off will be produced before the Commission.

Fourthly. The above arrangements pre-supposing an award in favor of the American Government on the main question, it is farther agreed that should the parties after such an award differ as to the means of giving it full & substantial effect, they will call upon the Emperor of Russia to lend his farther good offices as Umpire between them on all the means proper to be adopted.

In the foregoing memorandum it is only in the observations of Castlereagh that there is any mention of the fixing of an average value of the slaves; but it seems clear that it was well understood, for in his despatch of September 21 (D. S., 25 Despatches, Great Britain, No. 146), Rush wrote that he took the meaning of the British proposal to be "that an average value should be set upon each slave," to be "affixed by the commission, provided it be constituted as now proposed by him [Castlereagh]; otherwise to be determined by the Emperor of Russia," all of which is essentially Article 2 of this convention.

There seems, however, to have been some confusion or uncertainty as to the duties of the proposed commission in respect of the number of slaves. Obviously, any list of slaves prepared by the Government of the United States, whether the list of 1815 or any other, could not

be conclusive.   The question would remain whether the slaves on that list alleged to have been carried away had been in fact carried off; yet Rush wrote in the despatch mentioned:

Should we agree to such a commission, and the number of slaves be ascertained by a list to be furnished before it sits, it seems to follow, that its *only* duty when organized, would be to affix such average value.

However, while the conferences of 1820 in London did not reach a definitive or binding result, they did provisionally arrange in substance the procedural terms of this convention of July 12, 1822.

It may be added, indeed, that the result finally reached, although it required some years to reach it, involving further negotiations, another convention, and a subsequent act of Congress, was not essentially different from that which would have been reached under Castlereagh's first suggestion of August 22, 1820.   The average value of the slaves was fixed (although by localities) under this convention; a lump-sum payment was made by the British Government under the convention of November 13, 1826 (Document 53); and the distribution of that sum was made by the Government of the United States (see Moore, *op. cit.*, 382–90, and also the notes to Document 53).

EXECUTION OF THE CONVENTION

An account of the differences that gave rise to this convention and of the proceedings thereunder is in Moore, International Arbitrations, I, 350–90.

The presidential message of January 16, 1823 (American State Papers, Foreign Relations, V, 214–21), communicated to Congress the proclamation of the convention, with translations of its three annexes, and also the agreement of January 10, 1823, regarding the compensation of the commissioners and arbitrators, and other expenses, the text of which appears above in these notes.

By the act of March 3, 1823 (3 Statutes at Large, 763), an appropriation of $20,000 was made for "carrying into execution" this convention, and further appropriations were made by later acts (4 *ibid.*, 16, 91, 148, 214).

The board of Commissioners and Arbitrators under Article 2 of the convention reached unanimous agreement on September 11, 1824, regarding the amounts to be allowed as compensation for each slave carried away, namely, $580 for slaves taken from Louisiana; $390 for slaves taken from Alabama, Georgia, and South Carolina; and $280 for slaves taken from Virginia, Maryland, Mississippi, and elsewhere (Moore, *op. cit.*, 370; American State Papers, Foreign Relations, V, 801); but the cumbersome procedure for the determination of claims under Articles 3–6 of the convention broke down, and no result was reached except disagreement.

The final settlement between the two Governments was made by the convention of November 13, 1826 (Document 53), which provided for the payment to the United States by Great Britain of the sum of $1,204,960.

Treaty Series No. 361
8 Statutes at Large, 298–300
18 *ibid.*, pt. 2, Public Treaties, 768–70

45

TUNIS : FEBRUARY 24, 1824

*Convention Amending the Treaty of August 28, 1797, and March 26,
1799 (Document 21), signed at Bardo, near Tunis, February 24,
1824 (24 Jumada II, A. H. 1239). Original in English.
Submitted to the Senate December 15, 1824. (Message of December 13, 1824.) Resolution of advice and consent January 13, 1825.
Ratified by the United States between January 13 and 21, 1825. As
to the ratification generally, see the notes. Proclaimed January 21,
1825.*

Whereas Sundry articles of the Treaty of peace and friendship[1]
concluded between the United States of America and Hamuda
Bashaw, of happy memory, in the month of Rebia Elul in the year of
the Hegira 1212, corresponding with the month of August of the
Christian year 1797; have by experience been found to require alteration and amendment: In order therefore that the United States
should be placed on the same footing with the most favored Nations
having Treaties with Tunis, as well as to manifest a respect for the
American Government and a desire to continue unimpaired the
friendly relations which have always existed between the two Nations,
it is hereby agreed & concluded between His Highness Mahmoud
Bashaw Bey of Tunis, and S. D. Heap Esquire Chargé d'affaires of
the United States of America, that alteration be made in the Sixth,
eleventh, twelfth and fourteenth articles of said Treaty; and that the
said articles shall be altered and amended in the Treaty to read as
follows.

ARTICLE 6ᵗʰ

If a Tunisian Corsair shall meet with an American vessel & shall
visit it with her boat, two men only shall be allowed to go on board,
peaceably to satisfy themselves of its being American, who as well as
any passengers of other Nations they may have on board, shall go
free both them & their goods; and the said two men shall not exact
any thing, on pain of being severely punished. In case a slave escapes

---

[1] Document 21.

and takes refuge on board an American vessel of war he shall be free, and no demand shall be made either for his restoration or for payment.

ARTICLE THE 11th

When a vessel of war of the United States shall enter the port of the Goletta she shall be saluted with twenty one guns, which salute, the vessel of war shall return gun for gun only, and no powder will be given, as mentioned in the ancient eleventh article of this Treaty, which is hereby annulled.

ARTICLE THE 12th

When Citizens of the United States shall come within the dependencies of Tunis to carry on commerce there, the same respect shall be paid to them which the Merchants of other Nations enjoy; and if they wish to establish themselves within our ports, no opposition shall be made thereto, and they shall be free to avail themselves of such interpreters as they may judge necessary without any obstruction in conformity with the usages of other Nations; and if a Tunisian Subject shall go to establish himself within the dependencies of the United States, he shall be treated in like manner. If any Tunisian Subject shall freight an American vessel and load her with Merchandise, and shall afterwards want to unload, or ship them on board of another vessel, we shall not permit him untill the matter is determined by a reference of Merchants, who shall decide upon the case, and after the decision, the determination shall be conformed to.

No Captain shall be detained in port against his consent, except when our ports are shut for the vessels of all other Nations, which may take place with respect to merchant vessels, but not to those of war. The Subjects and Citizens of the two Nations respectively Tunisians and Americans, shall be protected in the places where they may be by the officers of the Government there existing; but on failure of such protection, and for redress of every injury, the party may resort to the chief authority in each country, by whom adequate protection and complete justice shall be rendered. In case the Government of Tunis shall have need of an American vessel for its service, such vessel being within the Regency, and not previously engaged, the Government shall have the preference on its paying the same freight as other Merchants usually pay for the same service, or at the like rate, if the service be without a customary precedent.

ARTICLE THE 14th

All vessels belonging to the Citizens and inhabitants of the United States, shall be permitted to enter the ports of the Kingdom of Tunis, and freely trade with the Subjects and inhabitants thereof on paying the usual duties which are paid by other most favored Nations at peace with the Regency. In like manner all vessels belonging to the subjects and inhabitants of the Kingdom of Tunis shall be permitted to enter the different ports of the United States, and freely trade with the Citizens and inhabitants thereof on paying the usual duties which are paid by other most favored Nations at peace with the United States.

Concluded, signed & sealed at the palace of Bardo near Tunis the 24th day of the Moon jumed-teni in the year of the Hegira 1239: corresponding the 24th of February 1824: of the Christian year; and the 48th year of the Independence of the United States; reserving the same nevertheless for the final ratification of the President of the United States by and with the advice and consent of the Senate.

(Signed)   S. D. HEAP
   Chargé d'affaires of the U. States of America at Tunis.

(Seal of MAHMOUD BASHAW.)
(Seal of HASSAN BEY.)

NOTES

The Department of State file of this agreement contains two documents only: the original proclamation and a copy of the convention, as the agreement is called in the proclamation.

Accordingly, the original signed convention is not available as a source text. The absence of the document from the archives cannot be satisfactorily explained, for it is certain that the original convention was received at Washington.

The negotiations for the revision of various articles of the earlier treaty with Tunis (Document 21) were carried on on behalf of the United States by Dr. Samuel D. Heap, then Chargé d'Affaires and Acting Consul at Tunis. His despatch of June 13, 1824, transmitting the original convention (copies of which he had forwarded earlier), was received at the Department of State on December 10, 1824 (D. S., 5 Consular Despatches, Tunis); another letter of the same date from Heap, transmitting another original document, is with that document in the same volume and is marked with the same date of receipt. Both letters came by the U. S. S. *Erie*, Captain Deacon.

There can thus be no doubt that the original convention was received at Washington on December 10, 1824, and that it was transmitted to the Senate with the presidential message dated three days later (Executive Journal, III, 395). This conclusion is supported by the statement in the annual message of President Monroe of December 7, 1824 (American State Papers, Foreign Relations, V, 354): "An advantageous alteration in our treaty with Tunis has been obtained by our Consular Agent residing there, the official document of which, when received, will be laid before the Senate"; and in an instruction to Heap dated August 27, 1824 (D. S., 2 Instructions to Consuls, 335), it was said that "the Treaty when received in the original will be submitted to the Senate for its advice and consent."

Presumably the original convention was returned to the President with the attested Senate resolution of advice and consent of January 13, 1825 (Executive Journal, III, 405). Possibly it was sent to Tunis as a part of the United States instrument of ratification; but there is no instruction or other record mentioning the transmittal of the ratification.

The papers which accompanied the presidential message of December 13, 1824, transmitting the convention to the Senate, comprised merely an extract from a despatch of Heap of January 24, 1824, and his despatch of March 4, which enclosed a copy of the convention (American State Papers, Foreign Relations, V, 430–32).

The attested Senate resolution of advice and consent of January 13, 1825, is in D. S., Miscellaneous Letters, January–March, 1825.

The Language

While the matter is not beyond doubt, it is fairly certain that the language of the convention was English. Heap's journal (D. S., 5 Consular Despatches, Tunis) shows that he submitted a draft of the desired alterations, which was certainly in English; among the entries of that journal are also the following:

[February 24, 1824, the recited date of signature of the convention.] Went to Bardo with the Treaty when the Bey informed me he had conceded all the alterations I had required.

March 2nd Sidi Assuna brought the Treaty signed and sealed by the Bashaw Bey, and the Bey.—Who informed me that the Turkish Secretary allways received a present for translating a Treaty.

The foregoing seems to imply a Turkish equivalent of the English; but it still leaves the question of the language of the original somewhat uncertain.

A despatch from Heap of March 4, 1824 (D. S., 5 Consular Despatches, Tunis), received at the Department of State August 14, 1824, enclosed a copy of the convention in English, which is with the despatch. Nothing is said as to any other language. According to the enclosed copy, the convention was signed by Heap but (which seems unlikely) not sealed by him; and it indicates two seals (but no

signatures) for Tunis, one of Mahmoud Pasha and one of Hassan Bey. This is confirmed in part by the journal entry above quoted; Hassan was the son of Mahmoud and succeeded as Pasha on the death of his father on March 28 or 29, 1824, only a few weeks after the date of the treaty (letter of Hassan to the President, March 29, 1824, *ibid.*).

In a letter to Commodore John Rodgers, dated at Tunis October 15, 1825, a copy of which was enclosed in a despatch of February 25, 1826, from Charles D. Coxe, then Consul at Tunis, to the Secretary of State (D. S., 5 Consular Despatches, Tunis), Coxe criticizes in considerable detail the alterations in the four articles of the earlier treaty which were made by this convention. In his strictures Coxe writes of the amended articles as if their text were in English, quoting the language of some phrases with substantial accuracy. But this is perhaps not very significant, particularly as Coxe similarly refers to certain clauses of the earlier treaty with Tunis (Document 21), where the English is unquestionably a translation.

The proclamation of January 21, 1825, says that certain alterations in the treaty of 1797 "were agreed upon . . . by the Articles in the words following"; this is consistent with an English original, and persuasive but perhaps not conclusive. According to the proclamation, the convention was signed and sealed by Heap and Sidi Mahmoud.

In the Department of State file is a copy of the provisions of the agreement, in English, written at Tunis, though in that copy is no mention of signatures or seals; and in the archives are two other copies from Tunis, also in English, sent in 1825 and 1826 (*ibid.*).

In the presidential message of February 2, 1825, communicating to Congress "copies of the alterations in the treaty of peace and friendship of August, 1797, between the United States and the Bashaw Bey of Tunis [Document 21], concluded at the palace of Bardo, near Tunis, on the 24th of February last," there is no hint of any language text other than English (American State Papers, Foreign Relations, V, 587–89).

On the whole, it can be said that the text of the agreement as proposed by Heap was in English, and there is nothing in the archives of the Department of State to indicate that the agreement, as signed by him, was in any language other than English. As far as the records go, they indicate an English text only.

THE SOURCE TEXT

There are various available sources from which the text of this document might be printed. Three of them are the three copies of the convention to be found in D. S., 5 Consular Despatches, Tunis. The first of those sources is the enclosure with Heap's despatch of March 4, 1824 (printed in American State Papers, Foreign Relations, V, 431). The second is the enclosure with the letter of C. D. Coxe (then Consul at Tunis) to Commodore John Rodgers of October

15, 1825, which Rodgers forwarded to the Secretary of State with his letter of May 13, 1826. The third is a copy of the above-mentioned letter and enclosure of Coxe to Rodgers, which Coxe enclosed with his despatch of February 25, 1826. A fourth possible source is the copy of the provisions of the agreement, in English like the other copies, but without mention of signatures or seals, which is in the Department of State file of this convention. The fifth is the text as copied in the original proclamation, which is the only other paper in the Department of State file. The sixth is the print of the text which was ordered by the Senate December 15, 1824 (Executive Journal, III, 395), and which was taken, it seems reasonable to suppose, from the original convention which was then before the Senate. A copy of that print is in Senate Confidential Document, 18th Congress, 2d session, December 15, 1824, Regular Confidential Documents, II, 5–7.

The three copies in D. S., 5 Consular Despatches, Tunis, and the copy of the provisions in the file, are all in the same handwriting—that of Ambrose Allegro, who served the United States Consulate at Tunis "since the commencement of 1801 . . . in the triple capacity of Chancellor, Secretary and Interpreter" (*ibid.*, Allegro to the Secretary of State, May 1, 1825, enclosure with Coxe's despatch of the same date). Numerous despatches and other papers from Tunis are also in the handwriting of Allegro, and it seems not improbable that the original convention was likewise in his handwriting. The two copies of the text enclosed in letters of Coxe are of later date than the transmittal of the original to the United States; but the copy enclosed by Heap in his despatch of March 4, 1824, was doubtless made from the original, which he had received, "signed and sealed by the Bashaw Bey, and the Bey," on March 2 (*ibid.*, Heap's journal). And, as has been observed, it seems that even the handwriting may be the same as that of the original.

The copy of the provisions of the agreement which is in the treaty file bears no endorsement as to its source or date of receipt; aside from the fact that it was made at Tunis by Allegro, nothing definite is known regarding its history. Heap states in his despatches of June 13 and June 26, 1824 (*ibid.*), that he sent one copy of the convention to the Department of State by way of Leghorn in April, 1824 (for March 26 Heap's journal contains the remark, "Despatched letters to Consuls Appleton and Anderson at Leghorn"), and another by way of Marseilles in May. That copy which accompanied the despatch of March 4, 1824 (*ibid.*), is the one sent by way of Marseilles in May; possibly the copy in the treaty file is the one sent by way of Leghorn in March or April.

The text of the convention as it appears in the original proclamation was copied in the press of the period (e.g., Niles' Weekly Register, XXVII, 355–57, February 5, 1825) and has been printed in treaty collections generally ever since. That text may possibly have been taken from the original convention; but it differs, in its indication of the signatures and seals, from the copy sent by Heap with his despatch of March 4, 1824, and from the Senate print.

The choice as to the source of the text to be printed is between the copy enclosed with Heap's despatch of March 4, 1824, and the Senate print, both of which were probably copied from the original. But if the original was in the handwriting of Allegro (an unusually accurate scrivener), as might be supposed, then the copy enclosed by Heap is doubtless more nearly like the original than is the Senate print, with its alterations of style.

Aside from matters of punctuation, capitalization, etc., the Senate print differs from the copy enclosed by Heap (and from all other available handwritten copies) in three places, which are almost certainly printer's changes or errors.

Accordingly, the copy enclosed by Heap with his despatch of March 4, 1824, has been adopted as the source text of the convention.

In all the possible sources available, the textual date of signature of the convention is given as February 24, 1824, and the corresponding date by the Mohammedan calendar as 24 Jumada II, A. H. 1239, which would be February 25, 1824, according to the chronological tables; see, however, the remarks as to the Mohammedan calendar in Volume 2, pages xxi–xxii.

THE RATIFICATION

While on the part of Tunis the agreement was doubtless complete upon its signature, ratification on the part of the United States appears to have been considered necessary. In the letter of Consul Coxe to Commodore Rodgers of October 15, 1825, which has been mentioned, Coxe wrote that on his arrival at Tunis (on December 11, 1824) "they [the officials of Tunis] were extremely anxious to know my opinion of their 'alterations,' and the probability of their being ratified"; and, in the case of the earlier treaty with Tunis, the United States instrument of ratification was duly delivered (see the notes to Document 21).

There has been found, however, no duplicate or other record of the United States instrument of ratification, nor is there any record that such a document was sent to Tunis. The fact that the convention had been ratified by the United States is recited in the proclamation, but the date of the ratification cannot be definitely stated. It was not earlier than January 13, 1825, the date of the Senate resolution of advice and consent; and it could not have been later than the following January 21, the date of the proclamation.

THE PROCLAMATION

The original proclamation, which is in the treaty file, is in rather unusual form, as it includes not only the text of the convention but also the text of Articles 6, 11, 12, and 14 as they appear in the earlier treaty (Document 21), according to the English translation thereof. The opening recital of the proclamation, which is printed in

full in American State Papers, Foreign Relations, V, 587–89, with
the presidential message of February 2, 1825, reads thus:

Whereas certain alterations in the Treaty of Peace and Friendship of August
1797, between the United-States and the Bashaw Bey of Tunis, were agreed
upon and concluded between His Highness Sidi Mahmoud, the Bey, and S. D.
Heap, Chargé d'Affaires of the United-States, at Tunis, on the twenty-fourth
day of February one thousand eight hundred and twenty-four, by the Articles
in the words following, to which are annexed the altered Articles as they were
in the Treaty before the alterations.

Following the preamble of the convention, the two texts of the four
articles are written in parallel columns in the proclamation, each
article in the left column having as part of its heading "As it now is"
and each article in the right column having as part of its heading
"As it was."

It is in the form of the proclamation that this convention has been
printed in treaty collections generally, though usually without the
clauses of the proclamation itself; but it seems certain that this was
not at all the form of the original convention; for all the four copies
written at Tunis by Allegro and sent to the Department of State,
and also the Senate print of the convention, to which reference has
been made, contain only the text of the articles as altered in 1824.

THE ALTERATIONS

The alterations of the earlier treaty with Tunis (Document 21)
which were made by this convention, were limited to Articles 6, 11,
12, and 14. It is to be remembered that three of those articles (11,
12, and 14) had previously been altered from the form in which they
were originally signed on August 28, 1797, by the changes made on
March 26, 1799, before the treaty was finally ratified by the United
States. In this connection the notes to Document 21 should be
consulted generally. Furthermore, as is indicated in those notes,
there had been, at least in respect of Article 14, some subsequent and
quite informal alterations agreed upon in 1807.

The 1824 negotiations were carried on by Heap without any full
power and without instructions from the Department of State (D. S.,
5 Consular Despatches, Tunis, March 4, 1824), but Heap must have
had before him at the time the instructions which had been given
to O'Brien, Cathcart, and Eaton, under date of December 18, 1798
(D. S., 5 Instructions, U. S. Ministers, 16–23; printed in part in American State Papers, Foreign Relations, II, 281–82), regarding the alterations of Articles 11, 12, and 14 then desired; for those instructions
were only partly carried out in 1799; and in respect of those three
articles the text of this convention follows those instructions with
precision. Article 14 and the latter part of Article 12 as proposed
in 1798 were embodied almost word for word in this convention, and
the further instructions then given as to Articles 11 and 12 were
accurately carried out. Only in regard to Article 6 did Heap go
outside of the instructions of 1798, and the improvement there made

in the treaty is, from the American point of view, both obvious and striking.

Accordingly, it seems unnecessary to review the criticism by Coxe of the alterations, to which reference has been made. In part those comments of Coxe complained of the fact that Heap acted without instructions; in part they relate to clauses of the treaty which were not altered by Heap; and, in general, they seem to have been written with the purpose of putting the course of Heap in an unfavorable light.

The criticism of Coxe, however, is interesting for another reason. It was written on October 15, 1825, and was submitted for the consideration of the Department of State with the despatch of Coxe of February 25, 1826 (D. S., 5 Consular Despatches, Tunis); this was more than one year after the convention had been ratified by the United States and proclaimed, and it shows that at that time Coxe had no knowledge of the action of this Government. Doubt as to whether the United States instrument of ratification was transmitted to Tunis must be increased by this circumstance.

Treaty Series No. 298
8 Statutes at Large, 302–5
18 *ibid.*, pt. 2, Public Treaties, 664–65

46

RUSSIA : APRIL 17, 1824

Convention Regarding Navigation, Fishing, and Trading, and Establishments on the Northwest Coast of America, signed at St. Petersburg (Leningrad) April 17, 1824 (April 5, Old Style). Original in French. Submitted to the Senate December 15, 1824. (Message of December 13, 1824.) Resolution of advice and consent January 5, 1825. Ratified by the United States January 7, 1825. Ratified by Russia May 22, 1824 (May 10, Old Style). Ratifications exchanged at Washington January 11, 1825. Proclaimed January 12, 1825.

[Translation]

Au Nom de la très Sainte et Indivisible Trinité.

Le Président des Etats-Unis d'Amérique, et Sa Majesté l'Empereur de toutes les Russies, voulant cimenter les liens d'amitié qui les unissent et assurer entre eux le maintien invariable d'un parfait accord, moyennant la présente Convention, ont nommé pour Leurs Plénipotentiaires à cet effet, savoir: le Président des Etats Unis d'Amérique, le Sieur Henry Middleton, Citoyen des dits Etats, et Leur Envoyé Extraordinaire et Ministre Plénipotentiaire près Sa Majesté Impériale: et Sa Majesté l'Empereur de toutes les Russies, Ses amés et féaux les Sieurs Charles Robert Comte de Nesselrode, Conseiller Privé actuel, Membre du Conseil d'Etat, Secrétaire d'Etat Dirigeant le Ministère des affaires

In the name of the Most Holy and Indivisible Trinity.

The President of the United States of America and His Majesty the Emperor of all the Russias, wishing to cement the bonds of amity which unite them and to secure between them the invariable maintenance of a perfect concord by means of the present convention, have named as their Plenipotentiaries to this effect, to wit: the President of the United States of America, Henry Middleton, a citizen of said States and their Envoy Extraordinary and Minister Plenipotentiary near His Imperial Majesty; and His Majesty the Emperor of all the Russias, his beloved and faithful Charles Robert, Count of Nesselrode, actual Privy Counselor, Member of the Council of State, Secretary

151

étrangères, Chambellan actuel, Chevalier de l'ordre de St Alexandre Nevsky, Grand Croix de l'ordre de St Wladimir de la 1.re classe, Chevalier de celui de l'aigle blanc de Pologne, Grand Croix de l'ordre de St Etienne d'Hongrie, Chevalier des ordres du St Esprit et de St Michel et Grand Croix de celui de la Légion d'honneur de france, Chevalier Grand-Croix des ordres de l'aigle noir et de l'aigle rouge de Prusse, de l'annonciade de Sardaigne, de Charles III d'Espagne, de St Ferdinand et du mérite de Naples, de l'Eléphant de Danemarc, de l'Etoile Polaire de Suède, de la Couronne de Würtemberg, des Guelphes de Hanovre, du Lion Belge, de la Fidélité de Bade, et de St Constantin de Parme, et Pierre de Poletica, Conseiller d'Etat actuel, Chevalier de l'ordre de Ste Anne de la 1.re classe et Grand Croix de l'ordre de St Wladimir de la seconde; lesquels apres avoir échangé leurs pleinpouvoirs, trouvés en bonne et due forme, ont arrêté et signé les stipulations suivantes.

ARTICLE PREMIER.

Il est convenu que dans aucune partie du Grand Océan, appelé communément Océan pacifique ou Mer du Sud, les Citoyens ou Sujets respectifs des hautes Puissances contractantes ne seront ni

of State directing the administration of foreign affairs, actual Chamberlain, Knight of the order of St. Alexander Nevsky, Grand Cross of the order of St. Vladimir of the first class, Knight of that of the White Eagle of Poland, Grand Cross of the order of St. Stephen of Hungary, Knight of the orders of the Holy Ghost and of St. Michael and Grand Cross of the Legion of Honor of France, Knight Grand Cross of the orders of the Black and of the Red Eagle of Prussia, of the Annunciation of Sardinia, of Charles III of Spain, of St. Ferdinand and of Merit of Naples, of the Elephant of Denmark, of the Polar Star of Sweden, of the Crown of Württemberg, of the Guelphs of Hanover, of the Belgic Lion, of Fidelity of Baden, and of St. Constantine of Parma; and Pierre de Poletica, actual Counselor of State, Knight of the order of St. Anne of the first class and Grand Cross of the order of St. Vladimir of the second; who, after having exchanged their full powers, found in good and due form, have agreed upon and signed the following stipulations.

ARTICLE 1

It is agreed that in any part of the Great Ocean commonly called the Pacific Ocean or South Sea, the respective citizens or subjects of the high contracting powers shall be neither disturbed nor re-

troublés, ni gênés, soit dans la navigation, soit dans l'exploitation de la pêche, soit dans la faculté d'arborder aux côtes sur des points qui ne seroient pas déjà occupés, afin d'y faire le commerce avec les Indigènes, sauf toutefois les restrictions et conditions déterminées par les articles qui suivent

Article Deuxième.

Dans la vue d'empêcher que les droits de navigation et de pêche exercés sur le grand Océan par les Citoyens et Sujets des hautes Puissances contractantes ne deviennent le prétexte d'un commerce illicite, il est convenu, que les Citoyens des Etats Unis n'aborderont à aucun point où il se trouve un établissement Russe, sans la permission du Gouverneur ou Commandant; et que réciproquement les Sujets Russes ne pourront aborder sans permission à aucun établissement des Etats-Unis sur la Côte nord ouest.

Article Troisième.

Il est convenu en outre, que dorénavant il ne pourra être formé par les Citoyens des Etats-Unis, ou sous l'autorité des dits Etats, aucun établissement sur la Côte nord ouest d'Amérique, ni dans aucune des îles adjacentes *au nord* du cinquante quatrième degré et quarante minutes de latitude septentrionale; et que de

strained, either in navigation, or in fishing, or in the power of resorting to the coasts, upon points which may not already have been occupied, for the purpose of trading with the natives, saving always the restrictions and conditions determined by the following articles.

Article 2

With the view of preventing the rights of navigation and of fishing exercised upon the Great Ocean by the citizens and subjects of the high contracting powers from becoming the pretext for an illicit trade, it is agreed that the citizens of the United States shall not resort to any point where there is a Russian establishment, without the permission of the governor or commander; and that, reciprocally, the subjects of Russia shall not resort, without permission, to any establishment of the United States upon the northwest coast.

Article 3

It is, moreover, agreed that hereafter there shall not be formed by the citizens of the United States, or under the authority of the said States, any establishment upon the northwest coast of America, nor in any of the islands adjacent, *to the north* of fifty-four degrees and forty minutes of north latitude; and that in the

même il n'en pourra être formé aucun par des Sujets Russes, ou sous l'autorité de la Russie, *au sud* de la même parallèle

Article Quatrième.

Il est néanmoins entendu que pendant un terme de dix années à compter de la signature de la présente Convention, les Vaisseaux des deux Puissances, ou qui appartiendroient à leurs Citoyens ou Sujets respectifs, pourront réciproquement fréquenter sans entrave quelconque, les mers intérieures, les golfes, hâvres et criques sur la Côte mentionnée dans l'article précédent, afin d'y faire la pêche et le commerce avec les naturels du pays.[1]

Article Cinquième.

Sont toutefois exceptées de ce même commerce accordé par l'article précédent, toutes les liqueurs spiritueuses, les armes à feu, armes blanches, poudre et munitions de guerre de toute espèce, que les deux Puissances s'engagent réciproquement à ne pas vendre, ni laisser vendre aux Indigènes par leurs Citoyens et Sujets respectifs, ni par aucun individu qui se trouveroit sous leur autorité. Il est également stipulé que cette restriction ne pourra jamais servir de prétexte, ni être alleguée, dans aucun cas, pour autoriser soit la visite ou la détention des Vaisseaux, soit la saisie de la

same manner there shall be none formed by Russian subjects, or under the authority of Russia, *south* of the same parallel.

Article 4

It is, nevertheless, understood that during a term of ten years, counting from the signature of the present convention, the ships of both powers, or which belong to their citizens or subjects respectively, may reciprocally frequent, without any hindrance whatever, the interior seas, gulfs, harbors, and creeks upon the coast mentioned in the preceding article, for the purpose of fishing and trading with the natives of the country.[1]

Article 5

All spirituous liquors, firearms, other arms, powder, and munitions of war of every kind, are always excepted from this same commerce permitted by the preceding article, and the two powers engage, reciprocally, neither to sell nor suffer them to be sold to the natives by their respective citizens and subjects, nor by any person who may be under their authority. It is likewise stipulated that this restriction shall never afford a pretext nor be advanced in any case to authorize either search or detention of the vessels, seizure of the merchandise, or, in fine, any measures of

---

[1] See the note regarding Article 4.

marchandise, soit enfin des mesures quelconques de contrainte envers les armateurs ou les equipages qui feroient ce commerce; les hautes Puissances contractantes s'étant réciproquement reservé de statuer sur les peines à encourir, et d'infliger les amendes encouruës en cas de contravention à cet article, par leurs Citoyens ou Sujets respectifs.

Article Sixième.

Lorsque cette Convention aura été duement ratifiée par le Président des Etats-Unis de l'avis et du consentement du Sénat, d'une part, et de l'autre par Sa Majesté l'Empereur de toutes les Russies, les ratifications en seront echangées à Washington dans le délai de dix mois de la date ci-dessous ou plutôt si faire se peut. En foi de quoi les Plénipotentiaires respectifs l'ont signée, et y ont fait apposer les cachets de leurs armes.

Fait à S⁺ Petersbourg le 17/5 Avril de l'an de grâce mil huit cent vingt quatre.

[Seal]
Henry Middleton
[Seal]
Le Comte Charles
de Nesselrode
[Seal]
Pierre de Poletica

constraint whatever towards the merchants or the crews who may carry on this commerce, the high contracting powers reciprocally reserving to themselves to determine upon the penalties to be incurred, and to inflict the punishments, in case of the contravention of this article by their respective citizens or subjects.

Article 6

When this convention shall have been duly ratified by the President of the United States with the advice and consent of the Senate on the one part, and on the other by His Majesty the Emperor of all the Russias, the ratifications shall be exchanged at Washington in the space of ten months from the date below, or sooner if possible. In faith whereof the respective Plenipotentiaries have signed this convention and thereto affixed the seals of their arms.

Done at St. Petersburg the 5/17 April of the year of grace one thousand eight hundred and twenty-four.

[Seal]
Henry Middleton
[Seal]
Le Comte Charles
de Nesselrode
[Seal]
Pierre de Poletica

NOTES

Unless otherwise stated, dates in the headnote and in these notes are in the New Style, or present calendar, which was then twelve days later than the Old Style.

THE FILE PAPERS

The file papers of this convention are complete, except for the attested resolution of advice and consent of the Senate of January 5, 1825 (Executive Journal, III, 403). The convention was executed in duplicate (American State Papers, Foreign Relations, V, 469); the original in the file, which was received in the Department of State on July 26, 1824, with the despatch of Henry Middleton, Minister at St. Petersburg, of May 24, 1824 (D. S., 10 Despatches, Russia), is within the duplicate United States instrument of ratification. The Russian instrument of ratification of May 22, 1824 (May 10, Old Style), is accompanied by a French translation certified by Baron de Tuyll, Russian Minister at Washington. The certificate of the exchange of ratifications on January 11, 1825, is in customary form, in duplicate, one written in French and one in English. The original proclamation of January 12, 1825, includes the French text of the convention and an English translation which appears to have been made in the Department of State. There is also in the treaty file a duplicate of that translation, in the same handwriting as that which is copied into the proclamation. The proclamation is printed in American State Papers, Foreign Relations, V, 583–84, with the presidential message of January 18, 1825, communicating it to Congress. It is the translation in the proclamation which is printed above and which is in the Statutes at Large and in treaty collections generally.

The papers accompanying the presidential message of December 13, 1824, transmitting this convention to the Senate, are in American State Papers, Foreign Relations, V, 432–71.

The attested resolution of advice and consent of the Senate of January 5, 1825, is in D. S., Miscellaneous Letters, January–March, 1825.

Regarding the exchange of ratifications at Washington on January 11, 1825, Secretary of State Adams wrote as follows (Memoirs of John Quincy Adams, VI, 465):

I went immediately to the office, and exchanged with Baron Tuyl the ratifications of the N. W. Coast Convention. Baron Maltitz was with him, and read the original treaty. I held the Russian ratified copy, Baron Tuyl ours, and Mr. Ironside the copy received from Baron Tuyl from his Government. We executed in French and English two certificates of the exchange.

THE RUSSIAN UKASE

The convention does not mention the Russian ukase, or edict, of September 4, 1821 (Old Style), which was the cause of the negotia-

tions from which the convention resulted and against which the United States promptly protested, following its communication to Secretary of State Adams by Pierre de Poletica, then Russian Minister at Washington, on February 11, 1822 (D. S., 1 Notes from the Russian Legation; the enclosure, in English, is entitled "Edict of His Imperial Majesty Autocrat of all the Russias. . . . Printed at St. Petersburg in the Senate, 7ᵗʰ September 1821"; accompanying it is the "Rules," a pamphlet of fourteen pages). As to that ukase, see Moore, International Arbitrations, I, 755–60; its text, with the rules above mentioned, in English translation, is in British and Foreign State Papers, IX, 472–82.

The Russian territorial claims are discussed at some length in the instructions of Secretary of State Adams to Henry Middleton, Minister at St. Petersburg, dated July 22, 1823 (D. S., 10 Instructions, U. S. Ministers, 54–60; American State Papers, Foreign Relations, V, 436–38), and in the enclosures therewith; they are also discussed in the instructions to Richard Rush, Minister at London, of the same date, from which the following statement regarding the Russian ukase is extracted (D. S., 10 Instructions, U. S. Ministers, 62; American State Papers, Foreign Relations, V, 446):

By the Ukaze of the Emperor Alexander of 4/16 September 1821 an exclusive territorial right on the North west Coast of America is asserted as belonging to Russia, and as extending from the Northern extremity of the Continent to Latitude 51, and the Navigation and fishery of all other Nations are interdicted by the same Ukaze to the extent of 100 Italian [or geographical] miles from the Coast.

In the Russian full power, however, the Russian ukase of September 16, 1821, is mentioned. In Middleton's despatch reporting the negotiations, under date of April 19, 1824, he wrote on the subject of the full powers as follows (D. S., 10 Despatches, Russia, No. 35; American State Papers, Foreign Relations, V, 458):

Having received an invitation from Cᵗ Nesselrode, I waited on him on Wednesday 20ᵗʰ Feby [Old Style] at one o'clock P. M. I found Mʳ Poletica with the Count, & a *rescrit* from the Emperor to these Gentlemen was exhibited to me, empowering them to treat and adjust a settlement of the differences which had arisen in consequence of His Majesty's Ukase of 4/16th Septʳ 1821. . . . I exhibited to them my Power from the President of the United States to the Same effect, & we exchanged Copies of the Same.

With that despatch was enclosed a copy of a certified translation, in French, of the Russian full power, which is dated February 12, 1824, Old Style. An English translation of the French is printed in American State Papers, Foreign Relations, V, 464. The substance of that full power as there printed, omitting the styles and titles there recited, is as follows:

We, Alexander the First, by the Grace of God Emperor and Autocrat of all the Russias, etc., etc., make known that, certain disputes having arisen between Our Government, that of His Majesty the King of the United Kingdom of Great Britain, and that of the United States of America, in consequence of Our ukase dated September 4/16, 1821, and having considered the necessity of terminat-

ing these disputes by means of an amicable negotiation, We have resolved to appoint, and do appoint, for Our Plenipotentiaries in the said negotiation, Our beloved and faithful Charles Robert, Count of Nesselrode, Our actual Privy Counselor, member of the Council of State, Secretary of State directing the administration of foreign affairs, etc., etc., and Pierre Poletica, Our actual Counselor of State, etc., etc., promising, on Our imperial word, to make good and ratify all the arrangements which the said Plenipotentiaries shall conclude and sign in regard to the objects above pointed out, with the Plenipotentiaries duly authorized to that effect by His Majesty the King of the United Kingdom of Great Britain, and by the United States of America.

In faith whereof We have signed the present full powers and have hereto caused to be affixed the seal of Our Empire.

In the American full power the Russian ukase is not in terms referred to; in general it is in the customary form of full powers issued by this Government, but it authorized either joint negotiations with British and Russian Plenipotentiaries or several negotiations with the latter. Its text follows (D. S., 1 Credences, 360):

James Monroe, President of the United States of America,

To all to whom these Presents may come, Greeting:

Know Ye, That reposing special Trust and Confidence in the Integrity, Prudence and Abilities of Henry Middleton, Envoy Extraordinary and Minister Plenipotentiary of the United States at the Court of His Imperial Majesty, the Emperor of all the Russias, I have invested him with full and all manner of Power, for and in the name of the United States to meet and confer with any person or persons furnished with like Powers on the part of His said Imperial Majesty, and with him or them to negotiate and conclude a Convention or Conventions, Treaty or Treaties, of and concerning the commerce and Navigation of the two Countries; of and concerning their respective Rights and Claims in respect to Navigation Fishery and Commerce on the North West Coast of America, and the Ocean and Islands thereto adjoining or appertaining: of and concerning the abolition of the African Slave Trade; and of and concerning the principles of Maritime War and Neutrality. And I do further invest him with full Power, also to meet and confer, on the said subjects with any Person or Persons furnished with like powers on the part of His Majesty the King of the United Kingdom of Great Britain and Ireland; and with the said Russian and British Plenipotentiaries jointly to conclude a Treaty or Treaties, Convention or Conventions, in relation to the respective rights and claims of the three Powers in and to the said Navigation, Fishery, Commerce and Territorial possessions, on the said North West Coast of America, and adjoining Ocean and Islands: or in relation to the abolition of the African Slave trade; or in relation to the principles of Maritime War and Neutrality—He the said Henry Middleton transmitting any and every such Convention or Treaty whether concluded jointly with British and Russian, or severally with Russian Plenipotentiaries to the President of the United States for his ratification, by and with the advice and Consent of the Senate of the United States if the same shall be given.

In Testimony whereof, I have caused the Seal of the United States to be hereunto affixed. Given under my hand at the City of Washington (L. S.) the twenty Ninth day of July A. D. 1823; and of the Independence of the United States of America, the Forty Eighth.

JAMES MONROE,

By the President,
JOHN QUINCY ADAMS,
    Secretary of State.

ARTICLE 4

During the negotiations at St. Petersburg between Henry Middleton and Count Nesselrode, a narrative of which is in American State Papers, Foreign Relations, V, 457–71, the form of Article 4 was much discussed and "became the subject of warm debate." As first agreed upon it contained a phrase to the effect that after a term of ten years "the reciprocal right granted by this article shall cease, on both sides." This seemed to Middleton to have "still too much the appearance of a substantive stipulation" and was changed to the language of the convention, which simply provides for the reciprocal privilege "during a term of ten years"; but a protocol, noting that the change did "not essentially alter the sense" of the earlier draft, and which was among the papers before the Senate, was signed by the three Plenipotentiaries (in French) on April 14, 1824, three days before the date of the convention.

The following French text is from the original protocol (D. S., 10 Despatches, Russia, No. 35, enclosure *r* with Middleton's despatch of April 19, 1824); the English is from a contemporary translation made in the Department of State and bound with the original; that translation is printed in American State Papers, Foreign Relations, V, 469.

[Translation]

Protocole.

Les Soussignés après avoir discuté dans plusieurs conférences un projet de convention proposé pour applanir tous les différens qui se sont élevés entre les Etats-Unis d'Amérique et la Russie à la suite d'un réglement publié par la dernière de ces Puissances, le 4/16 Septembre 1821, ont définitivement arrêté la rédaction des divers articles dont se compose cette convention, les ont revêtus de leurs paraphes et se sont engagés réciproquement à les signer tels qu'ils se trouvent annexés au présent Protocole.

En arrêtant le 4me de ces articles, les Plenipotentiaires de Russie ont rappelé qu'ils avoient proposé au Plénipotentiaire des Etats-Unis de rédiger le dit article dans les termes suivans:

"Article 4me. Il est néanmoins en-
"tendu que les vaisseaux des deux
"Puissances ou qui appartiendroient
"à leurs citoyens ou sujets respectifs,
"pourront réciproquement fréquenter
"sans entraves quelconques les mers
"intérieures, les golphes, havres et
"criques sur la dite côte, afin d'y faire
"la pêche et le commerce avec les

Protocol

The undersigned, after having discussed in several conferences a *projet* of a convention proposed for settling all the differences which arose between the United States of America and Russia in consequence of a regulation published by the latter of these powers on the 4/16 September, 1821, definitively drew up the different articles of which this convention is composed, added to them their sign manual, and mutually engaged to sign them as they are found annexed to the present protocol.

In drawing up the fourth of these articles the Plenipotentiaries of Russia recollected that they had proposed to the Plenipotentiary of the United States to arrange the said article in the following terms:

Article 4. "It is, nevertheless, understood that the ships of the two powers, or which belong to their citizens or subjects, respectively, may mutually frequent, without any hindrance whatever, the interior seas, gulfs, harbors, and creeks upon the said coast, for the purpose of there fishing and trading with the natives of the country. But

"naturels du pays, mais le droit "réciproque accordé par cet article, "cessera de part et d'autre après un "terme de dix ans à compter de la "signature de la présente convention."

Les Plénipotentiaires de Russie ont ajouté qu'après être tombé d'accord de cette rédaction, le Plénipotentiaire des Etats-Unis les avoit ensuite invités à changer la finale de ce même article et à l'arrêter tel qu'il se trouve consigné dans la convention; observant que cette seconde rédaction plus conforme à la lettre des instructions qu'il a reçues, est la seule qu'il se croie autorisé à signer; mais que d'ailleurs cette ré-daction ne change pas essentiellement le sens de celle qui avoit été proposée par les Plénipotentiaires de Russie, puisqu'à la fin du terme indiqué la stipulation devant cesser également par les deux rédactions, la faculté réciproque de faire le commerce, ac-cordée par cette stipulation, ne sauroit être prolongée au delà du dit terme que d'une mutuel accord.

Sur ces observations l'article en question a été paraphé avec la modi-fication que le Plénipotentiaire des Etats-Unis avoit demandé à y intro-duire.

Après quoi tous les autres articles ont pareillement été revêtus des para-phes respectifs, et il a été résolu de procéder à la signature de la conven-tion elle-même le cinq suivant.

fait à St. Petersbourg, le 14/2 Avril 1824.

HENRY MIDDLETON
NESSELRODE
POLETICA

the reciprocal right granted by this article shall cease, on both sides, after a term of ten years to be counted from the signing of the present convention."

The Plenipotentiaries of Russia added that, after agreeing to this arrange-ment, the Plenipotentiary of the United States had afterwards invited them to change the ending of this very article and agree to it as it is found signed in the convention, observing that this second arrangement, more conformable to the letter of the instruc-tions which he received, is the only one which he thinks himself authorized to sign; but, moreover, that this ar-rangement does not essentially alter the sense of that which had been pro-posed by the Plenipotentiaries of Rus-sia, because at the end of the term mentioned the stipulation ceasing equally by the two arrangements, the reciprocal power of trading granted by that stipulation cannot be prolonged beyond the said term but by mutual agreement.

Under these observations the article in question has been signed, with the modification which the Plenipotentiary of the United States had demanded to be there introduced.

After which, all the other articles were also signed respectively, and it was resolved to proceed to the signa-ture of the convention itself on the fifth [April 17, New Style] following.

Done at St. Petersburg the 2/14 April, 1824.

HENRY MIDDLETON
NESSELRODE
POLETICA

Upon the expiration of the ten-year period described in Article 4 the Government of Russia declined to renew its provisions. The question was discussed in the presidential message of December 3, 1838 (Richardson, III, 483, 487–88). The printed correspondence and other papers on the subject which were communicated to Congress with that message are in Senate Document No. 1, 25th Congress, 3d session, serial 338, pages 24–74.

A PROPOSED MODIFICATION

A proposal on the part of the Russian Government to explain and modify the convention was made at Washington shortly before the convention was submitted to the Senate. The conference on

December 6, 1824, between Baron de Tuyll, the Russian Minister at Washington, and Secretary of State Adams, is thus described by the latter (Memoirs of John Quincy Adams, VI, 435–37):

Baron Tuyl, the Russian Minister, wrote me a note requesting an immediate interview, in consequence of instructions received yesterday from his Court. He came, and, after intimating that he was under some embarrassment in executing his instructions, said that the Russian-American Company, upon learning the purport of the Northwest Coast Convention concluded last June [April] by Mr. Middleton, were extremely dissatisfied (a jetée de hauts cris), and, by means of their influence, had prevailed upon his Government to send him these instructions upon two points. One was, that he should deliver, upon the exchange of the ratifications of the Convention, an explanatory note, purporting that the Russian Government did not understand that the Convention would give liberty to the citizens of the United States to trade on the coast of Siberia and the Aleutian Islands. The other was, to propose a modification of the Convention, by which our vessels should be prohibited from trading on the Northwest coast north of latitude 57°. With regard to the former of these points, he left me a minute in writing.

I told him that we should be disposed to do everything to accommodate the views of his Government that was in our power, but that a modification of the Convention *could* be made no otherwise than by a new Convention, and that the construction of the Convention as concluded belonged to other Departments of the Government, for which the Executive had no authority to stipulate; that if on the exchange of the ratifications he should deliver to me a note of the purport of that which he now informally gave me, I should give him an answer of that import, namely, that the construction of treaties depending here upon the judiciary tribunals, the Executive Government, even if disposed to acquiesce in that of the Russian Government as announced by him, could not be binding upon the Courts, nor upon this nation. I added that the Convention would be submitted immediately to the Senate; that if anything affecting its construction, or, still more, modifying its meaning, were to be presented on the part of the Russian Government before, or at the exchange of, the ratifications, it must be laid before the Senate, and could have no other possible effect than of starting doubts, and perhaps hesitation, in that body, and of favoring the views of those, if such there were, who might wish to defeat the ratification itself of the Convention. This was an object of great solicitude to both Governments, not only for the adjustment of a difficult question which had arisen between them, but for the promotion of that harmony which was so much in the policy of the two countries, which might emphatically be termed natural friends to each other. If, therefore, he would permit me to suggest to him what I thought would be his best course, it would be to wait for the exchange of the ratifications, and make it purely and simply; that afterwards, if the instructions of his Government were imperative, he might present the note, to which I now informed him what would be in substance my answer. It necessarily could not be otherwise. But if his instructions left it discretionary with him, he would do still better to inform his Government of the state of things here, of the purport of our conference, and of what my answer must be if he should present the note. I believed his Court would then deem it best that he should not present the note at all. Their apprehensions had been excited by an interest not very friendly to the good understanding between the United States and Russia. Our merchants would not go to trouble the Russians on the coast of Siberia, or north of the fifty-seventh degree of latitude, and it was wisest not to put such fancies into their heads. At least, the Imperial Government might wait to see the operation of the Convention before taking any further step, and I was confident they would hear no complaint resulting from it. If they should, then would be the time for adjusting the construction or negotiating a modification of the Convention; and whoever might be at the head of the Administration of the United States, he might be assured that every disposition would be cherished to remove all causes of dissatisfaction, and to accommodate the wishes and the just policy of the Emperor.

The Baron said that these ideas had occurred to himself; that he had made this application in pursuance of his instructions; but he was aware of the distribution of powers in our Constitution, and of the incompetency of the Executive to adjust such questions. He would therefore wait for the exchange of the ratifications without presenting his note, and reserve for future consideration whether to present it shortly afterwards, or to inform his Court of what he has done, and ask their further instructions upon what he shall definitively do on the subject. He therefore requested me to consider what had now passed between us as if it had not taken place (non avenu); to which I readily assented, assuring him, as I had done heretofore, that the President had the highest personal confidence in him, and in his exertions to foster the harmony between the two countries. I reported immediately to the President the substance of this conversation, and he concurred in the propriety of the Baron's final determination.

The Invocation

This convention begins with the invocation, "In the name of the Most Holy and Indivisible Trinity." Some comments on the use of that invocation in treaties are in the notes to Document 55, the treaty with Sweden and Norway of July 4, 1827.

Execution of the Convention

Under date of May 19, 1828, there was enacted a statute "for the punishment of contraventions of the fifth article of the treaty between the United States and Russia" (4 Statutes at Large, 276).

Treaty Series No. 52
8 Statutes at Large, 306–21
18 *ibid.*, pt. 2, Public Treaties, 150–57

47

COLOMBIA : OCTOBER 3, 1824

Treaty of Peace, Amity, Navigation, and Commerce, signed at Bogotá October 3, 1824. Original in English and Spanish.
Submitted to the Senate February 22, 1825. (Message of February 21, 1825.) Resolution of advice and consent March 3, 1825. Ratified by the United States March 7, 1825. Ratified by Colombia March 26, 1825. Ratifications exchanged at Washington May 27, 1825. Proclaimed May 31, 1825.

General Convention of Peace, Amity, Navigation, and Commerce between The United States of America and The Republic of Colombia.

In the name of God Author and Legislator of the Universe

The United States of America and the Republic of Colombia desiring to make lasting and firm the friendship and good understanding, which happily prevails between both nations, have resolved to fix in a manner clear, distinct, and positive the rules which shall in future be religiously observed between the one and the other by means of a treaty or General Convention of peace, friendship, Commerce, and Navigation; For this most desirable object the President of the United States of America has conferred full powers on Richard Clough Anderson junior a citizen of the said States and their Minister

Convencion Jeneral de paz, amistad, navegacion y Comercio entre la republica de Colombia y los Estados Unidos de America. Año de 1824.

En el nombre de Dios Autor y Lejislador del Universo.

La republica de Colombia, y los Estados Unidos de America, deseando hacer duradera y firme la amistad y buena intelijencia que felizmente existe entre ambas Potencias, han resuelto fijár de una manera clara, distinta y positiva las reglas que deben observár relijiosamente en lo venidero, por medio de un tratado, ó convencion jenerál de paz, amistad, comercio y navegacion.

Con este muy deseable objeto, el Vice-Presidente de la republica de Colombia encargado del podér Ejecutivo, ha conferido plenos poderes a Pedro Gual, Secretario de Estado y del despacho de relaciones esteriores de la misma,

163

Plenipotentiary to the said Republic and the Vice President of the Republic of Colombia charged with the Executive power on Pedro Gual Secretary of State and of foreign Relations, who after having exchanged their said full powers in due and proper form have agreed to the following Articles

ARTICLE FIRST. There shall be a perfect, firm, and inviolable peace and sincere friendship between the United States of America and the Republic of Colombia in all the extent of their possessions and territories and between their people and Citizens respectively without distinction of persons or places

ARTICLE SECOND. The United States of America and the Republic of Columbia desiring to live in peace and harmony with all the other nations of the Earth, by means of a policy frank and equally friendly with all, engage mutually not to grant any particular favour to other nations in respect of commerce and navigation, which shall not immediately become common to the other party, who shall enjoy the same freely, if the concession was freely made, or on allowing the same compensation, if the Concession was conditional

ARTICLE THIRD. The Citizens of the United States may frequent all the coasts and Countries of

y el Presidente de los Estados Unidos de America a Ricardo Clough Anderson el menór, Ciudadano de dichos Estados, y su Ministro Plenipotenciario cerca de la dicha Republica; quenes despues de haber canjeado sus espresados plenos poderes en debida y buena forma, han convenido en los articulos siguientes.

ART? 1? Habra una paz, perfecta, firme, é inviolable y amistad sincera entre la Republica de Colombia y los Estados Unidos de America, en toda la estencion de sus posesiones y territorios, y entre sus pueblos y Ciudadanos respectivamente sin distincion de personas, ni lugares.

ART? 2? La republica de Colombia, y los Estados Unidos de America, deseando vivir en paz y harmonia con las demás Naciones de la tierra, por medio de una politica franca, é igualmente amistosa con todas, se obligan mutuamente á no conceder favores particulares á otras Naciones, con respecto á Comercio y navegacion, que no se hagan inmediatamente comunes á una ú otra, quien gozará del mismo libremente, si la concesion fuese hecha libremente, ó prestando la misma compensacion, si la concesion fuere condicional.

ART? 3? Los Ciudadanos de la republica de Colombia, podrán frecuentár todas las costas y

the Republic of Colombia and reside and trade there, in all sorts of produce, manufactures, and merchandize and shall pay no other or greater duties, charges, or fees whatsoever, than the most favoured nation is or shall be obliged to pay; and they shall enjoy all the rights, privileges, and exemptions in navigation and Commerce, which the most favoured nation does or shall enjoy, submitting themselves nevertheless to the laws, decrees, and usages there established and to which are submitted the subjects and citizens of the most favoured nations. In like manner the Citizens of the Republic of Colombia may frequent all the coasts and countries of the United States and reside and trade there, in all sorts of produce, manufactures, and merchandize, and shall pay no other or greater duties, charges, or fees whatsoever, than the most favoured nation is, or shall be obliged to pay; and they shall enjoy all the rights, privileges, and exemptions in navigation and commerce, which the most favoured nation does or shall enjoy, submitting themselves nevertheless to the laws, decrees and usages there established, and to which are submitted the subjects and Citizens of the most favoured nations

paises de los Estados Unidos de America, y residir, y traficar en ellos con toda suerte de producciones, manufacturas, y mercaderias, y no pagarán otros, ó mayores derechos, impuestos, ó emolumentos cualesquiera que los que las naciones mas favorecidas están ó estuvieren obligadas á pagar; y gozarán todos los derechos, privilejios y esenciones, que gozan ó gozaren los de la nacion mas favorecida, con respecto á navegacion y comercio, sometiendose no obstante á las leyes, decretos, y usos establecidos, á los cuales estan sujetos los subditos ó Ciudadanos de las naciones mas favorecidas. Del mismo modo los Ciudadanos de los Estados Unidos de America podrán frecuentar todas las costas y paises de la republica de Colombia, y residir y traficár en ellos con toda suerte de producciones, manufacturas, y mercaderias, y no pagarán otros ó mayores derechos, impuestos, ó emolumentos cualesquiera, que los que las naciones mas favorecidas, están ó estuvieren obligadas á pagár, y gozarán de todos los derechos, privilejios y esenciones, que gozan ó gozaren los de la nacion mas favorecida con respecto á navegacion y comercio, sometiendose, no obstante, á las leyes, decretos y usos establecidos, a los cuales estan sujetos los subditos ó Ciudadanos de las naciones mas favorecidas.

ARTICLE FOURTH. It is likewise agreed that it shall be wholly free for all merchants, Commanders of Ships, and other Citizens of both Countries to manage themselves their own business in all the ports and places subject to the jurisdiction of each other, as well with respect to the consignment and sale of their goods and merchandize, by wholesale or retail, as with respect to the loading, unloading, and sending off their Ships, they being in all these cases to be treated as Citizens of the Country in which they reside, or at least to be placed on a footing with the subjects or Citizens of the most favoured nation.

ARTICLE FIFTH. The Citizens of neither of the Contracting parties shall be liable to any Embargo, nor be detained with their Vessels, cargos, merchandizes or effects for any military expedition, nor for any public or private purpose whatever, without allowing to those interested a sufficient indemnification.

ARTICLE SIXTH. Whenever the Citizens of either of the Contracting parties, shall be forced to seek refuge or asylum in the rivers, bays, ports or dominions of the other with their Vessels, whether merchant or of War, public or private, through stress of weather, pursuit of pirates or enemies, they

ART° 4° Se conviene ademas, que será enteramente libre y permitido, a los Comerciantes, Comandantes de buques, y otros Ciudadanos de ambos paises el manejár sus negocios, por si mismos, en todos los puertos y lugares sujetos á la jurisdiccion de uno ú otro, así respecto á las consignaciones y ventas por mayor y menor de sus efectos y mercaderias, como de la carga, descarga y despacho de sus buques, debiendo en todos estos casos, ser tratados como Ciudadanos del pais en que residan, ó al menos puestos sobre un pie igual con los subditos ó Ciudadanos de las naciones mas favorecidas.

ART° 5° Los ciudadanos de una ú otra parte, no podrán ser embargados ni detenidos con sus embarcaciones, tripulaciones, mercaderias, y efectos comerciales de su pertenencia, para alguna espedicion militár, usos publicos, ó particulares cualesquiera q° sean, sin concedér á los interesados una suficiente indemnizacion.

ART° 6° Siempre que los ciudadanos de alguna de las partes contratantes se vieren precisados á buscár refujio, ó asilo en los rios, bahias, puertos, ó dominios de la otra, con sus buques, ya sean mercantes, ó de guerra, publicos, ó particulares, por mal tiempo, persecucion de piratas ó enemigos,

shall be received and treated with humanity, giving to them all favour and protection for repairing their Ships, procuring provisions, and placing themselves in a situation to continue their voyage without obstacle or hindrance of any kind

ARTICLE SEVENTH. All the ships, merchandize, and effects belonging to the citizens of one of the contracting parties, which may be captured by pirates, whether within the limits of its jurisdiction or on the high seas, and may be carried or found in the rivers, roads, bays, ports, or dominions of the other, shall be delivered up to the owners, they proving in due and proper form, their rights before the Competent tribunals; it being well understood that the claim should be made within the term of one year by the parties themselves, their attorneys, or agents of the respective governments

ARTICLE EIGHTH. When any vessel belonging to the Citizens of either of the contracting parties shall be wrecked, foundered, or shall suffer any damage on the coasts, or within the dominions of the other, there shall be given to them all assistance and protection, in the same manner, which is usual and customary with the Vessels of the Nation where the damage happens, per-

serán recibidos y tratados con humanidad, dandoles todo favor y proteccion, para reparar sus buques, procurár viveres, y ponerse en situacion de continuár su viaje, sin obstaculo ó estorbo de ningun jenero.

ART? 7? Todos los buques, mercaderias y efectos pertenecientes á los Ciudadanos de una de las partes contratantes, que sean apresados por piratas, bien sea dentro de los limites de su jurisdiccion, ó en alta mar, y fueren llevados, ó hallados en los rios, radas, bahias, puertos, ó dominios de la otra, serán entregados á sus dueños, probando estos en la forma propia y debida sus derechos ante los Tribunales competentes; bien entendido que el reclamo ha de hacerse dentro del termino de un año, por las mismas partes, sus apoderados o Ajentes de los respectivos Gobiernos.

ART? 8? Cuando algun buque perteneciente á los ciudadanos de alguna de las partes contratantes, naufrague, encalle, ó sufra alguna averia, en las costas, ó dentro de los dominios de la otra, se les dará toda ayuda y proteccion, del mismo modo que es uso y costumbre, con los buques de la nacion en donde suceda la averia; permitiendoles descargár el dicho buque (si fuere necesario de sus

mitting them to unload the said Vessel, if necessary, of its merchandizes and effects, without exacting for it any duty, impost or contribution whatever, until they may be exported

ARTICLE NINTH. The Citizens of each of the contracting parties shall have power to dispose of their personal goods within the jurisdiction of the other, by sale, donation, testament or otherwise, and their representatives being Citizens of the other party, shall succeed to their said personal goods, whether by testament or ab intestato, and they may take possession thereof, either by themselves or others acting for them, and dispose of the same at their will, paying such dues only as the inhabitants of the Country wherein the said goods are, shall be subject to pay in like cases: And if in the case of real estate, the said heirs would be prevented from entering into the possession of the inheritance on account of their character of Aliens, there shall be granted to them, the term of three years to dispose of the same, as they may think proper and to withdraw the proceeds without molestation and exempt from all rights of detraction on the part of the government of the respective States.

mercaderias y efectos,) sin cobrar por esto hasta que sean esportados, ningun derecho, impuesto ó contribucion.

ART⁰ 9⁰ Los Ciudadanos de cada una de las partes contratantes, tendrán pleno podér para disponér de sus bienes personales dentro de la jurisdicción de la otra, por venta, donacion, testamento, ó de otro modo; y sus representantes, siendo ciudadanos de la otra parte, succederan á sus dichos bienes personales, ya sea por testamento ó *ab intestato*, y podran tomar posecion de ellos, ya sea por si mismos, ó por otros, que obren por ellos, y disponer de los mismos, segun su voluntad, pagando aquellas cargas solamente, que los habitantes del pais en donde estan los referidos bienes, estuvieren sujetos á pagar en iguales casos. Y si en el caso de bienes raices, los dichos herederos fuesen impedidos de entrár en la posecion de la herencia por razon de su caracter de estranjeros, se les dará el termino de tres años, para disponér de ella como juzguen conveniente, y para estraér el producto sin molestia, y esentos de todo derecho de deduccion, por parte del Gobierno de los respectivos estados.

ARTICLE TENTH. Both the Contracting parties promise and engage formally to give their special protection to the persons and property of the Citizens of each other of all occupations, who may be in the territories subject to the jurisdiction of the one or the other, transient or dwelling therein, leaving open and free to them the Tribunals of Justice for their Judicial recourse on the same terms, which are usual and customary with the natives or Citizens of the Country in which they may be; for which they may employ in defence of their rights, such advocates, solicitors, notaries, agents and factors as they may judge proper in all their trials at law; and such citizens or agents shall have free opportunity to be present at the decisions and sentences of the tribunals, in all cases which may concern them, and likewise at the taking of all examinations and evidence which may be exhibited in the said trials.

ARTICLE ELEVENTH. It is likewise agreed that the most perfect and entire security of Conscience shall be enjoyed by the citizens of both the contracting parties in the countries subject to the jurisdiction of the one and the other, without their being liable to be disturbed or molested on account of their religious belief,

ART? 10º Ambas partes contratantes se comprometen y obligan formalmente á dar su proteccion especial á las personas y propiedades de los ciudadanos de cada una reciprocamente transeuntes ó habitantes de todas ocupaciones, en los territorios sujetos á la jurisdiccion de una y otra, dejandoles abiertos y libres los Tribunales de justicia, para sus recursos judiciales, en los mismos terminos que son de uso y costumbre para los naturales ó Ciudadanos del pais en que residan; para lo cual, podran emplear en defensa de sus derechos aquellos Abogados, Procuradores, Escribanos, Ajentes, ó · Factores que juzguen conveniente, en todos sus asuntos y litijios; y dichos ciudadanos ó Ajentes tendrán la libre facultad de estar presentes en las decisiones y sentencias de los Tribunales, en todos los casos que les conciernan, como igualmente al tomar todos los examenes y declaraciones que se ofrezcan en los dichos litijios.

. ART? 11º Se conviene igualmente en que los ciudadanos de ambas partes contratantes gozen la mas perfecta y entera seguridad de conciencia en los paises sujetos á la jurisdiccion de una ú otra, sin quedar por ello espuestos á ser inquietados ó molestados en razon de su creencia relijiosa, mientras que

so long as they respect the laws and established usages of the Country. Moreover the bodies of the Citizens of one of the contracting parties, who may die in the territories of the other, shall be buried in the usual burying grounds or in other decent and suitable places, and shall be protected from violation or disturbance.

ARTICLE TWELFTH. It shall be lawful for the Citizens of the United States of America and of the Republic of Colombia to sail with their Ships with all manner of liberty and security, no distinction being made who are the proprietors of the merchandizes laden thereon, from any port to the places of those who now are or hereafter shall be at enmity with either of the Contracting parties. It shall likewise be lawful for the citizens aforesaid to sail with the ships and merchandizes beforementioned and to trade with the same liberty and security from the places, ports, and havens of those who are enemies of both or either party, without any oposition or disturbance whatsoever, not only directly from the places of the enemy beforementioned to neutral places, but also from one place belonging to an enemy to another place belonging to an enemy, whether they be under the jurisdiction of one power or

respeten las leyes y usos establecidos. Ademas de esto, podrán sepultarse los cadaveres de los Ciudadanos de una de las partes contratantes, que fallecieren en los territorios de la otra, en los cementerios acostumbrados, ó en otros lugares decentes, y adecuados, los cuales, serán protejidos contra toda violacion ó trastorno.

ART⁰ 12⁰ Será licito á los Ciudadanos de la republica de Colombia, y de los Estados Unidos de America, navegár con sus buques, con toda seguridad y libertad, de cualquiera puerto á las plazas ó lugares de los que son ó fueren en adelante enemigos de cualquiera de las dos partes contratantes, sin hacerse distincion de quienes son los dueños de las mercaderias cargadas en ellos. Será igualmente licito á los referidos ciudadanos navegár con sus buques y mercaderias mencionadas y traficár con la misma libertad y seguridad, de los lugares, puertos y ensenadas de los enemigos de ambas partes, ó de alguna de ellas, sin ninguna oposicion, ó disturbio cualquiera, no solo directamente de los lugares de enemigo arriba mencionados á lugares neutros, sino tambien de un lugar perteneciente á un enemigo, á otro enemigo, ya sea que esten bajo la jurisdiccion de una potencia, ó bajo la de diversas. Y queda aqui estipulado, que los buques

under several. And it is hereby stipulated that free Ships shall also give freedom to goods, and that every thing shall be deemed to be free and exempt, which shall be found on board the Ships belonging to the Citizens of either of the Contracting parties, although the whole lading or any part thereof should appertain to the enemies of either, Contraband goods being always excepted. It is also agreed in like manner that the same liberty be extended to persons, who are on board a free ship, with this effect that although they be enemies to both or either party, they are not to be taken out of that free Ship, unless they are officers or soldiers and in the actual service of the enemies; Provided however and it is hereby agreed that the stipulations in this Article contained declaring that the flag shall cover the property, shall be understood as applying to those powers only, who recognize this principle, but if either of the two contracting parties shall be at war with a third and the other neutral, the flag of the neutral shall cover the property of enemies, whose governments acknowledge this principle and not of others.

Article Thirteenth. It is likewise agreed that in the case, where the neutral flag of one of the contracting parties shall pro-

libres, dan tambien libertad á las mercaderias, y que se ha de considerár libre y esento todo lo que se hallare á bordo de los buques pertenecientes á los Ciudadanos de cualquiera de las partes contratantes, aunque toda la carga ó parte de ella pertenezca á enemigos de una ú otra, eceptuando siempre los articulos de contrabando de guerra. Se conviene tambien del mismo modo, en que la misma libertad se estienda á las personas que se encuentren á bordo de buques libres, con el fin de que aunque dichas personas sean enemigos de ambas partes ó de alguna de ellas, no deban ser estraidos de los buques libres, á menos que sean oficiales ó Soldados en actual servicio de los enemigos: á condicion no obstante, y se conviene aqui en esto, que las estipulaciones contenidas en el presente articulo, declarando que el Pabellon cubre la propiedad, se entenderán aplicables solamente á aquellas potencias que reconocen este principio; pero si alguna de las dos partes contratantes, estuviere en guerra con una tercera, y la otra permaneciese neutrál, la bandera de la neutrál cubrirá la propiedad de los enemigos, cuyos Gobiernos reconozcan este principio y no de otros.

Art⁰ 13⁰ Se conviene igualmente que en el caso de que la bandera neutrál de una de las partes contratantes proteja las

tect the property of the enemies of the other, by virtue of the above stipulation, it shall always be understood that the neutral property found on board such enemies' Vessels, shall be held and considered as enemies' property, and as such shall be liable to detention and confiscation, except such property as was put on board such vessel before the declaration of war, or even afterwards, if it were done without the knowledge of it, but the contracting parties agree that two months having elapsed after the declaration, their Citizens shall not plead ignorance thereof. On the contrary, if the flag of the neutral does not protect the enemy's property, in that case the goods and merchandizes of the neutral embarked in such enemy's ships, shall be free

ARTICLE FOURTEENTH. This liberty of Navigation and Commerce shall extend to all kinds of merchandizes excepting those only which are distinguished by the name of Contraband and under this name of Contraband or prohibited goods shall be comprehended; first, Cannons, mortars, howitzers, swivels, blunderbusses, muskets, fusees, rifles, Carbines, pistols, pikes, swords, sabres, lances, spears, halberds, and granades, bombs, powder, matches.

propiedades de los enemigos de la otra, en virtud de lo estipulado arriba, deberá siempre entenderse, que las propiedades neutrales encontradas á bordo de tales buques enemigos, han de tenerse y considerarse como propiedades enemigas, y como tales, estarán sujetas á detencion, y confiscacion; eceptuando solamente aquellas propiedades que hubiesen sido puestas á bordo de tales buques antes de la declaracion de la guerra, y aun despues, si hubiesen sido embarcadas en dichos buques, sin tenér noticia de la guerra, y se conviene, que pasados dos meses despues de la declaracion, los ciudadanos de una y otra parte no podrán alegár que la ignoraban. Por el contrario, si la bandera neutrál, no protejiese las propiedades enemigas, entonces serán libres los efectos y mercaderias de la parte neutrál, embarcadas en buques enemigos.

ART⁰ 14⁰ Esta libertad de navegacion y comercio se estenderá á todo jenero de mercaderias, eceptuando aquellas solamente, que se distinguen con el nombre de contrabando, y bajo este nombre de *contrabando* ó efectos prohibidos se comprenderán;

1⁰ Cañones, morteros, obuces, pedreros, trabucos, mosquetes, fusiles, rifles, carabinas, pistolas, picas, espadas, sables, lanzas, chuzos, alabardas y granadas,

balls, and all other things belonging to the use of these arms; Secondly, Bucklers, helmets, breast plates, coats of Mail, infantry belts, and clothes made up in the form and for a military use; thirdly, Cavalry-belts, and horses with their furniture; fourthly, And generally all kinds of arms and instruments of iron, steel, brass, and copper or of any other materials, manufactured, prepared, and formed expressly to make war by sea or land

ARTICLE FIFTEENTH. All other merchandizes and things not comprehended in the articles of contraband explicitly enumerated and classified as above, shall be held and considered as free, and subjects of free and lawful commerce, so that they may be carried and transported in the freest manner by both the Contracting parties even to places belonging to an enemy, excepting only those places which are at that time beseiged or blocked up; And to avoid all doubt in this particular it is declared that those places only are beseiged or blockaded, which are actually attacked by a belligerent force capable of preventing the entry of the Neutral

bombas, polvora, mechas, balas, con las demas cosas correspondientes al uso de estas armas.

2º Escudos, casquetes, corazas, cotas de malla, fornituras y vestidos hechos en forma, y á usanza militar.

3º Bandoleras y caballos junto con sus armas y arneses.

4º Y jeneralmente toda especie de armas, ó instrumentos de hierro, acero, bronce, cobre, y otras materias cualesquiera, manufacturadas, preparadas, y formadas espresamente para hacér la guerra por mar, ó tierra.

ART.º 15º Todas las demas mercaderias, y efectos no comprendidos en los articulos de contrabando esplicitamente enumerados, y clasificados en el articulo anterior, serán tenidos, y reputados por libres, y de licito y libre comercio, de modo que ellos puedan sér transportados, y llevados de la manera mas libre, por los ciudadanos de ambas partes contratantes, aun á los lugares pertenecientes á un enemigo de una ú otra, eceptuando solamente aquellos lugares ó plazas, que están al mismo tiempo sitiadas ó bloqueadas: y para evitar toda duda en el particulár, se declaran sitiadas ó bloqueadas áquellas plazas, que en la actualidad estuviesen átacadas por una fuerza de un belijerante, capaz de impedir la entrada del neutrál.

ARTICLE SIXTEENTH. The articles of Contraband before enumerated and classified which may be found in a Vessel bound for an enemy's port, shall be subject to detention and confiscation, leaving free the rest of the cargo and the ship, that the owners may dispose of them as they see proper. No vessel of either of the two nations shall be detained on the high seas on account of having on board, articles of Contraband whenever the Master, Captain, or Supercargo of said Vessel will deliver up the Articles of Contraband to the Captor, unless the quantity of such Articles be so great and of so large a bulk, that they cannot be received on board the Capturing Ship without great inconvenience; but in this and in all other cases of just detention, the vessel detained shall be sent to the nearest convenient, and safe port for trial and judgement according to law

ARTICLE SEVENTEENTH. And whereas it frequently happens that Vessels sail for a port or place belonging to an enemy without knowing that the same is beseiged, blockaded, or invested, it is agreed that every vessel so circumstanced may be turned away from such port or place, but shall not be detained, nor shall any part of her cargo, if not Contraband, be confiscated

ART⁰ 16⁰ Los articulos de contrabando antes enumerados y clasificados, que se hallen en un buque destinado á puerto enemigo, estarán sujetos á detencion y confiscacion, dejando libre el resto del cargamento y el buque, para que los dueños puedan disponér de ellos como lo crean conveniente. Ningun buque de cualquiera de las dos naciones, será detenido, por tenér á bordo articulos de contrabando, siempre que el Maestre, Capitan, ó Sobrecarga de dicho buque quiera entregár los articulos de contrabando al apresador, á menos que la cantidad de estos articulos sea tan grande y de tanto volumen, que no puedan sér recibidos á bordo del buque apresadór, sin grandes inconvenientes; pero en este como en todos los otros casos de justa detencion, el buque detenido será enviado al puerto mas inmediato, comodo, y seguro, para ser juzgado y sentenciado conforme á las leyes.

ART⁰ 17⁰ Y por cuanto frecuentemente sucede que los buques navegan para un puerto ó lugár perteneciente á un enemigo, sin saber que aquél esté sitiado, bloqueado ó envestido, se conviene en que todo buque en estas circunstancias se pueda hacer volver de dicho puerto, ó lugar; pero no será detenido, ni confiscada parte alguna de su cargamento, no siendo contrabando; á

unless after warning of such blockade or investment from the commanding officer of the blockading forces, she shall again attempt to enter, but she shall be permitted to go to any other port or place she shall think proper. Nor shall any Vessel of either that may have entered into such port before the same was actually beseiged, blockaded, or invested by the other, be restrained from quitting such place with her cargo, nor if found therein after the reduction and surrender shall such vessel or her cargo be liable to Confiscation, but they shall be restored to the owners thereof.

ARTICLE EIGHTEENTH. In order to prevent all kind of disorder in the visiting and examination of the Ships and Cargos of both the Contracting parties on the high seas, they have agreed mutually that whenever a Vessel of War, public or private, shall meet with a neutral of the other Contracting party, the first shall remain out of Cannon shot, and may send its boat with two or three men only in order to execute the said examination of the papers concerning the ownership and Cargo of the vessel, without causing the least extortion, violence, or ill treatment, for which the Commanders of the said armed ships shall be responsible with

menos que despues de la intimacion de semejante bloqueo ó ataque, por el comandante de las fuerzas bloqueadoras, intentase otra vez entrar; pero le será permitido ir á cualquiera otro puerto ó lugár que juzgue conveniente. Ni ningun buque de una de las partes, que haya entrado en semejante puerto, ó lugár, antes que estuviese sitiado, bloqueado, ó envestido por la otra, será impedido de dejár el tal lugár con su cargamento, ni si fuere hallado allí despues de la rendicion y entrega de semejante lugár, estará el tal buque ó su cargamento sujeto á confiscacion, sino que serán restituidos á sus dueños.

ART⁰ 18⁹ Para evitár todo jenero de desorden en la visita, y examen de los buques y cargamentos de ambas partes contratantes en alta már, han convenido mutuamente, que siempre que un buque de guerra, publico ó particular se encontrase con un neutral de la otra parte contratante, el primero permanecerá fuera de tiro de cañon, y podrá mandár su bote, con dos ó tres hombres solamente, para ejecutár el dicho examen de los papeles concernientes á la propiedad y carga del buque, sin ocasionár la menor estorcion, violencia ó mal tratamiento, por lo que los comandantes del dicho buque armado serán responsables, con sus per-

their persons and property; for which purpose the Commanders of said private armed Vessels shall before receiving their commissions, give sufficient security to answer for all the damages they may Commit. And it is expressly agreed that the neutral party shall in no case be required to go on board the examining vessel for the purpose of exhibiting her papers or for any other purpose whatever

ARTICLE NINETEENTH. To avoid all Kind of Vexation and abuse in the examination of the papers relating to the ownership of the Vessels belonging to the Citizens of the two Contracting parties, they have agreed and do agree, that in case one of them should be engaged in War, the Ships and Vessels belonging to the Citizens of the other, must be furnished with sea-letters or passports expressing the name, property, and bulk of the Ship, as also the name and place of habitation of the Master or Commander of said Vessel, in order that it may thereby appear that the Ship really and truly belongs to the Citizens of one of the parties; they have likewise agreed that such Ships being laden, besides the said sea-letters or passports, shall also be provided with certificates containing the several particulars of the Cargo and the

sonas y bienes; á cuyo efecto los comandantes de buques armados por cuenta de particulares, estarán obligados antes de entregarseles sus comisiones ó patentes, á dar fianza suficiente para respondér de los perjuicios que causen. Y se ha convenido espresamente, que en ningun caso se exijirá á la parte neutrál, que vaya á bordo del buque examinadór con el fin de exibir sus papeles, ó para cualquiera otro objeto sea el que fuere.

ART° 19° Para evitár toda clase de vejamen y abuso en el examen de los papeles relativos á la propiedad de los buques pertenecientes á los ciudadanos de las dos partes contratantes, han convenido y convienen, que en caso de que una de ellas estuviere en guerra, los buques, y bajeles pertenecientes á los ciudadanos de la otra, serán provistos con letras de már, ó pasaportes, espresando el nombre, propiedad y tamaño del buque, como tambien el nombre y lugar de la residencia del Maestre, ó Comandante, á fin de que se vea que el buque, real y verdaderamente pertenece á los ciudadanos de una de las partes; y han convenido igualmente, que estando cargados los espresados buques, ademas de las letras de mar, ó pasaportes, estarán tambien provistos de certificatos, que contengan los pormenores del cargamento, y el

place whence the ship sailed, so that it may be known whether any forbidden or Contraband goods be on board the same; which Certificates shall be made out by the officers of the place, whence the Ship sailed in the accustomed form; without which requisites said Vessel may be detained to be adjudged by the Competent tribunal and may be declared legal prize, unless the said defect shall be satisfied or supplied by testimony entirely equivalent

ARTICLE TWENTIETH. It is further agreed that the stipulations above expressed relative to the visiting and examination of Vessels shall apply only to those which sail without Convoy, and when said Vessels shall be under Convoy, the verbal declaration of the Commander of the Convoy on his word of honour, that the Vessels under his protection belong to the Nation whose flag he carries, and when they are bound to an enemy's port, that they have no Contraband goods on board, shall be sufficient.

ARTICLE TWENTY FIRST. It is further agreed that in all cases the established Courts for prize Causes in the Country, to which the prizes may be conducted, shall alone take Cognizance of them. And whenever such tribunal of

lugar de donde salió el buque, para que asi pueda saberse, si hay á su bordo algunos efectos prohibidos ó de contrabando, cuyos certificatos serán hechos por los oficiales del lugár de la procedencia del buque, en la forma acostumbrada, sin cuyos requisitos el dicho buque puede ser detenido, para ser juzgado por el Tribunál competente, y puede ser declarado buena presa, á menos que satisfagan, ó suplan el defecto con testimonios enteramente equivalentes.

ART° 20° Se ha convenido ademas, que las estipulaciones anteriores, relativas al examen y visita de buques, se aplicarán solamente á los que navegan sin conboy y que cuando los dichos buques estuvieren bajo de conboy, será bastante la declaracion verbal del Comandante del conboy, bajo su palabra de honór, de que los buques que están bajo su proteccion pertenecen á la nacion, cuya bandera llevan, y cuando se dirijen á un puerto enemigo, que los dichos buques, no tienen á su bordo articulos de contrabando de guerra.

ART° 21° Se ha convenido ademas, que en todos los casos que ocurran, solo los Tribunales establecidos para causas de presas, en el pais á que las presas sean conducidas, tomarán conocimiento de ellas. Y siempre que seme-

either party shall pronounce judgement against any vessel or goods or property claimed by the Citizens of the other party, the sentence or decree shall mention the reasons or motives, on which the same shall have been founded and an authenticated copy of the sentence or decree and of all the proceedings in the case shall, if demanded, be delivered to the Commander or Agent of Said Vessel, without any delay, he paying the legal fees for the same

ARTICLE TWENTY SECOND. Whenever one of the Contracting parties shall be engaged in War with another State, no Citizen of the other Contracting party shall accept a commission or letter of Marque for the purpose of assisting or cooperating hostilely with the said enemy against the said party so at War under the pain of being treated as a pirate

ARTICLE TWENTY THIRD. If by any fatality, which cannot be expected and which God forbid, the two Contracting parties should be engaged in a War with each other, they have agreed and do agree, now for then, that there shall be allowed the term of Six months to the Merchants residing on the Coasts and in the ports of each other, and the term of one year to those who dwell in the Interior to arrange their business

jante Tribunal de cualquiera de las partes, pronunciase sentencia contra algun buque, ó efectos, ó propiedad reclamada por los Ciudadanos de la otra parte, la sentencia o decreto hará mencion de las razones ó motivos en que aquella se haya fundado, y se entregará sin demora alguna al comandante ó Ajente de dicho buque, si lo solicitase, un testimonio autentico de la sentencia, ó decreto, ó de todo el proceso, pagando por él los derechos legales.

ART? 22? Siempre que una de las partes contratantes, estuviere empeñada en guerra, con otro estado, ningun Ciudadano de la otra parte contratante, aceptará una comision ó letra de marca para el objeto de ayudár ó cooperar hostilmente con el dicho enemigo, contra la dicha parte que esté así en guerra, bajo la pena de ser tratado como pirata.

ART? 23? Si por alguna fatalidad, que no puede esperarse, y que Dios no permita, las dos partes contratantes se viesen empeñadas en guerra una con otra, han convenido y convienen de ahora para entonces, que se concederá el termino de seis meses á los comerciantes residentes en las costas y en los puertos de entrambas, y el termino de un año á los que habitan en el interior, para arreglár sus negocios, y

and transport their effects wherever they please, giving to them the safe conduct necessary for it, which may serve as a sufficient protection until they arrive at the designated port. The citizens of all other occupations, who may be established in the territories or dominions of the United States and of the Republic of Colombia, shall be respected and maintained in the full enjoyment of their personal liberty and property, unless their particular Conduct shall cause them to forfeit this protection, which in consideration of humanity, the contracting parties engage to give them

ARTICLE TWENTY FOURTH. Neither the debts due from Individuals of the one nation to the individuals of the other, nor shares, nor moneys which they may have in public funds nor in public or private banks, shall ever in any event of War or of National difference be sequestered or confiscated.

ARTICLE TWENTY FIFTH. Both the Contracting parties being desirous of avoiding all inequality in relation to their public communications and official intercourse have agreed and do agree to grant to the envoys, Ministers and other public Agents, the same favours, immunities and exemptions, which those of the most favoured nation do or shall enjoy; it being understood that

transportár sus efectos á donde quieran, dandoles el salvo conducto necesario para ello, que les sirva de suficiente proteccion hasta que lleguen al puerto que designen. Los Ciudadanos de otras ocupaciones, que se hallen establecidos en los territorios ó dominios de la republica de Colombia, ó los Estados Unidos de America, serán respetados, y mantenidos en el pleno goze de su libertad personal y propiedad, á menos que su conducta particular les haga perdér esta proteccion, que en consideracion á la humanidad, las partes contratantes se comprometen a prestarles.

ART? 24? Ni las deudas contraidas por los individuos de una nacion, con los individuos de la otra, ni las acciones ó dineros, que puedan tenér en los fondos publicos, ó en los bancos publicos, ó privados, serán jamas secuestrados ó confiscados en ningun caso de guerra, ó diferencia nacional.

ART? 25? Deseando ambas partes contratantes, evitár toda diferencia, relativa á etiqueta en sus comunicaciones, y correspondencias diplomaticas han convenido asi mismo, y convienen en concedér á sus Enviados, Ministros, y otros Ajentes Diplomaticos, los mismos favores, inmunidades, y esenciones de que gozan, ó gozaren en lo venidero los de las naciones mas favorecidas, bien

whatever favours, immunities or privileges, the United States of America or the Republic of Colombia may find it proper to give to the Ministers and public Agents of any other power, shall by the same act be extended to those of each of the Contracting parties

ARTICLE TWENTY SIXTH. To make more effectual the protection, which the United States and the Republic of Colombia shall afford in future to the navigation and Commerce of the Citizens of each other, they agree to receive and admit Consuls and Vice Consuls in all the ports open to foreign Commerce, who shall enjoy in them all the rights, prerogatives, and immunities of the Consuls and Vice Consuls of the most favoured Nation, each Contracting party however remaining at liberty to except those ports and places, in which the admission and residence of Such Consuls may not seem convenient.

ARTICLE TWENTY SEVENTH. In order that the Consuls and Vice Consuls of the two Contracting parties may enjoy the rights, prerogatives, and immunities, which belong to them by their public Character, they shall before entering on the exercise of their functions, exhibit their Commis-

entendido que cualquier favór, inmunidad ó privilejio, que la Republica de Colombia ó los Estados Unidos de America, tengan por conveniente dispensár á los Enviados, Ministros, y Ajentes Diplomaticos de otras Potencias, se haga por el mismo hecho estensivo á los de una y otra de las partes contratantes.

ARTọ 26ọ Para hacér mas efectiva la proteccion, que la republica de Colombia, y los Estados Unidos de America, darán en adelante á la navegacion y comercio de los Ciudadanos de una y otra, se convienen en recibir y admitir Consules, y Vice-Consules en todos los puertos abiertos al comercio estranjero, quienes gozarán en ellos todos los derechos, prerrogativas ó inmunidades de los Consules, y Vice-Consules de la nacion mas favorecida, quedando no obstante en libertad cada parte contratante, para eceptuar aquellos puertos y lugares en que la admision y residencia de semejantes Consules, y Vice-Consules no parezca conveniente.

Artọ 27ọ Para que los Consules, y Vice-Consules de las dos partes contratantes, puedan gozár los derechos, prerrogativas, ó inmunidades, que les corresponden por su caracter publico, antes de entrár en el ejercicio de sus funciones, presentarán su comision ó patente en la forma debida,

sion or patent in due form to the Government, to which they are accredited, and having obtained their Exequatur, they shall be held and considered as such by all the Authorities, Magistrates and inhabitants in the Consular district in which they reside

ARTICLE TWENTY EIGHTH. It is likewise agreed that the Consuls, their Secretaries, officers and persons attached to the service of Consuls, they not being Citizens of the Country in which the Consul resides, shall be exempt from all public Service and also from all kind of taxes, imposts, and contributions, except those which they shall be obliged to pay on account of Commerce or their property, to which the Citizens and inhabitants native and foreign of the Country in which they reside are subject, being in every thing besides, subject to the laws of the respective states. The Archives and papers of the Consulates shall be respected inviolably, and under no pretext whatever, shall any Magistrate seize or in any way interfere with them.

ARTICLE TWENTY NINTH. The said Consuls shall have power to require the assistance of the Authorities of the Country, for the arrest, detention, and custody of deserters from the public and private Vessels of their Country,

al Gobierno con quien esten acreditados, y habiendo obtenido el *exequatur*, seran tenidos, y considerados como tales, por todas las autoridades, majistrados y habitantes del distrito Consulár en que residan.

ART? 28? Se ha convenido igualmente, que los Consules, sus secretarios oficiales y personas agregadas al servicio de los Consulados (no siendo estas personas Ciudadanos del pais en que el consul reside) estarán esentos de todo servicio publico, y tambien de toda especie de pechos, impuestos, y contribuciones, eceptuando aquellas que esten obligados á pagár por razon de comercio, ó propiedad, y á las cuales estan sujetos los Ciudadanos, y habitantes naturales, y estranjeros del pais en que residen, quedando en todo lo demas, sujetos á las leyes de los respectivos Estados. Los archivos y papeles de los consulados serán respetados inviolablemente, y bajo ningun pretesto los ocupará majistrado alguno, ni tendrá en ellos ninguna intervencion.

ART? 29. Los dichos consules tendrán podér de requerir el auxilio de las autoridades locales, para la prision, detencion y custodia de los desertores de buques publicos y particulares de su pais, y para este objeto se dirijirán á los

and for that purpose, they shall address themselves to the Courts, judges, and officers competent, and shall demand the said deserters in writing, proving by an exhibition of the Registers of the Vessels, or Ships roll, or other public documents, that those men were part of the said Crews; and on this demand so proved, (saving however where the contrary is proved) the delivery shall not be refused. Such deserters when arrested shall be put at the disposal of the said Consuls, and may be put in the public prisons at the request and expense of those who reclaim them, to be sent to the Ships, to which they belonged or to others of the same nation. But if they be not sent back within two months, to be counted from the day of their arrest, they shall be set at liberty, and shall be no more arrested for the same cause.

ARTICLE THIRTIETH. For the purpose of more effectually protecting their Commerce and navigation, the two Contracting parties do hereby agree as soon hereafter as circumstances will permit them, to form a Consular Convention, which shall declare specially the powers and immunities of the Consuls and Vice Consuls of the respective parties.

ARTICLE THIRTY FIRST. The United States of America and the Republic of Colombia desiring

Tribunales, Jueces, y oficiales competentes, y pedirán los dichos desertores por escrito, probando por una presentacion de los rejistros de los buques, rol del equipaje, u otros documentos publicos, que aquellos hombres eran parte de las dichas tripulaciones, y á esta demanda asi probada (menos no obstante cuando se probare lo contrario) no se reusará la entrega. Semejantes desertores, luego que sean arrestados, se pondrán á disposicion de los dichos Consules, y pueden ser depositados en las prisiones publicas, á solicitud y espensas de los que los reclamen, para ser enviados á los buques á que corresponden, ó á otros de la misma nacion. Pero sinó fueren mandados dentro de dos meses contados desde el dia de su arresto, serán puestos en libertad, y no volverán á ser presos por la misma causa.

ARTº 30º Para protejér mas efectivamente su comercio y navegacion, las dos partes contratantes se convienen en formar luego que las circunstancias lo permitan, una convencion Consulár, que declare mas especialmente los poderes é inmunidades de los consules y Vice-Consules de las partes respectivas.

ARTº 31º La republica de Colombia y los Estados Unidos de America, deseando hacer tan du-

to make as durable as Circumstances will permit, the relations which are to be established between the two parties by virtue of this Treaty or general Convention of peace, amity, Commerce and Navigation, have declared solemnly and do agree to the following points; first, The present treaty shall remain in full force and virtue for the term of twelve years, to be counted from the day of the exchange of the ratifications, in all the parts relating to commerce and navigation; and in all those parts, which relate to peace and friendship, it shall be permanently and perpetually binding on both powers; secondly, If any one or more of the Citizens of either party shall infringe any of the articles of this treaty, such citizen shall be held personally responsible for the same, and the harmony and good correspondence between the two nations, shall not be interrupted thereby, each party engaging in no way to protect the offender or sanction such violation; thirdly, If (what indeed cannot be expected) unfortunately any of the articles contained in the present treaty, shall be violated or infringed in any other way whatever, it is expressly stipulated that neither of the contracting parties will order or authorize any acts of reprisal nor declare War against the other, on complaints of injuries or damages, until the

raderas y firmes, como las circunstancias lo permitan, las relaciones que han de establecerse entre las dos Potencias, en virtud del presente tratado ó convencion jenerál de paz, amistad, navegacion y comercio, han declarado solennemente y convienen en los puntos siguientes:

1º El presente tratado permanecerá en su fuerza y vigór por el termino de doce años contados desde el dia del canje de las ratificaciones, en todos los puntos concernientes á comercio y navegacion, y en todos los demas puntos que se refieren á paz y amistad, será permanente, y perpetuamente obligatorio para ambas potencias.

2º Si alguno, ó algunos de los Ciudadanos de una ú otra parte infrinjiesen alguno de los articulos contenidos en el presente tratado, dichos ciudadanos serán personalmente responsables, sin que por esto se interrumpa la harmonia y buena correspondencia entre las dos naciones, comprometiendose cada una á no protejér de modo alguno al ofensor, ó sancionár semejante violacion.

3º Si (lo que á la verdad no puede esperarse) desgraciadamente, alguno de los articulos contenidos en el presente tratado, fuesen en alguna otra manera violados, ó infrinjidos, se estipula espresamente que ninguna de las dos partes contratantes, ordenará, ó autorizará ningunos actos de

said party considering itself offended shall first have presented to the other a statement of such injuries or damages verified by competent proof, and demanded justice and satisfaction, and the same shall have been either refused or unreasonably delayed; fourthly, Nothing in this treaty contained shall however be construed or operate contrary to former and existing public treaties with other sovereigns or States. The present treaty of peace, Amity, Commerce and Navigation shall be approved and ratified by the President of the United States of America by and with the advice and consent of the Senate thereof, and by the President of the Republic of Colombia with the consent and approbation of the Congress of the same, and the ratifications shall be exchanged in the City of Washington within eight months to be counted from the date of the signature hereof, or sooner if possible

In faith whereof We the plenipotentiaries of the United States of America and of the Republic of Colombia have signed and sealed these presents.

Done in the city of Bogota on the third day of October in the

represalia, ni declarará la guerra contra la otra por quejas de injurias, ó daños, hasta que la parte que se crea ofendida, haya antes presentado á la otra una esposicion de aquellas injurias, ó daños, verificada con pruebas y testimonios competentes, exijiendo justicia y satisfaccion, y esto haya sido negado, ó diferido sin razon.

4º Nada de cuanto se contiene en el presente tratado, se construirá sin embargo, ni obrará, en contra de otros tratados publicos anteriores, y existentes con otros Soberanos ó Estados.

El presente tratado de paz, amistad, navegacion, y comercio, será ratificado por el Presidente ó vice-Presidente de la republica de Colombia, encargado del podér Ejecutivo, con consentimiento y aprobacion del Congreso de la misma, y por el Presidente de los Estados Unidos de America, con consejo, y consentimiento del Senado de los mismos; y las ratificaciones serán canjeadas en la ciudad de Washington dentro de ocho meses contados desde este dia, ó antes si fuese posible.

En fé de lo cual, nosotros los Plenipotenciarios de la republica de Colombia, y de los Estados Unidos de America hemos firmado y sellado las presentes

Dadas en la Ciudad de Bogota el dia tres de Octubre del año del

year of our Lord one thousand
eight hundred and twenty four;
in the forty ninth year of the
independence of the United States
of America, and the fourteenth of
that of the Republic of Colombia.
[Seal]
   RICHARD CLOUGH ANDERSON JR
[Seal]
   PEDRO GUAL.

Señor mil ochocientos veinticua-
tro, decimo cuarto de la independencia de la republica de Colombia y cuadrajesimo nono de la
de los Estados Unidos de America.

(L. S.)
   PEDRO GUAL.
(L. S.)
   RICHARD CLOUGH ANDERSON.

NOTES

The Republic of Colombia, with which this treaty was made, then included Venezuela and Ecuador, a union from which Venezuela withdrew in 1829 and Ecuador in 1830. There followed, in November, 1831, the founding of the "State of New Granada," which, in May, 1834, adopted as its official designation the title, "Republic of New Granada." In 1858 the title was changed to the "Granadan Confederation"; by a *Pacto de Unión* of 1861 the title was changed to the "United States of Colombia"; and in 1885 the present designation, the "Republic of Colombia," was adopted (Robertson, History of the Latin-American Nations, 359–84).

On February 20, 1821, Manuel Torres addressed the Secretary of State, enclosing his credentials as "Agent and Chargé des Affaires of the Republic of Colombia" and requesting recognition of his credentials and of the independence of Colombia (D. S., 1 Notes from the Colombian Legation, pt. 2). That note was not answered until May 23, 1822, when Secretary of State John Quincy Adams wrote as follows (D. S., 3 Notes to Foreign Legations, 104):

I have the honor of informing you, by direction of the President of the United States, that he will receive you in the character of Chargé d'Affaires from the Republic of Colombia, whenever it may suit your convenience, and be compatible with the state of your health to repair to this place for that purpose.

The formal act of recognition of the Republic of Colombia by the United States took place on June 19, 1822, when Secretary of State Adams presented Torres to President Monroe. That occasion is described in the Memoirs of John Quincy Adams, VI, 23–24.

The instructions to Richard Clough Anderson, jr., Minister to Colombia, regarding the negotiation of this treaty, were under date of May 27, 1823 (D. S., 9 Instructions, U. S. Ministers, 274–312; printed in part in American State Papers, Foreign Relations, V, 888–97). The following narrative of the events leading up to the

recognition of the Republic of Colombia by the United States on June 19, 1822, is extracted therefrom:

In the history of South American Independence there are two periods clearly distinguishable from each other. The first, that of its origin, when it was rather a War of Independence against France than against Spain; and the second from the restoration of Ferdinand the 7th. in 1814. Since that period the Territories now constituting the Republic of Colombia have been the only Theatre upon which Spain has been able to maintain the conflict offensively with even a probable colour of ultimate success. But when in 1815 she made her greatest effort in the expedition from Cadiz, commanded by Morillo, Mexico, Peru, and Chili were yet under her authority, and had she succeeded in reducing the Coast of Terra Firma, and New Grendada, the Provinces of La Plata divided among themselves, and weakened by the Portuguese occupation of Montevideo, would probably not have held out against her long. This at least was the calculation of her Policy, and from the Geographical position of these Countries, which may be termed the heart of South America, the conclusion might well be drawn, that if the Power of Spain could not be firmly reseated there, it must be on her part a fruitless struggle, to maintain her supremacy in any part of the American Continent.

The expedition of Morillo, on its first arrival was attended with signal success. Carthagena was taken. The whole coast of Terra Firma was occupied, and New Grenada was entirely subdued. A remnant of Patriots in Venezuela, with their leader Bolivar, returning from expulsion revived the cause of Independence, and after the Campaign of 1819, in which they reconquered the whole of New Grenada, the demonstration became complete, that every effort of Spain to recover the South American Continent, must thenceforward be a desperate waste of her own resources, and that the truest friendship of other Nations to her would consist in making her sensible that her own interest would be best consulted, by the acknowledgment of that Independence, which she could no longer effectually dispute.

.   .   .   .

The reconquest in the campaign of 1819 of New Grenada to the Patriot cause, was immediately followed by the formation of the Republic of Colombia, consisting of three great divisions of the preceeding Spanish Government, Venezuela, Cundinamarca [Colombia], and Quito [Ecuador]. It was soon succeeded by the dissolution of the Spanish authority in Mexico, by the Revolution, in Spain itself, and by the Military operations which resulted in the Declaration of Independence in Peru. In November 1820 was concluded the Armistice between the Generals Morillo and Bolivar, together with a subsequent Treaty stipulating that in case of the renewal of the War, the parties would abstain from all hostilities and practices, not consistent with the modern Law of Nations, and the humane maxims of civilization. In February 1821, the partial Independence of Mexico was proclaimed at Yguala, and in August of the same year was recognized by the Spanish Vice-Roy, and Captain General O'Donoju at Cordova.

The formation of the Republic of Colombia by the fundamental Laws of the 17th. December 1819 was notified to this Government by its Agent, the late Don. Manuel Torres on the 20th. February 1821, with a request that it might be recognized by the Government of the United States, and a proposal for the negotiation of Treaties of Commerce, and Navigation, *founded upon the bases of reciprocal utility and perfect equality*, as the most efficacious means of strengthening, and encreasing the relations of amity between the two Republics.

The request and proposal were renewed in a Letter from Mr Torres of the 30 November 1821, and again repeated on the 2^d January 1822. In the interval since the first demand, the General Congress of the new Republic, had assembled, and formed a Constitution [August 30, 1821], founded upon the principles of popular Representation, and divided into Legislative, Executive, and Judicial authorities. The Government under this constitution had been organized, and was in full operation; while during the same period, the principal remnant of the Spanish force had been destroyed by the battle of Carabobo, and its last fragments were confined to the two places of Porto Cabello and Panama.

Under these circumstances, a Resolution of the House of Representatives of the United States on the 30th. January 1822, requested of the President to lay before the House the communications from the Agents of the United States, with the Governments south of the United States which had declared their Independence; and those from the Agents of such Governments here, with the Secretary of State, tending to shew the political condition of their Governments, and the state of the War between them and Spain. In transmitting to the House the papers called for by this Resolution the President by his Message of the 8th. March 1822, declared his own persuasion that the time had arrived when in strict conformity to the Law of Nations, and in the fulfilment of the duties of equal and impartial justice to all parties, the acknowledgment of the Independence declared by Spanish American Colonies could no longer be withheld. Both houses of Congress having almost unanimously concurred with these views of the President, an appropriation was made by Law (4 May 1822) for such Missions to the Independent Nations on the American Continent, as the President should deem proper.

. . . . . .

On the 17ᵗʰ [19th] of June 1822 Mʳ Manuel Torres was received by the President of the United States as the Charge d'Affaires from the Republic of Colombia, and the immediate consequence of our recognition was the admission of the Vessels of the South American Nations under their own colours into the ports of the principal maritime nations of Europe.

There have been two views as to the date on which the existence of the Republic of Colombia began (Moore, International Arbitrations, IV, 3494, 3524–27, 3542–44). Two "fundamental laws" were enacted for the union of Venezuela and New Granada, one on December 17, 1819, and the other on July 12, 1821. It may be noted, however, that, as stated in the instructions above quoted, the first request for the recognition by this Government of the Republic of Colombia was made on February 20, 1821. Ecuador joined the constituted union in 1822.

The "Fundamental Law of the Union of the People of Colombia," dated July 12, 1821 (Spanish text in Cuerpo de leyes de la República de Colombia, 1–2; English translation in Niles' Weekly Register, XXI, 219–20), provided, among other things, that "the present congress of the republic will frame the constitution of the republic." The first constitution was accordingly drawn up and signed on August 30, 1821. The text thereof, in Spanish, is in Cuerpo de leyes de la República de Colombia, 3–21.

THE NEGOTIATIONS

The papers which accompanied the presidential message of February 21, 1825, transmitting this treaty to the Senate, are printed in American State Papers, Foreign Relations, V, 696–729. They include a somewhat detailed account of the negotiations at Bogotá.

In the instructions of May 27, 1823, above mentioned, it was asserted (D. S., 9 Instructions, U. S. Ministers, 307–8; American State Papers, Foreign Relations, V, 896) that in respect of the principle that free ships make free goods, Colombia was bound by the treaty of 1795 with Spain (Document 18):

How stands it between us and the Republic of Colombia on the ground of *Conventional* Law? By a Treaty between the United States and Spain concluded at a

time when Colombia was a part of the Spanish dominions, and so far as the *Spanish* Laws would admit enjoyed the benefit of its stipulations, the principles that free ships should make free goods was expressly recognized, and established. Is it asserted that by her declaration of Independence, Colombia has been entirely released from *all* the obligations by which as a part of the Spanish Nation she was bound to *other* Nations? This principle is not tenable. To all the engagements of Spain with other nations affecting their rights and interests, Colombia so far as she was affected by them, remains bound in honour and in justice. The stipulation now referred to, is of that character, and the United States besides the natural right of protecting by force in their vessels on the seas, the property of their friends, though enemies of the Republic of Colombia, have the additional claim to the benefit of the principle by an express compact with Spain made when Colombia was a Spanish Country. Again; by the late Treaty of 22 February 1819 [Document 41], between the United States and Spain it is agreed that the 15th. Article of the Treaty of 1795, in which it is stipulated that the flag shall cover the property, shall be so understood with respect to those powers who recognise the principle; but if either of the two contracting parties shall be at War, with a third party, and the other neutral, the flag of the neutral shall cover the property of enemies whose Government acknowledge the principle, and not the others.

This Treaty having been concluded after the Territories now composing the Republic of Colombia had ceased to acknowledge the authority of Spain, they are not parties to it, but their rights and duties in relation to the subject matter of it, remain as they had existed before it was made. Nor will she be affected by it at all, if she continues to acknowledge in her new national character, and with reference to the United States the principle that free ships make free goods which was the Conventional Law between them while Colombia was a part of Spain.

Anderson reported on August 20, 1824, that no occasion had then arisen to bring up "the question how far this Government was already bound by the stipulations of our treaty with Spain, made while Colombia was a component part of the monarchy" (American State Papers, Foreign Relations, V, 704); and it seems that it was not discussed during the negotiation, although the treaties between the United States and Spain were referred to by way of argument (*ibid.*, 708).

FORM OF THE TREATY

This agreement is frequently called a convention, following the wording of its heading, "General Convention of Peace, Amity, Navigation, and Commerce"; it is so styled in the presidential message of February 21, 1825, and in the Senate resolution of March 3 (Executive Journal, III, 416, 424), in both instruments of ratification, in the certificate of exchange of ratifications, and in the proclamation; but it might correctly have been called a treaty, as it is in the presidential message to Congress of December 6, 1825 (American State Papers, Foreign Relations, V, 761), and in various places in the agreement itself. The preamble speaks of "a treaty or General Convention," and in Article 31 the expression "this treaty" or "the present treaty" occurs six times. Considering this use of the word "treaty" in the document itself, and in view of the fact that the agreement has, in the strictest sense of the word, every form of a treaty, it is referred to as such in the headnote and in these notes.

In neither the English nor the Spanish text is the title of the treaty consistently given in the four places in each where it is mentioned. In the English text it is written "General Convention of Peace, Amity, Navigation, and Commerce" in the heading; "treaty or General Convention of peace, friendship, Commerce, and Navigation" in the preamble; and "Treaty or general Convention of peace, amity, Commerce and Navigation" and "treaty of peace, Amity, Commerce and Navigation" in Article 31.

This was the earliest treaty made between the United States and any country of Latin America. Its language became in large part a model for the future; the instance next in date is the treaty of December 5, 1825, with the Central American Federation (Document 50), thirty articles of which are taken almost literally from this treaty. Articles 3–5 of that treaty with the Central American Federation, however, constitute a basis in respect of trade, commerce, and navigation importantly different from that of this treaty (Article 3).

The File Papers

There were two originals of this treaty signed; and the principle of the *alternat* was duly observed, as the printed texts and signatures show; but one original was in English only, for the Government of the United States, and the other was in Spanish only, for the Government of Colombia. Certified copies of the respective originals were exchanged. A protocol of October 2, 1824 (original enclosed with the despatch of Anderson of October 8, 1824, D. S., 3 Despatches, Colombia, No. 19; printed in American State Papers, Foreign Relations, V, 729), thus states the procedure:

In compliance with what had been said at the close of the fifth conference, the two Plenipotentiaries presented in English & Castilian as previously agreed and corrected, the Treaty or General convention of peace, amity, navigation and commerce, in the terms in which it had been arranged, and having examined it carefully and compared the English with the Castilian Copy, they found them correct and conformable to the alterations and additions which had been respectively proposed in the course of the Negotiation, and thereupon they resolved to place their signatures and affix their seals the next day, that is to say, to two distinct originals, the one in the English, the other in the Castilian language, of which copies shall be interchanged mutually, certified and compared with the originals.

In the treaty file are the two documents mentioned, namely, the English original and a copy of the Spanish original certified by Pedro Gual, Colombian Secretary of State for Foreign Affairs, who signed the treaty on behalf of Colombia. The English original is written on one side of a large sheet of heavy paper, in size about twenty-six by forty inches, and now in very bad condition; it is embodied in the duplicate United States instrument of ratification of March 7, 1825. It is from the certified copy of the Spanish original that the Spanish text printed above is taken.

The treaty file is complete, including the attested resolution of the Senate of March 3, 1825 (Executive Journal, III, 424), which is

erroneously dated 1824. The certificate of exchange of ratifications at Washington on May 27 is in duplicate, English and Spanish, and notes the fact that the instrument of ratification on the part of Colombia includes the Spanish text only. The certificate was signed and sealed by Daniel Brent, Chief Clerk of the Department of State, and José Marie Salazar, Colombian Minister at Washington, and is in the following form in the English text:

We, the Undersigned, Daniel Brent, Chief Clerk in the Department of State of the United-States of America, in the absence of Henry Clay, Secretary, and José Maria Salazar LL.D. Fiscal of the high Court of Justice of the Republic of Colombia, and Envoy Extraordinary and Minister Plenipotentiary thereof near the Government of the United States of America, Certify,

That the Ratifications of the General Convention of Peace, Amity, Navigation and Commerce, between the said United-States and the said Republic, concluded at Bogota on the third day of October one thousand eight hundred and twenty four, accompanied with all suitable solemnities, and after due comparison, each with the other, and with the original examples of the Convention, have been exchanged by us this day:

But in the Ratification, on the part of the Government of the Republic of Colombia, the copy of the Convention being only in the Spanish Language, the said Daniel Brent desired that mention thereof should be made in the present Certificate, and that in accepting the Ratification, on the part of the Colombian Government, as aforesaid, he observes that the Convention, as concluded, was in the two Languages, and that the Ratification, herewith now delivered, on the part of the United-States, contains the Convention as so concluded:

In witness whereof we have signed this act in duplicates, and in both languages, and have sealed the same with our respective Seals, at the City of Washington, this twenty seventh day of May one thousand eight hundred and twenty five.

The original proclamation of May 31, 1825, which was communicated to Congress with the presidential message of December 6, 1825 (American State Papers, Foreign Relations, V, 760–74), includes both the English and Spanish texts. The English text, which precedes the Spanish, is that copy of the treaty which Anderson enclosed with his despatch of October 3, 1824 (D. S., 3 Despatches, Colombia, No. 17), the date of signature of the treaty. The Spanish text is a copy made in the Department of State.

The Full Powers

In this case the exchange of the full powers was "by means of compared copies of both" on May 25, 1824 (American State Papers, Foreign Relations, V, 720). The full power to Anderson, dated May 22, 1823, is in the usual form (D. S., 1 Credences, 357). A copy of that issued by the Republic of Colombia under date of May 18, 1824, was enclosed with Anderson's despatch of October 8, 1824 (D. S., 3 Despatches, Colombia, No. 19); it is printed in American State Papers, Foreign Relations, V, 725, in Spanish and in translation, the latter as follows:

Republic of Colombia: Francisco de Paula Santander, General of Division of the Armies of Colombia, of the Liberators of Venezuela and Cundinamarca, Decorated with the Cross of Boyaca, Vice President of the Republic Charged with the Executive Power, etc.

To all those to whom these presents shall come, Greeting:

Whereas the Government of the United States of America has constituted and appointed the Honorable Richard C. Anderson its Minister Plenipotentiary near that of the Republic of Colombia, giving him full power and authority to negotiate, arrange, conclude, and sign, in this capital, a treaty or treaties of friendship, commerce, and navigation, that may clearly establish and permanently secure the relations of perfect friendship and intercourse which happily exist between both powers: Therefore, having entire confidence in the ability, zeal, and integrity of the Honorable Pedro Gual, Secretary of State and of the Despatch of Foreign Affairs, I have conferred upon him, as by these presents I do confer on him, full power and authority to negotiate, arrange, conclude, and sign, with the aforesaid Minister Plenipotentiary of the United States of America, the above treaty or treaties of friendship, commerce, and navigation, obliging myself to its or their ratification, with the previous consent and approbation of the Congress of the said Republic of Colombia.

In faith of which I give and sign the present with my hand, sealed with the seal of the Republic of Colombia, and countersigned by the Secretary of State and of the Despatch of the Interior, in this city of Bogotá, the eighteenth of May of the year of our Lord one thousand eight hundred and twenty-four, fourteenth of independence.

[Seal]   FRANCISCO DE PAULA SANTANDER

By His Excellency the Vice President of the Republic charged with the executive power, the Secretary of State of the Despatch of the Interior:
JOSÉ MANUEL RESTREPO

EXECUTION OF THE TREATY

Commercial relations with Colombia under Articles 2 and 3 of the treaty were the subject of a message of President John Quincy Adams to Congress under date of March 30, 1826. The papers then transmitted (American State Papers, Foreign Relations, V, 910–16) included copies, in Spanish and in English translation, of a Colombian decree of January 30, 1826, having particular reference to the articles mentioned. An act to equalize the duties on vessels of the Republic of Colombia followed (April 20, 1826, 4 Statutes at Large, 154); among other provisions, it authorized the refund of all discriminating duties on vessels of the Republic of Colombia, and their cargoes, being of the growth, produce, or manufacture thereof, assessed since January 29, 1826.

In 1831 a "commercial arrangement" under Article 2 of this convention was made; the papers are printed in House Document No. 46, 22d Congress, 1st session, serial 217.

Following diplomatic exchanges at Bogotá which began on November 4, 1831, the American Minister, Thomas P. Moore, under date of November 21, wrote as follows (*ibid.*, 10):

The undersigned, Envoy Extraordinary and Minister Plenipotentiary of the United States, has had the honor of receiving the communication of the honorable Minister of Foreign Relations, enclosing the letter of the honorable Minister of Finance, in relation to the decision of the regulation, permitting the exaction of five per centum additional duty upon merchandize introduced from the United States in vessels of that country, the merchandize not being of the growth or manufacture of those States. In replying to that note, the undersigned says distinctly, that he is sufficiently authorized to state, explicitly, that

merchandize which may be imported into the United States, in Colombian vessels, going directly from Colombia, will be considered, in the payment of duties, as productions or manufactures of Colombia, whether they are the growth or manufacture of the Republic of Colombia or of any other country; in conformity with the 11th article of the treaty between Colombia and the United Provinces of Central America.

On the same day a Colombian decree was issued, Article 1 of which contained the following provisions (*ibid.*, 11):

The vessels of the United States of America, and their cargoes, whether of the growth or manufacture of the United States, or of any other country, proceeding directly from the ports of that Republic, shall pay, on being entered at the custom-houses of Colombia, no duties of import, anchorage, tonnage, or other, higher than those which are, or hereafter may be, laid on Colombian vessels, in conformity with the provisions expressed in the eleventh article of the treaty concluded between Colombia and the United Provinces of Central America.

With the presidential message to Congress of January 10, 1832 (*ibid.*, 1–2), there was transmitted a report of Secretary of State Livingston of the previous day which thus discussed the arrangement:

A case has arisen in our foreign intercourse, which will require the intervention of the Legislature, the circumstances of which, I have now the honor to lay before you, that if you deem it expedient, they may be made the subject of a communication to Congress.

By the second article of our treaty with the Republic of Colombia, the contracting parties "engage mutually, not to grant any particular favor to other nations in respect of commerce and navigation, which shall not immediately become common to the other party, who shall enjoy the same freely, if the concession was freely made; or, on allowing the same compensation, if the concession was conditional."

The *casus fadœris* under this article, arose by a treaty made between Colombia and Central America, by which it is understood to have been stipulated, that ships and their cargoes, whether consisting of domestic or foreign produce, or manufactures registered (cleared) in the customhouses of one of the contracting parties, shall not pay any higher duties on importation, anchorage, tonnage, or other impositions, than those which are, or may be, imposed on the national vessels, in the ports of the other.

Up to the date of the decree hereinafter mentioned, our commerce was subject, in the ports of Colombia, to a discriminating duty of five per cent. on all merchandize not the produce of manufacture of the United States; a duty from which the British commerce was exempt, as far as respected the East India and British goods, which must form part of every well assorted cargo. It became accordingly, an object of great importance to procure the benefit of the stipulations of the second article; which, by placing our commerce on the footing of that enjoyed by Central America, would take off this discrimination, and enable us to introduce the foreign merchandize, in our assorted cargoes, by paying no greater duties than those imposed on the nations of which they were the produce or manufacture. But, when application was made to this effect, it was justly and naturally answered that the privilege given to Central America, the more favored nation, was conceded on the condition of a reciprocal advantage; and that, by the terms of the article, we could not claim to enjoy it, without granting a reciprocal privilege to Colombian vessels in our ports. The justice of this was so apparent, that our Minister at Bogota, did not hesitate to make an arrangement for the reciprocal privilege required by the article, as a consideration for admitting our commerce on the same footing with that of Central America. In consequence of this, the Vice President of the Republic charged with the executive power, on the 21st November last, issued the decree, a translation of which is annexed to this report; by which it is declared, that "the vessels of the United

States and their cargoes, whether of foreign or domestic produce or manufacture, *which shall come direct from the ports of that nation,* shall pay in the customhouses of the Republic, no greater duties on importation, anchorage, tonnage, or any other kind that now are, or hereafter may be imposed on the national vessels, in conformity with the stipulations of the 11th article of the convention made between Colombia and the United Provinces of Central America."

Your proclamation, announcing these facts, would have been sufficient to carry this arrangement into full effect; but for the limitation in the decree, which restricts the privilege to vessels arriving direct from the ports of the United States—a restriction understood to be equivalent to the provision in the article of the convention between Colombia and Central America, requiring the cargoes to be registered in the customhouses of the nation to which the ships belong. However this may be, as the decree refers to the article in the convention with Central America, we must enjoy under it, all the advantages to which it entitles the contracting parties.

The laws of the 7th January, 1824, and of 24th May, 1828, which give the President power to issue his proclamation, declaring that no discriminating duties shall be levied on foreign vessels, only apply to those of such nations, as shall have taken off all discriminating duties upon vessels or goods without distinction of the place from whence they are imported. A law, therefore, seems necessary to authorize the declaration under the special circumstances of this case.

Copies of the documents, relating to the subject, which have been forwarded by the Minister of the United States in Colombia, are herewith transmitted.

There followed the act of May 19, 1832, "for giving effect to a commercial arrangement between the United States and the Republic of Colombia" (4 Statutes at Large, 515–16).

That arrangement, however, was of short duration; the Colombian decree of November 21, 1831, was repealed by that Government and the arrangement ceased to be in effect on December 17, 1832, so far as the Government of Colombia was concerned (D. S., 7 Despatches, Colombia, No. 47, May 21, 1832, and No. 62, March 7, 1833); but the privileges extended by the act of 1832 were not abrogated. Under date of April 15, 1835, Secretary of State Forsyth wrote (D. S., 1 Instructions, Venezuela, 7–9):

Under a just interpretation of the second article of the treaty with Colombia as it was affected by the treaties between Colombia and Central America and Colombia and Peru, our commerce and navigation with Colombia were placed upon a footing almost as liberal as we could have desired. By these Treaties, Colombian, and Central American and Peruvian vessels, proceeding directly from the ports of one party to those of another, are placed upon a like footing as it respects duties of tonnage and imposts on cargoes in the ports of either party; in other words, in these respects all are treated as national vessels. Under the second article of our treaty with Colombia, the United States claimed this favor from Colombia, and it being a conditional or reciprocal favor, the same compensation for it was offered in all the ports of the United States. The offer was accepted, and by a decree of the 21st November, 1831, the vessels of the United States and their cargoes, proceeding *directly* from ports of the United States, were placed in Colombian ports upon the same footing as national vessels. Very much to the surprize and dissatisfaction of the President, and contrary to the earnest remonstrances of our representative near the Government of Colombia, this decree was subsequently repealed, and discriminating duties collected upon all *foreign* goods imported into the Republic in vessels of the United States. The repeal of the decree was the more surprising, as it took place not at the instance or in consequence of the complaints of either Central America or Peru, but, as it is understood, of other powers who neither had extended, nor it is believed would

extend to the commerce and navigation of Colombia in their ports, the benefits secured to them in the ports of the United States by the Act of Congress of the 19th of May, 1832.   By that Act, (which reciprocates the provisions of the decree in question) the vessels of the Republic of Colombia and their cargoes, whether of foreign or domestic produce, coming direct from Colombian ports, are placed upon an equality with our vessels and their cargoes in the ports of the United States; and the President is authorized to take off the restriction of coming direct from a port in Colombia, so soon as he shall receive satisfactory evidence that a like restriction is taken off from the vessels of the United States in the ports of Colombia.   The Act also authorizes the President to abrogate by proclamation the privileges it secures to Colombia, whenever he shall be satisfied that the benefits secured to the United States by the decree, shall have ceased.   This decree was declared by the Treasury of New Granada to have been unauthorized, and it expired on the 17th of December, 1832, but the President, actuated by the hope that it would be renewed, has abstained from exercising the authority vested in him, and Colombian vessels and their cargoes still enjoy in the ports of the United States all the privileges secured to them by the Act of Congress referred to.

Negotiations for a commercial treaty, to " provide for the total suppression of all discriminating duties," were continued, with interruptions and without success, until the signature of the treaty with New Granada of December 12, 1846.

COLOMBIA : MARCH 16, 1825

*Convention for Adjusting Certain Claims, signed at Bogotá March 16,
1825. Original in English and (doubtless) in Spanish.
Not subject to ratification. Not proclaimed.*

On this sixteenth day of March in the year of our Lord one thousand eight hundred and twenty five, according to previous invitation, the Minister plenipotentiary of the United States, of America, and the Secretary of State and foreign Relations of the Republic of Colombia, having met for the purpose of adjusting certain existing claims on the part of the said United States, after a due Consideration of the points, relative to them, agreed to the following Articles—

ARTICLE FIRST. There shall be paid to the owners of the Cargo of the American Schooner Liberty, for the value of the said Cargo, for the loss of profit, injuries and damages, the sum of nine thousand, four hundred and Sixty one dollars and forty Cents, with interest at the rate of Six per Centum per annum, to be calculated from the fifth day of July in the year one thousand eight hundred and Seventeen.

ARTICLE SECOND. There shall likewise be paid to the owners of the Brig Josephine and Cargo, for the value of the said Vessel and Cargo, loss of profit, injuries and damages, the sum of twenty one thousand, seven hundred and fifty dollars, with interest thereon at the rate of six per Centum per annum from the twenty seventh day of January in the year one thousand eight hundred and nineteen.

ARTICLE THIRD. There shall likewise be paid to the owners of the American Schooner Minerva and Cargo, for the value of said Vessel, Cargo, loss of profit, injuries and damages, the sum of twenty thousand dollars with the like interest thereon of six per centum per annum to be calculated from the twenty seventh day of of June in the year one thousand eight hundred and twenty.

ARTICLE FOURTH. In like manner there shall be paid to the owners of the Cargo of the Brig America, for the part forfeited in Santa Martha and restored in Bogota, expenses of Condemnation, fees of advocates and demurrage of the Vessel, the sum of twenty one thousand four hundred and forty two dollars, with interest thereon at the rate of six per Centum per annum, to be calculated from the

twenty sixth day of February, in the year one thousand eight hundred and twenty one.

ARTICLE FIFTH. The sum of Seventy two thousand six hundred and fifty three dollars and forty Cents, to which the principal of the said several sums amounts, shall be paid in the United States, together with the interest thereon, to be calculated from the days respectively mentioned in the four preceding articles, up to the day on which shall be put in the hands of the Minister plenipotentiary of the United States, the corresponding bills of Exchange, drawn upon the Consul General of the Republic of Colombia in said States, payable at ninety days sight.

ARTICLE SIXTH. The Government of Colombia reserves to itself nevertheless, its rights and actions against any person or persons, whose irregular conduct may have been the cause of the claims, just settled.

R. C. ANDERSON JR
P. GUAL

NOTES

The only source text for this agreement is the copy of the articles, in English, which was enclosed with the despatch of Richard Clough Anderson, jr., Chargé d'Affaires at Bogotá, of March 18, 1825 (D. S., 3 Despatches, Colombia, No. 28). With that copy the text above printed has been collated. That there was also a Spanish text is hardly to be doubted; but none is available.

This agreement, while of a rather informal nature, is here called a convention, as it was in the note of Pedro Gual, Colombian Secretary of State, addressed to Anderson under date of March 18, 1825 (*ibid.*, No. 29, March 25, enclosure), and in the convention with Colombia of November 25, 1829 (Document 67); though Anderson seems to have regarded it merely as a "memorandum" of a conference (despatch of March 18, 1825, above cited).

The agreement is an early and interesting instance of an agreed settlement of claims of citizens of the United States against another Government, made by the Executive. No ratification was required on either part; there were no full powers; and the agreement was definitive upon signature; but it is to be noted that the amounts of the claims were not questioned; the calculations were according to the figures of the claimants; and ratification of such an agreement was *de facto* unnecessary as the bills of exchange for the payments were delivered two days after its date.

On the part of Colombia, the agreement was authorized to be made by the Executive by the "decreto" of March 9, 1825, in which is mentioned a communication of the previous January 20 to the

Congress on the subject (Codificación nacional de Colombia, II, 15–16).

In his first annual message to Congress, of December 6, 1825, President John Quincy Adams made this reference to the agreement (Richardson, II, 302):

It is with great satisfaction that I am enabled to bear witness to the liberal spirit with which the Republic of Colombia has made satisfaction for well-established claims.

THE CLAIMS SETTLEMENT

In the despatch mentioned of March 18, 1825, Anderson wrote:

I have delayed my departure from this place much beyond the time contemplated in my letter of the 19th of January, from a very great unwillingness to leave the Country, until I had brought to a final adjustment, the old claims of the Citizens of the United States, against this Government, entrusted to my management. I have now the satisfaction of informing you that I have arrived at a successful settlement in the cases of the Schooner Liberty and Cargo, the Schooner Tiger and Cargo, the Cargo of the Brig America, the Minerva and Cargo, and the Josephine and Cargo.

For the several sums due on these acknowledgments, bills have this day been given to me, drawn on the Colombian Consul General in the United States [certain of the bills were on London]. As it was impossible in some of the Cases to ascertain from any papers in my possession, to whom the money was really due, the bills have been drawn payable to my order. They will immediately on my arrival be deposited in your office, and endorsed under your direction for the benefit of those interested.

The memorandum of the Conference at which the Claims were admitted which is herewith transmitted, only shows the gross amounts assumed in each case, for vessel and Cargo; but the accompanying paper [now missing] marked (A) will show the different items, which, in the adjustment, were considered as composing the amount in each case. This paper will serve to regulate the distribution of the Money between the respective owners of the Vessel and Cargo.

Two of the claims stated in that despatch to have been adjusted, that for the schooner *Liberty* (not her cargo) and that for the schooner *Tiger* and cargo, are not mentioned in this agreement. The reason is doubtless that those two claims had previously been acknowledged by the Government of Colombia; formal certificates of indebtedness had been issued under date of June 26, 1823, for $6,000 in the one case and $28,219 in the other, with interest from July 5 and July 4, 1817, respectively (D. S., Colombian Claims, folder *Liberty*); and on March 18, 1825, Anderson received bills on London for £10,541 16s. 3d. in payment of the two obligations (D. S., 3 Despatches, Colombia, list of bills with No. 29).

All the claims settled arose from acts of various dates from 1817 to 1821, and thus during the period of the conflict with Spain for independence and prior to the recognition of Colombia by the United States on June 19, 1822 (see the notes to Document 47).

The schooner *Liberty*, of Philadelphia, William F. Hill, Master, was captured in the Orinoco River by a Venezuelan squadron under Admiral Luis Brion on July 10, 1817. The vessel and cargo were said to have been "condemned" for an alleged breach of blockade during

the previous January. The claim for the schooner had, as stated above, been admitted; the claim settled by this agreement was for the cargo. The schooner *Tiger*, of Salem, was captured by the same squadron at about the same time (D. S., Colombian Claims, folder *Liberty*, letter of Israel Sheldon, dated at Angostura September 29, 1817, and protest of September 25, 1817, before John Mitchell, Consul at Martinique).

The brig *Josephine*, of Philadelphia, John H. Hampton, Master, on her return voyage to Philadelphia from La Guayra, was taken on January 27, 1819, by the Venezuelan brig of war *Orinoco*, commanded by Vincent Dubois. The officers and crew of the *Josephine* were sent by an English schooner to St. Thomas, but nothing further appears in the papers regarding the disposal of the *Josephine* or her cargo, which consisted of cotton, coffee, and hides (D. S., Colombian Claims, folder *Josephine, passim*). The claim was for the vessel and cargo; but owing to an error of $13,500 in making up the figures in the *Josephine* case, that claim had a subsequent history; the notes to the convention with Colombia of November 25, 1829 (Document 67), should be consulted.

The schooner *Minerva*, of about 140 tons, William Wild, Master, was captured by a Venezuelan brig of war near Santiago, Cuba, on June 27, 1820, and taken into Savanilla in the River Magdalena for adjudication. The cargo was condemned as Spanish; the vessel, after delay, was ordered released, and the freight was ordered paid out of the sale of the cargo, but neither order was carried out. The claim was for the vessel, cargo, freight, and demurrage (D. S., Colombian Claims, folder *Minerva*, memorial of Joseph E. Read, February 8, 1821). A further claim in respect of the *Minerva* was presented to the Commission under the convention of February 10, 1864, with the United States of Colombia, but was adjudged not valid (Moore, International Arbitrations, II, 1418, case 35).

The claim regarding the cargo of the brig *America* was for certain merchandise landed at St. Martha in February, 1821, which was seized, condemned as "contraband," and sold. Appeal was taken and the sentence was revoked by the Tribunal of the High Board of the Treasury at Bogotá on November 21, 1821; judgment was there given for the claim and in the sum of $18,135.62½, with costs and demurrage of the brig, in all $21,442.06¼ (D. S., Colombian Claims, folder *America, passim*).

Execution of the Convention

The payments under this agreement were immediately made; on March 18, 1825, Anderson received bills of exchange for the amounts stated therein (D. S., 3 Despatches, Colombia, Nos. 28 and 29, March 18 and 25, 1825); and those bills were duly accepted and paid. In the archives of the Department of State are receipts for the various amounts; each of them is for the proceeds of a bill drawn by the Government of Colombia and accepted on June 1, 1825, at ninety days. The payments were all received through the Bank of the United States, and the receipts are essentially as follows:

1. Cargo of the schooner *Liberty*, September 3, 1825; signed by John A. Leamy for Ledlie and Leamy; $9,461.40 principal and $4,372.70 interest; total $13,834.10.

2. Brig *Josephine* and cargo, September 17, 1825; signed by the presidents of the Insurance Company of the State of Pennsylvania and the Marine Insurance Company of Philadelphia; $21,750 principal and $8,014.87 interest; total $29,764.87.

3. Cargo of the schooner *Minerva*, September 12, 1825; signed by the president of the Delaware Insurance Company of Philadelphia; $13,500 principal and $3,822.75 interest; total $17,322.75.

4. Schooner *Minerva*, freight, and demurrage, February 18, 1826; signed by Joseph E. Read; $6,500 principal and $1,840.59 interest; total $8,340.59.

5. Cargo of the brig *America*, September 3, 1825; signed by Charles H. Baker and John Rianhard; $21,442 principal and $5,221.12 interest; total $26,663.12.

RUSSIA : APRIL 19 AND 22, 1825

Exchange of Notes for the Settlement of the Claim in the Case of the Brig "Pearl." Original American note (April 19, 1825) in English. Original Russian note (April 22, 1825) in French. As to ratification, see the notes following the texts.

DEPARTMENT OF STATE,
Washington, 19 April, 1825.

The BARON DE TUYLL,
Envoy Extraordinary and Minister Plenipotentiary from Russia.
SIR:

I have understood, in the interviews with which you have honored me on the affair of the claim of the owners of the Brig Pearl, which sailed in January 1822 from the Port of Boston, bound on a trading voyage to the North West coast of America, and whose destination was changed, and the principal purposes of her voyage defeated, by the interposition of the Russian authorities, that His Imperial Majesty, without admitting the legality of the claim for indemnity set forth by the Government of the United States, in behalf of the owners of the said Brig, nevertheless being induced by a desire to afford a fresh proof of his friendly feelings towards the American Government, has determined to order compensation to be made for the loss referred to. Having sought for a measure to effect this object, without abusing the liberal and equitable intentions of His Imperial Majesty, I have now the honor to submit to your consideration the view which has presented itself to me of the claim.

From documents in this Department it appears that the original cost of the Brig, her Cargo and outfit, including Insurance and wages to her officers and crew, and excluding the cost of three boat frames which she delivered at Valparaiso to Cap⁺ Stewart of the American navy, was_____ $32, 541. 30

And that there has been realized, as the nett proceeds of the sale of the Brig and her Cargo, including return freight from the Sandwich Islands to Boston_____ } 15, 546. 61

Leaving therefore a loss of_____ 16, 994. 69

This loss was the result of a sacrifice, at the Sandwich Islands, to which the vessel was carried after she had been directed to leave the N. W. Coast of that portion of her Cargo which was designed for that coast.

The same documents would also tend to shew that if the Brig had not been compelled to abandon the chief object of her voyage, her owners would have realized a great profit upon their adventure, which has been estimated as high as one hundred per Cent.

Upon this state of the case, the three following standards of compensation present themselves.

1. That which is derived from a consideration of the profits which might have been made, if the change of the destination of the vessel had not been ordered; according to which the owners instead of sustaining a loss of $16,994.69 would receive double that sum vizt $33,989.38 with interest.

2. A simple replacement of the Capital sunk, by the payment of $16,994.69 with interest from January 1822 until the time of payment, and other charges. And,

3. The restoration of the capital, without interest or other charges, by the payment simply of a sum equal to $16,994.69.

The owners themselves probably expect an indemnity according to the first of those three standards. But I think myself it is too uncertain and speculative to be adopted, and I therefore reject it. The second corresponds better with what would seem to be proper; But being anxious to bring this matter to a close, and to present a proposition, conceived in a spirit of true moderation, I have the honor to submit the third to you, in the hope, that you will concur with me in thinking, that the sum which it expresses will not exceed the just and liberal intentions of H. I. M's Government. Should you accede to this proposal the payment of the before mentioned sum on the part of the Imperial Government, will be considered by the Government of the United States, as terminating the present transaction in a manner entirely satisfactory.

I avail myself of this occasion, to renew to you, Sir, the assurance of my distinguished consideration.

(Signed)   H. CLAY.

———

[Translation]

Le Soussigné, Envoyé extraordinaire et Ministre plénipotentiaire de Sa Majesté L'Empereur de toutes les Russies, a

The undersigned, Envoy Extraordinary and Minister Plenipotentiary of His Majesty the Emperor of all the Russias, has

reçu la note que Monsieur Clay, Secrétaire d'Etat des Etats Unis, lui a fait l'honneur de lui adresser le 19 Avril, renfermant la proposition, à laquelle le Gouvernement Américain s'est arrêté, en suite des conférences qui ont eu lieu relativement à la fixation du dédommagement que le Gouvernement de Sa Majesté Impériale a trouvé bon d'accorder aux propriétaires du navire La Perle, pour des pertes éprouvées par eux à l'occasion d'un voyage de ce bâtiment à la Côte Nord Ouest, entrepris dans l'année 1822.

Monsieur le Secrétaire d'Etat porte dans la note susmentionnée ce dédommagement à la somme de $16,994.69.; et il annonce simultanément, que le payement de la dite somme effectué d'après les ordres de la Cour de Russie, sera considéré par le Gouvernement des Etats Unis comme terminant la présente transaction d'une façon pleinement satisfaisante.

Le Soussigné a reconnu dans la manière dont le Cabinet de Washington a traité cette question, la même délicatesse de procédés, les mêmes dispositions satisfaisantes, dont il avait déja été à même de recueillir des témoignages en plus d'une occasion. Il s'est félicité de voir que le Gouvernement Américain de son coté apprécié justement les intentions bienveillantes qui

received the note which Mr. Clay, Secretary of State of the United States, did him the honor to address to him on the 19th of April, containing the proposition upon which the American Government have decided in consequence of the conferences which have taken place upon the subject of the assessment of the indemnity which the Government of His Imperial Majesty has thought proper to grant to the owners of the ship *Pearl* for losses sustained by them in a voyage made by that vessel to the northwest coast in the year 1822.

The Secretary of State, in the note above mentioned, fixes this indemnity at $16,994.69 and states at the same time that the payment of the said sum by order of the Court of Russia, will be considered by the Government of the United States as terminating this affair in a manner entirely satisfactory.

The undersigned has perceived in the manner in which the Cabinet of Washington has treated this question, the same delicacy of procedure, the same accommodating disposition, of which he has already received evidence on more than one occasion; and he is happy to see that the American Government on their part justly appreciate the benevolent motives which have influenced the deter-

ont de nouveau motivé les déter-
minations de l'Empereur en cette
occurrence.

Le Soussigné considérant la
proposition que vient de lui
adresser Monsieur le Secrétaire
d'Etat, comme conforme aux
principes d'équité et de modéra-
tion que les deux Gouvernemens
ont en vue, a l'honneur d'accepter
cette proposition; et il portera
sans perte de tems l'arrangement
dont on vient de convenir, à la
connaissance du Ministère de
L'Empereur Son Auguste Maître,
dans l'espoir qu'il obtiendra la
pleine approbation de Sa Majesté
Impériale, réquise pour la conclusion définitive de la présente
affaire.

Il a jugé devoir hésiter d'autant
moins à adopter l'opinion émise
par Monsieur Clay, qu'une autorité, qui aura toujours des droits
assurés à la déférence la plus
étendue de la part du Soussigné,
s'est prononcée d'une manière
favorable quant à la probité des
individus, aux assertions desquels
il a fallu nécessairement s'en rapporter en grande partie, pour l'es-
timations des pertes éprouvées
dans le voyage en question.

Le Soussigné saisit cette occasion pour offrir à Monsieur le
Secrétaire d'Etat l'expression de
sa considération très distinguée.

Washington, le 10/22 Avril
1825.

TUYLL.

À Monsieur CLAY,
       *Secrétaire d'Etat des Etats
       Unis, &c^a &c^a &c^a.*

mination of the Emperor on this
occasion.

The undersigned, considering
the proposition now made to him
by the Secretary of State as conformable to the principles of
equity and moderation which the
two Governments have in view,
has the honor to accept it, and
will, without loss of time, communicate the arrangement just
concluded to the Ministry of the
Emperor, his August Master, in
the hope that it will receive the
full approbation of His Imperial
Majesty, which is requisite for
the definitive conclusion of the
affair.

He has thought it proper to be
the more prompt in adopting the
decision of Mr. Clay, as an
authority which will always possess a most assured right to the
fullest deference on the part of
the undersigned has pronounced
favorably with regard to the
probity of the individuals upon
whose assertions it was necessary
to rely in a great measure as to
the estimate of the losses sustained in the voyage in question.

The undersigned seizes this
opportunity to offer to the Secretary of State the assurance of his
very distinguished consideration.

Washington, 10/22 April, 1825.

TUYLL.

NOTES

Unless otherwise stated, dates in the headnote and in these notes are in the New Style, or present calendar, which was then twelve days later than the Old Style.

The claim in the case of the American brig *Pearl* arose in 1822–23 as a result of the Russian interdiction of commerce on the northwest coast of America. In January, 1822, the brig *Pearl*, Samuel Chandler, Master, sailed from Boston on a trading voyage to the Sandwich Islands and the northwest coast. In August she arrived at the Sandwich Islands; and on September 19 she reached "Norfolk Sound," where she remained until October. On October 20 the master (then Charles Stephens) received peremptory orders from the Governor of the Russian settlement of New Archangel (Sitka) "to immediately leave the road and never again appear on that coast"; and on the following day he received similar orders from the commander of the Russian frigate *Apollo*. The *Pearl* thereupon returned to the Sandwich Islands, where her cargo was landed and a freight of oil taken on board. In March, 1823, she sailed for Boston, where she arrived the following August. Meanwhile the cargo left at the Sandwich Islands deteriorated; what remained of it was sold at auction in November, 1823.

The loss of capital in the venture, in consequence of the orders of the Russian authorities, was placed by Bryant & Sturges, part owners and agents for the *Pearl*, at \$16,994.69; and the total of lost capital and lost profits was estimated at about \$35,000.

A copy of a statement of the case by Bryant & Sturges under date of September 15, 1824, without address, is in D. S., Russian Claims, Miscellaneous, folder *Pearl*. An earlier statement was made in a letter of Bryant & Sturges to Secretary of State Adams of April 21, 1823, which enclosed the protest of the master and officers of the *Pearl*, sworn to on November 24, 1822. (That letter and protest have not been found in the archives of the Department of State, but they are printed in Fur Seal Arbitration: Proceedings of the Tribunal of Arbitration Convened at Paris, VII, 175–76.)

The action of the Russian authorities in ordering the *Pearl* off the northwest coast was taken in pursuance of the provisions of the Russian ukase of September 16, 1821 (September 4, 1821, Old Style; an English translation thereof is printed in American State Papers, Foreign Relations, IV, 857–61). Following the issuance of that ukase a Russian fleet had been despatched to the northwest coast to enforce its provisions (Hildt, "Early Diplomatic Negotiations of the United States with Russia," in Johns Hopkins University Studies in Historical and Political Science, XXIV, 160; D. S., 8 Despatches, Russia, No. 12, November 10, 1821).

To a certain extent the negotiations in the case of the *Pearl* paralleled those for the Northwest Coast Convention with Russia of April 17, 1824 (Document 46); John Quincy Adams was then Secretary of State.

In June and July, 1823, Adams was making a thorough study of the northwest coast question (Memoirs of John Quincy Adams, VI,159; Hildt, *op. cit.*, 169); on July 1 he finished a draft of instruc-

tions to Henry Middleton, Minister to Russia, on that question; on July 16 he wrote to Middleton regarding the case of the *Pearl* (D. S., 10 Instructions, U. S. Ministers, 52–53); and six days later he sent instructions to Middleton and to Richard Rush, Minister at London, relative to the northwest coast (*ibid.*, 54–68). The instructions of July 16, 1823, regarding the case of the *Pearl*, were as follows:

I have the honor of enclosing, herewith, Copies of a Letter from Mess.rs Bryant and Sturges of Boston, owners of the Brig Pearl, and of the Protest by the Captain of that Vessel against acts of hostility by officers of the Russian Government on the North west Coast of this Continent.

In presenting to the Russian Government the representation required by these transactions you will observe that course of proceeding which will best be calculated to obtain the reparation to these injured Citizens of the United States which the case eminently requires. With the most amicable and conciliatory forms, but with the firmness inspired by the clearest consciousness of right, you will urge the necessity of adequate indemnity to those suffering individuals. You will not forbear to state that after the communications which had passed between the Russian Government and you, upon the representations made by you, heretofore, this incident was as unexpected as it was varient from the friendly relations subsisting between the two Nations, and so sincerely cherished on the part of the United States; and you will give it distinctly to be understood, that while the Executive Government of this Country has not ceased to rely upon the sense of Justice which would ultimately mark the determinations of the Imperial Government, it cannot consistently with its duties overlook the aggression, which the rights of the Nation, as well as the interests of Individual citizens, in the perfect exercise of their rights have sustained.

Hitherto this subject has been under the exclusive direction, and control of the Executive. But unless some satisfactory prospect of its adjustment should appear from your communications to this Department, it will cease to be so at the next Session of Congress. I have to request therefore, your early attention to it, and information, as soon as may be, of the result of the steps which you will take concerning it. Should you receive assurances that suitable indemnity will be made, there may be no necessity for submitting the case to the consideration of the Legislature. It will otherwise be indispensable.

Doubtless the copy of the letter of Bryant & Sturges and the protest referred to in those instructions were the letter of April 21, 1823, and accompanying protest, already cited.

Pursuant to the instructions of July 16, Middleton presented the claim to the Russian Government in a note of November 20, 1823 (D. S., 10 Despatches, Russia, No. 33, December 13, 1823, enclosure *a*). But nearly three months later he had received no answer to that note, and "there was no appearance of a disposition to give a favorable reply" (*ibid.*, No. 34, February 17, 1824). On April 17, 1824, the date of signature of the Northwest Coast Convention (Document 46), however, Middleton again reminded Nesselrode of the case of the *Pearl;* and under date of May 4, 1824, Nesselrode replied that Baron de Tuyll, Russian Minister at Washington, had been authorized to negotiate (despatch No. 36, of May 5, 1824, with enclosures, which is missing from D. S., 10 Despatches, Russia, but is printed in Fur Seal Arbitration: Proceedings of the Tribunal of Arbitration Convened at Paris, VII, 178–80).

The negotiations were resumed in Washington, apparently in November, 1824 (D. S., 3 Notes to Foreign Legations, 196), and continued (*ibid.*, 204, March 25, 1825; Fur Seal Arbitration: Proceedings of the Tribunal of Arbitration Convened at Paris, VII, 177–78)

until April, 1825. On April 18 agreement was reached in conference between Secretary of State Clay and Baron de Tuyll (D. S., 1 Notes from the Russian Legation, April 19, 1825; Memoirs of John Quincy Adams, VI, 529–30, April 18, 1825); and under dates of April 19 and 22, respectively, Clay and Baron de Tuyll exchanged formal notes setting forth the terms of agreement.

The American note of April 19 and the Russian note of April 22, 1825, are printed above, the former from the record copy in D. S., 3 Notes to Foreign Legations, 217–18, and the latter, with its translation, from D. S., 1 Notes from the Russian Legation. The notes were submitted for consideration, on the one part and the other, before their delivery; and Clay wrote on April 19 that he "considers himself fully authorized by the owners of the Pearl to make the arrangement which was yesterday verbally agreed upon" (D. S., 3 Notes to Foreign Legations, 216).

Middleton was informed of the agreement in instructions of April 25, 1825 (D. S., 10 Instructions, U. S. Ministers, 295), which enclosed copies of the notes exchanged; and he was directed to collect the money in behalf of the claimants if the Emperor of Russia approved the agreement. Delay ensued, partly as a result of the death of the Emperor (see the comments of Secretary of State Clay in his instructions of April 21, 1826, 11 *ibid.*, 26). In July, 1826, the agreement received the approval of the Emperor of Russia; and in December, 1826, the money was paid over by the Russian Treasury to the banker appointed by the claimants to receive it (D. S., 11 Despatches, Russia, No. 67, December 7, 1826, and enclosures).

Treaty Series No. 39
8 Statutes at Large, 322–39
18 *ibid.*, pt. 2, Public Treaties, 95–103

50

CENTRAL AMERICAN FEDERATION
DECEMBER 5, 1825

Treaty of Peace, Amity, Commerce, and Navigation, signed at Washington December 5, 1825. Original in English and Spanish.
Submitted to the Senate December 15, 1825. Resolution of advice and consent December 29, 1825. Ratified by the United States January 16, 1826. Ratified by the Central American Federation July 29, 1826. Ratifications exchanged at Guatemala August 2, 1826. Proclaimed October 28, 1826.

General Convention of Peace, Amity, Commerce and Navigation between the United States of America and the Federation of the Centre of America.

The United States of America, and the Federation of the Centre of America desiring to make firm and permanent the peace and friendship which happily prevails between both nations, have resolved to fix, in a manner clear, distinct, and positive, the rules which shall in future be religiously observed between the one and the other, by means of a Treaty or general Convention of Peace, Friendship, Commerce and Navigation.

For this most desirable object, the President of the United States of America has conferred full powers on Henry Clay, their Secretary of State, and the Ex-

Convencion General de Paz, Amistad, Commercio y Navegacion entre la Federacion de Centro America, i los Estados Unidos de America.

La Federacion de Centro-America i los Estados Unidos de America deseando hacer firme i permanente la paz i amistad que felizmente existe entre ambas Potencias, han resuelto fijar de una manera clara, distinta y positiva las reglas que deben observar religiosamente en lo venidero, por medio de un Tratado ó Convencion general de paz, amistad, comercio y navegacion.

Con este muy deseable objeto, el Poder Executivo de la Federacion de Centro-America ha conferido plenos poderes á Antonio Jose Cañas, diputado de la Asem-

ecutive Power of the Federation of the Centre of America on Antonio Jose Cañas, a Deputy of the constituent National Assembly for the Province of San Salvador, and Envoy Extraordinary and Minister Plenipotentiary of that Republic near the United States, who after having exchanged their said full powers in due and proper form, have agreed to the following Articles:

ARTICLE 1st

There shall be a perfect, firm, and inviolable peace and sincere friendship between the United States of America and the Federation of the Centre of America, in all the extent of their possessions and territories, and between their people and Citizens respectively, without distinction of persons or places.

ARTICLE 2d

The United States of America and the Federation of the Centre of America desiring to live in peace and harmony with all the other nations of the earth, by means of a policy frank and equally friendly with all, engage mutually not to grant any particular favour to other nations in respect of commerce and navigation, which shall not immediately become common to the other party, who shall enjoy the same freely, if the concession was

blea nacional constituyente por la provincia de San Salvador, i Enviado Extraordinario i Ministro Penipotenciario de la aquella Republica cerca de los Estados Unidos, y el Presidente de los Estados Unidos de America à Henrico Clay, su Secretario de Estado, quienes despues de haber canjeado sus espresados plenos poderes en debida i buena forma, han convenido en los articulos siguientes:

ARTICULO 1º.

Habra una paz, perfecta, firme é inviolable y amistad sincera entre la Federacion de Centro-America i los Estados Unidos de America, en toda la estencion de sus posesiones i territorios, i entre sus pueblos i Ciudadanos respectivamente sin distincion de personas ni lugares.

ARTICULO 2º.

La Federacion de Centro-America, i los Estados Unidos de America, deseando vivir en paz i harmonia con las demas Naciones de la tierra, por medio de una politica franca, é igualmente amistosa con todas, se obligan mutuamente à no conceder favores particulares à otras naciones, con respecto a comercio i navegacion, que no se hagan inmediatamente comun à una ù otra, quien gozarà de los mismos libremente, si la concesion fuese hecha libremente,

freely made, or on allowing the same compensation, if the concession was conditional.

ARTICLE 3ᵈ

The two high contracting parties, being likewise desirous of placing the Commerce and Navigation of their respective Countries on the liberal basis of perfect equality and reciprocity, mutually agree that the Citizens of each may frequent all the coasts and countries of the other, and reside and trade there, in all kind of produce, manufactures and merchandize, and they shall enjoy all the rights, privileges and exemptions in navigation and commerce, which native Citizens do or shall enjoy, submitting themselves to the laws, decrees and usages there established, to which native Citizens are subjected. But it is understood that this article does not include the coasting trade of either Country, the regulation of which is reserved by the parties respectively, according to their own separate laws.

ARTICLE 4ᵗʰ

They likewise agree, that whatever kind of produce, manufacture or merchandize of any foreign country can be, from time to time, lawfully imported into the United States, in their own vessels, may be also imported in vessels of the Federation of the

---

ò prestando la misma compensacion, si la concesion fuere condicional.

ARTICULO 3°.

Las dos altas partes contratantes deseando tambien establecer el comercio y navegacion de sus respectivos paises sobre las liberales bases de perfecta igualidad y reciprocidad, convienen mutuamente que los ciudadanos de cada una podran frecuentar todas las costas y paises de la otra y residir i traficar en ellos con toda clase de producciones, manufacturas i mercaderias, i gozeran de todos los derechos, privilegios y esempciones con respecto à navegacion i comercio que gozan ò gozaren los ciudadanos nativos, sometiendose à las leyes, decretos è usos establecidos à que estan sujetos dichos Ciudadanos nativos. Pero debe entenderse que este articulo no comprende el comercio de costa de cada uno de los dos paises, cuya regulacion es reservada à las partes respectivamente, segun sus propias i peculiares leyes.

ARTICULO 4°.

Igualmente convienen, que cualquiera clase de producciones, manufacturas ò mercaderias estrangeras que puedan ser en cualquier tiempo legalmente introducidas en la Republica Central en sus propios buques, puedan tambien ser introducidas en los buques

Centre of America; and that no higher or other duties, upon the tonnage of the vessel, or her cargo, shall be levied and collected, whether the importation be made in vessels of the one country or of the other. And in like manner that whatever kind of produce, manufactures or merchandize of any foreign country can be, from time to time, lawfully imported into the Central Republic, in its own vessels, may be also imported in vessels of the United States; and that no higher or other duties, upon the tonnage of the vessel, or her cargo, shall be levied and collected, whether the importation be made in vessels of the one country or of the other. And they further agree that whatever may be lawfully exported or re-exported from the one country, in its own vessels, to any foreign country, may, in like manner, be exported or re-exported in the vessels of the other country. And the same bounties, duties and drawbacks shall be allowed and collected, whether such exportation or re-exportation be made in vessels of the United States or of the Central Republic.

ARTICLE 5.ᵗʰ

No higher or other duties shall be imposed on the importation into the United States of any articles, the produce or manufactures of the Federation of the

de los Estados Unidos; i que no se impondran ò cobraran otros ò mayores derechos de tonelada ò por el cargamento, ya sea que la importacion se haga en buques de la una ò de la otra. De la misma manera que cualesquiera clase de producciones, manufacturas ò mercaderias estrangeras que pueden ser en cualquier tiempo legalmente introducidas en los Estados Unidos en sus propios buques, puedan tambien ser introducidas en los buques de la Federacion de Centro America; i que no se impondran o cobraran otros ò mayores derechos de tonelada ò por el cargamento ya sea que la importacion se haga en buques de la una ò de la otra. Convienen ademas, que todo lo que pueda ser legalmente esportado ò re-esportado de uno de los dos paises, en sus buques propios para un pais estranjero pueda de la misma manera ser esportado ò re-esportado en los buques de el otro. Y los mismos derechos, premios ò descuentos se concederan i cobraran ya sea que tal exportacion ò re-exportacion se haga en los buques de la Republica central ò de los Estados Unidos.

ARTICULO 5º.

No se impondran otros ò mayores derechos sobre la importacion de cualquier articulo, produccion ò manufactura de los Estados Unidos en la Federacion de Centro-

Centre of America, and no higher or other duties shall be imposed on the importation into the Federation of the Centre of America of any articles, the produce or manufactures of the United States, than are or shall be payable on the like articles being the produce or manufactures of any other foreign country; nor shall any higher or other duties or charges be imposed in either of the two countries, on the exportation of any articles to the United States or to the Federation of the Centre of America, respectively, than such as are payable on the exportation of the like articles to any other foreign country; nor shall any prohibition be imposed on the exportation or importation of any articles, the produce or manufactures of the United States or of the Federation of the Centre of America, to or from the territories of the United States, or to or from the territories of the Federation of the Centre of America, which shall not equally extend to all other nations.

America, i no se impondran otros ò mayores derechos sobre la importacion de cualquier articulo, produccion ò manufactura de la Federacion de Centro-America en los Estados Unidos, que los que se pagan ò pagaren en adelante por iguales articulos, produccion ò manufactura de cualquiera pais estrangero; ni se impondran otros ò mayores derechos ò cargas en cualquiera de los dos paises sobre la esportacion de cualesquiera articulos para la Federacion de Centro-America ò para los Estados Unidos respectivamente, que los que se pagan ò pagaren en adelante por la esportacion de iguales articulos para cualquiera otro pais estrangero; ni se establecera prohivicion sobre la importacion ò esportacion de cualesquiera articulos, produccion ò manufactura de los territorios de la Federacion de Centro-America para los de los Estados Unidos, ò de los territorios de los Estados Unidos para los de la Federacion de Centro-America, que no sea igualmente estensiva à las otras naciones.

Article 6th.

It is likewise agreed that it shall be wholly free for all merchants, commanders of ships, and other Citizens of both countries, to manage, themselves, their own business in all the ports and places subject to the jurisdiction of each other, as well with respect to the

Articulo 6º.

Se conviene ademas, que serà enteramente libre i permitido, a los comerciantes, comandantes de buques, i otros Ciudadanos de ambos paises, el manejar sus negocios, por si mismos, en todos los puertos i lugares sujetos à la jurisdiccion de uno ù otro, asi

consignment and sale of their goods and merchandize by wholesale or retail, as with respect to the loading, unloading, and sending off their ships, they being in all these cases to be treated as Citizens of the country in which they reside, or at least to be placed on a footing with the subjects or Citizens of the most favoured nation.

ARTICLE 7th

The Citizens of neither of the contracting parties shall be liable to any embargo, nor be detained with their vessels, cargoes, merchandize or effects, for any military expedition, nor for any public or private purpose whatever, without allowing to those interested a sufficient indemnification.

ARTICLE 8th

Whenever the Citizens of either of the contracting parties shall be forced to seek refuge or asylum in the rivers, bays, ports or dominions, of the other, with their vessels, whether merchant or of war, public or private, through stress of weather, pursuit of pirates, or enemies, they shall be received and treated with humanity, giving to them all favour and protection for repairing their ships, procuring provisions, and placing themselves in a situation to continue their voyage without obstacle or hindrance of any kind.

respecto à las consignaciones i ventas por mayor i menor de sus efectos i mercaderias, como de la carga, descarga i despacho de sus buques, debiendo en todos estos casos, ser tratados como Ciudadanos del pais en que residan, ò al menos puestos sobre un pie igual con los subditos ò Ciudadanos de las naciones mas favorecidas.

ARTICULO 7º.

Los Ciudadanos de una ù otra parte, no podran ser embargados ni detenidos con sus embarcaciones, tripulaciones, mercaderias, i efectos comerciales de su pertenencia, para alguna espedicion militar, usos publicos ò particulares cualesquiera que sean, sin conceder à los interesados una suficiente indemnizacion.

ARTICULO 8º.

Siempre que los Ciudadanos de alguna de las partes contratantes se vieren precisados à buscar refujio, ò asilo en los rios, bahias, puertos, ò dominios de la otra, con sus buques, ya sean mercantes, ò de guerra, publicos ò particulares, por mal tiempo, persecucion de piratas ò enemigos, seran recibidos i tratados con humanidad, dandoles todo favor i proteccion, para reparar sus buques, procurar viveres, i ponerse en situacion de continuar su viaje, sin obstaculo ò estorbo de ningun genero.

Article 9th.

All the ships merchandize, and effects belonging to the Citizens of one of the contracting parties, which may be captured by pirates, whether within the limits of its jurisdiction or on the high seas, and may be carried or found in the rivers, roads, bays, ports, or dominions, of the other, shall be delivered up to the owners, they proving in due and proper form their rights before the competent tribunals; it being well understood that the claims should be made within the term of one year by the parties themselves, their attorneys, or agents of the respective Governments.

Article 10th.

When any vessel belonging to the Citizens of either of the contracting parties shall be wrecked, foundered, or shall suffer any damage on the coasts, or within the dominions of the other, there shall be given to them all assistance and protection in the same manner which is usual and customary with the vessels of the nation where the damage happens, permitting them to unload the said vessel, if necessary, of its merchandize and effects, without exacting for it any duty, impost, or contribution whatever, until they may be exported.

Articulo 9º.

Todos los buques, mercaderias i efectos pertenecientes à los Ciudadanos de una de las partes contratantes, que sean apresados por piratas, bien sea dentro de los limites de su jurisdiccion, ò en alta mar, i fueren llevados, ò hallados en los rios, radas, bahias, puertos, ò dominios de la otra, seràn entragados à sus dueños, probando estos en la forma propia i debida sus derechos ante los Tribunales competentes; bien entendido que el reclamo ha de hacerse dentro del termino de un año, por las mismas partes, sus apoderados ò Agentes de los respectivos Gobiernos.

Articulo 10º.

Cuando algun buque perteneciente à los Ciudadanos de alguna de las partes contratantes, naufrague, encalle, ò sufra alguna averia, en las costas, ò dentro de los dominios de la otra, se les dara toda ayuda i proteccion, del mismo modo que es uso i costumbre, con los buques de la nacion en donde suceda la averia; permitiendoles descargar el dicho buque (si fuere necesario) de sus mercaderias i efectos, sin cobrar por esto hasta que sean esportados, ningun derecho, impuesto ò contribucion.

ARTICLE 11th

The Citizens of each of the contracting parties shall have power
to dispose of their personal goods
within the jurisdiction of the
other, by sale, donation, testament, or otherwise, and their representatives, being Citizens of the
other party, shall succeed to their
said personal goods, whether by
testament or *ab intestato*, and they
may take possession thereof, either
by themselves or others acting
for them, and dispose of the same
at their will, paying such dues
only as the inhabitants of the
country, wherein the said goods
are, shall be subject to pay in like
cases: and if, in the case of real
estate, the said heirs would be
prevented from entering into the
possession of the inheritance, on
account of their character of
aliens, there shall be granted to
them the term of three years to
dispose of the same, as they may
think proper, and to withdraw
the proceeds without molestation,
and exempt from all duties of
detraction, on the part of the
Government of the respective
States.

ARTICLE 12th

Both the contracting parties
promise and engage, formally to
give their special protection to
the persons and property of the
Citizens of each other, of all occupations, who may be in the terri-

ARTICULO 11º.

Los Ciudadanos de cada una
de las partes contratantes, tendràn pleno poder para disponer
de sus bienes personales dentro
de la jurisdiccion de la otra,
por venta, donacion, testamento,
ò de otro modo; i sus representantes, siendo Ciudadanos de
la otra parte, succederàn à sus
dichos bienes personales, ya sea
por testamento ò *ab intestato*,
i podra tomar posesion de ellos,
ya sea por si mismos, ò por otros,
que obren por ellos, i disponer
de los mismos, segun su voluntad, pagando aquellas cargas solamente, que los habitantes del
pais en donde estan los referidos
bienes, estuvieren sujetos à pagar
en iguales casos. Y si en el
caso de bienes raices, los dichos
herederos fuesen impedidos de
entrar en la posesion de la
herencia por razon de su caracter de estrangeros, se les dará
el termino de tres años, para disponer de ella como juzguen conveniente, i para estraer el producto sin molestia, i esentos
de todo derecho de deduccion,
por parte del Gobierno de los
respectivos Estados.

ARTICULO 12º.

Ambas partes contratantes se
comprometen i obligan formalmente à dar su proteccion especial à las personas i propiedades
de los Ciudadanos de cada una
reciprocamente,   transeuntes   ò

tories subject to the jurisdiction of the one or the other, transient or dwelling therein, leaving open and free to them the tribunals of justice for their judicial recourse, on the same terms which are usual and customary with the natives or Citizens of the Country in which they may be; for which they may employ in defence of their rights such advocates, solicitors, notaries, agents, and factors, as they may judge proper, in all their trials at law; and such Citizens or agents shall have free opportunity to be present at the decisions and sentences of the tribunals, in all cases which may concern them, and likewise at the taking of all examinations and evidence which may be exhibited in the said trials.

habitantes de todas ocupaciones, en los territorios sujetos à la jurisdiccion de una i otra, dejandoles abiertos i libres los Tribunales de justicia, para sus recursos judiciales, en los mismos terminos que son de uso i costumbre para los naturales ò Ciudadanos del pais en que residan; para lo cual, podràn emplear en defensa de sus derechos aquellos Abogados, Procuradores, Escribanos, Agentes, ò Factores que juzguen conveniente, en todos sus asuntos i litigios; i dichos Ciudadanos ò Agentes tendràn la libre facultad de estar presentes en las decisiones i sentencias de los Tribunales, en todos los casos que les conciernan, como igualmente al tomar todos los examenes i declaraciones que se ofrezcan en los dichos litigios.

ARTICLE 13th.

It is likewise agreed that the most perfect and entire security of conscience shall be enjoyed by the Citizens of both the contracting parties in the countries subject to the jurisdiction of the one and the other, without their being liable to be disturbed or molested on account of their religious belief, so long as they respect the laws and established usages of the country. Moreover, the bodies of the Citizens of one of the contracting parties, who may die in the territories of

ARTICULO 13°.

Se conviene igualmente en que los Ciudadanos de ambas partes contratantes gozen la mas perfecta i entera seguridad de conciencia en los paises sujetos à la jurisdiccion de una ù otra, sin quedar por ello espuestos à ser inquietados ò molestados en razon de su creencia religiosa, mientras que respeten las leyes i usos establecidos. Ademas de esto, podràn sepultarse los cadaveres de los Ciudadanos de una de las partes contratantes, que fallecieren en los territorios de la otra,

the other, shall be buried in the usual burying grounds, or in other decent and suitable places, and shall be protected from violation or disturbance.

ARTICLE 14th

It shall be lawful for the Citizens of the United States of America and of the Federation of the Centre of America to sail with their ships, with all manner of liberty and security, no distinction being made, who are the proprietors of the merchandize laden thereon, from any port to the places of those who now are or hereafter shall be at enmity with either of the contracting parties. It shall likewise be lawful for the Citizens aforesaid to sail with the ships and merchandize beforementioned, and to trade with the same liberty and security from the places, ports, and havens, of those who are enemies of both or either party, without any opposition or disturbance whatsoever, not only directly from the places of the enemy, beforementioned, to neutral places, but also from one place belonging to an enemy to another place belonging to an enemy, whether they be under the jurisdiction of one power or under several. And it is hereby stipulated, that free ships shall also give freedom to goods, and that every thing shall be deemed to be free and exempt, which

en los cementerios acostumbrados, ò en otros lugares decentes i adecuados, los cuales seràn protejidos contra toda violacion ò trastorno.

ARTICULO 14º.

Sera licito a los Ciudadanos de la Federacion de Centro-America, i de los Estados Unidos de America, navegar con sus buques, con toda seguridad i libertad, de cualquiera puerto à las plazas ò lugares de los que son ò fueren en adelante enemigos de cualquiera de las dos partes contratantes, sin hacerse distincion de quienes son los dueños de las mercaderias cargadas en ellos. Serà igualmente licito à los referidos Ciudadanos navegar con sus buques i mercaderias mencionadas i traficar con la misma libertad i seguridad, de los lugares, puertos i enseñadas de los enemigos de ambas partes, ò de alguna de ellas, sin ninguna oposicion, ò disturbio cualquiera, no solo directamente de los lugares de enemigo arriba mencionados à lugares neutros, sino tambien de un lugar perteneciente à un enemigo, à otro enemigo, ya sea que esten bajo la jurisdiccion de una potencia, ò bajo la de diversas. Y queda aqui estipulado, que los buques libres, dan tambien libertad à las mercaderias, i que se ha de considerar libre i esento todo lo que se hallare à bordo de los buques pertenecientes à los

shall be found on board the ships belonging to the Citizens of either of the contracting parties, although the whole lading, or any part thereof, should appertain to the enemies of either, contraband goods being always excepted. It is also agreed, in like manner, that the same liberty be extended to persons who are on board a free ship, with this effect, that although they be enemies to both or either party, they are not to be taken out of that free ship, unless they are officers or soldiers, and in the actual service of the enemy: Provided, however, and it is hereby agreed, that the stipulations in this article contained, declaring that the flag shall cover the property, shall be understood as applying to those powers only who recognize this principle; but if either of the two contracting parties shall be at war with a third, and the other neutral, the flag of the neutral shall cover the property of enemies whose Governments acknowledge this principle, and not of others.

ARTICLE 15th

It is likewise agreed, that in the case where the neutral flag of one of the contracting parties shall protect the property of the enemies of the other, by virtue of the above stipulation, it shall always be understood that the

Ciudadanos de cualquiera de las partes contratantes, aunque toda la carga ò parte de ella pertenezca à enemigos de una ù otra, eceptuando siempre los articulos de contrabando de guerra. Se conviene tambien del mismo modo, en que la misma libertad se estienda à las personas que se encuentren à bordo de buques libres, con el fin de que aunque dichas personas sean enemigos de ambas partes ò de alguna de ellas, no deban ser estraidos de los buques libres, à menos que sean oficiales ò Soldados en actual servicio de los enemigos: à condicion no obstante, i se conviene aqui en esto, que las estipulaciones contenidas en el presente articulo, declarando que el Pabellon cubre la propiedad, se entenderán aplicables solamente à aquellas potencias que reconocen este principio; pero si alguna de las dos partes contratantes, estuviere en guerra con una tercera, i la otra permaneciese neutral, la bandera de la neutral cubrirà la propiedad de los enemigos, cuyos Gobiernos reconozcan este principio i no de otros.

ARTICULO 15°.

Se conviene igualmente que en el caso de que la bandera neutral de una de las partes contratantes protega las propiedades de los enemigos de la otra en virtud de lo estipulado arriba, deberá siempre entenderse, que las proprie-

neutral property found on board such enemy's vessels shall be held and considered as enemy's property, and as such shall be liable to detention and confiscation, except such property as was put on board such vessel before the declaration of war, or even afterwards, if it were done without the knowledge of it; but the contracting parties agree, that two months having elapsed after the declaration, their citizens shall not plead ignorance thereof. On the contrary, if the flag of the neutral does not protect the enemy's property, in that case the goods and merchandize of the neutral, embarked in such enemy's ships, shall be free.

ARTICLE 16th.

This liberty of navigation and commerce shall extend to all kinds of merchandize, excepting those only which are distinguished by the name of contraband, and under this name of contraband, or prohibited goods, shall be comprehended:—

1st. Cannons, mortars, howitzers, swivels, blunderbusses, muskets, fuzees, rifles, carbines, pistols, pikes, swords, sabres, lances, spears, halberds and granades, bombs, powder, matches, balls, and all other things belonging to the use of these arms;

dades neutrales encontradas à bordo de tales buques enemigos, han de tenerse i considerarse como propiedades enemigas, i como tales, estaràn sujetas à detencion i confiscacion; eseptuando solamente aquellas propiedades que hubiesen sido puestas à bordo de tales buques antes de la declaracion de la guerra, i aun despues, si hubiesen sido embarcadas en dichos buques, sin tener noticia de la guerra; i se conviene, que pasados dos meses despues de la declaracion, los Ciudadanos de una i otra parte no podràn alegar que la ignoraban. Por el contrario, si la bandera neutral, no protegiese las propiedades enemigas, entonces seran libres los efectos i mercaderias de la parte neutral, embarcadas en buques enemigos.

ARTICULO 16º.

Esta libertad de navegacion i comercio se estenderà à todo genero de mercaderias, eceptuando aquellas solamente, que se distinguen con el nombre de contrabando, i bajo este nombre de *contrabando* ò efectos prohibidos se comprenderàn:

1º. Cañones, morteros, obuces, pedreros, trabucos, mosquetes, fusiles, rifles, carabinas, pistolas, picas, espadas, sables, lanzas, chuzos, alabardas, i granadas, bombas, polvora, mechas, balas, con las demas cosas correspondientes al uso de estas armas.

2[ly] Bucklers, helmets, breastplates, coats of mail, infantry belts, and clothes made up in the form and for a military use;

3[ly] Cavalry belts, and horses with their furniture;

4[ly] And generally all kinds of arms and instruments of iron, steel, brass, and copper, or of any other materials manufactured, prepared, and formed, expressly to make war by sea or land.

ARTICLE 17th

All other merchandize and things not comprehended in the articles of contraband explicitly enumerated and classified as above, shall be held and considered as free, and subjects of free and lawful commerce, so that they may be carried and transported in the freest manner by both the contracting parties, even to places belonging to an enemy, excepting only those places which are at that time besieged or blockaded; and to avoid all doubt in this particular, it is declared that those places only are besieged or blockaded which are actually attacked by a belligerent force capable of preventing the entry of the neutral.

2.° Escudos, casquetes, corazas, cotas de malla, fornituras, i vestidos hechos en forma, i à usanza militar.

3.° Bandoleras, i caballos junto con sus armas i arneses.

4.° Y generalmente toda especie de armas, è instrumentos de hierro, acero, bronce, cobre, y otras materias cualesquiera, manufacturadas, preparadas, i formadas espresamente para hacer la guerra por mar, ò tierra.

ARTICULO 17°.

Todas las demas mercaderias, i efectos no comprendidos en los articulos de contrabando esplicitamente enumerados, i clasificados en el articulo anterior, seràn tenidos, i reputados por libres, i de licito i libre comercio, de modo, que ellos puedan ser transportados, i llevados de la manera mas libre, por los Ciudadanos de ambas partes contratantes, aun à los lugares pertenecientes à un enemigo de una ù otra, eceptuando solamente aquellos lugares ò plazas, que estan al mismo tiempo sitiadas ò bloqueadas: i para evitar toda duda en el particular, se declaran sitiadas ò bloqueadas aquellas plazas, que en la actualidad estuviesen atacadas por una fuerza de un beligerante capaz de impedir la entrada del neutral.

ARTICLE 18th.

The articles of contraband, before enumerated and classified, which may be found in a vessel bound for an enemy's port, shall be subject to detention and confiscation, leaving free the rest of the cargo and the ship, that the owners may dispose of them as they see proper. No vessel of either of the two nations shall be detained on the high seas on account of having on board articles of contraband, whenever the master, captain or supercargo of said vessel, will deliver up the articles of contraband to the captor, unless the quantity of such articles be so great and of so large a bulk, that they cannot be received on board the capturing ship without great inconvenience; but in this and in all other cases of just detention, the vessel detained shall be sent to the nearest convenient and safe port, for trial and judgment, according to law.

ARTICLE 19th.

And whereas it frequently happens that vessels sail for a port or place belonging to an enemy, without knowing that the same is besieged, blockaded, or invested, it is agreed, that every vessel so circumstanced may be turned away from such port or place, but shall not be detained, nor shall any part of her cargo, if not contraband, be confiscated, unless,

ARTICULO 18°.

Los articulos de contrabando, antes enumerados i clasificados, que se hallen en un buque destinado à puerto enemigo estaran sujetos à detencion i confiscacion; dejando libre el resto del cargamento i el buque, para que los dueños puedan disponer de ellos como lo crean conveniente. Ningun buque de cualquiera de las dos Naciones serà detenido, por tener à bordo articulos de contrabando, siempre que el Maestre, Capitan, ò Sobrecargo de dicho buque quiera entregar los articulos de contrabando al apresador, à menos que la cantidad de estos articulos sea tan grande i de tanto volumen, que no puedan ser recibidos à bordo del buque apresador, sin grandes inconvenientes; pero en este, como en todos los otros casos de justa detencion, el buque detenido será enviado al puerto mas inmediato, comodo, i seguro, para ser juzgado i sentenciado conforme à las leyes.

ARTICULO 19°.

Y por cuanto frecuentemente sucede que los buques navegan para un puerto ò lugar perteneciente à un enemigo, sin saber que aquel estè sitiado, bloqueado ò envestido, se conviene en que todo buque en estas circumstancias se pueda hacer volver de dicho puerto, ò lugar; pero no serà detenido, ni confiscada parte alguna de su cargamento, no

after warning of such blockade or investment from the commanding officer of the blockading forces, she shall again attempt to enter; but she shall be permitted to go to any other port or place she shall think proper. Nor shall any vessel of either, that may have entered into such port before the same was actually besieged, blockaded, or invested, by the other, be restrained from quitting such place with her cargo, nor if found therein after the reduction and surrender, shall such vessel or her cargo be liable to confiscation, but they shall be restored to the owners thereof.

Article 20th

In order to prevent all kind of disorder in the visiting and examination of the ships and cargoes of both the contracting parties on the high seas, they have agreed mutually, that whenever a vessel of war, public or private, shall meet with a neutral of the other contracting party, the first shall remain out of cannon shot, and may send its boat with two or three men only in order to execute the said examination of the papers concerning the ownership and cargo of the vessel, without causing the least extortion, violence or ill treatment, for which the commanders of the said armed ships shall be responsible with their

siendo contrabando; à menos que despues de la intimacion de semejante bloqueo ò ataque, por el comandante de las fuerzas bloqueadoras, intentase otra vez entrar; pero le sera permitido ir à cualquiera otro puerto ò lugar que juzgue conveniente. Ni ningun buque de una de las partes, que haya entrado en semejante puerto, ò lugar, antes que estuviese sitiado, bloqueado, ò investido por la otra, serà impedido de dejar el tal lugar con su cargamento, ni si fuere hallado alli despues de la rendicion i entrega de semejante lugar, estarà el tal buque ò su cargamento sujeto à confiscacion, sino que seràn restituidos à sus dueños.

Articulo 20º.

Para evitar todo genero de desorden en la visita, i examen de los buques i cargamentos de ambas partes contratantes en alta mar, han convenido mutuamente, que siempre que un buque de guerra, publico ò particular, se encontrase con un neutral de la otra parte contratante, el primero permanecerà fuera de tiro de cañon, i podra mandar su bote, con dos ò tres hombres solamente, para ejecutar el dicho examen de los papeles concernientes a la propiedad i carga del buque, sin ocasionar la menor estorcion, violencia ò mal tratamiento, por lo que los comandantes del dicho buque armado seràn responsables,

persons and property; for which purpose the commanders of said private armed vessels shall, before receiving their Commissions, give sufficient security to answer for all the damages they may commit. And it is expressly agreed, that the neutral party shall in no case be required to go on board the examining vessel, for the purpose of exhibiting her papers, or for any other purpose whatever.

con sus personas i bienes; à cuyo efecto los comandantes de buques armados, por cuenta de particulares, estaràn obligados antes de entregarseles sus comisiones ò patentes, à dar fianza suficiente para responder de los perjuicios que causen. Y se ha convenido espresamente, que en ningun caso se exigirà à la parte neutral, que vaya à bordo del buque examinador con el fin de exibir sus papeles, ò para cualquiera otro objeto sea el que fuere.

ARTICLE 21st

To avoid all kind of vexation and abuse in the examination of the papers relating to the ownership of the vessels belonging to the Citizens of the two contracting parties, they have agreed, and do agree, that in case one of them should be engaged in war, the ships and vessels belonging to the Citizens of the other must be furnished with sea-letters or passports, expressing the name, property, and bulk of the ship, as also the name and place of habitation of the master or commander of said vessel, in order that it may thereby appear, that the ship really and truly belongs to the Citizens of one of the parties; they have likewise agreed that such ships being laden, besides the said sea-letters or passports, shall also be provided with certificates containing the several particulars of the cargo, and the place whence

ARTICULO 21º.

Para evitar toda clase de vejamen i abuso en el examen de los papeles relativos à la propiedad de los buques pertenecientes à los Ciudadanos de las dos partes contratantes, han convenido i convienen, que en caso de que una de ellas estuviere en guerra, los buques, i bajeles pertenecientes à los Ciudadanos de la otra, seran provistos con letras de mar, ò pasaportes, espresando el nombre, propiedad i tamaño del buque, como tambien el nombre i lugar de la residencia del Maestre, ò Comandante, à fin de que se vea que el buque, real i verdaderamente pertenece à los Ciudadanos de una de las partes; i han convenido igualmente, que estando cargados los espresados buques, ademas de las letras de mar, ò pasaportes, estarán tambien provistos de certificatos, que contengan los por menores del

the ship sailed, so that it may be known whether any forbidden or contraband goods be on board the same; which certificates shall be made out by the officers of the place whence the ship sailed, in the accustomed form; without which requisites, said vessel may be detained to be adjudged by the competent tribunal, and may be declared legal prize, unless the said defect shall be satisfied or supplied by testimony entirely equivalent.

ARTICLE 22ᵈ

It is further agreed, that the stipulations above expressed relative to the visiting and examination of vessels, shall apply only to those which sail without convoy; and when said vessels shall be under convoy, the verbal declaration of the commander of the convoy, on his word of honour, that the vessels under his protection belong to the nation whose flag he carries—and when they are bound to an enemy's port, that they have no contraband goods on board, shall be sufficient.

ARTICLE 23ᵈ

It is further agreed that in all cases the established courts for prize causes, in the country to which the prizes may be conducted, shall alone take cognizance of them. And whenever

cargamento, i el lugar de donde salió el buque, para que asi pueda saberse, si hay à su bordo algunos efectos prohibidos ò de contrabando, cuyos certificatos serán hechos per los oficiales del lugar de la procedencia del buque, en la forma acostumbrada, sin cuyos requisitos el dicho buque puede ser detenido, para ser juzgado por el Tribunal competente, i puede ser declarado buena presa, à menos que satisfagan, ò suplan el defecto con testimonios enteramente equivalentes.

ARTICULO 22°.

Se ha convenido ademas, que las estipulaciones anteriores, relativas al examen i visita de buques, se aplicarán solamente á los que navegan sin conboy i que cuando los dichos buques estuvieren bajo de conboy, serà bastante la declaraciòn verbal del Comandante del conboy, bajo su palabra de honor, de que los buques que estan bajo su proteccion pertenecen a la nacion, cuya bandera llevan, i cuando se dirijen à un puerto enemigo, que los dichos buques no tienen à su bordo articulos de contrabando de guerra.

ARTICULO 23°.

Se ha convenido ademas, que en todos los casos que ocurran, solo los Tribunales establecidos para causas de presas, en el pais à que las presas sean conducidas, tomaràn conocimiento de ellas.

such tribunal of either party shall pronounce judgment against any vessel or goods, or property claimed by the Citizens of the other party, the sentence or decree shall mention the reasons or motives on which the same shall have been founded, and an authenticated copy of the sentence or decree, and of all the proceedings in the case, shall, if demanded, be delivered to the commander or agent of said vessel, without any delay, he paying the legal fees for the same.

Y siempre que semejante Tribunal de cualquiera de las partes, pronunciase sentencia contra algun buque, ò efectos, ò propiedad reclamada por los Ciudadanos de la otra parte, la sentencia ò decreto harà mencion de las razones ò motivos en que aquella se haya fundado, i se entregarà sin demora alguna al comandante ò Agente de dicho buque, si lo solicitase, un testimonio autentico de la sentencia, ò decreto, ò de todo el proceso, pagando por el los derechos legales.

ARTICLE 24th

Whenever one of the contracting parties shall be engaged in war with another State, no Citizen of the other contracting party shall accept a Commission, or letter of marque, for the purpose of assisting or co-operating hostilely, with the said enemy, against the said party so at war, under the pain of being treated as a pirate.

ARTICULO 24º.

Siempre que una de las partes contratantes estuviere empeñada en guerra, con otro Estado, ningun Ciudadano de la otra parte contratante aceptarà una Comision ò letra de marca para el objeto de ayudar ò co-operar hostilmente con el dicho enemigo, contra la dicha parte que estè asi en guerra, bajo la pena de ser tratado como pirata.

ARTICLE 25th

If, by any fatality which cannot be expected, and which God forbid, the two contracting parties should be engaged in a war with each other, they have agreed, and do agree, now for then, that there shall be allowed the term of six months to the merchants residing on the coasts and in the ports of each other; and the term of one year to those who dwell

ARTICULO 25º.

Si por alguna fatalidad, que no puede esperarse, i que Dios no permita, las dos partes contratantes se viesen empeñadas en guerra una con otra, han convenido i convienen de ahora para entonces, que se concederà el termino de seis meses à los comerciantes residentes en las costas i en los puertos de entrambas, i el termino de un año à los que habitan en el

in the interior, to arrange their business and transport their effects wherever they please, giving to them the safe conduct necessary for it, which may serve as a sufficient protection until they arrive at the designated port. The Citizens of all other occupations who may be established in the territories or dominions of the United States and of the Federation of the Centre of America, shall be respected and maintained in the full enjoyment of their personal liberty and property, unless their particular conduct shall cause them to forfeit this protection, which in consideration of humanity the contracting parties engage to give them.

ARTICLE 26th

Neither the debts due from individuals of the one nation to the individuals of the other, nor shares, nor moneys, which they may have in public funds, nor in public or private banks, shall ever, in any event of war, or of national difference, be sequestered or confiscated.

ARTICLE 27th

Both the contracting parties being desirous of avoiding all inequality in relation to their public communications and official intercourse, have agreed, and do agree, to grant to the Envoys, Ministers, and other public Agents, the same favours, immu-

interior, para arreglar sus negocios, i transportar sus efectos à donde quieran, dandoles el salvo conducto necesario para ello, que les sirva de suficiente proteccion hasta que lleguen al puerto que designen. Los Ciudadanos de otras ocupaciones, que se hallen establecidos en los territorios ò dominios de la Federacion de Centro-America, ò los Estados Unidos de America, seràn respetados, i mantenidos en el pleno goze de su libertad personal i propiedad, à menos que su conducta particular les haga perder esta proteccion, que en consideracion à la humanidad, las partes contratantes se comprometen à prestarles.

ARTICULO 26°.

Ni las deudas contraidas por los individuos de una nacion, con los individuos de la otra, ni las acciones ò dineros, que puedan tener en los fondos publicos, ò en los bancos publicos, ò privados, seràn jamas secuestrados ò confiscados en ningun caso de guerra, ò diferencia nacional.

ARTICULO 27°.

Deseando ambas partes contratantes, evitar toda diferencia, relativa à etiqueta en sus comunicaciones, i correspondencias diplomaticas, han convenido asi mismo, i convienen en conceder à sus Enviados, Ministros, i otros Agentes Diplomaticos, los mismos

nities, and exemptions, which those of the most favoured nation do or shall enjoy; it being understood that whatever favours, immunities, or privileges, the United States of America or the Federation of the Centre of America may find it proper to give to the Ministers and public Agents of any other power, shall by the same act be extended to those of each of the contracting parties.

ARTICLE 28th

To make more effectual the protection which the United States and the Federation of the Centre of America shall afford in future to the navigation and commerce of the Citizens of each other, they agree to receive and admit Consuls and Vice-Consuls in all the ports open to foreign commerce, who shall enjoy in them all the rights, prerogatives, and immunities, of the Consuls and Vice-Consuls of the most favoured nation; each contracting party, however, remaining at liberty to except those ports and places in which the admission and residence of such Consuls may not seem convenient.

ARTICLE 29th

In order that the Consuls and Vice-Consuls of the two contracting parties may enjoy the rights,

favores, inmunidades, i esenciones de que gozan, ò gozaren en lo venidero los de las naciones mas favorecidas, bien entendido que cualquier favor, inmunidad ò privilegio, que la Federacion de Centro America, ò los Estados Unidos de America, tengan por conveniente dispensar à los Enviados, Ministros, i Agentes Diplomaticos de otras Potencias, se haga por el mismo hecho estensivo à los de una i otra de las partes contratantes.

ARTICULO 28º.

Para hacer mas efectiva la proteccion, que la Federacion de Centro America, i los Estados Unidos de America, daràn en adelante à la navegacion i comercio de los Ciudadanos de una i otra, se convienen en recibir i admitir Consules, i Vice-Consules en todos los puertos abiertos al comercio estrangero, quienes gozaràn en ellos todos los derechos, prerrogativas è inmunidades de los Consules, i Vice-Consules de la Nacion mas favorecida, quedando no obstante en libertad cada parte contratante, para eceptuar aquellos puertos i lugares en que la admision i residencia de semejantes Consules, i Vice-Consules no parezca conveniente.

ARTICULO 29º.

Para que los Consules i Vice-Consules de las dos partes contratantes, puedan gozar los derechos,

prerogatives and immunities, which belong to them, by their public character, they shall, before entering on the exercise of their functions, exhibit their commission or patent, in due form, to the Government to which they are accredited; and having obtained their *Exequatur*, they shall be held and considered as such, by all the authorities magistrates, and inhabitants, in the Consular district in which they reside.

prerrogativas, è inmunidades, que les corresponden por su caracter publico, antes de entrar en el ejercicio de sus funciones, presentaràn su comision ò patente en la forma debida, al Gobierno con quien estan acreditados, i habiendo obtenido el *exequatur*, seràn tenidos, i considerados como tales, por todas las autoridades, majistrados i habitantes del distrito Consular en que residan.

ARTICLE 30th

It is likewise agreed, that the Consuls, their secretaries, officers, and persons attached to the service of Consuls, they not being Citizens of the country in which the Consul resides, shall be exempt from all public service, and also from all kind of taxes, imposts and contributions, except those which they shall be obliged to pay on account of commerce, or their property, to which the Citizens and inhabitants, native and foreign, of the country in which they reside are subject, being in every thing besides subject to the laws of the respective States. The archives and papers of the Consulates shall be respected inviolably, and under no pretext whatever shall any magistrate seize, or in any way interfere with them.

ARTICULO 30º.

Se ha convenido igualmente, que los Consules, sus secretarios, officiales i personas agregadas al servicio de los consulados (no siendo estas personas Ciudadanos del pais en que el Consul reside) estaràn esentos de todo servicio publico, i tambien de toda especie de pechos, impuestos, i contribuciones, eceptuando aquellas que esten obligados à pagar por razon de comercio, ò propiedad, i à las cuales estan sujetos los Ciudadanos i habitantes naturales, i estrangeros del pais en que residen, quedando en todo lo demas, sujetos à las leyes de los respectivos Estados. Los archivos i papeles de los consulados seràn respetados inviolablemente, i bajo ningun pretesto los ocuparà magistrado alguno, ni tendra en ellos ninguna intervencion.

Article 31ˢᵗ

The said Consuls shall have power to require the assistance of the authorities of the country for the arrest, detention, and custody of deserters from the public and private vessels of their country, and for that purpose they shall address themselves to the courts, judges, and officers competent, and shall demand the said deserters in writing, proving by an exhibition of the registers of the vessel or ship's roll, or other public documents, that those men were part of the said crews; and on this demand, so proved, (saving, however, where the contrary is proved,) the delivery shall not be refused. Such deserters, when arrested, shall be put at the disposal of the said Consuls, and may be put in the public prisons at the request and expense of those who reclaim them, to be sent to the ships to which they belonged, or to others of the same nation. But if they be not sent back within two months, to be counted from the day of their arrest, they shall be set at liberty, and shall be no more arrested for the same cause.

Article 32ᵈ

For the purpose of more effectually protecting their commerce and navigation, the two contracting parties do hereby agree, as soon hereafter as circumstances

Articulo 31°.

Los dichos Consules tendràn poder de requerir el auxilio de las autoridades locales, para la prision, detencion i custodia de los desertores de buques publicos i particulares de su pais, i para este objeto se dirigiràn à los Tribunales, Jueces, i oficiales competentes, i pediràn los dichos desertores por escrito, probando por una presentacion de los registros de los buques, rol del equipage, ù otros documentos publicos, que aquellos hombres eran parte de las dichas tripulaciones, i à esta demanda asi probada (menos no obstante cuando se probare lo contrario) no se reusarà la entrega. Semejantes desertores, luego que sean arrestados, se pondràn à disposicion de los dichos Consules, i pueden ser depositados en las prisiones publicas, à solicitud i espensas de los que los reclamen, para ser enviados a los buques à que corresponden, ò à otros de la misma nacion. Pero si no fueren mandados dentro de dos meses contados desde el dia de su arresto, seràn puestos en libertad, i no volveràn a ser presos por la misma causa.

Articulo 32°.

Para proteger mas efectivamente su comercio i navegacion, las dos partes contratantes se convienen en formar luego que las circumstancias lo permitan,

will permit them, to form a Consular Convention, which shall declare specially the powers and immunities of the Consuls and Vice Consuls of the respective parties.

ARTICLE 33ᵈ

The United States of America and the Federation of the Centre of America, desiring to make as durable as circumstances will permit, the relations which are to be established between the two parties by virtue of this Treaty or General Convention of Peace, Amity, Commerce and Navigation, have declared solemnly, and do agree to the following points:

1ˢᵗ The present Treaty shall remain in full force and virtue for the term of twelve years, to be counted from the day of the exchange of the ratifications, in all the parts relating to commerce and navigation; and in all those parts which relate to peace and friendship, it shall be permanently and perpitually binding on both powers.

2ˡʸ If any one or more of the Citizens of either party shall infringe any of the articles of this Treaty, such Citizen shall be held personally responsible for the same, and the harmony and good correspondence between the two Nations shall not be interrupted thereby; each party engaging in no way to protect the

una Convencion Consular, que declare mas especialmente los poderes é inmunidades de los Consules i Vice Consules de las partes respectivas.

ARTICULO 33°.

La Federacion de Centro-America i los Estados Unidos de America, deseando hacer tan duraderas i firmes, como las circumstancias lo permitan las relaciones que han de establecerse entre las dos Potencias, en virtud del presente tratado ò Convencion general de paz, amistad, comercio i navegacion, han declarado solennemente i convienen en los puntos siguientes:

1° El presente tratado permanecerà en su fuerza i vigor por el termino de doce años contados desde el dia del cange de las ratificaciones, en todos los puntos concernientes à comercio i navegacion, i en todos los demas puntos que se refieren à paz i amistad, serà permanente, i perpetuamente obligatorio para ambas potencias.

2° Si alguno ó algunos de los Ciudadanos de una ú otra parte infringiesen alguno de los articulos contenidos en el presente tratado, dichos Ciudadanos serán personalmente responsables, sin que por esto se interrumpa la harmonia i buena correspondencia entre las dos Naciones, comprometiendose cada una á no prote-

offender, or sanction such violation.

3^{ly} If, (which, indeed, cannot be expected,) unfortunately, any of the articles contained in the present Treaty shall be violated or infringed in any other way whatever, it is expressly stipulated, that neither of the contracting parties will order or authorize any acts of reprisal, nor declare war against the other, on complaints of injuries or damages, until the said party considering itself offended, shall first have presented to the other a statement of such injuries or damages, verified by competent proof, and demanded justice and satisfaction, and the same shall have been either refused or unreasonably delayed.

4^{ly} Nothing in this Treaty contained shall, however, be construed, or operate contrary to former and existing public Treaties with other Sovereigns or States.

The present Treaty of Peace, Amity, Commerce, and Navigation, shall be approved and ratified by the President of the United States of America, by and with the advice and consent of the Senate thereof, and by the Government of the Federation of the Centre of America, and the ratifications shall be exchanged in the City of Guatemala within eight

ger de modo alguno al ofensor, ó sancionar semejante violacion.

3º Si, (lo que á la verdad no puede esperarse) desgraciadamente, alguno de los articulos contenidos en el presente tratado, fuesen en alguna otra manera violados, ó infringidos, se estipula espresamente que ninguna de las dos partes contratantes ordenará, ó autorizará ningunos actos de represalia, ni declarará la guerra contra la otra por quejas de injurias, ó daños, hasta que la parte que se crea ofendida, haya antes presentado á la otra una esposicion de aquellas injurias, ó daños, verificada con pruebas i testimonios competentes, exigiendo justicia i satisfaccion, i esto haya sido negado, ó diferido sin razon.

4º Nada de cuanto se contiene en el presente Tratado, se construirá, sin embargo, ni obrará, en contra de otros Tratados publicos anteriores, i existentes con otros Soberanos ó Estados.

El presente Tratado de paz, amistad, comercio i navegacion, será ratificado por el Gobierno de la Federacion de Centro-America, i por el Presidente de los Estados Unidos de America con consejo i consentimiento del Senado de los mismos; i las ratificaciones seran cangeadas en la Ciudad de Guatemala dentro de ochos meses contados

months from the date of the signature hereof, or sooner if possible.

desde este dia, ó antes si fuese
posible.

In faith whereof, We, the Plenipotentiaries of the United States
of America and of the Federation
of the Centre of America, have
signed and sealed these presents.

En fe de lo cual nosotros los
Plenipotenciarios de la Federacion de Centro-America, i de
los Estados Unidos de America
hemos firmado i sellado las presentes.

Done in the City of Washington, on the fifth day of December,
in the year of our Lord one thousand eight hundred and twenty
five, in the fiftieth year of the
Independence of the United States
of America, and the fifth of that
of the Federation of the Centre of
America, in Duplicate.

Dadas en la Ciudad de Washington el dia cinco de Deciembre
del año del Señor mil ocho
cientos veinticinco, quinto de
la independencia de la Federacion de Centro-America i quinquagesimo de la de los Estados
Unidos de America, por duplicado.

H. CLAY.   [Seal]
ANTONIO JOSE CAÑAS   [Seal]

[Seal]   ANTONIO JOSE CAÑAS
[Seal]   H. CLAY

NOTES

This agreement, like the treaty with Colombia of October 3, 1824
(Document 47), is frequently called a convention, following the wording of its heading, "General Convention of Peace, Amity, Commerce
and Navigation"; it is so styled in the presidential message of December 15, 1825, and in the Senate resolution of December 29 (Executive Journal, III, 455, 468), in both instruments of ratification, in the
certificate of exchange of ratifications, and in the proclamation; but it
might correctly have been called a treaty, as it is in the presidential
message to Congress of December 5, 1826 (American State Papers,
Foreign Relations, VI, 208), and in various places in the agreement
itself.   The preamble speaks of "a Treaty or general Convention,"
and in Article 33 the expression "this treaty" or "the present treaty"
occurs six times.   Considering this use of the word "treaty" in the
document itself, and in view of the fact that the agreement has, in the
strictest sense of the word, every form of a treaty, it is referred to as
such in the headnote and in these notes.

The negotiations which resulted in this treaty were carried on in
Washington.   The immediate model of its provisions was the treaty
with Colombia of October 3, 1824 (Document 47), Articles 1, 2, and
4–31 of which are essentially the same as Articles 1, 2, and 6–33 of this
treaty; but Articles 3–5 of this treaty provide a commercial system

quite different from that of Article 3 of the treaty with Colombia, which is based on the principle of the most favored nation; here national treatment is accorded (except for the coasting trade) as to residence, trade, navigation, and commerce (Article 3); as to vessels and tonnage duties (Article 4); and the most-favored-nation clause of Article 5 relates to duties on, and prohibition of, imports and exports.

THE CENTRAL AMERICAN FEDERATION

The five constituent states of the Central American Federation are now the Republics of Costa Rica, El Salvador, Guatemala, Honduras, and Nicaragua. A declaration of the independence of the former provinces was issued on September 15, 1821; after internal differences, union was adopted by a national constituent assembly on July 1, 1823; and the definitive constitution of November 22, 1824, followed. Interstate dissensions tended to loosen the union in the following decade, and the congressional decree of May 30, 1838, granting to the states freedom of action in most important matters, brought about a practical dissolution of the union in 1839; and despite efforts to maintain or renew it, there was a complete termination of the Federation by 1847. The last diplomatic representative of the United States accredited to the Central American Federation was William S. Murphy, appointed "Special and Confidential Agent of the United States to Central America" on July 28, 1841, who arrived in the city of Guatemala on December 25, 1841, and took formal leave of the Government there in March, 1842. A "General Convention of Peace, Amity, Commerce and Navigation between the United States of America and the Federation of Central America" was signed at Guatemala on July 14, 1838; in substance it was a renewal of this treaty; but it did not go into force (see Richardson, III, 533–34).

There seems to have been a good deal of uncertainty in Washington as to the exact name to be used in describing the Central American Government.

Secretary of State John Quincy Adams relates that "Antonio José Cañaz, Envoy Extraordinary from the United Provinces of the Centre of America," was officially received by President Monroe on August 4, 1824 (Memoirs of John Quincy Adams, VI, 405–6).

The earliest official documents from the Central American Government were delivered by that Minister; one was his letter of credence, dated April 30, 1824, which is headed "El Supremo Poder Executivo de las provincias unidas del Centro de Amèrica," the inscription of the seal being similar: "Provincias Unidas del Centro de America" (original in D. S., 1 Notes from the Central American Legation, 22). His full power follows the same form (certified copy *ibid.*, 19); a translation thereof (*ibid.*, 21) follows:

The Supreme Executive Power of the United Provinces of the Center of America

To all who shall see these presents, Greeting:

Whereas the order of 8 July of last year, decreed by the Constituent National Assembly which at present rules, authorizes us to appoint envoys to foreign governments and to direct the diplomatic and commercial relations in which they should be occupied; and it suits the general good and prosperity of said Provinces to proceed in all preference to the appointment of a subject in whom are united the qualities of illustriousness, probity, distinguished patriotism, and zeal for their absolute independence and aggrandizement, near the Government of the United States of North America; and being convinced that the Citizen Antonio José Cañas, a deputy of the Constituent National Assembly for the Province of San Salvador, possesses these qualities in a superior degree, after having fulfilled the other requisites provided for these cases, we have appointed, and in fact do appoint, him Envoy Extraordinary and Minister Plenipotentiary near the Government of said Republic, that he may treat in the name of this, as far as may be proper for its good and prosperity, in those cases which may not afford time to wait for the orders of the Government, and in which the want of authority might impede a ready and correct performance thereof, guiding himself in everything else by the instructions which have been given, and hereafter shall be given, him, and that in virtue thereof he may propose, commence, conclude, and sign, in the name of the Nation which he represents, the stipulations and conventions which its interest and that of said Republic require, holding, as we hold, from this time, as ratified and valid, what he shall thus conclude, it being agreeable to the fundamental laws adopted, and others which are in force; and we offer, in the name of the same Nation, to observe and fulfil it and cause it to be scrupulously observed and fulfilled, urging and causing to be issued the letters of ratification in due form, and causing them to be delivered that they may be exchanged in the time agreed upon, entirely agreeable to the requisites established and usual in such negotiations.

In faith whereof we give these presents in the National Palace of Guatemala the thirtieth of March of the year of grace one thousand eight hundred and twenty-four, signed by us, sealed with the seal of the Nation, and countersigned by the Minister of State and of Despatch of Relations. With two individuals by the permission of the Assembly. With two individuals by the permission of the absence of the Citizen O-Horan, with the permission of the Assembly.

JOSÉ DEL VALLE, *President*
MANUEL J. ARCE   [Seal]

By order of the Supreme Executive Power:
MARCIAL LEBADUA
    Minister of State and Relations

The full power given to Henry Clay, Secretary of State, to conclude this treaty, which is dated November 22, 1825, and is in the usual form (D. S., 2 Credences, 29), used the style, "The Central Republic of America."

In the treaty itself the English text speaks throughout of "the Federation of the Centre of America" and the Spanish text of "la Federacion de Centro-America," except in Article 4, where the term "Central Republic" is used twice in the English and "Republica Central" twice in the Spanish. In other documents other forms are used. The instrument of ratification on the part of the Central American Federation has "Republica de centro-america" and also "Republica federal de centro-america." Both of those expressions are found in the full power from the Central American Government to Pedro Gonzalez to exchange the ratifications, a copy of which, dated August 1, 1826, is in the treaty file. In neither of the two documents last mentioned is the word "federacion." In the certificate of the exchange of ratifications at Guatemala on August 2,

1826, there is no consistency of expression, as may be seen from the text thereof, in English and Spanish, which follows:

We, the Undersigned, John Williams Chargé D'Affaires of the United States of America near the Government of the Federation of the Centre of Amirica, and Pedro Gonzales Chief officer of the Department of State, dispatch, War & Marine, Secretary of Legacion of the Republic of Central America near the Governments of South America, being fully and especially empowered.

Certify; That the Ratifications of the General Convention of Peace, amity, commerce and navigation, between the Said United States and the Said Federation of the Centre of America concluded at Washington, on the fifth day of December one thousand eight Hundred and twenty five, accompanied with all Suitable Solemnities, and after due comparison, each with the other and with the original example, of the Convention have been exchanged by us this day.

In witness whereof we have Signed this act in duplicates, and in both Languages, and have Sealed the Same with our respective Seals at the City of Guatemala this Second day of August one thousand eight Hundred & twenty six.

Los infrascriptos Pedro Gonzalez oficial mayor de la secretaria de estado y del despacho de guerra y marina y secretario de la legacion de la republica de centro-america cerca de los gobiernos de Sur-america autorizado especial y plenamente pᵃ verificar el cange de las ratificaciones de la convencion general de paz, amistad, comercio y navegacion, concluida en Washington el dia cinco de diciembre del año mil ochocientos veinte y cinco entre la republica de Centro-america y los estados unidos, y Juan Williams encargado de negocios de los mismos estados unidos cerca del Gobierno de dicha republica.

Certificamos: qᵉ las ratificaciones de la convencion general de paz, amistad, comercio y navegacion, entre la dicha federacion de centro-america y los estados unidos, concluida en la ciudad de Washington el dia cinco de diciembre de mil ochocientos veinte y cinco, rebertida de las solemnidades convenientes y debidamente colijada una con otra y con los originales de la convencion, han sido cangedas por nos en este dia

En fe de lo cual hemos firmado las presentes por duplicado y en ambos idiomas, y las hemos sellado con nuestros Sellos respectivos en la ciudad de Guatemala, el dia dos de agosto de mil ochocientos veinte y seis.

On December 22, 1825, John Williams, of Tennessee, was nominated to be Chargé d'Affaires "to the Federation of Central America" (Executive Journal, III, 461); and by instructions dated February 10, 1826 (D. S., 11 Instructions, U. S. Ministers, 5–9), addressed to "John Williams, appointed Chargé d'Affaires of the United States, to the Federation of the Centre of America," Williams was directed to proceed to his post "in the United States Corvette John Adams, now lying at Norfolk," and to exchange the ratifications of this treaty. The United States instrument of ratification accompanied those instructions, in the course of which were used such varying terms as "the Government of the Federal States of the Centre of America"; "the Government of the Central Republic"; "the Republic of Guatemala"; "the Republic of the Centre"; and "the Republic of the Centre of America." (See also Manning, Diplomatic Correspondence of the United States Concerning the Independence of the Latin-American Nations, II, 880, 886, 891.)

The relevant Central American constitutional provisions are to be found in the "Bases de constitucion federal," formulated by a national

constituent assembly on December 27, 1823 (Library of the Department of State, pamphlet endorsed as received August 5, 1824, from the "Minister from Guatemala"). Articles 2 and 3 of those "Bases" read as follows:

La forma de gobierno de las provincias unidas del centro de america, es *republicana representativa federal*.

La denominacion de estas provincias en lo succesivo: *estados federados del centro de america*.

Article 9 of the definitive constitution of November 22, 1824 (Constitucion de la república federal de Centro-América dada por la asamblea nacional constituyente en 22 de noviembre de 1824, official print), reads, "La República se denomina: *Federacion de Centro-américa*," but the inscription in the seal is "República Federal de Centro-América."

THE FILE PAPERS

Except for the attested resolution of advice and consent of the Senate (Executive Journal, III, 468), the treaty file is complete. The original signed treaty is written in English and Spanish, the former on the left pages, the latter on the right; and, as the printed texts show, the *alternat* was observed; the United States is named first in the English text and second in the Spanish text throughout, and the signature of Henry Clay, who signed on the part of the United States, is first following the English text and last following the Spanish text.

The duplicate United States instrument of ratification and the original proclamation are embodied in one rather unusual document; it begins with the preliminary paragraph of the ratification; at the top of the reverse of the same page and the obverse of the next page is attached a single sheet of paper (now cut in two) on which is written the first paragraph of the original proclamation; then follows the text of the treaty in English and Spanish, the English on the left pages and the Spanish on the right; following the treaty text is another sheet of paper, attached at the head of the next two pages in the same manner as before, on which appears the rest of the original proclamation; and beneath the proclamation is the conclusion of the instrument of ratification.

As the ratification is dated January 16, 1826, and the proclamation the following October 28, the latter document was affixed to the former in the fashion described, presumably on or about its date.

The proclamation was communicated to Congress with the presidential message of December 5, 1826 (American State Papers, Foreign Relations, VI, 207, 208, 269–76).

The instrument of ratification on the part of the Central American Government includes both texts in parallel columns, the Spanish on the left. It is dated July 29, in the year 1826, "the sixth of the independence and the fourth of the liberty of the Republic"; and it recites that the Federal Congress had ratified the "convention" by a decree dated June 28, 1826, approved by the Senate July 29.

The certificate of the exchange of ratifications at Guatemala on August 2, 1826, is in duplicate, one example in English and one in Spanish, the texts of which appear above.

The Exchange of Ratifications

The despatch of Chargé d'Affaires John Williams of August 3, 1826 (D. S., 1 Despatches, Central American Federation, No. 1), the day after the exchange of ratifications, appears to have enclosed the Central American instrument of ratification; the despatch is endorsed as received on October 28, 1826, and the proclamation is dated the same day. That despatch, from which the following is extracted, contains an account of the arrival of Williams in Guatemala on May 2, 1826, with the United States instrument of ratification, and of the delays encountered in executing the exchange of ratifications:

On the 19th [of May] I was officially presented to Mr. Arce the President. In the evening of the same day I addressed a note to Mr Sosa informing him that I was prepared to exchange the ratifications of the treaty between our Governments concluded & signed at Washington on the 5th of last December. To which on the next day he replyed that he had been only five days in official possession the treaty. And so soon as it was ratified by Congress he would proceed with me in the exchange of the ratifications. The constitution of this Republic requires that a treaty should be ratified by both houses of Congress. It is difficult to account for the unreasonable delay which has taken place. They have all been profuse in their professions of regard for the United States, & of esteem for me individually. In conversations with those in authority on the subject of the treaty, they expressed their unqualified approbation of it. Yet the President defered submitting it to Congress until a short period before the time fixed for the adjournment of the House of Deputies. And when all agreed there was not time to act on it. When a proposition was made in the House of Deputies to prolong the Sessions of that body from the first to the last June the friends of the President voted against it. And it was finally carried by the arrival of an absent member. Yet most of these Gentlemen voted for the treaty. In the secret discussions in the House of Deputies it was objected, that Altho the treaty on its face was reciprocal, there was in fact no reciprocity in it. Because this Government had no shipping. That by the terms of the treaty this Government would not have it in its power to grant peculiar concessions to Mexico & the other Spanish Republics. That there was no article stipulating for offensive & defensive cooperation in time of War, without which this Government ought not to treat, & for the want of such a stipulation it was said Mexico had refused to treat with the United States. And finally that treating with the U States ought to be refered to the Congress at Panama, or posponed for the decisions of that body. I met these objections in the best way I could. I have not heard from Mr Poinsett & cannot say what has been the course of the Mexican Government. On the day before the House of Deputies adjourned the friends of the treaty declared their sessions perpetual (equivalent to our previous question) & thereby put an end to the discussion. The Senate remained in Session after the House adjourned. And rec^d the treaty on the 3^d day of July & ratified it on the 29th of the same month. They had little else before them during all that time. I have not yet learned the precise objections in the Senate. I was not prepared to expect the delay which has occured. It is not ascribable as I persuade myself to any motive disrespectful or unfriendly to the U States, but to an inherent disposition for procrastination, & an undue caution in the transaction of business. They may not have duly appreciated the frank & generous of the U States towards them, & have supposed that some benefits might result from delay. I hastened them as much as propriety & decorum would permit. But could not procure an earlier decision. The ratifications were exchanged on yesterday. And Mr Marshall will set out with the treaty for the U States on next Saturday.

Treaty Series No. 65
8 Statutes at Large, 340–43
18 *ibid.*, pt. 2, Public Treaties, 167–70

51

DENMARK : APRIL 26, 1826

Convention of Friendship, Commerce, and Navigation, signed at Washington April 26, 1826. Original in English.
Submitted to the Senate April 28, 1826. Resolution of advice and consent May 4, 1826. Ratified by the United States May 6, 1826. Ratified by Denmark August 2, 1826. Ratifications exchanged at Copenhagen August 10, 1826. Proclaimed October 14, 1826.
Following the text of the convention are printed the note of Secretary of State Henry Clay to the Chevalier Pedersen, Minister Resident from Denmark, dated April 25, 1826, formally reserving certain claims on behalf of United States citizens, and also the answering note of the Danish Minister Resident, dated the following day.

General Convention of Friendship, Commerce and Navigation, between the United States and H. M. the King of Denmark.

The United States of America and His Majesty, the King of Denmark, being desirous to make firm and permanent the peace and friendship which happily prevail between the two nations, and to extend the commercial relations which subsist between their respective territories and people, have agreed to fix, in a manner clear and positive, the rules which shall in future be observed between the one and the other party, by means of a general convention of friendship, commerce and navigation—With that object, the President of the United States of America has conferred full powers on Henry Clay, their Secretary of State, and His Majesty, the King of Denmark, has conferred like powers on Peter Pedersen, His privy Counsellor of Legation, and Minister Resident near the said States, Knight of the Dannebrog, who, after having exchanged their said full powers, found to be in due and proper form, have agreed to the following Articles:

ARTICLE I.

The contracting parties, desiring to live in peace and harmony with all the other nations of the earth, by means of a policy frank and equally friendly with all, engage, mutually, not to grant any particular favour to other nations, in respect of commerce and navigation, which shall not immediately become common to the other party, who shall

enjoy the same freely, if the concession were freely made, or on allowing the same compensation, if the concession were conditional.

ARTICLE 2.

The contracting parties being likewise desirous of placing the commerce and navigation of their respective countries on the liberal basis of perfect equality and reciprocity, mutually agree that the Citizens and subjects of each may frequent all the coasts and countries of the other (with the exception hereafter provided for in the sixth Article) and reside and trade there in all kinds of produce, manufactures and merchandize, and they shall enjoy all the rights privileges and exemptions, in navigation and commerce, which native Citizens or subjects do or shall enjoy, submitting themselves to the laws, decrees and usages there established, to which native Citizens or subjects are subjected. But it is understood that this Article does not include the coasting trade of either country, the regulation of which is reserved by the parties, respectively, according to their own separate laws.

ARTICLE 3.

They likewise agree that whatever kind of produce, manufacture, or merchandize, of any foreign country, can be, from time to time, lawfully imported into the United States, in vessels belonging wholly to the Citizens thereof, may be also imported in vessels wholly belonging to the subjects of Denmark; and that no higher or other duties upon the tonnage of the vessel or her Cargo shall be levied and collected, whether the importation be made in vessels of the one country, or of the other. And, in like manner, that whatever kind of produce, manufacture or merchandize, of any foreign country, can be, from time to time, lawfully imported into the dominions of the King of Denmark, in the vessels thereof, (with the exception hereafter mentioned in the sixth article) may be also imported in vessels of the United States, and that no higher or other duties, upon the tonnage of the vessel or her cargo shall be levied and collected, whether the importation be made in vessels of the one country, or of the other. And they further agree that whatever may be lawfully exported or re-exported, from the one country in its own vessels to any foreign country, may, in like manner, be exported, or re-exported, in the vessels of the other country. And the same bounties, duties and drawbacks shall be allowed and collected, whether such exportation, or re-exportation, be made in vessels of the United States or of Denmark.

Nor shall higher or other charges of any kind be imposed, in the ports of one party, on vessels of the other, than are or shall be payable, in the same ports, by native vessels.

ARTICLE 4.

No higher or other duties shall be imposed on the importation into the United States of any article, the produce or manufacture of the dominions of His Majesty, the King of Denmark, and no higher or other duties shall be imposed on the importation into the said Dominions of any article, the produce or manufacture of the United States, than are or shall be payable on the like articles, being the produce or manufacture of any other foreign country. Nor shall any higher or other duties or charges be imposed in either of the two countries, on the exportation of any articles to the United States, or to the dominions of His Majesty, the King of Denmark, respectively, than such as are or may be payable on the exportation of the like articles to any other foreign country. Nor shall any prohibition be imposed on the exportation or importation of any articles the produce or manufacture of the United States or of the dominions of His Majesty, the King of Denmark, to or from the territories of the United States, or to or from the said dominions, which shall not equally extend to all other nations.

ARTICLE 5.

Neither the vessels of the United States nor their cargoes shall, when they pass the Sound or the Belts, pay higher or other duties than those which are or may be paid by the most favoured nation.

ARTICLE 6.

The present Convention shall not apply to the Northern possessions of His Majesty, the King of Denmark, that is to say, Iceland, the Ferroe Islands, and Greenland; nor to places situated beyond the Cape of Good Hope, the right to regulate the direct intercourse with which possessions and places, is reserved by the parties respectively. And it is further agreed that this Convention is not to extend to the direct trade between Denmark and the West India Colonies of His Danish Majesty, but in the intercourse with those Colonies, it is agreed that whatever can be lawfully imported into or exported from the said Colonies in vessels of one party from or to the ports of the United States, or from or to the ports of any other foreign country, may, in like manner, and with the same duties and charges, applicable to vessel and cargo, be imported into or exported from the said Colonies, in vessels of the other party.

ARTICLE 7.

The United States and His Danish Majesty mutually agree that no higher or other duties, charges or taxes of any kind shall be levied in the territories or dominions of either party, upon any personal property, money, or effects of their respective Citizens or subjects, on the removal of the same from their territories or dominions reciprocally, either upon the inheritance of such property, money, or effects, or otherwise than are or shall be payable in each State, upon the same, when removed by a Citizen or subject of such State, respectively.

ARTICLE 8.

To make more effectual the protection which the United States and His Danish Majesty shall afford, in future, to the navigation and commerce of their respective Citizens and subjects, they agree mutually to receive and admit Consuls and Vice-Consuls in all the ports open to foreign commerce; who shall enjoy in them all the rights, privileges and immunities of the Consuls and Vice-Consuls of the most favoured nation, each contracting party, however, remaining at liberty to except those ports and places, in which the admission and residence of such Consuls may not seem convenient.

ARTICLE 9.

In order that the Consuls and Vice-Consuls of the contracting parties may enjoy the rights, privileges and immunities which belong to them, by their public character, they shall, before entering on the exercise of their functions, exhibit their Commission or Patent in due form to the Government to which they are accredited; and, having obtained their Exequatur, which shall be granted gratis, they shall be held and considered as such by all the authorities, magistrates and inhabitants in the Consular District in which they reside.

ARTICLE 10.

It is likewise agreed that the Consuls and persons attached to their necessary service, they not being natives of the country in which the Consul resides, shall be exempt from all public service, and also from all kind of taxes, imposts and contributions, except those which they shall be obliged to pay, on account of commerce, or their property, to which inhabitants, native and foreign, of the country in which such Consuls reside, are subject, being in every thing, besides, subject to the laws of the respective States. The Archives and papers of the Consulate shall be respected inviolably, and, under no pretext, whatever, shall any magistrate seize or in any way interfere with them.

ARTICLE 11.

The present Convention shall be in force for ten years from the date hereof, and further until the end of one year after either of the contracting parties shall have given notice to the other of its intention to terminate the same, each of the contracting parties reserving to itself the right of giving such notice to the other at the end of the said term of ten years; and it is hereby agreed between them, that, on the expiration of one year after such notice shall have been received by either from the other party, this Convention and all the provisions thereof shall altogether cease and determine.

ARTICLE 12.

This Convention shall be approved and ratified by the President of the United States, by and with the advice and consent of the Senate thereof, and by His Majesty, the King of Denmark, and the ratifications shall be exchanged in the City of Copenhagen within eight months from the date of the signature hereof, or sooner if possible.

In faith whereof We the Plenipotentiaries of the United States of America and of His Danish Majesty have signed and sealed these presents.

Done, in triplicate, at the City of Washington on the twenty-sixth day of April, in the year of our Lord, one thousand eight hundred and twenty six, in the fiftieth year of the Independence of the United States of America.

H. CLAY   [Seal]

Pr PEDERSEN   [Seal]

The Chevalier PEDERSEN
Minister Resident from Denmark.

The undersigned, Secretary of State of the United States, by the direction of the President thereof, has the honor to state to Mr Pedersen, Minister Resident of His Majesty the King of Denmark that it would have been satisfactory to the Government of the United States if Mr Pedersen had been charged with instructions, in the negotiation which has just terminated, to treat of the indemnities due to citizens of the United States in consequence of the siezure, detention and condemnation of their property in the ports of His Danish Majesty. But, as he has no instructions to that effect, the undersigned is directed at and before proceeding to the signature of the Treaty of Friendship, Commerce and Navigation, on which they have agreed, explicitly to

declare that the omission to provide for those indemnities is not hereafter to be interpreted as a waiver or abandonment of them by the Government of the United States, which, on the contrary, is firmly resolved to persevere in the pursuit of them until they shall be finally arranged upon principles of equity and justice. And to guard against any misconception of the fact of the silence of the treaty, in the above particular, or of the views of the American Government, the undersigned requests that Mᴿ Pedersen will transmit this official declaration to the Government of Denmark. And he avails himself of this occasion to tender to Mᴿ Pedersen assurances of his distinguished consideration.

(signed)   H. CLAY.

DEPARTMENT OF STATE, WASHINGTON, *25. April, 1826.*

The Honorable HENRY CLAY,
> *Secretary of State of the United States.*

The undersigned Minister Resident of His Majesty the King of Denmark has the honor herewith to acknowledge having received Mᴿ Clay' official Note of this day, declaratory of the advanced claims against Denmark, not being waived on the part of the United States, by the convention agreed upon and about to be signed, which Note he as requested, will transmit to his Government; and he avails himself of this occasion to renew to Mᴿ Clay assurances of his distinguished Consideration.

Pᴿ PEDERSEN

WASHINGTON *26, April 1826.*

NOTES

This was the first treaty made between the United States and Denmark. While throughout the text it is called a convention, the note of Secretary of State Clay of April 25, 1826, refers to it as the "Treaty of Friendship, Commerce and Navigation."

Two of the three preliminary drafts of this convention which are in the treaty file refer to it as a "General Convention of *Peace*, Friendship, Commerce, and Navigation," and in the three places in the original document where the title is given, the word "peace" was first written and later erased or crossed out. This change was probably made just before the signature of the treaty, and certainly not much later, for the United States instrument of ratification of May 6, 1826, omits the word "peace" without erasure or alteration, and that word is also omitted from the Senate print of the treaty (Senate Confidential Document, April 28, 1826, 19th Congress, 1st session, Regular Confidential Documents, IV, 111–15).

The File Papers

Except for the attested resolution of the Senate of May 4, 1826 (Executive Journal, III, 536), the treaty file is complete. One original is in the file, as noted below, and a copy of the text is within the duplicate United States instrument of ratification, which is bound within the original proclamation. That instrument of ratification states the date of the Senate resolution incorrectly as the "third" of May, 1826, with a change in pencil to the correct date of the "fourth."

The instrument of ratification by the King of Denmark is written in the Danish language, except for the text of the convention therein included, which is in English only. The date of that instrument is August 2, 1826, although a despatch of John Rainals, Consul of the United States at Copenhagen, of July 29 (D. S., 3 Consular Despatches, Copenhagen), a duplicate of which is in the treaty file, states that he had on that day been informed by the Minister of Foreign Affairs that the King of Denmark "had yesterday ratified the Treaty of Commerce." With that instrument is an English translation thereof, made at Copenhagen and enclosed with a despatch of Rainals of August 11, 1826, which is also in the treaty file. The certificate of the exchange of ratifications, in English, which was signed in duplicate at Copenhagen on August 10 by Count E. H. Schimmelmann, the Danish Minister of Foreign Affairs, and by Rainals, was an enclosure with the same despatch.

The original proclamation does not have either within or appended to it, the notes of April 25 and 26, 1826, of Secretary of State Clay and the Chevalier Pedersen, respectively; but in the press of the period (e.g., Niles' Weekly Register, XXXI, 119–21, October 21, 1826) those notes were printed following the signature and countersignature of the proclamation, and the above-mentioned publication adds the notation, "Publishers of the laws of the United States will please to add the foregoing correspondence to the proclamation, accordingly, in their respective papers." The proclamation is printed, with the notes appended, in American State Papers, Foreign Relations, VI, 266–68, and the treaty text has been similarly printed with the notes appended in United States treaty collections since that time.

The Full Powers

The full power given to Secretary of State Clay under date of April 17, 1826, is in the usual form (D. S., 2 Credences, 46). A certified copy of that given to the Chevalier Pedersen was enclosed with his note dated April 4, 1825 (D. S., 1 Notes from the Danish Legation). The document was written in French and reads in translation as follows (certain titles and the certification omitted):

Frederic the Sixth, by the Grace of God King of Denmark, etc., etc.

Be it known by these presents that, having the desire to facilitate and to extend relations of commerce and of navigation which subsist at this time between Our states and the United States of America and desiring to establish those relations on bases reciprocally advantageous, We have to that end chosen and

named, as by these presents and in virtue of these full powers We choose and name, as Plenipotentiary on Our part, Our Privy Counselor of Legation, Pierre Pedersen, Knight of Our Order of the Danebrog and Our Minister Resident near the United States of America, authorizing him to enter into negotiations and to conclude and sign a convention for the object above expressed, with him or those whom the President of the United States of America shall name for the same object.

Promising on the faith and word of a King, for Us and Our successors, to accept and faithfully to accomplish that which Our above-mentioned Plenipotentiary shall have drawn up, concluded, and signed in virtue of these full powers, as well as to cause Our ratification thereof to be transmitted within the agreed term.

In faith whereof We have signed these full powers with Our hand and have caused to be affixed thereto Our royal seal. Given in Our royal residence at Copenhagen the thirteenth of October in the year of grace one thousand eight hundred and twenty-four and of our reign the seventeenth.

[Seal] FREDERIC

Full powers
    E. H. SCHIMMELMANN

THE ORIGINAL CONVENTION

The original convention, which was written in English only, was signed in triplicate, as stated in the final clause thereof. One original was retained in the Department of State, and the other two were delivered to the Chevalier Pedersen, who refers to "my Originals" and "the 2 originals sent to Denmark" in his note to Secretary of State Clay of May 10, 1826 (D. S., 1 Notes from the Danish Legation, 307).

The *alternat* was observed in the original in the Department of State file, in which the United States and Secretary of State Clay are named first and the signature of Henry Clay precedes that of the Chevalier Pedersen; but it appears from the note of the latter of May 10, 1826, above mentioned, that the *alternat* was not consistently observed in the two originals which were sent to Denmark:

The more I think on, and look at, the form of the 7th & 8th Arts of our Convention, where in my Originals also the U. S. are named before the King of Denmark, the more I feel apprehensive that difficulty on that account may be made by my Government, and I deeply regret we were so much hurried at the time of Signature as not to attend sufficiently to this formality, which could so easily have been prevented by leaving the transposition as Mr Ironside no doubt there had made it perfectly correct; some remedy has occurred to me, and that is, if you should approve of it, in sending the act of Ratification to Mr Raynals, he might be instructed by you, in case he should find that on this score alone there was a hesitation on the part of my Government to ratify and exchange, to declare, that there would be no objection on the part of the President, or the United States government if in the Kings ratification, or in the publication of the convention made in Denmark a transposition of the contracting parties should be adopted for the above mentioned 2 articles. I am perfectly aware that very little consequence if any here is attached to the circumstance but in Denmark it may be viewed differently; it might also inofficially be communicated to Mr Raynals how it happened, in fact the erazures and alterations are not yet so obliterated but that they still are visible in the 2 originals sent to Denmark.

In a note to the Secretary of State of May 12 (*ibid.*, 309) the Chevalier Pedersen proposed that "another Copy of the Treaty might be made out," signed, and sealed, "in which, in the 7th & 8th Arts the

King should be named before the United States, & subjects before Citizens, but in all other respects like the 2 Copies already sent to Denmark," in order to remove "any thing that might furnish a pretext for not immediately ratifying" the convention.

In his reply of May 12 to the two notes of the Danish Minister (D. S., 3 Notes to Foreign Legations, 267), Secretary of State Clay regarded the former's objections to the form of Articles 7 and 8 as of no consequence and refused to consider the making out and signing of another original of the convention, "seeing that the only point that I ever supposed had any value (that of the commencement and the signatures) was attended to."

It appears that no objection was made by the Danish Government to the form of the convention, and the inconsistencies as to the *alternat* in Articles 7 and 8 and elsewhere in the text remained uncorrected in the Danish instrument of ratification and in the official Danish print of the treaty, a copy of which Rainals enclosed with his despatch of August 22, 1826 (D. S., 3 Consular Despatches, Copenhagen).

THE EXCHANGE OF RATIFICATIONS

Article 12 of the convention provided that "the ratifications shall be exchanged in the City of Copenhagen" within eight months from the date of signature of the convention. The United States instrument of ratification, together with instructions under date of May 19, 1826 (D. S., 11 Instructions, U. S. Ministers, 75–76), was accordingly transmitted by a special messenger, Captain John Adams Dix, to John Rainals, Consul of the United States at Copenhagen, who was authorized and directed to execute the exchange of ratifications. Captain Dix delivered the ratification to Rainals on July 21, 1826 (D. S., 3 Consular Despatches, Copenhagen, July 24, 1826), and on August 10 the exchange of ratifications took place. The following day Captain Dix left for Washington with the Danish instrument of ratification (*ibid.*, August 15, 1826), and that document seems to have been received in the Department of State on October 14, 1826, the date of proclamation.

An omission of twelve words from the first sentence of Article 3 in the Danish instrument of ratification was noted after that document had reached the Department of State, and the error was made the subject of instructions to Rainals of October 31, 1826 (D. S., 11 Instructions, U. S. Ministers, 173). The omission of the words, "belonging wholly to the Citizens thereof, may be also imported in vessels," was purely a scrivener's error and was so regarded at that time (*ibid.*):

This omission is considered here, as altogether accidental, and, in no wise, affecting the Treaty, which will be regarded and fulfilled as if the omission had not occurred. The Treaty has been accordingly, officially promulgated, and its stipulations are now in full operation in the United States. You will be pleased to communicate the above particulars to Count Schimmelmann.

Acknowledging those instructions, Rainals wrote under date of January 30, 1827 (D. S., 3 Consular Despatches, Copenhagen):

I immediately communicated in writing the particulars you desired to Count Schimmelman the Minister for Foreign Affairs, and he has assured me that the omission was entirely accidental, and can in no shape affect the Treaty.

THE NOTES OF APRIL 25 AND 26, 1826

Following the text of the convention are printed the note of Secretary of State Clay to the Chevalier Pedersen, Minister Resident from Denmark, dated April 25, 1826 (D. S., 3 Notes to Foreign Legations, 265), formally declaring that this Government would "persevere in the pursuit of" certain "indemnities due to citizens of the United States in consequence of the seizure, detention and condemnation of their property in the ports of His Danish Majesty," and the answering note of April 26 (D. S., 1 Notes from the Danish Legation, 303), in which it was said that the American note would be transmitted to the Danish Government.

Copies of the notes exchanged were transmitted to the Senate with the presidential message of April 28, 1826 (American State Papers, Foreign Relations, V, 905–7); and when the proclamation of the convention was transmitted to Congress with the presidential message of December 5, 1826, copies of the notes accompanied it (*ibid.*, VI, 207–8, 266–68); but there is no mention of the notes or reference to them in either instrument of ratification or in the proclamation.

The claims in question had their origin in the Napoleonic wars. By Article 1 of the convention with Denmark of March 28, 1830 (Document 68), it was agreed by the United States to accept "Six-Hundred and Fifty Thousand Spanish milled Dollars" on account thereof. Regarding those claims and their settlement, see the chapter on "The Danish Indemnity" in Moore, International Arbitrations, V, 4549–73, and the authorities there cited, particularly American State Papers, Foreign Relations, III, 328–38, 521–36, 557–61; see also *ibid.*, VI, 384–85, 504–35, and Moore, Digest, I, 254.

The language of the note of April 25, 1826, was perhaps broad enough to reserve also the case of the three prizes seized by the Danish Government in 1779, after they had been taken into Bergen, Norway. As to that claim, see Moore, International Arbitrations, V, 4572–73.

EXECUTION OF THE CONVENTION

Under date of August 22, 1826, Rainals reported that the convention had been published in Copenhagen and that he considered it "now in full operation" (D. S., 3 Consular Despatches, Copenhagen); and in a later despatch (*ibid.*, January 30, 1827) there was enclosed a copy and translation of the Danish edict of September 28, 1826, abolishing retroactively from April 26 as to citizens of the United States, pursuant to Article 7 of the convention, all discriminatory removal taxes.

TAHITI : SEPTEMBER 6, 1826

Articles Agreed on with the King, Council, and Head Men of Tahiti (O Taheite), signed at Papeete September 6, 1826. Original in English and Tahitian. The date of the latter text is September 4, 1826.
As to ratification or approval on the part of the United States, see the notes. Not proclaimed and (semble) not published at the time.
Articles signed at Raiatea on September 18, 1826, by the King of Raiatea and Tahaa (two of the Society Islands) are described in the notes.

T. ap. C. Jones Esqʳ Comᵍ
U. S. Shᵖ Peacock

Articles agreed upon between the United States of North America, by Thomas ap Catesby Jones, their Representative, appointed to confer with the King, Council, and head men of Otaheite, and it's dependencies, for the purpose of arranging certain interesting matters with the said King and chiefs &c. &c. on the one part, and the undersigned Regency of the other part.

Te hoe mau parau i faa au hia e Pomare III te Arii o Tahiti &c &c, e o raua Thomas Ap Catesby Jones Esqʳ te auvaha parau no America ra.

ART: 1ˢᵗ The peace and friendship subsisting between the United States, and Their Majesties, the Queen Regent, and Pomare the III heir apparent to the Throne of Tahiti, Moorea &c. &c. and their subjects, and people, are hereby confirmed, and declared to be perpetual.

.1.

Te hinaaro nei tatou e ia hau. O Pomare III te Arii o Tahiti nei, e o tana mau Gavana tahi pae e o te mau matainaa o America ra, epiti ahuru ma maha atoa ra tahi pae; ei hau opa ore to tatou, e eiaha ia mure.

ART: 2. Their Majesties do hereby bind themselves to receive

.2.

Peneiae, ia tono mai to America ra to ratou auvaha parau e noho

and protect a Consul, or other Agent, whenever the United States shall see fit to send such a person to reside near them; and to guarantee the fullest protection of both person and property of such Consul, or Agent; and to allow to him all the rights, privileges, and immunities which are granted to Consuls of the most favoured nation.

ART: 3ʳᵈ. The ships and vessels of the United States (as well as their Citizens) within the Territorial Jurisdiction of Tahiti, together with all their property, shall be inviolably protected against *all* Enemies of the United States, in time of war.

ART: 4ᵗʰ. The contracting parties being desirous to avail themselves of the bounties of Divine Providence by promoting the commercial intercourse and friendship subsisting between the respective nations, for the better security of these desirable objects Their Majesties bind themselves to receive into their Ports and Harbours, all ships and vessels of the United States, and to protect, to the uttermost of their capacity, all such ships and vessels, their Cargoes, Officers, and crews, so long as they shall behave themselves peacefully, and not infringe the established laws of the land; the citizens of the United States being permitted to trade

i Tahiti nei, e ite maitai atu Pomare III nei e tana mau tavana iana. E paturuturu atu, tona tino, e tana mau taoa; e faa tia maite atu iana, i te mau peu atoa, e au ai te auvaha parau o te fenua e here hia tu e to Tahiti nei

.3.

Tiae ia noho mai te pahi America, e te hoe mau taata America i Tahiti: Ia riro Tahiti nei ei pare haabu raa ora ia ratou; e eiaha tatou e bubu noa tu ia ratou i te rima o te mau enemi no America ia tamai hia ra. E faaora ra rau i te mau fenua ê ê.

.4.

Ta horo mai hoi te hoe mau pahi no America e hoo te maa rii, e te taoa rii, e farii maitai atu Pomare III e tana mau Gavana ia ratou. E paruru maite taua mau pahi ra, te taoa i roto, te mau raatira, e te mau taata rii, eiaha ia rave ino hia tu. Eiaha ra te ati America e hoo te ava paepaa, eiaha e ofene te ture o te fenua nei

freely with the people of Tahiti in all foreign productions (spirituous liquors of every description only excepted.

ART: 5.th Their Majesties do further agree to extend the fullest protection, within their control, to all ships, and vessels of the United States, which may be wrecked on their shores; and to render every assistance in their power to save the wreck, and her apparel, and cargo; and as a reward for the assistance and protection which the people of Tahiti shall afford to all such distressed vessels of the United States, they shall be entitled to a salvage, or a portion of the property so saved; but such salvage shall, in no case, exceed one third of the value saved; which valuation is to be fixed by a commission of disinterested persons, who shall be chosen, equally, by the Parties.

ART: 6. Their Majesties do further agree, and bind themselves to discountenance, and use all practicable means to prevent, desertion from all American ships which visit the Ports of Tahiti; and to that end it shall be made the duty of all Governors, Magistrates, Chiefs of districts, and all others in authority, to apprehend all deserters; and to deliver them over to the Master of the vessel from which they have deserted; and for the apprehension of every such deserter,

.5.

Peneiae hoi ia parari tetahi pahi America i Tahiti nei e vaiho hoe maite Pomare III e tana mau Gavana hoi taua pahi i parari ra, Eiaha ia rave noa hia tu. E mea tia rahi ra ia haabutu maite te taata Tahiti te mau taoa atoa, o taua pahi ra i te vahi hoe. E ia bue maite ra a faa au ai te taoa e tiái i te feia e haabutu ra, e te au mau ra i te ture no te pahi i pa rari i te mau fenua atoa, o te reira te horoa hia tu na to Tahiti na te feia i haabutu ra o te rahi ra, na te feia pahi iho â ia.

.6.

Eiaha roa Pomare III, e tana mau Gavana e ite atu te taata America ia horo oia i tana pahi; e aruaru ra, e a faahoi atu ai i tana pahi ra. Tei te pae pahi taua taata ra i te roaa raa mai e vau dala ia:—Tei i o ê mai ra mai ia Taiarabu ra hoe ahuru epae dala Tei tehoe fenua taa ê ra, mai ia Moorea ra te roaa raa mai e piti ahuru e maha dala. Ia tae atu i nia te pahi ra, e horoa hia tu ai ia moni

who shall be delivered over, as aforesaid, the Master, owner, or agent, shall pay to the person or persons apprehending such deserter the sum of eight dollars if taken on the side of the Island near which the vessel is anchored; but if taken on the opposite side of the Island, the sum shall be sixteen dollars; and if taken on any other Island subject to Tahiti, the reward shall be twenty four dollars (and shall be a just charge against the wages of every such deserter).

ART: 7.th No Tonnage dues or Impost shall be exacted of any citizen of the United States, which is not paid by the citizens, or subjects of the nation most favoured in commerce with Tahiti; and the citizens, or subjects of Tahiti shall be allowed to trade with the United States, and her Territories upon principles of equal advantage with the most favoured nation.

Done in duplicate at Papeete in the Island of Otaheite this sixth day of September A. D. 1826.

THO⁹ AP CATESBY JONES [Seal]
POMARE [Seal]
TATI
UTAMI
RORA
VAIRAATOA } *Principal Chiefs*

.7.

Eiaha roa Pomare III e tana mau Gavana nei e titau hua tu ta to America ra pahi ia tipae mai io nei. Ia faite maite ra to ratou, e ta to te mau pahi i e atoa ra e tiái. Ei ture hoe to te mau pahi atoa ia tipae mai e aio ai. E mai tei reira atoa to America ra haapao raa ia hinaaro to Tahiti nei pahi te fano i reira.

I Papeete taua mau parau nei i te faatia raa hia i teienei maha no September 1826.

POMARE [Seal]

Principal Chiefs { UTAMI
TATI
RORA
VAIRAATOA

THO⁹ AP CATESBY JONES [Seal]
  Test,

J M OSMOND
CHA⁹ WILSON.

NOTES

The source text of these articles is the original in the archives of the Navy Department (Naval Records and Library); the document is with the "Report Of the Peacock's cruise to the Sandwich, Society and other Islands in the Pacific Ocean performed in the years 1826 and 27," dated May 14, 1827 (Cruises of U. S. S. *Cyane*, 1826 . . . U. S. S. *Peacock*, 1826–1827 . . .).

During that cruise the *Peacock* was under the command of Captain Thomas ap Catesby Jones, U. S. N., who signed, on behalf of the United States, the articles agreed on with Tahiti; at the time, the rank of Thomas ap Catesby Jones in the Navy was that of "Master Commandant," a title which was changed to "Commander" by the act of March 3, 1837 (5 Statutes at Large, 163).

As to the Tahitian text of the articles printed above, no more can be said than that it is believed to be very nearly correct; the illegible handwriting and the poor physical condition of the original, which is bound in a volume so that some of the stitches obliterate letters and even words, make a copy of certain accuracy impossible.

The Cruise of Captain Jones

Under date of January 18, April 29, and May 24, 1825, instructions were sent by the Secretary of the Navy, Samuel L. Southard, to Commodore Isaac Hull, commanding the United States naval forces in the Pacific, for a cruise to the Society Islands and the Sandwich Islands (Naval Records and Library, 15 Officers of Ships of War, 465; 16 *ibid.*, 39, 55–58; the instructions of May 24 are printed in House Report No. 92, 28th Congress, 2d session, serial 468). The three memorials mentioned in those instructions made representations regarding mutinies and desertions of the crews of American whaling vessels in the Pacific (printed *ibid.*). The instructions of May 24, 1825, read as follows:

I transmitted to you under date of the 18th January last, Copy of a Memorial signed by Sundry Merchants in Nantucket, in relation to the Mutineers of the Ship Globe; and on the 29th April last, copy of another Memorial from the same quarter in relation to our Commerce in the neighborhood of the Sandwich Islands.

I now transmit, copy of a Memorial to the President of the United States, by Citizens of New Bedford, in relation to their vessels, engaged in the Whale Fishery, and particularly to their interests at the Sandwich and Society Islands. It is the wish of the Executive that these several Memorials shall receive the attention to which their importance entitle them. The proper course for you to pursue as to the one first mentioned, was pointed out in the letter enclosing it.

I have now to instruct you as soon as you can, with propriety, leave the Coast of Peru and Chili, to proceed to the Sandwich Islands, touching at the Society Islands, and on your return passing down the Coast of California and Mexico.

The general objects of your cruise are explained in the Memorials; the manner in which you shall endeavour to accomplish them, must be left almost entirely to your own discretion and prudence. It is not possible for the Department to furnish you with more than an outline of your duties, and of the mode in which they are to be discharged.

Our Commerce is increasing with great rapidity in that region, to which your attention is directed, and it becomes necessary that the Government should be

provided with the most satisfactory information respecting it. You will therefore endeavor to gain the best acquaintance with it, that your situation will permit, and furnish to the Department, with the report of your cruise, a minute statement of facts which fall within your observation, as to its nature, extent and probable growth, and also such suggestions as may seem useful for its protection and encouragement. It is believed that you may procure much authentic and useful information.

You will afford to our Citizens, Vessels, and Commerce, the protection which may be found to be necessary, and to which they may be lawfully entitled. You will, every where, encourage the best feelings towards our Government, Nation, and interests, manifesting on all occasions, that kindness, moderation, and decision, which become your own character, and that of the Government which you represent.

One of the definite objects of your visits, is to make a proper disposition of the Seamen; (which are mentioned in the Memorial) at the Sandwich Islands. Such of them as are Citizens of the United States, are there in violation of their contracts, and of their public duties. And the safety of our commerce, as well as the peace and good order of these Islands, require that they should, in some proper way, be removed from scenes of the mischief they are promoting and perpetrating. You will inform yourself as perfectly as you can, of their numbers, character, and conduct, and the means by which they were brought thither. Being thus informed, you will make whatever communications to, and arrangements with, the Government may be necessary and proper, apprising it of your character, and views, and the friendly wishes of the Government of the United States. After which you will induce as many as you can, to enter on board your vessel, assigning such duty as they may be qualified to perform; and if it can be done without offence to the Government, existing on the Islands, you will take and bring away with you, all those American Citizens whose character and conduct are calculated either to disturb the peace of the Country, or endanger the interests of our vessels and commerce,—and such as have committed acts of a piratical character.

Should you bring with you Citizens of the United States, who are not willing to serve on board either our public, or merchant vessels, you will retain them, until a fit opportunity arises of sending them to the United States.

You will communicate to the Government of the Islands, the intention of sending occasionally, one of our public Ships there, with a view to the protection of our interests, and the cultivation of friendly relations with the Government, and inhabitants of the Islands.

It is supposed that a stay of two or three weeks will enable you to accomplish the objects of your visit.

On leaving the Coast, you will give to the Commanders of the Peacock, and Dolphin, full instructions for their Government during your absence.

The mission was entrusted by Commodore Hull to Captain Thomas ap Catesby Jones, U. S. N., Commander of the U. S. sloop of war *Peacock*, who sailed from Callao on May 30, 1826, and, proceeding by way of Guayaquil and the Gallapagos Islands to the Society Islands, arrived off Tahiti on August 6, 1826.

THE VISIT TO TAHITI

The following paragraphs regarding the visit to Tahiti, where Captain Jones remained for a month, are extracted from his report above cited:

The next morning [August 6, 1826] at daylight discovered Otaheite directly ahead, at a great distance: at 5 P. M. off Matavai Point, received James Williams (an Englishman) as Pilot, but the wind proving unfavourable, we lay off and on during the night, and at 9 A. M. Monday August 7th anchored in Matavai Bay. The range of low Islands which we had just passed through, must be considered

a very dangerous navigation, as imperfectly as they are at present known, and still more incorrectly placed on the charts, added to which they are all low, and some of them cannot be seen two leagues from the Deck of a common ship: all are surrounded by coral Reefs, with an unfathomable sea to the very brink— there is also a strong and irregular current found everywhere among them.

The Tahitians, as they call themselves, have for more than thirty years been under the instruction of Missionaries sent out by the London Foreign Missionary Society. Their labours for the first 12 or 15 years were almost fruitless, but subsequently, their success has more than equalled their first disappointment; and the Tahitians may now be classed, not only among the civilized, but the evangelical nations of the Globe. The Government is that of an hereditary Monarchy,— they have a Constitution and a code of Laws not differing in the main from those of Great Britain. Trial by jury, and other judicial proceedings are the same as in England. The Island is divided into Districts, each District has it's Governor, Cheif, Justices, Judges, Magistrates &c. &c. and military cheif, and in most cases a resident missionary. Annually, in May, there is a meeting of all the dignatories of the Island, at the grand Council House, as they call it, when all subjects of general political or local interest are discussed and acted upon.

Soon after anchoring at Matavai, the Rev^d Mr Wilson, Missionary of that district, accompanied by the Governor and Military Commander, came on board to pay their respects, and welcome our arrival; and in due season, the like ceremonies were performed by the cheifs of the neighbouring districts.

On my first interview with the cheif Justice of the Matavai district, whose name is Pawai, the following dialogue took place, which I give as the best evidence of the advanced state of civilization, and of the necessity of cultivating a friendly intercourse with the South Sea Islanders viz:—

Pawai. Who is President of the United States now?
Answer. Mr. Adams.
Pawai. What is his first name?
Answer. John Quincy (the name repeated by Pawai).
Pawai. What was the name of the predecessor?
Answer: James Monroe.
P. How long is the President elected for?
A. Four years.
P. Can he serve longer than four years?
A. Yes, as often as the people choose to elect him; but no President has yet served longer than two terms, making 8 years.

Pawai remained silent for some minutes, apparently absorbed in deep thought, which was broken by the following remark by him: "A Happy Country (America) governed without a King."

At my next interview with this cheif (whom I soon found to be a man of uncommon strength of mind, and of liberal education, well acquainted with all the operations of the English Laws and Government, and not altogether unacquainted with the superiority of our own national rights and liberties) he asked me if the U. States would not send a Consul to reside among them, adding that we have one from Britain, and would like very much to have one from America, as it would encrease our resources for obtaining political information," and begged me to ask Mr Adams to send them a Consul as soon as I returned to America. This request was frequently repeated by him, and universally concurred in by all the other cheifs with whom I had any intercourse; altho' it is generally admitted that Pawai is a very intelligent and sensible man, yet it is said he has many equals, and even some superiors.

Some of the cheifs also stated that many Renegade Botany Bay convicts, find their way to those Islands and undertake to advise them in the concerns of government, which they had sometimes followed, very much against their interests as afterwards proved, particularly as regarded American vessels—this, they said, could not be the case if we had a Consul there. To test the sincerity of these disclosures, and professions made repeatedly by the same and different persons almost daily for six weeks, I drew up a few simple regulations, designed to counteract the evil effects of the bad advice alluded to above, until the President's pleasure could be known, and submitted them, through the agency of the Mis-

sionaries, to the King in council, who readily approved them as Laws, to be henceforth observed by all.

(Note. I must here embrace the occasion to acknowledge the very kind, friendly, and hospitable attentions we received from the missionaries and their families during our sojourn at Tahiti, and visit to Timeo and Raiatea, who not only served us in their christian calling by preaching on board every sabbath, but were always ready to give information we required, or to accompany any of the officers on any little excursion about the Islands; and to the Rev^d Mr. Osmond of Timeo & Mr. Williams of Raiatea I am indebted for the translation of my correspondence with the Authorities of the Society Islands.)

THE ARTICLES

It thus appears that the seven articles or "simple regulations," as Captain Jones styles them, were submitted to the King or ruler of Tahiti and his Council through the agency of the resident missionaries.

Most of the provisions of the articles are obligations in favor of the United States and American citizens; there are, however, some in favor of Tahiti, such as the salvage clause of Article 5 and the payments for deserters in Article 6; such, in form, also, is the most-favored-nation clause of Article 7 regarding the trade of the subjects of Tahiti with the United States; but, in fact, that provision is hardly to be regarded as more than an illusory phrase.

In any case, it seems that Captain Jones regarded the articles, to the extent that they constituted an agreement, as provisional and operative only "until the President's pleasure could be known." So far as the records show, the pleasure of the President never was made known in the matter; no record appears of any official notice of the articles; and, so far as has been observed, they were not published at the time.

It is perhaps arguable whether the articles are properly to be considered an international act; but in any case they are of sufficient interest to be included as a document in this collection; and it seems the better view that the articles are to be regarded as an international act, even if deemed provisional. The wording used is that of agreement (see Article 4, "the contracting parties"); the authorities of Tahiti undoubtedly regarded the articles as binding; the Government of Tahiti was at the time independent of foreign control, although a British vice consul resided there and British influence, because of the missionaries, was important; and it is to be observed that Captain Jones, who gives substantial reasons for his view, regarded the Tahitians at the time as "among the civilized . . . nations of the Globe."

THE VISIT TO RAIATEA

From Tahiti Jones proceeded to Raiatea, one of the western or Leeward group of the Society Islands, in order to obtain the assent of the ruler there, Tamatoa, to articles like those adopted at Tahiti. In this effort Jones was only in part successful; it appears that Tamatoa was the grandfather of the young King of Tahiti and did not

"altogether acknowledge the sovereignty" of the latter. The following account is from the report above cited:

On the morning of the 7ᵗʰ of September [1826] put to sea and cruized off the Island. . . . At 2 P. M. of the 8ᵗʰ close in with Matavia Point bore up, and made all sail for Raiatea, passing close to Timeo and Huahine, anchored at the principal harbour of Raiatea at 2 P. M. the following day: Our reception here was quite as hospitable as at Tahiti (I ought to have mentioned before that every visit of a Cheif is accompanied by a considerable present of Hogs, Fowls, Fruit, Vegetables &c. &c: and that at Tahiti provisions are very abundant, of the above kind, to which may be added some Beef of a superiour quality, and Goat mutton scarcely inferiour to the best Wethers—the latter very abundant and cheap; also excellent water and plenty of Wood.)

The usual anchorage at Raiatea is abreast of the village, or rather settlement within the reef of coral, which, with the Island, forms one of the finest sounds the world can boast of; in length 6 or 7 leagues, and in breadth from one to two, affording good anchorage every where, and as smooth as a basin at all times. The shore of Raiatea, washed by this sound, is indented with many deep Bays, where ships of any dimensions may lay alongside the coral Banks, which form a natural wharf. The entrance to this harbour is through a narrow gap in the Reef, east of the settlement; the passage is very narrow, tho' deep enough for any ship, and perfectly free of danger, as you always have a leading breeze in, and large vessels always run through the sound and go out at the West passage, by which means you are sure of a commanding Wind in and out.

Raiatea, as well as all the Islands of the Society and Georgian Groups, acknowled the sovereignty of Pomarre II. of Tahiti; but since his death, Tamatoa; (the present King of Raiatea, whose daughter was married to Pomarre II. and who is the mother of Pomarre III. and another daughter of Tamatoa, is the present Queen Regent of Tahiti) does not altogether acknowledge the sovereignty in the young King, over Raiatea and Taha: and as the harbour above described affords every inducement for our Whale Ships to go there, and I was desirous to nip in the bud those evils which were encreasing at Tahiti, and which, at one time, had nearly driven our shipping from the Sandwich Islands, added to which the Hicksaw, an American Whale ship had, a short time before, been wrecked on one of the Society's, when the Master and crew were plundered of every thing they saved; a repetition of such acts, I wished, if possible, to guard against. To that end I submitted to Tamatoa a duplicate of the Regulations made with Pomarre III. My success in this instance was not so complete as in the first, but the explanations and talks which grew out of the effort, will, doubtless, have their good effects. The documents which passed between the Parties will speak best for themselves, and show what was accomplished. I did not urge the adoption of these articles on Tamatoa after I discovered the least objection on his part, because I doubted my authority to use the arguments with which the subject richly abounds, and which doubtless, would have been accepted, had I have been disposed to remain at Raiatea a few weeks; but I also knew that any arrangements not perfectly free and voluntary on his part would no longer be respected after our departure; and, considering his letter of the 18ᵗʰ of September a sufficient pledge for the observance of impartial justice, I determined to proceed in the further execution of my orders; and accordingly at 9.40 A. M. of the 19ᵗʰ [September, 1826] weighed anchor and put to sea. . . .

The Negotiations at Raiatea

The negotiations at Raiatea between Captain Jones and Tamatoa, "King of Raiatea and Taha [Tahaa], two of the Society Islands," as he is described, while of trifling importance then and now, are none the less of real interest.

Jones had presented to Tamatoa for signature articles identic with those signed at Tahiti, except for a reference in the preamble to the

Society Islands instead of "Otaheite" and other changes involved in
the mention of "His Majesty Tamatoa, King of Raiatea and Taha."
They were, however, accepted by Tamatoa only in part, following some
correspondence carried on with the aid of the Reverend J. Williams, a
missionary of the London Missionary Society.

Under date of September 16, 1826, Tamatoa submitted, in writing,
ten questions regarding the articles, which are thus translated:

DEAR FRIEND, GREAT CAPTAIN OF AMERICA.

We have received the various articles you presented to me & my Cheifs, we have
conversed over them, we now propose a few questions to you, if you will write
answers you will gratify our hearts

The first is, There is a British Consul at Tahiti does he know of *the articles*

The second—If he knows, what are his thoughts *upon them*

The third—In case of war between Britain & America are we to remain at
peace with America alone, or does the declaration of perpetual peace in (1ˢᵗ
Article) refer only to times of peace.

The fourth, In case of an American Consul being settled here, he treats us with
contempt he ridicules our religion, he distributes spirits he endeavors to revive
dances and other bad old customs we have abandoned as has been done by
Tahiti, will your great men hearken to a representation from me and my Cheifs.

The fifth, Is the proposition of settling a Consul here a pretext to the ultimate
settlement of other citizens of America on our lands.

The sixth, In case of the settlement of an American consul here will he interfere
with our Government, will he hoist American colors—is food, a house, land &c. to
be given or is he to purchase those things.

The seventh, What kind of protection is required by (Article 3) are we to fight
or is it to be word of mouth protection.

The eighth, In case of British vessels being in our harbours and the Americans
fight them (the ships and subjects of Great Britain,) are we to protect the British
or only the Americans (see Article 3).

The ninth, In case of women being taken away clandestinely and the laws of
our land otherwise broken by the citizens of America.   How are we to act.

The tenth, In case of breaking the Covenant with America after having
entered into it what punishment will America inflict on us.

Make known your thoughts on these questions I & my Cheifs will consider
again & present our determination to you

May you great Captain of America enjoy health & peace through Jesus the true
Lord.

Signed   TAMATOA

FEUUASSEHO

A literal translation
    J. WILLIAMS
    ROBERT BOURNE

RAIATEA. *16. Sepᵗ 1826*

Jones replied to those questions as follows:

Answer to 1ˢᵗ Quest: Mʳ Elby, the British vice consul residing at Tahiti, knew
that I was negotiating with the authorities of that Island; he representing a third
nation could have no part in the negotiation, and as I did not need his advice, he
was not consulted by me, tho' I did communicate to him (unofficially) my intentions; but as the articles agreed upon by Pomare and myself were several days in
the hands of the Missionaries, and before the cheifs, all of whom were accessible
to Mr Elby, it is most probable that he both saw and read them.

2ⁿᵈ Question answered by the above.

Answer to 3ʳᵈ Quest: Article 1ˢᵗ is designed to secure perpetual peace and
friendship so long as it can exist with mutual advantage to the contracting
Parties, and upon strict principles of international law; consequently, strict

neutrality, even should Great Britain and the United States be at open war, would be expected; and that the vessels and citizens of the United States will be placed on an equal footing with those of Great Britain or any other most favoured nation.

Answer to 4th Quest: Any consul or agent who may be sent to Raiatea by the United States, who should so far forget himself, his station, and the honor of his Country as to be guilty of any act enumerated in the 4th Query, or in any other way meddle with the constituted Authorities of the place, or Divine worship, would immediately be recalled upon the King's representation to the President of the United States.

Answer to 5th Quest: No.   The object of settling a consul at one of the Society Islands is to look after the interest of American shipping, citizens and their property that may, by accident or otherwise, be cast among the inhabitants of said Islands; as well as to guard the inhabitants against insult or injury from Americans who come among them for trade or refreshment.

1st Paragraph of Question 6th answered in reply to 4th Query.   With regard to hoisting colours, that rests entirely with the King, as does the finding of a house and food; but should these privileges, or either of them be allowed a British, or any other, Consul, then they would be required by the United States Consul.

Answer to 7th Quest: The best that is in your power to give; and as you would extend to the most favoured nation.   If the enemies of the United States were to attempt to capture a vessel inside of the reefs or to take American Citizens or property from your shores, it would be in violation of your territorial rights; and if you were able, you ought to repel such an act by force of arms.

Answer to 8th Quest: Article 3rd is not intended to give exclusive protection to American property; if Raiatea observes strict neutrality, she will extend her protection and friendship alike to British and American Vessels &c.

Answer to 9th Quest: In case any American citizen violates any law of Raiatea, or attempted to carry away *women* or people, he is amenable to, and must be judged by, the King's judges; and punished as one of the natives would be, under the same law.

Answer to 10th & last Quest: Treaties perfidiously violated is considered dishonourable by all, and is deemed a just cause of war between two powerful nations; but, in the present case, a violation of these articles would not lead to war, or other punishment, but be considered as a want of good faith on the part of the one who fails to comply with the covenant.

In the original articles of agreement with Tamatoa the preamble and Articles 4–7, inclusive, appear in English and Tahitian in the same form as the articles signed at Tahiti, *mutatis mutandis,* and are followed by the signature of Tamatoa, but by no other except that of the Reverend Mr. Williams as witness, under date of September 18, 1826; but opposite the column containing the English of Articles 1–3, inclusive, and written lengthwise of the column, is a paragraph of Tahitian, also signed by Tamatoa, and followed by this translation of Mr. Williams under date of September 12:

I with my Chiefs think these three Articles of great importance, I can not hastily agree to them, We are under the wing (protection) of England and do not wish to do any thing to offend her, we will obtain the opinion of British Government before we give our consent. to the 4th 5th 6th & 7th Arts I am perfectly agreeable & have signed my name

Thus the reservation or amendment made by Tamatoa deleted Articles 1–3.

Jones had proposed, under date of September 16, an additional article reading in substance that "the foregoing covenant shall cease and be of non effect after the 31st day of December 1830, unless

previously renewed or extended by mutual consent of Parties"; but this was not accepted, and the correspondence was concluded by the following letter from Tamatoa:

DEAR FRIEND, GREAT CAPT^N OF AMERICA.

Our hearts are much gratified by the explanations you have given to our queries. I earnestly desire to be on most friendly terms with America. Continue to sail your ships to Raiatea and Tahaa without the slightest suspicion. We will receive them well and treat them kindly. Should America be at war with any other lands we will be decidedly on the part of America. Should you at any time be at war with Great Britain our desire is to be at peace with both parties, but it is not suitable for us hastily to determine, we will enquire the thoughts of England before we finally agree to that.

Do not be offended at our not hastily agreeing to all your propositions. Wishing you health, and peace in your voyaging

TAMATOA

A correct Translation
    J. WILLIAMS *Missionary*

RAIATEA *18 Sep*. *1826*

On the next day, September 19, Captain Jones sailed from Raiatea for the Sandwich Islands, as the Hawaiian group was then called, and arrived off the bar of Honolulu on October 10, 1826. As to the visit of Jones to the Sandwich Islands, see the notes to Document 54.

THE SOCIETY ISLANDS

The Society Islands, an archipelago of the Pacific, in the eastern part of Polynesia, between 16° and 18° south latitude and 148° and 155° west longitude, have a total land area of about 731 square miles. The archipelago now belongs to France (Archipel de la Société). The islands are of volcanic origin and mountainous, Tahiti, the principal island, rising to a height of 8,500 feet.

The first recorded discovery of Tahiti was in 1767 by Wallis, who gave it the name George's Island. In 1769 Captain James Cook visited the island and preferred to use the native name, O Taheite, in referring to it. He discovered the northwestern group of islands to which he gave the name Society Isles. The native name has survived in the modified form, Tahiti, while the name Cook gave to the western islands was subsequently adopted for the whole archipelago of the Society Islands, and the eastern and western groups were called respectively the Windward Islands (Iles du Vent) and Leeward Islands (Iles sous le Vent).

In 1842 France concluded a treaty with Queen Pomare establishing a protectorate over the Society Islands, which did not, however, include the Iles sous le Vent. In 1880 France definitely annexed the Iles du Vent, and in 1888 the Iles sous le Vent were added to the colony. In 1903 the Society Islands were joined with other French possessions in the Pacific to form the governmental unit, Les Etablissements Français de l'Océanie, with its capital at Papeete on the island of Tahiti.

The population of the Society Islands is now about 20,000, of whom nearly half are inhabitants of Tahiti.

Treaty Series No. 115
8 Statutes at Large, 344–45
18 *ibid.*, pt. 2, Public Treaties, 308–10

53

GREAT BRITAIN : NOVEMBER 13, 1826

Convention for the Payment of $1,204,960 by Great Britain, signed at London November 13, 1826. Original in English.
Submitted to the Senate December 20, 1826. Resolution of advice and consent December 26, 1826. Ratified by the United States December 27, 1826. Ratified by Great Britain January 31, 1827. Ratifications exchanged at London February 6, 1827. Proclaimed March 19, 1827.

Difficulties having arisen in the execution of the Convention[1] concluded at St Petersburgh on the Twelfth day of July 1822, under the Mediation of His Majesty The Emperor of all the Russias, between the United States of America and Great Britain, for the purpose of carrying into effect the Decision of His Imperial Majesty upon the differences which had arisen between the said United States and Great Britain, on the true construction and meaning of the First Article of the Treaty of Peace and Amity[2] concluded at Ghent on the Twenty fourth day of December 1814:—The said United States, and His Britannick Majesty, being equally desirous to obviate such difficulties, have respectively named Plenipotentiaries to treat and agree respecting the same, that is to say:—

The President of the United States of America has appointed Albert Gallatin, Their Envoy Extraordinary and Minister Plenipotentiary to His Britannick Majesty:—

And His Majesty The King of the United Kingdom of Great Britain and Ireland, The Right Honourable William Huskisson, a Member of His said Majesty's Most Honourable Privy Council, a Member of Parliament, President of the Committee of Privy Council for Affairs of Trade and Foreign Plantations, and Treasurer of His said Majesty's Navy;—And Henry Unwin Addington, Esquire, late His Majesty's Chargé d'Affaires to the United States of America:—

Who, after having communicated to each other their respective Full Powers, found to be in due and proper form, have agreed upon and concluded the following Articles:—

---

[1] Document 44.　　　　　　　[2] Document 33.

ARTICLE I.

His Majesty The King of the United Kingdom of Great Britain and Ireland agrees to pay, and the United States of America agree to receive, for the use of the persons entitled to indemnification and compensation by virtue of the said Decision and Convention, the Sum of Twelve Hundred and Four Thousand, Nine Hundred and Sixty Dollars, Current Money of the United States, in lieu of, and in full and complete satisfaction for, all Sums claimed or claimable from Great Britain, by any person or persons whatsoever, under the said Decision and Convention.

ARTICLE II.

The object of the said Convention being thus fulfilled, that Convention is hereby declared to be cancelled and annulled, save and except the Second Article of the same, which has already been carried into execution by the Commissioners appointed under the said Convention; and save and except so much of the Third Article of the same, as relates to the definitive List of Claims, and has already likewise been carried into execution by the said Commissioners.

ARTICLE III.

The said Sum of Twelve Hundred and Four Thousand, Nine Hundred and Sixty Dollars shall be paid at Washington to such person or persons as shall be duly authorized, on the part of the United States, to receive the same, in two equal payments, as follows:—

The payment of the first half to be made Twenty days after official Notification shall have been made, by the Government of the United States, to His Britannick Majesty's Minister in the said United States, of the Ratification of the present Convention by the President of the United States, by and with the Advice and Consent of the Senate thereof.

And the payment of the second half to be made on the First day of August 1827.[1]

ARTICLE IV.

The above Sums being taken as a full and final liquidation of all Claims whatsoever arising under the said Decision and Convention, both the final adjustment of those Claims, and the distribution of the Sums so paid by Great Britain to the United States, shall be made in such manner as the United States alone shall determine;

---

[1] See the note regarding Article 3.

and the Government of Great Britain shall have no further concern or liability therein.

ARTICLE V.

It is agreed, that, from the date of the exchange of the Ratifications of the present Convention, the joint Commission appointed under the said Convention[2] of St Petersburgh, of the Twelfth of July 1822, shall be dissolved; and upon the dissolution thereof, all the Documents and Papers in possession of the said Commission, relating to Claims under that Convention, shall be delivered over to such person or persons as shall be duly authorized, on the part of the United States, to receive the same. And the British Commissioner shall make over to such person or persons, so authorized, all the Documents and Papers, (or authenticated Copies of the same, where the originals cannot conveniently be made over,) relating to Claims under the said Convention, which he may have received from his Government for the use of the said Commission, conformably to the Stipulations contained in the Third Article of the said Convention.

ARTICLE VI.

The present Convention shall be ratified, and the Ratifications shall be exchanged in London, in Six Months from this date, or sooner if possible.

In Witness whereof, the Plenipotentiaries aforesaid, by virtue of their respective Full Powers, have signed the same, and have affixed thereunto the Seals of their Arms.

Done at London, this Thirteenth Day of November, in the Year of Our Lord One Thousand Eight Hundred and Twenty Six.

[Seal] ALBERT GALLATIN

[Seal] WILLIAM HUSKISSON

[Seal] HENRY UNWIN ADDINGTON

NOTES

This convention and the payments made thereunder by Great Britain to the United States, aggregating $1,204,960, terminated as between the two Governments a dispute which had originated under the Treaty of Ghent (Document 33), the treaty of peace following the War of 1812, and which had been dealt with in two later agreements,

---

[2] Document 44.

the convention of October 20, 1818 (Document 40), and the convention signed on July 12, 1822, at St. Petersburg, under the mediation of the Emperor of Russia (Document 44).

By Article 1 of the Treaty of Ghent it was provided that "all territory, places, and possessions" taken by either party during the war (with an exception here immaterial) "shall be restored without delay and without causing any destruction or carrying away any of the Artillery or other public property originally captured in the said forts or places, and which shall remain therein upon the Exchange of the Ratifications of this Treaty, or any Slaves or other private property." The dispute between the two Governments arose from the fact that private property (chiefly slaves) had been carried away by the British forces; but it was contended by the British Government that the clause quoted was, in respect of private property, applicable only to such property remaining in "said forts or places" at the time of the exchange of ratifications and, accordingly, that the carrying away of the slaves in question (or most of them) was not a breach of the treaty. The Government of the United States held to the contrary and claimed indemnity. The respective contentions of the two Governments are set forth in Moore, International Arbitrations, I, 350–57.

It was agreed by Article 5 of the convention of October 20, 1818 (Document 40), that the question in dispute between the two Governments, as there described, should be referred to "some Friendly Sovereign or State"; and accordingly the question was submitted to the Emperor of Russia, whose decision (see Document 44) was in favor of the contention of the United States. Following that decision and under the mediation of the Emperor of Russia a convention (Document 44) was drawn up and signed at St. Petersburg on July 12, 1822, and in due course went into force. By that convention there was provided a quite elaborate procedure for determination by commissioners of the amount due from Great Britain to the United States.

Article 2 of that convention made it the duty of the commissioners and arbitrators to determine the average value of the slaves carried away. That task the commissioners and arbitrators performed; they fixed an average value of slaves for each of various localities. Under Articles 3–6 of that convention the two commissioners were to examine and determine the claims listed, and in event of their disagreement, they were, in each case, to call in by lot one of the two arbitrators respectively appointed by the two Governments, who was to be deemed, for that case, a commissioner.

As the procedure under Articles 3–6 of the convention of July 12, 1822, proved to be highly unsatisfactory and unworkable, Secretary of State Henry Clay then decided to seek an agreement "fixing upon some gross amount for all the indemnities which the convention promises"; and in the elaborate instruction of May 10, 1825, to Rufus King, Minister at London (D. S., 10 Instructions, U. S. Ministers, 314–30, printed in part in American State Papers, Foreign Relations, VI, 339–43), he reviewed the proceedings of the commissioners under

Articles 2–6 of the convention of July 12, 1822, estimated that the principal sum recoverable would be $886,000, added $265,800 as half the interest claimed, and so fixed $1,151,800 "as the minimum to which you can fall."

The expectation of Clay that an agreement would be reached with the British Government with "no difficulty" was not fulfilled; the negotiations were transferred from London to Washington, where they reached no result; the instructions to King were renewed to Albert Gallatin, who succeeded him at London; and the signing of this convention on November 13, 1826, followed the negotiations between Gallatin and George Canning, British Secretary of State for Foreign Affairs, the terms being not far from those first laid down by Clay the year before.

The papers transmitted to the Senate with the presidential message of December 20, 1826 (Executive Journal, III, 545–46), are in American State Papers, Foreign Relations, VI, 339–55; a list of the claims for slaves and other property is with the message to the House of Representatives of March 8, 1826 (*ibid.*, V, 800–29). For an account of the dispute from its origin to its conclusion, including the proceedings under the act of March 2, 1827 (4 Statutes at Large, 219–21), for carrying into effect this convention, see the chapter entitled "Difference as to the Treaty of Ghent" in Moore, International Arbitrations, I, 350–90, and the writings there cited.

The File Papers

It seems that this convention was executed in quadruplicate. Albert Gallatin, Minister at London, in his despatch of November 11, 1826, wrote that "four fair Copies of the Convention" were to be transcribed for signature two days later (D. S., 33 Despatches, Great Britain, No. 22; American State Papers, Foreign Relations, VI, 353).

There are two originals of the convention in the treaty file, both in the same handwriting. The differences between them are limited to three immaterial commas and a very few other matters of variant writing style, too trivial to mention.

The file also contains the duplicate United States instrument of ratification of December 27, 1826, the certificate of the exchange of ratifications at London on February 6, 1827, in duplicate, and the original proclamation of March 19, 1827, which is in customary form (American State Papers, Foreign Relations, VI, 637–38). Only the attested resolution of the Senate (Executive Journal, III, 553) is lacking.

The United States instrument of ratification and instructions under date of December 28, 1826 (D. S., 11 Instructions, U. S. Ministers, 225–26), were transmitted to London by a special messenger, Edward Wyer, who delivered them to Gallatin on January 26, 1827, "at 8 o'clock in the morning" (D. S., 33 Despatches, Great Britain, No. 53, January 29, 1827). The exchange of ratifications took place on February 6, between two and four o'clock in the afternoon, and the British instrument of ratification and the certificate of exchange, with

Gallatin's despatch of the same date, were entrusted to Edward Wyer for delivery. Wyer arrived in Washington on March 19, and the convention was proclaimed the same day (D. S., 11 Instructions, U. S. Ministers, 277, March 20, 1827):

Mr. Wyer arrived yesterday with the British ratification of the Treaty of indemnity; and it is promulgated by the Proclamation of the President, in the usual manner, in this day's papers.

The text included in the British instrument of ratification of January 31, 1827, shows that the *alternat* was duly observed in the respective originals.

The full power to Albert Gallatin dated May 10, 1826, is in the usual form (D. S., 2 Credences, 42). Nothing appears in the despatches or elsewhere regarding the full power to the British Plenipotentiaries who signed the convention; but, as mentioned above, the prior negotiations at London were in fact conducted on behalf of the British Government chiefly by the Secretary of State for Foreign Affairs, George Canning.

ARTICLE 3

Under the provisions of Article 3 it was contemplated that the first of the two payments of $602,480 each would be made prior to the exchange of ratifications; for under Article 3 the payments were to be made at Washington, and the first of them was to be made within twenty days after notice to the British Minister at Washington of the ratification of the convention by the United States, presumably immediately upon the ratification; but under Article 6 the exchange was to take place in London; and in the conditions of communication existing at the time an exchange of ratifications at London within twenty days after the execution of the United States instrument of ratification at Washington was not to be expected or thought of as possible.

The procedure and dates adopted were with the purpose of avoiding any question as to interest on the amount payable. The final proposal of Gallatin had been the sum of $1,204,960 payable on May 1, 1827, with interest at 6 per cent on any portion paid subsequently. While that proposal had been accepted, the question of dates was left open; and as the British Government did not wish to exceed the principal fixed, it was agreed, as suggested by Canning (D. S., 33 Despatches, Great Britain, No. 22; American State Papers, Foreign Relations, VI, 352, despatch of Gallatin of November 11, 1826):

that half the money should be paid after the ratification of the Convention by the President, but without waiting for that of the King. This would give us a sufficient pledge, if any indeed was wanting, that His ratification would certainly follow that of the President. The Second instalment they would pay on the first of August, which was as long after the first of May, as the probable time which would elapse between the payment of the first instalment and the last mentioned day, so as to make both together tantamount to a payment of the whole on the first of May, and therefore without interest. As they were ready to pay the money, they could not take into consideration the delay which might arise on account of the early adjournment of Congress; but they presumed that the Anticipated payment of the first half might also facilitate an anticipated provision

on our part for the adjustment of the claims.   The proposition considered, without reference to this last point, but only as connected with that of exchanging the ratifications in London, appeared to me sufficient, and I accordingly accepted it.

In fact the first payment of $602,480 was made at Washington on January 15, 1827, nineteen days after the ratification on the part of the United States, notice of which had been given on its date, December 27, 1826 (D. S., 3 Notes to Foreign Legations, 318–19).   The payment was thus made sixteen days before the ratification on the part of Great Britain and twenty-two days before the exchange of ratifications at London.

In the treaty file there is a *procès verbal* of that payment, signed by Secretary of State Henry Clay and by the Right Honorable Charles R. Vaughan, British Minister at Washington, which is printed in American State Papers, Foreign Relations, VI, 372–73, and which is as follows:

DEPARTMENT OF STATE
Washington 15 January 1827.

On this day, in consequence of an appointment made by an exchange of Official Notes between H. Clay, Secretary of State, and the Right Honourable Charles R. Vaughan, His Bratannic Majesty's Envoy Extraordinary and Minister Plenipotentiary, Mr. Vaughan, attended at the Department of State, and, in pursuance of the third article of the Convention, concluded and signed at London on the 13th day of November last, between the United States and Great Britain, paid to the Secretary of State the sum of Six hundred and two thousand, four hundred and eighty Dollars, being the first moietey of the gross sum which Great Britain, in the aforesaid Convention, stipulates to pay to the United States; which payment, in the presence of Charles Bankhead His Britannick Majesty's Secretary of Legation and Daniel Brent, Chief Clerk of the Department of State of the United States was made by a transfer of a check or order for that sum drawn by the Bank of the United States on its Office of discount and Deposite in the City of Washington, in favor of the said Vaughan.   Whereupon, the said Clay, Secretary of State as aforesaid, executed, in duplicate, a receipt for the said sum, and delivered it to the said Vaughan.

In testimony of all which this procès verbale has been made and signed by the said Clay and Vaughan.

H. CLAY
CHAS R. VAUGHAN

Done in presence of—
DANIEL BRENT.
CHARLES BANKHEAD.

The payment was thus made by a check of the Bank of the United States in favor of Vaughan and doubtless endorsed over by him; and in the treaty file is also a receipt signed by R. A. Smith, Cashier of the Bank of the United States, acknowledging the deposit of the payment to the credit of the United States and "subject to the order of the Congress of the United States."

President John Quincy Adams on the next day communicated the convention to Congress, so that proper legislative action might follow, although the proclamation of the treaty could not issue until Congress had adjourned; in his message (American State Papers, Foreign Relations, VI, 372) he wrote:

I communicate to both houses of Congress copies of a convention between the United States and Great Britain, signed on the 13th of November last, at London,

by the respective plenipotentiaries of the two Governments, for the final settlement and liquidation of certain claims of indemnity of citizens of the United States which had arisen under the first article of the treaty of Ghent. It having been stipulated by this convention that the exchange of the ratifications of the same should be made at London, the usual proclamation of it here can only be issued when that event shall have taken place, the notice of which can scarcely be expected before the close of the present session of Congress. But it has been duly ratified on the part of the United States; and by the report of the Secretary of State, and the accompanying certificate herewith also communicated, it will be seen that the first half of the stipulated payment has been made by the minister of his Britannic Majesty residing here, and has been deposited in the office of the Bank of the United States at this place, to await the disposal of Congress.

I recommend to their consideration the expediency of such legislative measures as they may deem proper for the distribution of the sum already paid, and of that hereafter to be received, among the claimants who may be found entitled to indemnity.

Congress accordingly passed a statute on March 2, 1827 (4 Statutes at Large, 219–21), for carrying the convention into effect. It had at that time gone into force by the exchange of ratifications at London on February 6, 1827, although the proclamation did not issue until March 19 and could not be communicated to Congress before the opening of the next session, December 4, 1827 (American State Papers, Foreign Relations, VI, 625, 637–38).

The second payment under the convention was duly made on August 1, 1827; a copy of the protocol of payment, similar in form to that of January 15, 1827, is in D. S., 3 Notes to Foreign Legations, 375.

THE CLAIMS COMMISSION

Under the act of March 2, 1827 (4 Statutes at Large, 219–21), a commission of three was duly appointed to pass on the claims for slaves and other property. That commission first met on July 10, 1827, and held its final meeting on August 31, 1828, an act of May 15, 1828 (*ibid.*, 269), having provided that the commission should not continue after September 1. The total amount of the awards, exclusive of interest, was $1,197,422.18; the remaining sum of $7,537.82 the commission ordered "to be distributed and paid ratably to all the claimants to whom awards have been made." For an account of the proceedings of the commission, see Moore, International Arbitrations, I, 382–90.

54

HAWAII : DECEMBER 23, 1826

Articles of Arrangement with the King of the Sandwich Islands (Hawaii), signed at Honolulu December 23, 1826. Original in English and Hawaiian.
As to ratification or approval on the part of the United States, see the notes. Not proclaimed.

Articles of arrangement made and concluded at Oahu between Thomas ap Catesby Jones appointed by the United States, of the one part, and Kauikeaouli King of the Sandwich Islands, and his Guardians, on the other part.

Na olelo keia i hooponoponoia'i a i hoopaaia'i i Oahu nei e Thomas ap Catesby Jones, kekahi, ko Amerika luna i hoounaia mai nei mai ka United States mai, a me ke alii o ko Hawaii nei pae aina o Kauikeaouli o laua me kona kahu, kekahi

ART: 1ˢᵗ

The peace and friendship subsisting between the United States, and their Majesties, the Queen Regent, and Kaiukiaouli, King of the Sandwich Islands, and their subjects and people, are hereby confirmed, and declared to be perpetual.

PAUKU 1.

Eia kekahi olelo, ke olelo pu nei kakou e hoopaa loa i ke kuikahi pu ana a me ke aloha pu ana o ko Amerika a me ko Hawaii kahu alii wahine a me ke alii nui o Hawaii nei o Kauikeaouli a me ko laua poe kanaka a me na makaainana a pau loa; eai ka hoailona e mau loa ai ua kuikahi nei.

ART: 2ⁿᵈ

The ships and vessels of the United States (as well as their Consuls and all other citizens within the territorial jurisdiction of the Sandwich Islands, together with all their property, shall be inviolably protected against *all* Enemies of the United States in time of war.

PAUKU 2.

Eia hou neia, a o ko Amerika poe moku mai a me ko laila Kanikele a me ko laila kanaka ma keia pae aina a me ko lakou waiwai a i hiki i ka wa kaua, e pau ia mau mea i ka malama pono ia e ko Hawaii nei i ko Amerika enemi a *pau loa*.

269

ART: 3rd

The contracting parties being desirous to avail themselves of the bounties of Divine Providence, by promoting the commercial intercourse and friendship subsisting between the respective nations, for the better security of these desirable objects, Their Majesties bind themselves to receive into their Ports and Harbours all ships and vessels of the United States; and to protect, to the uttermost of their capacity, all such ships and vessels, their cargoes, officers and crews, so long as they shall behave themselves peacefully, and not infringe the established laws of the land, the citizens of the United States being permitted to trade freely with the people of the Sandwich Islands.

ART: 4th

Their Majesties do further agree to extend the fullest protection, within their control, to all ships and vessels of the United States which may be wrecked on their shores; and to render every assistance in their power to save the wreck and her apparel and cargo; and as a reward for the assistance and protection which the people of the Sandwich Islands shall afford to all such distressed vessels of the United States, they shall be entitled to a salvage, or a portion of the property so saved; but such salvage shall, in no case, exceed one third of the value saved;

PAUKU 3.

Eia hou neia, e makemakeana keia mau poe e loaa mai ia lakou ka waiwai a ke Akua i haawi mai aiika hookuai pu ana a me ke aloha pu ana o na aina o ka poe nana keia olelo, no laila hoi, no ka paa pono ana o keia mau mea mahalo, e ae mai ua mai alii o Hawaii nei e pono ia laua e komo no i loko o ko laua awa a me ko laua mau wahi e ku ai ka moku, o na moku Amerika a pau, a e malama nui aku i ua mau moku la a me na ukana ma luna a me na alii a me na kanaka o ua mau moku la oi hana pono mai lakou a i haki ole ia lakou na kanawai o keia aina i kau ai, e kuai no hoi ko Amerika me ko Hawaii nei poe kanaka.

PAUKU 4

Eia hou neia ke olelo io nei ua mau alii nei e malama nui laua i ko Amerika poe moku ke ili mai ma ko laua pae aina e hooikaika pono aku laua i pakele ai ka moku ili a me kana mau mea a pau a me kona ukana. He pono no e loaa mai i ko Hawaii nei poe ka uku no ko lakou hooikaika ana i pakele ai ua moku ili la a i malama pono ia ai ka mau mea ana. Eia ka uku, he mau kala paha, a i ole ia, o kekahi puu o ka waiwai i hoopakele ia ai, ka uku. Ina e kolu puu waiwai ua like, hookahi puu paha ka uku aka aole loa e nui aku ko lakou uku i kekahi oua puu waiwai

which valuation is to be fixed by a commission of disinterested persons who shall be chosen equally by the Parties.

akolu la. A o ka mea nona ka moku a o ka poe i hoopakeleia ai ka waiwai e kuhikuhi pu lakou i kekahi mau kanaka e aole no lakou ka waiwai na lakou hoi e hoike mai i ka nui o ka waiwai i malama ia ai.

ART: 5ᵗʰ

Citizens of the United States, whether resident or transient, engaged in commerce, or trading to the Sandwich Islands, shall be inviolably protected in their lawful pursuits; and shall be allowed to sue for, and recover, by judgment, all claims against the subjects of His Majesty The King, according to strict principles of equity, and the acknowledged practice of civilized nations.

PAUKU 5.

A o ko Amerika poe kanaka e kuai ana ma ko Hawaii nei pae aina, ka poe e noho ana, a me ka poe e holoholo ana, e pau lakou i ka malama pono ia i ka lakou hana ana i ka mea i ku i ke kanawai. A he pono no lakou e hoopaa i ka poe lawehala ma ke kanawai, a ma ka ahaolelo e loaa mai ai ia lakou ka uku e pau ai ka aie pono a pau a na kanaka o ko Hawaii nei alii e like ai me ke kanawai pololei a me ka oihana a ka aina naau ao i ikea ai

ART: 6ᵗʰ

Their majesties do further agree and bind themselves to discountenance and use all practicable means to prevent desertion from all American ships which visit the Sandwich Islands; and to that end it shall be made the duty of all Governors, Magistrates, Cheifs of Districts, and all others in authority, to apprehend all deserters; and to deliver them over to the master of the vessel from which they have deserted; and for the apprehension of every such deserter, who shall be delivered over as aforesaid, the

PAUKU 6.

Eia hou neia, ke olelo io nei kealii nui laua o kona kahu i ka olelo i paa ai laua i ka hooikaika aku laua e pau ai ka mahuka ana mai o na kanaka o ko Amerika mau moku e hiki mai ana i ko Hawaii nei pae aina e alai aku no i ka mahuka ana mai. No ia mea he pono no na alii malama aina a me na kilo a me na kia-aina a me na kau alii a pau e hopu aku a paa ka poe mahuka a pau a e hoihoi aku i ka mea nona ka moku i haalele ia aku ai. A e uku ia mai ko onei poe i hopu aku e ka mea nona ka moku. Ina ma

master, owner, or agent, shall pay to the person or persons apprehending such deserter, the sum of six Dollars, if taken on the side of the Island near which the vessel is anchored; but if taken on the opposite side of the Island, the sum shall be twelve Dollars; and if taken on any other Island, the reward shall be twenty four Dollars, and shall be a just charge against the wages of every such deserter.

ka aoao o ka aina e kuai ka moku e paa ai ka mea i mahuka e ono kala ka uku. A ina ma kela aoao o ka aina e paa ai umi a me kumamalua kala ka uku—a ina ma ka aina e i moku i ke kai e paa ai a i hoihoi i kona moku, iwa kalua kala a me kumamaha ka uku, no loko pono keia uku o ka waiwai a ka mea mahuka i hoolimalimaia'i, ma laila e kau pono ia'i.

ART: 7ᵗʰ

No tonnage dues or impost shall be exacted of any Citizen of the United States which is not paid by the Citizens or subjects of the nation most favoured in commerce with the Sandwich Islands; and the citizens or subjects of the Sandwich Islands shall be allowed to trade with the United States, and her territories, upon principles of equal advantage with the most favoured nation.

PAUKU 7.

Eia hou neia; aole e oi aku ka uku mai no ka awa o ko Amerika poe kanaka i ko ka aina punahele kanaka e kuai ana ma ko Hawaii pae aina, aole kii hou ia aku ka uku nui ae o ko Amerika kanaka. A e kuai no ko Hawaii nei poe kanaka me ko Amerika e like ka oihana a me ka pono e pono ai ko ka aina punahele loa i ka kuai pu ana mai me ko Hawaii nei pae aina.

Done in council at Honolulu; Island of Woahoo, this 23ʳᵈ day of December in the year of our Lord 1826.

Ua hoopaaia i ka ahaolelo ma Honolulu i ka aina Oahu nei i keia la 23 o Detemaba i ka makahiki o ko kakou Haku 1826.

Tho⁸· ap Catesby Jones	[Seal]	Tho⁸ ap Catesby Jones	[Seal]
Elisabeta Kaahumanu	[Seal]	Elisabeta Kaahumanu	[Seal]
Karaimoku	[Seal]	Karaimoku	[Seal]
Poki	[Seal]	Poki	[Seal]
Howapili	[Seal]	Howapili	[Seal]
Lidia Namahana	[Seal]	Lidia Namahana	[Seal]

NOTES

The source text of these articles is the original in the archives of the Navy Department (Naval Records and Library); the document is with the "Report Of the Peacock's cruise to the Sandwich, Society and other Islands in the Pacific Ocean performed in the years 1826 and 27," dated May 14, 1827 (Cruises of U. S. S. *Cyane*, 1826 . . . U. S. S. *Peacock*, 1826–1827 . . .).

During that cruise the *Peacock* was under the command of Captain Thomas ap Catesby Jones, U. S. N., who signed, on behalf of the United States, the "articles of arrangement" with the Sandwich Islands, now Hawaii.

CHARACTER OF THE INSTRUMENT

Six of the articles here printed (1–4, 6, and 7) are in all essentials the same as six of those written with Tahiti three months earlier (Document 52, Article 1 and Articles 3–7); the Tahitian Article 2 was omitted as unnecessary for Hawaii, where the United States had had an "Agent for commerce and seamen" since 1820; and the Hawaiian Article 5 is new; but the similarity of the two instruments is noteworthy.

There is no record of any express recognition or approval of these articles by the Government of the United States; their text appears not to have been published or communicated to Congress at the time. The English text of the articles is printed in British and Foreign State Papers, XIX, 1430–32; that volume was published in 1834, and no earlier print of the agreement has been noticed.

The official view has been that this instrument of December 23, 1826, is to be regarded as an "unperfected" treaty because it was not ratified by the United States (see Haswell, 1343; Moore, Digest, I, 475–76; and the correspondence of December, 1842, between Secretary of State Webster and the Agents of the Hawaiian Islands, cited below); but there are considerations tending to a somewhat different conclusion.

In a report of the Committee on Foreign Affairs of the House of Representatives under date of February 4, 1845, is this statement (House Report No. 92, 28th Congress, 2d session, serial 468; the text of the articles is printed in that document):

Notwithstanding the difficulties which he had to encounter, Captain Jones was entirely successful. He negotiated a commercial arrangement with the authorities of the Sandwich islands, eminently beneficial to us; and he prevailed upon them to adopt a plan of raising a revenue to satisfy claims of our citizens, as novel and curious as it was successful. These two measures were the first essay of those islanders in negotiation and legislation; and it is believed the success of them tended to no small extent to generate in them a feeling of independence and self-reliance; which alone, it is more than probable, has prevented these islands from being numbered, by this time, among the colonial possessions of Great Britain. . . . The one has ever been regarded by all nations having intercourse with these islanders as a solemn treaty; has been respected as such; and been made the basis of all similar arrangements entered into with them.

The other was so efficient as to secure to our citizens some $500,000, the recovery of which, until it was adopted, had been despaired of.

In the "Report upon the Official Relations of the United States with the Hawaiian Islands from the First Appointment of a Consular Officer There by This Government," submitted February 9, 1893, by Andrew H. Allen, Chief of the Bureau of Rolls and Library of the Department of State (Foreign Relations, 1894, appendix II, 8–28), is the following just observation regarding the agreement:

This was the first treaty formally negotiated by the Hawaiians with any foreign power, and although it was never ratified by this Government, certain of its stipulations appear to have embodied friendly views and purposes of the United States which were considered morally binding by both parties.

While the view of Captain Jones as to the character of the articles signed at Tahiti and at Honolulu is not wholly clear, he writes of the former as "simple regulations" and of the latter as "regulations of general interest to our commerce in the Pacific," and adds that "the regulations received the signatures of the ruling Princes and chiefs." The form of the document is such that it may properly be called a "Treaty of Friendship, Commerce, and Navigation between the United States and the Sandwich Islands" (as in British and Foreign State Papers, XIX, 1430–32, published in 1834; and in the report of Andrew H. Allen, above cited); but Jones may have regarded the articles as being in the nature of national regulations of the Hawaiian Government which had received the assent of himself as the representative of the United States; for, while he considered the object of his mission to Hawaii as "of high national importance" and speaks of the great responsibility laid upon him, he writes that he was neither fully acquainted with the views of his Government nor "authorized to make treaties," and that he would have been successful in any undertaking of that character.

Such a view as that suggested, however, cannot be supported. The articles were clearly an international act, signed as such by the authorities of the then independent Hawaiian Government, and by a representative of the United States, whose instructions, while vague, must be regarded as sufficient authority for his signature, in view of the then remoteness of the region from the seat of Government and the general discretion which those instructions granted; indeed, the distinction between national regulations and such a document as that comprising these articles is to be seen in the negotiations which Jones conducted at Honolulu.

In his note of October 23, 1826, to the King of the Sandwich Islands, which is mentioned in his report, Jones states that he proposed to the Hawaiian Government certain regulations for the port of Honolulu, which that Government adopted and which, Jones wrote, "now form a part of their code." Those regulations, a copy of which is with his report, Jones did not sign; but a draft of these "articles of arrangement" as proposed by Jones, in the form in which they were signed, was transmitted with a note addressed by Jones to the King of the

Sandwich Islands under date of November 13, 1826, containing the following paragraphs:

The accompanied articles are submitted for Your Majesty's consideration. They are designed to place the good understanding and friendship happily subsisting between our respective nations upon a clear, firm, and lasting basis—there is nothing contained therein which is designed or calculated to give the United States advantages over any other nation. All she expects, and all she asks, is equal privileges with the *most favoured* in time of peace, and *strict neutrality*, in case of wars.

Should your Majesty approve of the Regulations submitted, and will convene your Chiefs and Counsellors, I will attend the meeting, and, in their presence, exchange signatures with you.

Neither in the correspondence nor in the report of Jones nor in the articles themselves is there any mention of the matter of ratification; and as this was the first international agreement ever made by the Hawaiian Government with a foreign power, it may well be that little, or perhaps nothing, was then known at Honolulu regarding ratification as a step in treaty-making procedure. So far as Hawaii was concerned, no ratification was required; the assent of the Hawaiian Government was complete upon signature; as a practical matter, this Government was warranted in regarding the paper as sufficient without further action; ratification was a step that could be taken later, if it should become desirable or essential; in the meantime the agreement was *de facto* in force at Hawaii and was doubtless there regarded as in force *de jure*.

This attitude was justified by the event; for the Hawaiian Government did not fail to live up to the agreement; under date of December 14, 1842, Agents of that Government wrote as follows to the Secretary of State, Daniel Webster (Foreign Relations, 1894, appendix II, 41–44):

The undersigned having been duly commissioned by His Majesty Kamehameha III, King of all the Hawaiian Islands, to represent his Government and promote its interests in the United States, wish to call the attention of your Government to the existing relations between the two countries.

In the year 1826 articles of agreement, in the form of a treaty, were entered into between His Majesty's Government and Thomas ap Catesby Jones, commanding the United States sloop of war *Peacock*. His Majesty has never received any notice of that treaty's being ratified, nor intimation that it was approved by the Government of the United States. His Majesty has, nevertheless, during the last sixteen years, governed himself by the regulations of that treaty in all his intercourse with citizens of the United States.

That communication of December 14, 1842, from which the foregoing extract is quoted, requested the negotiation of a treaty with the United States and elaborately argued that the state of "His Majesty Kamehameha III, King of all the Hawaiian Islands," should be "formally received into the general compact of sovereign nations"; the answer of December 19, 1842, was a refusal both of the negotiation of a treaty and of the "appointment or reception of diplomatic characters" (*ibid.*, 44–45); the correspondence was submitted to Congress with the presidential message of December 30, 1842 (*ibid.*,

39–41; House Document No. 35, 27th Congress, 3d session, serial 420).

A letter addressed to the King of the Sandwich Islands by the Secretary of the Navy on behalf of the President, was delivered in the year 1829 by Captain William Bolton Finch, U. S. N., commanding the U. S. S. *Vincennes;* in that letter, the text of which follows (from Naval Records and Library, 17 General Letter Book, 87–89), there is no direct reference to the articles of December 23, 1826:

To TAMEHAMEHA THE 3RD
   King of the Sandwich Islands.

NAVY DEP'MT. OF THE US.
City of Washington, 20. Jan'y. A. D. 1829.

By the approbation and direction of the President of the United States, I address you this letter, and send it by the hands of Captain William Bolton Finch, an officer in our Navy, Commanding the Ship of War Vincennes.

Captain Finch also bears to you from the President, certain small tokens of regard, for yourself, and the Chiefs who are near to you, and is commanded to express to you in his name, the anxious desire which he feels for your advancement in prosperity and in the arts of civilized life, and for the cultivation of harmony and good will between your nation and the people of the United States. He has heard with admiration and interest of the rapid progress which has been made by your people in acquiring a knowledge of letters, and of the True Religion—the Religion of the Christian's Bible. These are the best and only means by which the prosperity and happiness of Nations can be advanced and continued, and the President, and all men every where, who wish well to yourself and your people, earnestly hope that you will continue to cultivate them, and to protect and encourage those by whom they are brought to you.

The President also anxiously hopes that peace, and kindness, and justice will prevail between your people and those citizens of the United States who visit your Islands, and that the regulations of your government will be such as to enforce them upon all.

Our citizens who violate your laws, or interfere with your regulations, violate at the same time, their duty to their own government and country, and merit censure and punishment. We have heard with pain that this has sometimes been the case, and we have sought to know and to punish those who are guilty.

Captain Finch is commanded diligently to inquire into the conduct of our citizens, whom he may find at the Islands, and as far as he has the authority, to ensure proper conduct and deportment from them.

The President hopes, however, that there are very few who so act as to deserve censure or punishment; and for all others he solicits the kindness and protection of your government; that their interests may be promoted, and every facility given to them in the transaction of their business. Among others he bespeaks your favor to those who have taken up their residence with you to promote the cause of Religion and learning in your Islands. He does not doubt that their motives are pure, and their objects most friendly to the happiness of your people, and that they will so conduct themselves as to merit the protecting kindness of your government. One of their number, the Reverend Charles Samuel Stewart, who resided for a long time with you, has received the favor of his government in an appointment to an office of Religion in our Navy, and will visit you in company with Captain Finch.

The President salutes you with respect, and wishes you peace, happiness and prosperity.

SAM'L. L. SOUTHARD, *Secretary of the Navy.*

THE VISIT TO HAWAII

For the instructions regarding the cruise of the U. S. sloop of war *Peacock* in 1826–27, under the command of Captain Thomas ap

Catesby Jones, U. S. N., and some account of his mission, the notes to Document 52 should be consulted. From the report of that cruise, above cited, the following is extracted regarding the visit to Hawaii, where Jones remained nearly three months:

During the whole passage from the Society to the Sandwich Islands the wind hung uncommonly far to the North, which, together with a strong Westerly current, obliged us to make all the Easting we could, consequently we never set a studding sail on the passage, until the day Owhyhee was made. Notwithstanding, this passage, in the course of which we ran 3330 miles, was performed in less than twenty two days. Between the Latitudes of 2° and 6° N. we found a most rapid current. One day, our Chronometers, well regulated, gave us a current of 96 miles due West. Our lunar observations, prior and subsequently thereto, fully proved the accuracy of the Instruments; and upon enquiry at Woahoo of the Whalemen and others, I found it to have been universally experienced by those who had crossed the Line, in or near that Longitude, especially in the neighbourhood a little east of Fanning's Island (new Discovery.)

At 2 P. M. October 10th [1826] close in with the shipping at anchor off the bar of Honolulu, hauled off to speak a ship in the Offing. At 4 boarded the American Whaling Ship Foster of Nantucket.

This digression prevented our anchoring that evening; and the night was spent in laying off and on a little to windward of the Harbour. At 1 P. M. on the 11th with the first of the sea breeze, bore up, and made all sail for, the anchorage off the Bar. At 2.45 received a Pilot, and at 3.30 anchored in the inner harbour of Honolulu, Island of Woahoo, having crossed the bar with flowing sheets without ever anchoring outside. : : :

Honolulu is not only the best harbour of Woahoo, but it's equal has not yet been discovered in any of the other Islands of the Sandwich group: it is, also the residence of the present Royal Family; and all trade and commerce centre there. . . .

The object of my visit to the Sandwich Islands was of high national importance, of a multifarious character and left entirely to my own judgment as to the mode of executing it, with no other guide than a laconic order which the Government designed one of the oldest and most experienced Commanders in the Navy should execute; if then it shall appear that I have transcended the authority legally vested in me by the course I have pursued, whether as regards the arrangements made with the authorities of the several Islands or with respect to the exercise of judicial power over, and the removal of, Citizens of the United States from the scenes of their lawless practices, I once for all place my defence upon the grounds of imperious necessity, in a situation altogether novel and without precedent. For here we find flags of most commercial nations covering their ships richly laden, whilst their heterogeneous crews promiscuously intermix on shore without the constraint of law; which, if necessary to curb the inordinate propensities of Man in the best regulated Societies, what might we not expect of sailors who, from time immemorial, have been looked upon, tho' with great injustice, as the very refuse of the human species, when those who convey them there and who ought to set a better example declare that "there is no Law round Cape Horn" and that no act, however atrocious, committed by a foreigner at those Islands is cognisable, or can be punished by the Laws of the country to which the offender owes allegiance; and they even go farther and declare that the Rulers of the Islands have no authority to punish foreigners who trangress their Laws. Such were the judicial views of the foreign residents and traders at Woahoo when the Peacock arrived!! then may it be asked what guarantee had the American Merchants for the safety of five millions of their property, that enters the port of Honolulu annually, or the individual engaged in this commerce, for his life and liberty. The answer must be none!!! Again we see a great influx of English renegadoes from New South Wales into the Sandwich, as well as the Society Islands; and I was informed by the English Consul General for those Islands that his orders were not to molest these scape-gallows', who, as soon as out of reach of the halter, according to the views of the British Ministry, are fit subjects for encreasing His Majesty's influence, and even for giving Laws to the South Sea

Islanders. The missionaries at the Society Islands will bear testimony to the great evils Otaheite has already experienced by the interference of convicts who have escaped from Botany Bay, and found their way to that Island. Their number is quite sufficient now at the different Islands, and I know it to have been their design, in the event of War between the United States and England to fit out the small vessels of the Islands for the purpose of predatory warfare upon our defenceless commerce and Whale Fishery in the Pacific Ocean, which, with the assistance of the Islanders, they would have annihilated before protection could be sent to it's releif; hence the importance of strict neutrality on the part of all the South Sea Islanders in future wars between the United States and European powers.

Under so great a responsibility it was necessary for me to proceed with the greatest caution and to measure well every step before it was taken; consequently the first ten or fifteen days were devoted to the study and examination of the character and natural disposition of a people who are so little known to the civilized world, and with whom I had important business to transact. I however, at an early period after my arrival took an occasion to state verbally to the Cheifs &c that I should in a few days address them some communications designed to place upon a firm and permanent basis the friendly intercourse between our respective countries to which they answered "it will be well" or "it is good" which is the highest term of approbation their language admits of. At this time Karaimoku, the prime minister, a cheif of great talents and influence, was labouring under a severe dropsical attack, and Kaahumanu, in whom the Government of the Islands at present rests was absent, and whose approbation could alone render valid any arrangements that might be effected, consequently my principal communication was not made until the 13th of November; in the meantime preliminary notes were addressed to the King under dates of Oct'r 17th 23rd & 31st and November 4th 1826. The [port] regulations which accompanied the letter of the 23rd were immediately approved of by the Governor, Poki and the King, and were accordingly adopted; and now form a part of their code; while my desires expressed in that of the 31st if possible, met with a still more prompt execution, for at an early hour the morning after the note was written, I received notice that Govr Poki, the American and English Consuls with a large concourse of runaway sailors requested my presence at the examination. The rule suggested by myself and which was adopted on that occasion, with regard to citizens of the United States; and which ought never to be departed from, was, that all those sailors who had deserted, however remote the period, should be removed from the Island; and those who were there from any other cause who had not some visible means of making an honest livelihood should also be removed as well as all other foreigners who did not support a good character. The number of American deserters banished from the scenes of their iniquity (many of whom however had been driven to it by the oppression of their employers) on this occasion amounted to near thirty; most of them, were ultimately disposed of to the Whale ships in Port, while the remainder, with the exception of one or two who are of notorious bad character, were permitted to sign articles for, and now compose a part of the Peacock's crew.

My letter of the 4th of November related entirely to the private claims of American citizens: it produced the subjoined decree in council [printed below], which, on the 27th of December was officially promulgated at a general meeting of the inhabitants of Honolulu and the neighbouring villages, and environs of the Capitol, convened for that especial purpose.

The communication of the 13th of November which accompanied some regulations of general interest to our commerce in the Pacific [the articles above printed] was not less successful; and on the 23rd of December the regulations received the signatures of the ruling Princes and cheifs; in testimony of their approbation of them and as a pledge of their sincere friendship and confidence in the American Nation, and their earnest desire to remain neutral, and take no part in any foreign wars.

The Sandwich Islanders, as legislators, are a cautious, grave, deliberate people, extremely jealous of their rights as a nation, and are slow to enter into any treaty or compact with foreigners by which the latter can gain any foothold or claim to their soil. The Russians have ever longed for the sovereignty of the Sandwich

Islands, as well as of Otaheite, both of which, at different times, they have attempted, by various artifices, to possess themselves of. In 1823 under the colouring of friendship to Rihoho, late King of Sandwich, they erected a fort of considerable strength on Atoi and commenced landing ordnance with the intention of garrisoning the work with Russians, when the just suspicions of the Islanders put a stop to the clandestine encroachment of their false friends.

Aware of those traits of character in the Islanders with whom I had to negotiate, I determined to conduct my correspondence with them in such a manner as at once to remove all grounds of suspicion as to the object and views of the American Government, and to guard against misrepresentation and undue influence, as well as to give the cheifs and others in authority the means of understanding perfectly the nature of my propositions, I took the precaution to have all official communications translated into the Oahuan language, which translation always accompanied the original in English; if, as I have before stated, cautious deliberation is characteristic in the national councillors of Wuahoo, their abhorrence at impetuosity in any person with whom they have to transact business is no less remarkable; with a knowledge of the foregoing facts, my course was clearly marked out; and I made it an invariable rule never to press a point when I could discover the slightest disinclination on their part to discuss the subject—but by giving them their own time to canvass and consult together, I found no difficulty in carrying every measure I proposed; and could I have been fully acquainted with the views of my Government, or have been authorized to make treaties, I do not doubt but my success would have been complete in any undertaking of that character.

Whilst the work of negotiation was thus deliberately and harmoniously progressing, our best exertions were put forth to suppress insubordination and disorder among the shipping. . . .

Having on the 23ᵈ of December successfully closed my correspondence with the authorities of the Sandwich Islands, I had nothing more to detain me at Honolulu but the departure of several Whale ships and Indiamen which only waited a favourable time to put to sea; accordingly every preparation was made by us for sailing; but as the wind proved adverse for several days it was the sixth day of January 1827 before I found it expedient to leave Woahoo, when in the afternoon of that day, in company with the Parthian, Indiaman, and Convoy, trader, I crossed the Bar, leaving only one Whale ship, undergoing repairs, and three of the coast traders in port.

The *Peacock* proceeded to San Blas, where Jones remained from February 1 to March 9 in order to obtain news from the American Minister to Mexico, Joel R. Poinsett; he then sailed for Peru, and the cruise was concluded when the *Peacock* anchored in Callao Bay on May 14, 1827.

American Claims

During his visit to Hawaii Captain Jones dealt with certain claims of American citizens against that Government, which are not particularly described; it appears, however, that the amount involved, and which was recovered, was about $500,000 (House Report No. 92, 28th Congress, 2d session, serial 468, pp. 3, 22, 23). In the report of Jones of May 14, 1827, above cited, is the following reference to the subject:

My letter of the 4ᵗʰ of November related entirely to the private claims of American citizens: it produced the subjoined decree in council, which, on the 27ᵗʰ of December was officially promulgated at a general meeting of the inhabitants of Honolulu and the neighbouring villages, and environs of the Capitol, convened for that especial purpose.

The letter of November 4, 1826, and the text of that strange but effective "decree in council," follow; both are from copies with the original report of Jones of May 14, 1827, but the date and signatures of the decree, which are lacking in the copy with the report of Jones, have been supplied from the print in House Report No. 92, 28th Congress, 2d session, serial 468, pages 18–19.

PEACOCK UNITED STATES' SLOOP OF WAR.
Woahoo November 4th 1826.

Herewith I have the honor to lay before your majesty a list of the claims, with the amount due on each, in sandal wood and Dollars, under contracts with your predicessors: This list, however, I believe, does not embrace all that is lawfully due to my countrymen, some of the agents being absent at this time. I have not been able to obtain the particulars of their claims. As to the justice of these demands, I presume, there exists no doubt; indeed, I am officially informed that the greater part of them have been acknowledged by the principal cheifs, and assumed as a debt of the Kingdom, under promise of speedy payment, but that promise remains to be fulfilled.

It is my duty to remind your majesty that these debts are of long standing, and for value received, and ought, according to contract, to have long since been paid. The tardiness in the government to pay their just debts I am however more willing to attribute to casualties not within it's control; and more particularly, to the premature death of your lamented predecessor, and your own tender age, than to a want or just sense of the moral obligations which bind nations, as well as individuals, to observe undeviating punctuality in their intercourse with each other; and particularly those of a commercial character. By the Laws of the United States any person having a just claim against a citizen can recover the same in due course of law; and not only oblige him to pay the full amount of the original contract, but the *Interest* is also added; that is, for every hundred Dollars which remains unpaid one year, the Debtor has to pay six Dollars, which makes a debt of One Hundred, One Hundred and six Dollars at the end of the first year, and one Hundred and twelve at the end of the second year, and so on for every year until the debt is paid, to which is added the cost of suit, sometimes amounting to more than the original debt. Now as the United States have by their laws acted up to one of the wisest principles inculcated by our Divine Master, while on earth, that of doing unto all others as we would they should do unto us, she feels herself morally and politically bound to exact in behalf of her citizens corresponding facilities in commercial and friendly intercourse with every Nation: At the same time the United States do not pretend to dictate to any foreign power the mode by which this desirable object shall be obtained. *Certain* and *speedy justice* is all she asks, is what she has a right to expect, and what she has the *will* as well as the power to enforce, when other, and more pacific measures are disregarded, and fail in the cause of national and individual justice.

Your Majesty will readily percieve that expediency, as well as *justice*, demands your early attention to this subject. I must therefore request your *acknowledgement* of all just claims held by citizens of the United States against your Majesty's government and subjects; and to say, *positively*, when, and how they are to be settled.

I am, With the highest consideration, Yours &c &c &c

(signed)   THOˢ AP CATESBY JONES *Captain*

To HIS MAJESTY KAIKIOULI
King of the Sandwich Islands.

[Decree in Council]

Every man is to deliver half a Pecul of good sandal Wood to the Governor of the district to which he belongs on or before the first day of September 1827: in case of not being able to procure the sandal wood, four Spanish dollars or any property worth that sum will be taken in payment.

No person except those who are infirm or of too advanced an age to go to the mountains will be exempted from this tax.

Every woman of the age of 13 years or upwards is to pay a mat 12 feet long and 6 wide or Tapa of equal value (to such a mat) or the sum of one Spanish dollar; on or before the first day of September 1827.

The amount of these taxes to be deposited in houses appointed for that purpose and on no account is any part thereof to be removed or applied to any purpose except liquidating the debts due to the creditors of the Government.

All monies collected under this tax are to be deposited in a chest secured by Iron hoops and firmly nailed with a hole in the top sufficient to admit a dollar, this chest is to be placed under the charge of some trusty person and on no account is it to be opened without giving notice to the creditors.

All persons who intend to pay their taxes in Hogs are to pay on or before the last day of January 1827.

Every man who shall proceed to the mountains for Sandal wood shall be at liberty to cut one pecul and on delivering half a pecul to the person appointed to receive it, shall be entitled to sell the other half on his own account to whomsoever he may think proper.

After the public debts are paid, the remainder of the amount of this tax to be divided between the King and governors, one half to the Regency for the use of the King and the other half to be divided between the Governors in proportion to the amount collected from each Island.

The last day of each month is appointed for the purpose of receiving the taxes from such persons as may be desirous of paying before the final period before mentioned. Should that day happen to be on Sunday the day following to be considered the proper day for receiving payments.

The amount of these taxes as soon as money can be realized for the cloth & mats shall be paid to the different creditors in proportion to their respective debts at the end of every three months the sandal wood also to be divided in like proportions.

First payment the 1st day of April.
Second Dº the 1st day of July.
Third Dº the 1st day of September [October].

Given under our hands & seals at Oahu this 27th day of December, 1826. In the name and on the behalf of His Majesty.

> ELISABETA KAAHUMANU, *Queen Regent*
> KARAIMOKU, *Prime Minister*
> BOKI
> HOAPILI
> LIDIA NAMAHANA

RELATIONS WITH HAWAII

The annexation of Hawaii became complete on August 12, 1898, pursuant to the joint resolution of July 7, 1898 (30 Statutes at Large, 750–51). Relations with Hawaii prior to annexation, from 1820, are described in Moore, Digest, I, 475–520.

Numerous papers for the period 1820–95, including various Senate and House documents, are in Foreign Relations, 1894, appendix II.

Since June 14, 1900, Hawaii has been a territory of the United States under the act of April 30, 1900 (31 Statutes at Large, 141–62).

Treaty Series No. 348
8 Statutes at Large, 346–59
18 *ibid.*, pt. 2, Public Treaties, 736–42

55

SWEDEN AND NORWAY : JULY 4, 1827

*Treaty of Commerce and Navigation, with separate article, signed at
Stockholm July 4, 1827. Original in French.
Submitted to the Senate December 12, 1827. (Message of December
11, 1827.) Resolution of advice and consent January 7, 1828.
Ratified by the United States January 17, 1828. Ratified by Sweden
and Norway July 11, 1827. Ratifications exchanged at Washington
January 18, 1828. Proclaimed January 19, 1828.*

[Translation]

Au nom de la très Sainte et Indivisible Trinité.

Les Etats Unis d'Amérique et Sa Majesté le Roi de Suède et de Norvège, également animés du désir d'étendre et de consolider les relations commerciales qui subsistent entre leurs territoires respectifs, et convaincus, que ce but ne sauroit être mieux rempli, qu'en les plaçant sur la base d'une parfaite égalité et réciprocité, sont convenus, en conséquence, d'entrer en négociation pour un nouveau Traité de Commerce et de Navigation, et ont nommé à cet effet des Plénipotentiaires, savoir: le Président des Etats Unis d'Amérique, John James Appleton, Chargé d'Affaires desdits Etats à la Cour de Sa Majesté le Roi de Suède et de Norvège; et Sa Majesté le Roi de Suède et de Norvège, le sieur Gustave Comte de Wetterstedt Son Ministre d'Etat et des

In the name of the Most Holy and Indivisible Trinity.

The United States of America and His Majesty the King of Sweden and Norway, equally animated with the desire of extending and consolidating the commercial relations subsisting between their respective territories, and convinced that this object cannot better be accomplished than by placing them on the basis of a perfect equality and reciprocity, have in consequence agreed to enter into negotiation for a new Treaty of Commerce and Navigation, and to this effect have appointed Plenipotentiaries, to wit: the President of the United States of America, John James Appleton, Chargé d'Affaires of the said States at the Court of His Majesty the King of Sweden and Norway; and His Majesty the King of Sweden and

Affaires Etrangères, Chevalier Commandeur de Ses Ordres, Chevalier des Ordres de Russie de St André, de St Alexandre Newsky et de Ste Anne de la Première Classe, Chevalier de l'Ordre de l'Aigle Rouge de Prusse de la Première Classe, Grand' Croix de l'Ordre de Leopold d'Autriche, Un des Dix-huit de l'Académie Suédoise, lesquels, après avoir échangé leurs Pleins Pouvoirs, trouvés en bonne et due forme, ont arrêté les Articles suivans:

ARTICLE I

Les Citoyens et Sujets de chacune des Deux Hautes Parties Contractantes pourront, avec toute sûreté pour leurs personnes, vaisseaux et cargaisons, aborder librement dans les ports, places et rivières des territoires de l'autre, partout où le commerce étranger est permis. Ils pourront s'y arrêter, et résider dans quelque partie que ce soit desdits territoires, y louer et occuper des maisons et des magasins pour leur commerce, et jouiront généralement de la plus entière sécurité et protection pour les affaires de leur négoce, à charge de se soumettre aux lois et ordonnances des pays respectifs.

ARTICLE II

Les bâtimens Suédois et Norvégiens et ceux de l'île de S^t

Norway, the Sieur Gustave Count de Wetterstedt, his Minister of State and of Foreign Affairs, Knight Commander of his Orders, Knight of the Orders of St. Andrew, St. Alexander Newsky, and St. Ann of the first class of Russia, Knight of the Order of the Red Eagle of the first class of Prussia, Grand Cross of the Order of Leopold of Austria, one of the eighteen of the Swedish Academy; who, after having exchanged their full powers, found in good and due form, have agreed upon the following articles:

ARTICLE 1

The citizens and subjects of each of the two high contracting parties may, with all security for their persons, vessels, and cargoes, freely enter the ports, places, and rivers of the territories of the other, wherever foreign commerce is permitted. They shall be at liberty to sojourn and reside in all parts whatsoever of said territories, to rent and occupy houses and warehouses for their commerce, and they shall enjoy, generally, the most entire security and protection in their mercantile transactions, on condition of their submitting to the laws and ordinances of the respective countries.

ARTICLE 2

Swedish and Norwegian vessels, and those of the island of Saint-

Barthélemy, qui arriveront sur leur lest ou chargés dans les ports des Etats Unis d'Amerique, de quelque lieu qu'ils viennent, seront traités à leur entrée, pendant leur séjour et à leur sortie, sur le même pied que les bâtimens nationaux venant du même lieu, par rapport aux droits de tonnage, de fanaux, de pilotage et de port, ainsi qu'aux vacations des officiers publics, et à tout autre droit ou charge, de quelque espèce ou dénomination que ce soit, perçus au nom, ou au profit, du Gouvernement, des Administrations locales ou d'Etablissemens particuliers quelconques.

Et réciproquement les bâtimens des Etats Unis d'Amérique, qui arriveront sur leur lest ou chargés dans les ports des Royaumes de Suède et de Norvège, de quelque lieu qu'ils viennent, seront traités, à leur entrée, pendant leur séjour, et à leur sortie, sur le même pied que les bâtimens nationaux venant du même lieu, par rapport aux droits de tonnage, de fanaux, de pilotage et de port, ainsi qu'aux vacations des officiers publics, et à tout autre droit ou charge, de quelque espèce ou dénomination que ce soit, perçus au nom, ou au profit, du Gouvernement, des Administrations locales ou d'Etablissemens particuliers quelconques.

Barthélemy, arriving either laden or in ballast into the ports of the United States of America, from whatever place they may come, shall be treated on their entrance, during their stay, and at their departure, upon the same footing as national vessels coming from the same place, with respect to the duties of tonnage, lighthouses, pilotage, and port charges, as well as to the perquisites of public officers and all other duties or charges, of whatever kind or denomination, levied in the name or to the profit of the Government, the local authorities, or of any private establishments whatsoever.

And reciprocally, the vessels of the United States of America, arriving either laden or in ballast in the ports of the Kingdoms of Sweden and Norway, from whatever place they may come, shall be treated on their entrance, during their stay, and at their departure, upon the same footing as national vessels coming from the same place, with respect to the duties of tonnage, lighthouses, pilotage, and port charges, as well as to the perquisites of public officers and all other duties or charges, of whatever kind or denomination, levied in the name or to the profit of the Government, the local authorities, or of any private establishments whatsoever.

Article III

Tout ce qui pourra légalement être importé dans les Etats Unis d'Amérique, par bâtimens desdits Etats pourra également y être importé par bâtimens Suédois et Norvégiens, ou de l'île de St Barthélemy, de quelque lieu qu'ils viennent, sans payer d'autres ou plus hauts droits ou charges, de quelque espèce ou dénomination que ce soit, perçus au nom, ou au profit, du Gouvernement, des Administrations locales, ou d'Etablissemens particuliers quelconques, que si l'importation avoit lieu en bâtimens nationaux.

Et réciproquement, Tout ce qui pourra légalement être importé dans les Royaumes de Suède et de Norvège par bâtimens Suédois ou Norvégiens, ou de l'île de St Barthélemy, pourra également y être importé par bâtimens des Etats Unis d'Amérique, de quelque lieu qu'ils viennent, sans payer d'autres ou plus hauts droits ou charges, de quelque espèce ou dénomination que ce soit, perçus au nom, ou au profit, du Gouvernement, des Administrations locales ou d'Etablissemens particuliers quelconques, que si l'importation avoit lieu en bâtimens nationaux.

Article IV

Tout ce qui pourra légalement être exporté des Etats Unis d'Amérique, par bâtimens des-

Article 3

All that may be lawfully imported into the United States of America in vessels of the said States may also be thereinto imported in Swedish and Norwegian vessels, and in those of the island of Saint-Barthélemy, from whatever place they may come, without paying other or higher duties or charges, of whatever kind or denomination, levied in the name or to the profit of the Government, the local authorities, or of any private establishments whatsoever, than if imported in national vessels.

And reciprocally, all that may be lawfully imported into the Kingdoms of Sweden and Norway in Swedish and Norwegian vessels, or in those of the island of Saint-Barthélemy, may also be thereinto imported in vessels of the United States of America, from whatever place they may come, without paying other or higher duties or charges, of whatever kind or denomination, levied in the name or to the profit of the Government, the local authorities, or of any private establishments whatsoever, than if imported in national vessels.

Article 4

All that may be lawfully exported from the United States of America in vessels of the said

dits Etats, pourra également en être exporté par bâtimens Suédois et Norvégiens ou de l'île de S! Barthélemy, sans payer d'autres ou plus hauts droits ou charges, de quelque espèce ou dénomination que ce soit, perçus au nom, ou au profit, du Gouvernement, des Administrations locales ou d'Etablissemens particuliers quelconques, que si l'exportation avoit lieu en bâtimens nationaux.

Et réciproquement, tout ce qui pourra légalement être exporté des Royaumes de Suède et de Norvège par bâtimens Suédois et Norvégiens, ou de l'île de S! Barthélemy, pourra également en être exporté par bâtimens des Etats Unis d'Amérique, sans payer d'autres ou plus hauts droits ou charges, de quelque espèce ou denomination que ce soit, perçus au nom, ou au profit, du Gouvernement, des Administration locales, ou d'Etablissemens particuliers quelconques, que si l'exportation avoit lieu en bâtimens nationaux

States may also be exported therefrom in Swedish and Norwegian vessels, or in those of the island of Saint-Barthélemy, without paying other or higher duties or charges, of whatever kind or denomination, levied in the name or to the profit of the Government, the local authorities, or of any private establishments whatsoever, than if exported in national vessels.

And reciprocally, all that may be lawfully exported from the Kingdoms of Sweden and Norway in Swedish and Norwegian vessels, or in those of the island of Saint-Barthélemy, may also be exported therefrom in vessels of the United States of America, without paying other or higher duties or charges, of whatever kind or denomination, levied in the name or to the profit of the Government, the local authorities, or of any private establishments whatsoever, than if exported in national vessels.

Article V

Les stipulations des trois Articles précédens, sont dans toute leur plénitude, applicables aux bâtimens des Etats Unis d'Amérique, qui se rendront chargés ou non chargés, dans la Colonie de S! Barthélemy, aux Indes Occidentales, soit des ports des Royaumes de Suède et de Norvège,

Article 5

The stipulations contained in the three preceding articles are to their full extent applicable to the vessels of the United States of America proceeding, either laden or not laden, to the colony of Saint-Barthélemy in the West Indies, whether from the ports of the Kingdoms of Sweden and

soit de tout autre lieu quelconque, ou qui sortiront de la dite Colonie, chargés ou non chargés, pour se rendre, soit en Suède ou en Norvège, soit en tout autre lieu quelconque.

Norway or from any other place whatsoever, or proceeding from the said colony, either laden or not laden, whether bound for Sweden or Norway, or for any other place whatsoever.

Article VI

Il est expressément entendu que les Articles précédens Deux, trois et quatre, ne sont point applicables à la navigation de côte ou de cabotage d'un port des Etats Unis d'Amérique à un autre port desdits Etats, ni à la navigation d'un port des Royaumes de Suède ou de Norvège à un autre, ou à celle entre ces deux derniers pays, navigation que chacune des Deux Hautes Parties Contractantes se réserve.

Article 6

It is expressly understood that the foregoing second, third, and fourth articles are not applicable to the coastwise navigation from one port of the United States of America to another port of the said States, nor to the navigation from one port of the Kingdoms of Sweden or of Norway to another, nor to that between the two latter countries, which navigation each of the two high contracting parties reserves to itself.

Article VII

Chacune des Deux Hautes Parties Contractantes s'engage à ne donner dans ses achats, ou dans ceux, qui seroient faits par des Compagnies ou des Agens agissant en son nom, ou sous son autorité, aucune préférence aux importations faites par ses batimens, ou par ceux d'une nation tierce, sur celles faites dans les bâtimens de l'autre Partie Contractante.

Article 7

Each of the two high contracting parties engages not to grant in its purchases, or in those which might be made by companies or agents acting in its name or under its authority, any preference to importations made in its own vessels, or in those of a third power, over those made in the vessels of the other contracting party.

Article VIII

Les Deux Hautes Parties Contractantes s'engagent à ne pas établir sur la navigation entre leurs territoires respectifs, par les bâtimens de l'une ou de l'autre,

Article 8

The two high contracting parties engage not to impose upon the navigation between their respective territories, in the vessels of either, any tonnage or other

des droits de tonnage ou autres, de quelque espèce ou dénomination que ce soit plus hauts ou autres, que ceux qui seront établis sur toute autre navigation, excepté celle qu'elles se sont respectivement réservée par le sixième article du présent Traité.

Article IX

Il ne pourra pas être établi dans les Etats Unis d'Amérique sur les productions du sol ou de l'industrie des Royaumes de Suède et de Norvège et de l'île de S⁺ Barthélemy, aucune prohibition ou restriction d'importation ou d'exportation, ni aucuns droits, de quelque espèce ou dénomination que ce soit, qu'autant que ces prohibitions, ces restrictions, et ces droits, seroient également établis sur les objets de même nature provenant de toute autre contrée

Et réciproquement il ne pourra pas être établi dans les Royaumes de Suède et de Norvège, ni dans l'île de S⁺ Barthélemy, sur les productions du sol ou de l'industrie des Etats Unis d'Amérique, aucune prohibition ou restriction d'importation ou d'exportation, ni aucuns droits, de quelque espèce ou dénomination que ce soit, qu'autant que ces prohibitions, ces restrictions, et ces droits seroient également établis sur les objets de même nature provenant, dans le cas où l'importation ou l'exportation auroit lieu dans ou

duties of any kind or denomination, which shall be higher or other than those which shall be imposed on every other navigation except that which they have reserved to themselves, respectively, by the sixth article of the present treaty.

Article 9

There shall not be established in the United States of America, upon the products of the soil or industry of the Kingdoms of Sweden and Norway, or of the island of Saint-Barthélemy, any prohibition or restriction of importation or exportation, nor any duties of any kind or denomination whatsoever, unless such prohibitions, restrictions, and duties shall likewise be established upon articles of like nature, the growth of any other country.

And reciprocally, there shall not be established in the Kingdoms of Sweden and Norway, nor in the island of Saint-Barthélemy, on the products of the soil or industry of the United States of America, any prohibition or restriction of importation or exportation, nor any duties of any kind or denomination whatsoever, unless such prohibitions, restrictions, and duties be likewise established upon articles of like nature, the growth of the island of Saint-Barthélemy, or of any other place, in case such importa-

hors les Royaumes de Suède et de Norvège, de l'île de S̲ᵗ Barthélemy ou de tout autre endroit; et, dans le cas où l'importation ou l'exportation auroit lieu dans ou hors l'île de S̲ᵗ Barthelemy, des Royaumes de Suède et de Norvège ou de tout autre endroit

tion be made into or from the Kingdoms of Sweden and Norway; or of the Kingdoms of Sweden and Norway, or of any other place, in case such importation or exportation be made into or from the island of Saint-Barthélemy.

Article X

Toute faculté d'entrepôt et toutes primes et remboursemens de droits, qui seroient accordés dans les territoires d'une des Hautes Parties Contractantes, à l'importation ou à l'exportation de quelque objet que ce soit, seront également accordés aux objets de même nature, produits du sol ou de l'industrie de l'autre Partie Contractante et aux importations et exportations faites dans ses bâtimens.

Article 10

All privileges of transit and all bounties and drawbacks which may be allowed within the territories of one of the high contracting parties upon the importation or exportation of any article whatsoever, shall likewise be allowed on the articles of like nature, the products of the soil or industry of the other contracting party, and on the importations and exportations made in its vessels.

Article XI

Les Citoyens ou Sujets de l'une des Hautes Parties Contractantes arrivant avec leurs bâtimens à l'une des côtes appartenant à l'autre, mais ne voulant pas entrer dans le port, ou, après y être entrés, ne voulant décharger aucune partie de leur cargaison, auront la liberté de partir et de poursuivre leur voyage, sans payer d'autres droits, impôts ou charges quelconques pour le bâtiment ou la cargaison, que les droits de pilotage, de quayage et d'entretien de fanaux, quand ces droits sont perçus sur les natio-

Article 11

The citizens or subjects of one of the high contracting parties, arriving with their vessels on the coasts belonging to the other, but not wishing to enter the port, or after having entered therein, not wishing to unload any part of their cargo, shall be at liberty to depart and continue their voyage without paying any other duties, imposts, or charges whatsoever, for the vessel and cargo, than those of pilotage, wharfage, and for the support of lighthouses, when such duties shall be levied on national vessels in similar

naux dans les mêmes cas. Bien entendu cependant qu'ils se conformeront toujours aux réglemens et ordonnances concernant la navigation et les places ou ports dans lesquels ils pourront aborder, qui sont ou seront en vigueur pour les nationaux; et qu'il sera permis aux officiers des douanes de les visiter, de rester à bord et de prendre telles précautions, qui pourroient être nécessaires pour prévenir tout commerce illicite pendant que les bâtimens resteront dans l'enceinte de leur juridiction.

Article XII

Il est aussi convenu que les bâtimens de l'une des Hautes Parties Contractantes, étant entrés dans les ports de l'autre, pourront se borner à ne décharger qu'une partie de leur cargaison, selon que le capitaine ou propriétaire le desirera, et qu'ils pourront s'en aller librement avec le reste sans payer de droits, impôts ou charges quelconques, que pour la partie, qui aura été mise à terre, et qui sera marquée et biffée sur le manifeste, qui contiendra l'énumération des effets dont le bâtiment étoit chargé, lequel manifeste devra étre présenté en entier à la Douane du lieu où le bâtiment aura abordé.   Il ne sera rien payé pour la partie de la cargaison, que le bâtiment remportera et avec laquelle il pourra continuer sa route pour un ou plusieurs autres ports du même pays, et y disposer

cases.   It is understood, however, that they shall always conform to such regulations and ordinances concerning navigation and the places and ports which they may enter, as are or shall be in force with regard to national vessels; and that the customhouse officers shall be permitted to visit them, to remain on board, and to take all such precautions as may be necessary to prevent all unlawful commerce, as long as the vessels shall remain within the limits of their jurisdiction.

Article 12

It is further agreed that the vessels of one of the high contracting parties, having entered into the ports of the other, will be permitted to confine themselves to unloading such part only of their cargoes as the captain or owner may wish, and that they may freely depart with the remainder without paying any duties, imposts, or charges whatsoever, except for that part which shall have been landed, and which shall be marked upon and erased from the manifest exhibiting the enumeration of the articles with which the vessel was laden; which manifest shall be presented entire at the customhouse of the place where the vessel shall have entered.   Nothing shall be paid on that part of the cargo which the vessel shall carry away and with which it may continue its voyage

du reste de sa cargaison, si elle est composée d'objets dont l'importation est permise, en payant les droits qui y sont applicables, ou bien il pourra s'en aller dans tout autre pays. Il est cependant entendu que les droits, impôts ou charges quelconques, qui sont ou seront payables pour les bâtimens mêmes doivent être acquittés au premier port ou ils romproient le chargement, ou en déchargeroient une partie, mais qu'aucuns droits, impôts ou charges pareils ne seront demandés de nouveau dans les ports du même pays où lesdits bâtimens pourroient vouloir entrer après, à moins que les nationaux ne soient sujets à quelques droits ultérieurs dans le même cas.

to one or several other ports of the same country, there to dispose of the remainder of its cargo, if composed of articles whose importation is permitted, on paying the duties chargeable upon it; or it may proceed to any other country. It is understood, however, that all duties, imposts, or charges whatsoever, which are or may become chargeable upon the vessels themselves, must be paid at the first port where they shall break bulk or unlade part of their cargoes; but that no duties, imposts, or charges of the same description shall be demanded anew in the ports of the same country which such vessels might afterwards wish to enter, unless national vessels be in similar cases subject to some ulterior duties.

Article XIII

Chacune des Hautes Parties Contractantes accorde à l'autre la faculté d'entretenir dans ses ports et places de Commerce, des Consuls, Vice-Consuls ou Agens de Commerce qui jouiront de toute la protection et recevront toute l'assistance nécessaire pour remplir duëment leurs fonctions, mais il est expressément déclaré, que dans le cas d'une conduite illégale ou impropre envers les lois ou le Gouvernement du pays, dans lequels les dits Consuls, Vice-Consuls ou Agens Commerciaux résideroient ils pourront être pour-

Article 13

Each of the high contracting parties grants to the other the privilege of appointing, in its commercial ports and places, consuls, vice consuls, and commercial agents, who shall enjoy the full protection and receive every assistance necessary for the due exercise of their functions; but it is expressly declared that in case of illegal or improper conduct with respect to the laws or Government of the country in which said consuls, vice consuls, or commercial agents shall reside, they may be prosecuted and

suivis et punis conformément aux lois, et privés de l'exercice de leurs fonctions par le Gouvernement offensé, qui fera connoître à l'autre ses motifs pour avoir agi ainsi, bien entendu cependant que les Archives et Documens relatifs aux affaires du Consulat seront à l'abri de toute recherche, et devront être soigneusement conservés sous le scellé des Consuls, Vice-Consuls ou Agens Commerciaux et de l'Autorité de l'endroit où ils résideroient.

Les Consuls, Vice-Consuls et Agens Commerciaux, ou ceux qui seroient duëment autorisés à les suppléer, auront le droit comme tels, de servir de juges et d'arbitres dans les différens qui pourroient s'élever entre les capitaines et les équipages des bâtimens de la nation dont ils soignent les intérêts, sans que les Autorités locales puissent y intervenir, à moins que la conduite des équipages ou du capitaine ne troublât l'ordre ou la tranquillité du pays, ou que lesdits Consuls, Vice-Consuls ou Agens Commerciaux ne réquissent leur intervention pour faire éxécuter ou maintenir leurs décisions. Bien entendu que cette espèce de jugement ou d'arbitrage ne sauroit pourtant priver les parties contendantes du droit qu'elles ont à leur retour de recourir aux Autorités judiciaires de leur Patrie.

punished conformably to the laws, and deprived of the exercise of their functions by the offended Government, which shall acquaint the other with its motives for having thus acted; it being understood, however, that the archives and documents relative to the affairs of the consulate shall be exempt from all search and shall be carefully preserved under the seals of the consuls, vice consuls, or commercial agents, and of the authority of the place where they may reside.

The consuls, vice consuls, or commercial agents, or the persons duly authorized to supply their places, shall have the right, as such, to sit as judges and arbitrators in such differences as may arise between the captains and crews of the vessels belonging to the nation whose interests are committed to their charge, without the interference of the local authorities, unless the conduct of the crews or of the captain should disturb the order or tranquillity of the country, or the said consuls, vice consuls, or commercial agents should require their assistance to cause their decisions to be carried into effect or supported. It is, however, understood that this species of judgment or arbitration shall not deprive the contending parties of the right they have to resort, on their return, to the judicial authority of their country.

Article XIV

Lesdits Consuls, Vice-Consuls ou Agens Commerciaux seront autorisés à requérir l'assistance des Autorités locales pour l'arrestation, la détention et l'emprisonnement de déserteurs des navires de guerre et marchands de leur pays, et ils s'adresseront, pour cet objet, aux tribunaux, juges et officiers compétens, et réclameront, par écrit, les déserteurs susmentionnés en prouvant par la communication des registres des navires ou rôles de l'équipage, ou par d'autres documens officiels que de tels individus ont fait partie desdits équipages, et cette réclamation, ainsi prouvée, l'extradition ne sera pas refusée.

De tels déserteurs, lorsqu'ils auront été arrêtés seront mis à la disposition desdits Consuls, Vice-Consuls ou Agens Commerciaux, et pourront être enfermés dans les prisons publiques à la réquisition et aux frais de ceux qui les réclament, pour être envoyés aux navires, auxquels ils appartenoient, ou à d'autres de la même nation. Mais s'ils ne sont pas renvoyés dans l'espace de deux mois, à compter du jour de leur arrestation, ils seront mis en liberté, et ne seront plus arrêtés pour la même cause.

Il est entendu, toutefois, que si le déserteur se trouvoit avoir commis quelque crime ou délit, il pourra être sursis à son extradition, jusqu'à ce que le tribunal,

Article 14

The said consuls, vice consuls, or commercial agents are authorized to require the assistance of the local authorities for the arrest, detention, and imprisonment of the deserters from the ships of war and merchant vessels of their country; and for this purpose they shall apply to the competent tribunals, judges, and officers, and shall in writing demand said deserters, proving, by the exhibition of the registers of the vessels, the rolls of the crews, or by other official documents, that such individuals formed part of the crews, and on this reclamation being thus substantiated, the surrender shall not be refused.

Such deserters, when arrested, shall be placed at the disposal of the said consuls, vice consuls, or commercial agents, and may be confined in the public prisons, at the request and cost of those who claim them, in order to be sent to the vessels to which they belonged or to others of the same country. But if not sent back within the space of two months, reckoning from the day of their arrest, they shall be set at liberty and shall not be again arrested for the same cause.

It is understood, however, that if the deserter should be found to have committed any crime or offence, his surrender may be delayed until the tribunal before

nanti de l'affaire aura rendu sa sentence, et que celle-ci ait reçu son éxécution.

which the case shall be depending shall have pronounced its sentence and such sentence shall have been carried into effect.

Article XV

Dans le cas où quelque bâtiment de l'une des Hautes Parties Contractantes aura échoué, fait naufrage ou souffert quelqu'autre dommage, sur les côtes de la domination de l'autre il sera donné tout aide et assistance aux personnes naufragées, ou qui se trouveroient en danger, et il leur sera accordé des passeports pour retourner dans leur patrie. Les bâtimens et les marchandises naufragés, ou leur produit, s'ils ont été vendus, seront restitués, à leurs propriétaires ou ayant cause, s'ils sont reclamés dans l'an et jour, en payant les frais de sauvetage que payeroient les nationaux dans les mêmes cas. Et les compagnies de sauvetage ne pourront faire accepter leurs services que dans les mêmes cas et après les mêmes délais,qui seroient accordés aux capitaines et aux équipages nationaux. Les Gouvernemens respectifs veilleront d'ailleurs à ce que ces compagnies ne se permettent point de vexations ou d'actes arbitraires.

Article 15

In case any vessel of one of the high contracting parties shall have been stranded or shipwrecked or shall have suffered any other damage on the coasts of the dominions of the other, every aid and assistance shall be given to the persons shipwrecked or in danger, and passports shall be granted to them to return to their country. The shipwrecked vessels and merchandise, or their proceeds if the same shall have been sold, shall be restored to their owners or to those entitled thereto, if claimed within a year and a day, upon paying such costs of salvage as would be paid by national vessels in the same circumstances; and the salvage companies shall not compel the acceptance of their services, except in the same cases and after the same delays as shall be granted to the captains and crews of national vessels. Moreover, the respective Governments will take care that these companies do not commit any vexatious or arbitrary acts.

Article XVI

Il est convenu que les bâtimens qui arriveront directement des Etats Unis d'Amérique à un port

Article 16

It is agreed that vessels arriving directly from the United States of America at a port within

de la domination de Sa Majesté le Roi de Suède et de Norvège, ou des territoires de Sa dite Majesté en Europe, à un port des Etats Unis, et qui seroient pourvus d'un certificat de santé donné par l'officier compétent à cet égard du port d'où les bâtimens sont sortis, et assurant qu'aucune maladie maligne ou contagieuse n'existoit dans ce port, ne seront soumis à aucune autre quarantaine que celle qui sera nécessaire pour la visite de l'officier de santé du port où les bâtimens seroient arrivés, après laquelle il sera permis à ces bâtimens d'entrer immédiatement, et de décharger leurs cargaisons, bien entendu toutefois qu'il n'y ait eu personne à leur bord, qui ait été attaqué pendant le voyage d'une maladie maligne ou contagieuse, que les bâtimens n'aient point communiqué dans leur traversée avec un bâtiment qui seroit lui-même dans le cas de subir une quarantaine, et que la contrée d'où ils viendroient ne fut pas à cette époque si généralement infectée ou suspecte, qu'on ait rendu avant leur arrivée une ordonnance, d'après laquelle tous les bâtimens venant de cette contrée seroient regardés comme suspects et en conséquence assujétis à une quarantaine.

Article XVII

Les Articles deux, cinq, six, sept, huit, neuf, dix, onze, douze, treize, quatorze, quinze, seize,

the dominions of His Majesty the King of Sweden and Norway, or from the territories of His said Majesty in Europe, at a port of the United States, and provided with a bill of health granted by an officer having competent power to that effect at the port whence such vessels shall have sailed, setting forth that no malignant or contagious diseases prevailed in that port, shall be subjected to no other quarantine than such as may be necessary for the visit of the health officer of the port where such vessels shall have arrived; after which said vessels shall be allowed immediately to enter and unload their cargoes; provided always, that there shall be on board no person who, during the voyage, shall have been attacked with any malignant or contagious diseases; that such vessels shall not, during their passage, have communicated with any vessel liable itself to undergo a quarantine; and that the country whence they came shall not at that time be so far infected or suspected that, before their arrival, an ordinance had been issued in consequence of which all vessels coming from that country should be considered as suspected and consequently subject to quarantine.

Article 17

The second, fifth, sixth, seventh, eighth, ninth, tenth, eleventh, twelfth, thirteenth, fourteenth,

dix-sept, dix-huit, dix-neuf, vingt un, vingt deux, vingt trois et vingt cinq, du Traité d'Amitié et de commerce,[1] conclu à Paris le trois Avril mil sept cent quatre-vingt trois par les Plénipotentiaires des Etats Unis d'Amérique et de Sa Majesté le Roi de Suède, ainsi que les Articles Séparés un, deux, quatre et cinq qui furent signés le mêmes jour par les mêmes Plénipotentiaires, sont remis en vigueur et rendus applicables à tous les pays sous la domination des Hautes Parties actuellement Contractantes, et auront la même force et valeur, que s'ils étoient insérés textuellement dans le présent Traité. Bien entendu que les stipulations contenues dans les Articles précités seront toujours censées ne rien changer aux conventions conclues de part et d'autre, avec d'autres nations dans l'intervalle écoulé entre l'expiration dudit Traité de Mil sept cent quatre-vingt trois et la remise en vigueur desdits Articles par le Traité de Commerce et de Navigation [2] conclu, par les Hautes Parties actuellement Contractantes, à Stockholm le quatre Septembre mil-huit cent seize.

ARTICLE XVIII

Vû l'éloignement des Pays respectifs des Deux Hautes Parties

fifteenth, sixteenth, seventeenth, eighteenth, nineteenth, twenty-first, twenty-second, twenty-third, and twenty-fifth articles of the Treaty of Amity and Commerce [1] concluded at Paris on the third of April, one thousand seven hundred eighty-three, by the Plenipotentiaries of the United States of America and of His Majesty the King of Sweden, together with the first, second, fourth, and fifth separate articles signed on the same day by the same Plenipotentiaries, are revived and made applicable to all the countries under the dominion of the present high contracting parties and shall have the same force and value as if they were inserted in the context of the present treaty; it being understood that the stipulations contained in the articles above cited shall always be considered as in no manner affecting the conventions concluded by either party with other nations during the interval between the expiration of the said treaty of one thousand seven hundred eighty-three and the revival of said articles by the Treaty of Commerce and Navigation [2] concluded at Stockholm by the present high contracting parties on the fourth of September, one thousand eight hundred and sixteen.

ARTICLE 18

Considering the remoteness of the respective countries of the two

---

[1] Document 10.

[2] Document 36.

Contractantes, et l'incertitude, qui en résulte sur les divers événemens qui peuvent avoir lieu, il est convenu, qu'un bâtiment marchand appartenant à l'une d'Elles qui se trouveroit destiné pour un port supposé bloqué au moment du départ de ce batiment, ne sera cependant pas capturé ou condamné pour avoir essayé une première fois d'entrer dans ledit port, à moins qu'il ne puisse être prouvé que ledit bâtiment avoit pû et dû apprendre en route que l'état de blocus de la place en question duroit encore: mais les bâtimens qui après avoir été renvoyés une fois, essayeroient pendant le même voyage d'entrer une seconde fois dans le même port bloqué, durant la continuation de ce blocus, se trouveront alors sujets à être détenus et condamnés.

high contracting parties and the uncertainty resulting therefrom with respect to the various events which may take place, it is agreed that a merchant vessel belonging to either of them which may be bound to a port supposed, at the time of its departure, to be blockaded, shall not, however, be captured or condemned for having attempted a first time to enter said port, unless it can be proved that said vessel could and ought to have learned during its voyage that the blockade of the place in question still continued. But all vessels which, after having been warned off once, shall during the same voyage attempt a second time to enter the same blockaded port, during the continuance of said blockade, shall then subject themselves to be detained and condemned.

Article XIX

Le présent Traité sera en vigueur pendant dix années à partir du jour de l'échange des ratifications, et, si, avant l'expiration des neuf premières années, l'une ou l'autre des Hautes Parties Contractantes n'avoit pas annoncé à l'autre, par une notification officielle, son intention d'en faire cesser l'effet, ce Traité restera obligatoire une année au delà, et ainsi de suite jusqu'à l'expiration des douze mois qui

Article 19

The present treaty shall continue in force for ten years, counting from the day of the exchange of the ratifications; and if, before the expiration of the first nine years, neither of the high contracting parties shall have announced, by an official notification to the other, its intention to arrest the operation of said treaty, it shall remain binding for one year beyond that time, and so on until the expiration of the twelve

suivront une semblable notification à quelque époque qu'elle ait lieu.

months which will follow a similar notification, whatever the time at which it may take place.

Article XX

Le présent Traité sera ratifié par le Président des Etats Unis d'Amérique, par et avec l'avis et le consentement du Senat, et par Sa Majesté le Roi de Suède et de Norvège, et les ratifications en seront échangées, à Washington dans l'espace de neuf mois après la signature, ou plutôt si faire se peut.

En foi de quoi les Plénipotentiaires respectifs ont signé le présent Traité en duplicata, et y ont apposé le cachet de leurs armes. Fait à Stockholm le quatre Juillet l'an de Grace Milhuit cent vingt sept.

J. J. Appleton.
[Seal]
G, Comte de Wetterstedt
[Seal]

Article 20

The present treaty shall be ratified by the President of the United States of America by and with the advice and consent of the Senate, and by His Majesty the King of Sweden and Norway, and the ratifications shall be exchanged at Washington within the space of nine months from the signature, or sooner if possible.

In faith whereof the respective Plenipotentiaries have signed the present treaty, by duplicates, and have affixed thereto the seals of their arms. Done at Stockholm the fourth of July in the year of grace one thousand eight hundred and twenty-seven.

J. J. Appleton.
[Seal]
G, Comte de Wetterstedt
[Seal]

Article Séparé.

Des rapports de proximité et d'anciennes relations, ayant fait régler l'importation des productions des Royaumes de Suède et de Norvège dans le Grand Duché de Finlande, et celle des productions de la Finlande en Suède et en Norvège sur les bâtimens des pays respectifs, par des stipulations

Separate Article

Certain relations of proximity and ancient connections having led to regulations for the importation of the products of the Kingdoms of Sweden and Norway into the Grand Duchy of Finland, and that of the products of Finland into Sweden and Norway, in vessels of the respective coun-

spéciales d'un Traité [1] encore en vigueur, et dont le renouvellement forme un objet de négociation actuelle entre les Cours de Suède et Norvège et de Russie, sans que lesdites stipulations soient liées aux réglemens existans pour le commerce étranger en général, les Deux Hautes Parties Contractantes, voulant écarter de leurs relations commerciales toute espèce d'équivoque ou de motif de discussion, sont tombées d'accord, que les Articles huit, neuf et dix du présent Traité ne seront point applicables, ni à la navigation et au commerce susmentionnés, et par conséquent aux exceptions dans les Tarifs généraux des douanes et dans les réglemens de navigation qui en résultent, ni aux avantages spéciaux qui sont ou pourroient être donnés à l'importation du suif et des chandelles de Russie, motivés par des avantages équivalens accordés en Russie à des articles d'importation de Suède et de Norvège.

Le présent Article séparé aura la même force et valeur que s'il etoit inséré mot à mot, dans le Traité, signé aujourd'hui et sera ratifié en même temps.

En foi de quoi, nous Soussignés, en vertu de nos Pleins Pouvoirs respectifs, avons signé le présent

tries, by special stipulations of a treaty [1] still in force and whose renewal forms at this time the subject of a negotiation between the Courts of Sweden and Norway and Russia, said stipulations being in no manner connected with the existing regulations for foreign commerce in general, the two high contracting parties, anxious to remove from their commercial relations all kinds of ambiguity or motives of discussion, have agreed that the eighth, ninth, and tenth articles of the present treaty shall not be applicable either to the navigation and commerce above mentioned, nor, consequently, to the exceptions in the general tariff of custom-house duties and in the regulations of navigation resulting therefrom, nor to the special advantages which are or may be granted to the importation of tallow and candles from Russia, founded upon equivalent advantages granted by Russia on certain articles of importation from Sweden and Norway.

The present separate article shall have the same force and value as if it were inserted word for word in the treaty signed this day, and shall be ratified at the same time.

In faith whereof we, the undersigned, by virtue of our respective full powers, have signed the

---

[1] See the note regarding the separate article.

Article Séparé et y avons apposé le cachet de nos armes. Fait à Stockholm le quatre Juillet Mil huit cent vingt sept.

present separate article and affixed thereto the seals of our arms. Done at Stockholm the fourth of July, one thousand eight hundred and twenty-seven.

J. J. APPLETON.
[Seal]

G, COMTE DE WETTERSTEDT
[Seal]

J. J. APPLETON.
[Seal]

G, COMTE DE WETTERSTEDT
[Seal]

NOTES

This treaty was a renewal, with modifications, of the treaty of September 4, 1816, with Sweden and Norway (Document 36), and by Article 17 of this treaty, as by Article 12 of the earlier one, twenty-four articles of the treaty of April 3, 1783, with Sweden (Document 10), were revived and "put in force."

The treaty of September 4, 1816 (Document 36), had by its terms expired on September 25, 1826, eight years after the exchange of ratifications. Both Governments, however, continued to observe "the rule of the treaty" as far as possible; Baron de Stackelberg, Chargé d'Affaires from Sweden and Norway, under date of September 26, 1826, had stated (translation, D. S., 3 Notes from the Swedish Legation; American State Papers, Foreign Relations, VI, 367–68):

The late Treaty of Commerce with Sweden and Norway and the United States of America expiring, and nothing being yet stipulated between the two Governments for the renewal of the treaty, His Majesty the King of Sweden and Norway, to give a new proof of his sentiments of sincere friendship towards the Government of the United States of America, and in the intimate conviction that it will adopt on its part analogous measures, has resolved to maintain, with regard to American commerce, and till a new order, the dispositions of the late treaty, in order to have the power of concluding, in the interval, another treaty in its place, without there being, in this manner, any hindrance in the mutual relations. The undersigned having received orders from his Government to announce officially to His Excellency Mr. Clay, Secretary of State and of Foreign Affairs, the contents of this note, is also authorized to propose to the American Government to give similar orders in the ports of the United States in regard to the Swedish and Norwegian commerce.

In the answering note of Secretary of State Clay of October 31, 1826 (D. S., 3 Notes to Foreign Legations, 305–6), it was said "that the President . . . will recommend to the Congress of the United States to pass a Law for the observance of the rule of the Treaty, for the present on our part."

Accordingly, the message to Congress of President John Quincy Adams under date of December 5, 1826, included the following passage (American State Papers, Foreign Relations, VI, 207, 208):

In the course of the last summer, the term to which our last commercial treaty with Sweden was limited has expired. A continuation of it is in the contempla-

tion of the Swedish Government, and is believed to be desirable on the part of the United States. It has been proposed by the King of Sweden that, pending the negotiation of renewal, the expired treaty should be mutually considered as still in force; a measure which will require the sanction of Congress to be carried into effect on our part, and which I therefore recommend to your consideration.

The subject was discussed in the instructions of Secretary of State Clay to John James Appleton, Chargé d'Affaires at Stockholm, under date of January 12, 1827 (D. S., 11 Instructions, U. S. Ministers, 231–35; American State Papers, Foreign Relations, VI, 717–19), from which the following is extracted:

Having just indirectly heard of your arrival at Stockholm, I am directed by the President to call your immediate attention to the subject of the Treaty which was concluded at that Capital and signed on the 4th day of September 1816. The Treaty expired on the 25th of last September. It had been the President's wish, by a new negotiation, and by engrafting some further regulations upon it, to prevent the event which has occurred. The illness and subsequent death of your predecessor, and your engagement on another public service, together with the incidental delay of your arrival at Stockholm, have prevented, on our part, the opening of the negociation there. We had, moreover, some reason to believe that the Baron de Stackelberg would have been provided with instructions to negociate on that subject here. It was not until about the time of the expiration of the Treaty that we were disappointed in the fulfilment of these expectations. On the 26th day of September last, a note was received from the Baron, of which a copy, together with a copy of the answer which was returned to it, is herewith transmitted.

As he announced in that note the determination of the Government of Sweden to continue to observe the rule of the treaty notwithstanding it should expire without being renewed, he was informed that the President would recommend to Congress to provide by law for its observance on our part, until the issue should be known of the intended negociation. He has, accordingly, in his message to Congress [of December 5, 1826, American State Papers, Foreign Relations, VI, 207, 208], on the opening of its present session . . . recommended to that body, the enactment of the necessary law, to secure to the navigation and commerce of Sweden the benefit of the treaty, until the result of the negociation is known. A bill has been introduced into the H. of R. . . . to admit the vessels of Sweden upon the terms stipulated in the treaty, and making provision to refund any discriminating duties, should any such have been collected from Swedish vessels or their cargoes, between the 25th of September last, and the date of the law. No doubt is entertained of the passage of the bill, prior to the adjournment of Congress; nor is any inconvenience anticipated, before the renewal of the treaty, from the limitation of the law to the single object of the discriminating duties. The bill would have been shaped so as to comprehend all the regulations of the treaty, but for doubts which were felt by some members of Congress as to the competency of the legislative power to extend to some of the stipulations which were believed to appertain strictly to the treaty-making power. As it is hoped that the interval will not be long before the treaty is renewed, and that no intermediate prejudice will arise to Sweden, it was not considered important to press a decision on those doubts. Your knowledge of our Constitution will enable you to explain the reasons of the President's being unable, without the concurrence of Congress or of the Senate, to direct the enforcement of the provisions of the treaty in the same summary manner as has been done in the ports of Sweden. By the Act of the 7th day of January 1824 [4 Statutes at Large, 2] the vessels of Norway will continue, without any interruption, to enjoy an exemption in our ports from the payment of the discriminating duties.

The statute exempting Swedish and Norwegian vessels from discriminating duties is the act of February 22, 1827 (4 Statutes at Large, 206). It was communicated to Baron de Stackelberg on March 16

and to the Chargé d'Affaires at Stockholm with instructions under date of April 11, 1827 (D. S., 11 Instructions, U. S. Ministers, 287–88).

The "instructions and correspondence relating to the negotiation" of this treaty were communicated to the Senate with the presidential message of December 11, 1827, transmitting the treaty. They are printed in American State Papers, Foreign Relations, VI, 707–41.

THE FILE PAPERS

During the negotiations Appleton had suggested that "the Treaty might be sign'd on the 4th of July, the double anniversary of my Country's Independence and of the birth of the Prince Royal" (journal enclosed with Appleton's despatch of July 11, 1827, D. S., 5 Despatches, Naples and Sweden, No. 20; American State Papers, Foreign Relations, VI, 729); and while the final clause of the treaty states that it was signed "en duplicata," it appears that after the signature of the treaty on July 4, two originals were signed on July 9, both of which were for this Government. In the despatch of Appleton of July 11, 1827 (D. S., 5 Despatches, Naples and Sweden, No. 20; American State Papers, Foreign Relations, VI, 726–27), is the following account of the signature:

The Treaty which I carried to the conference of the 4th of July for signature having at that conference required some alterations to make it agree with that which the Count had prepared, not to lose the opportunity of signing it that day, we sign'd it notwithstanding its erasures and interlineations, intending subsequently to sign fairer copies without altering the date. The preparation of these copies, which I had committed to my secretary Mr Cucheval, was not completed until the 9th Instant. On that day, the document already sign'd was cancelled, and the new exemplifications sign'd and sealed. These two originals, are entrusted to Mr Cucheval with directions, to take charge of one to Washington and to leave the other with our Consul at Liverpool to be forwarded by the packet succeeding that in which Mr Cucheval will embark.

The two originals thus transmitted to Washington are now in the treaty file. Although they are in the same handwriting, they are not absolutely identical. Only one difference in wording is to be found; the first paragraph of Article 14 of the original with which the text here printed has been collated ends with "pas refusée," while the same paragraph of the other ends with "point refusée." There are also certain inconsistencies in capitalization and spelling, and some thirty-seven differences in punctuation have been noticed; almost all of them are matters of the insertion or omission of commas, and none of them appears to be in any way material.

The treaty file contains also the instrument of ratification of July 11, 1827, by the King of Sweden and Norway, written in Swedish, with a French translation; a certificate of the exchange of ratifications at Washington on January 18, 1828, in English; and the original proclamation of January 19, 1828, which includes the French text and an English translation of the treaty and of the separate article. These papers are in customary form. The attested resolution of the Senate of January 7, 1828 (Executive Journal, III, 589–90), is not in the file.

The proclamation was communicated to Congress with the presidential message of February 6, 1828 (American State Papers, Foreign Relations, VI, 829–35).

The translation included in the proclamation is that which has been printed in the Statutes at Large and treaty collections generally and which is printed above.

The file contains no contemporary duplicate or copy of the United States instrument of ratification; and various other treaty files of the period from 1827 to 1835 likewise lack that document, which should properly be found with every treaty that has gone into force.   There are numerous earlier instances of the correct practice, which was resumed about 1835 and has since been constantly maintained. There is now in the file of this treaty a facsimile of the original United States instrument of ratification, obtained from the Swedish archives. That instrument is in usual form and includes the treaty text in French only.

The Full Powers

Among the documents in the file is the original full power, under date of June 1, 1827, of the King of Sweden and Norway to Count de Wetterstedt, Minister of Foreign Affairs, to negotiate and sign the treaty.   The power is written in the Swedish language and is accompanied by a French translation.   Appleton mentions the exchange of full powers in the journal enclosed with his despatch of July 11, 1827 (D. S., 5 Despatches, Naples and Sweden, No. 20; American State Papers, Foreign Relations, VI, 731):

At this conference which took place on the 4th of July we compared our copies of the Treaty, and after exchanging our full Powers, signed and sealed the Treaty.

Thus the original full powers in this case were exchanged.   The full power given to Appleton under date of January 23, 1827 (D. S., 2 Credences, 57), is in customary form.   That given to the Plenipotentiary of Sweden and Norway reads thus (translation from the Swedish):

We, Charles John, by the grace of God King of Sweden, of Norway, of the Goths, and of the Wends, make known that, having judged proper for the welfare of Our faithful subjects to enter into negotiations with the United States of North America for the renewal of the Treaty of Amity and Commerce concluded under date of September 4, 1816, and having found the President of the United States likewise disposed to come to an accord with Us in that regard, for those reasons We have named and authorized, as We hereby name and authorize, Our beloved and faithful Gustave, Count de Wetterstedt, Our Minister of State and for Foreign Affairs, Knight Commander of Our Order, Knight of the Orders of Russia of St. Andrew, of St. Alexander Newsky, and of St. Anne of the first class; Knight of the Royal Prussian Order of the Red Eagle of the first class; Grand Cross of the Imperial Austrian Order of Leopold; one of the eighteen of the Swedish Academy, as Our Plenipotentiary to enter into negotiations with the Plenipotentiary or Plenipotentiaries named or to be named for that purpose by the President of the United States of North America and to draw up, conclude, sign, and seal a new treaty of amity and commerce.   It is Our will and We promise, moreover, in the manner the most efficacious possible, to confirm and accept and ratify all that Our Plenipotentiary above mentioned shall have agreed upon and concluded in Our name and in conformity with the instructions given to him.

In faith whereof We have signed the present full powers with Our own hand and have caused Our royal seal to be thereto affixed.

Done at the Palace of Stockholm the first day of the month of June in the year of grace one thousand eight hundred and twenty-seven.

[Seal] CHARLES JOHN

E. LAGERHEIM

THE LANGUAGE OF THE TREATY

Under date of September 11, 1827 (D. S., 11 Instructions, U. S. Ministers, 374–76), Secretary of State Clay acknowledged receipt of the treaty two days earlier and thus expressed regret that the treaty had been written only in French:

I regret that the Treaty has not been signed in the English, as well as in the French language, as was the case with the two former treaties which were made with Sweden. We ought always to insist upon the use of our own language, in forming our national engagements.

It is reasonable to suppose that if there had been an English text of the treaty there would also have been a Swedish text; and the statement that "the two former treaties" had English texts is surprisingly erroneous, for each of them (Documents 10 and 36) was signed in French only.

THE INVOCATION

At the beginning of this treaty appears the invocation, "In the name of the Most Holy and Indivisible Trinity." The use of such an invocation in treaties was at the time rather general among certain countries of Europe. The invocation appears in some other treaties of the United States, as, for example, the Treaty of Peace of September 3, 1783, with Great Britain (Document 11); the treaty of September 4, 1816, with Sweden and Norway (Document 36); the convention of July 12, 1822, with Great Britain, signed at St. Petersburg under the mediation of the Emperor of Russia (Document 44); the convention of April 17, 1824, with Russia (Document 46); the treaty of December 12, 1828, with Brazil (Document 64); and the treaty of December 18, 1832, with Russia (Document 75).

When the negotiations for this treaty had been substantially completed, it was proposed on behalf of the United States that the invocation be omitted. Appleton's report of the discussion at his conference with Count de Wetterstedt on June 30, 1827, and of the two letters exchanged the next day, is as follows (D. S., 5 Despatches, Naples and Sweden, No. 20; American State Papers, Foreign Relations, VI, 730):

At the close of this conference in which all the difficulties in the way of a conclusion of the Treaty had been surmounted, I expressed a wish that the invocation of the "Holy and Indivisible Trinity" placed at the head of M.ʳ Russels Treaty [Document 36] might in the present be retrench'd as no longer suited to the great variety of religious opinions existing in my Country, in relation to the dogme which it consecrates The Count did not approve of the change, but still promised to reflect upon it, and let me Know the result. The next day I received a letter from him, a copy of which you will find inclosed, . . . inviting me to withdraw my proposal in relation to the invocation. Persuaded that this letter

had not been written until after the Count had consulted the King upon the subject of it, and that it was therefore the personal wish of the King that it expressed, I thought it due to the spirit displayed by the King and his minister during the negociation not to shew myself inflexible upon a point to which, from respect to the prevailing opinion here, they were disposed to attach much importance, and I accordingly yielded, as you will see by the answer . . . which I sent to the Count.

Copies in French, of the two letters of July 1 written by the respective Plenipotentiaries were enclosures with Appleton's despatch of July 11, 1827 (D. S., 5 Despatches, Naples and Sweden, No. 20), and are printed in French in American State Papers, Foreign Relations, VI, 741. Extracts therefrom in translation follow, the first from the letter of Count de Wetterstedt:

Since yesterday I have deeply reflected on the omission of the invocation generally used at the head of treaties: "In the name of the Most Holy and Indivisible Trinity," and I fear that in omitting it we would have attributed to us motives rather personal than of a general interest. There is no question here of him who signs or even of the one who ratifies, but of the totality of one country which treats with another. Why lay aside now the usage generally received by the Christian powers, a usage accepted on the part of the United States of America in the treaty of 1816, countersigned then by the President of today [John Quincy Adams, who was Secretary of State when the treaty of 1816 was ratified]? If this formula may offend certain new doctrines, its omission for that reason would not fail to offend other doctrines which might be supported by precedent and the proprieties. The more freedom of religious opinion extends, the more must tolerance be its guide, for without that, it might easily fall into error in its independent progress, as does servile superstition in the midst of its burning fagots. Accordingly, let us make no innovation, above all in an act in which the individual who signs it, while preserving an ancient formula, proclaims no profession of faith and renounces no opinion, and in which he speaks in the name of the generality of his fellow citizens, Trinitarians as well as Unitarians. To substitute for that formula another which compromises with the various religious beliefs would be to fall in line with the Turks, which would not suit either constitutional Scandinavia or free America.

Pardon this little theological digression, which bears, I hope, the mark of the tolerant doctrine that I profess, but, above all, has been dictated by the most distinguished consideration. . . .

In the following reply Appleton yielded his proposal, but by way of conciliation only:

Without entirely accepting on behalf of my country the reasons which Your Excellency has set forth for not omitting at the head of the treaty the invocation heretofore used, I have too much desire to reciprocate the spirit of conciliation which has animated Your Excellency during the entire course of the negotiation, to refuse the pleasure of giving you a proof thereof by not pressing my request; and I take this course all the more readily since, as the treaty has not been drawn up under the eyes of my Government, it is not at all upon my Government, but only on its negotiator, that the responsibility for all matters of form can rest.

THE ISLAND OF SAINT-BARTHÉLEMY

The island of Saint-Barthélemy, or St. Bartholomew, mentioned in Articles 2–5 and 9 of this treaty, is one of the Leeward Islands in the French West Indies, situated in 17° 54' north latitude and 62° 50' west longitude, some 130 miles northwest of Guadeloupe. It is irreg-

ular in shape, of about nine square miles in area, and has a population of about three thousand. The island was occupied by France in 1648, ceded to Sweden in 1784, and in 1877 again acquired by France, pursuant to a treaty signed at Paris on August 10, 1877, with a protocol of October 31 (Von Martens, Nouveau recueil général de traités, 2d series, IV, 366–68). That treaty provided for the payment by France of a total of four hundred thousand francs, of which eighty thousand represented the value of certain public property.

The Separate Article

The separate article refers to "certain relations of proximity and ancient connections" between Sweden and Norway on the one part and Finland on the other; to the commerce between those countries; and to "a treaty still in force" regarding that commerce.

The history of Finland is closely connected with that of Sweden. Finland was independent until about the middle of the twelfth century, when it was conquered by Sweden. In 1716 Finland was overrun by Russia; and by the Treaty of Peace signed at Nystad in 1721, Russia, under Peter the Great, retained the province of Viborg (the eastern division of Finland) and certain other Swedish territory.

In 1808 war again broke out between Russia and Sweden; in March, 1809, the Swedish Government was overturned; and in September of that year the new Government accepted the peace dictated by Russia. This was the Treaty of Peace signed at Fredrikshamn (in southern Finland, the Finnish and official form being Hamina) September 17, 1809, by which Finland and the Åland Islands were given up to Russia.

The Treaty of Fredrikshamn was ratified by Sweden October 3, 1809, and by Russia October 13, 1809. The Swedish instrument of ratification, in French, and including the text of the treaty in French, is in Von Martens, Nouveau recueil de traités, I, 19–30.

Article 17 of the Treaty of Fredrikshamn provided that commerce between Sweden and Finland until October 13, 1811, should be carried on "exactly on the same footing as before the war"; and Article 20 provided for further negotiations on certain points.

The reference in the separate article to the "treaty still in force" is to the additional act to the Treaty of Fredrikshamn, which was signed at St. Petersburg on September 10, 1817. The text of that additional act, in French, is in American State Papers, Foreign Relations, VI, 739–40, and also in Von Martens, Nouveau recueil de traités, V, pt. 1, 137–45.

In his report of the negotiations of this treaty Appleton wrote as follows regarding the terms of the additional act to the Treaty of Fredrikshamn (D. S., 5 Despatches, Naples and Sweden, No. 20; American State Papers, Foreign Relations, VI, 730):

Besides reserving special advantages to the Trade between Sweden and Finland in Vessels of the two Countries it secures to the Tallow and Candles of *Russia* a preference over like articles brought to Sweden from any other place, in compensation of a similar favour accorded to the Herring, Stockfish and red lead of Sweden and Norway, in Russia. The Count of Wetterstedt stated that it was

the intention of this Government, to obtain in the Treaty now negociating with Russia a renewal of these reciprocal advantages. Russia had already proposed that the favour accorded to her Tallow and Candles should be extended to her Hemp and Duck.

By the terms of Article 16 of the additional act to the Treaty of Fredrikshamn, the duration of that agreement was limited to the beginning of the year 1826. It must be assumed, however, that it continued in force, as stated in the separate article of this treaty. The negotiations mentioned as being at the time in progress between Sweden and Norway and Russia resulted in the Convention of Commerce and Friendship which was signed at St. Petersburg on February 26, 1828. For the French text of that convention, see Von Martens, Nouveau recueil de traités, VII, pt. 2, 572–91, and British and Foreign State Papers, XV, 675–89.

EXECUTION OF THE TREATY

While the proclamation of this treaty was communicated to Congress with the presidential message of February 6, 1828 (American State Papers, Foreign Relations, VI, 829–35), no legislation for the execution of the treaty seems to have been deemed necessary, beyond general statutes, such as the act of May 24, 1828 (4 Statutes at Large, 308–9).

In his despatch of April 25, 1828, from Stockholm (D. S., 5 Despatches, Naples and Sweden, No. 27), Appleton wrote that on April 4 "this Government communicated officially to all the Foreign Ministers residing here its new Treaty of Navigation and Commerce with the United States"; and in a postscript of April 29 he added that a royal ordinance enjoining the execution of the treaty had been issued under date of April 10.

Treaty Series No. 116
8 Statutes at Large, 360–61
18 *ibid.*, pt. 2, Public Treaties, 310–11

56

GREAT BRITAIN : AUGUST 6, 1827

Convention Continuing in Force Article 3 of the Convention of October 20, 1818 (Document 40), signed at London August 6, 1827. Original in English.
Submitted to the Senate December 12, 1827. (Message of December 11, 1827.) Resolution of advice and consent February 5, 1828. Ratified by the United States February 21, 1828. Ratified by Great Britain March 29, 1828. Ratifications exchanged at London April 2, 1828. Proclaimed May 15, 1828.

The United States of America, and His Majesty The King of the United Kingdom of Great Britain and Ireland, being equally desirous to prevent, as far as possible, all hazard of misunderstanding between the Two Nations, with respect to the Territory on the North West Coast of America, West of the Stoney or Rocky Mountains, after the expiration of the Third Article of the Convention [1] concluded between Them on the Twentieth of October 1818; and also with a view to give further time for maturing measures which shall have for their object a more definite settlement of the Claims of each Party to the said Territory, have respectively named Their Plenipotentiaries to treat and agree concerning a temporary renewal of the said Article, that is to say:—

The President of the United States of America, Albert Gallatin, their Envoy Extraordinary and Minister Plenipotentiary to His Britannick Majesty:—

And His Majesty The King of the United Kingdom of Great Britain and Ireland, The Right Honourable Charles Grant, a Member of His said Majesty's Most Honourable Privy Council, a Member of Parliament, and Vice-President of the Committee of Privy Council for Affairs of Trade and Foreign Plantations;—And Henry Unwin Addington, Esquire:—

Who, after having communicated to each other their respective Full Powers, found to be in due and proper form, have agreed upon and concluded the following Articles:—

---

[1] Document 40.

ARTICLE I.

All the Provisions of the Third Article of the Convention concluded between the United States of America, and His Majesty The King of the United Kingdom of Great Britain and Ireland, on the Twentieth of October 1818, shall be, and they are hereby, further indefinitely extended and continued in force, in the same manner as if all the Provisions of the said Article were herein specifically recited.

ARTICLE II.

It shall be competent, however, to either of the Contracting Parties, in case either should think fit, at any time after the Twentieth of October 1828, on giving due notice of Twelve Months to the other Contracting Party, to annul and abrogate this Convention: and it shall, in such case, be accordingly entirely annulled and abrogated, after the expiration of the said term of notice.

ARTICLE III.

Nothing contained in this Convention, or in the Third Article of the Convention of the Twentieth of October 1818, hereby continued in force, shall be construed to impair, or in any manner affect, the Claims which either of the Contracting Parties may have to any part of the Country Westward of the Stoney or Rocky Mountains.

ARTICLE IV.

The present Convention shall be ratified, and the Ratifications shall be exchanged in Nine Months, or sooner if possible.

In Witness whereof, the respective Plenipotentiaries have signed the same, and have affixed thereto the Seals of their Arms.

Done at London, the Sixth day of August, in the Year of Our Lord One Thousand Eight Hundred and Twenty Seven.

[Seal] ALBERT GALLATIN
[Seal] CHA. GRANT
[Seal] HENRY UNWIN ADDINGTON.

NOTES

This convention and that which follows as Document 57 (continuing in force the convention of July 3, 1815, Document 35), were signed at London on the same day, August 6, 1827; but the two conventions were independent; one might have gone into force without the other; and either by its terms might be denounced without affecting the other.

Following the signature of the convention of November 13, 1826 (Document 53), the negotiations which proceeded between the United States and Great Britain and which, on the part of the United States, were conducted by Albert Gallatin, then Minister at London, resulted in three agreements between the two Governments, the two conventions of August 6, 1827, above mentioned, and the convention of September 29, 1827 (Document 58), for the submission to arbitration of the northeastern boundary question.

The British Plenipotentiaries who signed the three conventions were Charles Grant and Henry Unwin Addington. The former was appointed to the "Commission to negotiate with the United States" on or about July 6, 1827, in consequence of the retirement therefrom of William Huskisson, who with Addington had theretofore conducted the negotiations on the part of the British Government, under the direction of George Canning, British Secretary of State for Foreign Affairs (during part of the negotiations, Prime Minister), until his death on August 8, 1827. Two of the three conventions had been signed two days earlier. From about April 10, 1827, when Canning formed his administration, the Secretary of State for Foreign Affairs was Viscount Dudley, who became the Earl of Dudley September 24, 1827.

Nothing appears in the despatches or elsewhere regarding the full powers of the British Plenipotentiaries except the following statements, extracted from the protocols of the first and twelfth conferences, respectively, of the American and British Plenipotentiaries, held on November 15, 1826, and July 21, 1827 (D. S., 33 Despatches, Great Britain, No. 29, enclosure with Gallatin's despatch of November 25, 1826; 34 *ibid.*, No. 100, enclosure with Gallatin's despatch of July 29, 1827):

After the communication of the respective full powers, it was agreed that the negotiations should be conducted. . . .

In consequence of the retirement from the Commission of one of the former British Plenipotentiaries, and the appointment of a successor in his place, The Plenipotentiaries again examined and exchanged their full Powers.

The full power of Gallatin was dated May 10, 1826, the same day as his full power in respect of the convention of November 13, 1826 (Document 53). It is in the usual form, but the subject-matter of the negotiations was described in language sufficiently broad to include not only the provisions of the three conventions of 1827, but more (D. S., 2 Credences, 41):

To negotiate of and concerning the Commercial intercourse between the United States, and the British Dominions in general or with any part of them, and of all matters and subjects connected therewith, or with the general commerce of the two Nations; or in relation to the boundaries between the United States, and the British Possessions in North America; of and concerning the principles of Maritime Law and Neutrality, which may be interesting to the two Nations; and of and concerning the Navigation of the River S⟨t⟩ Lawrence; and to conclude and sign a Treaty or Treaties, Convention or Conventions upon all or any of the premises.

The three agreements with Great Britain were together submitted to the Senate with the presidential message of December 11, 1827. That message and the accompanying papers relating to the negotiations are printed in American State Papers, Foreign Relations, VI, 639–706.

THE EXCHANGE OF RATIFICATIONS

The exchange of ratifications of the three agreements took place concurrently in London on April 2, 1828, and they were all proclaimed on the following May 15; but the dates of the three ratifications on the part of the United States differ, and the dates of ratification on the part of Great Britain are not all the same. In the Senate the three conventions were separately considered, and the resolutions of advice and consent to their respective ratifications were adopted at various times.

Nothing was provided in any one of the three conventions regarding the place of the exchange of ratifications. The term allowed in each case was nine months from the date of signature. On February 7, 1828, Secretary of State Clay informed Charles R. Vaughan, the British Minister at Washington (D. S., 3 Notes to Foreign Legations, 429), that the Senate had given its advice and consent to the three conventions and that they would "be forthwith ratified by the President" (one of them, Document 57, had already been ratified on January 12); and he inquired whether Vaughan was empowered "to make the exchange" at Washington. Vaughan replied that he had no instructions regarding the exchange of ratifications "and that he was uninformed of the views of his Government upon that subject" (D. S., 12 Instructions, U. S. Ministers, 61–62, instructions to William B. Lawrence, Chargé d'Affaires at London, February 20, 1828).

The United States instruments of ratification of the three conventions, with instructions under date of February 20, 1828 (*ibid.*), were transmitted to Lawrence by a special "Bearer of despatches," Nathaniel B. Blunt, who delivered them to Lawrence on March 24 (D. S., 35 Despatches, Great Britain, No. 30, March 29, 1828). On the date of receipt of the instruments of ratification Lawrence addressed the British Secretary of State for Foreign Affairs, the Earl of Dudley, as follows (*ibid.*, No. 32, April 5, 1828, enclosure 1):

Though no one of these Conventions designates the place, where the Ratifications are to be exchanged, and though some delay might have been avoided, had Washington been selected for this purpose, yet, as it was understood, on enquiry, that the Minister of His Majesty in America had no instructions on the subject, the President has acquiesced in the presumed wish and expectation of the British Government, that the formal act necessary to give validity to the Treaties should be performed in England. The several Ratifications by the President of the United States of the three Conventions above referred to have been accordingly entrusted to the Undersigned, and he is authorized to exchange the same for those of the King, with any person duly empowered on behalf of the British Government.

That same despatch of April 5, 1828, reported that the exchange of ratifications of the three conventions had taken place three days earlier:

On the evening of the 1ˢᵗ, a note was sent to me by Mr. Grant and Mʳ Addington, the late Plenipotentiaries for negotiating with America, inviting me to a meeting on the ensuing day, at the Foreign Office, for the purpose of exchanging the Ratifications. Accordingly, this business was transacted, at the appointed time, with Messʳˢ Grant and Addington instead of the Secretary of State, as proposed in Lord Dudley's note. The several Ratifications of the British Government will be confided to Mʳ Blunt, who leaves London to-morrow to embark in the Packet of the 8ᵗʰ instant from Liverpool. The certificates of exchange are enclosed in the Treaties to which they respectively refer, and duplicates will be sent by the ordinary conveyance next week.

Under date of May 17, 1828, Secretary of State Clay informed Lawrence of the arrival of Blunt with the British instruments of ratification (D. S., 12 Instructions, U. S. Ministers, 102), which were received in the Department of State on May 14, one day before the date of proclamation.

The File Papers

At least one original of each of the two conventions signed on August 6, 1827, was transmitted with the despatches of Albert Gallatin, Minister at London, of August 6 and 7 (D. S., 34 Despatches, Great Britain, Nos. 102 and 103). Those despatches, with the enclosed conventions, were received in the Department of State on September 16, 1827.

It seems that this convention was executed at least in triplicate, for there are two signed originals in the treaty file. That original with which the text here printed has been collated has one immaterial comma in the preamble which the other lacks; and the other, which is in a different handwriting, is endorsed "Duplicate" in the upper left-hand corner of the first page; but, except for a few differences in capitalization, no other variances between the two documents have been noticed.

The file lacks the attested resolution of the Senate of February 5, 1828 (Executive Journal, III, 597). The other documents are in customary form; they include a facsimile of the United States instrument of ratification of February 21, recently obtained from the British archives; the British instrument of ratification of March 29; the certificate of the exchange of ratifications at London on April 2, in duplicate; and the proclamation of May 15, 1828, which was communicated to Congress with the presidential message of May 19 (American State Papers, Foreign Relations, VI, 999–1000).

The Northwest Territory

Article 3 of the convention of October 20, 1818, with Great Britain (Document 40) reads as follows:

It is agreed, that any Country that may be claimed by either Party on the North West Coast of America, Westward of the Stony Mountains, shall, together with it's Harbours, Bays, and Creeks, and the Navigation of all Rivers within the same, be free and open, for the term of ten Years from the date of the Signature of the present Convention, to the Vessels, Citizens, and Subjects of the Two

Powers: it being well understood, that this Agreement is not to be construed to the Prejudice of any Claim, which either of the Two High Contracting Parties may have to any part of the said Country, nor shall it be taken to affect the Claims of any other Power or State to any part of the said Country; the only Object of The High Contracting Parties, in that respect, being to prevent disputes and differences amongst Themselves.

Accordingly, the term of ten years mentioned in that article (indefinitely extended by this convention of August 6, 1827) was to expire on October 20, 1828; and with the provisions of that article should be read the provisions of Article 2 of the same convention, the effect of which was to provide that a line drawn due south from the northwesternmost point of the Lake of the Woods to the forty-ninth parallel of north latitude and thence due west along the said parallel, should form the boundary between the territories of the United States and those of His Britannic Majesty "from the Lake of the Woods to the Stony [Rocky] Mountains" (see the note regarding Article 2 of Document 40). While the point was perhaps never definitely decided, it was later assumed that "to the Rocky Mountains" meant to the summit of the Rocky Mountains; and the boundary with Canada westward from the point of termination under Article 2 of the convention of October 20, 1818, was, by Article 1 of the treaty of June 15, 1846, with Great Britain, fixed as continuing "westward along the said forty-ninth parallel of north latitude to the middle of the channel which separates the continent from Vancouver's Island; and thence southerly through the middle of the said channel and of Fuca's Straits to the Pacific Ocean."

Treaty Series No. 117
8 Statutes at Large, 361–62
18 *ibid.*, pt. 2, Public Treaties, 311–12

57

GREAT BRITAIN : AUGUST 6, 1827

Convention Continuing in Force the Convention of July 3, 1815 (Document 35), signed at London August 6, 1827. Original in English. Submitted to the Senate December 12, 1827. (Message of December 11, 1827.) Resolution of advice and consent January 9, 1828. Ratified by the United States January 12, 1828. Ratified by Great Britain February 14, 1828. Ratifications exchanged at London April 2, 1828. Proclaimed May 15, 1828.

The United States of America, and His Majesty The King of the United Kingdom of Great Britain and Ireland, being desirous of continuing in force the existing commercial regulations between the two Countries, which are contained in the Convention[1] concluded between Them on the Third of July 1815, and further renewed by the Fourth Article of the Convention[2] of the Twentieth of October 1818, have, for that purpose, named Their respective Plenipotentiaries, that is to say:—

The President of the United States of America, Albert Gallatin, their Envoy Extraordinary and Minister Plenipotentiary to His Britannick Majesty:—

And His Majesty The King of the United Kingdom of Great Britain and Ireland, The Right Honourable Charles Grant, a Member of His said Majesty's Most Honourable Privy Council, a Member of Parliament, and Vice President of the Committee of Privy Council for Affairs of Trade and Foreign Plantations;—And Henry Unwin Addington, Esquire:—

Who, after having communicated to each other their respective Full Powers, found to be in due and proper form, have agreed upon and concluded the following Articles:—

ARTICLE I.

All the Provisions of the Convention concluded between the United States of America, and His Majesty The King of the United Kingdom of Great Britain and Ireland, on the Third of July 1815, and further continued for the term of ten Years by the fourth Article of the

---

[1] Document 35. [2] Document 40.

Convention of the Twentieth of October 1818, with the exception therein contained, as to St Helena, are hereby further indefinitely, and without the said exception, extended and continued in force, from the date of the expiration of the said ten Years, in the same manner as if all the Provisions of the said Convention of the Third of July 1815, were herein specifically recited.

ARTICLE II.

It shall be competent, however, to either of the Contracting Parties, in case either should think fit, at any time after the expiration of the said ten Years, that is, after the Twentieth of October 1828, on giving due notice of Twelve Months to the other Contracting Party, to annul and abrogate this Convention:—and it shall, in such case, be accordingly entirely annulled and abrogated, after the expiration of the said term of notice.

ARTICLE III.

The present Convention shall be ratified, and the Ratifications shall be exchanged in Nine Months, or sooner if possible.

In Witness whereof, the respective Plenipotentiaries have signed the same, and have affixed thereto the Seals of their Arms.

Done at London, the Sixth day of August, in the Year of Our Lord One Thousand Eight Hundred and Twenty Seven.

[Seal] ALBERT GALLATIN
[Seal] CHA. GRANT.
[Seal] HENRY UNWIN ADDINGTON.

NOTES

This convention and that which precedes as Document 56 (continuing in force Article 3 of the convention of October 20, 1818, Document 40), were signed at London on the same day, August 6, 1827; but the two conventions were independent; one might have gone into force without the other; and either by its terms might be denounced without affecting the other.

As to the negotiations, the full powers, the submission of this convention to the Senate, the ratification thereof by the United States and by Great Britain, and the exchange of ratifications at London on April 2, 1828, see the notes to the preceding convention (Document 56).

THE FILE PAPERS

It seems that this convention was executed at least in triplicate, for there are two signed originals in the treaty file. That original

with which the text here printed has been collated has one immaterial comma in the preamble which the other lacks; and the other, which is in a different handwriting, is endorsed "Duplicate" in the upper left-hand corner of the first page; but, except for a few differences in capitalization, no other variances between the two documents have been noticed.

The file of this convention contains the attested resolution of the Senate of January 9, 1828 (Executive Journal, III, 590). All the documents are in the usual form; they include a facsimile of the United States instrument of ratification of January 12, recently obtained from the British archives; the British instrument of ratification of February 14; the certificate of the exchange of ratifications at London on April 2, in duplicate; and the proclamation of May 15, 1828, which was communicated to Congress with the presidential message of May 19 (American State Papers, Foreign Relations, VI, 999–1000).

THE CONVENTION OF 1815

The convention of July 3, 1815 (Document 35), by its terms was to be in force until July 3, 1819, or for four years from its date of signature, and by Article 4 of the convention of October 20, 1818 (Document 40), had been extended for ten years from that date, or until October 20, 1828. The further extension of the convention of 1815 by this convention of August 6, 1827, was indefinite, with the right of denunciation by either party on one year's notice; but the exception to the convention of 1815 regarding the island of St. Helena, expressly abrogated by Article 1 of this convention, had come to an end with the death of Napoleon on May 5, 1821, and the notice given by the British Government on the following July 30 (see the notes to Document 35).

Treaty Series No. 118
8 Statutes at Large, 362–65
18 *ibid.*, pt. 2, Public Treaties, 312–15

58

GREAT BRITAIN : SEPTEMBER 29, 1827

Convention for the Submission to Arbitration of the Northeastern Boundary Question, signed at London September 29, 1827. Original in English. Submitted to the Senate December 12, 1827. (Message of December 11, 1827.) Resolution of advice and consent January 14, 1828. Ratified by the United States February 12, 1828. Ratified by Great Britain March 29, 1828. Ratifications exchanged at London April 2, 1828. Proclaimed May 15, 1828.

Whereas it is provided by the Fifth Article of the Treaty of Ghent,[1] that in case the Commissioners appointed under that Article for the Settlement of the Boundary Line therein described, should not be able to agree upon such Boundary Line, the Report or Reports of those Commissioners, stating the Points on which they had differed, should be submitted to some friendly Sovereign or State, and that the Decision given by such Sovereign or State on such Points of Difference, should be considered by The Contracting Parties as final and conclusive:—That case having now arisen, and it having therefore become expedient to proceed to and regulate the reference as above described, The United States of America, and His Majesty The King of the United Kingdom of Great Britain and Ireland have, for that purpose, named their Plenipotentiaries—that is to say, The President of The United States has appointed Albert Gallatin, their Envoy Extraordinary and Minister Plenipotentiary at the Court of His Britannick Majesty: and His said Majesty, on His part, has appointed The Right Honorable Charles Grant, a Member of Parliament, a Member of His said Majesty's Most Honorable Privy Council, and President of the Committee of the Privy Council for affairs of Trade and Foreign Plantations; and Henry Unwin Addington Esquire—Who, after having exchanged their respective Full Powers, found to be in due and proper form, have agreed to and concluded the following Articles.

---

[1] Document 33.

ARTICLE I.

It is agreed that the Points of Difference which have arisen in the Settlement of the Boundary between the American and British Dominions, as described in the 5ᵗʰ Article of the Treaty of Ghent, shall be referred, as therein provided, to some friendly Sovereign or State, who shall be invited to investigate and make a decision upon such Points of Difference

The Two Contracting Powers engage to proceed in concert, to the Choice of such Friendly Sovereign or State, as soon as the Ratifications of this Convention shall have been exchanged, and to use their best endeavours to obtain a decision, if practicable, within two years after the Arbiter shall have signified his Consent to act as such.

ARTICLE II.

The Reports and Documents thereunto annexed of the Commissioners appointed to carry into execution the 5ᵗʰ Article of the Treaty of Ghent, being so voluminous and complicated, as to render it unprobable that any Sovereign or State should be willing or able to undertake the office of investigating and arbitrating upon them, it is hereby agreed to substitute for those Reports new and separate Statements of the respective cases severally drawn up by each of The Contracting Parties, in such form and terms as each may think fit.

The said Statements, when prepared, shall be mutually communicated to each other by The Contracting Parties, that is to say, by The United States to His Britannick Majesty's Minister or Chargé d'affaires at Washington, and by Great Britain to the Minister or Chargé d'affaires of The United States at London, within Fifteen Months after the Exchange of the Ratifications of the present Convention.

After such Communication shall have taken place, each Party shall have the Power of drawing up a second, and definitive, Statement, if it thinks fit so to do, in reply to the Statement of the other Party so communicated, which definitive Statements shall also be mutually communicated in the same manner as aforesaid, to each other, by The Contracting Parties, within Twenty One Months after the Exchange of Ratifications of the present Convention.

ARTICLE III.

Each of The Contracting Parties shall, within Nine Months after the Exchange of Ratifications of this Convention, communicate to the other, in the same manner as aforesaid, all the Evidence intended to

be brought in support of its Claim beyond that which is contained in the Reports of the Commissioners or Papers thereunto annexed, and other written documents laid before the Commission under the 5ᵗʰ Article of the Treaty of Ghent.

Each of The Contracting Parties shall be bound on the Application of the other Party, made within Six Months after the Exchange of the Ratifications of this Convention, to give authentick Copies of such individually specified Acts of a publick nature, relating to the Territory in question, intended to be laid as Evidence before The Arbiter, as have been issued under the Authority or are in the exclusive possession of each Party.

No Maps, Surveys or topographical Evidence of any description, shall be adduced by either Party beyond that which is hereinafter stipulated, nor shall any fresh Evidence of any description be adduced or adverted to by either Party, other than that mutually communicated or applied for as aforesaid.

Each Party shall have full Power to incorporate in, or annex to, either its first or second Statement, any portion of the Reports of the Commissioners or Papers thereunto annexed, and other written documents laid before the Commission under the 5ᵗʰ Article of the Treaty of Ghent, or of the other Evidence mutually communicated or applied for [1] as above provided, which it may think fit.

ARTICLE IV.

The Map called Mitchell's Map, by which the Framers of the Treaty of 1783 are acknowledged to have regulated their joint and official Proceedings, and the Map A which has been agreed on by The Contracting Parties, as a delineation of the Water courses and of the Boundary Lines in reference to the said Water Courses, as contended for by each Party respectively, and which has accordingly been signed by the above named Plenipotentiaries at the same time with this Convention, shall be annexed to the Statements of the Contracting Parties, and be the only Maps that shall be considered as Evidence mutually acknowledged by The Contracting Parties of the Topography of the Country.

It shall however be lawful for either Party to annex to its respective first Statement, for the purposes of general illustration, any of the Maps, Surveys or topographical delineations which were filed with The Commissioners under the 5ᵗʰ Article of the Treaty of Ghent—any

---

[1] The words "or applied for" are inserted with a caret in each of the two originals in the treaty file, and the initials of the three Plenipotentiaries who signed the convention are written in the margin opposite.

engraved Map heretofore published—and also a Transcript of the abovementioned Map A, or of a Section thereof; in which Transcript each Party may lay down the Highlands or other Features of the Country as it shall think fit, the Water courses and the Boundary Lines, as claimed by each Party, remaining as laid down in the said Map A.

But this Transcript, as well as all the other Maps, Surveys or topographical delineations, other than the Map A, and Mitchell's Map, intended to be thus annexed by either Party to the respective Statements, shall be communicated to the other Party, in the same manner as aforesaid, within Nine Months after the Exchange of the Ratifications of this Convention, and shall be subject to such objections and Observations as the other Contracting Party may deem it expedient to make thereto, and shall annex to his first Statement, either in the Margin of such Transcript, Map, or Maps or otherwise.

ARTICLE V.

All the Statements, Papers, Maps and Documents abovementioned, and which shall have been mutually communicated as aforesaid shall, without any addition, subtraction, or alteration whatsoever, be jointly and simultaneously delivered in to The Arbitrating Sovereign or State within Two Years after the Exchange of Ratifications of this Convention, unless The Arbiter should not, within that time, have consented to act as such; in which case, all the said Statements, Papers, Maps, and Documents shall be laid before him within Six Months after the time when he shall have consented so to act. No other Statements, Papers, Maps, or Documents shall ever be laid before The Arbiter, except as hereinafter provided.

ARTICLE VI.

In order to facilitate the Attainment of a just and sound decision on the part of the Arbiter, it is agreed that in case the said Arbiter should desire further elucidation, or evidence in regard to any specifick point contained in any of the said Statements submitted to him, the requisition for such elucidation or evidence shall be simultaneously made to both Parties, who shall thereupon be permitted to bring further evidence if required, and to make each, a written reply to the specifick questions submitted by the said Arbiter but no further; and such evidence and replies shall be immediately communicated by each Party to the other.

And in case the Arbiter should find the topographical Evidence laid, as aforesaid, before him, insufficient for the purposes of a sound and

just decision, he shall have the power of ordering additional Surveys to be made of any portions of the disputed Boundary Line or Territory as he may think fit; which Surveys shall be made at the joint expence of the Contracting Parties, and be considered as conclusive by Them.

ARTICLE VII.

The Decision of the Arbiter when given, shall be taken as final and conclusive: and it shall be carried without reserve into immediate effect by Commissioners appointed for that purpose by the Contracting Parties.

ARTICLE VIII.

This Convention shall be ratified, and the Ratifications shall be exchanged in Nine Months from the date hereof, or sooner if possible.

In Witness whereof We the respective Plenipotentiaries have signed the same, and have affixed thereto the Seals of Our Arms.

Done at London the Twenty Ninth day of September, in the Year of Our Lord One Thousand Eight Hundred and Twenty Seven.

[Seal] ALBERT GALLATIN
[Seal] CHA. GRANT.
[Seal] HENRY UNWIN ADDINGTON.

NOTES

The negotiations which were carried on in London in 1826 and 1827 resulted in three agreements between the two Governments, the two conventions signed on August 6, 1827 (Documents 56 and 57), and this convention of September 29, 1827, for the submission to arbitration of the northeastern boundary question. Those three agreements with Great Britain were together submitted to the Senate with the presidential message of December 11, 1827. That message and the accompanying papers relating to the negotiations are printed in American State Papers, Foreign Relations, VI, 639–706.

As to the negotiations, the full powers, the ratification of this convention, and the exchange of ratifications at London on April 2, 1828, see the notes to Document 56.

THE FILE PAPERS

It seems that this convention was executed at least in triplicate, for there are two signed originals in the treaty file. That original with which the text here printed has been collated is bound with a blue ribbon which passes under the original seals; the other is similarly bound with red yarn. The two originals are not entirely consistent as to capitalization and spelling, and a number of differences

in punctuation, most of which are the insertion or omission of commas and none of which appears to be in any way material, have been noticed.

The file lacks the attested resolution of the Senate of January 14, 1828 (Executive Journal, III, 592). It contains a facsimile of the United States instrument of ratification of February 12, recently obtained from the British archives; the British instrument of ratification of March 29; the certificate of the exchange of ratifications at London on April 2, 1828, in duplicate; a facsimile of the certificate of exchange in the British archives, which is in a different style; and the proclamation of May 15, which was communicated to Congress with the presidential message of May 19 (American State Papers, Foreign Relations, VI, 999–1002).

All the documents mentioned are in customary form. In neither instrument of ratification is there any reference to Mitchell's Map or to Map A, beyond those in the text of the convention.

The Northeastern Boundary

This convention was one of the steps taken toward the settlement of the "northeastern boundary question"—the dispute regarding the boundary between the United States and Canada from the source of the St. Croix River to the St. Lawrence River—which involved the boundary, in part, of the States of Maine, New Hampshire, Vermont, and New York.

While some of the bases of that controversy date far back of 1782, the dispute, as between the two Governments, had its origin in the language of Article 2 of the Preliminary Articles of Peace of November 30, 1782 (Document 7), which, as essentially repeated in Article 2 of the Definitive Treaty of Peace of September 3, 1783 (Document 11), is, as far as here material, as follows:

And that all disputes which might arise in future on the Subject of the Boundaries of the said United States, may be prevented, it is hereby agreed and declared, that the following are and shall be their Boundaries, Viz. From the North West Angle of Nova Scotia, viz. That Angle which is formed by a Line drawn due North from the Source of the Saint Croix River to the Highlands along the said Highlands which divide those Rivers that empty themselves into the River St Lawrence, from those which fall into the Atlantic Ocean, to the Northwesternmost Head of Connecticut River: Thence down along the middle of that River to the forty fifth Degree of North Latitude; From thence by a Line due West on said Latitude until it strikes the River Iroquois or Cataraquy; . . . East, by a Line to be drawn along the Middle of the River St Croix, from its Mouth in the Bay of Fundy to its Source; and from its Source directly North to the aforesaid Highlands, which divide the Rivers that fall into the Atlantic Ocean, from those which fall into the River St Lawrence; comprehending all Islands within twenty Leagues of any Part of the Shores of the United States, & lying between Lines to be drawn due East from the Points where the aforesaid Boundaries between Nova Scotia on the one Part and East Florida on the other, shall respectively touch the Bay of Fundy and the Atlantic Ocean, excepting such Islands as now are or heretofore have been within the Limits of the said Province of Nova Scotia.

A history of the northeastern boundary question is in Moore, International Arbitrations, I, 65–161, and in International Boundary

Commission: Joint Report upon the Survey and Demarcation of the Boundary between the United States and Canada from the Source of the St. Croix River to the St. Lawrence River, 269–336. A study of the subject by a Canadian geographer, James White, entitled "Boundary Disputes and Treaties," is in Canada and Its Provinces, VIII, 779–827; and "A Monograph of the Evolution of the Boundaries of the Province of New Brunswick," by William F. Ganong, which is printed in Proceedings and Transactions of the Royal Society of Canada, 2d series, VII, deals elaborately with the northwest angle of Nova Scotia. Further information on the subject of the northeastern boundary may be found in the notes to the Webster-Ashburton Treaty of August 9, 1842, and in the authorities there cited.

In Paullin, Atlas of the Historical Geography of the United States, are maps showing the various lines of the international boundary from time to time proposed and agreed upon, from the St. Lawrence River to the Bay of Fundy (plates 89, 90, 91A, 91C, 92A, 92B, 93A, and 93D). The relevant text in the work cited is at pages 52–62.

One essential point in the northeastern boundary was the source of the St. Croix River; and, as there was an early disagreement as to which of two rivers the St. Croix was, there was an important part of the northeastern boundary which could not possibly be finally delimited until the question of the St. Croix was settled. Pursuant to Article 5 of the Jay Treaty (Document 16), as modified by the explanatory article of March 15, 1798 (Document 22), a binding and accepted declaration as to the St. Croix was signed on October 25, 1798 (Document 23), and the source of that river was fixed by that decision, which "settled definitely the uncertain *terminus a quo* the northeastern boundary was to run" (Executive Journal, IV, 227). A complete history of that settlement is in Moore, International Adjudications, Modern Series, I and II.

With the source of the St. Croix determined, there came to be three separate features of dispute in the northeastern boundary question. The first and by far the most important was how far due north of the St. Croix was to be found that point in the "highlands" which was designated as "the North West Angle of Nova Scotia"; here was involved a large part of the boundary of Maine and, as between the conflicting claims, a territory later estimated at 12,027 square miles. The second was as to the northwesternmost head of the Connecticut River, involving part of the boundary of New Hampshire and, as between the conflicting claims, about 150 square miles of territory. The third was the location of the forty-fifth parallel of north latitude, which the Treaty of Ghent stated had not been surveyed but which had been surveyed between 1771 and 1774; but that survey, then supposed to be correct, in fact departed somewhat from the true line, running in places to the north and elsewhere to the south thereof; and here were involved "strips" along the northern boundary of Vermont and New York from the Connecticut River to the St. Lawrence.

The unratified convention of May 12, 1803, with Great Britain (American State Papers, Foreign Relations, II, 584–85) contained provisions (Articles 2 and 3) for the determination by a majority of three commissioners of the northwest angle of Nova Scotia and for the running of the line thither from the source of the St. Croix River and also for a similar determination of the northwesternmost head of the Connecticut River; but that convention failed to go into force owing to the rejection by the Senate of Article 5 thereof, which provided for a line from the Lake of the Woods to the source of the Mississippi (Executive Journal, I, 463–64). Clauses similar to those of 1803 regarding the northeastern boundary were proposed in 1807 (American State Papers, Foreign Relations, III, 162–65); but no agreement resulted.

In Article 5 of the Treaty of Ghent of December 24, 1814 (Document 33), provision was made for the determination and mapping of the northeastern boundary by two commissioners and, in the event of their disagreement, for a reference of the question "to a friendly Sovereign or State." That article reads as follows:

Whereas neither that point of the Highlands lying due North from the source of the River Sᵗ Croix, and designated in the former Treaty of Peace between the two Powers as the North West Angle of Nova Scotia, nor the North Westernmost head of Connecticut River has yet been ascertained; and whereas that part of the boundary line between the Dominions of the two Powers which extends from the source of the River Sᵗ Croix directly North to the abovementioned North West Angle of Nova Scotia, thence along the said Highlands which divide those Rivers that empty themselves into the River Sᵗ Lawrence from those which fall into the Atlantic Ocean to the North Westernmost head of Connecticut River, thence down along the middle of that River to the forty fifth degree of North Latitude, thence by a line due West on said latitude until it strikes the River Iroquois or Cataraquy, has not yet been surveyed: it is agreed that for these several purposes two Commissioners shall be appointed, sworn, and authorized to act exactly in the manner directed with respect to those mentioned in the next preceding Article unless otherwise specified in the present Article. The said Commissioners shall meet at Sᵗ Andrews in the Province of New Brunswick, and shall have power to adjourn to such other place or places as they shall think fit. The said Commissioners shall have power to ascertain and determine the points above mentioned in conformity with the provisions of the said Treaty of Peace of one thousand seven hundred and eighty three, and shall cause the boundary aforesaid from the source of the River Sᵗ Croix to the River Iroquois or Cataraquy to be surveyed and marked according to the said provisions. The said Commissioners shall make a map of the said boundary, and annex it to a declaration under their hands and seals certifying it to be the true Map of the said boundary, and particularizing the latitude and longitude of the North West Angle of Nova Scotia, of the North Westernmost head of Connecticut River, and of such other points of the said boundary as they may deem proper. And both parties agree to consider such map and declaration as finally and conclusively fixing the said boundary. And in the event of the said two Commissioners differing, or both, or either of them refusing, declining, or wilfully omitting to act, such reports, declarations, or statements shall be made by them or either of them, and such reference to a friendly Sovereign or State shall be made in all respects as in the latter part of the fourth Article is contained, and in as full a manner as if the same was herein repeated.

The relevant provisions of Article 4 of the Treaty of Ghent, referred to in Article 5 of that treaty, regarding the reference to arbitration, read thus:

It is further agreed that in the event of the two Commissioners differing upon all or any of the matters so referred to them, or in the event of both or either of the said Commissioners refusing or declining or wilfully omitting to act as such, they shall make jointly or separately a report or reports as well to the Government of His Britannic Majesty as to that of the United States, stating in detail the points on which they differ, and the grounds upon which their respective opinions have been formed, or the grounds upon which they or either of them have so refused declined or omitted to act. And His Britannic Majesty and the Government of the United States hereby agree to refer the report or reports of the said Commissioners to some friendly Sovereign or State to be then named for that purpose, and who shall be requested to decide on the differences which may be stated in the said report or reports, or upon the report of one Commissioner together with the grounds upon which the other Commissioner shall have refused, declined or omitted to act as the case may be. And if the Commissioner so refusing, declining, or omitting to act, shall also wilfully omit to state the grounds upon which he has so done in such manner that the said statement may be referred to such friendly Sovereign or State together with the report of such other Commissioner, then such Sovereign or State shall decide ex parte upon the said report alone. And His Britannic Majesty and the Government of the United States engage to consider the decision of such friendly Sovereign or State to be final and conclusive on all the matters so referred.

While Commissioners were duly appointed pursuant to Article 5 of the Treaty of Ghent, their labors resulted in disagreement (see Moore, International Arbitrations, I, 72–83). The final meetings of the Commissioners were held in April, 1822, and their respective reports were transmitted to the two Governments.

That disagreement brought into play the arbitral provisions of the Treaty of Ghent above quoted; but, as is stated in Article 2 of this convention, it had become impracticable for the provisions of the Treaty of Ghent to be carried out literally, as the reports and documents thereto annexed of the Commissioners under Article 5 of the Treaty of Ghent were "so voluminous and complicated, as to render it unprobable that any Sovereign or State should be willing or able to undertake the office of investigating and arbitrating upon them."

A list of the papers of the Commissioners under Article 5 of the Treaty of Ghent was transmitted to the Governor of Maine by Secretary of State Clay on May 7, 1827 (American State Papers, Foreign Relations, VI, 926–27), and in the covering letter it was said that to copy them "would require the services of two or three copyists for many weeks."

Delay had increased the difficulties. Maine had been admitted as one of the States of the United States pursuant to the act of March 3, 1820 (3 Statutes at Large, 544); and incidents in the regions particularly in dispute tended to increase, despite the fact that "by a common understanding between the Governments it was agreed that no exercise of exclusive jurisdiction by either party, while the negotiation was pending, should change the state of the question of right to be definitively settled" (message to Congress of President John Quincy Adams of December 4, 1827, American State Papers, Foreign Relations, VI, 626).

Any settlement of the northeastern boundary question by direct negotiation was impracticable at the time; and this convention, with its elaborate and well-drawn provisions regarding "Statements,

Papers, Maps, or Documents" to be submitted to the "Arbitrating Sovereign," was the means of agreement adopted instead.

But the provisions of this convention failed to accomplish their purpose, and the northeastern boundary question remained open for fifteen years more. It was by the provisions of the Webster-Ashburton Treaty of August 9, 1842, that the dispute between the Governments of the United States and Great Britain regarding the northeastern boundary was ended.

MITCHELL'S MAP

The following observations on Mitchell's Map are taken in large part from a draft of an unpublished book [1] by Colonel Lawrence Martin, Chief of the Division of Maps, Library of Congress, and formerly Geographer of the Department of State. Colonel Martin has also been good enough to read and assent to the text here printed. The examination of the copies of Mitchell's Map in the library of the Colonial Office in London was made in September, 1931, by Mr. Samuel W. Boggs, Geographer of the Department of State. The contribution of Mrs. Sophia A. Saucerman, Assistant Geographer of the Department of State, includes particularly the account of the copies of Mitchell's Map in the archives of the Department. Certain paragraphs are by the editor of these volumes. [2]

In the first paragraph of Article 4 of this convention mention is made of two maps which were to be annexed to the statements of the parties to be laid before the Arbiter and which were to be the only maps to "be considered as Evidence mutually acknowledged by The Contracting Parties of the Topography of the Country." The first of those two maps is "The Map called Mitchell's Map, by which the Framers of the Treaty of 1783 [Document 11] are acknowledged to have regulated their joint and official Proceedings."

The boundary provisions in the Definitive Treaty of Peace of September 3, 1783, with Great Britain (Document 11) were first

---

[1] "Mitchell's Map, an Account of the Origin and Uses of the Most Important Map in American History." This book was written by Colonel Lawrence Martin during the period from 1925 to 1933. Brief abstracts and excerpts from it have been published by him as follows: (1) "Mitchell's Map and American Diplomatic History," American Historical Review, XXXIII, 529, and Annual Report of the American Historical Association for the Years 1927 and 1928, 41, 47; (2) Lawrence Martin, Noteworthy Maps, Accessions 1925–26, 20–22; *ibid.*, No. 2, Accessions 1926–27, 17–21; *ibid.*, No. 3, Accessions 1927–28, 19–21; (3) "The Thirteen Original Colonies as They Appeared to Geographers and Makers of Maps at the Time of the Declaration of Independence," a broadside of eighty lines, with respect to Mitchell's Map, printed by the Library of Congress in 1926; (4) Report of the Librarian of Congress, 1926, 107, 109, 119, 121–22; *ibid.*, 1927, 90, 91; *ibid.*, 1928, 95; *ibid.*, 1929, 136, 151; *ibid.*, 1930, 174, 180; *ibid.*, 1931, 180, 189; *ibid.*, 1932, 130–31. The book deals not only with this map and its use in connection with important internal and external geographical problems of the United States and Canada, but also with the life and work of the author, Dr. John Mitchell.

[2] A facsimile reproduction of a copy of Mitchell's Map is in a pocket in the back cover of this volume.

written in the Preliminary Articles of Peace of November 30, 1782 (Document 7).

Aside from the statement in Article 4 of this convention, above quoted, there is abundant evidence of the use of Mitchell's Map in the negotiations at Paris of 1782 and 1783, beginning with the letter signed by Benjamin Franklin, John Adams, John Jay, and Henry Laurens, dated December 14, 1782 (Library of Congress, 58 C. C. Papers, folios 254, 255; Wharton, Diplomatic Correspondence, VI, 131–33), in which it is said, "The Map used in the Course of our Negotiations was Mitchells." Subsequent statements to the same effect are numerous.

In his testimony of August 15, 1797, in the St. Croix River arbitration (Moore, International Adjudications, Modern Series, I, 63), taken while he was President, John Adams said:

Mitchell's map was the only map or plan, which was used by the Commissioners at their public Conferences, though other maps were occasionally consulted by the American Commissioners at their lodgings. . . . Lines were marked at that time as designating the boundaries of The United States upon Mitchell's map.

In the deposition of John Jay of May 21, 1798, in the same arbitration (*ibid.*, 65), is the following:

Mitchell's Map was before them, and was frequently consulted for geographical information. . . .

By whom in particular that Map was then produced, and what other Maps, Charts and Documents of State were then before the Commissioners at Paris, and whether the British Commissioners then produced or mentioned an Act of Parliament respecting the boundaries of Massachusetts, are circumstances which his recollection does not enable him to ascertain. It seems to him that certain lines were marked on the copy of Mitchell's map, which was before them at Paris, but whether the Map mentioned in the Interrogatory as now produced, is that copy, or whether the lines said to appear in it are the same lines, he cannot without inspecting and examining it, undertake to judge.

In the letter of Benjamin Franklin addressed to Thomas Jefferson, Secretary of State, under date of April 8, 1790 (D. S., Papers Relative to the Commissioners under the Fifth Article of the Treaty with England, Northeastern Boundary, 1796, pt. 1, p. 5; Sparks, Works of Benjamin Franklin, X, 447–48), he wrote, nine days before his death:

I now can assure you that I am perfectly clear in the Remembrance that the Map we used in tracing the Boundary was brought to the Treaty by the Commissioners from England, and that it was the same that was published by Mitchell above 20 Years before. Having a Copy of that Map by me in loose Sheets I send you that Sheet which contains the Bay of Passamaquoddy, where you will see that Part of the Boundary traced. I remember too that in that Part of the Boundary, we relied much on the Opinion of Mr Adams, who had been concerned in some former Disputes concerning those Territories. I think therefore that you may obtain still farther Lights from him. That the Map we used was Mitchel's Map, Congress were acquainted, at the Time, by a Letter to their Secretary for foreign Affairs, which I suppose may be found upon their Files.

A letter of John Adams to Thomas Cushing, Lieutenant Governor of Massachusetts, under date of October 25, 1784 (Adams, Works of John Adams, VIII, 209–10), includes the statement that "it was Mit-

chell's map, upon which was marked out the whole of the boundary lines of the United States."

Finally, there may be quoted the very definite statement regarding the exclusive use of Mitchell's Map both in the negotiations of 1782 and in those of 1783, from the letter of John Adams to James Sullivan dated August 2, 1796 (*ibid.*, 519–20):

Mitchell's map was the only one which the ministers plenipotentiary of the United States, and the minister plenipotentiary of Great Britain, made use of in their conferences and discussions relative to the boundaries of the United States, in their negotiation of the peace of 1783, and of the provisional articles of the 30th of November, 1782. Upon that map, and that only, were those boundaries delineated.

There is no doubt whatever that more than one copy of Mitchell's Map was used during the negotiations of 1782; but the question of the identity of each of the various copies so used is one which is still somewhat obscure, despite all that has been written on the subject.

No mention of Mitchell's Map is made in the treaties of 1782 and 1783, and no copies of Mitchell's Map were signed by the Plenipotentiaries; the statement of the historian, George Bancroft (History of the United States of America, V, 580; and Histoire de l'action commune de la France et de l'Amérique pour l'indépendance des Etats-Unis, II, 246–47), that signed copies of Mitchell's Map were interchanged by the Plenipotentiaries, is without any known foundation whatsoever.

ORIGIN AND CHARACTER

Mitchell's Map was issued in 1755 with the approval and at the request of the British Government; it was dedicated to the Earl of Halifax, who was then President of the Board of Trade; it bears the endorsement of John Pownall, Secretary of the Lords Commissioners for Trade and Plantations, dated February 13, 1755; and in the printed text of the map is this statement:

This Map was Undertaken with the Approbation and at the request of the Lords Commissioners for Trade and Plantations [the Board of Trade]; and is Chiefly composed from Draughts, Charts and Actual Surveys of different parts of His Majesties Colonies & Plantations in America; Great part of which have been lately taken by their Lordships Orders, and transmitted to this Office by the Governors of the said Colonies and others.

It appears, moreover, from the text printed on the second edition of his map, that Mitchell had access not only to the records of the Board of Trade, but also to those of the British Admiralty, which he speaks of as "the Journals of our Ships of War kept in the Admiralty Office."

In general, Mitchell's Map is a political map, showing the division of eastern North America between the British and the French and the administrative subdivisions of the British North American Colonies. The map also has roads, however, and gives the positions of the principal Indian tribes, as well as extensive notes regarding the dates of various settlements, the nature of the country, and so forth.

Topographic features are roughly indicated, particularly in the Appalachian Mountains. It is especially worthy of note that, although a considerable portion of the territory of Louisiana is included, the boundaries of the maritime colonies are extended westward across the Mississippi River to the western border of the map. This is deliberate, for the parallel of 40° north latitude in the position of the present boundary between Nebraska and Kansas is denominated, "Bounds of Virginia and New-England by Charters, May 23. 1609 and Novr 3. 1620, extending from Sea to Sea, out of which our other Colonies were granted." Northwest of Lake Superior, in the present State of Minnesota, the same claim is repeated along the forty-eighth parallel in the words, "Northern Bounds of New England by Charter Novr 3 1620, extending to the South Sea's." Just off the present coast of Texas and just off the east coast of Florida the twenty-ninth parallel is marked "Bounds of Carolina by Charter" and "Bounds of Carolina by their Charter." North Carolina is carried westward beyond the Mississippi River to the western edge of the map by specific boundary symbols.

EDITIONS AND IMPRESSIONS

The question of identification of particular copies of Mitchell's Map is somewhat complicated by the fact, which has not always been recognized, that Mitchell's Map was published at various times and in various places. We know of two Dutch impressions, published in Amsterdam, with English titles; of at least eight French editions or impressions, some of them with titles and notes in German as well as in French; and of two Italian piracies published in Venice. All of these are on the scale of the original map and all but two include its whole area; and, while the dates of publication are not in all cases known, all of them except the latest French and Italian editions are prior to 1782.

More important are the English editions; for while it is certain that one of the French editions of Mitchell's Map was used in the conversations at Paris which Franklin and Jay had with Vergennes and with Aranda, it may be assumed that foreign editions of an English map were not used in the negotiations between the American and British Plenipotentiaries.

Up to 1782 four English editions of Mitchell's Map were published in London (the latest in 1775); and of the first edition there were three impressions and of the third edition, two, or seven impressions in all.

Colonel Lawrence Martin's classification of the English issues of Mitchell's Map, which does not attempt to include all the points of difference between the several issues, follows:

FIRST EDITION

First Impression. The line of print near the lower right corner, outside the neat line of the map, uses the letter *e* in place of the letter *a* in the words "Miller" and "Katherine."

Second Impression. Correctly uses the letter *a* in the words "Millar" and "Katharine" in the line of print mentioned above; but is like the first impression in showing two cities of Leicester and no city named Worcester in Massachusetts.

Third Impression. Shows the city of Worcester by name, but lacks the tables of text in the Atlantic Ocean.

SECOND EDITION

Has the tables of text in the Atlantic Ocean and still retains the name of Millar.

THIRD EDITION

First Impression. Carries the firm name of Jefferys and Faden as publishers; but has no printed boundary in Lake Ontario.

Second Impression. Has a printed boundary in Lake Ontario and still retains the words "and French Dominions" in the title.

FOURTH EDITION

Entitled "A Map of the British *Colonies* in North America. . . ."

Shortly after February 13, 1755, Dr. John Mitchell published in London the first edition of his "Map of the British and French Dominions in North America with the Roads, Distances, Limits, and Extent of the Settlements." Twenty years later the fourth English edition appeared in London with the title simplified by the substitution of the words "British Colonies" for "British and French Dominions." In the intervening years the map had been issued at least five times in England.

There are differences in latitudes and longitudes between the first and second, and in boundaries and place names between the second, third, and fourth English editions; in most of the reproductions of Mitchell's Map in various works, all such differences have been disregarded; it seems generally to have been assumed that any of the various English impressions of Mitchell's Map might be used indifferently to show the map or maps used in 1782 and 1783.

Mitchell's revisions for the second edition of his map, in respect of latitudes and longitudes, were based principally upon a study of the "Journals of our Ships of War kept in the Admiralty Office" and of the "Observations of Mr Chabert." Mitchell states in the columns of text which appear on the second and subsequent English editions: "From these Authorities we find but two Alterations necessary in our Map: 1. In the Latitude of Cape Race: 2. In the Longitude of Cape Sable." Cape Race, Newfoundland, was placed about half a degree farther south, and Cape Sable, Nova Scotia, about a degree farther east than as shown in the first edition. The locations of other points were adjusted in conformity with these alterations and on the basis of "the several Manuscript Maps, Charts, & Surveys, that have been lately made of our Colonies." The alterations perhaps most pertinent to the discussion of the northeastern boundary are the changed positions of the River St. Croix and of the line due north from its source, Lake Kousaki. In the first edition these lie entirely west of longitude 67° west from London, while in the second edition they lie entirely to the east of that meridian. The result is that whereas in

the first edition the due-north line passes about seventeen miles to the west of Lake Medousa, in the second edition it passes through the mouth of the Madawaska and, after following closely the course of that stream, passes through Lake Medousa, the location of the natural features in this portion remaining almost unchanged. The mouth of the St. Croix is represented about thirty-seven miles farther east in the second than in the first edition.

Mitchell's Map appeared in 1755 in eight sheets on the scale of 1:2,000,000, or an inch to about thirty-two miles; it covers the coast from Newfoundland and southern Labrador to Florida and Texas, extending on the west to what is now Oklahoma, Kansas, Nebraska, and South Dakota, and on the north to Hudson Bay. An insert map in the upper left corner of the main map is entitled, "A New Map of Hudson's Bay and Labrador," and includes part of the west coast of Greenland; and the Mississippi River extends up to and disappears beneath the neat line of the insert map. Thus the position of its supposed headwaters is omitted. The Lake of the Woods is shown a little to the east of the insert.

Dr. Mitchell published his map himself, as is indicated by the following words, printed outside the neat line at the bottom of the map: "Publish'd by the Author Feby 13th 1755 according to Act of Parliament, and Sold by And: Miller opposite Katherine Street in the Strand."

Here lies the distinguishing mark of the first impression of the first edition of Mitchell's Map, for the name of the dealer who sold the map was not "Miller" but "Millar." His name appears on the second impression as "And: Millar," and his address is there given as "Katharine Street."

The name of the engraver of the map is recorded by the words, "Tho: Kitchin Sculp. Clerkenwell Green."

The map bears an endorsement by John Pownall, Secretary of the Lords Commissioners for Trade and Plantations, dated "Plantation Office, Feby 13th 1755"; but this same date is printed on all the English editions and impressions of the map.

The second English edition is definitely designated as such; the third edition was published and sold by Jefferys and Faden, rather than by Millar; the fourth edition (published in 1775) is entitled, "A Map of the British Colonies in North America . . . ," the words "and French Dominions" having been omitted.

In the Division of Maps, Library of Congress, are copies of all the seven English impressions of Mitchell's Map except the first impression of the first edition (of which there is a photostat).

COPIES IN THE DEPARTMENT OF STATE ARCHIVES

There are in the Department of State six complete originals of Mitchell's Map and a separate sheet, herein designated "Franklin's Sheet," which is a part of an original Mitchell Map. Each complete map, as measured between the neat lines, is approximately 52 inches high and 75 inches wide. They are all constructed on the same

projection and on the same scale (1:2,000,000), and they are all of English editions. According to Colonel Lawrence Martin's criteria for distinguishing between the various English editions and impressions, the Mitchell Maps in the Department of State are classified as follows: two of the second edition; one of the second impression of the third edition; and four, including "Franklin's Sheet," of the fourth edition.

A list of the Mitchell Maps in the collection of the Department of State, with a description of each, follows.

1. Mitchell's Map inscribed on the back as "The copy used by the framers of the treaty of 1783."

A Map of the British and French Dominions in North America with [the] Roads, [Distances, Limits, and Extent of the] Settlements, Humbly Inscribed to the Right Honourable The Earl of Halifax, And the other Right Honourable The Lords Commissioners for Trade & Plantations, By their Lordships Most Obliged, and very humble Servant Jnọ Mitchell. Tho: Kitchin Sculp. Clerkenwell Green Publish'd by the Author Feby 13ᵗʰ 1755 according to Act of Parliament, and Sold by And: Millar opposite Katharine Street in the Strand.

This map is described by Lawrence Martin in Noteworthy Maps, Accessions 1925–26, 20, item 103, a pamphlet issued by the Library of Congress.

The map is dissected and mounted to fold to about 27 by 38 inches (69 by 97 cm.). It is without color. Except where the surface has peeled along lines of folding and in the title, it is legible.

This map is of the second English edition, revised by Mitchell himself and issued probably before 1762. The columns of explanatory text relating to revisions on the basis of new data and containing Mitchell's observation that his examination of all the information he could get, having in view the rendering of his map "as correct & usefull as possible," had "given occasion to this Second Edition," first appear on the maps of this edition, though they are reproduced on the maps of all subsequent English editions and impressions.

On this map a faint line, seemingly drawn with a lead pencil, but scarcely as noticeable as the impress of the pencil, and not continuously discernible, begins in the "highlands" (indicated by hill shadings) which lie between the source of the River Mitis, a tributary of the St. Lawrence, and Lake Medousa; passes to the north of Lake Nipissigouche, tributary to Lake Medousa from the northwest; continues southwesterly along the southern watershed of the St. Lawrence River basin; and ends a little to the west of the source of the northwest branch of the Connecticut River. An X marked in pencil appears just west of the portage leading from the north end of Ourangabena Lake, which lake empties into the St. John River.

The map is annotated on the back with the following inscription, lettered in ink on the original cloth mounting: "Mitchell's Map The copy used by the framers of the treaty of 1783." There is nothing to indicate when or by whom this was written; and there is no record as to when or from whom the map was received in the Department of State. When the map was remounted in July, 1926, the

inscription was left intact, and a statement to that effect, dated October 8, 1926, was written on a flap cut from the new mounting cloth, which opens to disclose the old inscription.

2. Mitchell's Map, not annotated, in eight sheets, unmounted, with a pale yellow border between the neat line and the outer line.

A Map of the British and French Dominions in North America with the Roads, Distances, Limits, and Extent of the Settlements, Humbly Inscribed to the Right Honourable The Earl of Halifax, And the other Right Honourable The Lords Commissioners for Trade & Plantations, By their Lordships Most Obliged, and very humble Servant Jnº Mitchell. Tho: Kitchin Sculp. Clerkenwell Green Publish'd by the Author Febᴿy 13ᵗʰ 1755 according to Act of Parliament, and Sold by And: Millar opposite Katharine Street in the Strand.

The map is in eight sheets, unmounted, each about 30 inches high and 20 inches wide (76 by 51 cm.).   Narrow bands of color emphasize political entities, which are not in any case represented in solid color.

This map is of the second English edition, issued probably before 1762.   New France is bounded on the south by a narrow band of color which runs along the lower St. Lawrence to Montreal, thence up the Ottawa River, and, departing therefrom, passes north of Lake Nipissing and in a westerly direction to the north shore of Lake Huron.   The boundary between Nova Scotia and New England extends north to the St. Lawrence and is not colored.   The bounds of Virginia, the Carolinas, and Georgia, as claimed under early charters and grants, extend across the Mississippi to the western limit of the map.   Florida is comprised entirely within the peninsula.

This map is one of five copies of Mitchell's Map which, on the suggestion of Judge John Bassett Moore, were purchased by the Department of State from B. F. Stevens, of London, in 1897.   Those five maps are listed and described in the bill for their purchase (Manuscript, Department of State Library, Bills, 1896–99) and in a paper referred to therein, entitled "A Collation or Comparison of the More Conspicuous Points of Variation in the Several Issues" (D. S., Manuscript); this map is "No. 2" of the bill of B. F. Stevens of November 4, 1897.

3. Mitchell's Map, not annotated, contained in a green box.

A Map of the British and French Dominions in North America with the Roads, Distances, Limits, and Extent of the Settlements, Humbly Inscribed to the Right Honourable The Earl of Halifax, And the other Right Honourable The Lords Commissioners for Trade & Plantations, By their Lordships Most Obliged, and very humble Servant Jnº Mitchell.   Tho: Kitchin Sculp Printed for Jefferys and Faden Geographers to the King at the Corner of Sᵗ Martins Lane Charing Cross London.   Publish'd by the Author Febᴿy 13ᵗʰ 1755 according to Act of Parliament.

The map is in eight sheets.   Each sheet, about 27 by 19 inches (68 by 49 cm.) in size, is dissected and mounted separately to fold to 4 by 6¾ inches (10 by 17 cm.).   They are contained in a green cardboard box, measuring 4¼ by 4¼ by 7½ inches, which is labeled, "Nortk America. 1755."   The label is of red leather, lettered and embellished in gold.

This map is not annotated.   It is of the second impression of the third English edition.

Canada, extending south to the Ohio and west to the Mississippi, is represented, in general, with boundaries described in the Quebec Act of 1774.   Its southern boundary runs, in part, from Chaleur Bay southwesterly along the southern watershed of the St. Lawrence River basin to a point south of Amaguntick Pond, thence southwest to the point where the parallel of 45° north intersects the east branch of the Connecticut River.   Nova Scotia and New England are separated by a line which runs along the St. Croix to Lake Kousaki, and from thence north through the mouth of the Madawaska (not named) and Lake Medousa to the southern boundary of Quebec. East and West Florida are distinguished from each other by color. Louisiana, west of the Mississippi and south of the Iberville–Lakes Maurepas and Pontchartrain line, is set off along its border by a wide yellow band edged in dark brown.

Nothing appears of record as to when or from whom this map was received by the Department of State.

4. Mitchell's Map in eight sheets, each folded once, and the whole bound loosely in atlas form.

A Map of the British Colonies in North America with the Roads, Distances, Limits, and Extent of the Settlements, Humbly Inscribed to the Right Honourable The Earl of Halifax, And the other Right Honourable The Lords Commissioners for Trade & Plantations, By their Lordships Most Obliged, and very humble Servant Jnᵒ Mitchell.   Tho: Kitchin Sculp   Printed for Jefferys and Faden Geographers to the King at the Corner of Sᵗ Martins Lane Charing Cross London.   Publish'd by the Author Febʳʸ 13ᵗʰ 1755 according to Act of Parliament

The map is in eight sheets, each 28 by 21 inches (71 by 53 cm.) in size.   The folded sheets were mounted on guards and bound. They appear to have been taken from an atlas and are still held loosely together by the sewed binding.   A green solid tint emphasizes the northern waters, and narrow bands of vivid colors on a ground without color mark the boundaries of political entities.   This map is of the fourth English edition, published in 1775.

The locations of a number of forts and missions are indicated by red dots, and the name of the Mission of St. Francis Xavier, west of Lake Michigan, and that of Fort St. Joseph, southeast of Lake Michigan, are underlined in red ink.   The word "Barrington" is added in handwriting in black ink north of Cape Sable, Nova Scotia; and various other annotations, in pencil and in ink, none of which, however, appears to have any bearing on the northeastern boundary question, are to be found on the map.

Canada, or Quebec, is represented with boundaries as defined by the Quebec Act of 1774.   Its southern boundary, southeast of the Quebec–Montreal area, differs somewhat from that shown on some other Mitchell Maps herein described, in that it follows the southern watershed of the St. Lawrence River basin all the way to the western headwaters of the River St. Francis, which enters the St. Lawrence just south of Trois Rivières, and then descends by the east branch

of the Connecticut to the parallel of 45° north, whereas, on other Mitchell Maps, the boundary lies some distance southeast of this line and passes in a southwesterly direction from Amaguntick Pond to the point where that parallel intersects the east branch of the Connecticut. The boundary between Nova Scotia and New England follows the St. Croix and the due-north line to the southern boundary of Quebec. The Floridas are distinguished from each other by colored border lines, and Louisiana, west of the Mississippi and south of the Iberville–Lakes Maurepas and Pontchartrain line, is set off by a border line in color.

This map is one of the five copies of Mitchell's Map which, as mentioned above, were purchased by the Department of State in 1897; it is "No. 5" of the bill of B. F. Stevens of November 4, 1897.

5. Mitchell's Map, a transcription of the heavily annotated "King George Map."

A Map of the British Colonies in North America with the Roads, Distances, Limits, and Extent of the Settlements, Humbly Inscribed to the Right Honourable The Earl of Halifax, And the other Right Honourable The Lords Commissioners for Trade & Plantations, By their Lordships Most Obliged, and very humble Servant Jnọ Mitchell. Tho: Kitchin Sculp Printed for Jefferys and Faden Geographers to the King at the Corner of Sṭ Martins Lane Charing Cross London. Publish'd by the Author Febṛy 13ᵗʰ 1755 according to Act of Parliament

This transcription of the King George Map is described by Lawrence Martin in Noteworthy Maps, Accessions 1926–27, 19, item 95, a pamphlet issued by the Library of Congress.

On the map a supplementary title, lettered in red ink and boxed in double red lines conforming to parallels and meridians, appears just above and to the right of the main title, as follows: "B. F. Stevens's Facsimile of the Red-Line-Map in the British Museum K118 d 26. the lines colourings and notes being reproduced on an uncoloured copy of the same issue of the original map. 22 June 1897."

The map is dissected and mounted to fold to about 13½ by 10 inches (34 by 25 cm.). In the upper right-hand corner and above the outer line on the face of the map is written in pencil, " 'K. G.' map." The map is in color. It is of the fourth English edition, published in 1775.

The map records international and other boundaries by annotated lines or bands in color, in accordance with treaties and other acts. It represents political subdivisions by means of border tints, over-all tints, or a combination of both.

The boundary of the United States is shown in its entirety as defined by the Treaty of Peace of September 3, 1783 (Document 11); and it may be noted here that of the original Mitchell Maps in the Department of State, this copy of the "King George Map" alone shows by means of one continuous line the entire bounds of the United States as defined by those articles.

The boundary is represented by a narrow red band or line annotated with the words, "Boundary as described by Mʳ Oswald," which

are written in red ink along the boundary at the north, the east, the south, and the west. On the east this annotation appears along that portion of the boundary defined as "East, by a Line . . . along . . . the River St Croix . . . ," and it appears twice along the line in the Atlantic "comprehending all Islands within twenty Leagues of . . . the Shores of the United States." The line along the Mississippi does not follow the middle of the stream, as specified by the treaty, but runs immediately to the east of earlier treaty lines which follow closely the left bank of that stream. The St. Marys River is not shown, but in that section the boundary is represented by a sinuous line which passes just north of Amelia Island and thence east into the Atlantic.

Other annotated lines on this map are the line of the Treaty of Utrecht according to both the English and the French construction, which is variously annotated along its several portions, and the line representing the bounds of the Hudson's Bay Company.

Quebec is shown according to the royal proclamation of 1763 and according to the Quebec Act of 1774. Its bounds, and the international boundary as well, in the region southeast of the Quebec-Montreal area, follow the southern watershed of the St. Lawrence River basin almost to the fork of the River St. Francis, south of Trois Rivières, and then descend the east branch of the Connecticut River to the parallel of 45° north. The Floridas are distinguished from each other by color. Louisiana, west of the Mississippi and south of the Iberville–Lakes Maurepas and Pontchartrain line, is shown in a color different from those of the Floridas.

This transcription of the King George Map was obtained by the Department of State in 1897; it is one of the five copies of Mitchell's Map which, as mentioned above, were then purchased on the suggestion of Judge John Bassett Moore; on the bill of B. F. Stevens of November 4, 1897, it is "No. 6."

6. Mitchell's Map, the "Steuben-Webster copy," with the title altered by a pasted slip bearing the words "United States."

A Map of the United States in North America with the Roads, Distances, Limits, and Extent of the Settlements, Humbly Inscribed to the Right Honourable The Earl of Halifax, And the other Right Honourable The Lords Commissioners for Trade & Plantations, By their Lordships Most Obliged, and very humble Servant Jn? Mitchell. Tho: Kitchin Sculp Printed for Jefferys and Faden Geographers to the King at the Corner of St Martins Lane Charing Cross London. Publish'd by the Author Feb^{ry} 13th 1755 according to Act of Parliament

This map is described by Lawrence Martin in Noteworthy Maps, Accessions 1926–27, 18, item 94, a pamphlet issued by the Library of Congress.

The map, which is in color, is dissected and mounted to fold to about 14 by 10 inches (36 by 25 cm.). The back bears two stamp marks which read, "Bureau of Rolls & Library Department of State Jul 20 1899 [?]." It is of the fourth English edition, published in 1775.

The title of the map was altered at an early date to read "United States" instead of "British Colonies"; that alteration was made by pasting over the words "British Colonies" a slip of paper upon which the engraved words "United States" are imprinted. On a similar slip of paper, which is pasted on a worn, red-marbled, pasteboard case that formerly contained and is now with that map, the words "United States" are imprinted, apparently from the same plate; and on the margin of that slip the autograph "J. W. Mulligan" is written in ink.

That autograph has led to the identification of the map as a copy purchased by Daniel Webster, referred to in a manuscript, in Webster's handwriting, in the possession of the New Hampshire Historical Society, and printed in The Writings and Speeches of Daniel Webster, XV, 217–18, an excerpt from which is quoted:

> I recollect purchasing various maps & charts—Some of them at high prices—one especially—which I had become acquainted with in 1838—& which I learned the British Consul then wished to buy—at almost any price, as it had a *red line* on it—supposed to have been placed there, by Mr. *Jay.* I bought this, at my own risk, in 1838—afterwards gave it to the agent of Maine, Mr. C. S. Davis [Daveis], who paid for it. At the time of the Treaty it was sent to the Dept—Mr. Davis was refunded what he had paid for it—& the map is now in the Dept
>
> My correspondence with Mr. Stubbs, & the papers will show how the account was settled. . . . See his letter to me.

Charles S. Daveis was a special agent cooperating with the Delegation of Maine in Congress (Northeastern Boundary Pamphlets, 1814–42, No. 5, p. 49). Mr. Stubbs was the disbursing agent in the Department of State (Curtis, Life of Daniel Webster, II, 282).

A Mr. Mulligan, of New York, doubtless John W. Mulligan, offered shortly before April 6, 1838, to sell to the British Consul General, Buchanan, at New York, a copy of Mitchell's Map "got from the library of the late Baron Steuben" (see Public Record Office, London, Foreign Office Records, America, series 2, now class 5, vol. 5, 325). In Friedrich Kapp, Life of Frederick William von Steuben, 591, 702, it appears that in 1791 Steuben made the acquaintance of a young man, John Mulligan, who became his secretary, and that in his last testament, dated New York, February 12, 1794, Steuben bequeathed "to John W. Mulligan . . . the whole of my library, maps and charts, and the sum of two thousand five hundred dollars to complete it."

The bounds of the United States represented by a brown line in juxtaposition with the tinted boundary line of the British possessions at the north and with that of the Spanish possessions at the west and the south, correspond with those described in the Preliminary Articles of Peace of November 30, 1782 (Document 7), and in the Definitive Treaty of Peace of September 3, 1783 (Document 11), except that no line is drawn in the Atlantic twenty leagues from shore and that, more noteworthy, the Maine boundary extends westwardly directly from the source of the St. Croix (the southern end of Lake Kousaki) instead of "due North" therefrom to the "Highlands." The line lies south of all tributaries of the River St. John, and the point of its departure from the line at the east lies some forty miles south of Mars Hill.

American, British, and Spanish areas are distinguished from each other by flat, soft tints, strengthened at the borders by distinctly deeper shades in corresponding colors. In the Spanish area the flat tint has a marginal band two or three inches in width which outlines the area and shades off inward almost imperceptibly into the ground tone. The United States is shown in buff or tan, Canada and Newfoundland in a reddish tone, and Louisiana and the Floridas in yellow. Attention may be called to the fact that the boundary lines match exactly in color and shade the border tints of these areas. The tint of the border between the neat line and the outer line of the map matches closely that of the American area.

This map was one of the two maps taken by Jared Sparks to Maine in May, 1842, in connection with the negotiations preceding the signature of the Webster-Ashburton Treaty on August 9, 1842 (see the letter of May 14, 1842, from Daniel Webster to Jared Sparks, in The Writings and Speeches of Daniel Webster, XVI, 371; and also Adams, The Life and Writings of Jared Sparks, II, 400–3).

7. Franklin's "Sheet which contains the Bay of Passamaquoddy," a sheet from Mitchell's Map. It is described by Lawrence Martin in Noteworthy Maps, Accessions 1926–27, 20–21, item 99, a pamphlet issued by the Library of Congress.

This sheet from the fourth edition of Mitchell's "Map of the British Colonies in North America," published in 1775, was sent by Benjamin Franklin to Thomas Jefferson, then Secretary of State, in response to a letter from Jefferson of March 31, 1790, requesting him "to communicate any Facts which your Memory or Papers may enable you to recollect, and which may indicate the true River the Commissioners on both sides had in their View, to establish as the Boundary between the two Nations" (Library of Congress, 9 Franklin Papers, Miscellaneous). Franklin said in his reply, dated April 8, 1790 (D. S., Papers Relative to the Commissioners under the Fifth Article of the Treaty with England, Northeastern Boundary, 1796, pt. 1, p. 5; Sparks, Works of Benjamin Franklin, X, 447–48), "I now can assure you that I am perfectly clear in the Remembrance that the Map we used in tracing the Boundary was brought to the Treaty by the Commissioners from England, and that it was the same that was published by Mitchell above 20 Years before. Having a Copy of that Map by me in loose Sheets I send you that Sheet which contains the Bay of Passamaquoddy, where you will see that Part of the Boundary traced." Additional evidence is found in Jefferson's letter to William Temple Franklin dated November 27, 1790, which reads, in part, as follows (Library of Congress, 58 Thomas Jefferson Papers): "Your grandfather sent me only one sheet of Mitchell's map, and it makes part of the testimony he was desired to give on the subject of the disputed river of St Croix, being referred to in his letter accompanying it."

The sheet has been recently remounted, and two flaps have been cut in the mounting cloth, one of which when opened reveals the words "Dr Franklin" written in pencil and the words "Dr Franklin Eastn boundy" written in ink; the other, the words "part of the

United States an odd sheet," written in ink. The writer of these words has not been identified; they appear to be in the handwriting of neither Benjamin Franklin nor Thomas Jefferson.

The bounds of Nova Scotia on the west and of Quebec on the south are represented by lines of different color, the trace of which follows the River St. Croix and the line due north from Lake Kousaki through the Madawaska and Lake Medousa and then, turning to the southwest, passes to the northwest of Amaguntick Pond and to the point where the parallel of 45° north intersects the east branch of the Connecticut River. No colored line runs through Lake Ontario.

COPIES FORMERLY IN THE DEPARTMENT OF STATE

Three copies of Mitchell's Map which were formerly in the archives of the Department of State were transferred to the Library of Congress in 1925 and 1926. One of these is "a colored printed copy of the third impression of the first English edition"; the second is the first impression of the third English edition; the third "is the second Dutch edition and contains three insert-maps,—plans of Quebec, Louisbourg, and Halifax" (see Lawrence Martin, Noteworthy Maps, Accessions 1925–26, 21, 22). A fourth copy, so transferred in 1932, is the second impression of the third English edition.

The two maps last mentioned were among the five copies of Mitchell's Map which were purchased at London in 1897 by the Department of State, as previously stated; they are respectively "No. 7" and "No. 4" of the bill of B. F. Stevens of November 4, 1897.

THE JAY COPY

Two existing copies of Mitchell's Map are, with some certainty, to be identified as directly connected with the negotiations of 1782.

One copy of Mitchell's Map which was certainly used during the earlier part of the negotiations of 1782 is that which is now in the archives of the New York Historical Society; that annotated copy of Mitchell's Map (the first impression of the third English edition), was continuously in the possession of the Jay family up to the year 1843. That map is colored to show Canada according to the Quebec Act, and it gives the whole boundary of the United States as proposed on October 8, 1782 (Wharton, Diplomatic Correspondence, V, 805–7), including the boundary of the St. John River (not the St. Croix), following the St. John up to the mouth of the Madawaska, thence up the Madawaska to Lake Medousa, thence by the highlands and the forty-fifth parallel to the St. Lawrence, and extending from the St. Lawrence to Lake Nipissing, and thence straight to the western edge of the map at 48° 45′ north latitude (which was taken to be the source of the Mississippi) rather than through the Great Lakes. It thus includes individual characteristics of the boundary provisions of October 8, 1782, as will be recognized. This map has St. Marys River drawn in with ink and denominated "Saint Marys River." It also carries a line drawn about twenty leagues off the coast from Florida to Maine.

On the boundary line of this copy of Mitchell's Map in thirteen places are written the words "Mr. Oswald's Line," and it was said in 1843 by Albert Gallatin (A Memoir on the North-eastern Boundary, 19) that those words had been "recognised by Mr. WILLIAM JAY, as being the handwriting of his father, the Hon. JOHN JAY." That is very strong evidence of the handwriting, coupled with the fact that the copy had continuously been in the possession of the Jay family; moreover, John Jay's name is written, in his own hand, on the back of this map; the boundary line of the map, "Mr. Oswald's Line," is the boundary of October 8, 1782, provisionally agreed to with Richard Oswald, the British Plenipotentiary; and that boundary is almost exactly that which Congress had proposed on August 14, 1779 (Journals, XIV, 958); it is possible that this copy was, at least in part, annotated in London; one author thinks that it was that sent by Oswald to London on October 8, 1782 (Fitzmaurice, Life of William, Earl of Shelburne, III, 273, note). A photostat of this copy is in the Division of Maps, Library of Congress (see Lawrence Martin, Noteworthy Maps, Accessions 1925–26, 21, item 104).

The placing of one of the thirteen repetitions of the words "Mr. Oswald's Line" is worthy of remark. The boundary clauses which were written at Paris early in October, 1782, contained the words, "East. by a Line to be drawn along the midle of St Johns River, from its Source to its mouth in the Bay of Fundy"; but with the articles [1] sent to London on October 8 was also written, "alteration. to be made in the inclosed Treaty, respecting the Boundaries of Nova Scotia. Viz at the Word East—the true Line shall be settled by Commissioners as soon as conveniently may be after the War." Nevertheless the words "Mr. Oswald's Line" appear along the portion of the boundary which follows the St. John River.

THE KING GEORGE MAP

Perhaps the most famous copy of Mitchell's Map is the King George Map, a transcription of which, made in 1897, is in the Department of State archives. That transcription has been described above (No. 5); the original is now in the British Museum. It is of the fourth English edition and is known as the "King George Map," as it was in the library of George III; and the boundary drawn on it, which, Lord Brougham said in the House of Lords on April 7, 1843, "entirely destroys our contention and gives all to the Americans" (Hansard, 3d series, LXVIII, 629), has written along it at various points (but not, as often stated, in the handwriting of George III), "Boundary as described by Mr Oswald." This copy of Mitchell's Map was exhibited at the Foreign Office in 1843 by Lord Aberdeen to Edward Everett, Minister at London, and is described in Everett's confidential despatch of March 31, in which he wrote (D. S., 50 Despatches, Great Britain):

---

[1] Quotations here are from a copy in the Public Record Office, London, in Oswald's hand (Foreign Office, 27, vol. 2, 665–76).

If the discovery of Mr Spark's Map at Paris was a singular incident, the bringing to light of Mr Oswald's at London is much more singular.   Lord Aberdeen assured me that he was not aware of its existence, till after the Conclusion of the Treaty, and the stir made about Franklin's map; and Lord Ashburton was equally ignorant of it till his return.   It was, however, brought from the British Museum to the Foreign Office in Lord Palmerston's time, and was known to him and to Mr Featherstonhaugh.   In whose custody it has been since the change of Ministry, so that it did not come to Lord Aberdeen's knowledge I was not told; very likely in that of Mr Featherstonhaugh himself, who has been employed till lately, as a sort of general Agent for the Boundary question.   Be this as it may, I was truly rejoiced at Lord Aberdeen's voluntary disclaimer of all previous knowledge of it, and so I said to him; for I could not have reconciled with that candor and good faith for which I have always given him credit, his repeated assurance to me, last summer, that there was no plan or map in their possession bearing on the question, not previously made known, had he all the time been aware of the Existence of this very remarkable Map, which I consider a far clearer and stronger Evidence in our favor, than any thing else of the kind which has ever been adduced.   I am perfectly persuaded that it is the map, on which the boundary established by the Treaty of 1783 was marked for the information of King George III. by Mr Oswald himself, or some one under his direction.   The line marked on this map and called in four [*sic*] different places the "Boundary described by Mr Oswald" is the line admitted by both parties to be the line of the Treaty as far as the two parties agree, and it gives to us the portion of the line on which we differ.

The ground on which it is here maintained that this map so marked, cannot be with certainty depended on as indicating the line of the Treaty is this.   We know historically that Mr Oswald, being deemed in the progress of the negotiation too yeilding, Mr Strachey, an Under Secretary of State, in the confidence of Mr Townsend, was sent out to assist him; and that a better line for England was obtained by him than had been agreed to by Mr Oswald.   So much is certain, and it has been suggested as possible that the line on King George the Third's map, called "the Boundary described by Mr Oswald" is that first line.

But it can be reduced to a certainty that such is not the case;—that the line on King George's map is not Mr Oswald's first rejected line; and it can be brought to the very highest degree of probability that this map contains the line of the Treaty as described by Mr Oswald himself.

On the 8th of October 1782 Articles of agreement were entered into, between Mr Oswald on the one hand, and Dr Franklin and Mr Jay on the other, (Mr Adams had not then arrived from Holland,) according to which the boundary on the *East* was to be the St Johns, from its Source to its mouth in the Bay of Fundy.   Our negotiators were aware that, on the principle of adhering to the old Charters, there was no ground, on the part of Massachusetts, to claim the St John's as the Boundary; and Mr Oswald appears to have obtained from them a promise to recede Westwardly from that river to the true boundary of Massachusetts according to the Old Charters, as the same should be afterwards ascertained.   In reference to this, the following note was appended to this plan of a treaty, vizt:—

"Alteration to be made in the Treaty respecting the Boundaries of Nova Scotia, vizt East, the true line between which and the United States shall be settled by Commissioners as soon as may be after the war."

By this same *projet* the States were to be bounded *North* by a line drawn from the North West Angle of Nova Scotia along the Highlands which divide those rivers which empty themselves into the St Lawrence from those which flow into the Atlantic Ocean, to the northernmost head of Connecticut River, thence down along the middle of that river to the 45th degree of North Latitude, and thence due West on the 45th degree to the Northwesternmost side of the river St Lawrence, thence straight to the South end of Lake Nipissing, and thence straight to the source of the Mississippi."

These Articles were sent over to London for the approbation of the King (see Franklin's Correspondence IV. p. 49.) and after a delay of two or three weeks, it having been thought that Mr Oswald was too yielding, (as has been already observed,) Mr Strachey was sent over to obtain more favorable terms in reference

to the Boundary and some other points. The Commissioners had "much contestation with him on the boundary and other articles," and a new agreement
was come to, which bore date 6th November. By this Second Set of Articles,
the *Northern* boundary, beginning as before at the North Western Angle of Nova
Scotia, and passing by the highlands to and down the Connecticut river to the
45th degree of North Latitude, was to run on that parallel to the Mississippi.
The *Eastern* boundary was the same as that which is contained in the Treaty
Actually concluded, with an immaterial difference in the phraseology.

In addition to this proposal, embodied in the second *projet* of a Treaty, it
appears from the history of the negotiation, that the American Commissioners
submitted a third, which Mr Strachey also took to London, which agreed with
the second as far as the Eastern boundary is concerned, but on the North substituted the line through the centre of the Lakes for the forty fifth degree of
Latitude. Messrs Oswald and Strachey considered, and justly, that either of
these lines was better than that agreed to by Mr Oswald on the 8th of October,
both as respects Canada and Nova Scotia.

After a short stay in London, Mr Strachey returned to Paris, bringing the
assent of his Government to the third proposal, which is the boundary of the
Treaty, as actually concluded.

It appears from the Correspondence that the United States Commissioners
were brought without difficulty, to recede from the St Johns to the St Croix, but
that they steadily refused the efforts of Messrs Oswald and Strachey to bring the
boundary west of the latter river.

Thus then it is certain that the line originally proposed by Mr Oswald and which
is described in the first projet of a Treaty of 8th October, made the St Johns the
boundary on the East, and a line from the South end of Nipissing to the Source
of the Mississippi the boundary on the North. There is no trace of any other
line agreed to by Mr Oswald and afterwards rejected.

The alternative lines as offered by the American Ministers as a second and
third proposal, giving a more favorable boundary than Mr Oswald's both as to
Nova Scotia and Canada, did so, in reference to Nova Scotia, by bringing the
Boundary westward from the St Johns to the St Croix, (in which respect the two
lines agreed,) and in substituting on the North, either the 45° of N. Latitude, or
the middle of the Lakes. The latter was adopted by England, and both were
better than the line of the first projet accepted by Mr Oswald.

It follows that the line found on King George the Third's map, and there
called "the boundary as described by Mr Oswald our Negotiator," is *not* the
line of Oct. 8th but one of the Alternative lines, of which the choice was obtained
by Mr Strachey, and is the line of the present Treaty.

This line is the line always claimed by the United States, which is thereby
shewn to be the true line by the map of Mr Oswald.

I humbly conceive that this train of argument is direct and unanswerable.

The above was chiefly written before I had seen Mr Oswald's map, which I
have since, by the kindness of Sir Robert Peel and Lord Aberdeen, been permitted
to do. It is a copy of Mitchell in fine preservation. The boundaries between the
British and French possessions in America, "as fixed by the Treaty of Utrecht,"
are marked upon it in a very full distinct line, at least a tenth of an inch broad,
and those words written in several places. In like manner, the line giving our
boundary as we have always claimed it, that is, carrying the North Eastern
[northwestern] Angle of Nova Scotia far to the North of the St Johns, is drawn
very carefully in a bold red line, full a tenth of an inch broad; and in four different
places along the line distinctly written "the boundary described by Mr Oswald."
What is very noticeable is, that a line narrower, but drawn with care with an
instrument, from the lower end of Lake Nipissing to the Source of the Mississippi,
as far as the Map permits such a line to run, had once been drawn on the map,
and has since been partially erased, though still distinctly visible.

It is to be observed that the only specific reference in the foregoing
despatch to any erasure on the King George copy of Mitchell's
Map is in the last sentence quoted. There mention is made of a

partially erased line running from the lower end of Lake Nipissing to the supposed source of the Mississippi.

On a facsimile of the King George copy of Mitchell's Map which was prepared by the late James White in 1926 in connection with the special reference to the Judicial Committee of the Privy Council of a question as to the location and definition of the boundary between Canada and Newfoundland in Labrador (The Times Law Reports, XLIII, 289–99), there is printed as a note the following statement, which is to be compared with the observation of Everett just mentioned and also with the comments on the despatch of Everett, written by James White in Canada and Its Provinces, VIII, 823–24 (a copy of that facsimile of the King George Map is in the Division of Maps, Library of Congress):

On the original map, there are faint red lines along the St. John river (N. B.), and on the line from the intersection of the 45th parallel with the river St. Lawrence to Lake Nipissing and, thence, westward. These lines were evidently added to the map to indicate proposals of the Commissioners for the United States, as reported by Oswald during the negotiations. When the present boundary was agreed upon, these lines were "washed out" as far as possible.

On the Stevens transcription of the King George Map, which is in the Department of State archives and which has been described above (No. 5), there is no indication of any erased lines.

This King George copy of Mitchell's Map is of undoubted authenticity; whether it was used at Paris during the 1782 negotiations or whether it was a map of reference used by George III and his ministers, as supposed by White ("Boundary Disputes and Treaties," 823), does not affect its evidentiary value; the red line drawn upon it is that of the treaty of November 30, 1782 (Document 7), not that of the tentative agreement dated October 8;[1] thus the line is that of the St. Croix, not that of the St. John; that line must have been drawn under the direction of Oswald or by him; it extends to the headwaters of the Lake Medousa of Mitchell's Map, later called Madawaska Lake and now Temiscouata Lake, and thus shows that no change from the tentative agreement dated October 8, 1782, was made or intended to be made by the negotiators in that portion of the east line which is drawn as running north from the mouth of the Madawaska to its source; and it accordingly supports in the strongest manner the view of Gallatin that both Congress in 1779 and the American negotiators in 1782 treated Nepissigouche (a small lake on Mitchell's Map near the head of Lake Medousa or Temiscouata) as the source of the St. John (see Moore, International Arbitrations, I, 95–96; Gallatin, The Right of the United States of America to the North-eastern Boundary, 66).

Indeed, as far as the negotiations of 1782 are concerned, the matter is now beyond debate or argument. In the tentative agreement dated October 8, 1782 (Wharton, Diplomatic Correspondence, V, 806), part of the boundary is "east by a line to be drawn along the middle of St. John's River from its source to its mouth"; that line is drawn on the Jay copy of Mitchell's Map to the source of the Mada-

---

[1] Strictly speaking that agreement was (*semble*) not dated; but October 8 is the date of Oswald's authentication.

waska, and as so drawn it is an east boundary, for it runs generally
north and south. In the treaty of 1782 the east boundary runs
north "to the aforesaid Highlands" at a point which had previously
been stated to be "the north west Angle of Nova Scotia"; and that
east boundary is also drawn on the King George Map to the source
of the Madawaska. In 1782 the northwest angle of Nova Scotia,
the source of the St. John River, and the northern point of the eastern
boundary of the United States were perfectly understood to be three
descriptions of the same spot, which was then marked on Mitchell's
Map due north of the source of the St. Croix River at the headwaters
of the Madawaska.

COPIES IN THE COLONIAL OFFICE

In the library of the Colonial Office, London, are seven copies of
Mitchell's Map, which were examined in September, 1931. In the
"Catalogue of the maps, plans and charts in the library of the Colonial
Office, 1910," under the heading "America (North and South),"
these are numbered 21 to 27, inclusive, and six of them (all but No.
24) bear rubber-stamp impressions indicating that they were formerly
in "Her Majesty's State Paper Office," now called the "Public
Record Office." These maps, with papers and documents, were
transferred to the Colonial Office in 1907–8.

Copy No. 22 is of special interest, as it is that copy which has been
referred to as the "Record Office Map." This copy is a first impression
of the first edition of Mitchell's Map. It has been mounted on paper
and backed with very heavy cloth. The edges have been taped, and
it is mounted on two sticks, one on each side rather than at the top
and bottom. The mounting is too heavy for the brittle paper of the
map itself; many small pieces have come off and others are coming loose.
The library has withdrawn the map from use, and it is kept rolled and
locked in a long box. There is no record that this map has ever been
photographically copied. The map is very badly faded and is now
dark brown in color; the edges are torn and fragments are missing.

The State Paper Office catalogue at one time stated that "This is
the identical map on which the Commissioners at Paris, 1783, traced
the Boundary between the British Dominions and the United States,
and was subsequently used by the Boundary Commissioners in the
year 1842."

It is, of course, *possible* that this copy was used at Paris in 1782 or
1783; but there is no evidence whatever that any boundary line was
then drawn on it, and indeed, there is now neither anything on the
map itself nor any documentary evidence to support the statement
that it was used at Paris during the negotiations of 1782 or 1783, a
statement which appears first to have been made in 1841 or 1842
(Fitzmaurice, The Life of William, Earl of Shelburne, III, 324;
Greville, A Journal of the Reign of Queen Victoria from 1837 to 1852,
II, 102).

Quite a number of place names and other additions to the map have
been made by hand; one of these, "Washington (D. C.)," is at least
as late as 1791.

The "red line" of the map appears on the River St. Croix, runs southwestwardly from Kousaki Lake to Chenbesec Lake, thence westwardly to a point near one of the headwaters of the Connecticut River, south to 45° north latitude, west on the forty-fifth parallel to the St. Lawrence; presumably following the St. Lawrence it is again discernible in crossing Lakes Ontario, Erie, Huron, and Superior, whence it goes to and across the Lake of the Woods and as far as the insert map.

The red line described above is rather closely paralleled throughout by a black pencil line, which diverges most noticeably in the northeast, near Lakes Kousaki and Chenbesec.

In any consideration of the "red line" of this map as bearing upon the northeastern boundary, it is to be remembered that that line from Kousaki Lake, the source of the St. Croix, does not run north at all, but runs somewhat south of due west.

This copy of Mitchell's Map was also shown to Edward Everett in 1843. However, in the paragraph which he wrote about it, which follows, and which was doubtless written after a somewhat casual examination, there are two errors. It does not give the northeastern boundary "as claimed by Great Britain," for, as mentioned above, the line runs south of due west from the source of the St. Croix; and the line is drawn in red ink, not in "red crayon" (D. S., 50 Despatches, Great Britain, March 31, 1843):

Lord Aberdeen shewed me, at the same time, another map alluded to by Sir Robert Peel, also a copy of Mitchell, which after Lord Ashburton left England was found in the State Paper Office. It is on rollers, and from having long been hung up, is much soiled and defaced. It gives the boundary as claimed by Great Britain. The line is faintly, but plainly drawn in red crayon, with a black lead pencil mark running by its side. There is nothing written on any part of the Map, to show by whom or when these lines were drawn; but I was informed that professional map-makers pronounced the lines to be ancient. To me the red crayon line appeared ancient, and the lead pencil modern.

THE STATEMENT OF EGBERT BENSON

Egbert Benson, one of the Commissioners under Article 5 of the Jay Treaty (Document 16) who on October 25, 1798, decided the question of the St. Croix River (Document 23), stated in his report to the President that "the" copy of Mitchell's Map used during the negotiations at Paris was offered in evidence in the course of the proceedings regarding the St. Croix. Referring to James Sullivan, the Agent of the United States in that arbitration, he wrote (Moore, International Adjudications, Modern Series, II, 382):

And he thereupon offered in Evidence : : : a Map of Mitchell, as the Identical Copy which the Commissioners had before them at Paris, having been found deposited in the Office of the Secretary of State for the United States, and having the Eastern Boundary of the United States, traced on it with a pen or pencil through the middle of the River Saint Croix, as laid down on the Map, to its source, and continued thence North, as far as to where most probably it was supposed by whoever it was done the highlands mentioned in the treaty are.

But the language actually used by James Sullivan in 1797 regarding that copy of Mitchell's Map was quite other than might be supposed from the statement of Benson (*ibid.*, I, 145):

Whether the Map on the Table is the same that was before the Commissioners at Paris in 1782 or not, cannot from the evidence in the case be precisely ascertained at this place, (Providence). It has been a Document in the archives of The United States and transmitted to their Agent by their Secretary with this notification,

By some documents which I shall send you next week you will see that the American & British Commissioners who negotiated the Treaty of peace at Paris used Mitchell's Map of North America. This will be considered as an important Document. I shall send you the Map, in which you will see traced our whole Boundary line. Whether it is the identical Map used at Paris I am not informed. You will please to preserve it that it may be returned to this office when your Agency shall be accomplished.

Perhaps Mr Adams or Mr Jay could not declare as witnesses that the map here produced is the copy had before the Commissioners at Paris in 1782, nor can it be important to prove that fact. All the lines marked are accurate, and there is but one river called the St Croix and it is proved by the testimonies of Mr. Adams and Mr. Jay that the River on that Map called Saint Croix was in fact agreed upon as a Boundary.

While that copy of Mitchell's Map was doubtless seen by Albert Gallatin in 1828 at the Department of State (Gallatin, A Memoir on the North-eastern Boundary, 48–49), subsequent efforts to find or identify it have been unavailing (Moore, International Arbitrations, I, 156–57); and while it is of course possible that it was a copy used at Paris in 1782 or 1783, it is clear that Secretary of State Timothy Pickering had no evidence to that effect in 1797.

CONCLUSION

Additions made to a map by hand are of two sorts. In the first place there are those which are added to the copies of an edition after they are printed but before they are issued. In former times it was a common practice to have parts of a map made by hand, particularly when in color, and the practice is still followed when the edition is too small to justify making color plates. Such additions are, of course, in the strictest sense a part of the map itself, upon its issuance. In the second place there are additions made by hand by those who obtain the issued map; these are properly to be regarded as subsequent annotations, and they may be of any nature according to the purpose and fancy of the owner of the map.

Regarding the evidentiary value historically or in the legal sense of annotations to a map, it is to be said that such value depends wholly upon evidence as to who made the annotations and, further, as to when they were made.

Mitchell's Map was widely circulated. It was a popular map, as is shown by the number of editions published. In the last four decades of the eighteenth century anyone in England or on the continent of Europe or in America who was interested in geography would be as likely to have a copy as such a person today would be

likely to have some popular atlas. It was very natural that the possessor of a copy of Mitchell's Map should, after the changes of 1783 in political geography, make some attempt to indicate those changes on his map; and unless we know something more about a "red line" drawn on a copy of Mitchell's Map than that it *is* a red line on such a copy, its historical significance is nil.

The fact that there are annotations on a copy of Mitchell's Map in a Foreign Office means in itself nothing at all other than that such annotations were probably made by someone in or connected with that Foreign Office and that they were certainly made at a date after the issuance of the map; the mere fact that a line seemingly intended to indicate a boundary is drawn on a copy of a map which is in the archives of a Foreign Office is in itself and without additional information, no evidence legally or historically that that government or any responsible official of that government considered that that boundary was even approximately indicated by that line.

So far as concerns the negotiations of 1783, there is no specific evidence to identify any particular copy or copies of Mitchell's Map as the one or the ones used; but while the boundary articles of the Definitive Treaty of 1783 are essentially identical with those of the Preliminary Articles of 1782, a number of geographical problems were discussed in 1783 by the negotiators, and it seems clear that some map must have been used; and there is the positive statement of John Adams that Mitchell's Map was used in 1783 as in 1782 (letter to James Sullivan of August 2, 1796, above quoted).

The conclusion is as follows: Only two copies of Mitchell's Map which were used at the time of the peace negotiations at Paris in 1782–83 can now be identified. The Jay copy (the first impression of the third English edition) in the archives of the New York Historical Society had to do with the tentative boundary agreement of October 8, 1782. The King George copy (fourth English edition) in the British Museum was certainly used in London during the peace negotiations of 1782, but probably not in Paris. Such other copies of Mitchell's Map as were used at Paris in the negotiations culminating on November 30, 1782, and September 3, 1783, are not now definitely known. The Department of State appears to have in its archives no map which can be proved to have been used at Paris in 1782 or in 1783.

JOHN MITCHELL

Mitchell's Map is the most important and the most famous map in American history. It is very aptly called Mitchell's Map, for not only was John Mitchell its author, but he made no other.

Dr. John Mitchell, of Virginia and England, was a distinguished and learned man of his time; he was a physician whose treatment of yellow fever became famous in 1793, a botanist of repute, the author of numerous works, and the maker of one map; but our knowledge of his life and career is strangely incomplete.

The place and date of Mitchell's birth are unknown. Although a Swedish authority, a contemporary, understood that Mitchell was

born in Virginia, it seems that he was born in the British Isles, since his more intimate friends said in 1746 that he "returned" to England and spoke of that return as his voyage "home." His ancestors and descendants have not been identified. He was married, but we do not know to whom. Where he was trained in medicine is not recorded. He is known to have received part of his botanical education at the University of Edinburgh, and he may have studied botany and medicine either at Leiden in the Netherlands or at Oxford or Cambridge in England. He probably had no formal training in the making of maps.

It cannot even be said when Mitchell came to America, though the unsupported statement that he reached Virginia in 1700 has often been printed. He spent some years (six at least) in Virginia, collecting plants, according to Linnæus; his residence was at Urbanna on the Rappahannock River. In October, 1735, the vestry of Christ Church parish gave him eight hundred pounds of tobacco for caring for the sick; on December 19, 1738, he was appointed a justice of the peace in Middlesex County, Virginia; in 1744 he visited Philadelphia, where he became a friend of Benjamin Franklin, with whom he corresponded thereafter. His writings were in part in Latin and, aside from those regarding botany, zoology, and medicine, bore chiefly on the theme that America should be British rather than French. His travels in America were limited to Virginia and the region north to Philadelphia. There is some ground for believing that Mitchell was a Quaker, but this is not at all certain.

Mitchell returned to England in 1746; hence we cannot actually prove that he spent more than eleven years in America.

After his return to England, he seems to have lived mostly in London; he was elected a Fellow of the Royal Society in 1747; he did not practice medicine and gradually gave up his botanical studies; but he wrote a number of scientific and historical papers; and he made Mitchell's Map.

Dr. Mitchell died on February 29, 1768, in or near London.

THE REPRODUCTION OF MITCHELL'S MAP IN THIS VOLUME

A facsimile reproduction of the Steuben-Webster copy of Mitchell's Map (which is in the archives of the Department of State and has been described above, No. 6), is contained in a pocket inside the back cover of this volume.

This reproduction is a reduced facsimile of the Steuben-Webster copy, made by photolithography. The reduction is to one half the scale of the original, namely, from the scale of 1:2,000,000 to the scale of 1:4,000,000. The colors have been made to match those on the Steuben-Webster Map in its present state as closely as possible; the colors on the Steuben-Webster copy, however, are somewhat uneven, due to their having been put on by hand. The original tone of the paper itself, as changed by lapse of time, but without color, appears on the ocean and the lakes, on a large portion of the territory west of the Mississippi River, and in the outer margins of the map.

There are cogent reasons for reproducing this particular copy of Mitchell's Map.

In the first place, the history of the Steuben-Webster copy is in large part known, and the influence of this map on public affairs has been important. It lies within the bounds of possibility that Baron Steuben acquired this map in July, 1783, when George Washington sent him to Canada to make plans for the taking over of the British posts on the St. Lawrence and the Great Lakes (Sparks, Writings of George Washington, VIII, 462–64). As already stated, the British Consul General at New York City attempted in 1838 to persuade the British Foreign Office to purchase this identical copy of Mitchell's Map because its indication of a northeastern boundary of the United States was thought to support the contention of the British Government. In the same year Daniel Webster purchased the map; subsequently he sold it to a special agent of the State of Maine; and still later he reacquired it for the Department of State. In 1842 Webster placed this map in the hands of Jared Sparks, who took it to Maine and used it in persuading the authorities there to cease their opposition to a conventional settlement of the northeastern boundary question. It would be unreasonable to assume that this map was not similarly before Senators of the United States from August 17 to 20, 1842, during the discussion of the Webster-Ashburton Treaty, for the other map which Sparks had taken to Maine was then before the Senate (Congressional Globe, XII, appendix, pp. 16, 61). No other copy of Mitchell's Map in the possession of the Department of State in 1932 is known to have an equally long and detailed history or has been shown to have had a more pronounced political influence.

Secondly, the Steuben-Webster copy of Mitchell's Map was thought to support the British contention with respect to the northeastern boundary of the United States; the King George copy of Mitchell's Map supports the American contention with respect to that boundary; since each of these maps failed to be produced and used during the negotiations between Webster and Ashburton, and since the Canadian Government has already reproduced the King George Map in facsimile, it now seems desirable to make available a facsimile of this Steuben-Webster Map.

MAP A

In the first paragraph of Article 4 of this convention mention is made of two maps as "Evidence mutually acknowledged":

The Map called Mitchell's Map, by which the Framers of the Treaty of 1783 are acknowledged to have regulated their joint and official Proceedings, and the Map A which has been agreed on by The Contracting Parties, as a delineation of the Water courses and of the Boundary Lines in reference to the said Water Courses, as contended for by each Party respectively, and which has accordingly been signed by the above named Plenipotentiaries at the same time with this Convention, shall be annexed to the Statements of the Contracting Parties, and be the only Maps that shall be considered as Evidence mutually acknowledged by The Contracting Parties of the Topography of the Country.

Map A was prepared for this convention.   It was made with "great labour and considerable difficulty," though Albert Gallatin, who signed this convention as Plenipotentiary of the United States, called it "only a skeleton" in his despatch of September 21, 1827, announcing agreement on the terms of the convention (D. S., 34 Despatches, Great Britain, No. 117), in which he wrote:

After a very arduous negotiation, we have at last agreed on the terms of the intended Convention, for regulating the proceedings of the reference to a friendly Sovereign or State of the North Eastern boundary, in conformity with the 5th Article of the Treaty of Ghent.   Some points of minor importance in the general Map, agreed on in lieu of the two conflicting that had been rejected by the Commission, remain alone to be adjusted.   This Map is only a skeleton containing the water courses, and connecting together the partial surveys filed with the Commissioners.   The contending lines are traced on it in reference to the water courses; but none of the highlands are delineated on it, this being in fact the main question at issue and on which we could not of course agree.

In his despatch of September 30, 1827 (*ibid.*, No. 122; American State Papers, Foreign Relations, VI, 696–99), transmitting the convention to Secretary of State Clay, Gallatin wrote more at length regarding Map A and Mitchell's Map:

I have the honour to transmit herewith a Convention with Great Britain for the regulation of the reference to Arbitration of the North East boundary Question, which after a long, protracted and arduous negotiation, was concluded yesterday.

Our attention was, in the first instance, drawn to the necessity of supplying the want of a general Map of the contested territory, those which had been prepared by the principal Surveyors of the two Governments respectively having been objected to, and neither of them admitted to be filed amongst the records of the late Commission.   We anticipated from the beginning that, as eventually happened, we would be unable to agree respecting the highlands, this being one of the main questions at issue.   But there was a great advantage to have, if practicable, a map mutually agreed on, which should connect together the partial surveys made under the late Commission, and to which all the arguments drawn from those surveys and from the relative situation of all the rivers and water courses might refer.   The work proved to be one of great labour and considerable difficulty.   It was the subject of several informal conferences and communications and occupied a great part of last spring whilst our official conferences were suspended.   The Map, with the exception of some details but lately settled, was completed towards the end of June.   As we were unable to agree on the highlands and some other points, it was from that time understood and has been made one of the provisions of the Convention, that each party might, on a transcript of the Map, delineate the highlands and other features of the Country according to its own view of the subject, and that the transcripts might be laid before the Arbiter, each being subject to the objections and observations of the other party.

It was also agreed that "Mitchill's Map" should, according to the evidence of the American negotiators of the treaty of 1783, be acknowledged as that by which the framers of that treaty had regulated their joint proceedings.   The Arbiter will therefore be enabled to compare the topography of the Country, such as it was understood by the framers of the treaty of 1783 with what from subsequent exploration it actually appears to be.   It fortunately happens that all the great features of the Country and specially the position of the River St John's and other waters, are so nearly similar in both that Map and the new one (A) which has been agreed on, that the arguments drawn from the intention of the parties are not at all affected by the particulars in which those two Maps differ.   To this there is but one exception.   It appears by Mitchill's Map, that the point of intersection of the North line drawn from the Source of the river S^t

Croix and of the highlands as contended for by the United States, (in other words the North West angle of Nova Scotia,) must have been presumed to be on the dividing ridge, which divides the rivers falling into the river St Lawrence from the tributary streams of the river St John's. It has been found by the survey of that north line, that the River Ristigouche, which empties into the Bay des Chaleurs penetrates farther inland or Westwardly than had been supposed by Mitchill, so that the said line crosses several of the upper branches of that river, and that the North West angle of Nova Scotia contended for by the United States is on the dividing ridge which divides the rivers emptying into the River St Lawrence from those which fall into the Gulf St Lawrence.

When I say that this is the only discrepancy, that may affect the argument, to be found between the two Maps or between the presumed intentions of the parties and what has turned out to be the fact, I must always be understood as excepting the question which has been raised by Great Britain respecting the Highlands. If, as she contends, (most erroneously in my opinion,) a continuous chain of conspicuous Mountains was meant by the term "Highlands," neither Mitchill's Map, nor that on which we have agreed throws any light on the subject. Whether such was the intended meaning of that expression, and, if it was, (which we deny,) whether the ground along which either of the two conflicting lines extends answers that description will be questions for the Arbiter to decide. The separate transcripts of the Map agreed on, which will be prepared by each party, are intended, as already stated, to enable each to delineate those highlands as he may think proper.

Map A was made in duplicate originals, one example for each of the two Governments, to "be annexed to the Statements of the Contracting Parties" to be delivered to the "Arbitrating Sovereign." One original is in the archives of the Department of State; measured between the neat lines, its dimensions are 63 by 62 inches (160 by 157 cm.); its scale, though not indicated, is approximately 8.2 miles to an inch (1 : 520,000). It is on heavy paper mounted on cloth and bound with green silk ribbon. Centered in its upper margin is a large letter A. The title of the map and its references are as follows:

A Map of The territory contained between the lines respectively contended for by The United States and Great Britain as being the North Eastern Boundary of The United States in conformity with the Treaty of Peace of 1783 embracing also the adjacent parts of the dominions of the two Powers

REFERENCES

A North-west angle of Nova Scotia as contended for by the United States.
B North-west angle of Nova Scotia as contended for by Great Britain.
D North-westernmost head of Connecticut River as contended for by the United States.
C North westernmost head of Connecticut River as contended for by Great Britain.

The green colour denotes the boundary line as claimed by the United States
The red colour denotes the boundary line as claimed by Great Britain

As stated in Article 4 of the convention, Map A was signed by the Plenipotentiaries. The certificate, with the signatures, follows:

We the Undersigned do hereby certify this to be the Map A, which, by the 4th Article of the Convention concluded this day between the United States and Great Britain, has been agreed on by the Contracting Parties, and which we have accordingly signed this 29th day of September 1827

ALBERT GALLATIN
CHA. GRANT
H. U. ADDINGTON.

That this original of Map A was that duly submitted to the Arbiter is shown by the fact that it has written on it, under a red *X* at the southwesternmost source of the River St. Francis, the words, "Le Ministre des Affaires Etrangères de S. M. le Roi des Paÿs Bas," followed by the signature (Verstolk de Soelen) of Baron Verstolk van Soelen, Minister of Foreign Affairs of the Netherlands. That letter *X*, so authenticated, marked on Map A a point on the Maine boundary as recommended and described in the award of the King of the Netherlands.

During the consideration of this convention in the Senate the following resolution was passed on January 7, 1828 (American State Papers, Foreign Relations, VI, 821, note):

Resolved, That the President of the United States be requested to communicate to the Senate, under such injunctions as he may judge proper, Mitchell's map, and also the agreed map, designated as map A, in the 4th article of the convention relating to the northeastern boundary of the United States.

On January 9 President John Quincy Adams responded with the following message (*ibid.*):

In compliance with a resolution of the Senate of the 7th instant, I transmit herewith Mitchell's map and the map marked A, as requested by the resolution; desiring that, when the Senate shall have no further use of them, they may be returned.

It seems that the Map A sent to the Senate was not the signed original map, but a copy transmitted with the above-mentioned despatch of Gallatin of September 30, 1827, for in that despatch he wrote:

I enclose the copy of the Protocols of our five last conferences and of the Map A. The original of this Map and of that of Mitchill procured here being both intended to be laid before the Arbiter will remain in the Archives of this Legation subject to your orders, according to the quarter of the world in which the Arbiter that will be selected may reside.

In the Department of State archives is a tracing of an original Map A, showing the signatures of the Plenipotentiaries, with that of Albert Gallatin first; it is fairly certain that the original from which this tracing was made is that described above; for while there are some very slight but noticeable differences in outline, in the placement of proper names, and in the size and spacing of the lettering, such variances may well occur in the making of a tracing.

By the terms of the second paragraph of Article 4 of this convention either party was permitted to submit to the Arbitrating Sovereign a transcript of Map A, "in which Transcript each Party may lay down the Highlands or other Features of the Country as it shall think fit, the Water courses and the Boundary Lines, as claimed by each Party, remaining as laid down in the said Map A."

In the archives of the Department of State is an example of the American transcript of Map A and a copy of the British transcript thereof. Both are on thin, transparent paper and of the same size and scale as the signed original Map A. Each transcript is in four sheets.

Regarding the preparation of the American transcript of Map A, Gallatin wrote on August 26, 1828, to Daniel Brent, Chief Clerk of the Department of State, as follows (D. S., Northeastern Boundary, envelope 8):

It is, under every circumstance, necessary that another transcript of the Map A, as correct as possible, should be prepared so as to be ready before November, on which I may delineate the highlands &ᵉ This will be the rough draft from which those additions will be transcribed, by the draughtsman who may be selected, on the two transcripts transmitted from London to your office and which are most perfect fac-similes of the original deposited in the Archives of the U. States mission at London. This original is the identical Map A signed by the negotiators and to be laid before the Arbitrator. The two transcripts or fac similes sent from London, will, with our delineations and additions transferred on them, be the two American transcripts of the same Map A contemplated by the Convention, one of which to be communicated to the British Minister on 1ˢᵗ of January next, and the other to be laid before the Arbiter.

The American transcript of Map A is unsigned. It is entitled "American Transcript of the Map A (agreed on by the Convention of 29 September 1827 as evidence mutually acknowledged of the Topography of the Country) with the Highlands and other features of the Country laid down in behalf of the United States." Then, following the references of the original Map A, is this notation:

N. B. The green colour has also been used in this transcript to designate the boundaries of States, and of Counties in the State of Maine; and the red colour to designate the boundaries of counties in the province of New Brunswick and of Districts in that of Lower Canada.

The dotted lines and the italic capitals E, F &ᶜ are inserted to elucidate references in the American statements.

The copy of the British transcript of Map A which is in the archives of the Department of State appears in outline and in the retention of the title and signed certificate, almost certainly to have been drawn from the original signed Map A which was for the British Government. It shows the signatures of the Plenipotentiaries; but the *alternat* was observed, for the signatures of the British Plenipotentiaries are above that of Gallatin; Great Britain is named before the United States in the title of the map and in the certificate; the "references" are transposed so that Great Britain is mentioned first; and the notation regarding the red line precedes that regarding the green. In its lower right corner this map is entitled "British Transcript of the Map A destined for general purposes of illustration as stipulated in Art. IV of the Convention of the 29ᵗʰ September 1827," and has the following explanatory notations or legend, the symbol colors of which are here described within brackets:

Rivers which empty themselves into the River Sᵗ Laurence____ [purple]
Rivers which fall into the Atlantic Ocean_____ [blue]
The line considered as the Most Favourable which Congress} thought could be obtained in 1782. viz. along the middle of the }[yellow] Sᵗ John River from its Source to its Mouth in the Bay of Fundy. }
Only Line of Communication between Great Britain and the} Canadas through the British Territory during Six Months of the }[brown] Year; and the Post Route to those Provinces, which has been} constantly used ever since the Peace of 1783. }

Fief of Madawaska originally established in 1683, under a Grant⎫
from the Government of Canada and uninterruptedly held of the ⎬[yellow-green
Government of Canada under the same title to the present Day. ⎭ flat tint]
  Madawaska Settlement commenced in 1783, and subject to the⎫
Jurisdiction of Great Britain from its establishment to the present⎬[blue-green
Day ⎭ flat tint]

The two major disputed areas are indicated on the British transcript of Map A by a reddish flat tint.

In North Eastern Boundary Arbitration, American Statements and Appendices (a printed volume, a copy of which is in the archives of the Department of State), is bound a copy of a map entitled "Map of the Northern Part of the State of Maine and of the Adjacent British Provinces, Shewing the portion of that State to which Great Britain lays claim. Reduced from the official Map A with corrections from the latest surveys by S. L. Dashiell. Washington 1830." The map has the inscription, "Engraved by B. Chambers." Within the neat lines this map measures 16 by 14½ inches. The scale, which is about 25 miles to an inch (1:1,584,000), is shown graphically. This Dashiell's Map of 1830 is a reduced engraving of the American transcript of Map A.

Dashiell's Map of 1830 was prepared under the direction of Albert Gallatin as one of the two maps to be "engraved and annexed to our Appendix, vizt a copy of part of Mitchell's and one reduced from Map A. Mr Deshiell received instructions respecting both" (D. S., Northeastern Boundary, envelope 8, letter of January 16, 1830, to Aaron Vail, of the Department of State). Gallatin considered the proof, proposed changes, and suggested the title of the map (*ibid.*, May 17, 1830, to the same).

It is Dashiell's Map which has sometimes been reproduced as the equivalent of Map A (as, e.g., in Senate Document No. 431, 25th Congress, 2d session, serial 318, where it is called Map A). Dashiell's Map is, of course, derived from Map A, and it similarly shows the boundary lines claimed by the two Governments, which are drawn in green for the United States and in red for Great Britain. A later edition of Dashiell's Map shows the boundary line of the Arbiter in yellow. It is that second edition, with the inscription, "B. Chambers, Engraver, Washington," which appears in the Senate document just mentioned; as the award of the King of the Netherlands was dated January 10, 1831, that edition must have been issued thereafter. A lithographed (approximate) reproduction of the second edition is in American State Papers, Foreign Relations, VI, between pages 820 and 821 (see also Moore, International Arbitrations, I, facing page 84).

There are various copies of both editions of Dashiell's Map in the archives of the Department of State.

EXECUTION OF THE CONVENTION

Various time limits, dating from the exchange of ratifications of the convention, April 2, 1828, were fixed by its terms.

Applications of either party to the other for authentic copies of public acts were to be made within six months (Article 3, paragraph 2); the transcripts of Map A and other maps and surveys, and all evidence aside from that within the reports and papers of the Commissioners under Article 5 of the Treaty of Ghent, were to be mutually communicated within nine months (Article 4, paragraph 3; Article 3, paragraph 1); the first statements of each party were to be mutually communicated within fifteen months (Article 2, paragraph 2); the second statements of each party were to be mutually communicated within twenty-one months (Article 2, paragraph 3); and all the statements, papers, maps, and documents were to be delivered to the Arbitrating Sovereign within two years, if by that time the Arbiter had consented to act (Article 5).

Pursuant to the act of April 17, 1828 (4 Statutes at Large, 262–63), Albert Gallatin, of Pennsylvania, and William Pitt Preble, of Maine, were appointed "Agents in the negotiation and upon the umpirage relating to the north-eastern boundary of the United States" (Executive Journal, III, 608–9; see also the act of March 2, 1829, 4 Statutes at Large, 344, making appropriation for the compensation of the two Agents).

The Arbiter was not named in the convention; and by Article 1 thereof the two Governments were to "proceed in concert, to the Choice of such Friendly Sovereign or State" as soon as the ratifications had been exchanged.

Agreement upon the Arbiter was reached at London. On February 20, 1828 (D. S., 12 Instructions, U. S. Ministers, 61–65), William B. Lawrence, Chargé d'Affaires at London, was authorized to agree to the Emperor of Russia, the King of Denmark, or the King of the Netherlands, and was instructed to exert himself to obtain the choice of one of those three sovereigns in the order in which they were named. In reporting the result in his despatch of June 22, 1828 (D. S., 35 Despatches, Great Britain, No. 45), Lawrence wrote that his own inquiries had also satisfied him "that, however equally unexceptionable might be the individual characters of the Sovereigns alluded to, there were in their different political positions, powerful considerations for inducing the United States to prefer Russia or Denmark to the Netherlands."

The procedure of choice made some difficulty. At the first conference that Lawrence had with Lord Dudley, British Secretary of State for Foreign Affairs, on the day of the exchange of ratifications, the latter suggested that Lawrence furnish him with a list from which the British Government might choose an arbiter. The instructions to Lawrence precluded him from agreeing to this method, and he proposed (*ibid.*):

that each of us should put on paper the name or names of one or two Sovereigns, (according as the one or other number might be agreed on,) and that our lists should then be compared and if it happened that the same power was selected by both, it should be the Arbiter, but, if otherwise, we should consider the Sovereigns or States selected by each to be in nomination and adopt such further proceedings, as might be expedient in order to effect a choice.

It seems that the question then went before the Cabinet, and a British counterproposal of procedure was made at the next meeting between Lawrence and Dudley, on May 12, as follows (*ibid.*):

That the names of all the powers of Christendom, from among whom there was any probability that a selection would be made, should be drawn from a box or glass and as they were respectively presented, we should each of us write on a separate piece of paper "yes" or "no," until we came to one in whom both concurred.

While the discussions were proceeding, Lord Aberdeen succeeded Lord Dudley at the Foreign Office, and the procedural agreement of June 14 and the choice resulting therefrom two days later are thus reported (*ibid.*):

Lord Aberdeen modified the proposition of Lord Dudley, so as to remove the objections which had hitherto prevented my acceding to it. This was effected by its being agreed that, on the first trial, each party should reserve himself till his first choice was drawn and that should both parties not have fixed in preference on the same Power, the operation should be repeated till a concurrence was obtained, it being understood that each party might continue to support the Sovereign or State in whose favour he had previously voted, but that he would not confine his assent, a second time, exclusively to one choice

As my instructions required, the Powers which were approved by me, on being drawn, were Russia and Denmark, though, contrary to my expectation, Lord Aberdeen negatived the Netherlands, both as his first and second choices, and indicated Sardinia and Austria, as the States which Great Britain was disposed to select.

After we had proceeded thus far, we were, as you will perceive, precisely in the same situation, as if my proposition made to Lord Dudley in the first instance had been acted on and, before a third ballot, I made an effort to induce an acceptance of one of the powers nominated by me, but without effect, Lord Aberdeen insisting on our proceeding according to the previous arrangement. On making another trial, we both signified our acceptance of the Netherlands, which thus became the Arbiter.

The agreement reached was referred to in an exchange of notes of June 17 and 18, 1828 (*ibid.*, enclosures 1 and 2).

The invitation to the King of the Netherlands was extended by similar notes on behalf of the two Governments, concurrently delivered to the Minister of Foreign Affairs of the Netherlands on January 12, 1829 (D. S., 8 Despatches, Netherlands, No. 4, January 22, 1829). The formal acceptance of the King of the Netherlands was under date of January 22 (*ibid.*, No. 5, January 23, 1829), following a verbal communication thereof by the King in person to Christopher Hughes, Chargé d'Affaires at Brussels, on the previous day (*ibid.*, No. 3, January 21, 1829).

The statements, papers, maps, and documents to be submitted by the two Governments to the Arbitrating Sovereign reached The Hague in March, 1830; and after "a careful scrutiny and collation of all the papers, maps, books, and documents" on both parts, they were on March 31 "simultaneously placed in the hands of the Secretary of State preparatory to their delivery to the King" of the Netherlands, in whose hands they were deposited by the representatives of the two Governments, Sir Charles Bagot, British Ambassador, and William

Pitt Preble, American Minister, on the following day, April 1, 1830 (D. S., 9 Despatches, Netherlands, No. 7, April 7, 1830), one day within the term of two years from the exchange of ratifications on April 2, 1828.

The "Statement on the Part of the United States of the Case Referred, in Pursuance of the Convention of 29th September, 1827, between the Said States and Great Britain, to His Majesty the King of the Netherlands, for His Decision Thereon" was "printed, but not published" at Washington in 1829; see Gallatin, The Right of the United States of America to the North-eastern Boundary, a work which was "principally extracted from the statements laid before the King of the Netherlands," and which was published at New York in 1840.

THE AWARD

The award of the Arbiter, or his "decision," as it is called in the convention, was rendered in French under date of January 10, 1831 and was delivered to William Pitt Preble, American Minister to the Netherlands (D. S., 9 Despatches, Netherlands, No. 30, January 16, 1831). An English translation thereof, in the handwriting of Aaron Vail, at that time a clerk in the Department of State, is with a copy of the award which Preble enclosed with his despatch of January 16 (*ibid.*) and is printed in the Senate document of December 7, 1831 (Senate Confidential Document, 22d Congress, 1st session, Regular Confidential Documents, I, 655–61). The text of the award, in French, printed literally from the original in the archives of the Department of State, with the translation from the Senate print above mentioned, is as follows:

[Translation]

Nous Guillaume, par la grace de Dieu, Roi des Pays-Bas, Prince d'Orange-Nassau, Grand Duc de Luxembourg, &ᵃ &ᵃ &ᵃ

Aÿant accepté les fonctions d'arbitrateur, qui Nous ont été conférées par la note du Chargé d'Affaires des Etats Unis d'Amérique, et par celle de l'Ambassadeur extraordinaire et plénipotentiaire de la Grande Bretagne, à Notre Ministre des Affaires Etrangères, en date du 12 Janvier 1829, d'après l'art: V du traité de Gand, du 24 Décembre 1814, et l'art: I de la convention conclue entre ces Puissances à Londres le 29 Septembre 1827, dans le différend, qui s'est élevé entre Elles au sujet des limites de leurs possessions respectives.

Animés du désir sincère de répondre par une décision scrupuleuse, et impartiale à la confiance, qu'Elles Nous ont témoignée, et de leur donner ainsi

William, by the grace of God King of the Netherlands, Prince of Orange Nassau, Grand Duke of Luxemburg, etc.

Having accepted the functions of arbitrator conferred upon Us by the note of the Chargé d'Affaires of the United States of America and by that of the Ambassador Extraordinary and Plenipotentiary of Great Britain to Our Minister of Foreign Affairs under date of the 12th January, 1829, agreeably to the fifth article of the Treaty of Ghent of the 24th December, 1814, and to the first article of the convention concluded between those powers at London on the 29th of September, 1827, in the difference which has arisen between them on the subject of the boundaries of their respective possessions;

Animated by a sincere desire of answering, by a scrupulous and impartial decision, the confidence they have testified to Us, and thus to give them a

un nouveau gage du haut prix, que Nous ÿ attachons.

Ayant à cet effet dûment examiné, et mûrement pesé le contenu du premier exposé, ainsi que de l'exposé définitif du dit différend, que Nous ont respectivement remis le premier Avril de l'année 1830 l'Envoÿé extraordinaire et Ministre plénipotentiaire des Etats Unis d'Amérique, et l'Ambassadeur extraordinaire et plénipotentiaire de Sa Majesté Britannique, avec toutes les pièces, qui ÿ ont été jointes à l'appui.

Voulant accomplir aujourd'hui les obligations, que Nous venons de contracter par l'acceptation des fonctions d'arbitrateur dans le susdit différend, en portant à la connaissance des deux hautes parties intéressées le résultat de Notre examen, et Notre opinion sur les trois points, dans lesquels se divise de leur commun accord la contestation.

Considérant, que les trois points précités doivent être jugés d'après les traités, actes et conventions conclus entre les deux Puissances, savoir le traité de paix de 1783, le traité d'amitié, de commerce et de navigation de 1794, la déclaration relative à la rivière Sᵗ Croix de 1798, le traité de paix signé à Gand en 1814, la convention du 29 Septembre 1827 et la carte de Mitchell, et la carte A citées dans cette convention.

Déclarons, que Quant au premier point, savoir la question, quel est l'endroit désigné dans les traités, comme l'Angle Nord-Ouest de la nouvelle Ecosse, et quels sont les highlands séparant les rivières, qui se déchargent dans le fleuve Sᵗ Laurent, de celles tombant dans l'Océan Atlantique, le long desquels doit être tirée la ligne de limites depuis cet Angle jusqu'à la source Nord Ouest de la rivière Connecticut.

Considérant: que les hautes parties intéressées réclament respectivement cette ligne de limites au midi et au nord de la rivière Sᵗ John, et ont indiqué chacune sur la Carte A la ligne, qu'elles demandent.

Considérant: que selon les exemples allégués, le terme highlands s'applique non seulement à un paÿs montueux, ou élevé, mais encore à un terrain, qui, sans être montueux, sépare des eaux coulant dans une direction différente,

new proof of the high value We attach to it;

Having to that effect duly examined and maturely weighed the contents of the first statement, as well as those of the definitive statement of the said difference, which have been respectively delivered to Us on the 1st of April of the year 1830 by the Envoy Extraordinary and Minister Plenipotentiary of the United States of America and the Ambassador Extraordinary and Plenipotentiary of His Britannic Majesty, with all the documents thereto annexed in support of them;

Desirous of fulfilling at this time the obligations We have contracted in accepting the functions of arbitrator in the aforesaid difference, by laying before the two high interested parties the result of Our examination and Our opinion on the three points into which, by common accord, the contestation is divided;

Considering that the three points above mentioned ought to be decided according to the treaties, acts, and conventions concluded between the two powers, that is to say, the Treaty of Peace of 1783, the Treaty of Friendship, Commerce, and Navigation of 1794, the declaration relative to the River St. Croix of 1798, the Treaty of Peace signed at Ghent in 1814, the convention of the 29th September, 1827, and Mitchell's Map and the Map A referred to in that convention;

We declare that, as to the first point, to wit, the question, Which is the place designated in the treaties as the northwest angle of Nova Scotia, and what are the highlands dividing the rivers that empty themselves into the River St. Lawrence from those which fall into the Atlantic Ocean, along which is to be drawn the line of boundary from that angle to the northwesternmost head of Connecticut River?—

Considering that the high interested parties respectively claim that line of boundary at the south and at the north of the River St. John and have each indicated upon the Map A the line which they claim;

Considering that, according to the instances alleged, the term "highlands" applies not only to a hilly or elevated country, but also to land which, without being hilly, divides waters flowing in different directions; and that thus

et qu'ainsi le caractère plus ou moins montueux, et élevé du paÿs, à travers lequel sont tirées les deux lignes respectivement réclamées au Nord et au Midi de la rivière St John, ne saurait faire la base d'une option entre elles.

Que le texte du second article du traité de paix de 1783 reproduit en partie les expressions, dont on s'est antérieurement servi dans la proclamation de 1763, et dans l'acte de Quebec de 1774, pour indiquer les limites méridionales du Gouvernement de Quebec, depuis le lac Champlain, "in fortÿ-five degrees of North latitude "along the highlands, which divide "the rivers, that emptÿ themselves "into the river St Lawrence, from "those, which fall into the Sea, & also "along the North coast of the baÿ des "Chaleurs."

Qu'en 1763, 1765, 1773 et 1782 il a été établi, que la nouvelle Ecosse serait bornée au Nord jusqu'à l'extrêmité Occidentale de la baie des Chaleurs par la limite méridionale de la province de Quebec, que cette délimitation se retrouve pour la province de Quebec dans la commission du Gouverneur Général de Quebec de 1786, où l'on à fait usage des termes de la proclamation de 1763, et de l'acte de Quebec de 1774, et dans les Commissions de 1786 et postérieures des Gouverneurs du nouveau Brunswick pour cette dernière province, ainsi que dans un grand nombre de Cartes antérieures, et postérieures au traité de 1783.

et que l'article premier du dit traité cite nominativement les Etats, dont l'indépendance est reconnue:

Mais que cette mention n'implique point l'entière coïncidence des limites entre les deux Puissances, réglées par l'article suivant, avec l'ancienne délimitation des provinces Anglaises, dont le maintien n'est pas mentionné dans le traité de 1783, et qui par ses variations continuelles, et par l'incertitude, qui continua d'exister à son égard, provoqua de temps à autre des différends entre les autorités provinciales.

Qu'il résulte de la ligne tirée par le traité de 1783 à travers les grands lacs à l'Ouest du fleuve St Laurent, une déviation des anciennes chartes provinciales, en ce qui concerne les limites.

the character more or less hilly and elevated of the country through which are drawn the two lines respectively claimed, at the north and at the south of the River St. John, cannot form the basis of a choice between them;

That the text of the second article of the treaty of 1783 recites, in part, the words previously used in the proclamation of 1763 and in the Quebec Act of 1774 to indicate the southern boundaries of the Government of Quebec from Lake Champlain, "in forty-five degrees of north latitude, along the highlands which divide the rivers that empty themselves into the River St. Lawrence from those which fall into the sea, and also along the north coast of the Bay des Chaleurs";

That in 1763, 1765, 1773, and 1782, it was established that Nova Scotia should be bounded at the north, as far as the western extremity of the Bay des Chaleurs, by the southern boundary of the Province of Quebec; that this delimitation is again found, with respect to the Province of Quebec, in the commission of the Governor General of Quebec of 1786, wherein the language of the proclamation of 1763 and of the Quebec Act of 1774 has been used, as also in the commissions of 1786 and others of subsequent dates, of the Governors of New Brunswick, with respect to the last-mentioned Province, as well as in a great number of maps anterior and posterior to the treaty of 1783;

And that the first article of the said treaty specifies by name the States whose independence is acknowledged; But that this mention does not imply (implique) the entire coincidence of the boundaries between the two powers, as settled by the following article, with the ancient delimitation of the British Provinces, whose preservation is not mentioned in the treaty of 1783 and which, owing to its continual changes and the uncertainty which continued to exist respecting it, created, from time to time, differences between the provincial authorities;

That there results from the line drawn under the treaty of 1783, through the Great Lakes west of the River St. Lawrence, a departure from the ancient provincial charters with regard to those boundaries;

Qu'on chercherait en vain à s'expliquer; pourquoi, si l'on entendait maintenir l'ancienne délimitation provinciale, l'on a précisément fait usage dans la négociation de 1783 de la carte de Mitchell, publiée en 1755, et par conséquent antérieure à la proclamation de 1763, et à l'acte de Quebec de 1774.

Que la Grande Brétagne proposa d'abord la rivière Piscataqua pour limite à l'est des Etats Unis, et ensuite n'accepta pas la proposition de faire fixer plus tard la limite du Maine, ou de Massachusetts baÿ.

Que le traité de Gand stipula un nouvel examen sur les lieux, lequel ne pouvait s'appliquer à une limite historique, ou administrative.

et que dès lors l'ancienne délimitation des provinces Anglaises n'offre pas non plus une base de décision.

Que la longitude de l'angle Nord-Ouest de la nouvelle Ecosse, laquelle doit coïncider avec celle de la source de la rivière St Croix, fut seulement fixée par la déclaration de 1798, qui indiqua cette rivière.

Que le traité d'amitié, de commerce et de navigation de 1794 mentionne le doute, qui s'était élevé à l'égard de la rivière St Croix, et que les premières instructions du Congrès lors des négociations, dont résulta le traité de 1783, placent le dit angle à la source de la rivière St John.

Que la latitude de cet angle se trouve sur les bords du St Laurent selon la carte de Mitchell, reconnue pour avoir réglé le travail combiné, et officiel des négociateurs du traité de 1783, au lieu qu'en vertu de la délimitation du Gouvernement de Quebec, l'on devrait la chercher aux highlands séparant les rivières, qui se déchargent dans la rivière St Laurent, de celles tombant dans la mer.

Que la nature du terrain à l'est de l'angle précité n'aÿant pas été indiquée dans le traité de 1783, il ne s'en laisse pas tirer d'argument pour le fixer de préférence dans tel endroit plutôt que dans un autre.

Qu'au surplus si l'on croÿait devoir le rapprocher de la source de la rivière St Croix, et le chercher par exemple à Mars hill, il serait d'autant plus pos-

That one would vainly attempt to explain why, if the intention was to retain the ancient provincial boundary, Mitchell's Map, published in 1755 and consequently anterior to the proclamation of 1763 and to the Quebec Act of 1774, was precisely the one used in the negotiation of 1783;

That Great Britain proposed, at first the River Piscataqua as the eastern boundary of the United States and did not subsequently agree to the proposition to cause the boundary of Maine, or Massachusetts Bay, to be ascertained at a later period;

That the Treaty of Ghent stipulated for a new examination on the spot, which could not be made applicable to an historical or administrative boundary;

And that, therefore, the ancient delimitation of the British Provinces does not either afford the basis of a decision;

That the longitude of the northwest angle of Nova Scotia, which ought to coincide with that of the source of the St. Croix River, was determined only by the declaration of 1798, which indicated that river;

That the Treaty of Friendship, Commerce, and Navigation of 1794 alludes to the doubt which had arisen with respect to the River St. Croix; and that the first instructions of the Congress at the time of the negotiations which resulted in the treaty of 1783, locate the said angle at the source of the River St. John;

That the latitude of that angle is upon the banks of the St. Lawrence, according to Mitchell's Map, which is acknowledged to have regulated the combined and official labors of the negotiators of the treaty of 1783, whereas, agreeably to the delimitation of the Government of Quebec, it is to be looked for at the highlands which divide the rivers that empty themselves into the River St. Lawrence from those which fall into the sea;

That the nature of the ground east of the before-mentioned angle not having been indicated by the treaty of 1783, no argument can be drawn from it to locate that angle at one place in preference to another;

That, at all events, if it were deemed proper to place it nearer to the source of the River St. Croix and look for it at Mars Hill for instance, it would

sible, que la limite du nouveau Brunswick tirée de là au Nord-Est donnat à
cette province plusieurs angles Nord-
Ouest, situés davantage au Nord, et à
l'Est selon leur plus grand éloignement de Mars hill, que le nombre de
degrés de l'angle mentionné dans le
traité a été passé sous silence.

Que par conséquent l'angle Nord-
Ouest de la nouvelle Ecosse, dont il
est ici question, aÿant été inconnu en
1783, et le traité de Gand l'aÿant
encore déclaré non constaté, la mention de cet angle historique dans le
traité de 1783 doit être considérée
comme une pétition de principe, qui ne
présente aucune base de décision,
tandis que si on l'envisage comme un
point topographique, eû égard à la
définition "viz, that angle, which is
"formed bÿ a line drawn due north
"from the source of the St Croix
"river to the highlands," il forme
simplement l'extrêmité de la ligne
"along the said highlands, which
"divide those rivers, that emptÿ
"themselves into the river St Law-
"rence, from those which fall into the
"Atlantic Ocean" extrêmité que la
mention de l'angle Nord-Ouest de la
nouvelle Ecosse ne contribue pas à
constater, et qui étant à trouver elle
même ne saurait mener à la découverte
de la ligne, qu'elle termine.

enfin que les argumens tirés des droits
de souveraineté exercés sur le fief de
Madawaska, et sur le Madawaska settlement, admis même que cet exercice
fut suffisamment prouvé, ne peuvent
point décider la question, par la raison
que ces deux établissemens n'embras-
sent qu'un terrain partiel de celui en
litige, que les hautes parties intéressées
ont reconnu le paÿs situé entre les lignes
respectivement réclamées par elles,
comme fesant un objet de contestation, et qu'ainsi la possession ne saurait
être censée déroger au droit, et que si l'on
écarte l'ancienne délimitation des provinces alléguée en faveur de la ligne réclamée au Nord de la rivière St John,
et spécialement celle mentionnée dans
la proclamation de 1763, et dans l'acte
de Quebec de 1774, l'on ne saurait
admettre à l'appui de la ligne demandée
au midi de la rivière St John, des
argumens tendant à prouver, que telle
partie du terrain litigieux appartient au
Canada, ou au nouveau Brunswick.

be so much the more possible that the
boundary of New Brunswick, drawn
thence northeastwardly, would give to
that Province several northwest angles,
situated farther north and east, according to their greater remoteness
from Mars Hill, from the fact that the
number of degrees of the angle referred
to in the treaty has not been mentioned;

That, consequently, the northwest
angle of Nova Scotia here alluded to
having been unknown in 1783, and the
Treaty of Ghent having again declared
it to be unascertained, the mention of
that historical angle in the treaty of
1783 is to be considered as a petition
of principle (pétition de principe),
affording no basis for a decision; whereas, if considered as a topographical
point having reference to the definition,
viz, "That Angle which is formed by a
Line drawn due North from the Source
of St. Croix River to the Highlands,"
it forms simply the extremity of the
line "along the said Highlands which
divide those Rivers that empty themselves into the River St. Lawrence,
from those which fall into the Atlantic
Ocean"—an extremity which a reference to the northwest angle of Nova
Scotia does not contribute to ascertain
and which, still remaining itself to be
found, cannot lead to the discovery of
the line which it is to terminate;

Lastly, that the arguments deduced
from the rights of sovereignty exercised over the Fief of Madawaska and
over the Madawaska settlement, even
admitting that such exercise were
sufficiently proved, cannot decide the
question, for the reason that those two
settlements only embrace a portion of
the territory in dispute, and that the
high interested parties have acknowledged the country lying between the
two lines respectively claimed by them
as constituting a subject of contestation, and that, therefore, possession
cannot be considered as derogating
from the right; and that, if the ancient
delimitation of the provinces be set
aside, which is adduced in support of
the line claimed at the north of the
River St. John and especially that
which is mentioned in the proclamation of 1763 and in the Quebec Act of
1774, no argument can be admitted in
support of the line claimed at the south
of the River St. John, which would
tend to prove that such part of the
territory in dispute belongs to Canada
or to New Brunswick;

Considérant: que la question dépouillée des argumens non décisifs tirés du caractère plus ou moins montueux du terrain, de l'ancienne délimitation des provinces, de l'angle Nord Ouest de la nouvelle Écosse, et de l'état de possession, se réduit en dernière analÿse à celles-ci, quelle est la ligne tirée droit au Nord depuis la source de la rivière St Croix, et quel est le terrain, n'importe qu'il soit montueux et élevé, ou non, qui depuis cette ligne jusqu'à la source Nord-Ouest de la rivière Connecticut, sépare les rivières se déchargeant dans le fleuve St Laurent, de celles, qui tombent dans l'Océan Atlantique; que les hautes parties intéressées ne sont d'accord, que sur la circonstance, que la limite à trouver doit être déterminée par une telle ligne, et par un tel terrain, qu'elles le sont encore depuis la déclaration de 1798 sur la réponse à faire à la première question, à l'exception de la latitude, à laquelle la ligne tirée droit au Nord de la source de la rivière St Croix doit se terminer, que cette latitude coïncide avec l'extrêmité du terrain, qui depuis cette ligne jusqu'à la source Nord-Ouest de la rivière Connecticut sépare les rivières, se déchargeant dans le fleuve St Laurent, de celles, qui tombent dans l'Océan Atlantique, et que dès lors il ne reste, qu'à déterminer ce terrain.

Qu'en se livrant à cette opération, on trouve d'un côté

d'abord, que si par l'adoption de la ligne réclamée au Nord de la rivière St John, la Grande Brétagne ne pourrait pas être estimée obtenir un terrain de moindre valeur, que si elle eut accepté en 1783 la rivière St John pour frontière, eû égard à la situation du paÿs entre les rivières St John et St Croix dans le voisinage de la mer, et à la possession des deux rives de la rivière St John dans la dernière partie de son cours, cette compensation serait cependant détruite par l'interruption de la communication entre le Bas Canada, et le nouveau Brunswick, spécialement entre Quebec et Fredericton, et qu'on chercherait vainement, quels motifs auraient déterminé la Cour de Londres à consentir à une semblable interruption.

Que si, en second lieu, en opposition aux rivières se déchargeant dans le fleuve St Laurent, on aurait convenablement d'après le langage usité en géographie, pu comprendre les rivières

Considering that the question, divested of the inconclusive arguments drawn from the nature, more or less hilly, of the ground, from the ancient delimitation of the Provinces, from the northwest angle of Nova Scotia, and from the actual possession, resolves itself in the end to these: Which is the line drawn due north from the source of the River St. Croix, and which is the ground, no matter whether hilly and elevated or not, which, from that line to the northwesternmost head of Connecticut River, divides the rivers that empty themselves into the River St. Lawrence from those which fall into the Atlantic Ocean?—that the high interested parties only agree upon the fact that the boundary sought for must be determined by such a line and by such a ground; that they further agree, since the declaration of 1798, as to the answer to be given to the first question, with the exception of the latitude at which the line drawn due north from the source of the St. Croix River is to terminate; that said latitude coincides with the extremity of the ground which, from that line to the northwesternmost source of Connecticut River, divides the rivers which empty themselves into the River St. Lawrence from those which fall into the Atlantic Ocean; and that, therefore, it only remains to ascertain that ground;

That, on entering upon this operation, it is discovered, on the one hand,

First, that if, by adopting the line claimed at the north of the River St. John, Great Britain cannot be considered as obtaining a territory of less value than if she had accepted in 1783 the River St. John as her frontier, taking into view the situation of the country situated between the Rivers St. John and St. Croix in the vicinity of the sea, and the possession of both banks of the River St. John in the lower part of its course, said equivalent would, nevertheless, be destroyed by the interruption of the communication between lower Canada and New Brunswick, especially between Quebec and Fredericton; and one would vainly seek to discover what motive could have determined the Court of London to consent to such an interruption;

That if, in the second place, in contradistinction to the rivers that empty themselves into the River St. Lawrence, it had been proper, agreeably to the language ordinarily used in geography,

tombant dans les baies de Fundÿ et des Chaleurs, avec celles se jettant directement dans l'Océan Atlantique, dans la dénomination générique de rivière tombant dans l'Océan Atlantique, il serait hasardeux de ranger dans l'espèce parmi cette catégorie les rivières St John et Ristigouche, que la ligne réclamée au Nord de la rivière St John sépare immédiatement des rivières se déchargeant dans le fleuve St Laurent, non pas avec d'autres rivières coulant dans l'Océan Atlantique, mais seules, et d'appliquer ainsi, en interprétant la délimitation fixée par un traité, où chaque expression doit compter, à deux cas exclusivement spéciaux, et où il ne s'agit pas du genre, une expression générique, qui leur assignerait un sens plus large, ou qui, étendue aux Scoudiac Lakes, Penobscot et Kennebec, qui se jettent directement dans l'Océan Atlantique, établirait le principe, que le traité de 1783 a entendu des highlands séparant aussi bien médiatement, qu'immédiatement, les rivières se déchargeant dans le fleuve St Laurent, de celles, qui tombent dans l'Océan Atlantique, principe également réalisé par les deux lignes.

Troisièmement, que la ligne réclamée au Nord de la rivière St John ne sépare pas même immédiatement les rivières se déchargeant dans le fleuve St Laurent, des rivières St John et Ristigouche, mais seulement des rivières, qui se jettent dans le St John et Ristigouche, à l'exception de la dernière partie de cette ligne près des sources de la rivière St John, et qu'ainsi pour arriver à l'Océan Atlantique les rivières séparées par cette ligne de celles se déchargeant dans le fleuve St Laurent, ont chacune besoin de deux intermédiaires, savoir les unes de la rivière St John, et de la baie Fundÿ, et les autres de la rivière Ristigouche, et de la baie des Chaleurs.

et de l'autre: qu'on ne peut expliquer suffisamment, comment si les hautes parties contractantes ont entendu établir en 1783 la limite au midi de la rivière St John, cette rivière, à laquelle le terrain litigieux doit en grande partie son caractère distinctif, a été neutralisée, et mise hors de cause.

Que le verbe "divide" parait exiger la contiguïté des objets, qui doivent être "divided.

to comprehend the rivers falling into the Bays of Fundy and des Chaleurs with those emptying themselves directly into the Atlantic Ocean in the generical denomination of rivers falling into the Atlantic Ocean, it would be hazardous to include into the species belonging to that class the Rivers St. John and Ristigouche, which the line claimed at the north of the River St. John divides immediately from rivers emptying themselves into the River St. Lawrence, not with other rivers falling into the Atlantic Ocean, but alone; and thus to apply, in interpreting the delimitation established by a treaty, where each word must have a meaning, to two exclusively special cases, and, where no mention is made of the genus (genre), a generical expression which would ascribe to them a broader meaning; or which, if extended to the Schoodiac Lakes, the Penobscot, and the Kennebec, which empty themselves directly into the Atlantic Ocean, would establish the principle that the treaty of 1783 meant highlands which divide, as well mediately as immediately, the rivers that empty themselves into the River St. Lawrence from those which fall into the Atlantic Ocean—a principle equally realized by both lines;

Thirdly, that the line claimed at the north of the River St. John does not divide, even immediately, the rivers that empty themselves into the River St. Lawrence from the Rivers St. John and Ristigouche, but only rivers that empty themselves into the St. John and Ristigouche, with the exception of the last part of said line, near the sources of the River St. John; and that hence, in order to reach the Atlantic Ocean, the rivers divided by that line from those that empty themselves into the River St. Lawrence, each need two intermediate channels, to wit, the ones, the River St. John and the Bay of Fundy, and the others, the River Ristigouche and the Bay of Chaleurs;

And, on the other hand, that it cannot be sufficiently explained how, if the high contracting parties intended in 1783 to establish the boundary at the south of the River St. John, that river, to which the territory in dispute is in a great measure indebted for its distinctive character, has been neutralized and set aside;

That the verb "divide" appears to require the contiguity of the objects to be "divided";

Que la dite limite forme seulement à son extrêmité occidentale la séparation immédiate entre la rivière Mettjarmette, et la source Nord Ouest du Penobscot, et ne sépare que médiatement les rivieres se déchargeant dans le fleuve St Laurent, des eaux du Kennebec, du Penobscot, et des Scoudiac Lakes, tandis que la limite réclameé au Nord de la rivière St John sépare immédiatement les eaux des rivières Ristigouche et St John, et médiatement les Scoudiac lakes et les eaux des rivières Penobscot et Kennebec, des rivières se déchargeant dans le fleuve St Laurent, savoir les rivières Beaver, Metis, Rimouskÿ, Trois pistoles, Green, du Loup, Kamouraska, Ouelle, Bras St Nicolas, du Sud, la Famine et Chaudière,

Que même en mettant hors de cause les rivières Ristigouche et St John, par le motif, qu'elles ne pourraient être censées tomber dans l'Océan Atlantique, la ligne Septentrionale se trouverait encore aussi près des Scoudiac lakes, et des eaux du Penobscot, et du Kennebec, que la ligne méridionale des rivières Beaver, Metis, Rimouskÿ et autres, se déchargeant dans le fleuve St Laurent, et formerait aussi bien que l'autre une séparation médiate entre celles ci, et les rivières tombant dans l'Océan Atlantique.

Que la rencontre antérieure de la limite méridionale, lorsque de la source de la rivière St Croix, on tire une ligne au Nord, pourrait seulement lui assurer un avantage accessoire sur l'autre, dans le cas, où l'une et l'autre limite réunissent au même degré les qualités exigées par les traités.

et que le sort assigné par celui de 1783 au Connecticut, et au St Laurent même, écarte la supposition, que les deux Puissances auraient voulu faire tomber la totalité de chaque rivière, depuis son origine jusqu'à son embouchure, en partage à l'une, ou à l'autre.

Considérant: Que d'après ce qui précède, les argumens allégués de part et d'autre, et les pièces exhibées à l'appui ne peuvent être estimés assez prépondérans pour déterminer la préférence en faveur d'une des deux lignes, respectivement réclamées par les hautes parties intéressées, comme limites de leur possessions depuis la source de la rivière St Croix jusqu'à la source

That the said boundary forms at its western extremity only the immediate separation between the River Mettjarmette and the northwesternmost head of the Penobscot and divides, mediately, only the rivers that empty themselves into the River St. Lawrence from the waters of the Kennebec, Penobscot, and Schoodiac Lakes; while the boundary claimed at the north of the River St. John divides immediately the waters of the Rivers Ristigouche and St. John, and mediately the Schoodiac Lakes and the waters of the Rivers Penobscot and Kennebec, from the rivers that empty themselves into the River St. Lawrence, to wit, the Rivers Beaver, Metis, Rimousky, Trois Pistoles, Green, Du Loup, Kamouraska, Ouelle, Bras St. Nicholas, Du Sud, La Famine, and Chaudière;

That, even setting aside the Rivers Ristigouche and St. John, for the reason that they could not be considered as falling into the Atlantic Ocean, the northern line would still be as near the Schoodiac Lakes and to the waters of the Penobscot and of the Kennebec, as the southern line would be to the the Rivers Beaver, Metis, Rimousky, and others that empty themselves into the River St. Lawrence, and would, as well as the other, form a mediate separation between these and the rivers falling into the Atlantic Ocean;

That the prior intersection of the southern boundary by a line drawn due north from the source of the St. Croix River could only secure to it an accessary advantage over the other, in case both the one and the other boundary should combine, in the same degree, the qualities required by the treaties;

And that the fate assigned by that of 1783 to the Connecticut, and even to the St. Lawrence, precludes the supposition that the two powers could have intended to surrender the whole course of each river from its source to its mouth to the share of either the one or the other;

Considering that after what precedes, the arguments adduced on either side and the documents exhibited in support of them cannot be considered as sufficiently preponderating to determine a preference in favor of one of the two lines respectively claimed by the high interested parties as the boundaries of their possessions from the source of the River St. Croix to the northwestern-

Nord Ouest de la rivière Connecticut; et que la nature du différend, et les stipulations vagues, et non suffisamment déterminées du traité de 1783 n'admettent pas d'adjuger l'une ou l'autre de ces lignes à l'une des dites parties, sans blesser les principes au droit, et de l'équité envers l'autre.

Considérant: que la question se réduit, comme il a été exprimé ci-dessus à un choix à faire du terrain séparant les rivières, se déchargeant dans le fleuve St Laurent de celles, qui tombent dans l'Océan Atlantique, que les hautes parties intéressées se sont entendues à l'égard du cours des eaux, indiqué de commun accord sur la Carte A, et présentant le seul élément de décision.

et que dès lors les circonstances, dont dépend cette décision, ne sauraient être éclaircies davantage, au moyen de nouvelles recherches topographiques, ni par la production de pièces nouvelles.

Nous sommes d'avis: Qu'il conviendra d'adopter pour limite des deux Etats une ligne tirée droit au Nord depuis la source de la rivière St Croix jusqu'au point, où elle coupe le milieu du thalweg de la rivière St John, de là le milieu du thalweg de cette rivière en la remontant jusqu'au point, où la rivière St Francis se décharge dans la rivière St John, de là le milieu du thalweg de la rivière St Francis en la remontant jusqu'à la source de sa branche la plus Sud Ouest, laquelle source Nous indiquons sur la Carte A par la lettre X, authentiquée par la signature de Notre ministre des affaires étrangères, de là une ligne tirée droit à l'Ouest jusqu'au point, où elle se réunit à la ligne réclamée par les Etats Unis d'Amérique, et tracée sur la Carte A, de là cette ligne jusqu'au point, où d'après cette Carte, elle coïncide avec celle demandée par la Grande Brétagne, et de là la ligne indiquée sur la dite carte par les deux Puissances jusqu'à la source la plus Nord Ouest de la rivière Connecticut.

Quant au second point, savoir la question, quelle est la source la plus Nord Ouest ./. North Western most head ./. de la rivière Connecticut.

Considérant: Que pour résoudre cette question, il s'agit d'opter entre la

most head of the Connecticut River; and that the nature of the difference and the vague and not sufficiently determinate stipulations of the treaty of 1783 do not permit to adjudge either of those lines to one of the said parties without wounding the principles of law and equity with regard to the other;

Considering that, as has already been said, the question resolves itself into a selection to be made of a ground dividing the rivers that empty themselves into the River St. Lawrence from those that fall into the Atlantic Ocean; that the high interested parties are agreed with regard to the course of the streams delineated by common accord on the Map A and affording the only basis of a decision;

And that, therefore, the circumstances upon which such decision depends could not be further elucidated by means of fresh topographical investigation, nor by the production of additional documents;

We are of opinion that it will be suitable (il conviendra) to adopt, as the boundary of the two states, a line drawn due north from the source of the River St. Croix to the point where it intersects the middle of the thalweg* of the River St. John; thence, the middle of the thalweg of that river, ascending it to the point where the River St. Francis empties into the River St. John; thence, the middle of the thalweg of the River St. Francis, ascending it to the source of its southwesternmost branch, which source We indicate on the Map A by the letter X, authenticated by the signature of Our Minister of Foreign Affairs; thence, a line drawn due west to the point where it unites with the line claimed by the United States of America and delineated on the Map A; thence, said line, to the point at which, according to said map, it coincides with that claimed by Great Britain; and thence, the line traced on the map by the two powers, to the northwesternmost source of Connecticut River.

As regards the second point, to wit, the question, Which is the northwesternmost head of the Connecticut River?—

Considering that, in order to solve this question it is necessary to choose

---

Thalweg, a German compound word: *Thal*, valley; *Weg*, way. It means here the deepest channel of the river.—TRANSLATOR.

rivière du Connecticut lake, Perry's Stream, Indian Stream, et Hall's Stream.

Considérant: Que d'après l'usage adopté en géographie, la source et le lit d'une rivière sont indiqués par le nom de la rivière attaché à cette source, et à ce lit, et par leur plus grande importance relative comparée à celle d'autres eaux, communiquant avec cette rivière.

Considérant: Qu'une lettre officielle de 1772 mentionne déjà le nom de Hull's brook, et que dans une lettre officielle postérieure de la même année du même inspecteur, on trouve Hall's brook représenté comme une petite rivière tombant dans le Connecticut.

Que la rivière, dans laquelle se trouve Connecticut lake, paraît plus considérable, que Hall's, Indian, ou Perry's stream, que le Connecticut lake, et les deux lacs situés au Nord de celui-ci, semblent lui assigner un plus grand volume d'eau, qu'aux trois autres rivières, et qu'en l'admettant comme le lit du Connecticut, on prolonge davantage ce fleuve, que si l'on donnait la préférence à une de ces trois autres rivières.

enfin que la Carte A ayant été reconnue dans la convention de 1827 comme indiquant le cours des eaux, l'autorité de cette Carte semble s'étendre également à leur dénomination, vu qu'en cas de contestation tel nom de rivière, ou de lac, sur lequel on n'eut pas été d'accord, eut pu avoir été omis, que la dite Carte mentionne Connecticut lake, et que le nom de Connecticut lake implique l'application du nom Connecticut à la rivière, qui traverse le dit lac.

Nous sommes d'avis: que le ruisseau situé le plus au Nord-Ouest de ceux, qui coulent dans le plus Septentrional des trois lacs, dont le dernier porte le nom de Connecticut-lake, doit être considéré comme la source la plus Nord-Ouest ./. North Western most head ./. du Connecticut.

Et quant au troisième point, savoir la question, quelle est la limite à tracer depuis la rivière Connecticut le long du parallèle du 45° degré de latitude Septentrionale, jusqu'au fleuve St Laurent, nommé dans les traités Iroquois, ou Cataraguÿ.

Considérant: que les hautes parties intéressées diffèrent d'opinion, sur la

between Connecticut Lake River, Perry's Stream, Indian Stream, and Hall's Stream;

Considering that, according to the usage adopted in geography, the source and the bed of a river are denoted by the name of the river which is attached to such source and to such bed, and by their greater relative importance as compared to that of other waters communicating with said river;

Considering that an official letter of 1772 already mentions the name of Hall's Brook, and that in an official letter of subsequent date, in the same year, Hall's Brook is represented as a small river falling into the Connecticut;

That the river in which Connecticut Lake is situated appears more considerable than either Hall's, Indian, or Perry's Stream; that Connecticut Lake and the two lakes situated northward of it seem to ascribe to it a greater volume of water than to the other three rivers; and that, by admitting it to be the bed of the Connecticut, the course of that river is extended farther than it would be if a preference were given to either of the other three rivers;

Lastly, that the Map A, having been recognized by the convention of 1827 as indicating the courses of streams, the authority of that map would likewise seem to extend to their appellation, since, in case of dispute, such name of river or lake, respecting which the parties were not agreed, may have been omitted; that said map mentions Connecticut Lake; and that the name of Connecticut Lake implies the applicability of the name of Connecticut to the river which flows through the said lake;

We are of opinion that the stream situated farthest to the northwest among those which fall into the northernmost of the three lakes, the last of which bears the name of Connecticut Lake, must be considered as the northwesternmost head of Connecticut River.

And as to the third point, to wit, the question, Which is the boundary to be traced from the River Connecticut, along the parallel of the forty-fifth degree of north latitude, to the River St. Lawrence, named in the treaties "Iroquois" or "Cataraguy"?—

Considering that the high interested parties differ in opinion as to the ques-

question de savoir, si les traités exigent un nouveau levé de toute la ligne de limite depuis la rivière Connecticut, jusqu'au fleuve St Laurent, nommé dans les traités Iroquois ou Cataraguÿ, ou bien seulement le complément des anciens levés provinciaux.

Considérant. que le cinquième article du traité de Gand de 1814, ne stipule point, qu'on levera telle partie des limites, qui n'aurait pas été levée jusqu'ici, mais déclare que les limites n'ont pas été levées, et établit, qu'elles le seront.

Qu'en effet ce levé dans les rapports entre les deux Puissances doit être censé n'avoir pas eû lieu depuis le Connecticut jusqu'à la rivière St Laurent, nommée dans les traités Iroquois ou Cataraquÿ, vu que l'ancien levé s'est trouvé inexact, et avait été ordonné non par les deux Puissances d'un commun accord, mais par les anciennes autorités provinciales.

Qu'il est d'usage de suivre en fixant la latitude, le principe de latitude observée, et que le Gouvernement des Etats Unis d'Amérique a établi certaines fortifications à l'endroit dit Rouse's point, dans la persuasion, que le terrain fesait partie de leur territoire, persuasion suffisamment légitimée par la ligne réputée jusqu'alors correspondre avec le 45e degré de latitude Septentrionale.

Nous sommes d'avis: Qu'il conviendra de procéder à de nouvelles opérations pour mesurer la latitude observée, afin de tracer la limite depuis la rivière Connecticut, le long du parallèle du 45e degré de latitude Septentrionale jusqu'au fleuve St Laurent nommé dans les traités Iroquois, ou Cataraguÿ, de manière cependant, qu'en tout cas à l'endroit dit Rouse's point, le territoire des Etats Unis d'Amérique s'étendra jusqu'au fort qui s'ÿ trouve établi, et comprendra ce fort, et son raÿon Kilométrique.

Ainsi fait et donné sous Notre sceau Roÿal à la Haye, ce dix Janvier de l'an de grace Mil Huit Cent Trente Un, et de Notre règne le dix-huitième.

GUILLAUME
Le Ministre des Affaires Etrangères.
VERSTOLK DE SOELEN

tion, Whether the treaties require a fresh survey of the whole line of boundary from the River Connecticut to the River St. Lawrence, named in the treaties "Iroquois" or "Cataraguy," or simply the completion of the ancient provincial surveys?—

Considering that the fifth article of the Treaty of Ghent of 1814 does not stipulate that such portion of the boundaries which may not have hitherto been surveyed shall be surveyed, but declares that the boundaries have not been, and establishes that they shall be, surveyed;

That, in effect, such survey ought, in the relations between the two powers, to be considered as not having been made from the Connecticut to the River St. Lawrence, named in the treaties "Iroquois" or "Cataraguy," since the ancient survey was found to be incorrect and had been ordered, not by a common accord of the two powers but by the ancient provincial authorities;

That in determining the latitude of places, it is customary to follow the principle of the observed latitude; and that the Government of the United States of America has erected certain fortifications at the place called Rouse's Point, under the impression that the ground formed part of their territory— an impression sufficiently authorized by the circumstance that the line had until then been reputed to correspond with the forty-fifth degree of north latitude;

We are of opinion that it will be suitable (il conviendra) to proceed to fresh operations to measure the observed latitude, in order to mark out the boundary from the River Connecticut, along the parallel of the forty-fifth degree of north latitude, to the River St. Lawrence, named in the treaties "Iroquois" or "Cataraguy," in such a manner, however, that in all cases, at the place called Rouse's Point, the territory of the United States of America shall extend to the fort erected at that place and shall include said fort and its kilometrical radius (raÿon kilométrique).

Thus done and given under Our royal seal at The Hague this tenth day of January in the year of Our Lord one thousand eight hundred and thirty-one, and of Our reign the eighteenth.

WILLIAM
The Minister of Foreign Affairs,
VERSTOLK DE SOELEN

Except for the definite opinion expressed (in favor of the British contention) as to the northwesternmost head of the Connecticut River, the award of the Arbiter was throughout a recommendation to the two Governments; it was accordingly not obligatory or within the language of Article 7 of the convention to the effect that the decision of the Arbiter, when given, should "be taken as final and conclusive" (see Moore, International Adjudications, Modern Series, I, lxiv–lxvi).

PROCEEDINGS FOLLOWING THE AWARD

Under date of June 1, 1829, William Pitt Preble, of Maine, who had been associated with Albert Gallatin in the preparation of the statements and evidence on behalf of the United States which were submitted to the Arbiter, was appointed Minister to the Netherlands. It was to Preble, on January 10, 1831, that the award of the King of the Netherlands was delivered (D. S., 9 Despatches, Netherlands, No. 30, January 16, 1831); and two days later, without instructions from his Government, Preble made a protest against the award (*ibid.*, enclosure; British and Foreign State Papers, XXII, 772–75).

It appears also that Preble communicated the import of the decision to the authorities of Maine even before the text of the award was received at Washington on March 16. A few days later (March 18) the decision was officially communicated to the Government of Maine by Secretary of State Van Buren (D. S., 24 Domestic Letters, 82–83); and in April the award and other documents were printed in American newspapers with an account of the proceedings of the Legislature of Maine (British and Foreign State Papers, XXII, 776–77).

The Legislature of Maine took action at an early date. The resolutions passed by that body on February 28, 1831 (Resolves of Maine, 1831, 242–46), do not specifically refer to the terms of the award but indicate that its substance at least must have been known. In part those resolutions are printed in Burrage, Maine in the Northeastern Boundary Controversy, 164–65. The text of the four resolves proper, omitting the preambles and argument, is as follows:

Resolved, That the territory bounded by a line running by the heads of the streams falling into the river St. Lawrence, and between them and streams falling into the river St. John, or through other main channels into the sea, until said line intersects a line drawn north from the source of the river St. Croix, is the territory of the State of Maine, wherein she has constitutional right and authority to exercise sovereign power; and the Government of the United States have not any power given to them by the Constitution of the United States, to prohibit the exercise of such right, and it can only be prohibited by an assumption of power.

Resolved, That the convention of September, 1827, tended to violate the Constitution of the United States, and to impair the sovereign rights and powers of the State of Maine, and that Maine is not bound by the Constitution to submit to the decision which is or shall be made under that convention.

Resolved, in the opinion of this Legislature, That the decision of the King of the Netherlands cannot and ought not to be considered obligatory upon the Government of the United States, either upon the principles of right and justice, or of honor.

Resolved further, for the reasons before stated, That no decision made by any umpire, under any circumstances, if the decision dismembers a State, has or can have any constitutional force or obligation upon the State thus dismembered, unless the State adopt and sanction the decision.

A letter of Governor Samuel E. Smith, of Maine, under date of March 2, 1831 (D. S., Northeastern Boundary, envelope 17, pp. 56, 57), transmitting a certified copy of those resolutions to the President, referred to a rumor on the authority of a London paper that by the decision of the Arbiter the territory in dispute had been divided. This was doubtless a reference to the report in the issue of February 28 of the Eastern Argus, of Portland, Maine (Burrage, *op. cit.*, 163).

On March 9 Secretary of State Van Buren acknowledged receipt of the letter of the Governor of Maine and said that an official account of the award of the King of the Netherlands had not yet been received (D. S., 24 Domestic Letters, 76). On March 18, as stated above, the text of the award, with a translation and other papers, was sent to the Governor of Maine by the Secretary of State. Those documents were communicated to the Legislature of Maine with a special message of the Governor of March 25. On March 31 the Legislature adopted a report of a special committee which supported the protest of the Minister at The Hague and concluded with the following paragraph:

In conclusion, your committee deem it to be their duty to the Legislature and to the State, to declare that in their opinion, in whatever light the document which emanated from the Arbiter may be considered, whether as emanating from an individual, and not from that *friendly Sovereign, Power,* or *State,* to whom the points in dispute were submitted by the parties, because he had long before the decision ceased to be such Sovereign; or whether it be considered as advice on two of the points submitted and a decision on the other; or whether it be considered a decision on all the three points submitted, inasmuch as the decision is not warranted by his situation and the authority which was given him, nor a decision of the questions submitted to him by the parties, the United States will not consider themselves bound, on any principle whatever, to adopt it. And further, should the United States adopt the document as a decision, it will be in violation of the constitutional rights of the State of Maine, which she cannot yield.

Under date of June 23, 1831, the Governor of Maine transmitted a certified copy of that report to the President (D. S., Northeastern Boundary, envelope 17, pp. 60, 62). All the papers mentioned were among those sent to the Senate with the presidential message of December 7, 1831, and are printed in the Senate document of that date (Senate Confidential Document, 22d Congress, 1st session, Regular Confidential Documents, I, 647–722).

The British Government had at once decided to accept the award of the King of the Netherlands, and Secretary of State Van Buren, who resigned on May 23, 1831, had, it seems, been verbally so informed by the British Minister at Washington. Formal instructions in that sense were given by Lord Palmerston, then British Secretary of State for Foreign Affairs, to Charles Bankhead, Chargé d'Affaires at Washington, under date of October 14. 1831, with somewhat elaborate arguments in favor of the adoption of that course by both Govern-

ments (British and Foreign State Papers, XXII, 780–83); but at the same time and in a separate communication it was suggested that modifications might be made in the boundary line of the award; and the British Chargé d'Affaires was thus instructed (*ibid.*, 783):

> You are nevertheless authorized to intimate privately to the American Minister, upon any suitable occasion, that His Majesty's Government would not consider the formal acceptance of the Award by Great Britain and The United States, as necessarily precluding the 2 Governments from any future modification of the terms of the arrangement prescribed in that Instrument, provided it should appear that any particular parts of the Boundary Line, thus established, were capable of being improved to the mutual convenience and advantage of both Countries; and you will state, that, after the Award shall have been formally acceded to by both Governments, His Majesty's Government will be ready to enter, with the Government of The United States, into the consideration of the best means of effecting any such modification by reciprocal exchange of concession.

This Government was formally notified of the decision of the British Government to accept the award by the following note of Bankhead, under date of December 20, 1831, which, with immaterial differences, is a copy of the first above-mentioned instructions of Lord Palmerston (D. S., 16 Notes from the British Legation):

> The Undersigned, His Britannic Majesty's Chargé d'Affaires, has the honour to acquaint M͏ʳ Livingston, the Secretary of State of the United States, that he has received His Majesty's commands to make the following communication to the Government of the United States.
>
> M͏ʳ Livingston is doubtless aware that his Predecessor in Office was informed, verbally, by M͏ʳ Vaughan, that the King, his Master, upon the receipt of the Instrument by which the Award of the King of the Netherlands was communicated to the British Government, had considered Himself bound, in fulfilment of the obligations which he had contracted by the terms of the Convention of Arbitration of 29ᵗʰ September 1827, to express to His Netherland Majesty, His Majesty's assent to that award.
>
> It appears to His Majesty's Government that the time is now arrived when a final understanding between the British and American Governments on the subject of that award, and on the measures necessary to be taken for carrying it into effect, ought no longer to be delayed: and the Undersigned is accordingly directed, in making to the Secretary of State the present more formal communication of the assent of His Majesty to the decision of His Netherland Majesty, to inquire of M͏ʳ Livingston, whether the Government of the United States are now ready to proceed, conjointly with that of Great Britain, to the nomination of Commissioners for marking out the Boundary between the possessions of His Majesty in North America, and those of the United States, agreeably to His Netherland Majesty's award.
>
> His Majesty's Government are not ignorant that the Minister of the United States of America residing at The Hague, immediately upon the receipt of the award of His Netherland Majesty, protested against that award, on the ground that the Arbitrator had therein exceeded the powers conferred upon him by the Parties to the Arbitration. But that protest was avowedly made without instructions from Washington, and His Majesty is persuaded that the Government of the United States, influenced, like His Majesty, by a sincere determination to give a fair and full effect to the spirit and intention of their engagements, no less than by an anxious desire to settle this long-pending difference between the two Governments, in the only way in which the experience of so many years has shewn to be practicable, will not hesitate to accept the award of His Netherland Majesty.
>
> In deciding to give His own assent to this award, for the reasons above stated, His Majesty was not insensible to the sacrifice which He was thus making of a most important portion of those claims, of the justice of which, in their full extent,

His Majesty continues to be, as He has always been, entirely satisfied. It was impossible for His Majesty to see without deep regret that on one branch of the British claims, the award deprived the British Crown of a large tract of Country to which it had long been held to be entitled; while on another branch of the claims, that award, at the same time that it pronounced in favour of the principle of demarcation for which Great Britain contended, introduced a special modification of that principle for the convenience and advantage of the United States, without offering to Great Britain any compensation for the loss thus occasioned to Her.

But these were not considerations by which His Majesty thought Himself at liberty to be influenced in deciding the question of His acceptance or rejection of the decision of His Netherland Majesty. In whatever degree His Majesty's wishes or expectations may have been disappointed by that decision, His Majesty did not hesitate to act upon the stipulation contained in the 7th Article of the Convention of Arbitration, that "The decision of the Arbiter, when given, shall "be taken as final and conclusive": and His Majesty fulfilled this duty with the greater cheerfulness, from the confident hope that in thus completing the engagement which He had contracted, He was finally setting at rest a dispute which had been so long and so hopelessly agitated between the two Governments, to the interruption of that perfect agreement and harmony on all points which it is His Majesty's sincere desire to see permanently established between Great Britain and the United States.

His Majesty would indeed be deeply grieved if He could suppose that the Government of the United States could hesitate to adopt the same course which His Majesty has pursued on this occasion. For what other prospect of an adjustment of this long-pending difference would then remain? Commissioners, since the Treaty of 1783, have found it impossible to reconcile the description of the Boundary contained in that Treaty with the real features of the Country ascertained by actual Survey; and the hopelessness of establishing absolutely, in favour of either Party, the point which has thus since the year 1783 been the subject of controversy between them, has now received a new confirmation by the solemn decision of an Arbitrator, chosen by both Parties, who has pronounced it to be incapable of being established in accordance with the Terms of the original Treaty; that Treaty having been drawn up in ignorance of the real features of the Country which it professed to describe.

Seeing, then, that there cannot be a settlement of the claims of either Party in strict accordance with the Treaty of 1783, what course would remain, even if the choice were now to be made, but that which was agreed upon by the Negotiators of the Treaty of Ghent; vizt the adjustment of the differences between the two Governments by means of an Arbitrator? and how unreasonable would it be to object to such an adjustment, because it aimed at settling by compromise, differences pronounced to be otherwise irreconcileable. That such an adjustment, and not a rigid adoption of one of the two claims, to the exclusion of all compromise, was the object of the Fourth Article of the Treaty of Ghent, will be manifest, upon referring to that Article; in which provision is made for a decision of the Arbiter which should be final and conclusive, even although the Arbiter, owing to the neglect or refusal of one of the parties, should have had before him only one of the two claims which it would be his province to adjust. Even the official correspondence of the United States furnishes proofs that such was the understanding in that Country, and among parties most interested in the subject, as to what would be the effect of the reference of this question to arbitration. "By arbitration "(says the Governor of the State of Maine in a letter to the President of the United States, dated May 19. 1827, and previously, of course, to the conclusion of the Convention,)"I understand a submission to some Foreign Sovereign "or State, who will decide at pleasure on the whole subject; who will be under no "absolute obligations or effectual restraint, by virtue of the Treaty of 1783" and it appears by a letter from the same Functionary dated the 18th April in the same year, that Mr Gallatin had used the following words in a Despatch to his Government on the same subject. "An Umpire, whether a King or a farmer, "rarely decides on strict principles of Law; he has always a bias to try, if possible, "to split the difference." And the Secretary of State of the United States in a letter to the Governor of Maine, written after the conclusion of the Treaty of Arbitration, (vizt on the 27th November 1827) adverting to the above-mentioned

exposition by Mᵣ Gallatin of the usual practice of Umpires, and to the objection which the Governor of Maine had thereupon stated to the mode of settlement by Arbitration, while he defends the Convention in spite of the objection of the Governor of Maine, admits that it *is* an objection to which the Convention is liable.

On every ground, therefore, His Majesty feels confident that the Government of the United States will not hesitate to enable the Undersigned to apprize His Majesty's Government of their acquiescence in the decision of the King of the Netherlands.

The grounds on which His Majesty's acceptance of that decision was founded, have been fully explained by the Undersigned, and he is commanded to add that among the motives which influenced His Majesty on that occasion, there was none more powerful than the anxious desire which His Majesty feels to improve and confirm the harmony which so happily exists on other subjects between Great Britain and the United States, by thus settling once for all a question of great difficulty, and for which His Majesty is unable to see any other satisfactory solution.

The Undersigned has the honour to renew to Mᵣ Livingston the assurance of his most distinguished consideration.

President Jackson, however, considered that the advice and consent of the Senate were a condition precedent to acceptance of the award by the United States, and accordingly he submitted the award to the Senate on December 7, 1831, although it seems that he himself favored acceptance. The British Chargé d'Affaires at Washington wrote on July 28, 1832, that he had "no reason to doubt that the President desired the fulfilment of the Award" (British and Foreign State Papers, XXII, 791); and it appears also that Jackson wished, after the event, that it had been accepted (Curtis, Life of Daniel Webster, II, 139). Sir Charles R. Vaughan, British Minister at Washington, reported under date of December 12, 1834, that Secretary of State Forsyth "expressed his regret that the Senate had not acquiesced in the Line of Boundary proposed by the King of The Netherlands" (British and Foreign State Papers, XXII, 881). Forsyth was a Senator from Georgia during the consideration of the award in the Senate and had voted for the award (Executive Journal, IV, 257); but he would hardly have expressed such an opinion more than two years later while Secretary of State if he had not known that it was in accord with the views of his chief, President Jackson. The negotiations with Maine, which are outlined below, also indicate that Jackson desired the acceptance of the award on the part of the United States.

On December 7, 1831, President Jackson submitted the award, which he called an "opinion," to the Senate with the following message of that date (Executive Journal, IV, 179–80). The text here printed includes a correction from the Senate print (Senate Confidential Document, 22d Congress, 1st session, Regular Confidential Documents, I, 647):

In my public message to both Houses of Congress I communicated the state in which I had found the controverted claims of Great Britain and the United States in relation to our northern and eastern boundary, and the measures which, since my coming into office, I had pursued to bring it to a close, together with the fact that on the tenth day of January last the sovereign arbiter had delivered his opinion to the plenipotentiaries of the United States and Great Britain.

I now transmit to you that opinion for your consideration that you may determine whether you will advise submission to the opinion delivered by the sovereign arbiter and consent to its execution.

That you may the better be enabled to judge of the obligation as well as the expediency of submitting to or rejecting the decision of the arbiter, I herewith transmit—

1. A protest made by the minister plenipotentiary of the United States after receiving the opinion of the King of the Netherlands, on which paper it may be necessary to remark that I had always determined, whatever might have been the result of the examination by the sovereign arbiter, to have submitted the same to the Senate for their advice before I executed or rejected it. Therefore, no instructions were given to the ministers to do any act that should commit the Government as to the course it might deem proper to pursue on a full consideration of all the circumstances of the case.

2. The despatches from our minister at the Hague, accompanying the protest, as well as those previous and subsequent thereto, in relation to the subject of the submission.

3. Communications between the Department of State and the governor of the State of Maine in relation to this subject.

4. Correspondence between the chargé d'affaires of His Britannic Majesty and the Department of State in relation to the arrest of certain persons at Madawasca under the authority of the British Government at New Brunswick.

It is proper to add that in addition to the evidence derived from Mr. Preble's despatches of the inclination of the British Government to abide by the award, assurances to the same effect have been uniformly [informally] made to our minister at London, and that an official communication on that subject may very soon be expected.

The papers with that message are printed in a confidential Senate document of seventy-six pages, dated December 7, 1831 (Senate Confidential Document, 22d Congress, 1st session, Regular Confidential Documents, I, 647–722). The list of the papers there given is incomplete and erroneous, and the documents are not arranged in any regular and consistent order.

On December 21 President Jackson sent to the Senate this second message regarding the award (Executive Journal, IV, 187):

Since my message of the 7th instant, transmitting the award of the King of the Netherlands, I have received the official communication, then expected, of the determination of the British Government to abide by the award. This communication is now respectfully laid before you for the purpose of aiding your deliberations on the same subject.

The "official communication" referred to in the above message is the note from the British Chargé d'Affaires at Washington of December 20, 1831, the text of which is printed above in these notes.

A presidential message of January 27, 1832 (Executive Journal, IV, 204), following a request of the Senate, transmitted papers including certain correspondence with the Governor of Maine from 1825 to 1829, correspondence with the British Minister at Washington, and three notes written at Brussels. Pursuant to an order of the Senate (ibid., 209), some of those papers, not there described with precision, were printed in a Senate document of February 8, 1832 (Senate Confidential Document, 22d Congress, 1st session, Regular Confidential Documents, VI, 275–91). In another Senate document of the same date (ibid., 271–74), are printed "certain proceedings and

resolutions of the Legislature of the State of Maine" transmitted with the presidential message of February 3 (Executive Journal, IV, 207). Those papers include a report by a joint committee of both branches of the Legislature of Maine under date of January 14, 1832, and a series of eight resolves adopted on the following January 19. A Senate resolution of January 9 asked for certain information and papers, which President Jackson sent with his message of February 13 (Executive Journal, IV, 211); but those papers, of seemingly minor importance, appear not to have been printed. A presidential message of March 29 (*ibid.*, 234) transmitted a report of the Secretary of State regarding negotiations that had been initiated between the Federal Government and the Government of Maine; this report was printed in a Senate document dated April 2, 1832 (Senate Confidential Document, 22d Congress, 1st session, Regular Confidential Documents, VI, 415–19). No more convenient reference to the papers mentioned than that which is given, has been found. Confidential Senate documents printed during this period were not numbered and are to be identified only by their dates.

In addition to the voluminous mass of papers before the Senate, the two volumes of maps and the volume of surveys which had been submitted to the Arbiter, and also Map A, were transmitted to the Senate by the Secretary of State (Executive Journal, IV, 208–9, 210).

On March 21, 1832, a majority of the Senate Committee on Foreign Relations reported at some length in favor of the acceptance of the award by the United States (*ibid.*, 226–30) and recommended the adoption of the following resolution. The words "United States" are omitted, obviously by error, in the original and in the printed Executive Journal; but they are in the printed report (Senate Confidential Document, 22d Congress, 1st session, Regular Confidential Documents, I, 629):

Resolved, That the Senate advise the President to express to his Majesty the King of the Netherlands, the assent of the United States to the determination made by him, and consent to the execution of the same.

Sentiment in the Senate was divided, but only a small minority favored the acceptance of the award. On the question of striking out all the resolution after the word "Resolved," the vote, on June 16, was thirty-five to eight (Executive Journal, IV, 257); but the majority included sixteen Senators out of the seventeen who five days later voted in favor of the proposal of amendment offered by Daniel Webster to the effect that "the Senate is not of opinion that this is a case in which the Senate is called on to express any opinion or give any advice to the President." The vote on Webster's proposal was seventeen to twenty-six (*ibid.*, 260).

Doubtless no resolution could have received a two-thirds vote in the Senate. The voting was not altogether consistent. The following proposed paragraph was accepted on June 21 by a vote of twenty-one to twenty and rejected on June 23 by a vote of fourteen to thirty (*ibid.*, 261, 263):

That the Senate advise the President to communicate to the British Government that the United States decline to "adopt" the boundary recommended by His Majesty the King of the Netherlands as being "suitable" between the dominions of His Britannic Majesty and those of the United States, because, in the opinion of the Senate, the King of the Netherlands has not decided the question submitted to him touching the northern and northeastern boundary of the United States.

A proposal to insert in the resolution the words, "two-thirds of the Senators present concurring," was negatived; and the following resolution, which was finally adopted by the Senate on June 23, passed by a bare majority of twenty-three to twenty-two (*ibid.*, 263):

Resolved, That the Senate advise the President to open a new negotiation with His Britannic Majesty's Government for the ascertainment of the boundary between the possessions of the United States and those of the King of Great Britain on the northeastern frontier of the United States, according to the treaty of peace of 1783.

The injunction of secrecy was removed from the proceedings and debates in the Senate on July 10, 1832 (*ibid.*, 272); and the votes were much discussed in subsequent diplomatic correspondence (British and Foreign State Papers, XXII, 787, 791, 847, 849–52, 855).

On July 21, 1832, the decision of this Government was formally made known in a note of Secretary of State Livingston to Charles Bankhead, British Chargé d'Affaires at Washington (D. S., 5 Notes to Foreign Legations, 199–201; British and Foreign State Papers, XXII, 788–90), as follows:

The Undersigned, Secretary of State of the United States, will now have the honor to fulfil to Mr Bankhead, His Britannic Majesty's Chargé d'Affaires, the promise which he made that, as soon as the action of the Senate should be known, on the reference made to that body, of the decision of the King of the Netherlands, the Undersigned would answer Mr Bankhead's note of the 20th of December last.

His Britannic Majesty's Government is too well acquainted with the division of powers in that of the United States to make it necessary to enter into any explanation of the reasons which rendered it obligatory on the President to submit the whole subject to the Senate for its advice. The result of that application is a determination, on the part of the Senate, not to consider the decision of the King of the Netherlands as obligatory, and a refusal to advise and consent to its execution—But they have passed a resolution advising "the President to open a new "negotiation with His Britannic Majesty's Government for the ascertainment "of the boundary between the possessions of the United States and those of Great "Britain on the northeastern frontier of the United States, according to the treaty "of Peace of 1783." This resolution was adopted on the conviction felt by the Senate that the Sovereign Arbiter had not decided the question submitted to him, or had decided it in a manner unauthorized by the submission.

It is not the intention of the Undersigned to enter into an investigation of the argument which has led to this conclusion,—the decision of the Senate precludes it, and the object of this communication renders it unnecessary,—but it may be proper to add that no question could have arisen as to the validity of the decision, had the Sovereign Arbiter determined on, and designated, any boundary as that which was intended by the treaty of 1783. He has not done so. Not being able, consistently with the evidence before him, to declare that the line he has thought the most proper to be established, was the boundary intended by the Treaty of 1783, he seems to have abandoned the character of Arbiter, and assumed that of a mediator, advising both parties that a boundary which he describes, should be

accepted, as one most convenient to them.   But this line trenches, as is asserted by one of the States of the Union, upon its territory, and that State controverts the constitutional power of the United States, to circumscribe its limits without its assent.   If the decision had indicated this line as the boundary designated by the treaty of 1783, this objection could not have been urged, because, then, no part of the territory to the north or the east of it, could be within the State of Maine: And however the United States, or any individual State, might think itself aggrieved by the decision, as it would, in that case, have been made in conformity to the submission, it would have been carried into immediate effect.   The case is now entirely different, and the necessity for further negotiation must be apparent, to adjust a difference which the Sovereign Arbiter has, in the opinion of a coördinate branch of our Executive Powers, failed to decide.   That negotiation will be opened and carried on by the President with the sincerest disposition to bring to an amicable, speedy, and satisfactory conclusion, a question which might otherwise interrupt the harmony which so happily subsists between the two countries, and which he most earnestly wishes to preserve.

The Undersigned is instructed to say, that even if the negotiators of the two Parties are unable to agree on the true line designated by the treaty of 1783, means will probably be found of avoiding the constitutional difficulties that have hitherto attended the establishment of a boundary more convenient to both parties than that designated by the treaty, or that recommended by His Majesty the King of the Netherlands,—an arrangement being now in progress, with every probability of a speedy conclusion, between the United States and the State of Maine, by which the Government of the United States will be clothed with more ample powers than it has heretofore possessed, to effect that end.   Should a negotiation be opened on this principal point, it will naturally embrace, as connected with it, the right of navigation of the River S⸮ John,—an object of scarcely less importance to the convenience and future harmony of the two nations, than the designation of the boundary,—it being the wish of the President, and, as he has the best reason to believe, that of His Britannic Majesty's Government, to remove all causes for misunderstanding between the two countries by a previous settlement of all points on which they might probably arise.

Presuming that the state of things produced by the resolution of the Senate above referred to, and the desire expressed by the President, to open, carry on, and conclude the negotiation recommended by that body, in the most frank and amicable manner, will convince His Britannic Majesty's Government of the necessity of meeting the offers now made with a correspondent spirit, the Undersigned is directed to propose for consideration the propriety of carrying on the negotiation at this place.   The aid which the negotiators, on both sides, would derive from being in the vicinity of the territory in dispute, as well as the information with respect to localities from persons well acquainted with them, which they might command, are obvious considerations in favor of this proposition.

Until this matter shall be brought to a final conclusion, the necessity of refraining, on both sides, from any exercise of jurisdiction beyond the boundaries now actually possessed, must be apparent, and will no doubt be acquiesced in on the part of the authorities of His Britannic Majesty's Province, as it will be by the United States.

The Undersigned avails himself of this occasion to renew to M⸮ Bankhead the assurance of his high consideration.

Thus the award failed of acceptance by the two Governments. On December 28, 1835, the British Government formally withdrew its offer to accept it (D. S., 18 Notes from the British Legation; British and Foreign State Papers, XXIV, 1179–84).   From that note of the British Chargé d'Affaires, Charles Bankhead, to Secretary of State Forsyth, the following is extracted:

And, first, with regard to the award of the King of the Netherlands.   The two Governments had agreed to refer to that Sovereign as Arbiter, the decision of three points of difference, and they pledged themselves beforehand to abide. by

the decision, which he might pronounce. The King of the Netherlands decided absolutely two points, out of the three; and with respect to the third, while he declared, that an absolute decision of that point was impossible, he recommended to the two parties, a compromise.

His Majesty's Government, on receiving the award of the King of the Netherlands, announced, without any hesitation, their willingness to abide by that award, if it should be equally accepted by the United States.

His Majesty's Government were, of course, fully aware that this award was not an absolute decision, on all the three points, submitted to reference; they were also quite sensible that in some important matters,—this award was less favorable to Great Britain, than it was to the United States; but the wish of His Majesty's Government for a prompt and amicable settlement of this question outweighed the objections, to which the award was liable, and for the sake of obtaining such a settlement, they determined to accept the award.

But their expectations were not realized. The Senate of the United States refused in July 1832, to subscribe to the award; and during the three years, which have elapsed since that time, although the British Government has more than once declared, that it was still ready to abide by its offer to accept the award, the Government of the United States has as often replied, that, on its part, that award could not be agreed to.

The British Government must now, in its turn, declare that it considers itself, by this refusal of the United States, fully and entirely released from the conditional offer, which it had made; and the Undersigned is instructed, distinctly, to announce to the President, that the British Government withdraws its consent, to accept the territorial compromise, recommended by the King of the Netherlands.

Discussions and correspondence between the two Governments continued, but none of the various proposals and offers made between 1832 and the negotiation of the Webster-Ashburton Treaty reached any result (Moore, International Arbitrations, I, 138–46; International Boundary Commission: Joint Report upon the Survey and Demarcation of the Boundary between the United States and Canada from the Source of the St. Croix River to the St. Lawrence River, 290–93; Ganong, *op. cit.*, 338–45).

NEGOTIATIONS WITH MAINE

The interest of Maine in the northeastern boundary dated from the admission of that State into the Union on March 15, following the act of March 3, 1820 (3 Statutes at Large, 544). A history of the relations of Maine to the controversy during this period is in Burrage, Maine in the Northeastern Boundary Controversy, chapters VI–X.

The State of Maine had from the beginning protested strongly against the acceptance of the award of the King of the Netherlands. The resolution of the Legislature of Maine of February 28, 1831, and the committee report adopted the following March 31, which were before the Senate, have been, in part, quoted above. Also before the Senate were the resolutions of January 19, 1832, which were transmitted with the presidential message of February 3 (Executive Journal, IV, 207); they read as follows (Resolves of Maine, 1832, 343–44; Burrage, *op. cit.*, 192–93):

Resolved, That the Constitution of the United States does not invest the General Government with unlimited and absolute powers, but confers only a special and

modified sovereignty, without authority to cede to a foreign power any portion of territory belonging to a State, without its consent.

Resolved, "That if there is an attribute of State Sovereignty which is unqualified and undeniable, it is the right of jurisdiction to the utmost limits of State Territory; and if a single obligation under the Constitution rests upon the Confederacy, it is to guaranty the integrity of this territory to the quiet and undisturbed enjoyment of the States."

Resolved, That the doings of the King of Holland, on the subject of the boundary between the United States and Great Britain, are not a decision of the question submitted to the King of the Netherlands; and that his recommendation of a suitable or convenient line of boundary is not obligatory upon the parties to the submission.

Resolved, That this State protests against the adoption, by the Government of the United States, of the line of boundary recommended by the King of Holland as a suitable boundary between Great Britain and the United States; inasmuch as it will be a violation of the rights of Maine,—rights acknowledged and insisted upon by the General Government,—and will be a precedent, which endangers the integrity, as well as the independence, of every State in the Union.

Resolved, That while the people of this State are disposed to yield a ready obedience to the Constitution and laws of the United States, they will never consent to surrender any portion of their territory, on the recommendation of a Foreign Power.

Resolved, That the Governor, with advice of Council, be authorized to appoint a competent Agent, whose duty it shall be, as soon as may be, to repair to the City of Washington, and deliver to the President of the United States a copy of the preceding Report and these Resolutions, with a request that he will lay the same before the Senate of the United States; and also deliver a copy to the Vice President, to each of the Heads of Departments, and to each Member of the Senate, and to our Representatives in Congress.

Resolved, That our Senators in Congress be instructed, and our Representatives requested, to use their best efforts to prevent our State from being dismembered, our territory alienated, and our just rights prostrated, by the adoption of a *new* line for our Northeastern Boundary, as recommended by the King of Holland.

Resolved, That the Agent to be appointed by the Governor and Council, be instructed to co-operate with our Senators and Representatives, in advocating and enforcing the principles advanced, and positions taken, in the foregoing Resolutions, and in supporting all such measures as shall be deemed best calculated to preserve the integrity of our State, and prevent any portion of our territory and citizens from being transferred to a Foreign Power.

Pursuant to that action of the Legislature of Maine, the Governor of that State appointed William Pitt Preble, formerly Minister to the Netherlands, as Agent of the State.

At the instance of President Jackson proposals were made for an agreement between the Federal Government and the State of Maine for compensation of that State in the event of the acceptance of the award. The attitude of the President is thus stated in the report of Secretary of State Edward Livingston of March 29, 1832, which was communicated to the Senate with the presidential message of that date and was printed in a Senate document of April 2, 1832 (Senate Confidential Document, 22d Congress, 1st session, Regular Confidential Documents, I, 637–41; D. S., 1 Special Missions, 58–60):

That the State of Maine having passed resolutions declaratory of their dissent to any acquiescence in the award made by the King of the Netherlands, and having appointed an agent to communicate the same to the President and both Houses of Congress, the President thought it proper to avail himself of the presence of the agent at the seat of Government, to make propositions for entering into such an arrangement, as, being confirmed by Congress, and by the

State of Maine, would satisfy the State for the loss of territory it might sustain, if it should be determined to confirm the award of the King of the Netherlands, either for reasons of expediency, or on the ground that the award, although it does not designate the boundary claimed by either party under the treaty of Ghent, is yet authorized by the submission. In either of which cases, it was thought that an indemnity would be due to the State of Maine.

In the first, because the advantage of settling the disputed question would have been purchased confessedly at the expense of Maine. In the second, because, although the United States had made a submission which authorized the arbiter to establish a line different from the one contemplated by the treaty of 1783, and the treaty of Ghent, and, although public faith might require a compliance with the award under it; yet the authority to make a submission which empowered the arbiter to dismember a State, might well be questioned.

If it should, on the other hand, be determined that the award should not be executed, the whole arrangement would be of course void.

The President gave no opinion on either of these points, but directed the Secretary of State to confer with Mr. Preble, the agent for the State of Maine, and to propose that some person should be appointed by the State to meet a person appointed by the President, to agree on an equivalent in land of the United States, as an indemnity in any case in which Congress might deem such compensation to be due.

In the same Senate document is a memorandum of the first conference held between the Secretary of State and the Agent of Maine on February 15, 1832. As a result thereof and of further discussions (Burrage, *op. cit.*, 194–203), the Legislature of Maine on March 3 passed the following resolutions (Resolves of Maine, 1832, 465–67; Senate Confidential Document, April 2, 1832, 22d Congress, 1st session, Regular Confidential Documents, I, 640):

Whereas information has been communicated by the Agent of this State at Washington, that it is proposed that Maine should cede to the United States her claim and jurisdiction over that portion of territory which lies Northerly and Easterly of the line recommended by the Arbiter, for an ample indemnity, in order that the United States may be enabled to make such an arrangement with Great Britain as may best comport with the interests and honor of the United States:

And whereas the Government of Maine has repeatedly declared, and now declares, that the right of soil and jurisdiction in said territory, according to the provisions of the treaty of 1783, is in the State of Maine, as a sovereign and independent State, and has denied and continues to deny, the right of the General Government to cede the same to any foreign power without the consent of Maine; and has communicated Resolutions to that effect to the General Government, and has claimed of that Government the protection guarantied to every State by the Constitution of the United States:

And whereas the Legislature of Maine is disposed to regard the proposition aforesaid as emanating from a disposition on the part of the General Government, to promote the interests, and to preserve the peace, of the nation, without violating the rights of Maine, or disregarding the obligation resting upon the whole Union to protect each State in the full enjoyment of all its territory and right of jurisdiction, and willing to meet the proposition in a like spirit in which it is believed to have been made:

Therefore Resolved, That upon the appointment by the President of the United States, of a person or persons to enter into negotiation with this State for the relinquishment, by this State to the United States, of her claim to said territory and for the cession of the jurisdiction thereof, on the one part; and for an ample indemnity therefor, on the other part, and notice thereof being communicated to the Governor, the Governor, with advice of Council, be and he is hereby authorized and requested to appoint three Commissioners on the part and in behalf of this State, to treat with such person or persons, so appointed by the President, on the subjects aforesaid; and any agreement or treaty, to be made in pursuance of this

Resolve, is to be submitted to the Legislature of Maine for approval or rejection; and until such agreement or treaty be so submitted to, and approved by, the Legislature of Maine, nothing herein contained shall be construed, in any way, as implying the assent of this State to the line of boundary recommended by the Arbiter, or to the right of the General Government to adopt or sanction that line instead of the line described in the treaty of 1783.

Resolved, That the Governor be requested forthwith to communicate the foregoing preamble and Resolution, confidentially, to the Agent of this State, at Washington, and also to the Executive of the Commonwealth of Massachusetts, to afford to that Commonwealth the opportunity of adopting such measures as she may consider expedient in relation to her interest in said territory.

The Commissioners appointed on the part of Maine under the foregoing resolutions were William Pitt Preble, Reuel Williams, and Nicholas Emery. To represent the United States President Jackson appointed Secretary of State Edward Livingston, Secretary of the Treasury Louis McLane, and Secretary of the Navy Levi Woodbury. The Commissioners of Maine were received by President Jackson on May 19; and it seems that the simple form of the Senate resolution as finally adopted on June 23 was due to the negotiations pending with Maine (Burrage, *op. cit.*, 204–11).

Following the action of the Senate an agreement was made between the Commissioners of the State of Maine and those appointed by President Jackson, although in the agreement itself mention is made only of conferences from May 18 to June 2. The form of the agreement appears to be substantially that which had been proposed by the Commissioners of Maine (*ibid.*, 212). The agreement, which was undated, was drawn up in duplicate; on July 25, 1832, the Commissioners appointed by President Jackson transmitted to the Commissioners of Maine an executed counterpart thereof, enclosed in a letter which reads as follows (D. S., 1 Special Missions, 69):

We have the honor to enclose, duly executed by us, a copy of the agreement which you had prepared, making a slight alteration, rendered necessary by the resolution of the Senate advising a further negotiation. You will please to send a counterpart, executed by you, as soon as possible, together with information at what time it will probably be placed under the consideration of your legislature, whose action on the subject would seem to be required before the matter can be submitted to Congress.

That original is in the State Library at Augusta, Maine, and bears also the signatures of the Maine Commissioners (see Burrage, *op. cit.*, facing page 214). A counterpart, executed by the Maine Commissioners, was forwarded by them to the Commissioners appointed by President Jackson with the following note of August 21 (D. S., Northeastern Boundary, envelope 17, p. 82):

We have had the honor to receive your note of the 25th ulto with the document which it enclosed. Agreeably to your request we now transmit a counterpart executed by us. The legislature of Maine will not be in session prior to next January and the subject cannot well come under their consideration until after the organization of the government shall have been completed. Should the state of the intended new negotiations in the opinion of the President render a postponement of the communication to our legislature desirable we would in that case suspend the communication on your suggestion until the first of February next.

The text of the agreement is printed as an appendix to Senate Document No. 431, 25th Congress, 2d session, serial 318. A record copy of the agreement is in D. S., 1 Special Missions, 63–68; there the agreement is preceded by a protocol, also undated, which seems to have constituted, with the text of the agreement, a record of the result of the discussions. The text which follows is from the original in the archives of the Department of State, which was signed by the Maine Commissioners only (D. S., Northeastern Boundary, envelope 17, p. 83):

The King of the Netherlands mutually selected as Arbiter by the King of the United Kingdom of Great Britain and Ireland, and the President of the United States, and invited to investigate and make a decision upon the points of difference which had arisen under the Treaty of Ghent of 1814, in ascertaining that point of the Highlands lying due North from the source of the River St Croix, designated by the Treaty of Peace of 1783, as the Northwest angle of Nova Scotia, and in surveying the Boundary line between the dominions of the United States and Great Britain from the Source of the River St Croix directly north to the above-mentioned Northwest angle of Nova Scotia, thence along the said Highlands, which divide those rivers that empty themselves into the River St Lawrence from those which fall into the Atlantic Ocean to the Northwesternmost head of Connecticut River, having officially communicated his opinion that it will be suitable to adopt for boundary between the two States (qu'il conviendra d'adopter pour limite des Etats) a line drawn due north from the Source of the River St Croix to the point where it intersects the middle of the thalweg of the River St John thence the middle of the thalweg of that River ascending to the point where the River St Francis empties itself into the River St John thence the middle of the thalweg of the River St Francis ascending to the Source of its Southwesternmost branch designated on map A by the letter X, thence a line drawn due west to the Highlands, thence along the said Highlands which divide those Rivers that empty themselves into the River St Lawrence from those that fall into the Atlantic Ocean to the Northwesternmost head of Connecticut River: And the Legislature of the State of Maine having protested and continuing to protest against the adoption by the Government of the United States of the line of boundary thus described by the King of the Netherlands, as a dismemberment of her Territory, and a violation of her constitutional rights: And the President of the United States having appointed the undersigned Secretaries of the Departments of State, of the Treasury, and of the Navy to meet with such persons as might be appointed by the State of Maine for the purpose of entering into a provisional agreement as to the quantity and Selection of lands of the United States, which the State of Maine might be willing to take and the President would be willing to recommend to Congress to give for a release on her part of all claim of jurisdiction to and of her interest in the lands lying North and East of the line so designated as a boundary by the King of the Netherlands—And the Governor of Maine by virtue of the authority vested in him having appointed the undersigned William Pitt Preble, Reuel Williams, and Nicholas Emery, Commissioners on the part of said State, to meet and confer with the said Secretaries of State, of the Treasury and of the Navy thus authorized as aforesaid with a view to an amicable understanding and satisfactory arrangement and settlement of all disputes which had arisen or might arise in regard to the North Eastern Boundary of said State and of the United States: And several Meetings and conferences having been had at Washington between the Eighteenth day of May and the Second day of June 1832. And the said Commissioners, on the part of the State of Maine having distinctly declared that said State did not withdraw her protest against the adoption of the line designated as a boundary by the King of the Netherlands, but would continue to protest against the same, and that it was the desire of the Legislature and Government of Maine, that new negotiations should be opened for the purpose of having the line designated by the Treaty of Peace of 1783 run and marked according to that Treaty, and if that should be found impracticable, for the establishment of such a new boundary between the dominions of the United States

and Great Britain as should be mutually convenient, Maine in such case to be indemnified, so far as practicable for jurisdiction and territory lost in consequence of any such new boundary, by jurisdictional and other rights to be acquired by the United States over adjacent territory and transferred to said State.   And for these purposes the undersigned Commissioners were ready to enter into a provisional agreement to release to the United States the right and claim of Maine to jurisdiction over the territory lying North and East of the line designated by the Arbiter: and her interest in the same the said State of Maine and the State of Massachusetts being owners of the land in equal shares.   Suggesting at the same time the propriety of suspending the Conferences until the Senate of the United States, whose advice it had become the duty of the President to take and before whom his message for that purpose was then under consideration should finally act in the matter in which suggestion the Secretaries of State of the Treasury and of the Navy concurred

And the Senate of the United States did on the Twenty third day of June 1832 pass a Resolution in the words following

Resolved That the Senate advise the President to open a new negotiation with his Britannic Majestys Government, for the ascertainment of the boundary between the possessions of the United States and those of Great Britain on the North East frontier of the United States according to the Treaty of Peace of 1783.

Whereupon the Secretaries of State, of the Treasury, and of the Navy did renew their communications with the Commissioners on the part of the State of Maine, and state it to be the wish and intention of the President to open a negotiation with the Government of Great Britain for the purposes mentioned by the said Commissioners, and also for making arrangements relative to the Navigation of the River St John and the adjustment of other points that may be necessary for the convenience of the parties interested: but deeming a Cession from the State of Maine of all her jurisdiction and right of soil over the territory heretofore described, and in the manner heretofore stated as indispensable to the success of such negotiation, The Secretaries of State, of the Treasury and of the Navy did declare and propose that in consideration of such cession The President will as soon as the state of the Negotiation with Great Britain may render it proper to do so, recommend to Congress to grant to the State of Maine an Indemnity for the release on her part of all right and claim to jurisdiction over and her interest in the Territory beyond the line so designated by the King of the Netherlands.   The said Indemity to consist of one Million Acres of land to be selected by the State of Maine and located in a square form as near as may be out of the unappropriated lands of the United States within the Territory of Michigan—the said lands to be surveyed and sold by the United States at their expense in the same manner and under the same regulations which apply to the public lands—And the whole proceeds without deduction to be paid over to the State of Maine as they shall be received.   But if in the result of any negotiation as aforesaid with Great Britain the State of Maine shall ultimately lose less of the territory claimed by her North and East of the Rivers St John and St Francis than she would according to the line designated by the King of the Netherlands, The aforesaid Indemnity shall be proportioned to the actual loss; and if any new territory contiguous to the State of Maine not now within her limits, shall be acquired by such negotiation from Great Britain, the same shall be annexed to and be made a part of said State And a further proportionate deduction shall be made from the indemnity abovementioned: But if such attempt on the part of the President to negotiate should wholly fail, and in that case, and not otherwise, the proper Authorities of the United States should on full consideration determine to acquiesce in the line designated by the King of the Netherlands and to establish the same as the North East Boundary of the United States the State of Maine shall be entitled to receive the proceeds of the said Million of Acres without any abatement or deduction which offer the undersigned Commissioners provisionally accede to, and on condition of the due performance of all and singular the things which by the declaration of the Secretaries of State, of the Treasury, and of the Navy and by the proposal before mentioned are to be performed or intended to be performed   They agree to recommend to the Legislature of the State of Maine to accept said indemnity and to release and assign to the United States all right and claim to jurisdiction and all her interest in the territory North and East of the line designated by

the King of the Netherlands.   But it is distinctly understood that until this agreement shall have been accepted and ratified by the Legislature of Maine nothing herein shall in any wise be construed, as derogating from the claims and pretensions of the said State to the whole extent of her territory as asserted by her Legislature.

Nor shall any thing herein contained be construed so as to express or imply on the part of the President any opinion whatever on the question of the validity of the decision of the King of the Netherlands, or of the obligation or expediency of carrying the same into effect.

Wᵐ P. Preble
Reuel Williams
Nicholas Emery

It was in Maine that the agreement failed.   During the session of 1833 the agreement was laid before the Maine Legislature, which reversed the action of the previous Legislature regarding the submission of such an agreement to that body, by the following resolution, approved March 4, 1833, which gave "a death blow to the proposal outlined in the agreement" (Resolves of Maine, 1833, 580–81; Burrage, *op. cit.*, 215–16).

Resolved, That so much of the Resolve passed the third day of March in the year of our Lord one thousand eight hundred and thirty two, entitled a "Resolve respecting the territory lying North and East of the Rivers St. Johns and St. Francis," as provides for the submission to the Legislature "for approval or rejection," of the agreement or treaty therein contemplated to be made by the Commissioners therein mentioned, be and the same is hereby repealed.

Resolved, That no arrangement, provisional agreement, or treaty, already made, or that may hereafter be made, under, or in pursuance of the Resolve to which this is additional, shall have any binding force, effect, or operation, until the same shall have been submitted to the people of this State, in their primary assemblies, and approved by a majority of their votes.

Treaty Series No. 157
8 Statutes at Large, 366–73
18 *ibid.*, pt. 2, Public Treaties, 400–3

59

THE HANSEATIC REPUBLICS : DECEMBER 20, 1827

Convention of Friendship, Commerce, and Navigation, signed at Washington December 20, 1827. Original in English and French.
Submitted to the Senate December 24, 1827. Resolution of advice and consent January 7, 1828. Ratified by the United States January 8, 1828. Ratified by Lübeck March 26, 1828; by Bremen April 3, 1828; and by Hamburg April 8, 1828. Ratifications exchanged at Washington June 2, 1828. Proclaimed June 2, 1828.

Original

Convention of Friendship, Commerce and Navigation between the United States of America, and the free Hanseatic Republics of Lubeck, Bremen, and Hamburg.

The United States of America, on the one part, and the Republic and free Hanseatic City of Lubeck, the Republic and free Hanseatic City of Bremen, and the Republic and free Hanseatic City of Hamburg (each State for itself separately,) on the other part, being desirous to give greater facility to Their commercial intercourse, and to place the privileges of Their navigation on a basis of the most extended liberality, have resolved to fix in a manner clear, distinct and positive, the rules which shall be observed between the one and the other, by means of a Convention of Friendship, Commerce and Navigation.

Original

Convention d'Amitié, de Commerce et de Navigation, entre les Républiques libres et Anséatiques de Lubeck, Bremen et Hambourg, et les Etats Unis d'Amérique.

La République et Ville libre et Anséatique de Lubeck, la République et Ville libre et Anséatique de Bremen, et la République et Ville libre et Anséatique de Hambourg, (chacun de ces Etats pour Soi séparément,) d'une part; et les Etats Unis d'Amérique, d'autre part; désirant accorder plus de facilités à Leurs relations commerciales, et établir les privileges de leur navigation sur les bases de la liberalité la plus étendue; sont convenus d'arrêter, d'une maniere claire, distincte et positive, par une Convention d'Amitié, de Commerce et de Navigation, les règles qui doivent être observées entre Eux.

387

For the attainment of this most desirable object, the President of the United States of America has conferred Full Powers on Henry Clay, Their Secretary of State; and the Senate of the Republic and free Hanseatic City of Lubeck, the Senate of the Republic and free Hanseatic City of Bremen, and the Senate of the Republic and free Hanseatic City of Hamburg, have conferred Full Powers on Vincent Rumpff, Their Minister Plenipotentiary near the United States of America; who, after having exchanged their said Full Powers, found in due and proper form, have agreed to the following articles:

ARTICLE I.

The Contracting Parties agree, That whatever kind of produce, manufacture, or merchandise of any foreign country can be, from time to time, lawfully imported into the United States, in their own vessels, may be also imported in vessels of the said free Hanseatic Republics of Lubeck, Bremen and Hamburg; and that no higher, or other duties upon the tonnage or cargo of the vessel, shall be levied or collected, whether the importation be made in vessels of the United States, or of either of the said Hanseatic Republics. And, in like manner, that whatever kind of produce, manufacture or merchandise, of any foreign country, can be, from time

Pour atteindre ce but désirable, le Sénat de la République et Ville libre et Anséatique de Lubeck, le Sénat de la République et Ville libre et Anséatique de Bremen, et le Sénat de la République et Ville libre et Anséatique de Hambourg, ont muni de Pleins Pouvoirs, Vincent Rumpff, Leur Ministre Plénipotentiaire près les Etats Unis d'Amérique; et le Président des Etats Unis d'Amérique a muni de Pleins Pouvoirs Henri Clay, Leur Secrétaire d'Etat; lesquels, après avoir echangé leurs dits Pleins Pouvoirs, trouvés en bonne et due forme, ont arrêté les articles suivans:

ARTICLE I.

Les Parties Contractantes conviennent que toutes sortes de productions, manufactures ou marchandises, provenant de quelque pays étranger que ce soit, qui, de temps à autre, pourront être légalement importées dans l'une desdites Républiques Anséatiques de Lubeck, Bremen et Hambourg, par leurs propres bâtimens, pourront aussi y être importées par les bâtimens des Etats Unis; et qu'il ne sera imposé ni perçu, sur le tonnage ou la cargaison du bâtiment, d'autres, ni de plus forts droits, soit que l'importation ait lieu par bâtimens de l'une des dites Républiques; soit par ceux des Etats Unis. Et pareillement, que toutes sortes

to time, lawfully imported into either of the said Hanseatic Republics, in its own vessels, may be also imported in vessels of the United States; and that no higher, or other, duties upon the tonnage or cargo of the vessel, shall be levied or collected, whether the importation be made in vessels of the one Party, or of the other. And they further agree, That whatever may be lawfully exported, or re-exported, by one Party, in its own vessels, to any foreign country, may, in like manner, be exported, or re-exported, in the vessels of the other Party. And the same bounties, duties and drawbacks shall be allowed and collected, whether such exportation or re-exportation be made in vessels of the one Party or of the other. Nor shall higher, or other, charges, of any kind, be imposed in the ports of the one Party, on vessels of the other, than are, or shall be payable, in the same ports, by national vessels.

de productions, manufactures ou marchandises, provenant de quelque pays étranger que ce soit, qui, de temps à autre, pourront être légalement importées dans les Etats Unis, par bâtimens des dits Etats, pourront également y être importées par les bâtimens desdites Républiques Anseatiques; et qu'il ne sera imposé ni perçu, sur le tonnage ou la cargaison du bâtiment, d'autres ni de plus forts droits, soit que l'importation ait lieu par bâtimens de l'une des Parties, soit par ceux de l'autre. Elles conviennent, en outre, que tout ce qui pourra être légalement exporté ou ré-exporté, pour quelque pays étranger que ce soit, par les bâtimens de l'une des Parties Contractantes, pourra également en être exporté ou ré-exporté, par ceux de l'autre Partie; et les mêmes droits, primes et remboursemens de droits, seront perçus et alloués, soit que l'exportation ou la ré-exportation ait lieu par bâtimens de l'une des Parties, soit par ceux de l'autre. Il ne sera imposé dans les ports de l'une des deux Parties, sur les bâtimens de l'autre, aucuns droits ou charges, de quelque nature qu'ils puissent être, plus forts ou autres que ceux qui seront imposés dans les mêmes ports, sur les bâtimens nationaux.

ARTICLE II.

No higher or other duties shall be imposed on the importation

ARTICLE II.

Il ne sera imposé d'autres ni de plus forts droits sur l'im-

into the United States, of any article, the produce or manufacture of the free Hanseatic Republics of Lubeck, Bremen and Hamburg; and no higher or other duties shall be imposed on the importation into either of the said Republics, of any article the produce or manufacture of the United States, than are, or shall be payable, on the like article being the produce or manufacture of any other foreign country; nor shall any other, or higher, duties or charges be imposed by either Party, on the exportation of any articles to the United States or to the free Hanseatic Republics of Lubeck, Bremen, or Hamburg, respectively, than such as are, or shall be, payable on the exportation of the like articles, to any other foreign country: nor shall any prohibition be imposed, on the importation or exportation of any article, the produce or manufacture of the United States, or of the free Hanseatic Republics of Lubeck, Bremen or Hamburg, to, or from, the ports of the United States; or to, or from the ports of the other Party, which shall not equally extend to all other nations.

portation dans les Républiques libres et Anséatiques de Lubeck, Bremen et Hambourg, des articles provenant du sol ou des manufactures des Etats Unis; et il ne sera imposé d'autres ni de plus forts droits sur l'importation dans les Etats Unis des articles provenant du sol ou des manufactures desdites Républiques, que ceux qui sont ou seront imposés sur les mêmes articles provenant du sol ou des manufactures de tout autre pays étranger. De même, il ne sera imposé, par l'une des Parties, sur l'exportation de quelque article que ce soit, pour les Républiques libres et Anséatiques de Lubeck, Bremen et Hambourg, ou pour les Etats Unis, respectivement, d'autres ni de plus forts droits, que ceux qui sont ou seront imposés sur l'exportation des mêmes articles, pour tout autre pays étranger. De même il ne sera imposé sur l'importation, ou sur l'exportation des articles provenant du sol ou des manufactures des Républiques libres et Anséatiques de Lubeck, Bremen et Hambourg, ou des Etats Unis, á l'entrée ou à la sortie des ports des Républiques Anséatiques, ou de ceux de l'autre Partie, aucune prohibition qui ne soit pas également applicable à toute autre nation.

ARTICLE III.

No priority or preference shall be given, directly, or indirectly,

ARTICLE III.

Il ne sera accordé, ni directement, ni indirectement, par l'une,

by any or either of the Contracting Parties, nor by any Company,
Corporation, or Agent, acting on
their behalf, or under their authority, in the purchase of any
article, the growth, produce, or
manufacture of their States, respectively, imported into the
other, on account of, or in reference to, the character of the
vessel, whether it be of the one
Party, or of the other, in which
such article was imported: it
being the true intent and meaning of the Contracting Parties,
that no distinction or difference
whatever shall be made in this
respect.

Article IV.

In consideration of the limited
extent of the territories of the
Republics of Lubeck, Bremen
and Hamburg, and of the intimate connection of trade and
navigation subsisting between
these Republics, it is hereby stipulated and agreed that any vessel
which shall be owned exclusively
by a Citizen, or Citizens of any,
or either of them, and of which
the master shall also be a Citizen
of any, or either of them, and
provided three fourths of the
crew shall be Citizens or Subjects
of any or either of the said Republics, or of any, or either of the
States of the Confederation of
Germany, such vessel, so owned,
and navigated, shall for all the
purposes of this Convention, be

ou par l'autre des Parties Contractantes, ni par aucune Com-
pagnie, Corporation ou Agent,
agissant en son nom, ou par son
autorité, aucune priorité ou préférence quelconque, pour l'achat
d' aucune production du sol ou
de l'industrie de leurs Etats respectifs, importée dans le territoire de l'autre, à cause, ou en
considération de la nationalité
du navire qui aurait transporté
cette production, soit qu'il appartienne à l'une des Parties,
soit à l'autre: l'intention bien
positive des deux Parties Contractantes étant qu'aucune différence ou distinction quelconque
n'ait lieu à cet égard.

Article IV.

En considération de l'étendue
limitée des territoires des Républiques de Lubeck, Bremen et
Hambourg, et de l'intime liaison
de Commerce et de navigation
subsistante entre ces Républiques;
il est ici stipulé et convenu que
tout navire appartenant exclusivement à un ou plusieurs Citoyens de l'une ou des autres desdites Républiques, et dont le Capitaine sera aussi Citoyen de l'une
desdites Républiques, pourvu que
les trois quarts de l'equipage se
composent de Citoyens ou Sujets
de l'une ou de plusieurs desdites
Républiques, ou d'un ou de plusieurs des Etats de la Confédéra-
tion Germanique; ledit navire
sera considéré pour tous les objets
de cette Convention, comme

taken to be, and considered as, a vessel belonging to Lubeck, Bremen, or Hamburg.

ARTICLE V.

Any vessel, together with her cargo, belonging to either of the free Hanseatic Republics of Lubeck, Bremen, or Hamburg, and coming from either of the said ports, to the United States, shall, for all the purposes of this Convention, be deemed to have cleared from the Republic to which such vessel belongs; although, in fact, it may not have been the one from which she departed; and any vessel of the United States, and her cargo, trading to the ports of Lubeck, Bremen, or Hamburg, directly, or in succession, shall, for the like purposes, be on the footing of a Hanseatic vessel, and her cargo, making the same voyage.

ARTICLE VI.

It is, likewise, agreed, That it shall be wholly free for all merchants, commanders of ships, and other Citizens of both Parties, to manage, themselves their own business, in all the ports and places subject to the jurisdiction of each other, as well with respect to the consignment and sale of their goods and merchandize, by wholesale or retail, as with respect to the loading, unloading, and sending off their ships, submitting themselves to the laws, decrees and usages there established, to

navire appartenant à Lubeck, Bremen ou Hambourg.

ARTICLE V.

Tout bâtiment, ainsi que sa cargaison, appartenant à l'une des Républiques Anséatiques de Lubeck Bremen et Hambourg, et venant de l'un des ports des susdites Républiques, aux Etats Unis, sera considéré, pour tous les objets de cette Convention, comme venant de la République à laquelle il appartient, quoique, dans le fait, ce port ne soit pas celui d'où il aurait fait voile: et tout bâtiment des Etats Unis, ainsi que sa cargaison, trafiquant directement ou successivement, avec les ports de Lubeck, Bremen et Hambourg, sera placé, pour ces mêmes objets, sur le même pied qu'un bâtiment Anséatique et sa cargaison faisant le même voyage.

ARTICLE VI.

Il est, en outre, convenu, que les négocians, capitaines de navires, et autres citoyens des deux Parties, pourront, eux-mêmes, diriger librement leurs propres affaires dans tous les ports et places soumis à la juridiction de chacune d'Elles, tant pour ce qui a rapport à la consignation, et à la vente, en gros et en détail de leurs denrées et marchandises, que por ce qui regarde le chargement, déchargement et expédition de leurs bâtimens; en se conformant aux lois, décrets et usages y éta-

which native Citizens are subjected; they being, in all these cases, to be treated as Citizens of the Republic in which they reside, or at least, to be placed on a footing with the Citizens or subjects of the most favored nation.

blis, auxquels les Citoyens de l'Etat sont assujettis: ils seront, dans tous ces cas, traités comme sujets de la République dans laquelle ils resideront; ou, du moins, ils seront placés sur le même pied que les Citoyens ou sujets de la nation la plus favorisée.

ARTICLE VII.

The Citizens of each of the Contracting Parties shall have power to dispose of their personal goods, within the jurisdiction of the other, by sale, donation, testament, or otherwise; and their representatives, being Citizens of the other Party, shall succeed to their said personal goods, whether by testament, or *ab intestato*, and they may take possession thereof, either by themselves or others acting for them, and dispose of the same, at their will, paying such dues only as the inhabitants of the country wherein said goods are, shall be subject to pay in like cases: and if, in the case of real estate, the said heirs would be prevented from entering into the possession of the inheritance, on account of their character of aliens, there shall be granted to them the term of three years to dispose of the same, as they may think proper, and to withdraw the proceeds, without molestation, and exempt from all duties of detraction, on the part of the Government of the respective States.

ARTICLE VII.

Les Citoyens de chacune des Parties Contractantes pourront disposer de leurs biens personnels, dans les limites de la juridiction de l'autre, par vente, donation, testament ou autrement; et leurs héritiers, etant Citoyens de l'autre Partie, succéderont auxdits biens personnels, soit en vertu d'un testament, soit *ab intestato;* ils pourront en prendre possession, soit en personne, soit par d'autres agissant en leur place; et ils en disposeront à leur volonté, en ne payant d'autres droits que ceux auxquels les habitans du pays où se trouvent lesdits biens, sont assujettis en pareille occasion. Et si, dans le cas de biens immeubles, lesdits héritiers ne pouvaient entrer en jouissance de l'heritage, a cause de leur qualité d'étrangers, il leur sera accordé un délai de trois ans, pour en disposer à leur gré, et pour en retirer le produit, sans obstacle, et exempt de tous droits de détraction de la part des Gouvernemens des Etats respectifs.

Article VIII.

Both the Contracting Parties promise and engage formally to give their special protection to the persons and property, of the Citizens of each other, of all occupations, who may be in the territories subject to the jurisdiction of the one or the other, transient or dwelling therein, leaving open and free to them the tribunals of justice for their judicial recourse, on the same terms which are usual and customary with the natives or Citizens of the country in which they may be; for which they may employ, in defence of their rights, such advocates, solicitors, notaries, agents, and factors, as they may judge proper, in all their trials at law; and such Citizens or agents shall have as free opportunity as native Citizens to be present at the decisions and sentences of the tribunals, in all cases which may concern them; and, likewise, at the taking of all examinations and evidence which may be exhibited in the said trials.

Article IX.

The Contracting Parties desiring to live in peace and harmony with all the other nations of the earth, by means of a policy frank and equally friendly with all, engage mutually not to grant any particular favor to other nations, in respect of Commerce and

Article VIII.

Les deux Parties Contractantes promettent et s'engagent formellement, d'accorder leur protection spéciale aux personnes et propriétés des Citoyens de chacune d'Elles, quelles que soient leurs occupations, qui pourraient se trouver dans les territoires soumis à leur juridiction, soit pour y voyager, soit pour y séjourner, leur accordant pleine liberté de recourir aux cours de justice, pour leurs affaires litigieuses, aux mêmes conditions qui seront accordées par l'usage, aux Citoyens du pays où ils se trouveront; et d'employer, dans leur procès, pour la défense de leurs droits, tels avocats, avoués, notaires, agens ou mandataires qu'ils trouveront convenable de choisir; et lesdits Citoyens, et leurs agents, jouiront de la même liberté que ceux du pays, d'assister aux décisions et sentences des tribunaux, dans tous les cas où ils s'y trouveront intéressés; ainsi qu'à l'examen des témoins qui seraient appelés dans lesdits procès.

Article IX.

Les Parties Contractantes désirant vivre en paix et harmonie avec toutes les nations de la terre, en observant envers chachune également une politique franche et amicale; s'engagent mutuellement à n'accorder aucune faveur particulière à d'autres

navigation, which shall not immediately become common to the other Party, who shall enjoy the same freely, if the concession was freely made, or on allowing the same compensation, if the concession was conditional.

ARTICLE X.

The present Convention shall be in force for the term of twelve years, from the date hereof, and further, until the end of twelve months after the Government of the United States, on the one part, or the free Hanseatic Republics of Lubeck, Bremen or Hamburg, or either of them, on the other part, shall have given notice of their intention to terminate the same; each of the said Contracting Parties reserving to itself the right of giving such notice to the other, at the end of the said term of twelve years; and it is hereby agreed between them, that, at the expiration of twelve months after such notice shall have been received by either of the Parties from the other, this Convention, and all the provisions thereof, shall, altogether cease and determine, as far as regards the States giving and receiving such notice; it being always understood and agreed, that if one or more of the Hanseatic Republics aforesaid, shall, at the expiration of twelve years from the date hereof, give or receive notice of

nations, en fait de commerce et de navigation, qui ne devienne aussitôt commune à l'autre Partie; et celle-ci jouira de cette faveur gratuitement, si la concession est gratuite; ou en accordant la même compensation, si la concession est conditionelle.

ARTICLE X.

La présente Convention sera en vigueur pendant douze ans, à dater de ce jour; et audelà de ce terme, jusqu'à l'expiration de douze mois après que l'un ou l'autre des Gouvernemens des Républiques Anséatiques de Lubeck, Bremen et Hambourg, d'une part; ou le Gouvernement des Etats Unis, d'autre part, aura annoncé à l'autre son intention de la terminer; chacune des Parties Contractantes se réservant le droit de faire à l'autre une telle déclaration, au bout des douze ans susmentionnés; et il est convenu entre Elles qu'à l'expiration de douze mois après qu'une telle déclaration de l'une des Parties aura été reçue par l'autre, cette Convention, et toutes les stipulations y contenues cesseront d'être obligatoires, par rapport aux Etats qui donneront ou recevront cette déclaration: bien entendu et convenu que si l'une ou plusieurs desdites Républiques Anséatiques, à l'expiration de douze ans, à dater de ce jour, donnent, ou reçoivent la déclaration de la cessation proposée de

the proposed termination of this Convention, it shall, nevertheless remain in full force and operation, as far as regards the remaining Hanseatic Republics, or Republic, which may not have given or received such notice.

ARTICLE XI.

The present Convention being approved and ratified by the President of the United States, by, and with the advice and consent of the Senate thereof; and by the Senates of the Hanseatic Republics of Lubeck, Bremen and Hamburg, the ratifications shall be exchanged at Washington, within nine months from the date hereof, or sooner if possible.

In faith whereof, We, the Plenipotentiaries of the Contracting Parties have signed the present Convention; and have thereto affixed our Seals.

Done in quadruplicates, at the City of Washington on the twentieth day of December, in the year of Our Lord, one thousand, eight hundred and twenty seven, in the fifty second year of the Independence of the United States of America.

[Seal]   H. CLAY
[Seal]   V. RUMPFF

cette Convention, ladite Convention restera, néanmoins, en pleine force et effet, par rapport à celle, ou à celles des Républiques Anséatiques qui n'aura, ou qui n'auront, ni donné ni reçu cette déclaration.

ARTICLE XI.

La présente Convention étant approuvée et ratifiée par les Sénats des Républiques Anséatiques de Lubeck, Bremen et Hambourg; et par le Président des Etats Unis, par, et avec l'avis et le consentement du Sénat desdits Etats, les ratifications en seront échangées à Washington dans l'espace de neuf mois, à dater de ce jour, ou plutôt, si faire se peut.

En foi de quoi les Plénipotentiaires des Parties Contractantes ont signé la présente Convention, et y ont apposé leurs Sceaux.

Fait par quadruplicata, en la Cité de Washington, le vingt Décembre, l'an de Grâce Mil huit cent vingt sept, et le cinquante deuxième de l'Indépendance des Etats Unis d'Amérique.

[Seal]   V. RUMPFF
[Seal]   H. CLAY

NOTES

This convention comprises three agreements. The Hanseatic Republics, Lübeck, Bremen, and Hamburg, contracted severally with the United States, as appears from the opening clause of the convention; and by Article 10 the right of termination after twelve years on twelve months' notice was several on both sides.

On November 7, 1827, Vincent Rumpff,[1] Minister Plenipotentiary of the Hanseatic Republics, was presented to the President by Secretary of State Henry Clay (D. S., 3 Notes to Foreign Legations, 399, November 6, 1827). President Adams wrote of the occasion as follows (Memoirs of John Quincy Adams, VII, 348):

> At one o'clock Mr. Clay came, and introduced Mr. Rumpff, who delivered to me three credential letters from the Senates of the Hanseatic cities of Hamburg, Lubeck, and Bremen, signed by the Burgomaster, President of Hamburg and Lubeck, and the President of the Senate of Bremen. He has the character of a Minister Plenipotentiary from the Hanseatic cities upon a special mission to negotiate a treaty of navigation and commerce. In delivering the letters, he addressed to me a very few words expressive of the desire of the Governments of the Hanseatic cities to cultivate the friendship of the United States and their Government, which I answered as briefly, by assuring him of our reciprocal feelings, of my own regard for the Hanseatic republics, and of my determination to foster and promote to the extent of my power our commercial intercourse with them.

The full powers of the three Republics to their Minister Plenipotentiary, the originals of which, in French, are in the treaty file, are separate instruments and of dissimilar wording, dated for Lübeck June 16, for Bremen June 30, and for Hamburg June 27, 1827. Similarly the Minister Plenipotentiary of the three Republics brought three separate letters of credence to the President, written also in French and of the same respective dates as his full powers; each of them follows a different diplomatic form and in each the Minister is spoken of as Minister of the three Republics to France (D. S., 1 Notes from the Hanseatic Legation). But the instrument of ratification on the part of the Hanseatic Republics is one document, separately executed on behalf of each on the respective dates stated in the headnote.

No papers accompanied this convention when it was transmitted to the Senate with the presidential message of December 24, 1827 (Executive Journal, III, 583; American State Papers, Foreign Relations, VI, 742–45).

In the final clause of the convention it is stated that the document was "done in quadruplicates." As only one original is in the treaty file, doubtless the other three were respectively for the Governments of the three Hanseatic Republics.

In the signed original in the file, as the printed texts show, the *alternat* was observed. The English text is written on the left pages and the French text on the right pages of that original; the United

---

[1] Mr. Rumpff was a son-in-law of John Jacob Astor.

States is named first in the English text and the Hanseatic Republics first in the French text throughout; and the signature of Henry Clay is first at the end of the English text and second at the end of the French text.

The treaty file is complete, including the attested resolution of advice and consent of the Senate of January 7, 1828 (Executive Journal, III, 589), except that there is no duplicate or copy of the United States instrument of ratification other than a facsimile of the original, recently obtained from the archives of the Senatskommission für Reichs- und Auswärtige Angelegenheiten, Lübeck. That document is in the usual form, including the text of the convention in both languages, with the English on the left pages.

The instrument of ratification on the part of the Hanseatic Republics is one document, signed and sealed for the three Republics on the respective dates stated in the headnote. It is written in French and includes both texts of the convention in parallel columns, the French on the left. In translation it reads as follows:

We, the Senates of the Republics and free and Hanseatic cities of Lübeck, Bremen, and Hamburg, make known to all those who shall see these presents that a Convention of Amity, Commerce, and Navigation having been concluded between us on the one part and the United States of America on the other part, signed at Washington the twentieth of December in the year of grace eighteen hundred and twenty-seven by our Plenipotentiary and by the Plenipotentiary of the President of the United States of America, authorized in that regard in due form, which convention, inserted here word for word, is of the following tenor:

[Here follows the text of the convention]

Having seen and examined the above-mentioned convention, we have approved, ratified, and accepted, and confirmed the same in all and each of its articles and clauses, and by these presents we approve, ratify, accept, and confirm the same as well for ourselves as for our successors, promising to fulfil and to observe inviolate and faithfully all that is contained in that convention, without permitting it to be contravened in any manner whatsoever.

In faith whereof the Burgomaster Presidents have signed these presents, and we have caused to be affixed the seals of our cities.

Done at Lübeck the twenty-sixth of March in the year of grace one thousand eight hundred and twenty-eight.

[Seal] C. H. KINDLER
Burgomaster President

Done at Bremen the third of April in the year of grace one thousand eight hundred and twenty-eight.

The President of the Senate
[Seal] J. M. NONNAN

Done at Hamburg the eighth of April in the year of grace one thousand eight hundred and twenty-eight.

The President of the Senate
[Seal] J. W. BARTELS, DR.

The certificate of the exchange of ratifications at Washington on June 2, 1828, is in English and in customary form; in the final clause thereof it is stated that it was signed in quadruplicate. One example is in the treaty file.

Like the ratifications, the original proclamation of June 2, 1828, includes the text of the treaty in both languages. The English is on the left pages. Attached to the document is the attested resolution

of advice and consent of the Senate. The proclamation is printed, with both texts of the treaty, at pages 178–87 of the Session Laws for the first session of the Twentieth Congress.

Copies of the proclamations of the convention and of the additional article thereto of June 4, 1828 (Document 63), including the texts in English and French, were transmitted to Congress with the presidential message of January 26, 1829 (Richardson, II, 425–26; House Document No. 92, 20th Congress, 2d session, serial 186).

The Full Powers

As has been mentioned, the treaty file contains the originals of the full powers given by the three Hanseatic Republics to their Minister Plenipotentiary to negotiate and sign the convention. Those three documents are signed by the respective Presidents of the Senates of the three Republics and are respectively under the seals of those Governments. In the treaty file are contemporary translations from the French of those three documents which read as follows:

[Lübeck]

The United States of North America having been pleased, on several occasions, to manifest their favorable dispositions respecting the relations of commerce and navigation desired to be kept up and promoted with the Republics and Free Hanseatic cities; and these said cities being animated with a mutual desire to negotiate and conclude with the said United States a treaty of commerce and navigation, calculated to give new and increasing activity to relations reciprocally advantageous:

The Senate of the Republic and Hanseatic city of Lübeck, reposing an entire confidence in the qualifications which distinguish the Sieur Vincent Rumpff, Minister of the free cities of Germany near His Majesty the King of France and Navarre, does, by these presents, appoint and constitute him its Plenipotentiary, to negotiate and conclude, in the name of Lübeck, with such person or persons as His Excellency the President of the aforesaid United States will be pleased to designate, a treaty of commerce and navigation common to the three Republics and Hanseatic cities, and likewise to sign the same on the part of Lübeck.

The Senate promises to confirm and ratify, within the term which shall be prescribed, all that the Plenipotentiaries thus appointed and constituted shall, accordingly, have agreed upon and signed.

In faith whereof the President of the Senate has signed the present full powers and caused the public seal to be hereunto affixed.

Done at Lübeck the sixteenth of June in the year of grace one thousand eight hundred and twenty-seven.

The President of the Senate of the Republic and Hanseatic city of Lübeck.

[Seal] A. H. Voeg

C. H. Gutschow
Secretary

[Bremen]

The Senate of the Republic and free Hanseatic city of Bremen, actuated by the desire of promoting, as far as in its power, the relations so happily existing between the United States of North America and the Republic of Bremen, and of drawing closer and closer the bonds of friendship and good intelligence between the said United States and the Hanseatic Republics, and convinced that nothing could contribute more to the attainment of this salutary end than the conclusion of a treaty of commerce and navigation between the said states, has, for this purpose, appointed, and by these presents does appoint the Sieur Vincent Rumpff, Min-

ister from this Republic to the Court of France, its Minister Plenipotentiary near the United States, to negotiate and conclude, in the name of the Republic of Bremen, with such person or persons as His Excellency the President of the aforesaid United States may be pleased, therefore, to designate, a treaty of commerce and navigation, and to sign such treaty in the name of the Republic and free Hanseatic city of Bremen.

The Senate promises to ratify, within the term which shall be prescribed, all that the said Plenipotentiaries shall have accordingly agreed upon and signed.

In faith whereof the presents have been signed by the President of the Senate and sealed with the seal of state.

Given at Bremen this thirtieth of June in the year of grace one thousand eight hundred and twenty-seven.

The Senate of the Republic and free Hanseatic city of Bremen.

> The President of the Senate
> [Seal] SMIDT

By the President:
BREULS

[Hamburg]

The Senate of the Republic and Hanseatic city of Hamburg

To all who shall see these presents, Greeting:

Anxious to promote and draw closer the bonds of friendship which connect the Hanseatic Republics, and particularly that of Hamburg, with the United States of North America, and convinced that nothing could more contribute to the accomplishment of this wished-for object than the conclusion of a treaty having for its object to fix in a more particular manner the commercial relations between the two countries: To this effect the Senate has appointed and by these presents does appoint the Sieur Vincent Rumpff, its Minister near His Majesty the King of France, its Plenipotentiary, authorizing him, for the purposes above mentioned, to enter into negotiations with such person or persons as His Excellency the President of the said United States will be pleased, therefore, to designate, and to sign such treaty as will result from said negotiations.

The Senate promises to ratify, within the prescribed term, all that shall have been agreed upon and signed by the said Plenipotentiaries.

In faith whereof these presents have been signed by the President of the Senate and sealed with the seal of the state.

Given at Hamburg the twenty-seventh day of June in the year of grace one thousand eight hundred and twenty-seven.

> The President of the Senate
> [Seal] WILLIAM AMSINCK

By the President:
E. BANKS
Secretary

The full power to Secretary of State Clay was dated November 26, 1827, and was in customary form (D. S., 2 Credences, 71).

ARTICLE 4

While this convention was several as to each of the three Hanseatic Republics, their commercial connection was recognized in Article 4 in the stipulations regarding vessels owned by the citizens of "any, or either of them." That article, also, in its limitations as to three fourths of the crews of such vessels, provided that they might be composed of citizens or subjects of any of "the States of the Confederation of Germany."

The German Confederation (Deutscher Bund) then existing, usually called the Germanic Confederation, was created at the Congress

of Vienna (see Treitschke, History of Germany in the Nineteenth Century, II, 122–36).　To the constitutive agreement of June 8, 1815, which was in part textually and in part by reference included in the Final Act of the Congress of Vienna of June 9, 1815, and the whole of which was annexed to that Final Act, there were thirty-eight parties. Its text, in German, with a French translation, is in British and Foreign State Papers, II, 114–36.　Under that federative act, which was elaborated at a conference held at Vienna in 1820 (Treitschke, *op. cit.*, III, 303–35), the Germanic Confederation was a rather loose form of union.　The federal diet had power to deal with certain relations of members of the Confederation *inter se;* but as to outside states, the members of the Confederation continued properly to be regarded as separate international entities.

While Austria and Prussia, "for all their possessions formerly belonging to the German Empire," were the leading members of the Germanic Confederation, it comprised all the then existing states of north and south Germany, including the three Hanseatic Republics; its thirty-nine members (the thirty-eight parties of 1815 and Hesse-Homburg from 1817) were the following (named in a somewhat arbitrary order):

Austria	Saxe-Gotha
Prussia	Saxe-Coburg
Bavaria	Saxe-Meiningen
Saxony	Saxe-Hildburghausen
Hanover	Oldenburg
Württemberg	Schwarzburg-Sondershausen
Baden	Schwarzburg-Rudolstadt
Electoral Hesse	Hohenzollern-Hechingen
Grand Duchy of Hesse	Hohenzollern-Sigmaringen
Hesse-Homburg	Liechtenstein
Holstein	Waldeck
Luxemburg	Reuss-Greiz
Brunswick	Reuss-Schleiz
Mecklenburg-Schwerin	Schaumburg-Lippe
Mecklenburg-Strelitz	Lippe
Nassau	Frankfort
Anhalt-Dessau	Lübeck
Anhalt-Bernburg	Bremen
Anhalt-Köthen	Hamburg
Saxe-Weimar	

Dynastic and territorial changes from time to time reduced the number of members of the Germanic Confederation.　The five Saxon duchies in 1826 became four (Saxe-Weimar, Saxe-Meiningen, Saxe-Coburg-Gotha, and Saxe-Altenburg); the three Anhalt duchies were united by 1863; and the two Hohenzollern principalities became part of Prussia in 1850.

The Germanic Confederation came to an end in 1866 as a result of the war between Austria and Prussia, following the dispute regarding Schleswig-Holstein, a war in which certain other German states took part.

The North German Confederation, which was formed following the war of 1866, and which continued until the creation of the German

Reich, 1870–71, comprised the German states north of the River
Main; but Hanover, Electoral Hesse, Nassau, Holstein (from which
the Duchy of Lauenburg was separated), Hesse-Homburg, and the
city of Frankfort were absorbed by Prussia. Austria and the small
principality of Liechtenstein were of course not within that confederation; Luxemburg did not become a member; but the North German
Confederation included all the twenty-six German states which later
formed the German Empire, except the Kingdoms of Bavaria and
Württemburg and the Grand Duchy of Baden, and in part (south of
the Main) the Grand Duchy of Hesse.

The Germanic Confederation (1815–66) was not in itself an economic unit. The relations between its members in commerce and
navigation were not governed by the federative act of June 8, 1815,
although mentioned in Article 19 thereof.

THE ZOLLVEREIN

The German Zollverein, or Customs Union, "formed by a series of
treaties and including seventeen states with a population of some
twenty-three millions, came into force on January 1st, 1834" (Ashley,
Modern Tariff History, 14). By 1836, with the accessions of Baden,
Frankfort, and Nassau, the area of the Zollverein was 8,252 square
miles with a population of over 25,000,000 (Weber, Der deutsche
Zollverein, 142). During the next few years there were additions of
various other, mostly small, German states, but including Brunswick
and Luxemburg (Weber, *op. cit.*, 143, 201–4). By 1842 the number
of German states without the Zollverein was very few; Austria never
was a party to the Zollverein; Hanover and Oldenburg were not
parties until 1851; but from that time on the only German states of
any importance outside the Zollverein, other than Austria, were the
two Mecklenburg grand duchies and the three Hanseatic Republics.

Following the war of 1866, the Zollverein was reconstituted.
From 1868 it included all the states of north and south Germany
except Hamburg and Bremen, and also included Luxemburg, which
was not a member of the North German Confederation. That
situation continued even after the formation of the German Empire.
From 1868 Lübeck was within the Customs Union, but Bremen and
Hamburg were not until 1888. As to the Zollverein, see generally,
Weber, Der deutsche Zollverein, and also Ashley, *op. cit.*, 1–49.

The preamble of the commercial convention between the United
States and the Zollverein signed on March 25, 1844 (which did
not go into force), begins with the following words descriptive of
the parties (D. S., Unperfected E3; Senate Confidential Document
No. 3, 29th Congress, 2d session, Regular Confidential Documents,
XX, 481–533):

The United States of America, on the one part and His Majesty the King of
Prussia, as well for himself, and as representing other sovereign States and parts
thereof included in the Prussian system of Customs and Impost, namely the
Grand-Duchy of Luxemburg, the Grand Ducal Mecklemburg enclaves Rossow,
Netzeband and Schoenberg, the Grand Ducal Oldenburg Principality of Birken-

feld, the Duchies of Anhalt-Coethen, Anhalt-Dessau, and Anhalt-Bernburg, the Principalities of Waldeck and Pyrmont, the Principality of Lippe, and the Landgrave Hessian Oberamt Meisenheim, as also in the name of the other members of the Germanic Association of Customs and Commerce, namely the Kingdom of Bavaria, the Kingdom of Saxony, the Kingdom of Württemberg for itself and representing the Principalities of Hohenzollern-Hechingen and Hohenzollern-Sigmaringen, the Grand Duchy of Baden, the Electorate of Hesse, the Grand Duchy of Hesse, for itself and representing the Landgrave Hessian Amt Homburg, the States forming the Thuringian Association of Customs and Commerce,—namely the Grand Duchy of Saxony, the Duchies of Saxe-Meiningen, Saxe Altenburg and Saxe Coburg and Gotha, and the Principalities of Schwarzburg-Rudolstadt and Schwarzburg Sondershausen, Reuss-Greitz, Reuss Schleitz, and Reuss-Lobenstein and Ebersdorf,—the Duchy of Brunswick, the Duchy of Nassau, and the free City of Frankfort, on the other Part. . . .

The report of Secretary of State Upshur of November 24, 1843, which accompanied the message to Congress of President Tyler of December 5, 1843, contains this statement regarding the Zollverein (Senate Document No. 1, 28th Congress, 1st session, serial 431, pp. 17–18):

The Zoll Verein or Customs Union at present consists of the following States:

States.	Population.
Kingdom of Prussia	14, 271, 530
Do. Bavaria	4, 315, 469
Do. Wurtemburg	1, 649, 839
Do. Saxony	1, 652, 114
Grand duchy of Baden	1, 277, 403
Electorate of Hesse	704, 700
Grand duchy of Hesse, (with Hamburg)	807, 671
Duchy of Nassau	386, 221
Thuringian Union	908, 478
Free city of Frankfort on the Maine	60, 000
Duchy of Brunswick	250, 000
Grand duchy of Luxemburg	400, 000
Principality of Lippe Detmold	106, 000
Total	26, 799, 000

The accession to the Union of the kingdom of Hanover, with nearly 2,000,000 of inhabitants, is in contemplation. This event would doubtless decide the smaller States of the north to join the Union; and in that case the whole of Germany, with the exception of the Austrian dominions, would be united, and would contain a population as is shown in the following table:

Table of population.

States.	Population.	Total.
Present population, as given in preceding table_____	_____	26, 799, 000
Hanover_____	2, 000, 000	
Grand duchy of Oldenburg_____	270, 000	
The duchies of Holstein and Luxemburg, (belonging to the King of Denmark)_____	481, 000	
The duchy of Mecklenburg Schwerin_____	490, 000	
The duchy of Mecklenburg Sterlitz_____	91, 000	
The Hanseatic cities of Lubeck, Hamburg, and Bremen_____	260, 000	
		3, 392, 000
All united in German Union_____	_____	30, 191, 000

The Negotiations

The archives of the Department of State furnish no material regarding the negotiations leading up to this convention; those discussions were verbal; detailed accounts of interest, including references to the instructions given to the Plenipotentiary of the Hanseatic Republics, are in Baasch, "Beiträge zur Geschichte der Handelsbeziehungen zwischen Hamburg und Amerika," 104–23 (Hamburgische Festschrift zur Erinnerung an die Entdeckung Amerika's, I), and in Lindeman, "Zur Geschichte des älteren Handelsbeziehungen Bremens mit den Ver. Staaten von Nordamerika" (Bremisches Jahrbuch, X, 124–46).

Treaty Series No. 202
8 Statutes at Large, 372–77
18 *ibid.*, pt. 2, Public Treaties, 474–76

60

MEXICO : JANUARY 12, 1828, AND APRIL 5, 1831

Treaty of Limits, signed at Mexico January 12, 1828, with additional article signed at Mexico April 5, 1831. Originals in English and Spanish.
Treaty submitted to the Senate April 21, 1828. Resolution of advice and consent April 28, 1828. Ratified by the United States April 30, 1828 (but as to this ratification, see the notes). Ratified by Mexico April 28, 1828. Treaty and additional article submitted to the Senate February 24, 1832. Resolution of advice and consent April 4, 1832. Ratified by the United States April 5, 1832. Ratified by Mexico January 14, 1832. Ratifications exchanged at Washington April 5, 1832. Proclaimed April 5, 1832.

Treaty of Limits between the United States of America and the United Mexican States.

The limits of the United States of America with the bordering territories of Mexico having been fixed and designated by a solemn treaty[1] concluded and signed at Washington on the twenty-second day of February, in the year of our Lord one thousand eight hundred and nineteen, between the respective Plenipotentiaries of the government of the United States of America on the one part and of that of Spain on the other: And whereas, the said treaty having been sanctioned at a period when Mexico constituted a part of the Spanish Monarchy, it is deemed necessary now to confirm the va-

Tratado de limites entre los Estados Unidos de Megico y los Estados Unidos de America.

Habiendose fijado y designado los limites de los Estados Unidos de America con los territorios limitrofes de Megico por un Tratado[1] solemne concluido y firmado en Washington á veinte y dos de Febrero de mil ochocientos diez y nueve entre los Plenipotenciarios respectivos del Gobierno de los Estados Unidos por una parte, y de España por la otra; por tanto, y en considecion á que dicho Tratado recibio su sancion en una epoca en que Megico formaba una parte de la Monarquia Española, se ha creido necesario al presente, declarar, y confirmar la validez de dicho

---

[1] Document 41.

lidity of the aforesaid treaty of limits, regarding it as still in force and binding between the United States of America and the United Mexican States.

With this intention, the President of the United States of America has appointed Joel Roberts Poinsett their Plenipotentiary; and the President of the United Mexican States their Excellencies Sebastian Camacho and José Ygnacio Esteva:

And the said Plenipotentiaries having exchanged their full powers, have agreed upon and concluded the following articles:

ARTICLE FIRST.

The dividing limits of the respective bordering territories of the United States of America and of the United Mexican States being the same as were agreed and fixed upon by the above-mentioned treaty of Washington concluded and signed on the twenty-second day of February in the year one thousand eight hundred and nineteen, the two high contracting parties will proceed forthwith to carry into full effect the third and fourth articles of said treaty, which are herein recited as follows:

Tratado considerandolo vigente y obligatorio entre los Estados Unidos de Megico y los Estados Unidos de America: en consecuencia han sido nombrados los respectivos Plenipotenciarios: á Saber.

El Presidente de los Estados Unidos de Megico á Sus Exêelencias los Señores Sebastian Camacho, y José Ygnacio Esteva: y el Presidente de los Estados Unidos de America al Señor, Joel Roberts Poinsett, su Enviado Extraordinario, y Ministro Plenipotenciario cerca del Gobierno de los Estados Unidos de Megico. Los que despues de haber cambiado sus plenos poderes, y hallados en buena, y debida forma han convenido y concluido los articulos siguientes:

ARTICULO PRIMERO

Siendo los limites divisorios de los Estados Unidos de Megico, y de los Estados Unidos de America en los terrenos colindantes de ambas Republicas los mismos que se acordaron, y fijaron en el dicho Tratado de Washington fño, á veinte y dos de Febrero de mil ochocientos diez y nueve, se procederá inmediatamente á poner en ejecucion entre las dos dichas partes contractantes los articulos tercero, y cuarto de dicho Tratado, que, á continuacion se insertan.

ARTICLE SECOND.

The boundary line between the two countries, west of the Mississippi, shall begin on the Gulf of Mexico, at the mouth of the river Sabine, in the sea, continuing north, along the western bank of that river, to the 32d degree of latitude; thence, by a line due north, to the degree of latitude where it strikes the Rio Roxo of Natchitoches, or Red River; then, following the course of the Rio Roxo westward, to the degree of longitude 100 west from London and 23 from Washington; then, crossing the said Red River, and running thence, by a line due north, to the river Arkansas; thence, following the course of the southern bank of the Arkansas, to its source, in latitude 42 north; and thence, by that parallel of latitude, to the South Sea. The whole being as laid down in Melish's map of the United States, published at Philadelphia, improved to the first of January, 1818. But if the source of the Arkansas river shall be found to fall north or south of latitude 42, then the line shall run from the said source due south or north, as the case may be, till it meets the said parallel of latitude 42, and thence, along the said parallel, to the South Sea: All the islands in the Sabine, and the said Red and Arkansas rivers, throughout the course thus described, to belong to the United

ARTICULO SEGUNDO.

La linea divisoria entre los dos países, al occidente del Misisipi arrancará del seno Megicano en la embocadura del rio Sabina en el mar, seguirá al Norte, por la orilla occidental de este rio hasta el grado 32. de latitud; desde allí, por una linea recta al Norte hasta el grado de latitud, en que entra en el rio Rojo de Natchitoche; *Red river*, y continuará por el curso del rio Rojo al Oeste hasta el grado 100. de longitud occidental de Londres, y 23 de Washington, en que cortará este rio y seguirá, por una linea recta al Norte, por el mismo grado hasta el rio Arkansas, cuya orilla meridional seguirá hasta su nacimiento en el grado 42. de latitud septentrional, y desde dicho punto se tirará una linea recta por el mismo paralelo de latitud, hasta el mar del Sur: todo segun el Mapa de los Estados Unidos de Melish publicado en Filadelfia y perfeccionado en 1818. Pero si el nacimiento del rio Arkansas se hallase al Norte, ó sur de dho, grado 42. de latitud, seguirá la linea desde el origen de dicho rio recta al Sur, ó Norte, segun fuese necesario, hasta que encuentre el expresado grado 42. de latitud, y desde alli por el mismo paralelo hasta el mar del Sur. Pertenecerán á los Estados Unidos todas las Yslas de los rios Sabina, Rojo de Natchitoches y Arkansas, en la extension de todo el curso,

States; but the use of the waters, and the navigation of the Sabine to the sea, and of the said rivers Roxo and Arkansas, throughout the extent of the said boundary, on their respective banks, shall be common to the respective inhabitants of both nations.

The two high contracting parties agree to cede and renounce all their rights, claims, and pretensions to the territories described by the said line; that is to say: the United States hereby cede to His Catholic Majesty, and renounce forever, all their rights, claims, and pretensions to the territories lying west and south of the above described line; and, in like manner, His Catholic Majesty cedes to the said United States, all his rights, claims, and pretensions to any territories east and north of the said line; and for himself, his heirs, and successors, renounces all claim to the said territories forever.

Article Third.

To fix this line with more precision, and to place the landmarks which shall designate exactly the limits of both nations, each of the contracting parties shall appoint a Commissioner and a Surveyor, who shall meet, before the termination of one year from the date of the ratification of this treaty, at Natchitoches, on the Red River, and proceed to run and mark the said line, from the mouth of the Sabine to the Red River, and

descrito; pero el uso de las aguas, y la navegacion del Sabina, hasta el mar, y de los espresados rios Rojo, y Arkansas, en toda la estension de sus mencionados limites en sus respectivas orillas será comun á los habitantes de las dos Naciones.

Las dos altas partes contratantes convienen en ceder, y renunciar todos sus derechos, reclamaciones y pretensiones sobre los territorios que se describen en esta linea, á saber, los Estados Unidos de America ceden á S. M. C. y renuncian para siempre todos sus derechos, reclamaciones, y pretensiones, á cualesquiera territorios situados al Oeste, y al Sur de dicha linea; y S. M. C. en igual forma, renuncia, y cede para siempre por sí y a nombre de sus herederos y sucesores todos los derechos que tiene sobre los territorios al Este y al Norte de la misma linea arriba descrita.

Articulo tercero.

Para fijar esta linea con mas precision, y establecer los mojones que señalen con ecsactitud los limites de ambas Naciones nombrará cada una de ellas un Comisario, y un Geometra que se juntarán antes del termino de un año Contado desde la fecha de la ratificacion de este Tratado, en Natchitoches, en las orillas del rio Rojo, y procederán á señalar, y demarcar dicha linea, desde la embocadura del Sabina hasta el

from the Red River to the river Arkansas, and to ascertain the latitude of the source of the said river Arkansas, in conformity to what is agreed upon and stipulated, and the line of latitude 42, to the South Sea: they shall make out plans, and keep journals of their proceedings, and the result agreed upon by them shall be considered as part of this treaty, and shall have the same force as if it were inserted therein. The two governments will amicably agree respecting the necessary articles to be furnished to those persons, and also as to their respective escorts, should such be deemed necessary.

Article Fourth.

The present Treaty shall be ratified, and the ratifications shall be exchanged at Washington, within the term of four months, or sooner, if possible.

In witness whereof, We, the respective Plenipotentiaries, have signed the same, and have hereunto affixed our respective seals.

Done at Mexico this twelfth day of January, in the Year of our Lord one thousand eight hundred and twenty eight, in the fifty-second year of the Independence of the United States of America, and in the eighth of that of the United Mexican States.

    J. R. Poinsett   [Seal]
    S. Camacho.   [Seal]
    J Y Esteva   [Seal]
56006°—33——28

rio Rojo, y de este hasta el rio Arkansas, y áveriguar con certidumbre el origen del expresado rio, Arkansas, y fijar segun queda estipulado, y convenido en este Tratado, la linea que debe seguir desde el grado 42. de latitud hasta el mar pacifico. Llevaran diarios, y levantaran planos de sus operaciones, y el resultado convenido por ellos se tendrá por parte de este Tratado, y tendrá la misma fuerza que se estuviese inserto en el, debiendo convenir, amistosamente los dos Gobiernos, en el arreglo de cuanto necesiten estos individuos y en la escolta respectiva que deban llevar siempre que se crea necesario.

Articulo cuarto.

El presente tratado será ratificado, y las ratificaciones serán cambiadas en Washington en el termino de cuatro meses .ó antes, si posible fuere.

En fe de lo cual, los respectivos Plenipotenciarios han firmado el presente, sellandolo con sus sellos respectivos.

Fecho en Megico, a los doce dias del mes de Enero, del año del Señor mil ochocientos veinte y ocho, octavo de la Independencia de los Estados Unidos de Megico, y 52° de la de los Estados Unidos de America.

    S. Camacho.   [Seal]
    J. Y. Esteva   [Seal]
    J. R. Poinsett   [Seal]

Additional Article to the Treaty of Limits concluded between the United States of America and the United Mexican States on the 12 day of January 1828.

The time having elapsed which was stipulated for the exchange of ratifications of the Treaty of Limits between the United Mexican States and the United States of America, signed in Mexico on the 12th of January 1828, and both Republics being desirous that it should be carried into full and complete effect with all due solemnity, the President of the United States of America has fully empowered on his part Anthony Butler a Citizen thereof and Chargé d'Affaires of the said States in Mexico. And the Vice-President of the United Mexican States, acting as President thereof, has in like manner fully empowered on his part their Excellencies Lucas Alaman, Secretary of State, and Foreign Relations, and Rafael Mangino Secretary of the Treasury, who after having exchanged their mutual powers found to be ample and in form have agreed and do hereby agree on the following article.

The ratifications of the Treaty of Limits concluded on the 12th January 1828, shall be exchanged at the City of Washington within the term of one year counting

Articulo adiccional al tratado de Limites celebrado entre los Estados Unidos Mejicanos y los Estados Unidos de America en 12. de Enero de 1828.

Habiendose pasado el tiempo señalado para el cambio de las ratificaciones del tratado de limites entre los Estados Unidos Mejicanos y los Estados Unidos de America firmado en Mejico el dia 12. de Enero de 1828, deseosas ambas Republicas de que el referido tratado tenga su mas puntual cumplimiento llenandose todas las formalidades necesarias, y habiendo revestido con sus plenos poderes el Vice Presidente en ejercicio del poder ejecutivo de los Estados Unidos Mejicanos á los Ecselentisimos Señores Don Lucas Alaman, Secretario de Estado y del Despacho de Relaciones interiores y esteriores y Don Rafael Mangino Secretario de Estado y del Despacho de Hacienda, y el Presidente de los Estados Unidos de America á Antonio Butler, Ciudadano de los mismos Estados y encargado de negocios de ellos en Mejico, despues de cambiar sus plenos poderes que se encontraron en buena y debida forma, han convenido y convienen en el articulo siguiente:

Las ratificaciones del tratado de limites celebrado el 12. de Enero de 1828, se cambiarán en la Ciudad de Washington dentro del termino de un año contado

from the date of this agreement and sooner should it be possible.

The present additional article shall have the same force and effect as if it had been inserted word for word in the aforesaid Treaty of the 12ᵗʰ of January of 1828, and shall be approved and ratified in the manner prescribed by the Constitutions of the respective States.

In faith of which the said Plenipotentiaries have hereunto set their hands and affixed their respective seals. Done in Mexico the fifth of April of the year one thousand eight hundred thirty one, the fifty fifth of the Independence of the United States of America, and the eleventh of that of the United Mexican States.

[Seal] A: BUTLER
[Seal] LUCAS ALAMAN
[Seal] RAFAEL MANGINO

desde la fecha de este convenio ó antes si fuere posible.

El presente articulo adiccional tendrá la misma fuerza y valor que si se hubiese incertado palabra por palabra en el tratado mencionado de 12. de Enero de 1828, y será aprovado y ratificado en los terminos que establecen las Constituciones de los respectivos Estados.

En fé de lo cual los referidos Plenipotenciarios lo hemos firmado y sellado con nuestros sellos respectivos. Fecho en Mejico á los cinco dias del mes de Abril de mil ochocientos treinta y uno, undecimo de la Independencia de los Estados Unidos Mejicanos, y quincuagesimo quinto de la de los Estados Unidos de America.

[Seal] LUCAS ALAMAN
[Seal] RAFAEL MANGINO
[Seal] A: BUTLER

NOTES

By Article 4 of this treaty it was provided that the ratifications thereof should be exchanged at Washington within the term of four months, or by May 12, 1828. The provision proved impossible of fulfilment, owing to the delay in the ratification on the part of Mexico, which was thus explained by Joel R. Poinsett, Minister to Mexico, in his despatch of April 24, 1828 (D. S., 4 Despatches, Mexico, No. 124):

The treaty of limits has been ratified by the house of Representatives and is now before the Senate. You will perceive, that it will be impossible to send the ratification of this government to Washington in time for the exchange of ratifications to take place within the term designated by the treaty.

This delay has originated from the extreme indolence of the person, who formerly filled the office of Secretary of State of this republic. He kept this treaty in his office upwards of two months without submitting it to Congress: altho I repeatedly represented to him, the prejudice that would result from this delay, especially to the Mexican government, which had already dispatched its commissioner to the frontiers.

In the meantime the treaty had been submitted to the Senate of the United States with the presidential message of April 21, and the usual resolution of advice and consent was passed on April 28 (Executive Journal, III, 604–6). Ratification by the United States followed not later than April 30; but the proceedings of the Mexican Congress were not completed until April 25, as appears from the despatch from Poinsett dated the next day (D. S., 4 Despatches, Mexico, No. 125):

The treaty of limits between the United States and Mexico concluded and signed on the 12ᵗʰ January last, was yesterday ratified by the Mexican Senate. The period fixed by the treaty for the exchange of ratifications being four months from the date of its signature, I shall not transmit the ratification of this government by express. It could not possibly arrive at Washington in time. I regret the delay which has occurred here, because I am aware it will render it necessary to submit the treaty a second time to Senate. This Congress despatched it with tolerable promptness. The delay, as I before observed, was occasioned by the dilatory habits of the former Secretary of State.

The Mexican instrument of ratification was in fact dated April 28, 1828, and it was not until August 2 that Secretary of State Clay was officially informed of the receipt of the Mexican ratification and the readiness of that Government to make the exchange (D. S., 1 Notes from the Mexican Legation). The reply of the same date (D. S., 4 Notes to Foreign Legations, 47–48) was to the effect that the treaty must again be submitted to the Senate, as the time for the exchange of ratifications had elapsed.

At the following session of the Senate, however, the treaty was not again sent to that body by President John Quincy Adams, presumably for the reason that the Treaty of Amity, Commerce, and Navigation of February 14, 1828 (American State Papers, Foreign Relations, VI, 952–62), had failed of ratification on the part of Mexico (D. S., 14 Instructions, American States, 149–71, October 16, 1829; House Document No. 351, 25th Congress, 2d session, serial 332; hereafter cited as "instructions of October 16, 1829"); and the policy of President Jackson was stated to be that this Treaty of Limits would be again submitted to the Senate when it was accompanied by a satisfactory treaty of commerce and navigation:

The Government of Mexico would do much to redress the past, and to remove well founded discontents in this country, by its speedy ratification of that treaty [of February 14, 1828], as it was agreed upon by its plenipotentiaries. The treaty of Limits now rests with the President. In consequence of the remissness on the part of Mexico in the transmission of its ratification to Washington, it has lost its obligatory character. The President intends, nevertheless, to submit it to the Senate, whenever he is enabled to accompany it with the treaty of Commerce and Navigation, now remaining before the Congress of Mexico, and which they have so long and so injuriously refused to act upon. But when he speaks of that treaty, and of his intention to submit it to the Senate with the treaty of Limits, he refers to it as containing the material provisions which were originally agreed to by the Executive Authority of Mexico. He is unwilling to believe that the Government of that country, after what has passed, can be induced to think it either just towards the United States, or respectful to itself, to send for consideration a mere skeleton of that Convention, with its most valuable stipulations expunged. It is not for him to say what the decision of the Senate of the United States, now free to act upon the whole subject as shall best comport with its views of the present interests of this country, would be, if both treaties were

presented in their original form. What the character of this decision may be, in the event of a refusal by the Government of Mexico to act upon the Commercial Treaty, or of a retrenchment of its most valuable provisions, there cannot be much room for doubt or conjecture.

Nearly three years elapsed after the ratification of the treaty by Mexico before the additional article of April 5, 1831, providing for the exchange of ratifications of the treaty within one year thereafter, was signed at Mexico. The treaty, with the additional article, was again submitted to the Senate by President Jackson on February 24, 1832 (Executive Journal, IV, 213); the usual resolution of advice and consent was passed unanimously on the following April 4 (*ibid.*, 237); and on the last day of the time limited, April 5, 1832, the ratifications were exchanged and the treaty proclaimed.

The adjournment of the exchange of ratifications from 1828 to 1832 is not, however, to be attributed to any single cause. A note of the Mexican Chargé d'Affaires at Washington, José Montoya, to Secretary of State Van Buren under date of April 16, 1829 (D. S., 1 Notes from the Mexican Legation), was to the effect that Mexico desired to carry out the Treaty of Limits and had invested him with full power to exchange the ratifications thereof; but this Government was still thinking of Texas and of a boundary different from that in the treaty (see Moore, Digest, I, 447–48, 454). The Jackson administration, which had come into office on March 4, 1829, desired to purchase Texas. Its project was formulated in the elaborate instructions of August 25, 1829, addressed to Poinsett (D. S., 1 Special Missions, 39–50); and the full power to Poinsett to negotiate regarding the matter is of the same date as the instructions (*ibid.*, 50–51); but Poinsett received word on December 9 that he was to be succeeded by Colonel Anthony Butler as diplomatic representative of the United States at Mexico with the rank of Chargé d'Affaires (D. S., 4 Despatches, Mexico, No. 193); and the instructions and full power of August 25 were delivered to him by Butler on December 22 (*ibid.*, December 23, 1829). The full power given by President Jackson to Butler under date of October 17, 1829 (D. S., 1 Special Missions, 53–54), followed the wording of that to Poinsett of August 25 and authorized him to treat "of and concerning the Limits between the territories of the United States of America, and those of the United Mexican States; and of and concerning a cession of part of the territory of the latter to the former; and to conclude a treaty or treaties touching the premises."

The Jackson project has been discussed by numerous writers; reference may be made to the chapter on "Texas and the Boundary Issue," in Manning, Early Diplomatic Relations between the United States and Mexico, 277–348, which deals particularly with the boundary question during the period 1822–30 and cites many other authorities. It need only be added here that the suggested acquisition met with no favor, but on the contrary met bitter opposition, in Mexico, where its general terms, including even the proposed purchase price of five million dollars, became public as early as January 9, 1830 (*ibid.*, 344).

Moreover, as has been said, the delay in the putting into force of this Treaty of Limits was connected with the negotiations for a treaty of amity, commerce, and navigation, which had been going on since 1825. In all, during the period 1826–31, four treaties with Mexico were signed, in chronological order as follows:

1. The Treaty of Amity, Commerce, and Navigation in thirty-five articles, with two additional articles, signed at Mexico on July 10, 1826. That treaty provided that its ratifications should be exchanged within eight months from the date of signature. It was submitted to the Senate on February 12, 1827, with the presidential message of February 8 (Executive Journal, III, 568–69); and the papers transmitted, including the text of the treaty and additional articles in English, are printed in American State Papers, Foreign Relations, VI, 578–613.

On February 26, 1827, the Senate consented to the ratification of that treaty, subject to certain amendments to Articles 3 and 16, the striking out of the first additional article, and the reduction of the term of the treaty from twelve years to six (Executive Journal, III, 570–71). The Mexican Chamber of Deputies, however, following an elaborate report from its Committee of Foreign Affairs recommending ratification subject to various amendments and conditions (instructions of October 16, 1829, where the time limited for the exchange of ratifications is mistakenly stated as ten months), on April 2, 1827, after the time limited for the exchange of ratifications but before the action of the United States Senate could have been known at Mexico, passed the following resolution (D. S., 3 Despatches, Mexico, protocol of January 8, 1828, enclosed in No. 118, March 8, 1828):

This House will not take into consideration the Treaty which the Government has concluded with the United States of America so long as it does not contain an article which shall renew the existence of the Treaty celebrated by the Cabinet of Madrid in the year 1819 with that of Washington, respecting the territorial limits of the two contracting parties.

Accordingly, that treaty of July 10, 1826, did not go into force. The negotiations leading up to its signature and the proceedings thereafter are carefully treated, with many citations, in Manning, Early Diplomatic Relations between the United States and Mexico, 205–33.

2. This Treaty of Limits of January 12, 1828. The presidential message of April 21, 1828, the text of the treaty in English and Spanish, and some of the papers stated to have been sent to the Senate therewith, are in American State Papers, Foreign Relations, VI, 946–50; but those papers relate almost wholly to the treaty next to be mentioned. Correspondence concerning the boundary (1825–36) is printed in House Document No. 42, 25th Congress, 1st session, serial 311.

3. The Treaty of Amity, Commerce, and Navigation signed at Mexico on February 14, 1828, in thirty-five articles with two additional articles. The text, in English and Spanish, without any other papers, is printed in American State Papers, Foreign Relations, VI,

952–62. That treaty provided that its ratifications were to be exchanged within six months from the date of signature.

Some of the correspondence relating to the treaty of February 14, 1828, is printed *ibid.*, 948–50; other papers are cited in the discussion of the negotiations in Manning, *op. cit.*, 234–42. As Poinsett reported under date of February 22, 1828 (*ibid.*, 239; American State Papers, Foreign Relations, VI, 948), in that treaty of February 14, 1828, all the alterations proposed by the Senate in respect of the treaty of July 10, 1826, had been introduced except that regarding its duration.

The treaty of February 14, 1828, was submitted to the Senate on April 25, 1828, with the presidential message of the previous day; it was accordingly before that body during the consideration of the Treaty of Limits of January 12, 1828; and it received the unanimous assent of the Senate on May 1 (Executive Journal, III, 605–7).

To the Mexican Congress, however, the treaty of February 14, 1828, was not acceptable. It was later said that "of that Treaty Seventeen Articles were rejected, and amongst these all that related to the principle of the flag protecting the Cargo" (D. S., 5 Despatches, Mexico, No. 19, August 20, 1831). More accurately, the action taken was that the lower House of the Mexican Congress rejected two articles of the treaty which the Mexican Senate also rejected, with twelve others; and when the treaty then went back to the other branch of the Legislature, it remained there without final action until late in 1829, nearly two years after the date of its signature, when the treaty was deemed to have failed (see Manning, *op. cit.*, 243–49, and the despatches of Poinsett, D. S., 4 Despatches, Mexico, No. 127, May 21, 1828, No. 156, November 15, 1828, with enclosure, and No. 174, July 22, 1829).

Accordingly, that treaty of February 14, 1828, did not go into force.

The three treaties above mentioned were negotiated at Mexico on behalf of the United States by Joel R. Poinsett, then Minister to Mexico. Toward the close of 1829 the mission of Poinsett ended; he took formal leave on December 25, 1829, and returned to the United States. His official conduct had not been disapproved, but his recall had been formally requested by the Mexican Government on October 17, 1829 (D. S., 1 Notes from the Mexican Legation; instructions of October 16, 1829, postscript of October 17; and see generally the chapter on "Public Attacks on Poinsett and his Recall," in Manning, *op. cit.*, 349–77). As its next diplomatic representative this Government sent Colonel Anthony Butler, with the rank of Charge d'Affaires; and to him, in a letter of March 24, 1831, President Jackson expressed his "impatience . . . for the conclusion of the Commercial Treaty" (D. S., 5 Despatches, Mexico, May 25, 1831).

4. The Treaty of Amity, Commerce, and Navigation signed at Mexico on April 5, 1831 (Document 70), which went into force.

The notes to Document 70 should be consulted. It is to be pointed out here, however, that the date of the signature of that treaty, April 5, 1831, is the same as the date of signature of the additional article to the Treaty of Limits; and in each case the term of one year from

the date of signature, or until April 5, 1832, was provided for the exchange of the ratifications. That treaty and this Treaty of Limits, with its additional article, were sent to the Senate by President Jackson on the same day, February 24, 1832 (Executive Journal, IV, 213); the United States instrument of ratification of the Treaty of Amity, Commerce, and Navigation was dated April 4 and the instrument of ratification of this treaty, April 5, 1832; on the latter date the ratifications of both agreements were concurrently exchanged and they were both proclaimed; and on May 1, 1832, they were communicated to Congress (Richardson, II, 573).

THE FILE PAPERS

The originals of the treaty and of the additional article which are in the file have the English text in the left columns and the Spanish in the right, and, as the printed texts show, the *alternat* was observed. Both documents are embodied in the original proclamation of April 5, 1832.

The file contains neither original nor copy of the first United States instrument of ratification of the treaty. Its date, April 30, 1828, is assumed from the note of Secretary of State Clay of that date to the Mexican Minister (D. S., 4 Notes to Foreign Legations, 15–16), in which he wrote that "the President . . . has ratified" the Treaty of Limits; the actual date may have been one or even two days earlier, but not more. The instrument of ratification on the part of Mexico under date of April 28, 1828, was not delivered; the date is stated in the Mexican instrument of ratification of the treaty and the separate article. That instrument is dated January 14, 1832, and includes the text in both languages, the Spanish in the left columns.

The treaty file contains no copy or duplicate of the United States instrument of ratification of April 5, 1832, other than a facsimile thereof recently obtained from the Mexican archives. The document is in customary form. Its reference to Senate action is only to the resolution of April 4, 1832.

Both attested resolutions of the Senate, that of April 28, 1828 (Executive Journal, III, 606), and that of April 4, 1832 (*ibid.*, IV, 237), are in the file; and there are three originals of the certificate of the exchange of ratifications, one in English and two in Spanish, and also a facsimile of a fourth example thereof, in English, which is in the Mexican archives. To each of these documents is appended a notation signed by the participants, Secretary of State Edward Livingston and Chargé d'Affaires José Montoya, which, in the English, is as follows:

In the Copy of the Treaty ratified by the Government of the United States, the word "Respectivos," in the Spanish translation, has been inserted between the fourth and fifth lines [of the preamble], and it is so noted previous to signing this certificate of exchange of ratification.

To the English original of the certificate of exchange is appended a second but unsigned "note" of differences between the original texts

and those contained in the instrument of ratification on the part of Mexico; but that notation is entirely erroneous and accordingly is not reproduced. It relates in fact to certain differences between the original texts of the Treaty of Amity, Commerce, and Navigation of April 5, 1831 (Document 70), and the Mexican instrument of ratification of that treaty. The error doubtless arose from the fact that the ratifications of the two treaties were concurrently exchanged on the same day, April 5, 1832, and the notation of discrepancies was written on the certificate of exchange of ratifications of this treaty as well as on the similar certificate of the other. On that other certificate the notation is signed, and it is quoted in full in the notes to Document 70.

The Full Powers

The full power issued to Joel R. Poinsett under date of March 14, 1825, was his authority for signing not only this treaty but also the unratified treaties of amity, commerce, and navigation of July 10, 1826, and February 14, 1828. By the terms of that full power (D. S.. 2 Credences, 3–4) authority was given

to meet and confer with any person or persons duly authorised by the Government of the United Mexican States, being furnished with like power and authority, and with him or them to agree, treat and consult, and negociate of and concerning the general commerce between the United States and the Government of the United Mexican States, and of, and concerning the limits and boundaries between the said United States of America, and the said United Mexican States, and of all matters and subjects connected therewith, which may be interesting to the two Nations; and conclude and sign a treaty or treaties, convention or conventions touching the premises; transmitting the same to the President of the United States, for his final ratification by and with the advice and consent of the Senate of the United States.

The additional article to this treaty and also the Treaty of Amity, Commerce, and Navigation of April 5, 1831 (Document 70), were signed by Anthony Butler pursuant to the authority granted by full power issued to him under date of October 17, 1829. One of the two full powers then issued to Butler has been referred to above; the one here in question (D. S., 2 Credences, 131) followed the language above quoted from the earlier full power to Poinsett.

The originals of the fourteen protocols of the conferences which preceded the signing of the unratified treaty of July 10, 1826, are in the file of that treaty (D. S., Unperfected E2); the English texts thereof are printed in American State Papers, Foreign Relations, VI, 583–608. In the first protocol, that of the conference of August 22, 1825, is the statement, "The Plenipotentiaries interchanged their respective powers," meaning that the original documents were exchanged. In the same treaty file is a portion of the original Mexican full power; the lower part of the document, with the signatures and seal, is lacking. The available text reads as follows (translation from the Spanish):

The President of the United States of Mexico

To all who shall see these presents, Greeting:

Know ye, that being desirous of establishing on a solid and stable basis the relations of friendship which exist between these States and the United States of

North America, and of regulating commerce and navigation between the two Republics in a manner advantageous to the mutual interests of neighboring and friendly countries and the harmony which should exist between them, and being fully satisfied of and having confidence in the enlightenment, integrity, and proven patriotism and zeal for the greater prosperity of this Republic, which characterize Mr. Lucas Alaman and Mr. Ignacio Esteva, both Secretaries of State, the former in the Department of Foreign and Domestic Relations and the second in the Treasury Department, I have appointed them to the end that, in the capacity of plenipotentiaries, clothed with all necessary authority, they may negotiate, settle, and conclude with Mr. J. R. Poinsett, Minister Plenipotentiary and Envoy Extraordinary of the United States of North America, or other person clothed with the same power and authority, a treaty of friendship, commerce, and navigation that may serve to attain such object, signing it in our name, as President of these States, binding myself and promising in the name of the Republic, that everything which the said Plenipotentiaries may negotiate and conclude, will be approved and ratified by me, after approval of the General Congress, in accordance with the Constitution, and offering to cause it to be fulfilled and observed, having the instruments of ratification executed in due form for this purpose, and ordering delivery thereof that they may be exchanged at the proper time and place.

In faith whereof I have caused this instrument to be drawn up, signed by my hand, sealed with the great seal of the Nation, and countersigned by the Secretary of Justice and Ecclesiastical Affairs. Done at the National Palace of Mexico on the eighth of August, one thousand eight hundred and twenty-five, the fifth year of independence.

Nothing further appears of record regarding Mexican full powers during this period except a note addressed to Butler and signed by the Mexican officials therein mentioned, Lucas Alaman and Rafael Mangino, under date of May 21, 1830, a copy of which, with a translation thereof, was an enclosure to the despatch of May 19 [21?], 1830 (D. S., 5 Despatches, Mexico). From that translation the following is extracted:

The undersigned Secretaries of State of Domestic and Foreign Affairs and of the Treasury have the honor of addressing Your Excellency, and to communicate that they are fully authorised by the Most Excellent the Vice President, exercising the executive power, to commence negotiating on the subject of the treaties pending between the United Mexican States and your Government.

Therefore the undersigned request Your Excellency will please to appoint a day for the first meeting on the aforesaid subject.

ARTICLES 2 AND 3

Regarding tne western boundary of the Louisiana Purchase, see Marshall, A History of the Western Boundary of the Louisiana Purchase, 1819–1841; and also Paullin, Atlas of the Historical Geography of the United States, plate 95A, the relevant text in that work at pages 66–68, and the authorities there cited.

Article 3 of the treaty of February 22, 1819, with Spain (Document 41), which went into force on February 22, 1821, had fixed the boundary between the United States and Spanish territory on this continent; but the *de facto* independence of Mexico, which dated from 1821, had made that boundary or any other that might be established, one between the United States and Mexico; and the provisions of Article 4 of that treaty with Spain for the demarcation of the boundary

were not executed. The United States recognized the independent Government of Mexico on December 12, 1822, when President Monroe received José Manuel Zozaya as Minister of Mexico at Washington (Manning, *op. cit.*, 12; Niles' Weekly Register, XXIII, 240, December 14, 1822).

The effect of this treaty was to make the provisions of Articles 3 and 4 of the treaty of February 22, 1819, between the United States and Spain (Document 41) definitive and specific as between the United States and Mexico; and to that end those two articles of the treaty with Spain are copied almost literally in this treaty as Articles 2 and 3 thereof.

For some comments on the provisions of the two articles and on the relations between the United States and Mexico during the first years of Mexican independence, the notes regarding Articles 3 and 4 of Document 41 should be consulted; and on the latter point see generally Manning, *op. cit.*, chapter IX. But the demarcation provisions (Article 3 of this treaty, Article 4 of Document 41), which had not been executed under the treaty with Spain, likewise remained unexecuted under this treaty.

The Government of Mexico took very early, indeed premature, steps towards the carrying out of the demarcation provisions of Article 3. As stated in the above-quoted despatch of Poinsett of April 24, 1828, that Government "had already dispatched its commissioner to the frontiers"; and under date of March 19, 1828, Secretary of State Clay had been informed that "General D. M. Teran" had been appointed "to perform the scientific operations and surveys necessary to proceed in the execution of the Treaty of Limits between the U. S. of America and the U. S. of Mexico" (D. S., 1 Notes from the Mexican Legation). That mission of General Manuel de Mier y Terán (styled in the writings of the time General Terán or Teran) had resulted from the proposal of the Mexican Government, made in 1825, for a joint commission. While that proposal had not been accepted by this Government, the Government of Mexico had in 1826 appointed a commission, headed by General Terán, which left the city of Mexico on November 10, 1827, before the signature of this treaty (see Manning, *op. cit.*, 291–92, 313–14); and while that commission proceeded on its course, it had an official Mexican status only and did not act under this treaty, which did not go into force until April 5, 1832.

Shortly after the treaty went into force an act was passed to carry it into effect (July 3, 1832, 4 Statutes at Large, 558–59); and William McRee and Robert Love were duly commissioned on May 30 and July 14, 1832, respectively, as commissioner and surveyor "to run and mark the dividing line between the United States and Mexico" (see Executive Journal, IV, 247–48, 278; as the two nominations were not confirmed by the Senate until July 14, the recorded date of the commission of McRee above given is perhaps erroneous).

Under date of April 27, 1832, the Mexican Chargé d'Affaires at Washington called the attention of Secretary of State Livingston to

Article 3 of the Treaty of Limits (D. S., 2 Notes from the Mexican Legation); and on July 20, 1832, Livingston wrote as follows (D. S., 5 Notes to Foreign Legations, 45–46):

The Undersigned Secretary of State of the United States, has the honor to transmit to Mr. Montoya Chargé d'Affaires from Mexico, the enclosed copy of an Act of the late session of Congress, entitled "an Act to provide for carrying "into effect the Treaty of Limits between the United States of America and "the United Mexican States" and to acquaint him that this Government is prepared to proceed, conjointly with that of Mexico, to the designation of the Boundary line between the Territories of the two Governments.

The Undersigned is instructed, therefore, by the President, to enquire of Mr. Montoya whether any arrangements have been made on the part of his Government, for proceeding conjointly with this, to the designation of the line contemplated or, if not, to request that he will ask the immediate attention of his Government to this subject.

The reply of the Mexican Chargé d'Affaires under date of July 31 (D. S., 2 Notes from the Mexican Legation) stated that no communication had been received from the Mexican Government in the matter, which was attributed "to the present interruption of communications between the Capital and the ports of Vera Cruz and Tampico," and added that the note had been forwarded to the Mexican Government, which would take the matter under consideration if arrangements had not already been made. The ensuing correspondence and the resulting delays are treated in Marshall, A History of the Western Boundary of the Louisiana Purchase, 1819–1841, 106–12.

No active steps were taken, however, to run and mark the line; the period of one year mentioned in Article 3 expired; and while that term was extended by the agreement of April 3, 1835 (Document 79, the notes to which deal further with the subject), which went into force on April 20, 1836, the changed status of Texas made the boundary no longer, except in part, one between the United States and Mexico. The independence of Texas was declared by a convention which met at the town of Washington in that state on March 2, 1836; the act of March 3, 1837 (5 Statutes at Large, 170), made appropriation for the salary of a diplomatic agent to the Republic of Texas; a Senate resolution of March 1 (Congressional Debates, XIII, 1014), had declared it expedient and proper that the independent political existence of Texas be acknowledged by the United States; President Jackson acquiesced in what he regarded "as a virtual decision of the question" in his message to the Senate of March 3, 1837, nominating Alcée La Branche to be Chargé d'Affaires to the Republic of Texas (Executive Journal, IV, 631); and on March 7 the commission of that official was issued by President Van Buren (D. S., 2 Credences, 262).

61

RUSSIA : MARCH 17, 1828

Settlement of the Claims for the Brig "Hector" and the Ship "Commerce." The terms of the settlement are stated in the note of Count Nesselrode, Russian Minister of Foreign Affairs, to Henry Middleton, Envoy Extraordinary and Minister Plenipotentiary of the United States, dated at St. Petersburg (Leningrad) March 17, 1828 (March 5, Old Style), which follows in the original French and in translation.

[Translation]

Le Soussigné a l'honneur de porter à la connaissance de Monsieur Middleton, Envoyé extraordinaire et Ministre plénipotentiaire des Etats-Unis d'Amérique, l'extrait ci joint d'un Oukase que Sa Majesté l'Empereur vient de signer au sujet de l'arrangement final de l'affaire relative aux réclamations des Négocians Américains Israel Thorndike, Eliphalet Loud et Samuel Bailey.

En vertu de cet Oukase et conformément à ce dont le Ministère des Finances est directement convenu tant avec Monsieur Middleton lui même, qu'avec les fondés de pouvoirs du Sr Israel Thorndike, il va être payé une somme de deux cent cinquante cinq mille sept cent trente et un Roubles vingt huit copeks en assignations, pour solde définitif de toute prétention que les dits réclamans auraient à former du chef de la capture faite en 1807,

The undersigned has the honor to bring to the knowledge of Mr. Middleton, Envoy Extraordinary and Minister Plenipotentiary of the United States of America, the enclosed extract of a ukase which His Majesty the Emperor has just signed on the subject of the final settlement of the affair relative to the claims of the American merchants, Israel Thorndike, Eliphalet Loud, and Samuel Bailey.

By virtue of this ukase and in conformity with what was agreed upon directly by the Ministry of Finance with Mr. Middleton himself, as well as with the representatives of Mr. Israel Thorndike, there will be paid the sum of two hundred and fifty-five thousand seven hundred and thirty-one rubles and twenty-eight kopecks, in drafts, as a definitive settlement of all claims which the said claimants may have on account of the capture in 1807 in

421

dans la Méditerranée, de leurs navires le *Hector* et le *Commerce*

En priant Monsieur Middleton de vouloir bien lui indiquer la personne qui sera autorisée à toucher la dite somme selon les dispositions du Ministère des finances, et à en donner quittance pleine et générale, le Soussigné se félicite sincèrement d'avoir à lui annoncer un résultat qui termine d'une manière satisfaisante une négociation dont il a été chargé, et dans laquelle Sa Majesté l'Empereur s'est plû à manifester les dispositions amicales qui l'animent à l'égard du Gouvernement des Etats-Unis.

Le Soussigné saisit avec empressement cette occasion de renouveler à Monsieur Middleton l'assurance de sa considération très distinguée.

St Pétersbourg, le 5 Mars 1828
Signé   NESSELRODE
c.o.c. H^y Mⁿ

the Mediterranean of their ships, the *Hector* and the *Commerce*.

In begging Mr. Middleton to be kind enough to indicate to him the person who will be authorized to receive the said sum according to the arrangements of the Ministry of Finance, and to give a full and general quittance therefor, the undersigned finds sincere pleasure in announcing to him a result which terminates in a satisfactory manner a negotiation with which he has been entrusted and in which His Majesty the Emperor has been pleased to manifest the friendly sentiments which animate him with regard to the United States.

The undersigned avails himself of this opportunity to renew to Mr. Middleton the assurance of his very distinguished consideration.

St. Petersburg, March 5, 1828.
NESSELRODE
c.o.c. H^y Mⁿ

NOTES

Unless otherwise stated, dates in the headnote and in these notes are in the New Style or present calendar, then twelve days later than the Old Style.

This settlement of the cases of the *Hector* and the *Commerce* was reported in the despatch of Henry Middleton, Minister to Russia, of April 2, 1828, from which the following is extracted (D. S., 11 Despatches, Russia, No. 75):

I have the honor to acquaint you that the long standing claim of Israel Thorndike for the brig Hector, and that of the Weymouth Importing Company for the ship Commerce, both captured by vessels under the Russian Flag in the Mediterranean Sea in the year 1807, have been at length admitted by this Government, and brought to a final settlement. On the 26 February of last year I addressed a note to Count Nesselrode on the subject of the first mentioned claim . . . from that time up to the present various communications both written and oral

have interpassed between the Minister of Foreign Affairs, and the Minister of Finance, and myself, until finally, on the 5ᵗʰ March of this present year I received an official note from the Minister of Foreign Affairs [printed above]. . . .

In explanation of the informal communications which were had on this affair it may suffice here to state that the claim of Mᴿ Thorndike for the cost of cargo and the value of the vessel amounted to 54,601 dollars 86 cents or about 273,000 roubles, which by the addition of freight charged and 10 per cent damages, was swelled to the sum of 325,000 roubles (exclusive of interest.) A counter-statement and valuation was produced on the other part which amounted to only 205,731 roubles 28 copeaks. I made several vain attempts to induce a reconsideration and alteration of this amount so as to divide at least the difference between the two statements. After due consideration, the Agent of Mᴿ Thorndike (Mᴿ I. Tilton Slade . . .) thought it would be most prudent to accept the sum offered, rather than abide the risk and delay of a new reference, and the said amount of Two hundred and five thousand seven hundred and thirty one Roubles twenty eight Copeaks has been paid over to him upon his producing a full power from Mᴿ Thorndike to recover and receive the proceeds of the Brig Hector or make any compromise for the same, and he has accordingly given a receipt in full of all demands.

In the course of the negotiation of the affair of the Hector, the claim for the Commerce coming into view, the Minister of Finance offered to settle the same by an allowance of 50,000 Roubles for the Weymouth Importing Company. No agent for that company being present, and being myself in possession of papers by which the claimants had formerly authorised Mᴿ Harris *to make the best terms he could* for them, I could not hesitate in accepting the offer, probably the best thing which could have happened for those concerned, as in this way they will receive the whole sum paid free of any charge or commission except the usual Banker's charge for paying and receiving.

I pray you therefore, Sir, to cause to be made known to the persons representing the proprietors of the Ship Commerce captured in the Mediterranean in the year 1807, by a privateer under the Russian Flag, that fifty thousand Roubles (or about ten thousand Dollars) have been deposited in the hands of Baron Stieglitz, Banker of this City & that the said amount will be paid over to their order whenever it shall be officially made known to me under the authority of the Secretary of State of the United States who are the persons legally entitled to receive the same, and to execute full and sufficient discharges for all demands on account of the claim for the capture of the Commerce as above stated.

I hope I shall be approved by the President for having obtained a settlement of the above claims, and that the persons concerned in them will be satisfied that all has been done which lay in my power.

A copy of the note of Count Nesselrode of March 5, 1828 (Old Style), which is printed above in French and in translation as stating the terms of the settlement, is enclosure B to the despatch of April 2, 1828, above cited. That note was formally acknowledged by Middleton on March 8, 1828 (Old Style); in the acknowledgment it was stated that the banker, Baron Stieglitz, had been authorized to receive the sum payable and to receipt therefor (*ibid.*, enclosure C).

THE HECTOR

Under date of January 13, 1808, Secretary of State Madison instructed Levett Harris, Consul of the United States at St. Petersburg, to "patronise the case" of the brig *Hector* "in the manner . . . most likely to obtain the justice demanded" (D. S., 1 Instructions to Consuls, 302–3), and suggested arguments which Harris embodied in his statement of the claim dated at St. Petersburg October 1,

1809 (D. S., Russian Claims, Miscellaneous, folder *Hector*, certified translation).

The facts in the case of the *Hector* as set forth in that statement of October 1, 1809, and presented by Harris to the Government of Russia, may be thus summarized:

The brig *Hector*, of 220 tons, "copper bottomed," Luke Thorndike, Master, owned by Israel Thorndike, merchant of Salem and Beverly, Massachusetts, sailed for Marseilles on March 23, 1807, with a cargo of sugar and coffee.   From Marseilles the *Hector* was despatched to Smyrna under new instructions; her clearance, dated May 17, 1807, was for Trieste.   On June 13 following, between Scio (Khios) and Tchesme (Cheshme) and thus about seventy miles' sail from Smyrna, the *Hector* was taken by the Russian frigate *Venus* and conducted to Tenedos, where condemnation for attempted breach of blockade followed, based, it seems, at least in part on the fact of clearance for Trieste.   The claimants denied knowledge of the blockade of Smyrna by the British and Russian fleets.   The claim as presented was for:

First cost of the cargo_____ $34, 601. 86
Value of the brig *Hector*_____ 20, 000. 00
Profit anticipated at Smyrna_____ 34, 878. 90
Profit anticipated on return cargo of cotton, Smyrna to Marseilles_ 62, 556. 00
                                                              _____
    Total_____ $152, 036. 76

THE COMMERCE

In October, 1809, Levett Harris presented the claim in the case of the ship *Commerce* to the Russian Government in a statement similar to that in the case of the *Hector;* but it appears that no copy of that statement was transmitted to the Department of State.   The facts in the case of the *Commerce*, Joseph Tirrell, Master, are thus stated in House Report No. 25, 19th Congress, 1st session, serial 141:

That Eliphalet Loud and Samuel Bailey, inhabitants of the town of Weymouth, Massachusetts, represent themselves as the principal owners of the Ship Commerce; that, in the year 1807, the said ship sailed from Boston to Leghorn, where she discharged her cargo; that she proceeded thence to Manfredonia, in the Gulf of Venice, and loaded with a cargo of wheat for Lisbon, under a contract with a merchant of Leghorn; that, on her passage from Manfredonia to Lisbon, the vessel was in distress by reason of the choaking of the pumps, and consequently attempted to put into the Island of Corfu; that, in so doing, she was captured by a Russian gun-boat, and condemned by a prize court sitting in Corfu, to which court neither the captain of the Commerce, nor any of the ship's company, nor counsel on their behalf, was admitted; that the ship's crew was left wholly destitute of money or means of return to America; that appeal was made from the decision of the prize court to the court of St. Petersburg, through Leavit Harris, Esq. the American Consul in that city; and that the successive ministers of the United States to the Court of St. Petersburgh have been charged, by the American Government, to present this case to the consideration of his Imperial Majesty the Emperor of all the Russias, for indemnity.

From other papers it appears that the date of the capture was June 13, 1807, which was also the date of capture of the *Hector*.   Both Manfredonia and Lisbon were neutral ports; at the time of the capture

of the *Commerce* "there was not the least pretention of a blockade, not even of paper," of those ports; but it seems that Corfu was then blockaded. The captors took over the ship, with her papers, and proceeded on the voyage to Lisbon. The claim made was for the ship, freight, and damage (but not for the cargo), in the sum of $22,500 (D. S., Russian Claims, Miscellaneous, folder *Commerce, passim*).

56006°—33——29

Treaty Series No. 294
8 Statutes at Large, 378–87
18 *ibid.*, pt. 2, Public Treaties, 656–60

62

PRUSSIA : MAY 1, 1828

Treaty of Commerce and Navigation, signed at Washington May 1, 1828.
Original in English and French.
Submitted to the Senate May 9, 1828. (Message of May 5, 1828.)
Resolution of advice and consent May 14, 1828. Resubmitted to the
Senate March 7, 1829. (Message of March 6, 1829.) Resolution of
advice and consent March 9, 1829. Ratified by the United States
March 12, 1829. Ratified by Prussia August 30, 1828. Ratifications
exchanged at Washington March 14, 1829. Proclaimed March 14,
1829.

Original.

Treaty of Commerce and Navigation between the United States of America, and His Majesty the King of Prussia.

The United States of America, and His Majesty the King of Prussia, equally animated with the desire of maintaining the relations of good understanding, which have hitherto so happily subsisted between their respective States, of extending, also, and consolidating the commercial intercourse between Them; and convinced that this object cannot better be accomplished, than by adopting the system of an entire freedom of navigation, and a perfect reciprocity, based upon principles of equity equally beneficial to both Countries, and applicable in time of peace, as well as in time of war,

Original.

Traité de Commerce et de Navigation entre Sa Majesté le Roi de Prusse, et les Etats Unis d'Amérique.

Sa Majesté le Roi de Prusse, et les Etats Unis d'Amérique, également animés du desir de maintenir les rapports de bonne intelligence qui ont si heureusement subsisté jusqu'ici entre Leurs Etats respectifs; et d'en étendre et consolider les relations commerciales; et convaincus que cet objet ne sauroit être mieux rempli qu'en adoptant le systême d'une entiere liberté de navigation, et d'une parfaite réciprocité, basé sur des principes d'équité également avantageux aux deux Pays, et applicables en temps de paix comme en temps de guerre; sont, en conséquence, convenus d'entrer en négociation, pour conclure un

427

have, in consequence, agreed to enter into negotiations for the conclusion of a Treaty of Navigation and Commerce, for which purpose the President of the United States has conferred Full Powers on Henry Clay, Their Secretary of State; and His Majesty the King of Prussia has conferred like Powers on the Sieur Ludwig Niederstetter, Chargé d'Affaires of His said Majesty near the United States; and the said Plenipotentiaries having exchanged their said Full Powers, found in good and due form, have concluded and signed the following Articles:

ARTICLE I.

There shall be between the Territories of the High Contracting Parties, a reciprocal liberty of commerce and navigation. The inhabitants of Their respective States shall, mutually, have liberty to enter the ports, places, and rivers of the territories of each Party, wherever foreign commerce is permitted. They shall be at liberty to sojourn and reside in all parts whatsoever of said territories, in order to attend to their affairs, and they shall enjoy, to that effect, the same security and protection as natives of the country wherein they reside, on condition of their submitting to the laws and ordinances there prevailing.

Traité de Commerce et de Navigation. A cet effet, Sa Majesté le Roi de Prusse a muni de Pleins Pouvoirs le Sieur Ludwig Niederstetter, Chargé d'Affaires de Sa dite Majesté, près les Etats Unis d'Amérique; et le Président des Etats Unis d'Amérique a muni des mêmes Pouvoirs Henri Clay, Leur Secrétaire d'Etat; lesquels Plénipotentiaires, après avoir échangé leurs dits Pleins Pouvoirs, trouvés en bonne et due forme, ont arrêté et signé les Articles suivans:

ARTICLE I.

Il y aura, entre les Territoires des Hautes Parties Contractantes, liberté et réciprocité de commerce et de navigation. Les habitans de Leurs Etats respectifs pourront, réciproquement, entrer dans les ports, places et rivieres des territoires de chacune d'Elles, partout où le commerce étranger est permis. Ils seront libres de s'y arrêter, et résider dans quelque partie que ce soit desdits territoires, pour y vaquer à leurs affaires; et ils jouiront, à cet effet, de la même sécurité et protection que les habitans du pays dans lequel ils résideront, à charge de se soumettre aux lois et ordonnances y établies.

ARTICLE II.

Prussian vessels arriving either laden or in ballast, in the ports of the United States of America; and, reciprocally, vessels of the United States arriving either laden, or in ballast, in the ports of the Kingdom of Prussia, shall be treated, on their entrance, during their stay, and at their departure, upon the same footing as national vessels, coming from the same place, with respect to the duties of tonnage, lighthouses, pilotage, salvage, and port charges, as well as to the fees and perquisites of public officers, and all other duties and charges, of whatever kind or denomination, levied in the name, or to the profit, of the Government, the local authorities, or of any private establishment whatsoever.

ARTICLE III.

All kind of merchandise and articles of commerce, either the produce of the soil or the industry of the United States of America, or of any other country, which may be lawfully imported into the ports of the Kingdom of Prussia, in Prussian vessels, may, also, be so imported in vessels of the United States of America, without paying other or higher duties or charges, of whatever kind or denomination, levied in the name, or to the profit of the Government, the local authori-

ARTICLE II.

Les bâtimens Prussiens arrivant, sur lest ou chargés dans les ports des Etats Unis d'Amérique; et, reciproquement, les bâtimens des Etats Unis, arrivant, sur lest ou chargés, dans les ports du Royaume de Prusse, seront traités, à leur entrée, pendant leur séjour, et à leur sortie, sur le même pied que les bâtimens nationaux venant du même lieu, par rapport aux droits de tonnage, de fanaux, de pilotage, de sauvetage et de port, ainsi qu'aux vacations des officiers publics, et à tout autre droit ou charge, de quelque espèce ou dénomination que ce soit, perçus au nom ou au profit du Gouvernement, des autorités locales, ou d'établissemens particuliers quelconques.

ARTICLE III.

Toute espèce de marchandises et objets de commerce, provenant du sol ou de l'industrie des Etats Unis d'Amérique, ou de tout autre pays, qui pourront légalement être importés dans les ports du Royaume de Prusse sur des bâtimens Prussiens, pourront également y être importés sur des bâtimens des Etats Unis d'Amérique, sans payer d'autres, ou plus forts droits ou charges, de quelque espèce ou dénomination que ce soit, perçus au nom ou au profit du Gouvernement, des au-

ties, or of any private establishments whatsoever, than if the same merchandise or produce had been imported in Prussian vessels.

And, reciprocally, all kind of merchandise and articles of commerce, either the produce of the soil or of the industry of the Kingdom of Prussia, or of any other country, which may be lawfully imported into the ports of the United States, in vessels of the said States, may, also, be so imported in Prussian vessels, without paying other or higher duties or charges, of whatever kind or denomination, levied in the name, or to the profit of the Government, the local authorities or of any private establishments whatsoever, than if the same merchandise or produce had been imported in vessels of the United States of America.

ARTICLE IV.

To prevent the possibility of any misunderstanding, it is hereby declared that the stipulations contained in the two preceding Articles, are, to their full extent, applicable to Prussian vessels, and their cargoes, arriving in the ports of the United States of America; and, reciprocally, to vessels of the said States and their cargoes, arriving in the ports of the Kingdom of Prussia, whether the said vessels clear directly from the ports of the country to which they respectively belong, or from the ports of any other foreign country.

torités locales, ou d'établissemens particuliers quelconques, que s'ils étoient importés sur des bâtimens Prussiens.

Et réciproquement, tout espèce de marchandises et objets de commerce, provenant du sol ou de l'industrie du Royaume de Prusse, ou de tout autre pays, qui pourront légalement être importés dans les ports des Etats Unis d'Amérique sur des bâtimens desdits Etats, pourront également y être importés sur des bâtimens Prussiens, sans payer d'autres ou plus forts droits ou charges, de quelque espèce ou dénomination que ce soit, perçus au nom ou au profit du Gouvernement, des autorités locales, ou d'établissemens particuliers quelconques, que s'ils etoient importés sur des bâtimens des Etats Unis d'Amérique.

ARTICLE IV.

Afin de prévenir tout mésentendu et équivoque possibles, il est declaré que les stipulations contenues dans les deux Articles précédens sont, dans toute leur plénitude, applicables aux bâtimens Prussiens et leurs cargaisons, arrivant dans les ports des Etats Unis d'Amérique; et réciproquement, aux bâtimens desdits Etats, et leurs cargaisons, arrivant dans les ports du Royaume de Prusse, soit que lesdits bâtimens viennent des ports du pays auquel ils appartiennent, soit de ceux de tout autre pays étranger.

ARTICLE V.

No higher or other duties shall be imposed on the importation into the United States, of any article, the produce or manufacture of Prussia; and no higher or other duties shall be imposed on the importation into the Kingdom of Prussia, of any article, the produce or manufacture of the United States, than are, or shall be, payable on the like article, being the produce or manufacture of any other foreign country. Nor shall any prohibition be imposed on the importation or exportation of any article the produce or manufacture of the United States, or of Prussia, to, or from, the ports of the United States, or to, or from the ports of Prussia, which shall not equally extend to all other nations.

ARTICLE VI.

All kind of merchandise and articles of commerce, either the produce of the soil or of the industry of the United States of America, or of any other country, which may be lawfully exported from the ports of the said United States, in national vessels, may, also, be exported therefrom in Prussian vessels, without paying other or higher duties or charges, of whatever kind or denomination, levied in the name, or to the profit of the Government, the local

ARTICLE V.

Il ne sera imposé d'autres ni de plus forts droits sur l'importation dans les Etats Unis, des articles provenant du sol ou de l'industrie du Royaume de Prusse; et il ne sera imposé d'autres ni de plus forts droits, sur l'importation dans le Royaume de Prusse des articles provenant du sol ou de l'industrie des Etats Unis, que ceux qui sont, ou seront imposés sur les mêmes articles provenant du sol ou de l'industrie de tout autre pays étranger. De même, il ne sera imposé sur l'importation ou sur l'exportation des articles provenant du sol ou de l'industrie des Etats Unis, ou du Royaume de Prusse, à l'entrée ou à la sortie des ports des Etats Unis, ou de ceux du Royaume de Prusse, aucune prohibition qui ne soit pas également applicable à toute autre nation.

ARTICLE VI.

Tout espèce de marchandises et objets de commerce provenant du sol ou de l'industrie des Etats Unis, ou de tout autre pays, qui pourront être légalement exportés des ports desdits Etats, sur des bâtimens nationaux, pourront également en être exportés sur des bâtimens Prussiens, sans payer d'autres ni de plus forts droits ou charges, de quelque espèce ou dénomination que ce soit, perçus au nom ou au profit du Gouvernement, des autorités locales, ou

authorities, or of any private establishments whatsoever, than if the same merchandise or produce had been exported in vessels of the United States of America.

An exact reciprocity shall be observed in the ports of the Kingdom of Prussia, so that all kind of merchandise and articles of commerce, either the produce of the soil or the industry of the said Kingdom, or of any other country, which may be lawfully exported from Prussian ports in national vessels, may also be exported therefrom in vessels of the United States of America, without paying other or higher duties or charges of whatever kind or denomination, levied in the name, or to the profit of the Government, the local authorities, or of any private establishments whatsoever, than if the same merchandise or produce had been exported in Prussian vessels.

ARTICLE VII.

The preceding Articles are not applicable to the coastwise navigation of the two Countries, which is, respectively, reserved, by each of the High Contracting Parties, exclusively, to Itself.

ARTICLE VIII.

No priority or preference shall be given, directly or indirectly, by either of the Contracting Parties, nor by any company, corporation,

d'établissemens particuliers quelconques, que si ces mêmes marchandises ou denrées avoient été exportées par bâtimens des Etats Unis d'Amérique.

Une parfaite réciprocité sera observée dans les ports du Royaume de Prusse, de sorte que toute espèce de marchandises et objets de commerce, provenant du sol ou de l'industrie du Royaume de Prusse, ou de tout autre pays, qui pourront être légalement exportés des ports dudit Royaume sur des bâtimens nationaux, pourront également en être exportés sur des bâtimens des Etats Unis d'Amérique sans payer d'autres ou de plus forts droits ou charges, de quelque espèce ou dénomination que ce soit, perçus au nom ou au profit du Gouvernement, des autorités locales, ou d'etablissemens particuliers quelconques, que si ces marchandises ou denrées avoient été exportées sur des bâtimens Prussiens.

ARTICLE VII.

Les Articles précédens ne sont pas applicables à la navigation de côtes, ou cabotage de chacun des deux pays, que l'Une et l'Autre des Hautes Parties Contractantes se réservent exclusivement.

ARTICLE VIII.

Il ne sera accordé, ni directement, ni indirectement, par l'Une ou par l'Autre des Parties Contractantes, ni par aucune com-

or agent, acting on Their behalf, or under Their authority, in the purchase of any article of commerce, lawfully imported, on account of, or in reference to, the character of the vessel, whether it be of the one Party, or of the Other, in which such article was imported: it being the true intent and meaning of the Contracting Parties, that no distinction or difference whatever, shall be made in this respect.

Article IX.

If either Party shall, hereafter, grant to any other nation, any particular favor in navigation or commerce, it shall, immediately, become common to the other Party, freely, where it is freely granted to such other nation, or on yielding the same compensation, when the grant is conditional.

Article X.

The two Contracting Parties have granted to each other the liberty of having, each in the ports of the other, Consuls, Vice Consuls, Agents, and Commissaries of their own appointment, who shall enjoy the same privileges and powers, as those of the most favored nations. But if any such consul shall exercise commerce, they shall be submitted to the same laws and

pagnie, corporation ou agent, agissant en Son nom, ou par Son autorité, aucune priorité ou préférence quelconque, pour l'achat d'aucun objet de commerce, légalement importé, à cause ou en considération de la nationalité du navire qui auroit importé lesdits objets, soit qu'il appartienne à l'Une des Parties, soit à l'Autre; l'intention bien positive des Parties Contractantes étant, qu'aucune différence ou distinction quelconque n'ait lieu à cet égard.

Article IX.

Si l'Une des Parties Contractantes accorde, par la suite, à d'autres nations, quelque faveur particuliere, en fait de commerce ou de navigation, cette faveur deviendra aussitot commune à l'Autre Partie, qui en jouira gratuitement, si la concession est gratuite; ou en accordant la même compensation, si la concession est conditionnelle.

Article X.

Les deux Parties Contractantes se sont accordé mutuellement la faculté de tenir, dans leurs ports respectifs, des Consuls, Vice-consuls, Agens et Commissaires de leur choix, qui jouiront des mêmes privilèges et pouvoirs dont jouissent ceux des nations les plus favorisées. Mais dans le cas où lesdits Consuls veuillent faire le commerce, ils seront soumis aux mêmes lois et usages, auxquels

usages to which the private individuals of their nation are submitted in the same place.

The Consuls, Vice consuls, and Commercial Agents shall have the right, as such, to sit as judges and arbitrators in such differences as may arise between the captains and crews of the vessels belonging to the nation whose interests are committed to their charge, without the interference of the local authorities, unless the conduct of the crews, or of the captain, should disturb the order or tranquillity of the country; or the said Consuls, Vice consuls, or Commercial Agents should require their assistance to cause their decisions to be carried into effect or supported. It is, however, understood, that this species of judgment or arbitration shall not deprive the contending parties of the right they have to resort, on their return, to the judicial authority of their country.

ARTICLE XI.

The said Consuls, Vice Consuls, and Commercial Agents, are authorised to require the assistance of the local authorities, for the search, arrest, and imprisonment of the deserters from the ships of war and merchant vessels of their country. For this purpose they shall apply to the competent tribunals, judges, and officers, and shall, in writing, demand said deserters, proving by the exhibi-

sont soumis les particuliers de leur nation, à l'endroit où ils résident.

Les Consuls, Vice consuls, et agens commerciaux, auront le droit, comme tels, de servir de juges et d'Arbitres dans les différens qui pourroient s'élever entre les capitaines et les équipages des bâtimens de la nation dont ils soignent les intérèts, sans que les autorités locales puissent y intervenir, à moins que la conduite des équipages ou du capitaine ne troublât l'ordre ou la tranquillité du pays; ou que lesdits Consuls, Vice consuls ou Agens commerciaux ne réquissent leur intervention pour faire exécuter ou maintenir leurs décisions. Bien entendu que cette espèce de jugement ou d'arbitrage ne sauroit, pourtant, priver les parties contendantes du droit qu'elles ont, à leur retour de recourir aux autorités judiciaires de leur pays.

ARTICLE XI.

Lesdits Consuls, Vice consuls, ou Agens commerciaux, seront autorisés à requérir l'assistance des autorités locales, pour la recherche, l'arrestation, la détention et l'emprisonnement des déserteurs des navires de guerre et marchands de leur pays; ils s'adresseront, pour cet objet, aux tribunaux, juges et officiers compétens, et reclameront, par écrit, les deserteurs sus-mentionnés, en

tion of the registers of the vessels, the rolls of the crews, or by other official documents that such individuals formed part of the crews; and, on this reclamation being thus substantiated, the surrender shall not be refused. Such deserters, when arrested, shall be placed at the disposal of the said Consuls, Vice Consuls, or commercial Agents, and may be confined in the public prisons, at the request and cost of those who shall claim them, in order to be sent to the vessels to which they belonged, or to others of the same country. But if not sent back within three months, from the day of their arrest, they shall be set at liberty, and shall not be again arrested for the same cause. However, if the deserter should be found to have committed any crime or offence, his surrender may be delayed until the tribunal before which his case shall be depending shall have pronounced its sentence, and such sentence shall have been carried into effect.

Article XII.

The Twelfth Article of the Treaty of Amity and Commerce,[1] concluded between the Parties in 1785, and the Articles from the Thirteenth to the Twenty-fourth, inclusive, of that[2] which was concluded at Berlin in 1799, with the exception of the last paragraph

prouvant, par la communication des régistres des navires, ou rôles de l'équipage, ou par d'autres documens officiels, que de tels individus ont fait partie desdits équipages; et cette réclamation ainsi prouvée, l'extradition ne sera point refusée. De tels déserteurs, lorsqu'ils auront été arrêtés, seront mis à la disposition desdits Consuls, Vice Consuls ou Agens commerciaux, et pourront être enfermés dans les prisons publiques, à la réquisition et aux frais de ceux qui les reclament, pour être envoyés aux navires auxquels ils appartenoient, ou à d'autres de la même nation. Mais s'ils ne sont pas renvoyés dans l'espace de trois mois, à compter du jour de leur arrestation, ils seront mis en liberté, et ne seront plus arrêtés pour la même cause. Toutefois, si le déserteur se trouvoit avoir commis quelque crime ou délit, il pourra être sursis à son extradition, jusqu'à ce que le tribunal saisi de l'affaire aura rendu sa sentence, et que celle-ci ait reçu son exécution.

Article XII.

L'Article douze du Traité d'Amitié et de Commerce,[1] conclu entre les Parties, en 1785; et les Articles Treize et suivans, jusqu'à l'Article Vingt-quatre, inclusivement, du Traité[2] conclu à Berlin, en 1799, en exceptant le dernier paragraphe de l'Article Dix-neuf,

---

[1] Document 13. [2] Document 24.

in the Nineteenth Article, relating to Treaties with Great Britain, are, hereby, revived with the same force and virtue, as if they made part of the context of the present Treaty; it being, however, understood that the stipulations contained in the Articles thus revived, shall be always considered as, in no manner, affecting the Treaties or Conventions concluded by either Party with other Powers, during the interval between the expiration[1] of the said Treaty of 1799, and the commencement of the operation of the present Treaty.

The Parties being still desirous, in conformity with their intention declared in the Twelfth Article of the said Treaty of 1799, to establish between Themselves, or in concert with other maritime Powers, further provisions to ensure just protection and freedom to neutral navigation and commerce, and which may, at the same time, advance the cause of civilization and humanity, engage again to treat on this subject, at some future and convenient period.

touchant les Traités avec la Grande Bretagne, sont remis en vigueur, et auront la même force et valeur que s'ils faisoient partie du présent Traité: il est entendu, cependant que les stipulations contenues dans les Articles ainsi remis en vigueur, seront toujours censées ne rien changer aux Traités et Conventions conclus de part et d'autre, avec d'autres Puissances, dans l'intervalle ecoulé entre l'expiration[1] dudit Traité de 1799, et le commencement de la mise en vigueur du présent Traité.

Les Parties Contractantes désirant toujours, conformément à l'intention déclarée dans l'Article Douze dudit Traité de 1799, pourvoir, entre Elles, ou conjointement avec d'autres Puissances maritimes, à des stipulations ultérieures qui puissent servir à garantir une juste protection et liberté au commerce et à la navigation des neutres, et à aider la cause de la civilisation et de l'humanité, s'engagent ici, comme alors à concerter ensemble sur ce sujet, à quelque époque future et convenable.

Article XIII.

Considering the remoteness of the respective Countries of the two High Contracting Parties, and the uncertainty resulting therefrom, with respect to the

Article XIII

Vû l'eloignement des Pays respectifs des deux Hautes Parties Contractantes, et l'incertitude qui en résulte sur les divers événemens qui peuvent avoir

---

[1] On June 22, 1810.

various events which may take place, it is agreed that a merchant vessel belonging to either of them, which may be bound to a port supposed, at the time of its departure to be blockaded, shall not, however, be captured or condemned, for having attempted, a first time, to enter said port, unless it can be proved that said vessel could, and ought to, have learnt, during its voyage, that the blockade of the place in question still continued. But all vessels which, after having been warned off once, shall, during the same voyage, attempt a second time to enter the same blockaded port, during the continuance of the said blockade, shall then subject themselves to be detained and condemned.

Article XIV.

The Citizens or subjects of each Party shall have power to dispose of their personal goods within the jurisdiction of the other, by testament, donation, or otherwise, and their representatives, being citizens or subjects of the other Party, shall succeed to their said personal goods, whether by testament, or *ab intestato*, and may take possession thereof, either by themselves, or by others acting for them, and dispose of the same, at their will, paying such dues only as the inhabitants of the country wherein the said goods are, shall be subject to pay in like cases. And in case of the

lieu; il est convenu qu'un bâtiment marchand, appartenant à l'Une d'Elles, qui se trouveroit destiné pour un port supposé bloqué, au moment du départ de ce bâtiment, ne sera cependant pas capturé ou condamné, pour avoir essayé une premiere fois d'entrer dans ledit port, à moins qu'il ne puisse être prouvé que ledit bâtiment avoit pû et dû apprendre en route que l'état de blocus de la place en question duroit encore: mais les bâtimens qui, après avoir été renvoyés une fois, essayeroient, pendant le même voyage d'entrer une seconde fois dans le même port bloqué, durant la continuation de ce blocus, se trouveront alors sujets à être détenus et condamnés.

Article XIV.

Les Citoyens ou Sujets de chacune des Parties Contractantes, auront, dans les Etats de l'autre, la liberté de disposer de leurs biens personnels, soit par testament, donation, ou autrement, et leurs héritiers, étant sujets ou citoyens de l'autre Partie Contractante, succéderont à leurs biens, soit en vertu d'un testament, ou *ab intestato*, et ils pourront en prendre possession, soit en personne, soit par d'autres agissant en leur place, et en disposeront à leur volonté, en ne payant d'autres droits que ceux auxquels les habitans du pays où se trouvent lesdits biens sont assujettis en pareille occasion.

absence of the representative, such care shall be taken of the said goods, as would be taken of the goods of a native, in like case, until the lawful owner may take measures for receiving them. And if question should arise among several claimants, to which of them said goods belong, the same shall be decided finally by the laws and judges of the land wherein the said goods are. And where, on the death of any person holding real estate, within the territories of the one Party, such real estate would, by the laws of the land, descend on a citizen or subject of the other, were he not disqualified by alienage, such citizen or subject shall be allowed a reasonable time to sell the same and to withdraw the proceeds without molestation, and exempt from all duties of *detraction*, on the part of the Government of the respective States. But this Article shall not derogate, in any manner, from the force of the laws already published, or hereafter to be published by His Majesty the King of Prussia to prevent the emigration of his subjects.

ARTICLE XV.

The present Treaty shall continue in force for twelve years, counting from the day of the exchange of the ratifications; and if twelve months before the expiration of that period, neither of the High Contracting Parties

En cas d'absence des héritiers, on prendra provisoirement desdits biens les mêmes soins qu'on auroit pris en pareille occasion des biens des natifs du pays, jusqu'à ce que le propriétaire légitime ait agréé des arrangemens pour recueillir l'héritage. S'il s'éleve des contestations entre différens prétendans ayant droit à la succession, elles seront décidées en dernier ressort, selon les lois et par les juges du pays où la succession est vacante. Et si, par la mort de quelque personne possédant des biens-fonds sur le territoire de l'une des Parties Contractantes, ces biens-fonds venoient à passer selon les lois du pays, à un citoyen ou sujet de l'autre Partie, celui-ci, si, par sa qualité d'étranger, il est inhabile à les posséder, obtiendra un délai convenable pour les vendre, et pour en retirer le produit sans obstacle, et exempt de tout droit de retenue de la part du Gouvernement des Etats respectifs. Mais cet article ne derogera en aucune maniere à la force des lois qui ont déja été publiées, ou qui le seront par la suite, par Sa Majesté le Roi de Prusse, pour prévenir l'émigration de ses sujets.

ARTICLE XV.

Le présent Traité sera en vigueur pendant douze années à compter du jour de l'échange des Ratifications; et si, douze mois avant l'expiration de ce terme, ni l'Une ni l'Autre des Hautes Parties Contractantes, n'annonce à l'autre,

shall have announced, by an official notification to the other its intention to arrest the operation of said Treaty, it shall remain binding for one year beyond that time, and so on, until the expiration of the twelve months which will follow a similar notification, whatever the time at which it may take place.

ARTICLE XVI.

This Treaty shall be approved and ratified by the President of the United States of America, by, and with, the advice and consent of the Senate thereof, and by His Majesty the King of Prussia, and the Ratifications shall be exchanged in the city of Washington, within nine months from the date of the signature hereof, or sooner, if possible.

In faith whereof the respective Plenipotentiaries have signed the above Articles, both in the french and english languages; and they have thereto affixed their seals: declaring, nevertheless, that the signing in both languages shall not be brought into precedent, nor in any way operate to the prejudice of either Party.

Done in triplicate at the City of Washington, on the First day of May, in the Year of Our Lord one thousand eight hundred and twenty eight; and the Fifty-second of the Independence of the United States of America.

[Seal]   H. CLAY
[Seal]   LUDWIG NIEDERSTETTER

---

par une déclaration officielle, son intention d'en faire cesser l'effet, ledit Traité restera obligatoire pendant un an audelà de ce terme, et ainsi de suite, jusqu'à l'expiration des douze mois qui suivront une telle declaration, à quelque époque qu'elle ait lieu.

ARTICLE XVI.

Le présent Traité sera approuvé et ratifié par Sa Majesté le Roi de Prusse, et par le Président des Etats Unis d'Amérique, par, et avec l'avis et le consentement du Sénat desdits Etats, et les Ratifications en seront échangées en la ville de Washington, dans l'espace de neuf mois, à dater de ce jour, ou plutôt, si faire se peut.

En foi de quoi les Plénipotentiaires respectifs ont signé les Articles ci-dessus, tant en françois qu'en anglois, et y ont apposé leurs sceaux; déclarant, toutefois, que la signature dans ces deux langues, ne doit pas, par la suite, être citée comme example, ni, en aucune maniere, porter préjudice aux Parties Contractantes.

Fait par triplicata en la Cité de Washington, le Premier Mai, l'An de Grâce Mil huit cent vingt-huit, et le Cinquante deuxieme de l'Indépendance des Etats Unis d'Amérique.

[Seal]   LUDWIG NIEDERSTETTER
[Seal]   H. CLAY

NOTES

In the final clause of the treaty is the statement that it was "done in triplicate." Presumably two originals were delivered to the Plenipotentiary of Prussia, as the treaty was signed at Washington and only one original is in the treaty file. That original has the English on the left pages and the French on the right; and, as the printed texts show, the *alternat* was observed; the United States is named first in the English text and second in the French, and the signature of Henry Clay is first following the English text and second following the French text. In the testimonium clause, where the signing in the two languages is mentioned, is the statement that "the signing in both languages shall not be brought into precedent, nor in any way operate to the prejudice of either Party." Similar language is to be found in the convention with France of September 30, 1800 (Document 25); and the expression mentioned was adopted in two later treaties with German states which were written in French as well as in English (Hanover, May 20, 1840, and Hesse, March 26, 1844).

The two attested resolutions of the Senate of May 14, 1828 (Executive Journal, III, 609), and of March 9, 1829 (*ibid.*, IV, 9), respectively, are attached to the original treaty. The second submission to the Senate arose from the delayed receipt of the Prussian instrument of ratification, which did not arrive at Washington until after the time limited for the exchange of ratifications, which (Article 16) was nine months from the date of signature, May 1, 1828 (D. S., 1 Notes from the Prussian Legation, February 6, 1829). President Jackson adopted the procedure of asking the advice and consent of the Senate to the exchange of ratifications in this message of March 6, 1829 (Executive Journal, IV, 7):

The treaty of commerce and navigation, concluded at Washington on the 1st of May, 1828, between the United States and the King of Prussia, was laid before the Senate, who, by their resolution of the 14th of that month, advised and consented to its ratification by the President.

By the 16th article of that treaty it was agreed that the exchange of ratifications should be made within nine months from its date.

On the 15th day of February last, being fifteen days after the time stipulated for the exchange by the terms of the treaty, the chargé d'affaires of the King of Prussia informed the Secretary of State that he had received the Prussian ratification, and was ready to exchange it for that of the United States. In reply, he was informed of the intention of the President, my late predecessor, not to proceed to the exchange, in consequence of the expiration of the time within which it was to be made.

Under these circumstances I have thought it my duty, in order to avoid all future questions, to ask the advice and consent of the Senate to make the proposed exchange.

I send you the original of the treaty, together with a printed copy of it.

The following resolution was unanimously agreed to in the Senate on March 9 (*ibid.*, 9):

Resolved (two-thirds of the Senators present concurring therein), That the Senate having re-examined the treaty of commerce and navigation, concluded at Wash-

ington on the first day of May, 1828, between the United States and the King of Prussia, do again consent thereto, and advise the President of the United States to proceed to the exchange of the ratifications of the same, notwithstanding the expiration of the time stipulated for this exchange by the terms of the treaty.

No accompanying papers (except perhaps copies of the revived articles of the treaties of 1785 and 1799) were sent to the Senate when the treaty was transmitted with the presidential message of May 5, 1828 (American State Papers, Foreign Relations, VI, 992–98; Executive Journal, III, 608).

The Prussian instrument of ratification is in French, including both treaty texts, the French in the left columns.

There is in the file no duplicate or copy of the United States instrument of ratification of March 12, 1829, other than a facsimile of the opening and closing pages thereof, obtained from the archives at Berlin. The document contains this recital:

And whereas the Senate of the United States, by their Resolutions of the fourteenth of May, 1828, and ninth of March, 1829, two thirds of the Senators then present concurring, did advise and consent to the Ratification of the said Treaty, and to the exchange of the said Ratification.

The other papers in the treaty file are in customary form; they include the original in English of the certificate of the exchange of ratifications at Washington on March 14, 1829, which was "executed in both languages," and the original proclamation, of the same date, which includes both texts of the treaty, the English on the left pages. The proclamation, including the text of the treaty in both languages, is printed in the Session Laws for the first session of the Twenty-first Congress.

The full power given to Secretary of State Clay for the negotiation and signature of this treaty was dated April 18, 1828, and was in customary form (D. S., 2 Credences, 81). Nothing appears of record as to the full power of the Prussian Plenipotentiary.

DISCRIMINATING DUTIES

By Articles 2 to 8 of this treaty national treatment, except as to the coasting trade, was mutually accorded to the vessels and cargoes of the two countries. Discriminating duties in respect of United States vessels and cargoes had been abolished by the Kingdom of Prussia on April 15, 1826; and a clause for the restitution of duties levied in the ports of the United States on Prussian vessels and their cargoes since that date had been proposed during the negotiations for this treaty.

The message to Congress of President John Quincy Adams of May 16, 1828, shortly after the signature of the treaty, recommended reciprocal application of the principle to Prussian vessels and cargoes, retroactive to April 15, 1826. The message (American State Papers, Foreign Relations, VI, 945–46) transmitted, in translation, a note of the Prussian Chargé d'Affaires of May 9, 1828, as follows:

The undersigned takes the liberty of again submitting to the consideration of His Excellency the Secretary of State a subject which, by order of his Government,

he has before had the honor of introducing at the conferences which have just ended in the conclusion of a treaty of commerce, etc. It regards the abolition of discriminating duties which, as relates to vessels of the United States and their cargoes, has taken place in the ports of the Kingdom of Prussia from the 15th of April, 1826, and been made applicable even to vessels not coming directly from the ports of the United States, but from any other country. This measure has been ordered by the Government of Prussia in the well-founded expectation that a project of a law framed for the same object, and at the same time before the Congress of the United States, would be put into operation. Thus has Prussia unhesitatingly granted, beforehand, the advantages enjoyed in her ports by national vessels and their cargoes, to vessels of the United States and their cargoes, without, so far, being admitted to that just reciprocity which she had expected in issuing this ordinance.

In the course of the conferences above referred to, the undersigned has readily acceded to the wishes of His Excellency, by renouncing the insertion in the said treaty of an article providing for the restitution of that part of the duties on tonnage, etc., which may have been levied in the ports of the United States on Prussian vessels and their cargoes since the 15th April, 1826, contrary to the principles of perfect reciprocity laid down in the said treaty, on condition that an arrangement to this effect would be made by a particular legislative act; and the undersigned has not hesitated to confide in the assurances given by His Excellency that he would make to the President of the United States the necessary recommendations of that object.

To complete the evidence of the measure adopted in Prussia, the undersigned has the honor to enclose a translation [printed *ibid.*, 946] of the order given to that effect on the 15th April, 1826, by the Minister of the Interior; and, at the same time, avails himself of the occasion to offer to His Excellency the Secretary of State the renewed assurances of his highest consideration.

An act of Congress in accord with the presidential proposal, and containing also provisions of a general nature in respect of discriminating duties, was passed on May 24, 1828 (4 Statutes at Large, 308–9).

ARTICLE 10

By the terms of Article 10 consuls were given certain jurisdiction in differences between captains and crews of vessels of their respective flags and might require the assistance of the local authorities "to cause their decisions to be carried into effect or supported." It seems that no question arose under those provisions until 1844. The annual message to Congress of President Polk of December 2, 1845 (Richardson, IV, 399), contains the following paragraphs:

A question has recently arisen under the tenth article of the subsisting treaty between the United States and Prussia. By this article the consuls of the two countries have the right to sit as judges and arbitrators "in such differences as may arise between the captains and crews of the vessels belonging to the nation whose interests are committed to their charge without the interference of the local authorities, unless the conduct of the crews or of the captain should disturb the order or tranquillity of the country, or the said consuls should require their assistance to cause their decisions to be carried into effect or supported."

The Prussian consul at New Bedford in June, 1844, applied to Mr. Justice Story to carry into effect a decision made by him between the captain and crew of the Prussian ship *Borussia*, but the request was refused on the ground that without previous legislation by Congress the judiciary did not possess the power to give effect to this article of the treaty. The Prussian Government, through their minister here, have complained of this violation of the treaty, and have asked the Government of the United States to adopt the necessary measures to prevent similar violations hereafter. Good faith to Prussia, as well as to other

nations with whom we have similar treaty stipulations, requires that these should be faithfully observed. I have deemed it proper, therefore, to lay the subject before Congress and to recommend such legislation as may be necessary to give effect to these treaty obligations.

An act "more effectually to provide for the Enforcement of certain Provisions in the Treaties of the United States," which recited a portion of Article 10 of the treaty, became law on August 8, 1846 (9 Statutes at Large, 78–79; Judicial Code, sec. 271; United States Code, title 28, ch. 10, sec. 393); a later statute is that of June 11, 1864 (13 Statutes at Large, 121–22; Revised Statutes, secs. 4079–81; now, as amended, United States Code, title 22, ch. 6, secs. 256–58).

ARTICLE 12

It seems that the provisions of Article 12 of this treaty for the revival of Article 12 of the treaty with Prussia of 1785 (Document 13) and Articles 13–24 of the treaty of 1799 (Document 24), were inserted in this treaty at the suggestion of President Adams, who recorded a conversation of April 22, 1828, with Secretary of State Clay on this subject as follows (Memoirs of John Quincy Adams, VII, 516):

> Mr. Clay called concerning the draft of a commercial treaty with Prussia that he had prepared. It consisted of fourteen articles, chiefly relating to the system of equalizing duties, with one article re-postponing the question of free ships free goods, but omitting all the maritime articles of the two former treaties.
>
> I recommended to Mr. Clay to insert one additional article, reviving all those of the former treaties which present circumstances render still useful. I observed that they might be all inserted in a single article, enumerating each of them by numbers. I thought the abandonment of all those articles would manifest an indifference to them which would be industriously used against us, and it would multiply the diversities of our treaties with different powers, while our policy is to assimilate as much as possible our obligatory treaties together.

Shortly prior to the exchange of ratifications of this treaty, but during the administration of President John Quincy Adams, which ended on March 4, 1829, notes were exchanged between the Prussian Chargé d'Affaires and the Secretary of State in explanation of the final clause of the first paragraph of Article 12. It is to be observed, however, that the notes thus exchanged were not submitted to the Senate. The portions of the Prussian note relating to the subject are as follows (D. S., 1 Notes from the Prussian Legation, February 8, 1829, translation):

> Another subject which the undersigned had the honor to introduce during the last interview, is of a nature simply explicative. It relates to this clause in the twelfth article of the said treaty: "it being, however, understood that the stipulations contained in the Articles thus revived, shall be always considered as, in no manner, affecting the Treaties or Conventions concluded by either Party with other Powers, during the interval between the expiration of the said Treaty of 1799, and the commencement of the operation of the present Treaty."
>
> The undersigned [Ludwig Niederstetter, Chargé d'Affaires of Prussia] is charged by His Excellency M. le Comte de Bernstorf, in order to prevent any possible misunderstanding on this subject, to address himself to His Excellency the Secretary of State, for the purpose of obtaining, before the exchange of the

ratifications, an official declaration of the intention and effect of this clause, and especially whether, in any case, it may influence the reciprocal rights guaranteed by this treaty to the vessels of the two contracting parties. M. le Comte de Bernstorf is of the negative opinion and thinks that Prussia could not conform to such an interpretation. The undersigned, in his last conversation with His Excellency the Secretary of State, had the satisfaction to find that the following explanation, which he has not ceased to maintain from the commencement of his negotiation, "that this clause had no other object than to assert the generally recognized principle, even without having been expressed, that the stipulations agreed on in the treaties of 1785 and 1799, and revived by the present treaty, ought not to be interpreted to the prejudice of a third power with which either of the contracting parties might have formed engagements anterior to the last, and that, in no event, could this clause be applied to the vessels of the two contracting parties," corresponds entirely to the views and intentions of the Government of the United States.

In this conformity of opinions entertained by the two respective Governments, the undersigned has now only to pray His Excellency to be pleased to acquaint him, in an ostensible form, with the expression of the intentions and interpretation of the above clause on the part of the Government of the United States, which His Excellency did him the honor to express to him in their last interview, for the purpose of enabling him to communicate it to his Government, for its complete satisfaction.

The reply of February 14, signed by Henry Clay as Secretary of State, was, on the point in question, in these terms (D. S., 4 Notes to Foreign Legations, 145–46):

The Undersigned having already communicated to Mr Niederstetter, in the above interview, the views which the President entertains in regard to the clause in the 12th Article of the Treaty which has been recited in the Note of Mr Niederstetter, takes pleasure, in conformity with his wishes, to repeat them on the present occasion. The clause, an explanation of which is required by His Excellency the Count de Bernstorf, is not universal or National compacts. It is inserted from abundance of caution to guard the national faith against the possible imputation or consequences of contracting incompatible engagements with different Powers. Thus, if the United States, or Prussia, reciprocally had entered into any treaty with a third Power, during the interval between the expiration of the Treaty of 1799 and the commencement of the operation of the Treaty of the 1st of May, 1828, which contained stipulations, inconsistent with the articles of the former treaties between the United States and Prussia, revived by the last mentioned Treaty, the engagements contracted with such third Power would have full effect, notwithstanding their incompatibility with the revived articles; But although the insertion of the clause was a necessary precaution, the President is not aware, nor is it believed, that there is any conflict between either of the provisions of the Treaty of the first of May last, and the stipulations of any other Treaty concluded between the United States and a third Power. On the particular point, referred to by Mr Niederstetter, of the mutual privileges of navigation, secured to American and Prussian Vessels by the Treaty of the first of May, the Undersigned is happy to be able to assure him that there is no impediment to the full enjoyment of those privileges by Prussian Vessels, in any of the Treaties of the United States with foreign Powers.

THE GERMANIC CONFEDERATION

When this treaty was made, Prussia was a member of the Germanic Confederation (Deutscher Bund), which was formed by the constitutive agreement of June 8, 1815, and which continued until 1866. The text of that federative act (in German, with a French translation), which formed part of the Final Act of the Congress of Vienna, is in

British and Foreign State Papers, II, 114–36; it was elaborated at a conference held at Vienna in 1820.

Of the Germanic Confederation there were (from 1817) thirty-nine members; it included not only Austria and Prussia, but also the other states of north and south Germany as they then existed. It is to be added, however, that Austria and Prussia were members only "for all their possessions formerly belonging to the German Empire"; accordingly, "the Prussian provinces of Prussia and Posen, and the Austrian territories in Galicia, Hungary, Milan, Venetia and Dalmatia, were not included in the [Germanic] Confederation" (Encyclopædia Britannica, 14th ed., X, 280). Prior to 1866 dynastic and other changes from time to time reduced somewhat the number of members of the Confederation.

That Confederation was a form of union which affected the relations of its members *inter se* but under which they remained separate entities as to outside states. When this treaty went into force, the United States had no other treaties in force with members of the Germanic Confederation except with the Hanseatic Republics (see Documents 59 and 63), for the earlier treaties with Prussia of 1785 and 1799 (Documents 13 and 24) had expired; but subsequently various treaties were made by the United States with other states, members of the Germanic Confederation, prior to 1866, when the Confederation came to an end as a result of the war between Austria and Prussia in which certain other German states joined. To one agreement, the Extradition Convention of June 16, 1852, with Prussia and other powers, twenty members of the Germanic Confederation were originally parties and six others later acceded.

Some further observations on the Germanic Confederation and on the German Zollverein or Customs Union (Deutscher Zoll- und Handelsverein), as well as on the North German Union, will be found in the notes to Document 59.

Treaty Series No. 158
8 Statutes at Large, 386–89
18 *ibid.*, pt. 2, Public Treaties, 403–4

63

THE HANSEATIC REPUBLICS : JUNE 4, 1828

Additional Article to the Convention of December 20, 1827 (Document 59), signed at Washington June 4, 1828. Original in English and French. Submitted to the Senate December 16, 1828. (Message of December 15, 1828.) Resolution of advice and consent December 29, 1828. Ratified by the United States between December 29, 1828, and January 14, 1829. Ratified by Lübeck August 13, 1828; by Bremen September 3, 1828; and by Hamburg September 13, 1828. Ratifications exchanged at Washington January 14, 1829. Proclaimed January 14, 1829.

Additional Article to the Convention of Friendship Commerce and Navigation[1] concluded at Washington on the twentieth day of December 1827, between the United States of America, and the Hanseatic Republics of Lubeck, Bremen and Hamburg.

The United States of America, and the Hanseatic Republics of Lubeck, Bremen and Hamburg, wishing to favour their mutual commerce, by affording, in their ports, every necessary assistance to their respective vessels, the Undersigned Plenipotentiaries have further agreed upon the following Additional Article to the Convention of Friendship, Commerce and Navigation, concluded at Washington, on the twentieth day of December 1827, between the Contracting Parties.

The Consuls and Vice Consuls may cause to be arrested the sailors, being part of the crews of

Article Additionel à la Convention d'Amitié de Commerce et de Navigation[1] conclue à Washington le vingt Décembre 1827, entre les Républiques Anséatiques de Lubeck, Bremen et Hambourg, et les Etats Unis d'Amérique.

Les Républiques Anséatiques de Lubeck, Bremen et Hambourg, et les Etats Unis d'Amérique, désirant favoriser mutuellement leur commerce, en donnant dans leurs ports, toute assistance nécessaire à leurs bâtimens respectifs, les Soussignés Plénipotentiaires sont convenus, de plus du suivant Article Additionel, à la Convention d'Amitié, de Commerce et de Navigation conclue à Washington le vingt Décembre Mil huit cent vingt-sept entre les Parties Contractantes.

Les Consuls et Vice-Consuls pourront faire arrêter les matelots faisant partie des équipages des

---

[1] Document 59.   447

the vessels of their respective countries, who shall have deserted from the said vessels, in order to send them back, and transport them out of the country. For which purpose the said Consuls and Vice-Consuls, shall address themselves to the Courts, judges, and officers competent, and shall demand the said deserters, in writing, proving, by an exhibition of the registers of the said vessels, or ship's roll, or other official document, that those men were part of said crews; and on this demand being so proved (saving, however, where the contrary is proved), the delivery shall not be refused, and there shall be given all aid and assistance to the said Consuls and Vice-Consuls, for the search, seizure, and arrest of the said deserters, who shall even be detained and kept in the prisons of the country, at their request and expense, until they shall have found opportunity of sending them back. But if they be not sent back within two months, to be counted from the day of their arrest, they shall be set at liberty, and shall be no more arrested for the same cause.

It is understood, however, that if the deserter should be found to have committed any crime or offence, his surrender may be delayed until the tribunal before which the case shall be depending, shall have pronounced its sentence, and such sentence shall have been carried into effect.

bâtimens de leurs pays respectifs, qui auraient déserté desdits bâtimens, pour les renvoyer et faire transporter hors du pays. Auquel effet lesdits Consuls et Vice-Consuls s'addresseront aux tribunaux, juges, et officiers compétens, et leur feront, par écrit la demande desdits déserteurs, en justifiant, par l'exhibition des régistres du bâtiment, ou rôle d'équipage, ou autres documens officiels, que ces hommes faisaient partie desdits équipages. Et sur cette demande ainsi justifiée, sauf, toutefois la preuve contraire, l'extradition ne pourra être refusée; et il sera donné toute aide et assistance aux dits Consuls et Vice-Consuls, pour la recherche, saisie et arrestation des susdits déserteurs, lesquels seront même détenus et gardés dans les prisons du pays, à leur réquisition et à leurs frais, jusqu' à ce qu'ils aient trouvé occasion de les renvoyer; mais s'ils n'étaient renvoyés dans le délai de deux mois, à compter du jour de leur arrêt, ils seront élargis, et ne pourront plus être arrêtés pour la même cause.

Il est entendu, toutefois, que si le déserteur se trouvait avoir commis quelque crime ou délit, il pourra être sursis à son extradition, jusqu' à ce que le tribunal nanti de l'affaire aura rendu sa sentence, et que celle-ci ait reçu on exécution.

The present additional article shall have the same force and value, as if it were inserted, word for word, in the Convention signed at Washington on the twentieth day of December One thousand eight hundred and twenty seven; and being approved and ratified by the President of the United States, by and with the advice and consent of the Senate thereof, and by the Senates of the Hanseatic Republics of Lubeck, Bremen, and Hamburg, the Ratifications shall be exchanged at Washington within nine months from the date hereof, or sooner, if possible.

In faith whereof, We, the Undersigned, by virtue of our respective Full Powers, have signed the present Additional Article, and have thereto affixed our Seals.

Done in quadruplicate, at the City of Washington, on the Fourth day of June in the Year of Our Lord One thousand eight hundred and twenty eight.

[Seal] H. CLAY
[Seal] V. RUMPFF

Le présent Article additionel aura la même force et valeur que s'il était inséré, mot à mot, dans la Convention signée à Washington le vingt Décembre Mil huit cent vingt-sept, et étant approuvé et ratifié par les Sénats des Républiques Anséatiques de Lubeck, Bremen et Hambourg; et par le Président des Etats Unis, par, et avec l'avis et le consentement du Sénat desdits Etats, les Ratifications en seront échangées à Washington dans l'espace de neuf mois, à dater de ce jour, ou plûtot, si faire se peut.

En foi de quoi, Nous Soussignés en vertu de nos Pleins Pouvoirs respectifs, avons signé le présent Article Additionel, et y avons apposé nos sceaux.

Fait par quadruplicata, en la Cité de Washington, le quatre Juin, l'An de Grâce Mil huit cent vingt-huit.

[Seal] V. RUMPFF
[Seal] H. CLAY

NOTES

This agreement, which is an additional article to the convention of December 20, 1827 (Document 59), was signed by the same representatives of the contracting parties who signed that convention. In the notes to Document 59 are some comments regarding the form and character of that convention and the relations of the three Hanseatic Republics *inter se* and with the other members of the Germanic Confederation (1815–66).

The negotiators of this additional article to the convention of 1827, which was signed two days after the exchange of ratifications of that convention, seem to have considered their full powers for the signing

of that convention as sufficient for the signature of this document, the opening sentence of which states that the Plenipotentiaries "have further agreed"; there is otherwise no reference to full powers except their mention in the testimonium clause.

No papers accompanied this convention when it was transmitted to the Senate with the presidential message of December 15, 1828 (Executive Journal, III, 622).

The File Papers

The treaty file of this agreement is complete except that it lacks a duplicate or copy of the United States instrument of ratification. While the exact date of that ratification cannot be stated, it was not earlier than December 29, 1828, the date of the Senate resolution of advice and consent, and not later than January 14, 1829, the date of the exchange of ratifications.

Like the convention of December 20, 1827 (Document 59), this agreement was "done in quadruplicate." Doubtless three of the originals were for the respective Governments of Lübeck, Bremen, and Hamburg; only one original is in the treaty file. As the printed texts show, the *alternat* was observed, as in the convention of 1827; the English and French texts are on opposite pages, the English on the left. The attested resolution of the Senate of December 29, 1828 (Executive Journal, III, 624–25), is attached to the original treaty. The ratification on the part of the Hanseatic Republics is a document similar in form to the ratification of the convention of 1827; it is written in French and includes both texts of the additional article, the French in the left column; it was signed and sealed on behalf of the respective Hanseatic Republics on the three dates stated in the head-note. The certificate of the exchange of ratifications on January 14, 1829, in the file, is in English and in customary form, except that it includes the phrase, "the said Anthony Charles Cazenove having previously communicated to the said Secretary of State his power and authority to that effect." The original proclamation, of the same date as the exchange of ratifications, includes a copy of the Senate print of the additional article, in both languages. As stated in the notes to Document 59, copies of the proclamations of the convention of 1827 and of this additional article were transmitted to both Houses of Congress with the presidential message of January 26, 1829, and were printed in House Document No. 92, 20th Congress, 2d session, serial 186. The proclamation of the additional article is also printed in British and Foreign State Papers, XV, 777–79.

Another document in the file is the original full power given to Antoine Charles Cazenove, Consul of Bremen and Vice Consul of Hamburg at Alexandria, Virginia (and "Swiss Consul for the District of Columbia and the Southern States"), to exchange the ratifications; the power is in French, joint in form but severally signed for the three Republics, under their seals, by the Burgomaster President of Lübeck on August 23, by the President of the Senate of Bremen on September 3, and by the President of the Senate of Hamburg on September 13, 1828.

Treaty Series No. 34
8 Statutes at Large, 390–98
18 *ibid.*, pt. 2, Public Treaties, 81–89

64

BRAZIL : DECEMBER 12, 1828

Treaty of Peace, Friendship, Commerce, and Navigation, signed at Rio de Janeiro December 12, 1828. Original in English and Portuguese. Submitted to the Senate February 27, 1829. (Message of February 26, read March 5, 1829; see Executive Journal, IV, 4.) Resolution of advice and consent March 10, 1829. Ratified by the United States March 17, 1829. Ratified by Brazil December 12, 1828. Ratifications exchanged at Washington March 18, 1829. Proclaimed March 18, 1829.

In the Name of the Most Holy and Indivisible Trinity.

The United States of America and His Magesty the Emperor of Brazil, desiring to establish a firm and permanent peace and friendship between both Nations, have resolved to fix in a manner, clear, distinct and positive, the rules which shall in future be religiously observed between the one and the other, by means of a Treaty or General Convention of Peace, Friendship, Commerce and Navigation.

For this most desireable object, the President of the United States has conferred full powers on William Tudor their Chargé d'Affaires at the Court of Brazil: and His Magesty the Emperor of Brazil on the Most Illustrious and Most Excellent Marquez of Aracaty, a Member of His Council, Gentleman of the Imperial Bed

Em Nome da Santissima e Indivisivel Trindade

Sua Magestade O Imperador do Brazil, e os Estados-Unidos da America, Dezejando estabelecer huma paz e amizade firme e permanente entre ambas as Nações, tem rezolvido fixar de huma maneira clara, distincta, e positiva, as regras que para o futuro se hão-de religiosamente observar entre huma e a outra, por meio de hum Tratado ou Convenção geral de Paz, Amizade, Commercio e Navegação.

Para este mui apreciavel fim Sua Magestade O Imperador do Brazil Deu Plenos Poderes aos Illustrissimos e Excellentissimos Senhores Marquez do Aracaty, do Seu Conselho, Gentil-Homem da Imperial Camara, Conselheiro da Fazenda, Grão Cruz da Ordem de Aviz, Senador do Imperio, Ministro e Secretario d'Estado

Chamber, Councillor of the Treasury, Grand Cross of the Order of Aviz, Senator of the Empire, Minister and Secretary of State for Foreign Affairs; and Miguel de Souza Mello e Alvim, a Member of His Council, Commander of the Order of Aviz, Knight of the Imperial Order of the Cross, Cheif of Division in the Imperial and National Navy, Minister and Secretary of State for the Marine, who after having exchanged their said full powers, in due and proper form, have agreed to the following articles:

dos Negocios Estrangeiros; e a Miguel de Souza Mello e Alvim, do Seu Conselho, Commendador da Ordem d'Aviz, Cavalleiro da Imperial do Cruzeiro, Chefe de Divizão da Armada Nacional e Imperial, Ministro e Secretario d'Estado dos Negocios da Marinha; e o Prezidente dos Estados Unidos da America, ao Senhor Guilherme Tudor, Encarregado de Negocios dos mesmos Estados na Corte do Brazil: os quaes depois de terem trocado os seus ditos Plenos Poderes, que forão achados em boa e devida forma, conviérão nos Artigos seguintes.

ARTIGO 1º

ART. 1st There shall be a perfect, firm and inviolable Peace and Friendship between the United States of America and their citizens, and His Imperial Magesty, his successors, and subjects throughout their possessions and territories respectively, without distinction of persons or places.

Haverà paz perfeita, firme, e inviolavel, e sincéra amizade entre Sua Magestade Imperial, e Seus Successores e Subditos, e os Estados Unidos da America, e Seus Cidadãos, em todas as suas possessoens e territorios respectivos, sem distincção de pessoas ou lugares

ARTIGO 2º

ART. 2^{d} The United States of America and His Magesty the Emperor of Brazil, desiring to live in peace and harmony with all the other Nations of the Earth, by means of a policy frank and equally friendly with all, engage mutually, not to grant any particular favour to other nations in respect of commerce and navigation, which shall not immediately become common to the other party,

Sua Magestade O Imperador do Brazil, e os Estados-Unidos da America, Dezejando viver em paz e harmonia com todas as outras Naçoens do Mundo por meio de huma Politica franca e igualmente amigavel com todas, concordão reciprocamente em não outorgar nenhum favor peculiar a outras Naçoens em materias de commercio e navegação, que se não torne immediatamente com-

who shall enjoy the same freely, if the concession was freely made, or on allowing the same compensation, if the concession was conditional It is understood however, that the relations and Conventions which now exist, or may hereafter exist between Brazil and Portugal shall form an exception to this article.

Art. 3. The two high contracting parties being likewise desirous of placing the commerce and Navigation of their respective countries, on the liberal basis of perfect equality and reciprocity mutually agree, that the citizens and subjects of each may frequent all the coasts and countries of the other, and reside and trade there in all kinds of produce manufactures and merchandize: and they shall enjoy all the rights, privileges and exemptions, in navigation and commerce, which native citizens or subjects do, or shall enjoy, submitting themselves, to the laws, decrees, and usages, there established, to which native citizens or subjects are subjected. But it is understood that this article does not include the coasting trade of either country, the regulation of which is reserved by the parties respectively, according to their own separate laws.

Art. 4th They likewise agree that whatever kind of produce,

mum á outra parte, se a concessão for feita livremente, ou sujeita à mesma compensação se a concessão for condicional.

Fica comtudo entendido que as relações e convençoens que agora existem, ou possão depois existir entre o Brazil e Portugal, formaráõ huma excepção a este Artigo.

Artigo 3º

As Duas Altas Partes Contractantes Dezejando igualmente pôr o commercio e navegação de seus respectivos Paizes, sobre a liberal baze de perfeita igualdade e reciprocidade, conviérão mutuamente que os Subditos e Cidadãos de cada huma d'ellas possão frequentar todas as Costas e Paizes da outra, rezidir e commerciar em todos os generos de productos, manufacturas, e mercadorias, e gozarão de todos os Direitos, Privilegios, e isençoens, em navegação e commercio, de que os Subditos ou Cidadãos naturaes gozão ou gozarem, submettendo-se às Leys, Decretos, e uzos estabelecidos, e a que se sujeitarem os Subditos ou Cidadãos naturaes. Fica porem entendido que neste Artigo não se inclúe o commercio de cabotagem de cada hum dos dous Paizes, o qual fica rezervado, conforme as Leys dos ditos Paizes, aos seus respectivos Subditos e Cidadãos.

Artigo 4º

Ellas concordão igualmente que quaes quer generos de producção,

manufactures, or merchandize, of any foreign country, can be, from time to time, lawfully imported into the United States, in their own vessels, may be also imported in vessels of Brazil: and that no higher or other duties upon the tonnage of the vessel and her cargo, shall be levied and collected whether the importation be made in the vessels of the one country or the other. And in like manner, that whatever kind of produce manufactures, or merchandize of any foreign country, can be, from time to time, lawfully imported into the Empire of Brazil, in its own vessels, may be also imported in vessels of the United States: and that no higher or other duties upon the tonnage of the vessel and her cargo, shall be levied or collected whether the importation be made in vessels of the one country, or of the other. And they agree that whatever may be lawfully exported, or re-exported from the one country in its own vessels, to any foreign country, may in like manner, be exported or re-exported in the vessels of the other country. And the same bounties, duties, and drawbacks, shall be allowed and collected, whether such exportation, or re-exportation, be made in vessels of the United States, or of the Empire of Brazil. The Gov-

manufactura, ou mercadoria de qualquer Paiz estrangeiro, que possão por certo espaço de tempo ser legalmente importados nos Estados-Unidos, em seus proprios navios, possão tambem importar-se em navios do Imperio do Brazil e que se não perceberáõ outros ou mayores Direitos sobre a Tonelagem do navio e sua carga, quer a importação se faça em navios de huma das Partes Contractantes, quer da outra. E similhantemente que qualquer genero de producção, manufactura, ou mercadoria de qualquer Paiz estrangeiro, que possa ser por certo prazo legalmente importado no Imperio do Brazil, em seus proprios navios, possa tambem ser importado em navios dos Estados Unidos e que se não exigiráõ ou perceberáõ nenhuns ou outros Direitos sobre a Tonelagem do navio e sua carga, quer a importação se faça em navios de huma Parte Contractante, quer da outra. Concordão outro sim que tudo o que possa ser legalmente exportado ou reexportado de hum dos Paizes, em seus navios proprios, para qualquer Paiz estrangeiro, possa de igual forma ser exportado ou reexportado em os navios do outro Paiz. E serão concedidos e percebidos os mesmos beneficios, direitos, e retornos [draw-backs][1] quer tal ex-

---

[1] The brackets in the Portuguese text of Articles 4, 31, and 33 of this treaty appear in the original Brazilian instrument of ratification, from which the Portuguese text here printed is taken.

ernment of the United States however considering the present state of the navigation of Brazil, agrees that a vessel shall be considered as Brazilian, when the Proprietor and Captain are subjects of Brazil and the papers are in legal form.

ART. 5th No higher or other duties shall be imposed on the importation into the United States, of any articles the produce or manufactures of the Empire of Brazil, and no higher or other duties shall be imposed on the importation into the Empire of Brazil, of any articles the produce or manufactures of the United States, than are or shall be payable on the like articles, being the produce or manufactures of any other foreign country: nor shall any higher or other duties, or charges be imposed in either of the two countries, on the exportation of any articles to the United States, or to the Empire of Brazil respectively, than such as are payable on the exportation of the like article to any other foreign country: nor shall any prohibition be imposed on the exportation or importation of any articles, the produce or manufactures of the United States, or of the Empire of Brazil, to or from

portação ou reexportação se faça em Navios do Imperio do Brazil, ou dos Estados-Unidos.

Dezejando porem o Governo dos Estados-Unidos attender à Navegação do Brazil, convem em que seja presentemente considerado navio Brazileiro aquelle, cujo Dono e Capitão forem Subditos Brazileiros, e cujos Papeis estiverem em forma legal.

ARTIGO 5º

Não se imporáõ outros ou mayores Direitos sobre a importação nos Estados-Unidos de quaes quer Artigos de producção, ou manufacturas do Imperio; e não se imporáõ outros ou mayores Direitos sobre a importação no Imperio do Brazil, de quaes quer Artigos ou manufacturas dos Estados-Unidos, do que são ou vierem a ser pagos sobre os mesmos Artigos, que forem de producção ou manufacturas de qualquer outro Paiz estrangeiro; nem se imporáõ outros ou mayores Direitos ou encargos em qualquer dos dous Paizes, sobre a exportação de quaes quer Artigos para o Imperio do Brazil, ou para os Estados-Unidos respectivamente, do que os que são pagos sobre a exportação de iguaes Artigos para qualquer outro Paiz estrangeiro, nem se imporà nenhuma prohibição sobre a exportação ou importação de quaes quer Artigos de producção ou manufacturas do Imperio do Brazil, ou dos Estados

the territories of the United States, or to or from the territories of the Empire of Brazil, which shall not equally etxend to all other Nations.

Unidos, para, ou dos territorios do Imperio do Brazil, para, ou dos territorios dos Estados-Unidos, que se não faça extensiva igualmente a todas as outras Naçoens.

Artigo 6º

Art. 6th It is likewise agreed, that it shall be wholly free for all merchants, commanders of ships, and other citizens or subjects of both countries, to manage themselves their own business, in all the pòrts and places subject to the jurisdiction of each other, as well with respect to the consignment and sale of their goods and merchandize by wholesale or retail, as with respect to the loading, unloading and sending off their ships; they being in all these cases to be treated as citizens or subjects of the country in which they reside, or at least to be placed on a footing with the subjects or citizens of the most favoured nation.

Concordou-se igualmente que todos os Negociantes, Commandantes de Navios e outros Subditos e Cidadãos de ambos os Paizes, tenhão toda a liberdade de dirigirem seus proprios negocios em todos os Portos e logares sujeitos à Jurisdicção de qualquer d'elles, tanto relativamente à consignação e venda de seus generos e mercadorias em grosso ou retalho, como relativamente à carga, descarga e remessa de seus navios, devendo elles ser tratados em todos estes cazos como Subditos ou Cidadãos do Paiz em que residirem, ou ao menos ser equiparados aos Subditos ou Cidadãos da Nação mais favorecida.

Artigo 7º

Art. 7th The citizens and subjects of neither of the contracting parties shall be liable to any embargo, nor be detained with their vessels, cargoes, or merchandize or effects, for any military expedition, nor for any public or private purpose whatever, without allowing to those interested, a sufficient indemnification.

Os Subditos e Cidadãos de qualquer das Partes Contractantes, não serão sujeitos a nenhum embargo, nem serão detidos com os seus navios, cargas, mercadorias, ou effeitos, para qualquer expedição militar, nem para serem empregados para objectos publicos ou particulares, quaes quer que sejão, sem se dar aos interessados huma sufficiente indemnização.

Art. 8th Whenever the citizens or subjects of either of the contracting parties shall be forced to seek refuge or asylum in the rivers, bays, ports or dominions of the other, with their vessels whether of merchant or of war, public or private, through stress of weather, pursuit of pirates, or enemies, they shall be received and treated with humanity, giving to them all favour and protection, for repairing their ships, procuring provisions, and placing themselves in a situation to continue their voyage without obstacle or hindrance of any kind.

Art. 9th All the ships, merchandize and effects belonging to the citizens or subjects, of one of the contracting parties, which may be captured by pirates, whether within the limits of its jurisdiction, or on the high seas, and may be carried, or found in the rivers, roads, ports, bays, or dominions of the other, shall be delivered up to the owners, they proving in due and proper form, their rights before the competent tribunals: it being well understood, that the claim should be made within the term of one year by the parties themselves, their attorneys, or agents of their respective governments.

ARTIGO 8º

Toda a vez que os Subditos ou Cidadãos de qualquer das Partes Contractantes, forem obrigados a buscar refugio ou asilo nos Rios, Bahias, Portos ou Dominios da outra, com seus navios mercantes, ou de guerra, publicos ou particulares, por força de temporaes, ou por serem perseguidos por piratas ou inimigos, serão recebidos e tratados com humanidade, dar-se-lhes ha todo o favor e protecção para concertarem seus navios, refazerem-se de viveres, e se pôrem em estado de continuar sua viagem, sem obstaculo ou estorvo de qualidade alguma.

ARTIGO 9º

Todos os navios, mercadorias, e effeitos pertencentes a Subditos ou Cidadãos de cada huma das Partes Contractantes, que hajão de ser tomados por piratas, quer dentro dos limites da sua jurisdicção, quer no mar alto, e sejão conduzidos ou se acharem dentro dos Rios, Enseadas, Bahias, Portos, ou Dominios da outra, serão restituidos aos Proprietarios, logo que elles provem em boa e devida forma seus Direitos, perante os competentes Tribunaes: ficando bem entendido que a reclamação deve ser feita dentro do prazo de hum anno pelas proprias partes, seus Procuradores, ou pelos Agentes de seus respectivos Governos.

Art. 10ᵗʰ When any vessel belonging to the citizens or subjects of either of the contracting parties, shall be wrecked, foundered, or shall suffer any damage on the coasts, or within the dominions of the other, there shall be given to them all assistance and protection, in the same manner which is usual and customary with the vessels of the nation, where the damage happens, permitting them to unload the said vessel, if necessary, of its merchandize and effects, without exacting for it any duty, impost or contribution whatever, until they may be exported, unless they be destined for consumption

Art. 11ᵗʰ The citizens or subjects of each of the contracting parties shall have power to dispose of their personal goods within the jurisdiction of the other, by sale, donation, testament or otherwise, and their representatives, being citizens or subjects of the other party, shall succeed to the said personal goods, whether by testament, or *ab intestato*, and they may take possession thereof, either by themselves, or others acting for them, and dispose of the same at their will, paying such dues only as the inhabitants of the country, wherin said goods are, shall be subject to pay in like cases: and if, in the case of real estate, the said

Artigo 10º

Se algum navio pertencente aos Subditos ou Cidadãos de huma das Partes Contractantes der á costa, for ao fundo, ou soffrer alguma deterioração nas Costas, ou dentro dos Dominios da outra, ser-lhe há dado todo o soccorro e protecção da mesma maneira que se uza e pratica com os navios da Nação onde acontecer a deterioração, permittindo-se que se descarreguem do dito navio, se for necessario, as mercadorias e effeitos, sem se exigir por isso nenhum Direito, Imposto, ou Contribuição qualquer, athé que sejão exportados, excepto se forem Despachados para consummo.

Artigo 11º

Os Subditos ou Cidadãos de cada huma das Partes Contractantes poderáõ dispôr de seus bens individuaes, dentro da Jurisdição da outra, por venda, doação, testamento, ou por qualquer outra forma: herdaráõ os ditos bens pessoaes, quer por testamento ou *ab intestato*, podendo tomar posse d'elles por si mesmos, ou por outrem em seu lugar, e dispôr dos mesmos à sua vontade, pagando somente aquelles Direitos a que são obrigados os habitantes do Paiz em que se acharem taes bens em cazos similhantes; e no cazo de serem bens de raiz, e que aos herdeiros, pela sua qualidade de estrangeiros, se obste de entrar na posse da herança, conceder-se-

heirs would be prevented from entering into the possession of the inheritance, on account of their character of aliens, there shall be granted to them the term of three years, to dispose of the same, as they may think proper, and to withdraw the proceeds without molestation, nor any other charges than those which are imposed by the laws of the country.

ART. 12th Both the contracting parties promise and engage formally to give their special protection to the persons and property of the citizens and subjects of each other, of all occupations who may be in their territories, subject to the jurisdiction of the one or the other, transient or dwelling therein, leaving open and free to them the tribunals of justice for their judicial intercourse, on the same terms which are usual and customary with the natives, or citizens and subjects of the country in which they may be; for which they may employ, in defence of their rights, such advocates, solicitors, notaries, agents, and factors, as they may judge proper in all their trials at law.

ART. 13th It is likewise agreed, that the most perfect and entire security of conscience shall be enjoyed by the citizens or subjects of both the contracting parties in

lhes-ha o prazo de trez annos para disporem da mesma como julgarem conveniente, arrecadando o producto sem embaraço, nem outros encargos, senão os que são impostos pela Ley do Paiz.

ARTIGO 12º

Ambas as Partes Contractantes promettem e se obrigão formalmente a prestar sua protecção especial às pessoas e propriedades de Seus respectivos Subditos e Cidadãos de todas as classes, que possão achar-se nos territorios sujeitos à Jurisdicção de qualquer dellas, seja transitoria ou fixamente, deixando-lhes francos e abertos os Tribunaes de Justiça para os seus recursos judiciaes, nos mesmos termos uzuaes e do costume praticados pelos Cidadãos naturaes, ou Subditos do Paiz em que se achem; para cujo fim elles poderão empregar em defesa de seus Direitos, aquelles Advogados, Procuradores, Tabelliaens, Agentes, e Correspondentes que julgarem convenientes, em todas as suas questoens judiciaes.

ARTIGO 13º

Conveio-se igualmente que os Subditos ou Cidadãos de Ambas as Partes Contractantes, gozarão da mais perfeita e inteira segurança de consciencia, nos Paizes sujeitos

the countries subject to the jurisdiction of the one and the other,
without their being liable to be
disturbed or molested on account
of their religious belief so long as
they respect the laws and established usages of the country.
Moreover the bodies of the citizens and subjects of one of the
contracting parties who may die
in the territories of the other,
shall be buried in the usual bury-
ing-grounds, or in other decent or
suitable places, and shall be protected from violation or disturbance.

ART. 14ᵗʰ It shall be lawful for
the citizens and subjects of the
United States of America, and of
the Empire of Brazil, to sail with
their ships, with all manner of
liberty and security, no distinction being made who are the proprietors of the merchandize laden
thereon, from any port to the
places of those who now are, or
who hereafter shall be at enmity
with either of the contracting parties. It shall likewise be lawful
for the citizens and subjects aforesaid, to sail with the ships and
merchandizes before mentioned,
and to trade with the same liberty
and security, from the places,
ports, and havens, of those who
are enemies of either party, without any opposition, or disturbance
whatsoever, not only directly
from the places of the enemy before mentioned, to neutral places,

à Jurisdicção de qualquer dellas,
sem que possão ser perturbados ou
molestados, por cauza de suas
crenças religiosas, em quanto res-
peitarem as Leis e usos estabelecidos do Paiz.

Outrosim serão os corpos dos
Subditos ou Cidadãos de huma
das Partes Contractantes que
venhão a fallecer nos territorios
da Outra, enterrados nos Cemi-
terios ordinarios, ou em outros
lugares decentes e apropriados,
e serão protegidos contra qualquer
perturbação, ou violação.

ARTIGO 14º

Serà licito aos Subditos do
Imperio do Brazil, e aos Cidadãos dos Estados-Unidos da
America, navegar os seus navios
com toda a liberdade e segurança
sem se fazer distincção de quem
são os proprietarios das mercadorias nelles transportadas de qualquer Porto para os Lugares das
Naçoens, que ora estão, ou para
o futuro vierem a estar em inimi-
zade com qualquer das Partes
Contractantes. Será tambem
licito aos mencionados Subditos
e Cidadãos, navegar os navios e
mercadorias referidas, e commerciar com a mesma liberdade e
segurança nas Praças, Portos,
e Enseadas das Naçoens que são
inimigas de cada huma das Partes
Contractantes, sem opposição ou
estorvo algum, não só indo directamente dos Portos do inimigo
referido para Portos neutros, mas

but also from one place belonging to an enemy to another place belonging to an enemy, whether they be under the jurisdiction of one power, or under several. And it is hereby stipulated, that free ships shall also give freedom to goods, and that everything shall be deemed to be free, and exempt, which shall be found on board the ships belonging to the citizens or subjects of either of the contracting parties, although the whole lading, or any part thereof should appertain to the enemies of either, contraband goods being always excepted. It is also agreed in like manner, that the same liberty be extended to persons who are on board a free ship, with this effect, that although they be enemies to both or either party, they are not to be taken out of that free ship, unless they are officers or soldiers, and in the actual service of the enemies: Provided however, and it is hereby agreed, that the stipulations in this article contained, declaring that the flag shall cover the property, shall be understood as applying to those powers only, who recognize this principle; but if either of the two contracting parties shall be at war with a third, and the other neutral, the flag of the neutral shall cover the property of enemies whose governments acknowledge this principle, and not of others.

tambem de hum Lugar que pertença a hum inimigo, para outro Lugar pertencente a outro inimigo, quer elles estejão sob a Jurisdicção de huma só Potencia ou de diversas. E estipula-se mais que os navios livres tambem libertaráõ as fazendas, e que se julgue livre e isento tudo o que se achar abordo de navios pertencentes a qualquer das Partes Contractantes, ainda que toda ou qualquer parte da carga pertencesse aos inimigos de cada huma d'ellas, exceptuando-se sempre generos de contrabando.

Tambem se convencionou da mesma forma, que a dita liberdade se extenda às pessoas que estiverem abordo de hum navio livre, afim de que, ainda quando ellas sejão inimigas de huma das Partes Contractantes, nunca sejão tiradas d'aquelle navio neutro, excepto se forem Officiaes ou Soldados, e em serviço actual dos inimigos.

Deve-se porem entender, e se ajustou outrosim que as estipulaçoens que contem este Artigo, declarando que a Bandeira cobre a carga, serão applicaveis unicamente àquellas Potencias que reconhecem este principio: porem se huma das duas Partes Contractantes estiver em guerra com huma terceira, ficando a outra neutra, a Bandeira da neutra cobrirà a propriedade dos inimigos, cujos Governos reconhecerem este principio, e não dos outros.

ART. 15ᵗʰ It is likewise agreed, that in the case where the neutral flag of one of the contracting parties, shall protect the property of the enemies of the other, by virtue of the above stipulation, it shall always be understood, that the neutral property found on board such enemy's vessels, shall be held and considered as enemy's property, and as such shall be liable to detention and confiscation, except such property as was put on board, such vessel before the declaration of war, or even afterwards, if it were done without the knowledge of it; but the contracting parties agree that four months having elapsed after the declaration, their citizens shall not plead ignorance thereof. On the contrary, if the flag of the neutral, does not protect the enemies property, in that case the goods and merchandize of the neutral, embarked in such enemy's ship shall be free.

Convencionou-se igualmente que, no cazo em que a Bandeira neutra de huma das Partes Contractantes proteja a propriedade dos inimigos da outra, em virtude da referida estipulação, se entenderà sempre que a propriedade neutra que se achar abordo d'aquelles inimigos, serà tida e considerada como propriedade do inimigo; e como tal serà sujeita à detenção e confisco, excepto se a dita propriedade for posta abordo d'aquelle navio antes da declaração da guerra, ou mesmo depois se o foi sem se ter essa noticia. Convencionárão porem as Duas Partes Contractantes em que tendo decorrido quatro mezes depois da declaração, não possão seus Subditos e Cidadãos chamarse à ignorancia d'ella. Pelo contrario se a Bandeira do neutro não proteje a propriedade do inimigo, então serão livres os generos e mercadorias do neutro, que estiverem embarcados naquelle navio inimigo.

ART. 16ᵗʰ This liberty of commerce and navigation shall extend to all kinds of merchandizes, excepting those only which are distinguished by the name of contraband, and under this name of contraband, or prohibited goods, shall be comprehended:

1ˢᵗ Cannons, mortars, howitzers, swivels, blunderbusses, muskets, fuzees, rifles, carbines, pis-

Esta liberdade de commercio e navegação se extenderà a todos os generos e mercadorias, excepto unicamente as que se distinguem pelo nome de contrabando, e neste nome, ou no de generos prohibidos se comprehenderão:

1º Artilheria, morteiros, obuzes, pedreiras, bacamartes, mosquetes, *rifles*, carabinas, espingardas, pis-

tols, pikes, swords, sabres, lances, spears, halberds, and granades, bombs, powder, matches, balls, and all other things belonging to the use of these arms:

2.ly Bucklers, helmets, breast-plates, coats of mail, infantry belts; and clothes made up in the form, and for a military use:

3.ly Cavalry belts and horses with their furniture;

4.ly And generally all kinds of arms and instruments of iron, steel, brass and copper, or of any other materials manufactured, prepared and formed expressly to make war by sea or land.

ART. 17th All other merchandize and things not comprehended in the articles of contraband, expressly enumerated and classified as above, shall be held and considered as free, and subjects of free and lawful commerce, so that they may be carried and transported in the freest manner by both the contracting parties, even to places belonging to an enemy, excepting only those places which are at that time beseiged or blockaded: and to avoid all doubt in this particular, it is declared, that those places only are besieged or blockaded, which are actually attacked by a force capable of preventing the entry of the neutral.

tolas, piques, espadas, sabres, lanças, venabulos, halabardas, granadas, bombas, polvora, mechas, ballas, e todas as outras couzas pertencentes ao uzo destas armas.

2º Escudos, capacetes, peitos de aço, saias de malha, boldriés, e roupa feita de uniforme, e para uzo Militar.

3º Boldriés de Cavalleria, e Cavallos ajaesados.

4º E geralmente toda a qualidade de armas, e instrumentos de ferro, aço, latão, e cobre, ou de quaes quer outros materiaes manufacturados, preparados, ou formados expressamente para fazer a guerra por mar ou por terra.

ARTIGO 17º

Todas as outras mercadorias e couzas não comprehendidas nos Artigos de contrabando, explicitamente enumerados e classificados acima, serão tidas e consideradas como livres e sujeitas ao commercio livre e legitimo, de maneira que poderão ser conduzidas e transportadas pela forma mais franca por ambas as Partes Contractantes, athé a Lugares que pertenção a hum inimigo, exceptuando-se somente aquelles Lugares que estiverem na mesma occazião sitiados ou bloqueados; e para evitar toda a duvida neste particular, declara-se que só estão sitiados ou bloqueados aquelles lugares que o estiverem effectivamente por

huma força capaz de impedir a entrada aos neutros.

Artigo 18º

Os Artigos de contrabando acima enumerados e classificados, que possão encontrar-se em hum navio, que se dirigisse para hum Porto inimigo, serão sujeitos à detenção e confisco, deixando-se livre o resto da carga e o navio, para que os proprietarios d'elles disponhão como lhes parecer.

Nenhum navio de qualquer das duas Naçoens serà detido no mar alto pelo motivo de ter a bordo artigos de contrabando, toda a vez que o Mestre Capitão ou Sobre-carga da dita Embarcação entregar os artigos de contrabando ao Captor, a não ser a quantidade dos ditos artigos tão grande, e de tão consideravel volume, que não possão ser recebidos a bordo do navio Captor sem grande inconveniente, porque neste, e em todos os outros cazos de justa detenção, serà o navio detido remettido ao Porto mais proximo, conveniente e seguro, a fim de ser processado, e julgado conforme a Ley.

Artigo 19º

E por quanto acontece frequentemente partirem navios para hum Porto ou Lugar pertencente a hum inimigo, sem saberém que o mesmo está sitiado, bloqueado ou investido conveio-se que o navio, que se achar naquel-

Art. 18ᵗʰ The articles of contraband, before enumerated and classified, which may be found in a vessel bound for an enemy's port, shall be subject to detention and confiscation, leaving free the rest of the cargo and the ship, that the owners may dispose of them as they see proper. No vessel of either of the two nations shall be detained on the high seas, on account of having on board articles of contraband, whenever the master, captain, or supercargo of said vessels will deliver up the articles of contraband to the captor, unless the quantity of such articles be so great, and of so large a bulk, that they cannot be received on board the capturing ship without great inconvenience: but in this and all the other cases of just detention, the vessel detained shall be sent to the nearest convenient and safe port, for trial and judgement according to law.

Art. 19ᵗʰ And whereas it frequently happens that vessels sail for a port or a place belonging to an enemy, without knowing that the same is besieged, blockaded, or invested, it is agreed, that every vessel so circumstanced, may be

turned away from such port or place, but shall not be detained, nor shall any part of her cargo, if not contraband, be confiscated, unless, after warning of such blockade or investment from any officer commanding a vessel of the blockading forces, she shall again attempt to enter; but she shall be permitted to go to any other port or place, she shall think proper. Nor shall any vessel of either that may have entered into such port before the same was actually besieged, blockaded, or invested by the other, be restrained from quitting such place with her cargo, nor if found therein, after the reduction and surrender, shall such vessel or her cargo, be liable to confiscation, but they shall be restored to the owners thereof. And if any vessel having thus entered the port before the blockade took place, shall take on board a cargo after the blockade be established, she shall be subject to being warned by the blockading forces to return to the port blockaded, and discharge the said cargo, and if after receiving the said warning the vessel shall persist in going out with the cargo, she shall be liable to the same consequences as a vessel attempting to enter a blockaded port after being warned off by the blockading forces

las circumstancias possa ser desviado d'aquelle Porto ou Lugar, mas não serà detido, nem parte alguma da sua carga, a não ser contrabando, serà confiscada huma vez que, depois de avisado da existencia do bloqueio ou assédio pelo Commandante de qualquer das Embarcações pertencentes as Forças bloqueantes, elle não tente de novo entrar; sendo-lhe porem permittido dirigir-se para qualquer outro Porto ou Lugar que lhe parecer.

Nenhum navio de qualquer das Partes Contractantes que possa ter entrado no dito Porto antes que elle estivesse effectivamente sitiado, bloqueado ou investido pela outra serà capturado por sahir daquelle Lugar com a sua carga, nem se for achado dentro, depois de rendido e tomado, serà tal navio e carga sujeito a confisco, porem sim serà restituido aos seus proprietarios.

E se tendo qualquer navio assim entrado no Porto antes que houvesse bloqueio, recebesse carga abordo depois da existencia do mesmo bloqueio, serà elle sujeito a ser avizado pelas Forças bloqueantes, a fim de voltar para o Porto bloqueado e descarregar a sua carga; e se depois de ter o dito navio sido avizado, persistir em sahir, incorrerà nas mesmas consequencias como hum navio que entrasse em hum Porto bloqueado depois de ter sido avizado **pela força bloqueante.**

ART. 20th In order to prevent all kinds of disorder in the visiting and examination of the ships and cargoes of both the contracting parties on the high seas, they have agreed mutually, that whenever a vessel of war, public, or private, shall meet with a neutral of the other contracting party, the first shall remain at the greatest distance compatible with making the visit under the circumstances of the sea and wind and the degree of suspicion attending the vessel to be visited, and shall send its smallest boat, in order to execute the said examination of the papers concerning the ownership and cargo of the vessel, without causing the least extortion, violence, or ill-treatment, for which the commanders of the said armed ships, shall be responsible with their persons and property; for which purpose the commanders of the said private armed vessels shall, before receiving their commissions, give sufficient security to answer for all the damages they may commit; and it is expressly agreed, that the neutral party shall in no case be required to go on board the examining vessel, for the purpose of exhibiting her papers, or for any other purpose whatever.

ART. 21st To avoid all kind of vexation and abuse in the exam-

ARTIGO 20º

Afim de evitar todo o genero de desordens na visita e exame dos navios e cargas de ambas as Partes Contractantes no mar alto, Ellas tem concordado mutuamente que, quando hum navio de guerra publico ou particular, encontrar hum neutro da Outra Parte Contractante, o primeiro se conservarà na distancia mayor que for compativel com a operação da vizita, attentas as circumstancias do már e vento, e gráo de suspeita do navio que se quer vizitar, e mandarà o seu bote mais pequeno para fazer o dito exame dos papeis relativos à propriedade e carga do navio, sem fazer a menor extorsão, violencia ou máo tratamento, pelo que serão responsaveis os Commandantes dos ditos navios armados, pelas suas pessoas e bens, dando para esse fim os Commandantes dos ditos navios armados particulares huma Fiança sufficiente para responderem por todos os damnos que commetterem; e se convenciona expressamente que a parte neutra não serà em nenhum cazo obrigada a hir a-bordo do navio examinador, para o fim de aprezentar os seus Papeis ou para outro qualquer objecto.

ARTIGO 21º

Para evitar todo o genero de vexame e abuzo no exame dos

ination of the papers relating to the ownership of the vessels belonging to the citizens and subjects of the two contracting parties, they have agreed, and do agree, that in case one of them shall be engaged in war, the ships and vessels belonging to the citizens or subjects of the other must be furnished with sea letters or passports, expressing the name, property and bulk of the ship, as also the name and place of habitation of the Master or Commander of said vessel, in order that it may thereby appear, that the ship really and truly belongs to the citizens or subjects of one of the parties; they have likewise agreed, that such ships being laden, besides the said sea letters or passports, shall also be provided with certificates, containing the several particulars of the cargo, and the place whence the ship sailed, so that it may be known, whether any forbidden or contraband goods be on board the same; which certificates shall be made out by the officers of the place whence the ship sailed, in the accustomed form; without such requisites said vessel may be detained, to be adjudged by the competent tribunal, and may be declared legal prize, unless the said defect shall be proved to be owing to accident, and be satisfied or supplied by testimony entirely equivalent.

Papeis relativos à propriedade dos navios pertencentes aos subditos e Cidadãos das Duas Partes Contractantes, Ellas conviérão e convem que, no cazo de huma dellas se empenhar em guerra os navios e vazos pertencentes aos Subditos e Cidadãos da Outra deveráõ munir-se dos Papeis de mar ou Passaportes, que expressem o nome, propriedade, e arqueação do navio; bem como o nome e lugar da habitação do Mestre ou Commandante do dito vazo, a fim de que por esse meio se conheça que o navio pertencia real e verdadeiramente aos subditos ou Cidadãos de huma das Partes Contractantes. Convencionárão mais que os ditos navios, se estiverem carregados, tenhão, alem dos ditos Papeis de mar ou Passaportes, certificados que contenhão as diversas partes da carga, e o lugar d'onde partio o navio, para que se possa saber se abordo ha algumas fazendas prohibidas, ou de contrabando; estes certificados serão feitos pelos officiaes do Lugar donde sahio o navio na forma ordinaria; e sem taes requizitos o navio serà detido para ser julgado pelo Tribunal competente, e serà declarado Presa legal huma vez que se não dê huma prova authentica de que aquella falta foi cauzada por algum accidente.

Art. 22ᵈ It is further agreed, that the stipulations above expressed, relative to the visiting and examining of vessels, shall apply only to those which sail without convoy: and when said vessels shall be under convoy, the verbal declaration of the commander of the convoy, on his word of honor, that the vessels under his protection belong to the nation whose flag he carries: and when they are bound to an enemy's port, that they have no contraband goods on board, shall be sufficient.

Art. 23. It is further agreed, that in all cases the established Courts for prize causes, in the countries to which the prizes may be conducted, shall alone take cognizance of them. And whenever such tribunal of either party, shall pronounce judgement against any vessel, or goods, or property claimed by the citizens or subjects of the other party, the sentence or decree shall mention the reasons or motives, on which the same shall have been founded, and an authenticated copy of the sentence or decree, and of all the proceedings in the case, shall if demanded, be delivered to the commander or agent of said vessel, without any delay, he paying the legal fees for the same.

Artigo 22º

He outrosim convencionado que as estipulações acima declaradas relativamente às vizitas e exames dos navios, se applicaráõ somente aos que navegarem sem comboy; pois que, quando os ditos navios forem comboiados, serà sufficiente a declaração verbal do Commandante do Comboy dando a sua palavra de honra que os navios que elle protege pertencem à Nação cujo Pavilhão tem içado, e se se destinarem a hum Porto inimigo, que elles não tem generos de contrabando abordo.

Artigo 23º

Convencionou-se mais que em todos os cazos, os Tribunaes estabelecidos para as Cauzas de Prezas nos Paizes a que as mesmas forem conduzidas, serão os que unicamente tomaráõ conhecimento d'ellas. E toda a vez que os ditos Tribunaes de qualquer das Partes Contractantes proferir Sentença contra qualquer navio ou fazendas, ou bens reclamados pelos Cidadãos da Outra Parte Contractante, na Sentença ou Decreto mencionaráõ as razoens ou motivos em que se fundárão, e sendo pedida, se darà huma copia authentica da Sentença ou Decreto, e bem assim de todo o Processo da questão ao Commandante ou Agente do dito navio, sem demora alguma e pagando-se pela mesma os emolumentos legaes.

Art. 24th Whenever one of the contracting parties shall be engaged in war with another State, no citizen or subject of the other contracting party, shall accept a commission, or letter of marque, for the purpose of assisting or co-operating hostilely, with the said enemy, against the said parties so at war, under the pain of being treated as a pirate.

Art. 25th If by any fatality, which cannot be expected, and which God forbid! the two contracting parties should be engaged in a war with each other, they have agreed, and do agree, now for then, that there shall be allowed the term of six months to the merchants residing on the coasts and in the ports of each other, and the term of one year to those who dwell in the interior, to arrange their business, and transport their effects wherever they please, giving to them the safe-conduct necessary for it, which may serve as a sufficient protection until they arrive at the designated port. The citizens and subjects of all other occupations, who may be established in the territories or dominions of the United States, and of the Empire of Brazil, shall be respected and maintained in the full enjoyment of their personal liberty and property, unless their particular con-

Artigo 24º

Quando huma das Partes Contractantes estiver em guerra com outro Estado, nenhum Subdito ou Cidadão da outra Parte Contractante acceitarà Commissão ou Carta de marca, com o fim de ajudar ou cooperar hostilmente com o dito inimigo contra as ditas Partes Contractantes que se achão em guerra, sob pena de ser tratado como Pirata.

Artigo 25º

Se por alguma fatalidade, que se não pode prever, e que Deos não permitta, as Duas Partes Contractantes declararem guerra entre sí, Ellas tem convencionado e convencionão agora para esse cazo, que serà outorgado o prazo de seis mezes aos negociantes que rezidirem nas Costas e nos Portos de cada huma d'ellas, e o prazo de hum anno aos que habitarem no interior, para arranjarem seus negocios, e transportarem seus bens para onde quizerem, dando-se-lhes o necessario salvoconducto para isso, o qual servirà de protecção sufficiente, athé que cheguem ao Porto designado. Os Cidadãos e Subditos de todas as outras occupaçoens, que estiverem estabelecidos nos territorios ou dominios do Imperio do Brazil, ou dos Estados-Unidos, serão respeitados, e mantidos no pleno gozo de sua liberdade pessoal e bens; excepto se a sua conducta particular lhes

duct shall cause them to forfeit this protection, which in consideration of humanity, the contracting parties engage to give them.

ART. 26th Neither the debts due from the individuals of the one nation, to the individuals of the other, nor shares nor money, which they may have in public funds, nor in public or private banks, shall ever in any event of war or national difference be sequestrated or confiscated.

ART. 27th Both the contracting parties being desirous of avoiding all inequality in relation to their public communications and official intercourse, have agreed and do agree, to grant to their envoys, Ministers, and other public agents, the same favours, immunities and exemptions, which those of the most favoured nation do, or shall enjoy: it being understood, that whatever favours, immunities, or privileges, the United States of America, or the Empire of Brazil may find it proper to give the Ministers and Public Agents of any other power, shall, by the same act, be extended to those of each of the contracting parties.

ART. 28th To make more effectual the protection which the

fizer perder esta protecção, a qual em consideração à humanidade, as Partes Contractantes se compromettem a prestar-lhes.

ARTIGO 26º

As dividas de individuos de huma Nação a individuos da outra, as Acçoens, ou Dinheiros que possão ter nos fundos publicos, ou em Bancos publicos, ou particulares, jamais serão sequestrados ou confiscados no cazo de sobrevir guerra ou dissenção entre as Naçoens.

ARTIGO 27º

Ambas as Partes Contractantes Dezejando prevenir toda a desigualdade relativamente ás suas communicaçoens publicas, e relaçoens officiaes, tem concordado e concordão em conceder aos Seus Enviados, Ministros, e outros Agentes Publicos, os mesmo favores, immunidades, e isençoens de que gozão ou vierem a gozar os da Nação mais favorecida; ficando entendido que quaes quer favores, immunidades, e privilegios, que o Imperio do Brazil, e os Estados-Unidos da America julgarem conveniente conceder aos Ministros e Agentes Publicos de qualquer outra Potencia, serão extensivos pelo mesmo acto aos de cada huma das Partes Contractantes.

ARTIGO 28º

Para tornar mais effectiva a protecção que o Imperio do Brazil,

United States and the Empire of Brazil shall afford in future to the navigation and commerce of the citizens and subjects of each other, they agree to receive and admit Consuls and Vice Consuls in all the ports open to foreign commerce, who shall enjoy in them all the rights, prerogatives, and immunities, of the Consuls, and Vice Consuls of the most favoured nation: each contracting party however, remaining at liberty to except those ports and places in which the admission and residence of such Consuls may not seem convenient.

ART. 29th In order that the Consuls and Vice-Consuls of the two contracting parties, may enjoy the rights, prerogatives, and immunities, which belong to them, by their public character, they shall before entering on the exercise of their functions, exhibit their commissions or patent in due form, to the government to which they are accredited: and having obtained their *exequatur*, they shall be held and considered as such, by all the authorities magistrates, and inhabitants, in the Consular district in which they reside.

ART. 30th It is likewise agreed, that the Consuls, their Secretaries, officers, and persons at-

e os Estados Unidos devem dar para o futuro à navegação e Commercio dos Subditos e Cidadãos de qualquer d'elles, concordão em receber e admittir Consules e Vice Consules em todos os Portos abertos ao commercio estrangeiro; os quaes gozarão de todos os Direitos, prerogativas, e immunidades dos Consules e Vice Consules da Nação mais favorecida: ficando comtudo cada huma das Partes Contractantes com a liberdade de exceptuar aquelles Portos e Lugares em que não julgar conveniente a rezidencia e admissão de taes Consules.

ARTIGO 29º

Para que os Consules e Vice Consules das Duas Partes Contractantes gozem dos direitos, prerogativas, e immunidades que lhes competem pelo seu caracter publico, antes de entrarem no exercicio das suas funcçoens, aprezentaráõ as suas Commissoens ou Patentes em devida forma, ao Governo junto ao qual são acreditados; e quando houverem obtido o seu *Exequatur*, serão tidos e considerados como taes por todas as Authoridades, Magistrados, e habitantes do Districto Consular, em que rezidirem.

ARTIGO 30º

Convencionou-se igualmente que os Consules, seus Secretarios, Officiaes e pessoas addidas ao

tached to the service of Consuls, they not being citizens or subjects of the country, in which the Consul resides, shall be exempt from all public service, and also from all kinds of taxes, imposts and contributions, except those which they shall be obliged to pay on account of commerce, or their property, to which the citizens or subjects and inhabitants, native and foreign, of the country in which they reside are subject: being in every thing besides subject to the laws of their respective States. The archives and papers of the Consulate shall be respected inviolably, and under no pretext whatever, shall any magistrate seize or in any way interfere with them.

Art. 31ˢᵗ The said Consuls shall have power to require the assistance of the authorities of the country, for the arrest, detention and custody of deserters from the public and private vessels of their country, and for that purpose they shall address themselves to the Courts, Judges, and officers competent, and shall demand the said deserters in writing, proving by an exhibition of the registers of the vessels or ships roll, or other public documents, that those men were part of said crews; and on this demand so proved, (saving however, where the contrary is proved) the delivery shall not be refused. Such

serviço Consular, se não forem Cidadãos do Paiz em que residir o Consul, sejão isentos de toda a qualidade de taxas, impostos, e contribuiçoens, excepto as que elles são obrigados a pagar por motivos de commercio, ou bens seus, a que os Subditos, ou Cidadãos e habitantes nacionaes e estrangeiros são sujeitos no Paiz em que elles rezidirem, sendo outrosim submissos em to-todas as couzas às Leys dos respectivos Estados.

Os Archivos e Papeis do Consulado serão respeitados inviolavelmente, e por nenhum pretexto qualquer Magistrado os aprehenderà ou por forma alguma terà nelles ingerencia.

Artigo 31º

Os ditos Consules serão authorizados para requerer a coadjuvação das Authoridades do Paiz para se arrestarem, deterem, e prenderem os desertores dos Navios publicos e particulares do seu Paiz, e para este fim se dirigirão aos Tribunaes, Juizes e Officiaes competentes, requisitando os ditos desertores por escripto, provando com a apresentação dos registros, matricula, ou outros documentos publicos da embarcação ou navio, que aquelles homens fazião parte das respectivas tripulações; e a pedido seu provado por esta forma [salvo comtudo quando se mostrar o contrario] se não negarà a entrega delles. Sendo prezos estes de-

deserters, when arrested, shall be put at the disposal of said Consuls, and may be put in the public prison at the request and expense of those who reclaim them, to be sent to the ships to which they belonged, or to others of the same nation. But if they be not sent back within two months, to be counted from the day of their arrest, they shall be set at liberty, and shall no more be arrested for the same cause.

ART. 32. For the purpose of more effectually protecting their commerce and navigation, the two contracting parties do hereby agree, as soon hereafter, as circumstances will permit them, to form a Consular Convention, which shall declare specially the powers and immunities of the Consuls and Vice Consuls of the respective parties.

ART. 33ᵈ The United States of America, and the Emperor of Brazil desiring to make as durable as circumstances will permit, the relations which are to be established between the two parties by virtue of this Treaty, or General Convention of Peace, Amity, Commerce and Navigation, have declared solemnly and do agree to the following points:

First. The present Treaty shall be in force for twelve years from the date hereof, and further until

sertores, serão postos à disposição dos ditos Consules, e poderão ser guardados nas prizoens publicas, a requerimento e a expensas de quem os reclamar, para serem enviados aos navios a que pertencião, ou a outros da mesma Nação. Porem se elles não forem transferidos no espaço de dous mezes, contados do dia da sua custodia, serão postos em liberdade, e não serão mais aprehendidos pela mesma cauza.

ARTIGO 32º

Com o fim de protegerem mais effectivamente o seu commercio e Navegação, as Duas Partes Contractantes concordão em que, tão depressa que as circumstancias permittirem, Ellas formarão huma Convenção Consular, a qual declarará especialmente os poderes e immunidades dos Consules e Vice Consules das Partes respectivas.

ARTIGO 33º

O Imperador do Brazil e os Estados-Unidos da America dezejando tomar tão duraveis quanto as circumstancias o permittirem, as relaçoens que se devem estabelecer entre as Duas Partes Contractantes em virtude deste Tratado, ou Convenção geral de Paz, Amizade, Commercio e Navegação, tem declarado solemnemente e concordado nos pontos seguintes

1º O presente Tratado deverá ficar em vigor por espaço de doze annos contados da sua data, e mais

the end of one year after either of the contracting parties shall have given notice to the other, of its intention to terminate the same: each of the contracting parties reserving to itself the right of giving such notice to the other, at the end of said term of twelve years: and it is hereby agreed between them, that on the expiration of one year, after such notice shall have been received by either, from the other party, this Treaty in all the parts relating to commerce and navigation, shall altogether cease and determine, and in all those parts which relate to peace and friendship, it shall be permanently and perpetually binding on both powers.

Secondly. If any one or more of the citizens or subjects of either party shall infringe any of the articles of this Treaty, such citizen or subject shall be held personally responsible for the same, and the harmony and good correspondence between the nations shall not be interrupted thereby; each party engaging in no way to protect the offender, or sanction such violation.

Thirdly. If (which indeed cannot be expected) unfortunately, any of the articles contained in the present Treaty, shall be violated or infringed in any way whatever, it is expressly stipulated, that neither of the contracting parties will order or

ainda athé o fim do anno que se seguir depois que as Partes Contractantes tiverem communicado huma à outra a sua intenção de conclui-lo, rezervando-se cada huma das Partes Contractantes o direito de fazer aquella participação à outra no fim do dito prazo de doze annos: E he mais convencionado entre Ellas, que, quando expirar o anno depois que huma das Partes Contractantes houver recebido aquella communicação da outra, cessarà inteiramente, e terminarà este Tratado em todas as partes relativas ao Commercio e Navegação, ficando porem nas outras partes que se referem à Paz e Amizade ligando permanente e perpetuamente ambas as Potencias.

2º Se algum ou alguns Subditos ou Cidadãos de huma das Partes Contractantes infringir qualquer Artigo deste Tratado, serà o dito Cidadão responsavel pessoalmente por isso, e a harmonia e boa correspondencia entre as Naçoens não serà por esse motivo interrompida, obrigando-se cada huma das Partes Contractantes a não proteger o criminozo, nem authorizar tal violação.

3º Se [o que certamente não se pode esperar] infelizmente alguns dos Artigos que contem o prezente Tratado for violado ou infringido por qualquer forma, estipulou-se expressamente que nenhuma das Partes Contractantes Ordenarà ou Authorizarà acto algum de

authorize any acts of reprisal, nor declare war against the other, on complaints of injuries or damages until the said party considering itself offended, shall first have presented to the other a statement of such injuries or damages, verified by competent proof, and demanded justice and satisfaction, and the same shall have been either refused, or unreasonably delayed.

Fourthly. Nothing in this Treaty contained shall however, be construed, to operate contrary to former and existing public Treaties with other Sovreigns or States.

The present Treaty of Peace, Amity, Commerce, and Navigation, shall be approved and ratified by the President of the United States by and with the advice and consent of the Senate thereof, and by the Emperor of Brazil, and the ratifications shall be exchanged within eight months from the date of the signature hereof, or sooner if possible.

In faith whereof we the Plenipotenciaries of the United States of America and of His Magesty the Emperor of Brazil have signed and sealed these presents.

Done in the City of Rio de Janeiro this twelfth day of the Month of December in the year of

represalia, nem declararà a guerra à outra por queixas de prejuizos ou damnos, antes que a dita Parte Contractante que se considera offendida, tenha primeiro aprezentado à outra hum relatorio daquelles prejuizos ou damnos, verificado com provas competentes, e reclamado justiça e satisfação, e tenha a mesma sido ou negada, ou desarrazoadamente demorada.

4º Nenhuma das estipulaçoens contidas neste Tratado terà comtudo huma interpretação ou effeito contrario aos precedentes Tratados públicos, que existão em vigor com outros Soberanos ou Estados.

O prezente Tratado de Paz, Amizade, Commercio e Navegação serà approvado e Ratificado pelo Imperador do Brazil, e pelo Prezidente dos Estados Unidos, com e pelo parecer e consentimento do Senado, e as Ratificaçoens serão trocadas no espaço de oito mezes contados da data da assignatura delle, ou antes se for possivel.

Em fé do que nós os Plenipotenciarios de Sua Magestade O Imperador do Brazil, e dos Estados-Unidos da America em virtude dos nossos Plenos Poderes, assignamos o prezente Tratado com os nossos punhos, e fizemos pôr o Sello das nossas Armas.

Feito na Cidade do Rio de Janeiro aos doze dias do mez de Dezembro do Anno do Nasci-

our Lord Jesus Christ one thousand eight hundred and twenty eight.	mento de Nosso Senhor Jezuz Christo de mil oito centos e vinte oito

[Seal]	W. TUDOR.	(L. S.)	MARQUEZ DO ARACATY.
[Seal]	MARQUEZ DO ARACATY	(L. S.)	MIGUEL DE SOUZA
[Seal]	MIGUEL DE SOUZA		MELLO E ALVIM
	MELLO E ALVIM	(L. S.)	GUILHERME TUDOR.

NOTES

This agreement has always and properly been called a treaty; it is so styled in both instruments of ratification, in the proclamation, in the presidential message to the Senate of February 26, 1829 (Executive Journal, IV, 4), and in the Senate resolution of March 10 (*ibid.*, 10); yet its language is for the most part copied from the agreement of December 5, 1825, with the Central American Federation (Document 50), which is often called a convention. Like that document it has in the preamble the wording, "Treaty, or General Convention of Peace, Friendship, Commerce and Navigation." This treaty, however, differing from the earlier agreement, has no heading; in lieu thereof is the invocation, "In the Name of the Most Holy and Indivisible Trinity." The notes to the treaty of July 4, 1827, with Sweden and Norway (Document 55), contain some observations regarding that phrase.

This treaty was signed in two languages, English and Portuguese, although no mention of that fact is made in its text. The procedure adopted was that duplicate originals were signed, one in English for this Government and one in Portuguese for the Brazilian Government; accordingly, each Government had the original text in its own language only. As the printed texts show, the *alternat* was duly observed.

However, no detailed statement regarding the signing of the treaty is available. In his despatch of December 11, 1828 (D. S., 6 Despatches, Brazil, No. 115), William Tudor, Chargé d'Affaires at Rio de Janeiro, wrote that he expected the signature of the treaty "the day after tomorrow" and that he would "accompany it with other despatches and the requisite explanations"; but his next despatch, No. 116, transmitting the treaty, is missing, and there is no copy of it in the archives of the American Embassy at Rio de Janeiro. That despatch must have arrived at Washington, and it seems that it was sent to the Senate; the message of President John Quincy Adams transmitting the treaty specifically mentions "a letter from Mr. Tudor elucidating some of its provisions" (Executive Journal, IV, 4); but no Senate order for printing the accompanying papers was made (*ibid.*). The Senate print of the time is of the English text of the treaty only (Senate Confidential Document, March 5, 1829, 21st Congress, special session of the Senate, Regular Confidential Docu-

ments, IV, 245–54). Despatch No. 117 from Tudor is in the archives (D. S., 6 Despatches, Brazil, December 13, 1828); and House Document No. 32, 25th Congress, 1st session, serial 311, which contains numerous despatches from Tudor, includes Nos. 115 and 117, but lacks No. 116. While the papers in that House document deal mostly with other matters, there are included therein various notes and despatches regarding the negotiation of this treaty.

Both the United States instrument of ratification of March 17, 1829, a facsimile of which, obtained from the Brazilian archives, is in the treaty file, and the original proclamation of March 18, 1829, include the English text only. That text in the latter document is a copy of the Senate print. The Brazilian instrument of ratification of December 12, 1828, the date of signature of the treaty, includes the Portuguese text only, and it is therewith that the Portuguese text above printed has been collated.

This treaty was submitted to the Senate by President John Quincy Adams with his message of February 26, received by the Senate February 27, 1829; but that message was not read in the Senate until March 5 (Executive Journal, IV, 4), during the following administration of President Jackson.

Certain papers accompanied the treaty when it was submitted to the Senate; but it appears that only the text of the treaty (in English) was printed (Executive Journal, IV, 4; Senate Confidential Document, March 5, 1829, 21st Congress, special session of the Senate, Regular Confidential Documents, IV, 245–54). The papers were "copies of the instructions under which it was negotiated, and a letter from Mr. Tudor, elucidating some of its provisions." The instructions to William Tudor, Chargé d'Affaires at Rio de Janeiro, were under date of March 29, 1828 (D. S., 12 Instructions, U. S. Ministers, 77–81; House Document No. 32, 25th Congress, 1st session, serial 311, pp. 14–17); "three different bases for an arrangement" were put forward; the principle of the treaty with the Central American Federation of December 5, 1825 (Document 50), was preferred; and with little change, even of wording, that treaty was the basis of this.

The attested Senate resolution of March 10, 1829 (Executive Journal, IV, 10), is attached to the original treaty.

The certificate of exchange of ratifications at Washington on March 18, 1829, was "executed in both languages," but the example thereof in the treaty file is in English only. It was signed and sealed by James A. Hamilton, Acting Secretary of State, and José Silvestre Rebello, Brazilian Chargé d'Affaires. As appears therefrom, the comparison of treaty texts usual upon an exchange of ratifications, was made only with "the original example in English"; there was then, as now, no original example in Portuguese at Washington. The certificate reads as follows:

We, the Undersigned, James A. Hamilton, Acting Secretary of State of the United States; and Jº Silvestro Rebello, Officer of tne Imperial Order of the Crosier, and Chargé d'Affaires of His Majesty the Emperor of Brazil, near the

said United States,—do hereby certify that the Ratifications of the Treaty, or General Convention of Peace, Friendship, Commerce and Navigation, signed at Rio de Janeiro, on the 12ᵗʰ of December 1828, between the United States of America, and His Majesty the Emperor of Brazil, have, this day, with all suitable solemnities and after due comparison with the original example in English of said Treaty, been exchanged by Us.

In witness whereof, we have signed this Act, executed in both languages, and have sealed the same with our respective seals, at the City of Washington, this eighteenth day of March, One thousand eight hundred and twenty nine.

[Seal] JAMES A. HAMILTON
[Seal] Jᵒ SILVESTRE REBELLO

James A. Hamilton, who signed that certificate, and also the certificate of exchange of ratifications of the treaty with Prussia of May 1, 1828 (Document 62), as Acting Secretary of State, was Secretary of State *ad interim* from March 4 to March 27, 1829. Martin Van Buren was commissioned Secretary of State on March 6 but did not enter upon the duties of his office until March 28. James A. Hamilton was the only individual who has been appointed from outside the Government service to serve as Secretary of State *ad interim*. Such an appointment was then lawful under the broad language of the act of February 13, 1795 (1 Statutes at Large, 415), which is no longer in force.

THE INSTRUCTIONS TO TUDOR

The instructions of March 29, 1828, to William Tudor, Chargé d'Affaires at Rio de Janeiro, which have been mentioned above, read as follows (House Document No. 32, 25th Congress, 1st session, serial 311, pp. 14–17):

The President is desirous that you should negotiate, in behalf of the Government of the United States, with the Government of Brazil, a treaty of friendship, commerce, and navigation. A similar desire is understood to be entertained by the Emperor on the part of his Government. Circumstances hitherto have not favored the execution of that object; but the time has now arrived when it is supposed it may be entered upon with advantage. The manufactures and productions of the United States have for some time sustained, in the ports of the Brazils, an unequal competition with similar productions and manufactures of other foreign countries. Whilst the former have been subjected, on entry into those ports, to a duty of 24 per cent. ad valorem, the latter have been admitted at the lower rate of only 15 per cent. Against this inequality your predecessor was instructed to remonstrate, as you also were, by your general instructions of the 3d day of October, 1827. Mr. Raguet's interposition was not attended with the desired effect, and we fear that yours may be equally unsuccessful. We hope an efficacious remedy may be found in the negotiation of a treaty. I had supposed that it might be most expedient to postpone opening such a negotiation until after you had made a satisfactory arrangement on the subject of indemnities due to citizens of the United States. Circumstances, however, on the on the spot, may recommend an earlier attempt to conclude a commercial treaty. It is submitted to your discretion to open a negotiation, at such time as may appear to you most expedient, keeping constantly in view the wish of the President to avoid unnecessary delay.

With respect to the commerce and navigation between the two countries, three different bases for an arrangement present themselves: the first is to be found in the fourth and fifth articles of the treaty between the United States and the Federation of the centre of America, signed at the city of Washington on the 5th

of December, 1825; the second is contained in the second article of the convention to regulate commerce between the territories of the United States and his Britannic Majesty, concluded at London on the 3d day of July, 1815; and the third you will meet with in the second and third articles of our treaty with Colombia, signed at Bogota on the 3d day of October, 1824.

According to the first-mentioned basis, no higher or other duties would be imposed, on the importation into the ports of one country of any articles the produce or manufacture of the other, than should be paid on the like articles being the produce or manufacture of any other foreign country.   Nor would any higher or other duties or charges be imposed in either of the two countries, on the exportation from the one to the other of any article of their respective produce or manufacture, than such as should be paid on the exportation of similar articles to any other foreign country.   Nor would any prohibition be imposed on the exportation or importation of any articles the produce or manufacture of either country, to or from their respective ports, which should not equally extend to all other nations.   Such would be the principle of the basis under consideration in respect to the commerce between the two countries.   It would leave each at perfect liberty, as each ought to be, to impose such duties as its wants or its policy might seem to require, whilst it would restrain either from laying upon the produce or manufactures of the other, higher duties than are exacted from other nations, on similar articles of their produce or manufacture.   It would consequently remove the existing inequality prevailing in the ports of the Brazils, to the disadvantage of the United States, of which we have more just cause to complain, since there is no similar inequality operating in our ports to the prejudice of the commerce of the Brazils.   What would the Government of the Brazils think, if we were to make a difference of nine or ten per cent. against the coffee of the Brazils in the ports of the United States?

As to the navigation between the two countries, the first basis is founded upon the most perfect equality and reciprocity.   According to its principle, whatever can be imported into or exported from the ports of one country, in its own vessels, without any regard to the place of its origin, may, in like manner, and upon the same terms and conditions, be imported or exported in the vessels of the other country.   This is the most perfect freedom of navigation.   We can conceive of no privilege beyond it.   All the shackles which the selfishness or contracted policy of nations had contrived, are broken and destroyed by this broad principle of universal liberality.   The President is most anxious to see it adopted by all nations.   Since the commencement of the present administration, besides the Gautemala treaty, the principle has been embraced in treaties concluded with Denmark, Sweden, and the free Hanseatic cities of Europe; in the two former instances with a slight modification, not at all, however, impairing its value.

2. The second basis which I have stated, found in the convention with Great Britain, in respect to commerce and duties, both on exportation and importation, is the same as that contained in the treaty with the Federation of the centre of America, and it would, therefore, secure to our produce and manufactures an admission into the ports of the Brazils upon as favorable terms as similar produce and manufactures of any other foreign country.   But there is a wide difference between the two treaties, in in relation to navigation: according to our convention with Great Britain, its privileges are limited to the importation of the produce and manufactures of the two countries respectively, neither being permitted to import into the ports of the other, goods from any other parts of the world.   Within those restricted limits, that convention secures a perfect equality and reciprocity between the vessels of the two countries.   It was a great improvement on the previous condition of the navigation of the two countries, but it falls far short of the comprehensive scope of the treaty with Central America.

3. The last basis which I have mentioned is that of the Colombian treaty, according to which the rule of the most favored nation has been adopted.   The objections to this principle are, in the first place, the difficulty of always clearly discriminating between that which is a gratuitous concession and what is granted upon equivalent; secondly, the difficulty of ascertaining the precise extent of commercial favors which may have been granted to all, or any one, the most

favored, of the commercial powers; and, thirdly, a grant by the United States of all the concessions which it has made to the most favored nation, in consideration of a similar grant from a foreign Power, might far transcend the limits of a just equivalent. The most favored nation, according to the commercial policy of some states, has its commerce and navigation loaded with burdens and restrictions; but the most favored nation, according to the liberal and enlightened policy of the United States, has its commerce and navigation freed from almost all burdens and restrictions.

Of the three bases which I have described, the first is entitled to a decided preference. You will therefore use your best endeavors to get it adopted. The treaty with Central America may be taken as a model, in all its articles, for one which you are authorized to conclude with the Government of the Brazils. If the assent of that Government can be obtained to the fourth and fifth articles of that treaty, you may agree to include or omit all or any of the other articles, according as you find the disposition of the other party.

Should the Government of the Brazils decline acceding to the principles of the treaty of Central America as a basis, your next endeavor will be to get that of the convention of Great Britain of 1815 adopted; and if that should be agreed to, you may propose to be connected with it the various articles of the treaty with Central America.

If you cannot prevail upon the Brazilian Government to negotiate on the basis of neither the treaty with Central America nor the convention with Great Britain, you will lastly propose the rule of the most favored nation, as contained in the treaty with Colombia; and you will offer to connect the other articles contained in the same treaty, most of which are identically the same as those contained in the treaty with Central America. That rule will at least secure to us equal competition with other foreign Powers in the trade with the Brazils.

Considering the present state, and the probable future extent, of the naval power of the United States, the opinion entertained by some is not without plausibility, that their interest is adverse to those liberal maritime principles for which they have ever contended since their origin as a nation. That opinion, perhaps, would be well founded if they were likely to be frequently involved in maritime wars: but their prosperity is so evidently connected with the preservation of peace, that it is to be hoped that they will but be rarely involved in war. Whatever may really be the pecuniary interest of belligerent maritime Powers, there can be no doubt that the general cause of humanity and civilization will be promoted by the adoption of those maritime principles which the United States have so perseveringly endeavored to establish.

It is in that view of the matter that the President wishes you to propose those articles which relate to that subject which you will find in the treaty with Central America, and to press them as long as there is any reasonable prospect of their being agreed to.

The principle of equality and reciprocity between the navigation of the two countries may be objected to, both in its more general and limited extent, upon the ground of the infancy of the mercantile marine of the Brazils, and its incompetency, therefore, to sustain an unequal competition with that of the United States; but if a competition cannot be maintained under a system of exemptions, how can it be under one of reciprocal restrictions? If one maritime Power, in its intercourse with another, endeavors to secure to its own navigation peculiar advantages, by laying burdens upon the navigation of that other, from which its own is free, countervailing legislation is the necessary consequence. Restriction begets restriction, until the parties, after a long course of irritating legislation and counter-legislation, find themselves arrived, in the end, at a point of equality it is true, but it is an equality either of mutual interdiction of all intercourse, or of burdensome restrictions essentially impairing the value of that intercourse. When that point is at last reached, the discovery is made by the contending parties that they had better have set out with equal and reciprocal freedom from burdens; and that each has injured himself as much if not more than the other, by the shackles which were attempted to be put upon his navigation. It is to be hoped that the Governments of the United States and the Brazils will avoid this unfriendly process of imposing burdens and restrictions upon the navigation

of each other, and, in their first treaty of commerce, exhibit to the world an example of equal justice and liberality worthy of imitation.

With respect to the duration of any treaty on which you may be able to agree, it may be fixed for a term of about ten or twelve years. It will be well to add a clause providing against the unintentional expiration of the treaty, whatever may be the term you fix upon, similar to the stipulation contained in the eleventh article of our late treaty with Denmark.

A full power is herewith transmitted to enable you to enter upon the negotiation, and to conclude the treaty to which you are authorized to agree.

The Full Powers

Another paper in the file is the original full power granted by the Brazilian Government to José Silvestre Rebello, Chargé d'Affaires at Washington, to exchange the ratifications of the treaty. It is dated December 12, 1828, the day the treaty was signed, and is in Portuguese.

The full power to William Tudor to negotiate and sign this treaty is dated March 29, 1828, and is in customary form (D. S., 2 Credences, 78). The original full powers were first exchanged and then returned; for the originals were substituted a duplicate original of the full power of Tudor and a certified copy of the full power of the Brazilian Plenipotentiaries (D. S., 6 Despatches, Brazil, No. 104, August 25, 1828, enclosures 1, 7, and 8 of second list; *ibid.*, No. 110, September 30, 1828, enclosure 1; House Document No. 32, 25th Congress, 1st session, serial 311, pp. 78, 81–83, 93). A copy of the certified copy of the Brazilian full power delivered to Tudor (enclosure 8 above cited) reads as follows (translation from the Portuguese):

I, Dom Pedro, by the grace of God and the unanimous acclamation of the peoples, Constitutional Emperor and Perpetual Defender of Brazil, etc., hereby make known to those who may see this my letter of general and special empowerment that, the Government of the United States of America having appointed as its Plenipotentiary William Tudor, its Chargé d'Affaires near the Court of Rio de Janeiro, in order to act in negotiating a treaty of commerce and navigation between this Empire and the United States of America, and as I likewise agree to appoint on My part a person or persons enjoying My imperial confidence who can enter immediately upon these negotiations, from which I expect the best results for the benefit of the interested parties, and particularly of this Empire, whose prosperity I am so earnestly endeavoring to promote; and inasmuch as the Marquis of Aracaty, of My Council, a Gentleman of My Imperial Chamber, Counselor of Finance, Commander of the Order of Avis, Senator of the Empire, Minister and Secretary of State for Foreign Affairs, and Miguel de Souza Mello e Alvim, of My Council, Chevalier of the Order of Avis and of the Imperial Order of the Southern Cross, Commander of Division of the Imperial and National Navy, Minister and Secretary of Marine, possess all the qualifications necessary for the proper discharge of so important a mission, I hereby deem fit to and hereby do appoint them as My Plenipotentiaries, so that by conferring with the Plenipotentiary appointed by the Government of the United States of America they may stipulate, conclude, and sign, preparatory to ratification, according to the instructions which they may receive directly from Me, any treaty or convention to which the negotiations may give rise, I hereby conferring upon them for this purpose all the full powers and general and special mandate necessary; and I promise, on the faith of My imperial word, that I shall consider firm and valid and shall ratify everything that may by My Plenipotentiaries *ad hoc* be thus stipulated, concluded, and signed in My imperial name together with the Plenipotentiary appointed by the Government of the United States of America, who is clothed with like full powers. In witness whereof I ordered the present instrument

drawn up, it being signed by Me, sealed with the great seal of the arms of the Empire, and countersigned as below by My Minister and Secretary of State. Given in the Palace at Rio de Janeiro on August 23, year of Our Lord Jesus Christ 1828, being the seventh year of Our independence and of the Empire.

(IMPERIAL ORDER, WITH FLOURISH)

José CLEMENTE PEREIRA

Letter whereby Your Imperial Majesty deems fit to appoint as your Plenipotentiaries the Marquis of Aracaty, of your Council, Gentleman of your Imperial Chamber, Counselor of Finance, Commander of the Order of Avis, Senator of the Empire, Minister and Secretary of State for Foreign Affairs, and Miguel de Souza Mello e Alvim, of your Council, Chevalier of the Order of Avis and of the Imperial Order of the Southern Cross, Commander of Division of the Imperial and National Navy, Minister and Secretary of State for the Marine, in order that by conferring with the Plenipotentiary appointed by the Government of the United States of America they may stipulate, conclude, and sign, preparatory to ratification, any treaty or convention to which the negotiations may give rise, all in the manner above set forth.

For Your Imperial Majesty's view.

Written by José JOAQUIM TIMOTHEO D'ARAUJO on the reverse.

A true copy.

BENTE DA SILVA LISBOA

MARGINAL NOTATIONS

On the signed original of the treaty, which is in the handwriting of William Tudor, are written, also in his handwriting, certain marginal notations, underscored; but these do not seem to have been deemed part of the agreement, as they appear neither textually nor by reference in either instrument of ratification or in the proclamation; nor are they in any official print of the treaty in the Statutes at Large or elsewhere. The marginal notes to this treaty in Haswell, for example, are those of the editor of that volume and are quite different in their language from the notations written in the original. The latter are here printed, with an indication of the article or paragraph to which they relate:

Article 1. Peace and Friendship.

Article 2. Agree not to grant any particular favours to other nations in respect of commerce not common to both. Portugal may form an exception.

Article 3. Mutual benefits in Trade and residence to be equally enjoyed. The coasting trade to be reserved.

Article 4. Each party may carry its own produce to the ports of the other. Equalization of duties to be established and to be the basis of all trade.

Article 5. Importations and Exportations to be on a reciprocal footing.

Article 6. Both parties free to manage their own business in either nation.

Article 7. Neither party to liable to embargo or detention without indemnification.

Article 8. Whenever the citizens or subjects of either party seek refuge in the dominions of the other &c. they are to be treated as friends.

Article 9. All ships &c belonging to the citizens, or subjects of either party, captured by pirates & found within the dominions of either to be delivered up to the owners.

Article 10. Assistance & protection to be rendered in case of wrecks &c within the dominions of each other.

Article 11. Citizens or subjects of each party to have power to dispose of their goods & effects within the jurisdiction of the other, by sale, testament, or otherwise.

Article 12. Complete protection in person and property in the territory of both nations, legal redress, &c.

Article 13. Liberty of conscience and rights of burial secured.

Article 14. Both parties at liberty to trade with those at enmity with either.
Free ships to make free goods.

All persons on board except those in the actual service of an enemy to be free.

Flag covering the property to be applied to those powers only who acknowledge the principle.

Article 15. Enemy's property to be protected by a neutral flag must be shipped two months before declaration of war.

Article 16. Contraband specified.

Article 17. Goods not contraband.

Definition of blockade.

Article 18. Contraband only liable to confiscation.

Article 19. In cases of blockade vessels to be notified but not detained.

Vessels entering before blockade may quit unmolested.

Vessels taking a cargo on board, after a blockade is established may be warned to go back & unload.

Article 20. During a visit at sea, armed vessels not to approach any nearer than absolutely necessary.

Neutrals not to go on board the examining vessel.

Article 21. In case of war, sea-letters, certificates of cargo &c. to be furnished expressing to whom the property belongs.

Article 22. Visiting regulations to apply only to vessels without convoy.

Article 23. Established Courts only to try prize causes.

Motives of condemnation to be stated.

Article 24. The neutral party not to accept a commission to cruize against the other.

Article 25. In case of war six months allowed to those on the coast and twelve for those in the interior, to remove effects &c.

Article 26. And no sequestration of money in bank or public funds.

Article 27. Official intercourse in relation to public Ministers &c. to be on a reciprocal footing.

Article 28. Each party permitted to have Consuls in each others ports.

Article 29. Commissions to be exhibited before exequatur is obtained.

Article 30. Consuls exempt from public service, their archives inviolate.

Article 31. Consuls may call on the public authorities to aid in securing deserters, who are not to be detained more than two months in prison.

Article 32. Consular Convention to be formed.

Article 33, Paragraph 1. The following points agreed to.

Paragraph 2. Treaty to remain in force twelve years.

Paragraph 3. Citizens or subjects responsible for infringing this article.

Paragraph 4. War not to be declared until remonstrance is made and satisfaction refused.

Paragraph 5. Other Treaties not to be contravened by this.

Paragraph 6. Ratification within eight months.

ARTICLE 2

An exception to the general principle of the most favored nation stated in Article 2 was "the relations and Conventions which now exist, or may hereafter exist between Brazil and Portugal." Authority to yield that point was contained in the instructions of March 31, 1828 (D. S., 12 Instructions, U. S. Ministers, 86), where it was thought that it might "be insisted upon, in consequence of the ancient political connexion between Portugal and the Brazils, and the present connexion between the reigning families of the two countries."

Dom Pedro, then Emperor of Brazil, was the elder son of Dom John VI, who in March, 1816, had succeeded to the throne of the United Kingdom of Portugal, Brazil, and the Algarves (Reino-Unido

de Portugal, e do Brasil, e Algarves), such having been the title of Portuguese sovereignty since December 16, 1815 (Pereira Pinto, Apontamentos para o direito internacional, I, 117–20). The independence of Brazil was proclaimed by Dom Pedro on September 7, 1822. That independence was recognized by the United States on May 26, 1824, when José Silvestre Rebello was received by President Monroe as Chargé d'Affaires (Memoirs of John Quincy Adams, VI, 354–55, 358–59), and by Portugal by a treaty between Brazil and Portugal of August 29, 1825 (British and Foreign State Papers, XII, 674–78). Soon after the death, on March 10, 1826, of Dom John VI, Dom Pedro abdicated the crown of Portugal in favor of his daughter, Dona Maria da Gloria, afterwards Queen Maria II, and completed that act of abdication on March 3, 1828 (British and Foreign State Papers, XV, 1153); but her uncle, Dom Miguel, brother of Dom Pedro, had obtained the throne of Portugal in 1828 and retained it until 1834. Dom Pedro I, Emperor of Brazil, abdicated in favor of his son, Dom Pedro II, in April, 1831.

Regarding the exception in Article 2 in favor of Portugal, Chargé d'Affaires William Tudor wrote under date of September 30, 1828 (D. S., 6 Despatches, Brazil, No. 110):

> The point however, respecting Portugal, I fear I shall be obliged to cede. It has been introduced into their Treaties with England, France, Austria, Prussia, the Hanse Towns, & one they are now concluding with Holland. They say their motive for it, is not so much as regards commerce, but to engage emigration from Brazil: (both the Ministers with whom I am treating are natives of Portugal, but they have passed more than half their lives in this country & their attachments are Brazilian) I told them I thought it would take place without it. They say however that the exception as yet, is merely in words, & probably will so continue; they shewed me the treaty with Portugal, in which there is no stipulation in favor of that nation over others, except perhaps the paying of 15 per Ct duties, which has since been introduced in other treaties, & finally extended by law to all nations; and that in the present aspect of affairs, Portugal is not likely to merit or obtain any peculiar favors, & they believed that the exception never would be made effective.

The treaty between Brazil and Portugal mentioned in that despatch is that above cited of August 29, 1825, the clause regarding duties of 15 per cent being Article 10 thereof.

Termination of the Treaty

In the presidential message of December 5, 1840 (Richardson III, 602, 605), is the following passage:

> The chargé d'affaires of Brazil having expressed the intention of his Government not to prolong the treaty of 1828, it will cease to be obligatory upon either party on the 12th day of December, 1841, when the extensive commercial intercourse between the United States and that vast Empire will no longer be regulated by express stipulations.

However, the notice given by the Brazilian Government on March 26, 1840, limited the termination of the treaty to "the articles relating to commerce and navigation," pursuant to clause 1 of Article 33 (see Moore, Digest, V, 325, 403–4).

65

BRAZIL : JUNE 15, 1829

Settlement of Claims. Confirmation of thirteen claims agreements and of an agreement regarding the rate of exchange, signed at Rio de Janeiro June 15, 1829. Originals in Portuguese. As to the agreements confirmed, see the notes.

[Translation]

Nos abaixo assignados Guilherme Tudor, Encarregado de Negocios dos Estados Unidos d'America junto de Sua Magestade o Imperador do Brazil, e Marquez do Aracaty do Conselho de Sua Magestade o Imperador, Ministro e Secretario d'Estado dos Negocios Estrangeiros, havendo examinado os Treze Convenios celebrados em differentes epocas entre os Commissarios Americanos e Brasileiros, nomeados pelos seus respectivos Governos, e devidamente authorizados, acerca das liquidações e ajustamentos das indemnisações de perdas, damnos, e prejuizos que soffrerão os donos e carregadores das Embarcações Americanos, Sarah-George — Rio — Ruth — Hero— Panther — Nile — Amity — Hussar — Pioneer — Spermo — Tell Tale—Hannah e Budget, que forão aprezadas e detidas pela Esquadra, e Authoridades Brazileiras; os approvamos, e confirmamos assim no geral, como em cada

We, the undersigned, William Tudor, Chargé d'Affaires of the United States of America near His Majesty the Emperor of Brazil, and the Marquis of Aracaty, of the Council of His Majesty the Emperor, Minister and Secretary of State for Foreign Affairs, having examined the thirteen agreements entered into at different times between the American and Brazilian Commissioners appointed by their respective Governments and duly authorized for the liquidations and settlements of the indemnities for losses and damages suffered by the owners of and shippers by the American ships *Sarah George, Rio, Ruth, Hero, Panther, Nile, Amity, Hussar, Pioneer, Spermo, Telltale, Hannah,* and *Budget,* which were seized and held by the Brazilian squadron and authorities: We approve and confirm the same, both in general and for each one of them in particular, and their respective

485

hum delles em particular, e seus respectivos Artigos e estipulações, e pela presente os damos por firmos e valiozos. Em testemunho e firmeza do sobredito, fizemos esta por nós assignada e sellada com os sellos de nossas Armas. Secretaria d'Estado dos Negocios Extrangeiros, aos 15 de Junho de 1829.

(seal.) W. Tudor.

(seal) Marquez do Aracaty.

articles and stipulations, and hereby declare them to be confirmed and valid. In testimony and confirmation of the above we have drawn up these presents, signed and sealed by us with the seals of our arms. Department of State for Foreign Affairs, June 15, 1829.

[Seal] W. Tudor.

[Seal] Marquez do Aracaty.

[Translation]

Nos abaixo assignados, Guilherme Tudor, Encarregado de Negocios dos Estados Unidos da America, e Marquez do Aracaty, do Conselho de Sua Magestade o Imperador, Ministro e Secretario d'Estado dos Negocios Estrangeiros, havendo visto, e examinado o Convenio celebrado, e assignado pelos Commissarios Americanos, e Brazileiros em 2 do corrente mez de Junho, e anno, em que ajustarão, e convierão o preço fixo, e determinado de mil e quinhentos reis por cada pezo forte, para por elles-liquidarem as quantias concedidas, qualquer que seja a sorte do agio na epoca do pagamento, em consequencia dos Convenios celebrados pelos mesmos relativamente as indemnisaçoens das embarcaçoens Sarah-George—Rio—Ruth—Hero—Panther—Hussar—Amity—Nile—Pioneer—Spermo—Hannah—Budget—e Tell Tale; approvamos e confirmamos o dito

We, the undersigned, William Tudor, Chargé d'Affaires of the United States of America, and the Marquis of Aracaty, of the Council of His Majesty the Emperor, Minister and Secretary of State for Foreign Affairs, having seen and examined the agreement entered into and signed by the American and Brazilian Commissioners on the second day of the current month of June of this year, wherein they settled and agreed upon the fixed and set rate of one thousand five hundred reis for each standard dollar, to apply in the liquidation of the amounts allowed, regardless of the rate of exchange at the time of payment, in accordance with the agreements entered into by the same with respect to the indemnities for the ships *Sarah George, Rio, Ruth, Hero, Panther, Hussar, Amity, Nile, Pioneer, Spermo, Hannah, Budget,* and *Telltale:* We approve and confirm the said

Convenio em todos os seus artigos, e o damos por firme e valioso. Em testemunho, e firmeza do sobredito, fizemos esta por nos assignada, e sellada com os sellos de nossas Armas. Secretaria d'Estado dos Negocios Estrangeiros aos 15 de Junho de 1829. (seal.) W. TUDOR. (seal) MARQUEZ DO ARACATY.

agreement in all its articles and hereby declare it final and valid. In testimony and confirmation of the above we have drawn up these presents, signed and sealed by us with the seals of our arms. Department of State for Foreign Affairs, June 15, 1829. [Seal] W. TUDOR. [Seal] MARQUEZ DO ARACATY.

NOTES

As the form in which this claims settlement was documented is quite peculiar, a somewhat particular account seems desirable. The printed source text for most of the relevant papers is House Document No. 32, 25th Congress, 1st session, serial 311 (hereafter cited as "published correspondence"). The originals of the despatches hereafter mentioned of William Tudor, Chargé d'Affaires to Brazil, are all in D. S., 6 Despatches, Brazil.

The claims of American citizens against Brazil which were the subject of the negotiations of 1828–29, arose for the most part during the period of the conflict between Brazil and Buenos Aires which began in December, 1825, and which ended following the preliminaries of peace signed on August 27, 1828; and while some of the claims involved questions other than blockade, their general character is thus described in an instruction to Tudor of October 23, 1827 (published correspondence, 9).

These claims originate chiefly from groundless allegations of breach of blockade, instituted by the Government of Brazil, and from injuries committed by the public vessels and cruisers of that Government. The principles of the law of blockade, invariably contended for by the United States, are discussed in the course of that correspondence, and appear to be substantially admitted by the Government of Brazil. According to those principles, no place can be considered as lawfully besieged or blockaded, which is not invested by a competent belligerent force, capable of preventing the entry of a neutral; and such neutral cannot be lawfully captured without having been notified of the existence of the blockade, and if he attempt to enter the blockaded port, being warned off.

The correspondence mentioned in the above quotation was that between Condy Raguet, Chargé d'Affaires at Rio de Janeiro, and the Government of Brazil (see American State Papers, Foreign Relations, VI, 1021–1121). Some of the expressions used by the Chargé d'Affaires were regarded by Secretary of State Henry Clay as "provoking or irritating"; and the correspondence ended upon the demand of Raguet for his passports on March 8, 1827 (*ibid.*, 1065, 1067). As to the mission of Raguet generally, see William R. Manning, "An Early Diplomatic Controversy between the United States and Brazil," in the American Journal of International Law, XII, 291–311, and also

Lawrence F. Hill, Diplomatic Relations between the United States and Brazil, 26–56.

The Chargé d'Affaires of Brazil at Washington was then José Silvestre Rebello; and the ensuing exchanges which took place at Washington terminated with a declaration made by him on June 1, 1827, "that he is authorized to assure the Government of the United States that the Government of Brazil will give just satisfaction for any violation of public law committed with respect to the property or persons of American citizens," and with a response by Secretary of State Clay on the following day that "relying upon the authorized assurance which your note contains, that, on the arrival at Rio de Janeiro of a successor to Mr. Raguet, a full and adequate indemnity will be promptly made for any injuries which have been committed upon the persons or property of citizens of the United States, in violation of the public law, under color of authority derived from his Majesty the Emperor of Brazil, such a successor will be accordingly sent" (quoted in the instruction of October 23, 1827, published correspondence, 8).

The instruction of October 23, 1827 (*ibid.*, 7–12), was directed to William Tudor, who, after service in Peru, had been appointed Chargé d'Affaires to Brazil; therein the claims were discussed, and as to the form and mode of settlement this was written:

There are several modes according to which the citizens of the United States who have suffered wrongs under color of authority from the Brazilian Government, in violation of the public law, may receive the indemnity to which they are entitled, in conformity with the assurances contained in Mr. Rabello's letters. The most direct and least expensive mode would be that of the Brazilian Government voluntarily rendering justice itself in each individual case. You are authorized to suggest that course, and if it should be adopted, you will afford to the respective claimants any official assistance in your power. In cases where the parties may differ about the quantum of indemnity, it will be easy to fix the amount by amicable arrangements, and by appeals to the judgment of impartial men.

Another and the simplest mode would be by a convention, in which the Government of Brazil should stipulate to pay a gross sum in full satisfaction of all claims of American citizens; which sum should be subsequently distributed amongst them under the direction of the American Government. The only difficulty which is perceived in adopting this mode, is that of arriving at an amount which would do justice to all parties. The data in the possession of this Department do not admit of the ascertainment of that amount. Perhaps you will be able, from the documents now transmitted to you, and from such other information as you may have it in your power to acquire from the parties themselves, or their agents, to fix on a proper sum. In that case, you are authorized to conclude a convention, stipulating its payment on the part of the Brazilian Government. But it may happen that you will neither be able to satisfy yourself on that subject, nor to agree with the Brazilian Government on the principles which should regulate the claims for indemnity. In that contingency, the only remaining mode of settlement which presents itself is that of concluding a convention by which a commission shall be instituted for the purpose of deciding the claims to indemnity. You are authorized to conclude such a convention, if, under all the circumstances of the negotiation with which you are charged, it shall appear the most expedient. A model for the appointment and organization of such a commission, which you may safely follow, is to be found in the sixth and seventh articles of the treaty with Great Britain in 1794, except that, instead of the commission being composed of five persons, as is provided for in those articles,

it would be best that it should consist of only three; and you may follow, in describing the instances in which indemnity is to be made, the language of the before-mentioned correspondence with Mr. Rebello. The place of the meeting of the commission may be fixed at Rio; and a reasonable time may be limited within which the claimants must present their demands for indemnity before the board. A full power, authorizing you to conclude a convention, in either of the two modes which have been suggested, is herewith transmitted. Should you conclude a convention, it will be executed in duplicate; and you will recollect, that in the counterpart which is transmitted to this Government, the United States must be first named, and your signature first placed to the convention, according to established usage; in that which shall be retained by the Brazilian Government, the opposite course will be pursued, agreeably to the same usage.

The full power to Tudor was under date of November 1, 1827, and in customary form. Authority was given "to agree, treat, consult and negotiate of and concerning claims of the Citizens and Subjects of the two Countries respectively upon the Governments of Brazil and the United States, and all matters and subjects connected therewith" (D. S., 2 Credences, 70).

Tudor, who arrived at Rio de Janeiro on June 22, 1828, carried on his negotiations for the ensuing twelve months with the Marquis of Aracaty, Brazilian Secretary of State for Foreign Affairs, who spoke English "extremely well," while Tudor was "unacquainted with the Portuguese." Those negotiations resulted in the Treaty of Peace, Friendship, Commerce, and Navigation of December 12, 1828 (Document 64), as well as in the settlement of certain claims.

Form of the Settlement

In the note of Tudor to Aracaty of July 5, 1828, the mode of adjustment is thus described (published correspondence, 39):

The Secretary of State suggests that, for adjusting the pending claims, the simplest mode and one least exposed to error, is that of settling each claim with the respective agents of it, with the intervention and assistance of the undersigned, which he need hardly assure your excellency will be attentively given, with the utmost disposition to facilitate the adjustment in the speediest and most equitable manner.

Even before the negotiations commenced, a decree of the Emperor of Brazil of May 21, 1828, had revised the sentences of the Supreme Court of Admiralty in respect of certain vessels (*ibid.*, 42–43); and one of the cases, that of the brig *Spark*, was soon settled quite informally, as thus reported (despatch No. 101, August 7, 1828, *ibid.*, 49):

The case of the Spark was finally settled to-day by Mr. Birkhead, the agent of the owner, receiving from the Minister of Marine the bonds of this Government, payable in six, twelve, and eighteen months, for the sum of 61,250,000 reis, being the amount of the original demand, $35,000, at the present rate of exchange, 1,750 reis to the dollar, the par being 800.

The case of the *Spark* was "that which occasioned the return of Mr. Raguet" and was particularly mentioned in the first instructions to Tudor of October 23, 1827. The *Spark* arrived at Rio de Janeiro

56006°—33——33

in March, 1827, from New York.   The following memorandum of the case was presented to the Brazilian Government by Tudor on July 21, 1828 (enclosure 1 to despatch No. 104, August 25, 1828, published correspondence, 58–59):

> Memorandum relating to the American brig Spark, actually the Quinze de Agosto, in the Imperial navy of Brazil.

> The brig Spark was formerly one of the navy of the United States, and was remarkable for being the fastest sailer in the service.   She was sold under a regulation adopted for reducing the navy to particular classes to which she did not correspond.

> The vessel was purchased by her late owners completely repaired in the most useful and substantial manner and at great expense; and, in consequence of encouragement received from Mr. Rebello and an officer of the Brazilian navy to send her to Brazil for sale, was despatched to Rio Janeiro with that object.   She had the most ample testimonials from several distinguished officers of the American navy, as to the character and condition of the vessel, accompanied by certificates of the Brazilian consul.   On her arrival in Rio de Janeiro she was generally admitted to be the handsomest vessel in the harbor.

> Pursuant to the original design, she was offered to the Brazilian Government at a less price by one-third than a vessel of the same description could have been procured if sent for expressly.   The Minister of Marine would not give the price asked, and the captain, disappointed in his expectations, was obliged to proceed further.   The vessel was then regularly cleared at the custom-house and sailed for Montevideo.

> In the mean time the Brazilian steamboat had proceeded out of the harbor in waiting for the Spark; and captured on leaving the harbor under the allegation that she was a pirate, although she had on board twelve respectable passengers, among them several females; a singular preparation for a piratical cruise.   Violence and insult were used towards the officers and crew, some of whom were put in irons, &c.   After a most rigid search, breaking up various parts of the vessel and destroying property, not the slightest evidence could be found, as in fact none ever existed, to justify the alleged suspicion.   Finding it in vain to procure a settlement, the captain made a protest, abandoned the vessel, and returned to the United States.

> After a time this brig was taken into the Brazilian navy, and has now for a year past borne the flag of his Imperial Majesty.

> The owner of this vessel is a man of irreproachable character, and his whole property is involved in her.

Two other claims (one, the *Spermo*, in part) were also informally adjusted, as follows (*ibid.*, 158–59):

> *Bonds of the Spermo.*—These bonds were executed at the time of the vessel's seizure at Pernambuco, and were given to allow her to depart for the United States.

> The amount was eight thousand milreas; according to my instructions their cancellation was insisted upon and obtained.

> *Brig Ontario.*—This vessel was bound from Bahia to Rio de Janeiro, having on board, as passengers, some deputies to the National Legislature.   On her passage she was spoken by an Argentine privateer, commanded by an American, a townsman of the supercargo of the Ontario.   The latter had the indiscretion to go on board the privateer to visit his countryman.   The privateersman examined the trunks of the Brazilian passengers, and rifled them of a considerable sum in gold, which those gentlemen were bringing to pay their expenses during the session of the Legislature.   To this visit of the supercargo they imputed their loss, supposing that he had given information to the commander of the corsair.   On arriving at Rio Janeiro the vessel was detained several days, the passengers wishing to make her answerable to them.   The amount claimed was partly for this demurrage and in part for the loss of profit in some passengers who were

engaged, but who went by another vessel. The whole amount claimed was $1,742.31.

The commissioners agreed with the agents to give milreas for dollars, which was quite as much as the claim was worth; the amount being so small was paid at once.

The remaining claims pressed were thirteen in number; as to these a more formal but quite unusual procedure was adopted; the Brazilian Government named two Commissioners for the settlement of the claims, Antonio Jozé da S. Loureiro, of the Foreign Office, and Diogo Soares da Silva de Bivar, an "eminent lawyer," who had "been employed as counsel by the same claimants in most of the cases"; the Commissioners opened their proceedings on August 28, 1828 (despatch No. 105, August 27, 1828, published correspondence, 83); various mercantile houses held powers of attorney from the respective claimants; those mandataries, by writings of the American Chargé d'Affaires, were duly authorized to treat; with the Brazilian Commissioners the respective agents of the American claimants agreed on terms and signed, at various dates from November, 1828, to June, 1829, thirteen several but similar *convénios*, each providing for the amount to be paid in the particular case. A description of the negotiations and procedure of settlement, written by William H. D. C. Wright, Consul of the United States at Rio de Janeiro at the time and until 1831, and agent in the cases of the *Rio, Pioneer, Telltale, Sarah George,* and *Nile,* is contained in a letter to Secretary of State Livingston of June 25, 1833, as follows (D. S., 4 Consular Despatches, Rio de Janeiro):

The Brazilian Government, after long discussions with Mr Tudor, agreeing to pay certain specified claims, appointed Snrs Bivar and Loureiro, as Commissioners, to meet such person or persons as should be duly authorized on the part of the claimants, to examine and adjust the several demands.

James Birckhead & Cº Merchants of this place held powers of Attorney in the cases of the Spark—Budget—Hannah—Spermo—Hussar—Amity and Ruth. Samuel Clapp & Cº held powers of Attorney in the cases of the Panther and Hero, and Maxwell Wright & Cº (in which house I am a partner) and myself individually held powers of Attorney in the cases of the Tell Tale, Pioneer—Sarah George—Rio and Nile—making together fourteen cases; which were all [except the *Ontario*], that were brought to a settlement by Mr Tudor.

Upon Messrs Birckhead, and Clapp, and Myself, calling on the Brazilian Commissioners, they remarked that they could view the settlement of the prize cases, in no other light, than as a National business, and therefore they could not treat with us, until we should present authorities from the U. States Legation. This being communicated to Mr Tudor, he, by written documents, authorized us respectively, to adjust the various cases, in which we, respectively, held powers of Attorney. Thus confirming, only, the claimants appointments of their own Attorneys. The adjustments being concluded, and the amounts reduced to the currency of this place, at the rate of fifteen hundred reis pr dollar, bonds were issued by the Brazilian Treasury, payable to the U. States Legation, in three instalments—on the 28th Feby 1830—28th August 1830—and 28th Feby 1831. These bonds were endorsed payable, and delivered to the respective Attorneys by Mr Tudor. And being punctually paid, as they fell due, no kind of responsibility could further rest upon our Government or its Agents.

I had no Agency in the adjustments, nor did I receive one cent of the awards, in my official capacity, as Consul of the United States. I like Messrs Birckhead and Clapp acted, entirely, by authority of powers of Attorney from the claimants.

On June 2, 1829, after the signature of those thirteen agreements, still another agreement, which fixed the rate of exchange for payment at fifteen hundred reis per dollar, was signed by the Brazilian Commissioners and by the agents of the various American claimants.

Those fourteen agreements were then, on June 15, 1829, confirmed by the two instruments the text of which is printed above. One of those instruments confirmed the thirteen claims agreements and the other the rate-of-exchange agreement.

Finally, the Brazilian Legislature having closed its session without passing the budget, the Emperor of Brazil on September 10, 1829, issued a decree for the issuance of the bonds provided as means of payment of the claims.

The Documents

From the foregoing account of the procedure adopted in respect of the claims adjusted by writings, it will be seen that this claims settlement comprised sixteen documents, aside from the Brazilian decree of September 10, 1829. These documents were the thirteen claims agreements between the Brazilian Commissioners and the respective agents of the American claimants, the rate-of-exchange agreement of June 2, 1829, signed by those Commissioners and agents, and the two confirmatory instruments of June 15, 1829, the text of which is printed above preceding these notes. All those sixteen documents were written in Portuguese only; none of the originals is in the archives of the Department of State; and there are available copies of only four of them.

Of the thirteen claims agreements, copies of but two are available, those in the cases of the *Sarah George* and the *Telltale*. There are three copies of the former; one was an enclosure to the despatch of Tudor of December 11, 1828 (D. S., 6 Despatches, Brazil, No. 115, enclosure 14; printed in published correspondence, 125–26); a second copy, seemingly enclosed with a duplicate of that same despatch, is in a volume entitled "Letters of William Tudor Minister U. S. to Rio de Janeiro"; and a third copy was enclosed with the letter of William H. D. C. Wright of June 25, 1833, above cited. The text, collated with the first of the three copies mentioned, and a translation, follow:

[Translation]

Os abaixos assignados Commissarios do Governo do Brazil, por hum parte, e o reclamante do Brigue Americano— Sarah George—e do sua carga por outra parte, representado pelo Sṝ W. D. C. Wright, devidamente authorizado para este effeito pelo Sṝ Guilherme Tudor, Encarregado de Negocios dos Estados Unidos d'America nesta Corte, em consecuencia de sus respectivos poderes, e instruccões para haverem de liquidar as perdas, damnos, e lucros cessantes, motivados pelo apresamento do referido Brigue—

We, the undersigned Commissioners of the Government of Brazil on the one hand, and the claimant of the American brig *Sarah George* and her cargo on the other hand, represented by Mr. W. D. C. Wright, duly authorized to this effect by Mr. William Tudor, Chargé d'Affaires of the United States at this Court, in accordance with their respective powers and instructions, in order to liquidate the losses, damages, and lost profits arising out of the seizure of the said brig *Sarah George*, Captain M. S. Gordon, have agreed and settled upon

Sarah George—Capt. M. S. Gordon tem convencionado e ajustado a referida liquidação pela maneira seguinte: a saber

Quanto ao Navio

Pelo valor do Casco, seus aparelhos, e pertences, segundo a estimaação dada (bona fide) Pezos fortes__	$11. 000.
Pelo freite na conformidade da Carta partida e conhecimento_____	3000.
Pelas soldadas, segundo a lista da equipagem (bona fide)_____	1923.
Pelas comedorias por arbitração_____	400.
Por ditas de Capt Gordon. idem_____	200.
Por despezas do Consulado e Justiça_____	66.
Por indemnisção de gastos extraordinarios, por arbitração_____	411.

São pezos fortes dezesete mil_____Pesos	17. 000.

Quanto a Carga.

Pelo que deveria produzir no Rio de Janeiro porto do destino_____	9. 458$000

São nove contos quatro centos cincoenta e oito mil e quarenta reis.

Conveio-se mais na indemnisação de hum juro sobre aquellas quantias, que será regulado da seguinte forma.

Pelo que pertence ao navio de seis por cento, contado desde 23 de Outubro de 1826, trinta dias depois da sua arrestação, até effectivo embolço do Capital. E pelo que pertence o Carga, hum juro de cinco por cento, contado desde 23 de Março de 1827 seis mezes depois da mesma arrestaçao até outro sem o pagamento do Capital.

O Governo dos Estados Unidos, pelo seu representante nesta Corte, ha de garantir ao do Brazil o pagamento a cada hum dos interesados nesta reclamação, de maneira que o Governo Imperial não ha de ficar a este respeito em nemhuma responsabilidade para com os mesmos interesados, por isso que as somas liquidadas serão postas a disposição do Governo dos Estados Unidos

A presente Convenção, e ajuste de liquidação fica em tudo dependente da

the said liquidation in the following manner, to wit:

For the Ship

For the value of the hull, its rigging and equipment, according to the estimate made (bona fide) standard dollars_____	$11, 000
For the freight, according to the charter party and bill of lading_____	3, 000
For wages, according to the roll of the crew (bona fide)_	1, 923
For provisions, as per arbitration_____	400
For the same for Captain Gordon, ditto_____	200
For consular and legal expenses_____	66
Compensation for extraordinary expenses, per arbitration_____	411

A total of seventeen thousand dollars____	$17, 000

For the Cargo

For what it should produce in Rio de Janeiro, the port of destination_____	9, 458, 040

Nine million four hundred and fifty-eight thousand and forty reis.

The payment of interest on the above amounts was also agreed to and shall be determined as follows:

With respect to the ship, at 6 per cent from October 23, 1826, thirty days after its seizure, until reimbursement of the capital is effected. And with respect to the cargo, interest at 5 per cent from March 23, 1827, six months after the said seizure, also until repayment of the capital.

The Government of the United States, through its representative at this Court, shall guarantee to the Government of Brazil the payment to be made to each of the parties concerned in this claim, in such a manner that the Imperial Government shall not be under any liability in this connection to the said interested parties because of the fact that the amounts liquidated will be placed at the disposal of the Government of the United States.

This liquidation agreement and settlement is in all respects subject to the

Approvação do Governo de S. M. o Imperador do Brazil.

É para que assim conste, nos Commissarios de huma e outra parte esta fizemos, assignamos, e sellamos, por duplicada no Rio de Janeiro aos seis de Novembro de mil oito centos e vinte oito.

(seal)
DIEGO SOARES DA SILVA DE BIVAR.

(")
ANTONIO JOZE DA S. LOUREIRO.

( )
W. H. D. C. WRIGHT

approval of the Government of His Majesty the Emperor of Brazil.

And in testimony thereof we, the Commissioners of both parties, have drawn up, signed, and sealed these presents in duplicate at Rio de Janeiro, November 6, 1828.

[Seal]
DIEGO SOARES DA SILVA DE BIVAR.

[Seal]
ANTONIO JOZE DA S. LOUREIRO.

[Seal]
W. H. D. C. WRIGHT

A copy of the agreement in the case of the schooner *Telltale*, which was signed May 13, 1829, was enclosed with the despatch of Wright, then Consul and acting Chargé d'Affaires of the United States at Rio de Janeiro, of December 22, 1830 (D. S., 7 Despatches, Brazil, No. 16). The text and a translation follow·

[Translation]

Os abaixo assignados Commissarios do Governo Imperial por huma parte, e por outra parte o Reclamante ou Reclamantes da Escuna Americana— Tell Tale—de New York, Mestre e Sobrecarga Munson Hinman, reprezentádos pelo Snr Guilherme Henrique de Courcy Wright, devidamente auctorisado pelo Sr Guilherme Tudor, Encarregado de Negocios dos Estados Unidos nesta Corte; em virtude de seus respectivos poderes, e instrucções para haverem de ajustar e liquidar as indemnizações pedidas pelo aprezamento e condemnação da dita Escuna— Tell Tale—tem ajustado e convencionado as referidas indemnizações pela maneira seguinte.

We, the undersigned Commissioners of the Imperial Government on the one hand, and on the other hand the claimant or claimants of the American schooner *Telltale*, of New York, Master and Supercargo Munson Hinman, represented by Mr. William Henry de Courcy Wright, duly authorized by Mr. William Tudor, Chargé d'Affaires of the United States at this Court, by virtue of their respective powers and instructions, in order to settle and liquidate the indemnities asked on account of the seizure and condemnation of the said schooner *Telltale*, have settled and agreed upon the said indemnities as follows:

Quanto ao Navio		For the Ship	
Pelo valor do seu casco e aparelhos, estimádo pᵣ arbitração	4. 500	Value of the hull and rigging, estimated by arbitration	$4, 500
Pelo frete constante dos Conhecimentos até Monte Video, e na sua volta pᵣ estimativa tudo	3. 000	Freight as shown on the bills of lading to Montevideo and return, all as per estimate	3, 000
Por despezas extraordinarias do Mestro durante a sua detenção, e gastos do processo, que serão repartidos proporcionalmente com a carga	600	Extraordinary expenses of the master during his detention, and costs of the lawsuit, which are to be shared in proportion to the cargo	600
Commissão ao Agente Americano, sobre o valor do Navio e frete somente a. 5%	375	Commission to the American agent, on the value of the ship and freight only, at 5 per cent	375
	$8. 475		$8, 475

Quanto á Carga		For the Cargo	
Pelo valor das Facturas apresentadas e conferidas com as que se achão no processo.	12. 130	Amount of the invoices submitted and compared with those which are found in the record	$12, 130
Premio sobre esta quantia, lucro esperádo por estimativa @ 15%	1. 819	Premium upon this amount, expected profit as per estimate, at 15 per cent	1, 819
Compensação ao Sobre-Carga pela perda das suas commissões @ 5%	606	Compensation to the supercargo for the loss of his commissions, at 5 per cent	606
Commissão ao Agente Americano sobre as importancias acima, a 5%	727	Commission to the American agent on the above amounts, at 5 per cent	727
	$15. 282		$15, 282

São quanto ao Navio, oito mil quatro centos e setenta e sinco, e quanto á Carga, quinze mil duzentos e oitenta e dois pezos fortes.

Conveio-se mais que sobre as indemnizacoes concedidas ao Navio pelo seu valor, e frete, isto é, sobre 7.500 pezos, e sobre ás concedidas á Carga, é dizer, sobre 14.555 pezos, se accumulára um juro, que sera regulado, quanto as primeiras á razão de 6 ℔ %, e quanto ás segundas á razão de 5% ao anno, contando se o vencimento da data de hoje em diante.

O Governo dos Estados-Unidos pelo seu Reprezentante n'esta Corte, ha de garantir ao do Brazil, o pagamento a cada um dos Interessados n'esta tranzacção, de maneira que o Governo Imperial, não ha de ficar á este respeito em nenhuma responsabilidade para com os mesmos interessados, por isso que as sommas liquidadas serão postas a disposição do Governo dos Estados Unidos.

A prezente Convenção e ajuste de liquidação fica em tudo dependente da Approvação e ratificação do Governo de Sua Magestade O Imperador do Brazil.

E para que assim conste, nós os Commissarios de uma parte, e os Reclamantes por seu Procurador da outra, este fizemos escrever, assignamos e sellamos por duplicado no Rio de Janeiro aos 13 de Maio de 1829.

(L S)   (signed)
DIOGO SOARES DA SILVA DE BIVAR
(L S)   (signed)
W. H. D'C. WRIGHT
(L S)   (signed)
ANTONIO JOZE DA Sᵃ LOUREIRO.

Total for the ship, eight thousand four hundred and seventy-five, and for the cargo, fifteen thousand two hundred and eighty-two standard dollars.

It was further agreed that the indemnities allowed for the value of the ship and freight, namely $7,500, and those allowed for the cargo, namely $14,555, will bear interest which shall be determined at the rate of 6 per cent on the former, and on the latter at the rate of 5 per cent annually, the interest period to run from this date.

The Government of the United States of America through its representative in this Court shall guarantee to the Government of Brazil the payment to each of the parties interested in this transaction, in such a manner that the Imperial Government shall not be under any liability in this respect to the said interested parties because of the fact that the liquidated amounts will be placed at the disposal of the Government of the United States.

This liquidation agreement and settlement is in all respects subject to the approval and ratification of the Government of His Majesty the Emperor of Brazil.

And in witness thereof we, the Commissioners on the one hand and the claimants through their attorney on the other, have had these presents drawn up and have signed and sealed them in duplicate at Rio de Janeiro, May 13, 1829.

[Seal]
DIOGO SOARES DA SILVA DE BIVAR
[Seal]
W. H. D. C. WRIGHT
[Seal]
ANTONIO JOZE DA Sᵃ LOUREIRO.

It may be presumed that the other eleven claims agreements were similar in form to the two of which the texts have been printed. A tabular statement of the amounts of the principal and interest in each case, under the heading, "List of the several amounts, principal and interest, awarded for American claims, and for which bonds have been received," was enclosure 13 to despatch No. 147 of Tudor of November 21, 1829 (published correspondence, 249). The figures there given are copied in the following table.

Case	Principal	Interest	Total
Telltale	Rs.35, 635, 500	Rs.2, 289, 350	Rs. 37, 924, 850
Pioneer	18, 000, 000	3, 134, 676	21, 134, 676
Sarah George	34, 958, 040	7, 514, 159	42, 472, 199
Rio	6, 733, 500	1, 347, 534	8, 081, 034
Panther	3, 000, 000	1, 229, 918	4, 229, 918
Hero	10, 305, 000	1, 743, 979	12, 048, 979
Nile	3, 000, 000	313, 178	3, 313, 178
Budget	29, 050, 500	1, 889, 493	30, 939, 993
Hannah	34, 978, 500	2, 219, 274	37, 197, 774
Spermo	74, 982, 600	17, 263, 203	92, 245, 803
Hussar	25, 504, 182	2, 823, 642	28, 337, 824
Amity	15, 030, 000	1, 892, 878	16, 922, 878
Ruth	24, 443, 949	4, 984, 491	29, 428, 440
Total (bonds)			364, 267, 546
For the brig *Ontario* (paid)			1, 742, 000
For the brig *Spark* (two thirds paid)			61, 250, 000
Total			Rs.427, 259, 546

At 1,500 reis to the dollar, the total of 364,267,546 reis would amount to \$242,845.03.

The text of the confirmation of the thirteen claims agreements which is printed above immediately after the headnote, is from the handwritten copy thereof which is enclosure 6 to the despatch of Tudor of July 2, 1829 (D. S., 6 Despatches, Brazil, No. 131; printed in published correspondence, 220).

While the text of the rate-of-exchange agreement is not available, its purport is stated in the confirmatory instrument of June 15, 1829, the text of which, collated with the handwritten copy which is enclosure 7 to despatch No. 131 above cited (printed in published correspondence, 220–21), appears above immediately preceding these notes.

The bonds delivered in settlement of the claims were duly paid (D. S., 4 Consular Despatches, Rio de Janeiro, June 25, 1833); the set for each claim was in three series, due, respectively, on February 28 and August 28, 1830, and February 28, 1831, in amounts which included the interest. For their form, in Portuguese and translation, and for the exact amount of each as listed in the receipts given by the

agents of the claimants, see published correspondence, 240, 249, 255–57 (the original receipts are in D. S., 6 Despatches, Brazil, No. 151. December 9, 1829, enclosures).

The Thirteen Claims

The nature of each of the thirteen claims adjusted by writings is stated more or less at length in the despatches, notes, and other papers (see American State Papers, Foreign Relations, VI, 1021–1121, *passim*, and published correspondence, *passim*). With his despatch of April 18, 1829, Tudor enclosed a "Statement of the claims of American citizens against the Government of Brazil, with *confidential* remarks on each case, divided into classes: 1. Claims finally liquidated. 2ᵈ Claims adjusted for liquidation. 3. Claims suspended. 4. Claims not presented" (D. S., 6 Despatches, Brazil, No. 125; only the first two classes are printed in published correspondence, 158–61). Regarding the settlement of six of the thirteen cases Tudor wrote in that statement as follows (published correspondence, 159–61):

Ship Panther.—This vessel called at Rio Janeiro in 1823 to obtain water and refreshments. By a mistake of the consignee (which he could have remedied by paying 150 mrs.) in entering the vessel at the customhouse in full, instead of *enfranquia*, it became necessary to declare her cargo, which in fact consisted of only a remnant of one or two articles of trifling value, and about $9,000 in specie, belonging to the captain and crew. The captain was ignorant of the blunder of the consignee, and acted with perfect good faith.

The vessel, however, was liable by their laws to seizure, the cargo to confiscation and payment of double the amount, and the captain to imprisonment, till all these demands were satisfied. The vessel and money were seized, and the captain imprisoned. Mr. Raguet, not aware of the facts in the case, and urged by feelings of humanity, and what he supposed to be justice, as well as equity, made the most strenuous efforts in the business, and after twenty-seven days' detention, the captain was released, and the property all restored, and the vessel sailed. The consignee, however, was to blame, and should have been justly responsible for all the damages. They proceeded according to their laws, though these are excessively harsh; but, as the captain was wholly blameless, and behaved with great firmness and propriety, I urged the claim on the ground of ill treatment of an American citizen. The award given was $2,000—1,500 to cover the demurrage, and 500 indemnity to the captain, with interest from August 6, 1823.

Schooner Hero.—This vessel sailed from Beunos Ayres during the blockade, with a cargo of nutria skins, &c., valued at 39,000 milrs. bound to the United States. Soon after sailing she sprang a leak, and was obliged to put into St. Catharine's in a sinking condition. The captain at first met with no obstruction, and repaired his vessel, but just before he was ready to sail, was accused of being a pirate, sent with his mate, both in irons, to Rio Janeiro, tried here immediately on their arrival, condemned as pirates, and put to work in irons on board the prison-ship. As soon as the consul, Mr. Wright, knew of their situation, he interfered, procured their release, and they were allowed to return to St. Catharine's. On arriving there he found the vessel had been robbed, and was not worth repairing, and he returned to the United States. His protest, with the strong language contained in the despatch No. 5 to me from the Department, enabled me to claim compensation for these injured men. The property, belonging to merchants of Beunos Ayres, (though Americans,) I should not have claimed, but as so much injustice and outrage had been practised, I thought the lesson might be more impressive if they paid something for it, and directed the agent to present the accounts. It is to be added that, besides the domicil of the owners, the super-

cargo, by the open part which he and others of his family had taken in rendering services to the Buenos Ayreans, was particularly obnoxious to the ill-will of this Government; the documents also were so loose and defective that they were really null; and further, the supercargo had barred all claims, by consenting to receive back the property. The commissioners settled it fairly, on principles of mercantile law, and all they could possibly be supposed to be answerable for was a proportion of the damage. They awarded $3,190 demurrage for the vessel, $1,000 to the captain, $800 to the mate, and $210 between them, for expenses, as indemnity for their ill treatment; and for indemnity on account of the cargo 10 per cent. of its value, equal to $1,670; whole amount of the award $6,870, with interest on the vessel and indemnities to the individuals from November 20, 1827, and on the cargo from same date. It is evident that no just claim existed in either this or the preceding case, except for the ill-treatment of the individuals commanding the vessels.

Brig Nile—was seized in the river Plate, coming from Canton, with a valuable cargo, bound to Buenos Ayres. She was detained 27 days, and then released. The claim was for demurrage, and interest on the value of the cargo. The documents were imperfect, but the facts of the case I knew to be well founded. The award was 3,000 milreas.

Brig Rio.—This vessel was detained at Montevideo 86 days, and then released. For this demurrage $2,150 were allowed for the vessel, and $2,339 for the cargo, in all $4,489.

Schooner Amity.—This was a small vessel, chiefly laden with lumber, and was burnt at the Salado. The documents and vouchers were of the most loose and imperfect description. The award was $6,900 on account of the vessel, freight, compensation to the captain, &c., and $2,710 for the cargo—with interest on the former from March 18, 1828, and on the latter from November 1, of the same year. Total $9,610.

Brig Hussar.—This vessel was also burnt at the Salado, just before the termination of the war—an English brig with a cargo of £25,000 being burnt at the same time. A very small part of the cargo belonging to the captain was claimed.

The award was $15,375 on account of the vessel and freight, and 2,441.583 rs. on account of the cargo; interest on the former from October 1, 1828, and on the latter from November 1, same year.

The case of the *Spermo* was one of those dealt with in the earliest instructions to Tudor of October 23, 1827. As already stated, the case was settled in part by an informal arrangement; regarding the final settlement Tudor wrote in his statement of the claims, above cited, as follows:

This ship was seized for an alleged breach of blockade at Pernambuco in 1824. The vessel was allowed to depart under bonds, (cancelled recently at my requisition,) acquitted in the first court, and finally condemned, after a long delay by the court of appeal in Rio Janeiro. The claim for the vessel was in behalf of the underwriters; for the cargo, for the owners. It has been settled by an award in milreas, valuing the dollar at 1,500 rs. (the par is 800.) This the agents, experienced merchants, considered more advantageous than a settlement in dollars. For the vessel, &c. 33,075.000 rs.; interest from January, 1827: cargo 41,907.000 rs.; interest from April 5, 1825.

The case of the *Ruth* was another of those dealt with in the instructions to Tudor of October 23, 1827. The facts are set forth in detail in American State Papers, Foreign Relations, VI, 1030–37. It appears that the brig *Ruth*, of Philadelphia, Jacob Jefferson, Master, sailed from Gibraltar on June 12, 1826, with a cargo, not contraband, bound to Buenos Aires, or if that port should be found to be in a state of blockade, then to Montevideo. The *Ruth* was captured on

August 5, 1826, about ninety miles out, and taken into Rio de Janeiro. There were allegations of serious mistreatment of the officers and crew. Regarding the settlement Tudor wrote in his statement of the claims, above cited, as follows:

This was one of the most unjustifiable of all the captures, without any pretext that was even specious; and the bad treatment received by the supercargo and captain, aggravated the injustice. After the case was settled, I told the minister that I could not sign the award, unless some compensation was given to the persons above mentioned. I proposed three thousand milreis, to which he assented; two-thirds to the supercargo, and the remainder to the captain; the former having suffered most.

The facts in the cases of the *Pioneer* and the *Sarah George* are thus set forth by Raguet in a note to the Brazilian Minister of Foreign Affairs of November 14, 1826 (American State Papers, Foreign Relations, VI, 1048):

The brig Pioneer, of Salem, Potter master, bound on a voyage from Havana direct to Montevideo, with a stipulation in the charter party to proceed to Buenos Ayres in case the blockade should, on arrival in the river Plate, be found to be raised, was captured on the 3d of September, off cape St. Mary's, by the squadron under the command of Admiral Pinto Guedes, and sent to the port of her destination, where she arrived on the 8th of that month, and where she still continued without a trial, as late as the 28th of October.

The brig Sarah George, of Portland, Gordon master, bound from Lima to Montevideo, was captured on the 23d of September, in or near the river Plate, by the imperial brig-of-war Coboclo, and sent into the latter port, where she arrived on the 26th of the same month, and where she still remained without a decision, on the 28th ultimo, the date of the last advices.

Regarding the settlement of these two cases Tudor wrote in his statement of the claims as follows:

Brig Sarah George.—The award in this case was very liberal; for the vessel, demurrage, &c. $17,000 dollars, and the cargo 9,458.040 rs. Interest on the vessel from October 26, 1826, and on the cargo from March 23, 1827.

Brig Pioneer.—The cargo of this vessel was English property, which was concealed from me till some time after the claim was presented. The commissioners objecting, on this account, I of course withdrew it, leaving it to be settled with the English demands. For the vessel, detention, &c. $12,000 were awarded. Interest from August 25, 1827.

In all the cases the interest on allowances for the vessel was at the rate of 6 per cent and for the cargo at the rate of 5 per cent.

It appears that the cases of the *Telltale*, the *Hannah*, and the *Budget* were also cases of condemnation for alleged breach of blockade and that the claimants abandoned the property under protest (published correspondence, 171, 177). It is said that the brig *Budget*, of Baltimore, was captured in August, 1828, near Montevideo, by the Brazilian squadron; and the following summary of the facts was written from the protest (*ibid.*, 20–21):

It appears that, after discharging a part of her cargo at Rio de Janeiro, she sailed with the residue, consisting of whiskey and tobacco, for Montevideo; that the Budget struck upon one of the banks going into the La Plata, in a violent gale, and lost her rudder; that in this crippled condition she remained several

days, until she had constructed a temporary rudder; that she was actually in sight of Montevideo, bound in, when she was taken possession of by the Brazilian squadron; and that if she was a few miles beyond the line of blockade it was owing to her unmanageable state, and to her being driven there by the violence of the winds and currents.

THE CASES OF THE "MATILDA" AND THE "PRESIDENT ADAMS"

In his "Statement of the claims of American citizens against the Government of Brazil," which was enclosed with his despatch of April 18, 1829, Tudor listed five claims as "cases suspended." Two of those cases, namely, that of the brig *Matilda* and that of the brig *President Adams*, were reconsidered and settled in 1833.

Regarding the seizure of the *Matilda*, Condy Raguet, Chargé d'Affaires at Rio de Janeiro, wrote on January 17, 1827, to the Brazilian Minister of Foreign Affairs as follows (D. S., 5 Despatches, Brazil, No. 24, February 7, 1827, enclosure A; American State Papers, Foreign Relations, VI, 1056):

> The American brig Matilda of New York, Marshall master, bound from that port to Monte Video, was captured on the 22d of November last, by the blockading squadron in the River Plate, and after having had the crew taken out, as in all the former cases in violation of the immunity of the American flag, was sent to this port, where she arrived on 26th Ultim'o.

In his statement of the claims, above mentioned, Tudor wrote regarding the case of the *Matilda* as follows:

> This vessel arrived in the Plate after a very long passage in which she had suffered greatly. She arrived in sight of Buenos Ayres without seeing any thing, where she met the blockading squadron, was captured & condemned. The reason given for the condemnation as she had received no previous warning, was, that, she would not heave to when fired at, & endeavoured to escape from the squadron & get into the blockaded Port. The case was finally condemned by a Council here, in which American, French & English vessels were acted upon, some being restored with damages, & others acquitted the Matilda being among the latter. The French & English have obtained a settlement of their cases, which is mentioned as a fact, not as a precedent. From the best opinion I can form, the property is American, but the vessel rendered liable to condemnation, by attempting to force her way into port. The amount of the claim, I think is greatly exaggerated, in the account presented to me. . . . If the President thinks the case ought to be insisted upon, they will no doubt agree to settle it.

Referring to the *Matilda* in a despatch of August, 1828 (D. S., 6 Despatches, Brazil, No. 102), Tudor wrote: "This vessel was finally condemned last June, by an Imperial decree which ordered the restoration of several others."

It appears from a protest of Albert P. de Valangin, Master of the *President Adams*, of Baltimore, dated at Montevideo July 21, 1827 (D. S., 1 Consular Despatches, Montevideo, August 1, 1827, enclosure), that on July 5, 1827, that vessel left the port of Montevideo, bound for Baltimore, and that on the following morning, some eighty or ninety miles from the Brazilian blockading squadron off Buenos Aires, she was captured by the Brazilian schooner *Rio* and

forced to return to Montevideo.   In his statement of the claims Tudor wrote of this case as follows:

> This vessel sailed from the Salado with a Cargo of country produce, was detained, sent to Monte Video, & before any trial took place, parted her cables in a gale, drove ashore & was totally lost. The papers presented to me, by her Captain, de Valangin, were extremely loose & imperfect. I told him it would be necessary to exhibit clear proof that the property was American. He then admitted that only a part of it was American, & the rest belonged to merchants in Buenos Ayres. I therefore suspended the case for further proof.

Thus it appears that Tudor, for want of proof in the two cases, agreed in 1829 to suspend consideration of them. Instructions from Secretary of State Van Buren to Tudor of February 10 and March 2, 1830, enclosed documents intended to establish the validity of the two claims (D. S., 14 Instructions, American States, 61–62, 63–64; published correspondence, 27–29); but owing to the death of Tudor on March 9, 1830, the claims were not pressed until after the arrival of his successor, Ethan A. Brown, nearly a year later.

Settlement was reached in the cases of the *Matilda* and the *President Adams* on March 4, 1833, when two agreements, similar in form to the agreements of 1828–29, were signed by a Brazilian and an American commissioner. A copy, in Portuguese, of the agreement in the case of the *Matilda*, was enclosed with the despatch of Ethan A. Brown, then Chargé d'Affaires at Rio de Janeiro, of May 6, 1833 (D. S., 9 Despatches, Brazil, No. 46, enclosure F). The text thereof and a translation follow:

[Translation]

Os abaixo assignados devidamente nomeados pelo Governo do Brazil e por parte do Governo dos Estados Unidos da America do Norte para liquidar as perdas, damnos, e lucros cessantes, provenientes da captura do Bergantim Americano Mathilda, que teve lugar no Rio da Prata em Novembro de 1826; pela Escudra Brasileira no bloqueio d'aqulle Rio; tendo examinado as contas e documentos da Reclamacão do dito Bergantim convencionacão a mesma Liquidação da maneira seguinte:

The undersigned, duly appointed by the Government of Brazil and on the part of the Government of the United States of North America to settle the losses, damages, and *lucrum cessans* caused by the capture of the American brigantine *Matilda*, which was made in the Rio de la Plata in November, 1826, by the Brazilian squadron in the blockade of that river, having examined the accounts and documents of the claim of the said brigantine, do agree upon the said settlement as follows:

Por indemnisação total do valor do Bergantim, Carregamento, fretos, lucros, despezas ordinarias e extraordinarias, soldadas, e comedorias ao capitão e Tripulacão, Cambios, juros &c R⁹ 24,000$000 cuja quantia de vinte e quatro contos de R⁹ deverá ser paga pelo Governo de Sua Magestade o Imperador do Brazil em Apolices do mesmo Governo pelo determinado preço de secenta e dois e meio por cento na conformidade da Resolução da assemblea Geral de 7 de Novembro de 1831.

As total compensation for the value of the brigantine, cargo, freight, profits, ordinary and extraordinary expenses, pay and subsistence for the captain and crew, exchange, interest, etc., Rs. 24,000$000, which amount of twenty-four contos of reis is to be paid by the Government of His Majesty the Emperor of Brazil in Government paper of the said Government at the fixed rate of 62½ per cent, in conformity with the resolution of the General Assembly of November 7, 1831.

O Governo dos Estados Unidos, pelo sua Representante nesta Corte ha de garantir ao do Brazil o pagamento a cada hum dos interessados na presente reclamacão de maneira que o Governo Imperial não ha de ficar à este respeito na menor responsabilidade para com os mesmos interessados por isso que a soma liquidada e convencionada será porto, do modo expressado á disposição do Governo dos Estados Unidos.

A presente convenção e ajuste de Liquidação fica em tudo dependente da aprovação e ratificação do Governo de Sua Magestade o Imperador do Brazil.

E para que assim conste nós os respectivos Commissarios liquidantes fezemos e assignamos a presente por duplicata.   Rio de Janeiro 4 de Marco de 1833.

João Miz Lourenço Vianna—
Commissario Brazeleiro.

Diogo Birckhead—
Commissario dos Estados Unidos.

The Government of the United States, through its representative at this Court, is to guarantee to the Government of Brazil the payment to each of the persons concerned in this claim, so that the Imperial Government shall not have the slightest responsibility in this regard toward the said interested persons because the sum settled and agreed upon be placed, in the way stated, at the disposal of the United States Government.

This liquidation agreement and settlement is in all respects subject to the approval and ratification of the Government of His Majesty the Emperor of Brazil.

And in witness thereof we, the respective liquidating Commissioners, have drawn up and signed these presents in duplicate.   Rio de Janeiro, March 4, 1833.

João Miz Lourenço Vianna
Brazilian Commissioner

James Birckhead
United States Commissioner

Following the copy of the Portuguese text above quoted is this statement:

The Liquidation and agreement in the case of the Brig President Adams is in the same terms, excepting the single difference that the sum liquidated in this case is sixty contos of Reis—R⁰ 60,000$000.

With Brown's despatch of March 16, 1833 (D. S., 9 Despatches, Brazil, No. 44), is a copy of a note of the Brazilian Minister of Foreign Affairs to Brown of March 5, 1833, signifying the approval of the agreements by the Brazilian Government; and it appears that within a few weeks after the signature of the agreements the amounts agreed upon were paid in certificates (*apólices*) of the funded dept (*ibid.*).

A further claim in the case of the *President Adams* was presented under the convention with Brazil of January 27, 1849, but was rejected (Moore, International Arbitrations, V, 4621, No. 16).

The Case of the "Adams"

Of the seventeen claims (including the two in the case of the *Spermo*) mentioned under the first two classifications (" Claims finally liquidated" and "Claims adjusted for liquidation") in Tudor's statement of the claims, above cited, only one was not settled during the negotiations of 1828–29, namely, the case of the schooner *Adams*.

The *Adams* was stopped by the blockading squadron on August 31, 1828, in the River Plata.   Her register was endorsed, "the only instance among all the captures" according to Tudor.   Thereupon, according to the protest of the master, Michael A. Parsons, she "got

under way for Monte Video" but was thereafter again stopped and ordered into that port. The schooner was condemned on the ground of deviation from the route to Montevideo with the intention of going to Buenos Aires (see D. S., 8 Despatches, Brazil, No. 29, June 21, 1832, enclosures B to L).

The case of the *Adams* was considered by the Brazilian Commissioners, who gave, under date of June 4, 1829, their reasons for not admitting the claim; and Tudor reserved it for the further consideration of his Government (published correspondence, 216–19).

An adjustment in the case of the *Adams* was reached on April 4, 1834, when an agreement, similar in form to the agreements of 1828–29, was signed by a Brazilian and an American commissioner. A copy of that agreement, in Portuguese, was enclosed with the despatch of Ethan A. Brown of April 7, 1834 (D. S., 9 Despatches, Brazil, No. 63, enclosure K). The text thereof and a translation follow:

Os abaixo assignados, Commissarios devidamente nomeados pelo Governo do Brazil e pelo Encarregado dos Negocios dos Estados Unidos d'America do Norte para Liquidar as perdas, damnos, e lucros cessantes provenientes da captura da Escuna Americana—Adams—, que teve lugar no Rio da Prata pela Esquadra Brazileira Bloqueadora no 1º de Setembro de 1828: tendo examinado o Processo da mesma Escuna e os papeis que lhe subministrarão; convencionarão esta Liquidação da maneira seg.te.

Pelo valor do casco	Pesos f	3, 500.	
Soldadas á Tripulação	"	446. 20	
Mantimentos	"	152.	
Frete	"	1, 051.	
	5, 149. 20 á 1,500 rs.		[1] 7, 723$810
Despezas do Navio em Monte Video	"	1, 138.	
Ditas do Capitão	"	186.	
Ditas da Tripulação	"	57.	
	1, 381.	"	2, 071$500
			9, 795$310
Juros de 5. annos á 6 por ^{100}			2, 938$590
Transporte			12, 733$900
Pelo valor de Carregam.to 5,907. á 1,500 rs		8860$500	
Juros de 5 annos, á 5 ℗. ^{100}		2215$125	
			11, 075$625
R.s			23, 809$525

Cuja quantia de Vinte e trez Contos oito centos nove mil quinhentos e vinte e cinco reis, deverá ser paga pelo Governo do Brazil em Apolices da Divida fundada, avencer juros da presente datta em diante, ao determinando preço de Sesenta e dois e meio por cento, na conformidade da determinação d'Assemblea Geral.

O Governo dos Estados Unidos pelo seu Representante n'esta Corte, ha de garantir ao do Brazil o pagamento á cada hum dos interessados na presente Reclamação, por isso que as somas liquidadas e convencionadas deverão ser postas do modo indicado ás disposições do mesmo Governo dos Estados Unidos.

---

[1] At 1,500 reis per dollar, $5,149.20 amounts to 7,723$800, not 7,723$810.

A presente convenção e ajuste de Liquidação fica em tudo dependente da Aprovação e ratificação do Governo de Sua Magestade o Imperador do Brazil.

E para que assim Conste, nós os respectivos Commissarios Liquidantes fizemos e assignamos a presente por duplicado. Rio de Janeiro 4 d'Abril de 1834.

(Signed by)   João Miz Lourⁿ Vianna *Commmissario Brazileiro.*
         Robert C. Wright *Commissario Americano.*

[Translation]

We, the undersigned Commissioners, duly appointed by the Government of Brazil and by the Chargé d'Affaires of the United States of America for liquidation of the losses, damages, and lost profits arising out of the capture of the American schooner *Adams*, which occurred on the Plata River by the Brazilian blockading squadron on September 1, 1828, having examined the case of the said schooner and the papers with which it was provided, agreed upon this liquidation as follows:

Value of the hull_____Standard dollars__	3, 500. 00	
Wages to the crew_____do____	446. 20	
Supplies_____do____	152. 00	
Freight_____do____	1, 051. 00	
	5, 149. 20 at 1,500 rs.,	[1]7,723$810
Expenses of the ship at Montevideo__do____	1, 138. 00	
The same for the captain_____do____	186. 00	
The same for the crew_____do____	57. 00	
	1, 381. 00 ____do____	2, 071$500
		9, 795$310
Interest for five years at 6 per cent_____		2, 938$590
Balance carried forward_____		12, 733$900
Value of the cargo, 5,907 at 1,500 rs_____ 8, 860$500		
Interest for five years at 5 per cent_____ 2, 215$125		
		11, 075$625
Total in reis_____		23, 809$525

Which amount of twenty-three million eight hundred and nine thousand five hundred and twenty-five reis must be paid by the Government of Brazil in certificates (*apólices*) of the funded debt bearing interest from the present date, at the agreed price of 62½ per cent, in accordance with the decision of the General Assembly.

The Government of the United States through its representative at this Court shall guarantee to the Government of Brazil the payment to each of the parties interested in the present claim, because of the fact that the amounts liquidated and settled are to be placed, in the manner indicated, at the disposal of the said Government of the United States.

This liquidation agreement and settlement is in all respects subject to the approval and ratification of the Government of His Majesty the Emperor of Brazil.

And in witness thereof we, the respective liquidating Commissioners, have drawn up and signed these presents in duplicate. Rio de Janeiro, April 4, 1834.

João Miz Lourⁿ Vianna, *Brazilian Commissioner*
Robert C. Wright, *American Commissioner*

There seems to have been no confirmation or ratification of that agreement by other authority, but shortly after the signature thereof

---

[1] See the footnote on p. 503.

a decree of the Brazilian Government directed the issuance of certificates (*apólices*) of the funded debt for the payment of the agreed amount (D. S., 9 Despatches, Brazil, April 26, 1834, and enclosures).

The Convention of 1849

In the "Statement of the claims of American citizens against the Government of Brazil" which was enclosed by Tudor with his despatch of April 18, 1829, cited above, five claims were listed as "suspended" and six as "not presented." Two of the claims there listed as suspended were settled in 1833, as stated above. Of the nine cases remaining, five were considered and allowed by the Commissioners under the convention with Brazil of January 27, 1849. The awards under that convention were less than the sums allowed, as the amount available under the convention, $322,535.98, was insufficient to meet the allowances, with interest. The total of the awards in those five cases, the *Felicidade*, the *Shilleleh*, the *Caspian*, the *Brutus*, and the *Amazon* (the last listed by Tudor as "South American Steamboat Association"), was $166,845 (see Moore, International Arbitrations, V, 4609–26; D. S., Record of the Proceedings of the Brazilian Commission).

56006°—33——34

Treaty Series No. 7
8 Statutes at Large, 398–401
18 *ibid.*, pt. 2, Public Treaties, 21–24

66

AUSTRIA : AUGUST 27, 1829

Treaty of Commerce and Navigation, signed at Washington August 27, 1829. Original in English and German; but "the English version is to decide the interpretation" (see the attestation clause).
Submitted to the Senate December 14, 1829. Resolution of advice and consent February 10, 1830. Ratified by the United States February 11, 1830. Ratified by Austria May 26, 1830. Question of the exchange of ratifications submitted to the Senate January 31, 1831. (Message of January 26, 1831.) Resolution of advice and consent to the exchange of ratifications February 3, 1831. Ratifications exchanged at Washington February 10, 1831. Proclaimed February 10, 1831.

Treaty of Commerce and Navigation between the United States of America, and His Majesty the Emperor of Austria.

The United States of America, and His Majesty the Emperor of Austria, King of Hungary and Bohemia, equally animated with the desire of maintaining the relations of good understanding which have hitherto so happily subsisted between their respective States, of extending, also, and consolidating the commercial intercourse between them, and convinced that this object cannot better be accomplished than by adopting the system of an entire freedom of navigation, and a perfect reciprocity, based upon principles of equity equally beneficial to both countries, have, in consequence,

Handels- und Schiffahrts Vertrag zwischen den Vereinigten Staaten von Amerika und Seiner Majestät den Kaÿser von Oesterreich.

Die Vereinigten Staaten von Amerrika und Seine Majestät der Kayser von Oesterreich, König von Ungarn und Böhmen beseelt vom gleichen Verlangen, die bisher zwischen beiden Mächten so glücklich bestandenen Freundschafts-Verhältnisse zu unterhalten; wie auch den Handels-Verkehr zwischen denselben zu erweitern, und zu befestigen, und uberzeugt dass diese Absicht am besten durch die Einführung einer gänzlichen Schiffahrts-Freiheit, und einer vollkommnen, auf Grundsätze, einer, beiden Staaten, gleich vortheilhaften Billigkeit, sich stützenden Reciprocität, er-

507

agreed to enter into negotiations for the conclusion of a Treaty of Commerce and Navigation, for which purpose the President of the United States has conferred Full Powers on Martin Van Buren, their Secretary of State; and His Majesty the Emperor of Austria has conferred like Powers on Lewis Baron de Lederer, His said Majesty's Consul for the port of New York, and the said Plenipotentiaries having exchanged their said Full Powers, found in good and due form, have concluded and signed the following Articles.

ARTICLE I.

There shall be between the Territories of the High Contracting Parties a reciprocal liberty of commerce and navigation. The inhabitants of their respective States shall mutually have liberty to enter the ports places and rivers of the Territories of each Party, wherever foreign commerce is permitted. They shall be at liberty to sojourn and reside in all parts whatsoever of said territories, in order to attend to their commercial affairs; and they shall enjoy, to that effect, the same security, protection and privileges as natives of the country wherein they reside, on condition of their submitting to the laws and ordinances there prevailing.

reicht werden könne, sind übereingekommen, Unterhandlungen zur Abschliessung eines Schiffahrts, und Handels Vertrag einzugehen, und zu dem Ende haben der Præsident der Vereinigten Staaten den Herren Martin Van Buren Secretär der auswärtigen Angelegenheiten, und seine Majestæt der Kayser von Oesterreich den Herrn Aloys Freiherrn von Lederer, Seiner Kaiserlichen Majestæt Consul zu New York mit den erforderlichen Vollmachten versehen, welche nachdem Sie ihre Vollmachten ausgewechselt, und richtig befunden, über nachstehende Artikel sich vereiniget haben

ART: I.

Es soll zwischen den Ländern der hohen contrahirenden Mæchte, eine wechselseitige Handels- und Schiffahrts-Freiheit bestehen. Die Einwohner beider Staaten, sollen gegenseitig alle Plätze, Häfen, und Flüsse des andern, in welchen der auswärtige Handel gestattet ist, besuchen dürfen. Sie sollen das Recht haben, in was immer fur einem Theile ihrer wechselseitigen Gebiethe zu verweilen und zu wohnen, um ihren Handels-Geschäften nachgehen zu können, und sie sollen zu diesem Zwecke dieselbe Sicherheit, denselben Schutz und Privilegien als die Einwohner des Landes, in welchem sie wohnen, geniessen jedoch mit der Bedingung, dass Sie sich allen daselbst

bestehenden Gesetzen und Verordnungen zu unterwerfen haben.

ARTICLE II.

Austrian vessels arriving, either laden or in ballast, in the ports of the United States of America; and, reciprocally, vessels of the United States arriving, either laden, or in ballast, in the ports of the dominions of Austria, shall be treated on their entrance, during their stay and at their departure, upon the same footing as national vessels coming from the same place, with respect to the duties of tonnage, light-houses, pilotage and port-charges, as well as to the fees and perquisites of public officers, and all other duties or charges of whatever kind or denomination, levied in the name, or to the profit of the Government, the local Authorities, or of any private establishment whatsoever.

ART: II.

Oesterreichishe Fahrzeuge, die entweder in Ballast, oder mit einer Ladung in irgend einen Hafen der Vereinigten Staaten von Amerika, und gegenseitig, nordamerikanische Fahrzeuge, die entweder in Ballast, oder mit einer Ladung in irgend einen Hafen der Dominien Seiner Kay: Königl: apostolischen Majestät anlangen: Sollen bey ihrem Einlaufen, während ihres Aufenthalts, und bei ihrer Abfahrt, sowohl in Rucksicht der Tonnen- Leuchtthurm- Lotsen und aller andern Hafen-Gebühren, als auch in Rücksicht anderer Abgaben und Taxen aller Art, sie mögen unter was immer für Benennung in Nahmen, und zum Vortheile der Regierung, der Orts-Behörden, oder irgend einer Privat-Anstalt erhoben werden, auf gleiche Weise wie die national Fahrzeuge behandelt werden, die von denselben Hafen kommen

ARTICLE III.

All kind of merchandise and articles of commerce, either the produce of the soil or the industry of the United States of America, or of any other country, which may be lawfully imported into the ports of the dominions of Austria, in Austrian vessels, may also be so imported in vessels of the

ART: III

Alle Gattungen Waaren und Handels-Artikel, solche mögen nun Grund- oder Industrie Erzeugnisse der Vereinigten Staaten, oder irgend eines andern Landes seyn, welche gesetzlich in den Häfen der oesterreichischen Monarchie, in oesterreichischen Fahrzeugen eingeführt werden kön-

United States of America, without paying other or higher duties or charges, of whatever kind or denomination, levied in the name or to the profit of the Government, the local Authorities, or of any private establishments whatsoever, than if the same merchandise or produce had been imported in Austrian vessels. And, reciprocally, all kind of merchandise and articles of commerce, either the produce of the soil or of the industry of the dominions of Austria, or of any other country, which may be lawfully imported into the ports of the United States, in vessels of the said States, may also be so imported in Austrian vessels, without paying other or higher duties or charges, of whatever kind or denomination levied in the name, or to the profit of the Government, the local Authorities, or of any private establishments whatsoever, than if the same merchandise or produce had been imported in vessels of the United States of America.

nen, sollen eben so in nord amerikanischen Fahrzeugen daselbst eingeführt werden dürfen, ohne höhere oder andere Abgaben und Zölle aller Art zu entrichten, was solche immer fur Benennung haben mögen, die im Nahmen oder zum Vortheile der Regierung, der Orts-Behörden, oder irgend einer Privat Anstalt erhoben werden, als diejenigen, welche dieselben Waaren oder Erzeugnisse zu entrichten hätten, wenn Sie in oesterreichishen Fahrzeugen eingefuhrt würden. Und gegenseitig alle Gattungen Waaren und Handels Artikel, solche mögen nun Grund- oder Industrie Erzeugnisse der oesterreichischen Monarchie, oder irgend eines andern Landes sein, welche gesetzlich in den nordamerikanischen Vereinigten Staaten, in nordamerikanischen Fahrzeugen eingeführt werden können, sollen eben so in oesterreichischen Fahrzeugen daselbst eingeführt werden dürfen, ohne andere oder höhere Abgaben und Zölle aller Art zu entrichten, was solche immer für Benennung haben mögen, die im Nahmen oder zum Vortheile der Regierung, der Orts-Behörden oder irgend einer Privat Anstalt erhoben werden, als diejenigen, welche dieselben Waaren oder Erzeugnisse zu entrichten hätten, wenn Sie in nordamerikanischen Fahrzeugen eingeführt würden.

Article IV.

To prevent the possibility of any misunderstanding, it is hereby declared that the stipulations contained in the two preceding Articles, are, to their full extent, applicable to Austrian vessels and their cargoes, arriving in the ports of the United States of America; and, reciprocally, to vessels of the said States and their cargoes arriving in the ports of the dominions of Austria, whether the said vessels clear directly from the ports of the country to which they respectively belong, or from the ports of any other foreign country.

Article V

No higher or other duties shall be imposed on the importation into the United States, of any article the produce or manufacture of the dominions of Austria; and no higher or other duties shall be imposed on the importatation into the dominions of Austria, of any article the produce or manufacture of the United States, than are, or shall be payable on the like article, being the produce or manufacture of any other foreign country. Nor shall any prohibition be imposed on the importation or exportation of any article the produce or manufacture of the United States, or of the dominions of Austria, to or

Art: IV.

Um eben der Möglichkeit eines Missverständnisses vorzubeugen, so wird hiemit erklärt, dass die, in den zwei vorhergehenden Artikeln enthaltenen, Bestimmungen, in ihrem vollen Umfange, auf oesterreichische Schiffe und deren Ladungen, die in irgend einem Hafen der Vereinigten Staaten anlangen, und gegenseitig, auf nordamerikanische Fahrzeuge, die in Oesterreichischen Häfen anlangen, anwendbar seyen, die genannten Schiffe mögen nun direct von einem Hafen des Landes kommen, zu welchen Sie gehören, oder von irgend einem Hafen eines andern Landes

Art: V.

Es sollen von sämmtlichen Artikeln, welche in den Staaten Seiner Majestät des Kaÿsers von Oesterreich erzeugt oder fabrizirt sind, bei der Einfuhr in die Vereinigten Staaten von Amerika, und von sämmtlichen Artikeln, welche in den vereinigten Staaten erzeugt oder fabrizirt sind, bei ihrer Einfuhr in die oesterreichischen Staaten, keine höhere oder andere Zölle bezahlt werden, als diejenigen, welche von denselben Artikeln, wenn Sie Erzeugnisse eines andern Landes sind, erlegt werden mussen. Auch soll kein Verboth, weder auf die Ein- noch Ausfuhr der oesterreichishen, oder nordamerikanischen Grund- oder

from the ports of the United States, or to or from the ports of the dominions of Austria, which shall not equally extend to all other Nations.

ARTICLE VI.

All kind of merchandise and articles of commerce, either the produce of the soil or of the industry of the United States of America, or of any other country, which may be lawfully exported, or re-exported from the ports of the said United States, in national vessels, may also be exported, or re-exported therefrom in Austrian vessels, without paying other, or higher duties or charges of whatever kind or denomination, levied in the name or to the profit of the Government, the local Authorities, or of any private establishments whatsoever, than if the same merchandise or produce had been exported or re-exported, in vessels of the United States of America.

An exact reciprocity shall be observed in the ports of the dominions of Austria, so that all kind of merchandise and articles of commerce either the produce

Industrie-Erzeugnisse, von oder nach den oesterreichischen Häfen, oder von und nach den Häfen der Vereinigten Staaten gelegt werden, wenn solches nicht zugleich auf dasselbe Erzeugniss anderer Länder ausgedehnt wird.

ART: VI.

Alle Gattungen Waaren und Handels-Artikel, solche mögen nun Grund oder Industrie Erzeugnisse der Vereinigten Staaten von America, oder irgend eines andern Landes, die gesetzlich von den nordamerikanischen Häfen, in national Fahrzeugen ausgeführt oder wieder ausgeführt werden können gleichfalls von oesterreichischen Fahrzeugen ausgeführt or wieder ausgeführt werden dürfen, ohne andere oder höhere Zölle oder Abgaben aller Art zu entrichten, Sie mögen unter was immer für Benennung im Nahmen und zum Vortheile der Regierung, der Orts Behörden, oder irgend einer Privat Anstalt erhoben werden, als diejenigen, welche dieselben Waaren oder Erzeugnisse zu bezahlen hätten, wenn Sie in Fahrzeugen der Vereinigten Staaten von Nord Amerika ausgeführt, oder wieder ausgeführt würden.

Eine vollkommne Reciprocität soll in dieser Rücksicht in den Häfen der oesterreichischen Monarchie beobachtet werden, so zwar dass alle Gattungen Waaren

of the soil or of the industry of the said dominions of Austria, or of any other country, which may be lawfully exported or re-exported, from Austrian ports, in national vessels, may also be exported or re-exported therefrom, in vessels of the United States of America, without paying other or higher duties or charges, of whatever kind or denomination, levied in the name or to the profit of the Government, the local Authorities, or of any private establishments whatsoever, than if the same merchandise or produce had been exported, or re-exported, in Austrian vessels.

And the same bounties and drawbacks shall be allowed, whether such exportation or re-exportation be made in vessels of the one Party, or of the other.

Article VII.

It is expressly understood and agreed that the coastwise navigation of both the Contracting Parties, is altogether excepted from the operation of this Treaty, and of every Article thereof.

und Handels-Artikel, solche mögen nun Grund oder Industrie-Erzeugnisse der Dominien Seiner K: K. Apostolishen Majestät, oder irgend eines andern Landes seyn, welche gesetzlich von den oesterreichischen Häfen in national Schiffen ausgefuhrt, oder wieder ausgeführt werden können dürfen auch in Schiffen der Vereinigten Staaten ausgeführt oder wieder ausgeführt werden, ohne andere oder höhere Zölle oder Abgaben aller Art zu entrichten, Sie mögen unter was immer für Benennung im Nahmen, und zum Vortheil der Regierung der Orts-Obrigkeiten, oder irgend einer Privat Anstalt erhoben werden, als diejenigen, welche dieselben Waaren oder Erzeugnisse zu bezahlen hätten, wenn Sie in oesterreichischen Schiffen ausgeführt, oder wieder ausgeführt würden.

Eben so sollen dieselben Prämien und Rückgaben von Zöllen bei Gelegenheit einer solchen Ausfuhr oder Wiederausfuhr erlaubt werden, Sie mag nun in Fahrzeugen der einen oder der andern Nation gemacht werden.

Art: VII.

Es ist ausdrücklich verstanden und bestimmt, dass die Küsten-Schiffahrt der beiden contrahirenden Mächte gänzlich von aller Wirkung dieses Tractats, und jedes Artikels desselben ausgeschlossen bleibt.

ARTICLE VIII.

No priority or preference shall be given, directly, or indirectly, by either of the Contracting Parties, nor by any company, corporation or Agent, acting on their behalf or under their authority, in the purchase of any article of commerce, lawfully imported, on account of, or in reference to the character of the vessel, whether it be of the one Party or of the other, in which such article was imported, it being the true intent and meaning of the Contracting Parties that no distinction or difference whatever shall be made in this respect.

ART: VIII.

Keine der contrahirenden Mæchte soll weder selbst, noch durch irgend eine unter ihrer Vollmacht, und zu ihren Behuf handelnde Privat- oder privilegirte Gesellschaft, oder Agenten, im Ankauf eines gesetzlich eingefuhrten Handels-Artikels irgend einen Vorzug, oder sonstige Priorität, wegen oder in Rücksicht des Characters des Schiffes zugestehen, das Schiff, in welchem der Artikel eingefürht wurde mag nun der einen oder der andern Partei zugehören. Indem es der ausdrückliche Wunsch, und die Absicht der beiden contrahirenden Mächte ist, dass kein Unterschied und keine Distinction, von was immer für Art in dieser Hinsicht gemacht werde.

ARTICLE IX.

If either Party shall hereafter grant to any other nation any particular favor in navigation or commerce, it shall immediately become common to the other Party, freely, where it is freely granted to such other nation, or on yielding the same compensation, when the grant is conditional.

ART[1]: IX.

Wenn immer in der Folge eine der beiden contrahirenden Mächte, eine besondere Begünstigung in der Schiffahrt oder im Handels-Verkehr einer andern Nation zugestehen sollte, so soll die andere Partei alsogleich derselben theilhaft werden, und zwar unentgeltlich, wenn Sie der andern Nation unentgeltlich bewilligt wurde, oder für dieselbe Entgeltung, wenn die Bewilligung bedingungsweise gemacht wurde.

ARTICLE X.

The two Contracting Parties hereby reciprocally grant to each other, the liberty of having, each

ART: X

Die beiden contrahirenden Mächte gestehen sich hiemit wechselseitig das Recht zu, in

in the ports of the other, Consuls, Vice-Consuls, Agents and Commissaries of their own appointment, who shall enjoy the same privileges and powers as those of the most favored nations. But if any such Consuls shall exercise commerce, they shall be subjected to the same laws and usages to which the private individuals of their nation are subject in the same place, in respect of their commercial transactions.

Article XI.

The Citizens or Subjects of each Party shall have power to dispose of their personal goods, within the jurisdiction of the other, by testament, donation, or otherwise; and their representatives, being citizens or subjects of the other Party, shall succeed to their personal goods, whether by testament, or *ab intestato*, and may take possession thereof, either by themselves or by others acting for them, and dispose of the same at their will, paying such dues, taxes or charges, only, as the inhabitants of the country wherein the said goods are shall be subject to pay in like cases. And in case of the absence of the representative, such care shall be taken of the said goods, as would be taken of the goods of a native in like case, until the lawful owner may take measures for re-

den Handelsplätzen des andern Staats Consule, Vice-Consule, Consular-Agenten und Commissäre aufzustellen, welche in Hinsicht ihrer Gerechtsame, Vorzüge und Freiheiten, mit jenem der meist-begunstigsten Nation ganz gleichgestellt werden sollen. Sollten jedoch Consule einen Handel treiben, so sollen Sie in Rücksicht ihrer Handelsgeschäfte denselben Gebräuchen und Gesetzen unterworfen bleiben, welche die Privat Einwohner ihrer Nation, die in denseben Platze wohnen, unterworfen sind.

Art: XI.

Die Unterthanen und Bürger jeder der contrahirenden Mächte, sollen das Recht haben, von ihrem persönlichen Vermögen, das Sie unter der Gerichtsbarkeit der Anderen besitzen, Kraft eines Testamentes, durch Schenkung, oder auf irgend eine andere Weise zu disponiren, und ihre Representanten, wenn sie Unterthanen oder Burger der andern Partei sind, sollen das Recht der Erbfolge in Hinsicht des persönlichen Vermögens, sowohl kraft eines Testaments als auch *ab intestato* geniessen, von denselben entweder Selbst oder durch einen Bevollmächtigten Besitz nehmen, und nach Wilkühr darüber schalten dürfen, wofür Sie bloss solche Abgaben oder Taxen zahlen sollen, als die Einwohner des Landes, in welchem das genannte Vermögen sich befindet, in einem

ceiving them. And if any question should arise among several claimants, to which of them said goods belong, the same shall be decided finally by the laws and Judges of the land wherein the said goods are. But this Article shall not derogate, in any manner, from the force of the laws already published, or hereafter to be published by His Majesty the Emperor of Austria, to prevent the emigration of his Subjects.

gleichen Falle zu zahlen hätten. Und im Falle der Representant abwesend wäre, so soll das Vermögen mit derselben Sorgfalt aufbewahrt werden, als in einem gleichen Falle, ein solches Vermögen für einen Einwohner des Landes aufbewahrt zu werden pflegt, bis der rechtmässige Eigenthümer, Massregeln für dessen Beziehung treffen kann. Und wenn die Frage sich erheben sollte, welchem von mehreren Individuen, die auf die Erbfolge Ansprüche machen, dieselbe zugehöre, so soll diese Frage von den Tribunalen, und nach den Gesetzen des Landes entschieden werden, in welchen das Vermögen sich befindet. Dieser Artikel soll jedoch auf keine Weise, der Kraft der schon bestehenden oder in der Zukunft von Seiner K. K: Apostolischen Majestæt zu erlassenden Gesetze, die zur Absicht haben, der Auswanderung Seiner Unterthanen vorzubeugen, den geringsten Eintrag thun.

ARTICLE XII.

The present Treaty shall continue in force for ten years, counting from the day of the exchange of the Ratifications; and if twelve months before the expiration of that period, neither of the High Contracting Parties shall have announced by an official notification to the other, its intention to arrest the operation of said Treaty, it shall remain binding for one year beyond that

ART: XII.

Gegenwärtiger Handels- und Schiffahrts Vertrag soll vom Tage der Auswechslung der Ratifications-Urkunde zehn Jahre in Wirksamkeit bleiben. Doch erlischt selber nach Verlauf dieses Zeitraums nur in dem Fall, wenn er von dem einen oder dem andern Theile zwölf Monate früher aufgekündiget wurde. Geschieht keine Aufkündigung zu der bestimmten Frist, so dauert der Vertrag auf

time, and so on, until the expiration of the twelve months which will follow a similar notification whatever the time at which it may take place.

ARTICLE XIII.

This Treaty shall be approved and ratified by the President of the United States, by and with the advice and consent of the Senate thereof; and by His Majesty the Emperor of Austria; and the Ratifications shall be exchanged in the City of Washington, within twelve months from the date of the signature hereof, or sooner, if possible.

In faith whereof the respective Plenipotentiaries have signed and sealed this Treaty, both in the English and German languages, declaring, however, that, it having been originally composed in the former, the English version is to decide the interpretation, should any difference in regard to it unfortunately arise.

Done in triplicate, at Washington, this twenty seventh day of August, in the year of Our Lord one thousand eight hundred and twenty nine.

[Seal] M. VAN BUREN

[Seal]

ALʸ FREYHERR VON LEDERER

unbestimmte Zeit fort, bis eine der contrahirenden Mächte ihn aufkündiget, wo sodann derselbe zwölf Monate nach erfolgter Aufkündigung aufzuhören hat, wenn immer diese Aufkündigung geschehen sollte.

ART: XIII.

Dieser Vertrag soll von den Presidenten der Vereinigten Staaten von Amerika, nach und mit der Zustimmung des Senats, und von Seiner Majestæt des Kaysers von Oesterreich genehmigt und ratifizirt werden, und die Ratifications-Urkunden sollen in Washington zwölf Monate nach dem Datum des Vertrags, oder wo möglich noch früher ausgewechselt werden.

Zu Urkund dessen haben die Bevollmächtigten dieses Instrument sowohl in der englischen als in der deutschen Sprache unterzeichnet und besiegelt jedoch mit der Erklärung, dass, indem dieser Vertrag ursprünglich in der englischen Sprache verfasst wurde, der englishe Text zur Richtschnur dienen soll wenn unglücklicher weise irgend ein Zweifel über dessen Auslegung sich erheben sollte.

So geschehen in Triplicat zu Washington am Sieben und zwanzigsten August im Jahre des Herrn Eintausend achthundert und neun und zwanzig.

[Seal] M. VAN BUREN

[Seal] L: BARON DE LEDERER

NOTES

In the final clause of this treaty is the statement that it was "done in triplicate." Presumably two originals were delivered to the Austrian Plenipotentiary, as the treaty was signed at Washington and only one original is in the treaty file. That original is written in English and German, with the English text on the left pages. It is to be observed, however, that in the attestation clause it is declared "that, it having been originally composed in the former, the English version is to decide the interpretation, should any difference in regard to it unfortunately arise." In both texts of that signed original the United States is named first throughout, and the signature of Secretary of State Van Buren precedes that of the Austrian Plenipotentiary at the end of each text.

The treaty file is complete, including the attested resolutions of the Senate of February 10, 1830 (Executive Journal, IV, 56), and February 3, 1831 (*ibid.*, 151). Various papers in the file are attached together; with the original treaty are the two attested Senate resolutions; those combined documents are attached to the duplicate United States instrument of ratification of February 11, 1830, which lacks the imprint of the Great Seal; and all the foregoing documents are embodied in the original proclamation of February 10, 1831. That proclamation includes, for the text of the treaty, a copy of the Senate print, which contains the English text only; and the proclamation as printed likewise includes the English only (House Document No. 129, 21st Congress, 2d session, serial 209).

The time allowed for the exchange of ratifications (Article 13) was twelve months from the date of signature or, in other words, until August 27, 1830. There was no delay in the ratification on either part; but the instrument of ratification on the part of the Emperor of Austria did not reach New York until September 8, 1830, there having been "a detention of that Document at the Austrian Embassy in London, occasioned by unavoidable events" (D. S., 1 Notes from the Austrian Legation, September 9, 1830, January 23, 1831).

In such case various methods of procedure have been adopted. At times an additional article to the treaty, extending the time for the exchange of ratifications, has been drawn up and signed, as in the case of the Treaty of Limits of January 12, 1828, with Mexico (Document 60); or, as in the case of the treaty of May 1, 1828, with Prussia (Document 62), the treaty itself may again be submitted to the Senate and a resolution of advice and consent to the treaty and also to the belated exchange of ratifications be given. In the present case the treaty had already been ratified by the United States, and President Jackson submitted to the Senate merely the question of the exchange of ratifications after the expiration of the time limited. The presidential message of January 26, 1831 (Executive Journal, IV, 146–47), reads as follows:

In pursuance of the advice and consent of the Senate as expressed in their resolution of the 10th February, 1830, the treaty of commerce and navigation

between the United States and Austria, concluded in this city on the 27th of August, 1829, was duly ratified by this Government on the 11th day of the same month of February; but the treaty itself containing a stipulation that the ratifications of the two parties to it should be exchanged within twelve months from the date of its signature, and that of the Austrian Government not having been received here till after the expiration of the time limited, I have not thought myself at liberty, under these circumstances, without the additional advice and consent of the Senate, to authorize that ceremony on the part of this Government. Information having been received at the Department of State from the Austrian representative in the United States that he is prepared to proceed to the exchange of the ratifications of his Government for that of this, the question is therefore submitted to the Senate for their advice and consent upon the occasion.

The Senate thereafter. on February 3, agreed to the following resolution (*ibid.*, 151):

Resolved (two-thirds of the Senators present concurring), That the Senate do advise and consent that the President of the United States be authorized to exchange the ratifications of the treaty of commerce and navigation with Austria, concluded at Washington the 27th of August, 1829, notwithstanding the expiration of the time designated in the said treaty for the exchange of the ratifications thereof.

Note was duly made of the matter in the certificate of the exchange of ratifications of February 10, 1831, which is in the following form:

We, the Undersigned, Martin Van Buren, Secretary of State of the United States of America, and Lewis, Baron de Lederer, Consul General of His Majesty the Emperor of Austria, in the said United States; do hereby certify that the Ratifications of the Treaty of Commerce and Navigation signed at Washington on the 27th day of August 1829, between the United States and His said Majesty have, this day, with all suitable solemnities and after due comparison each with the other, been exchanged by us; the Senate of the United States, by their Resolution of the 3d instant, and the Government of His Majesty the Emperor of Austria, having consented to such exchange, notwithstanding the expiration of the term within which, by a stipulation in the said Treaty, it was to have taken place.
In witness whereof we have signed this Act in duplicate, and affixed our respective Seals at Washington the 10th day of February 1831.

[Seal]   M. Van Buren
[Seal]   L. Baron de Lederer

The Austrian instrument of ratification contains the treaty text in both languages, the German in the left columns; and in both texts the Emperor of Austria is named first throughout. The document itself is written in Latin, which was then used as a language of diplomacy by the Government of Austria.

It appears that no accompanying papers were sent to the Senate with the presidential message of December 14, 1829, transmitting this treaty (Executive Journal, IV, 28).

The proclamation of this treaty was communicated to Congress with the presidential message of March 2, 1831 (Richardson, II, 542; House Document No. 129, 21st Congress, 2d session, serial 209).

The Full Powers

When the negotiations on the part of the Austrian Government were opened by Baron de Lederer, then Consul and later Consul

General of Austria, his note to Secretary of State Clay under date of August 31, 1828 (D. S., 1 Notes from the Austrian Legation, endorsed as received on July 31, 1828), enclosed a copy of his full power from the Emperor of Austria, written in Latin, dated March 18, 1828, and reading in translation as follows:

We, Francis I, by the favor of divine grace Emperor of Austria, King of Jerusalem, of Hungary, of Bohemia, of Lombardy and Venetia, of Dalmatia, of Croatia, of Slavonia, of Galicia, and of Lodomeria, Archduke of Austria, Duke of Lorraine, of Salzburg, of Styria, of Carinthia, of Carniola, of Upper and Lower Silesia, Grand Prince of Transylvania, Margrave of Moravia, Count of Habsburg and of Tyrol, etc., do, by the tenor of these presents, make known and declare to all and singular whom it may concern:

Since the Government of the Union of Free States of North America, by means of a declaration made by the Secretary of State for Foreign Affairs on the 20th day of December in the year 1825, has expressed its ready disposition to conclude with the Austrian Empire a convention of commerce and navigation, and We are led by an earnest desire, by means of a treaty based on the principle of perfect reciprocity, to strengthen the bonds of friendship flourishing between the two states and to establish and promote mutual commerce and navigation between their respective domains and subjects, with equitable consideration for the advantage of both parties:

The matter having been duly considered, We have determined to proceed to the conclusion of a solemn convention of commerce and navigation with the Government of the Union of Free States of North America. To that end We do furnish Our Consul, resident at New York, Lewis, Baron de Lederer, with the necessary instructions, and do confer upon him, by virtue of the present mandate, full authority to stipulate and to sign the terms of the said convention of commerce and navigation with the plenipotentiary or plenipotentiaries designated to this end by the President of the Union of Free States of North America, after negotiation with them, and We pledge Our imperial and royal word that We shall hold as wholly valid and acceptable all those things which Our aforesaid Plenipotentiary shall have done, concluded, and signed with the plenipotentiary or plenipotentiaries of the aforesaid President within the limits of the mandates.

In witness whereof We have signed with Our own hand this present instrument of Our full power and have ordered it to be confirmed by the affixing of Our imperial royal seal. Given in Our imperial city, Vienna, in Austria, on the eighteenth day of the month of March in the year one thousand eight hundred and twenty-eight, and of Our reign the thirty-seventh.

FRANCIS I [Seal]
PRINCE METTERNICH

By the special command of His Sacred Imperial and Royal Apostolic Majesty:
IGNATIUS BRENNER OF FELSACH, *Knight*

The negotiations then commenced had been suggested in a note of Secretary of State Clay of December 20, 1825 (D. S., 3 Notes to Foreign Legations, 245), and were concluded by his successor, Secretary of State Van Buren. Indeed, the treaty, although not signed until August 27, 1829, had more than eight months earlier "been prepared for signature by the Secretary of State and by the Baron de Lederer, intrusted with full powers of the Austrian Government" (Richardson, II, 409, message of December 2, 1828). Accordingly, two full powers were issued by this Government for the negotiation and signature of this treaty, each of them being in customary form. The first, to Secretary of State Clay, was dated October 24, 1828, and the second, to Secretary of State Van Buren, was dated August 11, 1829 (D. S., 2 Credences, 95, 128).

The first diplomatic representative of the United States at the Court of Austria was Henry A. Muhlenberg, of Pennsylvania, commissioned Envoy Extraordinary and Minister Plenipotentiary on February 8, 1838 (see the presidential message of December 5, 1837, Richardson, III, 373, 375).

DISCRIMINATING DUTIES

During the negotiations for this treaty, this Government was informed by a note of May 7, 1829 (D. S., 1 Notes from the Austrian Legation), that in respect of vessels of the United States "the discriminating duties levied . . . in the Austrian ports, are provisionally to cease from the first of January 1829." In his reply of May 11 (D. S., 4 Notes to Foreign Legations, 183–84) Secretary of State Van Buren said that this arrangement would "be met by a reciprocal arrangement, on the part of this Government, with respect to Austrian Vessels, in the ports of the United States, by a Proclamation, which he [the President] has directed to be prepared for that purpose, and which will be issued with all convenient despatch."

The promised proclamation under the act of January 7, 1824 (4 Statutes at Large, 2–3), was duly issued on the same day (*ibid.*, 816) and was followed by another of June 3, 1829 (*ibid.*, 814), under the act of May 24, 1828 (*ibid.*, 308–9).

THE GERMANIC CONFEDERATION

For some comments on the Germanic Confederation (1815–66), of which Austria was a member, see the notes to the convention of December 20, 1827, with the Hanseatic Republics (Document 59).

56006°—33——35

67

COLOMBIA : NOVEMBER 25, 1829

Convention for Adjusting Certain Claims, signed at Bogotá November 25, 1829. Original in English and Spanish.
Not subject to ratification by the United States. Ratified by Colombia February 5, 1830. Not proclaimed.

On this twenty fifth day of November in the year of our Lord One thousand eight hundred and twenty nine, the Minister Plenipotentiary of the United States of America and the Secretary of State and Foreign Relations of the Republic of Colombia, having met according to previous arrangement, for the purpose of adjusting certain claims, pending on the part of the said United States; after a due consideration of all the points relative to them, agreed to the following articles.

ARTICLE 1ST. It being agreed, that in consequence of an error committed in the office of the Department of State of the United States, the whole sum, to which the owners of the Brig Josephine and her cargo, or their assignees, were entitled, was not included in a Convention [1] concluded in this City of Bogotá on the sixteenth day of March, One thousand Eight hundred & twenty

Bogotá hoy día veinte y cinco de Noviembre del año del Señor, mil ochocientos veinte y nueve, habiendose reunido previa invitacion, el Ministro plenipotenciario de los Estados Unidos de America y el Secretario de estado y relaciones esteriores de la Republica de Colombia, con el fin de arreglar ciertos reclamos pendientes de dichos Estados Unidos, convinieron despues de la debida consideracion de todos los puntos relativos á los espresados reclamos en los articulos siguientes.

ARTICULO 1º Habiendose acreditado que por una equivocacion padecida en el Ministerio de estado de los Estados Unidos no se incluyó en el convenio[1] celebrado en esta ciudad de Bogotá el diez y seis de marzo de mil ochocientos veinte y cinco toda la suma á que eran acreedores los dueños del buque y cargamento del Bergantin Josefina, se abonará ahora a los propietarios ó á sus

---

[1] Document 48.

five, there is now allowed to said owners or their Assignees, the sum of Twenty thousand two hundred and fifty dollars, the amount then omitted, on account of loss of profit, injuries & damages; and this sum of Twenty thousand Two hundred and fifty dollars shall bear interest as stipulated in the said Convention, at the rate of six per centum per annum; to be calculated from the twenty seventh day of January, One thousand Eight hundred and nineteen, to the sixteenth day of March, One thousand eight hundred and twenty five, the date of the said Convention.

ARTICLE 2D. There shall be allowed also, to the owners of the Schooner Ranger or their assignees, for said vessel and part of the cargo which were confiscated, in contravention of the sixteenth article of the treaty between the United States and Colombia, for loss of profit, injuries and damages, the sum of Five thousand One hundred and thirteen Dollars 59^{100} with interest, at the rate of six per centum per annum, to be calculated from the second day of August, One thousand eight hundred and twenty five, until paid.

ARTICLE 3D. Any final agreement in relation to the claim, pending in the case of the Brig

sindicos (assignees) la cantidad de veinte mil doscientos cincuenta pesos a que ascienden la que dejo entonces de abonarseles y la perdida de ganancias, daños y perjuicios; y de esta suma de veinte mil doscientos cincuenta pesos se satisfará conforme á lo estipulado en aquel convenio el interes de un seis por ciento anual desde veinte y siete de enero de mil ochocientos diez y nueve hasta diez y seis de marzo de mil ochocientos veinte y cinco que es la fecha del mismo convenio.

ARTICULO 2° Se abonará igualmente á los propietarios ó sus Sindicos (Assignees) de la Goleta Ranger por el valor del buque y parte del cargamento confiscados en contravencion de lo estipulado en el articulo diez y seis del tratado entre los Estados Unidos y Colombia por perdida de ganancias, daños y perjuicios la cantidad de cinco mil ciento trece pesos cincuenta y nueve centavos con el interes de un seis por ciento desde el dos de agosto de mil ochocientos veinte y cinco hasta que les sea satisfecha.

ART$^\circ$ 3° Se suspende el convenio sobre el reclamo pendiente del Bergantin Morris hasta que se

Morris is suspended, until further information which is wanted and has been applied for, can be obtained.

ARTICLE 4TH. The sums to be paid respectively to the owners of the Brig Josephine and the Schooner Ranger, or to their assignees, shall be paid within six months; and the persons interested shall empower an Agent in this City, who may enter into such arrangements with the Minister of Finance, as may be necessary for their final adjustment and discharge.

ARTICLE 5TH. The Government of Colombia reserves to itself, its rights & actions, against any person or persons, whose irregular conduct, may have been the cause of the claims just settled.

ARTICLE 6TH. This Convention is to be submitted to His Excellency the Liberator President, for his approbation, without which, it shall not be executed.

ESTANISLAO VERGARA

T P MOORE In sighning this convention it is understood that I reserve to the owners of the Brig Josephine or their Assignees, the right of claiming of the Columbian Government, at any time hereafter any additional interest to which they may think themselves entitled on the sum herein agreed to be paid them

hayan recibido informes y datos que faltan y ya se han pedido.

ARTº 4º Las sumas correspondientes á los propietarios ó sus sindicos (Assignees) del bergantin Josefina y goleta Ranger se pagarán dentro de seis meses. Los interesados instruirán un apoderado en esta ciudad, que se entienda con el Señor Ministro de Hacienda sobre el pago y terminos en que deba verificarse.

ARTº 5º El Gobierno de Colombia se reserva sus derechos y acciones contra cualquiera persona ó personas, cuya conducta irregular haya sido causa de los reclamos que acaban de arreglarse.

ARTº 6º Este convenio queda sugeto á la aprobacion de S. E. el Libertador Presidente sin la cual no se pondrá en ejecucion

ESTANISLAO VERGARA

T P MOORE In sighning this convention it is understood that I reserve to the owners of the Brig Josephine or their assignees the right of claiming of the Columbian Government at any time hereafter any additional interest to which they may think themselves entitled on the sum herein agreed to be paid them.

NOTES

The original of this agreement, which is called a convention, is in D. S., 6 Despatches, Colombia, as an enclosure to despatch No. 9 of Thomas P. Moore, Minister at Bogotá, of November 28, 1829, from which the following is extracted:

I have the honor to inform you, that on the 25th instant, I concluded an arrangement with the Colombian Government, by which it undertakes to indemnify to a certain extent, the claimants in the cases of the Josephine & Ranger. The Convention, signed by the Minister of Foreign Relations and myself, one original in the English, and the other in the Spanish language, is herewith transmitted.

I have not succeeded in getting the claim, on account of the Josephine, allowed to the full extent. The Council of Government resisted the payment of any interest, later than the date of the agreement (the 16th March 1825) between Mr. Anderson and Mr. Gual [Document 48]. They contend, that the Government was at that time, willing and prepared to pay the whole amount, and its not having done so, being wholly imputable to an error, committed on the part of the Govt. of the United States, they consider any demand for interest, subsequently accruing, as unjust; and allege in support of this opinion, that the original convention of the 16th of March 1825, was concluded, in a spirit of amity and compromise, and not in consequence of any acknowledged obligation on the part of this Government, to indemnify the claimants.

Under these circumstances, I have thought it advisable to adjust those claims, as far as practicable; reserving as you will perceive, to those interested in the Josephine, the right of presenting a demand for additional interest, at any future period; though I am apprehensive, that such a demand will never be very successfully urged. Taking into consideration the instability of the government, and the deranged condition of the Treasury, I have effected as much perhaps, as could be reasonably expected. The present conjuncture is exceedingly unpropitious, to the liquidation of claims of any kind, and in this respect, no improvement can be expected, until the country becomes tranquil, and until its fiscal operations are conducted with more energy and system than at present.

Any further negotiation in regard to the Brig Morris has been suspended, until the Government can procure some explanations from the tribunal at Caracas, which took cognizance of the case, and which are conceived to be necessary, to elucidate some parts of the proceedings. I have reason to believe, that the claim will be ultimately allowed, and that the principle of payment, adopted in the other cases, will be applied to this.

The original document, with which the texts here printed have been collated, is in two papers, in English and Spanish respectively.

This convention is another early instance of an agreement adjusting claims of American citizens against another country, which, like the convention of March 16, 1825 (Document 48), was deemed not to require ratification on the part of the United States, which was not submitted to the Senate, and which was not proclaimed. Indeed, the text of the convention does not appear heretofore to have been printed, although it is mentioned by at least two authorities (Moore, Digest, V, 560; Wriston, Executive Agents in American Foreign Relations, 643). There is no mention of full powers in the convention; Moore, however, had a full power in customary form which included authority "to agree, treat consult and negotiate of and concerning general Commerce, and Claims of the Citizens of the two Countries respectively upon the Governments of Colombia, and the United States, and all matters and subjects connected therewith" (D. S., 2 Credences, 109, June 9, 1829).

It is to be observed, however, that in Article 6 of the convention is the provision that it should be submitted to the Liberator President of the Republic of Colombia "for his approbation."

As an enclosure to despatch No. 12, of February 6, 1830, there was transmitted by the Minister at Bogotá "a copy of a note of the Minister of Foreign Relations, advising me, that President Bolivar has approved the Convention of the 25th of November last, recognising certain claims of the citizens of the United States and providing for their payment" (D. S., 6 Despatches, Colombia). That copy which was enclosed is as follows (translation):

BOGOTÁ, *February 5, 1830*

HONORABLE THOMAS P. MOORE
  Envoy Extraordinary and Minister Plenipotentiary of the United States of America near the Government of Colombia

SIR: I have the honor to communicate to Your Excellency that the Liberator President has approved the convention regarding the claims which have been pending of certain citizens of the United States of America and has communicated the necessary instructions to the Minister of the Treasury in order that the stipulation in Article 4 of the said convention may be fulfilled.

With perfect respect and distinguished consideration, I am Your Excellency's very obedient servant,

DOMINGO CAYECEDO

The following statement regarding the convention was made in the presidential message of January 19, 1830 (Richardson, II, 466–67):

I deem the present a suitable occasion to inform you that shortly after my communication to Congress at the opening of the session dispatches were received from Mr. Moore, the envoy extraordinary and minister plenipotentiary of the United States to Colombia, stating that he had succeeded in obtaining the assent of the council of ministers to the allowance of the claims of our citizens upon that Government in the cases of the brig *Josephine* and her cargo and the schooner *Ranger* and part of her cargo. An official copy of the convention subsequently entered into between Mr. Moore and the secretary of foreign affairs, providing for the final settlement of those claims, has just been received at the Department of State. By an additional article [Article 3] of this convention the claim in the case of the brig *Morris* is suspended until further information is obtained by the Colombian Government from the Court at Carracas; and Mr. Moore anticipates its early and satisfactory adjustment. The convention only waited the ratification of the Liberator President, who was at the time absent from Bogota, to be binding upon the Colombian Government. Although these claims are not, comparatively, of a large amount, yet the prompt and equitable manner in which the application of Mr. Moore in behalf of our injured citizens was met by that Government entitles its conduct to our approbation, and promises well for the future relations of the two countries.

EXECUTION OF THE CONVENTION

The payments due under the convention were not made within six months, pursuant to Article 4. Political changes took place; by 1830 Venezuela and Ecuador had withdrawn from the Republic of Colombia; the obligations of the convention devolved upon the three successor Republics; and some delay in the adjustment of their relations *inter se* was inevitable. By the treaty between New Granada and Venezuela of December 23, 1834 (British and Foreign State Papers, XXIII, 1342–55), to which Ecuador subsequently acceded,

New Granada became responsible for 50 per cent, Venezuela for 28½ per cent, and Ecuador for 21½ per cent, of the debts of the Republic of Colombia; and the United States, while maintaining that the three Republics were "jointly and severally liable," was "willing to exonerate those governments from all further accountability in any particular case, upon payment of their proportions, according to the convention adverted to" (see Moore, Digest, V, 559–61).

Accordingly, the three cases mentioned in this convention—the *Josephine*, the *Ranger*, and the *Morris*—and their settlement became the subject of further negotiations with the three Republics of New Granada, Venezuela, and Ecuador; and years elapsed before the cases were closed.

ARTICLE 1

The case of the brig *Josephine* had been dealt with in the convention with Colombia of March 16, 1825 (Document 48). The amount there agreed on for the vessel and her cargo, and which was duly paid, was $21,750, with interest at 6 per cent from January 27, 1819; but in arriving at the figure then reached there was an error of calculation; in transcribing in the Department of State one of the sums claimed for the cargo it was written as $1,500 instead of $15,000; and the difference of $13,500, with damages of 50 per cent, as agreed on in 1825, made the sum of $20,250 agreed in this convention to be paid with interest from 1819.

A letter to the Secretary of State dated at Philadelphia June 25, 1822, and signed by the presidents of the Marine Insurance Company of Philadelphia and the Insurance Company of the State of Pennsylvania, gave the amount of insurance written by each company on the vessel as $5,000, or $10,000 in all, and on the cargo as $3,000 for the one company and $15,000 for the other, or $18,000 in all. In the copy of that letter which was sent to Richard C. Anderson, Minister to Colombia, $15,000 is written $1,500 (both the original and the copy showing the error are in D. S., Colombian Claims, folder *Josephine*).

It was on the basis of the figures received by Anderson that he had negotiated the settlement of the *Josephine* case in the agreement of March 16, 1825, namely, $10,000 for the vessel, $4,500 for the cargo, and 50 per cent, or $7,250, for damages, making a total of $21,750, plus interest. The settlement under this convention of November 25, 1829, was for the remaining $13,500 for the cargo, with 50 per cent for damages, or $20,250, with interest.

By Article 1, however, that interest ran only to the date of the earlier convention, March 16, 1825; the reservation written with the signature of Thomas P. Moore, Minister to Colombia, who signed this convention on behalf of the United States, left open the question of further interest (see the despatch of November 28, 1829, above quoted).

Thus in the case of the *Josephine* there were left for negotiation with each of the three successor Republics two points: One was the payment

of a share of the amount of approximately $27,700 here fixed, and the other was the item of further interest claimed.

In 1837 the Congress of New Granada made an appropriation of $13,849 and 2½ reals for the proportionate liability of New Granada under this convention in the case of the *Josephine*, and, pursuant to a verbal arrangement made by Robert B. McAfee, then Chargé d'Affaires, the Government of New Granada in 1837 and 1838 paid the sum mentioned in "macuquino" money (a silver currency then depreciated 4 to 6 per cent) in four instalments (D. S., 8 Despatches, Colombia, August 26, 1837; D. S., Colombian Claims, folder *Josephine*, the Secretary of State to the president of the Insurance Company of the State of Pennsylvania, August 28, 1837, and four receipts for the instalments).

By the convention with New Granada of May 16, 1846, that Government agreed to pay $6,569.14 in current money in final settlement of the *Josephine* case. The notes to that convention give some further details regarding that agreement, which was duly performed.

However, a further claim in respect of the *Josephine* was made before the Commission under the convention of February 10, 1864, with the United States of Colombia, but was adjudged not valid (Moore, International Arbitrations, II, 1418, case 23).

The proportionate share of Venezuela of the sum due under this convention in the case of the *Josephine* was duly paid on August 10, 1839, following an appropriation therefor made by the Venezuelan Congress; the amount paid, in specie, was $7,894.11 (D. S., 1 Despatches, Venezuela, Nos. 51 and 52, July 1 and August 6, 1839; letter of Simeon Toby, president of the Insurance Company of the State of Pennsylvania, of May 9, 1845, D. S., Miscellaneous Letters, April–July, 1845).

By the convention with Venezuela of November 16, 1846, that Government agreed to pay $5,453.75 "macuquinos" in final settlement of the *Josephine* case. The notes to that convention give some further details regarding that agreement, which was duly performed.

By Article 1 of the convention with Ecuador of June 15, 1849, the Government of Ecuador agreed to pay in full settlement of its liability in the case of the *Josephine* the sum of $5,955.20 Spanish, with interest at 6 per cent from May 5, 1830. The notes to that convention give some further details regarding that agreement, which was duly performed.

ARTICLE 2

The case of the *Ranger* is thus set forth in a "Statement of the cases of the Brig Josephine Sch: Ranger & Brig Morris" dated at Bogotá February 25, 1829, and "Drawn from the documents in the Archives of the U. S. Legation by Ed: T: Tayloe" (D. S., Colombian Claims, folder *Josephine*):

The Sch: Ranger, Capt. Jos: Seaward, sailed from Portsmouth, Va. in June, 1825, bound to Havana. Her cargo consisted in bread, flour, & gunpowder—the latter an article contraband of war. The Captain was aware of the risk he would encounter in meeting with cruisers under the Colombian Flag; but under an

entire confidence in the faith of the Treaty [Document 47] that had been ratified [proclaimed] at Washington on the 31st of May, between the United States & Colombia, a copy of which he carried with him, he was persuaded, that in fulfilment of the provisions of the 16th art. of that Treaty, he would, in such an event, lose the gunpowder, but that he should be allowed to proceed with his vessel & the balance of the cargo which was not contraband.

On the 2nd. of August, he fell in with the Colombian privateer schooner Represalia, who captured him, put on board a prize master & crew, & ordered her to Puerto Cabello. A few days after her arrival, the vessel & her cargo were condemned as good prizes, in violation of the stipulations of the Treaty, & of the principle that contraband articles do not vitiate those that are not contraband nor the vessel on which they are loaded.

The claimant now demands the value of the vessel & of the bread and flour—articles not contraband of war—with which she was in part laden—and damages, with interest.

The amount of the claim is stated in that paper as follows: for the vessel, $2,875; for the cargo and freight, $534.06; 50 per cent for damages, $1,704.53; total, $5,113.59.

As by Article 2 of this convention the amount due in the case of the *Ranger* was definitely fixed at the above sum of $5,113.59, with 6 per cent interest from August 2, 1825, until paid, the question left pending with the three successor Republics was merely the payment of their proportionate shares thereof.

The proportionate share of New Granada of the amount due in the case of the *Ranger* amounted on March 1, 1839, including interest, to $4,640.58½, of which $4,321 was then paid; and arrangement was made for the payment in September, 1844, of the small balance (D. S., 10 Despatches, Colombia, No. 26, July 26, 1844, and enclosure).

However, a further claim in respect of the *Ranger* was made before the Commission under the convention of February 10, 1864, with the United States of Colombia, but was adjudged not valid (Moore, International Arbitrations, II, 1418, case 45).

The proportionate share of Venezuela of the sum due under this convention in the case of the *Ranger* was duly paid in 1839, following an appropriation therefor made by the Venezuelan Congress. The exact amount paid does not appear (D. S., 1 Despatches, Venezuela, Nos. 51 and 52, July 1 and August 6, 1839).

By Article 2 of the convention with Ecuador of June 15, 1849, the Government of Ecuador agreed to pay, in full settlement of its liability in the case of the *Ranger*, the sum of $1,099.42 Spanish, with interest at 6 per cent from August 2, 1825. The notes to that convention give some further details regarding that agreement, which was duly performed.

ARTICLE 3

The whole case of the brig *Morris* was, by the terms of Article 3, left open. The case became the subject of negotiations with the successor Republics. The facts of the case and its settlement are considered in the notes to the convention with New Granada of November 5, 1844. See also the notes to the convention with Ecuador of February 9, 1850.

Treaty Series No. 66
8 Statutes at Large, 402–7
18 *ibid.*, pt. 2, Public Treaties, 170–73

68

DENMARK : MARCH 28, 1830

*Convention for the Settlement of Claims, signed at Copenhagen March
28, 1830. Original in French and English.
Submitted to the Senate May 28, 1830. (Message of May 27, 1830.)
Resolution of advice and consent May 29, 1830. Ratified by the
United States June 2, 1830. Ratified by Denmark April 2, 1830.
Ratifications exchanged at Washington June 5, 1830. Proclaimed
June 5, 1830.*

Convention entre les Etats-Unis d'Amérique et Sa Majesté, le Roi de Dannemarc. Signée à Copenhague, le 28 mars 1830.

Les Etats-Unis d'Amerique et Sa Majesté le Roi de Dannemarc—désirant également mettre fin aux discussions qui se sont élevées, de part et d'autre, à l'égard des réclamations et prétentions formées par les citoyens des Etats-Unis et les sujets du Dannemarc, ayant pour motif la saisie, détention, condamnation ou confiscation de leurs navires, cargaison ou propriétés quelconques, dans les territoires, ou sous l'autorité des Gouvernemens respectifs,—ont nommé à cet effet, et muni de Leurs pleins-pouvoirs:—à savoir le Président des Etats-Unis d'Amérique, par et avec l'avis et le consentement du Sénat, le Sieur Henri Wheaton, Chargé d'Affaires desdits Etats-Unis près la Cour de Sa

Convention between the United States of America and His Majesty the King of Denmark Signed at Copenhagen the 28th of March 1830.

The United States of America and His Majesty the King of Denmark, being equally desirous of terminating the discussions which have taken place between Them in respect to the claims and pretensions formed by the citizens of the United States and the subjects of Denmark, having for their object the seizure, detention, condemnation or confiscation of their vessels, cargoes or property whatsoever, within the territory or under the authority of the respective Governments,—have named, for this purpose, and furnished with Their full powers; that is to say, the President of the United States of America, by and with the advice and consent of the Senate, Henry Wheaton,

531

Majesté le Roi de Dannemarc, etc.; et Sa Majesté le Roi de Dannemarc, le Sieur Ernest-Henri Comte de Schimmelmann, Chevalier de l'Ordre de l'Eléphant, Grand-Croix de celui du Dannebrog, décoré de la Croix d'argent du même Ordre, Son Ministre intime d'Etat, Chef de Son Département des Affaires étrangères, etc., et le Sieur Paul-Chrétien de Stemann, Chevalier de l'Ordre de l'Eléphant, Grand-Croix de celui du Dannebrog, décoré de la Croix d'argent du même Ordre, Son Ministre intime d'Etat et de Justice, Président de Sa Chancellerie Danoise, etc.; lesquels Plénipotentiaires, après avoir échangé leurs pleins-pouvoirs, qui furent trouvés en bonne et due forme, ont arrêté et conclu les articles suivans.

Article I.

Sa Majesté le Roi de Dannemarc renonce aux indemnités qui pourroient être réclamées du Gouvernement des Etats-Unis d'Amérique, pour des sujets Danois, à cause des saisies, détentions, condamnations ou confiscations de leurs navires, cargaisons ou propriétés quelconques, sous l'autorité du-dit Gouvernement; et Sa Majesté S'engage en outre à payer au-dit Gouvernement la somme de Six-Cent-

Chargé d'Affaires of the said United States at the Court of His Majesty the King of Denmark, etc; and His Majesty the King of Denmark, the Sieur Ernest-Henry Count de Schimmelmann, Knight of the Order of the Elephant, Grand Cross of the Order of Dannebrog decorated with the silver Cross of the same Order, His Minister (:intime:) of State, Chief of His Department of foreign Affairs, etc., and the Sieur Paul-Christian de Stemann, Knight of the Order of the Elephant, Grand-Cross of the Order of Dannebrog, decorated with the silver Cross of the same Order, His Minister (:intime:) of State and of Justice, President of His Danish Chancery, etc; and the said Plenipotentiaries, after having exchanged their full powers, found in good and due form, have agreed upon and concluded the following Articles.

Article I.

His Majesty the King of Denmark renounces the indemnities which might be claimed from the Government of the United States of America, for the subjects of Denmark, on account of the seizure, detention, condemnation or confiscation of their vessels, cargoes or property whatsoever, under the authority of the said Government; and His Majesty engages moreover to pay to the said Government the sum of

Cinquante-Mille Piastres, en faveur des citoyens des Etats-Unis qui ont élevé des réclamations, au sujet de la saisie, détention, condamnation ou confiscation de leurs navires, cargaisons ou propriétés quelconques, par les vaisseaux de guerre et armateurs, ou par les tribunaux du Dannemarc, ou dans les Etats soumis au Sceptre Danois.

ARTICLE II.

L'acquittement de la somme de Six-Cent-Cinquante-Mille Piastres se fera de la manière et aux termes suivans:

Le 31 mars 1831—Deux-Cent-Seize-Mille-Six-Cent-Soixante-Six et deux tiers de Piastres.

Le 30 septembre 1831—Deux-Cent - Seize - Mille - Six - Cent - Soixante-Six, et deux tiers de Piastres.

Le 30 septembre 1832.—Deux-Cent - Seize - Mille - Six - Cent - Soixante-Six, et deux tiers de Piastres.

Au second terme de payement seront ajoutés les intérêts, pour cette somme, et pour celle à payer au dernier terme, de quatre pour cent par an, à compter depuis le terme du premier payement, du 31 mars 1831.

Au troisième terme seront également ajoutés les intérêts, pour cette dernière somme, de

Six-Hundred and Fifty Thousand Spanish milled Dollars, on account of the citizens of the United States, who have preferred claims relating to the seizure, detention, condemnation or confiscation of their vessels cargoes or property whatsoever, by the public and private armed ships, or by the tribunals of Denmark, or in the States subject to the Danish Sceptre.

ARTICLE II.

The payment, of the above sum of Six-Hundred and Fifty Thousand Spanish milled Dollars, shall be made in the times and manner following:

On the 31 March 1831—Two-Hundred and Sixteen-Thousand-Six Hundred and Sixty-Six Dollars and two thirds of a Dollar

On the 30 September 1831—Two-Hundred-and Sixteen-Thousand-Six Hundred-and Sixty-Six Dollars and two thirds of a Dollar.

On the 30 September 1832—Two-Hundred-and Sixteen Thousand-Six Hundred and Sixty-Six Dollars and two thirds of a Dollar.

To the second payment shall be added the interest for that and for the last payment, at four per centum per annum, to be computed from the first payment, on the 31 March 1831

To the third payment shall also be added the interest for that payment, at four per centum per

quatre pour cent par an, à compter du second terme du 30 septembre 1831.

Les sommes ci-dessus spécifiées en Piastres seront acquittées par des lettres de change, à quinze jours de vue, payables à Hambourg, pour le payement desquelles le Gouvernement Danois restera résponsable.

En même temps que le payement du premier terme, du 31 mars 1831, aura lieu, deux obligations, qui corrésponderont aux deux derniers termes ci-dessus-indiqués, pour le capital et les intérêts, seront émises par la Direction de la dette d'Etat et du fond d'amortissement du Dannemarc, à l'ordre du Département des Affaires étrangères du Dannemarc, et transportées au Gouvernement des Etats-Unis. En vertu de ces obligations Sa Majesté le Roi de Dannemarc Se reconnoîtra comme débiteur des sommes point encore payées au Gouvernement des Etats-Unis d'Amérique, et elles seront delivrées à celui ou à ceux qui seront dûment autorisés, à cet effet, par le-dit Gouvernement. Quand l'acquittement de ces obligations s'effectuera, dans les termes qu'elles sont remboursables de la part du Gouvernement Danois, la personne ou les personnes dûment autorisées par le Gouvernement des Etats-Unis pour recevoir le payement stipulé remettront en même temps ces

annum, to be computed from the second payment on the 30 September 1831.

The above sums, thus specified in Spanish milled Dollars, shall be paid in bills of exchange, at fifteen days sight, at Hamburg; for the payment of which the Danish Government shall be responsible.

At the time when the first payment shall be made on the 31 March 1831, two obligations, corresponding to the two last payments to be effected, for the capital and the interest thereof, shall be issued by the Direction for the public debt and the sinking fund of Denmark, to the order of the Department of foreign Affairs of Denmark, and assigned to the Government of the United States. By the said obligations His Majesty the King of Denmark shall acknowledge Himself debtor for the sums not yet paid, to the Government of the United States of America, and the same shall be delivered to such person or persons, as may be authorized to receive the same by the said Government; and when the said obligations are to be discharged according to the tenor thereof, by the Danish Government, the person or persons authorized by the Government of the United States to receive the stipulated payments, shall deliver up the said obligations, with receipts, for the

obligations munies des quittances du-dit Gouvernement.

Article III

Pour déterminer le montant précis et la validité des réclamations des citoyens des Etats-Unis mentionnées dans l'Article I, une Commission, composée de trois citoyens des Etats-Unis, sera nommée par le Président, par et avec l'avis et le consentement du Sénat; ces commissaires s'assembleront à Washington, et, avant que deux ans, à compter du jour de leur première séance, se seront écoulés, ils doivent avoir reçu toutes ces réclamations, et avoir examiné et décidé leur montant et leur validité, d'après les circonstances spéciales de chaque cas, la justice, l'équité et le droit des gens.

Les commissaires prêteront serment, ou donneront des affirmations, à insérer dans le journal de leurs procédés, qu'ils rempliront fidèlement et assidûment leurs devoirs.

En cas de décès, de maladie ou d'absence indispensable d'un des commissaires, sa place sera remplie par la nomination d'un autre commissaire, de la manière susmentionnée, ou, durant les vacances du Sénat, par le Président des Etats-Unis.

Les commissaires seront autorisés à se faire rendre compte et à examiner chaque question rélative à ces réclamations, et à se

amount thereof, from the said Government.

Article III.

To ascertain the full amount and validity of the claims mentioned in Article I. a Board of commissioners, consisting of three citizens of the United States, shall be appointed by the President, by and with the advice and consent of the Senate, who shall meet at Washington, and within the space of two years, from the time of their first meeting, shall receive examine and decide upon the amount and validity of all such claims, according to the merits of the several cases and to justice, equity and the law of nations.

The commissioners shall take an oath or affirmation, to be entered in the journal of their proceedings, for the faithful and diligent discharge of their duties.

In case of the death, sickness or necessary absence of any commissioner, his place may be supplied by the appointment of another commissioner, in the manner before mentioned, or, during the recess of the Senate, by the President of the United States.

The commissioners shall be authorized to hear and examine, on oath, or affirmation, every question relating to such claims,

faire donner, sous serment, ou affirmation, tous les témoignages convenables et authentiques qui les concernent.

Afin de faciliter les travaux de cette Commission, Sa Majesté le Roi de Dannemarc S'engage, lorsque la réquisition en sera faite, outre les documens déjà remis, à faire délivrer, à celui ou à ceux qui seront dûment autorisés, à cet effet, par le Gouvernement des Etats-Unis, tous les actes, documens, papiers de bord, et pièces de procès qui pourroient encore se trouver dans les Archives de la Haute Cour d'Amirauté, ou des Tribunaux de prises du Dannemarc, rélativement à la saisie, détention, condamnation ou confiscation des navires, cargaisons ou propriétés quelconques des citoyens des Etats-Unis d'Amérique, par devant ces tribunaux.

La dite Commission adjugera et fera distribuer entre les différentes parties, dont elle admettra les réclamations, les sommes mentionnées dans l'Article I et II, dans la proportion, et pro rata, à leurs réclamations respectives qui auront été ainsi admises.

Article IV.

Moyennant les rénonciations et payemens mentionnés dans l'Article I et II, de la part de Sa Majesté le Roi de Dannemarc, le Gouvernement des Etats-Unis dé-

and to receive all suitable, authentic testimony concerning the same.

In order to facilitate the proceedings of this Board, His Majesty the King of Denmark engages, when thereunto required, to cause to be delivered to any person or persons, who shall be duly authorized, for that purpose, by the Government of the United States, in addition to the papers already delivered, all the acts, documents, ship's papers and prize proceedings, which may still remain in the Archives of the High-Court of Admiralty or the Prize Tribunals of Denmark, relating to the seizure, detention, condemnation or confiscation of the vessels cargoes or property whatsoever belonging to the citizens of the United States of America before the said tribunals.

The commissioners shall award and cause to be distributed, among the several parties, whose claims shall be allowed by the Board, the sum mentioned in Article I and II, in a rateable proportion to the amount of the respective claims thus allowed.

Article IV.

In consideration of the renunciation and payments mentioned in Article I and II, on the part of His Majesty the King of Denmark, the Government of the United

clare qu'il Se regarde comme entièrement satisfait, non-seulement pour ce qui Le concerne, mais aussi pour ce qui concerne les citoyens des-dits Etats, à raison des réclamations mises en avant jusqu'ici, ou qui pourroient être élevées à l'avenir, ayant pour objet la saisie, détention, condamnation ou confiscation de leurs navires, cargaisons ou propriétés quelconques qui, dans la dernière guerre maritime du Dannemarc, ont eu lieu, sous le pavillon de Dannemarc, ou dans les Etats soumis au Sceptre Danois; et les-dites réclamations seront par conséquent régardées comme définitivement et irrévocablement terminées.

Article V.

L'intention des deux Hautes Parties Contractantes étant uniquement de terminer définitivement et irrévocablement toutes les réclamations qui jusqu'ici ont eu lieu, Elles déclarent expressement, que la présente Convention n'est applicable qu'aux cas désignés, et que n'ayant d'autre but, elle ne saura jamais, de part ou d'autre, dans l'avenir être invoquée comme un précédent, ou comme règle pour le futur.

Article VI.

La présente Convention sera dûment ratifiée par les Hautes Parties Contractantes, et les Ratifications seront échangées à Washington-

States declares Itself entirely satisfied, not only in what concerns the said Government, but also in what concerns the citizens of the said United States, on account of the claims hitherto preferred or which may hereafter be preferred relating to the seizure, detention, condemnation or confiscation of their vessels, cargoes or property whatsoever, which in the last maritime war of Denmark have taken place under the flag of Denmark, or in the States subject to the Danish Scepter; and the said claims shall consequently be regarded as definitively and irrevocably terminated.

Article V.

The intention of the two High Contracting Parties being solely to terminate definitively and irrevocably all the claims, which have hitherto been preferred, They expressly declare, that the present Convention is only applicable to the cases therein mentioned, and having no other object, can never hereafter be invoked, by one party or the other, as a precedent or rule for the future.

Article VI.

The present Convention shall be duly ratified by the High Contracting Parties, and the Ratifications shall be exchanged at

ington, d'ans l'espace de dix mois, ou plutôt si faire se peut.

En foi de quoi, et en vertu de nos pleins-pouvoirs respectifs, nous avons signé la présente Convention, et y fait apposer les Sceaux de nos Armes.

Fait à Copenhague, ce 28me jour de mars 1830.

HENRY WHEATON   [Seal]

Washington, in the space of ten months, or sooner if possible.

In faith thereof, and in virtue of our respective full powers, we have signed the present Convention, and have thereunto set the Seals of our Arms.

Done at Copenhagen, this 28th day of March 1830.

E. H. SCHIMMELMANN   [Seal]
STEMANN   [Seal]

NOTES

This convention was "executed in triplicate" (D. S., 1B Despatches, Denmark, No. 15, April 3, 1830, from Henry Wheaton, then Chargé d'Affaires at Copenhagen). There are two signed originals in the treaty file; in each of them the French text is in the left columns and the English in the right. The one of those two originals with which the text here printed has been collated is that which forms part of the duplicate United States instrument of ratification of June 2, 1830, to which is attached the attested Senate resolution of May 29 (Executive Journal, IV, 115–16). In each of those originals the order of the names of the parties and of the signatures is the same, the United States and its Plenipotentiary coming first throughout.

The instrument of ratification on the part of Denmark is written in Danish and includes the treaty text in both languages, the French in the left columns. In the text there recited the King of Denmark and the Danish Plenipotentiaries have precedence. The certificate of the exchange of ratifications at Washington on June 5, 1830, and the original proclamation of the same date are in customary form. The latter includes both texts of the convention, the French in the left columns, and copies thereof, in similar form, were transmitted to both Houses of Congress with the presidential message of December 10, 1830 (Richardson, II, 530; House Document No. 3, 21st Congress, 2d session, serial 206).

The full power to Henry Wheaton, Chargé d'Affaires at Copenhagen, for the negotiation and signature of this convention, was dated June 8, 1827, and is in customary form (D. S., 2 Credences, 67). Under date of January 12, 1829, Wheaton was officially informed of the appointment of the Danish Plenipotentiaries (D. S., 1B Despatches, Denmark, No. 6, January 31, 1829, enclosure). Nothing further appears regarding the full powers except the statement in the protocol of the conference of August 27, 1829 (*ibid.*, No. 9, October 17, 1829, translation of enclosure): "The Commissioners met, pursuant to agreement, and exchanged their full powers."

The presidential message of May 27, 1830, transmitting this convention to the Senate (Executive Journal, IV, 112), reads as follows:

It is gratifying to me to be able to communicate to the Senate, before the termination of its present session, for its advice and consent as to the ratification of it, a convention just received at the Department of State, between the United States and His Majesty the King of Denmark, which was negotiated on the part of the former by Mr. Henry Wheaton, their chargé d'affaires at the Court of Denmark, and on that of the latter by the Sieurs Henry Count de Schemmelman, his minister of foreign affairs, and Paul Christian de Stemann, president of his chancery, and concluded and signed by these plenipotentiaries at Copenhagen on the 28th of March of the present year.

The convention provides by compromise for the adjustment and payment of indemnities to no inconsiderable amount, long sought from the Government of Denmark by that of the United States in behalf of their citizens who had preferred claims for the same, relating to the seizure, detention, and condemnation or confiscation of their vessels, cargoes, or property by the public armed ships, or by the tribunals of Denmark, or in the states subject to the Danish scepter; and there is every reason to believe, as the Senate will infer from the correspondence which accompanies this communication, that the proposed arrangement will prove entirely satisfactory to them.

The accompanying correspondence appears not to have been printed at the time; according to the Executive Journal of the Senate, no order for printing was made; and the Senate resolution of advice and consent was adopted on the day following the receipt of the convention. Much of the relevant correspondence, however, will be found in House Document No. 249, 22d Congress, 1st session, serial 221.

In his message to Congress of December 6, 1830, President Jackson wrote as follows (Richardson, II, 500, 505):

You are apprised, although the fact has not yet been officially announced to the House of Representatives, that a treaty was in the month of March last concluded between the United States and Denmark, by which $650,000 are secured to our citizens as an indemnity for spoliations upon their commerce in the years 1808, 1809, 1810, and 1811. This treaty was sanctioned by the Senate at the close of its last session, and it now becomes the duty of Congress to pass the necessary laws for the organization of the board of commissioners to distribute the indemnity among the claimants. It is an agreeable circumstance in this adjustment that the terms are in conformity with the previously ascertained views of the claimants themselves, thus removing all pretense for a future agitation of the subject in any form.

THE SOURCE TEXT

There are a number of differences, mostly in punctuation (none in wording), between the two signed originals which are in the treaty file. Those in capitalization, spelling, the use of a symbol for the word "and," and matters of what may be called punctuation style, such as the use of a colon for a semicolon, are hardly worthy of mention. The remaining differences are nearly all cases of commas inserted in one original and omitted in the other, some in the French text and some in the English. None of them seems to be in any way material.

The Claims Settlement

For an account of the origin of the claims settled by this convention, the negotiations preceding it, and the proceedings of the Commissioners under Article 3, appointed pursuant to the act of February 25, 1831 (4 Statutes at Large, 446–47), see Moore, International Arbitrations, V, 4549–73.

The total amount realized from the payments duly made by Denmark under the convention was $670,654.70, including interest, and the total amount of claims allowed by the Commissioners was $2,154,-425 (*ibid.*, 4571). The proceedings of the Commissioners lasted from their first meeting on April 4, 1831, until their adjournment *sine die* on March 28, 1833.

The view of the United States Plenipotentiary, Henry Wheaton, of the settlement, was expressed in his despatch of March 29, 1830 (D. S., 1B Despatches, Denmark, No. 14), as follows:

The Convention will speak for itself, & seems to require little explanation. The amount agreed to be paid by the Danish Government, in addition to the renunciation of all the Claims of Danish subjects, is considerably more than the *minimum* which I was authorized by the general Agent of the Claimants to accept rather than break off the negotiation. [See D. S., 13 Instructions, U. S. Ministers, 81–82, January 13, 1830.]

The sum to be paid under the Convention, together with that received in 1827–8 on account of the seizures at Kiel [about $76,000; D. S., 1B Despatches, Denmark, No. 2, December 22, 1827, and No. 3, March 4, 1828], and the Danish claims now renounced, make altogether an amount exceeding three quarters of a million. In order to present a full view of the whole subject it may be found expedient to send to the Senate my correspondence relating to the cases of the Ariel, Fair-Trader, & Minerva Smyth [i.e., relating to the cargoes of the three vessels detained at Kiel in 1810].

I have not before me sufficient materials from which to form a judgment as to the real amount of the losses unjustly sustained by our citizens from Danish captures. You will find that Mr Erving [George W. Erving, Special Minister to Denmark, 1811–12] in his Correspondence estimates the actual loss at about $1,750,000, reckoning "about thirty five condemnations quite unjust," to use his own expressions. But supposing the real injury to have been considerably greater, the sum now recovered, considering the diminished resources of this exhausted Country, will, I trust, be considered as a tolerable salvage from this calamitous concern.

Treaty Series No. 267
8 Statutes at Large, 408–9
18 *ibid.*, pt. 2, Public Treaties, 583–85

69

TURKEY : MAY 7, 1830

Treaty of Commerce and Navigation (with separate and secret article which was not ratified), signed at Constantinople (Istanbul) May 7, 1830 (14 Zu'lkadah, A. H. 1245). Original in Turkish.
Submitted to the Senate December 9, 1830. (Message of December 10 [?], 1830.) Resolution of advice and consent, excepting the separate and secret article, February 1, 1831. Ratified by the United States February 2, 1831. Ratified by Turkey on or shortly before October 5, 1831. Ratifications exchanged at Constantinople October 5, 1831. Proclaimed February 4, 1832.
A facsimile reproduction of the Turkish text of the treaty, except for the seal, appears opposite page 542. Immediately following this headnote is printed the English translation which was proclaimed, followed by two other translations, French and English in parallel columns, which were also before the Senate. Thereafter is the translation of 1931, with annotations.
For the separate and secret article, see the notes, which follow the translation of 1931.

[Proclaimed translation]

The object of this firm Instrument, and the motive of this writing well drawn up, is that:

No Treaty or diplomatic and official convention, having, heretofore, existed, between the Sublime Porte of perpetual duration, and the United States of America; at this time, in consideration of the desire formerly expressed, and of repeated propositions which have, lately, been renewed by that Power, and in consequence of the wish entertained by the Sublime Porte, to testify to the United States of America, its sentiments of friendship, We the undersigned Commissioner, invested with the high Office of Chief of the Chancery of State, of the Sublime Porte existing forever, having been permitted by His very noble Imperial Majesty, to negotiate and conclude a Treaty, and having thereupon conferred with our friend, the Honorable Charles Rhind, who has come to this Imperial Residence, furnished with full powers, to negotiate settle and conclude, the Articles of a Treaty, separately and jointly, with the other two Commissioners, Commodore Biddle and David Offley, now at Smyrna, Have arranged, agreed upon and concluded, the following articles.

ARTICLE I.

Merchants of the Sublime Porte, whether Mussulmans or Rayahs, going and coming in, the countries, provinces and ports, of the United States of America, or proceeding from one port to another, or from the ports of the United States to those of other countries, shall pay the same duties and other imposts, that are paid by the most favored nations; and they shall not be vexed by the exaction of higher duties; and in travelling by sea and by land, all the privileges and distinctions observed towards the subjects of other Powers, shall serve as a rule, and shall be observed, towards the Merchants and subjects of the Sublime Porte. In like manner, American merchants who shall come to the well defended countries and ports of the Sublime Porte, shall pay the same duties and other imposts, that are paid by merchants of the most favored friendly Powers, and they shall not, in any way, be vexed or molested. On both sides, travelling passports shall be granted.

ARTICLE II.

The Sublime Porte may establish Shahbenders (Consuls) in the United States of America; and the United States may appoint their citizens to be Consuls or Vice-Consuls, at the commercial places in the dominions of the Sublime Porte, where it shall be found needful to superintend the affairs of commerce. These Consuls or Vice-Consuls shall be furnished with Berats or Firmans; they shall enjoy suitable distinction, and shall have necessary aid and protection.

ARTICLE III.

American merchants established in the well-defended states of the Sublime Porte, for purposes of commerce, shall have liberty to employ Semsars (brokers) of any nation or religion, in like manner as merchants of other friendly Powers; and they shall not be disturbed in their affairs, nor shall they be treated, in any way, contrary to established usages. American vessels arriving at, or departing from the ports of the Ottoman Empire, shall not be subjected to greater visit, by the Officers of the Custom-House and the Chancery of the Port, than vessels of the most favored Nations.

ARTICLE IV.

If litigations and disputes should arise, between subjects of the Sublime Porte and citizens of the United States, the parties shall not be heard, nor shall judgment be pronounced, unless the American

Dragoman be present. Causes, in which, the sum may exceed five hundred piastres, shall be submitted to the Sublime Porte, to be decided according to the laws of equity and justice. Citizens of the United States of America, quietly pursuing their commerce, and not being charged or convicted, of any crime or offence, shall not be molested; and even when they may have committed some offence, they shall not be arrested and put in prison, by the local authorities, but they shall be tried by their Minister or Consul, and punished according to their offence, following in this respect, the usage observed towards other Franks.

ARTICLE V.

American merchant vessels that trade to the dominions of the Sublime Porte, may go and come in perfect safety with their own flag; but they shall not take the flag of any other Power, nor shall they grant their flag to the vessels of other Nations and Powers, nor to vessels of Rayahs. The Minister, Consuls and Vice-Consuls of the United States, shall not protect, secretly or publicly, the Rayahs of the Sublime Porte, and they shall never suffer a departure from the principles here laid down, and agreed to, by mutual consent.

ARTICLE VI.

Vessels of war of the two contracting parties, shall observe towards each other, demonstrations of friendship and good intelligence, according to naval usage; and towards merchant vessels they shall exhibit the same kind and courteous manner.

ARTICLE VII.

Merchant vessels of the United States, in like manner as vessels of the most favored nations, shall have liberty to pass the canal of the Imperial Residence, and go and come in the Black sea, either laden or in ballast; and they may be laden with the produce, manufactures and effects, of the Ottoman Empire, excepting such as are prohibited, as well as of their own country.

ARTICLE VIII.

Merchant vessels of two Contracting Parties shall not be forcibly taken, for the shipment of troops, munitions and other objects of war, if the Captains or Proprietors of the vessels, shall be unwilling to freight them.

ARTICLE IX.

If any merchant vessel of either of the contracting parties, should be wrecked, assistance and protection shall be afforded to those of the crew that may be saved; and the merchandise and effects, which it may be possible to save and recover, shall be conveyed to the Consul, nearest to the place of the wreck, to be, by him, delivered to the Proprietors.

CONCLUSION.

The foregoing articles, agreed upon and concluded, between the Riasset (Chancery of State) and the above mentioned Commissioner of the United States, when signed by the other two Commissioners, shall be exchanged. In ten months, from the date of this *Temessuck* or instrument of Treaty, the exchange of the ratifications of the two Powers shall be made, and the articles of this Treaty shall have full force and be strictly observed, by the two Contracting Powers.

Given the 14 day of the moon Zilcaade, and in the year of the Hegira, 1245, corresponding with the 7 day of May of the year 1830, of the Christian Æra.

(Signed)   MOHAMMED HAMED
Reis-ul-Kutab (*Reis Effendi*)

[Other translations before the Senate]

L'objet de cet instrument et le motif de la rédaction de cet écrit est que, comme il n'a pas existé jusqu'à présent aucune sorte de traité et convention officielle et diplomatique entre la Sublime Porte, de perpétuelle durée, et la puissance des Etats-Unis d'Amérique; cette fois-ci, en considération du désir exprimé et des propositions réitérées antérieurement et dernièrement faites par cette puissance, et en conséquence du désir de la Sublime Porte de témoigner ses sentiments d'amitié à la puissance des Etats-Unis d'Amérique, nous, soussigné Commissaire, revêtu du haut rang de	The object of this instrument and the motive for drawing up this writing are that, whereas no treaty or official and diplomatic convention has hitherto existed between the Sublime Porte, of perpetual duration, and the Government of the United States of America; now, in consideration of the desire expressed and the propositions heretofore reiterated and lately renewed by the last-mentioned power, and in consequence of the wish entertained by the Sublime Porte to testify her friendly sentiments towards the Government of the United States of America, we, the under-

Chef du Ministère de la Chancellerie d'Etat de la Sublime Porte à jamais existante, ayant été autorisé par Sa Très Noble Majesté Impériale à traiter et régler cette affaire, ayant conféré à ce sujet avec notre ami l'honorable Commissaire et Plénipotentiaire des Etats-Unis d'Amérique, Charles Rhind, venu à cette Résidence Impériale muni de pleins pouvoirs pour traiter et conclure, en son propre nom ou conjointement avec les deux autres Commissaires, le Commodore Biddle et David Offley, qui sont maintenant à Smyrne, les articles du traité, nous avons entre nous réglé, arrêté, et conclu les articles dont suit la rédaction.

Article Premier

Les négociants Musulmans et rayas de la Sublime Porte, allant et venant dans les pays, provinces, ports, et échelles dépendants des Etats-Unis d'Amérique, ou allant d'une à une autre échelle, ou bien des échelles des Etats-Unis aux échelles d'autres états, payeront les droits de douane et autres droits comme les nations les plus favorisées, et ne seront molestés en exigeant d'eux des droits plus forts; et en voyageant par mer et par terre, tous les privilèges et distinctions qui sont en usage envers les sujets des dites puissances serviront de règle et

signed Commissioner, invested with the high rank of Chief of the Department of the Chancery of State of the ever-subsisting Sublime Porte, being authorized by His Most Noble Imperial Majesty to treat of and conclude that affair, having conferred on that subject with our friend, the Honorable Charles Rhind, Commissioner and Plenipotentiary of the United States of America, who has come to this Imperial Residence provided with full powers to treat and conclude, in his own name or jointly with the other two Commissioners, Commodore Biddle and David Offley, now at Smyrna, the articles of the treaty, we have settled, agreed upon, and concluded the articles of which the following is the tenor.

Article First

Mussulman merchants and rayas of the Sublime Porte, going and coming in the countries, provinces, ports, and seaport towns (*échelles*) in the allegiance of the United States of America, or going from one port to another, or from the ports of the United States to those of other states, shall pay the same customhouse and other duties as the most favored nations, and shall not be molested by the exaction of higher duties from them; and in traveling by sea or by land, all the privileges and distinctions usually granted to the subjects

seront absolument observés envers les sujets Ottomans. De la même manière ce sera pour les Américains. Les négociants Américains qui viendront dans les pays bien gardés, dans les ports et échelles de la Sublime Porte, payeront les mêmes droits de douane ou autres droits que payent les négociants des puissances amies les plus favorisées et ne seront vexés en aucune autre manière que ce soit; et, de part et d'autre, on accordera les documents nécessaires pour voyager.

of said powers will serve as a rule and be strictly observed towards Ottoman subjects. In like manner with regard to Americans; American merchants coming to the well-guarded countries, in the ports and seaport towns of the Sublime Porte, shall pay the same customhouse or other duties as are paid by the merchants of the most favored friendly powers and shall not be molested in any other manner whatever; and the documents necessary to travel shall be granted on either side.

Article Second

Il sera permis à la Sublime Porte d'établir des shehbenders (consuls) dans les pays des Etats-Unis d'Amérique; et, de même, il sera permis aux Etats-Unis d'établir des consuls et vice-consuls de leur nation dans les places de commerce de la Sublime Porte, où le besoin [en] sera démontré, pour soigner les affaires de commerce; et seront, à cet effet, délivré des firmans et bérats (diplômes consulaires), et [ils] jouiront des distinctions dues à leur caractère et de la protection et assistance nécessaires.

Article Second

The Sublime Porte shall be at liberty to establish shahbenders (consuls) in the territories of the United States of America; and, in like manner, the United States shall be at liberty to establish consuls and vice consuls of their nation in the commercial places of the states of the Sublime Porte, where it shall appear necessary, to take care of the affairs of commerce; and for that purpose firmans and berats (consular diplomas) shall be delivered to them, and they shall enjoy all the distinctions due to their character and the necessary aid and protection.

Article Troisième

Les négociants Américains établis dans les états bien gardés de la Sublime Porte pour affaires de commerce, pourront, à l'instar

Article Third

American merchants settled in the well-guarded states of the Sublime Porte for affairs of commerce, may, in the same manner as the

des négociants des susdites nations amies, se servir pour censeaux [1] d'individus de quelque nation et religion que se soit; et ne seront aucunement troublés dans leurs affaires, ni l'on agira envers eux contre les usages établis; et lorsque des bâtiments Américains viendront dans les échelles de l'Empire Ottoman, ainsi qu'à leur départ, ils ne seront visités par les préposés de la douane et de la chancellerie du port (appelée "liman") plus que les bâtiments des susdites nations.

merchants of the aforesaid friendly nations, employ as brokers persons of any nation or religion whatsoever; they shall in no wise be molested in their affairs, nor shall any one act towards them contrary to established usages; and when American vessels shall come into the ports of the Ottoman Empire, as also at their departure, they shall not be visited by the officers of customs or of the chancery of the port (called "liman") otherwise than the vessels of the aforesaid nations.

Article Quatrième

Si entre les rayas et dépendants de la Sublime Porte, et les dépendants des Etats-Unis, il arrivait des différends et des litiges, il ne sera pas accordé audience, et [ils] ne seront pas jugés sans que le drogman Américain y soit présent. Les causes qui excéderont la somme de cinq cent piastres seront portées à la Sublime Porte et y seront jugées d'après le droit et la justice. Les dépendants des Etats-Unis d'Amérique s'occupant tranquillement de leurs affaires de commerce et contre lesquels il n'aura pas été constaté aucun délit, ne pourront être molestés et troublés sans cause légitime; et quand même ils se seraient rendus coupables, ils ne seront arrêtés et mis en prison par les juges et les autorités locales,

Article Fourth

If any difference or litigation should arise between rayas and subjects of the Sublime Porte, and citizens of the United States, no hearing shall be granted, nor shall they be tried, unless the American dragoman be present. All cases exceeding the sum of five hundred piasters shall be carried before the Sublime Porte and shall there be tried according to right and justice. Citizens of the United States of America quietly engaged in their commercial affairs and against whom no offense shall have been proved, shall not be molested or interrupted without legal cause; and, even if guilty, they shall not be arrested or imprisoned by the judges or local authorities, but, as practiced towards other Franks, they shall be punished, in propor-

---

[1] So written as the plural of *censal*.

mais, d'après ce qui est pratiqué à l'égard des autres Francs, ils seront punis, à proportion de leurs délits, par leur ministre ou leurs consuls.

tion to their offenses, by their minister or consuls.

Article Cinquième

Les bâtiments marchands Américains qui vont et viennent pour affaires de commerce dans les états de l'Empire Ottoman pourront aller et venir en toute sûreté avec leur pavillon, et ne prendront et ne feront usage des pavillons d'autres puissances; de même les Etats-Unis n'accorderont leur pavillon aux bâtiments d'autres puissances et nations, ni aux navires des rayas (sujets de la Sublime Porte) et le ministre, les consuls, et vice-consuls d'Amérique ne délivreront des patentes aux sujets de la Sublime Porte et ne les protégeront secrètement ou publiquement, et il ne sera jamais permis de s'écarter d'aucune manière des principes qui ont été de commun accord convenus et établis à ce sujet.

Article Fifth

American merchant vessels going and coming for affairs of commerce in the states of the Ottoman Empire may go and come in full security under their flag, and shall neither take nor use the flags of other nations. In like manner, the United States shall not grant their flag to the vessels of other powers or nations, nor to the vessels of the rayas (subjects of the Sublime Porte); and the minister, consuls, and vice consuls of America shall not deliver any patents to the subjects of the Sublime Porte nor shall protect them either secretly or publicly, nor shall it ever be lawful to deviate, in any manner, from the principles which, with one common accord, have been agreed upon and established in this respect.

Article Sixième

Les bâtiments de guerre des deux états venant à se rencontrer rempliront les uns envers les autres, réciproquement, les égards d'amitié et de convenance établis par les règles de marine; et venant à rencontrer des bâtiments marchands de l'un et de l'autre état, auront envers eux des procédés bons et convenables.

Article Sixth

The ships of war of the two states which may happen to meet shall reciprocally fulfil towards each other the duties of friendship and propriety established by maritime regulations; and, when meeting with merchant vessels of either state, they will observe towards them friendly and suitable proceedings.

Article Septième

Les bâtiments marchands des Etats-Unis, soit sur lest ou bien chargés de produits de leurs pays ou de produits et marchandises non prohibés des pays de l'Empire Ottoman, pourront passer des parages de la Résidence Impériale et aller et venir dans la Mer Noire comme les susdites nations.

Article Seventh

The merchant vessels of the United States, either in ballast or laden with the productions of their countries or with productions and merchandise not prohibited of the countries of the Ottoman Empire, may pass from the waters of the Imperial Residence and go and come in the Black Sea like the aforesaid nations.

Article Huitième

Dès que les capitaines, les propriétaires des bâtiments marchands des deux états ne seraient disposés et contents de noliser leurs bâtiments, il ne sera pas permis de les prendre par force, d'y embarquer des troupes, ou y charger de la poudre, canons, et autres munitions de guerre.

Article Eighth

In case the captains and owners of the merchant vessels of either state should not be disposed or willing to charter their vessels, it shall not be lawful to take them by force, to embark troops therein, or to load them with powder, cannon, or other warlike stores.

Article Neuvième

Si quelque bâtiment marchand des deux états faisait naufrage et venait à se briser, il sera prêté assistance et protection aux personnes de l'équipage qui se seraient sauvées; et les marchandises et effets, quels qu'ils soient, qu'il aura été possible de retirer et recouvrer, on les fera parvenir, tels quels, aux consuls Américains plus proches du lieu du naufrage, pour être remis à qui de droit.

Article Ninth

In case any merchant vessels of the two states should be wrecked or stranded, there shall be given aid and protection to the persons composing the crew who may be saved; and the merchandise and effects, whatever they may be, which it will have been practicable to extricate and recover, shall be sent, untouched, to the American consul nearest the place of shipwreck, to be delivered to whom they may belong.

Conclusion

Les articles ci-dessus énoncés, arrêtés et conclus entre le Ministère du *Riasset* (c'est à dire, de la Chancellerie d'Etat et des Affaires Etrangères) et le Commissaire des Etats-Unis susmentionné, et ensuite signés aussi par les deux Commissaires absents, seront fermement observés et exécutés entre les deux puissances après l'échange des ratifications des puissances contractantes, lequel échange aura lieu, à peu près dans l'espace de dix mois, à compter de la date du jour de l'échange de l'instrument de ce traité.

Ecrit le quatorzième jour de la lune de Zileaadé Cherifé de l'année 1245 de l'Hégire; le septième mai, 1830.

Pour traduction exacte et littérale.

N. Navoni

Conclusion

The foregoing articles, agreed upon and concluded between the Minister of the *Riasset* (that is to say, of the Chancery of State and of Foreign Affairs) and the Commissioner of the United States, aforesaid, and subsequently signed likewise by the two absent Commissioners, shall be firmly observed and executed between the two powers after the exchange of the ratifications of the contracting parties, which exchange shall take place in about ten months, counting from the date of the day of the exchange of the instrument of this treaty.

Written on the fourteenth day of the moon of *Zileaadé Cherifé* in the year of the Hegira 1245; the seventh May, 1830.

An exact and literal translation.

N. Navoni

THE TRANSLATION OF 1931

The Turkish text of the treaty was translated in 1931 by Dr. J. H. Kramers, of Leiden, in collaboration with Professor C. Snouck Hurgronje. Dr. Kramers then compared his translation with those printed above and also with an annotated translation of the treaty made for the Department of State in September, 1873, by the Reverend Dr. Henry Augustus Homes. Dr. Homes, who wrote much upon oriental subjects and who had translated important Arabic and Persian works, was in Constantinople from 1837 to 1853. During the last three years of that period he was Assistant Dragoman of the American Legation. Subsequently Dr. Homes became Librarian of the New York State Library at Albany. He died in 1887.

The translation of Dr. Kramers, with his notes thereon, is printed below. Regarding the earlier translations and his own, Dr. Kramers writes:

The French translation of Navoni, besides being written in not very good French, is rather superficial and does not find really adequate expressions. It is an adaptation of the contents to western ideas. The proclaimed translation is in this last respect more precise but in various passages is erroneous.

The translation of Dr. Homes, however, is a real attempt to account for the true meaning and value of the terms and expressions used. It has been of great use to me in correcting my own translation, although I differ in some points with the view of Dr. Homes.

I have added to my translation some notes in which the meaning of several expressions is discussed and in which I give my reasons for those renderings that differ from those of Dr. Homes.

Article 4 has been annotated in more detail on account of its importance.

[Translation]

The reason of the writing of this document and the motive of the drawing up of this writ are as follows:

As there does not exist as yet any kind of official treaty between the everlasting Sublime Government and the Government of the United States of America, now, with regard to the wish and desire that are exhibited and manifested formerly and latterly by the said Government, and to the observance of a friendly and amical attitude by the Sublime Government towards the Government of the United States of America, we, the undersigned functionary, occupying the elevated degree of Chief of the Secretaries of the ever-stable Sublime Government and of the exalted Sultanate, eternally enduring, having been authorized by the Most Noble Imperial Excellence to negotiate and arrange this matter, there have been negotiations between us and our friend the Honorable Charles Rhind, who has been authorized and commissioned by the aforesaid Government with complete authority to conclude and fasten the matter of the treaty, separately by coming to the Gate of Felicity and jointly with the functionaries named Commodore Biddle and David Offley, now being in the town of Smyrna, as a result of which negotiations, have been drawn up and settled the articles that are mentioned and established hereafter.

The qualifications "everlasting," "ever-stable," etc., express at the same time wishes.

I have followed Dr. Homes throughout in his rendering of "Dewlet-i Aliye" by "Sublime Government." The term "Sublime Porte" really means the office of the Grand Vizier. Still, it is not wrong to use "Sublime Porte" for the Turkish Government, as this has been a constant usage, even among the Turks themselves.

"Chief of the Secretaries" (Reis-ul-Kuttab) is the title of the functionary who was practically the Minister of Foreign Affairs;

at the time this functionary was generally known as "Reis Effendi." Not long afterwards the title was abolished.

I think that my translation of the passage containing the words "separately" and "jointly" is grammatically correct, though it cannot be said to give a satisfactory sense. The fault is, however, with the Turkish text. The meaning is, obviously, that Rhind was authorized to treat separately, but that he needed the consent of his two colleagues in Smyrna. The French translation, "en son propre nom, ou conjointement avec les deux autres Commissaires" (in his own name, or jointly with the two other Commissioners), is in any case wrong.

The "Gate of Felicity" is a common expression for Constantinople.

FIRST ARTICLE

If the Mohammedan and subjected merchants of the Sublime Government visit the dominions, provinces, harbors, and ports under the authority of the American Government, or proceed from one port to another port or from American ports to ports of other dominions, they shall pay the custom and other duties in the same way as merchants belonging to governments that are granted a more favored treatment, and they shall not be troubled with higher demands.

On sea and on their other journeys, all exemptions and other privileges that are observed with regard to the said governments shall be observed and taken as the line of conduct with regard to the merchants and subjected people of the Sublime Government.

Likewise, the American merchants visiting the well-protected dominions and the harbors and ports of the Sublime Government for the purpose of commerce, shall pay their custom and other duties in the same way as the merchants belonging to those befriended governments that are granted a more favorable treatment, and they shall in no other wise be molested or interfered with. By both parties the required way-papers shall be given.

Here and afterwards "subjected" or "subjected people" stands for the Turkish "raya," meaning at that time the Christian and Jewish subjects of the Porte.

The corresponding Turkish word for "visit" is rendered in the former translations by "coming and going" or similar expressions. This is, indeed, the literal meaning of the Turkish expression, but I think the sense is better rendered by the verb "to visit."

"On sea and on their other journeys" is more literal than "by sea and by land," but this is of course the meaning.

As remarked by Dr. Homes, "way-papers" are the papers supplementary to a citizen's passport, which the Turkish authorities were accustomed to issue to all travelers.

SECOND ARTICLE

It shall be allowed to the Sublime Government to institute shah-benders in the dominions of America, and likewise to the American Government to appoint and institute, together with the imperial diplomas and orders, consuls and vice consuls belonging to their own kind, for the administration of their commercial affairs, in the localities that are commercial places and where the necessity has become manifest; with regard to them the suitable privileges and the necessary protection and guard shall be observed.

"Shahbenders" is the Turkish equivalent for "consuls." As the Turkish text uses this word only for Turkish consuls, while consuls of other nations are denoted as "konsolos," it seems better to maintain the difference in the translation.

"Diploma" renders the well-known Turkish word "berat," which is often translated also by "exequatur," though the real sense is larger, meaning an official document granting some privilege or exemption. The Turkish for "orders" is "ewamir," which is given as "firmans" in the proclaimed translation.

From the note of Dr. Homes regarding the word "kind" I extract the following: "The Turkish noun in this phrase is *jins*, which has much of the force of the word *genus* or class. . . . The use of the word in this connection appears extremely colloquial and almost contemptuous, and of equivocal meaning: seeing that the word *jins* might be interpreted by either *nation* or *religion*, and hence allowing natives to be appointed Consuls, for *jins* does not necessarily imply citizenship." While agreeing in general with those observations of Dr. Homes, I think that the word indicates any people belonging to the Christian nations of Europe and America, excluding all Turkish Mohammedan or other subjects. This meaning is also obvious in the treaties with Algiers and Tunis that I have examined. The Turks wanted to prevent the nominating as consuls of Turkish Christian subjects, which had led to many abuses in the foregoing century.

THIRD ARTICLE

The brokers whom American merchants residing for purposes of commerce in the well-protected dominions, just as the merchants belonging to other friendly governments, take into their service for their commercial affairs, to whatever community or creed they belong —this shall not be interfered with nor shall this be treated contrary to usage. American merchant ships coming to the ports of the well-protected dominions, and also at the time of their departure, shall not be searched by the functionaries of the customhouse and of the port to a greater extent than the ships of the aforesaid governments.

The translation of the first sentence is as literal as possible. The sentence appears to be grammatically incorrect.

"Community" renders Turkish "millet," which in not quite modern Turkish means one of the officially recognized religious communities in the Ottoman Empire. Nowadays "millet" means "a nation," but that translation would certainly be wrong for the time of the treaty; it is true, however, that even at that time these communities were sometimes improperly called nations. "Creed" stands for "medhheb," which in Turkish always designates a religious denomination.

Fourth Article

If disputes and litigations should occur between the subjects and subjected people of the Sublime Government and the subjects of the American Government, if their dragoman is not present, there shall be no hearing or decision of the matter. Those of their litigations which exceed five hundred piasters shall be transferred to the Threshold and be dealt with according to right and justice. As long as American subjects occupy themselves, within the limits of their position, with their commerce, while no accusation or crime is ascertained, they shall not be interfered with or molested without cause; and even if they come under accusation, they shall not be imprisoned by the authorities or the police officers, but, in the same way as other persons living under a peace treaty are treated, the suitable punishment shall be applied to them with the cognizance of their minister and consuls.

I have taken over the wording "disputes and litigations" from Dr. Homes; the expression is probably an attempt to include both criminal and civil affairs, which were not clearly distinguished from each other by the judicial practice of the Turks.

"Subjected people" is my translation of the word "raya," as in Article 1.

Dr. Homes, in his notes, explains why he has translated "dragoman" by "interpreter," but I cannot agree with him; "dragoman," indeed, has always been the title of a particular kind of functionary in the service of governments, embassies, and consulates in the Levant, and their function was much more extended than that of simple interpreting. Most of the other translations have kept to "dragoman."

"Threshold" is the literal translation of the Turkish word. It means the threshold of the imperial palace, and as such it may stand for that palace itself, but also for the whole capital, where the Sultan resides. Therefore I think that those translations that have "Capital" or even "Constantinople" are nearer to the truth than "Sublime Porte" or "Porte" (as has Dr. Homes), the idea being that such processes will be dealt with by the judicial authorities (whoever they be) in the capital.

"Right and justice" means that those processes shall not be judged according to the Mohammedan law, which is very un-

favorable to those who are not Moslems. "Equity and justice" (proclaimed text) is equally good. Dr. Homes' translation of the first word as "truth"— which sometimes may be the meaning— does not seem adequate. The Turkish word rendered "accusation" means in general "suspicion," and, as a judicial term, it can mean only that one is accused of or charged with a crime. Therefore the word "conviction," which is used by Dr. Homes and which is in some translations, seems to be too strong. It must be admitted, on the other hand, that the whole passage, "while no accusation or crime is ascertained," lacks precision.

"Persons living under a peace treaty" is an attempt to render still more precisely the idea of the word "muste'min," though I quite agree with the observations of Dr. Homes to the effect that the word means "those who demand protection" and who translates it "foreign residents." A "muste'min" is a foreigner belonging to a country with which the Mohammedan state can never be at constant peace; at the utmost there may be a truce or temporary treaty. The "muste'min" avails himself of such a treaty to live unmolested in a Mohammedan country. At the time of the treaty with the United States these medieval ideas had lost their practical meaning, but the word "muste'min" was still in use (see W. Heffening, Das islamische Fremdenrecht bis zu den islamisch-frankischen Staatsverträgen).

"Cognizance" renders the Turkish expression "ma'rifetile"; this has the literal meaning of "by the knowledge of," but it is used more often in the sense of "by the intermediary of." Therefore I think that "cognizance," which I have taken over from Dr. Homes, is admirable, as it has originally the same meaning, "knowledge," while used also as a judicial term. This translation, however, does not solve at all the problem of what is really meant by the text; but it is as far as possible from an interpretative translation, as is given, for example, by Navoni ("par") and by the proclaimed translation ("tried by"). In any case the text does not speak of the "trying" of foreign residents by their minister or consuls, but only of the "punishing."

Fifth Article

It has been decided that the American merchant vessels, visiting the well-protected dominions, may pass and travel with their own flags, in increased safety and security, provided that they do not take and use the flags of other governments; that they do not give the American flag to ships belonging to other governments or to other kinds of people, or to the boats of the subjected people; that their ministers, consuls, and vice consuls shall not deliver *patentas* to the subjected people of the Sublime Government or sustain them secretly and openly. It shall not be allowed in any way to behave and act contrary to these principles.

As to "kinds of people," see the foregoing notes to Article 2.

"Subjected people" stands again for "rayas."

"Patentas," as Dr. Homes explains, means "protection papers."

The literal meaning of the Turkish word rendered "sustain" would be "associate"; but as this association manifested itself in the form of protection, I have taken over Dr. Homes' translation by "sustain."

Sixth Article

If war vessels belonging to both parties meet with each other, they shall show friendship and recognition to each other, according to the sea rules. Equally, if they meet with merchant ships, both parties shall act in a friendly way.

Seventh Article

In accordance with the treatment of the above-mentioned friendly governments it shall be allowed to the merchant ships of the American Government, in case they are empty of cargo, and equally when laden with products of their own country or with non-prohibited wares and goods of the products of the well-protected dominions, to visit the Black Sea by passing through the Strait of the Imperial Abode of the Sultanate.

"Visit" is a translation of the same expression as in Articles 1 and 5.

Eighth Article

If the captains and owners of the merchant ships of both Governments, or their agents, do not wish to consent to the chartering of their ships with their free will and approbation, it shall not be allowed to take the ships from them in an illegal way to load them with soldiers, ammunition, and materials of war.

The Turkish word for "agents" means a person on whom one can rely, and I do not see why Dr. Homes translates it "consignees." The French translation and the proclaimed text do not translate the word at all.

"Chartering" is literally "to let."

Ninth Article

If a merchant ship belonging to one of the parties meets with disaster and is shipwrecked, those persons of the crew who may have escaped shall be protected, and the wares and goods belonging to the cargo which it has been possible to save, shall be delivered, as soon as they are found, to the nearest American consul, so that notice may be given to the persons entitled.

Only the American consul is here spoken of, though in the beginning of the article the ships of both parties are mentioned.

The last passage is much better translated in the French and in the proclaimed translation than by Dr. Homes, whose rendering is that the salvaged goods "shall be delivered up to whom the right belongs and sent to the nearest American consul"; so I cannot agree at all with the explanatory note of Dr. Homes to this article, which reads: "Wrecked property must be given up to persons appointed, either by the Turkish authorities or by the consul and then sent to him. *Proprietors* are not mentioned, as in the official copy."

Conclusion

It has been agreed upon in the form placed above between the office of the Chief (of the Secretaries) and the aforesaid functionary; after this treaty document shall have been undersigned by the two aforesaid functionaries, and after the exchange of the ratifications by both parties within ten months after the date of the exchange of this document, the established articles shall be observed and fixed between the two Governments.

Written on the fourteenth day of the noble month of Zu'lkadah of the year twelve hundred and forty-five.

He who beseeches the generous King for his assistance,

> MEHMED HAMID
> *Chief of the Secretaries*

The Turkish expression rendered here "the office of the Chief" denotes properly the function of the Reis Effendi (see the notes to the preamble). It is a widespread usage in Turkish official style not to mention functionaries themselves, but generally to employ the substantive denoting their function, though the person himself is really intended.

The date corresponds, according to the chronological tables, to May 7, 1830.

NOTES

The text of the treaty proper, without the separate and secret article, appears above in five forms. A facsimile reproduction of the Turkish text is opposite page 542. Following the headnote are printed three translations, the sources and content of which are discussed in these notes. Those three translations were all before the Senate. The first, which is the proclaimed English translation, is printed across the full width of the page; the other two translations are in parallel columns, French and English; and after those early translations is printed the translation of the Turkish made in 1931 by Dr. Kramers, with his annotations.

The documental history of this treaty with Turkey is a complex one, and much that has been written on the subject is erroneous. A somewhat detailed account is therefore necessary.

The despatches and other papers upon which the following notes are based are to be found, when no specific reference is given, in

D. S., 1 Despatches, Turkey, a volume which is now bound in two parts. In House Documents No. 250, 22d Congress, 1st session (there are two documents of that number relating to this treaty, both in serial 221; one, of May 29, 1832, is incorrectly headed "Treas. Dept."; the other, of July 14, 1832, is headed "Executive"), there are printed, of the papers of 1830, only the report of Rhind to President Jackson of May 10 (with some slight omissions), an extract from his despatch of June 1, and the despatch of Biddle and Offley of June 8, 1830.

THE NEGOTIATIONS

The negotiations were entrusted jointly and severally to Captain James Biddle, "Commander in Chief of the American Naval Forces in the Mediterranean," David Offley, and Charles Rhind. Their instructions, under date of September 12, 1829, are in D. S., 1 Instructions, Turkey, 196–202; their full power, of the same date (*ibid.*), contains the following as its clause of substance:

> Know Ye that reposing special trust and confidence in the integrity, prudence and abilities of James Biddle, a Captain in the Navy of the United States, commanding their Squadron in the Mediterranean, of David Offley, Consul of the United States at Smyrna and of Charles Rhind, a Citizen of the United States, I have appointed them and each of them, jointly and severally, Commissioners of the United States of America, for them and in their name to confer, treat and negotiate with the Sublime Porte, or with any person or persons duly authorized in its behalf, of and concerning all matters of navigation and commerce between the United States and the Turkish Dominions, with full power to conclude and sign a Treaty thereupon, or to give their assent to a capitulation therefor—transmitting the same to the President of the United States for his final ratification by and with the advice and consent of the Senate.

Rhind left New York on October 20, 1829, and proceeded by way of Gibraltar to Mahon, where he met Commodore Biddle and whence they proceeded to Smyrna, where Offley was Consul. It was agreed that Rhind should go on to Constantinople alone, which he did, arriving there on February 8, 1830. Rhind was an American merchant trading to the Levant and had been appointed Consul at Odessa on August 7, 1829. The entire negotiations which resulted in the treaty were conducted by Rhind with the Turkish representatives. Rhind spoke French. He had with him during the negotiations Nicholas Navoni, who was then American Dragoman. Navoni was a Levantine, of Neapolitan nationality (New York Historical Society, Bradish Papers, box 7, June 16, 1828); he was well versed in Turkish; his French was fluent but its style was foreign and not idiomatic; some of his letters are in English. In his letter of March 10, 1832 (D. S., 6 Despatches, Turkey), Navoni gives some account of his services from 1827, when he was employed by Luther Bradish, until 1831.

According to the report of Rhind of May 10, 1830, the full power of the Commissioners was exhibited to the Reis Effendi, or Turkish Minister of Foreign Affairs, on February 11, and copies in French and Turkish were then delivered; and as a successor in the Ministry of Foreign Affairs, Hamid Bey, was appointed a few days later, a copy

in Turkish of the full power was delivered again on February 28. There is nothing definitely stated in that report as to any Turkish full power.

The first draft written during the negotiations was that of Rhind in two short articles as "the Basis of a Treaty"; these articles were presented to Hamid Bey, Reis Effendi, on March 10, presumably in French, and perhaps also in Turkish. In English they are embodied in the report of Rhind to the President of May 10, 1830, as follows:

1st The United States to be received on the same footing in every respect, pay the same duties, & enjoy all the rights & privileges of the most favored Nations, particularly France & England.

2d That at all times hereafter the Navigation to and from the Black Sea shall be free and open to American Vessels, nor shall they be delayed in passing either to or from it, under any pretext whatever.

On March 17 Rhind was informed "that the business was finished on the basis of the two articles I [Rhind] had sent on the 10th March."

On March 22 Rhind offered to sign those two articles as a treaty; but this offer was declined by the Reis Effendi, who said that he had appointed an official to draw up a treaty and that it was "then making out" and suggested that Rhind "had better do the same, and after comparing & arranging them it should be immediately signed."

Rhind wrote that accordingly he drew up a treaty and that on March 26 it was "now prepared to be laid before the Divan." The language of the draft is not stated, but it was probably French.

Rhind reported that on April 13 he had a meeting with the Reis Effendi and other ministers and was informed that the Sublime Porte had ordered a treaty to be drawn up in strict conformity with the one submitted by Rhind and "that he [the Reis Effendi] had now the honor of presenting it." Presumably that document then presented was in Turkish, although this is not wholly certain; in his despatch of April 23 Rhind wrote as follows:

Finding some omissions and corrections which I wished to be made, it was returned, and became so obliterated that a new Copy had to be drawn out. this was immediately done, and I have been in daily expectation of receiving it for a week past, but the Members of the Divan have been thrown into such a ferment by the Greek Protocol that they can attend to nothing else; they make every apology, and have promised it from day to day—it now only requires to be read over by the Reis Effendi, the moment I receive and examine it I shall dispatch a Messenger with a Firman for my Colleagues.

Whether any such "new copy" was delivered to Rhind or not, and if so, when, his despatches do not definitely state; in any case, there was some delay, and Rhind changed his mind as to his procedure. In his report of May 10 he states that he sent a special message to the Reis Effendi to the effect that he wished the treaty to be signed and exchanged as soon as possible and that he would exercise the powers which he had and terminate the affair at once. The date of that message is not given; but it must have been later than April

23; and in his report of May 10 Rhind gives the following as the answer of the Reis Effendi to his proposal:

> H: E. was pleased with the proposition & promised to have Copies of the Treaty drawn up for Signature & Exchange, but notwithstanding my constant importunities it was not until the 6ᵗʰ May, when he said the Instruments were ready and he had appointed the next morning for Signing & Exchanging them— he intimated that I would be received in the usual style of Ambassadors on concluding a Treaty and that horses would be ready for myself and attendants at the landing place in Constantinople. Accordingly on the 7ᵗʰ of May I repaired to the Palace, where I found the Reis Effendi; the Secretary of State & the Drogoman of the Porte. The Reis Effendi after a short Conversation signed & sealed the Treaty in Turkish and I did the same with the French translation & we exchanged them. H. E. expressed nearly the same ideas he did on the Conclusion of the negotiation; and I reciprocated his friendly wishes, expressing my personal gratitude for the manner in which I had been received and treated since my arrival in Turkey.

It thus appears from the despatches which have been quoted or referred to above that there were three preliminary drafts: the text of the first, the two articles proposed by Rhind on March 10, has been quoted; next came the draft treaty of Rhind which was ready for presentation on March 26; and finally the draft (probably in Turkish) of the Reis Effendi, which Rhind received on April 13, and a "new copy" of which he was "daily" expecting to receive on April 23. Probably such a redraft was delivered to Rhind some time after April 23, though his despatches are silent on the point; clearly it was the Turkish draft of April 13, subject to whatever changes were made in it, which became the treaty text; and according to Rhind, he had been informed that the Turkish draft was in "strict conformity" with his own.

There is not now available any copy of either the Rhind draft treaty of March 26 or the Turkish draft treaty of April 13; the manuscript which has generally and mistakenly been supposed to be a draft of Rhind, is described below under the heading, "The Annotated French Translation."

It is specially to be noted that the despatches of Rhind written during the negotiations and even his long report to the President of May 10, 1830, do not allude to the separate and secret article; that article is nowhere mentioned prior to his brief despatch of May 7 to the Secretary of State, where it is said:

> To shew the Sultan, that he has made an acquisition, and obtained a consideration for his concessions, I have signed a *private* article—giving him the privilege "*of making Contracts for cutting Timber in the United States, and building Vessels, if he pleases.*"
> This is *all* I had to offer, but so highly is the *Boon* esteemed, that the new Administration have gained great credit by the circumstance.

One other statement of Rhind regarding the negotiations, though written some time after the event, is to be quoted (D. S., 1 Despatches, Turkey, August 8, 1831):

> During the Negotiation the Chancellor (who had been appointed by the Reis Effendi to aid in the minutiae of it) had only extended the *Articles* of the Treaty,

the Caption, and conclusion I never saw until the final copy was produced. In the preamble thereto, they stated the simple fact, that *Three* Commissioners having been appointed by the President to negotiate this Treaty & that I had come to the Capital, delivered my power, negotiated, and concluded the Treaty, the other *two* Commissioners being then in Smyrna, but were to repair here and sign it also.

The Signing of the Treaty

The statement of Rhind regarding the signature of the treaty has been quoted above. It is rather summary; the substance is merely that the treaty in Turkish was signed and sealed by the Reis Effendi and delivered to Rhind and that the French version, which Rhind calls a translation, was signed and sealed by him and delivered to the Reis Effendi.

Nothing is there said about the secret article, which in the Turkish was a separate document from the treaty proper, and doubtless was a separate document in the French also. Accordingly, there were delivered to Rhind two documents in Turkish signed and sealed; and he delivered the two equivalent documents in French signed and sealed by him.

Regarding the French version Rhind wrote in his private despatch of August 8, 1831 (D. S., 1 Despatches, Turkey):

As the Instructions required the utmost caution in translations I directed our excellent Drogoman, Mr Navoni, to make the French translation which we were to sign, as *literal* as he could from the Turkish, disregarding all niceties of style or construction—this he did very faithfully and satisfactorily (at least to me) & this translation was confirmed and certified by the Drogoman of the Porte

Under such circumstances the French version of the treaty and of the separate article had an official character. Even if it could not be said at that time that in the strictest sense there were two official texts of the agreement, one Turkish and one French, there was at least an official and agreed French translation of the Turkish; that French version had been signed and sealed by the American Commissioner; it had been assented to by the Turkish Government as correct; and it had been delivered to and accepted by the Turkish Government as the equivalent of the Turkish text. The fact that the American negotiator was known to be ignorant of the Turkish language makes the case for the official character of the French version all the stronger.

However, owing to the procedure subsequently followed by this Government, the French version lost entirely its official character and became merely a translation made at the time. It is a quite extraordinary circumstance that it was the Government of the United States which abandoned the French text and was accordingly constrained to rely and did rely in the future upon the Turkish as the text of the treaty, and upon the Turkish only.

As has been mentioned, the other two American Commissioners, Commodore James Biddle and David Offley, were in Smyrna; and following the signature of the treaty on May 7, 1830, Rhind requested them to come to Constantinople, as it was understood that

they were to add their signatures to that of Rhind. At about the same time Rhind delivered to Count Orlov, the Russian Minister at Constantinople, a copy of the treaty, doubtless without the secret article; and with a letter to Henry Middleton, then American Minister at St. Petersburg, dated May 10, 1830, he enclosed a copy in French of the treaty proper, but not of the secret article (D. S., 11 Despatches, Russia, No. 94, with Rhind's letter and the copy of the treaty as enclosures); but Rhind refused to permit a copy of the treaty to be given to the British Ambassador at Constantinople.

Even to his own colleagues, moreover, Rhind did not transmit a copy of the secret article; and although they arrived at Constantinople on May 24, it was not until May 28 that the secret article was communicated to them, despite the fact that, as Biddle wrote, they had all "been residing four days in the same house, had been constantly together, and almost constantly conversing upon the treaty."

In his private despatch of August 8, 1831 (D. S., 1 Despatches, Turkey), giving "an abbreviated account of my late mission to Turkey," Rhind defends his own course and violently attacks his colleagues. The following extract therefrom refers to his concealment of the secret article from Biddle and Offley; but it must be read at least with scepticism, as the statement that Rhind "actually forgot it" is incredible and impossible to believe:

> The private article (which was fully explained by me to the President, Secretary of State, and Committee of the Senate) being considered as of no importance in itself—but yet was a secret, I put it away among some private papers, and actually forgot it until they had consented to sign the Treaty—and Mᵣ Navoni reminded me of it. I however mentioned the nature of it in the Letter which I sent to them enclosing the Treaty. They now made a bold and open hold of this insignificant paper, (altho Mᵣ Navoni assured them that the Reis Effendi would tell them, that the President might burn it if he pleased) and finally insisted that the Treaty must be annulled! As it evidently had, from the moment they left Smyrna, been their determination to mar the Negotiation (for they even did not bring the money with them, but left it on board of the Java) and disgusted with this unworthy species of trifling in a case of such importance to the Nation, I wrote them a Note, stating, that as my powers were plenipotentiary, I had signed, sealed, and actually exchanged the Treaty,—that their names were not necessary to it; that I was perfectly willing to assume all the responsibility, and as their illiberal conduct rendered it necessary for me to sacrifice my individual interests, and return home to America, I forbade their further interference in the matter. On receipt of this Note, they concluded to sign the Treaty, to which I assented in order to comply with the wish of the President as expressed in the Instructions—this favor not only moved the muscles of the grave & reflecting Turk, but produced the ridicule of all the Diplomatists & Franks of Pera.

Owing chiefly to Rhind's concealment of the secret article, a violent quarrel broke out between him and his colleagues, and it was not long before he ceased to be on speaking terms with them, so that all communications between him and them were made in writing.

In the treaty proper Biddle, whose view was shared by Offley, saw nothing objectionable except "its bad French and the short period allowed for exchanging the ratifications"; but Biddle and Offley objected most strongly to the secret article, which they thought con-

flicted with their instructions and was at variance with the settled
policy of the United States. Biddle, taking Offley's advice (Offley to
Biddle, May 29), finally concluded, however, for reasons which he
states very forcibly in his despatch of May 31, that it was his public
duty to sign the secret article; and accordingly both he and Offley
signed it, as well as the treaty, on May 30, 1830; that is to say, they
added their signatures to the signatures of Rhind to the French translations of the treaty proper and of the separate and secret article; for
Rhind had signed nothing else; and on June 8 Biddle and Offley
received from the Porte Turkish duplicates of the treaty and of the
separate and secret article.

The original treaty and the original secret article in Turkish are
each written on a single sheet of heavy paper, and each of them is
sealed on the reverse, directly back of the signature. They were
transmitted to the President by Biddle and Offley with their letter of
June 8, 1830, by the U. S. S. *Lexington*, which arrived at Norfolk on
November 20 (Niles' Weekly Register, XXXIX, 222, November 27,
1830). The duplicates, also in Turkish, were forwarded with Offley's
letter of June 21 from Smyrna by the brig *Cherub*, which entered at
Boston on September 6 (the Boston Evening Daily Transcript,
September, 1830).

The Annotated French Translation

There is in the archives of the Department of State (1 Despatches,
Turkey) an annotated French version of the treaty proper, that is to
say, without the separate and secret article. It has heretofore been
supposed (supplementary note of Mr. Adee, quoted in Moore, Digest,
II, 669; Secretary of State Frelinghuysen to the Turkish Minister,
ibid., 687–88) that that paper is a copy of the Rhind draft treaty
which he mentions in his despatch of March 26, 1830, or at least a
copy of a draft submitted by Rhind during the negotiations. The
present editor is decidedly of another opinion, for which the reasons
will be given.

First of all it is to be said that there is nothing on the paper in
question by way of endorsement or signature to indicate its origin,
nor is there anything on it to indicate the date of its receipt by the
Department of State or its source. No despatch of the time mentions
it specifically as an enclosure. Its French is crude, as the literal
print of it below shows; the handwriting is not that of any other
contemporaneous document in the archives; in particular, the handwriting is not that of Navoni. The two sheets of paper on which
the writing appears are larger in size and thinner than any paper
used by, or for, the American Commissioners. The negative indi-
cations that the paper did not originate with any of the American
Commissioners or their staff are strong.

The paper is written throughout in the same angular hand, although
the notes, some of which are interlarded with the text of the articles,
are all in red ink. It appears that the scrivener was not familiar

with English, for he misspells the word "Commodore" and also the names "Biddle" and "Offley."

From the internal evidence it is clear that the paper is a translation from the Turkish language. It is highly improbable that a paper drawn up in French would contain such Turkish words as, for example, *sàhbenders, rayàs,* and *temessuk.* Certainly any draft made by Rhind must have been written first in French; and even if it had been put later into Turkish, the French would hardly have contained the Turkish words as there written in Articles 2 and 5 and in the conclusion.

Furthermore, the footnote to Article 2 which the paper contains is almost conclusive that it is not only a French translation but also that it is a translation of a document prepared by the Turkish Foreign Office. That footnote begins with this expression: "Le mot *gins* dont la Porte fait usage ici" (the word *gins* which the Porte uses here); that expression is a definite statement that the Turkish word is one used here (in the document) by the Turkish Government.

The date of the document is very significant. Strictly speaking, *and as a document,* it is undated; that is to say, there is no date given for the writing of the paper itself; but its final clause of execution contains the date of April 8, 1830. As that date is five days prior to the submission to Rhind of the Turkish draft on April 13, it seems to lend some force to the supposition that the paper might be a copy or translation of the earlier Rhind treaty draft of March 26; but it is highly improbable that Rhind's draft contained a date for its execution; and if it had, that date would not have been as late as April 8, for Rhind said in his despatch of March 26, where he referred to his draft, that he hoped "in a day or two to have the Treaty signed." He would not have put in a date for execution which was thirteen days later.

Very significant, moreover, is the fact that the date of April 8 in the final clause of the paper now considered is an error. That clause says that the treaty was (or was to be) executed on 15 Zu'lkadah, A. H. 1245, and gives the equivalent date as April 8, 1830; but the equivalent date in our calendar of 15 Zu'lkadah, A. H. 1245, is not April 8, but May 8, 1830, one day *after* the signature of the treaty on May 7. The scrivener wrote the date in the Mohammedan calendar, intended to add the equivalent date of our calendar, made a slip and wrote "April" instead of "May" (the mistake could not have been the other way around because April 8 was 14 Shawwal); so the equivalent date of execution given in the final clause should properly be May 8, 1830.

If the paper is not an American draft, neither is it a translation of a Turkish draft. A draft does not ordinarily have in it a date of execution; a draft leaves the date blank; and in this case it was not until May 6 that Rhind was informed that the treaty would be signed on the following day, Friday, May 7, 1830.

The document cannot well be anything other than a translation of the treaty made *after* its signature. The text of the provisions of the

treaty in this document is in general too similar in substance to the
text of the treaty proper for the paper now considered to be anything
else than a translation of the treaty. As mentioned above, this
document is beyond doubt a translation from the Turkish, and there
is no Turkish document other than the treaty itself of which it can
well be a translation. Moreover, the notes in the document read as
references to a treaty and not to a draft; they mention "this treaty,"
that "American ships are not to be subjected," and so on.

It is true that there are differences between this translation and
that of Navoni, for example, aside from matters of language and style;
but those of any importance are hardly more than two. One of these
is in Article 4, where the words referring to the trial of accused Americans before the American minister or consul (seront justiciables de
leurs Ministres ou Consuls) do not appear in the Navoni translation;
and the other is in Article 5, where the text of the document now considered omits the clause of Navoni's translation to the effect that
American ministers, consuls, and vice consuls shall not issue documents of protection to Turkish subjects (ne délivreront des patentes
aux sujets de la Sublime Porte.)

Assuming that the paper is a translation of the treaty, the question of its source remains. Only one source is indicated in the correspondence of the time. It was on May 13 that Biddle and Offley
received at Smyrna a letter from Rhind enclosing a copy of the
treaty. Leaving Smyrna, they arrived at Constantinople on May
24. According to Offley's despatch of June 2 they had an independent translation of the treaty made; Offley writes, "after examination
of the translation of the Treaty as negociated by Mr Rhind and procuring a translation to be made by another person with a view to
correct any misapprehensions or mistakes which might have been
made by Mr Navoni Com^r Biddle and myself determined to add our
signatures." Rhind also refers to that translation in one of his
protests, that of June 7, in which he wrote, "Messrs Biddle & Offley
had a free translation made of the Treaty, and on my challenging
them to shew any difference between that and the literal one, M^r
Offley (who alone knows French) confessed there was no difference
de facto"; and in his private despatch of August 8, 1831 (D. S., 1
Despatches, Turkey), Rhind wrote that Offley "had a translation
made by a very competent person."

While the proof cannot, after a century, be said to be conclusive,
all the evidence that there is indicates that this annotated French
translation was the translation of the treaty made for Biddle and
Offley by an unnamed individual. Every circumstance surrounding
the document is consistent with its being that translation, and various
circumstances are inconsistent with its being anything else. It may
even be conjectured that this annotated French translation was made
by the Russian Dragoman, as Rhind had given a copy of the treaty
to Count Orlov, the Russian Envoy, and his colleagues were aware of
that fact. And as far as the date is concerned, it is to be remembered
that the Turkish text of the treaty does not give *any* equivalent date

in our calendar for the date of execution; it contains merely the Mohammedan date, 14 Zu'lkadah, A. H. 1245; and the translator, who was doubtless also the scrivener, mistook 14 for 15 and then added the wrong equivalent.

The annotated French translation is copied below. The print is literal except that the annotations, which in the paper itself are written in red ink, are here put in parentheses. In view of the other translations of the treaty which are printed, it seems unnecessary to add a translation of the French of the treaty articles; however, a translation of the notes follows the print of the French.

[The annotated French translation]

Le motif et l'objet de la rédaction de cet instrument est que
Comme il n'a pas éxistè jusqu'à ce jour, aucune Convention officielle ou Traitè, entre la Sublime Porte, dont l'existence soit perpetuelle, et la Puissance des Etats Unis d'Amerique; ainsi la Sub⁹ Porte ayant eû maintenant égard au désir que la Puissance susmentionnée avait anterieurement et récemment manifestè à ce sujet, et voulant de son côtè temoigner aux Etats Unis d'amerique les sentimens d'une amitiè sincere, Nous soussignè qui occupont la place élevée du Ministére de Chef de la Chancellerie de la Sub⁹ Porte de perpetuelle durée, et son Commissaire ad hoc, en vertu de la permission qui nous a été conférée par Sa Majestè Imp⁹le, nôtre très auguste souverain, pour traiter et regler cette affaire; ayant conferè à ce sujet avec l'honorable Charles Rhind nôtre ami, expressem⁺ venû à cette Residence Imp⁹le de la part de la Puissance susmentioñée autorisè et muni de pleins pouvoir pour negocier, regler et conclure les articles du traitè, soit par lui seul, ou conjointement avec les deux autres Commissaires, le Commodor Bidle et David Ofley qui se trouvent maintenant à Smirne, nous avons entre nous deux réglè et arrêtè les articles suivans.

ARTICLE PREMIER

Les Negocians de la Sub⁹ Porte, Mussulmans, ou Rayàs allant et venant dans les pays, provinces, ports et Échélles sous la domination des Etats Unis d'amerique, d'une à l'autre des dites Échélles, ou bien des Échélles des Etats Unis, aux Échélles dépendentes d'autres Etats, payeront les droits de Douane, et autres impositions à l'instar des Negocians des Puissances les plus favorisées. Ils ne seront molestès par des pretensions de droits plus forts, et en voyageant par mer ou par terre jouiront de tous les priviléges, et de toutes les distinctions qui sont en usage envers les sujets des autres Puissances, qui auront lieu et serviront de regle de conduite envers les Negocians et Sujets de la Sub⁹ Porte. De même les Negocians Americains qui pour objet de Commerce parviendront dans les pays bien gardés, ports, et échelles de la Sub⁹ Porte payeront les droits de Douane, et autres impositions, à l'instar des Negoc⁹ des Puissances Amies les plus favorisées, et ne seront molestès, et véxès d'aucune autre maniere que ce soit. De part et d'autre on delivrera aux Voyageurs, les papiers de Voyage ou passeports necessaires.

ART⁹ SECOND

Il sera permis à la Sub⁹ Porte de faire résider des Sàhbenders (Consuls) dans les Etats Unis d'amerique. De même dans les places de Commerce, où le besoin est démontrè, les Etats Unis d'amerique pourront établir des Consuls ou Vice-Consuls, pour soigner et diriger les affaires Commerciales. Les dits Consuls ou V. Consuls (a) seront munis de Berats ou de Firmans, jouiront des distinctions convenables, et il leur sera prêtè l'assistance et protection necessaire.

(a) (Le mot *gins* dont la Porte fait usage ici, comme dans toutes les Capitulations et Traitès, pour marquer la qualitè qu'elle éxige par rapport à la Nationalitè des Consuls, est un mot génèrique, qui signifie éspéce et non pas Nation, et par consequent s'applique à tous les francs de quelque Nation qu'ils soient indistinctem⁺ à l'exclusion des Rayàs Sujets Ottomans.)

ART^e TROISIEME

Les Neg^s Americains établis pour objet de Commerce dans les états bien gardés, de la Sub^e Porte pourront employer à leur service pour leurs aff^s commerciales en qualitè de *Sanseaux* [1] ou Courtiers et agens de change à l'instar des Neg^s des autres Puissances amies, des individus de quelque nation, secte, ou religion que ce soit, lesquels ne seront troublès dans l'exercice de leurs fonctions, et ne seront éxposès à des procédés contraires aux usages établis. Les Batimens Americains, en entrant dans les ports et échelles de la Sub^e Porte, ou en partant, les preposés de la Douane et des ports, ne les visiteront pas plus que les Bat^s des susdites Puiss^s amies. (Puisque dans le pr^r art^e il est dit que les americains seront traitès comme les Neg^s des Puissances amies *les plus favorisées*, ainsi toutes les fois qu'il est mention de *Puissances amies*, la clause les plus favorisèes est toujours sous-entendûe, et par consequent les B^s am^s ne doivent être soumis qu'à la visite éventuelle dans le soupçon qu'il y ait à bord des *Rayàs*, c'est à quoi tous et les Russes eux mêmes sont sujets.)

ART^e QUATR^e

S'il arrivait quelque differend ou litige entre les dependans (turcs) et les Rayàs de la Sub^e Porte, et les dependans des Etats Unis d'am^e les Juges n'entendront les parties, et ne prononceront de Jugement si le Drogman n'est pas présent. Les Causes qui excederont la somme de Cinq Cent piastres seront portées à la Sub^e Porte, et seront jugées en toute équité et justice, comme de droit. (C'est à dire que l'on a droit, d'évoquer les causes qui excederont la dite somme des Tribunaux inferieurs à l'audience du G. Visir, et des Echelles à la Capitale.) Les personnes dependantes des Etats Unis d'amerique, qui en s'occupant tranquillement de leur Commerce, n'auraient pas été atteintes et convaincûes de quelque crime ou delit, ne seront pas molestées, sans cause legitime, et quand même ils se rendraient coupables, ils ne seront arrêtes et mis en prison par les Juges et les autoritès civiles, mais seront justiciables de leurs Ministres ou Consuls, qui les puniront à proportion du delit, suivant à cet égard le même procédè qu'on garde envers tous les autres francs en général. (Cette clause n'est pas toujours strictem^t observée. Les autorites arrêtent souvent des individus francs, que les Ministres Etrangérs, réclament et obtiennent, mais quelque fois avec beaucoup de peine.)

ART^e CINQ^e

Les Batimens Marchands americains qui pour objet de Commerce naviguent, vont et viennent dans les Etats de la Sub^e Porte pourront aller et venir en toute sûretè avec leur pavillon, et il est convenû à cet égard, qu'ils n'emprunteront le pavillon d'aucune autre Puissance et n'accorderont le leur à des Bat^s d'autres Puissances et Nations, ni à des Navires *Rayàs*, et ne protégeront non plus ni publiquem^t ni en secrèt des *Rayàs*, et il ne sera aucunem^t permis de s'écarter, et de permettre des procedés contraires aux principes ci-dessus enoncés, et établis d'un commun accord.

ART^e SIX^e

Les Batimens de guerre des deux parties contractantes, en se rencontrant rempliront reciproquement les uns envers les autres les égards d'amitiè et de bonne intelligence et civilitè, établis par les regles de marine; et venant aussi à rencontrer des Batimens Marchands ils garderont envers ceux-ci les mêmes égards d'amitiè et curtoisie.

ART^e SEPT^e

Les Batim^s Marchands des Etats Unis pourront aussi passer par le Canal, et rivage de cette Residence Imp^{le}, pour aller et venir à la Mer Noir sur leur lest, ou chargès de productions du crû de leurs pays, aussi bien que de productions, manufactures et objets non defendùs des Etats Ottomans, tout comme les Bat^s March. des Puissances amies susmentionnées.

---

[1] So written as the plural of *sansal*.

ART⸱ HUIT⸱

Les Batimens Marchands des deux Puissances ne pourront être pris par Elles par force afin d'y embarquer des troupes, des munitions et autres objets de guerre, si les Capitaines, proprietaires, ou recommandataires de ces Bat⸱ ne se contentent et ne sont pas disposés de leur plein grè de les noliser.

ART. NEUV⸱

Si quelque Bat⸱ Marchand des deux parties contractantes avait le malheur d'échouer et de se briser, les personnes qui se seraient sauvées, seront protegées, et les Marchandises et autres objets que l'on parviendrait à récouvrer, on les fera parvenir au Consul plus proche de l'endroit du Naufrage, pour être remis et consignès tels quels à qui de droit.

CONCLUSION

Tels sont les articles convenûs et arrêtès entre le Ministére du *Riᵤset* c'est à dire entre le Grand Chancelier et Ministre des affaires étrangéres, et le Commissaire Americain ci-dessus nommè. Dés que le *Temessuk*, l'instrument de ce Traitè sera aussi signè par les deux autres Commissaires, et sera échangè, et qu'en comptant du jour de la date de cet échange dans le terme de dix mois aura lieu l'échange des ratifications des deux Puissances, les articles de ce traitè auront force de chose conclûe et arretée, et seront exactement observés par les deux Puissances Contractantes.

Donnè le 15. de la Lune Zilcaade de l'année 1245. de l'hegire, et de N. S. le 8 avril 1830.

(N. B. Si le petit nombre des Art. de ce traitè, peut faire penser que tous les Cas possibles n'ont pas été prévûs, et que des details plus minutieux auraient été a désirer, j'observerai que la base du traitè, etant la Clause essentielle, d'être regardés comme les Nations les *plus favorisées*, cette clause donne droit à tout ce qui pourrait manquer, et par consequent à tous les privileges, usages, et distinctions actuellement en vigueur, ou qui pourraient être accordès par la suite à d'autres Puissances.)

[Translation of the notes to the foregoing document]

Article 2. The word *gins*, of which the Porte makes use here, as in all capitulations and treaties, to indicate the character which is required in respect of the nationality of consuls, is a generic word which signifies *kind* and not *nation* and consequently applies indifferently to all Franks, of any nation whatever, to the exclusion of rayas, Turkish subjects.

Article 3. Since in the first article it is said that the Americans will be treated as the merchants of *the most favored* friendly powers, accordingly, each time that mention is made of *friendly powers* the phrase "the most favored" is always understood, and consequently American ships are not to be subjected, under the suspicion that they have on board rayas, to other than the final visit to which all, including the Russians themselves, are subject.

Article 4, first note. That is to say that the right exists to transfer causes which exceed the said sum from the inferior tribunals to the hearing of the Grand Vizier and from the ports to the capital.

Article 4, second note. This clause is not always strictly observed. The authorities often arrest individual Franks, whom the foreign ministers demand and obtain, but sometimes with much difficulty.

Final Note. If the small number of the articles of this treaty causes it to be thought that all possible cases have not been provided for and that more minute details would have been desirable, I observe that as the basis of the treaty is the essential clause—that of being regarded as the *most favored* nations—that clause includes all which might be lacking, and consequently includes all the privileges, customs, and distinctions now in force or which may hereafter be accorded to other powers.

The Receipt of the Papers

It is not now possible to determine just when each of the various papers relating to this treaty and now in the archives of the Department of State was received; the date of receipt is noted on but few of the material writings.

It seems that the despatches of Rhind of May 7 and 10, reporting the conclusion of his negotiations, were received on August 6, for one of them is so endorsed; but it is a strange fact that those despatches of Rhind do not contain, either in whole or in part, the text of the agreement he made. He gives his views of the treaty; he mentions the secret article in his despatch to the Secretary of State of May 7, 1830, though not in his long report to the President of May 10; but in neither the one nor the other does he give the text, in any language, of what he signed. Neither of those despatches refers to an enclosure. He tells of his treaty but leaves its provisions to be gathered from his description. Not until his despatch of June 1 did Rhind enclose a copy of the treaty; that despatch was probably received on September 10, as another of the same date is so endorsed.

In his letter dated New York November 15, 1830 (D. S., 1 Despatches, Turkey), Rhind informed Secretary of State Van Buren that he had arrived from Smyrna on the evening before and that he would "proceed in a few days to Washington for the purpose of delivering to H: Exy The President, the Treaty which I have negotiated with the Sublime Porte." The copy of the treaty to which Rhind here referred was doubtless that which he mentions in his private despatch of August 8, 1831 (*ibid.*): "Mess.ʳˢ Biddle & Offley having taken away the original Treaty, I was under the necessity of applying [to the Reis Effendi] for a Copy, to carry home with me."

Perhaps the fact that a treaty had been negotiated at Constantinople first became public upon Rhind's arrival at New York with "four elegant Arabian horses" (Niles' Weekly Register, XXXIX, 220); but whatever papers Rhind may have brought, the official news of the treaty had preceded him; and Rhind certainly did not bring with him the originals in Turkish of the treaty and of the secret article, for those had, over his objection, been sent to the President with the despatch of Biddle and Offley of June 8 (D. S., 1 Despatches, Turkey), which was transmitted by the U. S. S. *Lexington;* and, as stated heretofore, that vessel arrived at Norfolk on November 20, 1830; and one of the letters of Biddle to the Secretary of State is endorsed as received on November 25.

Furthermore, the duplicates of the despatches of Biddle and Offley had been received at the Department of State some two months earlier, as they, with the Turkish duplicates of the treaty and of the secret article, had reached Boston on September 6, as above mentioned, and appear to have been received at the Department of State on September 19, for Offley's letter of June 21 from Smyrna is endorsed as received on that day.

Accordingly, there must have been available at Washington during September all the essential information as to the terms of the treaty and the negotiations.

The Senate Proceedings

On December 9, 1830, President Jackson submitted the treaty to the Senate with the following message, which through some error is dated December 10 (Executive Journal, IV, 126):

I submit for the consideration of the Senate a treaty of commerce and navigation, together with a separate and secret article, concluded at Constantinople on the 7th day of May last, and signed by Charles Rhind, James Biddle, and David Offley, as commissioners on the part of the United States, and by Mahommed Hamed, Reis Effendi, on the part of the Sublime Porte.

The French versions, herewith transmitted, and accompanied by copies and English translations of the same, are transcripts of the original translations from the Turkish, signed by the commissioners of the United States, and delivered to the Government of the Sublime Porte.

The paper in Turkish is the original, signed by the Turkish plenipotentiary, and delivered by him to the American commissioners. Of this a translation into the English language, and believed to be correct, is likewise transmitted.

While the message is not as explicit as it might be, there can be no doubt that there were eight documents transmitted with it, namely: (1) the Turkish original of the treaty; (2) the French version thereof; (3) an English translation of the French; (4) an English translation of the Turkish; (5) the Turkish original of the secret article; (6) the French version thereof; (7) an English translation of the French; and (8) an English translation of the Turkish.

It may be said at this point that none of those four English translations came from Constantinople. They were all written in Washington. The manuscripts of all of them are in the archives of the Department of State; the handwriting in each case is well known; and there are no other contemporaneous English translations in the archives at all.

The two Turkish documents transmitted to the Senate, the Turkish original of the treaty and the Turkish original of the separate and secret article, are in the treaty file. Each of those two Turkish documents is similarly sealed on the reverse, just back of the signature; but the seal in each case is somewhat blurred. Dr. Kramers remarks that the seal contains clearly the name Mehmed Hamid but is otherwise not very distinct. The Turkish original of the treaty is reproduced in facsimile above, except for the seal; but it has not been deemed necessary to reproduce the Turkish original of the separate and secret article.

Thus six documents which were written in French or English were sent to the Senate; and the first of the Senate documents relating to this treaty, which is dated December 9, 1830 (Senate Confidential Document, 21st Congress, 2d session, Regular Confidential Documents, I, 437–51), contains four of them. It includes the French version of the treaty, the French version of the separate article, and the respective English translations of the French.

As far as the treaty proper is concerned, it is those two translations thereof (French and English) which are printed above in parallel columns under the heading, "Other translations before the Senate." Something is now to be said as to each of those translations of the treaty proper.

The French is Navoni's translation. There is a manuscript of it in D. S., 1 Despatches, Turkey, signed by Navoni and dated at Pera June 2, 1830; that manuscript, however, cannot be the manuscript from which the Senate print was made, for the certificate at the end is in different form. However, the wording of the manuscript, except for the scrivener's and the printer's errors, is the same as that of the Senate print; and the Senate print (which includes the bracketed words in Articles 2 and 4) has here been used as the source text, subject to necessary slight corrections of spelling, punctuation, and accents.

That French text is unquestionably the same as that which was delivered on the signature of the treaty on May 7, 1830, then signed by Rhind and later (on May 30) by the other American Commissioners.

Another manuscript copy of Navoni's translation, in the handwriting of Rhind but without certification, is, as already mentioned, an enclosure with the despatch of Henry Middleton, Minister at St. Petersburg, of June 16, 1830 (D. S., 11 Despatches, Russia, No. 94); but it is clear that that copy, which shows some sixteen differences in wording (apparently scrivener's errors) from the manuscript signed by Navoni, could not have been the source of the Senate print.

The English translation from the French was made by Aaron Vail, who was then a clerk in the Department of State in Washington. His manuscript, which the Senate print followed, is also in D. S., 1 Despatches, Turkey. There is no question whatever that that manuscript is in the handwriting of Vail, who was for years in the Department of State, was afterwards Chargé d'Affaires at London, and who left many pages of his very clear penmanship in the archives. There is equally no question that the manuscript of Vail is the text of the Senate document; there is a difference of a word or so here and there and an occasional transposition, but in all essentials the two are the same.

The Senate print of December 9, 1830, is the source text for the Vail translation, which, with slight changes in spelling, capitalization, and punctuation, is printed above.

The next Senate document is dated December 16, 1830 (Senate Confidential Document, 21st Congress, 2d session, Regular Confidential Documents, I, 453–56). This contains two other papers transmitted with the above-quoted message of President Jackson, namely, English translations from (or said to be from) the Turkish of the treaty proper and of the separate article.

Referring now only to the treaty proper, there is again no question as to the origin of that English translation or as to its authorship. The manuscript thereof is in the treaty file as a part of the duplicate United States instrument of ratification of this treaty. It was written by William B. Hodgson, who was for years in the Department of

State and was reputed to know both Turkish and Arabic; he was in Washington at the time and is mentioned by name in a letter of Secretary of State Van Buren dated January 11, 1831, to which reference is made below. Many papers written by Hodgson are in the Department of State archives; indeed, it was Hodgson who was sent as a messenger to take to Commodore David Porter the ratification of this treaty and who accompanied Porter to Constantinople.

It was that translation of Hodgson in English which was adopted by this Government as its official translation of the treaty; it was included in the United States instrument of ratification; it was the text proclaimed; and it is the text which has been printed ever since, not only in the Session Laws, in the Bioren and Duane edition of the laws, and in the Statutes at Large, but also in treaty collections generally. It is the translation first printed above; that text is a literal copy of the manuscript written by Hodgson which is now in the treaty file as part of the duplicate United States instrument of ratification.

Mention has now been made of all the versions of the treaty proper of the period in question (1830–31), in either French or English, which are in the archives of the Department of State, except one. That manuscript is also in D. S., 1 Despatches, Turkey, and is in the handwriting of Hodgson. It is headed, in his handwriting, "Translation from the Original Turkish." It is, however, unquestionably not a translation from the original Turkish at all. Examination of its language shows conclusively that it is translated from Navoni's French. The text of that manuscript of Hodgson is not here reproduced.

That last-mentioned translation of Hodgson has been erroneously supposed to be a translation sent from Constantinople. Thus, in Mr. Adee's report of March 26, 1878 (D. S., 3 Notes from the Turkish Legation), the translation in question is called annex 1 to Rhind's despatch of June 1, 1830 (D. S., 1 Despatches, Turkey); but the translation of Hodgson, which is in his handwriting, could not possibly have been enclosed with Rhind's despatch, for Hodgson was in Washington. The copy of the treaty which Rhind transmitted cannot be positively identified because of the lack of endorsements on the papers of the period, but it was probably the French manuscript attested by Navoni at Pera June 2, 1830, which is in the same volume and which bears the heading, in Rhind's handwriting, "Original treaty as translated from the Turkish by N. Navoni Esqr American Dragoman." And, as Rhind discusses the secret article in the same despatch, it is very likely that that despatch also enclosed Navoni's manuscript translation of that article which is now in the treaty file. That translation, which is in Rhind's handwriting, bears the same date as the above-mentioned translation of the treaty proper and has a similar certificate of correctness.

Thus for the treaty proper, aside from the separate and secret article, there are in the Department of State archives five manuscript versions of the period, as follows:

1. The annotated French translation (printed above in these notes).

2. The French translation of Nicholas Navoni (there are two manuscripts of this version in the archives of the Department of State, one in the handwriting of Rhind and the other signed by Navoni; but the text printed above in the left column is from the Senate print, which was from still another but similar, manuscript, now missing).

3. Aaron Vail's English translation of Navoni's French (printed above in the right column).

4. Hodgson's English translation from, or said to be from, the Turkish (printed first above after the Turkish).

5. Hodgson's English translation which he stated was from the Turkish but which was in fact a translation from the French of Navoni (not printed).

Thus the Senate had before it three translations of the treaty proper, all of which were printed in Senate documents: the French of Navoni, the English of Vail, and the English of Hodgson. While there is nothing in the Senate records to indicate that the action of the Senate was based on one version or another, it seems reasonable to assume that reliance was placed chiefly, perhaps wholly, on the version of Hodgson, for it is that version which the administration adopted as the official translation; and in this connection it is to be remembered that the only question which seems to have been raised in the Senate regarding the treaty proper related to Article 7, concerning the Black Sea trade, and not to Article 4, which later became the subject of prolonged controversy.

Freedom of passage of the Straits to Russian merchant ships had been provided by the Convention of Ackerman of October 7, 1826 (the text in French is in Von Martens, Nouveau recueil de traités, VI, pt. 2, 1053–59), and, more particularly, in the Treaty of Adrianople of September 14, 1829 (*ibid.*, VIII, 143–51), in Article 7 of which there was even a declaration of freedom of passage to merchant ships of all countries at peace with the Sublime Porte. Mention is also to be made of the treaty between Spain and Turkey, signed at Constantinople October 16, 1827, "for permitting Spanish Merchant Vessels to navigate and trade in the Black Sea" (British and Foreign State Papers, XV, 762–69). A copy of that treaty was with the instructions to Biddle, Offley, and Rhind of September 12, 1829.

The question about the Black Sea trade was whether American vessels engaged in that commerce could be laden with products of countries other than the United States and Turkey. According to the Navoni translation this was somewhat doubtful. To the Senate the Committee on Foreign Relations on December 28, 1830, reported a clarifying proviso (Executive Journal, IV, 139), which seems not to have been pressed; and an amendment to the article which was offered on February 1, 1831, was defeated (*ibid.*, 149). The rendering of Article 7 by Hodgson was distinctly more favorable to the view of the United States than that of Navoni; and it may be inferred that the

Senate relied on the Hodgson text and considered the amendment superfluous.

The question of Article 7 of the treaty had been considered in the Department of State prior to the submission of the treaty to the Senate. In the treaty file is a draft in the handwriting of Vail of a long presidential message to the Senate transmitting the treaty; all but the opening paragraphs discuss the true meaning of Article 7 in the light of Navoni's translation. But the message of President Jackson as transmitted, which has been quoted above, embodied only the substance of the general opening paragraphs of the Vail draft.

On February 1, 1831, the Senate, by a vote of forty-two to one, passed a resolution of advice and consent to the ratification, "with the exception of the separate and secret article," which was thus rejected; and immediately thereafter the Senate passed another resolution for the prolongation of the time limited for the exchange of the ratifications, which reads as follows (Executive Journal, IV, 150):

Resolved (two-thirds of the Senators present concurring), That the Senate advise the President of the United States to exchange, and, on their part, consent that the ratifications of the treaty with the Ottoman Porte may be exchanged, at any time hereafter, within nine months, notwithstanding the period limited for the exchange of the said ratifications may have expired before the same can be effected, in conformity with the present provisions of the said treaty.

It is to be added that there were papers before the Senate other than treaty texts and translations; the Senate resolution of December 16, 1830, asked for "copies of the instructions given to the commissioner or commissioners who negotiated the treaty with Turkey, now before the Senate, together with copies of the commissions or letters of appointment, and of the communications of the commissioner or commissioners relating to the negotiation with the Porte, and the provisions of the treaty; and that the President be also requested to communicate to the Senate the time of appointment of our ministers or commissioners to the Sublime Porte" (*ibid.*, 130). The papers requested were furnished on December 20 (*ibid.*, 134); but they were not ordered printed, so far as the record shows (see *ibid.*, 139); and no print of them has been found. The report of Secretary of State Van Buren of December 18, 1830, which was with the papers furnished, is in D. S., 4 Report Book, 299; it includes the following paragraph:

In regard to so much of the resolution of the Senate as relates to the time of appointment of our Commissioners or Ministers to the Sublime Porte, the Secretary states for the information of the President, as relative to the subject matter of the resolution, and as would seem to be embraced by its general terms, that Commodore Rodgers was instructed, on the 7th February, 1825, though no formal commission was given to him to that effect, to sound the Captain Pacha, commander of the Naval forces of the Sultan in the Levant, upon the practicability of concluding a treaty with the Porte;—that a commission similar to that conferred upon Messrs. Biddle, Offley, and Rhind, was, on the 21st July, 1828, given to Commodore Crane and Mr Offley, empowering them to open with the Sublime Porte a negotiation for such a treaty, the result of which was received at this Department on the 14th of June, 1829, and that Messrs. Biddle, Offley, and Rhind were appointed on the 12th September following, as will be seen by the copy of their commission, herewith transmitted.

With the report mentioned is a list of the accompanying papers; those from Constantinople (all of 1830) were the despatches of Rhind of April 26 (extract), May 7, May 10, and June 1 (extract), his report to the President of May 10, the despatch of Biddle of May 31 (extract), the despatch of Offley of June 2 (extract), the letter of Biddle and Offley to the President of June 8 (extract), and a letter of Offley to Biddle of May 29. Elsewhere in these notes will be found reference to or quotation from each of those papers from Constantinople except the brief and unimportant despatch of Rhind of April 26.

The Separate and Secret Article

This was the first of the only two occasions in the history of this country when the President of the United States has submitted to the Senate a secret treaty engagement with another country.

No doubt seems to have been entertained as to the power of the United States to make such a secret engagement if it chose. The instructions to the American Commissioners of September 12, 1829 (D. S., 1 Instructions, Turkey, 196–202), had suggested a secret article regarding Turkish customs duties. The resolution proposed by the Senate Committee on Foreign Relations in its report of December 28, 1830, above mentioned, advised and consented to the ratification of the entire treaty, including the separate and secret article, although it contained a qualifying proviso in respect of that article. Two amendments to the separate and secret article were proposed in the Senate and withdrawn, and a third was defeated by a vote of twenty-two yeas to twenty-three noes, following which the article itself was rejected, yeas eighteen, noes twenty-seven (Executive Journal, IV, 142, 145, 148–49). The rejection of the separate and secret article by the Senate seems to have been due entirely to objections to its substance.

It has been seen that the despatches of Rhind were silent on the question of this article until its signature. In his despatch of June 1, 1830, he states that the article was proposed by the Turkish negotiators:

It was necessary to shew The Sultan that *something* had been granted for the concessions he had made, and our Turkish Friends suggested the private article. You will perceive that it is a *perfect nullity*, giving only the privilege of *consulting* with our Minister about the best mode of making a Contract to procure Ships or Ship Timber and moreover The Reis Effendi said that if The President was not disposed to sign the article, it would be of no consequence, and the Treaty would be ratified without it; but added that it would be pleasing, if the whole are accepted in order to lay them before The Sultan at the final ratification.

Like the treaty proper, the separate and secret article was signed in Turkish on May 7, 1830, by the Reis Effendi, and delivered to Rhind in exchange for the French version thereof signed by Rhind and which was later, on May 30, signed by his colleagues, Commodore Biddle and David Offley.

As stated above, the Turkish original of the separate and secret article is in the treaty file; like the Turkish original of the treaty, it is sealed on the reverse, just back of the signature, with a somewhat blurred seal containing the name Mehmed Hamid. It has not been deemed necessary to reproduce that document in facsimile.

In the archives of the Department of State there are two French versions of this article, similar and each attested by Navoni. They doubtless contain the French text which was signed by the Commissioners at Constantinople. One of those two manuscripts is in D. S., 1 Despatches, Turkey, and the other is in the treaty file. They are alike in all essentials. The certificate of the latter is dated June 2, 1830, and differs somewhat from that of the former; and it has a note at the end which may be translated as follows:

In the Ottoman Empire the prices which the Government pay are different from those paid by individuals. This is why the privilege of paying as the Government of the United States pays is requested, supposing that there exists that same difference in the United States.

When the treaty was submitted to the Senate with the message of President Jackson above quoted, one of the accompanying papers was the French version of Navoni of this article, and another was an English translation of the French, by Aaron Vail. The manuscript of the latter is also in D. S., 1 Despatches, Turkey; and the two, the French of Navoni and the English of Vail, are printed in the Senate document dated December 9, 1830.

With that message of Jackson there was also sent another English translation of the separate and secret article, made by Hodgson and stated (erroneously) to have been made direct from the Turkish. The manuscript of that translation, in Hodgson's handwriting, is also in D. S., 1 Despatches, Turkey. On January 11, 1831, Secretary of State Van Buren wrote to Senator Tazewell, Chairman of the Senate Committee on Foreign Relations, as follows (D. S., 4 Report Book, 302):

In the papers submitted to the Senate with the President's Message, communicating the Treaty lately concluded with the Sublime Porte, the separate and Secret Article attached to the same is described as being a translation from the original Turkish. At that time it was believed by the Department to be of that character; but it has recently been informed by Mr Hodgson, the clerk who made the translation of the treaty from the Turkish, that finding no material difference between the French and Turkish, with respect to the Secret Article, he had made his translation of it from the French, and through inadvertence, omitted to inform me of the circumstance. I think it is due to the Senate that the mistake should be corrected, and have to request the favor of you to do so, by submitting to it this official letter with its enclosure. This enclosure, a translation of the Separate Article from the Turkish, now made by Mr. Hodgson, will enable the Senate to decide whether there is any material difference between it and that from the French, already submitted.

Accordingly, that supposed translation of the separate and secret article from the Turkish by Hodgson was abandoned; in place thereof another English translation, again stated to have been made by Hodgson direct from the Turkish, was substituted; and that English

translation was printed in a Senate document dated January 12, 1831. No manuscript of that last translation has been found in the archives.

Accordingly, there were no less than four translations of the separate and secret article printed by the Senate, as follows: the French of Navoni and the English of Vail, printed in the Senate document dated December 9, 1830; the first English of Hodgson, printed in the Senate document dated December 16, 1830; and the subsequent English of Hodgson, printed in the Senate document dated January 12, 1831. For all of these except the last there is in the Department of State archives the equivalent manuscript, and for the first mentioned, the French of Navoni, there are two such manuscripts.

As the separate and secret article was rejected by the Senate, it is printed below as part of these notes. Three versions of it are printed. In parallel columns are the French of Navoni and the English rendering thereof by Vail; the French of Navoni has been collated with the manuscript signed by him which is in D. S., 1 Despatches, Turkey; the English of Vail has been collated with the Senate print of December 9, 1830. Following the parallel columns is the later translation of Hodgson, which has been taken from the Senate document dated January 12, 1831. All three translations are printed with some slight corrections of spelling, capitalization, accents, etc. The earlier translation of Hodgson (printed in the Senate document of December 16, 1830), which he said was from the Turkish but which was in fact from the French, is not printed.

It should be added that in the Senate document of December 9, 1830, the following words of the French of Navoni are omitted: "et que les frais de construction ne soient pas plus forts que les frais ordinaires des bâtiments de guerre des États-Unis"; there is a corresponding omission in Vail's English translation of the French, both in his manuscript and in the Senate print; but as the French omitted in the Senate print appears here as Navoni wrote it, the equivalent English has been inserted in the other parallel column in brackets.

[Translation]	[Translation]
### Acte Séparé Contenant un Article Secret	### Separate Act Containing a Secret Article
L'objet et le motif de la rédaction de cet écrit est que comme il n'a pas existé jusqu'à ce jour aucun traité ni convention officielle et diplomatique entre la Sublime Porte, de perpétuelle durée, et la puissance des Etats-Unis d'Amérique, nous, soussigné, revêtu du haut rang du *Riasset* de la Sublime Porte, à jamais existante (Ministère de la Chancellerie d'Etat), ayant été cette fois-ci autorisé par Sa Très Noble Majesté Impériale à entamer la négociation avec notre ami, l'Honorable Commissaire et Plenipotentiaire des Etats-Unis d'Amérique, Charles Rhind, venu à cette Résidence Impériale avec	The object and motive of the drawing up of this writing is that, whereas to this day there has not existed any treaty or official and diplomatic convention between the Sublime Porte, of perpetual duration, and the Government of the United States of America, we, the undersigned, invested with the high rank of *Riasset* of the ever-subsisting Sublime Porte (Department of the Chancery of State), having been, this time, authorized by His Most Noble Imperial Majesty to open a negotiation with our friend, the Honorable Charles Rhind, Commissioner and Plenipotentiary of the United States

pleins pouvoirs afin de traiter et conclure, séparément, ou conjointement avec les deux autres Commissaires et Plénipotentiaires, le Commodore Biddle et David Offley, qui sont a Smyrne, nous avons conclu et échangé entre nous les instruments contenant les articles du traité, qui a été ensuite également signé par les deux autres Commissaires et Plénipotentiaires susmentionnés.

En conséquence de ce traité, de la manière ci-dessus énoncée, nouvellement conclu, et en vertu des relations de la plus sincère amitié qui vient de s'établir entre les deux puissances, et des principes d'avantages réciproques qui en doivent résulter, il a été dressé cet article séparé et secret, par lequel, en considération de l'abondance et de la solidité du bois de construction dans les Etats-Unis d'Amérique et du prix plus convenable, et en témoignage éclatant de la sincère amitié de la puissance susmentionnée envers la Sublime Porte, il a été arrêté que toutes les fois que la Sublime Porte voudrait faire construire dans les Etats-Unis un nombre quelconque de vaisseaux à deux ponts, de frégates, corvettes, et bricks de guerre, le Ministère du *Riasset* (Chancellerie d'Etat et des Affaires Etrangères) s'adressant, et se concertant avec, le Ministre de la dite puissance près la Sublime Porte sur la manière de faire un contrat, qui contiendra les conditions convenues relativement aux frais de construction, à l'espace du temps convenable pour la conclusion de l'ouvrage, et aux moyens de les faire parvenir à Constantinople; afin que, en vertu de ce contrat, les bâtiments que l'on voudra faire construire, d'après les modèles qui seront remis par cette Amirauté Impériale, soient construits dans les Etats-Unis, aussi forts et solides que les bâtiments de guerre des Etats-Unis et que les frais de construction ne soient pas plus forts que les frais ordinaires des bâtiments de guerre des Etats-Unis. De même, si la Sublime Porte le desirait, les Commissaires des deux puissances se concerteront, afin que les bâtiments qui auront été construits, au lieu de partir sur lest, des Etats-Unis pour Constantinople, il soit chargé à bord de chaque bâtiment la quantité de bois nécessaire et suffisante pour la construction d'un autre bâtiment de la même forme et dimension, au

of America, who has come to this Imperial Residence with full powers to treat of and conclude, separately, or jointly with the other two Commissioners and Plenipotentiaries, Commodore Biddle and David Offley, now at Smyrna, we have concluded and exchanged between us this instrument, containing the articles of the treaty, which has, likewise, subsequently been signed by the other two Commissioners and Plenipotentiaries aforesaid.

In consequence of the treaty recently concluded in the manner above mentioned, and by virtue of the relations of the most sincere friendship which has just been established between the two powers, and the principles of reciprocal advantages which are to result therefrom, this separate and secret article has been framed, by which, considering the abundance and strength of ship timber in the United States of America and the more suitable price thereof, and as a signal proof of the sincere friendship entertained by the aforesaid power towards the Sublime Porte, it has been agreed that whenever the Sublime Porte may wish to cause to be built in the United States any number whatever of ships of two decks, frigates, sloops, and brigs of war, the Department of the *Riasset* (Chancery of State and of Foreign Affairs) may apply to, and concert with, the Minister of said power near the Sublime Porte, respecting the manner of making a contract, which shall contain the conditions agreed upon in relation to the cost of construction, the space of time for the completion of the work, and the means of having it conveyed to Constantinople; in order that, by virtue of such contract, the ships which may be ordered to be built agreeably to the models which will be furnished by this Imperial Admiralty, may be built, in the United States, as strong and solid as the ships of war of the United States [and that the costs of construction shall not be greater than the ordinary costs of ships of war of the United States]. In like manner, if the Sublime Porte should desire it, the Commissioners of the two powers will concert together, in order that instead of the vessels which may have been built sailing from the United States in ballast, there may be laden on board of each the necessary and sufficient quantity of timber for the construction of another vessel of the same form and dimensions,

même prix que le Gouvernement de la dite puissance aurait établi et payerait pour ses propres bâtiments, en le faisant couper et préparer sur les lieux d'après les mesures et dimensions données à qui de droit.

Les susmentionnés Commissaires et Plénipotentiaires, nos amis, ayant accepté et contracté cet engagement, il en a été dressé et signé un article séparé et secret, qui aura son exécution comme les autres articles du traité qui vient d'être conclu, qui doivent être en toute chose observés après l'échange des ratifications, qui aura lieu à peu près d'ici à dix mois, à compter du jour de la date de cet instrument.

Donné a Constantinople le quatorzième jour de Zilcaadé, de l'année 1245, et de l'ere Chrétienne le septième mai de l'année 1830.

Pour traduction éxacte et littérale.

N. Navoni

at the price which may have been fixed by the Government of said power to be paid for its own vessels, the timber to be cut and prepared on the spot according to the measures and dimensions given to whom it may belong.

The above-mentioned Commissioners and Plenipotentiaries, our friends, having accepted and contracted this engagement, there has been drawn up and signed a separate and secret article, which shall have its execution in the same manner as the other articles of the treaty just concluded, which shall in every respect be observed after the exchange of the ratifications, which shall take place in about ten months from this time, counting from the day of the date of this instrument.

Given at Constantinople the fourteenth day of Zu'lkadah in the year 1245, and of the Christian era the seventh May, 1830.

An exact and literal translation.

N. Navoni

[Translation]

The motive of this firm writing and the cause of this instrument, well drawn out, is that, no treaty or official and diplomatic convention having until now existed between the Sublime Porte, of perpetual duration, and the United States of America; at this time we, the undersigned, invested with the high rank of the *Riasset* (office of Reis Effendi) of the Sublime Porte, existing forever, having been permitted by His Very Noble Imperial Majesty to treat with the Honorable (firm) Charles Rhind, our friend, who has come to this Imperial Residence with full powers to negotiate and conclude a treaty, separately, and conjointly with the other two Commissioners, Commodore Biddle and David Offley, have concluded and exchanged the articles of a treaty, which are hereafter to be signed by the other two aforesaid Commissioners.

This new treaty having thus been concluded, sincere and increased friendship being thereby established, and mutual advantages secured, it is agreed by our friend aforesaid, in testimony of the pure friendship of the United States towards the Sublime Porte and on account of the abundance and durability of the timber and the cheapness of construction in the United States, that whenever the Sublime Porte may wish to build any number of *caiks*,[1] frigates, corvettes, or brigs of war in the United States, the *Riasset* shall take the counsel and advice of their Minister Resident near the Sublime Porte; and in whatever way it may be talked of and mentioned, as to the expense and time of construction and the mode of conveying the ships to the Imperial Residence, in that way it shall be fixed, according to a contract, so that the ships may be constructed by the models furnished from this Imperial Admiralty and be as well built as vessels of the United States, and at no greater cost.

So, also, again, if it be desired, the two Commissioners shall arrange that the ships built in the United States be not sent to the Imperial Admiralty (Constantinople) in ballast, but that each ship be laden with a quantity of timber sufficient for the construction of another ship of equal dimensions and of the same cost as similar ships of the United States, the timber having been cut in its place according to measures furnished therefor.

---

[1] "Caiks" or "caiques" here is erroneous. The Turkish is "kapaks," meaning "two-deckers."

After the above-mentioned treaty shall have been signed by the aforesaid Commissioners, this separate article, to be added to that treaty as a secret article, shall also be signed.

In ten months from the date of this *temessuck*, or instrument of treaty, the ratifications shall be exchanged.

He who asks assistance from God, the King, the Giver of Good,

MEHMED HAMID
Reis-ul-Kuttab (i.e., Reis Effendi)

Written the fourteenth day of Zu'lkadah the noble, and in the year 1245.

The separate and secret article has also been translated by Dr. Kramers (in 1931), whose rendering is printed below. As the preamble of the separate article is much like that of the treaty proper and as various other expressions in the two documents are similar, the notes of Dr. Kramers regarding the treaty proper should be consulted.

[Translation]

The reason of the writing of this document and the motive of the drawing up of this writ are as follows:

As there has not been concluded heretofore any kind of official treaty between the everlasting Sublime Government and the Government of the United States of America, now, as we, the undersigned functionary, occupying the elevated degree of Chief of the Secretaries of the ever-stable Sublime Government and of the exalted Sultanate, eternally enduring, have been authorized by the Most Noble Imperial Excellency, there have been negotiations between us and our friend Charles Rhind, who has been charged and commissioned with complete authority by the aforesaid Government, separately by coming to the Gate of Felicity and jointly with the functionaries named Commodore Biddle and David Offley, now being in the town of Smyrna.

The documents containing the treaty articles that have been drawn up and established as a result of these negotiations, have been exchanged and will be undersigned hereafter by the two aforesaid functionaries.

Now that in this way a new treaty and an increased friendship and amity have been established between the two Governments, in observance of the principles of mutual profit and common interest and with regard to the fact that in the state of America timber is abundant and strong and that the building expenses are there light and small, the aforesaid functionary, our friend, in confirmation of the sincere feelings of the said Government towards the glorious Imperial Sultanate, has contracted the obligation that, whenever the Sublime Government shall order the building and construction in the dominion of America of whatever quantity of war vessels, such as two-deckers, frigates, corvettes, and brigs, this shall be communicated and notified by the office of the Chief (of the Secretaries) to the functionary of the said Government who will be at that time at the Gate of Felicity; that there shall be drawn up a contractual document stating in which way it has been negotiated and agreed upon with regard to the building expenses, the time of construction, and also to the mode of sending and conveying to the Gate of Felicity, according to which contract the required ships shall be built and constructed after the design and model to be fixed and explained by the Imperial Arsenal, so as to be as strong and tight as the Government ships of the said Government, and provided that the building expenses be not higher than the expenses of the war ships of the said Government; and that, in case of an order being given, and so as to prevent the required ships from arriving empty at the Imperial Arsenal, there shall be negotiations between the functionaries of both parties, according to which there shall be laden and sent in each ship the timber necessary for the construction of another ship like that ship itself, provided that the price be in accordance with the official price of the said Government and that the material be calculated carefully and prepared in its place, after having been cut and well executed according to the measure.

This separate article, after having been signed by the two aforesaid functionaries, is destined to be a secret article and to be counted as a part of the mentioned treaty. By the exchange of the ratifications within ten months after the day of this document, it shall be observed in every way.

Written on the fourteenth day of the noble month of Zu'lkadah of the year twelve hundred and forty-five.

He who beseeches the generous King for his assistance,

MEHMED HAMID
Chief of the Secretaries

THE UNITED STATES RATIFICATION

A duplicate of the United States instrument of ratification is in the treaty file. The document is in rather poor condition and has been restored. It is under the Great Seal, signed by Andrew Jackson, and attested by Secretary of State Van Buren; otherwise (aside from the English translation annexed) it is in the handwriting of Aaron Vail. It is erroneously dated February 2, 1830, instead of February 2, 1831, and reads as follows:

Andrew Jackson President of the United States of America,

To all and singular who shall see these Presents,—Greeting.

Whereas a Treaty of Commerce and Navigation between the United States of America and the Ottoman Porte, whereof the original in the Turkish language, and a translation of the same in English are hereunto annexed, was concluded and signed at Constantinople by the respective Plenipotentiaries of the two Powers on the seventh day of May, in the year of our Lord one thousand eight hundred and thirty;—and whereas the Senate of the United States, by their Resolution on the first day of February one thousand eight hundred and thirty one, two thirds of the Senators then present concurring, did advise and consent to the ratification of the said Treaty

Now, therefore, I, Andrew Jackson President of the United States of America, having seen and considered the said Treaty, in pursuance of the aforesaid advice and consent of the Senate, by these presents accept, ratify and confirm the said Treaty, and every clause and Article thereof.

In faith whereof I have caused the Seal of the United States of America to be hereunto affixed.

Given under my hand, at the City of Washington, this second day of February, in the year of Our Lord one thousand eight hundred and [Seal] thirty; and of the Independence of the United States of America, the fifty fifth.

ANDREW JACKSON

By the President
  M. VAN BUREN
      Secretary of State.

With the duplicate instrument of ratification are the original treaty in Turkish—that is, the treaty proper without the separate and secret article—and also the manuscript of the Hodgson translation, in his handwriting, which was adopted by this Government as its official translation of the treaty. It is headed "Translation from the original Turkish, of the Treaty concluded between the United States and the Ottoman Porte."

There are also now (perhaps not originally) with the duplicate instrument of ratification, the two Senate resolutions of February 1, 1831, attested, on one sheet.

The Turkish Ratification

The Turkish instrument of ratification has also been examined by Dr. Kramers. The following observations and renderings are from his report.

The ratification was the act of the Sultan. The tughra (name sign), which is at the heading of the document, is that of Sultan Mahmud, son of Abdul Hamid. The Turkish sentence written to the right of the tughra is "According to this it has been ratified by my Imperial side," a further indication of the fact that the instrument was the act of the Sultan. The tughra takes the place of the seal or of the signature of the sovereign; and if this ratification bore a seal, a point now impossible to determine because of the condition of the document, the seal was that of the Grand Vizier, or of the Reis-ul-Kuttab (Chief of the Secretaries), and not that of the Sultan himself.

The document is dated in the last days of Rabia II, A. H. 1247. According to the chronological tables that month ended on October 7, 1831; so the dating is in accord with the despatch of Commodore Porter which stated that the exchange of the ratifications took place on October 5, 1831.

The opening clauses of the ratification run about as follows:

With the assistance of God . . . and of the Prophet . . . I, the ruler of . . . [a long list of countries and towns], am Sultan Mahmud, son of Sultan Abdul Hamid . . . [a list of imperial titles], whose residence is generally acknowledged as a place of refuge for all great rulers.

The paragraphs following have been given a literal translation. The functionary, Ahmed Khulusi Pasha, who is referred to as the Vizier, was at the time *locum tenens* (kaimmakam) of the Grand Vizier Reshid Pasha, who was not then in the capital.

Consequently, as there did not exist as yet any kind of official treaty between My everlasting Sublime Government and the Government of the United States of America, now, as the said Government had manifested the complete wish and desire to contract a treaty containing articles on commerce and relations with My eternally lasting Sublime Government, the said Government has given and granted complete authority to negotiate and conclude the said matter, separately to the model of the notable people of the Christian community, Charles Rhind—may his end be blessed—who has arrived at the Gate of Felicity, and jointly with the functionaries called Commodore Biddle and David Offley, being in the town of Smyrna, and after the treating of this affair had been approved of by Our crown-bearing Threshold, elevated to the sphere, there has been designated from the side of My illustrious Royalty, in order to negotiate the articles of the treaty, My former Chief of the Secretaries, the glory of the praiseworthy and noble people, Mehmed Hamid—may his praise endure—who, having negotiated with the said Plenipotentiary of the above-said Government, there has been reached an agreement on both sides, on nine articles and a conclusion.

The treaty instrument, written in Frengi [i.e., Frankish or European], as this was more convenient to the said functionary, having been presented with a translation to the foot of Our mighty Royal Throne, and having been approved of by Our noble-minded Lordship, has been exchanged; in consequence of which there has now arrived the ratification letter communicating the acceptance and confirmation of the said Government, which ratification having been presented and referred to the noble audience of Our Lordship by the noble Vizier and illus-

trious marshal and administrator of the world, who leads the state affairs with penetrating intellect and accomplishes the interests of humanity with striking insight, who lays the foundations of happy government and prosperity and fortifies the columns bearing felicity and illustriousness, who is surrounded by the accessories of the highest royal power, at present the *locum tenens* of My imperial stirrup, My Vizier Ahmed Khulusi Pasha—may God make him continually illustrious—this matter has become known to Our Sublime Imperial Highness, after which the articles of the said treaty have equally been confirmed and declared to be in force by Our exalted Royalty, and, with the view of making them respected and observed, wherever it shall be required, these articles are quoted and mentioned identically.

Then follows in the ratification the text of the treaty, that is to say, the nine articles thereof and the conclusion or final clause, ending with the equivalent of the words "between the two Governments." The preamble of the treaty is not repeated, but for the most part it appears in the clauses of the ratification above translated.

After the text of the treaty come the final clauses of the ratification, the translation of which is given below. There are, however, two gaps in the Turkish text. An effort has been made to complete these by comparison of the text with that of the Belgian treaty with Turkey of 1838, but so much of the translation below as is enclosed in brackets (representing the first gap) gives no more than the probable general sense, as the Belgian treaty is rather different at this point. The words in italics (representing the second gap) are in all probability correct, as in the corresponding sentence the Belgian treaty has nearly the same text.

The foregoing text was written in the treaty instruments that have been exchanged between the Plenipotentiaries of both parties, dated the fourteenth day of the noble month of Zu'lkadah of the year twelve hundred and forty-five. Now [that this has been agreed upon by the two Governments], as long as attention shall be paid to the rules of friendship and amity and to the observation of contractual obligations, there shall not be allowed [any infraction] by the Imperial Sublime Government, and, in order to confirm perpetually the bases of friendship and to *strengthen the foundations of sincere amity*, there shall be performance according to *this Our Imperial sign and* the full contents of Our *obligation, full of solicitude.*
Written in the last days of the month of Rabia el-Akhir of the year 1247.

The abode of the Sublime Sultanate,
Constantinople the well preserved.

The Exchange of Ratifications

The duty of exchanging the ratifications of this treaty was entrusted to Commodore David Porter, who was appointed Chargé d'Affaires at Constantinople (D. S., 2 Credences, 164, April 15, 1831). Long and detailed instructions were given to him under date of April 15, 1831 (D. S., 1 Instructions, Turkey, 211–25). The instructions referred to the fact that the time allowed by the treaty itself for the exchange of ratifications had elapsed; somewhat elaborately they gave reasons for the rejection of the separate and secret article by the Senate; and while Porter was not directed to make any representations regarding the interpretation of Article 7 at the time of the

exchange of ratifications, that article was discussed in the instructions, with some observations regarding the translations of the treaty, as follows:

The Treaty transmitted to this Department, was drawn up in the Turkish language, and signed by the Reis Effendi: A french translation made by the Dragoman, Mr Navoni, was signed by the United States Commissioners. This translation is not beleived to be in all respects a correct one, & a doubt has in consequence been raised by some about the interpretation of the 7th Article. According to the intention of this Government, and the understanding of its negotiators, and what is regarded here as the true construction of that article, the merchant vessels of the United States will be permitted to pass into, and return from the Black Sea, either in ballast or laden with any kind of Cargo, *permitted to the Merchant vessels of the most favoured nations*, whether the same consist of articles of the growth, produce or manufacture of the United States, or of the Ottoman Empire, or of any other country whatsoever; But it was feared by some that according to the french version of the article in question, as it was received from the Commissioners, the commerce of the United States would, in this regard, be restricted to the productions of the Ottoman Dominions, and the United States, while the vessels of other and more favored nations would not be so restricted. This latter construction is opposed by the tenor of the Treaty, and particularly of the 7th Article itself; by the friendly disposition manifested by the Turkish Government, and by what is stated to have been the express understanding of the Commissioners. A version of the Treaty into the English language, made by Mr Hodgson of this Department, sustains the interpretation of the commissioners, which asserts a free and unrestricted commerce, subject only to such conditions as are imposed on the vessels and their cargoes of the most favored nations. This privilege is expressly granted by the first clause of the 7th Article; and by the legitimate rule of interpreting Treaties, it could not be annulled by an ambiguous phrase in a subsequent clause, and is moreover the 7th article of the Treaty of Adrianople. The construction thus adopted by us, is, we have no doubt, the true meaning of the article in the Turkish original. You are therefore specially instructed, to claim for the United States the privilege of trade which it concedes; and to announce to the Imperial Ministry, if ever the right of the United States should be contested, that upon no other terms was the Treaty ratified by the President or assented to by the Senate.

Porter was told that one of the first of his duties would be to effect "with the Turkish Government an exchange of the ratification on the part of the President of the Treaty already referred to, which, in the English language, together with a french translation thereof, is herewith committed to your charge for that purpose, against one, on the part of the Sultan, of a similar character"; and also, in referring to the negotiations which resulted in the conclusion of the treaty, it was added: "an authentic and official translation whereof into the English language, accompanied by a french translation thereof, as already stated, both of which have been made here, received the sanction of the President, and to which his act of ratification is attached, is herewith transmitted to you, as above stated, to be delivered to the Turkish Government, in exchange for the ratification by the Sultan of the same Treaty, for this Government."

To Porter was also sent a letter from the President to the Sultan explaining the rejection of the separate and secret article, together with "an introductory letter from this Department, to the Reis Effendi, or minister of foreign affairs, at Constantinople."

All the papers were entrusted to William B. Hodgson, who also had a full power to exchange the ratifications, to be used in case

Commodore Porter did not accept the appointment as Chargé d'Affaires (D. S., 2 Credences, 165, April 15, 1831; 1 Instructions, Turkey, 227–28). Hodgson sailed on the U. S. S. *John Adams* in the latter part of April, 1831. He met Commodore Porter at Mahon and went on with him to Constantinople, where they arrived on August 11, 1831.

At Constantinople Porter met with difficulties, which were somewhat complicated by the fact that he soon came to distrust Navoni, who had received a formal appointment as "Drogoman or Interpreter of Languages to the Legation" under date of March 3, 1831 (D. S., 2 Credences, 162). Porter suspended Navoni from office, charging him with "infidelity and intrigues."

There seems at first to have been some dissatisfaction on the part of the Turkish Foreign Office with the rank of Commodore Porter as Chargé d'Affaires and not as Minister, but he was duly received on September 13. No particular question seems to have been made regarding the expiration of the period allowed for the exchange; but the Turkish Foreign Office was deeply concerned about the rejection of the separate and secret article and, according to the letter of Navoni to Porter of September 23, 1831 (D. S., 2 Despatches, Turkey, No. 20, September 23, 1831, enclosure), refused to accept the English translation of the treaty and insisted that, as the ratification was not based on the original French translation, the Turkish Government would accept nothing but ratification of the Turkish text alone.

On this last point Porter yielded; he signed a declaration, later called a "codicil," a copy of which is with his despatch of September 26 (*ibid.*, No. 22), as "a translation from the Turkish, of what I have agreed to sign," as follows:

Some expressions in the French translation of the Turkish instrument, exchanged between the Plenipotentiaries of the two Contracting Parties, and which contains the articles of the Treaty of Commerce concluded between the Sublime Porte and the United States of America, not being perfectly in accordance with the Turkish Original, a circumstance purely the effect of translation, and the Government of the United States being satisfied with the Turkish Treaty, and having accepted it, without the reserve of any word:

Therefore; on every occasion, the above Instrument shall be strictly observed; and if, hereafter, any discussion should arise between the Contracting Parties, the said Instrument shall be consulted by me and by my Successors, to remove doubts.

In faith of which, I have, officially signed the present copy, accurately compared, of the Turkish Instrument.

(Signed)   DAVID PORTER
Chargé d'Affaires

Constantinople
    Septr 26. 1831.

Translation from the Turkish Original

Wm B. HODGSON

It should be stated here, however, that an examination of the Turkish archives made in 1873, of which more will be said hereafter, disclosed the fact that the document signed and sealed by Porter was

written in the following very poor French, of which the foregoing text is a quite literal translation:

CONSTANTINOPLE *le 26ᵐᵉ de Septembre, 1831.*

Quoique quelques expressions de la traduction française de l'instrument turc, echangé entre les plenipotentiaires des deux parties contractantes, et qui contient les articles du traité de commerce, conclu entre la Sublime Porte et les États-Unis d'Amériques ne soit pas tout à fait, d'accord avec l'original turc, cette circonstance étant seulement le résultat de la traduction et le Gouvernement des États-Unis étant satisfait du Traité Turc et l'ayant accépté, sans réserve d'aucune mot: Pour cet effet, dans toutes les occasions, le susdit instrument sera strictement observé, et si dans l'avenir, quelque discussion s'élèvera entre les deux partiés contractantes, le susdit instrument sera consulté de ma part, et de la part de mes successeurs pour lever de doutes.

En foi de quoi j'ai signé officiellement la présente copiè collationnée du dit instrument turc.

(L. S.) Signé DAVID PORTER
Chargé d'affaires des Etats-Unis d'Amerique

In his despatch of October 23, 1831 (*ibid.*, No. 27), Porter states that he signed the document in French, but that it had been drafted originally in Turkish by the Reis Effendi:

In the paper, drawn up in Turkish by the Reis Effendi, to be translated into French for me to sign, copy of which I had the honour to send you on the 26ᵗʰ ult° this is admited; yet I am aprehensive of difficulties on the subject.

In respect of the separate and secret article Porter also yielded as far as he could; he describes his action in his despatch of September 26 as follows:

The rejection of the Separate Article, caused great irritation on the part of the Porte, and there is great reason to believe that, Mʳ Navoni has used every effort to keep it up, and aggravate it; but since his suspension from duty, which was on the 23ᵈ, the day on which I began to correspond with the Porte, without his intervention, I have reconciled them to the rejection of the article in question, by substituting in place of it, paper N° 2, which is in strict conformity with my instructions of the 15ᵗʰ of April last, and I hope will meet your approbation.

The only available text of that "paper No. 2" is that enclosed in the despatch of Porter. It is a rather extraordinary document, and it must be supposed that it was duly executed, although it was not mentioned as among the papers in the Turkish archives when they were examined in 1873. The text, as Porter gives it, is as follows:

Whereas; a Treaty of Amity and commerce, has been negotiated between the United States of America and the Sublime Porte, to which the Commissioner on the part of the United States, has, without authority, permitted to be added, a Separate Article, in favor of the Sublime Porte, which it is not in the power of the Government of the United States to execute, thus deceiving the Sublime Porte, and causing great embarrassment to the Government of the United States:

Now, I David Porter, Chargé d'Affaires acting for, and in behalf of, the United States, near the Sublime Porte, do, in conformity with the orders of the President of the United States, and as an *Equivalent* for the aforesaid rejected Separate Article, hold myself, at all times, ready to give my friendly council and advice, to the Sublime Porte, as to the best manner of obtaining ships of War, wood for their construction, and timber of every description, from the United States, and to obtain all the advantages contemplated by the said separate

article, without violating the Laws of the United States, or conflicting with their engagements with other Nations.

This concession is to be binding on the part of my successors.

In witness whereof I have hereunto placed my signature and seal of Office this   day of   of the year   in the City of Constantinople.

(Signed)   DAVID PORTER
Chargé d'Affaires

Done into French.
   W B. H.

As Porter justified his action in this regard by his instructions of April 15, 1831 (D. S., 1 Instructions, Turkey, 211–25), the following extract therefrom is quoted:

These grounds for the rejection of the separate and secret article, should not fail to be satisfactory to the Ottoman Ministry. They imply no want of good feeling on the part of this Government; for it cannot but see an advantage to our commerce in the building of vessels of war in the Ports of the United States of which it would be its duty and right to avail itself; and in this light you will present the subject to the Imperial Ministry. At the same time you will assure the Reis Effendi, that although this separate article was by the Senate deemed liable to the objections stated, or some of them, and was therefore unacceptable to that body, yet, that whenever the Sublime Porte may wish to construct Ships of War in the United States, your good offices will be rendered in the advice & counsel which your knowledge of the subject and experience may enable you to give it as to the best manner of accomplishing that object, thus securing to the Sublime Porte all the advantages contemplated by it from the article in question according to the version of it given by Mr Rhind.

Porter also promised the Reis Effendi, "in order to hasten the Exchange of Ratifications," that he would use his best offices to obtain from this Government for the Sultan something over and above the customary present; he hinted at a steamboat which might be used for the purpose of towing the Sultan's barges during his frequent excursions on the Bosporus. In his despatch of September 30 (D. S., 2 Despatches, Turkey, No. 24) Porter enlarges on the subject and gives some details of his idea. He says that it would be an affair of from five to ten thousand dollars, that the Sultan is exceedingly fond of such things, that something is due him "after the trick played on him" (referring to the separate article), that the snuffbox which he proposes giving to the Sultan would alone cost ten thousand dollars, and that he would substitute a steamboat of the proper kind if there were time; he thought it need not be larger in the essentials than the launch of a line-of-battle ship, but with additional ornaments for appearance and with a neat, small cabin; and he concluded: "The ornamental parts of the Boat might be made to resemble a Swan The head and neck fixed to bow, The wings to the Guards of the wheel and the Tail to the Stern."

It does not appear from the archives of the Department of State that the suggestion of Porter received any consideration.

The exchange of ratifications took place on October 5, 1831, and was reported by Porter in his despatch of that date (*ibid.*, No. 26), in which he wrote, "I transmit to you, by the hands of Mr Hodgson, the Turkish ratified Treaty in Exchange for the American copy, which was delivered to the Reis Effendi this morning."

Another account of the circumstances surrounding the exchange of ratifications is that of Navoni, written after his suspension from office, but at a time when he did not consider his employment definitively terminated (D. S., 1 Despatches, Turkey, October 10, 1831):

By his [Hodgson's] intrigues he has misled the Executive of the United States in making them believe that my translation of the Treaty was not correct & induced them to ratify a translation, which he pretended to have made, correct, or *more probably made up from mine*, this the Sublime Porte has refused to accept, saying that this acceptance of the Senate, not being in conformity with that deposited here & signed by the three Commissioners & by myself as Drogman or Interpreter of the United States, which translation was verified at the time by the Drogman of the Imperial Divan, who found it to be correct & Strictly according with the original Turkish, & consequently they could not accept or exchange ratifications on a translation so widely different from the real one.   Mʳ Hodgson thus seeing that his intrigues were about to be discovered, used every effort to have the exchange accomplished, & asserted that the Copy which had been Sent to the Government of the United States was not a correct one, nor did it conform to the one Signed by the Commissioners & left with the Sublime Porte, in consequence whereof a new translation became necessary, but that the Government of the United States being perfectly satisfied with the Turkish original, Monsieur le Chargé d'Affaires had no objection to signing *it* /e.e. the Turkish/ together with a declaration also in turkish, by which he will accept the Turkish Copy in all its parts /this offer was made to him by the Reis Efendi, who did not believe it possible, he would accede to such an unprecedented act/ and in this manner the ratifications have been exchanged.

It is evident that by this act, the ratification by the Senate has been made null and void, and it is the Chargé d'Affaires who has made the Treaty & ratified it himself.

Respecting the Separate or private article, which the Government of the United States would not ratify, Mʳ le Chargé d'Affaires has signed an obligation by which he agrees to accept it with the only difference that the Sublime Porte is not to expect to have vessels constructed at the same price as the American Government: a modification which amounts to nothing, and which certainly was not the motive which induced the Government to reject that article.   In addition to this Mʳ le Chargé d'Affaires has Solemnly promised that the United States will make a present to the ottoman Porte of a *Steam Vessel* or a *frigate* leaving it to the latter Government to make a choice of the two.   His Excellency the Reis Efendi told him that as regarded that proposition, & that as he possessed that authority, in place of waiting 6. or 8. months, he need only take the vessel of Mʳ Eckford, which gave great Satisfaction to the Sultan & thus make him the present at once.   Mʳ le Commodore finding himself a little embarrassed at this proposal replied, that this was a matter entirely separate from his concerns, that the vessel belonged individually to Mʳ Eckford & that he could not interfere—in answer to this it was remarked that neither the President nor Senate would construct the Ship which he had promised as a present, that the Government of the United States would have to purchase such as they might find ready built.

THE TRANSLATIONS OF HODGSON

There is a good deal of doubt as to whether William B. Hodgson at this time (1830–31) had sufficient knowledge of the Turkish language to be able properly to translate it.   As the suggestion is a serious one, involving Hodgson's good faith, it is only fair to state the evidence on both sides.

In connection with this treaty there are five translations made by Hodgson which he represented at the time to be translations made by him direct from the Turkish.   Those five translations are, first, his translation of the treaty proper, the manuscript of which is in D. S.,

1 Despatches, Turkey (not here printed); secondly, his other translation of the treaty proper which became the proclaimed translation (printed above), the manuscript of which is in the treaty file with the duplicate United States instrument of ratification; thirdly, his translation of the separate and secret article which was printed in the Senate document dated December 16, 1830, the manuscript of which is in D. S., 1 Despatches, Turkey (not here printed); fourthly, his later translation (printed above) of the separate and secret article which is in the Senate document dated January 12, 1831, the manuscript of which is not available; fifthly, his translation (printed above) of the so-called "codicil" of Porter, which is with Porter's despatch of September 26, 1831 (D. S., 2 Despatches, Turkey, No. 22).

It can fairly be said that three of those five translations are, at the least, very suspicious. One of them is admittedly so—Hodgson's first translation of the separate and secret article, which "through inadvertence" he omitted to say was from the French but which he headed as made from the Turkish. Another is that translation of his of the treaty proper, the manuscript of which is in D. S., 1 Despatches, Turkey, and which was, beyond all doubt, made from the French of Navoni; it follows that French in omitting the words of jurisdiction in Article 4, regarding *trial* by ministers and consuls, which Hodgson includes in his other translation; it also follows that French of Navoni in including in Article 5 the phrase about patents of protection which Hodgson omits from his other translation; yet it is headed in Hodgson's hand, "Translation from the Original Turkish." The third is his translation of the so-called "codicil" of Porter. That declaration, the text of which has been given, was signed in French, "collated with the said Turkish instrument." The English of Hodgson is almost literally the French, but it is signed by him as a "Translation from the Turkish Original."

The evidence against Hodgson in respect of his most important translation, the one of the treaty proper which was adopted by this Government as the official English version of the treaty, is strong. The annotated French translation in Article 4 contains words of jurisdiction which are not in the Turkish, and Hodgson puts the equivalent of those words into his English; the annotated French translation omits a phrase in Article 5 about protection papers which the Turkish includes, and Hodgson omits any equivalent of that phrase from his English; his rendering of Article 7 is very conveniently nearer to the wishes of his superiors than is the Turkish; and his Article 9 reads strikingly like a translation of Navoni's French. At the very least, Hodgson used the annotated French translation and the translation of Navoni in making his own, whether he was then able to read Turkish or not.

The only one of the five translations of Hodgson which looks as if it might have been made from the Turkish is his final translation of the separate article, which is printed above in these notes and which is in the Senate document dated January 12, 1831. Assuming that the final translation by Hodgson of that article was made by him from the

Turkish, a comparison of the result with the translation of Dr. Kramers would lead to the inference that Hodgson could read Turkish to some extent, but not completely, and that he could, in part and with errors, translate what he read.

On the other hand, it is true that Hodgson had been in Algiers for three years or so; and more significant is the fact that it was certainly believed at the Department of State that Hodgson knew Turkish. He is referred to by name in the letter of Secretary of State Van Buren to Senator Tazewell of January 11, 1831 (printed above), as the translator from the Turkish; Hodgson's translation of the treaty was accepted without question by the Department of State and adopted as the official translation of this Government; in the instructions which were given to Porter under date of April 15, 1831 (D. S., 1 Instructions, Turkey, 211–25), Hodgson is again referred to as the translator from the Turkish, and mention is made of his favorable translation of Article 7; and in the same instruction Hodgson is later spoken of in very high terms, the Secretary of State writing, "from his intelligence, discretion and experience, and his acquaintance with the Turkish character and habits, added to his knowledge of the Arabick and Turkish languages, acquired by his residence at Algiers, there is every reason to believe that you would find him very useful, and that you will be glad of the opportunity of having the benefit of his company and assistance." Indeed, Hodgson at the same time was given alternative powers to exchange the ratifications if Commodore Porter had declined or been unable to act (*ibid.*, 227–28).

It is very difficult to understand why such confidence was placed in Hodgson and in his linguistic abilities unless the Department had some evidence of the latter other than the representations of Hodgson himself.

It should be added, moreover, that Porter wrote of Hodgson's services to him in Constantinople in the highest terms; his despatch of September 26, 1831 (D. S., 2 Despatches, Turkey, No. 22), called them "incalculable"; and he suggested the appointment of Hodgson as dragoman, saying: "If the place is worth the acceptance of Mr Hodgson, the Government could not dispose of it better than by giving it to him; and the appointment would be highly gratifying to me, as I am well assured it would be to the Sublime Porte." Hodgson received that appointment under date of March 23, 1832 (D. S., 2 Credences, 183).

At the same time, Porter did not rely very strongly on the Hodgson or official translation of the treaty. The article which concerned him was Article 7, of which, according to his despatch of October 23, 1831 (D. S., 2 Despatches, Turkey, No. 27), he had three translations made, "by different persons here, and at different times"; and none of them, as Porter recognized, gave as much support to the American position regarding navigation "to and from the Black Sea" as did the Hodgson translation; as Porter put it, "the implication is smaller in the new translations, than in the one deposited at Washington."

There is other evidence from Constantinople on the subject. Navoni not only stated in his letter of October 25, 1831 (D. S., 1 Consular Despatches, Constantinople), that Hodgson was "entirely ignorant of the Turkish language," but transmitted various certificates of others to that effect.

While the bitter hostility between Hodgson and Navoni requires that any evidence from the latter be viewed with caution, it is of the utmost significance that Commodore Porter completely changed his mind about Hodgson within two years. On June 19, 1833, Porter wrote to Secretary of State Livingston that he (Porter) would prevent injury to the public interests by dispensing with the services of Hodgson as much as possible. Porter spoke of "his contumely and presumption, encouraged perhaps by the high estimation in which he has been held by the Department," and added, "His services have never been of any use, except when assisted by the Second Dragoman, and may be altogether dispensed with"; and his statement regarding Hodgson's knowledge of Turkish is as follows (D. S., 3 Despatches, Turkey, No. 111):

I do not say this to the injury of Mʳ Hodgson, who no doubt, since he has been here, has made much progress in the Turkish Language, as he has had little else to do but study it, but his ignorance of it cannot be denied at the time of his Appointment as Dragoman on my recommendation; for totally ignorant of the Language myself, and not knowing the difference between the Turkish and the Arabic, I took it for granted they were similar, but I now know that there is as great a difference between them, as between the English and French, and that his knowledge of it did enable him to do no more than translate from it imperfectly, by means of a dictionary.

Also to be quoted, as relevant, is the following extract from a despatch of Hodgson dated January 7, 1834, and thus written from Constantinople some three years after the proceedings on the treaty in the Senate (D. S., 6 Despatches, Turkey):

The want of Meninski was unfortunately felt, when I arrived at Washington [late in January, 1832], with Sultan Mahmoud's ratification of our Treaty with the Sublime Porte. Mʳ Livingston requested me to translate the instrument of ratification, to be published, after having been submitted to the Senate. I declined the translation, because I had not access to Meninski, to secure the correctness, and assume the responsibility of an official version. I however submitted to him an approximate translation, a copy of which, I have herewith the honor to enclose. The preamble is similar to that of other Ottoman treaties, published in Jenkinson's (Lord Liverpool) collection, and in de Martin's recueil de Traités.

Our Treaty with the Sublime Porte, was transmitted to Washington, for ratification, accompanied by a translation done into Perote french, by my predecessor Mʳ Navoni. The phraseology of the 7ᵗʰ and most important article, was not approved by Mʳ Van Buren, then Secretary of State, and by his instruction, I made a translation into English, of the entire Treaty, which was ratified by the Senate. This version was made with the aid of Meninski's invaluable Lexicon, which I, then, happily had at Washington, in my private library.

The passage of the Bosphorus, and the navigation of the Black Sea, are secured to us by the 7ᵗʰ article of our Treaty. Should this privilege ever be contested, by sophistry of language, some grammatical skill will be required by the Dragoman of this Legation. The Turkish original alone, can be referred to, in questions arising under the Treaty, the Reis Effendi having required of the Chargé d'Affaires, an additional article, consenting to such reference. A similar provision in

favor of the English language, was, I believe, made by M⟨r⟩ Clay, in appendix to the Austrian Treaty. The Porte in this case, has acted upon its established usage, in relation to which, Klüber (droit des gens p. 178) says, "La Porte Ottomane ne "s'estimant parfaitement obligée par un Traité, que lorsqu'il est conçu dans sa "langue vulgaire, et les gouvernemens des autres états européens ne voulant se "prêter à l'usage du turc, les traités conclus entre ces états et la Porte, sont tou- "jours expédiés en plusieurs langues." Hence the Treaty of *Kutchuk Kainardji* between Catharine II, and Sultan Abd-ul-Hamid, in 1774, by which Russia first acquired the free navigation of the Black Sea, was drawn up in Turkish, Italian and Russian.

From the despatch quoted it appears that Hodgson was unwilling, in 1832, to make an "official version" of a Turkish document unless he had the aid of the lexicon which he had used in the latter part of 1830 (the 1780 Vienna revised edition of the Lexicon Arabico-Persico-Turcicum of F. a Mesgnien Meninski, which was first published in 1680–87); but the statements made regarding the Hodgson transla-tion of the treaty are not very complete; to what is erroneously called the "established usage" of the Turkish Government is attributed its insistence on the Turkish original in this case, ignoring the fact that that Government, while it had accepted the Navoni French version of the treaty, was not willing to accept the Hodgson English version; the relative accuracy of the two versions is not discussed; and noth-ing is said as to the real question involved in the meaning of Article 7.

Moreover, it is stated in that despatch of January 7, 1834, that the "approximate translation" of the Turkish instrument of ratification therein enclosed was a copy of that submitted to Secretary of State Livingston in 1832. Examination of that enclosure shows that, while it conveys the general sense of the instrument of ratification, it is a very imperfect rendering of the Turkish, both in respect of errors and of omissions.

The great weight of evidence supports the view that Hodgson's knowledge of Turkish in 1830–31 was rather limited and was not quite sufficient for him to be trusted as a translator of that language.

THE PROCLAMATION

The statement in the despatch of William B. Hodgson of January 7, 1834, quoted above, to the effect that in 1832 Secretary of State Livingston desired a translation of the Turkish instrument of ratifi-cation for publication, "after having been submitted to the Senate," is of curious interest. The various despatches of Commodore Porter showed that the Turkish text had been accepted as solely authentic and that the English translation which had been before the Senate had been laid aside; and they also showed that Porter had signed a paper which, it might be argued, had qualified the rejection of the separate and secret article. A further consultation of the Senate, under such circumstances, would not have been without warrant; and the text of the Turkish ratification, in translation, would have been necessary, or at least desirable, for the purpose.

No such step was taken, however; the proclamation of the treaty issued in due course and contained the explicit statement that "the

ratification by the President of the said treaty in the Turkish language, and in a translation thereof into the English, annexed thereto, was exchanged"; one would certainly suppose from such language that the English version had been accepted by the Turkish Government.

The original proclamation is in the treaty file; it is in the handwriting of William S. Derrick, who was afterwards Chief Clerk of the Department of State at various times between 1843 and 1852, and reads as follows:

By the President of the United States

A PROCLAMATION.

Whereas a treaty of commerce and navigation between the United States of America and the Ottoman Porte was concluded and signed at Constantinople by the respective Plenipotentiaries of the two Powers, on the seventh day of May, in the year of our Lord one thousand eight hundred and thirty, and the said treaty was duly ratified, by the President, on the part of the said United States, on the second day of February, in the year of our Lord one thousand eight hundred and thirty-one, in pursuance of the advice and consent of the Senate, as signified by their resolution of the first day of that month: and whereas the ratification by the President of the said treaty in the Turkish language, and in a translation thereof into the English, annexed thereto, was exchanged at Constantinople, on the fifth day of Oct.ʳ 1831, by David Porter, the Chargé d'Affaires of the United States near the Sublime Porte, and Nejib Effendi, Reis Effendi of the Porte, for the ratification of the Sultan: which convention, as ratified by the President, in the English version, is, word for word, as follows:

[Here follows the proclaimed English translation of the treaty]

Now, therefore, to the end that the said treaty may be observed and performed with good faith on the part of the United States, I have caused the premises to be made public, and I do hereby enjoin all persons bearing office, civil or military, within the United States and all others, citizens or inhabitants thereof, or being within the same faithfully to observe and fulfil the said treaty, and every clause and article thereof.

In Testimony whereof, I have caused the seal of the United States to be hereunto affixed, and have signed the same with my hand.

        Done at Washington this fourth day of January, in the year of our [Seal] Lord one thousand eight hundred and thirty-two, and of the Independence of the United States the fifty sixth.

ANDREW JACKSON

By the President
  EDW LIVINGSTON
     Secretary of State.

While the proclamation is thus dated January 4, 1832, it was actually signed and sealed February 4, 1832. On the proclamation is the following memorandum dated February 9, 1832, written and signed by Daniel Brent, Chief Clerk:

The foregoing date of "January" was inadvertently used instead of "February" as the period of signing this Proclamation. It was signed on the 4th of the last mentioned month; and by direction of the Secretary, the Circumstance is thus noticed.

There seems to have been a curious perversity of fate about the misdating of documents relating to this treaty. The annotated French translation, the original United States instrument of ratifica-

tion, and the original proclamation are all wrongly dated; the presidential message transmitting the treaty to the Senate (Executive Journal, IV, 126), is dated December 10, 1830, although that message was received in the Senate on December 9; and the early pamphlet print of the proclamation of this treaty, a copy of which is in the treaty file, has on its front cover page as the date thereof, May 7, 1831, instead of May 7, 1830.

The treaty was communicated to Congress by President Jackson on February 7, 1832 (House Document No. 304, 22d Congress, 1st session, serial 221). The message mentions that "my ratification" had "been exchanged in due form on the 5th October, 1831, by our chargé d'affaires at Constantinople and that Government" (Richardson, II, 564).

Earlier official mention of the exchange of ratifications was made in a letter of Secretary of State Livingston to the Chairman of the Committee of Foreign Affairs of the House of Representatives, under date of January 18, 1832, asking for appropriation of $37,500 "to cover the expenses of the treaty with the Sublime Porte" (House Document No. 303, 22d Congress, 1st session, serial 221). The appropriation was duly voted (act of May 5, 1832, 4 Statutes at Large, 506, 513).

THE ORIGINAL DOCUMENTS

While the original documents in the Department of State file of this treaty have been heretofore described in some detail, a summarized account of them will also be given for convenience.

Five of the six documents properly to be found in the file of a bilateral treaty are present. The original signed treaty in Turkish (reproduced in facsimile above) is with the duplicate United States instrument of ratification, as is also the attested resolution of the Senate. That ratification also includes the manuscript of the Hodgson translation which was adopted by this Government as its official translation. The Turkish instrument of ratification and the proclamation are also in the file. The only customary document lacking is a certificate or protocol of the exchange of ratifications. It seems that no such document was executed. The date of the exchange is stated in Porter's despatch of the same date, October 5, 1831, which is quoted above.

Another original paper in the file is the Turkish original of the separate and secret article. It has not been deemed necessary to reproduce that document.

The Turkish instrument of ratification (not reproduced) was for many years not to be found in the archives of the Department of State. A memorandum in the file (undated, but probably written in 1888), says that a diligent search had been made for it and that it could not be found.

In 1927 the document was found in a sack or bag about four feet long. Evidently the sack came from the Turkish Government. A despatch from Constantinople of December 22, 1873, mentions that in the Turkish archives it was then the custom "to enclose each treaty

. . . together with all the relative documents thought worthy of preservation, in a separate sack." The sack has on it a sort of tassel which runs through a large lump of red wax about the size and shape of a small teacup, but solid and with the imprint of a seal on it. When found, the document was in quite a damaged condition. It has since been restored as far as possible, although there are some four or five blanks in it where scraps have been torn out. Perhaps the document itself was sealed; but if so, its restoration has hidden the seal.

It should be said further that the treaty file contains various other papers of contemporaneous or later dates, such as memorandums regarding the correspondence, subsequent translations of the treaty in whole or in part, prints of the Senate documents of December, 1830, and January, 1831, etc. Some of these papers have been mentioned above, but it is unnecessary even to list them all.

THE TURKISH ARCHIVES

On September 22, 1873, George H. Boker, then Minister at Constantinople, was instructed as follows (D. S., 2 Instructions, Turkey, 520–21):

There is at least an impression that there was more or less mystery about the negotiation and subsequent proceedings touching the treaty between the United States and Turkey of 1830, which is not satisfactorily accounted for by the papers on record or on file in this Department. For instance although there are two versions in French of that instrument on file, neither of them is signed by the negotiators; and it does not appear that any such version so signed was ever received at the Department. Under these circumstances you will apply to the Turkish foreign office for leave to inspect and to copy the signed version in French, which it is presumed they must have on their files. You will carefully compare the copy when made with the original and forward the same hither.

Under date of October 25, 1873 (D. S., 25 Despatches, Turkey, No. 158), Boker reported that he had "carefully examined all the copies of the Treaty among the archives at the Sublime Porte" and gave the result of his examination as follows:

I have not been able to find a French translation of the Treaty, whether signed or unsigned, and the Ottoman officials say that no such document is in existence. The Signed copy of the Treaty preserved at the Porte is in English, and it has attached to it an unsigned version in the Turkish language. I have collated the above mentioned English copy with the printed copy, to be found upon page 643 of the volume entitled "Treaties and Conventions concluded between the United States of America and other Powers," and I have found them to be identical.

. . . .

I also enclose a copy of a document in French, bearing the signature and the seal of David Porter, former *Chargé d' Affaires* of the United States, agreeing that in case any misunderstanding of the stipulations of the Treaty should arise between the contracting parties, he and his successors shall be bound to consult the Turkish version of the Treaty in order to solve all doubts as to the meaning of that instrument. This document was appended to the Turkish copy of the Treaty in the archives of the Sublime Porte; and as it is the first knowledge which I have had of the existence of such an agreement, it may have been also unknown to the present officers of the Government of the United States.

I beg the Department to bear in mind that this Legation is not responsible for the quality of the French used in the above mentioned instrument, of which the copy which I send is an accurate transcript.   I have searched the archives of the Legation without having been able to find in the correspondence with the Department of State any copy or mention of the agreement in question on the part of the Government.

The declaration in French of Porter of September 26, 1831, of which the foregoing despatch of Boker enclosed a copy, has been printed above, and also an English version thereof.

A further instruction was sent to Boker under date of November 20, 1873 (D. S., 3 Instructions, Turkey, 9–11).   It was there said that the despatch of October 25 had been "received with surprise."   It was assumed, erroneously, that when Boker wrote in his despatch of a signed copy of the treaty in English he meant one signed by the American Commissioners, whereas in fact he meant that he had seen the United States instrument of ratification with its English text.   Partly because of this misapprehension the instruction went on to say, "the whole affair appears still to be enveloped in a mystery which it is desirable should be cleared up" and suggested further attempts at Constantinople, "as all the actors on our side are believed to be dead."

Accordingly, Boker made a further examination, and his despatch of December 22, 1873 (D. S., 25 Despatches, Turkey, No. 174), deserves to be quoted in full:

In reply to despatch N⁰ 153, under date of November 20th, 1873, relating to the Treaty of 1830, I have the honor to say that I have caused a careful and exhaustive search for documents connected with that Treaty to be made at the Sublime Porte with the following result.

No paper of any description whatever, bearing the signatures of Messrs Biddle, Offley and Rhind, or of any of them, could be discovered.   The theory of the Ottoman officials is that the documents relating to the original negotiation were either destroyed, or removed to some unknown place of deposit, soon after the signature of the so-called "Codicil" by David Porter, agreeing to abide by the Turkish draft of the Treaty in all matters of disputed interpretation.   *Vide*, Enclosure 2 of Despatch N⁰ 158 [of October 25, 1873] from G. H. Boker to the Department of State.

No French version of the Treaty, however imperfect, nor of any Article thereof, can now be found among the archives of the Sublime Porte.

It is the custom at the Porte to enclose each treaty which the Ottoman government has negotiated, together with all the relative documents thought worthy of preservation, in a separate sack.   The only contents of the sack containing the Treaty of 1830, were as follows:

1. The ratified Treaty in English.
2. The Turkish text of the same, with the "Codicil," in French, attached.
3. A letter from President Jackson to the Sultan, explaining the reasons for the rejection of the "Secret Article."   *Vide*, D. S. despatch to Porter, No. 1, under date of April 15th, 1831.
4. A letter from Martin Van Buren, Secretary of State, to the *Reis ul Kutab* or Minister of Foreign Affairs.   *Vide*, enclosure C. of D. S. despatch N⁰ 2, under date of April 15, 1831.
5. Two copies, the one in English and the other in Turkish, of the "Secret Article" which was rejected by the Senate.

My opinion is that a further inquiry for documents relating to the Treaty of 1830 would be fruitless; for if any such papers exist, there is no intention at the Sublime Porte that they shall be opened to my inspection.   In saying this, I do not mean to be understood as asserting that any concealment has been practised. On the contrary, I have every reason to believe that all the documents have been exhibited to me which are now in possession of the Ottoman government.

It appears, therefore, from those two reports of Boker that in 1873 the documents in the Turkish archives, aside from the letter of President Jackson to the Sultan and the letter of Secretary of State Van Buren to the Turkish Minister of Foreign Affairs, were the following:

1. The United States instrument of ratification. It is true that in the later of the two despatches above quoted, Boker mentions separately "the ratified treaty in English" and "the Turkish text of the same"; but he says in his earlier despatch that "the signed copy of the treaty preserved at the Porte is in English, and it has attached to it an unsigned version in the Turkish language," so it is clear that reference is made to the United States instrument of ratification, in which it is said expressly that "the original in the Turkish language, and a translation of the same in English are hereunto annexed." Furthermore, when Boker speaks of the version in the Turkish language as being "unsigned," it is probable that he means unsigned by the American Commissioners, for that Turkish text was almost certainly a duplicate original, as will be seen.

2. A Turkish text and an English text of the separate and secret article. That Turkish text was also doubtless a duplicate original, and the English version was probably the one written by Hodgson, the manuscript of which, as stated above, is not to be found in the Department of State archives. It may be conjectured that Hodgson took the two documents with him to Constantinople. Certainly any English version of the separate and secret article originated at Washington and not at Constantinople.

3. The so-called "codicil," or declaration, in French, signed by Porter on September 26, 1831.

The Turkish originals of the treaty and of the separate article (both now in the treaty file) were enclosures to the despatch to the President of Biddle and Offley of June 8, 1830 (D. S., 1 Despatches, Turkey), a despatch which Rhind declined to sign (see also the letter of Biddle and Offley to Rhind of the same date, the despatch of Offley to the Secretary of State dated June 7, the protest of Rhind of June 8, and the postscript to the despatch of Rhind to the Secretary of State of June 11, *ibid.*).

The reasons for thinking that the Turkish of the treaty and the Turkish of the separate and secret article mentioned by Boker were duplicate originals are as follows: On June 8, 1830, Biddle and Offley received from the Porte duplicates of the treaty and of the separate article, which they transmitted to Rhind (their letter to Rhind of that date, *ibid.*). Rhind refused to receive them (Biddle to the Secretary of State, June 9, 1830, last paragraph, *ibid.*). The same despatch says that Offley was to forward those duplicates from Smyrna; and it appears that he did so from his letter to the Secretary of State of June 21, 1830 (*ibid.*), in which he wrote that he was sending from Smyrna duplicates of his despatches by the brig *Cherub*, of Boston, to the collector at that port, and enclosed a bill of lading for the parcel, stipulating the payment of twenty dollars as freight.

The duplicate of the treaty proper formed part of the United States instrument of ratification, which Boker saw in the Turkish archives.

The duplicate of the separate and secret article, also seen by him in the Turkish archives in 1873, was perhaps, as above suggested, taken back to Constantinople by Hodgson; it is difficult to account otherwise for the fact that it is not in the archives of the Department of State.

ARTICLE 4

It is well known that between this Government and the Turkish Government there continued for some decades from 1868 on, a difference of opinion as to the correct translation and the proper interpretation of Article 4 of this treaty. Any review of that prolonged diplomatic controversy would be outside of the scope of these notes. The correspondence exchanged between the two Governments from time to time is formidable in volume. Some of the pieces are quoted and others are cited in Moore, Digest, II, 668–714. One point only is to be noticed here. With a note of the Turkish Minister, Mavroyeni Bey, of August 24, 1888, there was transmitted to this Government an official Turkish translation of the Turkish text of Article 4, in French (D. S., 5 Notes from the Turkish Legation), which reads, with the English translation thereof made at the time in the Department of State, as follows (italics as in original):

[Official Turkish translation]

Au cas où un différend ou un procès surgissait entre des sujets Ottomans et des citoyens Américains, il ne sera ni entendu ni jugé sans la présence du drogman. Leurs procès dépassant cinq cents piastres seront référés à Constantinople et jugés suivant l'équité et la justice. Les citoyens Américains vaguant paisiblement aux affaires de leur commerce ne seront point molestés sans motif, tant qu'ils n'auront pas commis quelque délit ou quelque faute; même en cas de culpabilité, ils ne seront pas emprisonnés par les juges et les agents de la sûreté, *mais ils seront punis par les soins de leur ministre et consul a l'instar de ce qui se pratique à l'égard des autres Francs.*

[Translation]

In case a dispute or a lawsuit shall arise between Ottoman subjects and American citizens, it shall neither be heard nor tried unless the dragoman be present. Their suits in which more than five hundred piasters shall be involved, shall be referred to Constantinople and tried according to equity and justice. American citizens attending peaceably to the affairs of their commerce shall not be molested without cause, so long as they shall not have committed any offense or any fault; even in case of guilt, they shall not be imprisoned by the judges and police authorities or officers, but *they shall be punished through the agency of their ministers and consuls, just as is done in the case of other Franks.*

The earliest statute dealing with the extraterritorial jurisdiction of Article 4 was that of August 11, 1848, "An Act to carry into Effect certain Provisions in the Treaties between the United States and China and the Ottoman Porte, giving certain judicial powers to Ministers and Consuls of the United States in those Countries" (9 Statutes at Large, 276–80). The general subject is elaborately treated in Moore, Digest, II, 593–727.

Treaty Series No. 203
8 Statutes at Large, 410–29
18 *ibid.*, pt. 2, Public Treaties, 476–86

70

MEXICO : APRIL 5, SEPTEMBER 17, AND DECEMBER 17, 1831

Treaty of Amity, Commerce, and Navigation, with additional article (the second additional article was not ratified), signed at Mexico April 5, 1831, and with protocols signed at Mexico September 17 and December 17, 1831. Originals in English and Spanish.
Submitted to the Senate February 24, 1832. Resolution of advice and consent March 23, 1832. Ratified by the United States April 4, 1832. Ratified by Mexico January 14, 1832. Ratifications exchanged at Washington April 5, 1832. Proclaimed April 5, 1832.
The texts of the protocols of September 17 and December 17, 1831, follow the treaty texts.

The United States of America and the United Mexican States desiring to establish upon a firm basis the relations of friendship that so happily subsist between the two Republics have determined to fix in a clear and positive manner the rules which shall in future be religiously observed between both, by means of a Treaty of Amity, Commerce and Navigation. For which important object the President of the United States of America has appointed Anthony Butler a Citizen of the United States and Chargé d'Affaires of the United States of America near the United Mexican States with full powers. And the Vice President of the United Mexican States in the exercise of the Executive power having conferred like full powers on his

Los Estados unidos de America y los Estados unidos Mexicanos deseosos de afirmar sobre bases solidas las relaciones de amistad y comercio que felizmente ecsisten entre ambas Repúblicas, han resuelto fijar de una manera clara y positiva las reglas que han de observarse en lo succesivo religiosamente entre ambas por medio de un Tratado de amistad, comercio y navegacion. Para cuyo importante objeto el Presidente de los Estados unidos de America há conferido plenos poderes al Ciudadano de los mismos Estados Antonio Butler Encargado de negocios cerca de los Estados unidos Mexicanos y el Vice Presidente de los Estados unidos Mexicanos en ejercicio del Poder Ejecutivo al Ecselentisimo Señor Don Lucas Alaman Secretario de Estado y

Excellency Lucas Alaman Secretary of State for home and foreign Affairs, and his Excellency Raphael Mangino Secretary of the Treasury. And the aforesaid Plenipotentiaries after having compared and exchanged in due form their several powers as aforesaid have agreed upon the following Articles.

ARTICLE 1st.

There shall be a firm inviolable and universal peace, and a true and sincere friendship between the United States of America and the United Mexican States in all the extent of their possessions and Territories and between their people and Citizens respectively without distinction of persons or places.

ARTICLE 2nd.

The United States of America and the United Mexican States designing to take for the basis of their Agreement the most perfect equality and reciprocity engage mutually not to grant any particular favor to other Nations in respect of Commerce and Navigation which shall not immediately become common to the other party; who shall enjoy the same freely, if the concession was freely made, or upon the same conditions if the concession was conditional.

ARTICLE 3d.

The Citizens of the two Countries respectively shall have lib-

del Despacho de Relaciones esteriores é interiores y al Ecselentisimo Señor Don Rafael Mangino Secretario de Estado y del Despacho de Hacienda. Los cuales despues de haber cambiado sus plenos poderes han convenido en los articulos siguientes.

ARTICULO 1º

Habrá una firme inviolable y universal paz, y una sincera y verdadera amistad entre los Estados unidos de America y los Estados unidos Mexicanos en toda la estension de sus posesiones y territorios, y entre sus pueblos y Ciudadanos, respectivamente, sin distincion de personas ó lugares.

ARTICULO 2º

Los Estados unidos de America y los Estados unidos Mexicanos, deseando tomár por base de este convenio la mas perfecta igualdad y reciprocidad, se comprometen mutuamente á no conceder ningun favor particular á otras naciones, en lo respectivo á comercio y navegacion que no venga á ser inmediatamente comun á la otra parte la cual deberá gozarlo libremente, si la concecion fué hecha libremente, ó bajo las mismas condiciones, si la concesion fuese condicional.

ARTICULO 3º

Los Ciudadanos de los dos paises respectivamente, tendrán libertad,

erty freely and securely to come with their vessels and cargoes to all such places ports and Rivers of the United States of America and of the United Mexican States to which other Foreigners are permitted to come; to enter into the same, and to remain and reside in any part of the said Territories respectively; also to hire and occupy houses and Warehouses for the purposes of their Commerce, and to trade therein, in all sorts of produce, manufactures and Merchandize, and generally the Merchants and Traders of each nation shall enjoy the most complete protection and security for their Commerce.

And they shall not pay higher or other duties imposts or fees whatsoever than those which the most favored Nations are or may be obliged to pay, and shall enjoy all the rights, privileges and exemptions with respect to Navigation and Commerce which the Citizens of the most favored Nation do or may enjoy; but subject always to the Laws, usages, and Statutes of the two Countries respectively.

The liberty to enter and discharge the vessels of both Nations of which this article treats, shall not be understood to authorize the coasting trade, which is permitted to National vessels only.

56006°—33——40

franquicia y seguridad para ir con sus buques y cargamentos á todas las plazas puertos y rios de los Estados unidos de America y de los Estados unidos Mexicanos á los que á otros estrangeros es permitido ir, entrar y permanecer en cualquiera parte de los dichos Territorios respectivamente; asi como arrendar y ocupar casas y Almacenes para los fines de su comercio y comerciar en ellos en toda clase de productos manufacturas y mercancias; y en general, los comerciantes y negociantes de cada Nacion, gozarán la mas completa proteccion y seguridad para su comercio.

Y no pagarán otros ni mas altos derechos impuestos ó emolumentos, cualquiera que sean, que los que esten ó estuvieren obligadas á pagar las naciones mas favorecidas, y gozarán todos los derechos, privilegios y ecsenciones, con respecto á la navegacion y comercio, que los Ciudadanos de la Nacion mas favorecida gozen ó gozaren; pero sugetos siempre á las leyes, usos y estatutos de las dos naciones respectivamente.

La libertad de entrar y descargar los buques de ambas naciones de que habla este articulo, no se entenderá que autoriza el comercio de Escala y Cabotaje permitido solamente á los buques nacionales.

Article 4th.

No higher or other duties shall be imposed on the importation into the United Mexican States of any article the produce growth or manufacture of the United States of America, than those which the same or like articles the produce growth or manufacture of any other foreign Country do now or may hereafter pay, nor shall articles the produce growth or manufacture of the United Mexican States be subject on their introduction into the United States of America to higher or other duties, than those which the same or like articles of any other foreign country do now or may hereafter pay.

Higher duties shall not be imposed in the respective States on the exportation of any article to the States of the other contracting party, than those which are now or may hereafter be paid on the exportation of the like articles to any other foreign Country; nor shall any prohibition be established on the exportation or importation of any article the produce, growth or manufacture of the United States of America or of the United Mexican States respectively, in either of them which shall not in like manner be established with respect to other foreign Countries.

Articulo 4º

No se impondrán otros ni mayores derechos á la importacion en los Estados unidos de America de articulo alguno de producto natural, ó manufactura de los Estados unidos Mexicanos, que los que pagan ó en adelante pagaren los mismos ó semejantes articulos de producto natural ó manufactura de cualquiera otro pais estrangero. Los articulos de producto natural ó manufactura de los Estados unidos de America, no estarán sugetos en su introduccion en los Estados unidos Mexicanos, á otros ni mas altos derechos que aquellos que los mismos ó semejantes articulos de cualquiera otro pais estrangero paguen ahora ó puedan pagar en adelante.

No se impondrán mayores derechos en los Estados respectivos, á la esportacion de articulo alguno á los Estados de la otra parte contratante que los que ahora ó despues sean pagados en la esportacion de los mismos articulos á algun otro pais estrangero; ni ninguna prohivicion será establecida en la esportacion ó importacion de cualquier articulo producto natural ó manufactura de los Estados unidos de America ó los Estados unidos Mexicanos respectivamente en alguno de ellos, que del mismo modo no se establesca igualmente con respecto á otros paises estrangeros.

ARTICLE 5th.

No higher or other duties or charges on account of tonnage, light or harbor dues, pilotage, salvage, in case of damage or Shipwreck, or any other local charges shall be imposed, in any of the Ports of Mexico on Vessels of the United States of America, than those payable in the same ports by Mexican Vessels; nor in the ports of the United States of America on Mexican Vessels than shall be payable in the same ports on Vessels of the United States of America.

ARTICLE 6th.

The same duties shall be paid on the importation into the United Mexican States of any article the growth, produce or manufacture of the United States of America, whether such importation shall be in Mexican Vessels or in Vessels of the United States of America; and the same duties shall be paid on the importation into the United States of America, of any article the growth produce or manufacture of Mexico, whether such importation shall be in Vessels of the United States of America or in Mexican Vessels. The same duties shall be paid, and the same bounties and drawbacks allowed on the exportation to

ARTICULO 5º

No se impondrán otros ni mas altos derechos ni cargas por razon de Toneladas, Fanal, emolumentos de Puerto, Practico, derechos de salvamento en caso de perdida ó naufragio ni ningunas otras cargas locales, en ninguno de los Puertos de los Estados unidos de America á los buques de los Estados unidos Mexicanos, sino los que unicamente pagan en los mismos Puertos los buques de los Estados unidos de America; ni en los Puertos de los Estados unidos Mexicanos se impondrán á los buques de los Estados unidos de America otras cargas que las que en los mismos Puertos paguen los buques Mexicanos.

ARTICULO 6º

Se pagarán los mismos derechos de importacion en los Estados unidos de America por los articulos de productos naturales y manufacturas de los Estados unidos Mexicanos, bien sean importados en buques de los Estados unidos de America ó en buques Mexicanos; y los mismos derechos se pagarán por la importacion en los Estados unidos Mexicanos de cualquiera articulo de producto natural ó manufactura de los Estados unidos de America, sea que su importacion se verifique en buques Mexicanos ó de los Estados unidos de America. Los mismos derechos pagarán y gozarán las mismas franquicias y

Mexico, of any articles the growth, produce or manufacture of the United States of America, whether such exportation shall be in Mexican Vessels or in Vessels of the United States of America; and the same duties shall be paid, and the same bounties and drawbacks allowed on the exportation on any articles the growth produce or manufacture of Mexico to the United States of America whether such exportation shall be in Vessels of the United States of America or in Mexican Vessels.

descuentos concedidos á la esportacion á Mexico de cualquiera articulos de los productos naturales ó manufacturas de los Estados unidos de America sea que la esportacion se haga en buques Mexicanos ó en buques de los Estados unidos de America, y los mismos derechos se pagarán ye se concederán las mismas franquicias y descuentos á la esportacion de cualquiera articulos de producto natural ó manufactura de Mexico á los Estados unidos de America sea que la esportacion se haga en buques de los Estados unidos de America ó en buques Mexicanos.

ARTICLE 7th.

All merchants, Captains, or Commanders of Vessels, and other Citizens of the United States of America shall have full liberty in the United Mexican States, to direct or manage themselves their own affairs, or to commit them to the management of whomsoever they may think proper, either as broker, factor, agent or interpreter; nor shall they be obliged to employ for the aforesaid purposes any other persons than those employed by Mexicans, nor to pay them higher salaries, or remuneration than such as are in like cases paid by Mexicans: and absolute freedom shall be allowed in all cases to the buyer and seller to bargain and fix the prices of any goods wares or Merchandize

ARTICULO 7º

Todo comerciante, Comandante de buque y otros Ciudadanos de los Estados unidos de America gozarán de libertad completa en los Estados unidos Mexicanos para dirijir ó girar por si sus propios negocios ó para encargar su manejo aquien mejor les parezca sea corredor, Factor, Agente ó Interprete; y no se les obligará á emplear para estos objetos á ningunas otras personas que aquellas que se emplean por los mejicanos, ni estarán obligados á pagarles mas salario ó remuneracion que la que en semejantes casos pagan los mejicanos, y se concederá libertad absoluta en todos los casos al comprador ó vendedor para ajustar y fijar el precio de cualesquiera efectos

imported into or exported from the United Mexican States as they may think proper; observing the Laws usages and customs of the Country. The Citizens of Mexico shall enjoy the same privileges in the States and Territories of the United States of America, being subject to the same conditions.

ARTICLE 8th

The Citizens of neither of the contracting parties shall be liable to any embargo, nor shall their Vessels, cargoes, Merchandize or effects, be detained for any Military expedition nor for any public or private purpose whatsoever without a corresponding compensation.

ARTICLE 9th

The Citizens of both Countries respectively shall be exempt from compulsory service in the Army or Navy; nor shall they be subjected to any other charges or contributions or Taxes than such as are paid by the Citizens of the States in which they reside.

ARTICLE 10th·

Whenever the Citizens of either of the Contracting parties shall be forced to seek refuge or asylum in the Rivers, bays ports or dominions of the other with their Vessels, whether Merchant or of War, public or private, through stress

articulos ó mercancias importadas ó esportadas de los Estados unidos Mexicanos como lo crean conveniente observando las leyes, usos y costumbres establecidas en el pais. Los Ciudadanos de Mexico gozarán los mismos privilegios en los Estados y Territorios de los Estados unidos de America quedando sugetos á las mismas condiciones.

ARTICULO 8º

Los Ciudadanos de las partes contratantes no estarán sugetos á embargo, ni sus buques, cargamentos, mercancias ó efectos serán detenidos para ninguna espedicion militar ni para ningun otro objeto público ó privado cualquiera que sea, sin una compensacion correspondiente.

ARTICULO 9º

Los Ciudadanos de ambos paises respectivamente, estarán ecsentos de todo servicio militar forzoso en el Ejercito ó Armada; ni estarán sugetos á ningunas otras cargas contribuciones ó impuestos que aquellas q. son pagadas por los Ciudadanos de los Estados en que residen.

ARTICULO 10º

Siempre que los Ciudadanos de cualquiera de las partes contratantes se vean precisados á buscar refugio ó asilo en los rios, bahias, puertos ó dominios de la otra con sus buques ya sean mercantes ó de guerra ó armados en corso á

of weather, pursuit of pirates or enemies they shall be received and treated with humanity, with the precautions which may be deemed expedient on the part of the respective governments in order to avoid fraud giving to them all favor and protection for repairing their Vessels, procuring provisions and placing themselves in a situation to continue their Voyage without obstacle or hindrance of any kind.

Article 11th.

All vessels, Merchandize or effects belonging to the Citizens of one of the Contracting parties which may be captured by pirates, whether within the limits of its jurisdiction or on the high seas, and may be carried into or found in the Rivers, bays, ports or dominions of the other, shall be delivered up to the owners, they proving in due and proper form their rights before the competent Tribunal; it being well understood that the claim shall be made within one year counting from the Capture of said Vessels or Merchandize by the parties themselves or their Attornies, or by the Agents of the respective Governments.

Article 12th

When any Vessel belonging to the Citizens of either of the contracting parties shall be wrecked, foundered, or shall suffer any

causa de un temporal, persecucion de piratas ó enemigos, serán recibidos y tratados con humanidad previas las precauciones que se juzgen convenientes por parte del respectivo Gobierno para evitar el fraude, concediendoles todo favor y proteccion para reparar sus buques, procurar provisiones y ponerse en estado de continuar su viaje sin obstaculo ó impedimento de ninguna clase.

Articulo 11º

Todo buque, mercancia y efectos pertenecientes á Ciudadanos de alguna de las partes contratantes que sean apresados por piratas ya sea dentro de los limites de su jurisdiccion ó en alta mar, y que fueren conducidos ó encontrados en los rios, bahias, puertos ó dominios de la otra, serán entregados á sus dueños provando estos en debida forma sus derechos ante el Tribunal competente; bien entendido que el reclamo deberá hacerse dentro del termino de un año contado desde la captura de dichos buques ó mercancias por los mismos interesados, sus Apoderados ó por los Agentes de sus Gobiernos respectivos.

Articulo 12º

Cuando algun buque perteneciente á Ciudadanos de alguna de las partes contratantes naufrague vaya á pique ó sufra cualquiera

damage on the Coasts or within the dominions of the other, there shall be given to it all the assistance and protection in the same manner which is usual and customary with the Vessels of the Nation where the damage happens permitting them to unload the said Vessel if necessary, of its merchandize and effects, with the precautions which may be deemed expedient on the part of the respective Governments in order to avoid fraud, without exacting for it any duty impost or contribution whatever untill they be exported.

Article 13th.

In whatever relates to the succession of Estates either by Will or *ab intestato* disposal of such property of whatever sort or denomination it may be, by sale, donation exchange or testament or in any other manner whatsoever the Citizens of the two contracting parties shall enjoy in their respective States and territories the same privileges, exemptions, liberties and rights, as native citizens, and shall not be charged in any of these respects, with other or higher duties or imposts than those which are now or may hereafter be paid by the Citizens of the power in whose territories they may reside.

averia en las costas ó dentro de los dominios de la otra, se le dispensará toda la asistencia y proteccion del mismo modo que es de uso y costumbre con los buques de la Nacion en que acontece el daño, permitiendoles descargar las mercancias y efectos del mismo buque si fuere necesario con las precauciones que se estimen convenientes por parte de los Gobiernos respectivos para evitar el fraude, sin ecsigir por ello ningun impuesto ó contribucion cualquiera q. sean, hasta que sean esportadas.

Articulo 13º

Por lo que toca á la succesion de las propiedades personales por testamento ó ab-intestato y al derecho de disponer de la propiedad personal de cualquiera clase ó denominacion por venta, donacion, permuta ó testamento ó de otro modo cualquiera los Ciudadanos de las dos partes contratantes gozarán en sus respectivos Estados y Territorios los mismos privilegios, ecsenciones, libertades y derechos que si fueran Ciudadanos nativos; y no se les cargará en ninguno de estos puntos ó casos, mayores impuestos ó derechos que los que pagan ó en adelante pagaren los Ciudadanos nativos de la Potencia en cuyo Territorio residan.

ARTICLE 14ᵗʰ

Both the contracting parties promise and engage to give their special protection to the persons and property of the Citizens of each other of all occupations who may be in their territories, subject to the jurisdiction of the one or of the other, transient or dwelling therein, leaving open and free to them the tribunals of Justice for their Judicial recourse, on the same terms which are usual, and customary with the natives or Citizens of the Country in which they may be; for which they may employ in defence of their rights such advocates, Solicitors, Notaries, Agents and Factors as they may judge proper, in all their trials at Law; and the Citizens of either party, or their Agents shall enjoy in every respect the same rights and privileges either in prosecuting or defending their rights of person or of property, as the Citizens of the Country where the cause may be tried.

ARTICLE 15ᵗʰ

The Citizens of the United States of America, residing in the United Mexican States shall enjoy in their houses persons and properties the protection of the Government, with the most perfect security and liberty of conscience: they shall not be disturbed or molested, in any manner on account of their religion so

ARTICULO 14º

Ambas partes contratantes prometen y formalmente se obligan á conceder su especial proteccion á las personas y propiedades de los Ciudadanos de cada una de ellas en todas clases que puedan ecsistir en sus Territorios sugetos á la jurisdiccion de la una ó de la otra transeuntes ó radicados en ellos, dejandoles abiertos y libres los Tribunales de Justicia para sus recursos judiciales de la misma manera que es uso y costumbre con los nacionales ó Ciudadanos del pais en que residan á cuyo efecto podrán emplear en defensa de sus derechos, los Abogados, Procuradores, Escrivanos, Agentes y Factores que juzgen á proposito en todos sus juicios: y dichos Ciudadanos ó sus Agentes gozarán en todo los mismos derechos y privilegios en la prósecucion ó defensa de sus personas ó propiedades que disfrutan los Ciudadanos del pais en donde la causa sea seguida.

ARTICULO 15º

Los Ciudadanos de los Estados unidos de America residentes en los Estados unidos Mexicanos, gozarán en sus casos, personas y propiedades de la proteccion del Gobierno y continuando en la posesion en que están, no serán alterados, inquietados ni molestados de ninguna manera por motivos de su religion, con tal que respeten

long as they respect the Constitution, the laws and established usages of the Country where they reside; and they shall also enjoy the privilege of burying the dead in places which now are, or may hereafter be assigned for that purpose, nor shall the funerals or sepulchres of the dead be disturbed in any manner nor under any pretext. The Citizens of the United Mexican States shall enjoy throughout all the States and Territories of the United States of America, the same protection: and shall be allowed, the free exercise of their religion in public or in private, either within their own houses, or in the Chapels or places of worship set apart for that purpose.

Article 16th.

It shall be lawful for the Citizens of the United States of America, and of the United Mexican States respectively to sail with their Vessels with all manner of security and liberty, no distinction being made who are the owners of the Merchandize laden thereon, from any port to the places of those who now are, or may hereafter be at enmity, with the United States of America or with the United Mexican States. It shall likewise be lawful for the aforesaid Citizens respectively to sail with their Vessels

la de la Nacion en que residan y la Constitucion, leyes usos y costumbres de esta; asi mismo continuarán en la facultad de que gozan para enterrar en los lugares señalados ó que en adelante se señalaren á este objeto á los Ciudadanos de los Estados unidos de America que mueran en los Estados unidos Mexicanos y los funerales y sepulcros de los muertos no serán turbados de modo alguno ni por ningun pretesto.

Los Ciudadanos de los Estados unidos Mexicanos gozarán en todos los Estados y Territorios de los Estados unidos de America, de la misma proteccion, y podrán ejercer libremente su religion en público ó en privado dentro de sus casas ó en los Templos y lugares destinados al culto.

Articulo 16º

Será permitido á todos y cada uno de los Ciudadanos de los Estados unidos de America y de los Estados unidos Mexicanos poder navegar libre y seguramente con sus embarcaciones sin que haya la menor escepcion por este respecto aunque los propietarios de las mercaderias cargadas en dichas embarcaciones procedan de cualquiera puerto/y sean destinadas á cualquiera plaza de una potencia enemiga, ó que lo sea despues, asi de los Estados unidos de America, como de los Estados unidos Mexicanos. Se

and Merchandize, before mentioned and to trade with the same liberty and security from the places, ports and havens of those who are enemies of both or either party without any opposition or disturbance whatsoever, not only directly from the places, of the enemy beforementioned to neutral places, but also from one place belonging to an enemy, to another place belonging to an enemy, whether they be under the Jurisdiction of the same Government or under several; and it is hereby stipulated that free ships shall also give freedom to goods, and that every thing shall be deemed free and exempt; which shall be found on board the Vessels belonging to the Citizens of either of the contracting parties, although the whole lading or any part thereof should appertain to the enemies of either, contraband goods being always excepted. It is also agreed that the same liberty be extended to persons who are on board a free Vessel, so that although they be enemies to either party they shall not be made prisoners or taken out of that free Vessel, unless they are Soldiers and in the actual service of the enemy. By the stipulation that the flag shall cover the property the two contracting parties agree that this shall be so understood, with respect to those powers who recognize this principle; but if either of the two contracting parties shall be at

permitirá igualmente á los Ciudadanos respectivamente navegar con sus buques y mercaderias, y frecuentar con igual libertad y seguridad las plazas y puertos en las potencias enemigas de las partes contratantes, ó de una de ellas, sin oposicion ú obstaculo, y de comerciar no solo desde los puertos de dicho enemigo, á un puerto neutro directamente, sino tambien desde un enemigo á otro tal, bien se encuentre bajo su jurisdiccion, ó bajo las de muchos; y se estipula tambien que los buques libres asegurarán igualmente la libertad de las mercancias, y que se juzgarán libres todos los efectos que se hallasen á bordo de los buques que perteneciesen á Ciudadanos de una de las partes contratantes aun cuando el cargamento por entero ó parte de él fuese de los enemigos de una de las dos, bien entendido sin embargo que el contrabando se esceptua siempre. Se há convenido asi mismo que la propia libertad gozarán los sugetos que puedan encontrarse á bordo del buque libre, aun cuando fuesen enemigos de una de las dos partes contratantes; y por lo tanto no se podrá hacerlos prisioneros, ni separarlos de dichos buques, á menos que sean militares, y estén á la sazon empleados en el servicio del enemigo. Por la estipulacion de que la bandera cubre la propiedad, han convenido las dos partes contratantes en que esto se éntiende asi respecto de aquellas

War with a third party and the other neutral, the flag of the neutral shall cover the property of enemies whose Governments acknowledge this principle and not of others.

Article 17th

It is likewise agreed that in the case where the Neutral flag of one of the contracting parties shall protect the property of the enemies of the other, by virtue of the above stipulation it shall always be understood, that the neutral property found on board such enemies vessels shall be held and considered as enemies property, and as such shall be liable to detention, and confiscation, except such property as was put on board such vessel before the declaration of War, or even afterwards if it were done without the knowledge of it: but the contracting parties agree that four months having elapsed after the declaration their Citizens shall not plead ignorance thereof; On the contrary if the flag of the neutral does not protect the enemy's property in that case the goods and Merchandizes embarked in such Enemy's Vessel shall be free.

Article 18th

This liberty of Commerce and Navigation shall extend to all kinds of Merchandize excepting

potencias que reconozcan este principio; pero que si una de las dos partes contratantes estubiese en guerra con una tercera, y la otra neutral, la bandera de esta neutral cubrirá la propiedad de los enemigos cuyo Gobierno reconozca este principio y no de otros.

Articulo 17º

Se conviene tambien que en caso de que el pavellon neutral de una de las partes contratantes proteja la propiedad de los enemigos de la otra en virtud de la referida estipulacion, se entenderá siempre que la propiedad neutral encontrada á bordo de los referidos buques enemigos se tendrá y considerará como propiedad enemiga, y como tal estará sugeta á detencion y confiscacion, escepto aquella propiedad que haya sido embarcada en tal buque antes de declaracion de guerra, y aun despues si se há hecho sin noticia de tal declaracion; pero las partes contratantes convienen en que cuatro meses despues de la declaracion, sus Ciudadanos no alegarán ignorancia, al contrario si el pavellon del buque neutral no proteje la propiedad enemiga, en este caso los efectos y mercancias del neutral embarcados en tal buque enemigo serán libres.

Articulo 18º

Esta libertad de navegacion y comercio será estensiva á todo genero de mercancias esceptuando

those only which are distinguished by the name of contraband; and under this name of contraband or prohibited goods shall be comprehended, first Cannons, mortars, howitzers, swivels, blunderbusses, muskets, fusees, Rifles, carbines, pistols, pikes, swords, Sabres, lances, spears, halberts; and granades, bombs, powder, matches, balls, and all other things belonging to the use of these arms: secondly buckles, helmets, breastplates, coats of mail, infantry belts, and clothes, made up in a military form and for a military use; thirdly cavalry belts and horses with their furniture; fourthly and generally, all kinds of arms, and instruments of iron, steel, brass and Copper or of any other materials manufactured, prepared and formed expressly to make War by Sea or Land.

ARTICLE 19th.

All other Merchandize and things not comprehended in the articles of contraband expressly enumerated and classified as above, shall be held and considered as free and subjects of free and lawful Commerce, so that they may be carried and transported, in the freest manner by both the contracting parties, even to places belonging to an enemy, excepting only those places which are at that time besieged or blockaded; and to avoid all doubt in that particular it is declared

solamente las que se distinguen con el nombre de contrabando y bajo esta calificacion ó la de efectos prohividos se comprenderán primero: Cañones, Morteros, obuses, Pedreros, Trabucos, fusiles, Escopetas, Carabinas, comunes y rayadas, Pistolas, Picas Espadas, Sables, Lanzas, Arpones, Alabardas y granadas, Bonbas, Polvora, Mechas, Balas y otras cosas que pertenecen á el uso de armas; segundo: Escudos, Yelmos, Petos, Cotas de maya, cinturones de infanteria, y uniformes ó vestidos propios para la tropa, tercero: cinturones de Caballeria y caballos con sus arneces, cuarto: y generalmente toda clase de armas é instrumentos en hierro, acero, bronce y cobre ú otros materiales manufacturados preparados y formados aproposito para hacer la guerra por mar ó por tierra.

ARTICULO 19º

Cualesquiera otras mercancias y cosas no comprendidas en los articulos en contrabando enumerados y clasificados esplicitamente como queda dicho, se tendrán y considerarán libres y de libre y legal comercio, de modo que podrán llevarse y transportarse de la manera mas libre por ambas partes contratantes aun á parages pertenecientes á enemigos esceptuando solo aquellos que á la sazon estubiesen sitiados ó bloqueados, y para evitar toda duda en este particular, se declara

that those places only are besieged or blockaded, which are actually besieged or blockaded by a belligerent force capable of preventing the entry of the Neutral.

ARTICLE 20th.

The articles of contraband before enumerated and classified which may be found in a vessel bound for an enemy's port shall be subject to detention and confiscation, leaving free the rest of the Cargo and the vessel, that the owners may dispose of them as they see proper. No vessels of either of the two nations shall be detained on the high Seas on account of having on board articles of contraband whenever the Master Captain or Supercargo of said vessel will deliver up the articles of contraband to the Captor, unless the quantity of such articles be so great and of so large a bulk that they cannot be received on board the capturing vessel without great inconvenience; but in this and in all other cases of just detention the vessel detained shall be sent to the nearest convenient and safe port for trial and Judgement according to Law.

ARTICLE 21st.

And whereas it frequently happens that Vessels, sail for a port or place belonging to an enemy without knowing that the same is besieged blockaded or invested, it is

que solo se considerarán bloqueados ó sitiados aquellos puntos que se hallen sitiados ó bloqueados por una fuerza veligerante capaz de impedir la entrada á los neutrales.

ARTICULO 20º

Los articulos de contrabando enumerados y clasificados arriba que se encuentren en un buque que navega para puerto enemigo, estarán sugetos á detension y confiscacion dejando libre el resto del cargamento y el buque para que los dueños dispongan lo que les paresca. Ningun buque en ambas naciones será detenido en alta mar por conducir á bordo articulos de contrabando, siempre que el dueño, Capitan ó Sobrecargo del referido buque los entregue al apresador, á menos que la cantidad de estos articulos sea tan grande y abulte tanto que no pueda recibirlos el buque apresador sin grande inconveniente; pero en este y en todos los demas casos de justa detencion, el buque detenido se enviará al puerto mas cercano conveniente y seguro para ser juzgado con arreglo á las leyes.

ARTICULO 21º

Como sucede muy frecuentemente que los buques salen para un puerto ó plaza perteneciente al enemigo sin saber que se halla sitiado, bloqueado ó atacado, se

agreed that every Vessel so situated may be turned away from such port or place, but shall not be detained, nor shall any part of her Cargo if not contraband be confiscated, unless after warning of such blockade or investment from the commanding officer of the blockading force she should again attempt to enter the aforesaid port; but she shall be permitted to go to any other port or place she may think proper. Nor shall any Vessel of either of the contracting parties that may have entered into such port before the same was actually besieged, blockaded or invested by the other be restrained from quitting such place with her Cargo; nor if found therein after the surrender shall such Vessel or her Cargo be liable to confiscation, but she shall be restored to the owner thereof.

ARTICLE 22nd.

In order to prevent all kinds of disorder in the visiting and examination of the Vessels and Cargoes of both the contracting parties on the high seas, they have agreed mutually, that whenever a Vessel of War public or private should meet with a neutral Vessel of the other contracting party, the first shall remain out of cannon shot, and may send his boat with two or three men only in order to execute the said examination of the papers concerning the owner-

conviene en que á ningun buque que se halle en estas circunstancias se le permitirá entrar en el; pero no será detenido, ni será confiscada parte alguna de su cargamento, sino hubiere en el alguno de los efectos de contrabando; á menos que despues de ser prevenido del sitio ó bloqueo por el oficial comandante de las fuerzas bloqueadoras emprendiese de nuevo entrar en dicho puerto; pero se permitirá ir á cualquiera otro puerto ó lugar que crea conveniente; ni á buque alguno de las partes contratantes que hubiere entrado en tal puerto antes de ser bloqueado, sitiado ó atacado por alguna de ellas, se le impedirá salir del puerto con su cargamento y si se hallare en el despues de la redicion, ni el buque ni el cargamento serán confiscados sino debueltos á sus dueños.

ARTICULO 22º

Para impedir toda clase de desorden en la visita y ecsamen de los buques y cargamentos de ambas partes contratantes en alta mar, convienen mutuamente en que siempre que un buque de guerra nacional, ó armado en corso se encontrare con un buque neutral de la otra parte contratante, el primero se mantendrá fuera del tiro de cañon, y enviará su vote con solo dos ó tres hombres para verificar el referido ecsamen de los papeles relativos al dueño y cargamento del buque, sin causar la

ship and Cargo of the Vessel, without causing the least extortion violence or ill treatment for which the Commanders of the said Armed Vessels shall be responsible with their persons and property; and for this purpose the Commanders of said private armed Vessels shall before receiving their Commissions, give sufficient security to answer for all the damages they may commit. And it is expressly agreed, that the neutral party shall in no case, be required to go on board the examining Vessel for the purpose of exhibiting his papers or for any other purpose whatsoever.

Article 23ᵈ·

To avoid all kinds of vexation and abuse in the examination of papers relating to the ownership of Vessels belonging to the Citizens of the two Contracting parties, they have agreed, and do agree, that in case one of them should be engaged in War, the Vessels belonging to the Citizens of the other, must be furnished with Sea letters or passports, expressing the name property and bulk of the Vessel, and also the name and place of habitation of the Master or Commander of said Vessel in order that it may thereby appear that the said Vessel really and truly belongs to the Citizens of one of the contracting parties; they have likewise agreed that such Vessels

menor violencia, vejacion ó maltrato: para lo que los Comandantes de los espresados buques armados, serán responsables con sus personas y propiedades, á cuyo fin los Comandantes de dichos buques armados en corso por cuenta de particulares, darán antes de recibir sus patentes, fianzas suficientes para responder de los daños que puedan causar. Y se estipula espresamente que á buque neutral en ningun caso se le obligará ir á bordo del que registra á manifestar sus papeles ni algun otro objeto sea el que fuere.

Articulo 23⁹

Para evitar toda bejacion y abuso en el ecsamen de los papeles relativamente á los dueños de los buques que pertenescan á Ciudadanos de las dos partes contratantes, han convenido y convienen que en caso de hallarse una de ellas en guerra, los buques y navios que pertenescan á Ciudadanos de la otra, deberán ser provistos con patentes de mar ó pasaportes, que espresen el nombre, propiedad y dimensiones del buque, asi como el nombre del lugar en que habite el Capitan ó Comandante del buque para que aparesca real y verdaderamente que pertenece á Ciudadanos de una de las partes contratantes; y han convenido igualmente en que los referidos buques si condujesen cargamento

being laden, besides the said Sea letters or passports, shall also be provided with Certificates, containing the several particulars of the Cargo, and the place whence the vessel sailed, so that it may be known whether any forbidden or contraband goods be on board the same: which Certificate shall be made out by the Officers of the place whence the Vessel sailed, in the accustomed form, without which requisites the said Vessel may be detained, to be adjudged by the competent Tribunal, and may be declared legal prize, unless the said defect shall be satisfied or supplied by testimony entirely equivalent to the satisfaction of the competent Tribunal.

ademas de las patentes de mar ó pasaportes, seran provistos de certificaciones con espresion de cada uno de los articulos que comprende el cargamento y el lugar de su procedencia, para saber si á su bordo se hallan efectos de contrabando cuya certificacion se dará por las autoridades del lugar de donde salió el buque en la forma acostumbrada, sin cuyo requisito el referido buque podrá ser detenido para ser juzgado por tribunal competente, y podrá ser declarado buena presa, á menos que esta falta se satisfaga ó supla con testimonio equivalente á satisfaccion del Tribunal competente.

Article 24th

It is further agreed, that the stipulations above, expressed relative to visiting and examination of Vessels, shall apply only to those which sail without convoy, and when said Vessels are under convoy, the verbal declaration of the Commander of the Convoy or his word of honor that the Vessels under his protection belong to the Nation whose flag he carries, and when they are bound to an enemy's port that they have no Contraband goods on board shall be sufficient.

Articulo 24º

Convienen ademas en que las estipulaciones arriba espresadas relativamente al ecsamen y visitas de buques tendrán lugar solamente respecto de aquellos que navegan sin convoy y que cuando los dichos buques estubieren bajo convoy será bastante la declaracion berval del Comandante del convoy bajo su palabra de honor de que los buques que están bajo su proteccion pertenecen á la Nacion del pavellon que enarbola, y cuando van con destino á puerto enemigo, de que no llevan contrabando á bordo.

Article 25th.

It is further agreed that in all cases the established Courts for prize causes, in the country to which the prizes may be conducted shall alone take cognizance of them. And whenever such tribunal of either party shall pronounce judgment against any Vessel, or goods, or property claimed by the Citizens of the other party, the sentence or decree shall mention, the reason or motives on which the same shall have been founded; and an authenticated copy of the sentence or decree in conformity with the laws and usages of the Country, and of all the proceedings of the case shall if demanded be delivered to the Commander or Agent of said Vessel without any delay he paying the legal fees for the same.

Article 26th.

For the greater security of the intercourse between the Citizens of the United States of America and of the United Mexican States it is agreed now for then, that if there should be at any time hereafter an interruption of the friendly relations which now exist, or a war unhappily break out between the two contracting parties, there shall be allowed the term of six months to the merchants, residing on the coast, and one year to those residing in the interior of the States and Terri-

Articulo 25º

Se convienen ademas que en todos los casos los Tribunales establecidos para juzgar presas en el pais adonde estas sean conducidas tendrán ellos solos el conocimiento de estas causas, y cuando estos Tribunales de alguna de las partes pronunciasen sentencia contra algun buque, efectos ó propiedad que sea reclamada por Ciudadanos de la otra en la sentencia se hará mension de las razones ó motivos en que la haya fundado y se dará si la pidiere, una copia autentica de ella en conformidad con los usos y leyes del pais y de todos los procederes del caso al Comandante ó Agente del buque interesado sin demora alguna, pagando este las costas establecidas por la ley.

Articulo 26º

Para mayor seguridad en la comunicacion entre los Ciudadanos de los Estados unidos de America y los de Mexico, se conviene desde ahora para entonces que si acaeciese en lo succesivo alguna interrupcion en las relaciones amistosas que hoy ecsisten ó si desgraciadamente hubiere un rompimiento hostil entre ambas partes contratantes se les concederá el permiso de seis meses á los comerciantes que residan en las costas, y un año á los que esten en el interior de cada uno de los

tories of each other respectively to arrange their business, dispose of their effects or transport them wheresoever they may please, giving them a safe conduct to protect them to the port they may designate. Those Citizens who may be established in the States and Territories aforesaid exercising any other occupation or trade, shall be permitted to remain in the uninterrupted enjoyment of their liberty and property, so long as they conduct themselves peaceably, and do not commit any offence against the laws, and their goods and effects of whatever class and condition they may be, shall not be subject to any embargo or sequestration whatever nor to any charge nor tax other than may be established upon similar goods and effects belonging to the Citizens of the State in which they reside respectively; nor shall the debts between individuals, nor monies in the public funds, or in public or private banks nor shares in Companies, be confiscated embargoed or detained.

Estados y Territorios respectivos para arreglar sus negocios, disponer de sus bienes ó transportarlos adonde gusten dandoles un salvo conducto que los proteja hasta el puerto que ellos designen: á los Ciudadanos que se hallaren establecidos en los referidos Estados y Territorios ocupados en cualquier otro trafico ó ejercicio se les permitirá permanecer sin interrupcion en el goze de su libertad y propiedades mientras se comporten pacificamente y no cometan ofenza alguna contra las leyes, y sus bienes y efectos de cualquiera clase y condicion que sean no estarán sugetos á embargo ó secuestro alguno, ni á otro impuesto ni contribucion que los establecidos sobre efectos y bienes semejantes pertenecientes á los Ciudadanos de los Estados en que respectivamente residan; ni las deudas particulares, ni las cantidades en los fondos públicos, ó en los bancos públicos ó particulares, ni las acciones de las compañias podrán ser confiscadas, embargadas ni detenidas.

ARTICLE 27th·

Both the contracting parties being desirous of avoiding all inequality in relation to their public communications and official intercourse have agreed and do agree to grant to the Envoys, Ministers, and other public Agents, the same favors, immunities and exemptions which those of the most

ARTICULO 27º

Ambas partes contratantes deseando evitar toda desigualdad relativa á las comunicaciones públicas y oficiales, se han convenido y convienen en conceder á los Enviados, Ministros y otros Agentes públicos, los mismos privilegios ecsenciones é inmunidades que hoy goza y en lo suc-

favored nation do or may enjoy; it being understood that whatever favors immunities or privileges the United States of America or the United Mexican States may find proper to give to the Ministers and public agents of any other power shall by the same Act be extended to those of each of the contracting parties.

Article 28th.

In order that the Consuls and Vice Consuls of the two contracting parties may enjoy the rights prerogatives and immunities which belong to them by their character they shall before entering upon the exercise of their functions, exhibit their Commission or patent in due form to the Government to which they are accredited; And having obtained their Exequatur they shall be held and considered as such by all the authorities magistrates and inhabitants of the Consular district in which they reside. It is agreed likewise to receive and admit Consuls and Vice Consuls in all the ports and places open to foreign Commerce, who shall enjoy therein all the rights prerogatives and immunities of the Consuls and Vice Consuls of the most favored Nation, each of the contracting parties remaining at liberty to except those ports and places in which the admission and residence of such Consuls and Vice Consuls may not seem expedient.

cesivo pueda gozar la Nacion mas favorecida: debiendo entenderse que cualquier favor, inmunidad ó privilegio que los Estados unidos de America ó los de Mexico tengan por conveniente conceder á los Ministros ó Agentes públicos de cualquiera otra potencia, será ipso-facto estensivo á cada una de las respectivas partes contratantes.

Articulo 28º

Para que los Consules y Vice Consules de las dos partes contratantes puedan gozar de los derechos, prerrogativas ó inmunidades que por su caracter les corresponden, presentarán al Gobierno cerca del cual estén destinados su patente ó despacho en debida forma antes de entrar en ejercicio de sus funciones; y habiendo obtenido su execuatur, serán tenidos y considerados como tales por todas las autoridades, magistrados y habitantes del distrito Consular donde residan. Se convienen tambien en recibir y admitir Consules y Vice Consules en todos los puertos y lugares abiertos al comercio estrangero, quienes gozarán en ellos todos los derechos, prerrogativas ó inmunidades de los Consules y Vice Consules de la Nacion mas favorecida, quedando no obstante en libertad cada parte contratante para esceptuar aquellos puertos y lugares en que la admision y residencia de semejantes Consules y Vice Consules no parezca conveniente.

ARTICLE 29th·

It is likewise agreed that the Consuls, Vice Consuls their Secretaries officers and persons attached to the service of Consuls they not being Citizens of the Country in which the Consul resides, shall be exempt from all compulsory public service, and also from all kind of taxes, imposts and contributions levied specially on them except those which they shall be obliged to pay on account of Commerce, or their property to which the Citizens and inhabitants native and foreign of the Country in which they reside are subject; being in every thing besides subject, to the Laws of their respective States. The archives and papers of the Consulates shall be respected inviolably, and under no pretext whatever shall any magistrate seize or in any way interfere with them.

ARTICLE 30th·

The said Consuls shall have power to require the assistance of the authorities of the country for the arrest detention and custody of deserters from the public and private vessels of their Country; and for that purpose they shall address themselves to the Courts, Judges and Officers competent, and shall demand the said deserters in writing, proving by an exhibition of the register of the vessel, or Ships roll, or other public documents, that the man

ARTICULO 29º

Ygualmente se conviene que los Consules, sus Secretarios, los oficiales y personas agregadas al servicio de los Consules, no siendo estos Ciudadanos del pais en que el Consul resida, estarán esentos del servicio público compulsivo y tambien de toda clase de impuestos y contribuciones señaladas especialmente á ellos: esceptuando las que respecto de su comercio ó propiedad estarán obligados á satisfacer del mismo modo que los Ciudadanos y habitantes naturales y estrangeros del pais en que residan pagaren, estando en todo lo demas sugetos á las leyes de los Estados respectivos: los archivos y papeles oficiales de los Consules serán respetados inviolablemente y por ningun pretesto sea el que fuere podrán los magistrados embargarlos ni de ningun modo tomar conocimiento de ellos.

ARTICULO 30º

Los dichos Consules tendrán poder de requerir el aucsilio de las autoridades locales para la prision, detencion y custodia de los desertores de buques nacionales y particulares de su pais, y para este objeto se dirijirá á los Tribunales, Jueces y oficiales competentes, y pediran los dichos desertores por escrito, probando por una presentacion de los registros de los buques Roll del equipage ú otros documentos públicos que aquellos hombres eran parte de las dichas

or men demanded were part of said Crews; and on this demand so proved (saving always where the contrary is proved) the delivery shall not be refused. Such deserters when arrested shall be placed at the disposal of the said Consuls, and may be put in the public prisons at the request and expence of those who reclaim them, to be sent to the Vessels to which they belonged, or to others of the same Nation. But if they be not sent back within two months, to be counted from the day of their arrest, they shall be set at liberty and shall not be again arrested for the same cause.

Article. 31st.

For the purpose of more effectually protecting their Commerce and Navigation, the two contracting parties do hereby agree, as soon hereafter as circumstances will permit, to form a Consular Convention, which shall declare specially the powers and immunities of the Consuls and Vice Consuls of the respective parties.

Article 32d.

For the purpose of regulating the interior Commerce between the frontier territories of both Republics it is agreed, that the Executive of each shall have power by mutual agreement of determining on the route and establishing the roads by which such Commerce shall be conducted; and in all cases where

tripulaciones, y esta demanda asi provada (menos no obstante cuando se probare lo contrario) no se reusará la entrega. Semejantes desertores luego que sean arrestados, se pondrán á disposicion de los dichos Consules, y pueden ser depositados en las prisiones públicas á solicitud y espensas de los que los reclamen para ser enviados á los buques á que correspondan, ó á otros de la misma Nacion. Pero sino fueren mandados dentro de dos meses contados desde el dia de su arresto, serán puestos en libertad, y no volverán á ser presos por la misma causa.

Articulo 31º

Con objeto de protejer mas efiscasmente su comercio y navegacion las dos partes contratantes convienen: que tan luego como lo permitan las circunstancias formarán un convenio consular que declarará especialmente las facultades y prerrogativas de los Consules y Vice Consules de las partes respectivas.

Articulo 32º

Con el fin de regularizar el comercio Terrestre por las fronteras de ambas Repúblicas queda establecido que se fijarán por los Gobiernos de estas por mutuo convenio los caminos por donde este trafico há de ser conducido y en todos aquellos casos en que las caravanas que se forman para este comercio necesiten convoy y pro-

the Caravans employed in such commerce may require convoy and protection by military escort, the Supreme Executive of each nation shall by mutual agreement in like manner fix on the period of departure for such Caravans and the point at which the military escort of the two nations shall be exchanged. And it is further agreed that untill the regulations for governing this interior commerce between the two nations shall be established, that the Commercial intercourse between the State of Missouri of the United States of America and New Mexico in the United Mexican States shall be conducted as heretofore, each Government affording the necessary protection to the Citizens of the other.

ARTICLE 33rd.

It is likewise agreed that the two contracting parties shall by all the means in their power, maintain peace and harmony among the several Indian nations who inhabit the lands adjacent to the lines and Rivers which form the boundaries of the two countries; and the better to attain this object both parties bind themselves expressly to restrain by force all hostilities and incursions on the part of the Indian nations living within their respective boundaries so that the United States of America will not suffer their Indians to attack

teccion de la fuerza militar se fijará tambien del mismo modo por mutuo convenio de ambos Gobiernos el tiempo de la partida de tales caravanas y el punto en el cual se han de cambiar las escoltas de tropas de las dos naciones. Se há convenido ademas que entretanto se establecen las reglas que han de regir segun lo dicho en el comercio terrestre entre las dos naciones, las comunicaciones comerciales entre el Estado de Missouri de los Estados unidos de America y el Territorio de Nuevo Mexico en los Estados unidos Mexicanos continuará como hasta aqui concediendo cada Gobierno la proteccion necesaria á los Ciudadanos de la otra parte.

ARTICULO 33º

Se há convenido igualmente que las dos partes contratantes procurarán por todos los medios posibles mantener la paz y buena armonia entre las diversas Tribus de indios que habitan los terrenos adyacentes á las lineas y rios que forman los limites de los dos paises; y para conseguir mejor este fin se obligan espresamente ambas partes á reprimir con la fuerza todo genero de hostilidades é incurciones de parte de las Tribus indias que habitan dentro de sus respectivos limites: de modo que los Estados unidos de America no permitirán que sus

the Citizens of the United Mexican States, nor the Indians inhabiting their Territory; nor will the United Mexican States permit the Indians residing within their Territories to commit hostilities against the Citizens of the United States of America, nor against the Indians residing within the limits of the United States, in any manner whatever.

And in the event of any person or persons captured by the Indians who inhabit the Territory of either of the contracting parties, being or having been carried into the Territories of the other, both Governments engage and bind themselves in the most solemn manner to return them to their country as soon as they know of their being within their respective Territories, or to deliver them up to the Agent or Representative of the Government that claims them, giving to each other reciprocally timely notice, and the claimant paying the expences incurred in the transmission and maintenance of such person or persons who in the mean time shall be treated with the utmost hospitality by the local authorities of the place where they may be. Nor shall it be lawful under any pretext whatever for the Citizens of either of the contracting parties, to purchase or hold captive prisoners made by the Indians, inhabiting the Territories of the other.

indios ataquen á los Ciudadanos de los Estados unidos Mexicanos, ni á los indios que habitan su Territorio, y los Estados unidos Mexicanos no permitirán tampoco que sus indios hostilizen á los Ciudadanos de los Estados unidos de America ó á sus indios de manera alguna.

Y en el caso de que alguna ó algunas personas cojidas por los indios que habitan los Territorios de cada una de las partes contratantes, fuere ó hubiere sido llevada á los Territorios de la otra, ambos Gobiernos se comprometen y obligan del modo mas solemne á debolverlas á su pais tan luego como sepan que se hallan en sus respectivos Territorios, ó entregarlas al Agente ó encargado de mismo Gobierno que las reclame, dandose aviso oportuno reciprocamente, y abonandose por el que lo reclama los gastos erogados en la conducion y manutencion de la tal persona ó personas aquienes entretanto se dispensará por las autoridades locales del punto en que se encuentren la mas generosa hospitalidad. Ni será legitimo por ningun pretesto que los Ciud[os] de cualquiera de las partes contratantes compren ó retengan prisioneros cautivos hechos por los indios que habitan el Territorio de la otra.

Article 34th.

The United States of America and the United Mexican States desiring to make as durable as circumstances will permit, the relations which are to be established between the two parties by virtue of this Treaty or General convention of Amity commerce and Navigation have declared solemnly and do agree to the following points.

First. The present Treaty shall remain and be of force for eight years from the day of the exchange of the ratifications and untill the end of one year after either of the contracting parties shall have given notice to the other of its intention to terminate the same; Each of the Contracting parties reserving to itself the right of giving such notice to the other, at the end of said term of Eight years; and it is hereby agreed between them, that on the expiration of one year after such notice shall have been received by either of the parties from the other party, this Treaty in all its parts, relating to Commerce and Navigation shall altogether cease and determine, and in all those parts which relate to peace and friendship it shall be permanently and perpetually binding on both the Contracting parties.

Articulo 34?

Los Estados unidos de America y los Estados unidos Mexicanos, deseosos de hacer tan permanentes como lo permitan las circunstancias las relaciones que van á establecerse entre las dos partes en virtud de este Tratado ó convenio general de amistad, comercio y navegacion, han declarado solemnemente, y convienen en los puntos siguientes.

Primero. El presente tratado permanecerá y estará en todo su vigor y fuerza por el termino de ocho años que deberán contarse desde el dia del cambio de las ratificaciones, y terminados estos continuará rigiendo hasta el termino de un año contado desde el dia en que alguna de las dos partes contratantes haya dado noticia á la otra de su resolucion de poner fin á este convenio. Y cada una de las partes contratantes se reserva asi misma el derecho de dar este aviso á la otra al cabo del referido termino de ocho años, quedando ademas convenido entre ambas que al cabo de un año despues de recibido tal aviso por alguna de las partes contratantes de parte de la otra, este Tratado deberá cesar y acabar en todo cuanto tiene relacion con comercio y navegacion, quedando solo permanente y perpetuamente valedero y obligatorio á ambas partes contratantes en todo cuanto toca á la paz y amistad entre ambas.

Secondly. If any one or more of the Citizens of either party shall infringe any of the articles of this Treaty, such Citizens shall be held personally responsible for the same; and the harmony and good correspondence between the two Nations shall not be interrupted thereby: each party engaging in no way to protect the offender or sanction such violation.

Thirdly. If (what indeed cannot be expected) any of the articles contained in the present Treaty shall be violated or infracted in any manner whatever, it is stipulated that neither of the contracting parties will order or authorise any acts of reprisal nor declare War against the other on complaints of injuries or damages, untill the said party considering itself offended, shall first have presented to the other a statement of such injuries or damages verified by competent proofs, and demanded justice and satisfaction and the same shall have been either refused or unreasonably delayed.

Fourthly. Nothing in this Treaty contained shall however be construed to operate contrary to former and existing public Treaties with other Sovereigns or States. The present Treaty of Amity, Commerce, and Navigation shall be approved and ratified by the President of the United States of America, by and with the advice and consent of the

Segundo. Si uno ó mas Ciudadanos de alguna de las partes infringiere algun articulo de este Tratado, será personalmente responsable de ello; pero no por esto se interrumpirá la armonia y buena correspondencia entre las dos naciones á cuyo fin ambas partes respectivamente se comprometen á no protejer á el agresor, ni sancionar semejante infraccion.

Tercero. Si (lo que no es de esperar) alguno de los articulos del presente Tratado desgraciadamente fuere violado ó infringido de cualquiera otro modo se estipula que ninguna de las partes contratantes dispondrá ó autorizará ninguna clase de represalia, ni declarará guerra á la otra por queja de injuria ó daño hasta que la misma parte que se considera agraviada no haya presentado á la otra una relacion de las injurias ó daños competentemente comprobada, y sobre ello hubiese pedido justicia y satisfaccion, y esta hubiere sido negada ó sin razon demorada.

Cuarto. Nada de lo contenido en este Tratado podrá de manera alguna interpretarse ni obrará en contra de los tratados públicos celebrados anteriormente y ecsistentes con otros Soberanos y Estados.

El presente tratado de amistad, comercio y navegacion será aprobado y ratificado por el Presidente de los Estados unidos de America

Senate thereof, and by the Vice President of the United Mexican States with the consent and approbation of the Congress thereof; and the ratifications shall be exchanged in the City of Washington, within the term of one year to be counted from the date of the signature hereof or sooner if possible.

In witness whereof we the Plenipotentiaries of the United States of America and of the United Mexican States have signed and sealed these presents. Done in the City of Mexico on the fifth day of April in the year of our Lord One thousand eight hundred and thirty one, in the fifty fifth year of the Independence of the United States of America, and in the eleventh of that of the United Mexican States.

[Seal] A: BUTLER

[Seal] LUCAS ALAMAN
　　　　RAFAEL MANGINO

con la anuencia y consentimiento de su Senado, y por el Vice Presidente de los Estados unidos Mexicanos, previo el consentimiento y aprobacion del Congreso; y las ratificaciones serán cangeadas en la Ciudad de Washington en el termino de un año contado desde la fecha en que fueren firmados, ó antes si fuere posible.

En fé de lo cual los respectivos Plenipotenciarios lo hemos firmado y sellado con nuestros sellos respectivos. Fecho en Mexico á los cinco dias de Abril del año del Señor de mil ochocientos treinta y uno, undecimo de la Independencia de los Estados unidos Mejicanos y quinquagesimo quinto de la de los Estados unidos de America.

[Seal] LUCAS ALAMAN
　　　　RAFAEL MANGINO

[Seal] A: BUTLER

ADDITIONAL ARTICLE

1st.

Whereas in the present state of the Mexican Shipping it would not be possible for Mexico to receive the full advantage of the reciprocity established in the fifth and sixth articles of the Treaty signed this day, it is agreed that for the term of six years the stipulations contained in the said

ARTICULO ADICIONAL

1º

Por cuanto en el presente estado de la marina mejicana no seria posible que Mexico gozase de las ventajas que deberá producir la reciprocidad establecida por los articulos 5º y 6º del tratado firmado en este dia, se estipula que durante el espacio de seis años se suspen-

articles shall be suspended; and in lieu thereof it is hereby agreed, that untill the expiration of the said term of six years American Vessels entering into the ports of Mexico, and all articles the produce growth or manufacture of the United States of America imported in such Vessels shall pay no other or higher duties, than are or may hereafter be payable in the said ports by the Vessels and the like articles the growth produce or manufacture of the most favored nation; and reciprocally it is agreed that Mexican Vessels entering into the ports of the United States of America and all articles the growth produce or manufacture of the United Mexican States imported in such Vessels shall pay no other or higher duties than are or may hereafter be payable in the said ports by the Vessels and the like articles, the growth produce or manufacture of the most favored nation; and that no higher duties shall be paid or bounties or drawbacks allowed on the exportation of any article the growth produce or manufacture of either country in the Vessels of the other than upon the exportation of the like articles in the Vessels of any other foreign Country.

derá lo convenido en dichos articulos y en su lugar se estipula que hasta la conclucion del termino mencionado de seis años, los buques americanos que entren en los puertos de Mexico, y todos los articulos de producto, fruto ó manufactura de los Estados unidos de America importados en tales buques, no pagarán otros ni mayores derechos que los que se pagan ó en adelante se pagaren en los referidos puertos por los buques é iguales articulos de fruto, producto ó manufactura de la Nacion mas favorecida, y reciprocamente se estipula que los buques mejicanos que entren en los puertos de los Estados unidos de America y todos los articulos de fruto, producto ó manufactura de los Estados unidos Mexicanos importados en tales buques, no pagarán otros ni mayores derechos que los que se pagan, ó en adelante se pagaren en los mencionados puertos por los buques y semejantes articulos de producto, fruto ó manufactura de la Nacion mas favorecida; y que no se pagarán mayores derechos, ni se concederán otras franquicias y descuentos á la esportacion de cualquiera articulo de producto, fruto ó manufactura de cada uno de los dos paises en los buques del otro mas que á la esportacion de dichos articulos en buques de cualquiera otro pais estrangero.

The present additional article shall have the same force and value as if it had been inserted word for word in the Treaty signed this day. It shall be ratified and the ratification shall be exchanged at the same time.

In witness whereof we the respective Plenipotentiaries have signed and Sealed the same. Done at Mexico on the fifth day of April One thousand Eight hundred and thirty One.

[Seal]   A: BUTLER

[Seal]   LUCAS ALAMAN
        RAFAEL MANGINO

El presente articulo adicional tendrá la misma fuerza y valor que si se hubiera insertado palabra por palabra en el Tratado de este dia. Será ratificado y la ratificacion cambiada al mismo tiempo.

En fé de lo cual los respectivos Plenipotenciarios lo hemos firmado y sellado con nuestros sellos respectivos.

Fecho en Mexico á cinco de Abril de mil ochocientos treinta y uno.

[Seal]   LUCAS ALAMAN
        RAFAEL MANGINO

[Seal]   A: BUTLER

Protocol of a conference had on the 17.th of September 1831. between Anthony Butler, Plenipotenciary on the part of the United States of America, and their Excellency's Lucas Alaman and Raphael Mangino Plenipotentiaries for the United Mexican States.

The Undersigned Plenipotentiaries having assembled in the Office of the Secretary of State for foreign affairs proceeded to consider the articles 7.th and 13.th of the Treaty of Amity, commerce and navigation concluded by the undersigned Plenipotentiaries, and also that part of the 3^d article of the said Treaty contained in the following words, "to trade therein in all sorts of produce, manufactures and merchandize"; These articles 7th and 13th and that part of the 3^d abovementioned having been

Protocolo de una conferencia tenida el 17. de Septiembre de 1.831. entre los Ecsmos. Sres. d^n Lucas Alaman y d^n Rafael Mangino, Plenip^{os} por parte de los Estados unidos Mexicanos, y el Sor. d^n Antonio Butler, por los Estados unidos de America.

Habiendose reunido los Infrascritos Plenip^{os} en la Secret^a de Estado y del Despacho de relaciones esteriores procedieron á tomár en consideracion los art^{os} 7° y 13° del Tratado de Amistad, Comercio y Navegacion celebrados por los Infrascritos Plenipotenciarios, como asi mismo la parte del tercer articulo de dicho Tratado, espresada en los terminos siguientes: "el poder comerciar alli en toda especie de productos, manufacturas y mercancias." Estos articulos 7° y 13° y la parte del mencionado

suspended by the Chamber of Deputies of the Congress of the United Mexican States, untill the undersigned shall have determined upon the construction which the said articles shall receive in regard to the rights of Commerce that may be enjoyed by the citizens of each of the high contracting parties. After free and mature deliberation, the undersigned have agreed that the construction to be given to the above mention⁰ articles, shall in no manner restrain the power possessed by each nation respectively of regulating sales by retail of goods, wares and merchandize within their respective States and Territories. And to remove all doubts as to the object designed to be effected by the said Treaty in regard to the several branches which it embraces, The Plenipotentiaries agree that the abovementioned articles so far as they relate to the Commercial intercourse conduct⁰ by the citizens of their respective Countries, it shall be reciprocal and equal reserving however to the United States of America, and to the United Mexican States, full power and entire liberty to regulate commerce of retail, by means of their respective Legislatures in conformity with what each party may consider as the interest of their own citizens, without being restrained by any stipulation contained in the abovementioned Treaty of

art⁰ 3⁰ se han suspendido por disposicion de la Cámara de Diputados del Congreso de los Estados unidos Mexicanos, hasta tanto q. los Infrascritos determinen de comun acuerdo la interpretacion q. se debe dar á dhos. articulos por lo que respecta á los derechos del comercio de que deben gozar los subditos de las dos partes contratantes. Despues de una libre y madura deliberacion, los Infrascritos han acordado q. el objeto de los mencionados artᵒˢ por lo que respecta al comercio, no es el de restringir en manera alguna la facultad q. tienen sus naciones respᵛᵃˢ de arreglar la venta por menor de muebles, generos y mercancias dentro de sus respᵛᵒˢ Estados y Territorios y que ninguna duda puede ofrecer el objeto q. se há querido establecer por el referido Tratado con respecto á los varios ramos q. abraza. Los Plenipᵒˢ convienen en q. los citados artᵒˢ, en la parte en q. se refieren á las relaciones de Comercio q. se han de mantener y observar por los Ciudadanos de cada una de las naciones respectivamᵗᵉ, serán iguales y reciprocos tanto para los Estados unidos Mexicanos, cuanto pᵃ los Estados unidos de America, dejando á estas naciones en plena facultad y entera libertad para arreglar la parte llamada *Comercio al menudeo* por medio de sus legislaturas respᵛᵃˢ, conforme á lo que cada una de las partes considere convenᵗᵉ al in-

Amity, Commerce, and Navigation, provided that the Measures adopted by the Legislature of either party, shall be general in their operations and extend equally to the subjects and Citizens of all other nations who maintain Commercial relations with the high contracting parties in conformity with the principle of *"the most favoured Nation"* establishᵈ as a reciprocal basis in the Treaty of amity, commerce and navigation concluded by the undersigned Plenipotentiaries and signed on the 5ᵗʰ April of the present year, and of which Treaty the abovementionᵈ articles 3ᵈ 7ᵗʰ and 13. form a part.

In testimony of which the undersignᵈ have subscribed the present protocol in Mexico on the 17ᵗʰ Septᵉʳ in the year 1831.

A: BUTLER

LUCAS ALAMAN

RAFAEL MANGINO

Protocol of a conference held by their Excellencies the Secretaries of State for Home and Foreign Affairs, and of the Treasury, and Anthony Butler, Chargé d'Affaires of the United States of America, Plenipotentiaries respectively of these States and of those; for the celebration of Treaties of Amity, Commerce Navigation and boundary between both Republics, the 17ᵗʰ of Decbʳ 1831.

On the 17ᵗʰ of Decbʳ 1831, their Excellencies, Lucas Alaman,

teres de sus propios Ciudadanos, independⁱᵉ de cualquiera estipulacion contenida en el mencionado Tratado de Amistad, Comercio y Navegacion, siempre que las determinaciones de dichas Legislaturas se estiendan igualmⁱᵉ á los Ciudadanos y subditos de todas las demas naciones q. tienen relaciones de Comercio con las altas partes contratantes en conformidad con el principio de la *Nacion mas favorecida*, establecido como base de reciprocidad en el Tratado de Amistad, Comercio y Navegacion concluido por los Infrascritos Plenipᵒˢ y firmado el 5. de Abril del presⁱᵉ año, y de cuyo Tratado los mencionados artᵒˢ 7º 13º y 3º forman parte.

En testimonio de lo cual los Infrascritos firman el presente protocolo en Mexico á 17. de Septiembre de 1.831.

LUCAS ALAMAN

RAFAEL MANGINO

A: BUTLER

Protocolo de una conferencia tenida entre los Ecsmos. Sres. Secretarios de Estado y del Despacho de Relaciones y Hacienda y Antonio Butler Encargado de Negocios de los Estados unidos de America, Plenipotenciarios respectivamⁱᵉ de estos y aquellos Estados para la celebracion de Tratados de Amistad, Comercio, Navegacion y Limites entre ambas Repúblicas el dia 17. de Diciembre de 1.831.

El dia 17. de Diciembre de mil Ochocientos treinta y uno reunidos

Secretary of State for Home and Foreign Affairs, and Raphael Mangino Secretary of the Treasury, Plenipotentiaries appointed by the Vice President, in exercise of the executive power of these States, for the celebration of Treaties of Amity, Commerce and Navigation, and for the adjustment of a boundary with the United States of America, and Anthony Butler, Chargé d'Affaires of the said States, and Plenipotentiary appointed, for the same object, by the President of the said States, having met in the Office of the Secretary for Home and Foreign Affairs, the two former set forth, that the Treaty of Amity, Commerce and navigation, celebrated in this Capital by the undersigned Plenipotentiaries on the fifth of April of the present year, being approved by both Chambers of the General Congress of these States, with the exception of the 34th article, on the approval of which difficulties have occurred, that have caused the deliberation respecting it to be suspended and of the second additional article, which has been disapproved, having been considered unnecessary; and the additional article of the Treaty of Boundary, celebrated the 5th of April last, being also approved, the extraordinary Sessions of Congress had been closed, without a communication to the

en la Secretaria del Despacho de Relaciones interiores y esteriores los Ecsmos. Sres. D. Lucas Alaman Secretario del mismo Despacho y D. Rafael Mangino que lo es del de Hacienda Plenipotenciarios nombrados por el Vice Presid[te] en ejercicio del Poder Ejecutivo de estos Estados p[a] la celebracion de Tratados de Amistad, Comercio y Navegacion, y para el arreglo de limites con los Estados unidos de America y el Sr. Coronel D[n] Antonio Butler Encargado de negocios de los mencionados Estados y Plenipotenciario nombrado con el propio objeto por el Presidente de los mismos; espusieron los primeros q[e] estando aprobado por ambas Cámaras del Congreso general de estos Estados el Tratado de Amistad, Comercio y Navegacion celebrado en esta Capital por los Plenipotenciarios q. suscriben el dia 5. de Abril del corriente año á escepcion del articulo treinta y cuatro sobre cuya aprobacion han ocurrido dificultades q. han hecho suspender su deliberacion y el 2[o] adicional que há sido desaprobado por considerarse inecesario y estando aprobado tambien el articulo adicional al Tratado de limites celebrado el cinco de Abril de este año, se habian cerrado las sesiones estraordinarias del Congreso sin que se comunicase al Ejecutivo el Decreto de aprobacion solo detenido por las

Executive of the decree of approbation withheld solely by the difficulties which have occurred only with respect to the said 34th article; and the Plenipotentiaries, having conferred at large upon the particular, desirous on the one part and on the other, that no hindrance should be put to the conclusion of treaties, which, drawing closer the friendly relations that happily unite the two Republics, are equally beneficial to both, they agreed that, to remove every obstacle which might embarrass the attainment of this desired end, the before mentioned 34th article ought to be separated from the Treaty of Amity, Commerce and Navigation, it not having any necessary Connection with the other Stipulations of the said Treaty, and, in the place of it, ought to be substituted the 35th article, which would then become, by numerical order, the 34th and the last; and that, besides, in the copy which should be made for the exchange of ratifications and the publication of the Treaty, the second additional article which has been disapproved by the Congress of these States, should be suppressed.

And it having been thus agreed and settled, for the due and suitable proof of the same, it was equally settled that this Protocol should be written in duplicate, and be signed by the plenipoten-

dificultades que han ocurrido unicamente con respecto al citado articulo treinta y cuatro y habiendo conferenciado largamente sobre el particular los Plenipotenciarios, deseosos por una y otra parte de que no se embaraze la conclucion de estos Tratados que estrechan las relaciones amistosas que felizmente unen á las dos Repúblicas con igualmente beneficos á ambas convinieron en que para remover todo obstaculo que pudiera embarazar este deseado fin, debia separarse del Tratado de Amistad, Comercio y Navegacion el mencionado articulo treinta y cuatro que no tiene una conecsion necesaria con las demas estipulaciones del citado Tratado y en su lugar sustituirse el treinta y cinco que vendria á ser entonces por el orden numerico treinta y cuatro y último, y que ademas en la copia que se forme para el cange de las ratificaciones y publicacion del Tratado se suprimira tambien el articulo segundo adicional que ha sido desaprobado por el Congreso generalo de estos Estados unidos.

Y asi acordado y convenido para la debida constancia y formalidad, se convino igualmente se estendiese este Protocolo por copia duplicada firmado por los Plenipotenciarios, que asi lo veri-

tiaries; which they did accordingly in the day, month and year already mentioned.

A: BUTLER

LUCAS ALAMAN

RAFAEL MANGINO

ficaron en el citado dia mes y año.

LUCAS ALAMAN

RAFAEL MANGINO

A: BUTLER

NOTES

In this treaty as it was signed on April 5, 1831, there were thirty-five articles of the treaty proper and, following the treaty proper, two additional articles signed at the same time by the same Plenipotentiaries.

As the result of the proceedings in the Mexican Congress while the treaty was before that body and prior to its submission to the Senate of the United States, there were drawn up the two protocols, printed above, of September 17 and December 17, 1831. The first of these protocols is explanatory of a part of Article 3 and of Articles 7 and 13 of the treaty. By the second protocol, that of December 17, 1831, it was agreed that Article 34 of the treaty as signed, which had not been approved by the Mexican Congress, should be "separated" from the treaty, or, in other words, suppressed, and that Article 35 of the treaty as signed should be numbered 34. In that form of numeration, accordingly, are printed above the texts of the treaty in English and Spanish, with the omission of Article 34 of the treaty as signed on April 5, 1831, which reads as follows:

ARTICLE 34th

It is likewise agreed that in the case of any slave or Slaves escaping from their owners residing in the states or territories of one of the contracting parties and passing over into the States and territories of the other, it shall be lawful for the owner or owners of such slave or slaves or their lawful agents to require the assistance of the authorities of the country where such slave or slaves may be found for their arrest detention and custody; and for that purpose the proprietors or their agents shall address themselves to the nearest magistrate or competent officer. On such demand being made it shall be the duty of the Magistrate or Competent Officer to cause the said slaves to be arrested and detained; and if it shall appear that such slave or slaves be actually the property of the claimant the Magistrate or competent Officer shall, surrender he she or them to the proprietor or proprietors his her or their Agents to be conveyed back to the

ARTICULO 34º

Tambien se pacta que en caso de que algunos esclavos se huyan de sus Señores residentes en los Estados ó Territorios de una de las partes contratantes, y pasen á los Estados ó Territorios de la otra, puedan el amo ó amos de tales esclavos ó sus Agentes legitimos requerir la ayuda de las autoridades del pais en que se encuentren para su arresto, detencion y custodia; y para esto los amos ó sus Agentes se dirijirán á el Magistrado ú oficial competente mas inmediato. Cuando se haga tal solicitud, será el deber del Magistrado ú oficial competente hacer arrestar y detener á dichos esclavos, y si apareciere que los tales esclavos son actualmente una propiedad del reclamante, el Magistrado ú oficial competente los entre gará á los propietarios ó sus Agentes para que buelvan á llevarlos á el pais de que se huyeron pagando los reclamantes los gastos del arresto, detencion y custodia de los tales esclavos, y ningun otro.

Country from whence the slave or slaves had escaped, the claimant or claimants paying the expences incurred in the arrest, detention and custody of such slave or slaves and none other. And it is further agreed by the contracting parties that on mutual requisitions by them, respectively or by their respective Ministers or Officers authorised to make the same, they will deliver up to justice all persons who being charged with murder or forgery committed within the jurisdiction of either, shall seek an asylum within any of the Territories of the other; provided that this shall be done only on such evidence of criminality, as according to the laws of the place where the fugitive or person so charged, shall be found would justify his apprehension or commitment for trial, if the offence had been there committed. The expense of such apprehension and delivery shall be defrayed by those who make the requisition and receive the Fugitive.

And it is hereby agreed that the demand allowed by this article for fugitive slaves and malefactors shall in all cases be made within the period of one year from the date of such slave or malefactor having taken refuge within the Jurisdiction of the other party, after which time they will be entirely free.

Y estipulan ademas las partes contratantes que por los requerimientos mutuos que hagan respectivamente ellas ó sus respectivos Ministros ú oficiales autorizados al efecto entregarán á la justicia á todas las personas que acusadas de asesinatos, ó falsificacion, sometida en la jurisdiccion de cualquiera de ellas, busquen un asilo en cualquier pais de la otra, con tal que esto solo se haga por tal evidencia de criminalidad que segun las leyes del lugar donde se encuentre al fugitivo ó á la persona asi acusada pueda justificar su aprension y juicio en caso de que el delito se hubiere cometido alli. El gasto de esta aprension y entrega será de cuenta de los que hagan el reclamo y reciban al fugitivo.

Queda tambien establecido que los reclamos de esclavos y criminales fugitivos que por este articulo se facultan, se entiende que solo podrán hacerse dentro del termino de un año contado desde la fecha de la llegada de tales esclavos ó criminales á refugiarse en el territorio de la jurisdiccion de la otra parte, y pasado este termino quedarán enteramente libres.

The two protocols of September 17 and December 17, 1831, are printed above as part of the agreement; one of them explained and the other one amended the treaty as signed. In the presidential message of February 24, 1832, transmitting the treaty to the Senate, there is no mention of them, nor indeed of any accompanying documents whatever (Executive Journal, IV, 213); and the Senate print of February 24, 1832 (Senate Confidential Document, 22d Congress, 1st session, Regular Confidential Documents, IV, 527–50), includes only the treaty and additional articles, in English and Spanish, as originally signed on April 5, 1831. The protocols are not mentioned in the Senate resolution of advice and consent of March 23, 1832 (Executive Journal, IV, 232), which indeed speaks of "additional articles" and not "article"; the form of the attested resolution in the treaty file is the same. There is no doubt, however, that the two protocols were before the Senate; there is a note in the treaty file, dated at the office of the Secretary of the Senate May 2, 1832, and signed by one of the Senate clerks, which, although it mistakenly gives each of the two protocols the same date, is conclusive on the point. It reads as follows:

I herewith enclose, by the direction of the Secretary of the Senate, two Protocols of Conference, on the Treaties with Mexico, held by the Am⁹ Minister on the 17th Dec. 1831; and the Copy of the Treaty of Commerce, in Spanish, as approved by the Chamber of Deputies.

Furthermore, on the attested Senate resolution of March 23, 1832, which is in the treaty file, there is the pencil note, "call at the Senate's office and procure the protocoles which had been sent there, with the Treaty."

In his despatch of December 24, 1831 (D. S., 5 Despatches, Mexico, No. 29), Chargé d'Affaires Butler wrote regarding the two protocols as follows:

The protocol of the 17ᵗʰ September will serve to explain the limitation which the Congress design to impose on the operation of the 3ᵈ Article;—This article was objected to, 1ˢᵗ because it was more comprehensive in its terms than any article on the same subject to be found in their Treaties with other Nations: and 2ⁿᵈˡʸ Because as they had no intention of divesting themselves of the power to regulate the manner in which the interior Commerce of the Country should be carried on, the phraseology of that article might involve the two Nations in difficulties from the different construction that each party might give to it. I think it probable however that no inconvenience will ever arise from the limitation imposed by the construction put on the article in the protocol, because the general Government not only declare themselves opposed to the policy of prohibiting foreigners from engaging in the retail trade but some of the States have also expressed their opposition to the measure, as one not only illiberal in its character, but the inevitable effect of which at the present time would be to lessen the Revenue;—to deprive the Country of its usual supply of Merchandize, from the want of Capital on the part of the Native Merchant to furnish himself with stock equal to the current demand—And moreover by creating a monopoly whereby the Venders of Merchandize in the absence of that fair competition which the present system encourages, would have it in their power to exact from the consumer whatever price their avarice might prompt them to demand.

The Protocol of the 17ᵗʰ December was designed to explain and provide for the peculiar state of things which the disagreement between the two chambers had created, and by which the ratification of the Treaty would be indefinitely postponed. The Chamber of Deputies first acted on the Treaty, and by that body several articles were rejected, amongst which was the 34ᵗʰ relative to fugitive Slaves and Criminals. The Senate restored all the rejected articles except the second additional Article, and returned the Treaty to the Chamber of Deputies with their amendments, all which amendments were concurred in except that relating to fugitive Slaves and Criminals, the rejection of which was reaffirmed by a majority of two thirds as required by the Federal Constitution in all cases of Amendments made by one House to the proceedings of the other. At this point a difficulty arose between the two houses which was about to produce serious embarrassment and create additional delay. By a provision of the Federal Constitution of Mexico relative to the ordinary proceedings of the two Chambers, it is declared that whenever a measure originating in either branch of Congress shall be amended by the other, and upon the return of the proceeding to the Chamber whence it originated, and the Amendment of the other Chamber be rejected by two thirds, then in such case the original proposition shall stand and be final. Under this provision the deputies contended that as the Legislative action on the Treaty commenced with them, their modifications of the Treaty must be considered in the light of an original proceeding, and subject to all the rules which govern in such cases—and as an amendment made by the other branch could have no effect if the original proposition be reaffirmed by two thirds of that Chamber who proposed it, so the Amendments made to the Treaty by the Chamber of Deputies must be governed by the same Rule. The Senate denied the analogy, and contended that the proceedings on the Treaty could not be considered in the Character of an Original proposition by either branch of the

Congress, and that the decision made by the Deputies on their Amendments although sustained by a majority of two thirds could not be considered as final, but that the question must again be submitted to the Senate when if the Amendments made by them to the proceedings of the Chamber of deputies should be supported by a like Majority of two thirds of that body then the Article rejected by the deputies should be restored. This presented a new question to the Congress upon which it did not seem probable they would ever agree, and as the Session was fast drawing to a close, there was every appearance that they would adjourn and leave the Treaty unfinished—In this condition of affairs I had an interview with the Secretary of Foreign Affairs on the subject and after a very free interchange of opinions, I considered it the best course to suppress or withdraw the Article which had created the difficulty, and so leave the Congress no pretext for longer delaying the ratification—this proposition was made by me to the Secretary and assented to on his part: And I felt the more disposed to adopt this course because the rejection of the 34th Article did no more at last than merely annul the forms provided by which our fugitive Slaves might be reclaimed—And because the rejection of that provision neither impaired our rights, nor lessened the means of enforcing them; and if the Mexican Congress in their folly chose to leave open a question that it was much their interest as ours to put at rest, they must expect to meet the consequences, that a collision between the two Governments on that subject would unavoidably lead to.

By the protocol of December 17, 1831, it was further agreed that the second additional article, which had been disapproved by the Mexican Congress, should be suppressed; accordingly, the text of that second additional article is omitted from the texts above printed. It reads as follows:

2nd

For the purpose of giving an equal share of the reciprocal advantages mentioned in this Treaty to the Mexican Shipping; it is agreed that all Vessels shall be considered as Mexican Vessels, that are *bona fide* the property of a Mexican Citizen, and whose Commander and half the Crew are Mexicans, without regard to the place or Country in which such Vessel may have been built.

2º

Con el mismo objeto de hacer efectivas para la marina mexicana las ventajas reciprocas de este Tratado, queda convenido que se considerará como mexicano todo buque en cualquiera parte que haya sido construido que pertenesca bona fide á alguno ó algunos Ciudadanos mejicanos y cuyo Capitan y la mitad de la tripulacion sean mejicanos.

In the treaty as signed, the paragraph following the two separate articles naturally reads in the plural. The necessary change to the wording in the singular, as in the texts above, though not specifically mentioned in the protocol of December 17, was adopted in each instrument of ratification as following from the omission of the second separate article. As first signed the paragraph reads thus:

The present additional articles shall have the same force and value as if they had been inserted word for word in the Treaty signed this day. They shall be ratified and the ratifications exchanged at the same time.

Los presentes articulos adicionales tendrán la misma fuerza y valor que si se hubieran insertado palabra por palabra en el Tratado de este dia. Serán ratificados y las ratificaciones cambiadas al mismo tiempo.

Regarding the earlier treaties of amity, commerce, and navigation signed on July 10, 1826, and February 14, 1828, neither of which was ratified, and the full powers for the treaties of this period and also the

relation between this treaty and the Treaty of Limits of January 12, 1828 (Document 60), the notes to the Treaty of Limits should be consulted. It may be said here that the additional article to the Treaty of Limits, extending the time limited for the exchange of ratifications thereof, was signed at Mexico on April 5, 1831, the date of the signature of this treaty. The ratifications of the two treaties were concurrently exchanged on April 5, 1832, and on that day they were both proclaimed.

The File Papers

The file contains the original of the treaty, with its two additional articles, and the originals of the two protocols of September 17 and December 17, 1831. All those documents are in English and Spanish, the English in the left columns.

The original treaty, with the two additional articles, is embodied in the original proclamation of April 5, 1832; and a very crude method was adopted for making the texts as signed conform with the amended texts as proclaimed, that is to say, in respect of the omission of the original Article 34 and of the second additional article. In the original treaty as signed, Article 34 and the second additional article are crossed out in pencil and Article 35 is renumbered 34. Similarly, in the paragraph beginning "The present additional articles," which follows the two additional articles in the original treaty as signed, the plural has throughout been changed in pencil to the singular, "articles" to "article," "they" to "it," "ratifications" to "ratification," and so on. Those pencil changes conform to the wording adopted in each instrument of ratification as a result of the protocol of December 17, 1831, and that same wording, as heretofore explained, appears in the texts printed above.

It is to be observed, however, that various other pencil corrections throughout the original treaty, in both the English and the Spanish, some of which have been printed, with or without brackets, in previous treaty compilations, have been disregarded in collating the texts above printed.

Mention has been made of the attested resolution of the Senate; but the file contains no duplicate or copy of the United States instrument of ratification of April 4, 1832, other than a facsimile thereof recently obtained from the Mexican archives. In the Mexican instrument of ratification, which is in Spanish, the Spanish text of the treaty is in the left columns. As has been said, each instrument of ratification includes the texts as amended pursuant to the protocol of December 17, 1831—that is, with the omission of the original Article 34, the change in the number of the following article, the omission of the second additional article, and the change from the plural to the singular form in the paragraph following the latter article.

The file contains three originals of the certificate of exchange of ratifications of April 5, 1832, one in English and two in Spanish, and also a facsimile of a fourth example thereof, in English, which is in the Mexican archives. To each of those documents is appended a nota-

tion of differences between the texts in the Mexican instrument of ratification and those in the signed original. The notation is signed by the participants, Secretary of State Edward Livingston and Chargé d'Affaires José Montoya, and in the English reads as follows:

Note. In the ratified copy of the Treaty, by the Mexican Government, the following difference between the original, signed by the Plenipotentiaries who negotiated it, and that version of the same Treaty, were noticed before the signature of the foregoing certificate of Exchange, viz:
Article 4. English version, line 27ᵗʰ after "exportation of" the article *the* is left out.
Article 14. Spanish version, the word *de* instead of "en" in the original. (line 6ᵗʰ)
Article 34. English version, 19ᵗʰ line, the following words are left out, after the word "other," *of its intention to terminate the same, each of the contracting parties reserving to itself the right of giving such notice to the other.*
In the same article, English version, line 28ᵗʰ the word *the* instead of "its parts," as in the original.
The same article, line 86ᵗʰ English version, the word *Vice,* before that of "President," omitted.
The same article, 89ᵗʰ line *of the same,* instead of "thereof," as in the original.

Another paper which is now in the treaty file is also mentioned in the despatch of December 24, 1831 (D. S., 5 Despatches, Mexico, No. 29). In the final paragraph of that despatch Butler wrote:

I send you the copy of the Treaty in Spanish which passed through the chamber of Deputies—by this you will see their course and as the Copy was furnished me by the Secretary of Foreign Affairs himself there can be no doubt as to its genuineness.

That paper, as the above-quoted note of May 2, 1832, from the office of the Secretary of the Senate shows, was before the Senate. It is a copy of the Spanish text of the treaty with marginal notes showing the action of the Mexican Chamber of Deputies in respect of particular articles at various dates from August 17 to September 13, 1831. Most of the articles are noted as approved (*aprobado*); Article 21 is not noted; those marked rejected (*reprobado*) are Articles 16, 17, 19, and 34, and the second additional article. The other notations include a general approval of the preamble and, as to Articles 3, 7, and 13, indicate a suspension of the discussion as stated in the protocol of September 17, 1831, which was explanatory of those three articles; and, as mentioned in the despatch above quoted of December 24, 1831, the Mexican Senate restored three of the articles rejected by the Chamber of Deputies, namely, Articles 16, 17, and 19.

Negotiations at Mexico and at Washington

In his despatch of November 2, 1830, Colonel Anthony Butler, Chargé d'Affaires at Mexico, wrote "that the Treaty of Amity, Commerce and Navigation between the United Mexican States and the United States of America is at last concluded. The finishing hand was put to it this day " (D. S., 5 Despatches, Mexico); and various later despatches speak of the treaty as having been concluded on November 2 (or November 1); but the text at that time was unsigned and in English

only; the Spanish version was drawn up later and changes were proposed (*ibid.*, No. 9, February 19, 1831, and enclosures). The discussions of the treaty in the two Houses of the Mexican Congress were prolonged from April 7 to December 15 (*ibid.*, No. 24, October 25, 1831; *ibid.*, enclosure to the letter to President Jackson of December 23, 1831); indeed, it appears from the protocol of December 17, 1831, that the "decree of approbation" was not communicated to the Executive of the United Mexican States. The final difficulty was the article regarding fugitive slaves (original Article 34), which the Mexican Senate accepted but which the Chamber of Deputies rejected (*ibid.*, No. 27, November 23, 1831); and the suppression of that article, pursuant to the protocol mentioned, was essential; otherwise the treaty would have failed.

This was the third treaty of amity, commerce, and navigation signed by representatives of the two parties; but it was the only one of them to go into force (see the chapter on "Obstacles in the Way of Concluding a Commercial Treaty" and the writings there cited, in Manning, Early Diplomatic Relations between the United States and Mexico, 205–51). The earlier treaties of July 10, 1826, and February 14, 1828, failed for the reasons outlined in the notes to the Treaty of Limits of January 12, 1828 (Document 60); and, as there mentioned, there was a close relation between the Treaty of Limits and this treaty. The Treaty of Limits had not gone into force, and its additional article, which extended the time limited for the exchange of ratifications, was signed on the same date as this treaty; on February 24, 1832, the same day that this treaty was submitted to the Senate, the Treaty of Limits was again submitted with its additional article (Executive Journal, IV, 213); but the Senate acted first on this treaty, on March 23 (*ibid.*, 232); and in reply to the note of the Mexican Chargé d'Affaires of March 26 regarding the exchange of ratifications of both treaties (D. S., 2 Notes from the Mexican Legation), Secretary of State Livingston under date of March 30 (D. S., 5 Notes to Foreign Legations, 16) mentioned only the exchange of ratifications of this treaty. In the next Mexican note, of March 31 (D. S., 2 Notes from the Mexican Legation), Montoya wrote that he "was much surprised and grieved by the terms of this reply"; the correspondence continued; and in the final paragraphs of the note of April 3 (*ibid.*) the position of the Mexican Government was thus definitely stated (translation from the Spanish):

Consequently the Government of the undersigned, being convinced that there would not be the slightest difficulty on the part of that of the United States of America in the ratification of the additional article, considered itself justified in expecting that the exchange of both treaties would take place at the same time.

Therefore the undersigned finds it necessary to inform the Secretary of State that, according to his instructions, he cannot proceed to the exchange of ratifications of the Treaty of Amity, Commerce, and Navigation, unless that of the ratifications of the boundary treaty takes place at the same time.

The Senate resolution of advice and consent to the Treaty of Limits was voted unanimously on April 4 (Executive Journal, IV, 237);

on the following day, April 5, 1832, the last day of the time limited for the exchange of ratifications of both treaties, their ratifications were concurrently exchanged and the proclamation of each was issued; and on the following May 1 they were communicated to Congress (Richardson, II, 573).

ARTICLE 3

In the despatch of Chargé d'Affaires Butler of December 24, 1831 (D. S., 5 Despatches, Mexico, No. 29), is the following observation regarding the texts of Article 3 of the treaty:

I beg leave to point your attention to the last clause in the 3ᵈ article of the Treaty in which you will perceive a variation between the English and Spanish Text, by the introduction into the latter of the words "Comercio de Escala"—in the English text there is neither a translation nor an equivalent for these words—I can give no translation myself and the best scholars I have consulted declare that they are not susceptible of being translated—The meaning of the phrase is "that no Vessel shall be permitted to enter and land part of her Cargo at one port "and the remainder at another, but the whole shall be landed in the port where "the Vessel first enters." I resisted the introduction of these words into the Treaty, but unavailingly, although the only argument urged in their favor, was that so frequently made use of "We have the same provision in every other "Treaty entered into with Foreign powers,—it is our policy and we cannot "consent to change it" The restriction I believe affects our Commerce but very little if it all; Vessels from the United States never coming with assorted Cargoes so far as I am informed—It is the practice with the French and English to do so, and with whom this regulation is a subject of serious complaint.

ARTICLE 32

This article was intended to regulate the trade by the route of the Santa Fé Trail. See generally the chapter on "Diplomacy Concerning the Opening of the Santa Fé Trail" in Manning, *op. cit.*, 166–89, and the authorities there cited.

Treaty Series No. 88
8 Statutes at Large, 430–33
18 *ibid.*, pt. 2, Public Treaties, 245–47

71

FRANCE : JULY 4, 1831

Convention Regarding Claims and Regarding Duties on Wines and Cottons, signed at Paris July 4, 1831. Original in English and French. Submitted to the Senate December 7, 1831. (Message of December 6, 1831.) Resolution of advice and consent January 27, 1832. Ratified by the United States February 2, 1832. Ratified by France August 31, 1831. Ratifications exchanged at Washington February 2, 1832. Proclaimed July 13, 1832; but see the notes as to the original proclamation, which was first dated February 2, 1832.

The United States of America and His Majesty the King of the French, animated with an equal desire to adjust, amicably and in a manner conformable to equity as well as to the relations of good intelligence and sincere friendship which unite the two countries, the reclamations formed by the respective governments, have, for this purpose, named for their plenipotentiaries; to wit the President of the United States, by and with the advice and consent of the Senate, William C. Rives, Envoy Extraordinary and Minister Plenipotentiary of the said United States near His Majesty the King of the French, and His Majesty the King of the French, Count Horace Sebastiani, lieutenant-général of his armies, his Minister Secretary of State for the Department of Foreign Affairs &ᵃ &ᵃ—who, after having ex-

Les Etats Unis d'Amérique et Sa Majesté le Roi des Français étant animés d'un égal désir de régler à l'amiable et d'une manière conforme à l'équité aussi bien qu'aux relations de bonne harmonie et d'amitié sincère qui unissent les deux pays, les réclamations formées par les gouvernemens respectifs ont, à cet effet, nommé pour leurs plénipotentiaires; savoir, le Président des Etats Unis, de l'avis et avec le consentement du Sénat, Mʳ William, C. Rives, Envoyé Extraordinaire et Ministre Plénipotentiaire des dits Etats près de Sa Majesté le Roi des Français, et Sa Majesté le Roi des Français, Mʳ le Comte Horace Sebastiani Lieutenant général de ses armées, son Ministre Secrétaire d'Etat au Département des Affaires Etrangères &ᵃ &ᵃ Lesquels après avoir échangé leurs pleins pouvoirs

changed their full powers found in good and due form, have agreed upon the following articles:

ARTICLE 1ʳˢᵗ

The French government, in order to liberate itself completely from all the reclamations preferred against it by citizens of the United States for unlawful seizures, captures, sequestrations, confiscations or destructions of their vessels, cargoes, or other property, engages to pay a sum of twenty five millions of francs to the government of the United States who shall distribute it among those entitled in the manner and according to the rules which it shall determine.

ARTICLE 2.

The sum of twenty five millions of francs above stipulated shall be paid at Paris in six annual instalments of four millions, one hundred and sixty six thousand six hundred and sixty six francs sixty six centimes each, into the hands of such person or persons as shall be authorised by the government of the United States to receive it.

The first installment shall be paid at the expiration of one year next following the exchange of the ratifications of this convention, and the others at successive intervals of a year, one after another, till the whole shall be paid.

To the amount of each of the said instalments shall be added

ARTICLE 1ᵉʳ

Le gouvernement Français, à l'effet de se libérer complétement de toutes les réclamations élevées contre lui par des citoyens des Etats Unis, pour saisies, captures, séquestres confiscations et destructions illégales de leurs navires, cargaisons ou autres propriétés, s'engage à payer une somme de vingt cinq millions de francs au gouvernement des Etats Unis qui en fera la répartition entre les ayant droit suivant le mode et d'après les règles qu'il déterminera.

ARTICLE 2ᵉ

La somme de vingt cinq millions de francs stipulée ci dessus sera payée à Paris, en six termes annuels de quatre millions cent soixante six mille six cent soixante six francs, soixante six centimes, entre les mains de la personne ou des personnes que le gouvernement des Etats Unis aura autorisées à la recevoir.

Le premier paiement aura lieu à l'expiration de l'année qui suivra l'échange des ratifications de la présente convention; et les autres paiemens s'effectueront successivement d'année en année jusqu'à parfait acquittement de la somme entière.

Au montant de chacun des paiemens annuels ainsi reglés

interest at four per cent thereupon, as upon the other instalments then remaining unpaid, the said interest to be computed from the day of the exchange of the ratifications of the present convention.

ARTICLE 3.

The government of the United States on its part, for the purpose of being liberated completely from all the reclamations presented by France on behalf of its citizens or of the Royal Treasury (either for ancient supplies or accounts the liquidation of which had been reserved, or for unlawful seizures, captures, detentions arrests or destructions of French vessels, cargoes or other property) engages to pay to the government of His Majesty (which shall make distribution of the same, in the manner and according to the rules to be determined by it) the sum of one million five hundred thousand francs.

ARTICLE 4.

The sum of one million five hundred thousand francs stipulated in the preceding article shall be payable in six annual instalments of two hundred and fifty thousand francs, and the payment of each of the said instalments shall be effected by a reservation of so much out of the annual sums which the French government is bound, by the second article above, to pay to the government of the United States.

seront ajoutés les intérêts à quatre pour cent, tant du terme échu que des termes à échoir; ces intérêts seront calculés à partir du jour des ratifications de la présente convention.

ARTICLE 3ᵉ

De son coté, le gouvernement des Etats Unis, pour se libérer complétement de toutes les réclamations présentées par la France dans l'intérêt de ses citoyens ou du Trésor Royal, à raison, soit d'anciennes fournitures ou comptes dont la liquidation avait été reservée, soit de saisies, captures, détentions, arrestations et destructions illégales de navires, cargaisons ou autres propriétes Francaises s'engage à payer au gouvernement de Sa Majesté qui en fera la distribution aux ayant droit, suivant le mode et d'après les règles qu'il déterminera la somme de quinze cent mille francs.

ARTICLE 4ᵉ

La somme de quinze cent mille francs stipulée dans l'article précédent sera payable en six termes annuels de deux cent cinquante mille francs, et le paiement de chacun de ces termes aura lieu au moyen d'une retenue de pareille somme que le gouvernement Français exercera sur les versemens annuels qu'il s'est engagé par l'art : 2 ci dessus à effectuer entre les mains du gouvernement des Etats Unis.

To the amount of each of these instalments shall be added interest at four per cent upon the instalment then paid, as well as upon those still due, which payments of interest shall be effected by means of a reservation similar to that already indicated for the payment of the principal. The said interest shall be computed from the day of the exchange of the ratifications of the present convention.

Au montant de chacun de ces termes seront ajoutés les intérêts à quatre pour cent tant du terme échu que des termes à échoir au moyen d'une retenue analogue à celle qui vient d'être indiquée pour le paiement du capital. Ces intéréts seront calculés à partir du jour des ratifications de la présente convention.

ARTICLE 5.

As to the reclamations of French citizens against the government of the United States, and the reclamations of citizens of the United States against the French government which are of a different nature from those which it is the object of the present convention to adjust, it is understood that the citizens of the two nations may prosecute them in the respective countries before the competent judicial or administrative authorities in complying with the laws and regulations of the country, the dispositions and benefit of which shall be applied to them in like manner as to native citizens

ARTICLE 5ᵉ

Quant aux réclamations des citoyens Francais contre le gouvernement des Etats Unis et aux réclamations des citoyens des Etats Unis contre le gouvernement Français qui sont d'une autre nature que celles aux quelles la présente convention a pour objet de faire droit, il est entendu que les citoyens des deux nations pourront les poursuivre dans les pays respectifs auprès des autorités judiciaires ou administratives compétentes en se soumettant aux lois et réglemens locaux, dont les dispositions et le bénéfice leur seront appliqués comme aux nationaux eux mêmes.

ARTICLE 6.

The French government and the government of the United States reciprocally engage to communicate to each other, by the intermediary of the respective legations, the documents, titles or

ARTICLE 6ᵉ

Le gouvernement Français et le gouvernement des Etats Unis s'engagent réciproquement à se communiquer par l'intermédiaire des légations respectives les documens titres ou renseignemens

other informations proper to facilitate the examination and liquidation of the reclamations comprised in the stipulations of the present convention.

ARTICLE 7.

The wines of France, from and after the exchange of the ratifications of the present convention, shall be admitted to consumption in the States of the Union, at duties which shall not exceed the following rates by the gallon (such as it is used at present for wines in the United States)— to wit, six cents for red wines in casks; ten cents for white wines in casks, and twenty two cents for wines of all sorts in bottles. The proportion existing between the duties on French wines thus reduced and the general rates of the tariff which went into operation the 1st of January 1829, shall be maintained, in case the government of the United States should think proper to diminish those general rates in a new Tariff.

In consideration of this stipulation, which shall be binding on the United States for ten years, the French government abandons the reclamations which it had formed in relation to the 8th article of the Treaty of cession of Louisiana. It engages moreover to establish on the *long staple* cottons of the United States, which after the exchange of the ratifications of the present con-

propres à faciliter l'examen et la liquidation des réclamations comprises dans les stipulations de la présente convention.

ARTICLE 7

A partir de l'échange des ratifications de la présente convention les vins de France seront admis à la consommation dans les Etats de l'Union, à des droits qui ne pourront pas excéder par gallon (tel qu'il est actuellement usité pour les vins aux Etats Unis) savoir, six cents pour les vins rouges en futailles; dix cents pour les vins blancs en futailles, et vingt deux cents pour les vins de toutes sortes en bouteilles. Le rapport dans lequel les droits ainsi réduits sur les vins de France se trouvent avec les taxations générales du tarif mis en vigueur le 1er Janvier 1829, sera maintenu dans le cas où le gouvernement des Etats Unis jugerait à propos de diminuer dans un nouveau tarif ces taxations générales.

Au moyen de cette stipulation qui demeurera obligatoire pour les Etats Unis pendant dix années, le gouvernement Français abandonne les réclamations qu'il avait élevées relativement à l'exécution de l'article 8 du traité de cession de la Louisiane. Il s'engage en outre à établir sur les cotons *longue soie* des Etats Unis, qui à compter de l'échange des ratifications de la présente conven-

vention shall be brought directly thence to France by the vessels of the United States or by French vessels, the same duties as on *short staple* cottons

tion seront directement apportées de ce pays en France par navires des Etats Unis ou par navires Français, les mêmes droits que sur les cotons *courte soie*.

ARTICLE 8.

The present convention shall be ratified and the ratifications shall be exchanged at Washington in the space of eight months, or sooner, if possible.

In faith of which, the respective plenipotentiaries have signed these articles and thereto set their seals.

Done at Paris the fourth day of the month of July one thousand, eight hundred and thirty one.

[Seal]   W C RIVES.

ARTICLE 8ᵉ

La présente convention sera ratifiée et les ratifications en seront échangées à Washington dans le terme de huit mois, ou plus tot si faire se peut.

En foi de quoi, les plénipotentiaires respectifs l'ont signée et y ont apposé leurs cachets.

Fait à Paris le quatrième jour du mois de Juillet de l'année mil huit cent trente et un.

[Seal]   HORACE SEBASTIANI

NOTES

In the original signed convention in the treaty file, the English text is written in the left columns and the French in the right; as the texts above printed show, the United States is named first in the preamble and the American Plenipotentiary signed at the left. To that document are attached the attested Senate resolution of January 27, 1832 (Executive Journal, IV, 205), and the duplicate United States instrument of ratification. While the date of that instrument of ratification is February 2, 1832, the French Minister at Washington was informed by Secretary of State Livingston on February 1 that President Jackson "has ratified the Convention" (D. S., 5 Notes to Foreign Legations, 5–6); probably the document had been signed with the date in blank.

In the French instrument of ratification both texts are included, with the French in the left columns; in those texts the King of the French is named first throughout and the signature of the French Plenipotentiary is shown at the left.

The certificate of the exchange of ratifications at Washington on February 2, 1832, is in the usual form, signed and sealed by the participants, Secretary of State Edward Livingston and Louis Charles

Serurier, French Minister at Washington; but appended thereto is the following:

Upon the examination and comparison of the ratifications of the convention referred to in this certificate, it was discovered that the copy of that instrument ratified by His Majesty the King of the French, differs from the original, signed by the Plenipotentiaries of The two Governments which was used in collating those ratifications, in the following particulars. Viz:

Article II, french version, in the 5ᵗʰ line, the words " de l'échange" are added.

Article III, 12ᵗʰ line, french version, the word "repartition," instead of "distribution," as in the original; same article, and same line, the word "entre" instead of "aux"; In the same article, line 14ᵗʰ, the words "among those entitled," are added, in the English.

Article VIII. line 10ᵗʰ, the words, "de l'année" are omitted.

And, before signature, this circumstance is thus noted by the Parties to the said certificate, under their respective Hands, on the day and date of the same.

EDW LIVINGSTON   SERURIER

The papers accompanying the convention when it was transmitted to the Senate with the presidential message of December 6, 1831 (Executive Journal, IV, 179, where the convention is called a treaty), consisted of three despatches from William C. Rives, Minister to France (Nos. 75, 78, and 83, July 8, September 28, and October 9, 1831), which were ordered printed; it seems, however, that the only copy of that Senate document now available is one which is bound with the original despatch of Rives of July 8, 1831 (D. S., 25 Despatches, France, No. 75). Instructions and other correspondence were requested by the Senate on January 3, 1832 (Executive Journal, IV, 194), and were received on January 19 (*ibid.*, 200); the report of the Secretary of State in this regard, under date of January 17, with a list of the accompanying papers, is in D. S., 4 Report Book, 322–23; but no order for printing the report and papers is recorded. Eight days later the resolution of advice and consent was unanimously agreed to, a motion of Senator Henry Clay, of Kentucky, to strike out Article 7 having been withdrawn (Executive Journal, IV, 204–5).

The same portions of correspondence which were received by the Senate on January 19, 1832, were communicated, with perhaps ten additional despatches, to the House of Representatives with the presidential message of January 17, 1833, and were printed in House Document No. 147, 22d Congress, 2d session, serial 235.

To William C. Rives, Minister to France, were given two similar full powers, in customary form, for the negotiation and signature of this convention (D. S., 2 Credences, 114, 163); they are dated respectively June 10, 1829, and March 18, 1831; the latter was "adapted to the late change of Government in France" (D. S., 14 Instructions, France, 92) and so differs from the former in its mention of "His Majesty the King of the French" in lieu of "His Most Christian Majesty the King of France and Navarre." Nothing appears of record in the despatches or elsewhere regarding the full power of the French Plenipotentiary, Count Sebastiani, "Minister Secretary of State for the Department of Foreign Affairs."

The Proclamation

The final clause of the original proclamation reads thus:

Done in Washington, the second day of February, in the year of our Lord one thousand eight hundred and thirty two, and of the Independence of the United States, the fifty sixth.

That clause has been altered in pencil. The words "second" and "February" are marked out and written above them are "13th" and "July," and similarly the last word, "sixth," becomes "seventh," and in the margin in brackets is written "See Printed Copy." In a copy of that print, made at the time, which is in the file, the proclamation is dated July 13, 1832; and that is the date which has always been printed since in official editions of the statutes and in treaty collections generally.

It appears, accordingly, that while the proclamation, when signed, was dated February 2, 1832, it was not deemed to have been issued until the date of the statute passed for carrying the convention into effect, July 13, 1832 (4 Statutes at Large, 574–76).

The question as to the date of issuance of the proclamation of this convention is related to the question of its force as law *ex proprio vigore* in the United States, without the aid of a statute for carrying the convention into effect. Article 7, in part, was a tariff act; it prescribed for ten years specific maximum duties on French wines; whether it was "self-executing" or whether its effectiveness depended on subsequent legislative action was a question which had then and has since been much debated (see Crandall, Treaties, Their Making and Enforcement, 183–99).

In the Senate the question was raised by Henry Clay, then Senator from Kentucky, who moved to strike out Article 7 of the convention, but who later withdrew his motion and voted on January 27, 1832, for the adoption of the usual resolution of advice and consent, which was unanimously agreed to (Executive Journal, IV, 204–5). The striking out of Article 7 would have meant necessarily the end of the convention, which was a global settlement of disputed questions; and the views of Clay may perhaps be deemed to have been that this was an exceptional case, outside of the general principle. The motion that he offered on February 8 (*ibid.*, 209) and which resulted in no action, was as follows:

Resolved, That in advising and consenting to the ratification of the treaty concluded with France on the fourth day of July, 1831, the Senate were actuated by considerations peculiar to the nature of the provisions of that treaty, and entertained objections to the 7th article, which would have been decisive against the provisions of that article if it had stood alone.

Resolved, Therefore, that the Senate do hereby declare that in giving their advice and consent as aforesaid, they do not intend that the said 7th article shall be taken and held as a precedent in the future exercise of the treaty-making power.

In the meantime, on February 7, President Jackson communicated the convention to Congress for legislative action with the following message (Richardson, II, 564):

A convention having been entered into between the United States and the King of the French, it has been ratified with the advice and consent of the Senate; and my ratification having been exchanged in due form on the 2d of February, 1832, by the Secretary of State and the envoy extraordinary and minister plenipotentiary of the King of the French, it is now communicated to you for consideration in your legislative capacity.

You will observe that some important conditions can not be carried into execution but with the aid of the Legislature, and that the proper provisions for that purpose seem to be required without delay.

Thus it seems that the belief in the necessity of legislation in aid of the execution of the treaty caused the withholding of the proclamation from publication and gave it the later date of the statute. Conflicting views were expressed in a brief debate in the House of Representatives on the tenth section of the proposed law (55 Congressional Debates, VIII, pt. 3, 3347–48). That final section of the act of July 13, 1832 (4 Statutes at Large, 574–76), reads as follows:

And be it further enacted, That, for the term of ten years, from and after the second day of February, one thousand eight hundred and thirty-two, wines, the produce of France, shall be admitted into the United States on paying duties not exceeding the following rates on the gallon, (such as is at present used in the United States,) that is to say: six cents for red wines in casks, ten cents for white wine in casks, and twenty-two cents for wine of all sorts in bottles.

ARTICLE 7

"The tariff [on wines] which went into operation the 1st of January 1829" in the United States was that of the act of May 24, 1828 (4 Statutes at Large, 309); the duties on French wines by that statute were, per gallon, ten cents on red wine in casks, fifteen cents on white wine in casks, and, "in addition to the duty now existing on the bottles when thus imported," thirty cents on wine in bottles.

The act of July 13, 1832 (4 Statutes at Large, 574–76, sec. 10), prescribed the import duties on French wines at the rates stated in Article 7, as a maximum for ten years from February 2, 1832.

The different views which had been entertained by the two Governments regarding Article 8 of the Treaty for the Cession of Louisiana (Document 28) have been thus authoritatively described (Moore, International Arbitrations, V, 4457–58):

By the seventh article of the Louisiana treaty, the ratifications of which were exchanged at Washington October 21, 1803, it was provided that for a period of twelve years, beginning three months after notice of the exchange was given at Paris, the ships of France and Spain should be entitled to certain exclusive privileges in the ports of the ceded territory. By Article VIII. it was stipulated that "in future and forever after the expiration of the twelve years the ships of France shall be treated upon the footing of the most favored nation in the ports above mentioned." On the 15th of December 1817 M. Hyde de Neuville, the French minister at Washington, complained that French vessels were not treated in the ports of Louisiana on the footing of the most favored nation. The ground of this complaint was the fact that British and certain other foreign vessels, under reciprocal agreements between their governments and the Government of the United States, enjoyed in the ports of the United States, including of course those in Louisiana, certain exemptions from duty to which vessels of France and of other nations with which there was no such arrangement were not admitted. Under the eighth article France demanded for her vessels in the ports of Louisiana

the rate of duty conceded to the most favored nation.   The United States replied that neither British nor other foreign vessels enjoyed in Louisiana ports any gratuitous advantage; that the article in question did not contemplate the concession to France as a mere gift of what was accorded to other nations for a full equivalent; that France might obtain, not only in the ports of Louisiana, but in all other ports of the United States, the same advantage as was enjoyed by other vessels on the same condition, namely, reciprocity; and that a more extensive construction of the article would violate that clause of the Constitution which requires all duties, imposts, and excises to be uniform throughout the United States.

Correspondence on the subject from December 15, 1817, to November 29, 1824, is printed in American State Papers, Foreign Relations, V, 640–74; see also House Document No. 147, 22d Congress, 2d session, serial 235.

The Settlement

This convention was a global settlement of various questions pending between the Governments of the United States and France, the claims of American citizens against France being the chief.   Those claims were in the major part for "belligerent depredations" during the Napoleonic wars, subsequent to 1805.   On the other hand were certain claims of France or of French citizens against the United States and the reclamations of France in respect of Article 8 of the Treaty for the Cession of Louisiana (Document 28).   As between the two Governments, all these claims were settled and adjusted by this convention and the payments made and action taken thereunder. The claims against France were settled by payments of 25,000,000 francs and the claims against the United States by offsetting payments of 1,500,000 francs; the French construction of Article 8 of the treaty of April 30, 1803, was abandoned; the United States reduced the duties on French wines for ten years and France established the same duties on long-staple cottons of the United States as on those of short staple.

A detailed account of the origin of the American claims and their character, of the French claims, of the negotiations leading to this convention, and of the proceedings thereunder, with numerous citations, is in Moore, International Arbitrations, V, 4447–85.

The act of July 13, 1832 (4 Statutes at Large, 574–76), was passed to carry the convention into effect.   The Commissioners appointed thereunder to pass on the American claims pursuant to the statute and to Article 1 of the convention met first on August 6, 1832, and finally adjourned on December 31, 1835, the period allowed for their task, originally two years, having been twice prolonged (act of June 19, 1834, 4 Statutes at Large, 679, and act of March 3, 1835, *ibid.*, 778).   The claims presented aggregated $51,834,170.15, and those allowed (without interest) $9,352,193.47 (Moore, *op. cit.*, 4461–63). The amount available for their payment was $5,558,108.07 (*ibid.*, 4468); the sums received from France aggregated $5,224,619.78 (Senate Executive Document No. 38, 44th Congress, 2d session, serial 1720, pp. 48, 104).

The net amount to be paid by France (allowing for the offsetting payments of 1,500,000 francs) was 23,500,000 francs, plus interest, payable in six annual instalments from February 2, 1833, to February 2, 1838; but there was delay, and a serious diplomatic controversy resulted between the United States and France during which diplomatic relations between the two countries were suspended. Not until 1836 were the first four instalments paid (Moore, *op. cit.*, 4463–68; and see the messages of President Jackson on various dates from 1833 to 1836 in Richardson, III, 20–22, 100–7, 126–27, 135–45, 152–60, 178–85, 188–214, 215–22).

PORTUGAL : JANUARY 19, 1832

*Settlement of Claims.   Agreement signed at Lisbon January 19, 1832.
Original in English and Portuguese.
As to ratification, see the notes.   Not proclaimed.*

The interview designated by the undersigned His Excellency the Viscount of Santarem, Secretary of State of Foreign Affairs of Portugal, in his letter dated the 3ʳᵈ of this month to the undersigned Mʳ Thomas L. L. Brent, Chargé d'Affaires of the United States, having taken place on the 4ᵗʰ of the present month the Government of Portugal has agreed to pay to the United States the following indemnities for the prizes the: Ann, Galatea Gleaner, and Planter, made by the squadron of Portugal that blockaded the Island of Terceira.

For the Brig: Ann:__ $33. 744. 42 say: thirty three thousand seven hundred and forty four dollars, and forty two cents, in metal: according to the account presented.

For the: Galatea:___ $38. 063. 85 say: thirty eight thousand and sixty three dollars, and eighty five cents, in metal: according to the account presented.

For the: Gleaner:____ $7. 250. — say: seven thousand two hun-

Tendo se realisado no dia 4 do corrente mez a entrevista marcada pelo abaixo assignado S. Exᵃ o Visconde de Santarem Ministro e Secretario d'Estado dos Negocios Estrangeiros de Portugal na sua nota dirigida em 3 do mesmo mez ao Sʳ Thomas L. L. Brent, Encarregado de Negocios dos Estados Unidos; nella se conveio que o Governo de Portugal pagará aos Estados Unidos as seguintes indemnisações pelas prezas: Ann: Galatea, Gleaner: e Planter: feitas pela Esquadra Portugueza no bloqueio da Ilha Terceira.

Pelo Brigue Ann____ 26:995$600 isto he, vinte seis contos noventos e noventa e cinco mil e seis centos reis em metal, conforme a conta apresentada.

Pela: Galatea:_____ 30:450$900 isto he, trinta contos quatro centos e sincoenta mil e novecentos reis em metal, conforme a conta apresentada.

Pelo: Gleaner_____ 5 800$000 isto he, cinco contos e oito cen-

dred and fifty dollars, in metal: according to the account presented.

The account for the owners of the Brig Planter, not having been presented, it is to be made out, and is to be allowed upon the same principles of the former accounts; to be paid at the same periods, and in the same manner from the 19th of January of this year the day of this arrangement. Previous to its presentation to the Portuguese Government, it is to be examined and corrected by the Government of the United States, and examined also by the Government of His Most Faithful Majesty.

The terms of payment are fixed at the following periods, calculated from the 19th of January of this year; one fourth in three, one fourth in six, one fourth in nine, and one fourth in twelve months in Government bills on the Treasury: the funds for the payment of these indemnities will be there ready at the stipulated periods.

The interest of five per cent to be added to the amount of the indemnities of each vessel calculated from the 19th of January of this year.

As regards the indemnity for the Mariners of the Galatea, for the Clothes, double of the amount of the account presented will be paid: and since no precise amount has been claimed for the indemni-

tos mil reis em metal, conforme a conta apresentada.

Não se tendo ainda apresentado a conta dos Donos do Brigue Planter, ella deve ser formada e satisfeita debaixo dos mesmos principios das outras, a paga nos mesmos periodos, e da mesma maneira desde 19 de Janeiro deste anno, dia deste arranjamento. Antes da sua apresentação ao Governo Portuguez, deverá ser examinada e corrigida pelo Governo dos Estados Unidos, examinada tambem pelo Governo de Sua M. Fidelissima.

Os termos do pagamento são fixados nos periodos seguintes calculados desde 19 de Janeiro deste anno, uma quarta parte a trez mezes, outra quarta a seis, outra quarta a nove, e outra quarta a doze mezes, em Letras do Erario. Os fundos para pagamento destas indemnisações estarão aly promptos nos periodos estipulados.

Accrescentarse-ha o juro de cinco por cento as indemnisações de cada navio calculado desde 19 de Janeiro deste anno.

Pelo que respecta á indemnisação dos Marinheiros da Galatea pela sua roupa, se pagará o dobro da conta apresentada; e visto que nenhuma somma determinada se tem reclamado para sua

ties for them on account of their arrest and treatment during it, the Government of Portugal proposes to that of the United States that that amount shall be regulated according to some precedent, if to be found; observing towards the Mariners of the United States what this Government has done towards the mariners of other Powers under similar circumstances, considered in relation to their treatment during the arrest, for which purpose it is proposed to look without delay for some precedent.

For the indemnification of the articles of the Seamen of the Glaner and Planter, the double will be paid in conformity to the law of Prizes

Lisbon 19th of January 1832.
(Signed)
Visconde de Santarem
(Signed)
Thomas L. L. Brent.

indemnisação pela prisão e tratamento que nella tiverão, o Governo de Portugal propoê ao dos Estados Unidos que esta somma será regulada conforme algum precedente, se o houver, observandose para com os Marinheiros dos Estados Unidos o que o Governo tiver praticado com os Marinheiros das outras Nações em iguaes circumstancias, consideradas em relação ao seo tratamento em quanto estiverão prezos, para cujo fim propoe que se examine sem demora algum precedente.

Para indemnisação dos artigos dos Marinheiros do Gleaner, e do Planter se pagará o dobro em conformidade da Ley das prezas

Lisboa 19 de Janeiro de 1832.
(Assignado)
Visconde de Santarem
(Assignado)
Thomas L. L. Brent

NOTES

The source text of this agreement is a copy thereof, in English and Portuguese, enclosed with the despatch of Thomas L. L. Brent, Chargé d'Affaires at Lisbon, dated February 7, 1832, and reading as follows (D. S., 11 Despatches, Portugal, No. 182):

I have the honor to inform you that yesterday was reduced to writing the verbal arrangement which you will have learnt by my last despatch N° 181, dated the 21st of last month, I had on the 19th of the same month made verbally with this Government respecting the prizes. Although unremittingly pressing for it it was not until yesterday that I succeeded in having it reduced to writing, a copy of which is herewith transmitted . . . made both in english and portuguese.

To avoid any misunderstanding, in the agreement signed in portuguese the sums of the indemnities are expressed in the coin of this Country, the dollar calculated at 800 reis according to the agreement made on arranging the indemnities to be paid, and on liquidating the accounts.

On making out this writing I found that the Minister of foreign affairs did not consider that he had definitively decided to admit that the government bills upon the Treasury should be made receivable for duties, and although I made every effort in my power, and pressed very hard for it, and as far as I could with propriety, I could not overcome the objections made to that plan.

I mentioned also in my aforesaid despatch, that bills would in the meantime and previous to the presentation of the estimate for the Planter be made out for a certain sum for the first period, but this being very decidedly opposed, to avoid delay, and in order to be able to get this despatch to Madrid in time to go by Mr Randolph who does not return here, as he will have informed you, I have been reluctantly obliged to give up that point; but no inconvenience will I hope result to the owners, having written to you in my last despatch N° 181, dated the 21st of last month to request that I might be furnished with the estimate, it may be here more or less within the three months: besides, as you will perceive that as the interest from the 19th of last month is to be paid on the amount of indemnities of each vessel, not much inconvenience may result.

From the account of the Ann the sum of two hundred and ninety nine dollars and thirty cents has been deducted. In it the whole amount of the Invoice had been charged, whilst some articles had been taken from the cargo for the use of Captain Hammond at St. Michael. . . .

You will perceive that at the bottom of the account of the Galatea it is there expressed: "Add expenses yet to be incurred in obtaining reparation" but no sum having been carried out, the Minister made such strong objections, that to avoid any farther delay in the signing of our arrangement, so essential on every account, I could not succeed in having a sum allowed for that item, as I was very anxious to do.

By an American vessel sailing tomorrow morning early for Philadelphia I shall forward a duplicate of this despatch sent by Mr Randolph, and will at the same time transmit estimates of the owners of the vessels, which may also be found with my despatch N°. 159 dated the 12th of May, as stated in my last despatch. As regards the abstract of the circumstances of each claim, and my corrections and observations, the instruction that you have given me will be attended to in my next despatch.

By my letters to this Government dated the 12th of January and 10th of February of last year, I had presented the claim of indemnity for the articles purloined from the Seamen of the Gleaner and Planter, which, as you will perceive, is admitted. No accounts of the loss having been furnished this Legation from any quarter I take the liberty to request that they may be sent on to me.

I have the honor to transmit herewith a copy . . . of a letter I yesterday addressed the Minister of Foreign Affairs, respecting the declaration made by him, upon the subject of the arrest and treatment of the Mariners of the Galatea. As late as yesterday, that Minister informed me that he had not as yet been able to find among the correspondence of the Chargé d'Affaires of Portugal at Washington with him, the amount, if any, of the indemnity you may have claimed of that Chargé d'Affaires. Whatever supposed precedent may be found will be examined into and reported to you. This subject will not be lost sight of in my interviews with the Minister of foreign affairs and will receive all the attention on my part that its very high importance demands. At all events I should be pleased to learn from you at a convenient period the amount the Government of the United States positively demand for that indemnity; or your views as to what this Government in justice ought to make. Not having mentioned to me in your instructions by Mr Randolph whether any other satisfaction than that of indemnity for the treatment of the seamen of the Galatea was required, I had only spoken to this Government of indemnity in conformity to your said instructions.

You will also perceive by the aforesaid letter the motive of my abandonment of the claim for interest from the time of the capture of the vessels to the 19th of January of this year, the day of the arrangement.

It will be observed that the agreement was reached verbally on the day of its date, January 19, 1832, though not written and signed until February 6. For three claims, the cases of the *Ann*, the *Galatea*, and

the *Gleaner*, the respective amounts were stated, aggregating $79,058.27, to be paid at the stipulated rate of exchange, 800 reis to the dollar; but the figures of other indemnities admittedly due, chiefly for the brig *Planter*, but also for some personal belongings and for the arrest and treatment of the mariners of the *Galatea*, were left to be fixed at a later date.

The explanatory note addressed to the Portuguese Secretary of State for Foreign Affairs under date of February 6, 1832, which is mentioned in the despatch of Brent above printed, contains the following statements:

I have had the honor to inform your Excellency verbally that I would communicate to my Government that I had stated to this that I had considered the declaration made in the arrangement signed on the 19th of January respecting the arrest and treatment of the Seamen of the Galatea, as evidence of the desire of His Majesty's Government to arrange that affair to the satisfaction of the United States; but at the same time did not thereby mean to express any opinion as to whether the mode of regulating the amount of indemnities by precedent would be agreeable to the latter, or that it ought not to be regulated abstractedly upon the merits of the case itself.

I have had also the honor to inform Your Excellency that it was incumbent upon me to explain to my Government that the claim which I had presented to His Majesty's Government of the five per cent interest per annum upon the indemnity for the prizes made by His Majesty's Squadron, the Galatea, the Planter the Ann, and Gleaner, from the time of their capture until the day of the arrangement which I had the honor to conclude with His Majesty's Government, dated the 19th of January last, that claim of 5 per cent interest I say, had been abandoned by me in consideration of the allowance of the accounts for the Galatea, Gleaner and Ann as presented to His Majesty's Government; and in consideration of the arrangements made, that the account for the Planter should be made out and liquidated upon the same principles as those upon which the other accounts were framed and liquidated.

The agreement went into force from its date; ratification on the part of the Portuguese Government was not required, and in the formal sense ratification by the United States was unnecessary; under date of April 11, 1832, Secretary of State Livingston wrote to Brent "that the arrangement . . . which was concluded and signed by yourself and the Viscount Santarem, on the 19th of January last, is satisfactory to this Government, and that the President entirely approves of your conduct in the transaction" (D. S., 13 Instructions, U. S. Ministers, 288).

It appears that no publication of the agreement was made at the time; but the annual message to Congress of December 4, 1832, contains the following paragraph (Richardson, II, 591, 594):

The demands against Portugal for illegal captures in the blockade of Terceira have been allowed to the full amount of the accounts presented by the claimants, and payment was promised to be made in three [four] installments. The first of these has been paid; the second, although due, had not at the date of our last advices been received, owing, it was alleged, to embarrassments in the finances consequent on the civil war in which that nation is engaged.

The English text of the agreement is printed in British and Foreign State Papers, XIX, 1379–80, a volume which was published in 1834.

The claim in the case of the brig *Ann* was thus made up (D. S., 11 Despatches, Portugal, No. 183, February 7, 1832, enclosures C and D):

Value of the brig	$6, 000. 00
Cost of cargo, less deduction	8, 029. 09
Freight	2, 400. 00
Profits	8, 200. 00
Loss on 4,500 hides bought at Goree	5, 400. 00
Commissions and expenses	1, 150. 33
Property lost or stolen	144. 00
Detention of officers and seamen at varying rates	1, 971. 00
Provisions for the same	450. 00
Total	$33, 744. 42

The claim in the case of the ship *Galatea* was thus made up (*ibid.*, enclosure A; 10 *ibid.*, No. 159, May 12, 1831, enclosure G):

Value of the ship		$8, 000. 00
Value of her outfit		8, 000. 00
Oil which would probably have been obtained had the voyage been pursued, 2,300 barrels, say 72,450 gallons, at 30 cents a gallon	$21, 735. 00	
Bone which would probably have been obtained had the voyage been pursued, 20,000 pounds at 30 cents a pound	6, 000. 00	
	27, 735. 00	
Deduct for probable deterioration of ship and outfits on the voyage	6, 000. 00	
		21, 735. 00
Expenses		328. 85
Total		$38, 063. 85

The claim in the case of the schooner *Gleaner*, which was on behalf of the Manufacturers Insurance Company of Boston, amounted to $7,250, of which $3,500 was stated as the value of the vessel and $3,750 as the value of the cargo.

The claim in the case of the brig *Planter* was subsequently presented (and admitted) in the sum of $29,418.90; the claims presented for clothing in the various cases amounted to $630.10, which, being doubled, came to $1,260.20; and the indemnity for the arrest and treatment of the seamen of the *Galatea* was adjusted at 600 milreis, or, at the agreed rate of exchange, $750 (D. S., 11 Despatches, Portugal, No. 193, October 9, 1832, enclosures).

The claim in the case of the *Planter* was thus made up (*ibid.*):

Value of the brig	$6, 000. 00
Value of her outfit	6, 000. 00
Value of 700 barrels, or 22,050 gallons, of spermaceti oil at 73 cents a gallon	16, 096. 50
Expenses incurred in Portugal	481. 40
Captain's passage, Lisbon to Edgartown	50. 00
Detention of officers and seamen at varying rates	730. 00
Property taken	61. 00
Total	$29, 418. 90

ORIGIN OF THE CLAIMS

In 1816 Dom John VI succeeded to the then united thrones of Portugal and Brazil; his elder son, Dom Pedro, was proclaimed Emperor of Brazil in 1822 (shortly after the independence of Brazil was declared) and, upon the death of John VI on March 10, 1826, became Pedro IV of Portugal; by a decree of May 2, 1826 (British and Foreign State Papers, XIII, 1111–12), Pedro IV surrendered the Portuguese Crown to his daughter, Maria da Gloria (then seven years of age), contingent upon her marriage to Dom Miguel, her father's younger brother; the charter of 1826 (*ibid.*, 958–78) was proclaimed, Dom Miguel accepted it, was betrothed to his niece, and was appointed Regent; he reached Lisbon in February, 1828; Pedro IV definitively abdicated in favor of his daughter on March 3, 1828 (*ibid.*, XV, 1153); but Dom Miguel disregarded the charter of 1826, accepted the Crown from the Cortes, and took the oath as King on July 7, 1828.

The ensuing struggle between Dom Miguel and the adherents of Maria da Gloria (Queen Maria II, 1834–53) continued until May, 1834, when Dom Miguel surrendered to the allied forces (see *ibid.*, XXII, 1338–52; the allies were Great Britain, France, Spain, and the Government of Maria II; for the text, in English, Spanish, French, and Portuguese, of the Quadruple Alliance of April 22, 1834, see *ibid.*, 124–34).

During that conflict the adherents of Maria II were established in the island of Terceira, one of the Azores; a regency in the name of Queen Maria II was installed there on March 20, 1830 (*ibid.*, XVIII, 1364–65); notice of a blockade of Terceira had been issued by the Government of Dom Miguel on February 27, 1829 (*ibid.*, XVI, 1201); and while that island was blockaded by a Portuguese squadron, four American vessels, the *Gleaner*, the *Galatea*, the *Ann*, and the *Planter*, were captured in 1829–30. The claims settled by this agreement arose from those four captures.

The following observations on the facts of the cases and the proceedings therein are based on documents in the archives of the Department of State (9 and 10 Despatches, Portugal; 5 Consular Despatches, Lisbon; Portuguese Claims, Miscellaneous), including copies of the protests, of the records of the hearings, and of the decrees or sentences.

In no one of the four cases was there any substantial evidence of an attempted or even of an intended breach of blockade; but the result of the preliminary hearings of the court at Ponta Delgada on the island of St. Michael (São Miguel) was that three of the vessels were condemned as good prize, the *Ann* being acquitted; and all were condemned by the Supreme Council of Justice of the Admiralty at Lisbon, which appears to have been regarded in the technical sense as the court of first instance; "a sentence of the court at the Island must be submitted to the superior court here [Lisbon] as a matter of course, and without any appeal from the Captors or captured, and it is the judgment of the Admiralty court here which only constitutes a com-

plete sentence in the first instance" (D. S., 9 Despatches, Portugal, No. 150, January 12, 1831). Two of the cases, the *Ann* and the *Planter*, were again heard on appeal by the same court, with the same result.

The schooner *Gleaner*, of Portland, Maine, of 73 tons, Robert H. Thayer, Master, sailed from her home port on May 9, 1829, with merchandise for Madeira and other markets. On June 6 the *Gleaner* reached Terceira and her master went ashore, when he first learned of the blockade; and on June 7, while at anchor, the *Gleaner* was taken and ordered to St. Michael. There was no reason for attributing to the vessel any knowledge of the blockade, as she had touched at no port en route.

The ship *Galatea*, a whaler of New Bedford, Massachusetts, of 310 tons, Elihu Russell, Master, sailed from her home port on June 1, 1829, with orders to go to a port in Brazil if the whaling voyage was not wholly successful. The *Galatea* had no cargo or passengers and was putting into Terceira for supplies when she was captured on July 4, 1829, and taken to St. Michael. The master of the *Galatea* claimed ignorance of the existence of the blockade; and that a vessel of such a character and in the early stages of such a voyage should attempt to run a blockade is incredible. Some eleven of the crew were confined in prison at St. Michael and at Lisbon, charged (without reason) with sedition and mutiny with a view to escape, and while on the Portuguese frigate *Diana* were for a time in irons. They were released in December, 1829, after a confinement of some months, although condemned to pay costs. The second mate was wounded by a shot from a sentry of the prize crew on the *Galatea*.

The brig *Planter*, of Edgartown, Massachusetts, of 115 tons, John H. Pease, Master, sailed from her home port on May 25, 1829, with provisions for a whaling voyage of fifteen months; in July, while close in to Terceira, the vessel was boarded by a frigate of the blockading squadron and informed of the blockade; continuing to cruise near the island for several months, the *Planter* was a second time visited by a vessel of the squadron and her papers were once more examined. After cruising for some months and obtaining a part cargo of oil, the vessel was again some leagues off Terceira, when she was taken by the Portuguese frigate *Diana* on May 24, 1830, and ordered to St. Michael with a prize crew, apparently because of the lack of a passport.

The brig *Ann*, of Boston, Massachusetts, of 106 tons, John Hammond, Master and owner, sailed on April 29, 1830, from New Orleans with a cargo of tobacco, staves, and other merchandise on a trading voyage to Fayal, Madeira, Teneriffe, and Goree. On June 19 the *Ann* called at Fayal and on the same day sailed for Madeira, having a regular clearance and bill of health endorsed for that island. On the following day, June 20, the *Ann* was captured and taken into St. Michael by a prize crew from the Portuguese frigate *Diana*. There was no evidence which would warrant even a suspicion that the *Ann* was not *bona fide* on her course to Madeira at the time of her capture.

THE NEGOTIATIONS

The circumstances surrounding the negotiation of this claims agreement were somewhat unusual. At the beginning diplomatic intercourse between the two Governments was suspended; not until October 2, 1829, were the credentials of the Portuguese Chargé d'Affaires at Washington, Torlade d'Azambuja, received and the Government of Dom Miguel, King of Portugal, recognized by the United States (Moore, Digest, I, 134–37; and see the paragraph on the subject in the annual message of December 8, 1829, in Richardson, II, 445); and as that fact was not known at Lisbon until the latter part of November, the representations to the Portuguese Government during the year 1829 regarding the cases of the *Galatea* and the *Gleaner* were made by the American Consul at Lisbon, Israel Pemberton Hutchinson.

During the period in question (1829–32), the financial difficulties of the Government of Portugal were continuous; while the amounts involved in the American claims were not large, the Portuguese Treasury was then in no position to meet them.

Moreover, the political situation of the Government of Dom Miguel was also one of many troubles. That Government remained unrecognized by most of the powers of Europe; Secretary of State Buchanan wrote in 1848 that "the Pope, the Emperor of Russia, and President Jackson were the only authorities on earth which ever recognized Dom Miguel as King of Portugal" (quoted in Moore, Digest, I, 137, footnote; but Spain also recognized Dom Miguel; see British and Foreign State Papers, XVIII, 374); and by Great Britain and France, respectively, numerous complaints were made against the Government of Portugal because of incidents at Lisbon and elsewhere. To the British demands the Government of Portugal finally yielded in May, 1831, under threat of reprisals, supported by a British squadron off the Tagus; and the French demands were acceded to by a convention signed on July 14, 1831, following reprisals, brief hostilities, and the capture of various Portuguese ships of war by the French squadron (as to the British and French demands, respectively, see *ibid.*, 43–341, and 341–440).

The discussions regarding the American claims, which took place almost wholly at Lisbon, went on for some two years without result other than a somewhat belated offer to return the brig *Ann*, an offer which was declined.

In the meantime the blockade of Terceira and the capture of American vessels, in particular that of the *Galatea*, were matters of public discussion in the United States. On January 29, 1831, the House of Representatives adopted the following resolution (D. S., Miscellaneous Letters, January–March, 1831):

Resolved, That the President of the United States be requested to inform this House what measures have been taken by the Executive in relation to the Capture, on the Fourth of July, 1829, of the Ship Galatea, late of the port of New Bedford, by a Portuguese naval squadron, then blockading the Island of Terceira; and also in relation to the imprisonment and robbery of the crew of said ship; and to the capture of other American Vessels under the same order of blockade.

Resolved, That the President be requested to lay before this House any correspondence that may have been had touching this matter, within the knowledge or possession of the President, not incompatible with the public interest.

In response to the congressional request, President Jackson, with his message of February 15, 1831 (Niles' Weekly Register, XXXIX, 447; dated February 16 in Richardson, II, 535–36), informed the House of Representatives "that orders had before the introduction of the resolution referred to been given to fit out a ship of war for the more effectual protection of our commerce in that quarter"; he also transmitted a voluminous mass of papers; no less than 107 items are listed with the report of Secretary of State Van Buren of February 15, 1831, which also accompanied the messsage (D. S., 4 Report Book, 310–13). From that report the following paragraph is extracted:

It may be proper to remark, that, at the date of the capture of the Galatea, the diplomatic functions of the Chargé d'Affaires of the United States at Lisbon had been suspended in consequence of the change which had taken place in the Government of Portugal; and that it was owing to that circumstance that the first representations against the capture referred to, were addressed to that Government by the Consul, on whom, in the absence of a diplomatic representative of the United States devolved the duty of protecting the interests of their citizens: that before information was received at this Department of the seizure of the Galatea, the new Government of Portugal had been recognised by this, and that one of the first duties enjoined upon the Chargé d'Affaires of the United States, on resuming his diplomatic functions, was to make a formal demand upon Portugal for indemnity to the owner and crew of the vessel in question.

It appears, strangely enough, that the papers communicated with the presidential message were not printed; the Journal of the House of Representatives discloses no order for printing, and no print has been found.

Following the intimation of the presidential message of February 15, 1831, that an American war vessel was to be despatched to Portuguese waters, the Chargé d'Affaires of Portugal, J. F. Torlade d'Azambuja, addressed a note of considerable length to Secretary of State Van Buren under date of February 19, expressing "regret and anxiety" and concluding with the following paragraph (D. S., 3 Notes from the Portuguese Legation, translation):

The undersigned, in praying His Excellency Mr. Van Buren to make known to the President the aspect under which the projected expedition to the Azores seems to present itself and the evils which the undersigned cannot but apprehend from a measure which, besides, adds nothing to the true interests of the United States, neither to their glory or the strength of the reclamations which they may have to address to the Government of Portugal, is gratified to have it in his power to renew to His Excellency the solemn assurance of the just intentions of His Most Faithful Majesty of avoiding, on his part, and of repressing with energy, every act of injustice and arbitrary aggression against the innocent commerce of the United States, and to repair the wrongs which his tribunals will acknowledge that it may have unjustly suffered from his commanders, without, however, renouncing in a manner derogatory to his royal dignity and to the national honor, the rights secured to him by nature of supporting the interests of the Nation confided to his care by Providence, against all who may insult or injure them.

That note of the Portuguese Chargé d'Affaires was answered on March 8, 1831, in the following terms (D. S., 4 Notes to Foreign Legations, 373–76):

The Undersigned, Secretary of State of the United States, has received the Note which Mr Torlade d'Azambuja, Chargé d'Affaires of Portugal, addressed to him on the 19th of last month, in which he refers to a message of the President of the United States to the House of Representatives, dated the 15th of the same month, communicating certain information to that House, in pursuance of a previous Resolution on its part, in relation to the recent capture, detention and condemnation of several American Vessels, under the authority of the Portuguese Government, upon the ground of imputed attempt on their part to violate the existing blockade of the Island of Terceira; which Mr Torlade contends was instituted, and has ever since been maintained in strict conformity with the well established and universally admitted principles of National Law.

For the additional information of the House of Representatives upon that occasion, the President intimated, in the Message referred to, that it was his purpose to send a public Vessel to the Seas in which these interruptions had occurred, for the protection of the Commerce of the United States. The Undersigned under these circumstances, is at a loss to conceive how a declaration to that effect could be construed by Mr Torlade, or by his Government, as he seems to think it may be, into a menace of an interference, on the part of the United States against the Government of His Most Faithful Majesty, in the exercise of the undoubted rights secured to him by the usages of war and the Law of Nations in reference to the enforcement of the said Blockade;—numerous instances of analogous precautions by Neutral Nations, with a view to the protection of their legitimate commerce under similar circumstances, and at the same time to serve as checks upon the Merchant Vessels themselves, of those Nations, towards preventing any attempts at irregular proceedings on their part, not being wanting in the history of Maritime States to establish the fact, while a resort to such precautions on the part of Neutral Nations has been thus usual, it is confidently believed that, under the management of discreet and intelligent Officers, such a course is eminently calculated to do much good, in reference to all the legitimate rights of Belligerents and Neutrals; and the declaration of The President could have contemplated or referred to no other than an Officer of that character for the service alluded to, nor to any other orders to him than such as might comport with the fullest rights of the Portuguese Crown, in respect to the blockade in question. It is in this spirit and with these qualifications, therefore, that the Undersigned is instructed by the President to request Mr Torlade to interpret the declaration of the President in his Message to the House of Representatives, in the communications which he may make to his Government upon the subject.

From the earnest desire, however, which the President cherishes to obviate any unfavorable conclusions which might by possibility be drawn from the proposed armament, and to continue to cultivate relations of the best understanding between the United States and His Most Faithful Majesty, and relying, as the President relies in this instance, upon the solemn assurance made by Mr Torlade in behalf of His most Faithful Majesty, that he will repress with energy every act of injustice and arbitrary aggression on the part of his Naval forces against the innocent commerce of the United States, and that He will repair the wrongs which that commerce may already have suffered by erroneous decisions on the part of His Tribunals; The President has come to the determination of countermanding the directions which had been given upon this subject.

The Undersigned has been directed to communicate to Mr Torlade the decision of the President in this respect, and is happy in the opportunity of fulfilling this agreeable duty. He avails himself of it also to renew to Mr Torlade d'Azambuja the assurance of his very distinguished consideration.

The American claims remained unadjusted, notwithstanding the countermanding of the orders for the despatch of a vessel of war; and on October 19, 1831, the following instructions were sent to Brent by

Secretary of State Livingston (D. S., 13 Instructions, U. S. Ministers, 255–58):

Since my last communication, your despatches to N⁰ 168, inclusive, have been received; each one of which led us to indulge the hope that the Government of Portugal, duly appreciating the moderation of our conduct towards it compared with the energetic measures other powers have used to obtain justice, would have had its proper effect, and that your next succeeding communication would have announced that effectual measures had been taken to indemnify our fellow citizens for the injuries they had sustained. It is with great regret that the President has hitherto found these expectations disappointed, and that repeated promises are followed by repeated evasions of their performance; and, in one instance, by an offer of indemnity so totally inadequate to the injury received, as to cause its immediate rejection. The offer was, moreover, made in a style that rendered its acceptance inconsistent with the dignity of our Government; for it was attributed to the generosity of His Majesty when it was demanded as an act of justice. It is hoped rather than expected that this course of conduct will have changed before you receive this instruction. Should this not, however, be the case, you will state to the Ministry of Portugal, that the President, having long expected the accomplishment of the promises made for the indemnity of his fellow citizens, whose property and persons have been illegally seized on the high seas by His Majesty's cruisers, and finding that no effectual measures have been taken for that purpose, has been obliged, in the performance of an imperative duty, to send a messenger with special instructions to you to say, that relying as well on the justice of our demands as on the disposition frequently expressed by His Majesty's Ministers to acknowledge it, the President expects from His Majesty's justice, that, without further delay, the property thus illegally seized, may be returned, if still in the power of that Government, with a full indemnity for detention and loss, and for the personal ill treatment and imprisonment of our mariners. You will add that this positive demand results from no unfriendly feeling; that, on the contrary, the strongest desire is entertained of preserving and increasing the amicable political and commercial relations of the two countries: But injuries to our citizens, while they remain unredressed, are an obstacle to the adoption of measures for attaining these desirable ends; and that satisfaction for these injuries is the more strenuously urged, because it will enable him to pursue the ulterior and more important object of uniting in a common interest two nations who have no points of collision but those which an unenlightened policy creates. Something, you may urge, is due to the only nation except the immediate neighbor of Portugal, which has acknowledged the title of their King—much to the generous forbearance which ceased to urge our claims when other's were enforcing their's—not a little to the confidence in the good faith of the King, which omitted the ordinary precaution of sending an armed force to protect our commerce, on the positive assurance of his minister that it should not be injured—and every thing to the repeated promises of reparation made by the command of His Majesty himself.

Let it be well understood, that we neither ask, nor will accept, any thing not founded in strict justice. And that we do not urge the claims on account of their pecuniary value to the country, but because of the importance we attach to the support of every just demand of our citizens, and that we would urge them with the same force were they of less value.

Express, in the strongest terms, the regret the President feels that this comparatively small affair, stands in the way of his frank acceptance of the overtures that have been made of a commercial arrangement—and that full powers will be sent to enter on that negotiation, to be presented as soon as this preliminary objection is removed.

You may hint, too, in conversation, of what importance to Portugal the friendship of the United States would be on the occurrence of events which present prospects render quite probable, and of the injurious consequences that might result, should Congress, on the refusal to compensate our merchants and mariners, direct reprisals.

Should you find that the state of the Treasury is an obstacle to the immediate payment, you may urge the liquidation, and agree to receive for the amount, Government bills on the Treasury, payable at such reasonable periods as you think their resources will require—and, if you can, let them be made receivable for duties. The amount of the few vessels in question will not justify the expense of a mixed commission; you must, therefore, negotiate for a certain sum for each claim, as nearly to the amount as you can come—urging no unreasonable indemnity, and reducing exaggerated estimates to their just value.

In pursuance of the suggestion you are herein before authorized to make, a full power, with instructions for the formation of a commercial treaty, will shortly be sent out, which is not to be acted upon until a satisfactory arrangement of the claims is made.

Mr [Philip G.] Randolph, who takes out these instructions, has despatches for our Minister at Madrid. His stay in that place will be short, and on his return he will take from you the answer you may have received, which, you may state, will, if not satisfactory, be communicated to Congress, who will judge whether it be expedient to resort to reprisals for the indemnification of our citizens.

Mr Torlade has given me the translation of a despatch which he sends by Mr. Randolph; a copy of this paper is annexed, with a copy of my note in answer to that by which he communicated it.

It is the President's desire that you should be impressed yourself, and that you should impress strongly on the Portuguese Ministry, the necessity of bringing this business to a final issue by the return of Mr. Randolph.

Mr Torlade has presented several notes requesting a reduction and modification of the duties on Portuguese wine, and an abrogation of the discriminating tonnage [see the presidential message of April 13, 1832, Richardson, II, 572, and the act of May 25, 1832, 4 Statutes at Large, 517]—all of which, and other advantages to the commerce of that kingdom, will be favorably considered, as soon as the business of the claims is settled.

Whether you succeed in obtaining a settlement of these claims or not, send on an abstract of the circumstances of each, with the estimates of the parties, and your corrections and observations, to this Department.

In his annual message of December 6, 1831, President Jackson referred to the negotiations and to the instructions above quoted, in the following terms (Richardson, II, 544, 550):

In the late blockade of Terceira some of the Portuguese fleet captured several of our vessels and committed other excesses, for which reparation was demanded, and I was on the point of dispatching an armed force to prevent any recurrence of a similar violence and protect our citizens in the prosecution of their lawful commerce when official assurances, on which I relied, made the sailing of the ships unnecessary. Since that period frequent promises have been made that full indemnity shall be given for the injuries inflicted and the losses sustained. In the performance there has been some, perhaps unavoidable, delay; but I have the fullest confidence that my earnest desire that this business may at once be closed, which our minister has been instructed strongly to express, will very soon be gratified. I have the better ground for this hope from the evidence of a friendly disposition which that Government has shown by an actual reduction in the duty on rice the produce of our Southern States, authorizing the anticipation that this important article of our export will soon be admitted on the same footing with that produced by the most favored nation.

The instructions of October 19, 1831, were received by Brent on December 22; from his long despatch of January 7, 1832 (D. S., 11 Despatches, Portugal, No. 180), it appears that he read to the Portuguese Secretary of State for Foreign Affairs, Viscount de Santarem, the "greater part" thereof; the decided attitude of this Government,

as expressed in the instructions, was effective; and at a subsequent interview, on December 31, Brent was informed that the orders of the King had been obtained and that "the basis was accepted" (*ibid.*). The written agreement followed.

PAYMENT OF THE CLAIMS

As the payments were made in the money of Portugal, it will be convenient to give the figures in reis. The claims at the agreed amounts were as follows:

Item	Reis	Dollars
The *Ann*	26, 995$600	$33, 744. 42
The *Galatea*	30, 450$900	38, 063. 85
The *Gleaner*	5, 800$000	7, 250. 00
The *Planter*	23, 535$120	29, 418. 90
Clothing	1, 008$160	1, 260. 20
Arrest and treatment	600$000	750. 00
Total	88, 389$780	$110, 487. 37

On June 15, 1832, the Portuguese Government paid the first instalment of one quarter of the claims, but *only* in the cases of the *Ann*, the *Galatea*, and the *Gleaner*, as the amounts of the other items were not then fixed; that payment was accordingly of 15,811$625 reis (besides 59$575 reis treated as paid on account of interest and not distributed); the principal account was then as follows:

The *Ann*	20, 246$700
The *Galatea*	22, 838$175
The *Gleaner*	4, 350$000
The *Planter*	23, 535$120
Clothing	1, 008$160
Arrest and treatment	600$000
Total reis	72, 578$155

Nothing further was paid during 1832; and following authorization from this Government (D. S., 13 Instructions, U. S. Ministers, 326, November 13, 1832), the time for the payment of the balance was extended for two years, with interest at 5 per cent continuing, the Portuguese Government stipulating for the equalization of the import duty on American rice with that on rice from Brazil (which was then 15 per cent). Notes of January 7 and 8, 1833, were written to record the terms of this arrangement; copies thereof as follows, the former in translation, were enclosed with the despatch of Brent of January 12, 1833 (D. S., 11 Despatches, Portugal, No. 198):

Having laid before the Government of His Majesty the communication which you lately made to me on the part of the Government of the United States of America, that it agreed that the payment should be deferred for two years of the sums remaining to be satisfied of the indemnities that the Government of

His Most Faithful Majesty adjudged for the damages produced by the capture of some American vessels in the seas of the Azores, paying the legal interest of 5 per cent on the above sums until their final payment, I have the honor and the satisfaction to communicate to you that the King, my master, has recognized in this act another proof of the good dispositions with which the Government of the United States is animated towards Portugal; and the said August Lord desiring also to give on his part a proof of the desire he has to strengthen more and more the good intelligence and friendship that happily exists between the two Governments, has been pleased to order that the duties which the American rice pays in the customhouse of these Kingdoms be henceforth equalized with those which the rice of Brazil pays in the same, and that if the latter be hereafter diminished, an equal concession shall be made to the former.

I pray you, therefore, to be pleased to bring to the knowledge of your Government this concession of the King, my master, in favor of the American commerce, in which the same August Lord shows the consideration and esteem which he has for the Government of the United States of America.

God preserve you. Department of State of Foreign Affairs, 7th of January, 1833.

VISCONDE DE SANTAREM

Mr. THOMAS L. L. BRENT

LEGATION OF THE UNITED STATES
Lisbon January 8th 1833

His Excellency the VISCOUNT OF SANTAREM
SIR:

I have had the honor to receive your Excellency's official letter dated yesterday. It will be very gratifying to my Government to perceive that the extension of the credit on the remaining indemnities due has been appretiated in the manner it has been by His Most Faithful Majesty: as will also be the equalization announced to me of the duty on the rice of the United States with that of Brazil, with the stipulation that in the event of a reduction of the latter, the former shall be diminished in an equal proportion. I am, also, persuaded that the Government of the United States will set a just value on the expressions of the desire of His Most Faithful Majesty to strengthen still more the good intelligence and frienship existing between the two Governments as well as upon those of the esteem and consideration which His Majesty entertains for it.

I have the honor to renew to your Excellency the assurance of my very distinguished consideration

(Signed)   THOMAS L. L. BRENT

By the presidential message of December 3, 1833, Congress was informed of the arrangement for extension and of the stipulation regarding the Portuguese duty on rice (Richardson, III, 19, 24).

There was further delay, however, beyond the two-year period of extension; and in 1837 a new adjustment was reached, which included some other claims; this adjustment was negotiated by Edward Kavanagh, the successor of Thomas L. L. Brent as Chargé d'Affaires at Lisbon, with the aid of Israel Pemberton Hutchinson, Consul at Lisbon, who represented most of the claimants. The figures were then:

The claims as above	72, 578$155
Other claims	12, 287$565
Interest calculated to October 31, 1837, net	34, 614$205
Total reis	119, 479$925

Treasury notes or bills were received in settlement; but as these were payable at various dates up to June 30, 1839, further interest of

5,300$995 reis was added, making the total amount of the Treasury notes 124,780$920 reis. The despatches of Kavanagh of March 3 and March 18, 1837, with their enclosures (D. S., 13 Despatches, Portugal, Nos. 39 and 40), give a detailed account of the transaction. The Treasury notes (and the small balance of 59$575 reis remaining from the payment of 1832) were turned over on March 17, 1837, to I. Pemberton Hutchinson & Co. as agents for the claimants; the form of those notes is given in enclosure B to the despatch of March 3, 1837, above cited; they were payable to Edward Kavanagh, as Chargé d'Affaires of the United States, for indemnities due to citizens thereof, and were endorsed by him in his official capacity; and the receipt given to the Portuguese Government was in the following form (*ibid.*, No. 39, enclosure A):

LEGATION OF THE UNITED STATES OF AMERICA.
Lisbon 3ᵈ March 1837.

The Government of the United States of America having, through the Undersigned, their Chargé d'Affaires in Portugal, preferred against that of Her Most Faithful Majesty certain claims in behalf of Citizens of the said States:

And, the Government of Her said Majesty, through His Excellency, the Viscount de Sa'da Bandeira, President of the Council of Ministers, Minister and Secretary of State for Foreign Affairs, having engaged to pay to that of the United States the sum of One hundred and twenty four contos seven hundred and eighty nine mil nine hundred and twenty Reis, metal, which includes the principal of the claims now allowed, and interest thereon at the rate of five per cent per annum to the several periods of payment herein after stated, and which is to be distributed in due proportions among the owners of, and others interested in, the Ship Galatea, the Brigs Ann, Planter, Osprey, Quito, Perseverance, and the Schooner Gleaner: and also among the Seamen of the Galatea and Planter aforesaid:

And, the Undersigned having, this day, received from Her said Majesty's Government One hundred and forty seven Treasury Notes, or Bills, dated the 27th of February 1837, which are respectively numbered from *71* to *217* inclusive, and are payable to the Undersigned or his order, as follows; viz:

Nos.					
71 to 82,	inclusive, due on the	31st of October	1837, for	10,000$000
" 83 to 94	" "	31st of December "		10,000$000
" 95 to 106	" "	28th of February	1838, for	10,000$000
" 107 to 118	" "	30th of April "		10,000$000
" 119 to 130	" "	30th of June "		10,000$000
" 131 to 142	" "	31st of August "		10,000$000
" 143 to 154	" "	31st of October "		10,000$000
" 155 to 166	" "	31st of December "		10,000$000
" 167 to 178	" "	28th of February	1839	10,000$000
" 179 to 197	" "	30th of April "		17,000$000
" 198 to 217	" "	30th of June "		17,780$920

124,780$920

Now, it is agreed that the said Treasury Notes, or Bills, when paid to the proper holders thereof, at the times, and in the manner, therein specified, are to be a full discharge of the claims herein before enumerated.

As to all other reclamations of Citizens of the United States against the Government of Her Most Faithful Majesty, in pursuance of the distinct and explicit agreement made with His Excellency, the Minister of Foreign Affairs, it is understood that they are to be prosecuted without any prejudice whatever from this settlement.

In faith whereof, the Undersigned has hereto set his hand, at Lisbon, this 3ᵈ day of March 1837.

(Signed)   EDWARD KAVANAGH.

There were thus three claims included in the settlement of 1837 which were not within that of 1832.   Two of them were for differences in duty and were very small, amounting for the *Quito* to 129$525 reis and for the *Perseverance* to 118$040 reis.   The claim for the *Osprey*, with interest calculated to October 31, 1837, was thus stated:

12,000 arrobas of beef at 1,920 reis	23, 040$000	
Interest thereon for 14 years and 90 days	16, 412$050	
		39, 452$050
Amount received on account	11, 000$000	
Interest thereon	3, 106$295	
		14, 106$295
Total reis		25, 345$755

Official notice of the settlement of 1837 was given by the Department of State under date of May 12, 1837, as follows (Niles' Weekly Register, LII, 181, May 20, 1837, quoted from the Washington Globe):

Information has been received at the department from Mr. Kavanagh the charge d'affaires of the United States at Lisbon, that treasury notes of the government of Portugal, which will become due at various periods, from the 31st of October, 1837, to the 31st of June, 1839, for the claims of citizens of this country in the cases of the Planter, Perseverence and Quito, and for the remaining instalments due in the cases of the Galatea, Ann, Gleanor and Osprey, with interest on the several sums liquidated, have been received by him, and deposited for the benefit of those interested with the house of S. Pemberton, Hutchinson & Co. of Lisbon who are agents for most of the claimants.   This settlement includes an allowance to the seamen of the Galatea and Gleanor for their loss of clothes, and damages to the seamen of the Galatea for their imprisonment.

The treasury notes given by the Portuguese Government were duly paid (see the despatches of Kavanagh in D. S., 13 and 14 Despatches, Portugal, from that of November 11, 1837, No. 58, to that of November 18, 1839, No. 99, *passim*).

Treaty Series No. 40
8 Statutes at Large, 434-41, 456-57
18 *ibid.*, pt. 2, Public Treaties, 104-14

73

CHILE : MAY 16, 1832, AND SEPTEMBER 1, 1833

Treaty of Peace, Amity, Commerce, and Navigation, signed at Santiago May 16, 1832, with Additional and Explanatory Convention signed at Santiago September 1, 1833. Originals in English and Spanish. Treaty submitted to the Senate December 11, 1832. Resolution of advice and consent December 19, 1832. Additional and Explanatory Convention submitted to the Senate February 27, 1834. (Message of February 22, 1834.) Resolution of advice and consent April 24, 1834. Ratified by the United States April 26, 1834. Ratified by Chile November 5, 1833. Ratifications exchanged at Washington April 29, 1834. Proclaimed April 29, 1834.
Following the texts of the treaty and explanatory convention are printed the note of John Hamm, Chargé d'Affaires of the United States at Santiago, to Andrés Bello, Plenipotentiary of Chile, dated May 16, 1832, formally reserving certain claims on behalf of United States citizens, and also the answering note of the Chilean Plenipotentiary, of the same date.

General Convention of Peace, Amity, Commerce, and Navigation, between the United States of America and the Republic of Chile.

In the name of God, Author and Legislator of the Universe.

The United States of America, and the Republic of Chile, desiring to make firm and lasting the friendship and good understanding which happily prevails between both nations, have resolved to fix, in a manner, clear, distinct, and positive, the rules which shall in future be religiously observed between the one and the other, by means of a treaty or general convention of peace and friendship, commerce and navigation.

En el nombre de Dios Autor y Lejislador del Universo.

La República de Chile y los Estados Unidos de América, deseando hacer duradera y firme la amistad y buena intelijencia que felizmente existe entre ambas Potencias, han resuelto fijar de una manera clara, distinta y positiva las reglas que deben observar relijiosamente en lo venidero, por medio de un tratado o convencion jeneral de paz, amistad, comercio y navegacion.

671

For this most desirable object, the President of the United States of America, by and with the advice and consent of the Senate thereof, has appointed, and conferred full powers on John Hamm, a citizen of said States, and their Chargé d'Affaires near the said Republic; and His Excellency the President of the Republic of Chile has appointed Señor Don Andres Bello, a citizen of the said Republic.

And the said Plenipotentiaries, after having mutually produced and exchanged copies of their full powers, in due and proper form, have agreed upon and concluded the following articles, videlicet.

ARTICLE 1. There shall be a perfect, firm, and inviolable peace and sincere friendship between the United States of America and the Republic of Chile, in all the extent of their possessions and territories, and between their people and citizens respectively, without distinction of persons or places.

ARTICLE 2ᵈ The United States of America and the Republic of Chile, desiring to live in peace and harmony with all the other nations of the earth, by means of a policy frank and equally friendly with all, engage mutually, not to grant any particular favor to

Con este tan deseable objeto el Presidente de la República de Chile ha nombrado y conferido plenos poderes a Don Andres Bello, ciudadano de la misma, y el Presidente de los Estados-Unidos de América, con el dictamen del Senado de ellos al Señor Juan Hamm, ciudadano de los mismos estados, y su Encargado de Negocios cerca de la dicha República.

Y los espresados plenipotenciarios, habiendo presentado mutuamente y canjeado copias de sus plenos poderes en buena y debida forma, han acordado y convenido en los articulos siguientes; á saber:

ARTICULO I.

Habrá una paz, perfecta, firme é inviolable, y amistad sincera, entre la República de Chile y los Estados-Unidos de América, en toda la estension de sus posesiones y territorios, y entre sus pueblos y ciudadanos respectivamente sin distincion de personas ni lugares.

ARTUCULO II.

La República de Chile y los Estados-Unidos de América, deseando vivir en paz, y harmonía con las demas naciones de la tierra, por medio de una política franca, é igualmente amistosa con todas, se obligan mutuamente á no conceder favores particulares

other nations in respect of commerce and navigation, which shall not, immediately, become common to the other party, who shall enjoy the same freely, if the concession was freely made, or on allowing the same compensation, if the concession was conditional. It is understood, however, that the relations and conventions which now exist, or may hereafter exist, between the Republic of Chile and the Republic of Bolivia, the Federation of the Centre of America, the Republic of Colombia, the United States of Mexico, the Republic of Peru, or the United Provinces of the Rio de la Plata, shall form exceptions to this article.

ARTICLE 3ᵈ The citizens of the United States of America may frequent all the coasts and countries of the Republic of Chile, and reside and trade there, in all sorts of produce, manufactures, and merchandize, and shall pay no other or greater duties, charges, or fees, whatsoever, than the most favoured nation is or shall be obliged to pay; and they shall enjoy all the rights, privileges, and exemptions in navigation and commerce, which the most favoured nation does or shall enjoy, submitting themselves, nevertheless, to the laws, decrees, and usages there established, and to which are submitted the citizens

á otras naciones, con respecto á comercio y navegacion, que no se hagan inmediatamente comunes á una u otra, quien gozará de los mismos libremente, si la concesion fuese hecha libremente, ó prestando la misma compensacion, si la concesion fuese condicional. Bien entendido, que las relaciones y convenciones que actualmente existen, ó puedan celebrarse en lo futuro entre la República de Chile y la República de Bolivia, la federacion de Centro América, la República de Colombia, los Estados-Unidos de Méjico, la República del Perú, o las Provincias Unidas del Rio de la Plata, formaran escepciones a éste articulo.

ARTICULO III.

Los ciudadanos de la República de Chile podrán frecuentar todas las costas y paises de los Estados-Unidos de América, y residir, y traficar en ellos con toda suerte de producciones, manufacturas, y mercaderías, y no pagarán otros, ó mayores derechos, impuestos ó emolumentos cualesquiera que los que las naciones mas favorecidas están ó estuvieren obligadas a pagar; y gozarán todos los derechos, privilejios y esenciones, que gozan o gazaren los de la nacion mas favorecida, con respecto a navegacion y comercio, sometiendose, no obstante, a las leyes, decretos, y usos establecidos, á los cuales

and subjects of the most favoured nations.

In like manner the citizens of the Republic of Chile may frequent all the coasts and countries of the United States of America, and reside and trade there, in all sorts of produce, manufactures, and merchandize, and shall pay no other or greater duties, charges, or fees, whatsoever, than the most favoured nation is or shall be obliged to pay, and they shall enjoy all the rights, privileges, and exemptions in commerce and navigation, which the most favoured nation does or shall enjoy, submitting themselves, nevertheless, to the laws, decrees, and usages, there established, and to which are submitted the citizens and subjects of the most favoured nations. But it is understood, that this article does not include the coasting trade of either country, the regulation of which is reserved by the parties, respectively, according to their own separate laws.

ARTICLE 4. It is likewise agreed that it shall be wholly free for all merchants, commanders of ships, and other citizens of both countries, to manage, themselves, their own business, in all ports and places subject to the jurisdiction of each other, as well with respect to the consignment and sale of

estan sujetos los súbditos o ciudadanos de las naciones mas favorecidas. Del mismo modo los ciudadanos de los Estados-Unidos de América podran frecuentar todas las costas y paises de la República de Chile, y residir y traficar en ellos con toda suerte de producciones, manufacturas, y mercaderias, y no pagarán otros o mayores derechos, impuestos, o emolumentos cualesquiera, que los que las naciones mas favorecidas, están o estuvieren obligadas á pagar, y gozarán de todos los derechos, privilejios y esenciones que gozan o gozaren los de la nacion mas favorecida con respecto á navegacion y comercio, sometiendose, no obstante, a las leyes, decretos y usos establecidos, a los cuales están sujetos los súbditos o ciudadanos de las naciones mas favorecidas. Bien entendido que éste artículo no incluye el comercio de cabotaje de uno u otro pais, cuya regulacion se reservan las partes, respectivamente en conformidad de sus peculiares leyes.

ARTICULO IV.

Se conviene ademas, que será enteramente libre y permitido a los comerciantes, comandantes de buques, y otros ciudadanos de ámbos paises el manejar sus negocios, por si mismos, en todos los puertos y lugares sujetos a la jurisdiccion de uno u otro, asi respecto a las consignaciones y

their goods and merchandize, by wholesale and retail, as with respect to the loading, unloading, and sending off their ships, they being in all these cases to be treated as citizens of the country in which they reside, or at least to be placed on a footing with the citizens or subjects of the most favoured nation.

ARTICLE 5. The citizens of neither of the contracting parties shall be liable to any embargo, nor be detained with their vessels, cargoes, merchandize, or effects, for any military expedition, nor for any public or private purpose whatever, without allowing to those interested a sufficient indemnification.

ARTICLE 6. Whenever the citizens of either of the contracting parties shall be forced to seek refuge or assylum in the rivers, bays, ports, or dominions of the other, with their vessels, whether of merchant or of war, public or private, through stress of weather, pursuit of pirates, or enemies, they shall be received and treated with humanity, giving to them all favor and protection for repairing their ships, procuring provisions, and placing themselves in a situation to continue their voyage without obstacle or hindrance of any kind.

ventas por mayor y menor de sus efectos y mercaderías, como de la carga, descarga y despacho de sus buques, debiendo en todos éstos casos ser tratados como ciudadanos del pais en que residan, o al menos puestos sobre un pié igual con los súbditos o ciudadanos de las naciones mas favorecidas.

Articulo V.

Los ciudadanos de una u otra parte, no podran ser embargados ni detenidos con sus embarcaciones, tripulaciones, mercaderías, o efectos comerciales de su pertenencia, para alguna espedicion militar, usos públicos, o particulares cualesquiera que sean, sin conceder a los interesados una suficiente indemnizacion.

Articulo VI.

Siempre que los ciudadanos de alguna de las partes contratantes se vieren precisados a buscar refújio, o asílo en los ríos, bahías, puertos, o dominios de la otra, con sus buques, ya sean mercantes, o de guerra, públicos o particulares, por mal tiempo, persecucion de pirátas o enemigos, serán recibidos y tratados con humanidad, dándoles todo favor y proteccion, para reparar sus buques, procurar viveres, y ponerse en situacion de continuar su viaje, sin obstáculo, o estorbo de ningun jenero.

ARTICLE 7. All the ships, merchandize and effects belonging to the citizens of one of the contracting parties, which may be captured by pirates, whether within the limits of its jurisdiction or on the high seas, and may be carried or found in the rivers, roads, bays, ports, or dominions of the other, shall be delivered up to the owners, they proving in due and proper form their rights before the competent tribunals; it being well understood, that the claim should be made within the term of one year by the parties themselves, their attorneys, or agents of their respective governments.

ARTICLE 8. When any vessel belonging to the citizens of either of the contracting parties shall be wrecked, foundered, or suffer any damage on the coasts, or within the dominions of the other, there shall be given to them all assistance and protection in the same manner which is usual and customary with the vessels of the nation where the damage happens, permitting them to unload the said vessel, if necessary, of its merchandize and effects, without exacting for it any duty, impost, or contribution whatever, until they may be exported, unless they be destined for consumption in the country.

ARTICULO VII.

Todos los buques, mercaderias y efectos pertenecientes a los ciudadanos de una de las partes contratantes, que sean apresados por piratas, bien sea dentro de los límites de su jurisdiccion, o en alta mar, y fueren llevados, o hallados en los rios, radas, bahías, puertos o dominios de la otra, serán entregados a sus dueños, probando estos en la forma propia y debida sus derechos ante los tribunales competentes; bien entendido que el reclamo ha de hacerse dentro del término de un año por las mismas partes, sus apoderados o ajentes de los respectivos gobiernos.

ARTICULO VIII.

Cuando algun buque perteneciente a los ciudadanos de alguna de las partes contratantes, naufrague, encalle o sufra alguna avería, en las costas, o dentro de los dominios de la otra, se les dará toda ayuda y proteccion, del mismo modo que es uso y costumbre, con los buques de la nacion en donde suceda la avería; permitiendoles descargar el dicho buque (si fuere necesario) de sus mercaderías y efectos, sin exijir por esto ningun derecho, impuesto o contribucion, hasta que ellos puedan ser esportados, a menos que sean destinados para consumirse en el pais.

ARTICLE 9. The citizens of each of the contracting parties shall have power to dispose of their personal goods within the jurisdiction of the other, by sale, donation, testament, or otherwise, and their representatives, being citizens of the other party, shall succeed to their said personal goods, whether by testament or *ab intestato*, and they may take possession thereof, either by themselves or others acting for them, and dispose of the same at their will, paying such dues only as the inhabitants of the country, wherein the said goods are, shall be subject to pay in like cases: and if, in the case of real estate, the said heirs, would be prevented from entering into the possession of the inheritance, on account of their character of aliens, there shall be granted to them the term of three years to dispose of the same, as they may think proper, and to withdraw the proceeds without molestation, and exempt from any other charges than those which may be imposed by the laws of the country.

Los ciudadanos de cada una de las partes contratantes, tendran pleno poder para disponer de sus bienes personales dentro de la jurisdiccion de la otra, por venta, donacion, testamento, o de otro modo; y sus representantes, siendo ciudadanos de la otra parte, sucederán a sus dichos bienes personales, ya sea por testamento, *o ab intestato*, y podrán tomar posesion de ellos, ya sea por si mismos, o por otros, que obren por ellos, y disponer de los mismos, segun su voluntad, pagando aquellas cargas solamente, que los habitantes del pais en donde estan los referidos bienes, estuvieren sujetos a pagar en iguales casos. Y si en el caso de bienes raices, los dichos herederos fuesen impedidos de entrar en la posesion de la herencia por razon de su caracter de estranjeros, se les dará el término de tres años, para disponer de ella como juzguen conveniente, y para estraer el producto sin molestia, y esentos de cualesquiera otras cargas, sino es aquellas que se les impongan por las leyes del pais.

ARTICLE 10. Both the contracting parties promise and engage formally to give their special protection to the persons and property of the citizens of each other, of all occupations, who may be in the territories subject to the

Ambas partes contratantes se comprometen y obligan formalmente a dar su proteccion especial a las personas y propiedades de los ciudadanos de cada una reciprocamente, transeuntes o habitantes de todas ocupaciones,

jurisdiction of the one or the other, transient or dwelling therein, leaving open and free to them the tribunals of justice for their judicial recourse on the same terms which are usual and customary, with the natives or citizens of the country in which they may be: for which they may employ in defence of their rights such advocates, solicitors, notaries, agents, and factors, as they may judge proper, in all their trials at law; and such citizens or agents shall have free opportunity to be present at the decisions and sentences of the tribunals, in all cases which may concern them, and likewise at the taking of all examinations and evidence which may be exhibited in the said trials.

ARTICLE 11. It is likewise agreed that the most perfect and entire security of conscience shall be enjoyed by the citizens of both the contracting parties in the countries subject to the jurisdiction of the one and the other, without their being liable to be disturbed or molested on account of their religious belief, so long as they respect the laws and established usages of the country. Moreover, the bodies of the citizens of one of the contracting parties, who may die in the territories of the other, shall be buried in the usual burying grounds, or in other

en los territorios sujetos a la jurisdiccion de una u otra, dejandoles abiertos y libres los tribunales de justicia, para sus recursos judiciales, en los mismos términos que son de uso y costumbre para los naturales o ciudadanos del pais en que residan; para lo cual, podran emplear en defensa de sus derechos aquellos Abogados, Procuradores, Escribanos, Ajentes, o Factores que juzguen conveniente, en todos sus asuntos y litijios; y dichos ciudadanos o Ajentes tendrán la libre facultad de estar presentes en las decisiones y sentencias de los tribunales, en todos los casos que les conciernan, como igualmente al tomar todos los examenes y declaraciones que se ofrezcan en los dichos litijios.

ARTICULO XI.

Se conviene igualmente en que los ciudadanos de ambas partes contratantes gocen la mas perfecta y entera seguridad de conciencia en los paises sujetos a la jurisdiccion de una u otra, sin quedar por ello espuestos a ser inquietados o molestados en razon de su creencia relijiosa, mientras que respeten las leyes, y usos establecidos. Ademas de ésto, podrán sepultarse los cadáveres de los ciudadanos de una de las partes contratantes, que fallecieren en los territorios de la otra, en los cementerios acostumbrados o en otros lugares decentes, y adecuados, los cuales

deeent or suitable places, and shall be protected from violation or disturbance.

ARTICLE 12. It shall be lawful for the citizens of the United States of America and of the Republic of Chile to sail with their ships, with all manner of liberty and security, no distinction being made, who are the proprietors of the merchandize laden thereon, from any port to the places of those who now are or hereafter shall be at enmity with either of the contracting parties. It shall likewise be lawful for the citizens aforesaid to sail with the ships and merchandize before mentioned, and to trade with the same liberty and security from the places, ports, and havens, of those who are enemies of both or either party, without any opposition or disturbance whatsoever, not only directly from the places of the enemy, before mentioned, to neutral places, but also, from one place belonging to an enemy, to another place belonging to an enemy, whether they be under the jurisdiction of the one power, or under several. And it is hereby stipulated, that free ships shall also give freedom to goods, and that every thing shall be deemed to be free and exempt, which shall be found on board the ships belonging to the citizens of either of the contracting parties al-

serán protejidos contra toda violacion o disturbio.

ARTICULO XII.

Será lícito a los ciudadanos de la República de Chile, y de los Estados-Unidos de América navegar con sus buques, con toda especie de libertad y seguridad, de cualquiera puerto á las plazas o lugares de los que son o fueren en adelante enemigos de cualquiera de las dos partes contratantes, sin hacerse distincion de quienes son los dueños de las mercaderias cargadas en ellos. Será igualmente lícito á los referidos ciudadanos navegar con sus buques y mercaderías mencionadas y traficar con la misma libertad y seguridad, de los lugares, puertos y ensenadas de los enemigos de ambas partes, o de alguna de ellas, sin ninguna oposicion, o disturbio cualquiera, no solo directamente de los lugares de enemigo arriba mencionados a lugares neutrales, sino tambien de un lugar perteneciente á un enemigo, a otro lugar perteneciente á un enemigo, ya sea que estén bajo la jurisdiccion de una potencia, o bajo la de diversas. Y quéda aquí estipulado, que los buques líbres dan tambien libertad a las mercaderías, y que se ha de considerar libre y esento todo lo que que se hallare abordo de los buques pertenecientes á los ciudadanos de cualquiera de las partes con-

though the whole lading, or any part thereof, should appertain to the enemies of either, contraband goods being always excepted. It is also agreed, in like manner, that the same liberty be extended to persons who are on board a free ship, with this effect, that although they be enemies to both or either, they are not to be taken out of that free ship unless they are officers or soldiers, and in the actual service of the enemies: Provided, however, and it is hereby agreed, that the stipulations in this article contained, declaring that the flag shall cover the property, shall be understood as applying to those powers only who recognise the principle; but if either of the two contracting parties should be at war with a third, and the other neutral, the flag of the neutral shall cover the property of enemies whose governments acknowledge this principle, and not of others.

ARTICLE 13. It is likewise agreed, that in the case where the neutral flag of one of the contracting parties shall protect the property of the enemies of the other, by virtue of the above stipulation, it shall always be understood that the neutral property found on board such enemy's

tratantes, aunque toda la carga o parte de ella pertenezca a enemigos de una u otra, esceptuando siempre los articulos de contrabando de guerra. Se conviene tambien del mismo modo, en que la misma libertad se estienda a las personas que se encuentren á bordo de buques libres, con el fin de que aunque dichas personas sean enemigos de ámbas partes o de alguna de ellas, no deban ser estraidos de los buques libres, a menos que sean oficiales o soldados en actual servicio de los enemigos. Bajo la condicion, sin embargo, (y quéda aquí espresamente acordado) que las estipulaciones contenidas en el presente articulo, declarando que el Pabellon cubre la propiedad, se entenderán aplicables solamente a aquellas potencias que reconocen este principio; pero si alguna de las dos partes contratantes estuviere en guerra con una tercera, y la otra permaneciese neutral, la bandera de la neutral cubrirá la propiedad de los enemigos, cuyos gobiernos reconozcan este principio, y no de otro.

ARTICULO XIII.

Se conviene igualmente que en el caso de que la bandera neutral de una de las partes contratantes proteja las propiedades de los enemigos de la otra en virtud de lo estipulado arriba, deberá siempre entenderse que las propiedades neutrales encontradas á bordo de buques de tales enemigos

vessels shall be held and considered as enemy's property, and as such shall be liable to detention and confiscation, except such property as was put on board such vessel before the declaration of war, or even afterwards, if it were done without the knowledge of it; but the contracting parties agree, that four months having elapsed after the declaration, their citizens shall not plead ignorance thereof. On the contrary, if the flag of the neutral does not protect the enemy's property, in that case, the goods and merchandize of the neutral, embarked in such enemy's ship, shall be free.

ARTICLE 14. This liberty of commerce and navigation shall extend to all kinds of merchandises, excepting those only which are distinguished by the name of contraband, and under this name of contraband, or prohibited goods, shall be comprehended—

1ˢᵗ Cannons, mortars, howitzers, swivels, blunderblusses, muskets, fuzees, rifles, carbines, pistols, pikes, swords, sabres, lances, spears, halberds, and grenades, bombs, powder, matches, balls, and all other things belonging to the use of these arms;

2. Bucklers, helmets, breastplates, coats of mail, infantry

han de tenerse y considerarse como propiedades enemigas, y como tales estaran sujetas a detencion, y confiscacion; esceptuando solamente aquellas propiedades que hubiesen sido puestas á bordo de tales buques antes de la declaracion de la guerra, y aun despues, si hubiesen sido embarcadas en dichos buques, sin tener noticia de la guerra; y se conviene, que pasados cuatro meses despues de la declaracion los ciudadanos de una y otra parte no podrán alegar que la ignoraban. Por el contrario si la bandera neutral no protejiese las propiedades enemigas, entonces serán libres los efectos y mercaderias de la parte neutral embarcadas en buques enemigos.

ARTICULO XIV.

Esta libertad de navegacion y comercio se estenderá á todo jénero de mercaderías, esceptuando aquellas solamente, que se distinguen con el nombre de contrabando, y bajo este nombre de *contrabando* ó efectos prohibidos se comprenderán:—

1ʳᵒ Cañones, morteros, obuses, pedreros, trabucos, mosquetes, fusiles, rifles, carabinas, pistolas, picas, espadas, sables, lanzas, chuzos, alabardas, y granadas, bombas, polvora, mechas, balas, con las demas cosas correspondientes al uso de estas armas.

2ᵒ Escudos, casquetes, corazas, cotas de malla, fornituras, y

56006°—33——45

belts, and clothes made up in the form and for a military use.

3. Cavalry belts, and horses with their furniture.

4. And generally all kinds of arms and instruments of iron, steel, brass, and copper, or of any other materials manufactured, prepared and formed, expressly, to make war by sea or land.

ARTICLE 15. All other merchandise and things not comprehended in the articles of contraband explicitly enumerated and classified as above, shall be held and considered as free, and subjects of free and lawful commerce, so that they may be carried and transported in the freest manner by both the contracting parties, even to places belonging to an enemy, excepting only those places which are at that time beseiged or blockaded; and, to avoid all doubt in this particular, it is declared that those places only are beseiged or blockaded, which are actually attacked by a belligerent force capable of preventing the entry of the neutral.

ARTICLE 16. The articles of contraband, before enumerated and classified which may be found

vestidos hechos en forma, y para el uso militar.

3ro Bandoleras y caballos junto con sus armas y arneses.

4º Y jeneralmente toda especie de armas, e instrumentos de hierro, acero, bronce, cobre, y otras materias cualesquiera, manufacturadas, preparadas, y formadas espresamente para hacer la guerra por mar ó tierra.

ARTICULO XV.

Todas las demas mercaderías, y efectos no comprendidos en los articulos de contrabando esplícitamente enumerados y clasificados en el articulo anterior, serán tenidos y reputados por libres, y de lícito y libre comercio, de modo que puedan ser trasportados y llevados de la manera mas libre, por los ciudadanos de ambas partes contratantes, aun a los lugares pertenecientes a un enemigo de una u otra, esceptuando solamente aquellos lugares o plazas, que estan al mismo tiempo sitiadas o bloqueadas: y para evitar toda duda en el particular, se declaran sitiadas o bloqueadas aquellas plazas unicamente, que en la actualidad estuviesen atacadas por una fuerza de un belijerante capaz de impedir la entrada del neutral.

ARTICULO XVI.

Los articulos de contrabando antes enumerados y clasificados, que se hallen en un buque desti-

in a vessel bound for an enemy's port, shall be subject to detention and confiscation, leaving free the rest of the cargo and the ship, that the owners may dispose of them as they see proper. No vessel of either of the two nations shall be detained on the high seas on account of having on board articles of contraband, whenever the master, captain, or supercargo of said vessel will deliver up the articles of contraband to the captor, unless the quantity of such articles be so great, and of so large a bulk, that they cannot be received on board the capturing ship without great inconvenience; but in this and in all other cases of just detention, the vessel detained shall be sent to the nearest convenient and safe port, for trial and judgement according to law.

ARTICLE 17. And whereas it frequently happens that vessels sail for a port or place belonging to an enemy, without knowing that the same is beseiged, blockaded, or invested, it is agreed, that every vessel so circumstanced, may be turned away from such port or place, but shall not be detained, nor shall any part of her cargo, if not contraband, be confiscated, unless, after warning of such blockade or investment from any officer commanding a

nado a puerto enemigo, estarán sujetos a detencion y confiscacion; dejando libre el resto del cargamento y el buque, para que los dueños puedan disponer de ellos como lo crean conveniente. Ningun buque de cualquiera de las dos naciones, será detenido en alta mar, por tener á bordo artículos de contrabando, siempre que el maestre, capitan, o sobrecargo de dicho buque quiera entregar los articulos de contrabando al apresador, a menos que la cantidad de éstos articulos sea tan grande y de tanto volumen, que no puedan ser recibidos a bordo del buque apresador, sin grandes inconvenientes; pero en este, como en todos los otros casos de justa detencion, el buque detenido será enviado al puerto mas inmediato, que sea cómodo y seguro, para ser juzgado y sentenciado conforme a las leyes.

ARTICULO XVII.

Y por cuanto frecuentemente sucede que los buques navegan para un puerto o lugar perteneciente a un enemigo, sin saber que aquel esté sitiado, bloqueado o atacado, se conviene en que todo buque en estas circunstancias se pueda hacer volver de dicho puerto o lugar; pero no será detenido, ni confiscada parte alguna de su cargamento, no siendo contrabando; a menos que despues de la intimacion de semejante bloqueo o ataque, por el

vessel of the blockading forces, she shall again attempt to enter; but she shall be permitted to go to any other port or place she shall think proper. Nor shall any vessel of either, that may have entered into such port before the same was actually beseiged, blockaded, or invested, by the other, be restrained from quitting such place with her cargo, nor if found therein after the reduction and surrender, shall such vessel or her cargo be liable to confiscation, but they shall be restored to the owners thereof; and if any vessel having thus entered the port before the blockade took place, shall take on board a cargo after the blockade be established, she shall be subject to be warned by the blockading forces, to return to the port blockaded, and discharge the said cargo; and, if after receiving the said warning, the vessel shall persist in going out with the cargo, she shall be liable to the same consequences as a vessel attempting to enter a blockaded port, after being warned off by the blockading forces.

Article 18. In order to prevent all kinds of disorder in the visiting and examination of the ships and cargoes of both the contracting parties on the high seas, they have agreed, mutually,

Comandante de las fuerzas bloqueadoras, intentase otra vez entrar; pero le será permitido ir a cualquier otro puerto o lugar que juzgue conveniente. Ni a buque alguno de una de las partes que haya entrado en semejante puerto o lugar, antes que estuviese sitiado, bloqueado o atacado por la otra, se impedirá salir de dicho lugar con su cargamento, y si fuere hallado allí despues de la rendicion y entrega de semejante lugar, no estará el tal buque o su cargamento sujeto a confiscacion, sino que serán restituidos a sus dueños; y si algun buque habiendo entrado de este modo en el puerto antes de verificarse el bloqueo, tomase a su bordo algun cargamento despues de establecerse el bloqueo, se le podrá intimar por las fuerzas bloqueadoras que vuelva al puerto bloqueado y desembarque dicho cargamento; y si recibida esta intimacion persistiese salir con la carga, estará sujeto a las mismas consecuencias que la embarcacion que intenta entrar en un puerto bloqueado despues que por las fuerzas bloqueadoras se le ha intimado que se retire.

Articulo XVIII.

Para evitar todo jénero de desorden en la visita, y examen de los buques y cargamentos de ambas partes contratantes en alta mar, han convenido mutuamente que siempre que un buque de

that whenever a vessel of war, public or private, shall meet with a neutral of the other contracting party, the first shall remain at the greatest distance compatible with making the visit, under the circumstances of the sea and wind, and the degree of suspicion attending the vessel to be visited, and shall send its smallest boat in order to execute the said examination of the papers concerning the ownership and cargo of the vessel, without causing the least extortion, violence, or ill-treatment, for which the commanders of the said armed ships shall be responsible with their persons and property; for which purpose the commanders of the said private armed vessels shall, before receiving their commissions, give sufficient security to answer for all damages they may commit. And it is expressly agreed, that the neutral party shall, in no case, be required to go on board the examining vessel, for the purpose of exhibiting her papers, or for any other purpose whatever.

ARTICLE 19. To avoid all kind of vexation and abuse in the examination of the papers relating to the ownership of the vessels belonging to the citizens of the two contracting parties, they have agreed, and do agree, that in case one of them shall be engaged in war, the ships and

guerra, público o particular, se encontrase con un neutral de la otra parte contratante, el primero permanecerá a la mayor distancia compatible con la ejecucion de la visita, segun las circunstancias del mar y el viento, y el grado de sospecha de que esté afecta la nave, que va a visitarse, y enviará su bote mas pequeño a ejecutar el examen de los papeles concernientes á la propiedad y carga del buque, sin ocasionar la menor estorsion, violencia o mal tratamiento, de lo que los Comandantes del dicho buque armado serán responsables, con sus personas y bienes; a cuyo efecto los Comandantes de buques armados, por cuenta de particulares, estarán obligados, antes de entregarseles sus comisiones o patentes, a dar fianza suficiente para responder de los perjuicios que causen. Y se ha convenido espresamente, que en ningun caso se exijirá a la parte neutral, que vaya a bordo del buque examinador con el fin de exibir sus papeles, o para cualquiera otro objeto sea el que fuere.

ARTICULO XIX.

Para evitar toda clase de vejamen y abuso en el examen de los papeles relativos a la propiedad de los buques pertenecientes a los ciudadanos de las dos partes contratantes, han convenido, y convienen, que en caso de que una de ellas estuviere en guerra, los buques, y bajeles pertene-

vessels belonging to the citizens of the other must be furnished with sea-letters or passports, expressing the name, property and bulk of the ship, as also the name and place of habitation of the master or commander of said vessel, in order that it may thereby appear, that the ship really and truly belongs to the citizens of one of the parties; they have likewise agreed that, such ships, being laden, besides the sea-letters or passports, shall also be provided with certificates containing the several particulars of the cargo, and the place whence the ship sailed, so that it may be known whether any forbidden or contraband goods be on board the same; which certificates shall be made out by the officers of the place whence the ship sailed, in the accustomed form; without which requisites, said vessel may be detained, to be adjudged by the competent tribunal, and may be declared legal prize, unless the said defect shall be proved to be owing to accident, and be satisfied or supplied by testimony entirely equivalent.

ARTICLE 20. It is further agreed, that the stipulations above expressed, relative to the visiting and examination of vessels, shall apply only to those which sail without convoy; and

cientes a los ciudadanos de la otra serán provistos de letras de mar o pasaportes, espresando el nombre, propiedad y tamaño del buque, como tambien el nombre y lugar de la residencia del maestre, o Comandante, á fin de que se vea que el buque real y verdaderamente pertenece a los ciudadanos de una de las partes; y han convenido igualmente, que estando cargados los espresados buques, ademas de las letras de mar, o pasaportes, serán tambien provistos de certificados que contengan los pormenores del cargamento, y el lugar de donde salió el buque, para que asi pueda saberse, si hai a su bordo algunos efectos prohibidos o de contrabando; cuyos certificados serán espedidos por los oficiales del lugar de la procedencia del buque en la forma acostumbrada; sin cuyos requisitos el dicho buque puede ser detenido para ser adjudicado por el tribunal competente, y puede ser declarado buena presa, a menos que se pruebe que esta falta ha sido ocasionada por algun accidente, y se satisfaga o supla con testimonios enteramente equivalentes.

ARTICULO XX.

Se ha convenido ademas, que las estipulaciones anteriores, relativas al examen y visita de buques, se aplicarán solamente a los que navegan sin comboy, y que cuando los dichos buques estuvieren

when said vessels shall be under convoy, the verbal declaration of the commander of the convoy, on his word of honor, that the vessels under his protection belong to the nation whose flag he carries; and when they are bound to an enemy's port, that they have no contraband goods on board, shall be sufficient.

ARTICLE 21. It is further agreed, that in all cases the established courts for prize causes, in the country to which the prizes may be conducted, shall alone take cognizance of them. And whenever such tribunal of either party shall pronounce judgement against any vessel or goods, or property claimed by the citizens of the other party, the sentence or decree shall mention the reasons or motives on which the same shall have been founded, and an authenticated copy of the sentence or decree, and of all the proceedings in the case, shall, if demanded, be delivered to the commandant or agent of said vessel, without any delay, he paying the legal fees for the same.

ARTICLE 22. Whenever one of the contracting parties shall be engaged in war with another state, no citizen of the other contracting party shall accept a commission, or letter of Marque,

bajo de comboy, será bastante la declaracion verbal del Comandante del comboy, bajo su palabra de honor, de que los buques que va protejiendo pertenecen á la nacion, cuya bandera lleva, y si se dirijen a un puerto enemigo, que los dichos no tienen a su bordo articulos de contrabando de guerra.

ARTICULO XXI.

Se ha convenido ademas, que en todos los casos que ocurran, solo los tribunales establecidos para causas de presas, en el pais a que las presas sean conducidas, tomarán conocimiento de ellas. Y siempre que semejante tribunal de cualquiera de las partes pronunciase sentencia contra algun buque, o efectos, o propiedad reclamada por los ciudadanos de la otra parte, la sentencia o decreto hará mencion de las razones o motivos en que aquella se haya fundado; y se entregará sin demora alguna al Comandante o ajente de dicho buque, si lo solicitase, un testimonio auténtico de la sentencia o decreto, o de todo el proceso, pagando por él los derechos legales.

ARTICULO XXII.

Siempre que una de las partes contratantes estuviere en guerra con otro Estado, ningun ciudadano de la otra parte contratante aceptará comision o letra de marca para el objeto de ayudar o co-

for the purpose of assisting or co-operating hostilely, with the said enemy, against the said party so at war, under the pain of being treated as a pirate.

ARTICLE 23. If, by any fatality which cannot be expected, and which God forbid, the two contracting parties should be engaged in a war with each other, they have agreed, and do agree, now for then, that there shall be allowed the term of six months to the merchants residing on the coasts and in the ports of each other, and the term of one year to those who dwell in the interior, to arrange their business and transport their effects wherever they please, giving to them the safe conduct necessary for it, which may serve as a sufficient protection until they arrive at the designated port. The citizens of all other occupations who may be established in the territories or dominions of the United States of America, and of the Republic of Chile, shall be respected and maintained in the full enjoyment of their personal liberty and property, unless their particular conduct shall cause them to forfeit this protection, which, in consideration of humanity, the contracting parties engage to give them.

ARTICLE 24. Neither the debts due from the individuals of the

ARTICULO XXIII.

Si por alguna fatalidad, que no puede esperarse, y que Dios no permita, las dos partes contratantes se viesen empeñadas en guerra una con otra, han convenido y convienen de ahora para entonces, que se concederá el término des seis meses á los comerciantes residentes en las costas y en los puertos de entrambas, y el término de un año á los que habitan en el interior, para arreglar sus negocios, y transportar sus efectos a donde quieran, dandoles el salvo conducto necesario para ello, que les sirva de suficiente proteccion hasta que lleguen al puerto que designen. Los ciudadanos de otras ocupaciones, que se hallen establecidos en los territorios o dominios de la República de Chile, o los Estados-Unidos de América, serán respetados y mantenidos en el pleno goce de su libertad personal y propiedad, a menos que su conducta particular les haga perder esta proteccion, que en consideracion a la humanidad, las partes contratantes se comprometen a prestarles.

ARTICULO XXIV.

Ni las deudas contraidas por los individuos de una Nacion, con

one nation, to the individuals of the other, nor shares, nor money which they may have in public funds, nor in public or private banks, shall ever, in any event of war, or of national difference be sequestrated or confiscated.

ARTICLE 25. Both the contracting parties being desirous of avoiding all inequality in relation to their public communications, and official intercourse, have agreed, and do agree, to grant to their Envoys, Ministers, and other public agents, the same favors, immunities, and exemptions which those of the most favoured nation do, or shall enjoy; it being understood that whatever favors, immunities, or privileges the United States of America or the Republic of Chile may find it proper to give to the Ministers and public Agents of any other power, shall, by the same act, be extended to those of each of the contracting parties.

ARTICLE 26. To make more effectual the protection which the United States of America and the Republic of Chile shall afford in future to the navigation and commerce of the citizens of each other, they agree to receive and admit Consuls and Vice-Consuls in all the ports open to foreign com-

los individuos de la otra, ni las acciones o dineros que puedan tener en los fondos públicos o en los báncos públicos ó privados, serán jamas secuestrados o confiscados en ningun caso de guerra o diferencia nacional.

ARTICULO XXV.

Deseando ámbas partes contratantes evitar toda diferencia relativa a etiqueta en sus comunicaciones y correspondencias diplomaticas, han convenido asimismo y convienen en conceder a sus Enviados, Ministros y otros Ajentes diplomaticos los mismos favores, inmunidades y esenciones de que gozan o gozaren en lo venidero los de las naciones mas favorecidas; bien entendido que cualquier favor, inmunidad o privilejio que la República de Chile, o los Estados-Unidos de América, tengan por conveniente dispensar á los Enviados, Ministros y Ajéntes diplomáticos de otras potencias, se haga por el mismo hecho estensivo a los de una u otra de las partes contratantes.

ARTICULO XXVI.

Para hacer mas efectiva la proteccion, que la República de Chile y los Estados-Unidos de América, darán en adelante a la navegacion y comercio de los ciudadanos de una y otra, se convienen en recibir y admitir Cónsules y Vice-Cónsules en todos los puertos abiertos al comercio

merce, who shall enjoy in them all the rights, prerogatives, and immunities, of the Consuls and Vice-Consuls of the most favoured nations; each contracting party, however, remaining at liberty to except those ports and places in which the admission and residence of such Consuls may not seem convenient.

Article 27. In order that the Consuls and Vice-Consuls of the two contracting parties may enjoy the rights, prerogatives, and immunities, which belong to them, by their public character, they shall, before entering on the exercise of their functions, exhibit their commission or patent, in due form, to the government to which they are accredited; and having obtained their Exequatur, they shall be held and considered as such, by all the authorities, magistrates, and inhabitants, in the Consular District in which they reside.

Article 28. It is likewise agreed, that the Consuls, their secretaries, officers, and persons attached to the service of Consuls, they not being citizens of the country in which the Consul resides, shall be exempt from all public service; and, also, from all kind of taxes, imposts, and contributions, except those which

estranjero, quienes gozarán en ellos todos los derechos y prerogativas e inmunidades, que los Cónsules y Vice-Consules de la nacion mas favorecida, quedando no obstante en libertad cada parte contratante, para esceptuar aquellos puertos y lugares en que la admision y residencia de semejantes Cónsules y Vice-Consules no parezca conveniente.

Articulo XXVII.

Para que los Consules, y Vice-Consules de las dos partes contratantes puedan gozar los derechos, prerogativas e inmunidades que les corresponden por su caracter público, antes de entrar en el ejercicio de sus funciones, presentaran su comision o patente en la forma debida, al Gobierno con quien esten acreditados, y habiendo obtenido el Exequatur, serán tenidos, y considerados como tales, por todas las autoridades, majistrados y habitantes del distrito Consular en que residan.

Articulo XXVIII.

Se ha convenido igualmente que los Cónsules, sus Secretarios, oficiales y personas agregadas al servicio de los Consulados (no siendo estas personas ciudadanos del pais en que el Consul reside) estarán esentos de todo servicio público, y tambien de toda especie de pechos, impuestos, y contribuciones, escep-

they shall be obliged to pay on account of commerce, or their property, to which the citizens and inhabitants, native and foreign, of the country in which they reside are subject; being in every thing besides subject to the laws of their respective states. The archives and papers of the Consulate shall be respected inviolably; and, under no pretext whatever, shall any magistrate seize, or in any way interfere with them.

ARTICLE 29. The said Consuls shall have power to require the assistance of the authorities of the country for the arrest, detention, and custody of deserters from the public and private vessels of their country; and for that purpose they shall address themselves to the Courts, Judges, and officers competent, and shall demand the said deserters in writing, proving by an exhibition of the registers of the vessel's or ship's roll, or other public documents, that those men were part of said crews; and on this demand, so proved, (saving, however, where the contrary is proved) the delivery shall not be refused. Such deserters, when arrested, shall be put at the disposal of said Consuls, and may be put in the public prison at the request and expence of those who reclaim them, to be sent to the ships to which they belonged, or to others of the same

tuando aquellas que estén obligados a pagar por razon de comercio o propiedad, y a las cuales estan sujetos los ciudadanos y habitantes naturales y estranjeros del pais en que residen, quedando en todo lo demas sujetos á las leyes de los respectivos Estados. Los archivos de los Consulados serán respetados inviolablemente, y bajo ningun pretesto los ocupará majistrado alguno, ni tendrá en ellos ninguna intervencion.

ARTICULO XXIX.

Los dichos Cónsules tendrán facultad de requerir el auxilio de las autoridades locales para la prision, detencion y custodia de los desertores de buques, públicos y particulares de su pais, y para este objeto se dirijirán a los tribunales, jueces y oficiales competentes y pedirán los dichos desertores por escrito, probando por una presentacion de los rejistros de los buques, rol de la tripulacion, u otros documentos publicos, que aquellos hombres eran parte de las dichas tripulaciones, y a esta demanda asi probada (menos no obstante cuando se probare lo contrario) no se reusará la entrega. Semejantes desertores, luego que sean arrestados, se pondrán a disposicion de los dichos Cónsules, y pueden ser depositados en las prisiones públicas, a solicitud y espensas de los que los reclamen, para ser enviados a los buques á que co-

nation. But if they be not sent back within two months, reckoning from the day of their arrest, they shall be set at liberty, and shall no more be arrested for the same cause. It is understood, however, that if the deserter should be found to have committed any crime or offence, his surrender may be delayed until the tribunal before which the case may be depending, shall have pronounced its sentence, and such sentence shall have been carried into effect.

ARTICLE 30. For the purpose of more effectually protecting their commerce and navigation, the two contracting parties do hereby agree, as soon hereafter as circumstances will permit them, to form a Consular Convention, which shall declare, specially, the powers and immunities of the Consuls and Vice-Consuls of the respective parties.

ARTICLE 31. The United States of America and the Republic of Chile, desiring to make, as durable as circumstances will permit, the relations which are to be established between the two parties, by virtue of this treaty, or general convention of peace, amity, commerce, and navigation, have declared solemnly, and do agree to the following points:

1ˢᵗ The present treaty shall remain in full force and virtue

rresponden, o a otros de la misma nacion. Pero si no fueren enviados dentro de dos meses contados desde el dia de su arresto, serán puestos en libertad, y no volverán á ser presos por la misma causa. Bien entendido que si apareciere que el desertor ha cometido algun crimen u ofensa, se podrá dilatar su entrega hasta que se haya pronunciado y ejecutado la sentencia del tribunal que tomare conocimiento en la materia.

ARTICULO XXX.

Para protejer mas eficazmente su comercio y navegacion, las dos partes contratantes acuerdan en formar, luego que las circunstancias lo permitan, una Convencion Consular, que declare mas especialmente los poderes é inmunidades de los Consules y Vice-Consules de las partes respectivas.

ARTICULO XXXI.

La República de Chile y los Estados-Unidos de América deseando hacer tan duraderas y firmes, como las circunstancias lo permitan, las relaciones que han de establecerse entre las dos potencias, en virtud del presente tratado o convencion jeneral de paz, amistad, navegacion y comercio, han declarado solemnemente y convienen en los puntos siguientes:

1ʳᵒ El presente tratado permanecerá en su fuerza y vigor por el

for the term of twelve years, to be reckoned from the day of the exchange of the ratifications; and further until the end of one year after either of the contracting parties shall have given notice to the other of its intention to terminate the same; each of the contracting parties reserving to itself the right of giving such notice to the other, at the end of said term of twelve years: and it is hereby agreed between them, that, on the expiration of one year after such notice shall have been received by either, from the other party, this Treaty, in all the parts relating to commerce and navigation, shall altogether cease and determine; and in all those parts which relate to peace and friendship, it shall be permanently and perpetually binding on both powers.

2ᵈ If any one or more of the citizens of either party shall infringe any of the articles of this treaty, such citizen shall be held personally responsible for the same, and the harmony and good correspondence between the nations shall not be interrupted thereby; each party engaging in no way to protect the offender, or sanction such violation.

3ᵈ If, (which, indeed, cannot be expected,) unfortunately, any of the articles contained in the present treaty shall be violated or

término de doce años contados desde el dia del canje de las ratificaciones, y ademas hasta el cabo de un año despues que alguna de las partes contratantes haya dado noticia á la otra de su intencion de terminarlo; reservandose cada una de ellas el derecho de dar esta noticia a la otra al fin del espresado término de doce años: y se estipula por el presente articulo, que al espirar el año despues que una de ellas haya recibido esta noticia, cesará y terminará completamente este tratado en todas las partes relativas a navegacion y comercio; pero en lo concerniente a la paz y amistad, será permanente y perpetuamente obligatorio para ambas potencias.

2º Si uno o mas de los ciudadanos de una u otra parte infrinjiesen alguno de los articulos contenidos en el presente tratado, dichos ciudadanos serán personalmente responsables del hecho, sin que por esto se interrumpa la harmonía y buena correspondencia entre las dos naciones, comprometiendose cada una a no protejer de modo alguno al ofensor o a sancionar semejante violacion.

3ʳº Si (lo que a la verdad no puede esperarse) desgraciadamente alguno de los articulos contenidos en el presente tratado,

infringed in any other way whatever, it is expressly stipulated that neither of the contracting parties will order or authorize any acts of reprisal, nor declare war against the other, on complaints of injuries or damages, until the said party, considering itself offended, shall first have presented to the other a statement of such injuries or damages, verified by competent proof, and demanded justice and satisfaction, and the same shall have been either refused or unreasonably delayed.

4. Nothing in this treaty contained, shall, however, be construed to operate contrary to former and existing public treaties with other sovereigns or states.

The present treaty of peace, amity, commerce and navigation, shall be approved and ratified by the President of the United States of America, by and with the advice and consent of the Senate thereof, and by the President of the Republic of Chile, with the consent and approbation of the Congress of the same; and the ratifications shall be exchanged in the City of Washington within nine months, to be reckoned from the date of the signature hereof, or sooner if practicable.

In faith whereof, we, the underwritten Plenipotentiaries of the United States of America, and of the Republic of Chile, have signed, by virtue of our powers, the pres-

fuese en alguna otra manera violado o infrinjido, se estipula espresamente que ninguna de las dos partes contratantes ordenará, o autorizará ningunos actos de represália, ni declarará la guerra contra la otra por quéjas de injúrias o daños, hasta que la parte que se crea ofendida haya presentado a la otra una esposicion de aquellas injurias o daños, verificada con pruebas y testimonios competentes, exijiendo justicia y satisfaccion, y esta haya sido negada o demorada sin razon.

4º Nada de cuanto se contiene en el presente tratado se interpretará, sin embargo, ni obrará, en contra de otros tratados públicos anteriores y existentes con otros soberanos o Estados

El presente tratado de paz, amistad, navegacion y comercio, será ratificado por el Presidente de la República de Chile, con el consentimiento y aprobacion del Congreso de ella, y por el Presidente de los Estados-Unidos de América, con el dictamen y consentimiento del Senado de ellos; y las ratificaciones seran canjeadas en la Ciudad de Washington en el espacio de nueve meses contados desde el dia en que se firma este tratado, o antes si fuere practicable.

En fe de lo cual nosotros los infrascritos Plenipotenciarios de la Republica de Chile, y de los Estados-Unidos de América, hemos firmado y sellado, en virtud de

ent treaty of Peace, Amity, Commerce, and Navigation, and have hereunto affixed our Seals, respectively.

Done and concluded, in triplicate, in the City of Santiago, this Sixteenth day of the month of May—in the year of our Lord Jesus Christ one thousand eight hundred and thirty two; and in the fifty sixth year of the Independence of the United States of America, and the Twenty third of that of the Republic of Chile.

JNº HAMM   [Seal]
ANDRES BELLO   [Seal]

nuestros plenos poderes, el presente tratado de paz, amistad, navegacion y comercio.

Hecho y concluido por triplicado en esta Ciudad de Santiago de Chile, el dia dieziseis del mes de Mayo del año de Nuestro Señor Jesu-Cristo mil ochocientos treinta y dos, 23º de la Independencia de la República de Chile, y 56 de la de los Estados-Unidos de América."

ANDRES BELLO   (L. S.)
JUAN HAMM   (L. S.)

An additional and explanatory Convention to the Treaty of peace, amity, commerce and navigation concluded in the City of Santiago on the 16ᵗʰ day of May 1832 between the United States of America and the Republick of Chile.

Whereas, the time stipulated in the Treaty of amity, commerce and navigation between the United States of America and the Republick of Chile, signed at the City of Santiago on the 16ᵗʰ day of May 1832, for the exchange of ratifications in the City of Washington, has elapsed;—and it being the wish of both the contracting parties that the aforesaid treaty should be carried into effect with all the necessary solemnities, and that the necessary explanations should be mutually made to remove all subject of doubt in the sense of some of its articles, the

Por cuanto ha trascurrido el tiempo señalado para el cánje de las ratificaciones del tratado de paz, amistad, comercio y navegacion entre la República de Chile y los Estados Unidos de América, firmado en Santiago de Chile el dia dieziseis de Mayo de mil ochocientos treinta y dos; y deseando ambas partes contratantes que el referido tratado se lleve a cumplido efecto con todas las solemnidades necesarias, y que al mismo tiempo se hagan las convenientes esplicaciones para evitar todo motivo de duda en la intelijencia de algunos de

Undersigned Plenipotentiaries,viz, John Hamm, a citizen of the United States of America, and their Chargé d'Affaires, on the part, and in the name of the United States of America,—and Señor Don Andres Bello, a citizen of Chile, on the part, and in the name of the Republick of Chile, having compared and exchanged their full powers, as expressed in the treaty itself, have agreed upon the following additional and explanatory articles.

ARTICLE 1ˢᵗ It being stipulated by the 2ᵈ Article of the aforesaid Treaty, that the relations and conventions which now exist, or may hereafter exist, between the Republick of Chile and the Republick of Bolivia, the Federation of the Centre of America, the Republick of Colombia, the United States of Mexico, the Republick of Peru, or the United Provinces of the Rio de la Plata, are not included in the prohibition of granting particular favors to other nations which may not be made common to the one or the other of the contracting powers;— and these exceptions being founded upon the intimate connexion and identity of feelings and interests of the new American States, which were members of the same political body under the Spanish Dominion, it is mutually under-

sus artículos; los infrascritos Plenipotenciarios, es a saber, Don Andres Bello, ciudadano de Chile por parte y en nombre de la República de Chile, y el Señor Juan Hamm, ciudadano de los Estados-Unidos de América, y Encargado de Negocios de los mismos Estados, por parte y en nombre de los Estados-Unidos de América, habiendo comparado y canjeado sus respectivos plenos poderes, como se espresa en el mismo tratado, han convenido en los siguientes articulos adicionales y esplicatorios:

ARTICULO I.

Estipulandose por el articulo segundo del referido tratado, que las relaciones y convenciones que ahora existen o en adelante existieren entre la República de Chile y la República de Bolivia, la federacion de Centro-América, la República de Colombia, los Estados-Unidos Mejicanos, la República del Perú, o las Provincias Unidas del Rio de la Plata, no se incluyan en la prohibicion de conceder favores especiales a otras naciones, los cuales no se estiendan a la una o la otra de las partes contratantes; y fundandose estas escepciones en la íntima conexion e identidad de sentimientos e intereses de los nuevos estados americanos, que fueron miembros de un mismo cuerpo político, bajo la dominacion española; se entiende por una y otra parte que tendrán

stood, that these exceptions will have all the latitude which is involved in their principle;—and that they will accordingly comprehend all the new nations within the ancient territory of Spanish America, whatever alterations may take place in their constitutions, names, or boundaries, so as to include the present States of Uruguay and Paraguay, which were formerly parts of the ancient Vice-royalty of Buenos Ayres, those of New-Granada, Venezuella, and Equador in the Republick of Colombia, and any other States which may in future be dismembered from those now existing.

ARTICLE 2ᵈ It being agreed by the 10ᵗʰ article of the aforesaid treaty, that the citizens of the United States of America, personally or by their agents, shall have the right of being present at the decisions and sentences of the tribunals, in all cases which may concern them, and at the examination of witnesses and declarations that may be taken in their trials;—and as the strict enforcement of this article may be in opposition to the established forms of the present due administration of justice, it is mutually understood, that the Republick of Chile is only bound by the aforesaid stipulation to maintain the most perfect equality in this re-

dichas escepciones toda la latitud que corresponde al principio que las ha dictado, comprendiendo por consiguiente a todas las nuevas naciones dentro del territorio de la antigua América española cualesquiera que sean las alteraciones que esperimenten en sus constituciones, nombres y límites, y quedando incluidos en ellas los Estados del Vruguai y del Paraguai, que formaban parte del antiguo Virreinato de Buenos Aires, los de Nueva Granada, Venezuela y el Ecuador en la que fue República de Colombia, y cualesquiera otros Estados que en lo sucesivo sean desmembrados de los que actualmente existen.

ARTICULO II.

Estando acordado por el articulo diez de de dicho tratado que los ciudadanos de los Estados-Unidos de América, personalmente o por sus ajentes, tengan el derecho de estar presentes a las decisiones y sentencias de los tribunales, en todos los casos que les concierna, y al examen de testigos y declaraciones que ocurran en sus pleitos, y pudiendo ser incompatible la estricta observancia de este articulo con las reglas y formas establecidas al presente en la administracion de justicia; se entiende, por una y otra parte, que la República de Chile solo quéda obligada por esta estipulacion a mantener la mas perfecta igualdad bajo este

spect between American and Chilian citizens, the former to enjoy all the rights and benefits of the present or future provisions which the laws grant to the latter in their judicial tribunals, but no special favors or privileges.

ARTICLE 3ᵈ It being agreed by the 29ᵗʰ article of the aforesaid treaty that, *deserters* from the publick and private vessels of either party are to be restored thereto by the respective Consuls—And Whereas, it is declared by the Article 132 of the present Constitution of Chile that, "there are no slaves in Chile"; and, that, "slaves touching the territory of the Republick are free"—it is likewise mutually understood, that the aforesaid stipulation shall not comprehend slaves serving under any denomination on board the publick or private ships of the United States of America.

ARTICLE 4ᵗʰ It is further agreed, that the ratifications of the aforesaid Treaty of peace, amity, commerce and navigation, and of the present additional and explanatory Convention, shall be exchanged in the City of Washington within the term of Eight months, to be counted from the date of the present Convention.

respecto entre los ciudadanos chilenos y americanos, gozando estos de todos los derechos, remedios y beneficios que las presentes o futuras provisiones de las leyes concedan a aquellos en los juicios; pero no de favores o privilejios especiales.

ARTICULO III.

Estipulandose por el articulo veinte y nueve de dicho tratado que los desertores de los buques públicos y privados de cualquiera de las partes contratantes se restituyan y entreguen a los mismos por medio de sus respectivos cónsules; y estando declarado por el articulo ciento treinta y dos de la presente constitucion de Chile, "que en Chile no hai esclavos, y el que pise su territorio quéda libre"; se entenderá asimismo que la antedicha estipulacion no comprende a los esclavos que bajo cualquier titulo vinieren a bordo de los buques públicos o privados de los Estados Unidos de América.

ARTICULO IV.

Se acuerda y estipula asimismo que las ratificaciones del dicho tratado de paz, amistad, comercio y navegacion, y de la presente convencion, serán canjeadas en la Ciudad de Washington, dentro del término de ocho meses contados desde la fecha de la presente convencion.

This additional and Explanatory Convention, upon its being duly ratified by the President of the United States of America, by and with the advice and consent of the Senate thereof, and by the President of the Republick of Chile, with the consent and approbation of the Congress of the same, and the respective ratifications mutually exchanged, shall be added to, and make a part of, the Treaty of peace, amity, commerce and navigation, between the United States of America and the Republick of Chile, signed on the said 16th day of May 1832, having the same force and effect as if it had been inserted word for word in the aforesaid treaty.

In faith whereof, We, the undersigned Plenipotentiaries of the United States of America and the Republick of Chile, have signed by virtue of our powers, the aforesaid additional and explanatory Convention, and have caused to be affixed our hands and seals, respectively.

Done in the City of Santiago this first day of September 1833;—and in the 58th year of the Independence of the United States of America, and the 24th of the Republick of Chile.

JN[o] HAMM. [Seal]
ANDRES BELLO [Seal]

Esta convencion adicional y esplicatoria, ratificada que sea por el Presidente de la República de Chile, con el consentimiento y aprobacion del Congreso de ella, y por el Presidente de los Estados Unidos de América con el dictamen y consentimiento del Senado de ellos, y mutuamente canjeadas las respectivas ratificaciones, será considerada como una parte integrante del tratado de paz, amistad, comercio y navegacion entre la República de Chile y los Estados Unidos de América, firmado el dieziseis de Mayo de mil ochocientos treinta y dos, teniendo la misma fuerza y valor que si sus articulos se hallasen insertos palabra por palabra en el referido tratado.

En fé de lo cual los dichos Plenipotenciarios de la República de Chile y de los Estados-Unidos de América la hemos firmado y marcado con nuestros sellos respectivos. Fecha en la Ciudad de Santiago el dia Primero de Setiembre del año de mil ochocientos treinta y tres, veinte y cuatro de la libertad de Chile, y cincuenta y ocho de la independencia de los Estados Unidos de América.''

ANDRES BELLO (L. S.)
JUAN HAMM (L. S.)

LEGATION OF THE UNITED STATES OF AMERICA.
Santiago dè Chile.   May 16ᵗʰ, 1832.

The undersigned, Chargé d.'Affaires of the United States of America, near the government of Chile, has the honor to represent to Señor Don Andres Bello, that it would have been satisfactory to the government of the United States, if he had, also, been charged with instructions in the negotiation which has just terminated, to treat of the indemnities to the citizens of the United States, in consequence of the seizure and detention; and condemnation of their property and effects by the officers of the government in the ports of the Republic. But as Señor Bello has no instructions to that effect, the undersigned feels it to be his duty, at and before proceeding to the signature of the treaty of peace, amity, commerce and navigation, on which they have agreed, explicitly to declare, that the omission to provide for those indemnifications is not hereafter to be interpreted as being waved or abandoned by the government of the United States, which, on the contrary, it is firmly resolved to persevere in the prosecution of them, until they shall be finally adjusted to the satisfaction of both parties, upon the principles of justice and equity.

And, to guard against any misconception of the fact of the silence of the treaty, in the above particular, or of the views of the American government, the undersigned respectfully requests the favor of Señor Bello, that he will present this official notification to the government of the Republic of Chile.

In conveying these motives to Señor Bello, the undersigned is happy in an occasion of repeating sincere assurances of the sentiments of perfect personal esteem and respect, with which he has the honor to be his most obedient and most humble Servant. (Signed in Duplicate.)

JOHN HAMM

To Señor Don ANDRES BELLO,
Plenipotentiary of Chile.

———

[Translation]

SANTIAGO DE CHILE, *May 16th, 1832*

The undersigned, Plenipotentiary of the Government of Chile, has the honor to acknowledge the having received Señor Hamm's official notification, under date of the 16th instant, making his declaration of the claims of sundry citizens of the United States of America against the Republic of Chile, and that by the Treaty of Peace, Amity, Commerce, and Navigation as agreed upon and about to be signed, he

does not waive or abandon them on the part of the Government of the United States.

Agreeably to his request, the notification as aforesaid will be forthwith laid before His Excellency the President of the Republic.

The undersigned begs Señor Hamm to accept his salutations and assurances of his high respect and distinguished consideration.

ANDRÉS BELLO

To the Honorable Señor JOHN HAMM
  Chargé d'Affaires and Plenipotentiary of the United States of America, Santiago de Chile

NOTES

The treaty signed on May 16, 1832, and the Additional and Explanatory Convention of September 1, 1833, form together one agreement which was ratified by each of the two Governments in one instrument. While the two documents of the agreement (hereafter called, respectively, the treaty and the convention) were each signed in English and in Spanish, it is clear that the procedure adopted (no account of which is given in the despatches) was that originals were signed in English for the Government of the United States and originals were signed in Spanish for the Government of Chile. Accordingly, the United States instrument of ratification of April 26, 1834, a duplicate of which is in the treaty file, includes the English texts only of the treaty and the convention; and the Chilean instrument of ratification of November 5, 1833, includes the Spanish texts only of the treaty and the convention. It is from that Chilean instrument of ratification that the Spanish texts above printed are taken; and it is to be observed that in them the Republic of Chile is named first throughout; thus the *alternat* was observed.

The treaty, according to the final clause, was "done and concluded, in triplicate." One original thereof is in the treaty file, and another is with the despatch of John Hamm, Chargé d'Affaires at Santiago, of June 1, 1832, in D. S., 3 Despatches, Chile. One of those originals—it is not now certain which—was forwarded by Captain Ratcliff Hicks, of the ship *Edward*, of Providence, with the despatch of June 1, and was received at the Department of State in the early part of October, 1832 (D. S., 14 Instructions, American States, 267–68, October 8, 1832).

The two originals are not literally identical. From the internal evidence it is fairly certain that the one in the treaty file, with which the text here printed has been collated, was written first and that the other original, in D. S., 3 Despatches, Chile, was transcribed therefrom. Aside from matters of spelling and style of punctuation and writing, the two originals differ in a few cases of commas omitted or inserted; but all of these seem quite immaterial. In what is deemed the later-written original there are a few errors of wording. In

Article 3 "navigation" and "commerce" are transposed; in Article 7 and in Article 10 a "the" is omitted; in Article 17 an "a" is inserted; in Article 18 the word "and" is once repeated; in Article 23 the words "to those" are omitted; and in Article 31 the word "the" is inserted before "either"; but these differences are plainly errors of the scrivener.

The convention, it seems, was signed only in duplicate. The original in the file was brought to Washington by Chargé d'Affaires Hamm on his return to the United States in 1834.

The treaty file is complete. Besides the signed originals and the two instruments of ratification, it contains the attested Senate resolution of December 19, 1832, regarding the treaty (Executive Journal, IV, 288), and that of April 24, 1834, regarding the convention (*ibid.*, 389); the certificate (in Spanish) of the exchange of ratifications at Washington on April 29, 1834; and also the original proclamation of the same date. Each of the two documents last mentioned is in customary form; the certificate of exchange states that the ratifications were exchanged "after due comparison made of one with the other and of both with the original examples of the said conventions"; the proclamation includes the English texts only.

Like the treaty with Colombia of October 3, 1824, and that with the Central American Federation of December 5, 1825 (Documents 47 and 50), the treaty signed on May 16, 1832, has sometimes been called a convention, or, as in the heading, in the Senate resolution of December 19, 1832, in the United States instrument of ratification, and in the proclamation, a "general convention"; but "treaty," as in the Chilean instrument of ratification, seems strictly more correct, in view of the language in the preamble and Article 4 of the Additional and Explanatory Convention of September 1, 1833, and considering the fact that the agreement has, in the strictest sense of the word, every form of a treaty.

It appears that no papers accompanied this treaty when it was submitted to the Senate with the presidential message of December 11, 1832 (Executive Journal, IV, 280). The treaty was referred to the Committee on Foreign Relations on the day of its receipt; and the resolution of advice and consent was unanimously adopted eight days later, the day it was reported (*ibid.*, 288–89). The Senate print contains merely the English text of the treaty (Senate Confidential Document No. 1, 22d Congress, 2d session, Regular Confidential Documents, VI, 425–34).

When the Additional and Explanatory Convention was submitted to the Senate with the presidential message of February 22, 1834, it was accompanied by a report of the Secretary of State (Executive Journal, IV, 359), the text of which will be found later in these notes. The Senate print contains merely the English text of the convention (Senate Confidential Document No. 3, 23d Congress, 1st session, Regular Confidential Documents, II, 535–36).

It appears from the despatch of Hamm of May 30, 1832 (D. S., 3 Despatches, Chile), that the original full powers were exchanged, for

in that despatch it is stated that the power given to Andrés Bello by the Government of Chile is enclosed; but the enclosure is not now with the despatch and has not been found. The full power of Hamm to negotiate and sign the treaty was in customary form and dated October 15, 1830 (D. S., 2 Credences, 156). As the preamble to the Additional and Explanatory Convention states, the respective full powers for the treaty served also for the convention.

The treaty and convention were communicated to Congress with the presidential message of May 15, 1834 (Richardson, III, 51).

THE NOTES OF MAY 16, 1832

Following the texts of the treaty and explanatory convention are printed a note of Chargé d'Affaires Hamm to Andrés Bello, Plenipotentiary of Chile, of May 16, 1832, the same date as the treaty, formally declaring that this Government would "persevere in the prosecution of" certain "indemnities to the citizens of the United States, in consequence of the seizure and detention; and condemnation of their property and effects by the officers of the government in the ports of the Republic," and the answering note, of the same date, in which it was said that the American note would be laid before the President of Chile. The texts of those notes are printed from a duplicate of the note of the American Plenipotentiary and a translation of the note of the Chilean Plenipotentiary, which apparently were enclosed with the despatch of Hamm of May 30, 1832, though now bound with the despatch of May 28, 1832 (D. S., 3 Despatches, Chile).

There is no mention of the notes in either instrument of ratification or in the proclamation, and it appears that they were not before the Senate.

While the language of the notes is general, the American claims then particularly in mind were two in number; they are mentioned in the instructions to Hamm of October 15, 1830 (D. S., 14 Instructions, American States, 83–97). The first was because of the seizure in 1819 by Lord Cochrane, then an admiral in the Chilean Navy, of sums of money amounting to something over $140,000; those sums were derived from the sale of cargo of the American brig *Macedonian* and were in part seized on land and in part from the French brig *Gazelle*. In the despatches the claim is generally spoken of as the first case of the *Macedonian*; the facts in this claim are set forth in Moore, International Arbitrations, II, 1449–50; and it is to be distinguished from a later claim, also involving the brig *Macedonian*, which is dealt with in following pages of the work mentioned. For the settlement in the first case of the *Macedonian*, see the agreement with Chile of July 7, 1840.

The second claim arose out of the seizure and detention of the brig *Warrior* at Coquimbo in 1820, and the amount claimed was about $16,000. For the facts and the settlement in the case of the *Warrior*, see the agreement with Chile of December 10, 1840.

The American note reserving the claims is very similar in form to the note of Secretary of State Clay of April 25, 1826, which is printed following the text of the convention with Denmark of April 26, 1826 (Document 51).

The Additional and Explanatory Convention

The Additional and Explanatory Convention which was signed at Santiago on September 1, 1833, resulted from the action of the Congress of Chile, regarding which, on October 5, 1832, Hamm wrote as follows (D. S., 3 Despatches, Chile):

> The Two Houses of the Congress have, at last, got through with the consideration of the treaty which was submitted to them by the President early in June.
> They have ratified the whole of it as presented to them—but have annexed sundry *additions and explanatory articles* which renders it necessary for me to ask for new instructions from your Department before I can proceed further.
> Enclosed herewith you have a copy (translation) of those additions and explanations, which have been furnished me by the Chilian Plenipotentiary.
> The next Congress of this government will convene in this capital on the *first monday of June next*—and will, I learn, continue in session *but three months*. It is, therefore, important that yʳ instructions should be forwarded to me with as little delay as practicable so as to reach me before the expiration of that period— And more especially, to afford an opportunity to that Congress (if it should be necessary) to act on a new treaty, or otherwise, should it be the desire of the President of the United States to recommence the negotiation.

The "additions and explanations," a translation of which was enclosed with that despatch, are in substance the same as Articles 1, 2, and 3 of the Additional and Explanatory Convention signed the following September 1.

Under date of April 19, 1833 (D. S., 14 Instructions, American States, 317–19), Secretary of State Livingston wrote as follows:

> Your despatch of the 5ᵗʰ October last, should have been immediately answered with the instructions you request, in relation to the additional articles, proposed by the Chilean Government, to the treaty concluded, by you, with them, if the original articles, so proposed, had been forwarded; but having only a translation, and that not authenticated, the sense of the senate could not be taken on the subject.
> The treaty has been ratified by the President and Senate, but before the arrival of your notice of the additional articles, and as the time for the exchange of the ratifications has expired, it will be necessary (independent of the additional articles) that the treaty itself should again be submitted to both Governments in order to prolong the time limited for the exchange. The additional articles have been submitted to the President and he directs me to instruct you, in relation to the first explanation they give of the terms of the treaty, to use all proper means to procure a departure from the policy it sanctions of giving exclusive privileges, in trade, to the other nations of Spanish America. ; ; .You are, therefore, instructed to get it omitted, if possible. If, however, you find that they make a point of it, you may consent to its introduction.
> To the second explanatory article, there is no objection. The third is entirely unnecessary, because no *slave* can form a part of the crew of any American vessel.

Following those instructions, the Additional and Explanatory Convention was signed. On September 22, 1833, Hamm wrote that the

the treaty "is now, together with the additions and explanations, before that body [the Chilean Congress] for its constitutional ratification" (D. S., 3 Despatches, Chile).

Late in November, the Chilean ratification having been obtained, Hamm sailed in the brig *Lady Adams* for the United States, and wrote from Baltimore on February 4, 1834, that he had arrived after a passage of seventy days (*ibid.*). With him was Don Manuel Carvallo, the Chilean Chargé d'Affaires, who was duly authorized to exchange the ratifications.

The report of Secretary of State McLane to President Jackson regarding the Additional and Explanatory Convention, made under date of February 22, 1834, and which accompanied the convention when it was transmitted to the Senate (Executive Journal, IV, 359), contains the following (D. S., 5 Report Book, 77):

I have the honour to submit to you an additional and explanatory Convention to the Treaty of Peace, Amity, Commerce and Navigation between the United States and the Republic of Chile. The treaty was concluded at Santiago de Chile, on the 16th of May 1832, and it was stipulated, that the ratifications should be exchanged in this City within nine months from that period. The President and Senate of the United States ratified the Treaty in season to comply with that stipulation, but although the President of Chile laid the treaty before the congress of that Republic early in June 1832, it was not until October in that year, that they advised and consented to its ratification upon the condition, that certain supplementary articles which they annexed should be agreed to by the United States. Intelligence of this conditional ratification on the part of the Chilean Congress not having been received here until after the ratification of the treaty by the President and the Senate of the United States, nor until after the period stipulated for the exchange of the ratifications had elapsed, it became necessary to extend that period, as well as to signify the assent of the United States to the supplementary articles by a new convention which having been duly negotiated by the plenipotentiaries of the two powers and ratified by the Chilean Government now only needs your ratification by and with the advice and consent of the Senate to become a law.

RELATIONS WITH CHILE

The independence of Chile dates from September 18, 1810, though not finally secured until 1818. On February 12, 1818, independence was proclaimed by Bernardo O'Higgins, Director General of Chile (see Moore, International Arbitrations, IV, 4329–32); and the battle at the River Maipo on April 5, 1818, marked the final success of the revolutionary struggle. Recognition of the independence of Chile by the United States took place in January, 1822, according to opinions of the United States and Chilean Claims Commission under the convention of August 7, 1892 (see The Final Report of George H. Shields, 41–51, the Didier case; also Moore, International Arbitrations, IV, 4329, 4330, *note*); but no record of a definitive act of recognition has been found prior to January 27, 1823, when Heman Allen was commissioned Minister to Chile; and John Quincy Adams, who was Secretary of State from 1817 to 1825, says specifically that the reception of Manuel Torres as Chargé d'Affaires of the Republic of Colombia on June 19, 1822, was "the first formal act of recognition of an independent South American Government" (Memoirs of John Quincy Adams, VI, 23).

Early diplomatic relations between the United States and Chile are treated in W. R. Sherman, The Diplomatic and Commercial Relations of the United States and Chile, 1820–1914, 9–42. The following paragraphs are extracted from the instructions of October 15, 1830, to John Hamm, Chargé d'Affaires at Santiago (D. S., 14 Instructions, American States, 83–84):

Shortly after the recognition by this Government of the independence of the Spanish American States, those relations [with Chile] were opened on our part, by the appointment of Mʳ Heman Allen [commissioned January 27, 1823] as Envoy Extraordinary and Minister Plenipotentiary of this Government near that of Chile, who, in November of 1823, proceeded to Santiago. This first movement towards the establishment of regular intercourse was, in 1827, reciprocated by Chile, by the appointment, in the person of Mʳ Joaquin Campino, of a minister of the same rank, who continued to reside in the United States, in his public capacity, until May, 1829, when he took his leave of this Government, near which that of Chile has remained unrepresented ever since.

The principal objects of Mʳ Allen's mission, besides apprizing the Government near which he was accredited, of its recognition by this, were to arrange our commercial relations with that country upon a permanent and advantageous footing of reciprocity; to protect the persons and property of our citizens trading in that quarter, and to obtain from that Government the liquidation of several important claims of American merchants, for the capture and detention of their vessels. Circumstances which it is deemed unnecessary to detail, but which arose principally from the unsettled state of public Affairs in Chile, prevented the entire fulfilment of the views of this Government; and, in August, 1827, Mʳ Allen returned to the United States, leaving the care of our affairs there in the hands of Mʳ Samuel Larned, the Secretary of Legation, who was subsequently appointed Chargé d'Affaires, and continued to reside at Santiago in that character, until October, 1829, when he was transferred to Peru with a similar appointment. By the last mentioned gentleman, no further advance was made towards the accomplishment of the original objects of our mission to Chile, than receiving from its Government, in April, 1828, an invitation to commence a negotiation for a treaty of commerce. This invitation, although accepted by Mʳ Larned, was not followed by any measure on the part of the Chilean Government to move farther in the matter, until December, 1828, when the Minister of Foreign Relations informed Mʳ Larned that his Government had concluded to transfer the negotiation to Washington, and that Mʳ Campino had been authorized and instructed to that effect. Mʳ Campino having taken his leave without carrying this intention of his Government into effect, the subject has been at rest ever since, and will form one of the objects of your mission.

COMMERCIAL POLICY

The instructions of Secretary of State Van Buren to John Hamm on his appointment as Chargé d'Affaires near the Republic of Chile, under date of October 15, 1830 (D. S., 14 Instructions, American States, 83–97), contain a very interesting review of the commercial policy of the United States internationally during the two decades preceding this treaty and show also the interrelation in commercial affairs of statutory provisions and treaty clauses. Extracts from those instructions follow; and it is to be noted that in general this treaty with Chile, in its commercial clauses, follows the basis deemed least desirable at the time by this Government. In general this treaty is very similar to that with Colombia of October 3, 1824 (Document 47); there are certain additions here, as in Articles 2, 3, 17, and 29; but the changes otherwise, even in wording, are few and not very material.

It will be proper, in this place, briefly to allude to the principles which have governed the United States in the establishment of their commercial relations with all countries. These principles are seated upon the broadest basis of the most perfect equality and reciprocity. They have engaged the attention of our negotiators and legislators ever since the first year of our political existence, and have ever since been adhered to with the most undeviating fidelity. Upon this groundwork has been erected a system whose wisdom is daily exemplified by the advantageous commerce we are now carrying on with other nations, and by the eagerness with which almost all the governments which have commercial intercourse with us, and among them several of the great European Powers, have accepted the terms which it offers equally to all nations willing to reciprocate to us the benefits flowing from it.

Its leading features are embodied in our own legislation, of which the following is a brief recapitulation:

In 1815 [act of March 3, 1815, 3 Statutes at Large, 224], the United States repealed all their acts imposing discriminating duties of tonnage or impost upon foreign vessels, or upon the produce or manufactures of the *nation to which such foreign vessel might belong,* and which were imported therein; such repeal to take effect in favor of any foreign nation which should extend equal exemptions to the vessels and produce of the United States.

In 1817 [act of March 1, 1817, *ibid.,* 351–52]. They restricted importations into the United States, in foreign vessels, to the productions of the country to which such vessels belonged, or as could only be, or were most usually shipped, in the first instance, from such country; but confining the operation of that restriction to such nations only as enforced a similar one against the vessels of the United States and their cargoes.

In 1824 [act of January 7, 1824, 4 *ibid.,* 2–3], They declared the suspension of all discriminating duties, in respect to the vessels and productions of several European nations, and their territories in Europe, which had accepted the terms proffered by the Act of 1815; and conferred authority upon the President to allow similar privileges to all Nations which should thereafter comply with its requisitions.

In 1828 [act of May 24, 1828, *ibid.,* 308–9], They authorized the President to extend the exemption from alien duties, (which, by previous Acts, was restricted to the productions of the country to which the vessel belongs,) to those of any foreign country, imported into the United States in vessels of *any nation* which should allow us similar privileges [see also the act of May 31, 1830, *ibid.,* 425, and the act of July 13, 1832, *ibid.,* 578–79].

The effect of these various enactments has been to vest in the President of the United States the power of granting to any foreign nation willing to reciprocate the same benefit to us, the privilege of importing into, or exporting from, our ports, in its own vessels, the produce of its own soil or manufacture, or of the soil or manufacture of *any other* country, upon equal terms with those imported or exported in vessels of the United States.

These terms which are offered indiscriminately to all nations willing to reciprocate them, go as far as the principle of equalization of duties on vessels and cargoes can be carried. They have, either by treaty or separate legislation, been virtually accepted to their full extent, by Prussia [Document 62], Sweden [Document 55], Denmark [Document 51], Austria [Document 66], the Grand Dukedom of Oldenburg [proclamation of November 22, 1821, 3 Statutes at Large, 795], Central America [Document 50] and Brazil [Document 64]; and, in part, by Great Britain [see *infra*], Russia, the Netherlands, France [proclamation of June 24, 1822, Richardson, II, 183–84], Hanover [proclamation of July 1, 1828, 4 Statutes at Large, 815–16], the Roman States [proclamation of June 7, 1827, 11 *ibid.,* 768–69], and Colombia [Document 47. As to Oldenburg, Russia, the Netherlands, and Prussia, see also the act of January 7, 1824. The Hanseatic Republics might have been mentioned; see the act of January 7, 1824, and Document 59.]. The President is anxious that the wisdom of our policy should be appreciated by all nations; and would like to add Chile to the list of those which are now reaping, in common with ourselves, the unquestionable advantages it affords to general commerce.

The principle upon which you will first endeavor to negotiate with the Chilean Government, is that on which the Act of 1828 was predicated. You will find it unfolded in the 3d, 4th and 5th Articles of the Treaty concluded, in 1828, with Brazil [Document 64], which adopts our system in its full extent, as to the equalization of duties on tonnage and imposts, whatever may be the nature and origin of the cargoes, and from whence imported. You will not be at a loss to adduce arguments to prove the beneficial effects which such a liberal extension of commercial facilities must have upon the commerce of Chile. Its extent, and the profits it will yield, both to the native and foreign merchant, must ever be in proportion to the sphere it embraces, and to the facilities afforded in the means of transportation and exchange, while, on the other hand, the opposite system of burthensome restrictions, exclusive privileges, and monopolies, cramps the energy of the nation, checks individual enterprise, and although apparently granting to navigation a protection against foreign competition in its own ports, it as surely begets retaliatory measures in those of the other nations, which produce an equality of burdens and restrictions instead of one of facilities and advantages.

It is hoped that these principles are now too well understood throughout the commercial world, to require much discussion; but if you should find the authorities of Chile disposed to question their applicability to the present condition of that country, the next basis on which you are authorized to negotiate is that which is contained in the act of Congress of 1824, above alluded to, and which restricts importations to the produce of the country to which the vessels importing it may belong. Our Convention of 1815 with Great Britain [Document 35], continued in 1818 [Document 40], and again further continued in 1827 [Document 57], is predicated upon this principle, which has recently been extended to the trade with her American Colonial possessions. [The reference here is to the "arrangement" elaborately discussed in the message to Congress of President Jackson of December 6, 1830 (Richardson, II, 501–4); that arrangement was effected by unilateral legislative and executive acts on each part, namely, the British statute of July 5, 1825 (6 George IV, ch. 114), the order in council of July 27, 1826 (British and Foreign State Papers, XIII, 366–70), the act of May 29, 1830 (4 Statutes at Large, 419–20), the proclamation of October 5, 1830 (*ibid.*, 817–18), and the order in council of November 5, 1830. The negotiations resulting in the arrangement are set forth in British and Foreign State Papers XVII, 850–94, the text of the order in council of November 5, 1830, being the last paper there printed. It may be added that the printed correspondence and other papers regarding this arrangement are to be found in House Document No. 22, 21st Congress, 2d session, serial 206 (message of January 3, 1831), and Senate Documents Nos. 118, 121, and 132, 22d Congress, 1st session, serial 214 (messages of April 4, 9, and 20, 1832).] The second article of that Convention would afford a model for one of a similar import in the treaty which you are authorized to conclude. This basis, which could not afford any advantage to Chile, whilst it would impose a considerable restriction upon our trade and navigation between her ports and those of other foreign countries, is not to be proposed by you, until you shall have failed in your efforts to procure the adoption of the first.

Should you find the Chilean Government still so strongly wedded to the ancient and exploded systems, as to decline either of the two bases mentioned above, your last resort will be the principle of the most favored nation. This principle forms the basis of our Convention of 1824 with the Republic of Colombia [Document 47], and is contained in its second Article. It grants to the commerce and navigation of the United States in Colombian ports, advantages equal to those which are, or may hereafter be, granted to any other nation, upon our paying for them the same equivalent. This principle, without confining either Power to any particular system, however restrictive or liberal, leaves each at liberty to regulate its foreign intercourse by legislation, requiring only that it should preserve, in doing so, the principle of equality. It may, or it may not, at the election of one of the parties, lead to the adoption of liberal views; but our objection to it is, that it leaves the commercial intercourse exposed to that uncertainty which it is our object to remove, by establishing it upon the basis of treaty stipulations.

When the United States began to negotiate with the New American Republics, a disposition was manifested on the part of some of them to reserve to those States which were formed out of the former Spanish Colonies, certain privileges in commerce, from which they wished to exclude the United States. This disposition was strenuously, and with success, opposed by our negotiators; and the second Article in the Convention with Colombia, above referred to, was the result of that opposition on our part. It was subsequently inserted in the Convention of 1825 with Central America [Document 50], and of 1828 with Brazil [Document 64], although both of these recognised and adopted the principle of our Act of 1828. It exists in several others of our treaties, and will form an appropriate article in that which you may conclude with Chile. I need not say that if you should discover such a disposition on her part as was shown by others of her Sister States, you will resist it by all such arguments as these facts and your own judgment will easily suggest.

As to all other stipulations which you will find necessary to place our intercourse with Chile upon a friendly, liberal, and reciprocal footing, I need scarcely do more than refer you to the treaty with Brazil [Document 64], to which reference has already been made, and which embraces all the points on which it is expected that you may be called upon to treat. Its language may also be safely adopted by you, being that in which similar stipulations are expressed throughout our diplomatic code.

. . . .

The eleventh and twelfth articles of our Convention of the 4th July, 1827, with Sweden [Document 55], which have been omitted in that with Brazil of 1828 [Document 64], which is here presented to you as a model, contain stipulations which may find a very appropriate place in a compact intended, like the one you are expected to negotiate, to regulate the trade between countries so widely separated as the United States and Chile. They afford to vessels entering one port, the faculty of proceeding to another port or country without discharging the whole or any part of their cargoes, and without being subjected to the payment of higher charges than national vessels in the same case. It may frequently happen that a vessel sailing from our ports, although clearing for a specified port of Chile, may wish, on her arrival at the place of her destination, to proceed to a more favorable market, either with the whole or only part of her cargo: the faculty of paying the duty of tonnage once only, in the first port, and that of impost upon those goods alone which may be landed, affords advantages well worth the attention of the negotiator, and therefore recommends itself to your consideration in conducting the negotiation.

. . . .

It has hitherto been the policy followed by our negotiators to limit the duration of our treaties with other nations to a definite period, beyond which it is left to their choice, either to arrest their operation, or to continue it for an indefinite length of time, according as they may think fit. It is desirable that you should pursue the same course. The period of ten or twelve years, adopted in most of them, will, also, be proposed by you; and you will find, in the closing Article of our treaty with Brazil the form of a provision for its unlimited duration beyond that time, as long as neither of the parties shall express a desire to arrest its operation.

Treaty Series No. 362
8 Statutes at Large, 442–45
18 *ibid.*, pt. 2, Public Treaties, 771–72

74

THE TWO SICILIES : OCTOBER 14, 1832

*Convention to Terminate the Reclamations of the Government of the
United States for the Depredations Inflicted upon American Commerce
by Murat during the Years 1809, 1810, 1811, and 1812, signed at
Naples October 14, 1832. Original in English and Italian.
Submitted to the Senate December 17, 1832. Resolution of advice
and consent January 19, 1833. Ratified by the United States January 19, 1833. Ratified by the Two Sicilies June 2, 1833. Ratifications exchanged at Naples June 8, 1833. Proclaimed August 27,
1833.*

Convention between The Government of the United States of
America, and his Majesty the
King of the Kingdom of the
two Sicilies to terminate the
reclamations of said Government, for the depredations inflicted upon American Commerce, by Murat during the
years 1809, 1810, 1811, and
1812.

The Government of the United
States of America and His Majesty the King of the Kingdom of
the Two Sicilies, desiring to
terminate the reclamations advanced by said Government
against His said Majesty, in
order that the Merchants of the
United States may be indemnified for the losses inflicted upon
them by Murat, by the depredations, seizures, confiscations and
destruction of their Vessels and
cargoes, during the years 1809,
1810, 1811, and 1812. and His

Sua Maestà il Re del Regno
delle Due Sicilie ed il Governo
degli Stati Uniti di America
desiderando di porre finalmente
un termine alle reclamazioni avan-
zate dal detto Governo presso la
Maestà Sua, perchè i Negozianti
di essi Stati fossero rifatti delle
perdite recate loro da Murat per
le prede, sequestro, confische, e
distruzione dei bastimenti, e dei
carichi di loro proprietà negli
anni 1809. 1810. 1811. e 1812. e
volendo con ciò vieppiù stringere
la Maestà Sua col cennato Go-

711

Sicilian Majesty desiring thereby to strengthen with the said Government the bonds of that harmony, not hitherto disturbed; the said Government of the United States and His aforesaid Majesty, the King of the Kingdom of the two Sicilies have with one accord, resolved to come to an adjustment; to effectuate which they have respectively named and furnished with the necessary powers, viz, The said Government of the United States, John Nelson Esquire, a citizen of said states, and their Chargé d'Affaires near His Majesty the King of the Kingdom of the Two Sicilies; and His Majesty His Excellency D. Antonio Maria Statella, Prince of Cassaro, Marquis of Spaccaforno, Count Statella etc, etc, etc, His said Majesty's Minister Secretary of State for foreign affairs etc, etc, who after the exchange of their respective full powers, found in good and due form, have agreed to the following articles

verno degli Stati Uniti i legami di buona armonia non mai turbata per lo addietro, la prelodata Maestà Sua il Re del Regno delle Due Sicilie, ed il Governo degli Stati Uniti hanno concordemente risoluto di venire ad un aggiustamento, a terminare il quale hanno nominati, e muniti delle necessarie Plenipotenze, cioè:

Sua Maestà il Re del Regno delle Due Sicilie

Sua Eccellenza D. Antonio Maria Statella Principe di Cassaro, Marchese di Spaccaforno, Conte Statella, Gran Siniscalco ereditario di Sicilia, Grande di Spagna di prima Classe, Cavaliere Gran Croce dei Reali ordini di S. Ferdinando, e del Merito, di S. Gennaro, e di Francesco I. Cavaliere del Toson d'oro, e Gran Croce del Reale e distinto ordine Spagnuolo di Carlo III. Gentiluomo di Camera con esercizio di Sua Maestà il Re del Regno delle Due Sicilie, Suo Ministro Segretario di Stato degli Affari Esteri, Corriere Maggiore, &c: &c:

ed il Governo degli Stati Uniti di America:

Il Signor Giovanni Nelson Suo Incaricato di Affari presso questa Real Corte.

i quali dopo il cambio delle rispettive loro Plenipotenze, e queste trovate in buona, e debita forma, hanno convenuto dei seguenti Articoli:

ARTICLE 1ˢᵗ

His Majesty the King of the Kingdom of the Two Sicilies, with a view to satisfy the aforesaid reclamations, for the depredations, sequestrations, confiscations and destruction of the vessels and cargoes of the Merchants of the United States (and for every expense of every Kind whatsoever incident to, or growing out of the same) inflicted by Murat during the years 1809, 1810, 1811, and 1812, obliges himself to pay the sum of Two Millions, one Hundred and fifteen Thousand Neapolitan Ducats to the Government of the United States; seven Thousand six Hundred and seventy nine ducats part thereof, to be applied to reimburse the said Government for the expense incurred by it, in the transportation of American seamen from the Kingdom of Naples during the year 1810, and the residue to be distributed amongst the claimants by the said Government of the United States in such manner, and according to such rules as it may prescribe.

ARTICLE 2ᵈ

The sum of two Millions one Hundred and fifteen Thousand Neapolitan Ducats agreed on in article the 1ˢᵗ shall be paid in Naples, in nine equal installments of Two Hundred and Thirty five Thousand Ducats and with interest thereon at

ARTÍCOLO 1º

Sua Maestà il Re del Regno delle Due Sicilie, ad oggetto di far tacere le succennate reclamazioni per le prede, sequestro, confische, e distruzione dei bastimenti, e dei carichi dei Negozianti degli Stati Uniti, recata da Murat negli anni 1809. 1810. 1811. e 1812. (e per qualunque altra spesa incidente, o derivante dalle anzidette cagioni), si obbliga di pagare la somma di Ducati Napolitani due milioni cento quindici mila al Governo degli Stati Uniti, cioè settemila seicento settantanove Ducati, a titolo di rimborso al detto Governo per ispese da esso fatte per trasporto di diversi marinari Americani nell'anno 1810. dal Regno di Napoli nell'America, ed il rimanente da dividersi ai reclamanti dal succennato Governo degli Stati Uniti nel modo, e secondo che esso stimerà opportuno di determinare.

ARTÍCOLO 2º

La somma dei due milioni cento quindici mila ducati Napolitani convenuta nell'Articolo Iº sarà soddisfatta in Napoli in nove rate eguali, ciascuna di Ducati dugentotrentacinque mila, coll'interesse a scalare del quattro per cento, da percepirsi dall'epoca del cambio

the rate of four per centum per annum, to be calculated from the date of the interchange of the ratifications of this Convention, untill the whole sum shall be paid. The first installment shall be payable twelve months after the exchange of the said ratifications, and the remaining installments, with the interest, successively, one year after another. The said payments shall be made in Naples into the hands of such person as shall be duly authorised by the Government of the United States to receive the same

delle ratifiche di questa Convenzione, sino all'estinzione dell'intera somma. Il primo pagamento sarà fatto dodici mesi dopo il cambio di dette ratifiche, ed i rimanenti successivamente un anno dopo l'altro. Questi pagamenti saranno fatti in Napoli nelle mani di chi sarà all'uopo autorizzato dal Governo degli Stati Uniti.

ARTICLE 3ᵈ

The present Convention shall be ratified and the ratifications thereof shall be exchanged in this Capital in the space of eight months from this date or sooner if possible.

In faith whereof the parties above named have respectively subscribed these articles, and thereto affixed their seals. Done at Naples on the 14ᵗʰ day of October one Thousand eight Hundred and thirty two.

JNO. NELSON   [Seal]

THE PRINCE OF CASSARO   [Seal]

ARTÍCOLO 3º

La presente Convenzione sarà ratificata, e le ratifiche saranno cambiate in questa Capitale nello spazio di otto mesi da questa data, o più presto se fia possibile.

In fede di che, le Parti di sopra accennate hanno rispettivamente firmato questi Articoli, e vi hanno apposto i loro suggelli.

Data in Napoli a di 14. di Ottobre milleotto cento trentadue.

Firmato—

IL PRINCIPE DI CASSARO (L. S.)

Firmato

JNO. NELSON   (L. S.)

NOTES

The signed original of this convention which is in the treaty file is in English only; but the convention was signed in the two languages; under the procedure adopted, one of the two originals was in English, for the Government of the United States, and the other was in

Italian, for the Government of the Two Sicilies. Accordingly, the United States instrument of ratification of January 19, 1833, a facsimile of which, obtained from the archives at Rome, is in the file, includes the English text only; and the ratification on the part of the Two Sicilies of June 2, 1833, includes the Italian text only. It is from that latter document that the Italian text here printed is taken. It will be observed that the heading or title of the convention is there omitted. The *alternat* was observed, as the King of the Kingdom of the Two Sicilies is named first throughout the Italian text and the signature of the Prince of Cassaro is indicated first.

Other documents in the file are the attested resolution of the Senate of January 19, 1833 (Executive Journal, IV, 301), and the original proclamation of August 27, 1833, which includes the English text of the convention only.

The ratifications were exchanged at Naples on June 8, 1833. The *procès-verbal* of exchange was in English and Italian; a facsimile of the Italian original, obtained from the archives at Rome, is now in the file; and the English original is with the despatch of Auguste Davezac of June 20, 1833 (D. S., 1 Despatches, Italy: Naples, No. 2). Davezac, who was Chargé d'Affaires at The Hague, had a full power dated January 30, 1833, to treat "of and concerning the General commerce between the United States, and the Kingdom of the two Sicilies" (D. S., 2 Credences, 194) and also two letters of credence of the same date (*ibid.*, 195, 196) from President Jackson to the King of the Kingdom of the Two Sicilies, one relating to the exchange of ratifications of the convention and one to negotiations for a treaty of amity, commerce, and navigation. The instructions to Davezac in regard to a commercial treaty were under date of March 13, 1833 (D. S., 14 Instructions, Netherlands, 3–6). The *procès-verbal* is in general in customary form; but doubtless owing to the fact that each instrument of ratification included only one language text of the treaty, it omits any statement regarding the comparison of the texts and in lieu thereof reads: "the said ratifications having been read, [the undersigned] have exchanged the same in the manner adopted in such cases."

Also in the file is the original full power (in Italian) to conclude the convention, given by the King of the Two Sicilies under date of October 13, 1832, to Antonio Maria Statella, Secretary of State for Foreign Affairs. It reads in translation as follows:

Ferdinand II, by the Grace of God King of the Kingdom of the Two Sicilies, of Jerusalem, etc., Duke of Parma, Piacenza, Castro, etc., Grand Hereditary Prince of Tuscany, etc., etc.

As it is Our earnest desire finally to terminate the claims advanced by the Government of the United States of America, in order that the merchants of those States may be recompensed for the losses caused them by Murat, through the capture, sequestration, and destruction of vessels and cargoes owned by them, during the years 1809, 1810, 1811, and 1812; and as We desire thereby to strengthen the ties of friendship with the said Government, for the benefit of Our beloved subjects, whose welfare is always a matter of deep concern to Us; we have decided to arrive at a definitive agreement with it. Therefore, as the President of the United States of America has conferred full powers and authority for this pur-

pose on John Nelson, his Chargé d'Affaires near Our Court, and as We also have
confidence in the intelligence, experience, zeal, and love for Our royal service, of
you, Don Antonio Maria Statella e Naselli, Prince of Cassaro, Marquis of Spacca-
forno, Count Statella, and Grand Hereditary Seneschal of Sicily, Grandee of the
First Class of Spain, Knight of the Grand Cross of Our various orders of San
Ferdinando and of Merit, of San Gennaro, and of Francisco I, Knight of the
Golden Fleece, and Grand Cross of the royal and distinguished Spanish Order of
Carlos III, Gentlemen of Our Chamber in actual service, and Our Minister
Secretary of State for Foreign Affairs, Chief Courier, etc., etc., We have deemed
proper to give to and confer upon you full power and authority, as We hereby do,
to negotiate, adjust, stipulate, and draw up in good and due form the above-
mentioned convention, promising to hold as confirmed and valid, to carry out
precisely, and to ratify within the period which shall be reciprocally established
by agreement, everything that you agree upon and stipulate with the said Chargé
d'Affaires of the Government of the United States of America with regard thereto.
In faith whereof We have had the present special full power drawn up, signed by
Our hand, bearing the seal of Our royal arms, and countersigned by the undersigned, Our Minister Secretary of State for Foreign Affairs, Naples, October
13, 1832.

[Seal]   FERDINANDO

ANTONIO MARIA STATELLA

The full power of John Nelson, the Plenipotentiary of the United
States, was dated October 24, 1831, the date of his commission as
Chargé d'Affaires at Naples (D. S., 2 Credences, 171, 172); it was in
customary form, authorizing him "to agree, treat consult and negotiate of and concerning general Commerce between the United States
and the government of the Kingdom of the two Sicilies; and also on
the subject of Indemnities claimed by Citizens of the United States
from that Government, in reference to the sequestration and confiscation of their property within the Neapolitan dominions, and all
matters and subjects connected therewith, and to conclude and sign a
Treaty or Treaties, Convention or Conventions touching the premises"; but his instructions of October 27, 1831, precluded him from
negotiating in respect of a treaty of commerce until the conclusion of
an agreement regarding the American claims (Senate Document No.
70, 22d Congress, 2d session, serial 230; D. S., 13 Instructions, U. S.
Ministers, 260–68).

No papers accompanied this convention when it was transmitted to
the Senate with the presidential message of December 17, 1832 (Executive Journal, IV, 286); but in response to a resolution of the Senate
requesting all the relevant correspondence (*ibid.*, 292–93), papers
were transmitted with the following presidential message of January
16, 1833 (*ibid.*, 300):

In conformity with a resolution of the Senate of the 31st December last, I
herewith transmit copies of the instructions under which the late treaty of indemnity with Naples was negotiated, and of all the correspondence relative thereto.

It will appear evident from a perusal of some of those documents that they are
written by the agents of the United States to their own Government with a
freedom, as far as relates to the officers of that of Naples, which was never intended
for the public eye, and as they might, if printed, accidentally find their way
abroad and thereby embarrass our ministers in their future operations in foreign
countries, I respectfully recommend that in the printing, if deemed necessary,
such a discrimination be made as to avoid that inconvenience, preferring this
course to withholding from the Senate any part of the correspondence.

Some of those papers were printed and the injunction of secrecy removed therefrom (*ibid.*, 309); that print of February 9, 1833, is Senate Document No. 70, 22d Congress, 2d session, serial 230.

The convention was communicated to Congress with the presidential message of January 24, 1833 (Richardson, II, 633). The act to carry the convention into effect was passed on March 2, 1833 (4 Statutes at Large, 666–67), which, while after the date of ratification by the United States, was prior to the going into force of the convention, as the ratifications were not exchanged at Naples until June 8, 1833. Thereafter the convention was again communicated to Congress with the presidential message of May 13, 1834 (Richardson, III, 50).

THE KINGDOM OF THE TWO SICILIES

The Two Sicilies, Sicily proper and Sicily beyond the Faro, or the Kingdom of Naples, as commonly called, had at various times been united under one government. The Kingdom of the Two Sicilies with which this convention was made was proclaimed on December 8, 1816, by King Ferdinand IV of Naples (III of Sicily and I of the Two Sicilies). In 1860–61 the Kingdom of the Two Sicilies became part of Italy under King Victor Emmanuel II.

A diplomatic representative of the United States was first received at Naples in 1816 (see Moore, International Arbitrations, V, 4576–78); on February 28 of that year, William Pinkney, of Maryland, was nominated by President Madison as Minister to Russia, "with a special mission to the King of the Two Sicilies" (Executive Journal, III, 32). The nomination of Pinkney as Minister to Russia was confirmed on March 7, but in respect of the special mission to the King of the Two Sicilies it was rejected (*ibid.*, 35). On April 17 Pinkney was again nominated by the following presidential message (*ibid.*, 45, April 20):

It being presumed that further information may have changed the views of the Senate, relative to the importance and expediency of a mission to Naples, for the purpose of negotiating indemnities to our citizens for spoliations committed by the Neapolitan government, I nominate William Pinkney, Envoy Extraordinary and Minister Plenipotentiary to Russia, to be Minister Plenipotentiary to Naples, specially charged with that trust.

The nomination of Pinkney was duly confirmed by the Senate on April 23, 1816, by a vote of eighteen to fifteen (*ibid.*, 46); and he was commissioned on the same day.

MURAT

Murat (Joachim Murat, 1767–1815) is named in the heading, in the preamble, and in Article 1 of the convention, without title and without reference to his authority except that it was exercised during the years 1809–12. Murat was a distinguished cavalry leader in the French Army during the Napoleonic wars. In 1800 he married Caroline, the youngest sister of Napoleon Bonaparte. By the decree of Napoleon of July 15, 1808, he was appointed on August 1 to the

throne of Naples, which he held until 1815. He styled himself Joachim Napoleon, King of the Two Sicilies, but his rule was limited to the Kingdom of Naples and at no time extended to Sicily proper. After losing his throne, Murat returned with a hostile expedition, was captured and courtmartialed, and was shot at Pizzo, in Calabria, on October 13, 1815.

THE CLAIMS SETTLEMENT

An account of the claims settled by this convention and their origin, of the negotiations of 1816, of 1825–26, of those leading directly to this convention, and of the proceedings of the Commissioners appointed to examine the American claims pursuant to the act of March 2, 1833 (4 Statutes at Large, 666–67), and to Article 1 of the convention, will be found in Moore, International Arbitrations, V, 4575–89.

The proceedings of the board of Commissioners lasted from September 19, 1833, until March 17, 1835, when their report was made, the time allowed by the original act for their task having been extended (act of June 19, 1834, 4 Statutes at Large, 680). The total of their awards, including 20 per cent for interest, was $1,925,034.68 (Moore, *op. cit.*, 4581–89). A list of the awards is in House Document No. 242, 24th Congress, 1st session, serial 291.

Taking the Neapolitan ducat at 83 cents, the total amount of the indemnity (without interest), 2,115,000 Neapolitan ducats, would be $1,755,450 (see Moore, *op. cit.*, 4581); at the same rate, the amount reserved for the expenses of the Government of the United States, 7,679 ducats (Article 1), would be $6,373.57.

The nine annual instalments of this indemnity of 235,000 ducats each were, by the terms of the convention, payable at Naples on June 8 of each year from 1834 to 1842, inclusive, with interest; including the interest at 4 per cent, the total was 2,538,000 ducats, the instalments (with the interest) ranging from 319,600 ducats in 1834 to 244,400 in 1842.

The nine instalments were duly paid; papers showing in detail the collection of the first four instalments (1834 to 1837, inclusive) through bankers in Paris, are in Senate Document No. 351, 25th Congress, 2d session, serial 317; the aggregate amount thereof, as received at the Treasury after deduction of expenses, was $995,965.62 (*ibid.*, 75–76). In Senate Executive Document No. 38, 44th Congress, 2d session, serial 1720, pages 59, 104, are given the figures of the total receipts and expenditures under the convention. The receipts for the nine instalments, up to and including the amount reaching the Treasury in 1843, aggregated $2,049,033.12. The sum received under Article 1 was $6,235.34.

PROPOSED MODIFICATION AS TO PAYMENT

After the going into force of this convention efforts were made by the Government of the Two Sicilies to reach an agreement with the Government of the United States for a lump-sum payment in lieu of the annual instalments. The first offer to commute the payments

(at a discount of 25 per cent) was made under date of December 14, 1833, even before the first instalment was due (D. S., 1 Despatches, Italy: Naples, No. 6, January 20, 1834, enclosure). Considerable correspondence followed in 1834 and 1835 between the Secretary of State and Domenico Morelli, Consul General of the Kingdom of the Two Sicilies (D. S., 1 Notes from the Neapolitan Legation; 5 Notes to Foreign Legations). This Government at first declined to enter into any such arrangement, on the ground that it had no authority to do so "without the assent of those individuals entitled to share the indemnity" (*ibid.*, 197, March 17, 1834; see also Richardson, III, 98); and on March 3, 1835, an "act to authorize the Secretary of the Treasury to compromise the claims allowed by the commissioners under the treaty with the King of the Two Sicilies, concluded October 14, 1832," failed to become a law because of the veto of President Jackson, who stated his reasons in his message as follows (Richardson, III, 146):

> I respectfully return to the Senate, where it originated, the "act to authorize the Secretary of the Treasury to compromise the claims allowed by the commissioners under the treaty with the King of the Two Sicilies, concluded October 14, 1832," without my signature.
>
> This act is, in my judgment, inconsistent with the division of powers in the Constitution of the United States, as it is obviously founded on the assumption that an act of Congress can give power to the Executive or to the head of one of the Departments to negotiate with a foreign government. The debt due by the King of the Two Sicilies will, after the commissioners have made their decision, become the private vested property of the citizens of the United States to whom it may be awarded. Neither the Executive nor the Legislature can properly interfere with it without their consent. With their consent the Executive has competent authority to negotiate about it for them with a foreign government—an authority Congress can not constitutionally abridge or increase.

On December 23, 1835, the Consul General of the Two Sicilies communicated to the Secretary of State documents stated to contain the consents and signatures of all the claimants interested, to a single payment of 1,500,000 Neapolitan ducats in lieu of the seven instalments, aggregating 1,645,000 ducats principal, which then remained to be paid. Five days earlier Morelli had communicated an extract from his instructions, as evidencing his power to treat; these were somewhat vague as to the amount of reduction authorized to be accepted. Thereupon the following agreement (the original of which is in the file of Treaty Series No. 362) was signed on December 26, 1835:

> The claimants entitled to indemnity by the award of the Commissioners under the Convention with the Kingdom of The Two Sicilies, concluded on the fourteenth of October Eighteen Hundred and Thirty Two, having agreed to an arrangement proposed by the Consul General of the King of The Two Sicilies, to receive in full payment of the balance of the indemnity remaining unpaid under said Convention, One Million Five Hundred Thousand Neapolitan ducats, to be paid in Naples, on the eighth day of February Eighteen Hundred and Thirty six; and having authorised and requested the Government of the United States to adopt the measures necessary to accomplish that object; the President of the United States has empowered and directed the Secretary of State to make with the Chevalier Morelli, who has the instructions and powers of his Government for that purpose, the following arrangement:

On the deposite in the Treasury Department by the claimants under the Treaty of Indemnity of their several Certificates, the Secretary of the Treasury will give directions to the Agent of the United States, to apply in Naples for One Million Five Hundred Thousand Neapolitan ducats, on or after the eighth day of February Eighteen Hundred and Thirty Six, to His Sicilian Majesty's Government, which, if paid, will be considered by the United States as a full and complete execution of the said Treaty. The said One Million Five Hundred Thousand ducats shall be distributed *pro rata* among the claimants, according to the amount of their Certificates in the Treasury Department, as the several instalments would have been paid if this arrangement had not been made. The certificates shall be delivered to His Sicilian Majesty's Government, or such other disposition made of them as it shall direct. If the said sum of One Million Five Hundred Thousand Neapolitan ducats shall not be paid within forty eight hours after the demand so as aforesaid to be made by the Agent of the United States at Naples, this arrangement shall be void and of no effect.

Signed at the City of Washington, on the Twenty sixth day of December, A. D. 1835, by John Forsyth, Secretary of State, on the part of the United States, and the Chevalier Morelli, on the part of His Majesty the King of the Two Sicilies.

JOHN FORSYTH
Sc^v of State of the United States
THE CHEVALIER DOMENICO MORELLI
His Sicilian Majesty's Consul General at the U. S.

That agreement, however, was not approved by the Government of the Two Sicilies; and under date of May 16, 1836, Secretary of State Forsyth was so informed by a note of Consul General Morelli which contained the following (D. S., 1 Notes from the Neapolitan Legation, translation):

The undersigned, Consul General of the Two Sicilies, has the honor to inform the Honorable J. Forsyth, Secretary of State of the United States, that the Royal Government has not entirely approved the convention signed on the 26th December last for the payment of the million and a half of ducats in discharge of the sum due according to the treaty of 1832.

The Royal Government has communicated to the undersigned a decree by which arrangements were made for the immediate payment of 1,222,000 ducats by the Royal Treasury to the United States, in discharge of the obligations contracted by the said convention, with the interest from the 9th of June, 1835, ordering, moreover, that in case the offer of this sum should not be accepted by the claimants in the United States, it should be immediately withdrawn, and the Royal Government would merely make the payments as already agreed on at the appointed times.

The Royal Government will, therefore, on the 8th of June next, pay the third instalment of 235,000 ducats with the interest; and should it then please the Government of the United States to receive the 987,000 ducats making up the sum of 1,222,000 ducats offered for the payment of the whole as by the treaty of 1832, it will only have to give authority to its agents, to draw that amount from the Royal Treasury.

This new proposal of the Government of the Two Sicilies was therefore, after the payment of the third instalment of the indemnity with interest, to commute the remaining six instalments, or 1,410,000 ducats, for a single payment of 987,000 ducats, a reduction of just 30 per cent. The answering note of Secretary of State Forsyth of May 24 (D. S., 6 Notes to Legations of Italian States, 18) made no reference to that new proposal, but referred only to the statements that the convention of December 26, 1835, had not been approved

by the Government of the Two Sicilies and that the third instalment of the indemnity would be paid with interest on the following June 8.

The payments of the indemnity accordingly proceeded pursuant to the terms of the convention of October 14, 1832, and were made in each year up to 1842, when the ninth instalment was paid.

The agreement signed on December 26, 1835, has been printed in various treaty collections without note of the fact that that agreement was not approved by the Government of the Two Sicilies (e.g., Haswell, 1101–2; Malloy, II, 1805–6).

Treaty Series No. 299
8 Statutes at Large, 444–53
18 *ibid.*, pt. 2, Public Treaties, 666–70

75

RUSSIA : DECEMBER 18, 1832

Treaty of Navigation and Commerce, with separate article, signed at
St. Petersburg (Leningrad) December 18, 1832 (December 6, Old
Style). Original in English and French.
Submitted to the Senate February 22, 1833. Resolution of advice
and consent February 27, 1833. Ratified by the United States
April 8, 1833. Ratified by Russia January 8, 1833 (December 27,
1832, Old Style). Ratifications exchanged at Washington May 11,
1833. Proclaimed May 11, 1833.

In the name of the most Holy and indivisible Trinity

The United States of America, and His Majesty the Emperor of all the Russias, equally animated with the desire of maintaining the relations of good understanding, which have hitherto so happily subsisted between their respective States, and of extending, and consolidating the commercial intercourse between them, have agreed to enter into negotiations for the conclusion of a Treaty of navigation and commerce. For which purpose the President of the United States has conferred full powers on James Buchanan their Envoy Extraordinary and Minister Plenipotentiary near His Imperial Majesty; and His Majesty the Emperor of all the Russias has conferred like powers on the Sieur Charles Robert Count de Nesselrode, His Vice-Chancel-

Au nom de la très-Sainte et indivisible Trinité.

Les Etats-Unis d'Amérique et Sa Majesté L'Empereur de toutes les Russies, également animés du désir de maintenir les rapports de bonne intelligence qui ont si heureusement subsisté jusqu'ici entre leurs Etats respectifs, et d'en étendre et consolider les relations commerciales, sont convenus d'entrer en négociation pour conclure un traité de commerce et de navigation. A cet effet, le Président des Etats-Unis a muni de ses pleinspouvoirs le Sieur James Buchanan, Envoyé Extraordinaire et Ministre Plénipotentiaire des Etats-Unis près Sa Majesté Impériale, et Sa Majesté L'Empereur de toutes les Russies a muni des mêmes pouvoirs le Sieur Charles Robert Comte de Nesselrode, Son Vice-Chancelier, Chevalier des ordres

lor, Knight of the orders of Russia and of many others &c: and the said Plenipotentiaries having exchanged their full powers, found in good and due form, have concluded and signed the following Articles:

ARTICLE 1.

There shall be between the territories of the high contracting parties, a reciprocal liberty of commerce and navigation. The inhabitants of their respective States shall, mutually, have liberty to enter the ports, places, and rivers of the territories of each party, wherever foreign commerce is permitted. They shall be at liberty to sojourn and reside in all parts whatsoever of said territories, in order to attend to their affairs, and they shall enjoy, to that effect, the same security and protection as natives of the country wherein they reside, on condition of their submitting to the laws and ordinances there prevailing, and particularly to the regulations in force concerning commerce.

ARTICLE II.

Russ_an vessels arriving either laden or in ballast, in the ports of the United States of America; and, reciprocally, vessels of the United States arriving either laden, or in ballast, in the ports of the Empire of Russia, shall be treated, on their entrance, during their stay, and at their departure,

de Russie et de plusieurs autres &c:, lesquels Plénipotentiaires, après avoir échangé leurs Pleinspouvoirs, trouvés en bonne et due forme, ont arrêté et signé les articles suivans:

ARTICLE I

Il y aura entre les territoires des hautes parties contractantes, liberté et réciprocité de commerce et de navigation. Les habitans de leurs Etats respectifs pourront réciproquement entrer dans les ports, places et rivières des territoires de chacune d'elles, partout où le commerce étranger est permis. Ils seront libres de s'y arrêter et résider dans quelque partie que ce soit des dits territoires pour y vaquer à leurs affaires; et ils jouiront à cet effet de la même sécurité et protection, que les habitans du pays, dans lequel ils résideront, à charge de se soumettre aux lois et ordonnances y établies, et en particulier, aux réglemens de commerce en vigueur.

ARTICLE II.

Les bâtimens Russes, arrivant sur lest ou chargés dans les ports des Etats-Unis d'Amérique, et réciproquement les bâtimens des Etats-Unis, arrivant sur lest ou chargés, dans les ports de l'Empire de Russie, seront traités à leur entrée, pendant leur séjour, et à leur sortie, sur le même pied,

upon the same footing as national vessels, coming from the same place, with respect to the duties of tonnage. In regard to light house duties, pilotage, and port charges, as well as to the fees and perquisites of public officers, and all other duties and charges, of whatever kind or denomination, levied upon vessels of commerce, in the name or to the profit of the Government, the local authorities, or of any private establishments whatsoever, the high contracting parties shall reciprocally treat each other, upon the footing of the most favored nations, with whom they have not Treaties now actually in force, regulating the said duties and charges on the basis of an entire reciprocity.

Article III.

All kind of merchandise and articles of commerce, which may be lawfully imported into the ports of the Empire of Russia in Russian vessels, may, also, be so imported in vessels of the United States of America, without paying other or higher duties or charges, of whatever kind or denomination, levied in the name, or to the profit of the Government, the local authorities, or of any private establishments whatsoever, than if the same merchandise or articles of commerce had been imported in Russian vessels. And, reciprocally, all kind of merchandise and articles of commerce, which may be lawfully imported into the ports

que les bâtimens nationaux, venant du même lieu, par rapport aux droits de tonnage. Pour ce qui concerne les droits de fanaux, de pilotage et de port, ainsi que les vacations des officiers publics, et tout autre droit ou charge, de quelque espèce ou dénomination que ce soit, perçus des bâtimens de commerce au nom ou au profit du Gouvernement, des autorités locales ou d'établissemens particuliers quelconques, les hautes parties contractantes se traiteront réciproquement sur le pied des nations les plus favorisées, avec lesquelles elles n'ont pas de traité actuellement en vigueur, qui règle les dits droits et charges sur la base d'une entière réciprocité.

Article III.

Toute espèce de marchandises et objets de commerce qui pourront légalement être importés dans les ports de l'Empire de Russie sur des bâtimens Russes, pourront également y être importés sur des bâtimens des Etats-Unis d'Amérique, sans payer d'autres ou de plus forts droits ou charges, de quelque espèce ou dénomination que ce soit, perçus au nom ou au profit du Gouvernement, des autorités locales, ou d'établissemens particuliers quelconques, que s'ils étaient importés sur des bâtimens Russes. Et, réciproquement, toute espèce de marchandise et objets de commerce qui pourront légalement

of the United States of America, in vessels of the said States, may, also, be so imported in Russian vessels, without paying other or higher duties or charges, of whatever kind or denomination, levied in the name, or to the profit of the Government, the local authorities, or of any private establishments whatsoever, than if the same merchandise or articles of commerce had been imported in vessels of the United States of America.

ARTICLE IV.

It is understood that the stipulations contained in the two preceding Articles, are, to their full extent, applicable to Russian vessels, and their cargoes, arriving in the ports of the United States of America; and, reciprocally, to vessels of the said States and their cargoes, arriving in the ports of the Empire of Russia, whether the said vessels clear directly from the ports of the country to which they respectively belong, or from the ports of any other foreign country.

ARTICLE V.

All kind of merchandise and articles of commerce, which may be lawfully exported from the ports of the United States of America in national vessels may, also, be exported therefrom in Russian vessels, without paying other or higher duties or charges, of whatever kind or denomination, levied

être importés dans les ports des Etats-Unis d'Amérique sur les bâtimens des dits Etats, pourront également y être importés sur des bâtimens Russes, sans payer d'autres ou de plus forts droits ou charges de quelque espèce ou dénomination que ce soit, perçus au nom ou au profit du Gouvernement des Autorités locales ou d'établissemens particuliers quelconques, que s'ils étaient importés sur des bâtimens des Etats-Unis d'Amérique.

ARTICLE IV.

Il est entendu que les stipulations contenues dans les deux articles précédens sont, dans toute leur plénitude, applicables aux bâtimens Russes et leurs cargaisons, arrivant dans les ports des Etats-Unis d'Amérique; et, réciproquement aux bâtimens des dits Etats et leurs cargaisons, arrivant dans les ports de l'Empire de Russie, soit que les dits batimens viennent des ports du pays, auquel ils appartiennent, soit de ceux de tout autre pays étranger.

ARTICLE V.

Toute espèce de marchandises et objets de commerce, qui pourront être légalement exportés des ports des Etats-Unis d'Amérique sur des bâtimens nationaux, pourront également en être exportés sur des bâtimens Russes, sans payer d'autres ni de plus forts droits ou charges, de quelque espèce ou

in the name, or to the profit of the Government, the local authorities, or of any private establishments whatsoever, than if the same merchandise or articles of commerce had been exported in vessels of the United States of America. And, reciprocally, all kind of merchandise and articles of commerce, which may be lawfully exported from the ports of the Empire of Russia in national vessels, may also be exported therefrom in vessels of the United States of America, without paying other or higher duties or charges of whatever kind or denomination, levied in the name, or to the profit of the Government, the local authorities, or of any private establishments whatsoever, than if the same merchandise or articles of commerce had been exported in Russian vessels.

ARTICLE VI

No higher or other duties shall be imposed on the importation into the United States, of any article, the produce or manufacture of Russia; and no higher or other duties shall be imposed on the importation into the Empire of Russia, of any article, the produce or manufacture of the United States, than are, or shall be, payable on the like article, being the produce or manufacture of any other foreign country. Nor shall any prohibition be imposed on the

dénomination que ce soit, perçus au nom ou au profit du Gouvernement, des autorités locales, ou d'établissemens particuliers quelconques, que si ces mêmes marchandises ou denrées étaient exportées par des bâtimens des Etats-Unis d'Amérique. Et, réciproquement, toute espèce de marchandise et objets de commerce qui pourront être légalement exportés des ports de l'Empire de Russie, sur des bâtimens nationaux, pourront également en être exportés sur des bâtimens des Etats-Unis d'Amérique, sans payer d'autres ou de plus forts droits ou charges, de quelque espèce ou dénomination que ce soit, perçus au nom ou au profit du Gouvernement, des autorités locales, ou d'établissemens particuliers quelconques, que si ces marchandises ou denrées étaient exportées sur des bâtimens Russes.

ARTICLE VI.

Il ne sera imposé d'autres ni de plus forts droits sur l'importation dans les Etats-Unis des articles, provenant du sol ou de l'industrie de l'Empire de Russie; et il ne sera imposé d'autres ni de plus forts droits sur l'importation dans l'Empire de Russie, des articles provenant du sol ou de l'industrie des Etats-Unis, que ceux qui sont, ou seront imposés sur les mêmes articles provenant du sol ou de l'industrie de tout autre pays étranger. De même, il ne sera

importation or exportation of any article the produce or manufacture of the United States, or of Russia, to, or from the ports of the United States, or to, or from the ports of the Russian Empire, which shall not equally extend to all other nations.

Article VII.

It is expressly understood that the preceding Articles II, III, IV, V, and VI shall not be applicable to the coastwise navigation of either of the two countries, which each of the high contracting parties reserves exclusively to itself.

Article VIII.

The two contracting parties shall have the liberty of having, in their respective ports, Consuls, Vice-Consuls, Agents and Commissaries of their own appointment, who shall enjoy the same privileges and powers, as those of the most favored nations; but if any such Consul shall exercise commerce, they shall be submitted to the same laws and usages to which the private individuals of their nation are submitted, in the same place.

The Consuls, Vice-Consuls, and Commercial Agents shall have the right, as such, to sit as judges and arbitrators in such differences as may arise between the Captains and crews of the vessels

imposé sur l'importation ou sur l'exportation des articles provenant du sol ou de l'industrie des Etats-Unis ou de l'Empire de Russie, à l'entrée ou à la sortie des ports des Etats-Unis, ou de ceux de l'Empire de Russie, aucune prohibition, qui ne soit pas également applicable à toute autre nation.

Article VII.

Il est expressément entendu que les articles précédens II. III. IV. V. et VI. ne sont point applicables à la navigation de côte ou cabotage de chacun des deux pays, que l'une et l'autre des hautes parties contractantes se réservent exclusivement.

Article VIII.

Les deux parties contractantes auront la faculté d'avoir dans leurs ports respectifs des Consuls, Vice-Consuls, Agens et Commissaires de leur choix, qui jouiront des mêmes privilèges et pouvoirs dont jouissent ceux des nations les plus favorisées; mais dans le cas où les dits Consuls veulent faire le commerce, ils seront soumis aux mêmes lois et usages, auxquels sont soumis les particuliers de leur nation à l'endroit où ils résident.

Les Consuls, Vice-Consuls et Agens Commerciaux auront le droit, comme tels, de servir de juges et d'arbitres dans les différends qui pourraient s'élever entre les Capitaines et les équi-

belonging to the nation whose interests are committed to their charge, without the interference of the local authorities, unless the conduct of the crews, or of the captain, should disturb the order or the tranquillity of the Country; or the said Consuls, Vice-Consuls, or Commercial Agents should require their assistance to cause their decisions to be carried into effect or supported. It is, however, understood, that this species of judgment or arbitration shall not deprive the contending parties of the right they have to resort, on their return, to the judicial authority of their Country.

ARTICLE IX.

The said Consuls, Vice-Consuls, and Commercial Agents, are authorised to require the assistance of the local authorities, for the search, arrest, detention and imprisonment of the deserters from the ships of war and merchant vessels of their country. For this purpose they shall apply to the competent tribunals, judges, and officers, and shall, in writing, demand said deserters, proving by the exhibition of the registers of the vessels, the rolls of the crews, or by other official documents that such individuals formed part of the crews; and, this reclamation being thus substantiated, the surrender shall not be refused.

Such deserters, when arrested, shall be placed at the disposal of

56006°—33——48

pages des bâtimens de la nation, dont ils soignent les intérêts, sans que les autorités locales puissent y intervenir, à moins que la conduite des équipages ou du Capitaine ne troublât l'ordre ou la tranquillité du pays, ou que les dits Consuls, Vice-Consuls ou Agens Commerciaux, ne réquissent leur intervention pour faire exécuter ou maintenir leurs décisions; bien entendu que cette espèce de jugement ou d'arbitrage ne saurait pourtant priver les parties contendantes du droit qu'elles ont à leur retour, de recourir aux autorités judiciaires de leur pays.

ARTICLE IX.

Les dits Consuls, Vice-Consuls ou Agens commerciaux sont autorisés à requérir l'assistance des autorités locales pour la recherche, l'arrestation, la détention et l'emprisonnement des déserteurs des navires de guerre & marchands de leur pays, ils s'adresseront pour cet objet, aux tribunaux, juges et officiers compétens, et réclameront par écrit, les déserteurs susmentionnés prouvant par la communication des régistres de navires, ou rôles de l'équipage, ou par d'autres documens officiels, que de tels individus ont fait partie des dits équipages, et cette réclamation ainsi prouvée, l'extradition ne sera point refusée.

De tels déserteurs, lorsqu'ils auront été arrêtés, seront mis à

the said Consuls, Vice Consuls, or Commercial Agents, and may be confined in the public prisons, at the request and cost of those who shall claim them, in order to be detained until the time when they shall be restored to the vessels to which they belonged, or sent back to their own country by a vessel of the same nation or any other vessel whatsoever. But if not sent back within four months, from the day of their arrest, they shall be set at liberty, and shall not be again arrested for the same cause.

However, if the deserter should be found to have committed any crime or offence, his surrender may be delayed until the tribunal before which his case shall be depending shall have pronounced it's sentence, and such sentence shall have been carried into effect.

Article X.

The citizens and subjects of each of the high contracting parties shall have power to dispose of their personal goods within the jurisdiction of the other, by testament, donation, or otherwise, and their representatives, being citizens or subjects of the other party, shall succeed to their said personal goods, whether by testament or *ab intestato*, and may take possession thereof, either by themselves, or by others acting

la disposition des dits Consuls, Vice-Consuls ou Agens commerciaux, et pourront être enfermés dans les prisons publiques, à la réquisition & aux frais de ceux qui les réclament, pour être détenus jusqu'au moment, où ils seront rendus aux navires, auxquels ils appartenaient, ou renvoyés dans leur patrie par un bâtiment de la même nation ou un autre bâtiment quelconque. Mais s'ils ne sont pas renvoyés dans l'espace de quatre mois, à compter du jour de leur arrestation, ils seront mis en liberté et ne seront plus arretés pour la même cause.

Toutefois, si le déserteur se trouvait avoir commis quelque crime ou délit, il pourra être sursis à son extradition jusqu'à ce que le tribunal, nanti de l'affaire, aura rendu sa sentence, et que celle-ci ait reçu son exécution.

Article X.

Les citoyens et sujets de chacune des hautes parties contractantes auront, dans les Etats de l'autre, la liberté de disposer de leurs biens personnels, soit par testament, donation ou autrement; et leurs héritiers, étant citoyens ou sujets de l'autre partie contractante, succéderont à leurs biens, soit en vertu d'un testament, soit *ab intestato*, et ils pourront en prendre possession, soit en personne, soit par d'autres agis-

for them, and dispose of the same, at will, paying to the profit of the respective Governments, such dues only as the inhabitants of the country wherein the said goods are, shall be subject to pay in like cases. And in case of the absence of the representative, such care shall be taken of the said goods, as would be taken of the goods of a native of the same country, in like case, until the lawful owner may take measures for receiving them. And if a question should arise among several claimants, as to which of them said goods belong, the same shall be decided finally by the laws and judges of the land wherein the said goods are. And where, on the death of any person holding real estate, within the territories of one of the high contracting parties, such real estate would, by the laws of the land, descend on a citizen or subject of the other party, who by reason of alienage may be incapable of holding it, he shall be allowed the time fixed by the laws of the country, and in case the laws of the country, actually in force, may not have fixed any such time, he shall then be allowed a reasonable time to sell such real estate and to withdraw and export the proceeds without molestation, and without paying to the profit of the respective Governments, any other dues than those to

sant en leur place, et en disposeront à volonté, en ne payant, au profit des Gouvernemens respectifs, d'autres droits, que ceux, auxquels les habitans du pays, où se trouvent les dits bien, sont assujettis en pareille occasion. En cas d'absence des héritiers, on prendra provisoirement des dits biens les mêmes soins, qu'on aurait pris, en pareille occasion, des biens des natifs du même pays, jusqu'à ce que le propriétaire légitime ait pris des arrangemens pour recueillir l'héritage. S'il s'élève des contestations entre les différens prétendans ayant droit à la succession, elles seront décidées en dernier ressort, selon les lois et par les juges du pays où la succession est vacante. Et si, par la mort de quelque personne possédant des biens-fonds sur le territoire de l'une des hautes parties contractantes, ces bien-fonds venaient à passer, selon les lois du pays, à un citoyen ou sujet de l'autre partie, et que celui-ci, par sa qualité d'étranger, fût inhabile à les posséder, il jouira du délai fixé par les lois du pays, et dans le cas où les lois du pays actuellement existantes n'en fixeraient aucun, il obtiendra un délai convenable pour vendre ces biensfonds et pour en retirer et exporter le produit sans obstacle et sans payer au profit des Gouvernemens respectifs, d'autres droits que ceux, auxquels les habitans du

which the inhabitants of the country wherein said real estate is situated, shall be subject to pay, in like cases. But this Article shall not derogate, in any manner, from the force of the laws already published, or which may hereafter be published by His Majesty the Emperor of all the Russias: to prevent the emigration of his subjects.

pays où se trouvent les biens-fonds, sont assujettis en pareille occasion. Mais cet article ne dérogera en aucune manière à la force des lois qui ont déjà été publiées ou qui pourraient l'être par la suite, par Sa Majesté L'Empereur de toutes les Russies, pour prévenir l'émigration de Ses sujets.

Article XI.

If either party shall, hereafter, grant to any other nation, any particular favor in navigation or commerce, it shall, immediately, become common to the other party, freely, where it is freely granted to such other nation, or on yeilding the same compensation, when the grant is conditional.

Article XI.

Si l'une des parties contractantes accorde par la suite à d'autres nations quelque faveur particulière en fait de commerce ou de navigation, cette faveur deviendra aussitôt commune à l'autre partie, qui en jouira gratuitement, si la concession est gratuite, ou en accordant la même compensation, si la concession est conditionnelle.

Article XII.

The present treaty, of which the effect shall extend, in like manner, to the Kingdom of Poland, so far as the same may be applicable thereto, shall continue in force until the first day of January, in the year of our Lord one thousand Eight hundred and Thirty nine, and if, one year before that day, one of the high contracting parties, shall not have announced to the other, by an official notification, it's intention to arrest the operation thereof, this treaty shall

Article XII.

Le présent traité dont l'effet s'étendra également au Royaume de Pologne, pour autant qu'il peut lui être applicable, restera en vigueur jusqu'au 1er Janvier de l'an de grâce 1839. et si, un an avant ce terme, l'une des hautes parties contractantes n'avait pas annoncé à l'autre, par une notification officielle, son intention d'en faire cesser l'effet, ce traité restera obligatoire une année au delà et ainsi de suite, jusqu'à l'expiration de l'année qui commencera après

remain obligatory one year beyond that day, and so on, until the expiration of the year which shall commence after the date of a similar notification.

la date d'une semblable notification.

Article XIII.

The present Treaty shall be approved and ratified by the President of the United States of America, by and with the advice and consent of the Senate of the said States, and by His Majesty the Emperor of all the Russias; and the ratifications shall be exchanged in the City of Washington within the space of one year, or sooner if possible.

In faith whereof, the respective Plenipotentiaries have signed the present treaty in duplicate and affixed thereto the seal of their arms. Done at St Petersburg the sixth/Eighteenth December, in the year of Grace, One thousand Eight hundred and thirty two.

JAMES BUCHANAN [Seal]

Article XIII.

Le présent traité sera approuvé et ratifié par le Président des Etats-Unis d'Amérique, par et avec l'avis et le consentement du Sénat des dits Etats, et par Sa Majesté L'Empereur de toutes les Russies; et les ratifications en seront échangées en la ville de Washington dans l'espace d'un an, ou plutôt si faire se peut.

En foi de quoi, les Plénipotentiaires respectifs ont signé le présent traité en duplicata, et y ont apposé le cachet de leurs armes. Fait à Saint-Petersbourg le six/dix huit Décembre l'an de grace mil-huit-cent-trente-deux.

[Seal] CHARLES
COMTE DE NESSELRODE

SEPERATE ARTICLE

Certain relations of proximity and anterior engagements, having rendered it necessary for the Imperial Government to regulate the commercial relations of Russia with Prussia and the Kingdoms of Sweden and Norway by special stipulations, now actually in force, and which may be renewed hereafter; which stipulations are, in no manner, con-

ARTICLE SÉPARÉ.

Des rapports de voisinage et des engagemens antérieurs, ayant mis le Gouvernement Impérial dans le cas de régler les relations commerciales de la Russie avec la Prusse et les Royaumes de Suède et de Norvège, par des stipulations spéciales, actuellement en vigueur, et qui pourront être renouvelées dans la suite, sans que les dites stipulations soient liées aux régle-

nected with the existing regulations for foreign commerce in general: the two high contracting parties, wishing to remove from their commercial relations every kind of ambiguity or subject of discussion, have agreed, that the special stipulations granted to the commerce of Prussia, and of Sweden and Norway, in consideration of equivalent advantages granted in these countries, by the one to the commerce of the Kingdom of Poland, and by the other to that of the Grand Dutchy of Finland, shall not, in any case, be invoked in favor of the relations of commerce and navigation, sanctioned between the two high contracting parties by the present Treaty.

The present Seperate Article shall have the same force & value as if it were inserted, word for word, in the Treaty signed this day, and shall be ratified at the same time.

In faith whereof, we, the undersigned, by virtue of our respective full powers, have signed the present Seperate Article, and affixed thereto the seals of our arms.

Done at S! Petersburg, the 6/18 of December, in the year of Grace, one Thousand Eight hundred & thirty Two.

JAMES BUCHANAN   [Seal]

mens existans pour le commerce étranger en général, les deux hautes parties-contractantes, voulant écarter de leurs relations commerciales toute espèce d'équivoque ou de motif de discussion, sont tombées d'accord, que ces stipulations spéciales accordées au commerce de la Prusse, de la Suède et de la Norvège, en considération d'avantages équivalens, accordés dans ces pays, d'une part au commerce du Royaume de Pologne, de l'autre à celui du Grand-Duché de Finlande, ne pourront dans aucun cas être invoquées en faveur des relations de commerce et de navigation, sanctionnées entre les deux hautes parties contractantes par le présent traité.

Le présent article séparé aura la même force et valeur que s'il était inséré mot à mot dans le traité signé aujourd'hui, et sera ratifié en même temps.

En foi de quoi, nous Soussignés, en vertu de nos pleinpouvoirs respectifs, avons signé le présent Article séparé et y avons apposé le cachet de nos armes.

Fait à Saint-Pétersbourg le six/dix huit Décembre, l'an de grace mil-huit-cent-trente-deux.

[Seal]   CHARLES
COMTE DE NESSELRODE

NOTES

Unless otherwise stated, dates in the headnote and in these notes are in the New Style, or present calendar, which was then twelve days later than the Old Style.

THE FILE PAPERS

The treaty file is complete, including the attested resolution of advice and consent of the Senate of February 27, 1833 (Executive Journal, IV, 316–17). According to the testimonium clause of the treaty, it was signed in duplicate. One original of the treaty and one of the separate article (a separate document) are in the file; each is written in English and French, with the English on the left pages; and the two documents are bound with the duplicate United States instrument of ratification of April 8 and the original proclamation of May 11, 1833. There are two Russian instruments of ratification, one for the treaty proper and one for the separate article, each written in Russian and dated December 27, 1832 (Old Style), with the treaty texts in both languages, the French in the left columns. The certificate of the exchange of ratifications at Washington on May 11, 1833, is in customary form, in French and English, with the French on the left pages.

The only paper accompanying the treaty when it was transmitted to the Senate with the presidential message of February 22, 1833, was an extract from the long despatch of James Buchanan, Minister to Russia, under date of December 20, 1832 (D. S., 12 Despatches, Russia, No. 9), which enclosed the treaty; but from the Executive Journal (IV, 313–17) it appears that not even the text of the treaty was printed for the Senate at that time; and no Senate document of that period containing the text has been found. The treaty was before the Senate for only a few days; it was referred to the Committee on Foreign Relations on the day of its receipt, February 22, 1833, and the resolution of advice and consent was unanimously adopted on the day that it was reported, February 27 (*ibid.*).

THE FULL POWERS

James Buchanan was commissioned Minister to Russia on January 4, 1832. He was given two full powers, each in customary form and dated the following March 26; one was to treat "of and concerning the principles of Maratime War, and Neutrality" (D. S., 2 Credences, 175); the subject of the other, for the negotiation and signature of this treaty, was "the Commerce and Navigation of the two Countries" (*ibid.*, 184).

From the despatch of Buchanan of December 20, 1832 (D. S., 12 Despatches, Russia, No. 9, enclosure H), it appears that a certified copy of the full power of Count Nesselrode was sent by him to Buchanan with a note of December 15, three days before the signature of the treaty and after its terms had been agreed upon and written.

A copy of that certified copy, which is a translation from the Russian into French, is with the despatch mentioned. The original full power was signed by the Emperor of Russia, countersigned by Nesselrode as Vice Chancellor, and was also dated December 15 (December 3, Old Style). In substance, and omitting various titles, the copy reads as follows (translation):

We, Nicholas I, by the grace of God Emperor and Autocrat of all of the Russias, etc., etc., having resolved, in common accord with the Government of the United States of America, to regulate by a treaty of commerce and navigation the commercial relations between Our Empire and the said United States, We have chosen and appointed, as by these presents We choose and appoint as Our Plenipotentiary, Our beloved and faithful Charles Robert, Count Nesselrode, Our Vice Chancellor, Knight of the orders of Russia and of many others, authorizing him not only to enter into negotiations with him or them who shall be properly authorized in that regard on the part of the Government of the United States of America, but also to draw up, conclude, and sign with him or them such treaty of commerce and navigation as shall be judged the most appropriate to the end which the two Governments desire to reach, promising on Our imperial word to accept and confirm all that which shall have been drawn up, concluded, and signed by virtue of the present full power, and to give Our imperial ratification thereto. In faith whereof We have signed the present full power with Our own hand and have caused to be affixed thereto the seal of Our Empire. Given at St. Petersburg the third of December (December 15, New Style) in the year of grace one thousand eight hundred and thirty-two and the eighth year of Our reign.

The Negotiations and the Form

James Buchanan, who succeeded John Randolph, of Virginia, as Minister to Russia, arrived at St. Petersburg on June 2, 1832. Regarding the state of the negotiations theretofore conducted he reported as follows (D. S., 12 Despatches, Russia, No. 2, June 12, 1832):

I found that Mᵣ Randolph, during his short residence in this City, had applied himself with energy and despatch, to accomplish the purposes of his mission: Within a short period after his arrival, he had placed in the possession of the Russian Ministry, "every paper public and private," with which he had been entrusted, touching the negotiation which the President had instructed him to open with this Government. Notwithstanding this frankness, which was certainly the highest evidence of confidence and therefore the greatest compliment which could have been paid to the Imperial Ministry; and notwithstanding the earnest attempts made by Mᵣ Randolph whilst he remained here, and continued by Mᵣ Clay afterwards, under his direction, to obtain an answer to the propositions he had made in behalf of his Government, no intimation has yet been given, whether Russia would be willing to treat with us either upon the subject of Commerce and Navigation or that of Maritime Rights. Now although from all the circumstances attending the transaction, I am not disposed to attribute this omission to any want of proper respect towards the Government of the United States; yet I feel that it has placed me in an embarrassing situation. All my instructions, (with the exception of those you have given me which are merely supplemental) together with the projet of the Treaty concerning Maritime Rights, and a private letter of Mᵣ Van Buren to Mᵣ Randolph (a copy of which is on file in the Legation) are already in the possession of the Russian Ministry.

Other despatches in the same volume give a full account of the negotiations (see Curtis, Life of James Buchanan, I, 161–72; and, particularly, Moore, The Works of James Buchanan, II, 193–298, *passim*). The agreement as to the clauses of the treaty was reached first in their French text; regarding the form and language and the

events on the day of its signature, the despatch of Buchanan of December 20, transmitting the treaty, contains the following (D. S., 12 Despatches, Russia, No. 9):

Our interview on this occasion [December 13] was very long, and the time was chiefly spent in reading over the amended French projet, article by article, & in the observations which arose out of different minute alterations proposed by both parties. All that passed between us of any importance, you will find embraced in the remarks which I shall hereafter make on the several articles of the Treaty.

At this interview Count Nesselrode agreed, without hesitation, to the "alternate" form of Treaty, observing it was the common practise of Europe; but proposed to follow the precedent set by Mr Middleton [Document 46, the convention of April 17, 1824] of executing it solely in the French language. This proposition, however, was soon abandoned. Indeed, until he produced the original Treaty itself signed by Mr Middleton, and assured me that no counter-part in English had ever been executed, I was not convinced of the correctness of his first impression in this particular.

On the next morning (Friday 14th) I received a copy of his amended French projet which was the same as the Treaty afterwards signed, with the exception of two unimportant changes, the first proposed by myself, & the other by Count Nesselrode. . . .

Late in the evening I transmitted to the Count an English translation of the Treaty. In this I have followed, so far as it was applicable, the English of our Treaty with Prussia, not that I deemed it either literal or elegant; but because it is substantially correct, and any departure from it which I might have proposed would only have afforded occasion for new difficulties & delays. Throughout the negotiation this Treaty with Prussia [of May 1, 1828, Document 62] both in the French & in the English, has been resorted to by the Count as a standard.

. . . . : : : : : . .

On our interview the next day [December 16], the Baron [Sacken] informed me that the English translation of the Treaty was satisfactory to Count Nesselrode, who proposed that it should be signed at two o'clock on Tuesday, after the morning Levee of the Emperor. He then agreed, for the purpose of expediting the business, that whilst they were preparing one French copy at the Foreign Office, we should prepare an English copy at the American Legation; & that after these were exchanged, they should annex the French to the English copy furnished by us, whilst we were annexing the English to the French copy furnished by them. The whole was completed & the Treaty prepared for Signature on Monday evening. (the 17th)

On Tuesday morning (the 18th) we went to the Emperor's levee; and on this occasion a singular occurrence took place in relation to the Treaty.

The strictest secrecy had been preserved throughout the negotiation. Indeed I do not believe an individual, except those immediately concerned, had the least idea that negotiations were even pending. A rumor of the refusal of this Government to make the Treaty had circulated two months ago; and I was then repeatedly informed in conversation, that it was in vain for any nation to attempt to conclude a Treaty of Commerce with the Russian Government, whilst Count Cancrene continued to be Minister of Finance. Count Nesselrode had on one occasion intimated a desire that the British Government should not obtain a knowledge that negotiations were proceeding; and this was an additional reason on our part for observing the greatest caution. It ought to be remarked, however, that this intimation was given before information had reached St Petersburg of the conclusion of the late Treaty between France & England in relation to the Belgian question.

The Diplomatic Corps, according to the etiquette were arranged in a line to receive the Emperor and Empress, and Mr Bligh, the English Minister, occupied the station immediately below myself. You may judge of my astonishment when the Emperor accosting me in French, in a tone of voice which could be heard by all around, said, "I signed the order yesterday that the Treaty should "be executed according to your wishes": & then immediately turning to Mr Bligh asked him to become the interpreter of this information. He is a most

amiable man, and his astonishment and embarrassment were so striking, that I felt for him most sincerely.   This incident has already given rise to considerable speculation among the knowing ones of St Petersburg; probably much more than it deserves.

I ought to remark, that when I was presented to the Emperor I understood but little, I might almost say, no French; and there was then an interpreter present.   Supposing this still to be the case he must have thought that an interpreter was necessary;—and he was correct to a certain extent, for I have not yet had sufficient practice to attempt to speak French in the presence of the whole Court.   I trust this may not long be the case: but I still more ardently hope I may not very long continue in a situation, where it will be necessary to speak that language.

There can be no doubt but all that occurred was designed on the part of the Emperor; and what must have rendered it still more embarrassing to Mr Bligh was, that one object of Lord Durham's mission is understood to have been the conclusion of a commercial Treaty with Russia

After the Emperor had retired, Mr Bligh, in manifest confusion, told me he feared he had been a very bad interpreter and asked me what kind of a Treaty we had been concluding with Russia; to which I replied, it was a Treaty of Commerce.

Count Nesselrode was not present at the moment and from his manner when I informed him of this incident, I believe he had not previously received any intimation of the Emperor's intention to make such a disclosure.

The Count and myself afterwards proceeded from the Palace to the Foreign Office and there signed the Treaty.   The only persons present were Baron Brunnow and Baron Sacken.

On this occasion but little worthy of repetition occurred.   They all exhibited the greatest cordiality and good will and the Count emphatically declared that he believed we had that day completed a work which would result in benefits to both nations.

On taking my leave, I expressed no more than I felt, in thanking him for his kind and candid conduct throughout the whole negotiation; and he paid me some compliments in return.

Some comments as to the use of the invocation, "In the name of the Most Holy and Indivisible Trinity," which is at the beginning of this treaty, are in the notes to Document 55, the treaty of July 4, 1827, with Sweden and Norway.

As to the content of the treaty, the observations of Buchanan are, in part, as follows (*ibid.*):

The first Article is similar to that of our Treaty with Prussia [Document 62].

The second Article, like the same one in that Treaty, provides for a perfect reciprocity, so far as Tonnage duties are concerned; and places Light House duties and other Port charges upon the footing of the most favored nations, with whom the parties have not, at the present time, subsisting Treaties regulating them upon terms of entire reciprocity.

This last qualification was inserted for the purpose of reserving to the United States the power of levying the discriminating Light House duty of Fifty cents per ton on Russian vessels, should such a measure be deemed expedient.   It was confined to Treaties *now existing*, to deprive Russia of any pretext for granting favors of this kind hereafter which American vessels should not enjoy.

If Russian vessels had any portion of the carrying trade between the two countries, this discrimination would much more than counterbalance all the trifling advantages which they possess in their own Ports; and this Government might thus be brought to terms of entire reciprocity.   The excess of Light House duties which a single Russian vessel would then be compelled to pay in an American Port would more than ten times exceed the discriminations against an American vessel of the same burthen in the Port of Odessa; — the only one in the Empire, with which we shall probably have much intercourse, where any discriminations

exist. I should not, however, advise the adoption of such a measure, because it is certain, that so far as Navigation is concerned, no reciprocity can exist between the two Countries, except upon paper. In this respect the treaty is solely for the benefit of the United States.

In the Ports of St Petersburg and Archangel, no discriminating duties exist against our vessels. In that of Odessa, the Tonnage and Light House duties and all other charges upon an American vessel of 100 Lasts or nearly 200 tons burthen amount only to 235. paper Roobles and 20 Kopeks, or 47. dollars of our money; whilst the similar charges upon a Russian vessel of the same burthen are 160 Roobles and 20 Kopeks or 32 dollars. If I correctly understand the report of our consul at this port, made to the Department in November 1831, the present Treaty will reduce this discrimination from 15 to 5 dollars on such a vessel.

At the Port of Taganrock, on the sea of Asoph, all the charges on an American vessel of the same burthen amount to 153 Roobles 50 Kopeks, and on a Russian vessel to 90 Roobles and 50 Kopeks. Under the operation of the Treaty, this difference will be reduced to 45 Roobles or 9 Dollars.

The 3^d, 4th, 5th, 6th, 7th, 8th, 9th, 10th, 11th, 12th, & 13th Articles so nearly resemble the 3^d, 4th, 6th, 5th, 7th, 10th, 11th, 14th, 9th, 15th, & 16th, Articles of our Treaty with Prussia, as to render any comment upon them unnecessary. In relation to the 12th it may be proper merely to observe that it was thought advisable to make the termination of the Treaty, in any event, correspond with the end of the year.

THE EXCHANGE OF RATIFICATIONS

By Article 13 the rather long term of one year was allowed for the exchange of ratifications, doubtless because of the fact that the short session of Congress could not last beyond March 4, 1833; but the desire of Buchanan to have the exchange take place within the period of that Congress was not realized, owing to some delay in the transmittal of the Russian instrument of ratification to Washington. In his despatch of February 5, 1833 (D. S., 12 Despatches, Russia, No. 14), is this mention of the matter:

Having learned that the ratification of the Treaty had not yet been transmitted to Washington by this Government, I obtained an interview to-day with Count Nesselrode, for the purpose of requesting him to send it without further delay. I told him I had received the impression it had been forwarded some time since and was sorry to have been mistaken; because if the ratifications could have been exchanged before the fourth of March, the President would then have been furnished with a favorable opportunity of adverting to the Treaty, in his inaugural address, & of expressing his genuine feelings in regard to Russia. He replied, that as the Treaty had been concluded here, under the very eye of the Emperor, the President could not entertain the least doubt of its ratification, and expressed a hope that the delay would not prevent him from alluding to the subject. I observed I did not know how that might be, as the Treaty could not be published in the United States until after the exchange of the ratifications.

The treaty was communicated to Congress with the presidential message of May 12, 1834 (Richardson, III, 50).

THE SEPARATE ARTICLE

In the separate article as well as in Article 12 there is mention of the Kingdom of Poland, which means the so-called Congress Kingdom (1815-63), the remnant of the former Poland which was assigned at the Congress of Vienna to Russia, under the Emperor of Russia

as King of Poland. The Final Act of the Congress of Vienna of June 9, 1815 (French text in British and Foreign State Papers, II, 3–180), contains the agreements regarding the Congress Kingdom (see *ibid.*, 11, 56–74). In form the Congress Kingdom existed until 1863, but in all but form it was a Russian province from 1831.

The agreement then in force between Russia and Prussia regarding the commerce of the Kingdom of Poland was the Convention of Commerce and Navigation signed at Berlin March 11, 1825; its text, in French, is in British and Foreign State Papers, XII, 927–32.

The agreement then in force between Russia on the one hand and Sweden and Norway on the other, regarding the commerce of the Grand Duchy of Finland, was the Convention of Friendship and Commerce signed at St. Petersburg February 26, 1828; its text, in French, is in Von Martens, Nouveau recueil de traités, VII, pt. 2, 572–91, and in British and Foreign State Papers, XV, 675–89. Copies of those two agreements are enclosures E and F to the above-mentioned despatch of Buchanan of December 20, 1832 (D. S., 12 Despatches, Russia. No. 9).

Treaty Series No. 321
8 Statutes at Large, 454–56
18 *ibid.*, pt. 2, Public Treaties, 693–95

76

SIAM : MARCH 20, 1833

Treaty of Amity and Commerce, signed at Bangkok March 20, 1833.
Original in Siamese and English, with Portuguese and Chinese
translations.
Submitted to the Senate June 12, 1834. (Message of May 30, 1834.)
Resolution of advice and consent June 30, 1834. Ratified by the
United States January 3, 1835. Ratified by Siam April 14, 1836.
Ratifications exchanged at Bangkok April 14, 1836. Proclaimed
June 24, 1837.
The Siamese text of the treaty is first reproduced (in facsimile); then
follows the English text, with the clause of conclusion signed by Edmund
Roberts, reserving the treaty for the ratification of the President by and
with the advice and consent of the Senate; then is printed the Portuguese
translation as written in the original treaty document; and finally
there is a reproduction of the Chinese translation, also as there written;
but the form of the treaty document is so very unusual that its descrip-
tion in the notes should be consulted as explanatory of the arrangement
of the texts.

741

๏ สมเดจ์พระพุทธิเจ้าอยู่หัวณะกรุงพระมหา
นคร[ศ]รีอยุทธยา ทำหนังสือสัญญาทางไมตรีค้า
ขายต่ออิศกาโตอุนิโตกาอะเมริกะ แล้วสมเดจ์
พระพุทธิเจ้าอยู่หัวโปรดเกล้าโปรดกระหม่อม
ให้ท่านเจ้าพญาพระคลังเสนาบดีผู้ใหญ่ทำ
หนังสือสัญากับเอกแมนรอเบกขุนนางซึ่ง
อิศกาโตอุนิโตกาอะเมริกะเมืองมะริกันให้เข้ามา
แทนตัว ทำหนังสือสัญาเปนไมตรีรักใคร่
ด้วยน้ำใจชื่อตรงไว้ต่อกันทังสองฝ่าย ไทกับ

ษะคมะริกันจะได้ไปมาค้าขายถึงกันโดยสุจริต

สืบไปชั่วฟ้าแลดิน ไทกับษะคมะริกันทำหนัง

สือสญาณวันพุทเดือนสี่แรมสิบห้าค่ำ ศักราช

พันร้อยเก้าสิบสี่ปีมะโรงจัตวาศก ศักราช

ฝรั่งพันแปดร้อยสามสิบสามปี เดือนมาไซร

เขียนเปนอักษรไทฉบับหนึ่ง อักษรมะริ

กันฉบับหนึ่ง ไทไม่รู้จักอักษรมะริกัน

มะริกันไม่รู้จักอักษรไท จึ่งเขียนอักษรพุทเกษ

ฉบับหนึ่ง อักษรจีนฉบับหนึ่ง ไว้เปนพญาณ

เรื่องความ   อักษรไทอักษรมะริกันอักษรพุท

เกษอักษรจีนคั่งกัน ฝ่ายกรุง ฯ ลงชื่อท่านเจ้า

พญาพระคลังเสนาบดีผู้ใหญ่ ปิดตราบัวแก้ว

ประจำชื่อ ฝ่ายมะริกันลงชื่อเอกแมนรอเบคปิด

ตรารูปนกรูปดาวประจำชื่อเปนสำคัญให้ไว้ณกรุง ฯ

ฉบับหนึ่ง เอกแมนรอเบคเอาไปไว้ณเมืองมะริ

กันฉบับหนึ่ง ถ้าอิศดาโกอุปิโกคาอะเมริกะ

ปิดตราเข้ามาเปลี่ยน แล้วกรุง ฯ จะปิดตรา

พระอัยภพชเปลี่ยนให้ออกไป   ๚ะ๛

๏ ความสัญญาข้อหนึ่งว่า ไทกับฝรังษอมะริกัน

เปนไม้ตรีมีความภาบคาบค่อกันชั่วฟ้าแลดิน   ๚

๏ ข้อสองลูกค้าษอมะริกันจะเข้ามาค้าขายณะ

กรุงแลหัวเมืองขึ้นกับกรุง ๑ จะบันทุกสินค้า

สิ่งใดใดนอกจากฝิ่นเปนของต้องห้ามเข้ามาขาย

และจะซื้อสินค้าที่มีอยู่ณกรุง ๑ แลสินค้าจะมี

มาแต่หัวเมืองใดใดก็ดี เจ้าพนักงานในหลวง

จะไม่ขัดขวงแลตั้งราคาให้ลูกค้าษอมะริกัน

แลลูกค้ากรุง ๑ ได้ซื้อขายกันเองทังสองฝ่าย

 โดยสภาก ถ้ากำปั่นลูกค้าชตมะริกันลำใดใด

จำหน่ายสินค้าและบันทุกสินค้าการพังปวงเสร์

ข้าพะนักงานจะให้เบิกล่องไปโดยคล่องสภาก

ถ้าลูกค้าชตมะริกันจะบันทุกเครื่องสาตราๆ

เข้ามาจำหน่ายณกรุงไม่ขายให้กบผู้ใดผู้หนึ่ง

จะจำหน่ายให้ในหลวงให้สิ้น ถ้าในหลวงต้อง

การก็จะซื้อไว้ ไม่ต้องการก็ไม่ซื้อ แต่เข้าสาร

นั้นจะบันทุกเปนสินค้าออกไปไม่ได้ด้วยณกรุงๆ

ห้ามอยู่   ๚ะ ๑

๏ ข้อสามลูกค้าชาอะริกันจะเข้ามาค้าขาย
ณกรุง ฯ แลหัวเมืองซึ่งขึ้นกับกรุง ฯ ให้ได้
ซื้อขายกันโดยสดวก   แต่ค่าทำเนียมสิ่งใด
สิ่งหนึ่งนั้นให้ยกเสีย ให้เข้าพะนักงานวัดปาก
กำปั่น   ถ้ากำปั่นมีดาษฟ้าสองชั้น ให้วัดหลัง
ดาษฟ้าชั้นล่าง   ถ้ามีดาษฟ้าชั้นเดียว ให้วัด
หลังดาษฟ้าชั้นบน แต่ให้วัดกึ่งกลางโดย
ยาวกำปั่น   ชาอะริกันจะเสียค่าทำเนียม
ให้เหมือนปากกำปั่นที่มีสินค้าละพันเจ็ด

ร้อยบาท ที่ไม่มีสินค้ามีแต่สินเข้ามาซื้อ

สินค้าวาละพันห้าร้อยบาท ค้วยไม้วาที่กรุง ฯ

ยาวเจกสิบแปดนิ้วมะริกน นิ้วไทเก้าสิบหก

นิ้ว แลลูกค้าชาวมะริกนไม่ต้องเสียค่าทำ

เนียมเรือล่าเสียง แลค่าทำเนียมอื่นอื่นนอก

ทกค่าปากกำปั่นอีกเลย ถ้ากำปั่นชาวมะริกน

จะเกิกเหกุการในกลางชะเล เสากระโดง

เพลาใบหก แลขกสินค้าประเสบียงอาหาร

จะแวะเข้ามาเปลี่ยนเสากะโดงเพลาใบแลซื้อ

ขงกินณกรุง ฯ ก็ดี ชคมะริกันจะทอดกำปั่น

อยู่นอกบากน้ำ แก่ถ้าจะเข้ามาสืบสินค้าก็ดี

อย่าให้เรียกค่าทำเนียมแก่ชคมะริกัน ขะ๏

๏ ข้อสี่ถ้านานไปเบื้องหน้าค่าทำเนียมสลุบ

กำปั่นจะลดให้ประเทษใกภาษาใด น้อยมาก

ค่าทำเนียมซึ่งสญาไว้นี้ กรุง ฯ จะลดค่า

ทำเนียมให้ชคมะริกันตามประเทษนั้น ขะ๏

๏ ข้อห้าสลุบกำปั่นชคมะริกันจะเปนเหตุอัน

ตรายสิ่งใดในท้องชะเลในแขวงกรุง ฯ แลแขวง

หัวเมืองขึ้นกับกรุง ฯ จะมีคนและสิ่งของรอกทาก
อันกรายมากน้อยเท่าใด ให้ช่วยทำณุบำรุง
เลี้ยงดูเอาใจใส่ให้ที่อยู่อย่าให้ขัดสนได้ กว่า
จะได้กลับไปบ้านเมือง และเงินซึ่งกรุง ฯ
ได้เสียเปนค่ากินใช้สอยไปมากน้อยเท่าใด

อิศกาใกอปิใกกาอะเมริกะเมืองมิริกันจะใช้ให้ ฯะ

๑ ข้อหกฃฅมะริกันจะเข้ามาค้าขายณกรุง ฯ จะเปน
ฉี่สินอยู่ที่กรุง ฯ มากน้อยเท่าใด ลูกค้าที่
กรุง ฯ จะเปนฉี่สินฃฅมะริกันมากน้อยเท่าใด

คนซึ่งเปนลูกนี้มีสิ่งของมากยฆ้ยเท่าใดจะต้อง

ซื้อขายใช้นี้ให้กับเจ้านี้กว่าจะสิ้นของที่มี ถ้า

สิ้นของที่มีแล้วยังไม่ครบเงินที่ค้าง อย่าให้เอา

ลูกนี้ไปเปนค่าใช้สอยจำจองเฆี่ยนตีเร่งเอา

เงิน ให้ปล่อยลูกนี้ไปตามใจ ๚ะ๛

๏ ข้อเจกลูกค้าฆคมะริกันเข้ามาค้าขายณกรุงฯ

และหัวเมืองขึ้นกับกรุ ฯ ถ้าจะเช่าที่ขึ้นอยู่จะให้

เช่าที่ศึกหลวงอยู่ ฆคมะริกันจะเสียค่าเช่าให้

ตามทำเฆียม ถ้าจะขนสินค้าขึ้นค้าขายเข้าพะนักงาน

ต้องตรวดดูสิ่งของ อย่าให้เจ้าพะนักงานเรียก

เอาภาษีรังกอบ　　　　　　　ฯะ๑

๏ ข้อแปดสลุบกำปั่นชตมะริกันจะเข้ามาที่ประ

เทษใดใกลบประไวรผู้ร้ายสลัดสัตรูที่แห่งใด

คนร้ายจะทำร้ายแก่ชตมะริกันคณแลของจะตก

เข้ามาณกรุง ๑ แลหัวเมืองขึ้นกับกรุง ๑ กรุง ๑

จะช่วยชำระให้คืนกลับไป　　　　　ฯ๑

๏ ข้อเก้าชตมะริกันจะเข้ามาค้าขายณกรุง ๑ จะทำ

ตามกฎหมายหย่างทำเนียมณกรุง ๑ ทุกสิ่ง ฯะ๑

๑ ข้อสืบนานไปเบื้องหน้าฝรั่งชคใดภาษาใด

นอกจากพุทเกษ จะขอเข้ามาตั้งกงสุ่นณกรุง

ๆ กกรุง ๆ โปรดให้ตั้ง ชามะริกนจะตั้ง

กงสุ่น ตามฝรั่งชคซึ่งโปรดนั้น ฯะ๛

ตราหลวงพระไอยภพช

๏ ดวภท่านเจ้าพญาพระคลังเสนาบดีผู้ใหญ่
ณกรุงพระมหานคร   ศิอยุทยา

Treaty of Amity and Commerce between His Majesty the Magnificent King of Siam and the United States of America.

His Majesty the Sovereign and Magnificent King in the City of Siayuthia has appointed the Chau-Phaya Phraklang one of the first Ministers of State, to treat with Edmund Roberts, Minister of the United States of America, who has been sent by the Government thereof on its behalf, to form a Treaty of sincere friendship and entire good faith between the two nations. For this purpose the Siamese and the Citizens of the United States of America, shall, with sincerity, hold commercial intercourse in the Ports of their respective nations, as long as Heaven and Earth shall endure.

This Treaty is concluded on wednesday the last of the fourth month of the year 1194 called Pimarông chattavasok (or the year of the Dragon) corresponding to the twentieth day of March, in the year of our Lord 1833. One original is written in Siamese, the other in English; but as the Siamese are ignorant of English, and the Americans of Siamese, a Portuguese & a Chinese translation are annexed, to serve as testimony to the contents of the Treaty. The writing is of the same tenor & date in all the languages aforesaid: it is signed on the one part, with the name of the Chau Phaya Phraklang, and sealed with the seal of the Lotus flower of glass; on the other part it is signed with the name of Edmund Roberts, and sealed with a seal containing an Eagle and stars.

One copy will be kept in Siam, and another will be taken by Edmund Roberts to the United States. If the Government of the United States shall ratify the said Treaty, and attach the seal of the Government, then Siam will also ratify it on its part, and attach the seal of its Government.

ARTICLE I. There shall be a perpetual peace between the United States of America and the Magnificent King of Siam.

ARTICLE II. The Citizens of the United States shall have free liberty to enter all the Ports of the Kingdom of Siam, with their cargoes of whatever kind the said cargoes may consist; and they shall have liberty to sell the same to any of the subjects of the King, or others, who may wish to purchase the same; or to barter the same for any produce or manufacture of the Kingdom, or other articles that may be found there. No prices shall be fixed by the officers of the King on the articles to be sold by the merchants of the United States, or the merchandize they may wish to buy: but the trade shall be free on both sides, to sell, or buy, or exchange, on the terms and for the prices

the owners may think fit. Whenever the said Citizens of the United States shall be ready to depart, they shall be at liberty so to do, and the proper officers shall furnish them with passports—provided always there be no legal impediment to the contrary. Nothing contained in this article shall be understood as granting permission to import & sell munitions of war to any person excepting to the King, who if he does not require, will not be bound to purchase them: neither is permission granted to import opium, which is contraband, or to export rice, which cannot be embarked as an article of commerce. These only are prohibited.

ARTICLE III. Vessels of the United States entering any Port within His Majesty's dominions, and selling, or purchasing cargoes of merchandize, shall pay in lieu of import and export duties, tonnage, license to trade, or any other charge whatever, a measurement duty, only, as follows. The measurement shall be made from side to side, in the middle of the Vessel's length, and if a single-decked vessel, on such single deck,—if otherwise, on the lower deck. On every vessel selling merchandize, the sum of one Thousand Seven Hundred Ticals or Bats shall be paid, for every Siamese Fathom in breadth so measured,—the said Fathom being computed to contain Seventy Eight English or American Inches; corresponding to Ninety-Six Siamese Inches:—but if the said vessel should come without merchandize, and purchase a cargo with specie only, she shall then pay the sum of Fifteen Hundred Ticals, or Bats, for each and every fathom before described. Furthermore, neither the aforesaid measurement duty, nor any other charge whatever, shall be paid by any vessel of the United States that enters a Siamese Port for the purpose of refitting, or for refreshments, or to enquire the state of the market.

ARTICLE IV. If hereafter the duties payable by foreign vessels be diminished in favor of any other Nation, the same diminution shall be made in favor of the vessels of the United States.

ARTICLE V. If any vessel of the United States shall suffer shipwreck on any part of the Magnificent King's dominions, the persons escaping from the wreck shall be taken care of and hospitably entertained at the expense of the King, until they shall find an opportunity to be returned to their country; and the property saved from such wreck shall be carefully preserved and restored to its owners:—and the United States will repay all expenses incurred by His Majesty on account of such wreck.

ARTICLE VI. If any citizen of the United States coming to Siam for the purpose of trade shall contract debts to any individual of Siam, or if any individual of Siam shall contract debts to any citizen of the United States, the debtor shall be obliged to bring forward and sell all his goods, to pay his debts therewith. When the product of such bonâ fide sale shall not suffice, he shall no longer be liable for the remainder; nor shall the creditor be able to retain him as a slave, imprison, flog, or otherwise punish him, to compel the payment of any balance remaining due; but shall leave him at perfect liberty.

ARTICLE VII. Merchants of the United States coming to trade in the Kingdom of Siam, and wishing to rent houses therein, shall rent the King's factories, and pay the customary rent of the country. If the said merchants bring their goods on shore, the King's Officers shall take account thereof, but shall not levy any duty thereupon.

ARTICLE VIII. If any Citizens of the United States, or their vessels or other property, shall be taken by pirates, and brought within the dominions of the Magnificent King, the persons shall be set at liberty, and the property restored to its owners.

ARTICLE IX Merchants of the United States, trading in the Kingdom of Siam, shall respect and follow the laws and customs of the Country, in all points.

ARTICLE X. If hereafter any foreign Nation, other than the Portuguese, shall request and obtain His Majesty's consent to the appointment of Consuls to reside in Siam, the United States shall be at liberty to appoint Consuls to reside in Siam, equally with such other foreign Nation.

EDMUND ROBERTS [Seal]

Whereas the undersigned Edmund Roberts, a Citizen of Portsmouth, in the State of New Hampshire, in the United States of America, being duly appointed an Envoy, by Letters Patent, under the Signature of the President and Seal of the United States of America, bearing date at the City of Washington the twenty-sixth day of January AD. 1832,—for negotiating and concluding a Treaty of Amity and Commerce, between the United States of America and His Majesty the King of Siam;—Now Know Ye, that I, Edmund Roberts, Envoy as aforesaid, do conclude the foregoing Treaty of Amity and Commerce, and every Article and Clause therein contained, reserving the same, nevertheless, for the final ratification of the President of

the United States of America, by and with the advice and consent of the Senate of the said United States.

Done at the Royal City of Sia Yuthia (commonly called Bankok), on the twentieth day of March in the Year of our Lord one thousand eight hundred and thirty-three, and of the Independence of the United States of America the fifty-seventh.

EDMUND ROBERTS

[The Portuguese translation]

Tractado de Amizade, e Commercio entre Sua Magestade o Magnifico Rey de Siam e os Estados Unidos d'America.

Sua Magestade o Soberano Magnifico Rey da Cidade de Syayuthia faculta a Chau Phaya Phraklang primeiro Ministro do Estado, de tractar com Edmund Roberts Ministro dos Estados Unidos d'America, o qual enviou o Governo de parte de sua propria pessoa a fazer hum Tractado de sincera amizade, e fidelidade inteira entre ambas as Naçoens.

Por este effeito os Siamezes, e os Cidadaons dos Estados Unidos d'America poderáõ commerciar nos portos de huma, e outra Nação, com sinceridade, em quanto existir o Ceo, e a Terra.

Este Tractado foi feito no dia quarta feira, fim do quarto mez no anno de 1194, Pimarông Chattavasok, que corresponde a Era Christão dos vinte de Março de 1833. Hum original vai escripto em lingua de Siam, e outro em lingua Ingleza; e como os Siamezes ignorão a lingua Ingleza, e os Americanos ignorão a lingua de Siam, vai então huma copia em lingua Portuguesa, e outra em lingua China, para ser testimunha do tractado. O escripto nas ditas quatro linguas hé do mesmo theor, e data; e vai assignado com o nome de Chau Phaya Phraklang, e sellado com o sello, de flôr de trate de vidro;—e do outro lado vai assignado com o nome de Edmund Roberts, e sellado com o sello, que tem huma Aguia, e estrellas. Huma copia será guardada em Siam, e outra copia Edmund Roberts levará para os Estados Unidos. Se o Governo dos Estados Unidos ratificar o dito tractado, e pozer o sello do Governo, então Siam de sua parte ratificará, e pará o sello do seu Governo.

ARTIGO 1º Haverá perpetua Paz entre os Estados Unidos d'America, e o Magnifico Rey de Siam.

ARTIGO 2º Os Cidadaons dos Estados Unidos teráõ livre liberdade de entrar em todos os Portos do Reyno de Siam, com suas cargas, de qual quer qualidade de fazendas forem, ou consistão; e teráõ

a liberdade de vender as ditas fazendas a qual quer dos Vassallos do Magnifico Rey, ou outras quaes queis pessoas, que as quizerem comprar, ou troca-las por quaes queis outras da producção, ou manufactura do Reyno, ou outros quaes queis artigos, que se possão ali achar. Nenhum preço será fixado pelos officiaes do Rey sobre as fazendas, que se venderem pelos mercadores dos Estados Unidos, ou sobre as mercancias, que elles queirão comprar; mas o negocio será livre para ambas as partes, p.ª vender, ou comprar, ou trocar, a vontade, e pelos preços que os proprietarios julgarem proprio. Cada vez que os Cidadaons dos Estados Unidos tiverem seus navios promptos a partir, não tendo embaraço algum, poderáõ partir livremente, e os officiaes competentes daráõ seus passaportes immediatamente. Se os mercadores dos Estados Unidos d'America trouxerem armas, e polvora p.ª vender na Corte de Siam, não as poderáõ vender a nenhuma pessoa, senão ao Rey; Se Sua Magestade não tiver precizão dellas, as não comprará. Na Corte de Siam he somente prohibido importar anfião, que he contrabando, e arroz tão somente hé prohibido exportar: este não se poderá carregar como fazenda p.ª negocio.

ARTIGO 3º As Embarcaçoens dos Estados Unidos d'America, vindo commerciar no algum porto dos dominios de Sua Magestade, vendendo, ou comprando cargas de mercancias, pagaráõ em lugar de direitos, tonage, licença p.ª commerciar, ou outro qual quer imposto por importação, ou exportação tão sommente hum direito de medição de embocadura. Se a Embarcação fôr de duas cobertas, medir-se-ha em cima da coberta debaixo; e se ella fôr de huma só coberta medir-se-há sobre aquella coberta, no meio de seu comprimento. A embarcação que trouxer carga de fazendas pagará, por cada vara de largura de sua boca, mil e sette centos ticaes, ou bats; e a que não trouxer carga, tão somente pagará mil e quinhentos ticaes por cada vara: sendo a dita vara calculada conter settenta, e oito polegadas Inglezas que correspondem a noventa e seis polegadas de Siam. Alem disso, se algum navio dos Estados Unidos da America soffrer qual quer avaria no mar, quebrar vergas, ou mastros, ou tiver falta de comedorias, entrando na Corte de Siam, para reparar do seu damno e faltas que tiver, ou inquirir do commercio do paiz, não pagará o dito direito de medição, ou outro qual quer imposto de qual quer natureza fôr.

ARTIGO 4º Se para o futuro aquelles direitos que pagão os Navios Estrangeiros forem diminuidos em favor de qual quer nação, o Governo de Siam fará a mesma diminuição a favor dos Estados Unidos.

Artigo 5º Se alguma embarcação dos Estados Unidos naufragar em qual quer lugar sugeito ao magnifico Rey, as pessoas que escaparem de naufragio seráõ tractados com cuidado, e entretidos com toda a hospitalidade a custa de Sua Magestade, até que haja opportunidade para retornarem á seu paiz; e a propriedade salvada de taes naufragios será cuidadozamente prezervada, e entregar-se-há ao seu proprietario: e então o Governo dos Estados Unidos pagará exactamente o que houver despendido por Sua Magestade.

Artigo 6º Se algum Cidadão dos Estados Unidos vier contractar ou negociar em Siam, e contrahir dividas com alguma pessoa de Siam, ou se algũa pessoa de Siam contrahir dividas com algum Cidadão dos Estados Unidos, o devedor será obrigado appresentar, e vender todos os seus bens, pª delles pagar as suas dividas, e quando aquillo não chegue pª saldar as dividas; O acredor não poderá deter o devedor como escravo, ou po-lo em prizão, açouta-lo, ou castiga-lo, e constrange-lo a pagar o resto das dividas; mas o deixará em liberdade.

Artigo 7º Os Mercadores dos Estados Unidos d'America, que vierem commerciar no Reyno de Siam, querendo alugar casas pª ficar, alugaráõ as Feitorias do Rey, e pagaráõ o aluguel como o costume do paiz. Se os ditos mercadores descarregarem suas fazendas em terra, os officiaes do Rey tomaráõ conta dellas deš e barcadas, mas não exigiráõ sobre ellas algum direito.

Artigo 8º Se algum Cidadão dos Estados Unidos, ou suas embarcaçoens, ou outra propriedade fôr tomada por piratas, e troucerem a algum dos Portos dos dominios do Magnifico Rey, as pessoas seráõ postos em liberdade, e a propriedade restaurada aos seus donos.

Artigo 9º Os Mercadores dos Estados Unidos, vindo negociar no Reyno de Siam, respeitaráõ, e sugeitaráõ as Leys, e costumes do Paiz em todos os pontos

Artigo 10º Se para o futuro alguma nação estrangeira, excepto os Portugueses, vier pedir para residir Consul na Corte de Siam, e se Sua Magestade ceder, os Estados Unidos tambem poderão mandar Consules para residir no Reyno de Siam, igualmente como outra nacão.

[The Chinese translation follows]

暹羅國王與雅彌理駕合衆國
結通好貿易之約

暹羅國王特諭認丕雅帕坑大庫府
大臣會同

雅彌理駕合衆國特派差使臣義德
門羅百哂畢弄約馬兩國永結和
睦以便　進　雅二國人商客得
平和來往貿易事務於　暹國年號
壹千貳百玖拾肆壬辰年四月叁拾

56006°—33——50

年 叁 拾 叁 念 日 洄 十 壹 年 王 也 敕 即 日

章 二 書 謄 約 會 立 同 日 拾 貳 月 沿 馬

字 利 言 羗 用 所 國 雜 | 字 羅 進 馮 即

漢 言 郇 以 夫 識 譙 相 互 字 文 國 兩 綠

附 同 共 書 國 四 計 | 各 字 洋 彼 兼 字

畫 書 尾 約 其 | 則 義 詞 同 不 雖 字 統 |

達 玉 書 並 號 字 府 庫 大 於 拘 雖 正 詔

字 言 羅 門 德 義 羗 差 梼 國 雜 書 亦 信 即

章 言 約 其 也 信 印 呈 帶 鳥 鷹 大 差 上 號

當留在進國一章貴帝至雅國一章待後日
雅國統領定好上蓋國璽至進則進國
亦應上蓋王璽付回雅國共議將所議
會約則例列明於左

一　進羅與雅彌理嘉各省內國永交
和誼無息

二　雅彌理嘉國民人准許進入進國所
屬海口地方任意貿易買賣且准隨
便將各類貨物進出與商戶自定價

後亦准其與何人買賣各遁自意文
關官吏不得何樣阻滯進以之物除
鴉片例所樣外不論是何國所生出
之物不論是國內生成抑是外國等素
此可自買自賣而自定價值官員絕
不准理如船有齊備願去逆無官事
把持可保必既交畀收關准行惟至
買賣之物惟有雅國向船裝帶炮械
兵器各等至運俱准其賣與運國君

進口之貨物，獨有糧米一件，例禁不准帶出。且若誅求，姓曰買賣，至於出口之貨物，裕賣不買，不用所許，全不准帶出。

三、所有進口出口之貨物，俱照船隻闊狹丈量，理難照船之裝載舉凡納餉。亦非為貿易之官埠，納餉亦非。納何類進口出口貨物之稅，但定照船之闊窄丈量納稅，一餉如乞。其有船隻餉若干，就量其下艙，餉盡面若率。

設若墅者就在船者通竃之其墅通

艙短須墅在船之中半烏準墅之闊窄

者装貨物之船每進國尋當納進國

例銀壹十亦曰銖若空船入港等銀

前來買貨每尋當納例銀壹十伍曰銖

其墅船等貳計進國鈕玖拾陸烏壹尋

雜國鈕亦拾測烏壹尋院納此亦頭税係

外不准再征何樣税簡之又差雜國何船

或有何處達風夫桅夫舵游就進國所

魯地方修整或要探買食物等事抑

貳船來探問生理之先呈不便生理者起

各須起准進修整買食探問生理覓

納稅稅頭稅餉並外何樣規費兵

四所議官規例稅如日後有准別國從輕

議減者准暹國商船亦須從他國減稅

五暹國商船貳來進國海口遇風颶破所

有使船物國貨法回去而修整國統須修定

代書銀須以運達國止且破船所存貨運
國亦宜照顧至可交還本主也

六 雜國商客與運國商人交易兩國商
人如有欠賬賬者必須將所有之物
件賣去運銀賣已賣完仍不能設法
得將情人拘拿勒追以完好傍義因或
何樣刑乃須放其准其往憑差往

七 雜國商人至運國貿易准其往憑上
岸僱買祖官方岸往亦准自便買賣且

所有貨物准准官員驗看不得征收稅
餉

八 若有雅國人客或貨物或船被海所
拿奪等至遁國所屬地方官府須查
察放回其人而追還貨物交回本主也

九 雅國倘有各人等至遁國者須尊行
遁國之各法律

十 倘遁國日後有准西洋國外之何等國
設立公使在遁國地方居住雅國亦當設
立公使如他國一然

NOTES

This treaty, the first treaty made between the United States and the Kingdom of Siam, was negotiated by Edmund Roberts on the earlier of his two missions to the Far East as Special Agent of the United States.

The particular objects of that mission of Roberts were negotiations of treaties with Cochinchina, Siam, and Muscat; his first instructions, of January 27, 1832 (D. S., 1 Special Missions, 73–75), directed him to negotiate treaties with Cochinchina, Siam, and "the powers of Arabia on the Red Sea"; he was furnished with a certificate, signed by Secretary of State Livingston and dated the preceding day, which designated him as "Commissioner to the Governments of Cochin China, Siam and Muscat" (D. S., 2 Credences, 189); and he was given three full powers, also dated January 26, 1832, to negotiate, respectively, with those three Governments (*ibid.*, 189–91).

The letters of credence which Roberts received were in two forms, issued at different times. Doubtless those of the earlier form, which Roberts took with him when he sailed from Boston in March, 1832, were under date of January 26, 1832, and were directed to the three Governments mentioned; there is, however, no record copy of them; but in the book of Roberts (Embassy to the Eastern Courts of Cochin-China, Siam, and Muscat, 204) and in his manuscript report of his mission (D. S., 10 Special Agents, 47) are copies, certified by Roberts, of the letter of credence to the Emperor of Cochinchina. Those two copies are the same except for the dates. The printed copy is dated January 20, 1833, and the written copy January 26, 1833. In each case 1833 is a slip for 1832, and the date, as mentioned, was almost certainly January 26.

Further instructions were sent to Roberts under date of July 23 and October 28, 1832 (D. S., 1 Special Missions, 76–79).

The instructions of July 23 authorized him, at his discretion, to conclude treaties with powers other than Cochinchina, Siam, and Muscat. Japan, "the Birman Empire," and "the King of Acheen" were mentioned. Enclosed with the instructions were new letters of credence.

But it is to be observed that those instructions of July 23 did not reach Roberts until June 5, 1833, when the *Peacock*, then on the way from Siam to Muscat with Roberts on board, met the *Boxer* at Batavia (report of Roberts, D. S., 10 Special Agents, 66; despatch of June 22, 1833, *ibid.*, 20–21; Roberts, *op. cit.*, 327).

The instructions of October 28, 1832, contained further reference to negotiations with Japan: "if you find the prospect favorable, you may fill up one of the letters of credence with the appropriate title of the Emperor, and present yourself there for the purpose of opening a trade." Perhaps those instructions reached Roberts by the *Boxer*, but they were not specifically acknowledged; and in a despatch from Rio de Janeiro of January 17, 1834, Roberts wrote, "I have rec'd no Letters from your Department but those acknowledg'd at Batavia."

It appears that there were four letters of credence enclosed with the instructions of July 23, 1832. Record copies of them are in D. S., 1 Communications to Foreign Sovereigns and States, 69–72; two of those copies with the address blank and one addressed "To His Highness Syede Syede Bin Sultan" are dated January 31, 1832; all are in the same wording and state that the Great Seal was affixed. That to the Emperor of Japan is as follows:

Andrew Jackson, President of the United States of America,

To His Imperial Majesty, The Emperor of Japan.

Great and Good Friend,

This will be delivered to your Majesty by Edmund Roberts, a respectable Citizen of these United States, who has been appointed Special Agent on the part of this Government to transact important business with your Majesty. I pray your Majesty to protect him in the exercise of the duties which are thus confided to him, and to treat him with kindness and confidence, placing entire reliance on what he shall say to you in our behalf, especially when he shall repeat the assurances of our perfect amity and Good will towards your Majesty.

I pray God to have you always, Great and Good Friend under his safe and holy keeping.

In Testimony whereof, I have caused the Seal of the United States to be hereunto affixed. Given under my hand at the City of Washington the sixth day of June A. D. 1832; and of the Independence of the United States of America, the fifty Sixth.

ANDREW JACKSON,

By the President,

EDW LIVINGSTON, *Secretary of State.*

The earlier form, as it appears in the copy of the letter of credence to the Emperor of Cochinchina in the writings cited above, was then the customary one. It differed from the later form in that it omitted the Great Seal and had a clause of dating in lieu of the testimonium clause.

The change from the customary to the more elaborate form, which included the Great Seal, is in keeping with Livingston's statement that the new credentials were "made out in a form that . . . will be more acceptable to the powers with whom you are to negotiate." And in this connection it is interesting to note that Livingston was correctly informed, for Roberts, in his record of the negotiations with Siam (D. S., 10 Special Agents, 53), remarks that "considerable surprise was expressed at the President's letter having no seal attached."

In the first paragraph of the earliest of the instructions to Roberts, under date of January 27, 1832 (D. S., 1 Special Missions, 73), the general purpose of his appointment was thus stated:

The President having named you as his agent for the purpose of examining, in the Indian Ocean, the means of extending the commerce of the United States by commercial arrangement with the powers whose dominions border on those seas, you will embark on board of the United States Sloop of war, the Peacock, in which vessel (for the purpose of concealing your mission from powers whose interest it might be to thwart the objects the President has in view,) you will be rated as Captain's Clerk. Your real character is known to Captain Geisenger, and need not be to any other person on board, unless you find it necessary, for the purpose of your mission, to communicate it to others.

The instructions (*ibid.*, 75) included authority to Roberts to promise, either verbally or in writing, "that the usual presents shall be made on

the exchange of the ratification—of which you may settle a list of such things as may be most agreeable, not exceeding ten thousand dollars in value for each Power.''

To Roberts were given three similar full powers, of the same date, which named, respectively, the Governments of Cochinchina, Siam, and Muscat. The full power for a treaty with Siam, like that for one with Cochinchina, had a blank line in which the proper title might be filled in. It reads as follows (D. S., 2 Credences, 190):

Andrew Jackson, President of the United States of America,

To all whom these presents shall come, Greeting:

Know Ye, That reposing special trust and confidence in the integrity prudence and ability of Edmund Roberts, a citizen of the United States, I have appointed him Commissioner of the United States, to meet, confer, treat and negotiate with   and his government, or with any person or persons duly authorized in his or its behalf of and concerning all matters of Navigation and Commerce between the United States and the said Government of Siam, with full power to conclude and sign a treaty thereupon, transmitting the same to the President of the United States, for his final ratification by and with the advice and consent of the Senate.

In Testimony whereof, I have caused the Seal of the United States to be hereunto affixed. Witness my hand at the City of Washington this twenty Sixth day of January A. D. 1832; and of the Independence of the United States of America, the fifty Sixth.

ANDREW JACKSON.

By the President,
    EDW LIVINGSTON, *Secretary of State.*

There was also issued to Roberts under the same date (*ibid.*, 189) a certificate signed by Secretary of State Livingston, under the seal of the Department of State, which contained the following clause:

I Certify, That Edmund Roberts a much respected Citizen of the United States, has been appointed by the President of the said United States as their Commissioner to the Governments of Cochin China, Siam and Muscat, with all the privileges and authorities of right appertaining to that appointment.

Roberts succeeded in negotiating two treaties in the course of his mission, namely, this treaty with Siam and that with Muscat (Document 77).

The published story of that first mission of Roberts is in his book, issued in 1837, after his death, entitled "Embassy to the Eastern Courts of Cochin-China, Siam, and Muscat." That work contains much of interest regarding the countries visited and the conduct of the mission generally.

Roberts' official report of this mission is in D. S., 10 Special Agents, 38–67, entitled "*Records* of a *Mission* undertaken by order of the Department of State of the U. States for the purpose of effecting Com^{cl} Treaties with the Kingdoms of Cochin China, Siam & Muscat." On that report the account in these notes is based, with extracts therefrom.

On the U. S. sloop of war *Peacock* Roberts sailed from Boston on March 8, 1832; it was nearly a year later, on February 18, 1833, that the *Peacock* anchored in the Gulf of Siam off the mouth of the Menam

or "Mother of Waters," strictly the Menam Chao Phya, the two latter words being a title of honor. The voyage included stops at the Cape Verde Islands, Rio de Janeiro, Montevideo, Sumatra, Java, Manila, and Canton. From Canton Roberts proceeded to Cochinchina, where his mission was unsuccessful, and from Cochinchina to Siam.

THE KINGDOM OF SIAM

At the time of this treaty the extent of the territories of the Kingdom of Siam was, according to the description of Roberts, as follows (D. S., 10 Special Agents, 29, Roberts to the Secretary of State, Washington, May 14, 1834):

Siam proper extends from about the Latitude of 23? North, to the Gulph of that name, and is bounded West, by the Burman Empire, and East by the Lac (Lau) Mountains, this is the valley of the Menam, the "Mother of Waters," the Country of the true Siamese. This River after watering and manuring the low, flat land, by its annual deposites, empties itself by three channels into the Gulph of Siam. The boundaries of the Siamese Dominions on the Bay of Bengal extend from the Burman, (or more correctly speaking in the present day) the *English* Burmese Dominions, as far south as the Boundary line between the petty states of Perak and Quedah in the Straits of Malacca, in about the Latitude of 5? N. in which is included the valuable Island of Junk, Ceylon, or Salung, containing a vast body of Tin Ore. It then extends nearly East across the Malay Peninsula in about the same Latitude, between the Provinces of Tringano and Pakang, whose shores are bathed by the China Sea—it then extends north to the head of the Gulph of Siam. The Siamese government during the year 1832, brought under their immediate subjection nearly the whole of the tributary states in the Malay Peninsula. They possess also a large part of the late Kingdom of Lao, including the former Capital of the Empire called Lau-chang, situated on the great River Cambojo, in about the 16th degree of north latitude, and which is represented to be very populous. They hold also (with the exception of a small portion of the southern part) the province of Batabang in Camboja. Their Eastern boundary line is in about the Longitude of 105? and extends north to the Latitude of 15°, being the dividing line between Lao and Camboja, and extending South to the Siamese Gulph, the boundary being the Island of Kong (alias Ko Kong) situate in north latitude 10? 43′ and Longitude 103? 17′ east. Extending north on the east coast of the Gulph lies Chantabun, once a part of the ancient Kingdom of Camboja—it is well known as a rich and valuable possession of Siam.

THE NEGOTIATIONS

Of the negotiations in Siam Roberts gives a detailed account. They were opened by the following letter (D. S., 10 Special Agents, 51) written in Chinese and English, the address of which is explained by the fact that at that time Roberts knew neither the name nor the title of the Siamese Minister of Foreign Affairs:

To His Excellency, the SUPERINTENDANT-GENERAL OF FOREIGN AFFAIRS, COM-MERCE, &c. *Bankok.*

Edmund Roberts, Special Envoy from the United States of America, desires to inform your Excellency, that Andrew Jackson, President of the United States of America, wishing to open a friendly intercourse with the King of Siam, has sent the United States Ship of War Peacock, Captn David Geisinger, to His Majesty's dominions.

And the President of the said United S. of America has deputed me his special Envoy to His Majesty's court, clothing me with full powers to treat, on behalf of the President of the United States, for the special purpose of effecting a Commercial treaty between the two Countries.

I have now the honour to inform Your Excellency that I have arrived in the said U. S. Ship off the Coast of His Majesty's dominions. I therefore request your Excellency to make it known to His Majesty, that measures may be taken to ensure me, and the Officers and Servants who may accompany me (amounting in number to about 15 persons), a speedy arrival at Bankok, where I shall be enabled immediately to enter on the important business confided to me by the President.

Signed and Sealed on board the U. Ship of War Peacock, off the entrance of the River Menam, in the Gulf of Siam, this 18ᵗʰ day of February A D. 1833. and of independence the fifty-seventh.

(Signed) EDMUND ROBERTS (Seal)

In due course Roberts was conducted to Bangkok (more properly then, according to Roberts, *op. cit.*, 281, called Sia Yuthia). The former capital of Siam, now called Ayuthia, is situated some forty miles north of Bangkok; the present capital, established about 1770, was for some time called both Bangkok and Siayuthia; in the certificate signed by Roberts and written after the texts of the treaty, the document is dated "at the Royal City of Sia Yuthia (commonly called Bankok)." Roberts was accompanied by Captain Geisinger and other officers of the *Peacock* and also by John R. Morrison (son of the Reverend Dr. Morrison, of Canton), who was familiar with Chinese and who had come from Macao as interpreter (*ibid.*, 153, 169, 230), making, with servants, a party of fifteen. On the arrival of the mission at Bangkok on February 25, a house was assigned for their use; and on the following day Roberts had his first interview with the Phra Klang, one of the Siamese Ministers of State, charged with the direction of foreign affairs.

According to Roberts (*ibid.*, 302), a supreme council of seven officials (two posts being then held by one individual) was at the head of the Siamese administration (see Walter Armstrong Graham, Siam, I, 234); of that council "Chao-phaya praklang" (Chao Phaya Phra Klang), whose post seems to have been somewhat like that of Minister of Commerce and Foreign Affairs, was fourth in rank; of the words themselves Roberts writes:

> Chao-phaya is the first in order of the honorary titles. Praklang is said to signify, "lord of the store-houses," and is the title of the office. This signification corresponds with the title given to him by the Chinese, viz.: "Great minister of the treasuries or store-houses."

At that conference of February 26, 1833, the letter of President Jackson to the King of Siam and also Roberts' full power and passport were produced, with Chinese translations. The first two were translated verbally from English into Portuguese and then written in Siamese; this last version was then compared with the Chinese translation. It was decided that it would be unnecessary to translate the passport.

The discussions regarding the terms of the treaty, involving both its form and its substance, required some three weeks. There were two bases of discussion. One of them was the treaty which Siam had made with the British Government in 1826 and 1827; but there was

no copy in English of the British treaty available. From a copy in Siamese six articles were read and translated into Portuguese. Roberts gives the substance of them, "written down from memory," in his report. From that record it is clear that the six articles were those of January 17, 1827 (British and Foreign State Papers, XXIII, 1165–67), supplementary to the treaty of June 20, 1826 (*ibid.*, 1153–59).

The articles proposed by Roberts (D. S., 10 Special Agents, 54–55) constituted the other basis of discussion. Articles 1, 2, 4, 5, 7, 8, and 9 thereof were taken almost literally from the draft treaty furnished to Roberts by the Department of State (D. S., 1 Special Missions, 80–81), except for the provisions of Article 2 regarding munitions and rice, which were from the British articles.

In the result Articles 1, 2, 4, 5, 7, and 8 of the treaty were substantially and, to some extent, literally in accord with the draft prepared in the Department of State.

The American proposals included an article regarding the appointment of American consuls in Siam. It seems that at the time the only European consul in the country was from Portugal (see Roberts, *op. cit.*, 244, 268); Roberts wrote: "The chief, in fact the only argument against Consuls was the uselessness of the Portuguese Consul, who has held the appointment and had a treaty the Phra-Klang said, fifteen years, without having a Single Portuguese vessel to trade in Siam." The Siamese view seems to have been that the establishment of trade should precede the appointment of consuls; accordingly, Article 10 was written so as to permit the appointment of American consuls only in case the same privilege was granted to some country other than Portugal.

Regarding the treaty reported to have been made between Portugal and Siam about 1818, it may be said that in no treaty collection which has been examined is there any mention of such a treaty; in particular, in Wyke and Keuchenius, State Papers of the Kingdom of Siam, published in London in 1886 (see Myers, Manual of Collections of Treaties, 312), there is no mention of any treaty made between Siam and Portugal earlier than that of 1859.

There was, in fact, no such treaty in the strict sense. In 1820 Carlos Manuel da Silveira was sent to Siam as Portuguese Consul General; his mission was to establish commercial relations between Portugal and Siam and to negotiate a treaty; he was duly received and was given a title of rank; and under date of November 9, 1820, he was granted a tract of land for the consulate, part of which is still owned by Portugal and occupied as the Portuguese Consulate at Bangkok. No treaty was then concluded between Portugal and Siam, but the grant mentioned rights of commerce. The relations of that period between Portugal and Siam are recounted in Boletim da agência geral das colónias for March, 1931 (No. 69, pp. 58–70); in that narrative is included the text, in Portuguese, of the communication of the Prime Minister of Siam of November 9, 1820, which contained the grant and privileges mentioned.

In the discussions between Roberts and the Phra Klang the question of the language of the treaty was necessarily considered. It appears from Roberts' report that the Siamese Government required a Chinese translation to be included; Roberts in return required one in Portuguese, as being a language known in the United States; the result was four texts in all, the Siamese and the English with Portuguese and Chinese translations.

The Siamese Minister of Foreign Affairs also laid down the procedure regarding the signing of the treaty and the exchange of the ratifications which was finally adopted, although not then agreed to by Roberts, and which, so far as it related to the number of originals of the treaty, was discussed at some length thereafter. The conversation is thus reported (D. S., 10 Special Agents, 55):

> It was next stated by the Phra Klang, that it would be necessary to have two copies of the treaty, which would be sealed by the Phra-Klang and the Envoy: then one copy being kept in Siam, the other must be carried to the United States, and being there ratified, it shall be brought back to Siam, when the King will affix his seal to the other copy, and give it in exchange. This was objected to as being contrary to the general usage. It was answered that Captain Burnay [the negotiator of the British treaty] had done the same. The Envoy finding the Phra-Klang unwilling to give up the point, desired time for consideration.

On March 18, 1833, Roberts was accorded an audience by the King of Siam, a full account of which is in his report; and on the following day the provisions of the treaty were verbally agreed upon.

The language question was one of great difficulty, as the preamble to the treaty itself states, and interpreters were employed throughout the negotiations, the Portuguese and Chinese languages being used as intermediates between English and Siamese; but the proposals of Roberts had, of course, been first written in English; and it seems that the discussions of the text as far as he was concerned related to that language only, for he wrote that at the conclusion of his conference with one of the Siamese officials on March 19, when the terms of the treaty were agreed on, "the P'hra Klang had finally rejected almost all the changes he had previously adopted, & restored the Treaty, with the exception of a few alterations to what it had been originally proposed by the Envoy" (*ibid.*, 62).

The textual date of the signature of the treaty is March 20, 1833, and the entry for that day in the report of Roberts is as follows (*ibid.*, 63):

> The Treaty having been today presented to the King, and approved by him, the writing out of three Siamese copies was forthwith commenced, without further reference to the Envoy. In consequence of having today received the King's approval, the Treaty bears date from this day.

Much remained to be done, however, before the actual signing of the treaty on April 1. The preparation of a satisfactory Siamese text and of the Portuguese and Chinese translations proved to be no easy task; errors were found in the Portuguese as first drawn up; a draft of the Chinese version had to be entirely discarded and rewritten

with the aid of a Chinese merchant in the service of the Siamese Government; that examination of the Chinese text brought about, indeed, the clause in Article 2 for prohibiting the importation of opium; and, finally, the Siamese copies were found incorrect and had to be rewritten. On March 30 Roberts recorded the following in his report:

Today the three copies of the Treaty were completed, in the Siamese, English, Portuguese, and Chinese languages,—each language being written in opposite columns on the same sheet.

One more question arose, as to the number of originals to be executed. It had been agreed on March 11 and March 20 that three originals should be executed, two of which would be given to Roberts "in order to provide against accidents that might occur to a single copy,—by sending one to the United States by a different conveyance, while the other should be kept by the Envoy himself." But in the result only two originals were signed and sealed, and Roberts gives this account of the execution of the documents on April 1, 1833 (*ibid.*, 64):

The Envoy went to the P'hra-Klang's about noon, to sign and seal the Treaties. The preparations for this on the part of the Phra-Klang occupied some time. At length his name was signed & his seal attached to two Copies, which operation was performed, according to Siamese Custom, by his Secretaries. The Envoy enquired what was intended to be done with the third copy. The P'hra-Klang replied, that he had changed his mind on the subject, and found it impossible to give the Envoy more than one copy signed and sealed. The promise which he had previously made of giving two copies was adverted to, and the probability stated, of some accident happening to the vessel in the long cruize she had yet to make, by which the Treaty might be prevented ever reaching the United States. The P'hra Klang answered that it was impossible a man of war could be lost,—that the Envoy must not entertain the idea,—and that, finally, he could not have his seal and signature attached to a third copy. The Envoy again represented, that it could not be possible for him to sell the duplicate of the Treaty, and if it were possible, such Treaty could be of no use to its purchasers & that were he even to have fifty copies, they could not have any more effect whatever than a single one. This the P'hra-Klang admitted, and he consented so far as to say he would give two copies, provided they should both be brought back. This, he was told, could not possibly be promised, as the object of having two was to ensure the greater probability of one of them reaching the United States, by sending them by different vessels. The P'hra-Klang thereupon repeated, that he could not give another copy, for that it was contrary to custom to give more than one;—and enquired if the ratification would be sent out by an Agent of the Government, or how, & by whom, adding that it ought not on any account to be sent by a Merchant Captain. The Envoy told him, that he could not say by whom it would be sent out, and that in fact it was not unlikely, if a single copy only were given, that some accident would prevent its reaching the United States or being brought out at all. He pointed out also the folly of speaking of customs, when all their customs was merely derived from one or two Treaties with the British, and added that in any European or American Nation as many Copies would be given as might be desired. The P'hra-Klang, however, still persisted in his refusal; the Envoy therefore having signed and sealed the two copies only, took one of them, together with the one which still remained without seal or signature; and then took leave.

On April 6, 1833, Roberts sailed from Siam for Muscat to carry on his negotiations there, regarding which the notes to Document 77 should be consulted.

The Original Documents

The treaty as a document is unique, being, as first signed and delivered, twenty-one inches wide and nine feet long. This now single sheet of heavy paper was made up from seven sheets which were joined together; and on the reverse, at each junction of the sheets, there is an imprint of a Siamese seal and a stamp of the name of Edmund Roberts.

The texts are written from one end of the document to the other in parallel columns, the Siamese on the left, then the Portuguese, then the Chinese, and finally the English. As the Siamese language is written from left to right, its text, like that of the English and Portuguese, is read down the document; but in the column space given to the Chinese translation, the vertical lines of Chinese characters are written sideways of the document, beginning at the top of the space column and so as properly to permit the Chinese version, like the other three, to be read continuously from the top of the document to the foot, but so to be read only from one side of the document, as though it were a scroll.

Following the four columns of texts are the seals, the royal seal of Siam on the left, the seal of the Phra Klang or Siamese Minister of Foreign Affairs in the center, the first seal with one line and the second with two lines of Siamese script beneath (which are not strictly signatures, but which describe and identify the seals above), and the seal and signature of Edmund Roberts at the right. Following these, written across the document from one side to the other, is the concluding certificate reserving the treaty for the ratification of the President by and with the advice and consent of the Senate, signed by Edmund Roberts, but without his seal. This certificate is wholly in the handwriting of Roberts.

Such was the form of the treaty when first signed and delivered, except that on that occasion the document did not bear the royal seal and the line of script beneath it; they were added upon the delivery of the United States instrument of ratification; and at the same time there was added to the document a paper, more particularly described hereafter, which is at once the Siamese instrument of ratification and a certificate of exchange, and which makes the treaty document in its present form almost twelve feet long.

The Siamese text of the treaty is first reproduced above, with the two seals, the royal seal of Siam and the seal of the Phra Klang; then follows the English text, with the certificate of Edmund Roberts reserving the ratification of the treaty for the President of the United States by and with the advice and consent of the Senate; then is printed the Portuguese translation as written in the original treaty document; and finally there is a reproduction of the Chinese translation, the vertical lines of the Chinese characters running sideways of the pages, from top to foot of each page. The paper above mentioned which was added to the treaty document upon the delivery of the United States instrument of ratification, is not, as such, reproduced; it will now be described.

That paper, which has been called a ratification and certificate of exchange of ratifications, is about thirty-three inches long and was originally composed of two sheets; and on the reverse of the document, at the junction of those two sheets, as well as at the junction of the paper with the treaty proper, appear the same Siamese seal and stamp of the name of Edmund Roberts as on the reverse of the treaty.

The ratification and certificate of exchange of ratifications is written in Siamese, Portuguese, and English, in parallel columns; it bears the royal seal as well as the seals of the six chief Ministers of State of Siam, each with a line of Siamese script beneath it, descriptive of the seal above. The English version reads as follows:

This is to Certify; that Edmund Roberts a Special Envoy of the United States of America, delivered & exchanged a ratified Treaty on the day & date hereafter mention'd, & which was signed & sealed in the Royal City of Sia-Yuthia, (being the Capital of the Kingdom of Siam) on the twentieth day of March Anno Domini One thousand, eight hundred & thirty three; corresponding to the fourth month of the year of the Dragon.

In Witness whereof, We the Magnificent King of Siam do ratify and confirm the said Treaty, by affixing hereunto Our Royal Seal, as well as the Seals of all our great Ministers of State, at the City of Sia-Yuthia on the fourteenth day of the fifth month of the year called the Monkey, being the Sacarat or year Eleven hundred & ninety eight, & which corresponds to the fourteenth day of the month of April, being the year of Christ One thousand, eight hundred & thirty six.

The Portuguese version is fairly equivalent to the English; but it gives the year of the treaty erroneously as 1836 instead of 1833; and it does not include express words of ratification and confirmation. It reads as follows in translation:

I hereby certify that Edmund Roberts, Special Envoy of the United States of North America, delivered and exchanged a ratified copy of a treaty signed and sealed in the royal city of Siayuthia, the capital of the Kingdom of Siam, on the twentieth day of March, the year of our Lord one thousand eight hundred and thirty-six, which corresponds to the fourth month of the year eleven hundred and ninety-four, called Pi Marong chatava Sok, or year of the Dragon. In testimony whereof it is sealed with the royal seal of Siam and with the seals of all the great Ministers of State on the fourteenth day of the month of April, the year of our Lord Jesus Christ eighteen hundred and thirty-six, which corresponds to the fourteenth day of the fifth month of the year called the Monkey, being the sakarat or year eleven hundred and ninety-eight.

The form of the Siamese version is different, though its substance is about the same. It has been thus translated by the Siamese Legation at Washington:

On the second day of the week, tenth of the waning moon, fifth month of year 1198, the year of the Monkey, and eighth of the decade, Edmund Roberts, Envoy of the United States of America, brought back the treaty which he had come to negotiate in the fourth month of the year of the Serpent, fourth year of the decade, bearing the American seal, to exchange for the treaty bearing the royal seal. At the capital, Sri Ayuddhya, the royal seal Phra Ayaraboj, as well as seals of the responsible Cabinet Ministers, were affixed to the treaty on the sixth day of the week, fourteenth day of the waning moon, fifth month of year 1198, year of the Monkey, and eighth year of the decade, corresponding to Christian era 1836, fourteenth day of the month of April.

An error in the English version is disclosed by the foregoing translation of the Siamese; the Siamese date of the document is not "the fourteenth day of the fifth month," etc., but "the fourteenth day of the full moon, in the fifth month," etc., or, say, the twenty-ninth of that month; and information from the Naval Observatory confirms the Siamese text, for April 14, 1836, was the fourteenth day of the full moon.

Two other original documents are in the treaty file; one is the attested Senate resolution of June 30, 1834; the other is the proclamation of June 24, 1837; but the proclamation, though otherwise in the usual form, does not in fact include any text of the treaty, despite the phrase "which Treaty is, word for word as follows." Doubtless the treaty text was deemed to be constructively included in the original proclamation or annexed thereto, for the proclamation as printed at the time (e.g., in Niles' Weekly Register, LII, 398–99, August 19, 1837) contains the English text of the treaty proper and also the concluding certificate of Edmund Roberts.

In the file are also various facsimiles of documents in the Siamese archives. The first to be mentioned is a facsimile of the United States instrument of ratification of January 3, 1835, signed by President Jackson, attested by Secretary of State Forsyth, and under the Great Seal, the impression of which, according to the then practice, was enclosed in a box "of silver richly gilt" (D. S., 1 Special Missions, 122; see also the letter of Roberts to the Secretary of State of December 15, 1834, D. S., 10 Special Agents, 81). According to the recitals of the ratification, the original treaty was annexed thereto, meaning that original which was delivered to Edmund Roberts on April 1, 1833.

There is also a facsimile of the original treaty which is now in the archives of the Government of Siam; this is in all respects similar to the treaty document heretofore described, as first signed and delivered; it does not bear the royal seal of Siam and the line of script thereunder and does not have with it the document executed upon the exchange of ratifications.

The Exchange of Ratifications

The purpose of the second mission of Edmund Roberts to the Far East as Special Agent of the United States was, in part, to effect the exchange of ratifications of the treaties signed in 1833 with Siam and with Muscat (Document 77).

To that end Roberts was given letters of credence and authority, signed by President Jackson under date of March 20, 1835, attested by Secretary of State Forsyth, and addressed respectively to "the Magnificent King of Siam" and to "the Sultan of Muscat" (D. S., 1 Special Missions, 148–49; and see the notes to Document 77); and similar, but conditional, letters of credence and authority, under date of April 17, 1835, were given to Captain Edmund P. Kennedy, U. S. N., to be used "in case that Edmund Roberts, who is about to embark in the said vessel [the sloop of war *Peacock*], to whom the ratification of the said Treaty on the part of this Government is

delivered, and who is empowered to make the exchange of ratifications, should, from death or any other physical incapacity, be prevented from performing that service" (*ibid.*, 152–53).

Roberts had also elaborate instructions, under date of March 20, 1835, to negotiate a commercial treaty with Cochinchina and a similar treaty with Japan (D. S., 1 Special Missions, 131–36); and he was given full powers to treat with those two Governments and also letters (under the Great Seal, which is unusual) from the President of the United States to the Emperor of Wiet Nam and to the Emperor of Japan (*ibid.*, 146–48). The two full powers were similar and in customary form, running to "Edmund Roberts, a citizen of these United States," and giving authority "to negotiate conclude and sign a Convention or Conventions, Treaty or Treaties, of and concerning the friendship, commerce, and navigation of the two countries, and all matters and subjects connected therewith, which may be interesting to the two nations." The documents for Cochinchina were accompanied by translations into French and Portuguese and those for Japan by translations into Dutch and Latin.

As far as has been observed, those two documents in Latin, namely, the translation of the letter of President Jackson to the Emperor of Japan and the translation of the full power given to Roberts to treat with Japan, are the only two documents in Latin originating in the Department of State of which there is a record. One of them, the Latin version of the full power, is in the archives; and copies of both, with a blank for the name of Edmund Roberts and for the title of the Emperor of Japan, are in D. S., 10 Special Agents, 95.

The death of Roberts on June 12, 1836, at Macao, took place before he had been able to undertake any negotiations on this mission either with Cochinchina or with Japan.

The report of that mission is in D. S., 10 Special Agents, 114–17, entitled "Records of a Mission, and occurrences connected with a Mission, to the Courts of Muscat, Siam, Cochin China and Japan; undertaken by the Undersign'd by Instructions from the Department of State of the United States of America, on board the U. States Ship of War Peacock E. K. Stribling Acting Commander, under E. P. Kennedy Commodore." The final date of that report is April 20, 1836, and the following account, with extracts therefrom, is based thereon.

The *Peacock* sailed from New York on April 23, 1835, for Rio de Janeiro, thence to Zanzibar, and from Zanzibar to Muscat, where the mission in respect of the treaty with the Sultan of Muscat was accomplished (see the notes to Document 77).

Leaving Muscat for the further accomplishment of his mission on October 11, 1835, Roberts proceeded to Siam by way of Bombay, Colombo, and Batavia. On March 25, 1836, when in the Gulf of Siam and nearing the entrance to the Menam (or Me-nam), Roberts sent forward to Bangkok a letter dated the previous day and addressed to "His Excellency the Chao P'haya P'hraklang one of the first Ministers of State to His Magnificent Majesty the King of Siam," in which he wrote (D. S., 10 Special Agents, 115):

Edmund Roberts Special Envoy from the United States of America, has the honor to inform your Excel^cy, that he has arriv'd off the Bar of the Menam in the U. States Ship of War Peacock, commanded by Capt Stribling, accompanied by the Schn^r of War Enterprize, Capt Campbell; the Squadron being under the command of Commodore Kennedy.

The Envoy begs leave to state, that he has brought back the Treaty which he had the honor to conclude between His Majesty of Siam & the U. States of America on the 20th day of March in the year 1833, and which was ratified on the part of his Gov^t on the 30th day of June of the past year (1835) [meaning June 30, 1834, the date of the Senate resolution] and which is now return'd for the purpose of exchanging it for its counterpart in the possession of Siam, on its being duly ratified by his Majesty, and the Royal Seal of the Kingdom affixed to the articles of the Treaty, as well as to the necessary certificate of ratification.

The Envoy has also the honor to inform your Excel^cy, that he has brought with him the articles His Majesty of Siam & your Excel^cy requested should be sent by the U. S. Gov^t with the exception of the Stone Statues which could not be obtain'd; and also, the Trees, & plants & seeds which were destroyed on the passage, the Peacock having been unfortunately wreck'd about six months since on the Coast of Arabia—but the deficiency in the Statues has been repaired by purchasing an extra number of the most elegant & expensive Lamps together with some other articles.

Your Excl^cy is therefore requested to send a suitable vessel to receive the presents before alluded to, with an order directed to me for their delivery. Your Excl^cy is further requested to furnish the Envoy with convenient & proper vessels capable of protecting himself & the Officers & servants which may accompany him to the capital, to the number of twenty five persons from the inclemencies of the weather with as little delay as possible as the Envoy has to visit many kingdoms, & has a great many thousands of miles of ocean to traverse, which will necessarily occupy the space of at least twelve months to accomplish.

The exchange of ratifications of this treaty was an elaborate ceremony, very different from the usual formality of the mutual delivery of two instruments of ratification and comparison of texts; indeed, the proceedings lasted from April 11 to 18, inclusive, the textual date of the exchange being April 14.

The form which the exchange took was the delivery by Roberts of the instrument of ratification executed by President Jackson on January 3, 1835, with the original treaty which had been received by Roberts in 1833 annexed thereto, in exchange for the other original treaty executed in 1833; to that other original was affixed the royal seal and to it was appended a paper which included the ratification on the part of Siam and a certificate of the exchange, dated April 14, 1836, written in Siamese, Portuguese, and English, and sealed with the royal seal and with the seals of the six principal officers of state of Siam.

On April 6 Roberts reached Bangkok, some miles up the Menam, and he thus describes his reception and escort (*ibid.*, 115):

On the 5th at 4 P. M arriv'd a very handsome large three masted Boat of Ceremony (Pudade & Raymunde two interpreters being sent in her) to conduct us to Packnam, when she would be taken in tow by four other boats of ceremony. She was mounted with four long brass guns (forward & aft) which were inlaid about the breech with silver flowers—she had numerous red flags—& two rudders. On her anchoring she saluted with 13 guns which was return'd with 21. Embark'd on board of her the presents sent to His Magnificent Majesty of Siam & C. P. P'hraklang. . . .

There embark'd on board this vessel the Comod[r], and myself & twenty three officers belonging to the two vessells including my interpreter Mr Jacobs nine Musicians & four or five other servants.   We arriv'd about nine at Packnam & visited the Gov[r] and partook of a feast which had been prepared for us the day previous—presented him with a double barrelled fouling piece, caps &c and two cases of gin purchas'd at Batavia—breakfast ended we reimbark'd on the morning of the 6th and our boat was taken in tow by four other boats of ceremony having each double rudders & mann'd by 136 oars the rowers being clothed in red uniform the trowsers being short & embroider'd at the termination of the leg—the coats with sleeves button'd loosely in front at the upper part—& bound with copper lace—caps helmet shaped & of the same materials.   The rowers kept time by striking one foot on the deck & making loud shouts, which was regulated by a person who struck together two cylindrical pieces of bambu.   The five boats contain'd upwards of 300 men being mostly Malays—Burmese & C. Chinese Slaves belonging to the King & taken in various wars—they were all clothed in red thin wollen cloth, with the exception of the artillery men, who were dressd in blue coatees slash'd about the breast &c all wearing broad swords.   As soon as the boats began to move the band struck up "Hail Columbia" which brought forth a numerous population to the banks of the river.   The procession form'd a very gay scene & was very imposing in its appearance

On our arrival opposite the extensive fortifications at Packlat being about 8 miles above P-knam, we found the shores lined with thousands of people and the Governor of the place sent off per order of His Majesty several canoes laden with fruit, which was rec'd with suitable acknowledgments, the band playing various tunes.   We arriv'd about 8 & landed shortly after at the house furnish'd by the King—it was lighted with numerous glass Lamps, having tables, chairs & twenty two neat new bedsteads, with new mattresses & neat mosquito nets & the floors entirely matted, with crockery, glass &c.   It had also attach'd to it a bathing room & out house—several Siamese servants were there to attend to the ordinary duties of the house.   The King also furnish'd me with a large & suitable boat having ten rowers &c

Following various official courtesies and functions, the United States instrument of ratification and the treaty annexed thereto were delivered on April 11, in the following manner, according to Roberts' report (*ibid.*, 115):

I have omitted to notice early this day, of the delivery of the ratified Treaty on the part of the U S which was done at the request of His Majesty two days previous to its delivery.   Notice being sent by an officer that one of the Kings gilded barges had arriv'd with an officer & a band of music to receive it in due form, all the Officers present went in procession in full uniform—the box cont[g] it being carried in front of me & in the rear of the music & the U S Flag.   It was carried to the side of the barge & then handed by me to the proper officer; no servant being allowed even to carry it to the boat, or to touch it upon any occasion; such being the custom of Siam—it was then placed on a silver dish resting on a massive silver stand & placed on the raised seat within the gold embroider'd curtains—the "Hail Columbia was struck up on delivering it, and when ended, the Siamese band played a few notes expressive of joy on receiving it. Shortly after the delivery of the Treaty rec'd a written request to deliver the pair of Gold mounted Swords, having massive gold scabbards—the crest of the hilt being surmounted with a golden elephant being symbolical of Siam and the termination showing the Am[en] Eagle with out spreading wings looking down on the elegant blade on which was chased on the steel a Siamese elephant & pagoda & on the opposite side the flag drum, eagle & warlike instruments emblematical of our country.

The preparation of the certificate of the exchange of ratifications was an affair of some three days, and the report of Roberts gives this account of the proceedings (*ibid.*, 115–16):

This morning [April 12] I was requested to visit the Rajah or rather Vice Roy of Ligore, who commands the Kingdom of Ligore in the east part of the Malay peninsula, & which is subject to Siam—the object of the visit was to write the necessary certificate of ratification to the treaty in the possession of Siam having delivered a form for that purpose written in English & Portuguese some days previous, so that it might be translated into Siamese in due time. But it seem'd the interpreter had mistaken the proper time, the morrow being the day appointed. The worthy Rajah seem'd distress'd at our disappointment and repeatedly said, he hoped I was not offended.

. . . .

Visited at 8 this morning [April 13] the Rajah of Ligore. He appointed rather disappointed I had not come attended by all the Officers—but I observ'd to him, that as I attended for the sole purpose of doing business, it would be inconvenient to all parties to invite a greater number than were then present. The Rajah's eldest sons were there seated below their father. Breakfast was serv'd in the same elegant style as yesterday. It being ended, proceeded to business. The Rajah stated that the King's or Royal Seal of Siam could only be placed at the certificate of ratification—to which I replied—that the King in the preamble to the treaty had *promis'd* to affix the seal to the *articles* of the treaty; & therefore he would unquestionably comply with it; and furthermore it was indispensably necessary to place it to the certificate or else it would not be ratified. After some further discussions he at length yielded although "against his will" & said it should be completed entirely in accordance with my wishes. During the morning Prince Mom fa noi called & shook us heartily by the hand as usual. On his appearance the Rajah descended from his elevated seat & kneeled—the Prince taking the highest place. He said he called to see us a few minutes being on his way to visit his eldest brother who is a Talapoy & was sick—his brother being the head priest of a temple a short distance from thence. On the departure of the Prince the Rajah resumed his former station. Shortly after a most elegant dinner was serv'd on thirty six gold & silver dishes placed on as many salvers of the same metal the silver being very massive. The water was serv'd in massive pure gold bowls, placed within richly wrought stands of the same metal, & containing gold drinking cups—even the spittoons were of gold enamell'd with flowers & the teapots were of the same—the number of gold & silver utensils used at the dinner & the desert amounted to *fifty four*. All the variety of ways that ducks, fowls, pork, fish &c &c could be well serv'd in soup, curries, ragouts & plain roasted were serv'd in the nicest manner & the cookery surpass'd all entertainments I have seen in Asia excepting at the Prince Mom fa noi's. Wine—Tea & Cocoa Nut water with fruit in all the variety of the season completed this elegant entertainment. In the afternoon the Prince return'd for a short time, & the Rajah resumed the same humiliating posture.

The . . . certificate was then added to the Treaty being written in the English, Siamese & & Portuguese languages.

. . . .

This certificate being finish'd we took leave, promising to attend the following day at noon to see the Treaty will all the Seals affixed to it.

. . . .

Being about to visit the Rajah of Ligore this morning [April 14] we were inform'd that an error had occurred of one day in the Siamese certificate—it was therefore necessary the certificates in the three languages should re-written. I attended therefore in the afternoon when the mistake rectified in the new certificate. A feast as usual was serv'd & in the same style as before.

On April 16 Roberts was granted an audience by the King of Siam; and on the following day the instrument of ratification and exchange was duly completed, as thus described (*ibid.*, 116):

In the course of the day [April 17] the Rajah of Ligore was again visited & the Treaty was brought forth completed according to my request—the Royal Seal was affix'd to the treaty as well as to the certificate of ratification, together with the six seals of the Ministers of State. He stated that the treaty would not be ready for delivery 'till tomorrow (the box not being made in which it was to be deposited—and then it must be delivered to me on board the Boat of ceremony which was to convey us to the Ship, and that it ought not be landed again. I asked why it could not be relanded & carried to the house of the Mission until we were in readiness to embark. He replied, that the Siamese fully believ'd into whatever house it was carried, that house would be ever after unfortunate to the occupants, & that it would bring some dreadful misfortune upon the owner of it. I acquiesced of course in this *very reasonable* explanation with all due gravity & then took a last leave of the worthy & hospitable Rajah.

Roberts gives an account of the seven seals affixed to the instrument of ratification and exchange, stating their names, "with the names of the different officers of state & the peculiar duties belonging to each office, together with the different devices engraved on each Seal so far as they could be deciphered" (*ibid.*, 116–17). Two of those seals appear also at the foot of the treaty and are reproduced above at the conclusion of the Siamese text; the first is the royal seal and the other is that mentioned in the preamble of the treaty, "the seal of the Lotus flower of glass," which was that of the Chao Phaya Phra Klang or Minister of Foreign Affairs.

Finally, on April 18, the ratified treaty was delivered in state (*ibid.*, 117):

This being the day appointed to receive the Ratified Treaty on the part of Siam, we were notified about one in the afternoon that the Kings Barges were in sight on their way to the vessel of ceremony which was to conduct us to the Peacock.

The officers in full dress accompanied me in three boats having with us the band of music & our flag. We found the P'hya Phiphat Coss'a already there having with him three of the Kings golden barges cont^g about an hund^d men in each clothed in red exclusive of the officers & music. The curtains to each were of cloth of gold the ground being scarlet. One of the boats carried several Royal Chats or Holy Umbrellas of five tiers each diminishing in size to the top, being the same exhibited on each side the throne. The treaty was carried in the latter boat & was contain'd in a box covered with yellow stuff woven with golden materials of no great value, the inside being lined with crimson silk velvet, the box resting on a massive silver dish which was placed on a large salver of the same metal—it was placed under a canopy over which was placed the white or royal umbrella worn only by the King. On its removal of the Treaty to our vessel the Siamese band played soft music on pipes &c On its being placed under the canopy on deck it was placed on another stand sent for that purpose to remain so until it was delivered on board the Peacock. The P. P. C on its being brought on board perform'd one salam to it, because the Royal Seal was affix'd to the document—it was then handed to me which I elevated as high as my head in token of respect to the King, it was then placed on the stand & conveyed into the cabin. On its being received by me, our band struck up the national air of "Hail Columbia." The ceremony being ended we landed again.

On April 20 Roberts sailed on the *Peacock* for Cochinchina; but illness overtook him on the voyage; he died at Macao on June 12, 1836, and was buried there. His passing was reported to the Secretary of State by Commodore Kennedy, U. S. N., in a letter dated June 21 on board the U. S. flagship *Peacock*, off Canton (D. S., 10 Special Agents, 110). Commodore Kennedy wrote:

I regret to inform you of the decease of Edmund Roberts Esquire Special Agent of the United States, and a passenger on board this Ship, at Macao on the 12ᵗʰ instant. He died of dysentary which he contracted at Siam while exchanging the Treaty &c:

The Treaty with the Sultan of Muscat, was ratified on the 30ᵗʰ September [1835], and that with the King of Siam on the 18ᵗʰ April 1836. They are in my possession.

We were detained eight days at Turon Bay, but owing to Mʳ Roberts' severe illness, nothing could be done there, and we sailed for this Port on the 21ˢᵗ of May.

Our expedition to Japan also must be given up, and I have directed that the Presents be forwarded to the United States by the first Vessel directed to the State Department.

. . . .

I sail tomorrow for the Sandwich Islands on my way for the United States.

The treaty was communicated to Congress with the annual message of President Van Buren of December 5, 1837 (Richardson, III, 376).

ARTICLE 3

A tical or bat was then equal to a small fraction over sixty-one cents (despatch of Roberts of May 10, 1833, D. S., 10 Special Agents, 19). The measurement duty was thus, for each six feet and one half measured "from side to side, in the middle of the Vessel's length," slightly in excess of $1,037 for ships selling merchandise and about $925 for ships with specie only.

During the course of the proceedings for the exchange of ratifications of the treaty, an American merchant vessel which had arrived at Bangkok, the brig *Maria Theresa*, of Boston, was measured on April 17 by the Siamese officials, pursuant to Article 3 of the treaty. Some questions arose as to the exact method of measurement across the deck; but while Roberts had at first protested, it appeared that the "deviation from the strict letter of the treaty" was in favor of the vessel by some ten inches and, accordingly, to the satisfaction of her captain; so Roberts was perforce content also, though unwilling to sanction "any infraction of the treaty"; and he forbore comment when the Siamese authorities stated that the mode adopted would be the precedent for all American vessels in the future (report of Roberts, *ibid.*, 116).

In his letter to the Secretary of State dated at Washington May 14, 1834, with which were transmitted the original treaties with the King of Siam and the Ruler of Muscat (Document 77), Roberts estimated the difference "in exactions and impositions prior and subsequent to the conclusion of the treaty" for a vessel of 250 tons with a beam of 25 feet and a cargo of $40,000 (see also Roberts, *op. cit.*, 315–16). He calculated that the various charges in such a case prior to the treaty were not less than $35,275 and that the measurement duty of Article 3 of the treaty was $4,275, or a difference in favor of the treaty of at least $31,000, and he added (D. S., 10 Special Agents, 31):

The result is that the treaty has restored to us a valuable branch of commerce which was entirely destroyed and which will continue to increase vastly as the Siamese recover from the serious disasters which resulted from the inundation of

the valley of the Menam for upwards of three months, during the year 1831. By the latest accounts several American vessels had arrived at Bankok eager to take advantage of the first re-opening of our trade; and good voyages, I trust, will be the reward of their industry. The Siamese will (I am perfectly satisfied) faithfully fulfil every article of the treaty.

Article 6

A copy of the treaty was enclosed with the despatch of Roberts from Batavia of June 22, 1833, endorsed as received November 11, 1833 (D. S., 10 Special Agents, 20–22). Somewhat earlier, however, there had appeared in the American press (e.g., the Daily National Intelligencer, October 31, 1833) an article copied from the Singapore Chronicle of June 6, containing some account of the negotiation and of the treaty, though not its text. That account was particularly critical of Article 6, the wording of which was somewhat inaccurately stated. In his despatch of January 17, 1834, from Rio de Janeiro (D. S., 10 Special Agents, 26) Roberts referred in the following terms to the criticism of Article 6:

> Some of the A. Papers I see Sir, have commented in rather severe terms, upon a clause in the Siam Treaty relative to Siamese debtors. It was introduced by the intrigues of the Chuliahs & the Chinese who possess great influence, hoping thereby to defeat me altogether. It was not introduced by me into the original draft, as the Official Records of the Mission will show. It only related to Am^{en} debtors. All foreigners as well as natives (by the laws of Siam) may be sold as well as put to excruciating tortures, if they cannot pay their debts. I had no means of avoiding the objectionable clause, although every exertion was used. The Ship was in fact *very* short of provisions which could not be had excepting at Singapore or Batavia. I therefore was obliged to *push matters*, which might have ended differently if there had been sufficient time. It is not a matter of primary importance after all. Am^{cns} who trade there, must go upon the old & only correct system in such countries—Viz^t—to sell & receive payment at the moment of purchase. The objectionable clause can be rejected by the President & the Senate.

In the later published account of the mission (Roberts, *op. cit.*, 314) there appears this further discussion of the article:

> As foreigners were equally liable to the penalties with the natives, I deemed it most proper to guard against the barbarity, which gave the creditor in fact the power of life and death over his debtor, and therefore in the early stage of the negotiation, I proposed an article (which was agreed to) which released the American citizen only, from all pains and penalties, by delivering to his creditors all the property he possessed. About a fortnight after its conclusion, the minister inserted an additional clause, making it reciprocal, so that the Siamese debtor might receive the same benefit of the American creditor. He was told it would have an unequal operation, as it would very rarely occur that an American would incur a debt to a Siamese; but he insisted that it should remain as it was, although I proposed nullifying the whole article. But still if any American feels disposed to take advantage of a code of laws written in blood, it will readily suggest to him that a transfer of his debt to a responsible Siamese, will give him a free and unimpeded course to hunt down a prostrate victim.

The Siamese Calendar

There are valuable, though not wholly complete, accounts of the Siamese calendar in the works of Sir John Bowring (The Kingdom

and People of Siam, I, 155–57) and of Roberts (*op. cit.*, 309–10). Roberts writes:

> The Siamese week consists of seven days; the months, alternately, of twenty-nine and thirty days; and twelve months, or three hundred and fifty-four days, make a year. The year being solar, an intercalary month of thirty days is added every third year after the eighth month. The month is divided into a dark and a bright half, as the moon is upon the increase or the wane.

It should be said, however, that that year was not strictly solar; three solar years are about three days longer than thirty-seven lunar months; and the length of three years by the Siamese calendar, according to Roberts, as above, would be 1,092 days; three years of our calendar are either 1,095 or 1,096 days; obviously without further correction the dates of the Siamese calendar would recede, as compared with solar time, approximately one month every twenty-four years (see Walter Armstrong Graham, Siam, I, 367–69).

The Siamese civil calendar then (not now) in use dated its numbered years from the time "when the worship of Gautama was first introduced" (Roberts, *op. cit.*); Bowring gives the date as 638 A. D. (*op. cit.*).

One complexity of that Siamese calendar lay in the fact that along with the numbered years there were cycles of twelve named years, each one of the twelve being named for some kind of animal; and each year began with the fifth month and ended with the following fourth month.

Illustrations may be given from the dates of the treaty and of its ratification. In the preamble of the treaty it is said that it was concluded on March 20, 1833, and, according to the Siamese year, on the last day of the fourth month of the year 1194, the year of the Dragon (more properly Large Snake, the fifth year of the cycle of twelve). In the Siamese calendar that day was the last day of the numbered year 1194 and, accordingly, was also the last day of the year of the Large Snake.

The certificate of the exchange of ratifications of the treaty was dated April 14, 1836, and the Siamese date was the fourteenth day of the full moon in the fifth month of the year 1198, the year of the Monkey, or in other words, the twenty-ninth day of the fifth month of the year 1198, the year of the Monkey, which is the ninth year of the cycle of twelve; so that Siamese date is at the same time the twenty-ninth day of the numbered year 1198 and also the twenty-ninth day of the year of the Monkey.

The elapsed time between the two dates in each calendar corresponds. From March 20, 1833, to April 14, 1836, is 1,121 days. In the Siamese calendar the period was three years plus twenty-nine days. Now three years of the Siamese calendar comes to 1,092 days which, plus twenty-nine days, is 1,121 days.

The named years in the cycles of twelve were as follows: (1) Rat, (2) Cow, (3) Tiger, (4) Hare or Rabbit, (5) Large Snake (sometimes translated Dragon), (6) Small Snake, (7) Horse, (8) Goat, (9) Monkey, (10) Cock, (11) Dog, (12) Pig.

Treaty Series No. 247
8 Statutes at Large, 458–59
18 *ibid.*, pt. 2, Public Treaties, 528–30

77

MUSCAT (OMAN) : SEPTEMBER 21, 1833

*Treaty of Amity and Commerce, signed at Muscat September 21, 1833
(6 Jumada I, A. H. 1249). Original in Arabic and English.
Submitted to the Senate June 12, 1834. (Message of May 30, 1834.)
Resolution of advice and consent June 30, 1834. Ratified by the
United States January 3, 1835. Ratified by Muscat September 30,
1835. Ratifications exchanged at Muscat September 30, 1835; but as
to the ratification generally, see the notes. Proclaimed June 24, 1837.
The Arabic text of the treaty is first reproduced (in facsimile), with
the signature of the Ruler of Muscat but without the seal; then is printed
the English text with the signature and seal of Edmund Roberts,
followed by the clause of conclusion signed by Roberts, reserving the
treaty for the ratification of the President by and with the advice
and consent of the Senate. After the treaty texts is printed an
annotated translation of the Arabic. The original treaty document
is described in the notes.*

789

٤

بيان تصريح المكاتبة التي وقعت بين جناب المؤيد السيد السيد ابن السيد سلطان خامي مسقط بقوته

مع يونيتد ستات يعني بلدان الأمريكة   لأجل الألفة والمحبة وتجارة ماء البيع والشراء

المطلب الأول يبيع لأنه لا يزال   وأن مع بين جناب الغاليجا السيد ابن السيد سلطان

وجميع بلدان الأمريكة

المطلب الثاني   سكان بلاد الأمريك لهم رخصة الدخول في أي بندر كان بناد رجنا :

الغاليجا السيد ابن السيد سلطان خامي مسقط   مع كل نعمة   يكون معهم ولهم رخصة

في بيع المذكور على كل ما كان من متعينة جناب السيد أم غيرهم ممن لهم امرأة مشتري :

تلك النعمة أم معاوضة أم مبادلة بكل الذي يحصل اليهم من ضياع تلك البلاد :

والبضائع التي يصلون بها ناس نفسهم يحدذ ثمنها وقيمتها ولا يكون عديتها من جناب السلطان :

ولكن قيمة اسعار الثمن والقيمة على أموال التجار القاطنين في بلاد يونيتد ستات الأمريكا وكذلك

اذا ارادوا شرآء شيئ من البضايع فلا يكون تحديد القيمه والثمن والمذكوبين على كل الامم

بضآء ريكين شرآهما البضآ المذكوبين يكون البيع والشرآء من الطرفين والجانبين منتظم غير

منقطع والبيع والشرآء يكون سآلك وفي المعاوضته عند لاتفآق يكون كذلك اذا حصل

الوفق من صاحبتآل في المعاوضته واذا ما حصل الاتفآق فلامريكه سكان ينتاسبت

وان ارادوا الخروج لا يكون لهم آنع وان احد من اولاد السلطان ام من عمّال ه .

تعمل فعلاً يخالف هذه المكاتبته يجازى من السلطان بانهل الجزآء

.٠ واذا وصل شيئ من البارووت والرصاص والاتفاق لاجل البيع

.٠ والشرآء والمعاملة من بلدآن الامريكان لا يمكن ٠

.٠ يشترى الا السلطان خاصه دوته .

ما عداه من الرعيّة

المطلب الثالث لما كب يونتاست الامريكان اذا وصلوا ودخلوا البلدن التي هي

تحت حكم السلطان او كل بلد كانت تحت حكمه يكون لا يعلمهم من التسليم شيئ الا

العشور في كل مائة خمس على المال والبضائع والشحنة النازلة ولا عليهم

تكون شيء غير ما ذكرناه أبداً والعوض لا عليه شيء من ذلك بالكلية

أبداً وما كان شيء تبقى فالمال ولا ابتياع وأراد وايرجوا فعليه :

فالماه خمس وما عداها فلا عليه مغرم او غير ذلك :

من مراكب الأمريكان واذا ارادوا الدخول في كل بندر كان زياده

جناب السلطان لأجل منها الماء او اشترى طعاماً إلا لأجل تصليح مراكبهم او لا
أن يبيعوا ويسلوا عن سفراتي

المطلب الرابع تجار الأمريكان الساكنين بونيتاست لا يكون عليهم تسلط

الزايد فالعشور او تكون غير ذلك بل يكونوا مثل الطائفة اللتي في :
اقرب في المحبة

المطلب الخامس ان كان شيء من مراكب بونيتاست الأمريكان اصابه

حكم التلف او انكسر في شيء من بلدان السلطان او في كل بلد اللتي

هي تحت حكم السلطان فكل من يكسر مراكب المذكور .:

المنكسر يعتني ويحتم غاية الاهتمام وبما ينتج عليه

من المصرف فهو يسلمه السلطان لا ان تحصل له عبرة

يبعث بها الى موطنه ومسكنه وايضا السالم فالمركب المنكسر

من المال يحفظ حفظًا تامًا ويسلم بيد صاحبه او

او بيد الكونسل بونيتاستاتس اوكل مفوض يقبضها واذا ما على ذا الخطوط

المطلب السادس اهل يونيتاستاتس سكان بلاد الاميكيه اذا ارادوا

ان يصلوا الى احد بلاد ان السلطان لاجل البيع والشراء فنهم مخوصين .:

وفي تنزيل اموالهم ليبوا بمعارضين واذا ارادوا ان يسكنوا فلا عليهم منها السكن

ية ولا سلوم شيء بل يكونوا مثل الطائعة الله على احد في القوة

المطلب السابع اذا احد من بلاد يونيتاستاميكيه ام مركب من مراكبهم ام مال

فهو الحر أميته   وجنى به   لا أحد بلاد السلطا انكان رجل يخلص ف ايديم

ما نكان ما لام غير ذلك يخلص وحفظ لا حينا   و يقبض صاحبه

او الى الكونسل الذي   من يونيتاس   او الى الوكيل المفوض   ؛

المطلب الثامن   انا وصل احد   من مراكب السلطا او من الرعيته لا حد

بلاد ان   يونيتاس الأمريكا   فلا عليهم عشور زآيد   ولا غير ذلك والمجان

الآمثل ينالوا ما الطائفة   التي هي اقرب في المودة   والمحبنه

المطلب التاسع اكبير الذي في يونيتاس اسب رتبا يجعل انا نا وكلا ف احد في

بلاد ان السلطا الذي فيها البيع والشرا   ان صحتا المصالف والمنازعة ؛

بين الامريكا با نفسهم فالوكيل المذكور هو حافظ نا ظرهم وان صحتا المصالفة

بينهم والعرب نحكمهم راجع الى العرب   وكلا تنح المصالفة بينهم بانفسهم في

ث البيع   والشرا   وغير ذلك   فكل ذلك يرجع ؛ .

الا القائم المذكور من   جهتهم   واذا مات احد منهم ؛

وعَليْه شيئ إلى رَعيّته السلطا يُخْرِجُ الَّذي إلى رعِيّته
السلطا من ماله والكونسل والوكيل المذكور . لا يُحجَر
عليْه ولا يُمنَع ولا اموالهم يُحجَر عليْها ولا يُفتَح
مآ اغلقَ من ابوابهم وبيوتاتهم ولا يُهجَم عليْها
وان كان اوقَح ما الوكيل شيئٍ من التقصير بخلاف حكم
البلد يَتكى منه الى ولاةالامريكا حتى يعزِله بالحا

تمّت المطالبات المكه
صحيح دكتر عبد الرحمن عبد اللك

A Treaty of Amity and Commerce, between the United States of America and His Majesty Seyed Syeed Bin Sultan of Muscat and His Dependencies.

ARTICLE I. There shall be a perpetual Peace between the United States of America and Seyed Syeed bin Sultan and his dependencies.

2. The Citizens of the United States shall have free liberty to enter all the Ports of His Majesty Seyed Syeed bin Sultan, with their Cargoes of whatever kind the said cargoes may consist, & they shall have the liberty to sell the same, to any of the subjects of the Sultan, or others who may wish to buy the same, or to barter the same for any produce or manufactures of the Kingdom, or other articles that may be found there—no price shall be fixed by the Sultan or his Officers on the articles to be sold by the Merchants of the United States, or the merchandize they may wish to purchase—but the trade shall be free on both sides, to sell, or buy, or exchange on the terms, & for the prices the owners may think fit—and whenever the said Citizens of the United States may think fit to depart, they shall be at liberty so to do—and if any Officer of the Sultan shall contravene this Article, he shall be severely punished. It is understood & agreed however, that the articles of Muskets, Powder and Ball can only be sold to the Government in the Island of Zanzibar—but in all the other ports of the Sultan, the said munitions of war may be freely sold, without any restrictions whatever to the highest bidder.

3. Vessels of the United States entering any port within the Sultan's dominions, shall pay no more than Five per centum Duties on the Cargo landed; and this shall be in full consideration of all import & export duties, tonnage, license to trade, pilotage, anchorage, or any other charge whatever. Nor shall any charge be paid on that part of the cargo which may remain on board unsold, & re-exported—nor shall any charge whatever be paid on any vessel of the United States which may enter any of the Ports of His Majesty for the purpose of re-fitting, or for refreshments, or to enquire the state of the market.

4. The American Citizen shall pay no other duties on export or import, tonnage, license to trade, or other charge whatsoever, than the nation the most favored shall pay.

5. If any vessel of the United States shall suffer Shipwreck on any part of the Sultans Dominions, the persons escaping from the wreck shall be taken care of and hospitably entertain'd at the expense of the Sultan, until they shall find an opportunity to be return'd to their

country—for the Sultan can never receive any remuneration whatever for rendering succour to the distress'd—and the property saved from such wreck, shall be carefully preserv'd and delivered to the owner, or the Consul of the United States, or to any authorized Agent.

6. The Citizens of the United States resorting to the Ports of the Sultan for the purpose of trade, shall have leave to land, & reside in the said ports, without paying any tax or imposition whatever for such liberty, other than the General Duties on Imports which the most favored nation shall pay.

7. If any citizens of the United States, or their vessells, or other property shall be taken by Pirates, and brought within the Dominions of the Sultan, the persons shall be set at liberty, and the property restored to the owner if he is present, or to the American Consul, or to any authorized agent.

8. Vessels belonging to the subjects of the Sultan which may resort to any port in the United States, shall pay no other or higher rate of Duties, or other charges, than the nation the most favored shall pay.

9. The President of the United States may appoint Consuls to reside in the Ports of the Sultan where the principal commerce shall be carried on; which Consuls shall be the exclusive judges of all disputes or suits wherein American Citizens shall be engaged with each other. They shall have power to receive the property of any American Citizen dying within the Kingdom, and to send the same to his heirs, first paying all his debts due to the subjects of the Sultan. The said Consuls shall not be arrested, nor shall their property be seized. Nor shall any of their household be arrested, but their persons, and property, & their houses, shall be inviolate. Should any Consul however, commit any offence against the laws of the Kingdom, complaint shall be made to the President who will immediately displace him.

Concluded, Signed and Sealed, at the Royal Palace in the City of Muscat in the Kingdom of Aman [1] the twenty first day of September in the Year One thousand, Eight hundred, & Thirty three of the Christian Era, & the Fifty Seventh year of the Independence of the United States of America, corresponding to the Sixth day of the Moon called Jamada Alawel, in the Year of the Allhajra (Hegira) Twelve hundred and Forty Nine.

EDMUND ROBERTS   [Seal]

---

[1] Properly *Oman*.

Wheras the undersigned Edmund Roberts a Citizen of the United States of America, and a resident of Portsmouth in the State of New Hampshire, being duly appointed a Special Agent by Letters Patent, under the Signature of the President and Seal of the United States of America, bearing date at the City of Washington the twenty sixth day of January, Anno Domini, One thousand, eight hundred & thirty two, for negotiating & concluding a Treaty of Amity and Commerce between the United States of America, and His Majesty Seyed Syeed bin Sultan of Muscat. Now Know Ye, That I Edmund Roberts, Special Agent as aforesaid, do conclude the foregoing Treaty of Amity & Commerce, and every Article & Clause therein contain'd, reserving the same nevertheless, for the final Ratification of the President of the United States of America, by and with the advice & consent of the Senate of the United States.

Done at the Royal Palace in the City of Muscat, in the Kingdom of Aman, on the twenty first day of September in the Year of our Lord, One thousand, eight hundred & thirty three, and of the Independence of the United States of America, the Fifty Seventh, corresponding to the Sixth day of the Moon called Jamada Alawel, in the Year of Allhajra (Hegira) One thousand Two hundred and Forty Nine.

EDMUND ROBERTS

THE ARABIC TEXT

The Arabic and English texts of this treaty have been examined by Professor C. Snouck Hurgronje, of Leiden, whose report, with his translation of the Arabic and comments (including those in brackets) thereon, follows.

While the spelling, "Muscat," has been used for the sake of conformity with the English version of the treaty, the correct phonetical transliteration is "Maskat."

In the opening clause of the treaty the Ruler of Muscat is mentioned as "His Highness, . . . the Seyyid Sa'id bin as-Seyyid Sultan, Protector of Muscat and its dependencies." "Sultan" is the *proper name* of the father of Sa'id (which may be written "Sa'eed"), not his own title. "Seyyid" ("Sir" or "Lord") is the title of all the members of his family. Although the word "sultan" as denoting "ruler" in the general sense occurs in Article 2 and elsewhere, Sa'id never assumed this *title* for himself, but modestly called himself always simply the "Protector" (*ḥâmî*) of Muscat and its dependencies. The same modesty appears still more strikingly in his signature at the foot of the treaty.

The original meaning of the word "sultan" is "authority" in the abstract sense, then the person or persons representing authority and their delegates, "authorities," and later also the principal ruler of a country; but the Ruler of Muscat or Oman never took the word as a *title*.

The frequent use in the treaty of the word "sultan," where it seems to denote the person of the ruler of the country, requires it to be emphasized that this word is not and never has been used in Muscat for that purpose. Its use in this document may have been an accommodation to the fact that the American negotiators addressed Sa'id by that title, which might thus have seemed to the court officers of the Ruler of Muscat to be the most convenient term to use in a document destined for the United States.

As has been observed above, the simplicity of mind of this "Protector" of Muscat and its dependencies is most expressively illustrated by the way in which he signed the treaty. Here reference may be made to the note on the placing of seals by Eastern potentates in my comments on the treaty with Morocco (Document 14, Volume 2, p. 227). The Arabic adjectives "unworthy" and "needy" (*haqeer, faqeer*) are used in signatures of letters when the writer wishes to address his correspondent in a most humble manner.

The document was drawn up by a man who had enjoyed good calligraphical instruction but very little literary or grammatical education. He did his work rather carelessly, and he had a predilection for pleonastic expressions such as "price and value," "friendship and amity."

In a few places the Arabic text seems intentionally to have been made different from the English, as, for instance, in Article 2 concerning the import of war munitions and in Article 9 concerning the settling of disputes between Arabs and Americans.

There is nothing in the Arabic text corresponding to the final paragraph of the English which begins, "Concluded, Signed and Sealed"; nor is there anything in the Arabic corresponding to the clause of conclusion signed by Edmund Roberts reserving the treaty for the ratification of the President by and with the advice and consent of the Senate.

[Translation]

Statement of the wording of the treaty that has come to exist between His Highness, whom God may strengthen, the Seyyid Sa'id bin as-Seyyid Sultan, Protector [*hâmî*] of Muscat and its dependencies, and the United States [here and elsewhere in the treaty there are varying and not very successful attempts at spelling these words in the Arabic writing], which means the country of America, for the sake of peace and amity and to further the matter of commerce.

FIRST ARTICLE. There ought to exist perfect harmony between His Highness the Seyyid Sa'id bin as-Seyyid Sultan and all the lands of the Americans.

SECOND ARTICLE. The inhabitants of the American lands shall have liberty to enter all the ports of His Highness the Seyyid Sa'id bin as-Seyyid Sultan, Protector of Muscat, with all their merchandise, and they shall have liberty to sell the same to any of the subjects of His Highness the Seyyid Sa'id or to others who wish to buy that merchandise or to barter it or to exchange it for any merchandise of those [*sic*] lands [evidently the lands of Muscat] which may be obtainable by them. As to the articles they bring with them, they shall fix the price and value of them themselves, and there shall be no fixing by the "sultan" or his [its] officers with regard to the price or value of the goods of merchants inhabiting the United States of the Americans; and, likewise, if they wish to buy any merchandise, there shall be no fixing of price or value by the said [authorities] with regard to any merchandise which the said merchants wish to buy, in order that commerce may be permanent and not interrupted from both parts and sides and that commerce may be continuous [current]; the same rule shall prevail with regard to bartering, if there is common agreement, if the proprietor of the goods agrees to the barter. If there is no agreement from the side of the Americans, inhabitants of the United States, and they wish to depart, there shall be no prevention. If any of the servants or officers of the "sultan" shall act in contravention of this treaty, he shall be punished by the "sultan" with severe punishment.

If there arrives any powder or lead [ball], and the agreement is [*sic*] for the sake of buying and selling and negotiating from the lands of the Americans, nobody shall be authorized to buy it except the "sultan," with the exclusion of all his subjects. [There is no equivalent of "musket" in the Arabic text, nor any mention of Zanzibar nor of the liberty of selling munitions of war to the highest bidder in the other ports.]

THIRD ARTICLE. If there arrive vessels of the United States of the Americans and they enter the town under the rule of the "sultan" or any town under the rule of the "sultan" [*sic*], they shall have nothing to pay except the tithes [the word '*ushûr*, "tithes" or "tenth parts," has evidently acquired the sense of duties or taxes generally], five in a hundred on goods or merchandise or the cargo which is unloaded. They are not subject to any other payment but what we have mentioned, and nothing whatever shall be taken from the equivalent [the price]. If there remains a part of the goods unsold, and they wish to return, then five in a hundred [the meaning is evidently, "is to be paid on what has been sold"], and on the rest there is no paying. If there are other vessels of the Americans and they wish to enter any of the ports of His Highness the "sultan" to take water or to buy provisions or to repair their ships or, in passing by, to inquire the state of the market [the meaning is evidently, "then they have nothing to pay"].

FOURTH ARTICLE. The Arabic text fairly corresponds with the English.

FIFTH ARTICLE. The Arabic text has two differences from the English. The clause, "for the Sultan can never receive any remuneration whatever for rendering succour to the distress'd," is not in the Arabic; and at the end the Arabic has the addition, "and if there is any expense on the goods preserved, this shall be placed to the account of the people of the United States."

SIXTH ARTICLE. People of the United States living in the American lands, if they wish to come to any of the towns of the "sultan" for the purpose of commerce, they shall be permitted to do so and they shall not be prevented from unloading their goods, and if they wish to reside they shall have nothing to pay for residing, nor shall they have to pay anything whatever, but they shall be like the most favored nation [the nation nearest in amity].

SEVENTH ARTICLE. The Arabic text fairly corresponds with the English, but the style is most defective.

EIGHTH ARTICLE. The Arabic text fairly corresponds with the English. "Most favored" is rendered by "nearest in amity and friendship."

NINTH ARTICLE. The Chief who is in the United States may appoint a deputy [*wakeel*] in one of the towns of the "sultan" in which commerce is done. If there happen to be disputes or quarrels between the Americans themselves, the said deputy shall be present and consider their affairs. If there shall be a dispute between them and the Arabs, judgment shall be given by the Arabs. But whenever there shall be a dispute between themselves concerning the matter of commerce or other matters, in all such cases recourse shall be had to the officer [i.e., the deputy] above mentioned from their side. If one of them dies, being in debt to one of the "sultan's" subjects, that which he owes to the "sultan's" subjects shall be taken out of his estate, and the consul and the said deputy shall not sequester it or prevent [i.e., hinder the payment]. Their [evidently the Americans are meant] goods shall not be sequestered, nor shall their locked doors and houses be opened, nor shall there be done violence to them. Should there happen or be stated any shortcoming of the deputy, contrary to the law of the country, complaint shall be made to the ruler [*wâlî*] of the Americans in order that he may immediately displace him.

End of the said articles.

That has signed the unworthy, the needy SA'ID with his own hand.

[Seal]

NOTES

This treaty was negotiated by Edmund Roberts on the first of his two missions to the Far East as Special Agent of the United States.

The particular objects of that mission of Roberts were negotiations of treaties with Cochinchina, Siam, and Muscat; his first instructions,

of January 27, 1832 (D. S., 1 Special Missions, 73–75), directed him to negotiate treaties with Cochinchina, Siam, and "the powers of Arabia on the Red Sea"; he was furnished with a certificate, signed by Secretary of State Livingston and dated the preceding day, which designated him as "Commissioner to the Governments of Cochin China, Siam and Muscat" (D. S., 2 Credences, 189); and he was given three full powers, also dated January 26, 1832, to negotiate, respectively, with those three Governments (*ibid.*, 189–91).

With regard to the certificate above mentioned, the instructions, and the letters of credence which were furnished Roberts for this mission, see the first pages of the notes to the treaty of 1833 with Siam (Document 76).

The three full powers given to Roberts on the date mentioned were of similar tenor; that one of them which names the Government of Muscat reads as follows (D. S., 2 Credences, 191):

Andrew Jackson, President of the United States of America,

To all whom these presents shall come, Greeting:

Know Ye, That reposing special trust and confidence in the integrity, prudence and ability of Edmund Roberts, a citizen of the United States, I have appointed him Commissioner of the United States, to meet, confer, treat and negotiate with His Highness Syede Syede Bin Sultan, The Imaum of Muscat, and his Government, or with any person or persons duly authorized in his or its behalf of and concerning all matters of Navigation and Commerce between the United States, and the said Government of Muscat, with full power to conclude and sign a treaty thereupon, transmitting the same to the President of the United States, for his final ratification by and with the advice and consent of the Senate.

In Testimony whereof, I have caused the Seal of the United States to be hereunto affixed. Witness my hand at the City of Washington this twenty sixth day of January A. D. 1832; and of the Independence of the United States of America, the fifty Sixth.

ANDREW JACKSON,

By the President,
EDW LIVINGSTON, *Secretary of State.*

In the course of this mission, the published story of which is in his book, "Embassy to the Eastern Courts of Cochin-China, Siam, and Muscat," Roberts succeeded in negotiating two treaties, namely, the treaty with Siam of 1833 (Document 76) and this treaty with Muscat.

OMAN AND ZANZIBAR

At the time of this treaty the domains of Seyyid Sa'id bin Sultan, the Ruler of Oman and Zanzibar, were very extensive. In his letter to the Secretary of State dated at Washington May 14, 1834, transmitting the originals of this treaty and of that made with the King of Siam (Document 76), Roberts thus describes those possessions (D. S., 10 Special Agents, 33):

The Sultan of Muscat is a very powerful Prince. He possesses a more efficient Naval force than all the native Princes combined from the Cape of Good Hope to Japan. His resources are more than adequate to his wants—they are derived from Commerce, running himself a great number of Merchant vessels—from duties on foreign merchandize and from tribute money—and presents received from various Princes, all of which produce a large sum.

His possessions in Africa, stretch from Cape Delgado to Cape Guardafui—and from Cape Aden, in Arabia, to Ras el Haud—and from Ras el Haud they extend along the northern coast of Arabia (or the coast Aman) to the entrance of the Persian Gulf—and he claims also all the sea coast and islands *within* the Persian Gulf, including the Bahrein Islands and the Pearl Fishery contiguous to them; with the northern coast of the Gulf as low down as Scindy. It is true that only a small part of this immense Territory is garrisoned by his troops, but all are tributary to him.

In Africa he owns the ports of Monghow, or Mongallow, Lyndy, Quiloa, (Keelwah) Melinda, Lamo, Patta, Brava, Magadosha (alias Magadshe) and the valuable islands of Moufeea, or Mafeea, Zanzibar—Pemba—Socotra—alias Socotera &c &c.

An interesting biography of the Ruler of Muscat who made this treaty with the United States, entitled "Said bin Sultan (1791–1856), Ruler of Oman and Zanzibar," has been written by his grandson, Rudolph Said-Ruete. The dealings of Sa'id with the United States are there treated at some length. The following summary of the then importance of Oman and its ruler appears in the introduction to that work by Major General Sir Percy Cox:

It is true that the Arabs of the southern principalities of Arabia had from time immemorial been a maritime people. Every year with the advent of the north-east breeze their fleets of trading craft would speed southwards across the Indian Ocean, to return in the spring before the burst of the south-west monsoon. For centuries they enjoyed a practical monopoly of the carrying trade of the East, and, in fact, played in Indian seas the same rôle that the Phœnicians were playing in the Mediterranean. But it was left to the constructive ambition of Saiyid Said bin Sultan, as Ruler of Oman, to establish an Arab "Dominion Overseas" with its capital at Zanzibar, of which he became first Sultan, and which has often been called the Mecca of the African native. On this ground alone Saiyid Said is deserving of a niche in the portrait gallery of world history; while as regards this country the events of his long reign (1804–1856) give us particular reasons for holding his name in fragrant memory. His stalwart and fearless personality prompted him, at great moral and practical inconvenience, and even danger, to himself, to identify himself openly with Great Britain (who enjoyed no co-operation in the matter from other western powers at that time) in her determined efforts for the suppression of the African slave trade and the sinister activities of the famous Jowasmi pirates of the Upper Gulf; while the truly Oriental generosity which distinguished all his dealings with the Government and subjects of Great Britain was a household word in that generation.

THE NEGOTIATIONS

Success in the negotiations for a treaty with Muscat was easily attained, for the Ruler of Muscat had invited an agreement with the United States. In the instruction to Roberts of July 23, 1832 (D. S., 1 Special Missions, 76–78), Secretary of State Livingston had informed him that "with the Imaum of Muscat you will have no difficulty, as you will see by the enclosed document, which he directed to the President, and forwarded by one of our vessels lately trading in those seas." While that message from Muscat has not been found in the archives of the Department of State, it seems that it must have been a request or suggestion for a treaty with the United States. The letter from N. L. Rogers & Bros., dated at Salem June 27, 1832 (D. S., Miscellaneous Letters, April–June, 1832), which transmitted that

document to the Secretary of State, states that "we understand the Imaum is anxious to form a commercial treaty with the United States, as he has with England."

The official report of that first mission of Roberts is in D. S., 10 Special Agents, entitled "*Records* of a *Mission* undertaken by order of the Department of State of the U. States for the purpose of effecting Com^{cl} Treaties with the Kingdoms of Cochin China, Siam & Muscat." From that report the following summary is written.

After negotiating the treaty with Siam (Document 76), Roberts sailed from the Gulf of Siam on April 6, 1833, for Singapore, and thence for Batavia; he arrived at Mocha on August 31, and he reached Muscat on September 18.

Roberts' own account of his negotiations is quite brief:

On the 20 [September] in the afternoon visited by appointment Syed Syeed the Sultan and immediately entered upon the subject of a Commercial Treaty after delivering the President's letter which was translated by Captain Calfaun his Interpreter. He at once agreed that American Vessels should be admitted to all the ports of his dominions on the terms of the *most favoured Nations* by paying *Five* per cent duties on all merchandize landed & free of every other charge, whether on imports or exports, tonnage, anchorage, presents or any other expense, having liberty to sell or buy of any person whatever as set forth in the Treaty. Presented the day following the Articles of a Treaty which with very slight alterations was adopted as it is hereafter recorded. It was mutually agreed that it should bear date & go into operation on the 21st day of September (1833). On the 3^{d} of October copies of the Treaty written in Arabic & English were signed and sealed; a certificate being annex'd to each copy in the usual form, setting forth the necessity of its being ratified by the President and Senate.

It thus appears that the question of language made no difficulty, as the Court of Muscat had an interpreter of English; and it further appears that the treaty was in fact signed in duplicate on October 3, 1833.

However, the original treaty which is now in the Department of State file is not one of the duplicate originals signed on October 3, 1833; it is still another original which was drawn up at the time of the exchange of ratifications two years later and was signed and sealed on October 10, 1835. The circumstances which required such procedure are explained hereafter in these notes.

The terms of the treaty as finally written are substantially in accord with the draft furnished to Roberts by the Department of State (D. S., 1 Special Missions, 80–81).

It is difficult, however, to explain, except on the theory of a mistake on the part of the scriveners, the difference between the English and Arabic texts of Article 5. As stated above by Professor Snouck Hurgronje in his comments on that article, the clause in the English, "for the Sultan can never receive any remuneration whatever for rendering succour to the distress'd," is not in the Arabic. Moreover, a clause at the end of the article in the Arabic is to the effect that any expense on the salvaged goods should be placed to the account of the United States. This last clause is very similar to the wording of the draft made in the Department of State, which reads (Article 4), "the United States will pay all the expenses which they have incurred."

In his book (*op. cit.*, 360–61) Roberts gives the following account of the discussion of this article during his reception by the Ruler of Muscat on September 28, 1833:

When the fifth article of the proposed treaty was read, which related to ship-wrecked seamen, he at once objected to that part of it relating to a remuneration for expenses, which would be necessarily incurred in supporting and forwarding them to the United States, and said, the article he wished so altered as to make it incumbent upon him to protect, maintain, and return them to their own country, free of every charge. He remarked, that it would be contrary to the usage of Arabs, and to the rights of hospitality, which have ever been practised among them; and this clause was also inserted, at his request.

On October 4 the Ruler of Muscat visited the *Peacock* and was duly saluted and entertained. The presents were delivered to the Sultan and his officers, but those offered to Roberts were declined. On October 6 Roberts took leave and on his departure was given a letter from Sa'id to President Jackson under date of October 7, 1833 (22 Jumada I, A. H. 1249), couched in terms of the most cordial and affectionate friendship (translation in Roberts, *op. cit.*, 430; original in Arabic, with translation, in D. S., 10 Special Agents, 73–75). On October 7 Roberts sailed for Mozambique and thence to Cape Town and Rio de Janeiro, where he transferred to the U. S. S. *Lexington*, and reached Boston on April 24, 1834. He had been 424 days at sea and according to the log had traveled 45,178 miles (Roberts, *op. cit.*, 400).

The Original Documents

The treaty proper is written on both sides of two large sheets of parchment, about fifteen by twenty inches in size, the Arabic in the left columns and the corresponding English in the right. Beneath the Arabic text is the signature of the Ruler of Muscat with a seal of red wax, now much defaced, and beneath the English are the signature and seal of Edmund Roberts. Following the treaty text, running across the page and continuing to a third sheet, is the clause of conclusion reserving the treaty for the ratification of the President by and with the advice and consent of the Senate, signed by Edmund Roberts without his seal.

Then follows the certificate, in Arabic, of the delivery and exchange of the United States instrument of ratification on September 30, 1835, signed and sealed by the Ruler of Muscat (the seal of red wax having now almost disappeared), with an English version thereof written opposite in the right column as follows:

This is to Certify, that on the thirtieth day of September Anno Domini, One thousand, Eight Hundred and Thirty five, corresponding to the Sixth day of the Moon called Jamada Athani, in the year of Allhajra, One thousand, two hundred, & Fifty one—Edmund Roberts, a Special Agent of the United States of America, delivered and exchanged a ratified copy of a Treaty, sign'd at Muscat in the Kingdom of Aman on the twenty first day of September One thousand, eight hundred & thirty three of the Christian Era, corresponding to the Sixth day of the Moon called Jamada Alawell in the year Allhajra, One thousand, two hundred, & forty nine. In Witness whereof, I have hereunto set my hand & Seal at Muscat aforesaid, on the Sixth day of the Moon called Jamada Athani, in the year of

Allhajra, One thousand, two hundred, & fifty one, corresponding to the thirtieth day of September, One thousand, eight hundred & thirty five of the Christian Era.

The English version of that certificate of delivery and exchange was in fact the one first drafted (D. S., 10 Special Agents, 102, despatch of Roberts of October 23, 1835, from Bombay); and the following translation of the Arabic, made by Professor Snouck Hurgronje, shows that the Arabic version is a fair equivalent of the English:

Be it known that on the thirtieth day of the month of September of the year one thousand eight [the word "hundred" is omitted] thirty-five of the Christian era, corresponding with the sixth of the month Jumada al-Thani of the year one thousand two hundred fifty-one of the Hijrah [Hegira], Edmund Rabut [Roberts], deputy from the side of the Government [represented here by the Persian-Turkish word *serkâr*] of the Americans [United States], we have received, and I [*sic*] have exchanged for the treaty which I [*sic*] have signed in Muscat, one of the towns of Oman, on the twenty-first of the month of September, thousand eight hundred thirty-five [error for 1833] of the Christian era, corresponding with the sixth day of the month called Jumada al-Awwal in the year of the Hijrah thousand two hundred and forty-nine, and I have set thereon the genuine seal of my hand at Muscat on the [here is a space for the number of the day, which has not been filled] of the month Jumada al-Thani in the year of the Hijrah thousand two hundred fifty-one, corresponding to the date of the thirtieth of the month of September in the year thousand eight hundred thirty-five of the Christian era. That has signed the unworthy, the needy SA'ID with his own hand.

The Arabic text of the treaty is first reproduced above, with the signature of the Ruler of Muscat; then is printed the English text of the treaty with the signature and seal of Edmund Roberts, followed by the clause of conclusion signed by Roberts, reserving the treaty for the ratification of the President by and with the advice and consent of the Senate. The Arabic text of the certificate of the delivery and exchange of the United States instrument of ratification is not reproduced.

There is no duplicate of the United States instrument of ratification in the treaty file or other record thereof. It seems, however, that the date of the ratification was the same as that of the ratification of the treaty of 1833 with Siam (Document 76). That treaty and this were dealt with together. They were submitted to the Senate with the same presidential message (Executive Journal, IV, 412–13), and the Senate resolutions regarding them were passed on the same date (June 30, 1834; *ibid.*, 444; the attested Senate resolution is not in the file). The ratifications of both treaties were being prepared at the same time in the latter part of 1834, for in the instruction to Roberts of December 8, 1834 (D. S., 1 Special Missions, 122), Secretary of State Forsyth wrote:

The box in which the great seal of the United States attached to treaties is usually enclosed, is of silver richly gilt, with the American Eagle in raised work upon the lid. It is proposed to use the same box for holding the seal to be affixed to the treaties recently concluded with the King of Siam and the Sultan of Muscat, unless you should be of opinion that the gilding would offend the taste of those Eastern Sovereigns. You will please to state whether it would be likely to have that effect, and whether you think the silver alone would be more suitable.

To that letter Roberts replied, under date of December 15 (D. S., 10 Special Agents, 81), that the silver box, "richly gilt," would be

more suitable than the other and could not possibly give offense; and in a despatch from Bombay of October 23, 1835 (D. S., 10 Special Agents, 104), Roberts wrote regarding the instrument of ratification of this treaty that there had been "an error in the year, substituting 1834 (Jan^y) for 1835, which was corrected before the exchange was effected." There is some indication of a similar correction to be seen in the facsimile of the instrument of ratification of the treaty with Siam (Document 76). Accordingly, it is assumed that the two documents were dated on the same day, January 3, 1835.

The original proclamation of June 24, 1837, is in the treaty file; it is somewhat torn and in its present condition contains the usual opening and closing clauses of a proclamation but not the text of the treaty; but the print of the proclamation issued at the time includes the English text of the treaty and also the concluding certificate of Edmund Roberts, though stating the date of the exchange of ratifications erroneously as September 30, 1833, instead of 1835.

The Exchange of Ratifications

On his second mission to the Far East as Special Agent of the United States, the first duty of Edmund Roberts was to effect the exchange of ratifications of this treaty. To that end he was given a letter of credence and authority to exchange the ratifications, signed by President Jackson under date of March 20, 1835, attested by Secretary of State Forsyth, and addressed to "the Sultan of Muscat" (D. S., 1 Special Missions, 149); and a similar but conditional letter of credence and authority, under date of April 17, 1835, was given to Captain Edmund P. Kennedy, U. S. N., to be used "in Case that Edmund Roberts, who is about to embark in the said vessel [the sloop of war *Peacock*], to whom the ratification of the said Treaty on the part of this Government is delivered, and who is empowered to make the exchange of ratifications, should, from death or any other physical incapacity, be prevented from performing that service" (*ibid.*, 153).

The report of that second mission of Roberts is in D. S., 10 Special Agents, entitled "Records of a Mission, and occurrences connected with a Mission, to the Courts of Muscat, Siam, Cochin China and Japan; undertaken by the Undersign'd by Instructions from the Department of State of the United States of America, on board the U. States Ship of War Peacock, E. K. Stribling Acting Commander, under E. P. Kennedy Commodore." On that report the following account is based, with extracts therefrom.

Again sailing in the U. S. sloop of war *Peacock*, Roberts left New York on April 23, 1835, reaching Rio de Janeiro on June 12 and Zanzibar on September 2. Sailing for Muscat on September 8, the *Peacock* stranded on September 21 near "Mazeira" (Masirah or Mosera) Island near the southeast coast of Arabia in about 20° north latitude and 58° east longitude, some four hundred miles from Muscat, according to Roberts (actually two hundred miles as the crow flies). Roberts left the *Peacock* in a cutter with a midshipman

and six men to seek aid at Muscat, where he arrived on September 26. Help was offered and given, and there was even promised a vessel to take the Americans to the United States if their ship was lost; but the *Peacock* arrived, somewhat damaged, three days later.

Roberts then took up the question of the exchange of ratifications. He had with him the original treaty (one of the duplicate originals signed in 1833), annexed to the ratification of President Jackson; the desired procedure was to deliver that document in exchange for the other of the two originals which had been signed under date of September 21, 1833, with a certificate of the exchange appended thereto; but that other original was not at Muscat. The difficulty was gotten over by writing out still another original, as Roberts records:

> On the following day (being [September] the 30th) I applied to the Sultan to have the usual certificate appended to the Treaty which was in his possession, & to exchange it for the ratified Treaty brought by me from the U. S; and handed to (Capt Calfaun) the proper certificate and requested him to put it into Arabic—but to my surprize I found the Sultan had left it at Zanzibar; it therefore became necessary to write another, which was finish'd on my part on the next day, but it was not written in Arabic 'till the 9th of Octr and was sign'd & sealed by the Sultan & rec'd & exchanged on the next day. The . . . Certificate was written at the bottom of the Treaty, & sign'd & seal'd by him.

It thus appears that the delivery of the United States instrument of ratification and the signing of the certificate of exchange took place on October 10, 1835.

Thus, of the two originals of the treaty signed in fact on October 3, 1833, but under date of September 21, one, which Roberts had taken to the United States and which had been submitted to the Senate, and which was annexed to the United States instrument of ratification, was delivered by Roberts; the other had been taken from Muscat to Zanzibar and remained there. It was a third original, drawn up and signed and sealed for the occasion, which was delivered to Roberts on October 10, 1835 (under date of September 30), and which is now in the Department of State file.

The procedure of October 10, 1835 (under date of September 30), is rightly to be deemed an exchange of ratifications; there was no instrument of ratification signed or sealed on the part of Muscat and doubtless no ratification on that part was required; but the exchange of the documents, the delivery of one original treaty (with a certificate of the exchange appended) to the Agent of the United States and the concurrent delivery by him of the other original with the United States instrument of ratification, imported a ratification on behalf of Muscat; and accordingly it may properly be said that the treaty was ratified by Muscat on September 30, 1835, and the ratifications exchanged on that day, the textual and agreed date of the certificate which was signed ten days later.

As Roberts points out, it was fortunate that the Agent sent to make the exchange was the same Agent who had negotiated the treaty; he writes that some months would have elapsed before a

voyage to Zanzibar and return could have been made, as the northeast monsoon had commenced.

The English version of the certificate of the exchange and delivery of the United States instrument of ratification, which appears above in these notes, gives the date in the Mohammedan calendar corresponding to September 30, 1835, as the "Sixth day of the Moon called Jamada Athani," or 6 Jumada II, A. H. 1251; according to the chronological tables that date was September 29, 1835; but see the remarks as to the Mohammedan calendar in Volume 2, pages xxi-xxii.

THE ENTRY INTO FORCE OF THE TREATY

When the exchange of ratifications had been accomplished, discussions took place as to the date when the treaty was to be deemed to have gone into force; and it was agreed that June 30, 1834, the date of the resolution of advice and consent of the Senate, would be accepted as the effective date. A possible refund of duties from that date was thus provided for in favor of American vessels, sixteen of which, according to Roberts, had visited Zanzibar since the agreed date (D. S., 10 Special Agents, 102–4, despatch of Roberts of October 23, 1835, from Bombay). The report of Roberts on the point reads as follows:

On receiving the ratified Treaty, I asked at what period of time it was to take effect, whether on the 30th day of June of the past year when it was ratified by the Senate of the U. S &c, or on the 30th day of Sept. as set forth in the certificate of ratification sign'd by the Sultan. His Highness reply was, affix your own time, it is an immaterial matter to me; my revenues are *farm'd* out. I was unwilling to name a time, & refused repeatedly to do so—at length the Sultan urged it so strongly, that I finally named the 30th day of June 1834. He then requested me to write the letter which here follows & which he wish'd to send to Zanzibar to the Govr, so that if any American had paid any charges or higher rate of Duties since the 30th day of June 1834 than is set forth in the Treaty, he should be refunded for such overcharge, by the Banyan who pays an annual sum of 110,000 Dollars for its revenues.

The following is a copy of the letter address'd "To the Masters & Supercargoes of American Vessels at Zanzibar or other ports within the Dominions of His Highness the Sultan of Muscat.

MUSCAT, *10 Oct. 1835*

GENT. The Commercial Treaty effected by me on the part of the U. States with His Highness Seyed Seyeed bin Sultan (The Sultan of Muscat) having been ratified and exchanged between the contracting parties, it is understood and agreed between His Highness & the U. States, that the said Treaty went into effect on the 30th day of June 1834, being the day on which it was ratified by the President & Senate of the U. States. All vessels therefore, having paid any higher rate of duties than is set forth in the said Treaty, or any charges subsequent to the said 30th day of June aforesaid, are en-titled to be refunded by the Collectors of the Customs of the various ports of His Highness for such overcharge

Your very obd^t Servt

EDMUND ROBERTS
Special Agent of the U S to the Sultan of Muscat &c

The following letter was also written to Captain Hassan bin Abraham at Zanzibar, who was appointed an Agent for Foreign Commerce at that place about three years since by the Sultan, & has since that time done most of the business at that port for the Americans.

Muscat, *10 Oct. 1835*

Sir, I have the pleasure to inform you, that the Treaty concluded between His Highness, the Sultan of Muscat and the Gov^t of the United States, went into full operation on the 30th day of June 1834, being the day on which it was ratified on the part of the President & Senate of the U S All vessels or merchandize therefore (subsequent to that period) who have paid any higher rate of duties or charges than is set forth in the said Treaty (a copy of which being placed in your hands by the Sultan) will be refunded by the Collectors of the Customs of those ports for such over charge. I have written a similar letter to this (at the request of the Sultan) address'd to American Masters & Supercargoes, which will be forwarded to Zanzibar by the first conveyance.

Captain Hassan will please accept the good wishes of the undersign'd for his health, happiness & prosperity.

Edmund Roberts

One more letter was written by Roberts "at the *Special request* of His Highness the Sultan"; it was with regard to the blockade of Mombasa, addressed to American masters and supercargoes, and dated October 10, 1835. The text thereof follows:

His Highness Seyed Seyeed bin Sultan of Muscat, wishing to prevent any collision between the Gov^t of the U S and His Highness, has requested me to make known to all Masters & Supercargoes belonging to vessels of the U. States, that the port of Mombas in East Africa being in a state of blockade by His Highness's Ships of War, (the said place being in a state of rebellion) and that it will continue to be thus blockaded, until it is again reduced to submission, & therefore no vessels will be permitted to enter said port during the continuance of such blockade.

On October 11 Roberts sailed from Muscat to continue on his mission to Siam, regarding which the notes to Document 76 should be consulted.

The treaty was communicated to Congress with the annual message of President Van Buren of December 5, 1837 (Richardson, III, 376).

Article 3

By Article 3 of the treaty the maximum import duty on merchandise in vessels of the United States was fixed at 5 per cent "on the Cargo landed"; and Article 4 limited even this provision by its most-favored-nation clause. The contrast with earlier conditions is thus described by Roberts (D. S., 10 Special Agents, 34, letter to the Secretary of State dated at Washington May 14, 1834):

Previous to the conclusion of the Treaty, American vessels paid generally *seven* and an *half* p. c^t upon imports, and *seven* and an half pr. cent^m upon exports, with Anchorage money and presents. The Governors of the out ports claimed the right of pre-emption in both cases, and they resorted to the most nefarious practises to accumulate wealth.

The commerce of the United States under the treaty is entirely freed from *all* inconvenient restrictions and pays but *one* charge, namely *Five* per cent on all *merchandize landed*, and it is freed from the charge of pilotage, as every port has Pilots which are kept in pay by the Sultan.

Treaty Series No. 328
8 Statutes at Large, 460–63
18 *ibid.*, pt. 2, Public Treaties, 718–20

78

SPAIN : FEBRUARY 17, 1834

Convention for the Settlement of Claims, signed at Madrid February 17, 1834. Original in English and Spanish, except the "model or form" of inscription, which is in Spanish only.
Submitted to the Senate April 24, 1834. (Message of April 17, 1834.) Resolution of advice and consent May 13, 1834. Ratified by the United States May 15, 1834. Ratified by Spain July 23, 1834. Ratifications exchanged at Madrid August 14, 1834. Proclaimed November 1, 1834.

Original

Convention for the settlement of Claims between the United States of America and Her Catholick Majesty

The Government of the United States of America and Her Majesty the Queen Regent, Governess of Spain during the minority of Her August Daughter, Her Catholick Majesty Donna Ysabel the 2ᵈ, from a desire of adjusting by a definitive arrangement the claims preferred by each party against the other, and thus removing all grounds of disagreement, as also of strengthening the ties of friendship and good undestanding which happily subsist between the two nations, have appointed for this purpose, as their respective Plenipotentiaries, namely, the President of the United States, Cornelius P. Van Ness, a citizen of the

Original

Convenio para el arreglo de las reclamaciones entre S. M. Católica y los Estados Unidos de America

Deseando S. M. la Reina Regenta Gobernadora de España, durante la menor edad de S. M. Católica Doña Ysabel 2ª, Su Augusta Hija, y el Gobierno de los Estados Unidos de America, terminar por un arreglo definitivo las reclamaciones promovidas por una y otra parte, evitando, de esta manera, todo motivo de desavenencia, y estrechando los vinculos de amistad y buena inteligencia que existen felizmente entre ambas naciones; han nombrado, con este objeto, por sus respectivos Plenipotenciarios, á saber: S. M. la Reina Regenta Gobernadora, á nombre y en representacion de S. M. Católica

811

said States, and their Envoy Extraordinary and Minister Plenipotentiary near Her Catholick Majesty Donna Ysabel the 2ᵈ, and Her Majesty the Queen Regent, in the name and behalf of Her Catholick Majesty Donna Ysabel the 2ᵈ, His Exellency Don José de Heredia, Knight Grand Cross of the Royal American order of Ysabel the Catholick, one of Her Majesty's Supreme Council of Finance, ex-Envoy Extraordinary and Minister Plenipotentiary, and President of the Royal Junta of appeals of credits against France; who after having exchanged their respective full-powers, have agreed upon the following articles.

ARTICLE 1ʳˢᵗ

Her Majesty the Queen Regent and Governess, in the name and in behalf of Her Catholick Majesty Donna Ysabel the 2ᵈ, engages to pay to the United States, as the balance on account of the claims aforesaid, the sum of twelve millions of Rials *vellon*, in one or several inscriptions,—as preferred by the Government of the United States,—of perpetual rents on the great book of the Consolidated debt of Spain, bearing an interest of five per cent per annum. Said inscription or inscriptions shall be issued in conformity with the model or form annexed to this Convention, and shall be delivered in Madrid to such person or

Doña Ysabel 2ª, al Exmo Señor Don José de Heredia, Caballero Gran Cruz de la Real orden americana de Ysabel la Católica, del Consejo de S. M. en el supremo de Hacienda, Enviado Extraordinario y Ministro Plenipotenciario cesante, y Presidente de la Real Junta de apelaciones de creditos contra la Francia; y el Presidente de los Estados Unidos de América á Don Cornelio P. Van Ness, ciudadano de dichos Estados, y Enviado Extraordinario y Ministro Plenipotenciario cerca de S. M. Católica Doña Ysabel 2ª; los cuales, despues de haber cangeado sus respectivos plenos poderes, han convenido en los articulos siguientes:

ARTICULO 1ᵒ

S. M. la Reina Regenta Gobernadora, á nombre y en representacion de S. M. Católica Doña Ysabel 2ª; se obliga á pagar á los Estados Unidos, por saldo de las reclamaciones arriba mencionadas, la cantidad de doce millones de reales vellon, en una ó varias inscripciones, á eleccion del Gobierno de los Estados Unidos, de renta perpetua sobre el gran libro de la deuda consolidada de España, con el interes de cinco por ciento anual. Esta inscripcion ó inscripciones serán conformes al modelo ó fórmula de que va unida copia al presente convenio: y se entregarán en Madrid, cuatro meses despues del cange de sus

persons as may be authorized by the Government of the United States to receive them, within four months after the exchange of the ratifications. And said inscriptions, or the proceeds thereof, shall be distributed by the Government of the United States among the claimants entitled thereto, in such manner as it may deem just and equitable.

ARTICLE 2ᵈ

The interest of the aforesaid inscription or inscriptions shall be paid in Paris every six months; and the first half yearly payment is to be made six months after the exchange of the ratifications of this convention.

ARTICLE 3ᵈ

The high contracting parties in virtue of the stipulation contained in article first, reciprocally renounce, release and cancel, all claims which either may have upon the other, of whatever class, denomination or origin, they may be, from the twenty second of February one thousand eight hundred and nineteen untill the time of signing this convention.

ARTICLE 4ᵗʰ

On the request of the Minister Plenipotentiary of Her Catholick Majesty at Washington, the Government of the United States will

ratificaciones, á la persona ó personas que autorize el Gobierno de los Estados Unidos para recibirlas, el cual distribuirá las expresadas inscripciones, ó su producto, entre los reclamantes que tengan derecho á él, del modo que le parezca mas justo y conveniente.

ARTICULO 2ᵈᵒ

El pago de los intereses de la mencionada ó mencionadas inscripciones se verificará en Paris cada seis meses; y el primer semestre será pagado á los seis meses despues de verificado el cange de las ratificaciones del presente convenio.

ARTICULO 3º

Las altas partes contratantes, en virtud de lo que se estipula en el articulo primero, renuncian y dán reciprocamente por satisfechas y canceladas todas las reclamaciones, sean cual fuere su clase, titulo ú origen, que cualquiera de las dos tenga contra la otra, desde el dia veinte y dos de Febrero de mil ochocientos diez y nueve hasta la fecha de este convenio.

ARTICULO 4º

El Gobierno de los Estados-Unidos, á peticion del Ministro Plenipotenciario de S. M. Católica en Washington, le entregará,

deliver to him, in six months after the exchange of the ratifications of this convention, a note or list of the claims of American citizens against the Government of Spain, specifying their amounts respectively; and three years afterwards, or sooner if possible, authentic copies of all the documents upon which they may have been founded.

seis meses despues del cange de las ratificaciones de este convenio, una lista ó nota de las reclamaciones de los ciudadanos Americanos contra el Gobierno de España, con expresion de sus valores; y tres años despues, ó antes si fuese posible, copias autenticas de todos los documentos en que se hayan fundado.

ARTICLE 5th

This convention shall be ratified, and the ratifications shall be exchanged in Madrid, in six months from this time, or sooner if possible.

In witness whereof the respective Plenipotentiaries have signed these articles, and affixed thereto their seals.

Done in triplicate at Madrid this seventeenth day of February one thousand eight hundred and thirty four.

[Seal] C. P. VAN NESS
[Seal] JOSÉ DE HEREDIA

ARTICULO 5º

El presente convenio será ratificado, y las ratificaciones cangeadas en esta Corte en el termino de seis meses contados desde su fecha, ó antes si fuese posible.

En fé de lo cual los respectivos Plenipotenciarios lo han firmado y sellado con el sello de sus armas.

Fecho por triplicado en Madrid á diez y siete de Febrero de mil ochocientos treinta y cuatro.

[Seal] JOSÉ DE HEREDIA
[Seal] C. P. VAN NESS

Nº ------
Cupon de------
pesos fuertes de Renta
pagadero en ------ de
------ de 183
Cupon Nº 1º
	Renta perpetua de España
	pagadera en Paris
	á razon de 5 p % al año
	inscrita en el Gran libro de la Deuda
	consolidada
	
	Esta Inscripcion se expide á conse-
	cuencia de un Convenio celebrado en
	Madrid en de de
	entre S. M. Catolica la Reyna de España
	y los Estados unidos de America para el
	pago de las reclamaciones de los ciuda-
	danos de dichos Estados.
	
	Inscripcion Nº ------
	
	Capital. Renta
	
	Pesos fuertes----- Pesos fuertes
	ó sean francos---- ó sean Francos
	   El portador de la presente tiene derecho
	á una renta anual de ------ pesos
	fuertes, ó sea de ------ francos, paga-
	deros en Paris por semestres en los dias
	------ de y de por los
	Banqueros de España en aquella Capi-
	tal, à razon de 5. francos y 40. centimos
	por peso fuerte, con arreglo al Rl Decreto
	de 15. de Diciembre de 1825.
	   Consiguiente al mismo Real Decreto
	se destina cada año á la amortizacion de
	esta renta uno porciento de su valor
	nominal, a interes compuesto, cuyo im-
	porte será empleado en su amortizacion
	periodica al curso corrient por dichos
	Banqueros. Madrid de
	de
	El Secretario de Estado y del Despacho
	  de Hacienda.
	El Director de la Rl Caja de Amortizacion.	

En fé de lo cual nos los abajo firmados Plenipotenciarios de S. M. Catolica la Reyna de España, y de los Estados Unidos de America, hemos firmado la presente formula y hemos puesto en ella el sello de nuestras armas.

Fecho en Madrid á -------- de -------- de -----------

              [Seal]   José de Heredia
              [Seal]   C. P. Van Ness

[Translation]

No. _____
Coupon for _____
standard pesos of
bonded indebtedness,
payable _____, 183__
Coupon No. 1.
	Perpetual Bonded Indebtedness of Spain
	payable at Paris
	at the rate of 5 per cent per annum,
	inscribed in the great book
	of the consolidated debt
	
	    This inscription is issued in accordance with a convention concluded at Madrid on the _____ day of _____, between H. C. M. the Queen of Spain and the United States of America, for payment of claims of citizens of said States.
	
	Inscription No. _____
	
	Principal Interest
	
	Standard pesos____ Standard pesos____
	or francs_____ or francs_____
	    The bearer hereof is entitled to an annuity of _____ standard pesos or _____ francs, payable at Paris every six months, on the _____ and _____ of _____, by the bankers of Spain in that city, at the rate of 5 francs 40 centimes for each standard peso, in conformity with the royal decree of December 15, 1825.
	    In accordance with said royal decree, 1 per cent of the nominal value of this bonded indebtedness, at compound interest, shall be set aside each year for the amortization thereof, which amount shall be employed by the aforesaid bankers in its periodical amortization at the current rate.
	    Madrid, _____ of _____
	The Secretary of the Treasury Department
	The Director of the Royal Sinking Fund	

    In faith whereof we, the undersigned Plenipotentiaries of Her Catholic Majesty the Queen of Spain and of the United States of America, have signed the present form and have affixed our seals thereto.

    Done at Madrid this _____ day of _____

                [Seal]   José DE HEREDIA
                [Seal]   C. P. VAN NESS

NOTES

In the final clause of the convention it is said that it was "done in triplicate." Two of the three originals were for the Government of the United States; the United States Plenipotentiary, Cornelius P. Van Ness, Minister at Madrid, wrote in his despatch of February 18, 1834, transmitting the treaty (D. S., 31 Despatches, Spain, No. 72; Senate Document No. 147, 23d Congress, 2d session, serial 269, p. 85): "I have retained in my possession a Triplicate of the Convention, precisely like that forwarded to you." It does not appear that that original was transmitted to the Department of State.

One signed original is in the treaty file; the English text is written on the left pages and the Spanish on the right, the *alternat* being properly observed, as the printed texts show. Annexed to the document is the "model or form" of inscription mentioned in Article 1, which is written in Spanish only; a separate sheet in the file has a translation of the model; in substance that printed above is similar. The original convention is embodied in the original proclamation of November 1, 1834.

The Spanish instrument of ratification includes the text of the convention in both languages, with the Spanish in the left columns. It does not contain any translation of the form of inscription. There is also in the file the attested resolution of the Senate of May 13, 1834 (Executive Journal, IV, 403). The certificate of the exchange of ratifications (in Spanish) was enclosed with the despatch of Van Ness of August 14, 1834 (D. S., 32 Despatches, Spain, No. 85).

Other documents in the file, obtained from the archives at Madrid, are facsimiles of the United States instrument of ratification of May 15 and of the certificate (in English) of the exchange of ratifications signed at Madrid on August 14, 1834. The United States ratification is in customary form, and, like the Spanish ratification, includes no translation of the form of inscription. The English version of the certificate of the exchange of ratifications reads as follows:

The Undersigned having met together for the purpose of exchanging the Ratifications of the convention between His Majesty the Queen Regent and Governess, in the name of Her august Daughter Her Catholick Majesty, Donna Ysabel the 2ᵈ and the Government of the United States of America, concluded and signed at Madrid on the seventeenth day of February one thousand eight hundred and thirty-four, together with a formula thereunto annexed—And the respective Ratifications of the said instrument having been carefully perused, the said exchange took place this day in the usual form.

In witness whereof the have signed the present certificate of exchange. Done at Madrid the fourteenth day of August one thousand eight hundred and thirty four.

C. P. VAN NESS
FRANCISCO MARTINEZ DE LA ROSA

It appears that no papers accompanied this convention when it was transmitted to the Senate with the presidential message of April 17, 1834 (Executive Journal, IV, 389), and no papers are with the Senate print of the convention (Senate Confidential Document No. 5, 23d Congress, 1st session, Regular Confidential Documents, VI,

589–92); but in February, 1835, the Senate asked for papers. Some of the instructions and correspondence were transmitted with the presidential message of February 28, 1835 (Richardson, III, 145), and are printed in Senate Document No. 147, 23d Congress, 2d session, serial 269.

THE FULL POWERS

To Van Ness were given two full powers dated, respectively, October 1, 1829, and December 5, 1833 (D. S., 2 Credences, 124, 204). In substance they were similar, authorizing him "to agree, treat, consult and negotiate of and concerning the general Commerce between the United States and the Kingdom of Spain and its dominions or dependencies, and of all matters and subjects connected therewith which may be interesting to the two Nations; also of and concerning claims of indemnity for whatever cause, of Citizens of the United States, and subjects of Spain upon the Governments of Spain and the United States respectively, and to conclude and sign a treaty or treaties, Convention or Conventions touching the premises."

The full power dated December 5, 1833, was sent "as a precautionary measure," owing to the death of the King of Spain (D. S., 14 Instructions, Spain, 28–30); but the earlier full power was the one used. A copy of that full power is in the Spanish archives, and a facsimile of that copy is in the archives of the Department of State.

It thus seems that copies but not the originals of the full powers were exchanged. A copy of the Spanish full power given to Don José de Heredia is one of the enclosures to the despatch of Van Ness of February 18, 1834 (D. S., 31 Despatches, Spain, No. 72; printed in part in Senate Document No. 147, 23d Congress, 2d session, serial 269). It is accompanied by a translation as follows:

Doña Isabel the Second, by the grace of God Queen of Castile, of Leon, of Aragon, of the Two Sicilies, of Jerusalem, Navarre, Granada, Toledo, Valencia, Galicia, Majorca, Minorca, Seville, Sardinia, Cordova, Corsica, Murcia, Jaén, the Algarves, Algeciras, Gibraltar, the Canary Islands, the East and West Indies, the islands and terra firma of the ocean sea; Archduchess of Austria; Duchess of Burgundy, of Brabant, and Milan; Countess of Habsburg, of Flanders, Tirol, and Barcelona; Señora of Biscay and Molina, etc., and, in the royal name, and during the minority of Her Majesty, the Queen Regent: From a desire of bringing to a conclusion the question of the claims of the citizens of the United States of America, whatever may be their origin or denomination, dating from the 22d of February, 1819, until the signing of the convention which I have resolved shall be concluded for that purpose with Cornelius P. Van Ness, Esq., Envoy Extraordinary and Minister Plenipotentiary of the said United States near the person of My august daughter, I have thought fit to appoint a person who to intelligence and probity shall unite all the other qualities which the case requires. And reposing special confidence in you, Don José de Heredia, member of My Supreme Council of Finance, ex-Envoy Extraordinary and Minister Plenipotentiary, and Knight Grand Cross of the Royal American Order of Isabel the Catholic, I have determined to invest and I do hereby invest you with full power to sign with the aforesaid Cornelius P. Van Ness, and agreeably to the instructions with which you have been furnished, the aforesaid convention. And I hereby promise under My royal word that whatsoever you may so treat of, agree upon, and sign, I will hold for good and valid, and will observe and fulfil and cause to be observed and fulfilled, in the same manner as if I had Myself treated of, discussed, settled, and signed the same; for which purpose I confer on you in the most ample form all the

authority which may be requisite in law. In testimony whereof I have caused the present to be drawn up, which is signed with My hand, sealed with My secret seal, and countersigned by My Principal Secretary of State.

Given in My Palace of Madrid this 29th of January, 1834.

[Seal] I THE QUEEN REGENT

FRANCISCO MARTINEZ DE LA ROSA

ARTICLE 4

Regarding the provisions of Article 4 requiring the Government of the United States to deliver certain papers to the Spanish Minister at Washington within stated periods after the exchange of the ratifications of the convention, Van Ness wrote as follows in his despatch of February 18, 1834, above cited:

The documents to be furnished on our part under the 4th Article of the Convention can create no difficulty. The first will be merely a list of the names of the claimants, so far as they may be known at the time, with the sums claimed by them respectively, without reference to what may be actually due. The copies mentioned in the last clause of the Article, it is considered, are to be furnished after the close of the examination & liquidation of the Claims, & will, of course, shew the amount actually allowed & paid.

It is stated on the part of this Gov't that these papers are wanted for the purpose of calling to an account the Spanish officers who have directed or sanctioned the outrages for which compensation has been made. Some of them have become very rich from the plunder, & are now in this Country. I endeavoured to persuade M⯑ Heredia that the first list would be of no use, as it would furnish no just criterion for the purpose stated, but he was very tenacious, & as it will be but the work of an hour or two for one of your clerks, I consented rather than to waste time on so small a point.

The correspondence showing the fulfilment of those obligations of the United States is printed in House Executive Document No. 129, 48th Congress. 1st session, serial 2207, pages 9–13.

THE CLAIMS SETTLEMENT

An account of the origin of the American claims settled by this convention, of the negotiations leading thereto, and of the proceedings for the determination of the American claims under the act of June 7, 1836 (5 Statutes at Large, 34–36), is in Moore, International Arbitrations, V, 4533–47. The convention was communicated to Congress with the presidential message of May 21, 1834, prior to the exchange of ratifications (Richardson, III, 52).

The proceedings of the commissioner appointed to pass on the American claims pursuant to the statute mentioned, lasted from July 30, 1836, to January 31, 1838, the time allowed for the proceedings having been extended by the act of March 3, 1837 (5 Statutes at Large, 179). The total amount of the awards was $466,809.56; and to the amount of each award was added 28½ per cent thereof, making the total awarded to claimants $599,850.28 (Moore, *op. cit.*, 4538–46). The final report of the commissioner (printed *ibid.*) and the journal and other papers of the proceedings are in the archives of the Department of State.

PAYMENTS UNDER THE CONVENTION

Under Article 1 of the convention the nominal amount of the perpetual rents inscribed on the great book of the consolidated debt of Spain was twelve million "Rials *vellon*" or reals; that amount was considered to be the equivalent of $600,000; the annual interest at 5 per cent was thus $30,000, payable semiannually, on February 14 and August 14 of each year.

It will be observed from the "model" of the inscription that under a royal decree of December 15, 1825, there was also to be an amortization of 1 per cent annually at compound interest. That decree, however, related to the consolidated debt of Spain generally; a legalized copy of the decree is with the despatch of August 8, 1858, of Augustus C. Dodge, Minister to Spain (D. S., 41 Despatches, Spain, No. 85). It reads as follows (translation):

[Seal]

The Director of the Sinking Fund having, through the medium of you, reminded Me of the instability of the loan which in France is called the Royal Loan of Spain, contracted, in the year one thousand eight hundred and twenty-three, with the house of Mr. Louis Guebhard, of Paris, making known at the same time that the Royal Fund Office cannot continue the payment of this obligation, as it is not established in it according to its rules; and considering the damage which might ensue to the parties interested in said loan, if it should remain in its present form and condition, I have, in conformity to the opinion of My Council of Ministers, resolved, and do resolve, that the Guebhard obligations may be converted, at the will of the holders, into obligations of perpetual income, on the great book of the consolidated debt of the state, at 5 per cent interest, like them, and under the pledges, inviolability, and guaranty enjoyed by other credits which are inscribed. For this purpose, and in order to favor the interested parties who consent to the conversion, their capital will be increased 5 per cent, say ten and a half dollars of perpetual income for each obligation of two hundred hard dollars, instead of the ten hard dollars which it enjoys at present, which interest will be paid at Paris, in half-yearly maturities, at the house which is named and intrusted with the conversion, in which it shall remain for the payment of interest and the progressive redemption of the principal, converted with the 1 per cent at compound interest, according to the rules and instructions of the Fund Office. You will bear this in mind and give the appropriate orders for its fulfilment.

Rubricated by the royal hand

PALACE, *fifteenth of December, one thousand eight hundred and twenty-five*
To Don Luis Lopez Ballesteros

The provisions of that decree were never fulfilled in respect of the inscriptions issued under this convention; and Secretary of State Seward wrote as follows regarding its legal effect (D. S., 66 Domestic Letters, 336–37, October 7, 1864, to William Gray):

Attempts have been made to induce the Spanish Government to make provision for that redemption of the principal of the debt, for which the convention is supposed to stipulate. They contend, however, that the debt was meant to be perpetual, and the clause claimed to provide for the redemption seems to me so obscure as at least to afford some ground for their assumption. It is the intention of this Department, however, to review the whole subject at the earliest proper moment.

Correspondence concerning efforts made by the United States from 1849 to 1879 to effect payment of the principal of the debt is in House Executive Document No. 129, 48th Congress, 1st session, serial 2207, pages 78–115; but no agreement was reached in that regard with the Government of Spain.

Events in Spain brought about the suspension of the payments of interest under the convention soon after it went into force. The four semiannual payments due at Paris in 1835 and 1836, of $15,000 each, were met, but from that time until 1841 the payments were suspended; four years' interest (1837–40) was then in arrear.

Under date of April 2, 1841, a secret arrangement was made with the Spanish Government whereby "the Treasury of Cuba shall pay punctually and annually sixty thousand dollars to be applied by halves to the discharge of the interests, arrear and current of the debt above-mentioned until the entire payment of the interests due" (D. S., 33 Despatches, Spain, No. 21, enclosure; House Executive Document No. 129, 48th Congress, 1st session, serial 2207, p. 34). The annual payments of $60,000 made up in a few years the arrears of interest, and thereafter $30,000 was paid annually.

Another arrangement was then entered into by an exchange of notes under date of March 9, 1847, between the Spanish Minister at Washington, A. Calderon de la Barca, and Secretary of State James Buchanan, which was subsequently approved by the Queen of Spain; the text of those notes (the former in translation) follows (D. S., 12 Notes from the Spanish Legation; 6 Notes to the Spanish Legation, 150–51):

WASHINGTON, *March 9, 1847*

The undersigned Envoy Extraordinary and Minister Plenipotentiary of Her Catholic Majesty the Queen of Spain, in obedience with his instructions, and as the result of the various conferences which he has had with the Honorable James Buchanan, says—

1. That the Government of Her Catholic Majesty is disposed to locate permanently in Habana the payment of the interest to which the second article of the convention of 1834 refers.

2. That the amount of the said interest shall be annually remitted by the Treasury of Habana in bills of exchange guaranteed by it, of the same nature as those hitherto sent.

3. That to cover the expense of the acquisition of the said bills, that it may not fall upon Spain, 5 per cent, or $1,500, shall be deducted from the aforesaid amount.

4. That on receiving the bills, the Government of the United States will give Her Majesty's Legation in Washington the receipts and the usual order for the delivery of the coupons in the same manner and in the same form as has been practiced until now.

As soon as the undersigned shall receive an answer in conformity to this from the Honorable Secretary of State, he will make the corresponding communication to his Government and to the authorities at Habana.

In the meanwhile, etc.

A. CALDERON DE LA BARCA

DEPARTMENT OF STATE,
Washington, 9th March, 1847.

Don A. CALDERON DE LA BARCA, &c., &c., &c.,

The Undersigned, Secretary of State of the United States, has attentively considered the note just handed to him by His Excellency Mr Calderon de la Barca, Envoy Extraordinary and Minister Plenipotentiary of Spain, formally announc-

ing, in accordance with his instructions, and as the result of the various conferences which have recently taken place between them, that the Government of Her Catholic Majesty is willing to locate permanently at Havaña the payment of the interest to which the second Article of the Convention of 1834 refers; and agreeing, that the amount of the said interest shall be annually remitted to Washington by the Treasury of Havaña in bills of exchange guarantied by it,—first deducting from said amount five per cent, or $1500, to cover expenses accruing upon the remittance,—provided that, on receiving these bills, the Government of the United States will give Her Majesty's Legation in this city, the acquittances and usual order for the delivery of the Coupons at Paris, in the manner and form heretofore observed.

The Undersigned has the honor to inform Mr Calderon, in reply, that having communicated with the holders of the certificates of this debt, and become acquainted with the views of a large majority of them in relation to an arrangement of the kind offered, he feels himself authorized to assent to that proposed by Mr Calderon; in the understanding that the said annual remittance of interest, in bills of Exchange, is to be made on the 14th day of August of each successive year, or at latest, one month or forty days thereafter, if, from imperative or unforeseen circumstances, it should occasionally prove impossible to make it by the day named. In this understanding, Mr Calderon's proposition, as set forth in his note above mentioned, is hereby accepted.

The Undersigned avails himself of the occasion to renew to Mr Calderon the assurance of his distinguished consideration.

JAMES BUCHANAN.

The convention was thus modified in various respects. Instead of the stated semiannual payments to be made at Paris, the amount agreed on was $28,500 payable annually by bills remitted from Habana to Washington. The notes exchanged under date of March 9, 1847, and correspondence from 1835 to 1879, are printed in House Executive Document No. 129, 48th Congress, 1st session, serial 2207.

The annual payments of $28,500 thus agreed upon were duly made up to and including 1907. Under the Legal Tender Act of February 25, 1862 (12 Statutes at Large, 345–48), the payments due were made in currency, a practice approved by an opinion of the Attorney General of June 10, 1869 (House Executive Document No. 139, 41st Congress, 2d session, serial 1417). The events of 1898 caused only a comparatively brief postponement of the current payments of the interest.

On August 12, 1907, the Government of Spain made tender of $570,000 in payment of the principal of the debt under the convention of February 17, 1834. After due consideration and on obtaining the assent of a large majority in amount of the parties in interest, this Government accepted the tender and the fund was in due course received and distributed by the Treasury Department (Annual Report of the Secretary of the Treasury, 1908, 152).

Treaty Series No. 204
8 Statutes at Large, 464–67
18 *ibid.*, pt. 2, Public Treaties, 486–87

79

MEXICO : APRIL 3, 1835

Convention for a Second Additional Article to the Treaty of Limits of January 12, 1828 (Document 60), signed at Mexico April 3, 1835. Original in English and Spanish.
Submitted to the Senate December 22, 1835. (Message of December 17, 1835.) Resolution of advice and consent January 26, 1836. Ratified by the United States February 2, 1836. Ratified by Mexico April 7, 1835. Ratifications exchanged at Washington April 20, 1836. Proclaimed April 21, 1836.

A Treaty[1] having been concluded and signed in the City of Mexico on the 12ᵗʰ day of January 1828 between the United States of America and the Mexican United States for the purpose of establishing the true dividing line and boundary between the two Nations the 3ᵈ article of which Treaty is as follows "To fix this "line with more precision and to "place the land marks which shall "designate exactly the limits of "both Nations each of the con- "tracting parties shall appoint a "Commissioner and a Surveyor "who shall meet before the ter- "mination of one year from the "date of the ratification of this "Treaty at Natchitoches on the "Red River, and proceed to run "and mark said line from the "Mouth of the Sabine to the Red "River and from the Red River

Habiendose concluido y firmado en la Ciudad de Mejico a los 12 dias del Mes de Enero de 1828 un Tratado[1] entre los Estados Unidos Mejicanos y los Estados Unidos del Norte con el fin de establecer la verdadera linea divisoria y los limites entre las dos Naciones; y habiendose estipulado en el articulo 3º del mencionado Tratado lo sigᵗᵉ. "Para fijar esta linea con "mas precision y establecer los "mojones que señalen con exacti- "tud los limites de ambas na- "ciones nombrará cada una de "ellas un Comisario y Geometra "q. se juntaran antes del termino "de un año contado desde la fecha "de la ratificacion de este Tratado "en Natchitoches en las Orillas "del Rio Rojo y procederán a "señalar y demarcar dicha linea "desde la embocadura del Sabina "hasta el Rio Rojo y de este hasta

---

[1] Document 60.

"to the River Arkansas and to
"ascertain the latitude of the
"source of said River Arkansas in
"conformity to what is agreed
"upon and stipulated and the line
"of Latitude 42. to the South
"Sea. They shall make out plans
"and keep journals of their pro-
"ceedings and the result agreed
"upon by them shall be considered
"as part of this Treaty and shall
"have the same force as if it were
"inserted therein. The two Gov-
"ernments will amicably agree
"respecting the necessary articles
"to be furnished to those persons
"and also as to their respective
"escorts should such be deemed
"necessary": And the ratifications of said Treaty having been
exchanged in the City of Washington on the 5th day of April in
the year of 1832 but from various
causes the contracting parties
have been unable to perform the
stipulations contained in the
abovementioned 3ª Article, and
the period within which the said
stipulations could have been executed has elapsed:—and both
Republics being desirous that the
said Treaty should be carried into
effect with all due solemnity; The
President of the United States of
America has for that purpose
fully empowered on his part
Anthony Butler a Citizen thereof
and chargé d'Affaires of said
States in Mexico, and the acting
President of the United Mexican
States having in like manner

"el Rio Arkansas y averiguar con
"certidumbre el origen del espre-
"sado Rio Arkansas y fijar segun
"queda estipulado y convenido en
"este Tratado la linea q. debe
"seguir desde el grado 42 de lati-
"tud hasta el Mar pacifico. Lle-
"varan diarios y levantaran pla-
"nos de sus operaciones; y el
"resultado convenido pᶠ ellos se
"tendrá pᶠ parte de este Tratado
"y tendra la misma fuerza q. si
"estuviese inserto en el, de-
"biendo convenir amistosamente
"los dos Gobiernos en el arreglo
"de cuanto necesiten estos indivi-
"duos y en la escolta respectiva q.
"deban llevar siempre q. se crea
"necesario." Y habiendose cangeado las ratificaciones del mencionado Tratado en la ciudad de
Washington a los 5 dias del Mes
de Abril del año del Sõr 1832; no
habiendo podido las partes contratantes cumplir por varias causas
las estipulaciones contenidas en el
mencionado articulo 3º habiendo
espirado el termino dentro del
cual debian ejecutarse y deseando
ambas Republicas, q. el referido
Tratado tenga su mas puntual
cumplimᵗᵒ llenandose todas las
formalidades necesarias; el Presidente interino de los Estados
Unidos Mejicanos ha revestido
con sus plenos poderes para este
objeto á los Exelentisimos Srẽs, D.
José Mª Gutierrez de Estrada
Sriõ de Estado y del despacho de
Relaciones interiores y. exteriores
y D. José Mariano Blasco Sriõ de

fully empowered on his part their Excellency's José Maria Gutierrez de Estrada Secretary of State for home and Foreign Affairs and José Mariano Blasco Secretary of the Treasury; and the said Plenipotentiaries after having mutually exchanged their full powers, found to be ample and in form, they have agreed and do hereby agree to the following second additional article to the said Treaty.

Within the space of one year to be estimated from the date of the exchange of the ratifications of this said additional article, there shall be appointed by the Government of the United States of America and of the Mexican United States each a Commissioner and Surveyor, for the purpose of fixing with more precision the dividing line, and for establishing the Land marks of boundary and limits between the two Nations, with the exactness stipulated by the 3^d Article of the Treaty of limits concluded and signed in Mexico on the 12th day of January 1828 and the Ratifications of which were exchanged in Washington City on the 5th day of April 1832. And the present additional article shall have the same force and effect as if it had been inserted word for word in the abovementioned Treaty of the 12th of January 1828, and shall be approved and ratified in the manner prescribed by the Constitutions of the respective States.

56006°—33——54

Estado y del despacho de Hacienda, y el Presidente de los Estados Unidos del Norte al Honorable Señor Antonio Butler encargado de Negocios de aquella Republica en Megico: y los referidos Plenipotenciarios despues de haber cambiado sus plenos poderes q. se encontraron en buena y debida forma han convenido y convienen en el siguiente segundo articulo adicional. "Se prorroga p^r el espacio de un año contado desde la fecha del cange de las ratificaciones del presente articulo adicional, el termino q. para el nombram^{to} de los Comisarios y Geometras encargados p^r los Gobiernos de Megico y de Washington de fijar con mas precision la linea divisoria y establecer los mojones q. señalen con exactitud los limites de Ambas Naciones estableció el Articulo 3° del Tratado de limites concluido y firmado en Megico a los 12 dias del mes de Enero de 1828, y cuyas ratificaciones fueron cangeadas en la Ciudad de Washington á los 5 dias del mes de Abril de 1832." El presente 2° articulo adicional tendrá la misma fuerza y valor q. si se hubiese insertado palabra p^r palabra en el Tratado mencionado de 12 de Enero de 1828 y será aprobado y ratificado en los terminos q. establecen las Constituciones de los respectivos Estados.

In faith of which the said Plenipotentiaries have hereunto set their hands and affixed their respective seals. Done in the City of Mexico on the third day of April in the year of our Lord one thousand Eight hundred and thirty five in the fifty ninth year of the Independence of the United States of America and of the fifteenth of that of the United Mexican States.

En fée de lo cual los referidos Plenipotenciarios lo hemos firmado y sellado con nuestros sellos respectivos, fecho en Megico á los tres dias del mes de Abril de mil ocho cientos treinta y cinco decimo quinto de la Independencia de los Estados Unidos Megicanos y quincuagesimo noveno de la de los Estados Unidos de America.

A: BUTLER   [Seal]
J. M. GUTIERREZ
         DE ESTRADA   [Seal]
JOSÉ MARIANO BLASCO   [Seal]

J. M. GUTIERREZ
         DE ESTRADA   [Seal]
JOSÉ MARIANO BLASCO   [Seal]
A: BUTLER   [Seal]

NOTES

The file of this convention is complete. The signed original in the file has the English text in the left columns; and, as the printed texts show, the United States of America has precedence in the English text and the United Mexican States in the Spanish. That original is embodied in the original proclamation of April 21, 1836, to which is attached the duplicate United States instrument of ratification of February 2.

All the papers are in the usual form, including the attested Senate resolution of January 26 (Executive Journal, IV, 507), the certificate of exchange of ratifications, in English, of April 20, and the Mexican instrument of ratification, in Spanish, of April 7, 1835. The latter document includes both texts, the Spanish in the left columns.

In the treaty file is also an explanatory declaration or protocol, signed and sealed on behalf of the respective Governments on the day of the exchange of ratifications, April 20, 1836, by Secretary of State John Forsyth and Don Manuel Eduardo de Gorostiza, Mexican Minister at Washington. The text of that document which was not before the Senate, follows:

The exchange of the ratifications of the Convention concluded on the third of April, 1835, for a second additional article to the Treaty of Limits between the United States of America and the United Mexican States being this day to be made by John Forsyth, Secretary of State of the United States and J. M. de Castillo y Lanzas, Chargé d'Affaires of the Mexican Republic to the United States; and Don Manuel Eduardo de Gorostiza, Envoy Extraordinary and

Debiendose verificar en el dia de la fecha por Don Joaquin Maria de Castillo y Lanzas Encargado de Negocios de la Republica Mexicana y Juan Forsyth Secretario de Estado de los Estados Unidos de America, el cange de las ratificaciones de la convencion celebrada en 3. de abril de 1835, entre la Republica Mexicana y dichos Estados Unidos para en 2º articulo adicion! al Tratado de limites, y hallandose Manuel Eduardo de Gorostiza, Enviado

Minister Plenipotentiary of the Mexican Republic to the United States, having full power from his Government to negotiate any addition that might be thought necessary to carry into full effect the intention of the parties if the terms of the said second additional article were not sufficiently comprehensive and explicit, on a full, official, and unreserved conference between the said Secretary of State and the said Envoy Extraordinary and Minister Plenipotentiary, it has been found that both Governments coincide in putting the same construction on the said second additional article, giving to it all the force and effect of the third article of the said Treaty of Limits, and that therefore no addition is necessary: Nevertheless as the said second additional article is not clearly expressed, although the intention is not doubtful, to prevent the possibility of misconception in giving full effect to the intention of the parties, it is thought expedient that the said Secretary of State and the said Envoy Extraordinary and Minister Plenipotentiary should declare, and they do declare in behalf of their respective Governments, that the stipulation in the said second additional article for the appointment of Commissioners and Surveyors to run and mark the boundary line between the two countries, is expressly understood and is to be construed to impose the obligation on the Commissioners and Surveyors to meet within the time and at the place prescribed by the said third article of the Treaty of Limits, namely, at Natchitoches and within one year from this date and to proceed to carry into full effect the stipulations of the said third article.

In testimony whereof, this instrument is executed in duplicate and is mutually delivered prior to the exchange of the ratifications of the Convention for a second additional article to the Treaty of Limits, duly ratified by our respective Governments.

Done at Washington this twentieth day of April, one thousand eight hundred and thirty six.

JOHN FORSYTH   [Seal]
    Scy of State U S. of A.
MANᴸ E. DE GOROSTIZA   [Seal]

Extraordinario y Ministro Plenipotenciario de la expresada Republica Mexicana con Plenos Poderes de su Gobierno para negociar cualquiera adicion que pueda jurgarse necesaria para llevar á entero efecto las intenciones de las Altas partes contratantes siempre que los terminos en que esta concebido el referido segundo articulo adicional no fuesen suficientemente comprehensivos y explicitos, há resultado de una conferencia amplia franca y oficial, tenida entre el expresado Enviado extraordinario y Ministro Plenipotenciario y el expresado Secretario de Estado, que los dos Gobiernos coinciden exactamente en la misma idea y construccion del indicado segundo articulo adicional, dandole toda la fuerza y sentido del tercer articulo del precitado Tratado de Limites, y de consiguiente que no es necesaria adicion Alguna. Pero como la redaccion del segundo articulo adicional no es bastantemente clara aun cuando su intencion no sea dudosa; con el fin de evitar toda posibilidad de mala inteligencia al llevar a efecto cuanto de propusieron entonces ambas Partes, se há creido conveniente que el citado Enviado extraordinario y Ministro Plenipotenciario y el citado Secretario de Estado declaren, como lo hacen por la presente, en nombre de sus respectivos Gobiernos que lo estipulado en el mencionado segundo articulo adicional respecto del nombramiento de los Comisarios y Geometras que deben señalar y demarcar la linea divisoria entre los dos paises se entiende expresamente y debe interpretarse que impone la obligacion á dichos Comisarios y Geometras de reunirse en el lugar y termino prescritos en el articulo tercero del Tratado de Limites á saber: en Natchitoches y en el termino de un año contado desde esta fecha y de proceder á dar entero cumplimiento a lo estipulado por el insinuado tercer articulo.

En fe de lo cual y antes del cange de las ratificaciones de la Convencion del Segundo articulo adicional al Tratado de limites debidamente ratificado por los respectivos Gobiernos, se extiende por duplicado el presente documento firmado y sellado por los Infrascritos, el cual se cangeara igualmente por ellos.

Fecho en Washington á los veinte dias del mes de abril del año de un mil ochocientos treinta y seis.

MANᴸ E. DE GOROSTIZA   [Seal]
JOHN FORSYTH   [Seal]
    Scy of State U. S. of A.

The reason for the foregoing declaration is to be found in the fact that the second additional article, while containing a provision for the appointment of the officials therein named by each Government within a year from the date of the exchange of ratifications, contains no provision for the time of the meeting of the commissioners and surveyors.

By Secretary of State Forsyth on the one part and the Mexican Minister, Don Manuel Eduardo de Gorostiza, on the other, various notes were written regarding the declaration. These are printed in House Document No. 42, 25th Congress, 1st session, serial 311, pages 83–94. The Mexican Minister would have preferred "that another second additional article should be drawn up," for which purpose he had a full power, but he accepted the procedure proposed by Forsyth in the note of April 1, 1836:

> The second additional article to the treaty of limits, although not so comprehensive in its terms as was desirable, was laid before the Senate by the President, in the belief that, as the third article of the treaty had ceased to be of any force or effect, in consequence of the expiration of the time within which its stipulations were to have been fully carried into execution, and as it was the intention of both parties to provide, by the second additional article, for effecting the same object as was provided for by the third article, the stipulation for the appointment of commissioners and surveyors to run and mark the boundary line between the two countries, should be construed to impose the obligation on the commissioners and surveyors to meet within the time prescribed by the third article. It is presumed that the Senate acted under the same belief in giving its advice and consent to the ratification of the second additional article.
>
> If this view be correct, to prevent the possibility of misconception in giving full effect to the intention of the parties, it will be sufficient for their respective agents, at the time of the exchange of the ratifications of the second additional article, to mark, by a joint explanatory note, the explicit understanding of the two Governments. Should Mr. Gorostiza concur in this opinion, and find himself authorized to adopt that course, the undersigned is instructed to agree with him upon the necessary arrangements.

It was further agreed that while the authority of the Mexican Minister was sufficient for him to sign a declaration, his powers did not authorize him to exchange the ratifications of the convention for the second additional article. Accordingly, in the exchange the Mexican Chargé d'Affaires, J. M. de Castillo y Lanzas, acted for that Government, the declaration being signed at the same time by the Mexican Minister.

The Full Powers

The full power given to Anthony Butler, Chargé d'Affaires at Mexico, was dated January 16, 1834 (D. S., 2 Credences, 205–6), and contained the following:

> Know Ye, that, whereas, by the third Article of the Treaty of Limits concluded between The United States of America and The United Mexican States on the 12th day of January 1828, it was stipulated, that each of the contracting parties should appoint a Commissioner and a Surveyor, who should meet before the termination of one year from the date of the ratification of the Treaty at Natchitoches, on the Red River, and proceed to run and mark the Boundary line between the Territories of the said contracting parties; but, whereas, for various causes,

the said Commissioners and Surveyors failed to meet, within the period stipulated by the said third article, yet, being still desirous of carrying into effect the intentions of the said Contracting parties with regard to the object of the said Treaty of Limits, and reposing special trust and confidence in the integrity prudence and abilities of *Anthony Butler*, Chargé d'affaires of The United States near the Goverment of The said United Mexican States, I have invested him with full and all manner of power and authority, for and in the name of The United States to meet and confer with any person or persons duly authorized by The Government of The United Mexican States, being furnished with like power and authority, and with him or them to agree treat consult and negotiate of and concerning a second additional article to the said Treaty of limits between the said United States of America and the said United Mexican States, stipulating for an extension of the time prescribed, by the said Treaty, for the meeting of the said Commissioners and Surveyors, as aforesaid, and to conclude and sign a treaty or treaties convention or conventions touching the premises, transmitting the same to The President of The United States, for his final ratification, by and with the advice and consent of The Senate of The United States.

It appears that the original full powers were exchanged, as that given by the Government of Mexico under date of March 30, 1835, to negotiate and conclude the convention, is in the treaty file. It reads as follows in translation:

Miguel Barragan, President of the United Mexican States

To all who may see these presents, know ye:

That, in view of the expiration of the period of one year designated in Article 3 of the boundary treaty concluded between these United [Mexican] States and the United States of North America in 1832 for the meeting, at Natchitoches, of the commissioners and geometers of the two Governments who are to proceed to mark out the boundary line of the two Nations in accordance with the said treaty, and as I am desirous of overcoming this difficulty and cherish a desire that this meeting of the commissioners should take place as soon as possible in order that they may begin their labors, I have seen fit, by virtue of the powers conferred upon me by the Federal Constitution, to grant full powers to Messrs. José María Gutierrez Estrada and José Mariano Blasco, the former, Secretary of Foreign Affairs, and the latter, Secretary of Finance, and both of whom enjoy my full confidence, owing to their intelligence, integrity, and patriotism, for the purpose of proceeding, in conjunction with the plenipotentiary or plenipotentiaries duly appointed by the Government of the United States of North America, to extend the period mentioned in Article 3 of the boundary treaty of 1832, for such length of time as may be considered sufficient in order that the meeting of the commissioners and geometers of the two Governments may take place, and I promise on behalf of these [United Mexican] States to regard as valid and to carry out and cause to be carried out whatever they may stipulate by virtue of the authority that I hereby confer upon them, after complying with the requirements stipulated by the Federal Constitution.

In faith whereof I have caused to be issued to them the present full powers, signed by my hand, authenticated by the national seal, and countersigned by the Secretary of War and Navy on March 30, 1835, being the fifteenth year of the independence of these States.

[Seal]   M. BARRAGAN

JOSE MARIA TORNEL

Also in the file are the original and a copy of the full power given under date of April 7, 1835, to Don Joaquin Maria del Castillo y Lanzas, Chargé d'Affaires at Washington, to exchange the ratifications.

THE BOUNDARY DEMARCATION

By Articles 3 and 4 of the treaty of February 22, 1819, with Spain (Document 41), the boundary between the United States and Spanish possessions in North America was fixed and provision was made for its demarcation. Mexican independence rendered the demarcation provisions of that treaty obsolete as to Spain, and they were not executed. In the Treaty of Limits of January 12, 1828, with Mexico (Document 60), was incorporated the language of Articles 3 and 4 of the treaty with Spain of 1819; but while the treaty of 1828 went into force on April 5, 1832, its similar demarcation provisions had not been carried out. Further details will be found in the notes to Documents 41 (Articles 3 and 4) and 60. In instructions to Butler of January 13, 1834, Secretary of State McLane wrote as follows (D. S., 15 Instructions, Mexico, 14–16):

You are aware that the period fixed by the third article of the treaty of limits with Mexico and the article additional thereto for the meeting of the commissioners and surveyors provided for by that treaty, expired on the 2nd of April, last [correctly, April 5, 1833], and that in consequence of the omission of the Mexican Government timely to appoint the commissioner and surveyor on their part, no such meeting took place. The appointment of the of the Commissioner on the part of the United States was made on the 30th May, 1832, and publicly announced in the Globe newspaper at Washington on the 19th of July, 1832, and notice was given to Mr Montoya, the Mexican Chargé d'Affaires, on the 20th of the same month, that this Government was prepared to proceed conjointly with that of Mexico to the designation of the boundary line, and, though Mr. Montoya was requested, at the same time, to state whether any arrangement had been made on the part of his government for that object, and, if not, to request the immediate attention of his government to the subject, this Department remained wholly without information as to the appointment of a commissioner and surveyor on the part of Mexico, until the 4th ultimo, when I was informed by Mr Castillo, the Mexican Chargé d'Affaires, under date of the 2nd of the same month, that the Mexican commissioner and surveyor had been appointed. I learn verbally from Mr Castillo that he has not been advised as to the time of their appointment, but by a Report made by the Minister of Foreign Affairs to the Congress of Mexico on the 20th of May, last, I perceive that no such appointment, had, then, been made; on the contrary, the minister speaks of the Commission as yet to be created by each Government.

Under these circumstances, the treaty of limits cannot be carried into full effect without a new convention between the two governments providing for that object.

The President directs, therefore, that you will conclude a new convention with the Mexican Government, consisting of a single article, stipulating for an extension of the time prescribed by the third article of the treaty for the meeting of the commissioners and surveyors, and authorizing them to meet for the performance of their duties at any time within one year after the exchange of the ratifications of the new convention. And to enable you to execute these instructions, the necessary powers are herewith transmitted to you. The new convention which you are now instructed to conclude, must be ratified by the Mexican Government previously to submitting it for the ratification by the United States, and provision must also be made for the exchange of the ratifications at Washington within one month after it shall be ratified by the United States. It is the wish of the President, therefore, that as soon as the treaty shall be ratified by the Mexican Government, you will ask for your audience of leave and return home, bringing the ratified treaty with you.

The previous ratification of the new treaty by the Mexican Government, is a necessary precaution against impediments similar to those which have heretofore

baffled the efforts of the President finally to close this subject, and when it is considered that these have arisen chiefly if not entirely from the neglect of the Mexican Government, she cannot with any propriety decline complying with the terms now presented.

The effect of this convention was to extend the time for the commencement of the demarcation of the boundary between the United States and Mexico until April 20, 1837; but events intervened. Hostilities between Mexico and Texas began in October, 1835; before this agreement went into force the independence of Texas was declared at a convention which met at the town of Washington in that state on March 2, 1836; in the Battle of San Jacinto on April 21, 1836, the Texan forces defeated those under the command of Santa Anna; and before the one-year limit of this convention had expired, the decisive step toward recognition of Texas by the United States had been taken. Alcée La Branche was commissioned Chargé d'Affaires to Texas by President Van Buren on March 7, 1837 (D. S., 2 Credences, 262), after his nomination by President Jackson on March 3, when the following message was sent by the latter to the Senate (Executive Journal, IV, 631; see also the message to Congress of December 21, 1836, Richardson, III, 265–69):

In my message to Congress of the 21st of December last I laid before that body, without reserve, my views concerning the recognition of the independence of Texas, with a report of the agent employed by the Executive to obtain information in respect to the condition of that country. Since that time the subject has been repeatedly discussed in both branches of the Legislature. These discussions have resulted in the insertion of a clause in the general appropriation law passed by both Houses providing for the outfit and salary of a diplomatic agent to be sent to the Republic of Texas, whenever the President of the United States may receive satisfactory evidence that Texas is an independent power and shall deem it expedient to appoint such minister, and in the adoption of a resolution by the Senate, the constitutional advisers of the Executive on the diplomatic intercourse of the United States with foreign powers, expressing the opinion that "the State of Texas having established and maintained an independent government, capable of performing those duties, foreign and domestic, which appertain to independent governments, and it appearing that there is no longer any reasonable prospect of the successful prosecution of the war by Mexico against said State, it is expedient and proper, and in conformity with the laws of nations and the practice of this Government in like cases, that the independent political existence of said State be acknowledged by the Government of the United States." Regarding these proceedings as a virtual decision of the question submitted by me to Congress, I think it my duty to acquiesce therein, and therefore I nominate Alcée La Branche, of Louisiana, to be chargé d'affaires to the Republic of Texas.

This convention was communicated to Congress with the presidential message of May 6, 1836 (Richardson, III, 226; see also *ibid.*, 238); and notwithstanding the events in Texas and the attitude of Congress in 1837 toward the recognition of the Republic of Texas, by the act of March 3, 1837 (5 Statutes at Large, 172), an appropriation was made "to enable the President to cause the southwestern boundary line of the United States to be run"; and a commissioner and surveyor were nominated by President Van Buren by a message of

March 6, 1837 (Executive Journal, V, 14); but the Senate on March 8 concurred in the following report of the Committee on Foreign Relations (*ibid.*, 22):

The Committee on Foreign Relations, to which was referred the nomination of Hiram G. Runnels, of Mississippi, to be commissioner, and that of John R. Conway of Arkansas, to be surveyor, to run the southwestern boundary line of the United States, report:

That by the treaty of January the 3d [12th], 1828 [Document 60], the boundary line was fixed between the United States and Mexico, but the provision which was made for running and marking the line was not carried into execution within the time limited by its terms. To remedy this omission a convention was concluded at the City of Mexico on the 3d April, 1835, between the contracting parties, under which each of them engaged to appoint a commissioner and surveyor to run and mark this boundary line within one year from the exchange of its ratifications, which took place at the city of Washington on the 20th April, 1836. It was doubtless for the purpose of executing this convention that a clause was inserted by Congress in the bill to provide for the civil and diplomatic expenses of the Government for the year 1837, appropriating the salary and expenses of a commissioner and surveyor; and the President of the United States has therefore felt it to be his duty to send nominations of these officers to the Senate.

Your committee believe, however, that the recognition of the independence of Texas by the United States has entirely changed the aspect of this affair. Mexico has no longer any control over the boundary in question; Texas has now become the party interested in its adjustment. If the United States should appoint a commissioner and surveyor, and they should be met by a commissioner and surveyor appointed by Mexico, this would be a violation of the rights of Texas, whose independence has just been recognized by the Government of the United States.

The committee are sensible that, under the laws of nations, Texas, which was a part of Mexico when the treaty of 1828 was concluded and ratified, is not released from executing its provisions in consequence of having since become an independent state. They deem it more politic and wise, however, under existing circumstances, to permit the question to rest for the present. The mode and manner of executing the treaty of 1828, in regard to the boundary line, will properly become a subject of negotiation between the United States and Texas in case the latter should maintain her independence.

The committee therefore recommend the adoption of the following resolution:

Resolved, That the appointment of Hiram G. Runnels to be commissioner, and that of John R. Conway to be surveyor, to run the southwestern boundary line of the United States, be laid upon the table.

The independence of the Republic of Texas gave to that country a long frontier which marched with that of the United States—from the mouth of the Sabine River in the Gulf of Mexico north along that river to the parallel of latitude 32, thence due north to the Red River, thence west along the Red River to the degree of longitude 100 west from London, and thence, according to the claim of Texas as against Mexico, north to the Arkansas, along that river to its source, north to latitude 42°, and west to the meridian which passes through the source of the Rio Grande (Laws of the Republic of Texas, I, 133–34, December 19, 1836). But the boundaries of Texas with Mexico were wholly undetermined and remained so during the existence of the independent Republic of Texas. The claim of Texas was the Rio Grande to its source (in southern Colorado) and thence due north to the parallel of latitude 42. With the admission of Texas into the Union in 1845, the boundary question between Texas and Mexico became

one between the United States and Mexico, determined, as far as the international boundary was concerned, by the Treaty of Guadalupe Hidalgo of February 2, 1848. Questions then remaining as to the boundaries of Texas became thereupon domestic and as between the United States and Texas were settled by the Compromise of 1850 (9 Statutes at Large, 446–52, 1005–6, September 9, 1850, December 13, 1850).

The notes to Document 85, the convention with Texas of April 25, 1838, contain some further observations regarding the boundaries of Texas.

O